RENAISSANCE
STUDIES IN HONOR OF HANS BARON

Hans Baron

Library of Congress Catalog Card Number: 71-148726
ISBN 0-87580-022-x
Printed in Italy

CONTENTS

PREFACE

It has been our intention that the present collection of studies in honor of Hans Baron reflect the achievements of a generation of scholars younger than his own— a generation which has been influenced and enormously stimulated by his work. We are most grateful to three distinguished senior colleagues, Denys Hay, August Buck and Eugenio Garin for their introductory essays on Baron's contributions to Renaissance studies. We also wish to express our appreciation to Mr. Bernard Wilson of The Newberry Library and Professor Anne Jacobson Schutte of Lawrence University for invaluable advice and assistance at every stage of this undertaking.

This book is affectionately dedicated to Hans Baron on his seventieth birthday.

Anthony Molho
John A. Tedeschi

COLLABORATORS

Denys Hay	*University of Edinburgh*
August Buck	*University of Marburg*
Eugenio Garin	*Università di Firenze*
John A. Tedeschi	*Newberry Library; University of Chicago*
Andrew W. Lewis	*Harvard University*
Giles Constable	*Harvard University*
Richard C. Trexler	*University of Illinois*
William M. Bowsky	*University of California (Davis)*
Anthony Molho	*Brown University*
T. C. Price Zimmermann	*Reed College*
Marvin B. Becker	*University of Rochester*
Ronald Witt	*Duke University*
Neal W. Gilbert	*University of California (Davis)*
Julius Kirshner	*University of Chicago*
Donald Wilcox	*University of New Hampshire*
Giovanni Ponte	*Università di Genova*
Donald Weinstein	*Rutgers University*
Sergio Bertelli	*Università di Perugia*
Cecil Grayson	*Oxford University*
Carlo Pincin	*Università di Torino*
Randolph Starn	*University of California (Berkeley)*
Paul F. Grendler	*University of Toronto*
Riccardo Scrivano	*Università di Padova*
John Hale	*University of London*
R. Burr Litchfield	*Brown University*
Eric Cochrane	*University of Chicago*
Charles G. Nauert, Jr.	*University of Missouri*
Lewis W. Spitz	*Stanford University*
Gerald Strauss	*Indiana University*
Eugene F. Rice, Jr.	*Columbia University*
Samuel Kinser	*Northern Illinois University*
George Huppert	*University of Illinois*
Donald R. Kelley	*State University of New York (Binghamton)*
Werner L. Gundersheimer	*University of Pennsylvania*
William J. Bouwsma	*Harvard University*
Theodore K. Rabb	*Princeton University*

STUDIES CONCERNING HANS BARON

DENYS HAY

THE PLACE OF HANS BARON IN RENAISSANCE HISTORIOGRAPHY

Renaissance scholarship has been transformed in the course of the last thirty-odd years. Among those who have contributed most to the change Hans Baron is certainly to be numbered. What are the ways in which he has influenced the development of historical scholarship in this field?

To answer this question involves recalling the general state of Renaissance studies before the Second World War and this is far from easily done. I propose to meet the difficulty by using as a stalking horse the treatment of the subject in the two last volumes of the *Cambridge Medieval History*. In volume VII (published in 1932) and in volume VIII (1936) there are chapters by Arthur A. Tilley, dealing respectively with 'The early Renaissance' and 'The Renaissance in Europe'[1]. By the 1930s Tilley, a French don at Cambridge who had written extensively on the Renaissance in France[2], was an elderly man but I believe that the synoptic chapters in the *Cambridge Medieval History* represent a fairly up to date (for the period) view of the subject. His bibliographies are not among the fullest in these uneven volumes[3], but one observes that he recorded Giuseppe Toffanin's *Che cosa fu l'umanesimo?* (1928) and clearly tried to keep abreast of the times. I shall now try to summarise his summary.

« The early Renaissance » begins, in effect, with Petrarch, who was « the first modern man » and was rightly

---

[1] VII, 751-776, VIII, 773-802.

[2] *The Literature of the French Renaissance: An Introductory Essay* (Cambridge, 1885); *The literature of the French Renaissance*, 2 vols. (Cambridge, 1904); *The Dawn of the Renaissance* (Cambridge, 1918).

[3] *Cambridge Medieval History*, VII, 966-8; VIII, 1004-6.

termed the first humanist, for he was the first to find in ancient literature a larger measure than elsewhere of that learning and training in virtue which are peculiar to man [4]. The resulting devotion to the Latin classics encouraged the existing Italian impulse to discover new manuscripts and form libraries. In this activity Petrarch was aided by Boccaccio, who excelled him in Greek. Tilley records Salutati's appointment as 'Latin secretary' at Florence and has a word on Luigi Marsili before touching on developments at Padua. There then follows a couple of pages on the study of Greek before we encounter Leonardo Bruni, whose « chief service to learning was the translation into Latin of works by Plato, Plutarch and Aristotle » [5]. We have a few lines on a number of scholars — Marsuppini, Manetti, Traversari — before a rather more elaborate account of Poggio and his discoveries, which leads to a further discussion of libraries, this in turn demanding some account of the manuscript book trade. The description of Guarino's and Vittorino's educational programme comes next, explicitly based on the works of Woodward. Some patrons are now put before the reader: Nicholas V (with particular reference to Filelfo, Biondo, who represented a 'higher' type of humanism, and Valla), Alfonso V (Fazio and Beccadelli). The humanists' faults derived from that « inordinate desire for fame » which characterised the period, but on the whole they were Christians except for Marsuppini. The chapter concludes with a brief description of development in the arts at Florence — much less confident than the rest of the section [6]. It leads on to the observation

---

[4] *Op. cit.* VII, 754.

[5] *Ibid.*, 760.

[6] *Ibid.*, 773: « The study of man ... leads to the study of individual man and ... portraiture rapidly develops. Yet during the first half of the fifteenth century avowed portraits of living persons were rare at Florence ». In vol. VIII there is a separate chapter by W. G. Constable on the arts (down to the beginning of the fifteenth century as far as Italy is concerned).

that secular art owed much to the way the « despots » had broken away from the « tutelage of the Church » in the cities of Northern Italy.

The contribution by Tilley to volume VIII begins abruptly with a catalogue of the popes after Nicholas V, and the affair of Pomponio Leto leads on to a description of the academies of Naples and Florence, the latter in turn involving a discussion of Ficino, Pico and Politian. Then, without warning, we are presented with the invention of printing and its diffusion in Italy. There then follows a brief description of Italian art in the fifteenth century[7] which ends with a couple of pages on « a third Renaissance feature of much of the Italian art of this time ... its scientific spirit »[8]; here Leonardo stands supreme. The author then deals *seriatim* with the spread of the Renaissance from Italy to other parts of Europe: France, the Low Countries and Germany, Hungary, Spain and England, taking the story down to the beginning of the sixteenth century, but not beyond; Reuchlin's quarrel with his obscurantist critics, « this memorable struggle between the forces of conservatism and those of progress, between medieval theology and humanism », belonged to modern history not to medieval[9]. In each of these national parts of the essay we are presented with the great figures of scholarship: « The restorer of classical studies in Spain was Antonio de Nebrija » is a not unrepresentative sentence[10].

It is, of course, easy enough to see the literary ancestry of Tilley's approach. This lay, as one would expect, in Voigt, Burckhardt and Symonds, that closely related group of scholars whose views, on the whole mutually compatible, had dominated learned discussion from the

---

[7] See previous note.

[8] *Cambridge Medieval History*, VIII, 779.

[9] *Ibid.*, 790.

[10] *Ibid.*, 795.

end of the nineteenth century onwards. This dependence is even more clearly revealed if Tilley's major generalisations are considered. The Renaissance is « the transition from the medieval to the modern world » which has « special features which distinguish it from other historical periods ». « If humanism is rightly defined as the cult of antiquity ... ». « These ardent humanists suffered from more than a touch of that pedantry which regards language and literature as having little relation to real life ». « Such was the Renaissance — not a rebirth, not a sudden transformation from darkness to light, but a gradual transition from the medieval to the modern world ... stimulated by the advent of a new spirit — a spirit of enthusiasm, of adventure, of pride in the dignity of man, a belief in individual effort, of criticism of old tradition, of search for new knowledge, a spirit guided and sustained by intercourse with the great writers of antiquity — poets, philosophers, historians — many of whom had been disinterred from dust-laden repositories, and who were all studied with a new reverence and a more enlightened understanding »[11].

Looking back on this presentation of the Renaissance the most striking feature is its desultory character. Scholarship since the 1880s was slotted unhappily into the Burckhardt framework with small regard for the logical, let alone the aesthetic, form of the master's work. The result tended to become an amalgam of assertions of broad principles with antiquarian observation of detail, in which the structure of society and politics was all but ignored and (for example) no distinction was drawn between the cultural developments to be found in republics, principates, monarchies. It is true that the « primacy » of Florence is mentioned by Tilley more than once[12]. It is also true that there are fugitive references in his pages to moral

[11] *Ibid.*, VII, 751, 769, 770, 775.
[12] *Ibid.*, VII, 771, VIII, 778.

or ethical questions [13]. But these hints do not provide an argument. They are not integral to an understanding of the individual scholars and artists who are successively dealt with. In short, the Renaissance is neither explained nor interpreted. It is treated as a collection of self-evident phenomena, ultimately requiring no justification.

If, with recent scholarship behind us, we find Tilley's account jejune, fragmented and detached from a solid social and political background, we should not be too severe on the author, nor reprove the editor's choice of a literary historian [14]. Looking at Tilley thirty-five years on, I find him more sophisticated than the actual teaching on the subject which I experienced in the 1930s when these Cambridge volumes were being prepared. At secondary school, where I read Burckhardt with great excitement in 1931, the Renaissance was firmly treated as the curtain-raiser to the drama of the Reformation. At Oxford, when I expressed a desire (I suppose this must have been in 1936) to study « The Italian Renaissance » as my « special subject », I was told by my tutor that only girls did that: I was to concentrate on the manly Middle Ages [15].

Now on what is our contemporary view of the Renaissance based? I suppose that most of us accept the Renaissance as a period which is worth studying in its own right rather than a lengthy « transition » from Middle

---

[13] *Ibid.*, VII, 754: « Petrarch ... was the first to find in ancient literature a larger measure than elsewhere of that learning and training in virtue which are peculiar to man ». VIII, 801: «... In England as in France the Renaissance at the close of the fifteenth century had a profoundly serious and ethical bias ... ».

[14] Cf. the account of the early Renaissance given at exactly the same time by E. P. Cheyney in the « Rise of Modern Europe » series: *The Dawn of a New Era* (New York & London, 1936). The next volume in the series is by Myron Gilmore. It appeared in 1952 and is called the *World of Humanism*. Note the syntactical consequences of emulating Michelet !

[15] That girls tended more than young men to study the Renaissance at Oxford in those days was, I suspect, because the subject was taught by a don at a woman's college, Miss Cecilia M. Ady.

Ages to modernity while we also have a distinctly more sceptical attitude to « periods » as such, realising their subjective quality. Beyond that we have lately grown accustomed to treating the changes which we summarise in the word « Renaissance » as serious factors in the public life of earlier times — matters (that is to say) to be digested by the « general » historian as well as by the art historian, or the historian of ideas. And if the Renaissance is to be treated seriously then it clearly revolves round the moral imperatives and the political urgencies of the period of its development. It was, at any rate in my own case, only when I read some of Hans Baron's articles published just before the War that I realised just how profoundly important the Renaissance had been in the evolution of the conscience and the consciousness of Europe [16].

There are a number of these papers prepared and published by Baron when he was in that unhappy interval between Germany and a new career in the States. I think in particular of two of them: the essay on « Cicero and the Roman Civic Spirit » and that on « Franciscan Poverty and Civic Wealth », both published in 1938 [17]. These articles were, of course, not the first indication of his novel approach. The edition of Leonardo Bruni's humanistic and philosophical works (1928) and the article in the *Historische Zeitschrift* (1933) on historical thought point forward, though perhaps more towards the post-war synthesis of the *Crisis* than expressly to the questions of morality raised in the essays to which I have referred. There is no need to provide a summary here of these two remarkable pieces of scholarship which are now part of

---

[16] I did not read these articles until just after the war, when preparing Edinburgh lectures on the later Middle Ages.

[17] « Cicero and the Roman Civic Spirit in the Middle Ages and Early Renaissance », *Bulletin of the John Rylands Library*, XXII (1938), 72-97; « Franciscan Poverty and Civic Wealth as Factors in the Rise of Humanistic Thought », *Speculum*, XIII (1938), 1-37.

the canon of Renaissance historiography [18]. To one reader at any rate they gave an entirely new dimension to the processes of intellectual change and went a long way to make plain why the Renaissance was important and why it developed in Italy as it did.

To begin with Baron was working within a framework which emphasised the chronological prominence and priority of Tuscany and above all of Florence in the evolution of new social and moral attitudes. This was a very important adjustment to the conventional Burckhardtian picture (part I of the *Civilization of the Renaissance in Italy* deals with tyrannies before it turns to republics), and it had parallels in the tendency discernible between the wars to relate the origins of the Renaissance to the development of capitalism. The principal result was the important distinction between « civic » humanism and its later princely manifestations. This basic notion has proved methodologically extremely rewarding and has been generally adopted in post-war surveys of the period and its problems [19].

Beyond that, Baron's interpretation was important in other ways. First of all he showed that a great mass of humanistic literature was to be taken seriously and not dismissed, as much of it had been by Burckhardt, Voigt and their successors, as empty vapourisings, stylish manipulation of Latin as an end in itself, the mere emulation of antiquity. The most immediately impressive feature of Baron's work was indeed the way in which it was solidly anchored in the literature of the period — these articles

[18] Cfr. Wallace K. Ferguson, *The Renaissance in Historical Thought* (Boston, 1948), pp. 231-38; Ferguson here discusses Baron briefly on pp. 228-9, but deals at greater length with his work in « The Interpretation of Italian Humanism: The Contribution of Hans Baron », *Journal of the History of Ideas*, XIX (1958), 14-25.

[19] For example E. Garin in his well-known work on Italian humanism which first appeared in a German version at Bonn in 1947. I have already pointed out the prophetic observation in G. Voigt's *Wiederbelebung* (1859), that Salutati secured « Bürgerrecht », for humanism in Florence; cf. my *The Italian Renaissance in its Historical Background* (Cambridge, 1961), p. 121.

hardly refer to any secondary authorities, for the simple reason that the author could find little prior work that was relevant to his purposes, and knew his texts so well that he could with confidence base his argument on the original materials. Secondly, this acceptance of a basic seriousness in much of the literature, especially the Latin literature, suggested that there were good practical reasons lying behind the patronage of the humanist by the Florentine bourgeoisie. And this was even more strongly suggested by the argument that the humanist had justified a moral position (the compatibility of the active life and of wealth with the demands of Christian citizenship) which afforded a long overdue adjustment between the demands of official doctrine and the practical possibilities of ordinary life. The conscience of the literate citizen was gradually eased by a growing conviction that his normal pattern of life was not as offensive to God as he had been taught to think it was.

Moreover the urgencies of these readjustments involved looking at classical antiquity with new eyes, stripping away from the writers of Greece and Rome the garb which had clothed them in the Middle Ages, and which had in some ways been furbished up in the fourteenth century. If, as Baron argued, Aristotelian values were to be dominant in the successful acceptance of the Renaissance we are faced with the paradox that the century when Aristotle was most thoroughly studied in western Europe was the thirteenth. In fact the Aristotle and the Cicero of the schoolmen had been strangely transmogrified in earlier centuries. No passage in Baron's work is more telling than that in which he discussed Petrarch's discovery of Cicero's letters to Atticus and draws out its consequences for the poet and moralist, who « shrank back in horror » from the revelation of Cicero's profound and permanent interest in political power [20]. Later writers were to become

[20] « Cicero and the Roman Civic Spirit », pp. 16-17.

aware of an unavoidable distinction between their own days and the days of the ancient world. From this was to spring both the sense of identity with classical civilization and the sense of anachronism. These two elements in the cultural scene of the late fifteenth and sixteenth century were sometimes at war with one another. But that the first reinforced the new educational curriculum there can be no doubt, nor that the second was the mainspring in the evolution of a new historiography.

And, finally, this moral readjustment could easily be absorbed and applied in societies quite different from that of republican Florence, which had seen the new ideas emerge and had nourished them. If we substitute *subditus* for *civis* we are still left with the burden of the older tradition. Service of a prince, management of farms and estates was just as much involvement in the world as the activity of counting house and guild. But the arguments supporting the active life and wealth which had been evolved by humanists were not limited to republican situations but were equally applicable in the courts of popes, dukes and kings, in Italy and in the rest of Europe. Thus the educational innovations and the moral adjustments of the civic humanism of Florence could be readily received in the princely and monarchical parts of Italy and elsewhere, that is to say, in most of the Continent. As Baron said himself, in connection with the problem of wealth, « the internal connection between the new Aristotelianism and the spirit of the Renaissance becomes wholly evident when an attempt is made to look beyond the history of Italy » [21]. Had the innovations of the Renaissance been restricted to republics they would never have attained, as they did, the power to change the ethical, literary and artistic assumptions of the whole of Europe.

Burckhardt, product himself of an educational system which had its birth in the Renaissance, had scarcely felt

[21] « Franciscan poverty », p. 36.

the need to account in any chronological or narrative sense for the emergence of the new ideas but had sought rather to identify and analyse them. The notions of individualism, of modernity, of scepticism and *virtù*, of naturalism in art and the intellectual importance of the physical sciences were all as self-evident as a school curriculum based on Latin and Greek. « Causation », as Professor Wallace Ferguson sums it up, « was not his major interest » [22]. And in so far as Burckhardt fell back on Hegelian concepts such as the « spirit of Italy » he was both frustrating rational examination and inviting others to that vague impressionism of which he was seldom guilty himself. In writing in this way I do not mean to suggest an opposition which hardly exists. Baron would probably in the end be prepared to argue that Burckhardt's basic approach was correct and he has in fact suggested that, as sociology comes increasingly to influence historical research, so « the core of the Burckhardtian conception of the Renaissance ... may still prove superior to the competing views about the nature of the transition to the modern age » [23].

This last observation is taken from Baron's retrospective appraisal of Burckhardt which was published in 1960 on the centenary of the first publication of the *Civilization of the Renaissance in Italy* [24]. In this he stressed the existence long before Burckhardt of schemes of historical evolution which included the Renaissance, and argued that what Burckhardt contributed to this prior pattern was on the one hand a denial that the movement was to be received as an anticipation of the Enlightenment and on the other « rebuttals » of the « classicist belief » that the revival of ancient letters played a causal role. Likewise Burckhardt's

---

[22] *Renaissance in Historical Thought*, p. 189.

[23] Hans Baron, « Burckhardt's *Civilization of the Renaissance* a Century after its Publication », *Renaissance News*, XIII (1960), 222.

[24] *Ibid.*, pp. 207-222.

stress on individualism had a lengthy ancestry. None the less the synthesis had « solidity and vastness ». The main criticism to be levelled at its work (said Baron) was its neglect of « the rudimentary sociology of city-state life already prepared by the historians of the Enlightenment and of Romanticism » and this neglect was a consequence of Burckhardt's well-established aversion to « the rising democratic trend »[25]. When he wrote this Baron had already published in 1955 the *Crisis* with its supporting *Humanistic and Political Literature*[26]. The subtitle of the *Crisis* — « Civic humanism and Republican Liberty in an age of Classicism and Tyranny » — is one authoritative statement of the essence of these volumes. Another is to be found in the dedication of the *Crisis* to Walter Goetz, who taught the author « that history should be a study of both politics and culture ». In these volumes Baron expressly attempted the investigation of the connection between society and culture, between political situations and concomitant developments in historiography, political and educational theory.

It was, of course, the case that Burckhardt had treated the political situation in Italy as the background against which he placed his analysis of the spiritual and intellectual state of the peninsula. But it is also the case that he did not really discriminate between the moral and cultural pressures exerted by the different kinds of states to be found in Italy — republics, tyrannies and the two curious monarchies — the nonhereditary papacy and the kingdom of Naples, which was hereditary but with a tradition of dramatic dynastic fractures. Nor did Burckhardt really justify the title of the first section of the *Civilization of*

---

[25] *Ibid.*, p. 218.

[26] *The Crisis of the Early Italian Renaissance* (Princeton, 1955), 2 vols.; *Humanistic and Political Literature in Florence and Venice at the Beginning of the Quattrocento: Studies in Criticism and Chronology* (Cambridge, Mass., 1955). A completely revised and in part rewritten edition of the *Crisis* in one volume was published at Princeton in 1966.

the Renaissance in Italy, « The State as a work of art », as we can see when we look at the transition to the next section, part II « The development of the individual », where the first chapter begins « In the character of these states, whether republics or despotisms, lies not the only but the chief reason for the early development of the Italian ». Despotism, Burckhardt goes on to claim, particularly favoured individuality, in both the tyrant and his « tools » — ministers, courtiers and so on; but even in republics the precarious nature of governments meant that « the individual was led to make the utmost of the exercise and enjoyment of power »; while « the private man, indifferent to politics » but cultivating intellectual interests was thrown up in both tyrannies and republics [27]. This was to ignore the plain fact that the first clear statements of the new moral attitudes and the first novel creations in painting, sculpture and architecture are to be found, not in the tyrannies, but in republican Florence in the years adjacent to 1400.

Baron had long been working his way towards the position he was to take up in the *Crisis*. There is a bold indication of his future programme in 1938 [28], when the threat of Visconti conquest was advanced as the main reason for the emergence of a new outlook among Florentine patricians and humanists, in alliance with one another. What is equally important, he himself regarded this approach as continuing an existing, though weak, tradition, faintly discernible in the writings of David Hume and Adam Ferguson but with a more unequivocal spokesman in Paolo Emiliani-Giudici, who published his

---

[27] I quote from the Middlemore translation in the 1929 London edition, pp. 143-5. It is worth while pointing out that this handsome volume (published by Harrap) was the first time that an English version had appeared with illustrations. It was *remaindered* when I acquired my copy in 1933. The great *popular* interest in the Renaissance comes after the Second World War.

[28] « The Historical Background of the Florentine Renaissance », *History*, new ser. XXII (1938), 315-327.

Storia delle belle arti in Italia in 1844. This last book, « undoubtedly ... familiar to Burckhardt », certainly does contain some pregnant observations on the connections between politics and cultural changes in those quotations to which Baron draws our attention [29], but it seems a small and uncertain link between the hints of the Edinburgh philosophers of the eighteenth century and Baron's own confident and finely integrated thesis of 1955, with its re-examination of the composition and dating of many of the major texts.

Is Baron right in his interpretation of the cultural consequences of the Florentine-Milanese struggle at the time of Giangaleazzo, and the subsequent threat to Tuscan states of Ladislas of Naples and Filippo Maria Visconti? He has been criticised because, by making the Florence of Salutati and Bruni the turning point of the humanist story (as it so evidently is in the evolution of the arts), he has unduly depreciated the significance of Petrarch. To this he has himself replied [30]: Petrarch was more original, pointed more dramatically forwards, in his earlier than in his later days, and could not take the final step towards the New World of which he was in many ways the prophet. And in this same reply he goes on to indicate the telling fact that the political-cultural relationship had been successfully used as a framework for enquiry by other recent writers besides himself [31]. Further Baron's influence and the general acceptance of his interpretation are also witnessed by that form of flattery which consists in animadversion. The exchanges between Seigel and

---

[29] « Burckhardt's *Civilization* », p. 217.

[30] « Moot Problems of Renaissance Interpretation: An Answer to Wallace K. Ferguson », *Journal of the History of Ideas*, XIX (1958), 26-34, esp. pp. 28-9.

[31] Referring to his chapter on « Fifteenth-century Civilization and the Renaissance » in the *New Cambridge Modern History*, I (1957), 50-75 and the note on p. 73; he names Garin, von Albertini, Renaudet, Spongano, and Ferguson.

Baron in *Past and Present* are now matters of record, and it seems to the present writer that Hans Baron has the better of the debate [32]. What lies behind much of the hostile reaction is a pejorative view of classical rhetoric. This is, in many ways, a revival of the judgment of Burckhardt, Voigt and others, who were prepared to tolerate stylish Latin in poetry, oratory and letters, but who condemned it in serious prose; who regretted the urbanity (« how insipid and conventional ») of Bruni's history (for example) and compared it unfavourably with Giovanni Villani or Machiavelli writing history in the vernacular [33]. Classical rhetoric, which determined the structure of most of the serious Latin writing of the *quattrocento* and the *cinquecento*, came in time to dominate vernacular composition in Western European countries down to the nineteenth century. It is dangerous, therefore, to condemn classical rhetoric as such or regard as mere exercises the works written according to its rules. A work must be judged by its contents. « What so effectually proclaims the madman », asked Cicero himself, « as the hollow thundering of words — be they never so choice and resplendent — which have no thought or knowledge behind them? » [34]. Rhetoric is a means of communicating and of persuading. Modern vernaculars permit these functions still to be performed, though the rules have not been formulated.

Finally, it has been urged that the oligarchy of Florence in the period after the Ciompi rising was very narrow and lacked all « democratic » content, was, in short, little different from the personnel to be found in the princely courts. (This is an argument which harks back again to

---

[32] J. E. Seigel, « 'Civic Humanism' or Ciceronian Rhetoric? The Culture of Petrarch and Bruni », *Past and Present*, no. 34 (1966); Hans Baron, « Leonardo Bruni: 'Professional Rhetorician' or 'Civic Humanist'? », *Past and Present*, no. 36 (1967). For other critics see P. J. Jones' review of the second edition (1966) of the *Crisis* in *History*, LIII (1968), 410-13.

[33] Burckhardt, *Civilization* (1929), pp. 247-8.

[34] Cicero, *De Oratore*, I. XII. 51; trans. Sutton, Loeb ed., I. 39.

Burckhardt). Here too Baron is well-enough aware of the manipulation of power by the great families in Florence, but, as Professor Molho has shown recently, the « political class » of Florence, called on to man not only the nine-man signoria every other month, but the many other commissions and offices of the state, was in fact a relatively large body: « one would not be too far wrong in asserting that the Florentine oligarchy during the last two decades of the Trecento numbered some 2000 men »[35]. Likewise Professor Rubinstein has shown how cautiously fifteenth-century Medici leaders had to move, how uncertain they sometimes were of getting their own way, how in basic structure Florence remained a republic until the sixteenth century[36].

Cataloguing Baron's writings and defending him from criticism in the way I have done above gives, of course, an unbalanced view of his place in Renaissance historiography. As for the criticism, he can take care of himself very well and needs no help from me or anyone else. It would, however, be absurd to suggest that in his generation his has been the only major reassessment of fundamental questions regarding the Renaissance. There has been a great deal of other, independent work of profound importance, notably in the field of educational and philosophical ideas: the names of Cassirer, Kristeller and Garin impose themselves. And in art history, in literary history and in history *simpliciter* there have been and are many other equally important and equally independent researches.

Yet it is my impression that the possibilities for synthesis afforded by Baron's thesis are attracting the

---

[35] Anthony Molho, « The Florentine Oligarchy and the Balìe of the Late Trecento », *Speculum*, XLIII (1968), 27; and see the same writer's paper on « Politics and the Ruling Class in Early Renaissance Florence », *Nuova rivista storica*, LII (1968), 401-420. Cf. also Lauro Martines, *Lawyers and Statecraft in Renaissance Florence* (Princeton, 1968), pp. 388-9.

[36] Nicolai Rubinstein, *The Government of Florence under the Medici, 1434 to 1494* (Oxford, 1966).

attention of scholars in many fields. After all the social and political structures of our own day evidently affect our cultural preoccupations and ambitions. There is every reason to suppose that, at a few rare and exciting moments, these social and political factors may induce innovations in the moral and ideological pattern which in the long run can transform art, letters and certain aspects of public life. This enunciation of principle has to be expressed with great circumspection if it is to avoid both Marxist and other forms of determinism or the absurd conclusion that such occasions involve total transformations of every aspect of public life. I am myself not persuaded that those cultural innovations we summarise in the word Renaissance had much consequence for the *spiritual* history of the *quattrocento*. And the influence of humanism on government was not much greater: it helped on an existing trend towards the employment by princes in administration and diplomacy of literate laymen rather than clergy — an important but not a catastrophic development [37]. But surely there is no doubt that in many other respects what happened in Florence in the decades round 1400 was to colour deeply the whole picture of Europe in the course of the sixteenth century. This would have been impossible at the level of mere ratiocination or decoration. It represents fundamental ethical, educational and cultural motivation in the governing classes of virtually the whole continent which was largely supplied by the new attitudes adopted in Florence in the days of Salutati, Bruni, Masaccio, Brunelleschi and all the other heroes and their patrons.

Now this irradiation of European life could only happen when Florentine republicanism had ceased to be an enve-

---

[37] On this cf. F. Chabod's contribution to *Actes du colloque sur la Renaissance, Sorbonne 1956* (Paris, 1958). For diplomats see the book by Hans Baron's great friend (the second edition of the *Crisis* is dedicated to his memory) Garrett Mattingly, *Renaissance Diplomacy* (London, 1955).

lope round the fructifying ideas which were otherwise welcome in a society predominantly agrarian, where princes, courtiers and gentry were the cultural pace-setters. I am therefore sometimes inclined to feel that Hans Baron's careful investigation of the ethical world, of the gradual change from a formal acceptance of renunciation to a formal acceptance of the active life and of wealth, may in the end of the day prove to be a more enduring inspiration and influence than his equally careful investigation into the climate which encouraged such a development. At any rate I can only repeat my own sense of nourishment from both the rich feasts with which he has regaled us.

« Both the rich feasts ... » As I write this I realise how inadequately the figure two enumerates the Renaissance subjects with which Baron has passed so many creative years. There are his many studies of works of literature not directly related to the themes on which I have touched above — notably the major papers on Petrarch and Machiavelli — which are discussed elsewhere in this volume by Professor Buck [38]. And there are a whole series of investigations into Renaissance historiography ranging over a period of about forty years [39]. And what will he do next?

---

[38] See pp. XXXI-LVIII.

[39] From the Bruni studies of 1928 and « Das Erwachen des historischen Denkens im Humanismus des Quattrocento », *Historische Zeitschrift*, CXLVII (1933), down to a volume of collected essays, *From Petrarch to Leonardo Bruni* (Chicago, 1968), especially those on Dati and the « Early Renaissance Venetian Chronicles ».

AUGUST BUCK

HANS BARON'S CONTRIBUTION TO THE LITERARY HISTORY OF THE RENAISSANCE

Aside from the fact that Italian literature of the Renaissance in its entirety is permeated with the humanistic spirit, Italian humanism has also produced a specific literature which by virtue of its content and form can lay claim to a special chapter in literary history [1]. In general, the originality of humanistic literature is not found in the neo-Latin poetry, where the humanists tried to compose, in all conceivable poetic forms, innumerable encomiums, epithalamiums, and occasional verse in order to show off their knowledge of Latin prosody and their scholarship. Among the neo-Latin poets only a few had real talent. Even the Latin poetry of a person like Petrarch — his unfinished epic *Africa*, his *Epistolae metricae*, and his *Bucolicum carmen* — is poor in real poetic inspiration. All humanistic efforts to renew the Latin epic in the footsteps of Virgil and the Latin tragedy after the model of Seneca produced no works of high poetic stature.

It is only when the humanists, in dialogue with authors of antiquity, developed their own ideas in the « open forms » of the letter and the dialogue [2], two styles so favored by them, that they produced original creations in which the humanistic turn of mind found adequate expression. Of course, we also encounter in this aspect of humanistic literature mere repetitions of the train of thought of antiquity. But we should not dismiss the majority of the problems dealt with by the humanists as

---

[1] E. Garin has recently presented « La letteratura degli umanisti » from the death of Petrarch to the end of the fifteenth century in *Storia della letteratura italiana*, III: *Il Quattrocento e l'Ariosto*, (Milan, 1966), pp. 5-353.

[2] Letters and dialogues for the most part take the place of treatises.

« elegant variations on commonplaces » [3], as even a person like Ernst Robert Curtius has done. Whenever the humanists had recourse to ancient *topoi*, *dicta*, and sentences (which often happened) they debated such commonplaces from the perspective of their own anthropology, with the intention of illuminating the essence of man, his character, and his conduct in the light of his surroundings and of deriving from this process inferences for a new rule of life. This rule of life was supposed to point the way to an improvement of the personality and also to regulate interhuman relations in society. The importance to the modern world of this humanistic anthropology (first pointed out by Wilhelm Dilthey) [4] has been demonstrated in detail in the research of the last decades, thanks to a penetrating study of sources. This has nothing to do with philosophy in the strict sense of the word: The humanists were not, and did not want to be, philosophers. On the contrary, they had a pronounced antipathy to scholastic philosophy and its methods. The thing that distinguishes the unsystematic reflections of humanistic anthropology is a new self-knowledge of man, who, aware of his creative talents, gives to himself the form suitable to that awareness, and at the same time, as a shaping power, recasts his environment. In this way the humanists appear as the spiritual spokesmen for the Renaissance — the epoch which was the prelude to modern times.

Baron's work has been a decisive factor in the formation of this opinion about the historical role of the Italian humanists. He has analyzed the writings of a certain group of humanists under various aspects and in minute detail. From this basis he has succeeded in developing a new

---

[3] E. R. Curtius, *Gesammelte Aufsätze zur romanischen Philologie*, (Bern, 1960), p. 467.

[4] W. Dilthey, « Auffassung und Analyse des Menschen im 15. und 16. Jahrhundert », in his *Gesammelte Schriften, II: Weltanschauung und Analyse des Menschen seit Renaissance und Reformation*, (Leipzig, 1914), pp. 1-89.

conception of humanism, and in so doing he has brought about a fundamental revision of the traditional ideas in this branch of scholarship. In his research of more than forty years and in numerous individual investigations and three comprehensive books [5] Baron has with admirable consistency strengthened his thesis (once it had been established) by the citation of further examples and the use of new arguments, and has successfully defended it against critical objections [6].

If, more than any other, Baron has devoted his whole energy to the investigation of Italian humanism, he must have received valuable suggestions during his evolution as a scholar both in the subject and in the methods of his research. In the dedication of his chief work, he explains that Walter Goetz had introduced him to the Renaissance and taught him « that history should be a study of both politics and culture » [7]. With this, Baron subscribes to cultural history in the sense that Goetz understood it: a view which sees politics and culture not as opposites, but rather studies them in their reciprocal action. While using this method, Goetz dealt with themes from Italian history of the Middle Ages and the Renaissance and in so doing touched upon problems which were to be of interest to his pupil: the importance of the cities as political and cultural centers of medieval Italy, and in this connection the question of the education of the layman; further, the influence of antiquity in the Middle Ages and the Renaissance, and the genesis of the modern idea of

---

[5] *Humanistic and Political Literature in Florence and Venice at the Beginning of the Quattrocento, Studies in Criticism and Chronology*, (Cambridge, 1955); *The Crisis of the Early Italian Renaissance, Civic Humanism and Republican Liberty in an Age of Classicism and Tyranny*, (Princeton, 1955, 2 vols.); *The Crisis ... Revised One-Volume Edition with an Epilogue*, (Princeton, 1966).

[6] « Leonardo Bruni: 'Professional Rhetorician' or 'Civic Humanist'? », *Past and Present*, 36 (1967), 21-37. Italian version in *Critica storica*, 7 (1968), 1-19.

[7] *The Crisis*, 1955, dedication.

the Renaissance, and in particular a coming to terms with Jacob Burckhardt's *Kultur der Renaissance in Italien*[8].

Goetz, with all his appreciation of Burckhardt (who grasped « the characteristic content of the whole period [the Renaissance] » and who called attention to « new and modern elements »)[9], nevertheless found that Burckhardt had not satisfactorily solved a series of questions. For example, the relationship between the humanistic historian and his models in antiquity was by no means that of slavish dependency; in the Florence of the fifteenth century, original historical thinking developed from the « connection between the writing of history and political activity »[10]. This remark of Goetz sounds today like a cue which the teacher gave the pupil for his appearance before the scholarly world. For Baron began his research with the humanist Leonardo Bruni, the most prominent exponent of a fruitful union between the writing of history and activity in the service of the city-state Florence in the Quattrocento. Baron's introduction to the edition of Bruni's humanistic and philosophical writings[11] already develops a new conception of humanism, which corrects and completes the current image of humanism that goes back to Burckhardt.

When Jacob Burckhardt in his *Kultur der Renaissance in Italien* expresses his opinion about the position of the

---

[8] *König Robert von Neapel (1309-1343). Seine Persönlichkeit und sein Verhältnis zum Humanismus*, (Tübingen, 1910); *Italien im Mittelalter*, (Leipzig, 1942), 2 vols.; *Quellen zur Geistesgeschichte des Mittelalters und der Renaissance, hrsg. von W. Goetz* (*Veröffentlichungen der Forschungsinstitute an der Universität Leipzig. Institut für Kultur- und Universalgeschichte*). Goetz was the director of this institute. For Goetz's concept of cultural history, see his « Geschichte und Kulturgeschichte », *Archiv für Kulturgeschichte*, 8 (1910), 4-19.

[9] Goetz, *Italien im Mittelalter*, II, 156.

[10] *Ibid.*, II, 197 f.

[11] Leonardo Bruni Aretino, *Humanistisch-philosophische Schriften, mit einer Chronologie seiner Werke und Briefe, hrsg. und erläutert von Hans Baron*, (Leipzig, 1928). (Veröffentlichungen der Forschungsinstitute an der Universität Leipzig. Quellen zur Geistesgeschichte des Mittelalters und der Renaissance, hrsg. von Walter Goetz, 1. Bd.).

humanists in society, he calls them « a crowd of a hundred shapes which today displays one face and tomorrow another »; and further « a new element of civic society » [12], which was regarded as such by the period and by the humanists themselves. In Burckhardt's opinion the forerunners of the humanists were the wandering clerics of the twelfth century who had led « the same unstable existence » and represented « the same free and more than free view of life » [13].

The etymology of the word *humanista* (in Italian *umanista*) shows [14] that it was coined during the second half of the fifteenth century in university circles, in analogy with expressions like *legista*, *jurista*, *canonista*, and *artista*, as a designation first of all for a teacher of the *studia humanitatis*, and later for a scholar of antiquity in general. At the same time this word designated the way of life of those humanists who went as wandering teachers from university to university, representatives of a freely soaring intelligence, without social ties. A similar unstable existence was led by those humanists who earned their living as secretaries in the courts of secular and spiritual princes; they often changed masters and lent their facile pens to anyone — foreshadowing the modern journalist.

This kind of humanist has largely determined the idea which posterity has come to have of the group as a whole. It is still current today, as is shown by the following quotation from Hauser's much-read *Sozialgeschichte der Kunst und der Literatur*: « The social disinterestedness of the humanist is alienation, a flight from the present, a lack of responsibility. He refrains from all political activity so as

---

[12] Jacob Burckhardt, *Die Kultur der Renaissance in Italien, ein Versuch. Durchgesehen von Walter Goetz*, (Stuttgart, 1952), p. 185.

[13] *Ibid.*

[14] P. O. Kristeller, « Humanism and Scholasticism in the Italian Renaissance », *Byzantion*, 17 (1945), 346-374; A. Campana, « The Origin of the Word ' Humanist ' », *Journal of the Warburg and Courtauld Institutes*, 9 (1946), 60-73.

not to be tied down, but through his passivity he only strengthens the wielders of power in their position »[15]. Although it cannot be denied that there were politically indifferent humanists who were concerned only with the cultivation of their own personality (and even occasionally devoted themselves to a boundless enjoyment of life because of a misunderstanding of epicureanism), nevertheless the personal records and works of these humanists do not justify the stigmatizing of all humanists as characterless, uprooted men of letters.

Although Baron concedes that the humanism of the Quattrocento outside of Florence was almost everywhere a literary movement borne up by a « politically and socially unstable class of journalistic elements », he objects to the idea that this movement is considered « the type of the totality of Italian humanism in the Quattrocento »[16]. For, a broad and penetrating study of sources had brought Baron to the realization that there was a firmly established humanism in the Florence of the fifteenth century, whose rule of life was determined by a combination of literary and political development. This enlisted literary culture in the service of the state; it was a *Bürger-Humanismus*, as Baron has aptly called it. This term, devised in 1928, has since that time passed into the terminology of humanistic scholarship, in the Anglo-Saxon world as « civic humanism », and in Italy as « *umanesimo civile* ».

While Baron was investigating the relationship between politics and humanism in the city-state Florence, he discovered an intellectual tradition not previously noticed: the political consciousness of the medieval commune whose effect continued into the Renaissance. This political consciousness had arisen as an expression of the economic power enjoyed by the medieval Italian city-states and of

---

[15] A. Hauser, *Sozialgeschichte der Kunst und Literatur*, (Munich, 1953), I, 363.

[16] Bruni, *Humanistisch-philosophische Schriften*, p. XII (introduction).

the relative independence which this entailed. For this reason the development of Florence was quite typical. The first half of the fourteenth century saw the collapse of the leading class of wholesale merchants and bankers, which had arisen from the fusion of the middle class and the gentry, and to which the city at first owed its economic prosperity. Now a new society which owed its living primarily to the wool industry seized power. It was a society oriented toward power and full of self-assurance, open to the new ideas of humanism. If Baron has shown in detail the part played by this society as the social foundation of the Renaissance [17], he recognizes (analogously to the teachings of the historical sociology of a Max Weber) that culture is bound up not only with political but also with social development: « Intellectual life ... cannot be interpreted as an isolated process » [18].

At the end of the fourteenth and the beginning of the fifteenth century the Florentine middle class began to come to terms with the realm of humanistic ideas. This happened at a period in which Florence was most seriously threatened in its continuance as an independent city-state by the expansionist politics of Milan. Humanism gained political relevance under the influence of this « crisis ». The *virtus* and *libertas* of Rome came alive in the self-reliance of the city struggling for independence. When Florence defended middle-class freedom from the threatening tyranny of the Visconti, it was continuing the tradition of the Roman Republic and creating the prerequisite for the flowering of culture, which can thrive only in a freely organized civic situation: in the *polis* of antiquity and in its modern reincarnation, the city-state Florence.

---

[17] « A Sociological Interpretation of the Early Renaissance in Florence », *The South Atlantic Quarterly*, 38 (1939), 427-448; « The Social Background of Political Liberty in the Early Italian Renaissance », *Comparative Studies in Society and History*, 2 (1959-60), 440-451.

[18] « A Sociological Interpretation ... », p. 427.

Baron has been able to set forth convincingly the development of the new convictions of civic humanism by means of two themes: the change in the image of Cicero, and the altered attitude toward wealth [19]. In both instances observation starts with Petrarch. For Baron, Petrarch is the prototype of the literary humanist, who arranged his life in the seclusion of Vaucluse partly according to the ideal of the stoic manner and partly according to that of the Christian monk [20]. When Petrarch discovered Cicero's Atticus letters and hence opened up a new approach to Cicero's personality, he deplored the intervention of the aged Cicero in everyday political disputes: A false glitter of fame had blinded Cicero; it would have been much more useful to him if he had devoted himself to philosophical meditation in the quiet of the country [21].

Cicero's political involvement, for which Petrarch had no understanding, could gain its proper evaluation only in connection with the « rebirth of Roman political ethics ». Coluccio Salutati, who, although a pupil of Petrarch, had nevertheless through his activity as chancellor of Florence become the first civic humanist, admired Cicero the politician and approved of his active intervention in the struggle for Roman freedom, since in doing so he was

---

[19] « La Rinascita dell'etica statale romana nell'umanesimo fiorentino del Quattrocento », *Civiltà moderna*, 7 (1935), 21-49; « Cicero and the Roman Civic Spirit in the Middle Ages and Early Renaissance », *Bulletin of the John Rylands Library*, 22 (1938), 72-97; « Franciscan Poverty and Civic Wealth as Factors in the Rise of Humanistic Thought », *Speculum*, 13 (1938), 1-37.

[20] Baron's detailed investigations of Petrarch (« The Evolution of Petrarch's Thought: Reflections on the State of Petrarch Studies », *Bibliothèque d'humanisme et Renaissance*, 24 (1962), 7-41, reprinted in H. Baron, *From Petrarch to Leonardo Bruni, Studies in Humanistic and Political literature*, (Chicago, 1968), pp. 7-50; « Petrarch's *Secretum*: was it Revised — and why? The Draft of 1342-43 and the Later Changes », *Bibliothèque d'humanisme et Renaissance*, 25 (1963), 489-530, reprinted in *From Petrarch to Leonardo Bruni*, pp. 51-101) and his numerous observations about Petrarch in various other places leads us to hope that Baron will write a book about Petrarch.

[21] Petrarch, *Le familiari, edizione critica per cura di Vittorio Rossi* [*ed Umberto Bosco*], (Florence, 1933-42) [Edizione nazionale delle opere di Francesco Petrarca, 10-13], Liber XXIV, 3 (vol. 4, pp. 226 f.).

only fulfilling an obvious civic duty [22]. The same view is expressed in Leonardo Bruni's biography of Cicero, the *Cicero novus*, which he, as the most important of the Florentine civic humanists, intended as a replacement for Plutarch's presentation of Cicero in the *Parallel Lives*. Bruni thought of Cicero the philosopher and Cicero the politician as a single entity. Philosophical ideas had determined his political attitude; philosophy and politics joined in the service of the *respublica*. The very fact that Cicero was able to perform outstandingly in both fields made him an exalted model for posterity.

Matteo Palmieri, « the citizen closest to Bruni in thought and feeling » [23], derived inspiration from Cicero's moral philosophy in the writing of an educational program for citizens — his treatise *Della vita civile*. It culminates in an apotheosis of the *vita activa politica*; the wording is modelled closely on Cicero's *Somnium Scipionis*: « Resta dunque che in terra non si faccia niuna cosa più cara nè più accetta a Dio, che con iustizia reggere e governare le congregazioni e moltitudini d'uomini, unitamente con iustizia ragunati: per questo promette Iddio a' giusti governatori delle città, e conservatori della patria, in cielo determinato luogo, nel quale eternalmente beati vivono co' suoi santi ... » [24].

The self-sufficient existence of an *otium cum litteris* in solitude, which Petrarch opposed to Cicero's political activity, also determined his attitude toward possessions and wealth. Here we again encounter both stoic and Chri-

---

[22] Salutati, *Epistolario, a cura di Francesco Novati*, (Rome, 1891-1905) (Fonti per la storia d'Italia, 15-18). Libro 8, no. 7, vol. 2, p. 389; libro 9, no. 3 and 4, vol. 3, pp. 25 f. and 50.

[23] Baron, « Franciscan Poverty », p. 22.

[24] Palmieri, *Della vita civile ... a cura di Felice Battaglia*, (Bologna, 1944), p. 45. Cf. Cicero, *De re publica*, VI, 13. Baron has pointed out the lack of an analysis of *Della vita civile* (*Crisis*, 1955, II, 576). A. Buck has attempted such an analysis in a chapter of his *Die humanistische Tradition in der Romania*, (Bad Homberg v. d. H., 1968), pp. 253-270: « Matteo Palmieri als Repräsentant des Florentiner Bürger-Humanismus ».

stian elements: The stoical disdain for *bona externa*, and the Franciscan ideal of poverty. Since the social position of the literary humanists was precarious, they regarded their existence as justified in the stoic way, by its indifference to public opinion and to material possessions. So far as they relied on *exempla paupertatis* in Roman history, it is significant that as early as the fourteenth century Florentine humanists began to become aware of the political aspects which the admiration for poverty had taken on in certain Roman authors. For them, poverty had been equivalent to the simple life of the Roman citizen of the early period, the *exemplum virtutis* of later generations.

The actual change in attitude toward wealth was first introduced by Leonardo Bruni in fifteenth-century Florence. Having translated the *Nichomachean Ethics* and the *Economics* of pseudo-Aristotle, he found in Aristotle a confirmation of the idea that the individual person is bound by duty to do service in the community; he also found there a moral justification for wealth. Citing Aristotle, he proclaimed that man as a creature made up of body and soul needs material as well as spiritual possessions and may enjoy them both. Stoic asceticism seemed inhuman to him. With conscious opposition to the *stoa*, Matteo Palmieri emphasized the positive significance of *utile* for civic social life in the city-state. The need to gain wealth through honorable labor is a completely legitimate one. It is only after the citizen has this wealth that he is in a position to exercise such a virtue as generosity, as well as to support the *respublica*, and to heighten the splendor of his city by erecting buildings: « ... però che lo sprezzare l'utile, il quale iustamente si può conseguitare, merita biasimo, nè in alcuno modo si confà a chi è virtuoso »[25].

For Leon Battista Alberti's ideal head of a family the retention or increase of fortune becomes a sacred duty. Under the influence of Xenophon's *Oeconomicus*, which

---

[25] Palmieri, *Della vita civile*, p. 129.

had been known in Italy since 1427, Alberti drafted a program of thrifty household management with a balanced budget, which helped the citizen to gain wealth and thereby gave him the possibility of acquiring esteem. Wealth is therefore by no means to be disdained, provided that the rich man can be moderate in his demands. So far as research [26] into Alberti's first attempts at a theory of capitalism has been able to establish, the justification of wealth developed within the framework of Florentine civic humanism retained its influence beyond the Quattrocento and into the modern period: « When in the sixteenth century ' divitiae ' had finally regained their vindication in European thought, the period of Florentine civic history which had been the first condition for the emergence of the new valuation of life was already at an end » [27].

Civic humanism, which began about 1400 with the « crisis of the early Italian Renaissance », attained full maturity in the Florence of the first half of the Quattrocento. The principle from which the educational ideal of civic humanism proceeded had already been expressed in diaries and autobiographies written by Florentine merchants: the education of youth as a function of the *civitas*, the city-state [28]. As to the need for such a civic and political education, the civic humanists cited Aristotle and Cicero as principal witnesses [29]. These were the two an-

---

[26] W. Sombart, *Der Bourgeois; zur Geistesgeschichte des modernen Wirtschaftsmenschen*, (Munich, 1913). For Sombart, Alberti embodies « the perfect type of the ' bourgeois ' during the Quattrocento » (p. 136). A. Fanfani, *Le origini dello spirito capitalistico in Italia*, (Milan, 1933).

[27] « Franciscan Poverty », p. 36.

[28] C. Bec, *Les marchands écrivains; affaires et humanisme à Florence 1375-1434*, (Paris, 1967), a study that confirms Baron's achievements and supplements it in some points.

[29] For Florentine studies of Aristotle, see Baron, *Crisis*, 1966, entry « Aristotle » in the index (p. 565). E. Garin, *La cultura filosofica del Rinascimento italiano*, (Florence, 1961), pp. 60-71 (« La fortuna dell'etica aristotelica nel Quattrocento »). For Cicero's posthumous fame, see Baron, « Cicero and the Roman civic spirit ».

cient philosophers who most forcibly taught the virtues that maintain the state, by which the citizen should be guided in social affairs.

A study which serves to develop civic virtues can only be carried out in close contact with society. In Bruni's words: « And here ... I must rectify the mistake made by many ignorant people. They believe that nobody is a student who does not bury himself in solitude and leisure. Among the stay-at-homes, withdrawn from human society, I have never seen one who could count up to three. A lofty and distinguished mind does not need such fetters ... To stand aside from social intercourse is characteristic of those whose inferior minds are incapable of understanding anything »[30]. In Baron's opinion, « the civic spirit of fifteenth-century Florence could not have found more characteristic expression ... »[31]. As to the various branches of learning, it is obvious that the civic humanist preferred moral to natural philosophy, being here in agreement with the general humanistic concept of knowledge. Both Bruni and Palmieri are convinced that the part of philosophy devoted to the knowledge of nature is far less profitable than the philosophy which is most especially concerned with man himself and which is to guide him throughout his life[32].

History is at least as important as moral philosophy. The special interest in the study of history as a source of political experiences is characteristic of the ideology of

---

[30] « ... mi giova riprendere l'errore di molti ignoranti, i quali credono, niuno essere studiante, se non quelli, che si nascondono in solitudine ed in ozio; ed io non vidi mai niuno di questi camuffati e rimossi dalla conversazione delli uomini che sapesse tre lettere. Lo 'ngegno alto e grande non ha bisogno di tali tormenti ... Sicchè stranarsi e levarsi dalla conversazione è al tutto di quelli, che niente sono atti col loro basso ingegno ad imprendere ». Bruni, *Humanistisch-philosophische Schriften*, p. 53. (The English version is from Baron, « A sociological interpretation », pp. 447-448).

[31] « A sociological interpretation », p. 448.

[32] Bruni, *Humanistisch-philosophische Schriften*, p. 21. Repeated almost word for word in Palmieri, *Della vita civile*, pp. 24-25.

civic humanism[33]. Bruni, in his scheme of study, *De studiis et litteris*, attaches special importance to the knowledge of history: « Dirigit enim prudentiam et consilium praeteritorum notitia, exitusque similium coeptorum nos pro re nata aut hortantur aut deterrent »[34]. Alluding to the *topos*, *veritas filia temporis*, which goes back to Aulus Gellius, Palmieri explained « veritatis profecto cognitionem dant tempora » and concludes from this the necessity for historical studies as *civilis disciplina*[35]. As Machiavelli interpreted Palmieri at a later date, the political experience of the present and that part of the past which has been deposited in history are the two sources to which he owed his knowledge.

If the practical life of every Florentine citizen was to be shaped according to the image aspired to by the civic humanist, this goal could be attained only to the extent that people were prepared to use not only Latin, but also the Italian language, the *volgare*, to propagate the ideology of civic humanism. When the civic humanists, on the basis of this insight, used the *volgare* they resolved a problem which was to have far-reaching consequences for the history of Italian ideas and literature. On the one hand, it was the beginning of the so-called vulgar humanism, that is, the spread of humanistic ideas throughout a public that was ignorant of Latin. On the other, the structure of the Italian literary language was changed under the influence of humanists writing in Italian. To a certain extent the stylistic laws of humanistic rhetoric were carried over into the vernacular. Even before the publication of the first version of Baron's *Crisis* (1955) the idea of an insurmountable prejudice of the Florentine humanists against the *volgare* had been given up; in place of this there

---

[33] Baron, « Secularization of Wisdom and Political Humanism in the Renaissance », *Journal of the History of Ideas*, 21 (1960), 141 f.

[34] Bruni, *Humanistisch-philosophische Schriften*, p. 13.

[35] Palmieri, *De captivitate Pisarum*, preface. Cited from Baron, « Secularization of Wisdom », p. 142.

appeared the conception that the humanistic and vernacular traditions had permeated one another during the course of the Quattrocento [36]. Baron was able to explain this process of the gradual rapprochement of Latin and the *volgare* ideologically when he connected this process with the formation of civic humanism.

In the eyes of the Florentine citizens the works in the vernacular of Dante, Petrarch, and Boccaccio represented a claim to glory for their city-state. When Giovanni da Prato proclaimed his eulogy of the mother tongue (which was ennobled by the « tre corone fiorentine ») he addressed himself expressly to his fellow citizens, « who devote their entire time and attention to the affairs of our hallowed republic so as to maintain it in its precious freedom » [37]. The acknowledgement of the outstanding qualities of the *volgare* is therefore a thing which concerns the responsible citizen: « ... l'edioma fiorentino è sì rilimato e copioso che ogni astratta e profonda materia si puote chiarissimamente con esse dire, ragionarne e disputarne » [38].

When Giovanni da Prato wrote down this proposition (in 1425-26, according to Baron's new dating of the *Paradiso degli Alberti*) the reconciliation between the humanists and the vernacular tradition had already been going on for a considerable period of time. This is indicated by Bruni's attitude. Under the influence of the civic humanism that was awakening within him he altered his opinion about Dante, at the highpoint of the crisis in the struggle against Milan. In the first of the *Dialogi ad Petrum Paulum Histrum* (newly dated before autumn 1401 by Baron)

---

[36] R. Spongano, *Un capitolo di storia della nostra prosa d'arte* (*la prosa letteraria del Quattrocento*), (Florence, 1941); reprinted in his *Due saggi sull'umanesimo*, (Florence, 1964), pp. 37-78; A. Buck, *Italienische Dichtungslehren vom Mittelalter bis zum Ausgang der Renaissance*, (Tübingen, 1952), pp. 97-112.

[37] Giovanni da Prato, *Il paradiso degli Alberti, ritrovi e ragionamenti del 1389, romanzo, a cura di Alessandro Wesselofsky*, (Bologna, 1867), II, 2.

[38] *Paradiso degli Alberti*, III, 84.

he still sharply criticized Dante. But in the second dialogue (which Baron dates, very probably correctly, autumn 1405) he has changed his mind and now expresses himself in positive terms about the poet of the *Divina commedia*. In the *Laudatio Florentinae Urbis*, written after 1402, he celebrates Florence not only for its leading position in the field of *studia humanitatis* but also as the city where the purest Italian is spoken.

Bruni made the decisive step in the recognition of Italian as a literary language when he himself began to write in the *volgare* after 1420. Even the first example of this, the *Canzone morale, nella quale si tratta della felicità, referendo l'oppinioni de' filosofi* [39], in which he discusses a question often dealt with in humanistic ethics, indicates that he considered the *volgare* capable of rendering the same subject content as Latin. The answer which Bruni gave to the question is in accord with the affirmation of the *vita activa politica* through civic humanism: « La virtù piena e perfetta operando ci assetta nello stato felice desto mondo » [40].

Bruni's most important achievement in the field of Italian literature is *Le vite di Dante e di Petrarca* [41], which Baron has re-interpreted in the perspective of civic humanism. In connection with his evaluation of Dante, Bruni establishes the equivalence of Latin and Italian: « Lo scrivere in istile litterato o vulgare non ha a fare al fatto, nè altra differenza è, se non come scrivere in greco od in latino. Ciascuna lingua ha sua perfezione e suo suono e suo parlare limato e scientifico ... » [42]. And with this, the use of the vernacular in Dante's work seemed justified against all humanistic criticism. Dante's life is a model for the citizen who fulfills his duties to his family and to

---

[39] Bruni, *Humanistisch-philosophische Schriften*, pp. 149-154.
[40] *Ibid.*, p. 154.
[41] *Ibid.*, pp. 50-69.
[42] *Ibid.*, p. 61.

the state without allowing these duties to interfere with his learned studies. Rejecting Boccaccio's criticism of Dante's marriage, which according to Boccaccio may have hindered his intellectual labor, Bruni strengthens his concept of man as an *animale civile*, a social creature, for whom the primary form of association, marriage, is completely adequate, and which assures the growth of the state.

Bruni took the writing of Petrarch's biography as an occasion for developing a thesis fundamental to his concept of history: the dependence of cultural development on civic life in the history of Italy. Latin literature and learned studies had flowered in the period of the Roman Republic and declined with the loss of freedom under the tyrannical emperors. Inversely, cultural life in medieval Italy could only develop when, after the invasion of the barbarians, the Italian communes regained their old freedom. Only after political progress had taken place in the free city-states was the revival of *litterae*, that began with Petrarch, possible; Bruni equates the cultivation of letters completely « with cultural flowering » [43].

Bruni continued what Petrarch had started. Palmieri celebrated Bruni as the « padre e ornamento delle lettere » who had restored to his fellow man the « dolcezza della latina lingua » [44]. Significantly, he did this in a treatise written in Italian, *Della vita civile*, during a digression in his presentation of a plan of studies for rising citizens. This is an indication that, for Palmieri, the humanistic and vernacular traditions had been extensively merged in the developmental ideal of civic humanism.

L. B. Alberti (next to Bruni probably the most important Florentine humanist in the Quattrocento) again raised the question as to the literary stature of the vernacular in his *Libri della famiglia*, written at about the same time

---

[43] *Ibid.*, p. XVII.

[44] Palmieri, *Della vita civile*, p. 37.

as Palmieri's *Vita civile*. Regardless of his esteem for Latin, in which he himself wrote both prose and poetry, he recognized that the future must belong to the vernacular, which had no need to feel inferior to Latin: « Ben confesso quella antiqua latina lingua essere copiosa molto e ornatissima, ma non però veggo che sia la nostra oggi toscana tanto d'averla in odio, che in essa qualunque benché ottima cosa scripta ci dispiaccia » [45]. Italian will assume the same rank as Latin, provided that the scholars (that is, the humanists) espouse its cause. « E sia quanto dicono quella antica apresso di tutte le genti pieno d'autorità, solo perché in essa molti dotti scrissero, simile certo sarà la nostra s'e' dotti la vorranno molto con suo studio et vigilie essere elimata e polita » [46].

Setting the example, Alberti himself preceded his contemporaries along this path: In the *Books About the Family* and in other treatises he offered specimens of an Italian prose that was fashioned according to the humanistic feeling for form. He wrote poetry in Italian; organized the *certame coronario*, a poetical competition for Italian poets; and very probably wrote the *Regole della lingua fiorentina* [47], which subjugated the use of the vernacular to norms determined from Latin models. The program of the development of Italian to a literary language equivalent to the classical languages was based on the principle, set forth by the *Regole*, of the derivation of the vernacular grammar from that of Latin. This program was formulated by Pietro Bembo in the sixteenth century, and he and his contemporaries put it into practice.

The process of mutual permeation of humanistic and vernacular traditions introduced by civic humanism continued in Florence even after the *Signoria* of the Medici

---

[45] L. B. Alberti, « I libri della famiglia, proemio del libro terzo », in his *Opere volgari, a cura di Cecil Grayson*, (Bari, 1960), I, 155.

[46] *Ibid.*, pp. 155 f.

[47] L. B. Alberti, *La prima grammatica della lingua volgare ... a cura di Cecil Grayson*, (Bologna, 1964).

had taken the place of the liberal republican order of the city-state. Lorenzo de' Medici derived from the classical literary languages the four conditions which, in his opinion, a language must fulfill before its dignity and perfection can be recognized: adequate expressional capability, harmonic form, general usefulness for the subjects dealt with, and universal diffusion. The Florentine language met the first three conditions, as, above all, the three great writers of the Trecento, Dante, Petrarch, and Boccaccio, had shown; they could measure up to the classical authors. The fulfillment of the fourth requirement depends not only on its inner quality but also on external circumstances. And here Lorenzo, following in this point the tradition of civic humanism, establishes the connection with politics: the Florentine language, still quite new, will spread all the more quickly if « qualche prospero successo ed augmento al fiorentino imperio » should favor such an extension [48].

Even this ideal continuity in the language question indicates that by no means all of the developmental tendencies of civic humanism that had emerged in the first decades of the Quattrocento had been interrupted by the establishment of the *Signoria*. Although Cosimo de' Medici had a constantly growing influence on the government of the city, he allowed the republican constitution to continue in force, and in this way the transition to the *Signoria* was gradually accomplished. Both Cosimo and Lorenzo il Magnifico were able to give the citizenry the impression that it was still participating in a city-state. To be sure, this participation shifted from practical politics into the sphere of philosophical and literary discussions, such as had been customary in the circles of intellectual citizens in Florence since the Trecento.

---

[48] Lorenzo de' Medici, « Comento del Magnifico Lorenzo de' Medici sopra alcuni de' suoi sonetti », in his *Opere, a cura di Attilio Simioni*, (Bari, 1939), I, 21.

In this social framework the ideal of life of civic humanism encountered the tendency (which arose with the *Signoria*) toward an unpolitical existence devoted to philosophical meditation, as represented by the Platonism revived by Marsilio Ficino. The dialogue between the representatives of these two intellectual attitudes in Cristoforo Landino's *Disputationes Camaldulenses* (« a confrontation of two clearly differentiated phases of humanism »)[49] reflects the theoretical arguments that arose between these two attitudes. Landino, who, like the civic humanists, harmonized the humanistic and vernacular traditions (« è necessario essere Latino chi vuole essere buono Toscano »)[50], and who wrote Italian commentaries on Dante's *Commedia* and Petrarch's *Canzoniere*, considered *vita activa* and *vita contemplativa* to be complementary; he emphasized a point of view that linked the ways of life: Whoever exercises political power must of necessity use power correctly because of insights gained from meditation. This interpretation of the *Disputationes*[51] confirms the mediating role which Baron ascribes to Landino.

If in this work Landino's aim was to lecture Lorenzo de' Medici, the lecture was little heeded. For Lorenzo showed no inclination in his personal regime to respect the traditional *Florentina libertas*. In his dialogue *De libertate*[52], Alamanno Rinuccini bitterly complained about the suppression of free opinion by the Medicean tyrannies

---

[49] E. Müller-Bochat, *Leon Battista Alberti und die Vergil-Deutung der Disputationes Camaldulenses; zur allegorischen Dichter-Erklärung bei Cristoforo Landino*, (Krefeld, 1968), p. 7.

[50] Baron, *Crisis*, 1966, pp. 353, 539. Cf. also, A. Buck, « Dichtung und Dichter bei Cristoforo Landino, ein Beitrag zur Dichtungslehre des italienischen Humanismus », *Romanische Forschungen*, 58-59 (1947), 233-246.

[51] Müller-Bochat, *Leon Battista Alberti.*

[52] A. Rinuccini, *Dialogus de libertate, a cura di F. Adorno*, (Florence, 1958). Cf. also V. R. Giustiniani, *Alamanno Rinuccini, 1426-1499; Materialien und Forschungen zur Geschichte des florentinischen Humanismus*, (Cologne, 1965), pp. 243 ff.

and evoked as a contrast the free communes of the Middle Ages. Thus, the tradition of civic humanism continued to survive even under the *Signoria* of the Medici, but it did not of course become politically effective. It was not until after the overthrow of the Medici in 1494 that a political discussion nourished by civic-humanistic ideas flared up again. This continued even during the restoration of the Medici (1512-1517), and did not die out until 1530, when the Florentine Republic ceased to exist[53].

A focus of political discussions (echoing the individuality of Florentine intellectual life) was the private meetings in the palace and garden of a distinguished citizen, Bernardo Rucellai[54] (the *Orti Oricellari*), where, rather than drawing up the image of an ideal state, they discussed realizable reforms on the basis of concrete historical actuality. Machiavelli was also a participant in these discussions during the very years when he was working on his *Discorsi* and when he was writing the dialogues on the *Arte della guerra*. The latter dealt with a theme that also occupied the *Orti Oricellari*[55], and for this reason the scene of the book was logically laid in this place.

This connection with the *Orti Oricellari* reveals how closely Machiavelli was imbued with the ideology of civic humanism. The author of *Il principe* and the *Discorsi*, commonly regarded as the founder of modern political science, is thus in accord with the realization to which Leonardo Bruni had come eight decades earlier in his preface to the translation of Aristotle's *Politics*: « ... nulla

---

[53] R. von Albertini, *Das florentinische Staatsbewusstsein im Übergang von der Republik zum Prinzipat*, (Bern, 1955). According to Baron, Albertini has clearly recognized « the close connection between Bruni's civic humanism and the historical philosophy of early-sixteenth-century Florence ... » (*Crisis*, 1966, p. 465).

[54] F. Gilbert, « Bernardo Rucellai and the Orti Oricellari, a Study on the Origin of Modern Political Thought », *Journal of the Warburg and Courtauld Institutes*, 12 (1949), 101-131.

[55] Albertini, *Das florentinische Staatsbewusstsein*, p. 82.

profecto convenientior disciplina homini esse potest, quam, qui sit civitas et quid res publica, intelligere et, per quae conservetur intereatque civilis societas, non ignorare »[56]. In agreement with Bruni, Machiavelli admired the civic consciousness of the Roman Republic as an expression of the *virtù* that upholds the state, and deplored its destruction by the Empire. Besides, an empire offers an unfavorable culture-medium for political talent. In a reversal of Dante's statement that an empire represents a necessity because a multitude of kingdoms is an evil[57], Machiavelli explained: « ... dove è assai potestadi, vi surga assai valenti uomini; dove ne è poche, pochi »[58]. Through the same interpretation of Roman history Bruni and Machiavelli drew the same conclusions for modern times. Bruni, in his treatise *De militia*, set up the ideal of the *civis armatus* who defends the fatherland and in this way makes the state self-sufficient[59] — an ideal which Palmieri also subscribed to[60]. Similarly, Machiavelli, in his *Dell'arte della guerra*, turned against the use of mercenaries and called for a citizen army[61].

Considering this ideological connection with civic humanism, it is not surprising that Baron extended the field of his research to include Machiavelli[62]. In contrast to

---

[56] Bruni, « Praemissio quaedam ad evidentiam novae translationis Politicorum Aristotelis », in his *Humanistisch-philosophische Schriften*, p. 73.

[57] Dante, *De monarchia*, I, V-XV.

[58] Machiavelli, « Dell'arte della guerra », in his *Opere, a cura di Antonio Panella*, (Milan, 1939), II, 540.

[59] C. C. Bayley, *War and Society in Renaissance Florence; the De militia of Leonardo Bruni*, (Toronto, 1961).

[60] Buck, *Die humanistische Tradition*, p. 266.

[61] Even when the ideal of the *vita activa politica* had faded in Florence, the aversion to mercenaries persisted. Cf. Baron, *Crisis*, 1966, pp. 435 f.

[62] « The *Principe* and the Puzzle of the Date of the *Discorsi* », *Bibliothèque d'humanisme et Renaissance*, 18 (1956), 405-428; « Marvell's ' An Horatian Ode ' and Machiavelli », *Journal of the History of Ideas*, 21 (1960), 450-451; « Machiavelli on the Eve of the *Discourses*: the Date and Place of his *Dialogo intorno alla nostra lingua* », *Bibliothèque d'humanisme et Renaissance*, 23 (1961), 449-476; « Machiavelli: the Republican Citizen and the Author

an opinion that is widespread in the scholarship on this subject, Baron is convinced that any attempt to harmonize the political ideas of *Il principe* and the *Discorsi* is inevitably doomed to failure because the conception of the two works is fundamentally different. Baron convincingly demonstrates that no parts of the *Discorsi* were written before *Il principe*, but that the whole of the *Discorsi* was written afterwards. In this way he can account for the difference between them from the development of Machiavelli's historical-political thinking. *Il principe* represents the results of experiences and reflections of a first phase in Machiavelli's intellectual development, which at that time was under the influence of the struggles of the great powers for control of Italy, a struggle that was provoked by the French invasion. In *Il principe* Machiavelli wanted to offer to the longed-for liberator of Italy from foreign domination a practical technique for political action. The *Discorsi*, on the other hand, grew out of Machiavelli's contact with the tradition of civic humanism in the *Orti Oricellari* and affirm a liberal, republican government.

With the *Istorie fiorentine* Machiavelli's historical-political thinking entered its third and final stage of development. « In the melancholy light » [63] of a changed historical perspective, Machiavelli resignedly established that the freedom of Florence had consumed itself in the centuries-long partisan struggles, and that the domination of the Medici represented the natural result of this process. The resulting re-interpretation of the old concept of freedom under the sign of the principality of the Medici was formulated at the end of the century by Gian Battista Guarini. In his *Trattato della politica libertà*, freedom no longer means the citizen's participation in politics and hence in the state.

---

of *The Prince* », *The English Historical Review*, 76 (1961), 217-253; « Machiavelli's Development: a propos of the New Edition of Ridolfi's *Vita di Niccolò Machiavelli* », *Bibliothèque d'humanisme et Renaissance*, 26 (1964), 253-255.

[63] Baron, « Machiavelli: the Republican Citizen », p. 250.

By freedom Guarini understands the protection of private existence by the state which provides for peace and order. The free citizens of the city-republic Florence had become subjects of the Grand Duke of Tuscany [64].

Baron's creative interpretation of the intellectual history of the Quattrocento on the basis of Florentine civic humanism is linked to a conception of the Italian Renaissance which precedes Burckhardt, and the outlines of which first became visible with J. C. L. Sismondi [65]. This conception, reduced to a formula, states: Civic freedom liberated the creative powers which produced the civilization of the Renaissance. Florence owes to the union of politics and humanism its position of supremacy in the cultural life of the fifteenth century.

Leonardo Bruni was probably more aware of this cultural primacy than any other of his contemporaries, and he expressed this awareness in various passages in his work, most impressively in the *Laudatio Florentinae Urbis*, to which Baron has given special attention for a long time, and the first edition of which he has recently published [66]. The *Laudatio*, inspired by the *Panathenaikos* of the Greek rhetorician Aelius Aristides, is an example of the creative *imitatio* characterizing the outstanding performances of humanistic literature, which in the process of competing with its model creates something altogether new. On the basis of the historical parallelism between the ancient *polis* and the modern city-state, Bruni compares the cultural primacy of Florence in Italy with that of Athens in Greece. Florence, which plays a leading role both in *studia humanitatis* and in the vernacular literature, has the rank of a modern rival to Athens and Rome. As

---

64 Albertini, *Das florentinische Staatsbewusstsein*, pp. 293 ff.

65 J. C. L. Simonde de Sismondi, *Histoire des républiques italiens du moyen âge ... 4. éd.*, (Brussels, 1826), 12 vols.; *Histoire de la liberté en Italie*, (Brussels, 1841).

66 *From Petrarch to Leonardo Bruni*, pp. 217-263. For an interpretation of the *Laudatio*, see *Crisis*, 1955, I, 163-189, and *From Petrarch ...*, pp. 151-171.

the geometrical center of the surrounding countryside and thanks to the harmony of its inner structure, Florence realizes the ideal of the perfect city envisioned by the Renaissance.

Bruni's *Laudatio* of the flowering of Italian culture in the Quattrocento under the aegis of Florence is confirmed by Baron's research. The Florentine civic humanism, which prevented a hegemony of Milan and preserved freedom, thus created the prerequisite for the development of cultural potentialities which, under the tyranny of the Visconti, could not have happened to the same extent and in the same way. Parallel to the Latin and Italian literature initiated by civic humanism, there was a flowering of fine arts and a beginning of natural science; the latter had by no means stagnated in the Quattrocento, as is occasionally asserted [67]. With this evaluation which Baron has been able to make from the abundance of his new insights into the intellectual structure of the century, he has been a pioneer in its rehabilitation. For a long time the Quattrocento had been little noticed, and De Sanctis's statement about the supposedly « religious, moral, and political indifference » [68] of the fifteenth century was generally accepted without demur. But Renaissance scholarship of the last decades in increasing measure has become interested in this epoch and has recognized its importance [69]. This importance stands and falls with Florentine civic humanism.

---

[67] Baron, « Towards a More Positive Evaluation of the Fifteenth-Century Renaissance », *Journal of the History of Ideas*, 4 (1943), 21-49. Cf. also J. Gadol, « The Unity of the Renaissance: Humanism, Natural Science, and Art », in *From the Renaissance to the Counter-Reformation; Essays in Honor of Garrett Mattingly, Edited and with an Introduction by Charles H. Carter*, (New York, 1965), pp. 29-55; and A. Buck, « Der humanistische Beitrag zur Ausbildung des naturwissenschaftlichen Denkens », in his *Die humanistische Tradition*, pp. 165-180.

[68] F. De Sanctis, *Storia della letteratura italiana, a cura di P. Arcari*, (Milan, 1930), I, 290.

[69] The first to be named among the Italian scholars engaged in a re-evaluation of the Quattrocento is Eugenio Garin with his numerous competent writings, above all his *L'umanesimo italiano, filosofia e vita civile nel Rina-*

Baron has demonstrated the function of the Quattrocento within the Italian Renaissance. The course of the Renaissance he conceives of as taking place in three stages, which correspond roughly to the three centuries, 1300 to 1600 — the Trecento, the Quattrocento, and the Cinquecento. With Petrarch, there emerges together with the newly awakened love of antiquity a new feeling for life. But Petrarch still vacillates irresolutely between the old and the new. He finds himself in the position of Moses, « first to see a new land, but not granted to enter it »[70]. Like Petrarch, his century still stands between the Middle Ages and the Renaissance, a century of transition.

The actual inception of the Renaissance, as a clear break with medieval tradition, Baron transfers to the beginning of the Quattrocento. The change of epochs is brought about by Florentine civic humanism under whose sign stand the most important culturally productive accomplishments of the century. The end of *Florentina libertas* followed by the decline of *Libertas Italiae* does not indeed mean that the cultural flowering of the Renaissance withered; instead, it changed from a civic to a courtly culture which then prevailed in the Cinquecento. At court, under the shadow of absolute princes, humanism was separated from politics, formalized, and put into the service of the developmental program of a social class recruited principally from the nobility: the ideal of the perfect citizen was replaced by the perfect courtier, the *cortegiano*. The esthetic and ethical postulates embodied in the *cortegiano* — the preservation of moderation — influenced the way of life of a social elite in all of Europe for centuries.

---

scimento, (Bari, 1952) (new edition, Bari, 1965), and *Scienza e vita civile nel Rinascimento italiano*, (Bari, 1965). In addition, see C. Varese, *Storia e politica nella prosa del Quattrocento*, (Turin, 1961); and F. Tateo, *Tradizione e realtà nell'umanesimo italiano*, (Bari, 1967).

[70] Baron, « Moot Problems of Renaissance Interpretation: An Answer to Wallace K. Ferguson », *Journal of the History of Ideas*, 19 (1958), 28.

The Renaissance, during its third and last phase, began to have its effect beyond the borders of Italy in other countries as the « prototype of life and thought in the modern world »[71]. When Baron characterizes the historical role of the Italian Renaissance with these words he finds himself in agreement with Jacob Burckhardt[72]. The thing that distinguishes him from Burckhardt is the fundamental perception that the culture of the Quattrocento developed from the base of the city-state Florence.

In the new image of the Renaissance which Baron was able to trace out on the basis of this perception, contemporary literature also appears in a new light. To the extent that literary history is and must be intellectual history as well, humanistic literature, thanks to Baron, now is felt to be essential for an understanding of the Renaissance.

(Translated by Bernard Wilson)

---

[71] Baron, « Burckhardt's 'Civilization of the Renaissance' a Century after its Publication », *Renaissance News*, 13 (1960), 221.

[72] In writing the *Kultur der Renaissance in Italien* Burckhardt called Italy « the mother and the home-land of modern man » (W. Kaegi, *Jacob Burckhardt, eine Biographie*, [Basel, 1947-67], III, 664); for him, the Italians were « the first-born among the sons of modern Europe » (*Die Kultur der Renaissance in Italien*, p. 123).

EUGENIO GARIN

LE PRIME RICERCHE DI HANS BARON SUL QUATTROCENTO E LA LORO INFLUENZA FRA LE DUE GUERRE

Senza alcun dubbio la vasta produzione di Hans Baron è destinata a costituire un contributo decisivo per la comprensione storica del Quattrocento italiano e, più in generale, del Rinascimento nei suoi valori di civiltà. La sua ricerca, infatti, ancorché addensata intorno ad alcuni punti precisi, viene a investire, nelle sue direzioni come nei suoi resultati, un complesso di questioni di portata assai ampia, con risonanze interpretative d' insieme. Ovviamente metterla a fuoco nei suoi temi centrali, o discuterla nelle sue motivazioni documentarie, non è possibile senza un'analisi puntuale dei dati, costantemente connessa con una consapevole disamina dei metodi d'indagine e dei loro presupposti teorici. Non di questo si vuole qui trattare, bensì, e in modo conciso e dimesso, dell' incidenza che gli scritti del Baron hanno avuto, nel periodo anteriore alla seconda guerra mondiale, su ricerche condotte in campi analoghi in Italia. Non si vuole con questo, è chiaro, pagare una sorta di debito di gratitudine; si vuole piuttosto indicare, da un lato, l'efficacia di un orientamento che non aveva ancora fissato i suoi resultati in interpretazioni definite; si intende, dall'altro, individuare convergenze non prive di valore in quello che fu senza dubbio un singolare momento di crisi.

Ovviamente, anche qui, un discorso, per essere esaustivo, dovrebbe cominciare da un confronto di metodi e di climi culturali: Italia e Germania fra le due guerre, e tutto quello che importava e significava, allora, un certo tipo di ricerche. È strano che studiosi che sottolineano, e giustamente, la necessità di non affrontare mai un documento del secolo XIV o XV senza rendersi conto esattamente del contesto culturale e politico in cui si colloca, non facciano altrettanto qualora si tratti di alcuni decenni addietro. È giusto non caricare la *libertas* o la *iustitia* di cui si legge nelle orazioni del Quattrocento dei significati che quei termini assunsero in seguito; ma è altrettanto giusto non dimenticare il modo in cui certi problemi storiografici vennero affrontati in Europa intorno agli anni trenta. Né questo importa alcuna degradazione scientifica per una produzione che muoveva, ed era avvivata, da un alto pathos ideale. Quella passione più d'ogni altra cosa giovava a comprendere il passato, sempre che non facesse difetto una sorvegliata coscienza critica. Gaetano Salvemini soleva ripetere, con quel suo gusto della battuta paradossale, che nelle sue scelte iniziali lo storico obbedisce sempre a prevenzioni, pregiudizi e passioni; ma che il suo rigore e la sua misura di studioso entrano in giuoco non a quel punto, ma nel concreto dell' indagine, nel corso della verifica « sul terreno », nella coerenza logica delle conseguenze. D'altra parte è pur vero che, senza quella « attuale » coscienza dei problemi, troppe porte resterebbero chiuse. Si potrebbe forse sostenere addirittura che il livello di penetrazione del passato è direttamente proporzionale al livello di apertura al presente, anche se proprio nella misura in cui venga evitata ogni reciproca influenza deformante. Goethe osservò — e Salvemini ricordava [1] — che « la storia deve esser riscritta di quando in quando, non solo perché si sono scoperti nuovi fatti, ma sopra tutto perché ogni generazione viene avanti con nuovi interessi e nuovi modi di considerare le cose, e per conseguenza osserva il passato da angoli visuali diversi da quelli di prima », scoprendone così aspetti inediti e rapporti impensati.

Non sembri inutile tutto questo. Non a caso nella *Crisis* del '55, col nome di Hitler, conservato nell'edizione del '66, compariva anche quello di Mussolini, poi soppresso. Vi compariva a proposito dell'opera dell' Emerton *Humanism and Tyranny*, e del tentativo dall'Autore compiuto nel 1925 « to interpret the development of the early Renaissance as

[1] G. Salvemini, *Storia e scienza*, Firenze, La Nuova Italia, 1948, p. 47.

a parallel to that of Italy in the beginning of the Fascist era ». Molto giustamente il Baron, nel '55, sottolineava come l'opera dell' Emerton, « a cicerone to the political problems of the early Renaissance » per gli studiosi di lingua inglese durante più di venticinque anni, fosse fondata essenzialmente sul *De Tyranno* del Salutati (e quale l'aveva ripresentato l' Ercole, di cui sono ben note le inclinazioni politiche). « Today — concludeva il Baron nel '55 — the time has come indeed for reconsideration ». Nel '66 muta l' intera nota, e il riferimento all' Italia di Mussolini scompare.

Libertà e tirannide, dignità dell'uomo e umanesimo, Medioevo Rinascimento e origini del mondo moderno, nell' Europa fra le due guerre non erano argomenti neutri, né sfoghi solitari di voglie erudite: l'eco destata dalla lettura di certi testi di un Bruni o di un Rinuccini aveva un timbro oggi non facilmente recuperabile. Qualcosa di simile avveniva del resto anche nei confronti dell'antichità classica o dell'età illuministica quali emergevano da certe opere di Jaeger o di Cassirer, che anche a questo dovettero la loro fortuna in Italia. Né è un caso che Baron abbia dedicato a Jaeger uno dei suoi volumi più importanti [2].

Altro punto da non trascurare è l'orientamento allora prevalente negli studi italiani sul Rinascimento, dominati dalla preoccupazione dei grandi problemi di continuità col Medioevo, di pietà o empietà, cristianesimo o paganesimo, averroismo o retorica, e così via: di idee generali, insomma, o meglio di formule, come qualcuno ha osservato [3], e

---

[2] A Jaeger è dedicato il volume del '55 *Humanistic and Political Literature in Florence At the Beginning of the Quattrocento* (« To Professor Werner Jaeger / in gratitude for the inspiration / which my studies of the Renaissance owe / to his work »).

[3] Così G. Sasso, « *Florentina libertas* » *e Rinascimento italiano nell'opera di Hans Baron* (*A proposito di due opere recenti*), « Rivista Storica Italiana », LXIX, 1957, pp. 250-276 (si utilizza qui di seguito anche G. Radetti, *Le origini dell'umanesimo civile fiorentino nel Quattrocento*, « Giornale Critico della Filosofia Italiana », XXXVIII, 1959, pp. 98-122; ma v. W. C. Ferguson, *The interpretation of Italian humanism: the contribution of Hans Baron*, « The Journal of the History of Ideas », XIX, 1958, pp. 14-25).

proprio parlando del Baron e della sua indagine, tanto consapevole di questa problematica quanto sdegnosa di genericità e rivolta alle cose, alla precisione dei testi e dei dati. Va aggiunto che gli studi italiani sul Rinascimento fra le due guerre, fortemente influenzati dalle ricerche e dalle idee del Gentile, guardavano in particolare al pensiero filosofico, e proprio là dove si era venuto svolgendo nelle grandi costruzioni di metafisica platonica destinate a incidere fino a Bruno e Campanella, e alle origini della cosiddetta rivoluzione scientifica. Lo stesso Cassirer col suo far centro su Cusano sembrava ribadire una veduta che in Italia era di casa — si pensi al Fiorentino — spostando l' interesse dalle origini al Quattrocento avanzato, a Ficino e alla cerchia ficiniana, a cui non a caso comincerà a dedicare i suoi sforzi così fecondi proprio negli anni trenta Paul Oskar Kristeller.

Di proposito si è ricordato il Kristeller; in quegli anni, infatti, il suo nome fu spesso unito a quello del Baron, a proposito, appunto, del Ficino e del Pico, e della discussione sull'astrologia. Era noto in Italia lo studio del Baron, del '27, su *Willensfreiheit und Astrologie bei Marsilio Ficino und Pico della Mirandola*, uscito in una miscellanea per Walter Goetz, e nel *Supplementum ficinianum* del '37 il Kristeller ringrazierà il Baron per avergli ceduto il materiale per l'edizione dei testi ficiniani sull'astrologia. Si trattava, forse, della questione più importante dibattuta nel secolo sul terreno delle scienze della natura e del loro metodo. Attraverso quella problematica si profilavano tutti i temi del rapporto uomo-natura. Probabilmente è tuttora di lì che si deve partire, se si vuole giungere correttamente alla comprensione del pensiero cinquecentesco nei suoi aspetti più significativi. Orbene, mentre il Kristeller legava la propria indagine al platonismo del Ficino e alla sua enorme influenza, orientandosi verso una esplorazione delle filosofie sistematiche in senso tradizionale, il Baron risaliva a monte, per mettere a fuoco sempre meglio l' indissolubile nesso fra cultura e politica. Di qui una prospettiva tutta diversa nei due studiosi, e alla fine una assai diversa concezione d' insieme. Facile fare due nomi che indicano anche gruppi di ricercatori diversi: Ernst Cassirer e Walter Goetz. Nomi ovviamente insufficienti a definire orientamenti e metodi, anche se non andrà dimenticato che Baron, dopo il saggio offerto a Goetz nel '27, dedicherà la *Crisis* del '55 « to Walter Goetz my teacher and friend / who introduced me to the Renaissance / and taught me that history / should be the study of both politics and culture ».

Politica e cultura: fu questo il tema di ricerca più ricco di echi nell' Italia degli anni trenta, su cui più feconde furono le convergenze: avviava nuove letture di testi già classici, quali quelli di un Landino o di un Ficino; spostava a un tempo l'attenzione verso l' inizio del secolo, verso gli umanisti-cancellieri. Dopo gli studi del Von Martin su Salutati, o del Walser su Poggio, l'attenzione si concentrava ora su Bruni, alla cui conoscenza il Baron offrì un primo contributo fondamentale col volume del 1928 [4]. Leonardo Bruni era un nodo importante; la scelta era singolarmente felice. L' indagine si collocava fra l'età di Salutati e le profonde trasformazioni politico-culturali di una Firenze in cui si attuava l'ascesa medicea. Sul terreno delle idee Bruni significava da un lato una sempre crescente conoscenza di Platone, e dall'altro la scoperta di un « nuovo » Aristotele. Gli anni dell'Aretino sono quelli che dividono la scoperta di Quintiliano da parte di Poggio dalla sua utilizzazione veramente « rivoluzionaria » da parte del grande avversario di Poggio, Lorenzo Valla. È il momento della formazione di una « nuova retorica » (Quintiliano a confronto con Cicerone), carica di un significato filosofico profondo e rinnovatore, che sembra sfuggire tuttora a non pochi studiosi. Ma il richiamo a Bruni era

---

[4] Leonardo Bruni Aretino, *Humanistisch-philosophische Schriften*, mit einer Chronologie seiner Werke und Briefe herausgegeben und erläutert von Dr. Hans Baron, Leipzig-Berlin, Teubner, 1928 (v. anche *Forschungen über Leonardo Bruni Aretino. Eine Erwiderung*, « Archiv für Kulturgeschichte », XXII, 1932, pp. 352-371).

anche altro: era l'avvío a una più attenta considerazione della storiografia umanistica, spesso sepolta sotto il peso di giudizi convenzionali; era il nodo fra storia, politica e retorica; era, appunto, il nesso fra politica e cultura.

Contemporaneamente, le prime puntualizzazioni cronologiche unite ai testi invitavano con discrezione a riaffrontare in concreto tutte le questioni generali intorno ai caratteri e ai momenti del rinnovamento umanistico. Se via via, almeno in parte, le dispute tradizionali sulle « formule » capaci di definire in blocco tutto il Rinascimento si sono attenuate, ciò si deve anche all'accoglimento dell' invito, che veniva dalle pagine del Baron, a riprendere le questioni nei loro termini precisi, nei « tempi brevi », nei confronti puntuali.

Ma, giova ripeterlo, fu innanzitutto quell'energica insistenza sul nesso fra « politica e cultura » negli umanisti, almeno in alcuni, e particolarmente fiorentini, che più incise su molti studi italiani intorno agli anni trenta, contribuendo a spostare sensibilmente il centro degli interessi. Non a caso, del resto, due saggi molto importanti del Baron comparvero proprio in Italia rispettivamente nel '35 e nel '38. Il primo su *La rinascita dell'etica statale romana nell'umanesimo fiorentino del Quattrocento* vide la luce nel '35 su « Civiltà Moderna », la rivista di Ernesto Codignola, ove si presentava come parte di un'opera storica su *Lo spirito comunale dell'Umanesimo fiorentino, secondo la « Vita civile » di Matteo Palmieri ed altre fonti*. Il saggio, che contiene *in nuce* non poche delle concezioni poi trasformate e ampiamente sviluppate, si conclude su una vivace polemica col Gundolf che aveva detto « gli umanisti, con poche eccezioni, ... espressamente apolitici ». Di contro il Baron rivendicava, almeno per l'umanesimo fiorentino, l' influenza della « rinata etica statale romana », lo « spirito politico della Respublica romana », e un « pensiero storico che diventò la creazione maggiore e più durevole dello spirito fiorentino ». Né esitava, nel corso della trattazione, a tracciare una linea di continuità fra il Bruni e il Machiavelli (una « pagina della storia del pensiero fiorentino al cui termine sta il nome di Machiavelli »). Nel '38, nel primo volume de « La Rinascita », la rivista del Centro Nazionale di Studi sul Rinascimento di Firenze, il Baron pubblicava, arricchito nelle note, il saggio su *Lo sfondo storico del Rinascimento fiorentino*, edito in Inghilterra su « History », in cui si sottolineava con forza l'ethos dell'umanesimo del primo Quattrocento fiorentino nel suo stretto legame con le « concezioni classiche della fusione dell' individuo con la sua *Polis* o *Civitas* ». Si aggiungeva che « il cittadino non si poté liberare dal passato medievale se non stringendosi alle idee classiche del civismo »; e questo secondo una tematica sviluppata dall'Autore nell'altro studio *Cicero and the Roman Civic Spirit in the Middle Ages and Early Renaissance*, presentato nel medesimo anno a Manchester come preliminare a un libro *The Legacy of Cicero and the Formation of Humanism* [5].

Nel '39, negli Stati Uniti, raccogliendo le prime conclusioni delle sue ricerche e definendone il metodo, il Baron dichiarava che « l' indirizzo sociologico della ricerca storica » aveva « profondamente cambiato » le prospettive dell'età rinascimentale: l'umanesimo, non più considerato come puro moto di riforma degli indirizzi educativi, svelava nuovi aspetti di pensiero, nei suoi agganci con la storia economica e politica. Il centro della ricerca sulla cultura del Rinascimento, spostandosi verso la prima metà del Quattrocento, anzi sempre più puntualmente fra la fine del Trecento ed i primi anni del Quattrocento, sostituiva un'analisi ravvicinata alla discussione su « formule » o idee generali. Nello sforzo di mettere a fuoco i personaggi nei loro contesti

---

[5] Come si vede dai titoli delle opere progettate, se era già ben chiaro nella mente del Baron l'orientamento, non era ancora definito l'ambito dell'opera in formazione. Per i lavori di questo periodo v. ancora: *Franciscan Poverty and Civic Wealth as Factors in the Rise of Humanistic Thought*, « Speculum », XIII, 1938, pp. 1-37. Importante, sulla trasformazione del pensiero storico: *Das Erwachen des historischen Denkens im Humanismus des Quattrocento*, « Historische Zeitschrift », CXLVII, 1933, pp. 5-20.

reali sempre meglio si induceva a legare i fatti « letterari » agli eventi reali, gli uomini alle cose; la cultura, appunto, alla politica. Con questo, in Italia, le indagini del Baron vennero ora a sollecitare e rinnovare, ed ora a confermare ed arricchire ricerche sul pensiero politico, su retorica e politica, su vita attiva e contemplativa, oltrepassando la tematica d'uso. Per fare qualche esempio, basti pensare alle pagine di Lamberto Borghi su Salutati, del '34, con la cui « interpretazione generale » il Baron dichiarava, subito nel '35, di consentire. Nel '37, uno studio di Delio Cantimori comparso nel « Journal of the Warburg Institute », recava un titolo che suonava, insieme, affermazione di principio e programma: *Rhetoric and Politics in Italian Humanism*. Fra i primi scritti citati dal Cantimori si trova il testo del Baron del '35, su *La Rinascita dell'etica statale romana nell'umanesimo fiorentino del Quattrocento* [6].

Dopo, nelle sue maggiori opere del '55 (e del '66-'68) il Baron ha colorito il suo disegno; ha posto al centro di una prospettiva singolarmente ricca l'età del Bruni; ha dato, oltre a contributi di vasta portata, una lezione di metodo. Intorno a taluni nodi si avvia oggi una discussione vivace, quale conviene a ogni concezione originale e feconda. È tuttavia auspicabile che non vadano dimenticati gl' insegnamenti che emersero già negli anni trenta da quei primi contributi, la cui genesi e le cui ragioni non devono essere perdute di vista. L' « umanesimo civile » non deve considerarsi una formula o, peggio, una sorta di schema politico-culturale: da accettare o respingere programmaticamente; è il riconoscimento del legame strettissimo, nel Quattrocento, fra alcune prese di posizione teoriche e precise situazioni politiche; è l' invito a non scindere impegno politico e manifestazioni letterarie e filosofiche, ad abban-

[6] Il saggio del Cantimori si trova nel « Journal of the Warburg Institute », I, 1937, pp. 83-102. Del Baron v. *A Sociological Interpretation of the Early Renaissance in Florence*, « The South Atlantic Quarterly », XXXVIII, 1939, pp. 427-448.

donare la riduzione dell' Umanesimo a vicenda letteraria cortigiana, o a episodio scolastico.

Uno degli stimoli più fecondi derivanti dall'opera del Baron è proprio l' invito a cogliere in tutta la loro fresca originalità le concezioni dell'uomo elaborate dagli umanisti: la loro visione della vita associata, morale e politica, e insomma la loro filosofia. Il che non può farsi senza rendersi conto con chiarezza di quello che fu per loro la « retorica » intesa come nuovo strumento da opporsi e sostituirsi alla « dialettica ». Chi si avvicini alle questioni che le ricerche del Baron sollecitano, senza un'adeguata messa a fuoco di quella nuova « retorica », non potrà evitare una serie di affermazioni poco pertinenti parlando, come già si è fatto, di subordinazione della filosofia alla retorica, o di sostituzione e opposizione [7]. Solo quando si colga il senso di una cultura che vuol rinnovare nei metodi e nei fondamenti le scienze dell'uomo, che vuole rendere rigorosi gli strumenti della persuasione, che vuol capire i procedimenti propri dei vari campi e delimitarli nei loro caratteri (uomo e natura), solo allora si potrà affrontare adeguatamente la questione del « nuovo » Aristotele, del « nuovo » Platone, di Cicerone a confronto con Quintiliano: o il rapporto che Valla pone tra retorica e teologia con la sua condanna, così rigorosamente argomentata, della « filosofia » scolastica.

Come si vede, il discorso avviato dal Baron viene di lontano e porta lontano: implica non solo una valutazione globale del contributo recato alla cultura dalla rinascita umanistica; implica una discussione approfondita di alcuni punti centrali nello sviluppo del pensiero moderno, quali il senso della crisi della Scolastica sul terreno delle varie discipline. Implica l' idea che una profonda trasformazione

---

[7] V. in particolare J. E. Seigel, *Rhetoric and Philosophy in Renaissance Humanism*, Princeton University Press, 1968, p. 137 e sgg., 165 e sgg.; ma cfr., invece, Ch. Perelman, *Rhétorique et philosophie*, « Les Études Philosophiques », N. S., XXIV, 1969, pp. 19-27.

della cultura e dell'educazione, quale nessuno può negare nei secoli dell'umanesimo, non è neppure concepibile al di fuori di un mutamento della visione del mondo e della società. Con questo, fatalmente, la discussione non può non spostarsi sul terreno « filosofico », perché non di divergenze parziali, o su singoli punti, si tratta, o non solo di queste, ma del modo stesso d' intendere la cultura umana, la sua storia e la sua funzione, e tutti i suoi maggiori problemi.

JOHN A. TEDESCHI - ANDREW W. LEWIS

BIBLIOGRAPHY OF THE WRITINGS OF HANS BARON 1924-1969

The entries will be arranged in the following manner: 1) books; 2) editions; 3) articles and bibliographical review articles; 4) book reviews; 5) encyclopedia pieces and short notes.

The bibliography does not include Professor Baron's contributions to the *Monatsberichte*, a student publication of the University of Berlin, which printed six or more of his communications in the years 1920 and 1921.

1924

1. *Calvins Staatsanschauung und das konfessionelle Zeitalter.* (Beiheft I der Historischen Zeitschrift, Berlin and Munich, 1924). Pp. viii, 121.

2. *Ernst Troeltsch, Spektator-Briefe, Aufsätze über die deutsche Revolution und die Weltpolitik 1918-22. Mit einem Geleitwort von Friedrich Meinecke, zusammengestellt und herausgegeben von H. Baron.* (Tübingen: J. C. B. Mohr, 1924).
The editor's « Vorwort »: pp. ix-xiii.

3. « Justus Mösers Individualitätsprinzip in seiner geistesgeschichtlichen Bedeutung », *Historische Zeitschrift*, 130 (1924), 31-57.

1925

4. *Aufsätze zur Geistesgeschichte und Religionssoziologie von Ernst Troeltsch, herausgegeben von Dr. Hans Baron.* (Gesammelte Schriften von Ernst Troeltsch, 4; Tübingen: J. C. B. Mohr, 1925).
The editor's « Vorbericht »: pp. v-xx.

5. *Ernst Troeltsch, deutscher Geist und Westeuropa. Gesammelte kulturphilosophische Aufsätze und Reden, herausgegeben von Hans Baron.* (Tübingen: J. C. B. Mohr, 1925).
The editor's « Vorbemerkung »: pp. iii-ix.

6. « Zur Frage des Ursprungs des deutschen Humanismus und seiner religiösen Reformbestrebungen. Ein kritischer Bericht über die neuere Literatur », *Historische Zeitschrift*, 132 (1925), 413-446.

7. Review: F. Engel-Jánosi, *Soziale Probleme der Renaissance* (Stuttgart, 1924), in *Historische Zeitschrift*, 132 (1925), 136-141.

8. Review: A. M. Schwindt, *Hans Denck, ein Vorkämpfer undogmatischen Christentums, 1495-1527* (Habertshof, n. d.), in *ibid.*, 117-119.

1926

9. « ‘ Christliches Naturrecht ’ und ‘ Ewiges Recht ’. Eine Erwiderung », *Historische Zeitschrift*, 133 (1926), 413-432.

10. « Literarische Wegweiser durch die italienische Geschichtsforschung der Gegenwart », *ibid.*, 325-334.
Discussion of: P. Egidi, *La storia medioevale* (Rome, 1922); A. Solmi, *La storia del diritto italiano* (Rome, 1922); L. Tonelli, *La critica* (Rome, 1920); G. Fumagalli, *La bibliografia* (Rome, 1923).

1927

11. « Willensfreiheit und Astrologie bei Marsilio Ficino und Pico della Mirandola », in *Kultur- und Universalgeschichte. Walter Goetz zu seinem 60. Geburtstage dargebracht von Fachgenossen, Freunden und Schülern* (Leipzig: B. G. Teubner, 1927), pp. 145-170.

12. « Literaturbericht: Renaissance in Italien », *Archiv für Kulturgeschichte*, 17 (1927), 226-256.

1928

13. *Leonardo Bruni Aretino. Humanistisch-philosophische Schriften mit einer Chronologie seiner Werke und Briefe.* (Veröffentlichungen der Forschungsinstitute an der Universität Leipzig. Institut für Kultur- und Universalgeschichte. Quellen zur Geistesgeschichte des Mittelalters und der Renaissance hrsg. von Walter Goetz. 1. Bd.; Leipzig and Berlin: B. G. Teubner, 1928). Pp. XL, 243.

1929

14. « Humanismus », *Jahresberichte für deutsche Geschichte, 3. Jahrgang 1927* (Leipzig, 1929), 440-454.

15. Discussion of recent Machiavelli research, under the « Notizen und Nachrichten » rubric in *Historische Zeitschrift*, 139 (1929), 418-419.

16. Review: *Vorträge 1922-1923 der Bibliothek Warburg* I (Leipzig, 1924), in *ibid.*, 393-395.

17. Review: H. Gmelin, « Personendarstellung bei den florenti-

nischen Geschichtschreibern der Renaissance », *Beiträge zur Kulturgeschichte des Mittelalters und der Renaissance, hrsg. von W. Goetz*, Bd. 31 (Leipzig, 1927), in *Historische Zeitschrift*, 140 (1929), 459-460.

18. Review: W. Rehm, *Das Werden des Renaissancebildes in der deutschen Dichtung vom Rationalismus bis zum Realismus* (Munich, 1924), in *ibid.*, 107-109.

19. Review: P. Smith, *Erasmus. A Study of his Life, Ideals and Place in History* (New York and London, 1923), in *ibid.*, 362-365.

1930

20. « Staatsanschauungen des späteren Mittelalters », *Jahresberichte für deutsche Geschichte, 4. Jahrgang 1928* (Leipzig, 1930), 328-331.

21. « Staatsanschauungen des 16. und 17. Jahrhunderts », *ibid.*, 331-337.

22. « Renaissance und Humanismus », *ibid.*, 348-370.

23. Review: G. Saitta, *Filosofia italiana e umanesimo* (Venice, 1928), in *Historische Zeitschrift*, 141 (1930), 138-141.

24. « Leonardo Bruni », *Encyclopaedia of the Social Sciences*, III (1930), 19.

1931

25. « Machiavelli und Morus », in P. R. Rohden and G. Ostrogorsky, eds., *Menschen die Geschichte machten. 4000 Jahre Weltgeschichte in Zeit- und Lebensbildern* (Vienna, 1931), II, 212-218.

26. « Literaturbericht: Renaissance in Italien », *Archiv für Kulturgeschichte*, 21 (1931), i: 95-128, ii: 215-239, iii: 340-356.

1932

27. « Forschungen über Leonardo Bruni Aretino. Eine Erwiderung », *Archiv für Kulturgeschichte*, 22 (1932), 352-371.

28. « Staatsanschauung und allgemeine Geschichte des geistigen Lebens. Frühes und hohes Mittelalter (bis 1300) », *Jahresberichte für deutsche Geschichte, 6. Jahrgang 1930* (Leipzig, 1932), 544-567.

29. Review: H. Haustein, « Die Frühgeschichte der Syphilis 1495-1498. Historisch-kritische Untersuchung auf Grund von Archivalien und Staatsdokumenten », *Archiv für Dermatologie und Syphilis*, 161 (1930), 255-388, in *Historische Zeitschrift*, 145 (1932), 643-644.

1933

30. « Das Erwachen des historischen Denkens im Humanismus des Quattrocento », *Historische Zeitschrift*, 147 (1933), 5-20.

1935

31. « La rinascita dell'etica statale romana nell'umanesimo fiorentino del Quattrocento », *Civiltà moderna*, 7 (1935), 21-49.

1937

32. « Religion and Politics in the German Imperial Cities during the Reformation », *English Historical Review*, 52 (1937), 405-427, 614-633.

1938

33. « Cicero and the Roman Civic Spirit in the Middle Ages and Early Renaissance », *Bulletin of the John Rylands Library*, 22 (1938), 72-97.
Republished 1968, see no. 104; see also no. 96.

34. « Franciscan Poverty and Civic Wealth as Factors in the Rise of Humanistic Thought », *Speculum*, 13 (1938), 1-37.
Reprinted in part, no. 96.

35. « The Historical Background of the Florentine Renaissance », *History*, n. s., 22 (1938), 315-327.
See no. 36.

36. « Lo sfondo storico del Rinascimento fiorentino », *La Rinascita*, 1 (1938), 50-72.
Italian translation of no. 35 with additional notes. See nos. 77 and 88 a.

1939

37. « Calvinist Republicanism and its Historical Roots », *Church History*, 8 (1939), 30-42.
Portions of this article are to be reprinted in a volume on whether Calvinism was a source of modern democracy being prepared by Robert M. Kingdon and Robert Linder for the D. C. Heath series, *Problems in European Civilization.*

38. « Imperial Reform and the Habsburgs, 1486-1504: A New Interpretation », *American Historical Review*, 44 (1938-39), 293-303.

39. « A Sociological Interpretation of the Early Renaissance in Florence », *South Atlantic Quarterly*, 38 (1939), 427-448.

40. Review: E. Müller, ed., *Die Abrechnung des Johannes Hageboke über die Kosten der Belagerung der Stadt Münster 1534-1535* (Münster, 1937), in *English Historical Review*, 54 (1939), 175.

1940

41. Review: G. Kallen, *Aeneas Silvius Piccolomini als Publizist in der 'Epistola de Ortu et Auctoritate Imperii Romani'* (Cologne and Stuttgart, 1939), in *American Historical Review*, 45 (1939-40), 453.

1941

42. Review: G. Weise, *Die geistige Welt der Gotik und ihre Bedeutung für Italien* (Halle and Saale, 1939), in *American Historical Review*, 46 (1940-41), 621-623.

1942

43. Review: N. Elias, *Über den Prozess der Zivilisation: soziogenetische und psychogenetische Untersuchungen*, 2 vols. (Basel, 1939), in *Journal of Modern History*, 14 (1942), 224-227.

1943

44. « Toward a More Positive Evaluation of the Fifteenth-Century Renaissance », *Journal of the History of Ideas*, 4 (1943), 21-49.
Reprinted in Karl H. Dannenfeldt, ed., *The Renaissance: Medieval or Modern?* (Problems in European Civilization; New York: D. C. Heath & Co., 1959), pp. 35-38, 64-75.

45. Review: G. E. Waas, *The Legendary Character of Kaiser Maximilian* (New York, 1941), in *American Historical Review*, 49 (1943-44), 93-94.

1944

46. « Articulation and Unity in the Italian Renaissance and in the Modern West », in *The Quest for Political Unity in World History, Edited for the American Historical Association by Stanley Pargellis* (Washington: United States Government Printing Office, 1944), pp. 123-138. (Volume III of the Annual Report of the American Historical Association for the Year 1942).
Revised German translation, no. 110.

1945

47. Review: F. C. Lane, *Andrea Barbarigo, Merchant of Venice, 1418-1449* (Baltimore, 1944), in *American Historical Review*, 50 (1944-45), 787-789.

1946

48. « Studies on Humanism and the Florentine Commonwealth in the Renaissance », *Year Book of the American Philosophical Society* (Philadelphia, 1946), pp. 183-186.

1947

49. « New Light on the Political Writers of the Florentine Renaissance », *Journal of the History of Ideas*, 8 (1947), 241-248.
Discussion of R. Ridolfi, *Opuscoli di storia letteraria e di erudizione. Savonarola-Machiavelli-Guicciardini-Giannotti* (Florence, 1942).

50. Review: B. W. Bates, *Literary Portraiture in the Historical Narrative of the French Renaissance* (New York, 1945), in *American Historical Review*, 52 (1946-47), 499-501.

1950

51. « The First History of the Historical Concept of the Renaissance », *Journal of the History of Ideas*, 11 (1950), 493-510.
Apropos of W. K. Ferguson, *The Renaissance in Historical Thought: Five Centuries of Interpretation* (Boston, 1948).

52. Review: W. K. Ferguson, *The Renaissance in Historical Thought*, in *American Historical Review*, 55 (1949-50), 864-866.

1951

53. « Aulius Gellius in the Renaissance and a Manuscript from the School of Guarino », *Studies in Philology*, 48 (1951), 107-125. (Newberry Library Ms. 90.5).
This article and no. 54 were republished together in revised form with a new title in no. 102.

1952

54. « The Scribe of the Newberry Gellius of 1445: A Supplementary Note », *Studies in Philology*, 49 (1952), 248-250.
Postscript to no. 53, reprinted in no. 102.

55. « The Anti-Florentine Discourses of the Doge Tommaso Mocenigo (1414-23): Their Date and Partial Forgery », *Speculum*, 27 (1952), 323-342.
Reprinted as ch. ix of no. 64.

56. « Erasmus-Probleme im Spiegel des Colloquium ‘ Inquisitio de Fide ’ », *Archiv für Reformationsgeschichte*, 43 (1952), 254-263.
Part 1. Das Apostolische Symbol und die Einigung der Konfessionen. Part 2. Der Humanismus und die thomistische Lehre von den « gentiles salvati ».
Apropos of *Inquisitio de Fide, a Colloquy by Desiderius Erasmus Roterodamus, 1524. Edited by Craig R. Thompson* (New Haven, 1950).

57. « Survey of Periodical Literature in the United States, 1945-1951: Articles in Non-religious Journals », *Archiv für Reformationsgeschichte*, 43 (1952), 99-103.

58. « Die politische Entwicklung der italienischen Renaissance », *Historische Zeitschrift*, 174 (1952), 31-54.
Discussion of: L. Simeoni, *Le Signorie* (Milan, 1950); N. Valeri, *L' Italia nell'età dei principati dal 1343 al 1516* (Verona, 1950).

59. Announcement of the completion of *The Crisis of the Early Italian Renaissance*, in *Renaissance News*, 5 (1952), 85.

1953

60. « A Struggle for Liberty in the Renaissance: Florence, Venice, and Milan in the Early Quattrocento », *American Historical Review*, 58 (1952-53), 265-289, 544-570.

61. Review: L. Simeoni, *Le Signorie* (Milan, 1950); N. Valeri, *L'Italia nell'età dei principati dal 1343 al 1516* (Verona, 1950); P. Pieri, *Il Rinascimento e la crisi militare italiana* (Turin, 1952), in *ibid.*, 891-893.

1954

62. « Library News: Newberry Library », *Renaissance News*, 7 (1954), 146-150.
Report on notable acquisitions.

1955

63. *The Crisis of the Early Italian Renaissance: Civic Humanism and Republican Liberty in an Age of Classicism and Tyranny.* (Princeton: Princeton University Press, 1955). 2 vols. Pp. xxix, 656. See nos. 99, 111.

64. *Humanistic and Political Literature in Florence and Venice at the Beginning of the Quattrocento: Studies in Criticism and Chronology.* (Cambridge: Harvard University Press, 1955). Pp. x, 223. Reissued 1968, see no. 103.

65. « Dekadenz im Italien des Quattrocento », *Bibliothèque d'humanisme et renaissance*, 17 (1955), 421-437.
Discussion of E.-R. Labande, *L'Italie de la Renaissance: Duecento-Trecento-Quattrocento. Évolution d'une société* (Paris, 1954).

66. Review: P. Huber, *Traditionsfestigkeit und Traditionskritik bei Thomas Morus* (Basel, 1953), in *Archiv für Reformationsgeschichte*, 46 (1955), 261-264.

1956

67. « The *Principe* and the Puzzle of the Date of the *Discorsi* », *Bibliothèque d'humanisme et Renaissance*, 18 (1956), 405-428.

68. Communication to the Editor of the *American Historical Review*, in *American Historical Review*, 61 (1955-56), 1088-1089.
A reply to a letter by R. S. Lopez, *ibid.*, 1087-1088. Both are reprinted in Dannenfeldt, *The Renaissance: Medieval or Modern?*, pp. 62-63.

69. Review: H. Baeyens, *Begrip en Probleem van de Renaissance. Bijdrage tot de Geschiedenis van hun Ontstaan en tot hun Kunsthistorische Omschrijving* (Louvain, 1952), in *Historische Zeitschrift*, 182 (1956), 115-120.

70. Review: E.-R. Labande, *L'Italie de la Renaissance: Duecento-Trecento-Quattrocento. Évolution d'une société* (Paris, 1954), in *American Historical Review*, 61 (1955-56), 385-387.

71. « Manuscript Acquisitions in 1955 », *The Newberry Library Bulletin*, 4 (1956), 78-83.
Professor Baron's unsigned reports on The Newberry Library's acquisitions in Continental History and Literature are dispersed in the « Library Notes » and « Notable Accessions » sections of *The Newberry Library Bulletin.* See Ser. II, no. 8 (1952), pp. 249-251; III (1952-1955), 62-67, 249-250, 251-254; IV (1955-1958), 49-55, 143-150, 256-267; V (1958-1962), 58-66, 133-142, 245-253, 326-333; VI (1962-1965), 40-45, 140-149.

1957

72. « Fifteenth-Century Civilisation and the Renaissance », *The New Cambridge Modern History*. I. *The Renaissance 1493-1520* (Cambridge, 1957), pp. 50-75.

73. Review: R. von Albertini, *Das florentinische Staatsbewusstsein im Übergang von der Republik zum Prinzipat* (Bern, 1955), in *American Historical Review*, 62 (1956-57), 909-911.

1958

74. « Moot Problems of Renaissance Interpretation: An Answer to Wallace K. Ferguson », *Journal of the History of Ideas*, 19 (1958), 26-34.
In reply to Ferguson's « The Interpretation of Italian Humanism: The Contribution of Hans Baron », *ibid.*, 14-25.

Pp. 31-34 are reprinted in Dannenfeldt, *The Renaissance: Medieval or Modern?*, pp. 110-112.

75. Review: H. Treinen, *Studien zur Idee der Gemeinschaft bei Erasmus von Rotterdam und zu ihrer Stellung in der Entwicklung des humanistischen Universalismus* (Saarlouis, 1955) and S. A. Nulli, *Erasmo e il Rinascimento* (Turin, 1955), in *American Historical Review*, 63 (1958), 947-949.

1959

76. « The *Querelle* of the Ancients and the Moderns as a Problem for Renaissance Scholarship », *Journal of the History of Ideas*, 20 (1959), 3-22.
Reprinted 1968, see no. 106.

77. « Lo sfondo storico del Rinascimento fiorentino », in A. Saitta, ed., *Antologia di critica storica*, II, *Problemi della civiltà moderna* (Bari, 1959), pp. 47-62.
Reprinting of no. 36 without notes.

78. Review: G. Sasso, *Niccolò Machiavelli: Storia del suo pensiero politico* (Naples, 1958), in *American Historical Review*, 64 (1958-59), 952-954.

1960

79. « Burckhardt's *Civilization of the Renaissance* a Century After its Publication », *Renaissance News*, 13 (1960), 207-222.
See nos. 108, 113.

80. « The Social Background of Political Liberty in the Early Italian Renaissance », *Comparative Studies in Society and History*, 2 (1960), 440-451.

81. « Secularization of Wisdom and Political Humanism in the Renaissance », *Journal of the History of Ideas*, 21 (1960), 131-150.
Discussion of E. Rice, *The Renaissance Idea of Wisdom* (Cambridge, Mass., 1958).

82. « Marvell's *An Horatian Ode* and Machiavelli », *ibid.*, 450-451.
Discussion of J. A. Mazzeo, « Cromwell as Machiavellian Prince in Marvell's *An Horatian Ode* », *ibid.*, 1-17.

83. Review: E. Hassinger, *Das Werden des neuzeitlichen Europa, 1300-1600* (Braunschweig, 1959), in *American Historical Review*, 65 (1959-60), 354-355.

1961

84. « Machiavelli on the Eve of the *Discourses*: The Date and Place of his *Dialogo intorno alla nostra lingua* », *Bibliothèque d'humanisme et Renaissance*, 23 (1961), 449-476.

85. « Machiavelli: The Republican Citizen and the Author of *The Prince* », *English Historical Review*, 76 (1961), 217-253.
Pp. 247 ff. appear in Italian in F. Fido, *Machiavelli* (Palermo, 1965), pp. 278-281, and in *Niccolò Machiavelli, Il Principe, con una scelta dei Discorsi. Introduzione, note e antologia della critica a cura di E. N. Girardi* (Brescia, 1967), pp. 487-492.

86. Review: J. R. Hale, *Machiavelli and Renaissance Italy* (New York, 1960), in *American Historical Review*, 67 (1961-62), 128-129.

1962

87. « The Evolution of Petrarch's Thought: Reflections on the State of Petrarch Studies », *Bibliothèque d'humanisme et Renaissance*, 24 (1962), 7-41.
Revision in no. 102.

88. « A British Symposium on Italian Renaissance Civilization », *Journal of the History of Ideas*, 23 (1962), 143-146.
Discussion of E. F. Jacob, ed., *Italian Renaissance Studies: A Tribute to the Late Cecilia M. Ady* (London, 1960).

88a. « Lo sfondo storico e l'ambiente sociale del Rinascimento », in *Civiltà letteraria d'Italia: Saggi critici e storici presentati da Vittore Branca e Cesare Galimberti* I (Florence, 1962), pp. 571-579.
Reprint without most of the notes of no. 36.

89. Review: T. Helton, ed., *The Renaissance: A Reconsideration of the Theories and Interpretations of the Age* (Madison, 1961), in *Journal of Modern History*, 34 (1962), 187.

90. Review: E. F. Jacob, ed., *Italian Renaissance Studies: A Tribute to the Late Cecilia M. Ady* (London, 1960), in *English Historical Review*, 77 (1961), 358-359.

1963

91. « Petrarch's *Secretum*: Was it Revised — and Why? The Draft of 1342-43 and the Later Changes », *Bibliothèque d'humanisme et Renaissance*, 25 (1963), 489-530.
Revision in no. 102.

1964

92. « Machiavelli's Development: A Propos of the New Edition of Ridolfi's *Vita di Niccolò Machiavelli* », *Bibliothèque d'humanisme et Renaissance*, 26 (1964), 253-255.
Discussion of Ridolfi's *The Life of Niccolò Machiavelli*, translated by C. Grayson (Chicago, 1963).

93. Review: D. Hay, *The Italian Renaissance in Its Historical Background* (Cambridge, 1961), in *Journal of Modern History*, 36 (1964), 186-187.

94. Review: R. Ridolfi, *The Life of Niccolò Machiavelli*, translated by C. Grayson (Chicago, 1963), in *American Historical Review*, 69 (1963-64), 764-766.

1965

95. « A Forgotten Chronicle of Early Fifteenth-Century Venice », in Heinz Bluhm, ed., *Essays in History and Literature Presented by Fellows of The Newberry Library to Stanley Pargellis* (Chicago, 1965), pp. 19-36.
Revision with a new title in no. 102.

96. « The Problem of Civic Activity and Wealth », in Denys Hay, ed., *The Renaissance Debate* (New York, 1965), pp. 98-105.
Brief selections from nos. 33 and 34.

97. Review: C. Clough, « Yet Again Machiavelli's Prince », *Annali dell'Istituto universitario orientale*, Naples: *Sezione romanza*, 5 (1963), 201-226, in *English Historical Review*, 80 (1965), 587-588.

98. Review: C. Pincin, « La prefazione alla prima parte dei *Discorsi* », *Atti dell'Accademia delle scienze di Torino*, 94 (1959-60), 506-518, and « I Discorsi sopra la prima deca di Tito Livio », *ibid.*, 96 (1961-62), 71-178, in *English Historical Review*, 80 (1965), 826-827.

1966

99. *The Crisis of the Early Italian Renaissance. Civic Humanism and Republican Liberty in an Age of Classicism and Tyranny. Revised One-Volume Edition with an Epilogue.* (Princeton: Princeton University Press, 1966). Pp. xxviii, 584.
Revision of no. 63.

1967

100. « Leonardo Bruni: 'Professional Rhetorician' or 'Civic Humanist'? » *Past & Present*, no. 36 (April, 1967), 21-37.
See no. 105.

101. Review: E. Garin, *Italian Humanism: Philosophy and Civic Life in the Renaissance*, translated by Peter Munz (New York, 1965), in *American Historical Review*, 72 (1966-67), 631-633.

1968

102. *From Petrarch to Leonardo Bruni: Studies in Humanistic and Political Literature.* (Chicago: Published for The Newberry Library by The University of Chicago Press, 1968). Pp. vii, 269.
Collection of new and revised papers.
Contents: « The Evolution of Petrarch's Thought: Reflections on the State of Petrarch Studies » (no. 87); « Petrarch's *Secretum*: Was it Revised — and Why? » (no. 91); « Chronology and Historical Certainty: The Dates of Bruni's *Laudatio* and *Dialogi* »; « A Crucial Date in the History of Florentine Historiography: The Composition of Dati's *Istoria di Firenze* in 1409 »; « Imitation, Rhetoric and Quattrocento Thought in Bruni's *Laudatio* »; « Early Renaissance Venetian Chronicles: Their History and a Manuscript in The Newberry Library » (no. 95); « Aulus Gellius in the Renaissance: His Influence and a Manuscript from the School of Guarino » (nos. 53, 54); « Bruni's *Laudatio Florentinae Urbis* » (First Printed Edition).

103. *Humanistic and Political Literature in Florence and Venice at the Beginning of the Quattrocento: Studies in Criticism and Chronology.* (New York: Russell & Russell, 1968). Pp. xii, 223.
Reprint of no. 64 with added introductory note.

104. « Cicero and the Roman Civic Spirit in the Middle Ages and the Early Renaissance », in F. L. Cheyette, ed., *Lordship and Community in Medieval Europe* (New York, 1968), pp. 291-314. Slightly revised version of no. 33.

105. « Leonardo Bruni: ' Retore di professione ' o ' Umanista civile '? » *Critica storica*, 7 (1968), 1-19. Translation of no. 100.

106. « The *Querelle* of the Ancients and the Moderns as a Problem for Renaissance Scholarship », in Paul Oskar Kristeller and Philip P. Wiener, eds., *Renaissance Essays from the Journal of the History of Ideas* (New York and Evanston: Harper Torchbooks, 1968), pp. 95-114. Slightly revised version of no. 76.

107. Review: P. O. Kristeller, *Renaissance Philosophy and the Medieval Tradition* (Latrobe, Pa., 1966), in *American Historical Review*, 74 (1968-69), 575-576.

1969

108 « Critica dell' ' individualismo ' burckhardtiano: elementi politici e sociali nel concetto di Rinascimento », *Il pensiero politico*, 2 (1969), 39-53. Thorough revision and translation of no. 79.

109. Review: C. Clough, *Machiavelli Researches*, (Pubblicazioni della Sezione romanza dell' Istituto universitario orientale. Studi, 3; Naples, 1967), in *English Historical Review*, 84 (1969), 579-582.

At the time of compilation (July, 1969), the following publications have been scheduled:

(1969)

110. « Politische Einheit und Mannigfaltigkeit in der italienischen Renaissance und in der Geschichte der Neuzeit », a revision and translation of no. 46 with a « Nachtrag » written in 1968, to appear in A. Buck, ed., *Wege der Forschung*, Bd. 204: *Zu Begriff und Problem der Renaissance* (Darmstadt).

(1970)

111. An Italian translation of *The Crisis of the Early Italian Renaissance*, with a new Introduction, to be published by Casa Editrice G. C. Sansoni, Florence.

112. « Petrarch: His Inner Struggles and the Humanist Discovery of Man's Nature », to appear in a volume of essays in medieval and Renaissance history edited by J. G. Rouse and W. H. Stockdale, to be presented to Wallace K. Ferguson.

113. « Burckhardt's *Civilization of the Renaissance* a Century After its Publication », a slight revision of no. 79, to appear in an anthology of Renaissance and Reformation papers edited by A. G. Dickens to be published by Pitman Publishing Corp., New York.

STUDIES IN EUROPEAN
HISTORY AND LITERATURE

6.

GILES CONSTABLE

THE POPULARITY OF TWELFTH-CENTURY SPIRITUAL WRITERS IN THE LATE MIDDLE AGES *

* For help and advice in the preparation of this article, the author is indebted to Professors P. O. Kristeller (Columbia University), Paul Nyhus (Bowdoin College), Heiko Oberman (University of Tübingen), and Eugene Rice (Columbia University).

The life of the mind and the life of the spirit seem at certain times in history to go their own ways and to draw on different sources; and in the fourteenth and fifteenth centuries, when men were finding new ideas and mental attitudes in the works of classical antiquity, their religious sentiments remained true to medieval themes and were nourished by traditional works of spirituality, especially those written in the twelfth century. The writings of Anselm, Bernard, Hugh and Richard of St Victor, and of less well-known Cistercian and Victorine authors (many of whose works circulated under the names of Augustine, Bernard, and Hugh) were widely read in the late Middle Ages and may in the long run have exercised an even greater influence than the didactic writings of Peter Lombard, Gratian, and Peter Comestor. These spiritual texts formed a distinct literary genre in the twelfth century, of which the importance has been stressed by several recent scholars [1]; but their later popularity and influence has been relatively little studied. The purpose of this article is to indicate some of the ways of investigating this question. In particular, it will deal with bibliographical evidence and with individual writers whose works either exercised influence or show the influence of twelfth-century spirituality. I shall deal in another article with some of the distinctive spiritual themes and devotional attitudes which developed in the late eleventh and twelfth centuries and which shaped the religious sentiments of the late Middle Ages [2].

---

[1] See especially the many works of Jean Leclercq. On the distinction of spirituality from exegesis and theology in the twelfth century, see Henri de Lubac, *Exégèse médiévale* (Théologie, 41-2, 59; Paris, 1959-64) II . 1, 423-29 and II . 2, 487-88, who also comments (II . 1, 379) on the great success and influence of twelfth-century didactic works.

[2] Delivered as a lecture at the Southeastern Institute of Medieval and Renaissance Studies in 1969 and to be published in volume V of its *Medieval and Renaissance Studies*.

I.

The clearest indication of the popularity of twelfth-century spiritual writers in the late Middle Ages is the number of manuscripts copied at that time, especially in the fifteenth century. The figures in the appendix are taken from available recent editions containing lists of dated manuscripts. Although the works are arbitrarily chosen, and the lists of manuscripts probably incomplete and inaccurate [3], there are an impressive number of fifteenth-century copies of various characteristic texts. Dom Wilmart remarked, for instance, that the *Jubilus* attributed to St Bernard had its greatest success in the fifteenth century [4] and that there seems to have been a revival of interest at the same time in the *Scala claustralium* of Guigo II of La Chartreuse. He could find no obvious reason for this revival. « What happened in the fifteenth century to bring about this change? » he asked. « Was the interest in spiritual things found in certain young and fervent circles sufficient to make the advice of a wise ascetic appreciated and fashionable? Perhaps. I have found nothing to give an adequate reply » [5]. The same question might be asked about the long and tedious commentary on the Benedictine Rule which was written by Stephen of Paris in 1191/4 but which survives only in late medieval manuscripts, mostly from southern Germany [6]. The answer appears to be that given by Bernards with regard to the manuscript figures of the *Speculum virginum*, which he compared with those of John *Homo Dei's De ordine vitae*: « It is thus again established that the piety

---

[3] In evaluating the figures, the greater chance of late copies surviving must be taken into consideration. Manuscripts dated to more than one century have been listed in the appendix under the later century.

[4] André Wilmart, *Le « Jubilus » dit de saint Bernard* (Rome, 1944) p. 51.

[5] André Wilmart, *Auteurs spirituels et textes dévots du moyen âge latin* (Paris, 1932) p. 231.

[6] Clm 3029 (Andechs, dated 1466), 4308 (St Ulrich, Augsburg, dated 1495), and 18155 (Tegernsee, dated 1472), Melk 285 (XIV/XV), Bamberg 151 (Ed. II. 4) (XV), and Epinal 12 (St Peter, Sens, XV). This information was kindly supplied by Dr Caroline Bynum.

of the fifteenth century attached itself in its devotional literature to the writings of the twelfth century » [7].

Such figures are hard to establish for long and very popular works, for which the lists of manuscripts are either old or incomplete. Although editors now mostly agree that *recentiores* are not necessarily *deteriores* from a textual point of view, it is still sometimes forgotten that even *deteriores* are a valuable indication of the popularity of a text and of the forms in which it was read. The available figures for one popular text, the *De miseria humanae conditionis* by Innocent III, of which over five hundred manuscripts are known, show that four-ninths of the dated copies are of the fifteenth century [8]. Of the works of Anselm, Bernard, and Hugh and Richard of St Victor there are literally thousands of manuscripts [9]. Leclercq inspected almost fifteen hundred manuscripts of Bernard's works, of which about forty-two percent were twelfth century, twenty-nine percent thirteenth, twelve percent fourteenth, and seventeen percent fifteenth and later [10]. Of the uninspected manuscripts, most were late and unimportant, but even these figures suggest that there was a rise of interest in Bernard's works in the fifteenth century.

This impression of the continued and growing popularity of twelfth-century texts in the late Middle Ages is confirmed

---

[7] Matthäus Bernards, *Speculum virginum* (Forschungen zur Volkskunde, 36-8; Cologne-Graz, 1955) p. 10.

[8] Innocent III, *De miseria humane conditionis*, ed. Michele Maccarrone (Thesaurus mundi; Lugano, 1955) pp. x-xx; Michele Maccarrone and Keith V. Sinclair, « New Manuscripts of Lotario's Treatise 'De miseria humane conditionis' », *Italia medioevale e umanistica*, IV (1961) 167-73; and Donald Howard, « Thirty New Manuscripts of Pope Innocent III's 'De miseria humanae conditionis' », *Manuscripta*, VII (1963) 31-35.

[9] It might be worth investigating the existence of manuscript collected editions of these authors' works. There was a collected edition of Bernard's works, as of Augustine's, in the twelfth century: see Joseph de Ghellinck, « Une édition ou une collection médiévale des Opera omnia de saint Augustin », *Liber Floridus: Mittellateinische Studien* (Festschrift Paul Lehmann) (St Ottilien, 1950) pp. 63-82, and Jean Leclercq, *Études sur saint Bernard et le texte de ses écrits* (Analecta sacri ordinis cisterciensis, IX . 1-2; Rome, 1953) pp. 124-136. I have no information, however, on late medieval collected editions.

[10] Leclercq, *Études*, p. 12, from whose exact figures I have derived the approximate percentages.

by the manuscript figures for less exclusively spiritual, but still non-scholastic, works. More manuscripts of the works of Rupert of Deutz, for instance, were copied in the fifteenth than in the fourteenth century [11]. Fourteen manuscripts of the letters of Peter the Venerable were copied in the fifteenth century, as compared with five in the fourteenth, ten in the thirteenth, and eight in the twelfth [12]. Over half of the approximately two hundred known manuscripts of the letters of Peter of Blois date from the fifteenth century [13]. The text-history of Richard of St Victor's *Liber exceptionum*, which was very popular in the late twelfth and early thirteenth century, shows the same pattern. « The fourteenth century was not much interested in it », wrote Châtillon, « and if it enjoyed a new favor in the fifteenth century, this was doubtless owing more to the taste of this period for ancient works than to any true or deep interest » [14]. Pure antiquarianism was not the only reason for the revival of interest in these works, however. Indeed, interest in twelfth-century theological works seems to have declined at the very time spiritual texts were becoming more popular [15]. As Lefèvre wrote of the *Elucidarium* of Honorius *Augustodunensis*, which was widely read even though neglected by teachers and theologians: « The Christian people from the twelfth to the fifteenth century were content with the *Elucidarium* because it was sufficient for their aspirations » [16].

---

[11] Rhaban Haacke, « Die Überlieferung der Schriften Ruperts von Deutz », *Deutsches Archiv*, XVI (1960) 427, and Hubert Silvestre, « La tradition manuscrite des oeuvres de Rupert de Deutz », *Scriptorium*, XVI (1962) 343. Of the total of 202 dated manuscripts, 99 are twelfth century, 58 thirteenth, 18 fourteenth, 22 fifteenth, and 5 sixteenth.

[12] *The Letters of Peter the Venerable*, ed. Giles Constable (Harvard Historical Studies, 78; Cambridge, Mass., 1967) II, 48-74.

[13] Information supplied by Miss Ethel Cardwell.

[14] Richard of St Victor, *Liber Exceptionum*, ed. Jean Châtillon (Textes philosophiques du moyen âge, 5; Paris, 1958) p. 81. Of the 171 known manuscripts (see pp. 14-51), 17 are twelfth century, 100 thirteenth, 21 fourteenth, 23 fifteenth (mostly from central Europe), 2 later, and 8 undated.

[15] Cf. Richard of St Victor, *De trinitate*, ed. Jean Ribaillier (Textes philosophiques du moyen âge, 6; Paris, 1958) p. 72. Ribaillier commented on the distinction between Richard's theological and spiritual works and their relative popularity in the late Middle Ages.

[16] Yves Lefèvre, *L'Elucidarium et les lucidaires* (Bibliothèque des Écoles françaises d'Athènes et de Rome, 180; Paris, 1954) p. 337. Almost half

The popularity of these texts outside learned circles is also shown by the number of translations. Nearly all the many translations of the works of St Bernard, according to Leclercq, were made in the late Middle Ages [17]. Hugh of St Victor was translated in the fourteenth and fifteenth centuries into French, German, Flemish, Italian, and Czech [18]. The library of King Charles V of France included translations of works by Hugh, Innocent III, Elizabeth of Schönau, Aelred of Rievaulx, and other twelfth-century authors [19]. The *Scala claustralium* was translated into Middle English [20]; the *Speculum virginum* into various languages in the fifteenth and sixteenth centuries [21]; and the works of John of Fécamp (under the name of St Augustine) into German, Italian, and Dutch before 1500 and later into English, Spanish, Polish, French, Swedish, and Greek [22].

Many of these works are listed in late medieval library catalogues. Charles V, for instance, in addition to the translations mentioned above, owned manuscripts of spiritual works by Bernard and Hugh, and on one occasion he gave a copy of Guigo's *Meditationes* to the Dominicans at Troyes [23]. The papal library at Avignon in 1369 included works by Aelred, Anselm, Bernard, Guigo, Hugh, Joachim, and Richard. [24]. Works by

---

of the known French manuscripts of the *Elucidarium* are fourteenth and fifteenth century, although in this case there are more fourteenth- than fifteenth-century copies: *ibid.*, pp. 48-49; cf. Valerie I. J. Flint, « The Original Text of the *Elucidarium* of Honorius Augustodunensis from the Twelfth Century English Manuscripts », *Scriptorium*, XVII (1964) 91-94.

[17] Leclercq, *Études*, p. 12, n. 4.

[18] Roger Baron, *Science et sagesse chez Hugues de Saint-Victor* (Paris, 1957) pp. 238-39.

[19] Léopold Delisle, *Recherches sur la librairie de Charles V* (Paris, 1907) I, 85-88 (263-64), 118 (224-27), 235-36, and 259; II, 67* (no. 379), 88-89* (no. 519), and 126* (no. 776).

[20] *The Cloud of Unknowing*, ed. Phyllis Hodgson (Early English Text Society, 218; London, 1944) p. LXXVI, mentioning three manuscripts.

[21] François Vandenbroucke, in Jean Leclercq, François Vandenbroucke, and Louis Bouyer, *La spiritualité du moyen âge* (Paris, 1961) p. 553.

[22] Stephen A. Hurlbut, *The Picture of the Heavenly Jerusalem in the Writings of Johannes of Fécamp* (Washington, 1929-43) VI, 8-12, and VII, 10.

[23] Delisle, *Recherches*, I, 124 and 330, n. 1; II, 307, 309, 310.

[24] Franz Ehrle, *Historia bibliothecae Romanorum pontificum*, I (Rome, 1890) 366 (Aelred), 311-13 (Bernard), 332 (Guigo), 302-3 (Hugh and Richard), 314 (Joachim), and others s. n. in index.

Anselm, Bernard, Hugh, and Richard also appeared in the inventory of books drawn up by Pope Nicholas V at the request of Cosimo de' Medici [25] and were prominent in the libraries of the Augustinian hermits, which were formed and catalogued in the fourteenth and fifteenth centuries [26].

The mere existence of books in libraries, however, is no evidence that they were read. The newly-formed humanist libraries, as might be expected, were less rich in twelfth-century spiritual texts than the old ecclesiastical collections. The Malatesta at Cesena appear to have had only one late manuscript of Bernard [27]; and in spite of the inventory drawn up by Nicholas V, all except one of the fifty-two books found in his own room after his death were classical texts [28]. But this was not universally the case. Petrarch showed his interest in the twelfth century not only by his well-known sympathy for Abelard but also by owning and reading works by Bernard, Hugh, Richard, and other twelfth-century writers [29]. The Urbino manuscripts now in the Vatican included works by Anselm, Bernard, Bernard of Cluny (Morval), Gilbert of Hoyland, Guigo, Hugh, Hugh of Fouilloy, Peter Damiani, Richard, and William of St Thierry, in addition to several anonymous twelfth-century works [30]. Pico della Mirandola also had manuscripts of works by Anselm, Bernard, Gilbert of Hoyland, Hugh, Joachim, and

---

[25] Giovanni Sforza, « La patria, la famiglia e la giovinezza di Papa Niccolò V », *Atti della Reale Accademia Lucchese di Scienze, lettere ed arti*, XXIII (1884) 365.

[26] David Gutiérrez, « De antiquis ordinis eremitarum sancti Augustini bibliothecis », *Analecta Augustiniana*, XXIII (1954) 186, 200, 207, 214, 221, 232, 243, 245, 247, 275, 277, 278, 303, 306, 307 (Bernard), 229, 244, 274, 307 (Anselm), 212, 221, 243, 255, 275, 302, 307 (Hugh and Richard), 215, 302 (Hugh of Fouilloy), 275, 276 (Innocent III).

[27] J. M. Mucciolo, *Catalogus codicum manuscriptorum Malatestianae Caesenatis bibliothecae* (Cesena, 1780-84) I, 56.

[28] Sforza, in *Atti*, XXIII, 385-91.

[29] Pierre de Nolhac, *Pétrarche et l'humanisme* (Bibliothèque littéraire de la Renaissance, N. S. 1-2; Paris, 1907) II, 217-24 (Abelard) and 224-25 (Bernard), I, 113, and II, 208, 216 (Hugh), I, 104, 113, and II, 216-17 (Richard), I, 61-62 (life of Peter Damiani), I, 113, and II, 218 (Stephen of Tournai), II, 207, 216 (Fulbert of Chartres).

[30] Cosimo Stornaiolo, *Codices Urbinates Latini* (Rome, 1902-21) s. n. in index.

Ralph of Flavigny [31], although there is no evidence in his own writings that he ever read any of these authors [32].

The reading habits and interests of humbler folk, and of those involved in late medieval religious movements, are shown by lists of recommended reading. Gerard Groote, Florentius Radewyns, and the Deventer canons urged their followers to read such « devout », « simple », and « moral » works as the *Speculum monachorum* by Arnulf of Bohéries and the *Epistola ad fratres de Monte Dei* (the so-called « Golden Letter ») by William of St Thierry [33]. In addition to these and other short texts, which were mostly attributed to Augustine and Bernard, Jean Mombaer recommended various works by Bernard, Richard, Hugh, and Letbert of St Rufus in his *Rosetum* [34], which has been described as a « spiritual arsenal of the end of the fifteenth century » [35]. A century later, the same works appeared in the rules drawn up for Jesuit novices in 1573/80, who were instructed to read, among other works, those of Bernard, Hugh, Innocent III, Peter Damiani, and Richard, and also the less common *De miraculis* by Peter the Venerable, which reflects the spirituality of Cluny in the first half of the twelfth century [36].

Among the best-known of these texts was an anonymous poem *De contemptu mundi*, which was thought to be by Bernard and was found with several other twelfth-century texts in a

---

[31] Pearl Kibre, *The Library of Pico della Mirandola* (New York, 1936) nos. 708 (Anselm), 690 and 1141 (Bernard), 714 (Gilbert), 691 (Hugh), 461 (Joachim), and 948 (Ralph).

[32] P. O. Kristeller, « Giovanni Pico della Mirandola and his Sources », *L'opera e il pensiero di Giovanni Pico della Mirandola nella storia dell'umanesimo* (Florence, 1965) I, 35-133.

[33] Thomas à Kempis, *Opera omnia*, ed. H. Sommalius (Lyons, 1623) pp. 957 (*Vita D. Florentii*, XXIV, 3), 964-5 (letter of Radewyns), 920 (*Vita Gerardi Magni*, XVIII, 11); « Propositum cujusdam canonici », *Collationes Brugenses*, XIV (1909) 8-9; cf. Marcel Viller, « Le *Speculum monachorum* et la 'Dévotion moderne' », *Revue d'ascétique et de mystique*, III (1922) 45-56; and Pierre Debongnie, in *Dictionnaire de spiritualité*, III (Paris, 1954-57) 741-42.

[34] Pierre Debongnie, *Jean Mombaer de Bruxelles, abbé de Livry: Ses écrits et ses réformes* (Université de Louvain: Recueil de travaux publiés par les membres des conférences d'histoire et de philologie, II, 11; Louvain-Toulouse, 1928) pp. 320-31.

[35] Viller, in *Revue d'ascétique*, III, 47.

[36] Joseph de Guibert, *The Jesuits: Their Spiritual Doctrine and Practice*, tr. William Young, ed. George Ganss (Chicago, 1964) pp. 216-17.

widely used textbook entitled *Auctores octo*, of which the manuscript history can be traced back to the thirteenth century and which appeared in at least thirty printed editions before 1500 [37]. The other works in this collection were less pious, but the fact that one of Erasmus's earliest poems, written while he was a schoolboy at Deventer, was modeled on the twelfth-century comedy *Pamphilus de amore* shows the established position of twelfth-century texts in late medieval education [38]. Young clerics in particular were advised to study devout and simple works like the treatises of Bernard rather than lofty and difficult texts, and the demand for such works among the parish clergy helps account for the large number of early printed editions of such works [39].

The works of many eleventh- and twelfth-century spiritual writers were printed before 1550: Adam of St Victor, Amadeus of Lausanne, Anselm, Bernard, Bruno of Cologne, Elizabeth of Schönau, Guigo I and II, Hildegard, Hugh, Hugh of Fouilloy, Innocent III, Joachim, John of Fécamp, Peter Damiani, Peter the Venerable, Richard, and William of St Thierry [40]. Bernard's works alone appeared in almost three hundred printed editions

---

[37] E. Ph. Goldschmidt, *Medieval Texts and Their First Appearance in Print* (Supplement to the Bibliographical Society's Transactions, 16; London, 1943) pp. 29-30.

[38] Augustin Renaudet, *Préréforme et humanisme à Paris pendant les premières guerres d'Italie (1494-1517)* (Bibliothèque de l'Institut français de Florence, I, 6; Paris, 1916) p. 262; cf. the additional note in the second ed. (Paris, 1953) p. 735. On the early editions of the *Pamphilus*, see Goldschmidt, *Medieval Texts*, p. 3, n. 1.

[39] Friedrich Oediger, *Über die Bildung der Geistlichen im späten Mittelalter* (Studien und Texte zur Geistesgeschichte des Mittelalters, 2; Leiden-Cologne, 1953) pp. 19 and 121.

[40] In addition to the works listed by Goldschmidt, *Medieval Texts*, pp. 122-25, and Jean Dagens, *Bibliographie chronologique de la littérature de spiritualité et de ses sources (1501-1610)* (Paris, 1952), see Amadeus of Lausanne, *Huit homélies mariales*, ed. G. Bavaud, Jean Deshusses, and Antoine Dumas (Sources chrétiennes, 72; Paris, 1960) p. 48; Renaudet, *Préréforme*, pp. 104, 472, 500; *Letters of Peter the Venerable* (cited n. 12 above) II, 45-47; Wilmart, *Auteurs spirituels* (cited n. 5 above) p. 231; Hurlbut, *Heavenly Jerusalem* (cited n. 22 above) VII, 8; Guigo of La Chartreuse, *Meditationes*, ed. André Wilmart (Études de philosophie médiévale, 22; Paris, 1936) pp. 41-42; and William of St Thierry, *Epistola ad fratres de Monte Dei*, ed. M.-M. Davy (Études de philosophie médiévale, 29; Paris, 1940) p. 29.

before 1500 [41], and twenty-two editions of Innocent III's *De miseria humanae conditionis* were printed before 1520 [42]. The selection of these works by fifteenth- and sixteenth-century printers was dictated, according to Goldschmidt, by « the current vogue for mystical contemplation and edification » among both clerics and laymen. « The demand for the mystical Christian writers », he said, « was so compelling in the period 1450-1550 that it resulted in the publication of practically every work in this class which we now consider to be of importance and value » [43].

II.

Of individual twelfth-century writers whose works were widely read in the late Middle Ages, St Bernard was by far the most important. Bernard and Augustine, according to Renaudet, were « the two great masters of the interior life and divine love » for the fifteenth century [44]. Wilmart wrote that, « St Augustine himself, who left many more works [than Bernard] ... did not, by far, have a comparable fate » [45]. And Bremond referred to Bernard as « that extraordinary man, off whom we live today at least as much as off St Augustine » [46]. An interesting special study should be written on the *Nachleben* of Bernard. It was by no means restricted, as Le Bail implies in his brief account of Bernard's influence in the *Dictionnaire de spiritualité*, to the four schools of the Franciscans, the nuns of Helfta, the *Devotio moderna*, and the French sixteenth- and seventeenth-century mystics [47]. Châtillon has shown that Bernard's influence on scholastic thought in the twelfth and thirteenth centuries was « more

---

[41] Leopold Janauschek, *Bibliographia Bernardina* (Xenia Bernardina, 4; Vienna, 1891) pp. 3-74.

[42] *De miseria*, ed. Maccarrone (cited n. 8 above) pp. XX-XXI.

[43] Goldschmidt, *Medieval Texts*, p. 51.

[44] Renaudet, *Préréforme*, pp. 70-71.

[45] Cited by Jean Leclercq, « L'édition de saint Bernard: Problèmes et perspectives », *Revue d'histoire ecclésiastique*, XLV (1950) 715.

[46] Henri Bremond, *Histoire littéraire du sentiment religieux en France* (Paris, 1915-32) III, 26.

[47] Anselme Le Bail, in *Dictionnaire de spiritualité*, I (Paris, 1932-37) 1495-98.

real, more profound, and more durable than is generally said » [48]. And Bremond has traced his influence through the early modern French school to Auguste Comte, who included Bernard's *De diligendo Deo* in his *Bibliothèque positiviste* on account of its stress on disinterested love of God and renunciation of self, which paralleled the Positivist belief in altruism [49].

« The letters, sermons, meditations, and various opuscula of St Bernard were the only works in the entire Latin patrology that seem to have enjoyed constant favor », said Renaudet [50]. The most influential among his authentic works in the fourteenth and fifteenth centuries were the sermons and some of the treatises, especially the *De consideratione* [51]. But among other widely read works cited under his name were the *Golden Letter* by William of St Thierry, the *Scala claustralium* by Guigo II, and the *Speculum monachorum* by Arnulf of Bohéries. Almost two hundred known apocryphal works, in both prose and verse, helped to spread the celebrity of his name [52]. No less than seven out of the nine treatises in the 1491 edition of Bernard's works were spurious [53]. Some of these apocrypha were anonymous twelfth- and early thirteenth-century works. Others were reworkings or extracts from authentic works. The famous *Meditationes vitae Christi*, for instance, which was written by a Franciscan in Tuscany in the second half of the thirteenth century, depended

---

[48] Jean Châtillon, « L'influence de S. Bernard sur la pensée scolastique au XIIe et au XIIIe siècle », *Saint Bernard théologien* (Analecta sacri ordinis cisterciensis, IX, 3-4; Rome, 1953) pp. 268-88 (quoted passage on p. 269). Châtillon suggests that Bernard exercised a comparable influence on canon law and stresses the difficulties of continuing his study into the fourteenth and fifteenth centuries (p. 269, n. 1). Cf. also Martin Grabmann, *Die Geschichte der scholastischen Methode* (Freiburg-im-Br., 1909-11) II, 107; Robert Linhardt, *Die Mystik des hl. Bernhard von Clairvaux* (Diss. Munich; Munich, 1923) pp. 240-41; and the articles on Bernard and Aquinas cited in Jean de la Croix Bouton, *Bibliographie Bernardine, 1891-1957* (Commission d'histoire de l'ordre de Cîteaux, 5; Paris, 1958) nos. 149, 152, 258.

[49] Bremond, *Histoire litt.*, III, 26.

[50] Renaudet, *Préréforme*, p. 253; cf. pp. 250, 369, 408, commenting on the many editions of Bernard's works printed at Paris.

[51] Leclercq, *Études* (cited n. 9 above) p. 38.

[52] Janauschek, *Bibliographia*, pp. IV-XIV; Ferdinand Cavallera, in *Dictionnaire de spiritualité*, I, 1499-1502.

[53] Wilmart, *Auteurs spirituels*, pp. 76-77.

heavily and in places literally on Bernard [54]. Most of them, however, were composed in the fourteenth and fifteenth centuries and were attributed to Bernard owing to the humility of the author, the desire to enhance the work's prestige, or a similarity with Bernard's real works [55].

The influence and popularity of Bernard's writings can be attributed not only to their content, especially their teaching on contemplation, love, and the humanity of Christ, but also to their style and the example of Bernard's own life. His « prerogative of mellifluous words » was cited by Gertrude of Helfta, who died in 1302, as the reason for her special devotion to Bernard [56]. This was also doubtless a major reason for his popularity with preachers, such as the Franciscans Bernardino of Siena and John of Capistrano in Italy [57] and the Dominican John Bromyard in England, where Bernard's influence on preaching can be traced through the Reformation to Latimer and even Bunyan [58]. Clichtove in his introductory letter to the 1508 Paris edition of Bernard's works particularly praised the sweetness and elegance of his style and « the wrapping of Sacred Scripture » in which Bernard presented his works, and which doubtless appealed to the religious reformers of the period [59].

Clichtove also praised Bernard's erudition and the sanctity of his life. In particular, the combination of action and contemplation found in his life and teaching had a special attraction

---

[54] Columban Fischer, « Die 'Meditationes Vitae Christi': Ihre handschriftliche Ueberlieferung und die Verfasserfrage », *Archivum franciscanum historicum*, XXV (1932) 458-64, and *Meditations on the Life of Christ*, tr. and ed. Isa Ragusa and Rosalie Green (Princeton, 1961) pp. XXI, n. 2 (on the author) and XXVI-XXVII.

[55] Cf. P. Pourrat, *Christian Spirituality in the Middle Ages*, tr. S. P. Jacques (London, 1924) p. 293, and Leclercq, *Études*, p. 12.

[56] Gertrude of Helfta, *Legatus divinae pietatis*, ed. L. Clement (Salzburg, 1662) p. 596 (IV, 50).

[57] Cf. Bernardino of Siena, *Opera omnia* (Quaracchi, 1950 ff.) V, 432-34, for references to Bernard's works in Bernardino's sermons; Johannes Hofer, *Johannes Kapistran: Ein Leben im Kampf um die Reform der Kirche*, 2nd ed. (Bibliotheca Franciscana, 1; Rome-Heidelberg, 1964) II, 32 and 161.

[58] G. R. Owst, *Literature and Pulpit in Medieval England*, 2nd ed. (Oxford-New York, 1961) pp. 99, 108, and s. n. « Bernard » in index.

[59] F. 22 v of the 1508 Paris edition of Bernard's sermons and other works. An exception to this generally expressed admiration of Bernard's style was voiced by Erasmus as a young man: Renaudet, *Préréforme*, p. 264.

for the late Middle Ages. Gerson's ideal of the « ambidextrous » prelate who is at the same time active and contemplative was attributed to Bernard and derived specifically from the *Golden Letter* of William of St Thierry [60]. Gerard Groote admired Bernard's combination of asceticism and apostolic activity and saw in his dispute with Peter the Venerable, and in the esteem and affection between the two protagonists, an example for his own struggle against the degeneracy of the Mendicants [61]. Gerlach Petri, who has been called « the other Thomas à Kempis », closely followed Bernard's teaching on Mary and Martha, saying that to minister like Martha was good, to be idle for God like Mary was better, and to be proficient in both was best [62]. Groote, Radewyns, Mombaer, and other writers of the school of the *Devotio moderna* recommended works by and attributed to Bernard as guides to a virtuous and well-ordered life [63]. Mombaer's doctrine of solitude and the cell derived from the *Golden Letter*, which he believed to be by Bernard, and from Petrarch's *De vita solitaria* [64]. Petrarch himself admired Bernard, and a chapter of the *De vita solitaria* is derived from the *Vita prima* of Bernard written by William of St Thierry [65].

It may have been this combination of action and contemplation in Bernard's life and teaching that endeared him to Dante, though the exact significance of Bernard's role in the *Paradiso*, where he acted as Dante's final guide, has been much debated

---

[60] André Combes, *La théologie mystique de Gerson: Profil de son évolution* (Spiritualitas, 1-2; Rome, 1963-64) I, 384.

[61] Heinrich Gleumes, « Gerhard Groot und die Windesheimer als Verehrer des hl. Bernhard von Clairvaux », *Zeitschrift für Aszese und Mystik*, X (1935) 90-95.

[62] *Ibid.*, 103, comparing Bernard's sermon on the Assumption 3, 3 (Gaume ed. [Paris, 1839] I, 2146-47) with Gerlach Petri's soliloquy 19 (ed. J. Strange [Cologne, 1849] pp. 68-69).

[63] See n. 33 above.

[64] Debongnie, *Mombaer* (cited n. 34 above) p. 136.

[65] Petrarch, *De vita solitaria*, in *Prose*, ed. G. Martellotti a. o. (Milan-Naples, 1955) pp. 460-62; cf. de Nolhac, *Pétrarche* (cited n. 29 above) II, 224-225, and P. O. Kristeller, « Augustine and the Early Renaissance », *Review of Religion*, IX (1944) 346, where he said that, « Petrarch's religious tracts show some connection with the popular religious literature of the Middle Ages ».

by scholars [66]. Vossler, for instance, saw the dualism of Bernard's life, his impelling of man's will towards two goals at once, acceptance and denial of the world, as an expression, for Dante, of the highest religious function [67]. « So from contemplation to desire and to volition », said Vossler, « all the way over and back, Bernard is to guide the pilgrim » [68]. For other scholars, however, Bernard's role in the *Divine Comedy* is simply as an exponent of mystical theology [69]. According to Gilson, Bernard was « the man whom love has transfigured into the image of Christ » and « the personification of the ecstasy caused by loving contemplation of God » [70].

Bernard's doctrine of affective contemplation and his devotion to the humanity of Christ were certainly the principal sources of his appeal to men in the late Middle Ages. According to Reinerius in his *Contra Waldenses*, even heretics like the Ortliebi, who condemned Bernard's writings along with those of Jerome, Augustine, and Ambrose, declared that Bernard was saved, while the others were damned, « because he was converted from his error and was saved, as they said » [71]. Their reason for this view is unclear, but the context suggests that like the Evangelists, whose authority the Ortliebi accepted, Bernard wrote with his heart. The same quality emerges from an episode in the life of John Whethamstede, the humanist abbot of St Albans, who

---

[66] Cf. the articles, of very uneven value, cited by de la Croix Bouton, *Bibliographie*, p. 156. On the whole, Bernard's role has been discussed far less than that of Dante's previous guide, Beatrice. P. Mandonnet, *Dante le théologien* (Paris, 1935), for instance, hardly assigns any role at all to Bernard. On the importance for Dante of some of Bernard's works, see Erich Auerbach, « Figurative Texts Illustrating Certain Passages of Dante's *Commedia* », *Speculum*, XXI (1946) 474-89, esp. 478 and 489.

[67] Karl Vossler, *Mediaeval Culture: An Introduction to Dante and His Times*, tr. W. C. Lawton (New York, 1929 [reprint 1958]) I, 72-73.

[68] *Ibid.*, II, 384.

[69] Cf. Edmund Gardner, *Dante and the Mystics* (London, 1913) p. 135 and Augustin Renaudet, *Dante humaniste* (Les classiques de l'humanisme; Paris, 1952) pp. 56 and 105, who also emphasized the « humanist » elements in Bernard (pp. 22 and 174-76). Edward Moore, *Studies in Dante: Second Series* (Oxford, 1899) pp. 62-63, considered that Bernard's main importance for Dante lay in his teaching on the Virgin Mary.

[70] Étienne Gilson, *Dante and Philosophy* (Harper Torchbook, 1089; New York, 1963) pp. 48 and 238.

[71] *Maxima bibliotheca veterum patrum* (Lyons, 1677) XXV, 267 FG (c. VI).

became ill on his way to Rome in 1423 and fell asleep after making his will. « And when he woke up », wrote the St Albans annalist, « he was somewhat restored in his body and recounted how St Bernard seemed to have come to him in a dream and to have promised him his life if henceforth he would love his books and adhere to them with ardent zeal ». The abbot then recovered « more by the aid of this saint than by the cure of doctors », according to the story, which is reminiscent of Jerome's famous dream and suggests that Bernard recalled Whethamstede from his worldly humanism to a proper love of God [72].

These aspects of Bernard's influence are found particularly in the *Devotio moderna*. De la Croix Bouton's *Bibliographie bernardine* lists several articles on Bernard and Groote, Ruysbroeck, Thomas à Kempis, and the Windesheim canons [73], in addition to the general studies by Gleumes and Mikkers, who stressed both the number of citations from Bernard by writers of the school of the *Devotio moderna* and the number of manuscripts of his works in their libraries [74]. They found in Bernard's works many spiritual themes which corresponded to their own religious attitudes: a concentration on inner spiritual development, a personal ideal of a mixed life of action and contemplation culminating in a mystical union with God, and a devotion to the humanity of Christ which included not only the example of his life and sufferings but also his role in the mystical marriage of union with the Word. In the works of this school, and above all in the *Imitatio Christi*, these themes were expressed in a form suited to the spirituality of that age. « Gerard Groote received and magnified », said de Lubac, « while modifying it somewhat, the current of affective piety issuing from St Bernard and St

---

[72] John Amundesham, *Annales monasterii S. Albini*, ed. Henry Riley (Rolls Series, 28; London, 1870-71) I, 151; cf. E. F. Jacob, *Essays in the Conciliar Epoch*, 2nd ed. (Manchester, 1953) pp. 45 and 192 and R. Weiss, *Humanism in England during the Fifteenth Century*, 3rd ed. (Oxford, 1967) p. 32.

[73] De la Croix Bouton, *Bibliographie*, nos. 711 and 779 (Ruysbroeck), 287, 302, and 491 (Thomas à Kempis), and others.

[74] Edmond Mikkers, « Sint Bernardus en de Moderne Devotie », *Cîteaux in de Nederlanden*, IV (1953) 149-86, esp. 154-58 and 180-86. According to Mikkers, this influence came through reading Bernard's own works and not intermediary Bernardine texts.

Francis of Assisi »[75]. The very fact that serious scholars have argued that the *Imitatio Christi* was written by a Benedictine abbot in the early thirteenth century shows its spiritual compatibility with that period[76]. « St Bernard, Hugh and Richard of St Victor », wrote Jacob, « to these the *Imitatio* owes most, especially to Bernard's Sermons on the *Cantica Canticorum* »[77].

Similar themes are found in the works of other twelfth-century writers, whose influence also deserves further study. In a recent article on Hugh of St Victor, Roger Baron cited a long list of writers who were influenced either directly or indirectly by Hugh[78]. Châtillon and Ribaillier have shown that Richard of St Victor was hardly less important. « His *Benjamins* became classic works », said Ribailler, « and played in the history of spirituality approximately the same role as the *Sentences* of Peter Lombard in theology »[79]. Much of Richard's influence was exercised through other works, such as the *Explanacio* of Thomas Gallus, which was written in 1242-45 and which in the fifteenth century, according to Javelet, « inspired the anti-intellectualist current in the Carthusian and Benedictine abbeys

[75] De Lubac, *Exégèse* (cited n. 1 above) II . 2, 496; cf. the view expressed by Gilson in his introduction to M.-D. Chenu, *La théologie au douzième siècle* (Études de philosophie médiévale, 45; Paris, 1957) p. 9: « Il ne fait pour nous aucun doute que la *devotio moderna*, dont le sens nouveau est d'être une réaction contre la scolastique du XIIIe siècle, continue simplement un courant plus ancien opposé d'avance à des méthodes théologiques dont, même vers la fin du XIIe siècle, le développement futur n'était pas encore prévisible ».

[76] Cf. J. Mahieu, « Le bénédictinisme de l'Imitation de Jésus-Christ », *Ephemerides theologicae Lovanienses*, XXII (1946) 376-94, who (while clearly accepting its fifteenth-century authorship and denying its Benedictine character) accepts, with Dom Berlière, that it contains Benedictine elements (pp. 389-90).

[77] Jacob, *Essays*, p. 151, who throughout this essay on the *Imitatio* (pp. 139-53) stresses the influence of these three writers.

[78] Roger Baron, « L'influence de Hugues de Saint-Victor », *Recherches de théologie ancienne et médiévale*, XXII (1955) 56-71; cf. de Lubac, *Exégèse*, II . 1, 427, on his importance in establishing a distinct discipline of spirituality.

[79] Ed. cited n. 15 above, p. 72; cf. *Liber exceptionum* (cited n. 14 above) p. 81; Renaudet, *Préréforme*, pp. 73 and 521. I have not seen the article on Richard by J. M. Schallij cited by Vandenbroucke, *Spiritualité*, p. 471, who gives other examples of Richard's influence (pp. 271, 503-4, 526, 571).

in southern Germany »[80]. In a different field, the prophetic writings of Joachim of Flora were highly influential right down to the eighteenth century[81].

John of Fécamp is a writer whose importance (and even whose identity) was more or less discovered by Wilmart, who considered him the most remarkable and characteristic medieval spiritual writer before Bernard[82]. His works circulated under various attributions. Hurlbut in particular has traced the process of transformation of his *De contemplativa vita* into, first, the *Liber supputationum* and later, probably in the late fourteenth or early fifteenth century, into the famous *Liber meditationum sancti Augustini*, which was widely read by both Catholics and Protestants up at least until the seventeenth century and of which new editions and translations, for devotional purposes, have appeared in modern times[83].

William of St Thierry is another author whose influence on later medieval spirituality deserves to be studied[84]. Although his *Golden Letter* was commonly attributed to Bernard, and he was Bernard's first biographer, recent scholars have emphasized the distinctive nature of his thought and doctrine[85]. The *Golden Letter* in particular influenced the *Devotio moderna*. Radewyns recommended it to one of the Windesheim canons as a work

---

[80] Robert Javelet, « Thomas Gallus et Richard de Saint-Victor mystiques », *Recherches de théologie ancienne et médiévale*, XXIX (1962) 206.

[81] Cf. Morton Bloomfield, « Joachim of Flora: A Critical Survey of His Canon, Teachings, Sources, Biography and Influence », *Traditio*, XIII (1957) 294-307, and B. Hirsch-Reich, « Eine Bibliographie über Joachim von Fiore und dessen Nachwirken », *Recherches de théologie ancienne et médiévale*, XXIV (1957) 33-35 and 38.

[82] Wilmart, *Auteurs spirituels* (cited n. 5 above) p. 127; cf. Jean Leclercq and Jean-Paul Bonnes, *Un maître de la vie spirituelle au XIe siècle: Jean de Fécamp* (Études de théologie et d'histoire de la spiritualité, 19; Paris, 1946) pp. 9 and 103.

[83] Hurlbut, *Heavenly Jerusalem* (cited n. 22 above) VI and VII; cf. Dagens, *Bibliographie* (cited n. 40 above) p. 42.

[84] Wilmart, *Auteurs spirituels*, p. 249.

[85] Viller, in *Revue d'ascétique et de mystique*, III (1922) 78; J.-M. Déchanet, *Aux sources de la spiritualité de Guillaume de Saint-Thierry* (Bruges, 1940) *passim*, esp. p. 22; Robert Javelet, *Image et ressemblance au douzième siècle de saint Anselme à Alain de Lille* (Diss. Strasbourg, 1967) I, XVII. Wilmart, *Auteurs spirituels*, p. 252, on the other hand, is of the opinion that William follows « assez fidèlement » the spiritual doctrine of Bernard.

where he could learn where he was deficient and proficient in virtue [86]. Its influence on Ruysbroeck, John of Schonhaven, and Gerlach Petri has been studied in an unpublished thesis by Réance Ruypens [87]; and Pinard de la Boullaye showed it was used by Vincent Ferrer and possibly also by Ignatius Loyola [88]. Its popularity among those with mystical inclinations was apparently so great that Gerson in one of his sermons warned against its teaching on the union of the contemplative soul with God, saying that, « Bernard [i. e., William] should be read with caution on this matter » [89]. But Combes has shown that Gerson himself was deeply influenced by the *Golden Letter*, from which he derived his ideal, mentioned above, of the « ambidextrous » Christian who is at the same time active and contemplative [90].

Even short works by obscure authors were not without readers in the late Middle Ages. Three examples may be cited. The treatise *De spiritu et anima*, which may have been written by Alcher of Cîteaux about 1160, and which depended heavily on the works of Hugh of St Victor and Isaac of L' Étoile, circulated widely under the name of Augustine and was cited with approval by Albertus Magnus, Thomas Aquinas, and particularly Bonaventura, who was attracted by its doctrine on the simplicity of the soul [91]. In the fifteenth century it was used not only by the Benedictine mystic John of Kastl in his *De adhaerendo Deo*

---

[86] See n. 33 above.

[87] Cited by Wilmart, *Auteurs spirituels*, p. 249.

[88] H. Pinard de la Boullaye, « Aux sources des Exercises: Guillaume de Saint-Thierry et Vincent Ferrer », *Revue d'ascétique et de mystique*, XXVI (1950) 327-46.

[89] Gerson, *Opera omnia* (Antwerp, 1706) III, 1125. This warning has been echoed by later writers, including Pourrat, who was accused by Viller (*Revue d'ascétique*, III, 80) and Wilmart (*Auteurs spirituels*, p. 249, n. 6) of having been imposed upon by Gerson with regard to William's orthodoxy, which they strongly defended.

[90] Combes, *Théologie* (cited n. 60 above) I, 159-60, cf. II, 560 and 597-98 for other examples of William of St Thierry's influence on Gerson.

[91] Wilmart, *Auteurs spirituels*, pp. 174-77; cf. Bernhard Blumenkranz, « La survie médiévale de saint Augustin à travers des apocryphes », *Augustinus magister: Congrès international augustinien (Paris, 21-24 Septembre 1954)* (Paris [1955]) II, 1010, who remarked with surprise that the work should ever have been taken as by Augustine.

(which was itself long attributed to Albertus Magnus) [92] but also, and more surprisingly, as Kristeller has recently shown, by the humanist Pier Candido Decembrio in his unpublished treatise on the immortality of the soul [93]. Decembrio followed it so closely, according to Kristeller, only because he believed it was by Augustine; but he evidently found a congenial spiritual doctrine in this twelfth-century Cistercian treatise. The *Scala claustralium* of Guigo II also went under a variety of names, including Augustine, Anselm, Bernard, and Bonaventura. It was widely admired in the fifteenth century, among others by d'Ailly, and was printed by the Brethren of the Common Life in 1482 [94]. The *Speculum monachorum* of Arnulf of Bohéries was popular in the circle of the *Devotio moderna*, as mentioned above, and was recommended by Radewyns to a canon of Windesheim as a work « in accordance with which you can order all your actions » [95].

III.

These and other twelfth-century spiritual texts were therefore an important source of religious teaching for late medieval writers, including some whose intellectual temperament was far removed from that of the pre-scholastic period. Work after work of popular spirituality in the fourteenth and fifteenth centuries show the influence of twelfth-century writers. Important parts of *The Cloud of Unknowing* came from Richard of St Victor, and perhaps also the *Scala claustralium* and the *De institutione novitiorum* by Hugh of St Victor [96]. Another anonymous fourteenth-century English mystical treatise, *A Stodye of Wysdome*,

---

[92] Martin Grabmann, « Der Benediktinermystiker Johannes von Kastl, der Verfasser des Büchleins *De adhaerendo Deo* », *Theologische Quartalschrift*, CI (1920) 234.

[93] P. O. Kristeller, « Pier Candido Decembrio and His Unpublished Treatise on the Immortality of the Soul », *The Classical Tradition: Literary and Historical Studies in Honor of Harry Caplan* (Ithaca, 1966) pp. 536-58.

[94] Wilmart, *Auteurs spirituels*, pp. 230-31. It was translated into Middle English in the fourteenth century and may have been the source of ch. 35 of *The Cloud of Unknowing* (see n. 20 above).

[95] See n. 33 above.

[96] *Cloud of Unknowing* (cited n. 20 above) pp. LXXIII-LXXVII.

has been called « a short Middle English version of the *Benjamin minor* »; and *A Tretis of Discrescyon of Spirites* is « partly a paraphrase of two of St Bernard's sermons » [97]. A lifetime of scholarship could be spent unravelling the twelfth-century sources of these and other works.

D'Ailly and Gerson in particular were called by Renaudet « the heirs of St Bernard and the Victorines » [98]. D'Ailly, said Renaudet, « was inspired neither from Germany nor from the Low Countries [and] ignored Eckhart and Ruysbroeck. It was above all following Richard of St Victor that he described the three classic stages of the spiritual life ... and following St Bernard that he strove to discover in the *Song of Songs* the symbols of the love of the soul and of Christ » [99]. He composed among other things a pendant to a series of extracts he had made from the *Scala claustralium* [100]. Combes in his volumes on the mystical theology of Gerson also stressed the influence, mentioned above, of Bernard, Hugh, Richard, and William of St Thierry [101]. The same authors appear again in the works of writers educated by the Brethren of the Common Life, such as Nicholas of Cusa [102], and in Italy in the works of Bernardino of Siena, who cited Anselm, Bernard, Guigo II, Hugh, Hugh of Fouilloy, Richard, and William [103], and in South Germany in John of Kastl's *De adhaerendo Deo* [104]. Almost all late medieval religious writers were influenced to some extent by these sources and cannot be fully understood outside this context of religious themes and attitudes going back to the late eleventh and twelfth centuries.

---

[97] *Deonise Hid Diuinite*, ed. Phyllis Hodgson (Early English Text Society, 231; London, 1955) pp. XXXV-XXXVI, cf. XLIII-XLVI.

[98] Renaudet, *Préréforme*, p. 113.

[99] *Ibid.*, p. 73.

[100] Wilmart, *Auteurs spirituels*, p. 231.

[101] Combes, *Théologie*, I, 63, 103, 121; II, 53-54, 97, 129-36, 196-99, 566; cf. Renaudet, *Préréforme*, pp. 74 and 76.

[102] Edmond Vansteenberghe, *Le cardinal Nicolas de Cues (1401-1464): L'action — la pensée* (Lille, 1920) pp. 42, 262, 423-25.

[103] Bernardino, *Opera* (cited n. 57 above) indices auctorum: V, 421; VII, 577; VIII, 345; IX, 346 (Anselm); V, 432-34; VII, 581-82; VIII, 347; IX, 448 (Bernard); V, 457; VII, 588; VIII, 350; IX, 452 (Hugh); V, 472; VII, 593; VIII, 355; IX, 456 (Richard).

[104] Grabmann, in *Theol. Quartalschrift*, CI, 186-235.

Finally, some clues to this spiritual correspondence between the twelfth and fifteenth centuries can be found in their use of various ancient and patristic sources. Already in 1920, for example, Vansteenberghe wrote that Nicholas of Cusa « rediscovered Platonism, usually purged by St Augustine, sometimes also changed by the Alexandrians and [John] Scotus Erigena, in [the works of] St Anselm, St Bernard, and the mystics of the Rhine valley » [105], but he suggested only the possibility of a direct connection with the Platonists at Chartres [106]. This was subsequently established by Klibansky, who wrote that:

> The influence of the masters of Chartres, latent for two centuries, revives in the doctrines of Nicholas of Cusa, who, more perhaps than any other individual thinker, contributed to the formation of the so-called modern cosmology. This connection between the Renaissance philosopher, in the judgement of contemporaries the « grande Platonista », and the Platonists of the twelfth century is a striking instance of the continuity of Platonic tradition [107]

— and also of the philosophical and spiritual affinity of the twelfth and fifteenth centuries. Twelfth-century Platonism was not restricted to the school of Chartres but was found also, as Chenu and Javelet have shown, in the centers of monastic spirituality [108]. And in the fifteenth century not only Nicholas of Cusa but also Ficino and the broad circle of Renaissance Platonists were indebted to the twelfth-century revival of Platonism [109].

The question of the interest of twelfth-century spiritual writers in Christian Greek works needs further study. Déchanet showed that three-quarters of William of St Thierry's treatise

---

105 Vansteenberghe, *Nicolas de Cues*, p. 423.

106 *Ibid.*, p. 431.

107 Raymond Klibansky, *The Continuity of the Platonic Tradition during the Middle Ages* (London [1950]) pp. 28-29, cf. p. 9.

108 M.-D. Chenu, « Platon à Cîteaux », *Archives d'histoire doctrinale et littéraire du Moyen Age*, XXI (1954) 99-106 (studying the Platonism in the letters of Nicholas of Montiéramey and Peter of Celle) and *Théologie* (cited n. 75 above) pp. 108-141; Robert Javelet, « Psychologie des auteurs spirituels du XIIe siècle », *Revue des sciences religieuses*, XXXIII (1959) 266.

109 Klibansky, *Continuity*, pp. 35-36, who argues (p. 35) that « the prevailing theory of a definite break between mediaeval and Renaissance Platonism ... cannot be maintained on closer inspection of the facts ».

De anima is derived from Gregory of Nyssa [110], and von Ivánka in his review of Déchanet's work stressed more generally the influence on Cistercian and other twelfth-century writings of translations from the Greek made in Hungary [111]. Among the Christian Greek authors read in western monastic circles at that time were not only Gregory of Nyssa but also John of Damascus, Epiphanius, Maximus the Confessor and above all pseudo-Denis and Origen [112]. Javelet has recently suggested a series of parallels between some of these writers and their twelfth-century « counterparts »: William of St Thierry and Gregory of Nyssa, Hugh and pseudo-Denis, and Richard and Origen [113].

The revival of interest in Origen is of particular interest because he also attracted attention in the fifteenth century [114]. The number of manuscripts of Origen's works grew rapidly in the twelfth century, especially in Cistercian libraries; and he had a marked influence on Bernard (some of whose short works are said to be indistinguishable from those of Origen), Richard, William, and the treatise *De spiritu et anima* [115]. Origen's images and his psychological approach to the interpretation of Scripture, especially the Song of Songs, were clearly congenial to the religious temperaments of both the twelfth and the fifteenth century, when Pico della Mirandola among others expressed his admiration for Origen [116]. Whether or not there was any specific connection between the Origenism of the two periods, however, could be established only by detailed research.

The use of Latin authors also needs to be studied. The recipient of this *Festschrift*, for instance, has shown in his article on « Cicero and the Roman Civic Spirit in the Middle Ages and the Early Renaissance » that the medieval attitude towards

---

[110] Déchanet, *Sources* (cited n. 85 above) pp. 25-59, esp. 55.

[111] E. von Ivánka, « Griechische Einflüsse im westlichen Geistesleben des XII. Jahrhunderts », *Egyetemes Philologiai Közlöny*, LXIV (1940) 216-17.

[112] Jean Leclercq, « Origène au XIIe siècle », *Irénikon*, XXIV (1951) 425-39.

[113] Javelet, *Image* (cited n. 85 above) I, 51 and 148-49.

[114] See Leclercq, in *Irénikon*, XXIV, 425-39, and de Lubac, *Exégèse* (cited n. 1 above) I. 1 *passim* (esp. ch. 4).

[115] G. Bardy, « Saint Bernard et Origène? », *Revue du moyen âge latin*, I (1945) 420-21, and Jean Leclercq, « Saint Bernard et Origène d'après un manuscrit de Madrid », *Revue bénédictine*, LIX (1949) 183-95.

[116] Kristeller, in *L'opera di Pico* (cited n. 32 above) pp. 79-80.

Cicero began to change, at least in Italy, in the late twelfth and early thirteenth century [117]; but there is no evidence for any dependence of later Ciceronianism on the twelfth century. With regard to Augustine, the case is unclear [118]. His influence was strong in the eleventh and twelfth centuries, and it is certainly no accident that so many spiritual works written at that time circulated under his name [119]. This influence seems to have declined somewhat in the thirteenth and fourteenth centuries, owing in part to the strength of Aristotelianism; but it then revived in the early Renaissance, according to Kristeller, who stressed the interest in Augustine both of humanists like Petrarch and Ficino and of writers in the school of the *Devotio moderna* [120]. This « graph of interest » in Augustine can also be traced in the histories of individual works like the *Confessions*, in which there was a marked interest in the twelfth century and then again at the end of the Middle Ages [121]. The fact that Augustine and his works clearly appealed to the religious sensibilities of both periods confirms the view that behind the popularity of twelfth-century spiritual works in the late Middle Ages lay a basis of shared religious interests and attitudes.

---

[117] First published in 1939 and revised in *Lordship and Community in Medieval Europe*, ed. Fredric Cheyette (New York, 1968) pp. 291-314.

[118] Cf. Paul Vignaux, « Influence augustinienne », *Augustinus Magister* (cited n. 91 above) III, 265-69.

[119] Cf. Ferdinand Cavallera, in *Dictionnaire de spiritualité*, I, 1130-35. Cf. also the collected edition cited in n. 9 above.

[120] Kristeller, in *Review of Religion*, IX, 39-58.

[121] Pierre Courcelle, *Les Confessions de saint Augustin dans la tradition littéraire* (Paris, 1963) (pp. 265-305 on the twelfth century).

APPENDIX

Century	11th	12th	13th	14th	15th	16th ff.
Aelred (all works) [1]	—	21	57	17	28	7
—, *De Iesu puero* [2]	—	—	6	6	11	—
Amadeus of Lausanne, *Homelies* [3]	—	—	1	—	2	—
Anselm, *Prayers* [4]	—	3	1	2	3	—
Bernard of Morval, *De contemptu mundi* [5]	—	—	5	6	1	1
Conrad of Hirsau, *De mundi contemptu* [6]	—	1	—	—	1	—
De quadripartito exercitio [7]	—	—	1	1	1	—
Guigo I, *Meditationes* [8]	—	3	—	1	7	1
Innocent III, *De miseria* [9]	—	—	96	161	204	9
Isaac of l' Étoile, *Sermons* [10]	—	—	4	1	2	—
Ivo, *Ep. de caritate* [11]	—	—	3	6	10	—
John of Fécamp, *De contemp. vita* [12]	2	6	5	1	1	1

---

1 Anselme Hoste, *Bibliotheca Aelrediana* (Instrumenta patristica, 2; Steenbrugge-The Hague, 1962) *passim*.

2 Aelred of Rievaulx, *De evangelica lectione cum factus esset Jesus annorum duodecim*, ed. A. Hoste (Sources chrétiennes, 60; Paris, 1958) pp. 33-38.

3 Amadeus, *Homélies* (cited n. 40 above) pp. 46-48.

4 Wilmart, *Auteurs spirituels*, pp. 168-69.

5 Bernard of Morval, *De contemptu mundi*, ed. H. C. Hoskier (London, 1929) pp. XXII-XXIII.

6 Conrad of Hirsau (?), *Dialogus de mundi contemptu vel amore*, ed. R. Bultot (Analecta mediaevalia Namurcensia, 19; Louvain-Lille, 1966) pp. 30-34.

7 Wilmart, *Auteurs spirituels*, pp. 240-248.

8 Guigo, *Meditationes* (cited n. 40 above) pp. 41-42.

9 See n. 8 to text.

10 Isaac of l'Étoile, *Sermons*, ed. A. Hoste, I (Sources chrétiennes, 130; Paris, 1967) pp. 70-73.

11 Ivo of Chartres, *Epistola ad Severinum de caritate*, and Richard of St Victor, *De IV gradibus violentae caritatis*, ed. Gervais Dumeige (Textes philosophiques du moyen âge, 3; Paris, 1955) pp. 9-17.

12 Hurlbut, *Heavenly Jerusalem* (cited n. 22 to text) V, 17-18.

Century	11th	12th	13th	14th	15th	16th ff.
—, *Liber supputationum* [13]	—	—	—	6	31	1
—, *Meditationes* [14]	—	—	—	—	10	2
John *Homo Dei, De ordine* [15]	1	6	4	8	19	1
Jubilus [16]	—	1	24	16	41	6
Peter of Blois, *De amicitia* [17]	—	—	2	5	5	—
Richard of St Victor, *De IV gradibus* [18]	—	4	8	6	19	1
Scala claustralium [19]	—	—	1	1	4	—
Speculum virginum [20]	—	8	6	6	31	2
William of St Thierry, *Epistola* [21]	—	9	20	34	42	—
—, *De contemplando Deo* [22]	—	6	13	12	8	—

[13] *Ibid.*, VI, 4.

[14] *Ibid.*, VII, 8-10.

[15] Wilmart, *Auteurs spirituels*, pp. 83-5 and 583.

[16] Wilmart, *Jubilus* (cited n. 4 to text) pp. 7-47.

[17] M.-M. Davy, *Un traité de l'amour du XIIe siècle: Pierre de Blois* (Paris, 1932) p. 35.

[18] Ed. cited n. 11 above, pp. 89-99.

[19] Wilmart, *Auteurs spirituels*, pp. 85, 230, n. 2, and 236, n. 1, who mentions knowing about 100 manuscripts in all but uses these 6.

[20] Bernards, *Speculum* (cited n. 7 to text) p. 10.

[21] William of St Thierry, *Epistola* (cited n. 40 to text) pp. 21-31.

[22] William of St Thierry, *De contemplando Deo*, ed. J. Hourlier (Sources chrétiennes, 61; Paris, 1959) pp. 53-54.

RICHARD C. TREXLER

DEATH AND TESTAMENT IN THE EPISCOPAL CONSTITUTIONS OF FLORENCE (1327) *

* A grant from the American Philosophical Society and a fellowship at the Harvard University Center for Italian Renaissance Studies enabled me to write this article. My friend Julius Kirshner insisted I read the law and the lawyers. My thanks conceal no usurious depravity: the mistakes are mine.

In the year of Our Lord 1372, the Bishop of Florence, Angelo Ricasoli, called together his cathedral canons to discuss a matter of import to the church of Florence. Certain circles in the city were, it seems, questioning the legality of the bishopric's synodal constitutions. The official *liber constitutionum*, displayed publicly in the cathedral so that ignorance of the law could not be pleaded by the bishop's subjects, lacked notarial signatures. On this basis, « nonnulli scholastici volentes contra doctrinam apostolicam plus sapere quam opporteat », said that the see in fact had no law, and that there could be no prosecution on the basis of these constitutions [1].

Since the curia in Florence as elsewhere was one of the prime judicial founts of the city, this was no small matter. Ricasoli, counselled by the canons, reaffirmed the validity of the existing law on his own authority and that of his counsellors.

The ecclesiastical law of the diocese of Florence has not drawn the attention of historians. And yet the signs of its vitality and its essential part in the total legal frame-work of Florentine society are everywhere.

Originally, synodal law in Florence was more concerned with clerical conduct than with that of the society at large [2]. Synodal legislation of this early type tended in Florence to be

---

[1] *A*(rchivio) *A*(rcivescovile), *F*(irenze), *Fondo Mazzei*, « Constitutiones Angeli Ricasoli », 14 Jan. 1372 (all dates modern style unless otherwise designated).

[2] I. a San Luigi, *Etruria Sacra*, I (Florence, 1782) printed synodal decrees of 1055, 1073, and 1139 (pp. 928-931). In 1279 the Cardinal Latino published a set of constitutions intended for Tuscany and for other parts of his legation; J.-D. Mansi, *Sacrorum Conciliorum nova et amplissima collectio* (Florence, Venice, 1759-1798), XXIV, cc. 245-254. Then in February 1327 the legate Orsini republished certain of these with some additions. The legatine constitutions, like the synodal, mostly concern clerical activity. The ten constitutions of Orsini became part of the Florentine constitutional canon; *I Capitoli del Comune di Firenze* (eds. C. Guasti and A. Gherardi) II (Florence, 1893), 50-56.

brief, responding to a more or less immediate exigency. The first full set of constitutions for the diocese, published 13 August 1310 by Antonio d'Orso Biliotti, marked a departure [3]. The attention given to the condition of the clergy remained strong, but here we find a new concern with lay behavior. The framework of the constitutions is that of the *Liber extra* (the Decretal collection of Gregory IX, 1234), whereas the content is often particularly Florentine. Marriage, confession and communion, testaments, usury legislation, popular customs: all received the attention of the bishop.

These constitutions, enlarged and refined by Antonio's successor, represented the beginning — late by Italian standards — of the « canonical » tradition of synodal constitutions in the diocese of Florence. Certain additions were incorporated into these basic tenets, but the wording of the constitutions, in their enlarged form, remained almost identical throughout the Trecento and Quattrocento [4]. Archbishop Cosimo Pazzi reissued

---

[3] Contained in an unpublished codex along with the first surviving constitutions of the see of Fiesole of 1306, *A*(rchivio) *V*(escovile), *F*(iesole), *sezione XXVI*, reg. 1.

[4] Slight emendations to this body of law were made:

1) In a republication by Bishop Angelo Acciaiuoli between 1342-1352 (exact date unknown); text in Mansi, XXVI, cc. 23-70. I find no authority for the various dates for their publication given by past writers. They were never notarized. The communal law books of 1354 speak of episcopal constitutions edited 3 April 1351; *A*(rchivio) di *S*(tato), *F*(irenze), *Provv. XLI*, ff. 14 rv. A few days before (19 March), at least one monetary penalty had been increased (in preparation for the publication?), *B*(iblioteca) *N*(azionale), *F*(irenze), II . I . 347, f. 8 r.

2) In the edition of Cosimo Pazzi at the synod of 8-9 Nov. 1508, printed the following January at Florence: *Constitutiones synodales cleri florentini* (Florence, 1509). A collation of these emendations to the text of 1327 is to be found in *Etruria Sacra*, pp. 1-59.

Further additions to the basic constitutions absorbed into the tradition were as follows:

1) Twelve Constitutions of the same Acciaiuoli (a strong statement of episcopal and curial rights vis-à-vis other courts); Mansi, *ibid.*, cc. 71-74.

2) Four Constitutions of Angelo Ricasoli dated 5 Feb. 1372 reaffirming the validity of Acciaiuoli's synodal constitutions and regulating canonical distributions and absenteeism; cf. n. 1 above.

3) Five Constitutions of Bishop Onofrio dello Steccuto (3 July 1393): proclaiming the feast of the four Doctors of the Church (*Etruria Sacra*, pp. 52 f); listing the feast days on which the curial court was not in session

them, with slight modifications, in 1508. Only as a result of the Fifth Lateran Council (1511-17) was a new set of constitutions issued, and even these incorporated many of the rubrics of the traditional statutes.

From the early Trecento we find, therefore, synodal legislation regulating communal religious behavior, with special attention to municipal law touching spiritual matters. A canon was then developed which, with certain additions, subsisted till the Cinquecento.

This pattern of unchanging constitutions in the later Middle Ages was common to Italy. Does this suggest they were outmoded? Certainly not. But to determine their effectiveness, we would have to examine the court records of the curias of Florence and nearby Fiesole. A careful perusal of communal legislation touching on the diocesan law would also help us answer this question.

This paper is meant to be a beginning. We will examine an early point in the « canonization » of these statutes, the enlargement and legal refinement carried out by Bishop Francesco da Cingoli in August, 1327. Why were these constitutions written? From what historical background do they emerge? What was the reaction of the secular authorities to them? How were the commune and the faithful affected by their pronouncement? Finally, was this body of law, even the episcopal curia itself, relevant to the social history of the commune?

Three essential factors conditioned or explained the decision of Cingoli to modify earlier synodal legislation: development

---

(*ibid.*, pp. 46 f); regulating notarial fees (*ibid.*, pp. 47 f); organizing curial judicial procedure (unpublished); ordering payment of clerical debts to laymen (unpublished). The best ms. for Acciaiuoli's constitutions and those of Onofrio is *BNF*, *Fondo principale*, II . I . 347. Onofrio's unpublished constitutions: ff. 31 v-37 v, 38 v-39 r.

4) A Constitution of Amerigo Corsini again arranging notarial fees; *Etruria Sacra*, p. 53 (date 1411-20).

5) One Constitution of Antonino Pieruzzi ordering a synod each year; *ibid.*, pp. 53 f (22 April 1446).

Finally, one significant set of constitutions did *not* find its way into what I have called the canon or traditional mss. These are synodal constitutions of ca. 1415 regulating the organization of the *clerus florentinus*. They are central to an understanding of the constitutional structure of the diocesan clergy; *BNF*, ms. Cl. XXXII, cod. 31. For some general remarks on Duecento synodal legislation in northern Italy, see R. Brentano, *Two Churches* (Princeton, 1968), pp. 190-193.

within the canon law, the financial condition of the Florentine church, and finally, the relationship between Pope John XXII and the commune of Florence.

The canon law with which we will be concerned deals with the testamentary process. The *Liber extra* of Gregory IX had codified the right of the secular clergy to certain legacies of testators who were not buried in their parish churches [5]. Then the constitution *Quamquam* (1274) stringently regulated the disposition of the bodies and estates of usurers [6]. These seemingly different laws were in fact inextricably related, since the great churches of the Mendicants were the final resting place of most of the rich merchant families of Florence and received large sums of money in the form of legacies — often tainted monies, as the realistic Florentines knew and the Mendicants themselves preached. In 1300 came the bull *Super cathedram*, with which Boniface VIII attempted to maintain the financial viability of the secular clergy while preserving the religious utility of the friars: if a testator elected burial among the Mendicants, they would return to his parish church a quarter of all legacies left them. Incorporated into the Clementines [7], this decretal was fiercely denounced and defended throughout the 1320's. The canon lawyers of the period had, however, another task: to make the law clear and utile. It was accomplished with great difficulty, for there was perhaps no body of church law so open to interpretation as, on the one hand, the law covering testamentary legacies (immeasurably complicated by the *lex nova* of *Super cathedram*) and on the other the law flowing out of *Quamquam*, attempting to define a manifest usurer and determine the disposition of his body and goods. Legal *consilia* on these subjects attracted a wide audience, from notaries through communal officials to the individual bourgeois Christian faced with the writing of a testament. On the eve of the publication of these constitutions, the famed canonist of Bologna, Giovanni d'Andrea,

---

[5] *Corpus iuris canonici*, X . III . 28 . 1, 4, 8-10. Subsequent citations will be to *CIC*.

[6] Subsequently incorporated in the *Liber sextus* (VI . V . 5 . 2). On restitution, see B. Nelson, « The Usurer and the Merchant Prince: Italian Businessmen and the Ecclesiastical Law of Restitution, 1100-1500 », *Journal of Economic History*, VII (1947), supplement, pp. 104-122.

[7] *Dudum a Bonifacio; Clem.*, III. 7. 2.

published what quickly became the standard gloss on the Clementines, and therewith glossed *Super cathedram* [8]. Internal evidence suggests that Cingoli and his lawyers had knowledge of it, along with *consilia* by the same Giovanni d'Andrea, Federigo da Siena, Oldradus de Laude, Matteo Romano, and perhaps Guillaume de Montlauzun and Paolo de' Liazarii, as well as information on the synodal statutes of other Italian sees. Cingoli published these constitutions therefore in an unsettled legal situation, but with all possible legal data at hand.

The financial condition of the bishop and the secular churches of the diocese was not uncertain, however. Systematic analysis of surviving testaments will show that legacies *super altari* to parish churches were declining, while in Florence the friars had cut deeply into testamentary legacies to churches and monasteries. *Super cathedram* was thus heartily welcomed by the secular clergy. The unusual fanfare and solemnity with which the bull was diffused in Florence are a case in point: in the presence of four clerical witnesses a like number of clerical syndics and procurators of the Florentine secular clergy proceeded first to a chapter meeting at the Dominican convent of S. Maria Novella, then to Santa Croce. The bull was read aloud to the friars. Then a copy was furnished each convent. A solemn record was finally made in the bishop's register [9]. This bull, the secular clergy doubtless thought, represented a turn for the better in its financial fortunes.

Taxing of the clergy during the 1320's had been very severe. Military pressure against the commune was building on all sides. And with this pressure came increased demands on the local clergy to support the cause of Florentine independence and Guelphic orthodoxy. A heavy impost on the clergy of the diocese of Florence of 1323 had brought on sequestrations of clerical property, anguished appeals to Avignon, and threats of John XXII to the commune [10]. The matter of some 5000 florins which the commune, apparently illegally, retained from

---

[8] J. F. von Schulte, *Die Geschichte der Quellen und Literatur des canonischen Rechts von Gratian bis auf die Gegenwart*, II (Stuttgart, 1877), 217.

[9] *ASF*, *Not. antecos.*, L 76 (1298-1327), ff. 17 v-19 v (22 April 1300).

[10] See the correspondence of John to the commune in *I Capitoli*, II, 480. Also R. Davidsohn, *Forschungen zur Geschichte von Florenz*, IV, (Berlin, 1908), 451.

decima money owed the pope from 1321 on, remained a point of friction between the pope and Bishop of Florence on the one side, and a recalcitrant commune on the other [11]. All through these years the commune stood under the threat of a stipulated but unpublished interdict, since it insisted on levying on the clergy the *gabella dei contratti* [12]. Indeed the communal taxation of the clergy through the illegal means of gabelle was so pressing that the Florentine clergy had instructed its proctors in September 1326 to obtain an authoritative judgement from the vicar as to whether it should continue to celebrate divine office, given these vexations [13].

Perhaps the bishop thought the moment politically propitious for the publication of the constitutions. Florence was ruled at that time of military stress by the high Guelf Duke of Calabria, himself surrounded by clerical bureaucrats. The heavy taxation did bring expressions of regret, even protest, from John XXII, who averred in one letter to the commune that it was taxing the churches at a time when even the pope would not dream of imposing a *decima* [14]. John admonished the commune, and the clergy appealed repeatedly in these years. But only with the disappearance of Castruccio from the scene, the removal of the Tarlotti bishop of Arezzo, and the return of Louis the Bavarian to Germany do we find the pope ready to oppose seriously the will of the commune in tax matters. As we shall see, there is no present evidence that he opposed it in the question of the bishop's constitutions.

---

[11] There is extensive documentation on the problem of the 5,000 florins. In 1333-4, the bishop was involved in a lengthy court case before curia officials trying to obtain the sums: *A*(rchivio) *S*(egreto) *V*(aticano), *Collectores*, 414, ff. 1-35 v.

[12] We possess letters permissory of John XXII and his successor allowing Cingoli to enter the city to say Mass and offices, despite the unpublished interdict:

Jean XXII (1316-1334), Lettres Communes (ed. G. Mollat), n. 25, 441 (22 May 1326).

Benoît XII (1334-1342), *Lettres Communes* (ed. J.-M. Vidal), n. 3770 (26 Sept. 1336).

Benoît XII (1334-1342), Lettres Closes, Patentes et Curiales se rapportant à la France (ed. G. Daumet), n. 1934 (29 July 1338).

[13] *ASF*, *Not. antecos.*, G 106 (1326-30), f. 1 r (2 Sept. 1326); R. Davidsohn, *Storia di Firenze*, IV (Florence, 1960), 1067.

[14] *ASV*, *R*(eg). *V*(at)., 114, f. 248 r.

The secular clergy could look with even less hope of redress to the papal legate, Gianni Orsini. He had made a dramatic entrance into Florence as legate in June of 1326, « quasi come papa », said Villani [15]. But he immediately busied himself in the acquisition of the commend of the Badia Fiorentina [16] and soon after, in the attempt to acquire the rich *pieve* of Impruneta [17]. That he published a series of constitutions regulating clerical life in February of 1327 [18] must have been a matter of indiffe-rence to the clergy. They were not particularly new, nor did they address themselves to the pressing needs of the clergy: redress in matters of taxation, regulation of testamentary matters and so forth. Why should they have? He was receiving a princely sum for his sustenance from the commune [19], and he chose Santa Croce, the Franciscan church, for the proclamation of his admonishments.

The Bishop of Florence was not present during the publication at Santa Croce. But his lawyers were evidently at work during this spring and summer on an extensive revision and elaboration of the constitutions of his predecessor, Antonio d'Orso Biliotti. These were published in synod to the diocesan clergy on 7 August 1327 [20].

They received the immediate attention of communal lawyers and raised a storm with many citizens. Just a week later, on the 15th, the city councils agreed to send four experts to the cardinal legate to appeal against the constitutions [21]. In April 1328 we hear more of this legation when certain of its members received their salary [22]. At this time instructions were

---

[15] *Cronaca*, VIII, 353.

[16] *ASV*, *RV* 114, f. 226 r (17 Sept. 1327); *RA* (vinionensia) 29, f. 108 v (18 Sept. 1327).

[17] The conflict over Impruneta is best followed in *ASF*, *Not. antecos.* B 1346 (1330-31); cf. Villani, X, 178 on the resolution of the conflict.

[18] Cf. n. 2 above.

[19] *ASF*, *L*(ibri) *F*(abarum), XIII, parte 1, f. 36 r (26 Nov. 1326); *Provv.*, XXIII, f. 56 r (4 Feb. 1327).

[20] *Capitoli*, II, 1-47.

[21] « Constitutio syndicorum ad defendendum iura comunis Florentie et ad appellandum a quibusdam constitutionibus noviter factis per dominum episcopum florentinum »; *LF*, XIII, parte 2, f. 17 r.

[22] « Occasione appellationis facte per comune Florentie causa constitutionum olim factarum per episcopum florentinum »; *Provv.*, XXIV, f. 53 r.

given to the communal camera to expend monies in the court of the legate and wherever else necessary until the resolution of the appeal. By the sixth of July, the commune stood ready to send a formal ambassador, Ser Giusto di Bartolommeo da Pistoia, to the court of Orsini.

The instructions given the emissary were the following: he was ordered to expose to the legate the harm suffered by the commune and by single persons through the edition of the constitutions [23]. The commune, in appealing against certain and all of the constitutions, asked the legate to appoint as judges delegate the abbots of Monte Scalario and of Vallombrosa as well as the priors of the Dominican and Franciscan convents of Prato.

We do not know what the legate's response was to this appeal. In fact, our source for the content of the appeal is, as we shall see, the revision of the constitutions and not any state document or legal *consilia* which I have been able to discover. In any case, we do not lose track of the appeal in the records. On 18 July the notary Ser Giusto di Bartolommeo da Pistoia received a salary for his part in a legation to Orsini [24]. One year later, in July 1329, another syndic was appointed by the priors «ad petendum revocari constitutiones hactenus facte per dominum episcopum florentinum » [25].

If the details of the appeal remain practically unknown, two things are certain: the commune was determined to bring about a change in the constitutions and considered this of great importance. Second, the commune, urged on by many citizens, was successful. For on 1 August 1330, the bishop, after extensive consultations with the *sapientes* at his disposal, removed from the constitutions certain of the rubrics which had brought on lay opposition [26]. While the constitutions

---

[23] *ASF*, *Missive*, III, f. 57 r.

[24] Giusto was definitely involved in the appeal against the constitutions, but also on other ecclesiastical business. This salary entry states simply he went to the Tuscan legate; *Provv.*, XXV, f. 5 r.

[25] *LF*, XIV, f. 16 r. The following Oct. 24th, an embassy of twelve was sent to Avignon « in quibuscumque causis quas dictum comune Florentie habet cum quibuscumque personis coram summo pontifice ... ». The group was led by the Florentine canons Simone Sapiti and Filippo dell'Antella; *ibid.*, f. 32 r.

[26] The text of the revision is in *Capitoli*, II, 47-49.

had been originally published legally and after much thought, the bishop now acted to remove the « incommoda et pericula » to which the faithful had been subject, and acceded « ad Comunis Florentie instantiam et rogamen supplicantium, ut in hiis salubri et opportuno remedio occurramus » [27].

The commune for its part was satisfied. Its procurator, present at the ceremony in the bishop's palace along with witnesses who had been continuously involved in the appeal by the commune from 1327, renounced in the name of the commune all appeals against the constitutions [28]. The copy of the constitutions kept in the statutory archive was corrected by communal notaries [29]. The commune, having attained modification of the constitutions, was now bound by them.

What were these modifications? They all dealt in one way or another with the rights of individuals, the state, and the bishopric in testamental matters. An examination of these articles will aid us in capturing a whiff of the aroma of death and testament in early Trecento Florence, at that moment, that is, when some sentimental writers have seen even medieval corporative man, « standing alone face to face with his creator ». It will tell us as well something about the operation of the episcopal court and camera at this date.

The examination will be divided into four parts: 1. the law regulating the apparatus of the deathbed; 2. the preparation of the testament; 3. the execution of testaments; 4. the communal duties to the episcopal curia in *cause spirituales*. To allow an overview of the development of diocesan law, in examining each segment I will consider first any applicable constitution of Bishop Antonio d'Orso, then the original constitution of Cingoli, its revision, and finally add as a footnote the subsequent development in the constitutions of Bishop fra Angelo Acciaiuoli (1342-52) and those of Archbishop Cosimo Pazzi (1508).

---

[27] *Ibid.*, pp. 47 f.

[28] *Ibid.*, p. 49.

[29] This document (*ASF*, *Capitoli*, XI, ff. 1-19) was written and signed by Ser Benedetto di Maestro Martino da Firenze, the most important episcopal notary of this period. An examination of the marginalia is most instructive, since they indicate by varied signs precisely those areas of the constitutions which the communal lawyers felt questionable.

I. *The Apparatus of the Deathbed*

« There is nothing more due men, than that they be able to write their last will with a free hand » [30].

« Mankind has no greater right than the liberty of disposing of its own goods » [31].

This long-standing religious feeling on the part of men who have sought immortality through the control of capital (monetary or spiritual), and specifically of those medieval men who fully expected to keep watch after death over the execution of their wills, and who knew that one could sin against the dead as well as against the living, was enshrined in the constitutions of the see of Florence from 1310 on. It is in the name of this freedom that Bishop Antonio, and Cingoli after him, castigated those who, preferring temporal gain to spiritual health, did not permit their friends and relations to dispose their wills freely. The results were often intestations in which a soul passed into eternity without having restituted that which he had stolen or procured by usury. In the Antonine and Cingoli constitutions, the authors of such pressures and their supporters were stricken with excommunication [32].

But whereas Bishop Antonio was satisfied with the statement of non-interference, his successor proceeded to spell out just how a free testament might be guaranteed. Whenever a person of the diocese became sick («aliqua infirmitate corporea contigerit aggravari»), he was before all to call his spiritual doctor, his own parish priest, and confess fully to him. Cingoli further prohibited any physician from visiting a sick person more than twice unless the invalid had fully confessed. The doctors were to consult the parish priest before making the visit [33].

---

[30] « Cum nihil magis debeatur hominibus quam ut supprime voluntatis liber sit stilus ... »; *AVF*, sez. XXVI, 1 (s. p.), *de usuris*; *Capitoli*, II, 25, 54. Cf. *Corpus iuris civilis*, C. 1. 2. 1.

[31] « Nichil est quod humano generi magis debeatur, quam libertas de bonis propriis disponendi .... »; *ibid.*, p. 26.

[32] *AVF*, *ibid.*, *de testamentis*; *Capitoli*, II, 25.

[33] « De hoc fidem habeant a proprio sacerdote »; *ibid.*, p. 45. The absolution of a negligent doctor was reserved to the bishop or his vicar, except in article of death.

To most of this the commune of Florence had no objection at all. It was certainly the duty of the republic to look after the spiritual health of its citizens and subjects. The notaries' statutes of 1314 had enshrined the duty of doctors in order to remind the gravely ill of their need to confess [34]. Some years later the commune went further and took over the above-mentioned content of the bishop's constitutions regarding doctors. They were not to visit a sick person more than twice without confession, and they were each year to swear to this before the *esecutore della giustizia* [35]. Only in one matter was Cingoli forced to modify these provisions. In the revision of 1330, the bishop allowed the invalid to call in some other confessor if he first obtained the license of his parish priest [36]. The defense of the revenues of the parish priest vis-à-vis those of the friars is obviously here in question, but this provision touches on the bishop's prerogatives, and we will examine it in that light at a later point.

To ensure the presence of the parish priest at the deathbed, still another provision had been made. Cingoli had ordered that a notary was not to prepare any testament without the parish priest being present. (This did not apply if the priest was prevented from being present) [37]. The penalty for the negligent notary was excommunication. Again, the commune forced the bishop to strike this provision. The motivation for this is clear: while the republic had an interest in seeing that the dying sinner had the spiritual comfort of the priest and the sacraments of the church, it could also see that this procedure would result in numerous intestations. Beyond that, it was

---

[34] The doctor was to state openly to the sick person or to others present: « Ego teneor nomine sacramenti monere, et consulere talem infirmum summere penitentiam de commissis »; R. Ciasca (ed.), *Statuti dell'Arte dei Medici e Speziali* (Florence, 1921), p. 50.

[35] Matteo Villani, *Cronaca*, VII, 92 (August 1357).

[36] « Decernentes insuper, ut ecclesiarum nobis subiettarum parrocchiani suis sacerdotibus, vel de ipsorum licentia alteri sacerdoti, possint libere confiteri »; *Capitoli*, II, 48. N. B. that Acciaiuoli, in republishing these constitutions, retained the words « proprius sacerdos » with no mention of a license to confess to another. This uncertainty may reflect the wavering interpretation of the bull *Super cathedram*.

[37] « Notarius prefata [testamenta, codicillos vel alias ultimas voluntates] scribere non audeat, nisi habeatur prius presentia proprii sacerdotis, si sine periculo adesse poterit »; *Capitoli*, II, 25.

aware that the presence of the priest was not, in fact, as the church knew, the best guarantee in all cases for a « freely » dictated last will and testament, i. e. one that could be at variance with what he had told his confessor [38]. Let us examine more carefully the procedure after the arrival of the priest, notary, and perhaps, doctor to gain more light on this point.

The very first thing to be accomplished at the deathbed was *not* the writing of the testament, but the general confession [39]. Secret of course, but limitedly so. Aside from the problems of overhearing by relatives, the common practice of medieval priests of retelling the secrets of the confessional in story form, and indeed the different concept of secrecy shared by that earlier age, there were institutional hindrances to secrecy. If the dying person was a «manifest usurer», he was obliged by the canon law and by the constitutions to sign a long public *cautio* in which he recognized his usury and the length of time he had practiced it, and stipulated funds from his estate to make restitution; in fact he obligated, along with his *fideiussor*, his whole estate to cover eventual claims of his debtors [40]. Only then, according to d'Orso's and Cingoli's constitutions, was a priest permitted to give him last sacraments or a notary to take down his testament [41]. This

---

[38] The Ravennan Constitutions of 1286 are the only ones up to this time in Mansi containing such a provision for North Italian sees; the presence of the priest, however, was mandatory only for the testament of a usurer; Mansi, XXIV, c. 621.

[39] « Primo et ante omnia ... sacerdotem convocet et sibi ... confiteatur »; *Capitoli*, II, 45. It should be cautioned that there is no specific and direct mandate *sub pena*.

[40] This *cautio* is given in the constitution *de usuris* of Antonio d'Orso: *AVF*, *ibid.*, *de usuris*; Cingoli: *Capitoli*, II, 40 f. This is the law; the reality in Florence was different. *Cautiones* were prolific, but of 63 dictated to the bishop's notary within the two years 1336-7, only two fulfilled all these conditions. I hope to publish a paper on the prosecution of usury in the near future.

[41] Here are the key terms: « ... nullus notarius testamento alicuius publici usurarii ... adesse presumat, nec suum testamentum aut ultimam voluntatem quamcumque conscribere, nisi ... caverit ... ». « Nec aliquis sacerdos ... nobis subiettus ... quemquam usurarium manifestum seu hoc crimen confitentem admittat ... ad ecclesiasticam sepulturam, seu illi ecclesiastica conferat sacramenta, nisi ... satisfactione premissa, seu cautione ... »; *Capitoli*, II, 39. N. B. the different terms « public » and « manifest ». Cingoli was in fact more cautious than I suggest in the text. What exactly was stipulated

meant in effect that the manifest usurer had stipulated by a legal instrument in a penitential process, and before any eventual testament or codicil to an existing testament, specific sums for restitution and had obligated his whole estate.

Since secrecy *in foro penitentiali* was prized because it encouraged admission of guilt before God if not man, one can say that the *cautio* itself was a violation of secrecy, since it presupposed expiation (restitution or promise to do so) *before* confessional declaration of guilt. For, to repeat, the manifest usurer could not be absolved if he did not first publicly make or promise restitution.

To all of these provisions touching manifest usurers the commune evidenced no objection [42]. But if we reconstruct the same process, after the arrival of the notary and priest, for those who were not defined in the constitutions as manifest usurers, we will see clearly the danger involved for the estates of very large and respectable segments of Florentine society by the lack of secrecy called for by the constitutions.

As we have seen, the constitutions prescribed that:

primo et ante omnia fide posita in domino Iesu Christo, qui potens est sanare langores, spiritualem anime medicum, qui eum possit solvere et ligare, scilicet proprium sacerdotem, convocet, et sibi sua integraliter et omnia confiteatur peccata [43].

The priest, « cuius est sui peccatoris secretam noscere voluntatem » [44], had of course to decide if the confessed person was contrite. Our constitutions examine this problem:

---

is: the notary could not, without a *cautio*, write a testament of a man who on open table had dealt at usurious rates; a priest could not confess or bury one who had the *fama* or who could be proved by an examination of his books to have practiced usury. Cingoli thus avoided unnecessary conflict with notarial traditions, while entering by the back door: for if a dead man was shown to have been usurious, his testament, without *cautio*, became *ipso iure* invalid. Cf. the following *consilium* on the difference between public, manifest, notorious and famous usury; F. Petrucci, *Disputationes, Questiones, Consilia* (Siena, 1488), q. 8.

[42] These provisions were new with Cingoli; they were then retained into the Cinquecento.

[43] N. 33 above.

[44] *Capitoli*, II, 25.

1. If absolution was not obtained, ecclesiastical burial was to be refused [45].

2. If the priest was prevented from going to the bedside, this penalty did not pertain [46].

3. If the penitent was not « in tali dispositione » to receive penance, i. e. in the necessary spiritual state, he was to be refused absolution [47].

4. If, however, the dying man disposed or would dispose of (« decreverint ») anything that defrauded episcopal rights or those of any church, he was to be refused ecclesiastical burial [48].

5. If then a priest refused ecclesiastical burial for this reason, he would swear to the ordinary authority that the testator had so disposed or was suspected to have so disposed or had admitted that he had so disposed (and thus been refused absolution since not *in dispositione*), and the bishop was to accept this oath of the priest [49].

6. If any secular or religious cleric admitted to ecclesiastical burial one who did so dispose, he was sentenced to a fine of five lire [50].

To make sense of the above: if ecclesiatical burial was refused because of fraud, the priest was to swear that this had been the

---

[45] « Si infirmus masculus vel femina sic decesserit, confessione et absolutione, [ut premittitur, non habitis], et etiam non condito testamento (ad quod condendum omnes rettores ecclesiarum omnes masculos et feminas inducant sollicite et fideliter), et nisi in condendo testamento causa rationabilis eos excuset; si preditta non observaverint, eos privamus ecclesiastica sepultura, et rettores ecclesiarum nostro arbitrio relinquimus puniendos »; *ibid.*, p. 45. The bracketed statement is not in the one ms. of Cingoli's constitutions. This must be a clerical error since otherwise the sentence seems senseless. The addition is found in all subsequent mss.

[46] *Ibid.*, p. 25.

[47] « Quod in confectione testamentorum nuncupativorum, seu alterius ultime voluntatis, proprium advocent sacerdotem, cuius est sui peccatoris secretam noscere voluntatem, prius penitentia recepta, si in tali dispositione fuerint constituti: alioquin ipsi testantes ecclesiastica careant sepultura »; *ibid.*, p. 25.

[48] « Si autem ipsi disponentes circa defraudationem iuris episcopalis vel ecclesie cuiuscumque aliquid in testamento vel alia dispositione legitima decreverint, eadem careant sepultura: quod credatur, cum iuramento proprio, sacerdoti »; *ibid.*

[49] This is the sense of the above quotation.

[50] *Capitoli*, II, 25.

reason. If on the other hand the person was buried canonically, but the bishop then claimed fraud, only two interpretations of this fact were possible:

a. either the priest had absolved the person knowing the latter intended to defraud the bishop, and had thus opened the door to ecclesiastical burial (penalty L. 5) or had even encouraged him to defraud the bishop (the same and excommunication)[51]; or

b. the confessed in his *secreta voluntas* had not intended to defraud the bishop.

Thus, barring complicity of the priest in fraud, any reading of the will which defrauded the rights of the bishop was being interpreted incorrectly. But in the absence of a prosecution of the priest by the bishop for complicity or fraud it would have to be assumed that any conflict between *secreta voluntas* and a will would have to issue either in another interpretation of the will or in its nullity, since either the testator had meant to defraud, and consequently his will was not to be given credence, or the testator had given his secret will to his confessor and had stated it publicly, but it had been incorrectly recorded by the notary.

The unabsolved penitent could not be buried in sacred ground. This meant in effect that one could be buried in sacred ground only if one stated to his confessor that he did not intend to defraud the bishop (barring fraud of the priest). Did this statement have any legal weight? Could a testament which « defrauded the rights of the bishop » be contested by the ecclesiastical authorities on the grounds that the dying man had necessarily confessed to the priest, « cuius est sui peccatoris secretam noscere voluntatem », not to have violated these rights? The « secret desire » of the penitent might have a legal force outweighing any merely oral (*nuncupativus*) will. Perhaps in this interpretation the very burial of the dead man in sacred ground would be evidence that his true will had not offended these rights. These are the types of questions — allowed by the unsettled canonical tradition — which the communal lawyers posed as they pored over the constitutions.

---

[51] *Ibid.*

There is in this paragraph of the constitutions [52] a blurring (intentional?) of the penitential and testamental process which makes it difficult to interpret it with complete satisfaction. But it seems quite clear that the priest's oath to the bishop — or the lack of one — represented a use of the confessional to determine in law the true will of the testator.

The bishop was trying, in fact, to create a process for the normal Christian deathbed penitent (for what Italian man of affairs felt on his deathbed that he had not stolen without restitution?) [53] which was a corollary to that of the manifest usurer: confession before last will and testament, statements of restitution or respect for the prerogatives of the bishop within the penitential process. We will soon see that all references to « the rights of the bishop » meant his right to have and dispose of sums left by testators for the restitution of usury or *male ablata* to unknown persons, as well as his asserted right to dispose of a portion of all monies left to unspecified parties for pious purposes.

What is the balance of our question? Why did the commune object to the priest being present at the writing of the testament? Answer: as the procedure was formulated in the constitutions, the presence of the priest, to whom the testator had just confessed, would place the testator under moral duress, since testamentary dispositions at variance with the previous confession would be personally difficult, if not legally questionable, given the quality of the confessor as the intimate of the « secret will » of the confessed. Such duress would cause an increase in the number of unabsolved deceased — violating the moral imperative of the commune — and bringing in its wake numerous testamentary lawsuits and a decrease in receipts from the contract gabelle.

From the point of view of the bishop, however, the free will of the testator was obviously best guaranteed by a testament which coincided with the « secret will » of the testator as expressed to his confessor.

---

[52] Texts above, nn. 47, 48.

[53] Statutory evidence of this self-understood societal or structural guilt is found in the Ravenna constitutions of 1317: anyone not leaving *male ablata incerta* in his testament was refused ecclesiastical burial; Mansi, XXV, c. 617.

The upshot of the dispute was that the required presence of the priest at the writing of the testament was struck from the constitutions [54]. Thereafter the notary could record a testament without the presence of the priest. On the other hand the injunction to call the confessor and the refusal of ecclesiastical burial to those irresponsibly failing to confess and be absolved remained in force [55].

The doctor, the notary, and the priest had arrived at the bedside of the invalid. The confession had been heard. And now the bishop announced one of his strongest measures: a testament *will* be written, « illam particulam que ad confectionem testamentorum subditos coartabat ... » [56]. All church rectors were to preach with solicitude the necessity of preparing a testament to all men and women under their jurisdiction [57]. If without good cause one was not prepared, the deceased was to be refused ecclesiastical burial [58]. This was a strong measure, even a dangerous one, considering the commonplace of intestation on the widest variety of grounds. Cingoli obviously had his reasons for imposing such a law on the diocese of Florence.

These reasons were not just those already stated: that when one died intestate, all sorts of robberies remained unrestituted, and consequently the soul of the Christian was gravely endangered. Practical difficulties arose for the bishop in the case of intestation. Intestation meant that the estate passed to the natural heirs. They of course in accepting the estate had to accept the obligations or debts which the decedent left behind. But how was one to prove that the testator's estate was indebted through usury taken by the decedent? A most difficult undertaking, the probation of which might lie finally only in the books of

---

[54] Text struck is given above, n. 37.

[55] This state of affairs remains in Pazzi.

[56] This statement is contained in the modification of 1330; *Capitoli*, II, 48. The text of the constitutions (cf. n. 45 above) does not contain this mandate. One must suppose that it was suspended by the bishop *before* the extant ms. was written. The text marginalia do contain, however, this conclusive statement: « Factio testamenti tollatur »; *Capitoli*, II, 45.

[57] Above, n. 45.

[58] *Ibid.* Other dioceses required a testament and, failing this, refused ecclesiastical burial; G. Lebras, *Institutions ecclésiastiques de la Chrétienté médiévale*, I (Paris, 1959), 144.

the decedent. But if the dying man had neither admitted usury to his confessor, nor stated it to the notary in the will, nor given permission for his books to be examined, it would have been costly for a creditor of the estate to prove usury, and as difficult for the bishop, the father of the poor of the diocese, to obtain *iura* or *bona* over any part of the estate [59]. The only practical alternative was to refuse ecclesiastical burial, and this was a highly unpopular and dangerous practice.

In short, it was in this bishop's eyes all-important that if certain usury (i. e. against known parties for known amounts) had been committed, it be declared in a written instrument; further, it was important that the natural, secret will of the penitent to « liberate his soul » from usury or *male ablata* taken from unknown persons by making money available for the poor of Christ, be fixed in legal form. Finally it was desirable that the penitent declare openly this desire to obligate his whole estate to cover usuries or other extortions that might be claimed and proved by his debtors after his death. The reasons were sufficient to make the commune insist on the revocation. The faithful dying intestate could be henceforth buried in sacred ground if they had confessed and been absolved [60].

II. *The Content of the Will*

Let us examine now the purport of the constitutions in the matter of the will itself. Certainly the groups of the population which pressured the commune — if pressure was needed — for revision were accustomed normally to preparing wills rather than leaving all to their natural heirs through intestation. It is consequently in the will which was written, and in the bishop's pro-

---

[59] The difficulties are well illustrated in a later case (1389) where a deceased, « tempore sue vite fenerator », had signed no *cautio*. His heirs denied that he had been a pawnbroker. Two witnesses were called by the Fiesolan vicar charged with overseeing testamentary execution and restitution of usury and *male ablata*, and they testified the deceased had in fact been of good and honest *conversatio*. The testator was then perforce declared by the vicar « non fuisse usurarium publicum vel manifestum, nec eum mutuasse ad fenus »; *AVF*, sez. XIII-B, reg. a, ff. 62 r, 81 v, 82 r.

[60] *Argumentum ad silentium*. This is preserved in Pazzi.

visions regarding it, that we find the core of these constitutional questions. The insistence on the priest's presence, the insistence on a will: both, pointing to the *content* of the will, signalized a departure from previous communal practice.

Bishop Antonio d'Orso had been silent on the actual content of the wills of all but manifest usurers. Cingoli's edition touched on only two points, but the first at least is a key one. We have mentioned it before without elaborating: it concerns the « defraudationem iuris episcopalis vel ecclesie cuiuscumque » [61]. In what could this consist?

Aside from his unquestioned right to the administration of restitution of usuries committed by manifest usurers [62], apart from his authority to take in and distribute to the poor monies left by testators for the restitution of *incerti* [63], the bishop when speaking of his *ius* in these rubrics referred most specifically to another category of legacy: that *ad pias causas* in the interest of the soul of the testator. Exactly, the bishop stated that he had a right to one-third of any sum or sums left in the hands of *fideicommissarii* to be distributed at the discretion of these executors to the poor, ecclesiastical persons, or places [64].

For clarity, let us abstract a typical will of the period made by other than a manifest usurer and isolate all legacies of a « moral » nature. 1. The testator leaves his soul to God, or to Him and some particular saint or saints. 2. The testator names the church to which he leaves his body. 3. The testator then states, in the majority of cases, that his estate must be responsive to the claims of any legal creditor. 4. The testator leaves a stipulated sum « pro incertis ». This « legacy » represented an estimate of sums which the testator felt might not have belonged to him, but rightful owners of which

[61] Text above, n. 48.

[62] Anchored in the canon *Quamquam*; *CIC*, VI . V . 5 . 2.

[63] The authority of the bishop over *incerti* left in testaments was assumed at this time. Giovanni d'Andrea represented just this position for a majority of canonists. For a summation of the question, cf. fra Antonino, *Summa Theologica* (Venice, 1477-80), p. 2, t. 2, c. 4.

[64] « Videlicet, quod tertia pars sic relittorum indistinte pro anima sua ad pias causas, nobis et nostro episcopatui exsolvatur, alia vero tertia pars rettori parrochiali, unde corpora assumuntur, detur et exsolvatur »; *Capitoli*, II, 25.

were unknown to him. These *incerti* or *male ablata incerta*, often confounded with certain usury, might represent even the testator's estimate of the dishonesty of his father or any other person, part of whose estate, including ill-gained goods [65], he may have received. They may represent no more than a monetary estimate of involuntary guilt, that is the unjust earnings made in a society based on a market which produced money rather than simply used it [66].

All the above categories were restitutive in nature. Justice was involved. But legacies *ad pias causas* for the soul of the testator were not restitutive, but rather largess: « largito sunt ex supererogationis consilio » [67]. Such legacies might, it was conceded, contain « forte bona incerta » [68]. But any *incerti* contained therein were assumed to arise from legal contracts, as against usurious ones, and were uncertain, rather than certain. They were a matter of conscience at most, and not of justice [69].

To complete our table, then, let us add this category:

5. The testator leaves sums to pious causes for his soul.

a. He leaves certain specified sums to specified persons or pious institutions (churches, monasteries, convents, hermitages, hospitals, etc.), which are called *distincte* in chancery documents [70] and in the constitutions.

b. He stipulates a certain sum to a category (*ad pias causas* to *pauperibus* or *miserabilibus personis* or *ecclesiasticis locis, religiosis personis* etc.), the final disposition being left to executors

---

[65] *Male ablata* retained their sinful character whatever their disposition by their illegal holder. If transferred, they continued to « produce » sin in their new holder. See the Dominican Giordano da Rivalto's sermon of 1306 meant for the ears of unsuspecting sons of usurer fathers; *BNF*, *Fondo principale*, II . IV . 145, ff. 17 v-18 r.

[66] Perfectly expressed by Dardano di fu Tingho degli Acciaiuoli in a testamentary slip (cedula) left to the prior of SS. Apostoli: « Anche voglio che sia restituito del mio L. 500 d'incerto e quali me pare avere siccome io non debbo »; *AAF*, *Libro di Contratti*, 1335, ff. 10 rv.

[67] Antonino, *ibid.*, p. 2, t. 2, c. 7, § 3, part. 2.

[68] *Ibid.* On the inclusion of *incerti* in legacies *pro anima testatoris*, cf. below, n. 78.

[69] This type of contract was called *conformata*; Antonino, *ibid.*

[70] « Certis distinctis et nominatis personis »; *AAF*, *ibid.*, ff. 163 rv.

appointed for this purpose (« fideicommissarii »). These were called *indistincte* [71].

We have now completed a summary statement of « moral » categories in the wills of average Florentines of the first half of the Trecento. Now we must examine the initiatives taken by the bishop in regard to numbers four and five. Let us first examine the latter, since this is where the force of innovation was greatest, and the social and economic import the most decisive.

Large sums left to *indistincte* categories were a marked feature of testaments of the time. They could assume quite massive proportions [72]. Legally they belonged to the *universitas pauperum* or to yet unnamed ecclesiastical or pious entities. Practically they were under the authority of the *fideicommissarii*. Realistically, indistinct legacies such as these were those least controllable and enforceable. A century later, the republic stated that the majority of pious *lasci* were not in fact ever paid out to their rightful owners, i. e. the poor and the pious [73]. It was precisely this indistinct sum within the will where, in the bishop's mind, the greatest defraudation of the poor and the churches and of his fisc, as father of the poor, took place. The mandate that one-third of such sums be remitted to him for distribution and that another third was to go to the parish church of the deceased is striking in its directness.

If we immediately ask who would have been negatively affected by this constitution, we answer in part: which forces in the city were most angered by its institution? They were four: the *fideicommissarii*, usually a combination of the wife, certain close relatives, and sometimes a religious person (usually a friar); the religious clergy itself; pious confraternities; and finally

---

[71] The term refers in chancery documents as a rule to a specific sum left to a category to be distributed by executors as they saw fit. I have found one case, however, where a grant was called « indistincte » because the recipients were not mentioned in the will, although the testator had specified recipients, if not amounts, to his sister; *ibid.*, ff. 147 rv.

[72] The highest I have found is contained in the will of Gualtiere di Jacopo de' Bardi, who left « 1,000 de auro florenorum pro anima sua pauperibus et piis locis, arbitrio et voluntate fideicommissariorum suorum »; *ibid.*, ff. 36 rv (protocol of 12 April 1336 regarding the will).

[73] *ASF*, *Catasto* 2, f. 72 v (11 May 1431); quote below, p. 54.

hospitals. Let us look at the investment of each of these four in this indistinct sum. First, the *fideicommissarii*. Clearly, any automatic disposition of two-thirds of the *indistincte* out of their hands would effectively remove any major right of disposition over that money. The final third was small consolation.

The interest of the latter three categories in this *indistincte* is just as obvious: with two-thirds of the *indistincte* absorbed by the secular clergy, or at a minimum put at its disposition for further division, few hospitals and confraternities, and least of all monks, friars and nuns outside the jurisdiction of the bishop, could expect to be adequately provided for. Certainly, no guardian of the Franciscan convent of Santa Croce could have imagined the bishop assigning part of that *indistincte* to the Franciscans.

One might well ask the elemental question: why in the first place did so many testators leave such very substantial sums with no specific ordinance for their distribution? The answer is varied, depending on whether this *indistincte* is–and was– considered an investment or a transmitted income.

Any legacy to a pious cause was considered an investment by the medieval testator. The common understanding was that if a proper confession and absolution had been effectuated before death, this ritual act [74] would lead the sinner to purgatory and not to hell. These legacies *ad pias causas* were then critical investments in reducing retribution in purgatory. But the fructifying ability of such investments depended on the spiritual quality of the individual who was the recipient of such money or goods. Thus, leaving money to the poor could be fully accomplished only if a pauper received it. He was of course charged with praying for the soul of the dead, and his prayers were more efficacious than those of most because they were humble. But aside from the eventual prayers of a pauper, his very poverty was fructifying [75]. Aiding the sick was fructifying not only because they

---

[74] Conscience, of course, might be said to form a non-ritual segment of the *opera* of the avoidance of hell, but the medieval mind reified conscience into visible signs, so that proper charity in the testament was an earnest of inner contrition.

[75] Poverty was that condition which insured that the giver's aims were altruistic; cf. Luke 6.20-38, especially « And if you do good to those who do good to you, what credit is that to you? » (33).

would pray for one, but also because of their very sickness. Finally, subventing a friar was fructifying not only because of his prayers, but also because he was a member of a religious order; that is, he belonged to a group within the fabric of Christian society which was « saintly » by corporative definition. If then a tax-paying citizen received poor money, a healthy man slept in a hospital bed bearing a donor's arms, or a vagabond friar or uncloistered nun was the recipient of such bequests, their corporative effectiveness would be negated, and their propitiative effectiveness would be no greater than that issuing from the cultic sacrifice of the priest. But how were the dead to control the corporative identity of a recipient? Doubtless best by leaving these large sums in the hands of fiduciaries who would continually have, as the curial chancery occasionally put it at the time, an « interest » in the soul of the dead [76]. In this way, the money could be invested on the spot, with a higher probability of successful intercession [77].

Still, considering these legacies as investments, we can understand that many testators, wanting to obviate raids on their estate, would avoid mentioning *male ablata*, usurious or not, certain or uncertain, as such in their testaments. They would rather stipulate it as *indistincte* for the poor and the cult [78].

These considerations of the *indistincte* as an investment have the advantage of assuming the sincerity of the testator. He wanted

---

[76] *AAF*, *Libro di Contratti*, f. 135 v.

[77] We see this principle at work in testamentary legacies to specific priests through the intermediary of a *fideicommissarius* who was to pay a certain sum to the priest if, and only if, he performed a required service, e. g. an anniversary Mass for the dead. But the indistinct legacy had the advantage of guaranteeing not only cultic but moral correctness.

[78] This approach was very widespread. In the constitutions of the archbishop of Ravenna of 1317 we find the following:

> Quorumdam fraudibus legis praevaricatorum occurrere intendentes, qui dum male ablata habent, de quibus ignoratur cui sit restitutio facienda, quae essent per locorum episcopos aut ipsorum auctoritate inter pauperes provide dispensanda, legant vel legare procurant, male ablatorum praetextu, de illis non facta mentione, aliquam pecuniae quantitatem per executores seu alios, excluso fraudulenter ordinario episcopo, dispensandam .... Statuimus, quod... quaelibet persona, quae restituere seu restitui voluerit aliqua male ablata incerta ... in suo testamento, codicillo, vel ultima voluntate,

to save his soul, and these *indistincte* were the fashion he chose. But we have already stated that « defrauding of the poor » was extremely widespread. From the beginning, the Florentine law books are full of provisions aiding confraternities, convents, hospitals, and churches in the collection of pious bequests from reluctant executors. The most common loophole was to dispute the right of a confraternity's syndic to collect a legacy because the confraternity was not a *persona morale*, i. e. was unrecognized by the republic or bishop as a legal entity. In this case only a minimum of two-thirds of its members meeting together could appoint a syndic, rather than the captains of the confraternity appointing him [79]. Again, the peculiar ecclesiastical position of a Franciscan house — as a group of propertyless men who, because of their poverty, were in law incapable of forming a corporation since they had no «corpo» — caused the commune at an early stage to appoint a communal official to act as syndic for Santa Croce [80]. In the very interlude of struggle over these constitutions (30 March 1329), twelve companies came forward in a body to the city councils and demanded machinery for collecting these unpaid *lasci* [81]. Clearly, what the *catasto* officials said in 1431 when talking of those obligated to pious places — « la maggior parte di tali cittadini sono in indugio per loro colpa et difecto in hedificare et satisfare dicte gravezze » — was already problematical (or had always been) in 1327. Not only was the bishop determined to force observance of wills in *re indistincte* [82],

---

> expresse dicat et clare: «Relinquo istud vel illud, seu tantum de male ablatis incertis, seu restitutione ipsorum »; nec dicat: « Relinquo pro remedio animae meae, seu parentum meorum ».

The bishops' revenues from *incerti* were here obviously decreasing: the bishop forbade ecclesiastical burial to a testator not leaving *incerti*; Mansi, XXV, c. 617. Cf. Nelson, *op. cit.*, p. 111.

[79] The earliest example I have found of such legislation is in favor of the confraternity of Or San Michele; *ASF*, *Provv.*, XVI, ff. 15 rv (22 Jan. 1319).

[80] *Statuti della repubblica fiorentina* (Florence, 1921), II (Podestà), 166 f.

[81] It is significant that the societies stressed in their petition that the fraud perpetrated by many heirs and executors (« malitiam fideicommissariorum ») of legacies (« legata et relicta ipsis societatibus et alicui earumque de facili sciri non possunt ») worked to the « defraudatio pauperum »; *ASF*, *Diplomatico*, S. Maria Nuova, 30 March 1329.

[82] The question of whether the bishop's motivations were essentially fiscal or charitable is unanswerable. Since not only bread but cult was in the interest of the poor; since the bishop was the administrator as well as

but the confraternities and hospitals and religious entities also had a like interest.

If we now state our question as to why such sums were left in the first place, we will see that to speak only of the remissness of heirs will not do. Clearly, the testators knew these sums often remained undistributed. It remains now to ask: where did certain testators *actually* intend such monies to go? Such *indistincte* must at times have had some other purpose for astute Florentine businessmen, eager as we have seen to continue their business investments after death.

The answer probably lies in the area of tax law. The *gabella de' contratti*, laid on all notarial instruments, struck transfers of money and goods effectuated in last wills and testaments. But pious *lasci* were in a special category. By placing a sizable, but fairly realistic property in the legal hands of *indistincte*, though in the disposition of trustees, these sums, so difficult for their legal owners to collect [83], could be used to transmit income without the gabelle, which attained 10% of the instrument, having to be paid.

This explanation is hypothetical. The lack of evidence on the operation of the *gabella de' contratti* at this early date precludes demonstrable proof. Posterior evidence of the use of such *lasci* is such, however, as to make it the most reasonable explanation for an otherwise inexplicable phenomenon [84]. Its weak point

---

the father of the poor; since certain of the see's lands were considered to be in law of the poor, if administered by the bishop; since the bishop sued for the poor as procurator, Cingoli could respond as the procurator of the estate of the poor to obvious testamental fraud in the best of conscience. And though the lay charitable institutions insisted that « continue dantur pauperibus » (*ibid.*) the accumulation of capital from goods left to the poor, as well as the diversion of poor money to other sections of the economy (e. g. forced loans to the state for war) was a commonplace of the whole society. On the bishop's right as procurator of the poor to poor money for cult on behalf of the poor, cf. the summation of canonical tradition in Antonino, *Summa*, p. 2, t. 2, c. 4. Cingoli as administrator and father of the poor: *AAF*, *Libro di Contratti*, at date 20 Jan. 1336 and *passim*. An example of land belonging to the poor, *ibid.*, ff. 279 rv. Cingoli sued as procurator to establish the rights of the poor to an uncovered coin hoard; *ibid.*, ff. 33 v-35 r.

[83] Cf. n. 81 above.

[84] A law of 22 Feb. 1363 makes it clear, for example, that *distincte* and *indistincte* were handled differently by the governors of the gabelle; at that date *lasci* to churches, religious, and ecclesiastical persons were exempt,

is that, in the earliest gabelle legislation known to me, blood relatives — but not the wife — were excluded from the gabelle if legacies were made to them. Thus under this hypothesis the desired inheritor of these sums would have had to have been either the wife (who was very commonly a fiduciary) or an outside party. Further research on early communal tax law will probably be able to resolve this. I offer the hypothesis in this state because it begins to explain the size of these *indistincte* in a society which knew how often they were not pious in their disposition.

A contemporary modification of testamental law may also explain the popularity of these grants. In the thirteenth century, the civil law *Si quis ad declinandam* (Cod. I. 3. 48) had been interpreted to exclude any apportionment by the legal heir of grants to the poor (including poor churches). But the decretal *Si pater* of Boniface VIII's *Liber sextus* (1298: VI. 3. 11. 1) implied that heirs could withhold a portion from grants to the poor *if* the distribution to the poor was entrusted to a fiduciary. Giovanni d'Andrea seems to have been the first to champion this interpretation. We know that the courts were filled with litigant heirs trying to retain a portion of such poor grants. Baldus notes he had counselled « an infinite number of times » against Giovanni's interpretation. Perhaps this legal firmness explains the contemporary decline of this type of grant in Florence (ca. 1370). In the meantime, testators may have had reason to utilize this indistinct grant, which preserved a legal and financial right of the heir [84 bis].

---

but those « inter pauperes, seu miserabiles personas, seu amore Dei, seu pro anima, seu pro elemosina » left with a *fideicommissarius* with a « distributionis commissio » were taxed. The latter, not being to the honor of the commune, was waived, if it could be proved that the *fideicommissarius* gave the money to the genuinely poor: the proof consisted in producing two witnesses from the *popolo* in question swearing the recipient was in fact poor. In short, the different tax categories resulted from the fraud that easily could be perpetrated in *indistincte; Provv.*, XLIX, 22 Feb. 1362 (s. f.) taken over literally in the *Statuta* of 1415; *Statuta populi et communis Florentiae* (Freiburg, 1778), II, 117 f. Tax fraud resulting from the institution of *fideicommissarii* is explained *ibid.*, pp. 111 f. Fraud from *lasci* to relatives where obligation to a third party existed is regulated *ibid.*, p. 106.

84 bis For brevity's sake I have telescoped the legal problem. It should be mentioned, however, that the subjects of both laws are inheritances of

To sum up, there were reasons for these large *indistincte*. The first was that they offered a better means of saving the soul. The second was that their very uncertainty and their tax status permitted circumvention of the communal fisc and also of the poor and pious places. All pious entities had an interest in forcing executors to distribute these *lasci*, but only the secular church could have benefited from the disposition of Cingoli.

Cingoli's demand for equal thirds for the episcopal and parochial fisc was tied to a refusal of ecclesiastical burial until the executors or *fideicommissarii* handed over one-third of the total to the bishop [85]. It is not clear how the testator himself could neglect to observe this mandate, since its observance in any case rested with the executors of the will. Perhaps the bishop desired that the testator specify in his will that two-thirds were to be distributed in the above fashion, or that the testator settle accounts with the bishop before his death. In any case, it must have seemed intolerable to the citizenry for the bishop to refuse ecclesiastical burial for such reasons. A summary examination of the canons and glosses on ecclesiastical portions and quarters will show on what weak grounds Cingoli stood, asserting as he did that his mandate was in conformity with those canons.

Monies or goods traditionally owed to the bishop through testaments were the following (excluding usury and *male ablata*):

1. Those left directly to him or to the see.

2. A portion of that left to those churches or monasteries under his ordinary authority [86].

3. A portion of the money or goods which a parish church

---

the poor through substitution. For Giovanni d'Andrea's viewpoint, see his *Commentarius libri VI. Bonifacii VIII* (Mainz, 1476), c. *Si pater; Novelle super sexto decreto Codicis* (Pavia, 1484), *de testamentis* c. *Si pater*. Baldus' dissent: *In primum, secundum, et tertium cod. lib. commentaria* (Venice, 1577), c. 44 va.

[85] « Si quis autem presentem nostram constitutionem neglexerit observare, preter peccati penam quam incurrit, tamdiu ecclesiastica careat sepultura, donec ipsius defunti heredes, fideicommissarii et executores, secundum mandatum nostrum vel vicarii nostri, preditta sic salubriter ordinata cum effettu curaverint adimplere »; *Capitoli*, II, 25.

[86] *CIC*, X . III . 26 . 15.

under his authority received from a burial church when a parishioner was buried away from his parish [87].

As a result of the bull *Super cathedram*, the bishop was able in some cases to collect a portion of the more liberal portion accorded the parish church from the burial church (Franciscan and Dominican, later other Mendicant orders) by that bull [88].

In all cases, the bishop was to receive this estate from the parish church or monastery under his authority, and not from the heirs or *fideicommissarii*. Only in the case of *proven* fraud [89] could the bishop make demands on the executors. Three different legal *consilia* written in these years, two by Giovanni d'Andrea [90] and one anonymous [91], hammered away at this point. Cingoli — though not alone — was legislating something clearly beyond the authority of the canons [92].

The canonists' main objection to this procedure was that before the distribution by the *fideicommissarii* took place, there was no surety as to just what sums made up a portion. For example, if these executors gave a sum of the *indistincte* to exempt

---

[87] Cf. the distinction between episcopal and parochial portions made at the time by Matteo Romano and later paraphrased by Francesco de Zabarellis, *Super Clementinas* (Venice, 1481), *de sep. Super cathedram*, § verum, q. 24. The canonist Petrucci later characterized this as « a quarter of the quarter »; q. 6 (a. d. 1341).

[88] Petrucci ascribed this view to Giovanni d'Andrea. *Super cathedram* does not mention the bishop's rights to a portion, but the rector's right. But, Giovanni d'Andrea is paraphrased: the bishop's right referred to that which his rector took in, not to the original destinatee of the grant. Thus if by the new law of *Super cathedram* a parish rector took in a portion from exempt friars, the bishop had a claim on that income, « nam ratione mutationis personarum alteratur natura rei »; *ibid.*

[89] *Collegio di Spagna*, Bologna, ms. 126, ff. 78 r-80 r, *solutio*.

[90] *Ibid.*, ms. 126, ff. 87 v-89 r; ms. 83, f. 145 r (in collaboration with Francesco di Umberto, *decretorum doctor*). I would date these *consilia* certainly in the 1320's, probably before his gloss on the Clementines (ca. 1322), which goes unmentioned.

[91] Above, n. 89. The date of this anonymous *consilium* can be closely approximated: *Dudum a Bonifacio* is mentioned (1311-2). The gloss of Giovanni d'Andrea on the Clementines is not (ca. 1322). The author uses argumentation quite similar to that of Giovanni d'Andrea.

I owe these references to the kindness of Domenico Maffei and Antonio Garcia y Garcia.

[92] On the necessary relationship of episcopal constitutions to the canon law, cf. Petrucci, *Consilium* 64.

persons or groups, or for Masses to be said, or for the fabric fund of a church, or to the poor, no portion could be demanded either by the rector or by the bishop [93]. The bishop's rights, if there were any, depended consequently on who received the money from the executors.

The case for a flat episcopal third on *indistincte* cannot be stated with precision in a few words. On the one hand, it was based on a flimsy reading of the beginning of the canon *Requisisti* in the *Liber extra* [94]. On the other, it logically flowed out of the interpretations put on the bull *Super cathedram* in the first third of the Trecento. The drift of one school of jurisprudence commenting on parochial and episcopal rights during this period allowed this extreme statutory mandate of Cingoli [95].

If the canonical tradition was weak, the fiscal tradition in the dioceses of Florence and Fiesole also offered little obvious precedent. An examination of the fragmentary surviving *mensa* records has turned up no entries from *indistincte* and few if any for quarter portions of legacies by testators to parish churches.

---

[93] Oldradus de Laude († 1335), an outspoken supporter of the friars in the matter of portions, best represents a point of view which strictly limited the categories taxable for a portion; cf. his *Consilia et questiones* (Rome, 1472), q. 61, written shortly after the gloss of Giovanni d'Andrea, which gives a forceful, vibrant picture of the assault by the secular clergy on the orders through the use of *Super cathedram*. Cf. also *Collegio di Spagna*, ms. 83, f. 145 r.

[94] « Et quidem regulariter verum est, quod episcopus debet de his [quae testator pro anima sua legat in ultima voluntate] secundum diversas consuetudines tertiam vel quartam portionem habere »; *CIC*, X, III. 26. 15.

[95] The Bishop of Perugia ca. 1320 warned *fideicommissarii* « qui relicta ad pias causas illis praedictis, quibus debent solvere, et executioni demandare cum effectu, et nobis quartam, nobis debitam, ex eis a die notitiae mortis testatoris debeant »; Mansi, XXV, c. 645. This may be a partial precedent for Cingoli. But the rubric probably means: pay a quarter on those *relicte* where a quarter is owed. This interpretation is suggested in the constitutions of Pistoia of 1308 in the rubric *de solvendo quartam legatorum*: the bishop warns all who receive a legacy (n. b. *not* the *fideicommissarius*): « de quo nobis quarta debetur, quatenus infra unum mensem ... solvere debeat ... »; F. Zaccharia, *Anecdotorum Medii Aevi* (Turin, 1755), pp. 136-149, n. 23. Nonetheless, Cingoli clearly did not act alone; the three *consilia* mentioned above show that different Italian bishops were trying to tax *indistincte* directly. I have uncovered no evidence that they, like Cingoli, so legislated in synod. I will examine the canonical tradition on portions more extensively in a future note.

What, on the contrary, has been uncovered is evidence that certain *pievi* took in quarters from oblations left to parish churches. That is, fragmentary evidence has verified a tradition for pievan, but not diocesan, reception of legacy money [96].

Cingoli may have seen the futility of insisting on *incerti* in each will as had the Archbishop of Ravenna (cf. n. 53 above). Certainly he was well aware of the complexity of collecting small sums from individual *lasci* to individual churches. Since he saw the real financial import of *indistincte* as they were being inserted in wills by Florentines at this time, and saw the fraud of the poor and of the cult that was being perpetrated, he perhaps conceived this plan as practicable. But he was forced to strike the whole paragraph in the rubric *de testamentis*. In the modifications of 1330, he pointedly leaves his claimed third to the «Iuri comuni», i. e. to the disposition of the *fideicommissarii*. Florentines, who in their testaments between 1327 and 1330 seem to have carefully refrained from leaving these large sums, now returned to their previous practice. No future bishop dared make another statutory bid for increasing the episcopal incomes.

Having examined in some detail the problem of *indistincte* and the bishop's asserted right to them, we now proceed to the last point touching the actual content of the testament which was unacceptable to the commune. It concerns number four in the abstracted will of the other-than-manifest usurer given above; namely, the legacy of a sum for *incerti*. No uncertain usuries or uncertain *male ablata* exceeding two lire were to be distributed by any person, without the express license of the bishop [97].

Precisely this provision had been included in the constitutions

---

[96] In December 1300, *pievano* Rainerio of Impruneta warned the clergy and lay of his *pieve* against withholding from him the « quarte decimarum, mortuariorum cappezalis et mortuorum oblationum », as well as not inviting him to festivals and anniversaries of the dead; *ASF*, *Not. antecos.*, B, 1341 (1300-1340), ff. 100 v, 101 r. Also *ibid.*, B, 1340 (1296-1347), f. 245 r (1308).

[97] « Monemus igitur omnes et singulos laicos Florentine civitatis et diocesis, ut predittas usuras et male ablata [usurarum et male ablatorum incertorum], undecumque ad eos pervenerint, sine nostra licentia et consensu, a XL soldis supra restituere sive distribuere non presummant »; *Capitoli*, II, 42.

of Antonio d'Orso of 1310 [98]. And the same text is found in Acciaiuoli's edition a generation later [99], as well as in Cosimo Pazzi's edition of 1508 [100]. The commune had taken no great umbrage at an earlier period. Why did it now object? The bishop explained in his revisions of 1330:

non obstante quod aliter vel alio modo ditta constitutio forsitan legeretur, possint illi qui ad restitutionem incertorum tenentur, illa dum vixerint restituere seu distribuere; nec talis restitutio dum tamen illam fideliter fecerint, intelligatur deinceps eis viventibus per constitutionem huiusmodi interditta. In aliis vero ditta constitutio in sua firmitate persistat [101].

Two remarks may be made. The acceptability of this point in 1310 makes its dubiousness to the lawyers of 1328 and '29 an indication of the distrust with which Cingoli and his lawyers were viewed. Second, what was conceded by the bishop must be well understood: *incerti* might be restituted by the living. Nothing is said in the revision which weakened the bishop's right to distribute or license the distribution of *incerti* by executors, and nothing there compromised the ordinary's rights to supervise restitution of usury. Restitution to entities and the poor of doubtful goods whose true owner was unknown could be conceded by the bishop to the living without endangering the episcopal fisc (although it would cost him the income from licenses). The normal recipients of such goods in any case would be the poor friars and « miserabiles persone ». Further, this would not preclude a further legacy for *incerti* in a codicil or another testament on the deathbed. For *incerti* were supposed to be just that: *incerti*, a matter of conscience demanding purification, rather than bad contracts demanding justice. And how could one finally quantify conscience [102] — un-

---

[98] *AVF,* sez. XXVI, 1, *de usuris*; the same stipulation is contained in Antonio d'Orso's Fiesolan constitutions of 1306; *ibid., de usuris.*

[99] Mansi, XXVI, c. 65.

[100] Pazzi, *de usuris.*

[101] *Capitoli,* II, 48.

[102] Cf. the case of Guccio di fu Tetto da Vezzano who, having given a *cautio* once and restituted usuries, later signed another for restitutions up to 500 florins. He also left 50 florins *incerti* to the bishop to distribute

less, of course, a potential testator paid the bishop a certain sum for *incerti* in exchange for a solemn liberation from any further rights or demands of the bishop to *incerti*? This would be financially advantageous to the bishop, since it would reduce the administrative costs of collecting *incerti* from heirs, while removing only a legal block, not one of conscience [103].

What is not modified, although it might seem to be, is the necessity of a license to make restitution for usury. Why the bishop could not concede this seems certain: to make restitution for usury was to make usury manifest. And a manifest usurer's restitution was canonically a part of the office of the ordinary [104]. But it would be best to draw back from the legal abyss of « manifestness » for now, as we have consistently done in this article.

We have completed an examination of revisions brought about in regard to the content of the testament itself: the canonical portion from *indistincte* was dropped, and the right of the Christian to « return » *incerti* to the poor while alive was asserted. It is even more important to keep in mind what had not been struck, or effectively questioned. None of the provisions in the constitutions regarding manifest usurers was touched; the bishop's curia remained the proper forum for the adjudication of restitution. Testaments were invalid unless they contained a formal *cautio* to make restitution. As we will see subsequently, it is just a question of whether, as we have perhaps suggested in this article, the manifest usurer was an outsider in society, a statistically insignificant portion of mercantile testators.

But before broaching this question, let us proceed to the third part of our inquiry, that touching upon the bishop's law regarding the execution of the testament.

III. *The Execution of the Will*

« Seeing in natural and divine law that multiplicity is subordinate to unity, we are not a little amazed at the presumption

---

among the poor: this all « ex superhabendanti [sic] et ad cautelam et ad suam conscientiam serenandam »; *AAF*, *Libro di Contratti*, ff. 116 v-117 r.

[103] There are many examples of this practice in the late '30's. Cf., for example, *ibid.*, f. 48 r.

[104] *Quamquam* is explicit on this point: *CIC*, VI . V . 5 . 2.

of those who, largely ignoring their spiritual father the bishop and his role in distributing restituted usuries and *male ablata incerta* to pious places and the poor, thoughtlessly distribute these monies themselves ».

This prologue, a copy of Antonio d' Orso's, is a succinct statement of the minor part bishops had played in the execution of testaments. At the same time it announced a successful thrust forward in this area [105].

It will be remembered that immediately after disposing of his soul the testator had ordered where his body was to be laid to rest. And we have also seen that the punishment for failure to fulfill many of the debated points in these constitutions was the prohibition of burial in sacred ground. Execution of the will started with burial, usually the day after death. And yet there can be no doubt that the denial of ecclesiastical burial was a common event in Florence. We have seen that the commune accepted the disposition that if the deceased had not confessed and been absolved, he was not to be buried in sacred ground — always barring unforseen circumstances where confession had been impossible. Further, records of usury *cautiones* from 1336-8 of the diocese of Florence, as well as extensive records of 1350, 1385, 1388-89, 1450-53 of the diocese of Fiesole, show that if a a man died and was said to have committed usuries, but had not given *cautio*, ecclesiastical burial was delayed until relatives or friends came forward to guarantee for the dead man [106]. This direct evidence is supplemented by dozens of legal *consilia*, glosses, and commentaries of the canonists concerning the problem of ecclesiastical burial. Clearly, unpopular as this was among the laity, it was fairly commonplace. Here, as in so many other

---

105 *Capitoli*, II, 42; *AVF*, sez. XXVI, reg. 1, *de usuris*, « cum tam iure ».

106 A selection of cases where the *fideicommissarius* came forward to give *cautio* for deceased « nondum ecclesiastice traditis sepulture »: *Libro di Contratti*, ff. 91 r, 112 r, 165 r, 212 v. Sacchetti tells the story of a Pazzi whom Antonio d'Orso refused to bury until his relatives gave *cautio*. The relatives complained that lack of correct burial was bad for the family name and for the soul of the deceased. But they were at first reluctant to give *cautio*, since that would hurt the family reputation as well, being as it was an admission of usury. Finally they gave it, and then between the benignity of the bishop and the virtù of S. Giovanni Boccadoro, the Pazzi was laid to rest ecclesiastically; Sacchetti, *Novelle*, 128.

areas of Italian life, the picture of ruthless signori or priors always having their way before a weak and corrupt church will have to be redone, using a brighter palette to restore the force of traditional piety and dogma to our view of the Italian city-state.

In our examination, we have seen the bishop attempt this punishment not only against those who lacked general confession and absolution, not only to manifest usurers who had not given *cautio*, but also to a much broader category unknown in the constitutions of Cingoli's predecessor. Any testator not calling his parish priest before making a testament was thus punished. If one died intestate without reasonable cause, the same punishment pertained [107]. If any provision of the will defrauded the bishop, the deceased could not be ecclesiastically buried. Here were such broad categories as to elicit their rejection by the commune [108]. How could a man die tranquilly when, as noted, a presumption of usury was sufficient grounds for refusing burial? Where the bishop seemed to exceed the *ratio* of usury or lack of absolution, well anchored in the law of the church, the commune of Florence was quick to challenge. Again, it must be said that the authoritative canonists of the period were opposed to the sense of these rubrics. The lawyers present a strong line against those who injudiciously deny ecclesiastical burial or, exceeding the authority conceded by the canon law to prohibit ecclesiastical burial in certain cases, extend this punishment [109].

Now to the disposition of the estate. The bishop's version in this matter can be pieced together from his mandates and the practice in the curia in these years. Immediately upon the death of the testator, the priest was to inform

---

[107] Clerks regular or secular admitting such a person to ecclesiastical burial were sentenced to a fine of L. 5. Small enough. The bishop, however, had the option of exhuming the body if the case was flagrant.

[108] A glance at the document itself shows that refusal of ecclesiastical burial was a prime concern of the commune. The lawyers made marginal marks for almost every case where this was the penalty; *ASF*, *Capitoli*, XI, ff. 1-19 *passim*.

[109] Cf., e. g., Giovanni d'Andrea's cautious circumscription of refusal of burial to usurers; *Novelle super sexto decreto Codicis* (Pavia, 1484), c. *Quamquam*.

the executors and heirs that, in line with diocesan law, they were forbidden, under pain of excommunication, to distribute any part of the legacy until bequests to pious causes for the soul had been completely disposed of [110]. With this mandate delivered, the machinery of the curia went forward. The notary present at the disposition of the testator had been obligated to carefully record all information from the testament concerning *male ablata*, certain and uncertain, and all legacies *ad pias causas* [111]. Promises or *cautiones* made by a testator to restore usuries or *male ablata* were to be forwarded to the bishop by notaries before death if possible, and for certain within one month of death [112]. A *cedula* of any *relicte ad pias causas* was to be made available on request by the notary [113]. The priest present at the testation was to inform the curia of the pious bequests within fifteen days if they were made in the city, and within a month if in the contado [114].

With this material at his disposal, the vicar of the bishop « super executione testamentorum et ultimarum voluntatum et restitutionibus usurarum » [115] would await or summon the *fidei-*

[110] « Item statuimus, volumus et mandamus, quod quilibet sacerdos confestim post obitum testatoris, ipsius fideicommissarios et heredes adeat, eisdem instanter notificando, et pro nostra parte mandando, quod ad distributionem et solutionem omnium fattorum in testamento vel qualibet alia ultima voluntate, nullo modo procedat, nisi ipsorum relitta pro anima et ad pias causas prius satisfecerint integraliter ». *Capitoli*, II, 26.

[111] *Capitoli*, II, 24 f.

[112] « Presenti etiam constitutione firmamus, ut quotienscumque a manifestis usurariis quisquam notarius cautionem de restituendis usuris vel male ablatis receperit vel scripserit in infirmitate vel sanitate, nobis vel nostro vicario ante obitum talis usurarii exhibeat talem cautionem, si commode potest: alioquin post obitum eius infra mensem, formam ditte cautionis hostendat »; *Capitoli*, II, 40.

[113] « ... et de omnibus relittis ad pias causas dittus notarius ditto sacerdoti in cedula copiam, si ab eo petita fuerit, debeat exhibere »; *ibid.*, p. 25.

[114] « Qui quidem sacerdos de predittis nobis vel nostro vicario, si fuerit civitatensis infra XV dies, si comitatinus infra mensem, fidem facere teneantur »; *ibid.*, p. 26.

[115] The vicar is not mentioned with this title in the constitutions. However, the office was a long-standing one found in several dioceses from the latter Duecento on. When the vicar was handling *incerti* or legacies, he was referred to minus the phrase « et restitutionibus usurarum ». This was added whenever the business at hand involved a *promissio* or *cautio* promising restitution of usuries; *Libro di Contratti*, *passim*.

10.

commissarii. If the testator had admitted certain usury and promised restitution, the executors would appear in curia to effect probation of usury. *Incerti* left in a will meant the executors would appear to pay it to the bishop as *pater et administrator pauperum Christi* or at least gain his license to distribute it themselves. *Indistincte* left in a will meant, in line with the bishop's projected, but never activated, innovation, that the same *fideicommissarii* would appear to give over one-third to the bishop, and present an instrument showing that another third had been paid to the parish priest, while proving pious distribution of the remaining third. Finally, to complete the various types of appearances before the vicar, the executors would in the normal course of events appear with proof that they had executed all the *distincte*, that is those legacies in specific amounts to specific persons or entities. If all this process had been in order, the estate would be cleared of any further claims on those grants or restitutions mentioned above [116].

This process, in keeping with the canons, had to be completed within one year of death, barring specific types of grants the disbursing of which extended over a longer period, or a circumstantial grant (e. g. one for the crusade « when and if the general passage is made »). In these cases, liberations of the estate could proceed if proof were given that the sums in question were on deposit for their eventual use [117]. But in any case, execution of the will beyond the one-year period rested with the authority of the bishop, and any executive actions beyond those of the bishop or with his license were *ipso iure* null. [118]

The law here is not very different from that in the constitutions of Antonio d'Orso. He in fact had ordered any notary writing a will to submit a full list of usuries and legacies within one month [119], whereas Cingoli avoided this. Antonio, too, took

---

[116] One example among many was the «absolutio» of Domenico di Giunto Borghi from *incerti* 4 Nov. 1337 and from usuries on the following 8 Dec.; *ibid.*, ff. 245 r, 255 r.

[117] « Deponitum est in loco congruo et securo »; *ibid.*, ff. 180 rv.

[118] There are several cases of this in the *Libro* here being used. Most interesting was the bishop's assumption of execution of the will of Donna Margherita di fu Messer Stoldo de' Frescobaldi. The distribution was done directly by the bishop, meaning that he disposed of parts of the estate; *ibid.*, ff. 147 rv; other cases ff. 52 v-53 r, ff. 181 rv.

[119] *AVF*, sez. XXVI, reg. 1, *de testamentis*.

over execution after one year. Both bishops, like all subsequent ones, fulfilled their office of overseeing the execution of pious legacies. Cingoli's innovations were two. He wanted to impede execution of the will until pious bequests were executed. And proper assignment of two-thirds of *indistincte* to the ordinary and *parroco*, foreign to his predecessor's constitutions, was a part of this execution. These passages were struck.

What this meant in practical terms is evident: since the executors, after the revisions of 1330, could alienate parts of the estate to fulfill secular *lasci*, the bishop found his vicar burdened with the task of attaching properties to force fulfillment of religious *lasci*. If the commune had not balked, it would have meant an end to fraud in pious *lasci*, and a sizable increase of the *mensa's* revenues.

We have reached the end of our examination of the execution of the testament. And with it that major section of the modifications touching the process of death and burial. There remains, however, one significant modification carried through by the commune which must be examined, since it provides the background for many of the particulars we have already examined.

IV. *Church and State*

In one of the few mandates in these constitutions directed specifically to the government of the city, the bishop ordered the *podestà*, the *capitano del popolo*, the *executore della giustitia*, and the priors to remit for the examination of the curia within three days of its reception any « attum, propositum sive exceptum [que] fuerit dirette vel indirette de usuris ... » or generally any spiritual business. They were forbidden in any way to pursue the usury case in question. Excommunication was the sentence *ipso facto* if this mandate was contravened [120].

The reader will recognize in this provision the one rubric which touches the field of church-state relations per se. Usury was of course prohibited by municipal law, but historians of the period well know how widespread the prac-

---

[120] *Capitoli*, II, 34.

tice of municipal licensing of *feneratores* was in Italy [121]. What exactly was the bishop attempting to regulate? Why did he move into this sensitive area? The easiest explanation is contained in the rubric *de usuris* of Antonio d' Orso. If opposition to an allegedly usurious contract was made before any official of the commune, the curia was to be notified as above:

> Ad hoc quia creditores feneratores contra debitores diversa nituntur invenire commendate. Et accederit plerumque quod pro modico rebus magni valoris feneratorum versutias debitores fraudantur [122].

Perhaps the bishop had wider goals in mind — stopping, for example, prosecution of usury in the secular courts, or even halting the licensing of pawnbrokers by the commune. It is just as possible that the explanation of Antonio d' Orso is sufficient and that the bishop wanted to halt the crasser practices of the *feneratores*. In fact, Antonio followed his explanation with this striking command:

> Statuimus ne creditor aliquis usurarius rem sibi pignoratam vel obligatam mobiliam vel immobiliam vendere vel alio quovis titulo alienare presumat, nisi prius iuris solempnitate servata. Quod si contrafecerit sententiam excommunicationis incurrat, et quod egerit, careat firmitate [123].

This mandate is missing from Cingoli's constitutions, probably because his curia could not enforce it. But how did the commune deal with this law (canonically highly questionable), which would have made it thoroughly incompetent in matters of usury?

The republic of Florence did not merely quash the paragraph, asserting the natural and unnegotiable demands of the territorial state, as some modern historians might lead us to suspect, the commune marching onward to the ideal of the desa-

---

[121] M. Becker, « Gualtieri di Brienne e la regolamentazione dell'usura a Firenze » and « Nota dei processi riguardanti prestatori di danaro nei tribunali fiorentini dal 1343 al 1379 », *Archivio storico italiano*, CXIV (1956), 734-748, containing general literature p. 735.

[122] *AVF*, *ibid.*, *de usuris.*

[123] *AVF*, *ibid.*

cralized state. Nor did it ignore it. Rather, without questioning or limiting the authority of the bishop to jurisdiction in cases of usury, it simply required the bishop himself to write a letter inhibitory to the officials in question. Thus, rather than the commune being the initiator, the bishop was. With the insertion of those words, « Post inhibitionem per nos vel vicarium nostrum fattam ... », the constitution remained in force at least through the reign of Cosimo Pazzi (1508-1513) [124].

I do not want to pursue the whole problem of the administration of cases of usury, but the point mentioned above must be stressed: the commune of Florence did not dispute the right of the bishop's court to the trial of cases of usury. It only sought to prevent the misuse of any court, including the episcopal curia, by debtors seeking to avoid payment by claiming usury. In the very years of the constitutional question considered here, the commune passed a law ordering that before a debtor could go ahead with any prosecution of usury *in aliqua curia*, he was obliged to deposit to the Mercanzia a sum equal to the debt called usurious. If within one month he could not prove usury, the deposit was then used to pay the debt [125]. The bishops were of course just as concerned to prevent the discrediting of their curia by such debtors. Cingoli's successor drafted into the law of the diocese a specific rubric « ad refrenandum malitias multorum, qui causas usurarias movent in nostra curia in fraudem » [126]. The assertion that at the beginning of the Quattrocento it had become « virtually impossible to prosecute anyone on a charge of usury in an ecclesiastical court » [127] dangerously misjudges the func-

---

[124] « Ut post inhibitionem per nos vel vicarium nostrum fattam, iudices seculares ad illud quod ditta constitutio precipit teneantur »; *Capitoli*, II, 48. Thus the relevant phrases now read: « ... quoquo modo illa absque difficultate aliqua ad nostrum examen vel nostri vicarii, seu nostrae curiae omnino in tertiam diem post inhibitionem per nos, vel vicarium nostrum factam remittere teneantur, et se de illis nullatenus intromittere »; Mansi, XXVI, c. 55 (Acciaiuoli's constitutions).

[125] *Provv.*, XXIII, f. 31 v (26 Nov. 1326).

[126] Mansi, XXVI, c. 73.

[127] M. Becker, « The Florentine Territorial State and Civic Humanism in the Early Renaissance », in N. Rubinstein (ed.), *Florentine Studies* (London, 1968), p. 111. Becker arrives at this startling statement by referring to the *Statuta* of 1415, essentially the same law as the one mentioned above of 1326. The law was not new (coming full-blown from the head of the

tion of the church in late medieval and Renaissance Italy. There are dozens and dozens of cases for usury in the fragmentary episcopal records. More self-evident, the new constitutions of the see in 1517 have extensive rubrics on the trial of cases of usury in the curial court [128].

I have said that this last rubric and the additional provisions of 1330 give a tone to the larger problems touched in this paper. That is, the commune assiduously avoided conflict wherever possible. It left untouched all provisions in these constitutions concerning manifest usurers. It objected and attained revisions only where innovations by the bishop disturbed the serenity of the deathbed and perhaps the treasuries of various pious corporations, and where the bishop had placed himself in shallow canonical waters. It responded not so much to challenges to its authority, as it did to the pressures of its constituent groups. It recognized the authority of the episcopal curia over the execution of pious legacies (maintained unbroken into the seventeenth century) and left unhindered the pursuit of usurers in ecclesiastical courts.

What the commune did do was to refuse precedence to claims on pious legacies. Where the commune did innovate was in the constant licensing or punishment of usurers.

Since this essay set out to examine the modifications of the constitutions of 1327, it would be well to return to an early remark: the commune, having agreed to the revisions, was bound by the constitutions. This needs no particular evidence. But note: while the commune forced the deletion of certain objectionable — and canonically weak — passages, a series of innovations was being introduced which put the see of Florence statutorily in a much strengthened position. One small example is Biliotti's constitutions which spoke only of the last will and testament. By adding the phrase « in infirmitate vel sanitate », and again

---

mature territorial state) but was at least ninety years old. His reading of the statute, that if a client won in ecclesiastical court he *forfeited* the deposit, is wrong. Text: « Et si infra mensem a die facti depositi non probaverit opposita vera esse, dictum depositum convertatur in debitum petitum extenuandum, et ulterius puniatur ... »; *Statuta Populi et Communis Florentiae*, I, 124.

[128] Mansi, XXXV, cc. 276-280. Nelson notes this continuity; *op. cit.*, p. 109.

« in ultimis voluntatibus *vel aliter* », [129] Cingoli extended the whole gamut of episcopal rights over testaments and codicils « corpore sane », with extremely significant results on the process of transferring property as legacy. Beyond this hint we will not go. The law of the church in Florence was, in 1327, first being defined in all clarity.

Let us pose one further question. Just what relation did these constitutions have to those being written elsewhere in northern Italy? If we knew, this would help us put these constitutions in their proper historical perspective.

An examination of Mansi's *Acta* allows us to state the historical problem to which Florence responded: how was the Italian bishop to maintain his revenues from *incerti* or from canonical portions in the face of the popularity of the friars and the « malevolence » of testators or heirs? Everywhere we find the bishop commanding either notary or priest to inform him within one month of all sums left for *incerti* and *pias causas* (Lucca, 1308; [130] Ravenna, 1311; [131] Pistoia, 1308; [132] Milan, 1287), [133] or acting to avoid the defraudation of the bishop (Pistoia, 1308; [134] Perugia, 1320) [135], or of the poor (Florence, 1310), [136] or of the local rector (Milan, 1287). [137] Ravenna had commanded notaries not to write the testaments of usurers without the presence of the parish priest, this with the specific aim of guaranteeing the carrying out of *Quamquam,* the Lyon decree regulating the testaments of usurers. [138]

But the problems must have seemed insuperable from this line of attack. The difficulty of collecting traditional quarters or portions of certain *lasci* has already been described. The situation with *incerti* was no better. We have also seen that testators in Ravenna were avoiding classifying *incerti* as such so as

---

[129] *Capitoli,* II, 40, collated with *AVF, ibid., de usuris.*
[130] Mansi, XXV, c. 188.
[131] *Ibid.,* XXV, c. 474.
[132] F. Zaccharia, *Anecdotorum Medii Aevi* p. 140 (n. 23).
[133] Mansi, XXIV, cc. 878 f.
[134] Zaccharia, p. 140.
[135] Mansi, XXIV, c. 643.
[136] *AVF, ibid., de testamentis.*
[137] Mansi, XXIV, c. 879.
[138] *Ibid.,* XXIV, c. 621 (1286).

to prevent episcopal administration [139]. The Perugian ordinary in 1320 stated that *incerti* belonged by *ius commune* to the administration of the bishop, but then turned around and stated that (while it would be best for the sinner wanting to restitute *incerti* to the poor while alive to give it to the bishop) if he or his executors were determined to do it themselves, they should at least inform him and have his *continentia* [140]. Hardly stated from a position of strength. And we have seen that the Bishop of Florence was ready to allow restitution of *incerti*, if not of certain usuries, to the living. The relative innovation introduced in Florence was to largely ignore these traditional avenues in favor of the increasingly large *indistincte*. They clearly contained *incerti*, i. e. goods of the poor, and the bishop might hope that legal opinion would come down on his side. It did not do so.

We have now attempted to view our constitutions as emerging from a given statutory tradition. There is, however, one other strand of historical development within which these constitutions must be seen. I have spoken before of the legal abyss on the question of manifest usury. From necessity my approach has been to isolate « ordinary sinners » from the manifest usurers. But abyss or not, the constitutions cannot ultimately be seen as if outside the developing canonical tradition on this problem. These constitutions emerge, that is, from a certain legal and moral comprehension of the nature of an overtly evil act: usury.

Let me point up two striking observations noted in comparing our constitutions:

1. Both Ravenna [141] and Aquileia [142] give specific definitions of manifest usury. Florence both in 1310 and in 1327 does not.

2. Florence (1310 and 1327) *alone* among the constitutions in Mansi for the period 1250-1350 gives a notarial formulary for the *cautio* demanded of the manifest usurer [143].

---

[139] Cf. above, n. 78.

[140] « Item de iure communi distributio ... incertorum ... inter pauperes vel pia loca sunt distribuenda ad ordinarium pertinere noscantur. Monemus ... etiam ... testamentorum executores vel fideicommissari[os] ... ne de praemissis dispensandis ... sine nostra scientia et continentia speciali, sed potius ea ad episcoporum eroganda deferat [sic] et per eius providentiam in pauperes, et alias pias causas »; Mansi, XXV, c. 644.

[141] Mansi, XXV, cc. 613-616 (1311).

[142] *Ibid.*, c. 1120.

[143] *AVF*, *ibid.*, *de usuris*; *Capitoli*, II, 40 f.

How should we interpret these facts? First we may note that the definition of a manifest usurer had been hotly debated by the canonists up to this time. The authority of one canonist, however, was determinate in the Italy of this period. And the opinion of Giovanni d'Andrea on this question was rigorous: if the deceased stood in the *fama* of usury, he was judiciable and suspect; if the deceased was proven in the court of the bishop to have committed usury *once*, he was and had been a manifest usurer [144].

Given the position of the great jurisprudent at Bologna, Cingoli, in his attempt to clarify and strengthen the diocesan law, may have avoided such a sweeping definition of manifest usury. Sticking closely to the decree *Quamquam* rather than to the glosses would make his provisions against manifest usurers unassailable. If this was his intent, he succeeded. The long *cautio* formula in the constitution *de usuris* suggests, without going any farther, a limited interpretation of manifest usury.

Cingoli therewith gained communal approval of his authority over restitutions of manifest usurers. But who was manifest? Here the law was on the side of the bishop. Since legal opinion made *fama* with probation of usury post-mortem proof of manifestness, increasing numbers of individuals stood under the threat of being found manifest. And, as all knew, the testament of a manifest usurer without a *cautio* was invalid. By then creating a parallel process for other than individuals publicly and notoriously usurious (absolution conditional on respect for rights of bishop over *incerti* and *indistincte*, with the threat of lack of ecclesiastical burial), Cingoli forced a situation whereby testators of means might have to pay high to minimize the danger of prosecution for usury.

Though the bishop was unsuccessful in his attempt on a third of *indistincte*, the point was made: it was simply too dangerous for a well-to-do merchant to die without either insuring

---

144 « Poterit autem episcopus eos publicare si convicti fuerunt vel confessi coram ipso vel si contra eos fecit probatio testium vel sint certa argumenta cum fama ... »; *Apparatus in libro sexto Decretalium* (1476), *de usuris*, § manifestos. He answers yes to the question: « si sint manifesta forsan cum uno solo contraxerit et manifesta est quantitas quam extorsit »; *Novella, de usuris, c. Quamquam*. Manifest usury was at this time much more broadly understood than Nelson suggests; *op. cit.*, pp. 107-109.

that all his past debtors renounced eventual charges for usury [145] or coming to terms through a *cautio* with the bishop before death. If the testator would run the risk, his executors and heirs would not. They would quickly sign a *cautio* to obtain burial of the deceased and to protect the estate. In the two years 1336 and 1337, sixty-two Florentines, most of them prominent merchants, were guaranteed or guaranteed themselves for their usuries before the officers of the bishop [146]. The usurer in the period before the plague was no petty bourgeois social outcast. That « merchant princes » admitted their usury was in part the result of Cingoli's skill as a legislator.

The framework which I have tried to build around this constitutional struggle is complete. It has been argued that the bishop's law is incomprehensible apart from the history of the canon law. To put it most forcibly, papal decrees (*Quamquam*, *Super cathedram*), but also the authority of the *consilia*, glosses, and commentaries of the renowned canonists of the day, impinged directly on the social history of the merchant city of Florence. Finally, but most importantly, the episcopal constitutions of the see of Florence were in 1327, and remained thereafter, part and fiber of the *leges* of the *civitas*. They created norms which remained law for the subjects of the bishop and conditioned their actions. They asserted rights which the commune recognized and enforced.

---

[145] This process is clearly observable in a series of 35 notarializations of 27, 29, 31 Dec. 1319 by which Niccolò di fu Guilicante da Monte Rapoli was « liberated » by potential plaintiffs of eight different *popoli; ASF*, *Not. antecos.*, G 106 (1319-1325), ff. 14 v-19 r.

[146] *Libro di Contratti.*

WILLIAM M. BOWSKY

CITY AND CONTADO: MILITARY RELATIONSHIPS AND COMMUNAL BONDS IN FOURTEENTH-CENTURY SIENA *

* The author gratefully acknowledges the fellowships from the John Simon Guggenheim Memorial Foundation and the Social Science Research Council that made possible the necessary archival research in Italy. The unpublished documents referred to below are housed in the Archivio di Stato of Siena. A reference in a footnote to a work in press may refer to the text to which that note belongs.

One of the most exciting and potentially fruitful group of questions posed in recent decades by historians of communal Italy concerns the relations that existed between a dominant city-state and its contado in the late middle ages and early Renaissance. In particular they have sought to discover whether, or to what extent and in what ways, communes exploited the populations of the contado — that large portion of a state outside of the city and its boroughs most directly and completely subject to communal jurisdiction [1]. These historical investigations have treated primarily problems of demography, taxation, communal food policies, changing juridic, economic, and territorial rights in the contado, and political and diplomatic issues [2].

The contado was indeed a source of food supplies for a city and of raw materials and manpower for urban industry, a font of taxation for a commune, and an area to be safeguarded and developed for the promotion of commerce. And it was more: the inhabitants of the contado (*contadini*) and their communities played an essential role in the military defense and in the expansion of an Italian city-state. The military relationships that were established between dominant communes and their contadi, and the significance of those relationships, have yet, however,

---

[1] For a definition and discussion of the nature of the contado, see esp. Giovanni de Vergottini, «Origini e sviluppo storico della comitatinanza», *Studi senesi*, XLIII (1929), 347-481. The Sienese state contained, however, another juridic entity even more closely bound to the commune than the contado: a group of communities immediately adjacent to the city and its boroughs that was known as the Massa or the Masse and Cortine; for this see, e. g., William M. Bowsky, *The Finance of the Commune of Siena, 1287-1355* (Oxford, 1970), Ch. II n. 83, and *idem*, « Medieval Citizenship: The Individual and the State in the Commune of Siena, 1287-1355 », *Studies in Medieval and Renaissance History*, IV (1967), 193-243, pp. 227-230.

[2] For a summary of the historiography of the problem of city-contado relationships and the varying results achieved to date, see Bowsky, *Finance*, Chapter XI, and also, for Siena, *idem*, « Medieval Citizenship », *passim*.

to become the object of modern historical examinations and to take their place within a total analysis of city-contado relations.

From 1287 to 1355 the Tuscan commune of Siena was dominated by the mercantile-banking oligarchy known as « the Nine », from the bimensal magistracy of the Nine Governors and Defenders of the Commune and People of Siena. The Noveschi, or families whose members served in that office, were of both burgher and noble origin, while by law (if not always in fact) they could not include judges, notaries, physicians, and members of the *casati* — specifically designated magnate houses [3].

This government, like those of other communes, could draw upon a great variety of sources for the military manpower necessary for the defense of the state or for military adventures. Florence was but one Tuscan republic whose citizens had not lost their « civic zeal » and allowed their citizen militia to deteriorate by the early fourteenth century, content to have their liberties defended by hired mercenaries alone [4]. In Siena, too, well-to-do citizens and certain other residents of the city served in person as mounted cavalry, while others fought as infantry (some specialized in the use of the crossbow) in the military companies of the commune [5]. Siena could also count upon the aid of the soldiery in the official « families » of the leading foreign magistrates, especially the Podestà, the Captain of the People, and, from approximately 1323 on, the War Captain — who ordinarily had a following of about fifty cavalry and one

---

[3] See William M. Bowsky, « The *Buon Governo* of Siena (1287-1355): A Mediaeval Italian Oligarchy », *Speculum*, XXXVII (1962), 368-381.

[4] This has been amply demonstrated in a most interesting article by Daniel Waley, « The Army of the Florentine Republic from the Twelfth to the Fourteenth Century », in Nicolai Rubinstein, ed., *Florentine Studies* (London, 1968), pp. 70-108.

[5] For the Sienese military companies, see William M. Bowsky, « The Anatomy of Rebellion in Fourteenth-Century Siena: From Commune to Signory? », in Lauro Martines, ed., *Violence and Civil Disorder in Italian Cities, 1200-1500* (Los Angeles and Berkeley, 1970). I will treat the Sienese « cavallate » and other aspects of Sienese military history separately in a forthcoming volume on the history of Siena under the government of the Nine.

hundred infantry [6]. Varying numbers of mercenary « constables » with their *masnade* or troops of infantry or horsemen ordinarily supplemented these forces.

The contado, too, provided an essential and large element of the Sienese military forces. In March 1292 no less than three thousand contado infantry were ordered assembled for action [7]. As many as seven thousand contado infantry may have participated in a campaign of 1318 against the commune of Massa Marittima [8]. Nor were *contadini* used only against foreign ene-

---

[6] See, e. g., Biccherna [B], 149, ff. 111 r, 125 v, 165 v. Most pertinent is Statuti, Siena, 26, Dist. IV, r. 87, f. 213 r: « De electione Capitanei Guerre. Rubrica. Domini Novem una cum ordinibus civitatis adiuncta viginti bonorum hominum per terzerium eligendorum per ipsos Novem et ordines supradictos et cum paziariis civitatis citandis omnibus ad consilium fiendum pro electione Capitanei Guerre pro ut citabuntur dicti viginti per terzerium in quo consilio ad minus triginta de dictis paziariis esse debent. Eligant singulis sex mensibus de mense Junii et Decembris unum bonum nobilem et probum virum ac expertum in armis generalem Capitaneum Guere [sic] civitatis et comitatus sen. cum salario pactis modis et condictionibus que per dictum consilium firmabuntur. Cuius Capitanei offitium perpetuo sit in civitate sen. Et habeat et habere debeat et tenere continue toto tempore sex mensium in civitate sen. unum sufficientem judicem duos notarios et quinquaginta equites cum quinquaginta equis armigeris et vigintiquinque ronzinis et ultra predictos habeat pro sua persona duos equos sufficientiores et unum palafredum. Habeat etiam centum famulos pedites sub uno capitaneo in ipsorum numero conputato. Pro quibus omnibus et aliis quos se cum ducere et habere voluerit pro sue persone honore maxime duobus tubatoribus uno nachereno et una trombecta et pro expensis temporibus sex mensium et ventus et syndicatus trium dierum et recessus habeat pro suo salario decem milia librarum denariorum senensium minutorum, habeat etiam ultra predictum salarium expensis comunis decentem habitationem pro se et sua familia quam ad suum cibum et potum tenuerit, quam habitationem procurent domini Novem invenire et concedere Capitaneo antedicto prope Campum fori et palatium ipsorum ubi eis videbitur convenire ». See also *ibid.*, r. 88, f. 213 r-v, « De arbitrio et jurisdictione Capitanei Guerre ». For Statuti, Siena, 26, a major constitutional redaction of the late 1330s, see Bowsky, « Medieval Citizenship », pp. 239-243. For the « paziarii » or « paciarii », see *idem*, « The Medieval Commune and Internal Violence: Police Power and Public Safety in Siena, 1287-1355 », *American Historical Review*, LXXIII (1967), 1-17, p. 12 [hereafter cited as « Police Power »].

[7] Consiglio Generale, Deliberazioni [CG], 43, ff. 40 v-41 r. These troops were raised « per pleberia et vicariatos ... ».

[8] The chronicle of Agnolo di Tura del Grasso [hereafter cited as « Agnolo »], in Alessandro Lisini and Fabio Iacometti, eds., *Cronache Se-*

mies. In 1302 a special force was created of two thousand men of the contado, « *fidelibus* and lovers of the sacrosanct Roman church and of the pacific state of the city of Siena », chosen from among the nine vicariates, or military districts, of the contado. They were not only to assist in crushing any uprisings in the contado, but to come to the city of Siena at the bidding of the Nine at times of internal turmoil. Their number was increased to five thousand in 1310, probably in view of the impending struggle with the Emperor-elect Henry VII — their special task then being defined as going to Siena « in the service and defense of the office of the lords Nine and of the pacific state of the city of Siena ». (This force was supplemented by a far smaller one recruited from the towns of the Masse)[9]. Contado contingents even participated in the restoration of order following the crisis of October 26, 1318 — the most serious rebellion to face the government of the Nine prior to its final overthrow in 1355 [10].

The contado was organized into three separate vicariates in the mid-thirteenth century. The constitution redacted in 1262 informs us that there then existed the vicariates of San Quirico in Osenna, Orgia, and Montagutolo Ardenghesca, whose commanders or vicars were paid in part by the principal commune of each vicariate and in part by the remaining communities of those districts [11]. We unfortunately lack further accurate infor-

---

nesi, in *Rerum Italicarum Scriptores*, n. s., XV Part VI (Bologna, 1931-37) [hereafter abbreviated *C. S.*], p. 371. Ordinarily Agnolo and other chroniclers fail to distinguish between contadini and city residents serving with the Sienese infantry. E. g., 3,000 to 4,000 infantry are reported to have served with the Angevins at the ill-fated battle of Montecatini in 1315 (Agnolo, p. 351; anon. chronicle, *C. S.*, p. 169). They similarly report a force of some 4,000 footsoldiers under the joint command of the Sienese War Captain, Guidoriccio dei Fogliani of Reggio, and the Noveschi noble, messer Francesco di messer Mino Accarigi, in an army sent against the Aldobrandeschi counts of Santa Fiora in 1331 (Agnolo, p. 503; anon. chronicle, *C. S.*, p. 145).

[9] Bowsky, « Anatomy of Rebellion », n. 34. For the expedition of Henry VII, see *idem*, *Henry VII in Italy. The Conflict of Empire and City-State, 1310-1313* (Lincoln, Nebraska, 1960).

[10] For the rebellion of Oct. 26, 1318, see Bowsky, « Anatomy of Rebellion », esp. n. 61.

[11] Lodovico Zdekauer, ed., *Il constituto del comune di Siena dell'anno 1262* (Milan, 1897), Dist. III, r. CCCXXXVIIII, p. 382; cf. *idem*, « La vita pub-

mation concerning the vicariates during the immediately following decades [12].

We do not even know that the vicariates enjoyed a continuous existence. A City Council deliberation of February 22, 1292 reveals that general measures were then approved ordering the arrangement of « in what way and how the communities of the Sienese contado are to be separated by vicariates and must serve the Sienese commune in general armies and cavalry expeditions and when they are to be so ordered by the Sienese commune ... », but the deliberation does not contain the contents of those provisions [13]. I suspect that following some major campaigns the very system of vicariates was abandoned, for early in 1303 — shortly after the conclusion of a war against the Aldobrandeschi counts of the Maremma — the City Council debated whether or not the contado should be separated into vicariates. Of special significance in several respects is the session of January 9, 1303 [14].

On that Wednesday the Podestà asked the councillors whether they wished to approve certain ordinances drawn up by a commission selected by the Nine:

---

blica dei Senesi nel Dugento », *Commissione senese di storia patria nella R. Accademia dei Rozzi. Conferenze*, III (Siena, 1897), pp. 75-191, p. 94 n. 1.

[12] Giugurta Tommasi, *Dell'Historie di Siena*, 2 vols. in one (Venice, 1625-26), II, 130, relates that in 1289 the Sienese « armarono tutto il Contado, distinguendolo per vicariati, ... a ciascuno assegnando per Capitano, un Cittadino buon popolano, e Guelfo. A tutta questa milizia [including the contadini of the vicariates] diedero Capitano generale il Capitano del Popolo, e l'intitolarono Capitano del Comune, e del popolo, e difensore delle compagnie, e de' Vicariati ». I have not found documentary substantiation for these statements, and, in fact, Tommasi errs in assigning the Captain of the People this title so early. He only obtained the title of « Capitaneus comunis et populi, defensor societatum et vicariatuum Civitatis sen. » in May 1314 (Statuti, Siena, 8, f. 160 r; cf. Capitano del Popolo, 1, f. 35 v). I will deal with the problems related to the history of the office of the Captain of the People separately in my volume on the history of Siena under the Nine. See for the present, Bowsky, « Anatomy of Rebellion », n. 88.

[13] CG, 43, f. 34 r, esp. « quomodo et qualiter comunitates comitatus sen. sortiantur per vicariatos et servire debeant comuni sen. in exercitibus et cavalcatis et quando mandebitur eis per comune sen. ».

[14] CG, 62, ff. 30 v-32 v.

concerning ordering and distinguishing the entire Sienese contado by vicariates and concerning making statutes and ordinances through which the highways and roads of the contado may be held in safety, and through which highwaymen may be captured and turned over to the power of the Sienese commune ... [15].

It is not without interest that the commission dealt at one and the same time with the military problem of creating military vicariates and with the essentially police problem of safeguarding the contado roads.

Magnates and Noveschi participated in the debate that rapidly centered upon an issue vital to the very nature of the communal state: the proper relationship that should obtain between the jurisdiction of the commune in the contado and its right to call upon all of its subjects for military assistance, as balanced against the claims of private and feudal jurisdictions that still existed within the contado.

Messer Frederigo di messer Renaldo Tolomei, a leading member of one of Siena's wealthiest and most influential *casati* [16], and a man who generally supported the government in City Council deliberations, advised that the provisions be approved, with the addition that the Nine place within one of the vicariates any « villa or land » that was omitted, unless it was subject to a « natural lord (*domino naturali*) ». But, he added, if any land or villa now on the list of communities included within the vicariates was subject to a natural lord, the rights of that lord were not thereby to be prejudiced. Messer Frederigo further proposed that the captains to be selected for each vicariate be no less than twenty-five nor more than sixty years old [17].

His kinsman, the even more powerful messer Tavena di messer Deo Tolomei, also counselled approval, but with the stipulation that the provisions « do not remove or give any

[15] *Ibid.*, f. 30 v, « ... super ordinando et distinguendo universo comitatu Sen. per vicariatos et super faciendo statuta et ordinamenta per que strata et vie comitatus Sen. in securitate teneantur et per que malefactores in stratis capiantur et in fortiam comunis Sen. deducantur ... » The deliberation does not include the text of these provisions.

[16] For the Tolomei see Bowsky, *Finance*, Ch. I n. 19; *idem*, « Anatomy of Rebellion », *passim*, and esp. n. 49 ff.

[17] CG, 62, f. 31 r.

right to the Sienese commune or to [any] special person »[18], but that the lands of the contado remain in the juridic condition in which they had been. Still another member of the same family apparently wished to whittle down the provisions one by one, eliminating those that he found objectionable. Messer Mozzo Tolomei advised the Council to reconsider the provisions individually, and allow but a single speaker for and against each[19].

Still more adamant was a member of perhaps the wealthiest of the Sienese *casati*, Benuccio di messer Benuccio Salimbeni. He wanted the entire matter to be postponed, and then re-examined at another meeting of the City Council to be held either that same evening or the following morning — at which time the Council could act on each separate item in whatever manner it wished[20]. Messer Guccio Malavolti, whose wealthy *casato* was almost to monopolize the bishopric of Siena for nearly a century, wanted to scrap the provisions and start anew. He proposed that the Nine secretly choose a new commission to revise the provisions and present its own proposals to the City Council. That commission, moreover, could include no one who had served on the commission that had prepared the ordinances then being debated, and the names of the new commissioners were to be kept secret[21].

Noveschi, too, spoke to the question — and not with a single voice. Jacomo Tommasi, a burgher and merchant, suggested that the Nine select two or three men from each Terzo. (The Terzi were the three major divisions of the city)[22]. These six or nine men would revise the present ordinances, and, at the same time, receive any petitions that private individuals might wish to submit to them — presumably in defense of their rights as natural lords. The City Council would then receive that commission's recommendations on the following Monday, January 14[23].

---

[18] *Ibid.*, f. 31 v, esp. « ... non tollant ne dent aliquid ius Comuni Sen. vel spetiali persone ... ».

[19] *Ibid.*, f. 32 v.

[20] *Ibid.*, f. 31 v.

[21] *Ibid.*, f. 32 r.

[22] These were the Terzo of Camollia in the north, the Terzo of Città in the southwest, and the Terzo of San Martino in the southeast.

[23] CG, 62, f. 32 v. For Jacomo Tommasi and his membership on the Nine, see Bowsky, « *Buon Governo* » [cited above, n. 3], p. 374.

Tuccio Alessi was a councillor who had served on Sienese signories from at least the early 1280s, and on the Nine in 1293. His sons and even a grandson were also to hold seats on the Nine [24]. Yet he did not support the passage of the provisions. Rather, he counselled that the Nine select two men per Terzo to revise and correct them and to present their revisions to the City Council [25].

The wealthy Noveschi noble Viva di Viviano di Guglielmo Vignari, whose family was to have at least ten members on the Nine [26], did not agree. He put forth the radical proposal that the Podestà and the Nine be permitted to leave the present meeting and go to dinner, posting a guard at the door of the council chamber who was not to allow the councillors to depart until they reached an agreement on the provisions under consideration [27].

At the close of this lengthy debate a secret vote was taken. By a vote of 168 to 44 the Council approved the provisions, with the additions that had been proposed by Frederigo Tolomei [28]. The result, therefore, was a compromise — and a partial victory for the government. For although the rights of the natural lords were to be protected in that their communities would not be added to the vicariates, the provisions for the vicariates were approved and all lands held by such lords that had been included within those vicariates were not to be removed. Nor will it have escaped notice that whereas the members of the *casati* recognized that this arrangement (general and uniform military service for the commune by the contado communities) threatened their feudal lordships, nevertheless those families, and even members of the same family, had differed in the extent of their opposition. Whether they did so from principle or because they did not believe that they could muster a majority for their most extreme claims we do not know.

A City Council session held almost two months later, on February 27, 1303, put the finishing touches on this legislation

[24] Bowsky, *Finance*, Ch. VII n. 13.
[25] CG, 62, f. 31 v.
[26] Bowsky, « *Buon Governo* », p. 372.
[27] CG, 62, f. 32 v.
[28] *Ibid.*, f. 32 v.

with little difficulty [29]. The only speaker to address himself to this measure, the Noveschi judge messer Meo di Tigo di Leo (Tigolei), advised approval; and it was obtained by a vote of 175 to 25 [30]. This legislation makes it clear that there were three vicariates, though no longer those of the mid-thirteenth century. The principal seats of the vicariates now were Castelfranco di Paganico and Prata, both in the Maremma, and Buonconvento, southeast of Siena bordering the major highway, the so-called Via Francigena [31].

Even more interesting than this re-orientation in the direction of Siena's more recent economic and political concerns, is the notice that each vicariate was to be captained by a knight in the family of the Podestà — one of whom was the « *scorridore* » of the highways — rather than being placed in the jurisdiction of the Captain of the People. For these members of the Podestà's official family were essentially police officials, men entrusted with keeping the peace and suppressing crime in the contado [32].

Thus the newly organized military districts of the vicariates now were fused — or perhaps better, confused — with police administration. And at least at this juncture such a combination probably seemed most convenient and posed no major difficulties or contrasts in the minds of the councillors. This arrangement was maintained for about seven years, and is the one that was included within the constitutional redaction of 1309-10 [33].

It probably was the approaching warfare with the forces of the Emperor-elect, Henry VII, that compelled the government to re-examine its state of military preparedness and the support that it might expect from the communities of the contado. In

---

[29] *Ibid.*, ff. 83 v-84 v.

[30] For messer Meo, cf. William M. Bowsky, « The Constitution and Administration of a Tuscan Republic in the Middle Ages and Early Renaissance: The *Maggior Sindaco* in Siena », *Studi Senesi*, LXXX (1968), 7-22, p. 16.

[31] For these communities and the Via Francigena, see Bowsky, *Finance*, Ch. II nn. 16, 18-23, 38.

[32] For the Podestà's knights in the contado see Bowsky, *Finance*, Ch. IX n. 54, X n. 11. For the scorridore in particular, see, e. g., Alessandro Lisini, ed., *Il costituto del comune di Siena volgarizzato nel MCCCIX-MCCCX*, 2 vols. (Siena, 1903) [hereafter cited *Const. 1309-10*], Dist. I, r. XXXVIII-XLVII. This office was eliminated Dec. 18, 1308: Statuti, Siena, 15, f. 368 v.

[33] *Const. 1309-10*, Dist. I, r. XXXVIII-XLVII.

the course of this re-examination the government became aware that the problem of violence and of military strength in the contado was not a single one, but had to be dealt with in two separate jurisdictional categories: the police problem of crime in the contado, and the military problems related to the utilization of armed *contadini* for the protection of the state. The decision was made to separate the police from the military administration of the contado, with the former remaining within the jurisdiction of the Podestà and those of his knights and their small bands of infantry assigned to various contado districts.

The contado itself was viewed as too populous, widespread, and unwieldy to be apportioned among only three vicariates. On May 26, 1310 the contado was separated into nine vicariates that contained within them a total of some 289 communities [34].

Table 1. The Vicariates of May 26, 1310.

Vicariate	Number of Communities within each Vicariate
1. Castelfranco di Maremma [Paganico]	24
2. Sant'Angelo in Colle	41
3. Monticiano	36
4. Menzano	44
5. Berardenga	45
6. Scialenga	36
7. Valdichiana	13
8. San Quirico [in Osenna]	11
9. Percena	39

[34] For the legislation of May 26, 1310 see Capitano del Popolo, 1, ff. 23 r-34 v, 24 rubrics. Rubric 14, ff. 26 v-31 v, contains the lists of the vicariates and the names of the communities within each. Cf. Romolo Caggese, « La Repubblica di Siena e il suo contado nel secolo decimoterzo », *Bullettino Senese di Storia Patria*, XIII (1906), 3-120, p. 103. It is possible that the noble discord that threatened the maintenance of order in the contado contributed to the decision to make this new arrangement. See, e. g., Agnolo, p. 307; also Orlando Malavolti, *Dell'Historia di Siena*, 3 vols. in one (Venice, 1599), II, 63 v-64 v, who, like Caggese, is not entirely accurate.

The vicariates were placed under the general supervision of the Captain of the People. Within four years, in fact, his official title was so expanded as to take note of this role as well as to recognize his function with respect to the military companies of the city [35].

It was in 1310, too, that the government decided that instead of foreign knights of the Podestà, Sienese urban *popolani* would command each of the vicariates [36]. A volume recording the income and expenditures of the Biccherna, the principal Sienese financial magistracy, notes a salary payment made on March 26, 1311 to the vicars of seven vicariates, at the rate of forty *soldi* (two *lire* of account) each per day of service. Far more interesting than the fact that only six of those vicariates appear in the legislation of May 26, 1310 — indicating that the government continued to experiment with the new administrative arrangement — are the names of those vicars themselves. Of the seven, four definitely and two almost certainly were Noveschi [37]. The leadership and supervision of these contado military districts thus was assigned not merely to Sienese *popolani*, but to those persons most trusted by and loyal to the very core of the ruling oligarchy.

During the following three decades the system of vicariates was further modified and refined. Nine of them, totaling 299 communities in all, were listed in the major constitutional redaction of the late 1330s [38]. And if we compare these with the police districts assigned to the knights of the Podestà in a measure of April 14, 1332 [39] it will be seen that although there was great overlap the two jurisdictions were by no means exactly the same.

---

[35] See above, n. 12.

[36] For the term « popolano » and the organization of the Popolo in Siena during the regime of the Nine, see Bowsky, « Anatomy of Rebellion », nn. 15-17, 88 ff.

[37] B, 125, f. 102 r. Listed are: 1) Tino di ser Nino (Sant'Angelo in Colle); 2) Lucca Viviani (San Quirico in Osenna); 3) Masso di Ranuccio [« Ranuccii »] (Percena); 4) Neri di Buonaventura di Agostino (Scialenga); 5) Guccio di Gregorio [« Gregorii »] (Berardenga); 6) Tici di Buonaventura Patrizi (Montefollonico); 7) Conticino Guicciardini (Monticiano). The Noveschi are Nos. 3-6, and almost certainly Nos. 2, 7.

[38] Statuti, Siena, 26, Dist. III, r. 383-392, ff. 189 v-193 r.

[39] Statuti, Siena, 23, ff. 381 r-391 v.

Table 2. Vicariates and Podestarile Districts.

Vicariates	Communities in Each	Podestarile Districts [40]	Communities in Each
1. Castelfranco [di Paganico]	24	Corsignano	40
2. Sant'Angelo in Colle	43	Valdichiana	11
3. Monticiano	37	Scialenga	24
4. Menzano	47	Berardenga	38
5. Berardenga	45	Querciagrossa	20
6. Scialenga	37	Menzano	18
7. Valdichiana	13	Monticiano and Prata	26
8. San Quirico in Osenna	11	[Castelfranco di] Paganico	12
9. Percena	42	The Baths [Petriolo and Macereto]	30
	299		219

The differences in these lists probably reflect more than the changing number of contado communities. They also suggest that differing types and amounts of criminality, and the need to safeguard particular areas, did not necessarily correspond with military exigencies and the varying quantities of manpower available throughout the contado.

By the end of 1347 there were at least two additional vicariates, making eleven in all. The actual composition of those eleven vicariates constituted a combination of some districts assigned to knights of the Podestà for police purposes, some of the earlier vicariates, and the new vicariates of Asciano and Arcidosso. Most revealing is a deliberation of the signory that took place on December 22, 1347. From it we learn that the leaders of those vicariates (now called « captains » rather than

[40] On June 25, 1335 it was decided to appoint a knight of the Podestà to a district centered about Castiglione di Valdorcia: Statuti, Siena, 23, ff. 475r-476 v, esp. ff. 475 v-476 r.

« vicars »), and of the three vicariates of the Masse, were selected by the Nine and the other Orders [41] of the city for six-month terms of office — in this particular case terms that began on January 1, 1348. All eight of the captains who can be identified by family were Noveschi. Oligarchical control over the military districts had not slackened [42].

Table 3. Vicariates of 1348 and their Captains [43].

Terzo of Città
The Massa of the Terzo of Città: Barnaba di Renaldo
Baths of Petriolo and Macereto: Baldera di Ghino di Baldera
Arcidosso: Jacomo di Vannuccio (« Vannuccii »)
Paganico: Andreoccio di Vannuccio (« Vannuccii »)
Monticiano: Giovanni di Niccolo Benzi

Terzo of San Martino
The Massa of the Terzo of San Martino: « Cherius Chole »
Asciano: Jacomo di messer Griffolo
Corsignano: Francesco di Mino di Vincenzo (« Vincentii »)
Corsignano [44]: Francesco Petrucci

Terzo of Camollia
The Massa of the Terzo of Camollia: Jacomo di Goro Monaldetti
Castiglione di Valdorcia: Pietro di Bindo di Manuccio (« Manuccii »)
Querciagrossa: Pietro di Guido Frederighi
Menzano: Ciampolo Baglioni
Berardenga: Buonfigliolo di Biagio (« Blaxii »)

[41] Those Orders, that together with the Nine formed the commune's highest signory, were the Four Provveditori of the Biccherna, the Consuls of the Mercanzia (Merchant Guild), and the Captains of the [Guelf] Party or Consuls of the Knights as these last also were called.

[42] Concistoro, 2, f. 62 r-v.

[43] The chronicle of Agnolo di Tura (p. 519), apparently referring to the early part of 1338, reports that there then were twelve vicariates; but it only lists eleven: Corsignano, Sinalunga, Asciano, Querciagrossa, Berardenga, Menzano, Monticiano, Paganico, [Castiglione di] Valdorcia, Bagni [the Baths, of Petriolo and Macereto], and Arcidosso.

[44] The notary of the Nine erroneously listed Corsignano twice, thus omitting the name of one vicariate. (That notary was one Bartolomeo del fu Ciardino, a Sienese citizen: Concistoro, 2, f. 1 r).

Some of the most valuable data concerning the vicariates are to be found in the constitution of the late 1330s. They tend to confirm the picture that we have thus far obtained. The constitution specifically ordered that « all of the Sienese contado is to be divided and separated [into nine vicariates] and ... perpetually kept so divided ... » [45]. For each vicariate the Nine and the other Orders of the city were to select a captain « *de popularibus civitatis senarum* », and to choose a notary and a messenger for each captain. The captains were to serve for six months, or more or less at the wish of the Nine and the other Orders. They further were commanded to spend at least six days of each month in the lands of their vicariates. Thus, unlike the knights of the Podestà assigned to the contado, these officials of the vicariates were not expected to remain constantly at their posts, but rather generally to supervise the military situation. Their assignments included all matters that within the city would fall within the purview of the captains, standard-bearers, and councillors of the military companies [46]. And like the companies of the city, each vicariate received a banner from the Captain of the People [47]. The captains of the vicariates, their notaries, messengers, and « *familiares* » (whose number is unspecified), as well as those same officials of the Masse and Cortine, were subject to « syndication » or official review of their actions by the Maggior Sindaco at the close of their terms of office [48].

All of the communities of the vicariates, and the persons within them, were to swear allegiance to the captains, who could fine anyone who failed to comply up to twenty-five *lire*. Within ten days of the passing of such sentences the captains in turn were to assign the fines to the Sienese Captain of the People [49].

Like the men of the urban companies, those of the vicariates, and especially the select corps of five thousand, could be called upon to hasten well-armed to guard the city of Siena at times of « *rumor* ». But anyone not in the vicariates was to remain in his own district at such a time. Disobedience could mean

---

[45] Statuti, Siena, 26, Dist. III, r. 383, f. 189 v.

[46] *Ibid.*, Dist. III, r. 380, f. 189 r. For the officials of the companies and their assignments, see Bowsky, « Anatomy of Rebellion », nn. 22, 24 ff.

[47] Statuti, Siena, 26, Dist. III, r. 405, f. 194 v.

[48] *Ibid.*, Dist. III, r. 397, f. 193 v.

[49] *Ibid.*, Dist. III, r. 394, f. 193 r-v.

a fine of one hundred *lire*, and the amputation of a foot if it was not paid within a month. If anyone went to a place other than Siena in the service of a private individual at a time of « *rumor* » he would be fined twenty-five *lire* [50]. The rubric in which these matters are defined makes it clear that not all of the inhabitants of the communities of the contado vicariates were members of those military districts. And while it is not explicitly stated, I suspect that only persons from the same classes that served in the urban companies, or at least those of whose loyalty the Sienese government could feel relatively secure, were members of the vicariates.

Any community of a vicariate that failed to send armed men to Siena or elsewhere as commanded by the Nine or the Captain of the People acting with the knowledge of the Nine or the captains of the vicariates was subject to an enormous fine: a sum equal to that community's entire annual contado gabelle taxation. Disobedience of any other orders of the Nine could cost a community of the vicariates up to one hundred *lire* [51].

Authority was not so neatly apportioned, however, as might appear from an initial reading of the constitution of the late 1330 s. The problem of overlapping and conflicting jurisdictions that plagued other aspects of government had not been completely solved with respect to the vicariates either. While rubrics of that constitution assigned the general supervision of the vicariates to the Captain of the People (especially when trouble arose within the city of Siena itself), that same document shows us that when specific military expeditions were organized, either in general or limited campaigns, it was the traditional commander of the Sienese armies, the Podestà, who exercised the highest jurisdiction — and this although the War Captain was specifically designated as the leader of Siena's armies in the rubrics that defined *his* office [52].

The constitutional rubrics concerning the relation of the Podestà to contado military service date from no later than 1304, as he was fully responsible for the enforcement of a measure of

---

[50] *Ibid.*, Dist. III, r. 396, f. 193 v.

[51] *Ibid.*, Dist. III, r. 395, f. 193 v; for the contado gabelle, see Bowsky, *Finance*, Chapter IX.

[52] See, e. g., Statuti, Siena, Dist. IV, r. 88, f. 213 r-v (cf. above, n. 6).

September 16, 1304 that was incorporated almost verbatim into the constitution of the late 1330s [53]. One *ad tempus* provision, not recopied into the constitution, ordered the Nine to select officials for each Terzo to prepare a list of all males aged twenty to sixty in each contado community, and to arrange them into groups of ten or fifty, or in some other suitable fashion, so that their names would be available when Siena called for contado troops [54]. Would that such a draft list was still extant!

The 1304 regulations concerning contado infantry ordered into Sienese service that were incorporated into the communal constitution stated that the Nine themselves, the Podestà, the Captain of the People, or other designated officials, could command contado communities to dispatch footsoldiers to Siena or elsewhere. A disobedient community incurred a fine of sixty *soldi* for each absent trooper for the first day of his absence, and twenty *soldi* for every other day's absence. Nor could this fine be evaded easily, for the payments were to be made « *in pecunia numerata* ». In addition the delinquent trooper himself had to pay twenty *soldi* for the first day of his absence, and thereafter ten *soldi* a day.

Nor could contado communities fulfill their military obligations to Siena with foreign mercenaries. They were categorically ordered to send men from their own communities or jurisdictions — aged at least twenty but not over sixty. Any man sent who did not meet these requirements would cost the community to which he was accredited a fine of forty *soldi*. These troops, moreover, and those provided by the towns of the Masse, had to be fully equipped with the offensive and defensive weapons and gear carefully set forth in the regulations. Each man had to have at least a headpiece and neckguard, a shield, knife, short spear (*spontone*), axe (*manaria*), long lance, and a light throwing lance (*spedo*) or a crossbow. An incompletely equipped soldier cost the community sending him a five *soldi* fine.

Of particular interest are the troopers' stipends, for although they were paid by their own communities, those contado towns

---

[53] See Statuti, Siena, 15, ff. 242 r-243 v, and Statuti, Siena, 26, Dist. I, r. 335-338, f. 75 v. (R. 338 is quoted in full in Bowsky, *Finance*, Ch. IX n. 56).

[54] Statuti, Siena, 15, ff. 242 v-243 r.

could deduct such expenses from the annual gabelle taxation that they owed Siena. In practise, however, they did not always have to resort to this expedient. On some occasions at least the Sienese commune directly reimbursed the contado communities in cash [55].

In addition to the provisions that it carried over from the legislation of 1304 the constitution ordered the Podestà to impose on the contado communities the various fines set forth above within fifteen days after the stipulated military service was to have been completed, and to collect them within a month of their imposition. And as with the fines that he had to impose upon Sienese citizens who failed to perform their military service, so, too, in the case of these fines against contado communities and soldiers, the Podestà himself was subject to a one hundred *lire* fine to be levied against him by the Maggior Sindaco if he was negligent in their imposition and collection [56].

The Italian city-states of the late middle ages and early Renaissance were not so unified juridically as are most modern states. Portions of what we might consider the Sienese « state » had not yet been incorporated into the contado. Lords and lands subject to Siena, but not within the contado, had their service to the commune defined by special pacts and acts of submission or capitulations, generally known as « *capituli* ». A prominent part of such capitulations defined the military obligations owed Siena by those lords and communities. And while such service could be considerable, Siena was, of course, at the disadvantage of being unable unilaterally to change at will the terms of that service.

The commune of Montepulciano, for example, agreed in its pacts of capitulation of June 13, 1294 that whenever Siena fielded a general army Montepulciano would contribute five hundred infantry — of her own subjects — at her own expense, and would maintain them in the field so long as the Sienese army was in existence. When Siena fielded a partial army, by Terzi, Montepulciano would contribute and support two hundred of her own subjects as footsoldiers [57]. A submission of the Maremma

---

[55] See Bowsky, *Finance*, Ch. II n. 102.

[56] Cf. Statuti, Siena, 26, Dist. I, r. 341, f. 76 r.

[57] Giovanni Cecchini, ed., *Il Caleffo Vecchio del Comune di Siena*, 3 vols. (Fonti di Storia Senese; Florence, 1932-34, Siena, 1940), No. 992, vol. III,

community of Travale concluded on November 27, 1317[58] included the stipulation that Travale would hold Siena's friends as its friends and Siena's enemies as its enemies, and would accept Sienese troops in the castle of Travale for making war whenever Siena so desired. When Siena raised a full general army (*pro comuni* [*Sen.*] *fiet exercitus*) Travale would contribute to that army forty well-armed infantry, and fifteen if the army was raised « *pro terzerio vel pro parte ipsius civitatis* [*Senensis*] ». « And if the army is made for pay or at the stipend of the Sienese commune [i. e., is only a foreign mercenary force] and Siena wishes any infantry of the castle of Travale », then Travale was to supply twenty well-armed footsoldiers who were to be maintained at Sienese expense. The submission of the Maremma commune of Perolla of December 6, 1331 saw that community pledge to send and maintain at its own expense ten well-armed footsoldiers from its own district whenever and for so long as Siena fielded an army by Terzi. Perolla further promised to provide twenty-five infantry whenever Siena had an army in certain parts of the Maremma[59].

---

pp. 1387-1393, esp. p. 1389: « Item quod comune Montispultiani faciet exercitum per comune hoc modo et forma, videlicet quod quando comune Senense faceret exercitum per comune, tunc comune Montispultiani mictet et mictere teneatur et debeat in dictum exercitum quingentos homines pedites bonos et sufficientes et bene munitos de habitatoribus assiduis terre vel districtus Montispultiani, et quod stabunt et morabuntur in dictum exercitum expensis comunis Montispultiani tantum quantum staret et moraretur exercitus comunis Senensis. Et quod quando comune Senense faceret exercitum per terzeria, tunc comune Montispultiani mictet et mictere teneatur et debeat in dictum exercitum CC. homines pedites bonos et sufficientes et bene munitos de habitatoribus assiduis terre vel districtus Montispultiani, et quod morabuntur et stabunt in dicto exercitu expensis comunis Montispultiani tantum, quantum staret et moraretur ibi exercitus comunis Senensis ».

[58] Travale did not on this occasion become a part of the Sienese contado. For this submission, see Bowsky, « Medieval Citizenship », p. 221; cf. *ibid.*, pp. 218-219.

[59] Diplomatico Riformagioni, No. 1498, Dec. 6, 1331. See esp., « ... quotienscumque fieret exercitus per dictum comune Sen. pro terzerio mictere et tenere in eodem exercitu toto tempore quo durabit decem pedites bene armis munitos expensis propriis eorundem comunis et hominum de Perolla ». (MS B 22, an unpaginated « spoglio » of a portion of the series of the Diplomatico Riformagioni, wrongly dates this parchment manuscript as Dec. 6, 1321).

In certain cases Siena succeeded almost completely in imposing its will concerning military service. On November 26, 1289 Count Ranerius, son of the late Count Manuele of Elci, submitted to Siena for himself and his heirs in perpetuity. The pacts then concluded contained the promise:

> That the said lord count and his sons and heirs in perpetuity will hold as friends the friends of the commune of Siena and as enemies the enemies of the commune of Siena. And that they will make war and peace and armies and cavalry expeditions through themselves and their vassals (*fideles*) and from their lands at the will (*ad voluntatem*) of the lord Podestà and of the commune of Siena and of the lords Nine and of the other officials who will then exist for the regimen of the City of Siena for the Sienese commune (*qui essent pro comuni Sen. ad Regimen Civitatis Senarum*) [60].

Even such once mighty lords as Siena's ancient foes, the Aldobrandeschi counts of Santa Fiora, could not obtain favorable terms. In the submission of August 18, 1345 (made through their proctor, the Noveschi Conte di messer Manno Squarcialupi) Pietro, Binduccio, Giovanni, and Enrico, sons of the late Count Enrico of Santa Fiora, agreed to hold Siena's friends as their friends, her enemies as their enemies, and to make war and peace « *secundum et sicut et qualiter et quomodo comuni sen. videbitur et placebit* ». They promised to receive Sienese armed forces into their lands and to allow them to enter and leave unmolested — though the document does not contain a promise to permit Siena to garrison Aldobrandeschi forts and castles. The counts further pledged not to receive any rebel of Siena after they obtained official notification « that such and such is a rebel » [61]. Their military obligation included the commitment that:

> If it befalls the said commune [of Siena] to make an army from the Orcia river southwards, in which army there are the insignia of the commune of Siena and citizens of the said city, [the said counts] are held to and must, at the petition of the said commune or of the

---

[60] Capitoli, 2, ff. 541 r-542 v; quotation on f. 541 r.

[61] For this submission and the documents relating to it, see Bowsky, « Medieval Citizenship », p. 220. The text cited here is that in Capitoli, 3, ff. 205 v-209 r; the quotation is on f. 206 r.

lords Nine who then will be in office, send six well-armed cavalrymen and twenty-five well-equipped and able infantry at their own expense. And [they] must hold them there in the said army at their own expense until and as long as the insignia of the said Sienese commune and citizens of the said city of Siena remain and will be there [62].

The inhabitants of the contado and of other portions of the Sienese state had come to play a significant role in the defense, expansion, and military structure of the commune. It was the first decade of the fourteenth century in particular, as we have noted, that witnessed a marked advance in the systematization and definition of military service. *Ad hoc* military and administrative arrangements then gave way to nearly universal military obligations imposed upon the entire contado through the permanent institution of those military districts known as vicariates. The government of the commune believed that the time was ripe, and its own control over the contado was sufficiently well established, for it to impose upon the communities of the contado a uniform system of military service — and one in which the contado contingents were rigidly supervised and led by urban Sienese *popolani*, and especially by those men most loyal to and trusted by the ruling oligarchy: the Noveschi themselves.

The leaders of the commune demonstrated a new and higher degree of administrative and political sophistication and awareness. They now recognized that the suppression of violence and crime in the contado entailed problems different than those related to its military organization. They saw for the first time that police and military administration of the contado were two distinct and separate spheres of activity. For their control and supervision they created two separate jurisdictions, leaving police matters largely in the hands of the Podestà and assigning the military administration in large part to the Captain of the People, now a purely communal official rather than the leader of a semi-autonomous organization of the *Popolo*. A medieval state thereby was slightly transformed in the direction of its modern counterpart.

To recognize the problems created by overlapping and interweaving jurisdictions was not, however, to resolve them

[62] Capitoli, 3, f. 206 v.

fully. Control over contado military forces still remained somewhat divided and lines of authority somewhat blurred. Here, as in other areas of government, the commune now recognized the need to clarify and distinguish the various spheres of its competence; and although further refinements still were necessary Siena undertook important measures towards achieving this goal.

Examination of the course of this progress towards the military integration of the contado also reveals that at this stage in its development the commune did not yet have the capability of completing this process and creating an absolutely uniform system of military obligations and service performed for it by the entire population or state outside of the city proper. The government did, however, perceive and directly confront the limitations upon its freedom of action imposed by time-honored private jurisdictions and privileges.

In the contado it faced the obstacles posed by the existence of « natural lords » who controlled certain local communities — feudal lords whose claims were not consonant with the obligations that those communities owed to the dominant Sienese commune. In the struggle over this issue in the City Council many urban magnates strove with varying zeal to protect the special exemptions and privileges of natural lords by preventing the contado towns from being incorporated into vicariates. This makes all the more significant the government's ability partially to withstand this pressure. While the commune agreed not to add to the communities of the vicariate any land subject to a natural lord, it did not remove those already included within the vicariates but rather limited its concession to a general promise that the rights of natural lords were not to be prejudiced by the inclusion of their lordships within the vicariates. This partial success over some of the wealthiest, most powerful, influential, and essential members of the Sienese citizenry occurred in part because of divisions among the magnates themselves — and even among members of the same clans. But it also is an indication that the commune had come just a little closer to attaining what later would be called its sovereignty.

That sovereignty was far from complete on the eve of the Renaissance. This is nowhere more manifest than in the respect that the commune found itself obliged to render to the special pacts and rights of those lords and towns that had been able to remain apart from the contado even though they capitulated and submitted to the Sienese commune. These limitations of its authority that the commune was forced to recognize within a part of its « force, district, and jurisdiction » reveal that the Italian city-state was not yet a completely unified and homogeneous political unit, but still was composed of several separate and distinct juridic entities bound in differing degrees of closeness and obligation to the central government.

Despite all such quite apparent limitations, anomalies, exceptions, and qualifications, fourteenth-century Siena did make considerable advances in the definition and formalization of the military role of the contado, and it succeeded in creating a permanent system of contado military service. And this sure indication of the increasing power and sophistication of communal government marks one step in the transition from the medieval to the modern state.

It is hoped that this brief investigation of contado-city military relationships will prove useful for more than what it discloses about the single Tuscan commune of Siena or the changing nature of one Italian city-state in that hazy zone marked by the transition from the late middle ages to the Renaissance. It may perhaps also serve as a pilot study, and encourage further scholarly examination of an aspect of history that has been too long neglected.

ANTHONY MOLHO

A NOTE ON JEWISH MONEYLENDERS IN TUSCANY IN THE LATE TRECENTO AND EARLY QUATTROCENTO

I should like to thank Dottoressa Francesca Morandini, Director of the Archivio di Stato of Arezzo, for her help.

On 23 March 1398/99 the communal council of Arezzo considered a petition submitted to it by a Gaius, *ebreus*, son of the late master Angelo of Siena. Gaius had requested permission to settle in Arezzo so that he might exercise *artem et ministerium usuratus*. Concurrently, he submitted a draft of the conditions which, in his estimation, the city of Arezzo should grant him so that he might settle in the city. The communal council proceeded to empower the priors of the city and a small number of other notables to examine Gaius's petition and reach terms honourable to the government and satisfactory to him [1]. The importance, one can even say urgency, of the matter is reflected in the fact that 23 March 1398/99 was Palm Sunday, and that the committee appointed to negotiate with the Jewish petitioner had to exercise its function during Holy Week — rather a strange time for the authorities of a Christian community to have dealings with a Jew who, of all things, was requesting permission to practice usury in their midst [2]. Be that as it may, on Tuesday after Easter, 1 April, the committee submitted its report to the communal council: it consisted of a copy of the terms reached with the petitioner, and of the recommendation that the request be granted [3]. After a brief discussion, the details of which unfortunately are not reported in the surviving documents, the council approved the petition of Gaius, adding to it one *proviso*: that neither the community of Arezzo nor any of its citizens would be responsible for defending him if the Florentine authorities, which in any case were responsible for ratifying this agreement, decided to impose any taxes on him or on the members of his entourage [4].

---

[1] *A(rchivio di) S(tato di) A(rezzo)*, *Provvisiones*, III, f. 186 v.

[2] A. Cappelli, *Cronologia, cronografia, e calendario perpetuo* (Milan, 1930), p. 52.

[3] *ASA*, *Provvisiones*, IV, ff. 187 r-188 r.

[4] Appendix of this essay, note b.

As Arezzo had been incorporated into the Florentine territory in 1384, the final authority for the ratification of this agreement rested with the government of Florence. Gaius, during his negotiations with the representatives of Arezzo, had agreed to bear the expenses which would be incurred during the process of ratification. Sometime in early April, therefore, Arezzo sent one of its most eminent citizens, and a lawyer of wide repute, Francesco degli Albergotti, to Florence entrusting him with the task of convincing the priors and colleges of that city to waive the traditional ban against the presence of the Jews in the Florentine territory and allowing Gaius, his family and business associates to settle in Arezzo. Though the Aretine ambassador *narravit, exposuit et supplicavit* during the course « of many days » it was not until the arrival of a second Aretine ambassador, Carolo de Mignano, who *eleganter* presented the petition of his government that the priors and colleges of Florence finally acted favorably upon the request of their subject city [5]. Thus, on 28 April, about five weeks after Gaius had originally submitted his petition to the government of Arezzo, he was finally allowed to settle in this Tuscan town.

What were the terms reached between Gaius on the one hand, and the authorities of Arezzo and Florence on the other? They can be divided in two general categories, one regulating Gaius's and his associates' business activities, the other elaborating the personal and legal status of the petitioner before the civil authorities of the city. To begin with, then, Gaius was authorized for the following twenty years to settle in Arezzo, there to operate a pawnshop (*bottega di presto a usura*). Pawns not redeemed within thirteen months and three days of their deposit were to become the property of the pawnbroker who could sell them at will. Gaius was authorized to accept pawns of any kind, from any person at all; this clause probably exempted him from the usual prohibition of accepting as pawns the animals of farmers, or arms of soldiers in the hire of the city. The maximum rate of interest which he could charge was set at thirty per cent per annum (six *denari* per *lira* per month), while

---

[5] *A(rchivio di) S(tato di) F(irenze), Signori e Collegi — Deliberazioni Fatte in Ordine di Speciale Autorità*, VIII, ff. 103 v-107 r. The deliberation of the priors and colleges is reproduced in whole in the appendix of this essay.

it was made amply clear that the account books kept by the scribes of his shop could be used as legal evidence in the communal courts. In any case, the city's magistrates and judges were ordered to treat him and his colleagues in legal cases just as if they were citizens of the city (*sieno tractati nele loro ragioni come cittadini della detta città in civili et criminali*). Finally, the pact provided that, as long as Gaius settled in the city within three months of its ratification, no other Jewish pawnbrokers would be allowed to settle in Arezzo. When the document was submitted to the priors and colleges of Florence for their approval an additional clause was inserted in it, stating that Gaius and his associates could not accept as pawns stolen property. This addition, as we shall shortly see, was contested both by Gaius and by the authorities of Arezzo.

More interesting, at least from the point of view of social history, are the provisions defining Gaius's personal status in the city. He and his associates, because they were considered to be foreigners, were exempt from all taxes, direct or indirect, imposed by the Florentine or Aretine governments. They were allowed to celebrate the Sabath as well as all the other Jewish holidays, *secondo la loro legge*, keeping their shop closed, even if a Christian wished to deposit or redeem a pawn on any of these days. They could freely congregate in their synagogue, and were finally allowed to purchase any type of land, in the city or countryside, being able to convert some of their land holdings into suitable cemeteries. The Florentine government, while approving the general content of this section of the document added certain clauses which clarified the financial responsibility of Gaius and his entourage toward the state: though reiterating the general tax exemption granted by the Aretine authorities it declared that Gaius was subject to paying the *gabella portarum*, the *gabella dei contratti* for real estate transactions (except for purchases of land destined to become the Jewish burial ground), and the *gabella degli feneratori*, an old tax normally assessed on all pawnbrokers and usurers practicing their trade in the Florentine territory. Moreover, the priors and colleges of Florence decreed that neither Gaius, nor any of his associates could be forced to wear the distinctive yellow mark, customarily worn by the Jews.

Finally, the government of Arezzo, obviously wishing to demonstrate its willingness to respect the terms of the pact, offered to post a surety of one thousand florins. Proof that any of the above provisions had been violated would result in the forfeiting of the surety, half of which was to be awarded to Gaius, the other half to the magistrate adjudicating the case. Thus, the stage was set for the safe introduction of a small number of Jewish moneylenders into Arezzo. Whether they had ever been allowed into that city before is not quite clear; that this was the first Jewish usurer permitted to exercise his trade in Arezzo since its submission to Florence in 1384 seems fairly clear from the language of the document.

On 7 May Gaius, either personally or more probably through a representative, *expresse consensit* to the terms of the treaty between himself and Arezzo. However, on the following 16 May the communal council of Arezzo received yet another request from him: wishing to avoid any *dampno vel detrimento* to his business activities Gaius was now requesting that the amendment of the original pact, inserted in the document by the Florentine authorities, which dealt with the acceptance and disposition of stolen pawns be cancelled. No pawn, he insisted, could be taken away from his shop unless the full sum which he had originally given to the depositor and the required interest had been fully paid (*ei sit solutum de vera sorte et de usura*). Gaius's new petition, having been introduced by one of the most prominent Aretine politicians, Cecco di Giovanni Boscoli, was approved by a 37-3 vote [6]. Having thus been satisfied that the conditions established for him were sufficiently satisfactory and attractive, Gaius, on 21 May submitted to the Florentine Signory a list of nine men who would accompany him to Arezzo, and would be his business associates. All, according to the terms of the agreement with the government, would be accorded the same treatment that was promised to him.

Though the nature of the documentation is such so that it becomes rather difficult to trace the affairs of Gaius during the following years, it is fairly clear that shortly after the final ratification of his petition he settled in Arezzo where he opened his pawn shop. In 1403 he is recorded as having made his annual

[6] Appendix, note c.

payment of ninety florins for his assessment of the *gabella degli feneratori*, while concurrently he also seems to have obtained permission to exercise his trade in Castello San Giovanni, where he also opened a shop [7]. His expected twenty-year stay in Arezzo, however, was interrupted in 1406 when the Florentine government in an attempt to protect the inhabitants of the *contado* and *districtus* against the malpractices perpetrated by Jewish and gentile usurers, attempted to regulate the activities of the Christian pawnbrokers more closely and limit their profits, and also ordered the expulsion of all Jews from territory which it controlled. No doubt, a measure of antisemitic prejudice contributed to the drastic ban imposed on the Jews who, in the legislative enactment expelling them from the Florentine territory, were described as *inimici crucis, domini nostri Yhesu Christi, et omnium christianorum, et excercent usuras contra mandatum ecclesie sancte* [8]. The indiscriminate ban on the Jews, however, was strongly protested by the governments of the local communities whose inhabitants had often profited by the services of the Jewish moneylenders. One of the most vocal protests was expressed by the Aretine government which sent an embassy to Florence entrusted with *prochurandum circha facta judeorum existentium in civitate Aretii ad fenerandum* [9]. The eventual abrogation of the ban, brought about by the constant pressure of the subject communities [10], did not seem to help Gaius and his business associates who, during the interval between the insti-

---

[7] *ASF, Camera del Comune — Provveditori — Entrata e Uscita*, XIX, f. 274 r.

[8] *ASF, Provisioni — Registri*, LXXXXIV, ff. 232 v-233 v (28 January, 1405/06). The portion of this law dealing with the Jews was printed by Umberto Cassuto, *Gli ebrei a Firenze nell'età del rinascimento* (Florence, 1918), pp. 362-363.

[9] *ASA, Provvisiones*, IV, f. 79 r (7 May 1406).

[10] *ASF, Libri Fabarum*, XLVIII, f. 116 r (27 May 1406), f. 118 r (7 June), 119 r (8 June), 121 r (16 June). Finally, on 6 August it was passed by a narrow vote of 145-72 and 109-50, ff. 132 r-133 r. The text of the law is in *Provisioni — Registri*, XCV, ff. 140 r-v. The preamble reads as follows: « Actendentes ad ea que a pluribus mensibus citra cum magnis querelis exponita pluries fuerunt per oratores que plurium comunium et locorum super reformatione et provisione edita de mense Januarii proxime preterite inter alia disponente quod nullus judeus vel ebreus posset fenerari ... et auditis dannis, incomodis et iacturis que inde resultant ipsis comunibus et locis secundum narrationes ipsorum oratorum ... ».

tution and abrogation of the ban, must have been forced to flee from the Florentine territory. In fact, a few days after the lifting of the ban, upon the petition of the Aretine council, the Florentine Signory granted a license to another Jew, Salomon Lucci de Arezzo, to open a pawnshop in that city. In his petition Salomon requested that all provisions that had been incorporated in the pact between Gaius and Arezzo be also inserted in his license, so that he would enjoy the same privileges and immunities as his predecessor [11]. Interestingly, two of the business associates of Salomon Lucci had worked in the pawnshop which Gaius had previously operated in Arezzo.

And Gaius? What happened to him? He reappears in the Florentine documents in the fall of 1421, saying that he had been in Siena, whence his father hailed, and now asking for permission to open a pawnshop in Colle Val d' Elsa, yet another of the subject communes in the Florentine *contado* [12]. Permission granted, he probably continued exercising his trade offering his services to the poorer inhabitants of the Florentine territory who, through the 1420s and '30s were experiencing some of the most difficult and depressed economic conditions since the onslaught of the Black Death in 1348 [13].

The case of Gaius, involving as it does the treatment which he was afforded by the Florentine and Aretine authorities, his undoubtedly bitter experience during his first stay in Florentine territory, and his eventual return to it, was not untypical for the members of the Jewish community settled in Italy during the late fourteenth and early fifteenth centuries. In this brief note I should like to present two problems connected with the activities of the Jewish moneylenders during that period. These problems merit fairly careful analysis by students of that period who are linguistically capable of reading contemporary docu-

---

[11] *ASF*, *Capitoli* — *Appendice*, XXVIII, ff. 8 r-11 r. Unfortunately, the public documents of Arezzo for the months of July and August simply have blank pages, the scribe having omitted to record the legislation enacted during those months.

[12] *Ibid.*, ff. 74 r-76 v.

[13] I am about to publish a monograph in which I have gathered some information on economic conditions in Florence during the third and fourth decades of the Quattrocento.

ments written in Hebrew. My own lack of knowledge of that language prevents me from doing more than suggesting the nature of these problems as revealed from my study of certain political and economic developments of that period.

The first such problem involves the foundations of the seeming economic prosperity of the Italian Jewish community. From what sources were the Jewish businessmen able to derive their considerable capital which they made available to their clients? No doubt should exist regarding the motivation of communal governments to extend invitations to Jewish moneylenders to practice their trade in their midst: the issue was cash, which governments of small and large communes and principalities felt that the Jewish moneylenders commanded in abundant supplies. Particularly acute was the shortage of liquid wealth in rural areas. In Tuscany, at least in that portion controlled by Florence, the Jews, while until 1431 being banned from settling in the capital city, were continuously invited to settle in the smaller, rural and more economically depressed areas.

Economic conditions in the Florentine *contado* were particularly depressed in the second half of the fourteenth and the first half of the fifteenth centuries. The massive and systematic exploitation of its *contado* by Florence — an exploitation more often than not taking the form of exorbitant tax assessments — had resulted in the transfer of the more affluent inhabitants to the city, the flight of agricultural workers who were in arrears with their tax payments and the consequent increase of the tax burden borne by those left behind. Thus, at the very moment when economic incentives should have been offered by the capital city to its subject territories to enable them to rehabilitate their economies, the tax burden imposed on them was so great so as to make impossible their economic recovery [14]. The most immediate problem confronting these subject communities was finding the necessary cash with which to pay their tax assessments. Often, they resolved it by borrowing from important Florentine bankers at rates which often exceeded twenty

---

[14] *Ibid.*, Chapter 3, which deals with the Florentine policy of taxation of the *contado*.

per cent per annum [15]. Thus, the slender cash resources of these localities were steadily absorbed by the economy of the mother city. The end result was that cash needed for the daily operations of the economies of these communes was in extremely short supply, and that those least able to afford it were driven in the direction of the moneylenders. It would seem to me that the admission of the Jews into the Florentine territory is explicable precisely on the grounds that they commanded sources of capital which were not available to gentile moneylenders. The petition submitted by the authorities of Pistoia in 1427 to the Florentine Signory was fairly typical: Imitating the example of many other cities under the jurisdiction of Florence the Pistoiesi were asking for permission that would allow the Jews in their city. The justification which they offered was the following:

> Quod debitis temporibus non valent oneribus publicis nec etiam privatis necessitatibus et debitis respondere ex quo necessario compelluntur gravissimis penis subici ac etiam persepe carceribus opprimi, que omnia evitarent si in civitate predicta esset aliquis qui ad pignus mutuaret et eorum indigentiis cum pignore subveniret ... [16]

The officials of Cortona, when submitting a similar demand in 1431 used almost precisely the same language, referring to the benefits that would accrue to the *pauperes persone* from the admission of the Jews into their city [17]. A measure of the great need which the local Tuscan communities had of the capital available to the Jewish moneylenders is the fact that from 1406, after the abrogation of their ban, until 1410 the Florentine government issued licenses to Jews to practice in at least nine localities of the *contado* [18].

---

[15] For a few examples: *ASF*, *Diplomatico*, *Castiglion Fiorentino*, 26 July 1411; *ibid.*, *Monte Comune*, 13. .; *Camera del Comune — Provveditori — Entrata e Uscita*, LIII, ff. 42 r, 56 r.

[16] *ASF*, *Provisioni — Registri*, CXVII, f. 86 v (6 June 1427).

[17] *ASF*, *Capitoli — Appendice*, XXVII, f. 1 r.

[18] *Ibid.*, XXVIII, ff. 1 r-3 v (Pescia); 4 r-7 r (S. Miniato); 8 r-11 r (Arezzo); 11 v-14 v (Prato); 15 r-18 r (Castro Collis); 18 v-21 r (Castiglion Fiorentino); 21 v-25 r (Montepulciano); 25 v-29 r (Volterra); 29 v-32 v (San Gimignano).

It seems, therefore, that the presence of the Jews in the Florentine territory was an economic necessity brought about by the particular relations which had developed between the capital city and its subject territories. Research among a few surviving account books of these moneylenders would provide one with rather interesting information regarding their clientele, the rates of interest which they charged, the types of pawn deposited in their shops and the like. Apparently the fact that the great majority of their clients belonged to the most indigent and oppressed social classes does not detract from the importance of their services to the Florentine and Tuscan economy [19]. It may well be that their presence in the Florentine territory accomplished a twofold end: it released other sources of capital, controlled by gentile businessmen, for investment in more acceptable and honourable channels; concurrently, it placated pressing economic demands of the most indigent rural and urban classes, and in so doing muted tendencies to rebellion which may have existed among them [20].

The first important question, therefore, which calls for considerable additional study, particularly on the surviving account books of the Jewish moneylenders, is the sources of their income and capital.

The second question, partly related to the first, and one on which I can offer almost no information at all except for a conjecture is the organization of the Italian Jewish community during the high Middle Ages and the Renaissance. Several decades ago Roberto Cessi had promised the publication of a detailed monograph on this subject, but to the best of my knowledge that promise has remained unfulfilled [21]. Further investigation of this general topic might reveal some information

---

[19] David Herlihy, *Medieval and Renaissance Pistoia* (New Haven, 1967), p. 161.

[20] It might be suggested that an additional motivation underlying the admission of the Jews into the Florentine territory was the income which the government derived from the imposition of the *tassa degli feneratori*. The income from this tax, however, never exceeded 2,000-3,000 florins, and for this reason it seems to me that such an explanation would miss the compelling reason which induced the government to invite the Jews into its territory.

[21] Roberto Cessi, « Le condizioni degli ebrei banchieri in Padova nel secolo XIV », *Bollettino del Museo Civico di Padova*, X (1907), p. 201, note 1.

regarding the business connections between Jewish moneylenders practicing in various Italian regions, the business training of young Jewish businessmen (how, for example, did the *cursus* which they had to follow differ from that established in the late thirteenth and early fourteenth centuries for young Christian males?) [22], the assistance which they might have offered each other during times of persecution by their Christian hosts. Two of Gaius's business associates, we already noticed, were hired by Salomon Lucci in 1406 when he was granted the license to establish his pawnshop in Arezzo in 1406. Five years later these two, Manovello and Sabatuccio di Abram de Perusio in association with a third Jewish businessman, a Daterio di Manovello de Monte Alcino, were granted a license to practice usury in Cortona [23]. This single example obviously does not enable one to formulate any kind of generalization on the social structure of the Jewish community of Tuscany in the late fourteenth and early fifteenth centuries. But it may be indicative of a certain situation in which close ties between various Jewish settlements were consciously cultivated, younger sons of families in one location became apprentices in the shops of other businessmen situated away from home, eventually establishing their own businesses. It might be interesting to know if, in addition to the training which they received as apprentices, they might also have been aided by their master by being given some capital with which to undertake their own careers.

In short, what one would like to have available is a social and economic history of the Italian Jewish community of those centuries. A scholar willing to investigate this topic and prepared to face the linguistic and paleographic problems which undoubtedly he would encounter in his study, would command the gratitude and respect of historians of late mediaeval and Renaissance Italian institutions.

---

[22] As described in Armando Sapori, *Le marchand italien au moyen âge* (Paris, 1947).

[23] For their license in Cortona, *ASF*, *Capitoli — Appendice*, XXVIII, ff. 33 r-37 r.

APPENDIX

From: *Archivio di Stato di Firenze, Signori e Collegi - Deliberazioni Fatte in Ordine di Speciale Autorità*, VIII, ff. 103v-107r. [Portions of this document were first published in « Documenti tratti dall'archivio segreto di Todi », *Archivio Storico Italiano*, sez. 3ª, XXI (1875) pp. 188-190].

Pro Comuni Aretii et pro Gaio Iudeo. 103v

In dei nomine Amen. Anno incarnationis domini nostri Yesu Cristi Millesimo trecentesimo nonagesimo nono, indictione septima, secundum cursum et morem florentinorum, die vigesimo octavo mensis Aprilis.

Magnifici et potentes domini, domini priores artium et vexillifer justitie populi et comunis florentie una cum offitiis gonfalonierorum societatis populi, et duodecim bonorum virorum comunis predicti. Benigne audita et diligenter intellecta narratione et petitione eis facta super his de quibus inferius disponetur pro parte comunis civitatis Aretii, primo per nobilem virum Franciscum de Albergottis civem aretinum et oratorem dicti comunis Aretii qui iam multis diebus coram eis super his narravit, exposuit et supplicavit, et hodie presenti die audito nobili viro Carolo de Mignano etiam oratore dicti comunis Aretii similiter et eleganter narrante et exponente ac infrascripta petente fieri et instantissime postulante. Et audita relatione facta per duos de dictis collegiis qui de mandato dictorum dominorum super his pluries praticam habuerunt et examinationem fecerunt. Et volentes dicto comuni Aretii in omnibus complacere et habito super his pluries ad invicem colloquio sequentesque dictam relationem per dictos duos de collegio factam et promisso et solemniter celebrato inter ipsos dominos priores et vexilliferum justitie et gonfaloneriis socie-tatum populi et duodecim bonos viros comunis predicti in numeris sufficientibus invicem congregatos in palatio populi florentini civitatis florentie solemni et secreto scrutineo et obtento partito ad fabas nigras et albas secundum ordinem dicti comunis vigorem auctoritatis et potestatis eis concesse et competentis, et omni via, modo, causa et jure quibus melius et efficacius potuerunt providerunt, ordinaverunt et disposuerunt omnia et singula infrascripta, videlicet. Imprimis quidem auditis et intellectis capitulis et pactis quorum tenor inferius describetur productis coram eis tam pro parte dicti comunis Aretii quam etiam pro parte infrascripti Gay, et modo et forma predictis ad approbationem ipsorum cum certis correctionibus, mutationibus et additionibus et aliis nomis, capitulis disponendo et ordinando procedere intendentes, ponito primo tenore ipsorum sic productorum que talis est in vulgari sermone prout exhibita fuerunt, videlicet.

Questi sono e capitoli et pacti che Gaio del maestro Agnolo Judeo per se et per chi nominasse suo compagno o compagni et
104r loro figliuoli, fratelli, et fattori, et garzoni // e ministri domanda al comune d'Arezo.

In primi di potere prestare et fare prestare a bottega di presto a usura et d'altro mestiere che fare volesse nela detta città d'Arezzo per quel modo et forma che a lloro piacerà per tempo e termine di venti anni. E i pegni che fossono impegnati che non si ricolgliessono fra 'l tempo d'uno anno, uno mese et tre dì che a loro sia licito venderli et alienarli come loro proprie cose, passato il detto termine, e non prima per alcuno modo, e di ciò niuno si possa richiamare ne domandare niente.

Ancho che durante il detto tempo di venti anni s' intendano et sieno exenti et liberi et immuni da tutte et qualunche altre spese et factioni reali et personali et mixte che per lo comune di Firenze o per lo comune d'Arezo sono imposte o per lo tempo s' imponessono, et per le dette factioni per niuno modo possano essere gravati. Ne eziandio per cagione di qualunche represaglie che fossono concedute o che si concedessono per li tempi ne per alcuna altra cosa così per lo comune di Firenze come per qualunche spetiale persona si concedesse per lo detto comune non possano essere gravati nela detta città di Firenze, ne suo contado et distretto.

Ancho che a lloro sia licito guardare il Sabato et altre loro feste secondo la loro legge sanza fare alcuno mestiere, ne di prestare ne di rendere alcuno pegno. E di non fare alcuna altra cosa contro a lloro volere più che si vogliano, e fare loro scole in sinagoghe secondo loro volere.

Ancho che possano comperare vigne, terre, case, et vendere, et maximamente per fare loro sepulture, pagando al comune di Firenze la gabella de' contratti secondo gli ordini dela detta gabella de' contratti così dentro nela città come di fuori. //

104v Ancho che a lloro sia licito di potere prestare sopra ogni cosa et a ogni persona come sarà di loro piacere et volontà senza alcuna contradictione.

Ancho che a loro libri et scripture si dia piena fede, e sieno tractati nele loro ragioni come cittadini dela detta città in civili et criminali e in altrimenti niuno di qualunche conditione si sia li possa gravare.

Ancho che niuno altro Judeo possa prestare ne presto fare durante el tempo et termine di venti anni nela detta città d'Arezo, salvo che quelli dela detta compagnia o loro fratelli, o figliuoli, factori, garzoni, o ministri. E che al detto Gaio sia licito specificare et chiarire suoi compagni coloro che a llui piacerà durante el tempo di venti anni come dichiarato è di sopra.

Ancho che tutte le predette cose sieno ferme et rate, e il detto comune prometta d'attenere et observare sotto la pena di fiorini mille d'oro, la quale pena in ogni lato si possa adomandare, e la metà sia del detto Gaio e di compagni, e l'altra metà sia del rettore inanzi al quale s'adomandasse, e ogni legge, statuto et riformagione che fosse contro ale dette cose, o che si facessono per l'avenire sieno casse et vane et sanza alcuno valore et inverso di loro non si debbia ne possa procedere sotto la detta pena.

Ancho che le predette cose sieno ferme et rate et dichiarate a senno del savio del detto Gaio non mutando la forma del contratto.

Ancho ch'al detto Gaio et suoi compagni sia licito potere prestare a ragione di soldi due el fiorino, et danari sei la lira il mese. E se li stesse il pegno meno d'uno mese ala loro discretione. E s'elli togliesse più vuole essere tenuto ala restituzione di quello, gli togliesse più et ala pena del doppio. // [a].

Et audito et intellecto quod dicta capitula fuerunt approbata in 105r
civitate Aretii et ibidem firmata per consilium ipsius civitatis additis etiam certis aliis verbis post capitula suprascripta maxime de veniendo ad exercendum infra tres menses a die approbationis predictorum et de exercendo durante dicto tempore et de aliis de quibus et prout et sicut dicitur contineri in scripturis inde factis per ser Antonium Venture, notarium aretinum [b], voluerunt, ordinaverunt, delibera-

---

[a] At this point, the original pact has the following chapter, omitted from the document as ratified by the Florentine authorities: *Archivio di Stato di Arezzo, Provvisiones*, III, f. 187 v:

Ancho che tutte le predette cose s'entendano essere approvate et approvare si dieno fra ei signori et collegi del popolo et comune di Fiorenza alle spese del detto Gaio et dei compagni sopradetti. Et etiamdio della gabella essere d'accordo cum lo comune de Fiorenza e cum chi spetasse la detta gabella a ogni loro spesa.

[b] At the time of the approval of this pact the following clause was inserted in the text of the treaty: *Ibid.*, f. 188 r:

Quod comune Aretii et vel singulares homines et persone dicti comunis Aretii nullo modo, jure, causa et seu forma teneantur et seu obligati sint et vel esse intelligantur ad conservandum dictum Gaium et seu suos sotios, factores et seu ministros et seu alterum ipsorum in dannos et secundum damno et seu modo aliquo defendere aut penam aliquam incurrere occasione maxime dictorum capitulorum si per dictum tempus et dicto tempore durante

verunt et disposuerunt quod ipsa suprascripta capitula prout et sicut approbata et firmata fuerunt in civitate Aretii intelligantur esse et sint approbata et confirmata, et ipsa approbaverunt et confirmaverunt prout et sicut in civitate Aretii approbata et confirmata fuerunt ut per scripturas dicti ser Antonii dicitur apparere. Salvis tamen exceptis et reservatis infra scriptis, et cum additionibus, detractionibus, correctionibus et aliis de quibus inferius describetur qua omnia infrascripta providerunt, ordinaverunt, et deliberaverunt prout inferius continetur, videlicet.

In primis quod predictus Gaius et eius sotius et sotii et eorum filii, fratres, factores et ministri quicunque non possint in dicta civitate Aretii eodem tempore pro fenerando et alium mi[ni]sterium faciendo habere, facere et tenere nisi unam apotecam et stationem inter omnes vigore capitulorum suprascriptorum et infrascriptorum.

Item quod de et pro pignoribus furatis super quibus predicti mutuaverint observentur statuta et ordinamenta civitatis Florentie et fiat et fieri et observari debeat prout et sicut in talibus et pro talibus observatur in civitate Florentie [c].

---

viginti annorum per comune Florentie aut eius collegia et seu consilia et vel quoscunquos rectores et offitiales dicti comunis Florentie aliqua gravedo et seu onus reale et vel personale et seu mixtum indiceretur et seu quocunquo modo imponeretur dicto Gaio et seu suis sotiis, ministris et factoribus antedictis aut alteri eorum.

[c] On 16 May the following petition of Gaius was voted upon by the communal council of Arezzo: *Ibid.*, f. 194 r:

Tertio [provisionem] cum Gaius Judeus veniat ad mutuandum pecuniam magnam ad usuras in civitate Aretii et petat a dicto comuni quod non vult teneri, cogi, artari vel molestari quoquo modo ad restituendum vel reddendum aliquod pignus vel pignora quod vel que ponerentur sub usuris suo presto que fuisset vel essent furata et ablata quoquo modo, nisi primo ei sit solutum de vera sorte et de usura dicto Gaio, non tamen obligando comune Aretii per presentem capitulum in aliquo, et super petitione dicti Gay cuius tenor et forma talis est, videlicet: Coram vobis magnificis viris dominis prioribus populi civitatis Aretii nec non capitaneis partis guelfe et consilio oportuno civitatis prefate. Gaius judeus quondam maestri Angeli de Senis reverenter exponit et dicit quod cum ipse venire intendit ad fenerandum sive mutuandum pecunias ad usuras in civitate Aretii super pignoribus, videlicet ad panuciam, et ut dictam artem suam sine periculo, dampno vel detrimento ipsius vel sotiorum, factorum, discipulorum vel ministrorum sui et suorum possit et valeat facere et secure, libere exercere, petit humiliter prefatus Gaius nomine quo supra per vos dominos priores et capitaneos prefatos et vestrum consilium oportunum reformare, deliberare et stantiare et reformari facere stantiari et deliberari quod dictus Gaius et sotii sui non possint vel debeant ullo modo directe vel indirecte artari, cogi, inquietari, cogi, molestari vel detineri quoquo modo per aliquem rectorem, pre-

Item quod verba ponita supra in secundo vulgari capitulo que sunt ista: ne per altra cosa et cetera, intelligantur pro guerris, discordiis et dissensionibus que essent vel evenirent inter comune florentie et aliud quidcunque comune, dominum vel principem aut tirannum et pro his inde in ipsis guerris et discordiis sequerentur. Et etiam quod non obstante predictis ipse Gaius et sotii, filii, fratres, factores et ministri teneantur et debeant solvere gabellam portarum prout quicunque alii.

Item quod capitulo quarto supra ponito, in quo continetur quod possint // emere et vendere et cetera, addatur et additum esse intel- 105v
ligatur et sit quod pro bonis immobilibus que emerent teneantur et debeant solvere et subire onera et factiones prout et sicut tenerentur et deberent illi de civitate aut comitatu Aretii a quibus emerent. Salvo quod huiusmodi onera et factiones non teneantur solvere vel subire pro terrenis que emerent pro eorum sepulturis.

Item quod ubicunque supra in capitulis de sotiis fit mentio intelligatur de sotiis nominandis per dictum Gaium hinc ad per totum mensem Octobris proxime secuturum et non de alio vel aliis. Salvo tamen quod si aliquis vel aliqui demum discederent a societate predicta possit per dictum Gaium loco cuiuslibet tali sotii a sua sotietate discedentis alius nominari etiam quandocunque durante dicto tempore viginti annorum et quilibet talis loco alterius qui discesserit a societate nominatus succedat in predictis et infrascriptis loco illius talis qui discesserit ut prefertur. Eo expresse declarato quod quilibet ex dictis sotiis nominandis debeat nominari et de eo nominatu fieri solummodo penam scribam reformationum civitatis florentie et non alibi et per eum seu eius coadiutorem inde scriptura fieri et non per alium, maxime pro evidentia veritatis, et ut in uno loco appareant qui sint sotii Gaii predicti et quid in predictis secus fieret non valeat.

Item quod dictus Gaius et seu eius sotii, fratres, vel eorum aut alicuius eorum filii, ministri vel factores vel aliquis ipsorum non teneantur portare aliquam vestem vel aliquod signum quoquo modo

---

sidem vel offitialem dicte civitatis Aretii ad reddendum vel restituendum dicta pignera vel pignus que fuissent furtiva, subtracta, accepta vel ablata vel subtractum, aceptum vel ablatum quoquo modo, qua fuissent pignerata dicto Gaio vel illis quorum nomine petit ut supra, nisi primo ei vel dictis suos sotiis nominibus quibus petit fuerit et sit de vera sorte et puro capitali solutum et integraliter satisfactum et quod pro predictis vel predictorum occasione et ullo usquam tempore puniri et seu quo ius modo procedi valeat contra eos. Ut altissimus vos conservet in statu prospero et felici.

On that same day, f. 195 r, the petition was approved by a 37-3 vote, having been introduced and supported by Cecco di Giovanni Boscoli, one of the communal councillors. I was not able to determine whether this amendment was also submitted for approval to the Florentine authorities.

nisi prout et sicut de ipsa processerit libera voluntate. Et quod aliquis episcopus, judex vel prelatus aut offitialis ecclesiasticus vel secularis vel alia persona non possit nec debeat ullo modo ipsos Gaium et eius sotios, fratres, aut filios ipsorum vel alicuius eorum aut eorum factores vel ministros gravare, requirere vel aliquo modo cogere ad portandum vel tenendum in dorsum vel ad dorsum aut supra se aliquod signum vel vestem ullo modo contra voluntatem eorum, et seu nisi prout et sicut de ipsorum libera voluntate processerit. Nec propterea vel occasione tali directa vel indirecte, tacite vel expresse contra eius vel aliquem eorum aut in eorum gravamen aliquid facere vel fieri facere quoquo modo. //

106r Item quod cum dicatur quod dictus Gaius convenerit et in concordia sit cum emptoribus gabelle feneratorum pro solutione florenorum nonaginta auri pro quolibet anno quo durat tempus emptionis per dictos emptores de dicta gabella facta a comuni florentie deliberaverunt, voluerunt et disposuerunt quod talis conventio et concordia facta pro dicta quantitate pro anno duret prout facta est pro dicto tempore quo durat dicta emptio gabelle, quod tempus est, ut dicitur, trium annorum proximorum futurorum a die primo mensis May proximo futuro. Et etiam postea pro tribus aliis annis pro dicta gabella solvatur comuni florentie aut ei qui ex inde jus haberet ab ipso comuni ipsa quantitas florenorum nonaginta auri. Et pro supradictis predictis temporibus quibus exercerent predicta in dicta civitate Aretii dictus Gaius et eius sotii, fratres, filii, factores et ministri ad solvendum maiorem gabellam vel maiorem quantitatem non teneantur nec cogantur ullo modo. Sed elapsis dictis sex annis pro tempore secuturis ex inde usque ad completum tempus dictorum viginti annorum pro tempore quo predictum ministerium exercerent in dicta civitate Aretii predicti Gaius et sotii, factores, fratres, filii et ministri intelligantur esse et sint taxati et ipsos taxerunt pro dicta gabella ad solvendum pro dicta gabella pro quolibet anno dicti temporis florenos centum quinquaginta auri et quod sic solvere debeant dicto comuni florentie vel habenti jus ab eo ordinaverunt, deliberaverunt et disposuerunt. Et quod pro maiori quantitate pro gabella predicta non possint nec debeant cogi vel gravari pro tali tempore.

Item quod supra disponita provisa et ordinata et contenta cum modis, effectibus et conditionibus suprascriptis valeant et teneant pleno jure. Et quod tam pro comune florentie quam etiam pro comune Aretii prout et sicut ad num quodque ipsarum comunium spectata et pertinet, et secundum predicta requiratur et pro recta observantia debetur possint et debeant observari, manuteneri et executioni mandari. Et quod quilibet capitaneus, et potestas et quilibet alius offitialis civitatis Aretii presens et futurus, et quilibet alius cuiuscunque dignitatis vel conditionis existat, possit, teneatur et

debeat ipsa omnia et singula observare et manutenere, et facere per
quemlibet effectualiter observari omni contradictione et oppositione
cessante, penitus et remota. Et quod nulla persona etiam cuiuscunque
dignitatis, auctoritatis vel gradus existat // audeat vel presumat quo- 106v
quo mode contra predicta facere vel venire directe vel indirecte tacite
vel expresse.

Acta disponita et ordinata, provisa et deliberata fuerunt suprascripta, modo et forma predictis in civitate florentie in palatio supradicto residentie dictorum magnificorum dominorum, dominorum priorum artium et vexilliferum justitie, presentibus ser Junta Francisci, notario florentino et Taddeo domini Francisci de civitatis Castelli, preceptore dictorum dominorum priorum et vexilliferi, testibus ad predicta adhibitis et vocatis.

Item post predicta, anno et indictionem predictis die septimo mensis May.

Supradictus Gaius auditis et ut asseruit intellectis omnibus suprascriptis ipsis omnibus expresse consensit prout in ipsas continetur.

Acta in palatio suprascripto presentibus ser Dino ser Scarfagni, ser Johanne ser Francisci et Particino Johannis, civibus florentinis testes ad predicta vocatis.

Item, postea, anno et indictionem predictis, die vigesimo primo mensis May.

Supradictus Gaius pro predictis et vigorem predictorum nominavit pro suis et in suos sotios ad predicta et in predictis, reservata sibi potestate etiam alios nominandi secundum et prout sibi competentur per capitula suprascripta.

Consiglum Datteri Consigli de Senis,
Sabatum Datteri Consigli de Pisis et Musettum eius filium,
Manuellum et
Bonaventuram — Abrami Datteri de Perusio, habitantes in civitate Castelli,

Deodatum Abrae Deodati de Perusio, habitantem in civitate Castelli,
Genettanum magistri Angeli de Perusio,
Salomonem et
Sabattinum — Vitalis de Montepoliciano.

Acta fuerunt predicta Florentie in dicto palatio presentium ser Dino ser Scarfagni et ser Johannem ser Francisci predictos, et Bartolo Angeli de civitatem Castelli testes ad suprascripta adhibitos et vocatos.

T. C. PRICE ZIMMERMANN

CONFESSION AND AUTOBIOGRAPHY IN THE EARLY RENAISSANCE

This paper was written during a term as a fellow of the Reed College Humanities Institute funded by the Rockefeller Foundation. I should like to acknowledge the many suggestions received in conversations with colleagues in the Institute and on the faculty, with visitors to the Institute and with other friends upon whom I have imposed for advice.

Nel principio della sua conversione, mandò a Firenze per uno libretto composto da messer Francesco Petrarca intitolato, *De conflictu curarum suarum*; dove in forma di dialogo egli si confessa de' peccati sua all'onnipotente Iddio; e santo Agostino, così è opinione, risponde al Petrarca dolendosi de' sua errori. E così con infinite lacrime il Petrarca si confessa de' sua peccati all'onnipotente Iddio, e ne domanda perdonanza.

VESPASIANO DA BISTICCI, *Life of Francesco de Lignamine*

In the course of transition from one historical epoch to another institutions are as often adapted as supplanted, as often transformed as discarded. The argument that follows is an attempt to construe the emergent Renaissance *genre* of autobiography as a transmogrification of the mediaeval practice of confession. While critical interest in autobiography has tended to center on the periods of its greatest flowering, which were subsequent to the Renaissance, the earlier era is of paramount interest from an aetiological standpoint, since during its primary stages autobiography betrays more clearly the evidence of its origins.

Ideally practiced, autobiography involves the formulation of a coherent interpretation of the self from a particular viewpoint in time. What distinguishes it from memoirs, diaries, journals, recollections and other forms of « autobiographical » writing is the author's viewing of his past life in an effort to construe it as a whole [1]. Through the process of reflection there emerges an interpretation of past experience which attempts to clarify the development of the self. Because of the nature of the involvement in taking one's self as object, autobiography

[1] These points are made at length in Roy Pascal, *Design and Truth in Autobiography* (Cambridge, 1960), ch. 1. Autobiography is thus to be distinguished from *ricordanze* and such-like.

constitutes an essentially distinct undertaking from biography, as well as from memoirs and the like.

Given the intrinsic characteristics of autobiography it is not difficult to find antecedents for it in the Christian confessional [2]. Beyond inducing the habit of alleviating guilt by confessing it — the obvious antecedent of the confessional-type autobiography — the mediaeval institution of the confessional created a formal system of introspection. Historically, this introduction of a mode of introspection was probably the crucial contribution of confession to autobiography, for as a function of guilt mechanisms in the psyche, whether in a religious or secular guise, the confessional urge is more or less continually present and may or may not be operative as the motive for autobiographies. Of greater import for the evolution of autobiography was the form that the expression of guilt had taken at the moment when new inducements were being offered to expanding self-awareness [3].

Within the mediaeval Church confession had been a chief means to self-knowledge. Man's being, his provenance, the overall lineaments of his nature — these were clearly-enough

---

[2] The debt of autobiography to the Christian confessional has been variously noted, e. g. Pascal, *op. cit.*, p. 181. Misch sees a long development in which the introspection of the religious is eventually transformed into the poetic introspection of nineteenth - century romantic poetry. *Geschichte der Autobiographie, Zweiter Band, Das Mittelalter, Erster Teil: Die Frühzeit* (Frankfurt a/M., 1955), I, 11 ff.

[3] In an unpublished essay on autobiography and psychoanalysis Bruce Mazlish, while noting that Rousseau used his *Confessions* as a means for expiating his sins, nevertheless draws a clear distinction between autobiography proper and « soul-searching of the religious ». An extreme example of the latter, a life story arranged as confession of sins, is afforded by a work of St. Ephraim the Syrian. Misch puts a low value on this mere self-dissection of sin compared with Augustine's sophisticated psychology. Georg Misch, *History of Autobiography in Antiquity*, tr. E. W. Dickes (Cambridge, 1951), II, 582. Although such an autobiography may provide a coherent interpretation of the self (from a restricted point of view) it would not qualify as autobiography in the modern sense, lacking a historical notion of the self as a developing entity. Modern autobiography arose when to the religious penchant for self-analysis was added a new historical sense coupled with an interest in humanistic philosophy and literature. In his study of mediaeval autobiography Misch notes the religious origin of confession but also its tendency to acquire ' societal ' overtones when incorporated into literature. Misch, *Geschichte*, II, 483.

known. When the individual wanted to know what he himself was, however, it was necessary to search his own conscience in terms of the obligations laid upon him by his human nature and Christian faith. Since these were the same for all Christians, a primary individuating factor among men, apart from the recognized categories of temperament and physique, was the degree and particularity of their involvement in sin [4]. While on the one hand the autonomy and responsibility of the individual will provided a clear basis for individuation, the tendency to regard personality in terms of capacities shared by all men militated against the evolution of the sorts of conceptions now attached to personality. Confession can therefore be closely linked to mediaeval notions of individuality.

By prescription of the Lateran Council of 1215 the Christian was obligated to perform the ritual of confession at least once a year. A strong inducement was thus given to undertake periodic self-examination, while formulas were provided for the exercise through the agency of the clergy. A bit of ecclesiastical doggerel from the late Middle Ages describes the qualities of a good confession: « It should be simple, a good confession, humble, pure, faithful, true, frequent, naked, tearful, rapid, whole and prepared beforehand » [5]. Many of these qualities are pertinent to autobiography as well. While not necessarily tearful and rapid, a good autobiography is certainly faithful, true and whole. Even more importantly, it is produced by the sort of reflection implied in premeditation. Among ecclesiastical writers there was a growing emphasis on an antecedent review, culminating in the canon promulgated at the Council of Trent which officially prescribed it [6]. Fra Domenico Cavalca, a fourteenth-century preacher, recommended a daily review [7]. Saint Bernardino, the

---

[4] See Ewart Lewis, *Mediaeval Political Ideas* (New York, 1954), I, 201.

[5] « Sit simplex, humilis confessio, pura, fidelis, vera, frequens, nuda, lacrimabilis, accelerata, integra, et sit patere parata ». Domenico Cavalca (d. 1342), *Lo specchio de' peccati*, Biblioteca Nazionale, Firenze, MS. Pal. 91, fol. 25 r. In variant forms the formula was widespread, e. g. Jacopo Passavanti (1300-1357), *Lo specchio di vera penitenza* (Florence, 1925), p. 183.

[6] H. C. Lea, *A History of Auricular Confession and Indulgences in the Latin Church* (London, 1896), II, 413.

[7] Domenico Cavalca, *Trattato della mondizia del cuore* (Rome, 1846), p. 29. Some doubt exists about the attribution of this particular tract to Cavalca.

greatest preacher of the early-fifteenth century, suggested to his auditors that they retire to some closet and there examine themselves [8]. A formula for confession found in a fifteenth-century manuscript of the Biblioteca Riccardiana included the sin of not having examined one's self sufficiently prior to confession [9]. Although many of the faithful were accustomed to confess frequently, the Church was quite familiar with the dilatory confessant who appeared once a year, or once a decade. For such a person confession became a review of large sections of his life. In this event, Jacopo Passavanti, a great Dominican preacher of the Trecento, recommended bringing written notes to the confessional [10]. There is, moreover, a more than casual similarity between the man who all at once is overcome by repentance for long years of sin and the type of autobiographer who at some point is suddenly struck by the desire to examine, analyze and narrate his past life. Some autobiographers have in fact spoken of the catharsis that has come through writing their autobiographies, the feeling of relief deriving from greater understanding.

More significant for the process of transformation than motive or content, however, was the legacy of system and form. It was the systematic nature of the self-examination which was of the greatest import for the evolution of autobiography. Writers on confession agree that the confessor should not be interested in hearing superfluous details nor the penitent in relating them [11]. Penitents are enjoined not to ramble or gossip but to stick to the point. Confession is for recounting sins, not one's life-story. While omitting no sin, it must include no irrelevant details. Such strict insistence on prescribed form inculcated the idea of a fixed principle by which one's life was to be viewed (in this case the ecclesiastical taxonomy of sin) and it is the sense of

---

[8] St. Bernardino of Siena (1380-1444), *Le prediche volgari inedite* (Siena, 1935), p. 472. See also his emphasis on premeditation in the *Trattato della confessione 'Renovamini'*, *Operette volgari* (Florence, 1938), pp. 94-95.

[9] Biblioteca Riccardiana, Firenze, MS. 1511, fol. 12 r.

[10] Passavanti, *Lo specchio*, p. 178.

[11] Strictures against prolix or unnecessarily detailed confessions are almost universal, e. g. Alain of Lille, *Liber poenitentialis*, in Migne, *Pat. Lat.*, CCX, 286, « Sed non debet ad minutias descendere ... ».

organization and purpose which distinguishes true autobiography from garrulous recollections.

In mediaeval practice the questions to be asked during confession and the review preceding it can be summed up in the handy distich,

> Who, what, where, by whom, how often, why, in what manner, when,
> Whosoever should ask who gives the soul its medicine [12].

The metaphor of the priest as physician, healing the soul by prescribing penance is a very old one. It is found as early as Origen [13]. In terms of this metaphor the autobiographer becomes the physician who undertakes to cure himself. Although the interrogatory of the confession was aimed at uncovering the nature and extent of sin, the seriousness of the sin was gauged in part objectively, in part in relation to the sinner himself. Hence the practice of the confessional involved a distinct notion of individuality. The priest « should consider the quality of the sin », advises the pseudo-Augustine, « in respect of the place and time when it was committed, the sinner's perseverance in it, the variety of person, how he was tempted and whether he repeated the sin » [14]. Under the question *quis* a primitive psychology was even evolved. Alain of Lille, for example, advises the priest to note the sinner's appearance and complexion in order to assay his disposition: « One man is more impelled to a certain sin than another; a choleric person is more driven to wrath, a melancholy one to hatred, a sanguine or phlegmatic

---

[12] « Quis, quid, ubi, per quos, quotiens, cur, quomodo, quando, Quilibet observet, animae medicamina dando ». Passavanti, p. 173. The jingle is frequently encountered.

[13] John T. McNeill, *Mediaeval Handbooks of Penance* (New York, 1938), p. 7.

[14] « Consideret qualitatem criminis, in loco, in tempore, in perseverantia, in varietate personae, et quali hoc fecerit tentatione, et in ipsius vitii multiplici exsecutione. Oportet enim poenitere fornicantem secundum excellentiam sui status aut officii, et secundum modum meretricis, et in modo operis sui, et qualiter turpitudinem suam peregit ». *De vera et falsa poenitentia*, Migne, *Pat. Lat.*, XL, 1124. Although wrongly attributed to Augustine, the treatise had great influence on the mediaeval confessional tradition.

one to lust »[15]. In general, interrogation was in terms of some fixed scheme, identifying first the sinner, and then the sin and his motives for it. Manuals produced for priests as well as laymen in Italy during the fourteenth and fifteenth centuries often turn into lists of specific questions regarding various sins. St. Bernardino authored one such guide, divided into twelve principal « rules » of confession, which provide interrogations in respect of the seven deadly sins, the ten commandments, the five senses of the body, the twelve articles of faith, the seven works of mercy, the seven virtues, and the seven gifts of the Holy Spirit [16]. The sort of reflection such rules prescribed was nothing if not systematic.

The close of the Middle Ages in Italy and the beginning of the Renaissance witnessed a proliferation of these vernacular handbooks of penance both for laymen and priests. Probably not since the early Middle Ages had there been such a significant output. As guides to the examination of the individual conscience these penitentials were, in fact, the matrix of early Renaissance autobiography. In conformity with the general trend of late mediaeval scholasticism they laid an increasing stress on systematic analysis of the will; and as the centuries progressed they became increasingly rhetorical in tone. Whereas early mediaeval handbooks were legalistic in tenor, the confessional works of popular preachers like Cavalca, Passavanti or San Bernardino were particularly successful in shifting emphasis from the nature of the sin to the conscience of the sinner, their object being to encourage periodic and systematic examination by the layman of his acts and motives. Confessors were instructed to ascertain whether the sinner wished to do what he did or understood what he was doing, and whether he intended to sin without actually carrying out his intentions. « All sins proceed from the will », declared an anonymous manual of the Quattrocento, « whence one has the desire to do ill » [17]. « First

---

[15] « ... unus magis impellitur ad aliquod peccatum, quam alius, quia si cholericus est, magis impellitur ad iram, si melancholicus, magis ad odium; si sanguineus, vel phlegmaticus, ad luxuriam ». *Liber poenitentialis*, Migne, *Pat. Lat.*, CCX, 287.

[16] *Operette volgari* (Florence, 1938), pp. 215-261.

[17] « ... In perciò che tutti i pechetti procedono dalla voluntà onde chi a voluntà del mal fare ... » Biblioteca Nazionale, Firenze, MS. Pal. 73, 132 v.

think of the sins you have committed », counselled St. Bernardino in a sermon preached at Siena in 1425:

> the worse you have sinned the more you should think. And if you want me to instruct you — you that have been twenty years without confessing yourself — hold to this manner if you want to be saved, because otherwise you never will be. Don't go at the point of death or on Good Friday, but prepare yourself beforehand, and so you will begin to recollect your misdeeds [18].

Thus during the late Middle Ages and early Renaissance the particular form of self-awareness represented by the practice of confession was brought to a high state of development. When to this type of self-knowledge were added the new modes of self-awareness revealed by the classical revival the resultant was the form of introspection known as autobiography, an adaptation, in its early Renaissance stages, of mediaeval formalism under the influence of humanist-rhetorical interest in ancient philosophy, history and literature. By a process analogous to the secularization of wisdom during the same period the ancient institution of confession was adapted to serve new purposes in a progressively humanistic context [19].

First in the line of Renaissance autobiographers was Petrarch, whose autobiographical writings illustrate the fusing of the

---

In a paper read to the 1969 San Diego-Salk Institute Symposium on Renaissance historiography, Rosalie Colie, on the basis of work on confession now in progress at Toronto, noted that « by the fifteenth century there was a noticeable change in the form in which cases of conscience were expressed. They were no longer simply applications of the *regulae* of canon law to particular instances of moral misdemeanors; rather they began to be, sometimes, set up as problems for the confessor dealing with the individuated sins of his penitents ».

[18] « In prima, pensare ne' peccati che hai fatti: quanto peggio hai fatto, tanto pensa più. E se vuoi che io t'insegni, o tu che se' stato già venti anni senza confessione, tiene questo modo se ti vuoi salvare, altrimenti mai non ti salvarai. Non ti condùcere al capezzale o al venardì santo, ma fatti innanzi al tempo, e così cominciarai a vedere e fatti tuoi ». *Prediche volgari inedite* (Siena, 1935), p. 470.

[19] For arguments relating to the secularization of wisdom see Eugene Rice, *The Renaissance Idea of Wisdom* (Cambridge, 1958) together with the commentary of Hans Baron, *Journal of the History of Ideas*, XXI (1960), 131-150.

two traditions, Christian and classical. That Petrarch left no autobiography in a « modern » format only attests to the still rudimentary nature of the fusion, since no doubt can exist as to the autobiographical nature of several of his works in the strict sense of the term. One feature of Petrarch's autobiographical writings need only be acknowledged in passing and that is the extent to which they may have been expressions of a confessional urge, therapeutic acknowledgements of error before the tribunal of conscience. Given Petrarch's proximity to the mediaeval Christian tradition it is hardly surprising that some element of the expiation of guilt would not be present in his self-analysis. Of greater significance for the development of autobiography, however, was his adapting of the form of mediaeval confession in conjunction with the expanded self-awareness stemming from his classical studies to evolve a new type of self-analysis, the forerunner of modern autobiography [20].

Beginning with Nolhac's fundamental study, the extent to which Petrarch's culture and outlook were enriched by his classical studies has accounted for a large body of scholarship, and his self-awareness has received extensive treatment recently in an interesting study by Arnaud Tripet [21]. Further interpretations of the *Secretum*, the « Letter to Posterity » or the « Ascent of Mt. Ventoux » (*Fam.* IV, 1) can provide little additional information. A few words, however, concerning their significance in the evolution of autobiography may not be amiss. Of the three works, the *Secretum* was the first to have been composed (at least in the main), while, as Hans Baron has shown, *Fam.* IV, 1 and the epistle *Posteritati* date from the 1350 's [22]. Through them run the various themes of Petrarch's self-discussion: his appearance and tastes, his love of the classics and disgust with the present, his love of Laura, his desire for glory and his need of solitude to explore the inner motions of his spirit. What

---

[20] Francesco Tateo concedes the elements in the *Secretum* of a « sincere confession » but stresses the autobiographical aspects. *Dialogo interiore e polemica ideologica nel Secretum del Petrarca* (Florence, 1965), p. 35. Vespasiano evidently thought they were confessions (see leading quotation).

[21] Pierre de Nolhac, *Pétrarque et l'Humanisme* (Paris, 1907); Arnaud Tripet, *Pétrarque ou la connaissance de soi* (Geneva, 1967).

[22] Hans Baron, *From Petrarch to Leonardo Bruni* (Chicago, 1968), chs. 1 & 2.

chiefly interest us are the means by which he conducted the exploration. It is probably wise to adopt at the beginning the view that Petrarch never achieved a wholly convincing synthesis of the classical and Christian elements in his culture [23]. His classical studies revealed to him attitudes accepted as normal with which he felt himself in deep sympathy but which were suspect to his Christian background. The first fruits of an expanded self-awareness, therefore, were a heightened crisis of conscience. Hence it is scarcely surprising that his self-examination should take a form so closely resembling the Christian confessional. Not only did he have sins to confess, not only was the habit of confessing strong, but the preparatory meditation for the confessional was the only form of systematic self-analysis available.

Interpretations of the identities of the *Secretum*'s two interlocutors have ranged from regarding Franciscus as Petrarch and Augustine as Reason to regarding both as aspects of Petrarch's own nature, his better and worse selves. Probably the most perceptive of these interpretations is Hans Baron's suggestion that Augustine is the representative of Petrarch's own conscience, whose role is to « uncover those secret trends of Petrarch's mind which he tries to hide from himself » [24]. Such an interpretation allows for both the Christian and classical components of the dialogue. It is not pure confession, where Augustine would have to represent a wholly ecclesiastical voice, but rather self-exploration where the conscience sets about examining the self in the fashion of a Christian confessor with classical sensibilities. Christian and classical forms are freely intermingled. On the one hand the situation is that of the Christian confessional, with Petrarch the penitent, Augustine the confessor and Truth the symbol of the Deity. Franciscus is interrogated by Augustine in terms of the Gregorian system of pride and the seven deadly sins. Tripet has pointed to Petrarch's need to reveal himself before authoritative witnesses before whom he is what he is and not what he would like to be, and such a need can be related without difficulty to the psychological

---

[23] Natalino Sapegno, « Petrarca », *Storia della letteratura italiana*, vol II, *Il Trecento* (Milan: Garzanti, 1965), p. 258.

[24] Baron, *From Petrarch*, p. 72.

habit of the confession. The Christian exomologete requires a confessor [25]. On the other hand, as Sapegno has observed, literature was the form of Petrarch's intelligence and the center of his humanity. From the reading of classical literature he also found models for classifying the « movements of his soul » [26]. Hence the interlocutors speak in Ciceronian Latin and cite the classics, as in Roman prototypes of the dialogue. The *Secretum* opens with a literary vision modelled somewhat on Boethius, and Truth is hailed by Franciscus with lines from the *Aeneid* (I, 327-328). Close study of the content of the dialogue, moreover, has revealed the extent to which Christian ideas such as the freedom of the will were expanded and developed in a Stoic setting. Tateo has shown how Petrarch's sense of *accidia* was deepened by Cicero's notion of *aegritudo* and Tripet has demonstrated how Ciceronian and Senecan philosophical positions led him close to Pelagianism [27].

Ancient philosophy and literature were thus factors in the adaptation of confession to autobiography. What about history? A record of self-development, a history of the self is certainly central to the modern practice of autobiography. Here it must be acknowledged that Petrarch's endeavor in the *Secretum* represents autobiography *im werden*, for there is little presentation of the idea of the self's growth and development [28]. In the sub-

---

[25] Tripet, pp. 153, 166. If, as social psychologists have suggested, the origin of self-consciousness is the awareness that one is regarded as an object by others, then the priest represents the ' other ' under whose scrutiny the first steps are taken toward self-consciousness. Since autobiography is an outgrowth of self-consciousness, confession would thus be a natural antecedent. Tripet stresses the manner in which, by dividing himself between the two speakers, Petrarch undermines the essentially antagonist situation of the confessional. But this is part of the adaptation process. *Ibid.*, pp. 104, 168.

[26] Sapegno, p. 257.

[27] Tateo, pp. 1, 48-49; Tripet, p. 163.

[28] From youth to old age, Tripet has asserted (p. 86), Petrarch saw his essential character (or perhaps his ideal self) as stable. Such a conception need not be a-temporal, however. Apropos of Montaigne, Sheldon Wolin has called attention to the sense of time as lateral movement. Petrarch may have given us an image of himself where the movement of the self is from one situation to another laterally rather than forward in time. Time would thus be subsumed rather than made the organizing principle of self-development.

sequent two autobiographical works, however, the historical principle is more fully employed. *Fam.* IV, 1 narrates the ascent as an incident in a deepening sense of the author's true identity. Ruminating on the distant prospect of Italy Petrarch is carried back in thought to his student days at Bologna. The idea which, as he puts it, « took possession of my mind, leading it from the contemplation of space to that of time » is of the changes in his moral habits since those days [29]. Review of the previous decade then yields to the famous passages preparing his resolutions for the decades ahead. When he came to write the unfinished letter *Posteritati* Petrarch seems to have resolved to give a chronological account of the chief events of his life. It is interesting to observe that even here, in this very self-consciously formalized version of his life he still felt compelled to analyze himself in respect of the cardinal sins.

An important question in regard to Petrarch's autobiographical writing is the precedent of Augustine's *Confessions.* How great a component in the adaptation process were they? Could Petrarch have simply been imitating the *Confessions* rather than adapting the mediaeval confessional practice? Certainly Augustine represented for Petrarch the continuation of ancient philosophy and culture in a Christian setting and was, accordingly, a unique precedent and guide [30]. In 1333 Petrarch had been given a pocket copy of the *Confessions* by Dionigi da Borgo San Sepulchro which he carried with him everywhere [31]. This was the volume he claimed to have drawn out and read on the summit of Mt. Ventoux. In the *Confessions,* he said, he saw not another's wandering, but his own [32]. Hence there is no doubt of the influence of the *Confessions* on Petrarch's thought. Great as are the similarities between the *Confessions* and the *Secretum*, however, the differences are not less significant, and when these are not owing to classical precedents they can more often than not be laid to the more proximate influence of the mediaeval confes-

---

[29] « The Ascent of Mt. Ventoux », tr. Hans Nachod, in Cassirer et al., eds., *The Renaissance Philosophy of Man* (Chicago, 1948), p. 42.

[30] Tateo, p. 45.

[31] B. L. Ullman, *Studies in the Italian Renaissance* (Rome, 1955), pp. 52, 132. *Fam.* X, 3 mentions the *Soliloquies* as well. Nolhac, II, 211.

[32] *Petrarch's Secret*, tr. W. H. Draper (London, 1911), p. 21.

sional tradition [33]. To begin with, the *Confessions* and the *Secretum* are very different works in character. Written in 397, when Augustine was forty-three, the *Confessions* were the outgrowth of a turning point in the Saint's life after he became bishop of Hippo Regius. Girding himself for his new tasks, Augustine found that, whatever the effects of Christian renewal, he could not jettison the memory of his youth. The same self still linked the mature bishop to the young man. Augustine's response to this predicament was to try to understand the young man in the light of God's purposes [34]. From his extraordinarily sensitive account of his emotional state in the period prior to his conversion it is apparent that Augustine was preoccupied in the same fashion as Luther by what Erikson calls « meaning it » [35]. He could not approach his conversion easily because instinctively he recognized that for him conversion would mean a total surrender to Christian doctrine, along with a complete change in his way of life. Conversion would not and could not be a halfway affair. Just how completely Augustine girded himself in his new role the *Confessions* bear eloquent witness.

Petrarch's *Secretum* (or the first version of it) was completed in 1342, during a period of religious crisis, when the poet was thirty-eight years of age. He had returned to France after his coronation in Rome in 1341 when evidently he began to suffer an attack of distress over the style of his past life. The themes of the dialogue are, as Hans Baron has summarized them, « a

---

[33] Petrarch's misinterpretations of Augustine are usually significant ones. For example, he misinterprets Augustine's conversion through laying too great stress on the self-sufficiency of the will, the effect probably of stoic philosophy. He has Augustine cite the classics in wholly uncharacteristic fashion. Augustine himself certainly never refers to the « heavenly » Plato. The « repose » the Saint finds in bitterness (*Conf.*, IV, 6) is through a genuine loathing of things previously loved and not the sort of *accidia* Petrarch describes. In these and other departures Petrarch seems affected by classical influences. Siegfried Wenzel sees Petrarch's *accidia* as a secularized or humanized form of the capital sin « Petrarch's *Accidia* », *Studies in the Renaissance*, VIII (1961), 36-48. On the other hand, his descriptions of Hell and death in *Secretum* I seem to derive from the mediaeval tradition (but cf. Tateo, pp. 30, 32).

[34] For interpretations of the *Confessions* as autobiography see Peter Brown, *Augustine of Hippo* (Berkeley and Los Angeles, 1967), and Misch, vol. II, ch. 3.

[35] Erik H. Erikson, *Young Man Luther* (New York, 1958), ch. 6.

striving for dominion over man's passions, for triumph over worldly dissipations, and a spiritual conversion under the influence of Augustine »[36]. Devoutly as Petrarch may have wished for these consummations, however, he never achieved them. That complete dedication of heart and will to God which marks the saint, by Petrarch's own confession, he could not approach. His refractoriness in regard to his love of earthly glory persists to the very end of the *Secretum*. When at the conclusion of the tenth book of the *Confessions* Augustine lists the temptations which still beset him one is nevertheless confident that here again God will « lift his foot out of the snare ». No such confidence, however, pervades the concluding passages of the *Secretum*, with the uneasy prayers of the two interlocutors for Petrarch's reformation. Petrarch is still, in fact, in the state described by Augustine, where past actions are determining the present. Much as he may want to he still does not « mean it ». The *Secretum* is not a *confessio* in the full Augustinian sense, that is, a confession of God as well as to God. Nor has the self been found in God. The *Secretum* is rather an exercise in self-examination of the mediaeval confessional sort. Petrarch was still striving for self-mastery and using confession in the mediaeval mode as a weapon both for self-analysis and self-improvement. What makes the *Secretum* such a difficult document to interpret is that Petrarch's self-analysis led him to conclusions about his personality which were incompatible with self-betterment in the traditional Christian sense. His discovery, for example, reinforced by his classical culture, that a desire for glory was a component of his personality induced a persistent recalcitrance toward the admonitions of his spiritual guide. Petrarch's repentance on this score was at best the sort of « hangman's repentance » which the penitent hopes that God will turn into true repentance by means of the sacrament.

Mirroring the substantive differences between the *Confessions* and the *Secretum* are those of form. In brief these can be summarized by observing that whereas the *Confessions* are cast in the form of a protracted prayer to God, the *Secretum* takes the form of a dialogue based partly on classical, partly on confessional practice, and that whereas Augustine evolved his own literary

---

[36] Baron, p. 20.

style, wishing to avoid the connotations of classic prose while still writing in a literate fashion, Petrarch was assiduously attempting to imitate classical Latin. One additional circumstance which ties Petrarch's *Secretum* more closely to the mediaeval tradition than to Augustine is indicated by its title; as its name implies, Petrarch's little work was intended to be kept secret throughout his life. « So, little book », he charged it,

> I bid you flee the haunts of men and be content to stay with me, true to the title I have given you of ' My Secret ': and when I would think upon deep matters, all that you keep in remembrance that was spoken in secret you in secret will tell to me over again [37].

In Augustine's day open confession was a common practice, in the sense both of confession and profession. Augustine relates his admiration for the distinguished citizen, Victorinus, who, upon being converted to Christianity, spurned the offer of a private ceremony and made his profession of faith publicly [38]. A public pronouncement had a decisive and fixing effect. In the *Confessions* Augustine wished, he declares to God, to do truth « before Thee in confession: and in my writing before many witnesses » [39]. In the tradition of the ancient Church he revealed himself in order to share his joy and to elicit the prayers of his « fellow citizens » and « fellow pilgrims », and by way of so doing he was more than willing to make an open confession of his sins. Petrarch, by contrast, availed himself of the tradition of secret confession adopted by the mediaeval Church. While Augustine was glad to make public his *Confessions* as a confession of God, Petrarch might well have hesitated before publishing what was only a self-analysis. Again, it is evident that the *Secretum* represents a mid-point between confession itself and autobiography written as a literary *genre* [40].

---

[37] Ed. *cit.*, p. 6.

[38] *Conf.*, VIII, 2; McNeill, pp. 10-14.

[39] *Conf.*, X, 1.

[40] One of the requirements of autobiography as a literary *genre* is that it convey the impression of sincerity. Part of the literary art consists in appearing to be open and sincere. Hence the ecclesiastical practice is the antecedent of the literary form. Sapegno has observed (« Petrarca », p. 250) that Petrarch never speaks of himself spontaneously but only after reflection.

The same tendencies that are found in the *Secretum* are found as well in *Fam.* IV, I, the same independence of Augustine, the same adaptations of Christian self-knowledge under the influence of classical self-awareness. In one famous passage, for example, Petrarch describes how, upon reaching the summit, he opened his copy of the *Confessions* and chanced to read there Augustine's reproach:

> And men go abroad to admire the high mountains, the vast floods of the sea, the huge streams of the rivers, the circumference of the ocean, and the revolutions of the stars, and desert themselves [41].

At once he realizes his folly in seeking to scale the heights of Mt. Ventoux, recalling Seneca's contention, « Nothing is admirable besides the mind; compared to its greatness nothing is great ». Yet Augustine in the passage cited is not issuing an invitation to admire the greatness of the mind, nor even to turn inward in meditation, as Petrarch straightway does. The passage occurs in book X, where Augustine is attempting to determine with what faculty we know God. He discovers that there are great regions in man, of which memory is the most wonderful:

> Great is the power of memory, a fearful thing, O my God, a deep and boundless multiplicity; and this thing is the soul and this am I myself. What am I then, O my God? What nature am I? A life various and manifold, and exceedingly immense [42].

Yet, Augustine finds, one must go beyond even this power to find knowledge of God, since God was not in the memory before Augustine learned of him. The saint's conclusion — and

---

While the relationship of spontaneity to sincerity is by no means a necessary one, the spontaneous is more apt to pass for genuine. The more a confession is premeditated the less spontaneous it becomes. Naturally the priest is there to penetrate the defenses of the sinner. The autobiographer, on the other hand, has only his own conscience as censor. Dr. Thomas Greening has made the interesting observation that psychoanalysts tend to make unsatisfactory autobiographers because their training enables them to suppress precisely the data which, when given spontaneously, would be most revealing.

[41] Ed. *cit.*, p. 44. The passage is from *Conf.*, X, 8.

[42] *Conf.*, X, 8.

it is a foregone one — is that the soul must reach entirely outside of itself to find God. In his admiration for « the height of human contemplation » Petrarch is closer to the neo-Platonic type of uplift than to Augustine's version of the Christian experience [43]. As the content of Petrarch's introspection was a mixture of Christianity and classicism mediated somewhat by Augustine, so he can be said to have used a confessional type of introspection as the mode of his self-analysis, modified somewhat by the example of Augustine and enlarged by his knowledge of classical literature.

Adaptation of the confessional type of analysis begun by Petrarch was continued by his professed disciple and the next important autobiographer of the Renaissance, Giovanni da Ravenna. In a sense, Petrarch's contributions are put into perspective by the younger man's work, as the fusion of various elements, particularly the historical, is made more solid. The *Rationarium Vitae*, or « account book of my life », was put together during the author's second sojourn in Padua, while chancellor. Exactly when it was begun is not clear, but it was cast in its final form during the difficult months in Giovanni's life toward the end of 1400, when he had just returned from a long and vexatious mission to Rome, only to have the plague carry off two of his young children, one after the other [44]. The work ends with a lament for the children and the resolve to offer to God the years that remain to him:

> Grant, therefore, Lord, that Thou wilt complete what Thou hast accomplished in us, as in Thy holy temple, in order that if any time remains to me beyond this fifty-sixth year, I may be devoted entirely to Thee and with my whole heart meditate more freely on Thy commandments, which are the lantern of my feet and the light of my paths, spending my remaining days in the eternal praise of Thy name, so that in the present moment I may begin the task of the court of heaven, which is to praise Thee, world without end, amen [45].

---

[43] On the differences between Augustine and neo-Platonism on this matter see Misch, II, 634.

[44] Remigio Sabbadini, *Giovanni da Ravenna* (Como, 1924), p. 86.

[45] « Confirma igitur (Domine Deus), quin perfice quod operatus es in nobis a templo sancto tuo, quatenus, siquid ultra hunc quinquagesimum et sextum annum michi residet, impendere tibi totum et toto corde meditari

The *Rationarium* gives the impression of having been generated during one of those periods when, under the pressure of external or internal events, one is made to question the sort of existence he has been leading. « For what is your endless labor, my little man? » begins the ' account book '.

How long will you work for others and never for yourself? You burn to read the deeds of old, to listen to those of the present day. Does it make sense to consume your time in the care of external things and never your own? [46]

From these opening sentences the impression is gained of a man approaching old age, tired, overworked, who is suddenly forced to take stock of his life, his accomplishments, and who finds that his career has been far less satisfying than he would have desired, his achievements fewer than he had hoped.

In what terms, then, in what context did the autobiographer construe the crisis? In religious terms, clearly, and here the link to confession becomes most apparent. Having posed himself the foregoing questions as to the meaning of his activity, Giovanni continues with a Biblical parable: « The wicked fear the voice of the overseer at any time, saying, ' Thou evil servant, turn in the accounts of thy stewardship ' » (Luke, XVI, 2). Here is the key to the author's conception of his enterprise. As the title declares, these will be the account books of his life, which he turns over to his master, the Lord. His self-examination, therefore, will be in the light of God's expectations of his servants. « You have served a long time », Giovanni reminds himself,

What have you accomplished, or rather, at what have you not failed?... Begin, at length, your own work, recall the years of your

---

liberius in mandatis tuis, que sunt lucerna pedibus meis et lumen semitis meis, postrema autem consumare in sempiterni laude tui nominis valeam, ut in presenti celestis aule negocium incipiam, quod est laudare te in secula seculorum. Amen ». *Ibid.*, p. 173.

[46] « Quo diuturnus iste labor, homuncio? Quousque te aliis impendes et nunquam tibi? Veterum gesta legere, audire presentia ferves. Siccine temporis abuti consilium est, ut una externorum cura detineare et nunquam tua? » *Ibid.*, p. 127.

life in the bitterness of your heart, recount your adverse fate in a style neither faulty nor false. For no one knows anything better than he knows himself, no one is a truer witness of his own life, as long as blind error does not deceive his awareness nor tenacious shame dull it. Speak a little about yourself, therefore; withdraw; give yourself back to yourself; write what you can read, in order that what you read you can correct, what you have corrected you can love, and what you have loved you can follow. Let self-love cease, do not exaggerate praise nor conceal faults, lest your quest for earthly favor make you straightway unworthy of heavenly favor. Speak to yourself that you may weep, speak to the world that it may know, speak to God that he may pardon. For so sings the psalmist, « I shall confess my iniquity to the Lord, and thou, O God, in thy mercy shalt pardon my sins », and the apostle teaches that if we judge ourselves we shall not be judged of God [47].

Assailed by a sudden crisis of meaning in his life, Giovanni instinctively embraces the modes of confession in order to divest himself of the effects and consequences of error, rediscover his true self and consecrate it to the wholesome existence he now wills for it. The sincerity of his efforts at self-confession have been attested to by Remigio Sabbadini, who in comparing Giovanni's own account with external sources became convinced of its « incontrovertible » veracity [48]. In format the *Rationarium* is a personal history, interrupted by digressions on various subjects, places and people, and punctuated by prayers to God in the Augustinian manner. Giovanni was familiar with the *Confessions* and the stylistic allusions to them are unmista-

[47] « ... villicasti diu: quid perfecisti vel quid potius non defecisti? num tue negligentior quam vite singulorum? Impartire tandem operam tibi, excute annos tuos in amaritudine anime tue, adversa fata recense stilo non mendoso nec mendaci. Nemo enim quam se quemquam melius novit, vite nemo verior testis dum conscientiam nec cecus error fallit nec tenax pudor obtundit. De te igitur paululum fare, sequestra, redde te sibi, scribe que legas, ut que legeris corrigas, que correxeris ames, que amaveris sequaris. Absistat amor proprius, laudes ne mendacio fuces nec mendas verecundia subtrahas, quatenus, terrestri dum favore grataris, prorsum indignus celesti fias. Dic ergo tecum ut fleas, dic mundo ut agnoscat, dic Deo ut ignoscat; monet psaltes dixi confitebor iniusticiam meam domino et tu remisisti in pietatem peccati mei; monet apostolus si nos iudicaremus non utique iudicaremur a domino ». *Ibid.*, *loc. cit.*; Balliol College, MS. 288, fol. 1 r.

[48] Sabbadini, p. 4.

kable [49]. As the confessional overtones of the *Rationarium* suggest, the self is analyzed in terms of Christian ethics, while the influence of classical culture is apparent in the prose, in the presence of philosophic ideas deriving from stoicism, and particularly in the sense of a historical approach to the development of the self. Although the *Rationarium* is not exactly a *confessio* in the two-fold Augustinian sense, Giovanni's charge to himself, « Tell the world that it may apprehend, tell God that he may pardon », is close to Augustine's professed desire to do truth « before Thee in confession, and in my writing before many witnesses » [50]. Reinforcing this religious urge is a strengthened sense of the value of autobiography as literature, particularly in its didactic and rhetorical aspects. The reader is reminded of Giovanni's discipleship of Petrarch by the opening lines of the *Rationarium*, an unmistakable allusion to Augustine's first demands in the *Secretum*, which the *Rationarium* follows in sincerity of self-examination [51]. In its greater attention to historical detail the *Rationarium* takes its departure from the epistle *Posteritati*, while in its broadened conceptions of the self deriving from ancient philosophy it assumes the generalized legacy of Petrarchan humanism. Overall it displays the marks of that adaptation of confession in the context of ancient literature which is the genesis of modern autobiography.

---

[49] For citations from the *Confessions* in Giovanni's correspondence see F. Novati, ed., *Epistolario di Coluccio Salutati* (Rome, 1891-1905), IV, 307, 316. As an example of stylistic allusion cf. « Tibi ergo deus meus vita mea salus mea tibi dicam ignorancias meas et delicta iuventutis meae », Balliol MS. 288, fol. 1 r. Another example of a prayer in the style of Augustine occurs on fol. 8 rv. Giovanni's contention in the passage cited that the self is the object of surest knowledge is reminiscent of Augustine's establishment of self-knowledge as the foundation for philosophizing, in the *Soliloquies*, II, 1. See Misch, II, 630.

[50] Sabbadini, p. 127; *Conf.*, X, 1.

[51] Cf. the passages cited in n. 42 with Augustine's opening demands to Petrarch in the *Secretum*, « Quid agis humuncio? quid somnias? quid expectas? miserarium ne tuarum sic prorsus oblitus es? An non te mortalem esse meministi? » Through his small circle of friends Petrarch's works were rapidly disseminated in his lifetime, even, it would appear, the *Secretum*. A particular admirer of the latter was Giovanni da Ravenna's correspondent and friend, Francesco Zabarella, who actively encouraged the reading of it. Giuseppe Billanovich, *Petrarca letterato: I, Lo scrittoio del Petrarca* (Rome, 1947), pp. 376-377, 381, 443.

One final point regarding the religious matrix of Giovanni's autobiographical thought: In his opening paragraph he alludes to a passage from Isaiah XXXVIII, 15, *Recogitabo tibi omnes annos meos et in amaritudine animae meae*. His allusion takes this form, *Excute annos tuos in amaritudine animae tuae*, substituting the more vigorous and, incidentally, more classical word *excutio* for *recogito* [52]. It is interesting that this phrase from Isaiah, which is taken by St. Bernardino as the text for a sermon on confession, and which also appears in Passavanti's *Mirror of True Penitence*, is rarely encountered in the mediaeval writers and appears in the *Confessions* in an almost unrecognizable form [53]. On one occasion Augustine employs the phrase *et requiescebam in amaritudine*; on another he uses *in amaritudine recogitationes meae*, but in neither instance does he take the whole sense of the phrase as Giovanni da Ravenna does [54]. Isaiah was one of Augustine's favorite authors; he had been given the prophet to read by Ambrose after his conversion, but it does not appear that Augustine introduced this highly appropriate phrase into confessional literature [55]. The supposition must be that Giovanni da Ravenna picked up the phrase either from his own reading of Isaiah, or, more probably, from the confessional literature of his own day. Were this, indeed, the case, an important link would be established between the vernacular confession manuals and the first fully-developed Renaissance autobiography.

---

[52] Sabbadini, p. 127.

[53] St. Bernardino, *Prediche volgari inedite*, p. 469; Passavanti, p. 102; the phrase also appears in Riccardiana MS. 1511, fol. 2 v.

[54] *Conf.*, IV, 6; II, 1.

[55] He does not seem to have used it in any of his major works. Nor does the phrase appear in the pseudo-Augustine. Eventually it made its way into the Tridentine canon *de poenitentia*: « Si quis dixerit, eam contritionem, quae paratur per discussionem, collectionem et detestationem peccatorum, qua quis recogitat annos suos in amaritudine animae suae ... », *Conc. Trid.*, t. VII, *actorum pars* IV, vol. I, p. 358, sess. XIV.

MARVIN B. BECKER

TOWARDS A RENAISSANCE HISTORIOGRAPHY IN FLORENCE *

* Prepared for presentation at the Symposium in Renaissance Studies held at La Jolla, California, May, 1969. I have concentrated, almost exclusively, upon vernacular historical literature in order to suggest that Trecento Florentines anticipated much that was to be essential to Quattrocento Latin humanist historiography. This paper, being in the nature of an essay, the footnotes are intended only as suggestions for further discussion.

James Watson: « Worrying about complications before ruling out the possibility that the answer was simple would have been damned foolishness. Pauling never got anywhere by seeking out messes ».

Wallace Stevens: « The most marvellous bishops of heaven were those that made it seem so ».

The visitor to Florence may be most impressed by its heroic civic art and architecture. Perhaps he will share something of my feeling for the unique character of the fifteenth-century Florentine physical creation. If I suggest that this Renaissance city, really so esthetically integrated, emerged as a tribute to a mythical aspiration, one may be curious — even sympathetic. What remains impressive is the play of citizen energy when confronting the task of constructing a sacred collectivity. This work was viewed by Florentines through the lenses of a variety of literary metaphors. The one very frequently in use, appearing most appropriate, was the image of the polis as Biblical ark. From anonymous poet, to Neoplatonist, to the civic-minded Savonarola, the image spoke for the divine election of the Republic. Sacred shelter against the « sword of God », or holy polis summoned to introduce a new Christian era, this collectivity was destined to serve as sacred vessel. Savonarola's favorite image of the Arno republic as the « umbilicus of Italy » even recognized something of the geographic configuration of this valley city [1].

---

[1] E. Garin, *Ritratti di umanisti* (Florence, 1967), pp. 112-83; L. Firpo, « Il pensiero politico del Rinascimento e della Controriforma », in *Grande Antologia Filosofica*, Vol. 10, pp. 190-224. In Savonarola's sermons during Lent in 1494 he began by preaching on the Flood. He spoke of the construction of an ark out of the Christian virtues. In each subsequent sermon he added a new virtue as a plank for his symbolic ark until completed by Easter. All were urged to enter the vessel while there was yet time. When Charles VIII (*gladius Domini*) arrived, the Dominican announced that the

A speech delivered by a member of the government's advisory council in July of 1431 deserves to be quoted: « God is the Republic, and whoever governs the Republic does the work of God. Likewise, God is justice, and whoever makes justice *facit Deum* » [2]. The priorate was « savior » of the city in 1362, just as Lorenzo de' Medici would be « salvator mundi » a century later. His ancestor Salvestro was to bear the same appellation in the continuation of a poem where the wars of Florence were likened to the labors of Hercules [3]. Poets readily mixed the sacrifices of Christ with the patriotic deeds of antique Romans; Scipio's costly heroism paralleled the sufferings of *il nostro Salvatore* [4]. Again, in the advisory councils, speakers combined maxims from Roman history with doctrine from the story of Job to instill civic confidence in their audience. The psychic formula proffered was that only in adversity can one prove his

---

ark was closed, and his audience was struck dumb with terror. The diarist Luca Landucci wrote, « Fra Girolamo preached and said and testified that the Virgin Mary had revealed to him that after going through much trouble, the city of Florence was to be the most glorious, the wealthiest, and the most powerful that ever existed, and he promised this absolutely. All these things he spoke as a prophet, and the greater part of the people believed him ». Particularly relevant is D. Weinstein's, « The Myth of Florence », *Florentine Studies*, ed. N. Rubinstein (London, 1968), pp. 15-44. Landucci's dispirited comment after Savonarola had confessed that he was no prophet is worth quoting:

« My heart was grieved to see such an edifice fall to the ground on account of having been founded on a lie. Florence had been expecting a new Jerusalem, from which would issue just laws and splendour and an example of righteous life, and to see the renovation of the Church, the conversion of unbelievers, and the consolation of the righteous; and I felt that everything was exactly contrary, and had to resign myself with the thought: *In voluntate tua Domine omnia sunt posita* ».

Cf. *A Florentine Diary from 1450 to 1516*, trans. A. Jervis (London, 1927), p. 139.

[2] Quoted in F. Pellegrini, *Sulla repubblica fiorentina a tempo di Cosimo il Vecchio* (Pisa, 1880), appendix, document 58. Cf. E. Garin's, *Science and Civic Life in the Italian Renaissance*, recently translated by P. Munz (New York, 1969), especially the chapter entitled « The Ideal City », pp. 21-48.

[3] F. Sacchetti, *Il libro delle rime*, ed. A. Chiari (Bari, 1936), p. 210 (CXCIV). See also G. Capponi, *Cronichette antiche di vari scrittori* (Florence, 1753), p. LI, where the author tells Salvestro, « che salva hai fatto con nobil savere la patria tua ».

[4] F. Sacchetti, *Sposizioni di vangeli*, ed. A. Chiari (Bari, 1938), pp. 277-82. Cf. also F. Ferri, *La poesia popolare in Antonio Pucci* (Bologna, 1909), pp. 75-78.

virtus. « The ' soul ' cannot be conquered unless the will is subdued ». The adverb most energetically employed was « viriliter », and the citizen was exhorted to act with a « virile soul » (*agere virili animo*) [5].

By the fifteenth century civic counselors, poets, and historians were elevating the polis by infusing the profane world with sacred idiom; where once mythologizing had been limited to the transcendent, now it was bestowed upon the everyday. What was furnished by artist and historian was a civic landscape wherein monumental deeds of heroism and villainy could achieve lasting dignity or opprobrium. Only by relating the single act to the destiny of the city could it gain ultimate acknowledgment. If these later-day Florentines were bent upon placing the discreet act in a political arena whose munificence guaranteed lasting regard for political virtue and vice, not so their literary forebears. Earlier writers had not used classical strategies and topoi to lend *virtù* or *inganno* a public dimension; for them the civic world was less sure than the interior realm of conscience. Their literary talents rested in their ability to dramatize those costly public choices the Christian pilgrim must make during his secular odyssey. The demands of politics, society, and business were frequently incommensurate with requirements for individual salvation. Medieval chronicler and poet gave full regard to this tension by entertaining the dual options of earthly and heavenly obligation. Neither was denigrated, and the equality of the contest became the crux for historical drama; because the choices were expensive, the pathos of the reader must be great. That men were defeated in the temporal world was no reason for deprecating their struggle; it was not to be the occasion, however, for celebrating the public forum in which the struggle occurred.

What we shall be interested in are two types of historical sensibility: the first, emerging in late medieval Florence, appre-

[5] *Commissioni di Rinaldo degli Albizzi per il Comune di Firenze*, ed. C. Guasti (Florence, 1867-1873), I, 11, 27, 413; II, 146, 149. A reading of the surviving records of the advisory councils shows the durability of civic faith throughout the period treated in this study. Only in the late Quattrocento does this confidence begin to erode with appeals to divine providence and invocations for remission of sin appearing in the minutes of these councils.

ciated the secular struggles of spiritual men, while the second, out of the early Renaissance, ensured the dignity of this contest by elevating the terrain on which it was to transpire. Perhaps it can be restated thusly: Medieval poets and chroniclers dramatized the civic odyssey of moral types animated by imperatives of conscience, while Renaissance historians sought to furnish them with a public arena that would endow civic victory and defeat with *dignitas* and *gravitas*. For just a brief time, in the early Quattrocento, medieval and Renaissance aspirations were fused in the art of the young Donatello and Masaccio, with the claims of conscience being satisfied in a morally hospitable public world.

I.

Elsewhere, I have suggested that a significant transvaluation of values occurred in the city from the thirteenth through the fifteenth century. This alteration involved the transferal of ideals pertaining to expectations of *renovatio* (spiritual renewal) [6]. To employ historical shorthand, we could subsume the aspirations of medieval Florence under the rubric of personal renewal. The primary intellectual and artistic quest focused upon the dramatization of this personal odyssey; one recalls Dante or Guido Cavalcanti or the young Boccaccio or Giotto placing their characters against a metaphysical or moral landscape. Careful reckoning is made of « the movements of the human soul ». Stress is placed upon the struggles, torments, and triumphs of the individual as he confronts a metaphysical dilemma, a vexing intellectual abstraction, or the force of divine providence. The significant concern of the artist was with the spiritual condition of his subject. Much of the same order of generalization can be advanced for that remarkable group of Florentine historians from Brunetto Latini through Giovanni Villani in the mid-fourteenth century [7]. To this talented company

---

[6] See M. Becker, *Florence in Transition*, 2 vols. (Baltimore, 1967-68) for extensive bibliography. Also L. Green's valuable article, « Historical Interpretation in Fourteenth-Century Florentine Chronicles », *Journal of the History of Ideas*, XXVIII (1967), 161-78.

[7] Raffaello Morghen in his « La storiografia fiorentina del Trecento » makes relevant comparisons between Lombard historiography at the time

we must of course add Dante, whose historiographical contribution and influence cannot be slighted. Among the early achievements of this assemblage was the creation of new secular types who could now be included in the growing cast of characters in the Florentine chronicles. I am well aware that the first European burgher chronicles came out of Genoa in the mid-twelfth century, and that we must also acknowledge the sophisticated historiographical creations from Padua as well as the civic Christian epics from Pisa. Indeed, were we surveying Italy in the late Middle Ages, we would be compelled to underscore the fact that its literature was intensely absorbed in the rendition of contemporary affairs. Were we to travel backward in time, we would see that the peninsula was most hospitable to historical writings and, with but a few exceptions, they were local in content and form, with annals rather than universal histories prevailing. Even in the ninth century we have robust expressions of commitment to civic poetry. To generalize about the Italian Middle Ages, especially in the north, is to stress the public nature of this culture with its concentration upon practical sciences, legal studies, and history. Italian contributions to metaphysics, theology, and the refinements of aesthetics and stylistics were marginal. Even in the thirteenth century its most eminent theologians found the intellectual terrain of north Europe more hospitable. Italian universities were lay in their origins, and medieval scholasticism was a very late development.

All this suggests that the public world had a greater hold upon the cultivated imagination of Italy than did other levels of the medieval experience. We should also recognize that, with a few exceptions, dynasties and feudal courts were not crucial for Italian historiography, so that the focus of historical obser-

---

of Frederick I and later-day Florentine developments, with differences in cultural premises and language being notable. The Florentine chronicles are of course in the vernacular and more spontaneous. Their Lombard counterparts display a more reserved, courteous tone, a deeper sense of the role of contingency in all human affairs, and are less attracted to inflated idealism. Few commentators can match the political passion and breadth of interests of a Malispini, a Compagni, or a Villani. Morghen's essay is published in *Libera cattedra di storia della civiltà fiorentina: Secoli vari ('300-'400-'500)* (Florence, 1958), pp. 69-93.

vers tended to be communal and vernacular[8]. This is especially relevant for the Florentine experience, since ideal types originating in the life styles of a courtly nobility could not serve so effectively as models for constructing historical characters. Indeed, if we consider the literary creations of Dante, Villani, or Boccaccio, we observe that their nobles are urbanized and exhibit both the strengths and insecurities of their order. No one was better aware of the self-isolating pride of the nobility or the psychic costs of clan loyalty than Dante. Boccaccio, whose contribution to historical writing has been so slighted because he was a novelist, presents a rounded portrayal of the part-burgher, part-noble, whose character and interests are defined by the intersection of two worlds: the noble who inadvertently becomes a good rate payer and the bourgeois who is seized by a grand passion. One is not immune to prudence, while the other is vulnerable to the lure of romance and adventure. It is the increase in the permutations of character traits that allows the chronicler to give dimension to his depiction of the social scene. Villani was to employ thematically the magnate as a figure whose very virtues precluded the possibility of his giving the city effective leadership. Not only did his martial qualities and pride disqualify him for a public role, but they placed his mortal soul in jeopardy. In this way, a social problem can become a spiritual question lending moral texture to historical narrative.

If we compare the vivid chronicle of Salimbene, the Franciscan from Parma, with Florentine literary equivalents, we are impressed by the multiplication of types housed in the works of the Florentines. Anecdotes, humor, vivid description, and sensibility for speech patterns make Salimbene's work a treasure. But, commitment to transposing Biblical passages, fondness for enumeration and stock etymologies, as well as the employment

---

[8] With Dante we observe how painful human identity can be when experienced in all the anguish of its selfhood and separation from God. On this earth, where most of his contemporaries merit the Inferno, « one's identity is the heaviest of burdens ». In *Purgatorio* this identity is refined, but only in *Paradiso* is it transhumanized, becoming « a source of joy ». His fellow medievals whom he values are defined by a fixed sense of selfhood coupled with a yearning for release and for God. Cf. Thomas Greene's « Dramas of Selfhood in the *Comedy* », in *From Time to Eternity*; *Essays on Dante's Divine Comedy* (New Haven, 1967), pp. 132 ff.

of specific numbers of causes which determine a particular event, render his work formalistic [9]. Also telling, despite his wide urban experience, are the limited sets of personality types from the secular world that find their way into his chronicle. Not only are they models from an older literary imagination, but the adjectives used to define clerics and nobles differ little from the language of the chivalric romances. Similar observations can be made concerning the rhetorical histories of the thirteenth century. Even the scientific school at Padua utilized familiar conventions in constructing historical types. The outstanding *Ecerinis*, the first historical tragedy to be composed since antiquity, saw its author, Albertino Mussato, dramatize the plight of a collectivity: the people of the commune served as chorus and moral conscience in a struggle against a rapacious tyrant [10]. The energies of leading chroniclers were devoted, for the most part, to discovering new principles for organizing and making meaningful the experience of a collectivity. Older schema originating in the eleventh and twelfth centuries, whereby cohesion was lent civic experience by relating town history to the imperial or papal cause, was losing effectiveness as a metaphor for structuring narratives of contemporary life [11].

These were also problems for the Florentines, but they were

---

[9] See G. Duby's discussion of the unpublished thesis of Jacques Paul, « The Diffusion of Cultural Patterns in Feudal Society », *Past and Present*, no. 39 (1968), pp. 3-10. The classic studies remain Attilio Momigliano's « Motivi e carattere della ' Cronica ' di Salimbene », *Cinque Saggi* (Florence, 1945), pp. 71-108, and C. Violante's « Motivi e carattere della Cronica di Salimbene », *Annali della Scuola Normale Superiore di Pisa, Lettere, Storia e Filosofia*, Ser. II, vol. XXII (1953), 108-34. Yet another figure, a leading poet-historian of the twelfth century, Moses of Bergamo, brings to his writing a culture which is an amalgam of the cult of the *decoro cavalleresco* and of *virtù guerriere* combined with intensive doctrinal study. Cf. G. Cremaschi, *Mosè del Brolo e la cultura a Bergamo nei secoli XI e XII* (Bergamo, 1945).

[10] E. Raimondi, « L' ' Ecerinis ' di Albertino Mussato », in *Studi ezzeliniani* (Rome, 1963), pp. 192 ff.

[11] The thirteenth-century chronicler Gerardo Maurisio best illustrates the dilemma of writers whose loyalties are both communal (to Vicenza) and dynastic (to the Da Romano family). Since the citizen state develops in a feudal milieu, we should expect vacillations in perspective as the writers' allegiances shift, pendulum-like, from citizen magistrate and podestà to feudal overlord or signore. Cf. G. Arnaldi's excellent monograph, *Studi sui cronisti della Marca Trevigiana nell'età di Ezzelino da Romano* (Rome, 1963).

able to project a larger cast of historical types, as well as an historical backdrop, whose moral dimensions were more commensurate with the personalities strutting and fretting their hour upon the urban scene. The earliest Florentine chronicle (*Chronica de origine civitatis*), written in the late twelfth or early thirteenth century, represented the search of a collectivity for civic identity and historical dignity [12]. Such a quest could not possibly be satisfied by the *Annales I* and *Annales II*, which were little more than a listing of consuls and podestà. The author recapitulated the story of the origins of Florence and neighboring Fiesole, combining this narrative with legends of Catiline, authenticated by occasional references to Sallust's *Bellum Catilinarium*. To these antiquarian investigations were added choice details of more recent vintage. Municipal history was depicted under the beneficent eye of progress, with periodization commencing with the founding of the city by Caesar, its destruction five hundred years later, its rebuilding, and ultimate triumph over its arch rival Fiesole. Roughly, the same spirit informed the next of the city's historians — the jurist Sanzanome. His *Gesta Florentinorum* also regarded the destruction of Fiesole (1125) as crucial; indeed, he projected this imperialistic contest back into the republic's Roman past until it became the single key designed to unlock all ancient mysteries [13]. This survey of events between 1125 and 1231 dwelled lovingly upon Florence's glorious victories over her neighbors. It was the conquest of the environs (*contado*) that was the elevated theme of this panegyric to civic expansion. Never did he moralize or criticize while justifying these major triumphs. Ricordano Malispini, in his *Storia fiorentina*, displayed an identical, univocal stance toward the Florentine experience [14]. No moral dimension intruded into his

---

[12] O. Hartwig, *Quellen und Forschungen zur Ältesten Geschichte der Stadt Florenz* (Marburg, 1875), part I, pp. 57-60.

[13] O. Hartwig, *Quellen*, pp. 2-3, 6, 9. N. Rubinstein, « The Beginnings of Political Thought in Florence », *Journal of the Warburg and Courtauld Institutes*, V (1942), 198-227.

[14] Articles on this chronicle are legion, as are scholarly controversies. Cf. A. Del Monte, « La storiografia fiorentina dei secoli XII e XIII », *Bullettino dell'Istituto storico italiano per il medio evo*, LXII (1950), 175-282; R. Morghen, « Note malispiniane », *ibid.*, XL (1921), 105-26; C. Davis, *Dante and the Idea of Rome* (Oxford, 1957), pp. 244 ff.

writing because no tension existed between private morality and public policy. What did emerge was the capacity to empathize with an older nobility and its presumed commitment to chivalric life styles. Indeed, an epic tone colored his work as he evoked the deeds of exemplary figures from the world of Frederick II to the ill-fated Manfred.

Up to this point we have been observing historical conceptualizations activated by patriotic impulse and memory of grandeur. Surely, one cannot discern ideas of *renovatio* or traces of moral dimension in the sparse literature of that time. Not until the age of Dante do we observe the multiplication of that list of historical types soon to give variety and texture to the writings of Florentine chroniclers and literati. Before entering this lush terrain we might step back to note certain features of the society, economy, and politics of this polis. Most striking was the phenomenal growth of the city; its population increased by 300 percent within a century. As of 1278 it stood at 73,000 inhabitants. It is not, however, with the fact of number that we should be concerned, but rather with the curious character of the attendant social change. This was a startlingly nouveau society, and the greater share of its leading families were, as the chroniclers put it, « men of recent origins ». Equally relevant to our inquiry is the gradual undermining of the feudal nobility. At approximately the same time almost half of the urban nobles were scions of wealthy businessmen. Meanwhile, the seventy-four *consorterie* of the *contado* were substantially reduced in prestige and power. Our concern is not with the pursuit of social data but rather to attempt to assess the cultural consequences of this burgeoning and oddly mixed society. First, we must consider briefly the implications of this democratization for spiritual life. If there is any single generalization concerning upper-class bourgeois behavior in the thirteenth century, it would treat the alacrity with which the *popolani grassi* sought to participate in religious life. Over a third of the churches in the city were in the hands of laity; the populace had already joined the clergy in ousting the simoniacs. Now Florence became the first Italian town where the companions of St. Francis were to preach. In 1218 they were given a fixed establishment under the protection of Cardinal Ugolino (the hospital of San Gallo); three years later the convent of the Clares was founded at Monticelli. Florence was the first center for lay monasticism with the establishment of the Third Order of the Franciscans. In 1221 the chapter of the Cathedral gave the Dominicans the church of Santa Maria Novella; only seven years later the Franciscans were to receive Santa Croce. For the next century and a half democratization of spiritual life proceeded with an intensity difficult to match in any part of Europe. No single explanation will cover this multi-faceted phenomenon, but surely the fact that the city had no proper nobility to monopolize the spiritualities was a prime cause. A visit to Santa Croce reveals the high rate of religious investment that Florentine burghers made when given an unrivaled opportunity to enter the sacred portals and bury their dead.

The burgher conscience was informed by the popularizings of Dominicans and Franciscans, and nurtured by a socioeconomic milieu in which they could continue to participate in the benefits of a religious community. The absence of a « true » nobility allowed for the quickening of lay spirituality, and this in turn prompted new dimensions in historical writing. It was possible for chronicler and poet to dramatize the conflict between private ethics and the demands of the public world. For example, we find mounting doubts projected by literary men, from Dante to Giovanni Villani, concerning the morality of Florentine imperialism. Villani questioned the harsh program of dominating the *contado*, while at the same time being keenly aware of the imperatives of civic pride [15]. Dante challenged the entire notion of urban expansion, placing himself in mortal opposition to a spiritually bankrupt foreign policy, yet, few were more aware of the roots of civic identity than the exiled poet [16]. Villani

---

[15] See his condemnation on the Florentine seizure of the Castle of Montebuono owned by the nobles of the Buondelmonti family: « and so the commune of Florence started her expansion more by force than by reason, augmenting her rural domains and subjecting to her jurisdiction every noble in it and destroying their fortresses ». *Cronica*, ed. F. Dragomanni (Florence, 1844-45), IV, 36. Cf. also *Cronica*, IV, 7. G. Aquilecchia in his « Dante and the Florentine Chroniclers », *Bulletin of the John Rylands Library*, XLVIII (1965), 30-55, shows Villani's indebtedness to Dante for key historical concepts so that the poet's direct contribution to fourteenth-century Florentine historiography is secure.

[16] Scholarly monographs on Dante and these themes are of course le-

commenced his chronicle as a civic panegyric to Florence, daughter of Rome, whose splendor outshone that of the Eternal City. Soon, however, tension mounted, and in the midst of celebrating the « unimagined wealth » of the republic, he descended into a morass of Christian recrimination. Never was this medieval merchant able to furnish justification for capitalism or capitalists without invoking religious metaphor.

The Golden Age for Dante was a hundred years or so before when his ancestor Cacciaguida lived and crusaded for Florence [17]. Simple, rustic values dominated the poet's vision as he lyricized the virtues of a tightly knit commune governed by a compact aristocracy. Faction and avarice had entered the city with the numerous immigrants over the last hundred years. Yet, this disdainful poet was well aware of the self-defeating virtues of the nobility. Clan pride contributed to the terrible isolation of Farinata, and from this stemmed the bitterness and the sin of partisanship. In the *Purgatorio*, Guido del Duca tells us how his blood was full of envy so that now he reaps his reward. « Oh race of men why do you set your heart where needs be exclusion of partnership? » The bloody landscape of poem and chronicle was a tragic tribute to the vendetta. A very different temperament was Giovanni Villani's, but he, too, was able to dramatize the plight of his merchant heroes. The golden age for this chronicler was the time of *Il Primo Popolo* (1250-60), during his father's prime, when merchant and magnate governed a thriving republic [18]. Only later did history betray this memory of a concord of the orders when, as a consequence of magnate violence and merchant avarice, the guild government Villani had eulogized sold the republic into bondage.

These two remarkable commentators on the urban scene provided their world with that moral dimension stemming from

---

gion, but see especially the sensitive presentation by A. P. d'Entrèves, *Dante as a Political Thinker* (Oxford, 1952).

[17] C. Davis, « Il buon tempo antico », *Florentine Studies*, ed. Rubinstein, pp. 45-69. Cacciaguida, Dante's great-great-great-grandfather's celebrated speech is found in *Paradiso*, XV-XVI.

[18] In extolling *Il Primo Popolo*, the chronicler fails to acknowledge the contributions of earlier regimes or the continuities involved. Thus he accentuates the mythical structure of the decade of the 1250's when virtue prevailed. Cf. Y. Renouard, *Les villes d'Italie de la fin du Xe siècle au début du XIVe siècle* (Paris, 1963), pp. 253-66.

a search for modes to dramatize the distance between historical ideal and political reality. They portrayed this separation by employing the conventions of « realistic » medieval literature, while entertaining at the same time ideal schema from theology, metaphysics, and ethics. Historical personality was delineated as a consequence of this irreconcilable tension. To put this in another way: the social element of human experience was quintessential, so that it could not be dissipated no matter how forceful might be the pull of overarching abstraction. What was created were a series of historical types that permitted the commentator to display unprecedented empathy for the imperatives of the secular world, while retaining a firm grasp upon the demands of immutable moral law. A gallery of memorable portraits of secular heroes emerged: Villani's and Dante's depiction of Brunetto Latini as public man par excellence and private sinner extraordinary was, I believe, the first such civic rendition in medieval literature [19]. Villani was willing to sketch the personalities of Giano della Bella or Dante himself with full regard for those qualities that could not be subsumed under any traditional abstract definition of historical personality. Dante easily shifted perspective from an humanistic orientation to a providential view, yet the reader's involvement in the historical plight of his characters was not diminished. Neither Paolo nor Francesca nor Ulysses are lessened by our knowledge of their ultimate moral failure [20].

The chronicler Dino Compagni, the other member of this artful triad, sustained the drama of his narrative by juxtaposing details of everyday life against a looming backdrop of moral outrage. Even the villains in his work were permitted quirks and eccentricities. Essentially, this realism was a product of a literary democratization whereby the author defined his characters in terms of those virtues and vices shared by the majority of his readers. In this way the line between the techniques of history and poetry, and even the *novella*, became blurred. Both author and audience were able to share the historical fate of the characters. If there is a progression in the literary develop-

---

[19] G. Villani, *Cronica*, VIII, 10; Dante, *Inferno*, XV.

[20] E. Auerbach, *Dante, Poet of the Secular World*, trans. R. Manheim (Chicago, 1961), p. 86.

ment of major writers like Dante and Boccaccio, it is the transition from abstract schema to intense particularization. Dante's appropriation of Virgil's style differed from all previous medieval writers in that he acquired techniques for participating psychologically in the character's history or destiny. Similes served to express inner conflict while symbolically announcing the character's future fate [21]. This sympathetic-empathetic posture allowed Dante to share the emotions of his characters and yet communicate his reactions to his readers. We observe the young Boccaccio's ready acceptance of rhetorical devices and willingness to assume a cold, almost dehumanized, scientific stance in his early work, the *Fiammetta*. With the *Decameron*, however, representation of personal experience does not yield to familiar paradigms as private history replaces intellectual analysis.

With leading Florentine chroniclers, too, the tendency was to prove all doctrines through appeals to personal experience. Despite those instances where such experiences did nothing to validate theories, the chronicler persisted. Dino Compagni's writing was permeated by blinding moral outrage as he came to recognize the damage done by political factions. Repeatedly, history confirmed the infinite vitality of man to violate ethical schema. What was dramatized in this masterful chronicle were two facets of the author's consciousness: a sense of cultural shock at the persistence of evil, and a need to communicate an untainted, durable, virtuous self. Like Dante, he sought to project his private sufferings upon a universal historical screen. Although the materials of his chronicle were not easily tractable to the imperatives of any familiar ethical system, he could not readily be dissuaded. For an ideology that would validate the righteousness of his personal experience it was necessary for the chronicler to invoke a divine agent. He closes the narrative by summoning the Holy Roman Emperor to punish political transgressors and vindicate his personal vision of justice, and this solution is polemical rather than ethical in tone.

Giovanni Villani began his monumental task with the blitheness of an untroubled, young spirit. Committed to a view

---

[21] On Virgil, see Antonio La Penna's « Virgilio e la crisi del mondo antico » that introduces *Tutte le opere*, ed. E. Cetrangolo (Florence, 1966), pp. XI-CIV and Brooks Otis', *Virgil. A Study in Civilized Poetry* (Oxford, 1963), a work true to its title.

of civic grandeur that saw Florence as surpassing mother Rome, he pridefully embarked upon his life's literary work. He would also dramatize men's moral fate through scrupulous regard for their individual history. He would seek the locus of progress and decline in the hearts of men. Like the *Divine Comedy*, this chronicle abounds with moral anecdotes intended to dramatize the retribution that must follow excess. The terrain of this history runs through those human souls whose fate is emblematic of a society [22]. At the next level this morality is epitomized in the behavior of social classes. Here Villani, like Dante, viewed the corrupting influence of wealth as the hallmark of immigrant peoples. He also regarded the imperialistic struggle against Fiesole as a contest between the progeny of law-abiding Roman settlers (Florence) and the descendants of Etruscans and factious Catilinarians. At first, he wished to attribute all manner of political evil to the mixture of good Roman with vile Etruscan blood. Looking back, he posited a golden age for his own pure-blooded, merchant ancestors. Very soon, however, this lyricism receded; successively, each social class demonstrated a penchant for corruption. What began as a panegyric to wealth and industry, culminated in a moral diatribe, not unlike that of a Dante or a Compagni.

Persistently, the dignity of the public world failed as did traditional historical arguments formulated to support Florentine immunity from the laws of moral decay. Chroniclers and poets tended to apply single, absolute ethical measure to private and public life. Those leaders appearing most likely to effect the political salvation of the city were found invariably to be fatally flawed. The Christian conception of *hubris*, coupled with the rigorous application of oligarchical standards to the individual political act, meant that the exceptional man must stand condemned for the sin of pride. Parenthetically, literary men will not diminish the grandeur of this temporal moment when the flawed hero confronts his fate. The failings of secular leadership were repeatedly dramatized so that pathos was evoked from the reader as he observed the limitations of human moral striving when seen under a transcendent perspective. In each

---

[22] Cf. the episodes of Count Ugolino (*Cronica*, VII, 21), Matteo Visconti (*Cronica*, VIII, 61), or the generalized statement in *Cronica*, X, 177.

instance, however, the values of the collectivity and the promptings of the Christian ethic were summoned to prove the incapacity of the secular hero to deliver his people from a catalogue of evils. At the same time, Roman models of civic virtue were paraded before a greedy audience to assure Florentines that once a saintly breed of senatorial apostles had made the world fit for His coming. Civic art, history, and political theory affirmed a psychology wherein the purity of patriotism was exalted. Love of country was affectionately associated with the Christian virtue of *caritas*. Yet, in this world of luminescent moral possibilities, the men of the present could only stand accused of pride, avarice, and envy.

The field of ideology also had its drama. The historically minded subscribed to notions of an open society where talent and deeds, not birth and privilege, would triumph. Yet, these self-same chroniclers continued to harbor deep prejudices against the newcomer. Similarly, devotion to the traditional liberties of the church and immunities of the aristocracy ran counter to dedication to the supremacy of communal law. As we have observed, recognition of the need for leadership was challenged by a corporate oligarchical ethic fearful of the emergence of any civic hero whose personality transcended the narrow limits of class or guild interest. Likewise, we see the robust postulation of the possibility of acts of civic unselfishness by a Brunetto Latini or a Dante subverted by rigorous application of Christian notions of *superbia*. From late thirteenth century on, with Latini and Giovanni Villani, we have a fuller appreciation of the historical obstacles confronting secular reformers, but the same schematic criteria were employed to judge their political handiwork [23]. Chroniclers were insistent in their call for citizen sacrifice and the stern application of juridical norms, while simultaneously excoriating public magistrates for performing

[23] For example, Latini depicts Cicero not in traditional fashion as a philosophic authority, but as a civic hero — the wise leader who defended his city against her enemies. Further, Latini reveals a deeper social insight than his predecessors when discussing the difficulties confronting the Roman orator, who was, after all, a « new man » in a world of aristocrats — a « cittadino di Roma nuova e di non grande altezza ». Giovanni Villani offers identical observations. Cf. C. T. Davis, « Brunetto Latini and Dante », *Studi medievali*, Ser. 3, VIII (1967), p. 424.

routine bureaucratic tasks because they impinged upon ancient immunities and liberties.

Firmly committed to a non-elitist view of culture, these historians and poets assumed the righteous role of civic prophet. Knowledge was not an arcane preserve but a field for popularizing. Few generations of writers had a higher estimate of the educability of their fellow citizens than did these Florentines. From the humble materials of everyday burgher life they created a formidable company of historical types. Despite their abiding sympathy with these laic personalities, they could only despair for the soul of the collectivity and the ultimate plight of political leaders. Dante, Compagni, and Giovanni Villani each closed his work on an apocalyptic note. The image of Dante can be generalized, for we watch the historian's world recede until the struggles of men pale on this « little threshing floor of earth ». What is left to us is the possibility of individual salvation at the expense of collective humiliation. The irony is that few bands of historians hoped for so much for the individual, loved their *patria* so well, and yet were victims of their own outraged sense of community.

If the political fate of the individual was exquisitely dramatized with a patient reverence for the details of his history, not so the collectivity. If individual historical identity was virtually non-eradicable, not so the collective claims of the polis. Here we note that the chronicler's concern was with securing a position for Florence that was immune from the flux of change and time. In order to establish a theory of urban progress, it was essential to fix the destiny of the republic to a religious agency whose claim to temporal immunity rested with the Divinity. It was this sacramental bond that communal experience must affirm if the cycle of civic decline was to be thwarted. Since the lives of men demonstrate that success engenders pride, and pride goeth before the fall, and all states are subject to the fatal cyclical law, then the salvation of the community must depend upon a transcendent power. But in the poetry of Dante and the chronicles of Compagni and Giovanni Villani, Florentine experience demonstrated precisely that the regenerative agencies — papacy and empire — had failed. Therefore, the focus must again be on the individual as he travels his earthly pilgrimage through a historical world in disarray. The agencies of spiritual regeneration are ultimately seen as ineffectual so that *renovatio* becomes a private rather than a public possibility. We should pay tribute to the fact that the historical heroes in the *Divine Comedy* and the two chronicles are the authors themselves, and that the pilgrimages we witness are their exile from the earthly polis. It is their moral odyssey that is dramatized.

II.

At mid-fourteenth century we observe the beginnings of a single historical perspective. The likelihood diminishes that an author will attempt to assess the eschatological significance of a particular historical act. Instead, the probabilities are in favor of the act being evaluated in terms of its contribution to the well-being or misery of men in this world. The tendency is to recognize the temporal limits of historically acquired knowledge separating this area that treats *res mutabilia* from those disciplines concerned with *res eternae*. The transcendent is never insignificant for the chronicler, only unknowable; perhaps the term historical fideism would be appropriate in describing this trend [24].

In the 1350's Matteo Villani argued that the justification for Guelfism (pro-papal policy) rested not in the realization of any transhistorical purpose (as earlier chroniclers contended), but in the promotion of communal liberty through resolute defense against tyranny. Patterned interpretations delineating the historical contest between good and evil were being displaced by a mounting sensitivity to the immediate psychological and

---

[24] Cf. M. Becker, *Florence in Transition*, Vol. 2, pp. 16-18. We observe in the historical writing of Coluccio Salutati (c. 1330-1406), Petrarch's disciple and chancellor of the city of Florence, the beginnings of that distinction between God's creation and the world that men were making. Humanist historians were frequently to accentuate the fact that knowledge of *res humanae* was more certain than that of *res naturales*. This felicitous distinction was to find its most effective protagonist in the philosopher-historian Vico, who employed it to distinguish between *factum* and *verum*. Because the former was man's doing, knowledge of it was more sure; therefore, the historical quest for intelligibility and structure was to be particularly prized. Cf. E. Cassirer, *The Individual and the Cosmos in Renaissance Philosophy*, trans. M. Domandi (New York, 1964), pp. 42 ff.

moral dimension of a political act. Like his contemporary, Paolo da Certaldo, Matteo saw war and civic strife as primary threats [25]. In the eyes of both men this blight stood condemned on humanitarian grounds rather than in the name of any ethical absolute derived from historical study. History was the bellicose stage for human suffering, and the chronicler could only depict the personal motives of « war-lovers ». Ultimate questions must be left unanswered; nor was there any remission extended. What is made to assail the reader are these facts: That slain innocence cannot be restored to life; that raped virgins cannot regain their chastity; and that pillaged cities cannot recover their liberty. One can never know what grace « warlovers » can find in the eyes of God. The public dimension of historical acts tended to be featured while a priori ethical implications were neglected.

Freud, in his essay on wit, discusses that energy normally occupied in maintaining inhibition; when it is freed for celebration, we see the restoration of vitality. The restraints of awe and respect are no longer sufficient; further outpourings of

---

[25] Christian Bec's *Les marchands écrivains, affaires et humanisme à Florence, 1375-1434* (Paris-The Hague, 1967) is valuable for its discussion of many of the chroniclers treated in my study. On Paolo da Certaldo, see his third chapter, pp. 95-111. Cf. also M. Villani, *Cronica*, VIII, 24; XI, 1.

At mid-Trecento we observe that history is becoming a testing ground for personality among Florentine literary men. Boccaccio stands as the most expert practitioner of this perspective; moments of extreme passion (*amore*) and times of severe reversal become the highest measure and proof of the capacity of man. The author dramatizes the uses to which men put their gifts and abilities when confronted by *amore* and *fortuna*. In this way the psychological element of the contest is highlighted. Cf. V. Branca's edition of Boccaccio's *Rime* (Bari, 1938), pp. 326 ff. and his *Boccaccio Medievale* (Florence, 1956), p. 16. This literary stance persists and is enhanced; with the mature Machiavelli, *fortuna* is depicted not so much as a mysterious force or transcendent mythical personification capable of working its will in history, but rather as a limit implicit in human nature itself. Its locus is in an obscure and non-virtuous area of the human psyche preventing men from dominating determined historical situations. For example, the inability of the individual to forget past injuries makes him incapable of exerting his powers to shape the future, just as his insatiable need for security renders him victim of events rather than master. Relevant to our discussion is the persistent elaboration of the psychological dimension in leading Renaissance historians. Cf. G. Sasso, « Sul VII capitolo del *Principe* », *Rivista storica italiana*, LXIV (1952), 205-7.

this energy follow when the individual observes that once-forbidden claims can be satisfied without punishment. If we adopt this commonsensical psychological construct in our discussion of Florentine chroniclers from mid-Trecento on, we may become more sensitive to the release of those energies once absorbed by reverence for empire and church. Indeed, we notice that in the last books of Giovanni Villani's chronicle, his own Guelf commitment to the papacy as divine intermediary between the historical and eternal worlds had deteriorated. The structure of his chronicle was such that it was dependent upon charismatic figures and sacred events. The books were given form by the rehearsal of moments of supreme medieval spirituality. The luminaries were, of course, the churchmen and the successors of Charlemagne.

With his brother Matteo, continuator of the chronicle, we witness a steady erosion of commitment to the efficacy of redemptive institutions. No longer will church or empire be viewed as being capable of bridging the chasm between the natural and supernatural realms. If divine providence did act, it was surely not through the anti-Florentine policies of a papacy bent upon exerting her dominion in north Italy or an avaricious empire so absurd in the view of men as it must be in the eyes of God. If divine providence did continue to exercise its sway over human affairs, its agencies could be neither of these medieval sacral vessels. Instead, a new form of election, more direct and sure, must exist: divine providence, without benefit of intermediary, was to select « the daughter of Rome » — the Arno republic herself as the anointed. Matteo engaged in a tortuous argument as to the reasons why the « translatio imperii » was only provisional and must revert back to those Italian republics who had « maintained the rights and liberties given them by the antique Romans » [26]. Without pursuing the theme of the need to validate Florence's divine Roman inheritance, let me

[26] N. Rubinstein, « Florence and the Despots: Some Aspects of Florentine Diplomacy in the Fourteenth Century », *Transactions of the Royal Historical Society*, ser. V, II (1952), 31-32. Matteo's Guelfism is transitional and does not possess the exclusivistic characteristics soon to hedge Florence's dominant role. For Matteo, Guelfism is validated by the predominance of independent and sovereign communes united by their opposition to tyrants and arbitrary rule.

suggest that vernacular chroniclers continued to identify divine providence with the politics, piety, and historical aspirations of the Florentine people [27]. Perhaps the following instances can suggest the thrust of this identification. We observe a progressive decline in the capacity of chroniclers and literati to criticize the foreign policy objectives of the republic no matter how imperialistic. Gone is the rigorous application of Christian standards to the lust for dominion over the *contado*. War against the Ubaldini feudatories elicits oratorical rhetoric from the usually conservative Giovanni di Pagolo Morelli. He will observe that God caused the sun to blind the infamous Pisans when warring with Florence in 1363. Gino di Neri Capponi devoted his *Commentari* to that sublime moment in Florentine history when the republic defeated Pisa and gained access to the sea [28]. The outstanding vernacular poet, Antonio Pucci, sees Florence exercising her authority, almost paternalistically, over « castella o cittade » as she seeks to restore liberty throughout Tuscany. In 1369 he celebrates the freeing of Lucca from « Babylonian captivity » after he has just speculated as to why the papacy

---

[27] We also observe a striking decline in traditional millenarian political poetry after mid-Trecento. The focus shifts from those time-honored engines of spiritual regeneration — the papacy and empire — to the polis. The one-time Ghibelline poet, the Florentine, Fazio degli Uberti, renounced his role as poet protagonist for the imperial position after witnessing the failure of Charles IV's expedition to the Eternal City. In his poems « Firenze » and « Fiesole » he projected the Arno city into the aggressive role of heir to imperial Rome. Florence, under the sign of Mars, was charged with defending Italy from the tyrant. R. Renier, *Liriche edite ed inedite di Fazio degli Uberti* (Florence, 1883), pp. 120-277. Cf. D. Weinstein, « The Myth of Florence », pp. 28-29. Historical defenses of traditional attachments to the church and the once venerated Guelf cause became even more bizarre. Cf. R. Davidsohn, « Tre orazioni di Lapo da Castiglionchio », *Archivio storico italiano*, ser. V, T. XX (1897), 225-46. Clearly, Petrarch's justly celebrated break with the views of medieval chroniclers, who saw history as continuous and regarded the Holy Roman Empire as the heir of imperial Rome, was publicized at a time when a sense of alienation from a universalized past was mounting. Cf. T. Mommsen, « Petrarch's Conception of the Dark Ages », *Speculum*, XVII (1943), 226-49.

[28] Capponi (Gino di Neri), « Commentari dell'acquisto di Pisa e tumulto dei Ciompi », in *Cronichette antiche di vari autori del buon secolo della lingua toscana*, ed. D. M. Manni (Milan, 1844). For Morelli, see V. Branca's edition of the *Ricordi* (Florence, 1956).

continued to protect the enemies of Florence [29]. If Pucci has a peer as an historical poet, it is Franco Sacchetti who will compare the twelve labors of Hercules with the glories and victories of Florence [30]. The war against the church, from 1375-78, literally resulted in the apotheosis of the Florentine republic; the *Diario d'Anonimo Fiorentino*, probably read in public to large audiences, speaks of the citizenry as « true Christians elected by God » [31].

Again, commencing with the chronicle of Matteo Villani, we find the tendency to lend dignity to the public world. Over the course of his narrative he realizes that trade and merchants are indeed the lifeblood of the republic [32]. The enemies of a thriving mercantile metropolis are the representatives of the old discredited orders — the once formidable allies of the papacy and the intransigent aristocracy. It is this world of merchants and artisans that is to be resolutely celebrated, first in the chronicles and later in the Latin letters of the humanists [33]. From Morelli to Gregorio Dati in the early fifteenth century we note that the physical setting of the city is spiritualized. When Morelli depicts the surrounding countryside it is in the glowing tones of a Fra Angelico or Botticelli. In this idyllic setting « la Bel-

---

[29] Florence was depicted by Pucci as a conquering polis always exercising authority paternalistically. When she triumphed over Pisa in 1364, the poet announced that soon his polis would subject all of Tuscany to her benevolent rule. Consolation was proffered to the vanquished Pisa by Pucci, who quoted Scripture: « chi si umilierà sarà esaltato ». Cf. F. Ferri, *La poesia popolare in Antonio Pucci* (Bologna, 1909), p. 75.

[30] Cf. footnote 3. Also, in the volume cited there, see sonnet CLXXXIX, « Florentina civitas Dei et Domina Libertatis ». It is worth recalling that Antonio Pucci's « Centiloquio », composed at this time, is a rendition of substantial portions of Giovanni Villani's chronicle done in *terzarima*. Also, Pucci composed an historical poem celebrating Florence's victory over Pisa. Cf. *Delizie degli Eruditi Toscani*, ed. F. Ildefonso di San Luigi (Florence, 1785), Vol. 6, pp. 189-266.

[31] *Diario d'anonimo fiorentino dall'anno 1358 al 1389*, ed. A. Gherardi (Florence, 1876), pp. 308, 315-22.

[32] M. Villani, *Cronica*, XI, 1: « I popoli liberi intenti a loro arti e mercatanzie moltiplicano in ricchezze magnificando la faccia di loro cittadi con ricchi e nobili edificii, e per li sicuri matrimoni cresce e moltiplica il numero de' cittadini con aspetto lieto e pieno di festa ».

[33] Here we can observe that humanists of the caliber of Coluccio Salutati transfer to Latin literature themes already anticipated by vernacular chroniclers. Cf. E. Garin, « I cancellieri umanisti della repubblica fiorentina da Coluccio Salutati a Bartolomeo Scala », *Rivista storica italiana*, LXXI (1959), 199.

lezza » is expressed through nature and personality. The world is accorded that elegance which Boccaccio conferred upon his ethereal landscape. Yet this world is much more or much less than a « locus amoenus », for Morelli would combine profit with that « clear and manifest beauty » of the civic landscape. This is a countryside furnishing Florence with wine, wood, grain, and troops; Morelli decries the fact that fifty years ago 10,000 men-at-arms were drawn from this region, now only six to 8,000 are extracted [34].

The contemporary world achieved a dignity, the city was divinely elected, and now Gregorio Dati endowed its physical structure with a regularity and order that lent the polis historical immortality unprecedented in vernacular writing [35]. Gino di Neri Capponi and the anonymous chronicle, once attributed to Piero di Giovanni Minerbetti, had already voiced a confidence in the durability of the state, willingly condoning its expansion and affirming the righteousness of its claims to dominion over Pisa [36]. Capponi was cognizant of those trying moments in public life when a citizen might be forced to jeopardize his Christian salvation for the good of the commonwealth. Later, Guicciardini

---

[34] See Christian Bec's telling remarks on the tonality of Morelli's language and its relationship to the lyric prose of Boccaccio in his *Les marchands écrivains*, pp. 72-74.

[35] As Hans Baron has shown, humanist culture was no retrograde movement and developments in Latin historiography were not inimical to tendencies evident in vernacular writings. Bruni, in his *Laudatio urbis florentinae*, projected a geometric plan of Florence as a city consisting of four concentric circles. At the center stands the Palazzo Vecchio whose tower dominates the rural environs. *The Crisis of the Early Italian Renaissance* (Princeton, 1955), Vol. 1, pp. 169-70.

[36] *Cronica volgare di anonimo fiorentino dall'anno 1385 al 1409 già attribuita a Piero di Giovanni Minerbetti*, ed. E. Bellondi in *Rerum Italicarum Scriptores*, XXVII, part 2 (Città di Castello, 1915). This chronicler does not view history providentially nor is he given to excessive moralizing; instead, he dwells upon the senseless brutality, corruption, and bloodshed of the times. Omens, portents, and heavenly constellations are not regarded as significant influences upon the unfolding of human history. The chronicler assumes a stance toward the events of his age wherein treachery, and the thousand evils flesh is heir to, have their origins in the human condition. He is, then, prompted to search for remedies for these ills in the realm of the phenomenal rather than the transcendent. What is relevant is that which is « useful for Christians », or « the inhabitants of the city of Florence ».

interpreted these writings to indicate that Capponi was well aware that « it is not possible in this day and age to rule domains and states according to the precepts of the Christian law » [37]. An historical tradition emerged describing the governors of Florence during the war against the papacy as the « Otto Santi della Balia del popolo di Dio ». With Dati this transvaluation of communal, political thinking culminates in a *laudatio florentinae urbis*, where the state is presented as a living entity capable of self-definition. Transcendent and overarching, its splendor does not depend upon the magnificence of corporate bodies, the grandeur of social orders, or the heroism of its citizens [38]. The state is not a passive receptacle for virtue, but rather the active agency for conferring nobility, wealth, and even immortality upon its devoted sons. John the Baptist stands as « champion and advocate », proclaiming the primacy of « virtù attiva », while « a melody so sweet ascends to the sky and moves the saints to love that city and defend it from anyone wishing to ruin so peaceful and tranquil a community ». It is the many citizens with their prayers and alms and holy works (« sante operazioni ») who win for the polis the « misericordia » of God. His love for the « buoni » has preserved and advanced our republic over all the states in Italy. Joined to this sacral representation of the city is the next leading motif: the second symbol of Florence was the gold florin. Victory over her enemies, defense of liberty, acquisition of empire, all these depended upon an abundance of merchant wealth. Proudly, Dati itemized the public debt accumulated for waging war between 1375 and 1406. How, he asks, after expending 10,500,000 florins, can the merchants still be men of substantial patrimony? The ready answer was that war brings increased prosperity and new territories to the thriving metropolis.

We observe that gradually a political orthodoxy replaced the dissent of the medieval chronicler. Morelli, Capponi, and Dati were anxious to establish impeccable political credentials.

---

[37] R. Sereno, « The *Ricordi* of Gino di Neri Capponi », *American Political Science Review*, LII (1958), 1118-22.

[38] G. Dati, *L'Istoria di Firenze*, ed. L. Pratesi (Norcia, 1904), pp. 140 ff., and especially p. 171. On the dating and later additions to the text, see H. Baron, *Humanistic and Political Literature in Florence and Venice at the Beginning of the Quattrocento* (Cambridge, Mass., 1955), pp. 63-69.

The perspective soon adopted was that of the public world. A city divinely elected, possessed of a lifestyle of its own, and capable of conferring honor upon its denizens could not be challenged lightly. Acts of piety and charity tended to be externalized so that they fostered a more civic spirituality. New models combining patriotism with Christian commitment were projected onto this comely civic scene. From the experience of the 1370's and 1380's emerged historical types markedly different from those structured out of the conventions of an earlier time by Dante and Giovanni Villani. A new form of reassurance, civic consolation, if you will, was being proffered by the historically minded during the last decades of the Trecento. These new creations surfaced in a milieu where sympathy for a citizen's earthly pilgrimage was intensified, not without substantial cost, however. Perhaps we can sense something of the quality of this new filter through which experience was to be passed if we recall some graphic lines from Matteo Villani written in the early 1360's. Sympathetically, he described the elegance and measured style of a great statesman and Florentine citizen who served as principal advisor to the Queen of Naples. He could not fault this paragon, Niccolò Acciaiuoli, whose soul was that of a noble knight; and yet, despite his virtues of magnanimity and tranquillity of spirit, he must accept voluntary exile because his very grandeur constituted a threat to the liberty of the city [39]. Around him conspiracies might be fomented, so, like the good Scipio Africanus, this man, « onesto e di bella maniera », must be banished. This, then, represented something of the cost exacted by the new moral filter. The exigencies of public law, the collectivity, and of course the *patria* triumphed over older private virtues of the spirit. Yet to believe that ideals were lacking in the new historiography is to misunderstand the nature of the new heroism.

A clue as to its character can be gleaned from the writings of civic-minded clerics during the 1370's. They displayed a warm sympathy for the earthly pilgrimage of civic politicians and burghers. Recognizing that public choices were cruel, sometimes even jeopardizing integrity and salvation, this generation of writers posited the first set of urban characters who success-

[39] *Cronica*, X, 22.

fully could fuse love of country with love of God. Guido del Palagio, leading politician of his day, is progenitor of a lofty succession of civic heroes whose personalities were shaped by dedication to God and the Republic. From the chronicler Buonaccorso Pitti to the humanist Coluccio Salutati, this reassuring image won currency. Palagio was « il santo e l'amico di Dio », who everyday gained the love of « grandi, mezzani, e minori », so that all citizens, good and evil, honored his work [40]. A second creation, whose place was secure in the Florentine historical tradition, was the civic-minded priest. Luigi Marsili epitomizes this character of history and legend, recognizing as he did in the 1370' s that men who do not fight for their country forfeit a part of their higher nature, becoming little more than beasts. The centrality of this patriot-priest, with his deep appreciation of the need for citizen identity, was assured by two generations of Florentine historians who ascribed to him genius on such varied topics as the defense of the Florentine vernacular and mastery of the intricacies of scientific historical researches. Hans Baron has shown that some of this reconstruction of the intellectual details of Marsili's life is an anachronistic fifteenth-century fiction. While one might argue that the writings of Giovanni da Prato, one of the creators of this civic mythology, still depended upon anterior sources, yet, agreement with Baron merely strengthens the observation that such figures were ideal types constructed out of conventions that reinforced the citizen ego by projecting the image of civic piety [41]. Finally, we could take the

---

[40] On Palagio, Marsili, and Giovanni da Prato, see M. Becker, *Florence in Transition*, Vol. 2, pp. 55-61.

[41] H. Baron, *Humanistic and Political Literature*, pp. 13-37; N. Rubinstein, « Il Poliziano e la questione delle origini di Firenze », in *Il Poliziano e il suo tempo* (Florence, 1957), pp. 101-04. It might be worthwhile to consider such sculpture as Donatello's marble David of 1408-9, and his terracotta Joshua, 1410, under the rubric of *civic piety*. Here we have figures symbolizing the proud accommodation of public *virtù* and Christian piety. Likewise, Ghiberti's and Brunelleschi's reliefs done for the competition of 1401,wherein the knife is about to be plunged into Isaac's throat when the angel of the Lord appears, has recently been interpreted in political terms.Not only do these reliefs of the sacrifice prefigure that of the Redeemer, but also the aspiration for salvation of the state from the dread Visconti menace. Cf. F. Hartt, « Art and Freedom in Quattrocento Florence », *Essays in Memory of Karl Lehmann* (New York, 1964), p. 124.

personages of Carlo and Roberto di Battifolle, Counts Guidi, as exemplars of the new nobility imbued with *carità* and *amore* who followed «their father the commune». Again, if we think upon center-city Florence between the Palazzo della Signoria and the Duomo, the world of civic statuary comes alive. Exactly in these years do we see the creation of a new breed of civic heroes. From Nanni di Banco through the young Donatello we observe purposeful public men combining Christian piety with civic devotion. Donatello's statue of the youthful David stands staring out into space above the severed head of the tyrant. He wears the hero's crown used by Thetis to cover the grave of Achilles, and the inscription below reads: « To those who bravely fight for the fatherland the gods will lend aid even against the most terrible foes ». Three years later, Brunelleschi, in his designs for the Ospedale degli Innocenti, created the appropriate civic space for the new citizen heroes: there it would be comely to hold sacred discourse about the *patria*. For the human realm to become secure, space must be intelligible [42].

The interpretations promulgated by chroniclers were becoming increasingly favorable to the setting of public figures in a civic space. History disclosed its own workings in two particular ways: through the operation of the human will and the resultant clash of voluntaristic impulses. The first successful rendition of this species of historiography was to be found in

---

[42] The *Giovannino Martelli* of Donatello is an early example of this symbolism combining new worldliness with spirituality. St. John, the symbol of Florence, is not depicted as a free and happy young man strolling in the desert; instead, his hands spasmodically clutch at the cross and scroll which his fingers press into his body. This is the boy who suffers penitence after meeting Christ and learning the meaning of His life and passion. M. A. Lavin, « Giovannino Battista: A Study in Renaissance Religious Symbolism », *Art Bulletin*, XXXVII (1955), pp. 90-91. Cf. also H. W. Janson, *The Sculpture of Donatello* (Princeton, 1957), 2 vols. A recent commentator on Brunelleschi notes the architect's belief in a new, finite, and imminent reality having its base in the experimental certainty of perspective with space capable of exact measurement. Confidence in perspective is joined with adherence to classical plastic values. Since space is no longer problematic, the earthly city and secular events can be represented in their full lyrical felicity. E. Luporini, *Brunelleschi: Forma e ragione* (Milan, 1964), p. 79. Cf. also the sensitive appraisal of P. Hendy, *Piero della Francesca and the Early Renaissance* (New York, 1968), pp. 24-25. (I wish to thank Professor Bruce Cole for this reference).

the chronicle of Stefani. Writing in the early 1380s, without confidence in traditional ideological scaffolding, he saw the bounds of historical personality as defined by the clash of those human wills engaged in an interminable struggle for power. No possibility of *renovatio* here; man's historical nature was already irrevocably fixed. Indeed, the Renaissance historian's belief in an immutable human essence was already in embryo in this late medieval chronicle. *Carità*, *amore*, *cortesia*, and *renovatio* played little part in this urban world as the chronicler defined men in terms of their thirst for power and will to dominate. Money, family, or authority of party are summoned to ensure predominance and prestige to individuals, clans, and states. The sense of the historical is projected by depicting the force of immutable appetites and the play of interests.

This extreme voluntaristic historicism is the antithesis of earlier medieval presentations of moral yearnings for renewal or the decrying of the malfunction of regenerative agencies. Yet the new historiography does not lack spiritual dimension. Again, we can turn to Boccaccio, whose *Decameron* had been exemplary in lending sublimity and elegance to the civic landscape. The individual was without traditional supports and historical commitments that would protect him against the buffets of *fortuna*. Confronted by forces that might overwhelm him, the individual testified to the difference between fortuitous nobility and *that* virtue conquered in continuous struggle always open to sudden and grave risks. In the *Decameron* the bourgeoisie became exalted protagonists in a now democratized spiritual drama. From Matteo Villani to Stefani we observe a quest for essential historical traits. These are disclosed through the individual as history tests the weakness and steadfastness of his purpose. How did citizens satisfy their ambitions? How were their appetites thwarted? What provision was made to forestall adversity? Even governments could be judged according to their ability to take the prudential course. The forces of self were directed outward toward the world of obstacles and dangers. The effects of an act or a policy were judged insofar as they promoted or thwarted human well-being. Neither asceticism nor renunciation were effective historical responses, but rather *ingenio*, *virtù*, or self-restraint were appropriate to this voluntaristic, civic man. What in Dante's generation were historical types intruding into the chronicler's narrative frame became secular models to be imitated, even venerated. Shortly thereafter, Giovanni Cavalcanti in his *Istorie fiorentine* clothed the historical figure of Cosimo de' Medici in the vestments appropriate to Christ. In the sequel to this work, the *Seconda Storia*, the deity proves to be a false messiah [43].

By the early fifteenth century the Florentine vernacular chronicle approached the salient characteristics soon to be made explicit in the classicized histories of the Renaissance. Extreme voluntarism, the dissipation of medieval political ideologies, an historical fideism, wherein the author acknowledged his limited ability to know transcendent purposes, projection of the ideal of an overarching political construct — the state — to which all must render homage, dwindling criticism of the use of statal power, blatant subscription to expansionist policies, and a firm espousal of the norms of public law were but a few of the motifs ensconced in the vernacular chronicle. With it all, however, the personalities in the chronicles of Matteo Villani, Stefani, and Morelli were so vulnerable, just as the *persona* of the author was so fragile. Their ultimate validation could not be achieved in a medieval frame, for this perspective did not allow the author to distance himself from his characters and their milieu. The classical canons of « decorum » and « suitability » permitted Bruni to treat human weakness (*imbecilitas umana*) and the « cross-grained » nature of man as historical constants not to be penetrated or even criticized. Human nature was essentially unchanged and unchangeable, and, therefore, only amenable to a superficial behavioristic psychology. Gone was the moral *angst* of Dante's generation; dissipated, too, was the metaphoric language of spiritual decline and renewal. In its stead was a new magic idiom expressing confidence in the values of the public world

[43] Giovanni Cavalcanti's writings have not attracted the interest of modern scholars. To a considerable measure his relevance stems from his talent for flooding the profane world with sacred and classical imagery. The ultrarational bias of present-day historians toward the Quattrocento has encouraged neglect of irrational energies and aspirations that were central to historiography and art. For the limited bibliography on Cavalcanti, see Guido di Pino's introduction to his edition of the *Istorie fiorentine* (Milan, 1944). The older edition by F. Polidori (Florence, 1839), however, remains the only complete one.

and linking the new Brunelleschian space with the polis of antiquity, wherein the true progenitors of the Florentines had gained secular immortality. If human nature was a constant, why not this apotheosis in a contemporary setting?

Florentine history was becoming a public enterprise, and Latin writers, from Bruni to Poggio, allowed their audience to glimpse the possibilities implicit in this new undertaking: History could aspire to save men and their deeds from the ravages of time. The Florentine government responded generously to this religious impulse by commissioning the sculptor Bernardo Rossellino to create a statesman's tomb for Florence's most consoling historian. If *condottieri* were rewarded with inexpensive painted replicas of marble monuments on church walls, not so Leonardo Bruni Aretino. According to one account, the sculptor placed a carving of Bruni's immortal *History of the Florentine People* on his effigy, another reports that it was the *Laudatio Florentinae urbis*. What pleasant alternatives for the citizen ego. The first merely promised the Florentines control of Tuscany, whereas the other contended that domination of the world belonged to the Arno city.

RONALD WITT

THE REBIRTH OF THE CONCEPT OF REPUBLICAN LIBERTY IN ITALY

In attempting to discuss the intellectual history of the Middle Ages, a period in which there were relatively few writers and from which only a percentage of what was set down has survived, the scholar should be wary of 'discovering' pioneers. This is especially true in the case of the present problem of republican liberty in Italy, since it is well-known that the word *libertas* was the most popular word in the political vocabulary of Northern and Central Italy from the time of Frederick I: much must have been written about it and more expressed verbally than we can know. The purposes of the present article, consequently, are to discuss what appear to have been the major obstacles in terms of intellectual traditions preventing a clear articulation of a republican concept of *libertas*, to offer the earliest texts known to me which contribute to the genesis of that idea and to suggest that the early years of the Quattrocento saw its articulation.

In 1375 the commune of Florence declared war on the Roman Papacy in a war allegedly intended to defend *libertas*, not only her own but that of other people [1]. A red banner marked with that word was designed to broadcast as succinctly as possible this war aim [2]. As the communes under ecclesiastical control one after the other revolted against Church authority, the Florentines

---

[1] Arch. Stato Firenze, Signoria, I Cancelleria, *Missive* XV, 40 v and 69 v. These are merely two examples. The claim to be fighting for *libertas* is found throughout *Missive* XV, XVI and XVII.

[2] *Cronaca fiorentina di Marchionne di Coppo Stefani*, ed. N. Rodolico (« Rerum Italicarum Scriptores », T. XXX, p. 1, Città di Castello, 1904), rub. 753: « Questi otto (the Otto di Balia designated to supervise the prosecution of the war) fecero una bandiera, la quale era tutta rossa con lettere a traverso, come quelle di Roma; ma questa bandiera dicea 'Libertà' lettere bianche. E molte Terre che si rubellavano si voleano dare alli Fiorentini, e mai niuna ne vollero, ma mandavano la bandiera della Libertà, e facevanle libere ». The Otto's decision to imitate the banner of the contemporary Roman municipal government was very probably inspired by a desire to establish Florence's relationship with ancient Rome and its tradition of liberty.

sent similar banners to each in order to emphasize the supposedly common goal. Bologna received hers in March 1376 after a bloodless revolt in which the former top judicial official of the Papacy was asked to remain on in the post with the new government and the papal legate, after a few days spent under house arrest for his own safety, departed laden with gifts and a present of a thousand gold florins [3]. This war fought in defense of *libertas* was the occasion for the first known attempt to analyze the term in all its senses and to determine what the populace meant when it rebelled against the Church's authority.

To the mind of one intelligent, if prejudiced observer of the proceedings, however, Bologna had lost, rather than gained her liberty in the course of these exciting days. A professor of canon law, Giovanni da Legnano was a Lombard by birth who received his first appointment in the Bolognese *studium* not perhaps coincidentally in the very months when the Pepoli regime was replaced by that of the Visconti in 1350 [4]. Yet, judging from his writings, it would be unfair to regard Giovanni as a Visconti partisan. His deepest loyalties were to the Church and more particularly to the Roman Papacy. A famous canonist by the time of the War with the Papacy, Giovanni was already known for his defense of papal prerogatives vis-a-vis the temporal powers. His *Somnium* composed in 1373 served very likely as one of the major sources of inspiration for the *Somnium Vi-*

---

[3] The banner « una insegna ricchissima, frangiata d'oro, nella quale era una sbarra azurrina con lettere d'oro, che dicevano *Libertas* » was brought from Florence after the conclusion of the pact between the two cities and was presented to the newly-elected rulers of the city (C. Ghirardacci, *Della Historia di Bologna*, Bologna, 1657, pt. 2, 342). In the initial stages of the Bologna rebellion the populace was called together and required to shout: « Vivat populus et libertas ». The slogan was also painted on the walls of various buildings (Giovanni da Legnano, *De iuribus ecclesiae in civitatem Bononiae*, Bibl. Marciana Venice, Lat. V, 16 (2653), 14 r.a). For the details of the rebellion see Ghirardacci, pp. 342-3.

[4] A fairly complete bibliography of Giovanni's writings and secondary material relating to his life and thought is found in John P. McCall, « The Writings of John of Legnano with a List of Manuscripts », *Traditio*, 23 (1967), 415-437. G. Ermini [« I Trattati della Guerra e della Pace », *Studi e Memorie per la storia dell'Università di Bologna*, 8 (1924), 8] suggests a link between Giovanni and the Visconti while McCall (p. 416, n. 7) seems to think it dubious.

ridarium written in France a few years later [5]. During the years when Florence led the alliance against the Papacy, he was to act as the chief emissary between the Bolognese and Gregory XI and to him belongs much of the credit for effecting a reconciliation between Pope and Commune in 1377. Thereafter, he served as papal representative in Bologna for a time and until his death in 1383 remained one of the most respected political personages in the city.

The rebellion of Bologna against the papal rule in 1376 inspired Giovanni to compose a political tract known as the *De juribus ecclesiae in civitatem Bononiae* [6]. Internal evidence shows that it was probably written after the re-establishment of papal authority in the city in 1377 [7]. Only a portion of the tract survives and it is possible that it remained incomplete. The repetition of a long anecdote about Alexander and Diogenes in two different chapters would imply that the whole was never revised for circulation [8]. Contained in only one manuscript, it would appear that the work was very little-known in its own time [9]. Yet for the history of political ideas Giovanni's *De juribus ecclesiae* is significant because it constituted the first attempt by a political theorist of the Middle Ages to offer a comprehensive definition of the concept of *libertas*. The tract provides the modern scholar

---

[5] G. W. Coopland, « An Unpublished Work of John of Legnano, the 'Somnium' of 1372 », *Nuovi Studi Medievali*, II, fasc. 1, 65-88, and especially 84-7.

[6] This tract (see above, n. 3) was partially edited by L. Rossi, *Dagli scritti inediti giuridico-politici di Giovanni da Legnano* (Bologna, 1898), pp. 25-59.

[7] Giovanni's reference to the « hodiernam libertatem » as compared with the servitude under the rebel government (14 r.a) suggests a time after the return of papal authority. Gregory XI, who died in 1378, moreover, was still alive (8 v.b).

[8] *De iuribus*, 14 r.a and 22 r.a-b.

[9] Giovanni da Ravenna shows signs in his *Dragmalogia*, largely devoted to proving that « eam libertatem quam unius non multorum iustitia dispenset quam solidior quidem et tranquilior », that he was acquainted with Giovanni da Legnano's work (Bibl. Nationale Paris, Lat. 6494, 15 v). A reference to the struggle of the communes against the Papacy in the War of the Eight Saints on behalf of their 'libertas', introduces a long discussion on the nature of true liberty (35 v). In the course of the tract, moreover, Giovanni da Ravenna uses two anecdotes from the life of the Bolognese jurist to illustrate his points (10 r-v and 36 v).

with something like a summary of the thinking on this question in the third quarter of the fourteenth century[10].

The author briefly declared the purpose for his writing in the opening paragraph:

> It has become an increasingly common thing in Italy, especially in the temporal patrimony of the Holy Roman Church, for peoples and territories subjected to its power and authority to withdraw their obedience and with the cry « Long live the people and liberty » set up a popular government. That this shout, which appears so attractive from the sound of the words and so in accord with natural law and which is in fact detestable and contrary to all law, not be permitted to lead peoples through error to their destruction in the future because no one has spoken out against it, I have decided to devote a special tract to this matter ... [11]

He followed this statement with an outline of his method of procedure. It was his intention to discuss (1) what powers the Church had over the lands subjected to its control and especially over Bologna; (2) why Bologna's rebellion was detestable and illegal; (3) in what way the shout « Long live the people and liberty » meant not liberty but servitude, not life but death; (4) how no territory in Italy was without a master; (5) under what conditions a popular government could enjoy autonomy; (6) what was the best regime; and (7) whether it was by divine judgment or the stars or both that the present trouble of the

---

[10] The tract was apparently unknown to Herbert Grundmann [« Freiheit als Religiöses, Politisches und Persönliches Postulat im Mittelalter », *Historische Zeitschrift*, 183 (1957), 23] » ... in der kaum übersehbaren Traktaten-Literatur des Mittelalters habe ich keine Schrift über die Freiheit, auch nicht über die *Libertas ecclesiae* endeckt, abgesehen von Traktaten über die Willens-freiheit, *De libero arbitrio*, als moraltheologisch-philosophisches Problem ». Grundmann cites Alamanno Rinuccini's *De libertate* as the first known to him (p. 23). Besides Legnano's work, the *Dragmalogia* finished in 1404 and Francesco de Zabarella's *De libertate ecclesiastica et eius immunitate* of 1389 (Arch. Prov. di Stato Aquila, S . 34, as mentioned in P. O. Kristeller, *Iter Italicum*, London, 1963, I, 1) should be added to the list of early treatments of *libertas*.

[11] *De iuribus*, 1 r.a; Rossi, p. 31.

Church in governing its lands had come about. Of the projected analysis only parts one, two, three and six survive [12].

In the first section Giovanni attempted to prove that Bologna owed obedience to the Pope as its temporal ruler not merely on the basis of special rights which the Emperor and the Bolognese themselves had previously recognized but also because the Pope was the « dominus plenus spiritualium et temporalium » [13]. Although originally men had been free of any superior authority but that of God « qui (principatus) nuncupatur ecclesiasticus », with Noah, who « exercised the office of priest », the Creator instituted human ecclesiastical government [14]. By inheritance this authority passed down through patriarchs and priests until the time of Christ, « who was true and natural lord of the whole world in both spiritual and temporal » [15]. All other governments, the temporal empires of history, were established illegitimately and with violence. Only by recognizing Christianity as the true religion and the Vicars of Christ as « true lords of the world » could the Roman Emperors succeed in purging their power of the stain of violence: « through recognition of the Vicar of God, those possessions violently usurped returned

---

[12] What was originally intended to be part six seems to have become part four in the text as we have it: « Circa quartum scilicet de multiplici genere monarchiae » (21 r.a). Rossi believed that this chapter, rather than being a part of the *De iuribus*, was the beginning of another treatise. His reasoning here was based primarily on the following points: « ... in questo quarto punto non si fa parole mai nè della Chiesa nè di Bologna ... » and « ... la parte che tratta della guerra navale, che pure è abbastanza lunga, non ha alcuna attinenza con l'argomento » (pp. 51-2). On the first point he overlooked the clear reference of 21 v.b in which Giovanni stressed the need for unity in the state « sicud in hac alma civitate Bononie de qua nunc sermonem ». As for the second argument, it is important to remember that Giovanni in part four was following closely (in some passages almost word for word) the treatment of politics of Aegidius Colonna in his *De regimine principum*. Because Aegidius treated war in the third book with his consideration of the best form of government, it is likely that Giovanni simply imitated him in this as in other aspects of the problem. I see, therefore, no reason for arguing that « l'amanuense aveva lasciato incompleto il primo scritto, e poi un altro amanuense, o lo stesso dopo qualche tempo, vi ha aggiunto un quarto punto appartenente a un'opera sulla politica aristotelica ».

[13] *De iuribus*, 1 v.a; Rossi, p. 33.

[14] *Ibid.*, 7 v.a; Rossi, pp. 39-40.

[15] *Ibid.*, 1 v.a; Rossi, p. 33.

to their true lord, that is the Vicar of God, who owned and owns all things » [16].

The conclusion of the second, much briefer section, was that Bologna's withdrawal of obedience from the Papacy had been nefarious because (1) of the crimes committed in the course of the action; (2) of the general right of the Papacy to rule over temporal and spiritual matters; and (3) of the special relationship which Bologna as part of the Papal States had with the Papacy: « this implies, as I have said, the total extinction of peace in the commonwealth. It implies, moreover, an enormous ingratitude and, I might add, a raving mind » [17].

Once the justice of the Church's claims to Bologna and the extent of the city's error in rebelling against its rightful ruler were established, Giovanni came to the major objective of the tract, to analyze what the slogan « Long live the people and liberty » could mean [18]. He gave nine senses of *libertas*, but for the purpose of clarity the various definitions of the word will be taken up in a somewhat different order from that followed in the tract itself.

The *libertas* of types three, four, five and six related to legal status of persons: (3) the man who is not a slave is free; (4) the manumitted slave is in a certain sense free; (5) the manumitted slave is in another sense not free; and (6) anyone involved in a condition of personal dependency could be considered as not of the ranks of the *liberi*. Closely following the *Corpus iuris civilis* and the accepted interpretation of previous civilian commentators, the Bolognese canonist recognized that in the first age after creation all men were free of any human jurisdiction. Slavery and property were products of the *ius gentium*, which Giovanni seems to feel had been introduced because of the problems arising in a society where all men were free and property common [19]. In the four senses considered here, *libertas*

---

[16] *Ibid.*, 8 r.b; Rossi, p. 41; «per recognitionem vicarii Dei, res violenter usurpate pervenerunt ad verum dominum, scilicet vicarium Dei, cuius omnia fuerant et sunt ».

[17] *Ibid.*, 11 r.b; Rossi, p. 48.

[18] *Ibid.*, 13 r.a; Rossi, p. 49.

[19] *Ibid.*, 1 r.b; Rossi, pp. 32-33. Actually Giovanni only explained the origin of property specifically in this way; he said nothing about the reason for slavery except that it was created by the introduction of the *ius gentium*. But,

had meaning only after the creation of legal classifications of persons. When the people of Bologna cried for *libertas*, however, they certainly could not have had any of these meanings in mind according to the author: every *paterfamilias* in Bologna was fully free as a citizen of the city and, consequently, had no need to demand what he already had [20].

Nor did the Bolognese canon lawyer appear to take seriously the possibility that the people in their rebellion sought a *libertas* defined as freedom from sin [21]. In any case, after initially listing it as the ninth sense of the term, he did not subsequently return to this particular meaning. On the other hand, although it was equally evident that the slogan « Long live the people and liberty » was not a demand for *libertas* in the eighth sense, that is, for freedom of choice as a power of the human will, nevertheless, Giovanni devoted a large portion of the treatise to a discussion of this particular definition [22]. Doubtless, *libertas arbitrii* was for him the most important of all the various freedoms. It was « by use of free choice » that men were « free with a freedom exclusive of human jurisdictional control » at the beginning of creation [23]. Although the *ius gentium* had been introduced « on account of the various necessities of men », human beings were still free in the sense that they possessed reason (« erant liberi libertate facultatis naturalis inductiva ») and freedom of choice (erant liberi libertate ad utrumlibet progressiva et necessitatis arbitrii humani exclusiva »). Whereas those who exer-

---

since the *ius gentium* itself was the product of these problems, it is fair to assume that he would have seen slavery and property as rising from similar causes. It is interesting to note that Giovanni does not mention the origins of these institutions in relationship to sin.

The various types of liberty involved under this rubric were defined as follows (13 r.a): « Tertio, sumitur libertas pro exlusione vinculi servilis ... hec libertas non competit servo; immo illam servitus excludit e contra ... Quarto modo sumitur libertas et hec competit liberto manumisso ... Quinto modo sumitur libertas pro exclusione libertinitatis et vinculi patronalis ... De sexto modo sumitur libertas pro exclusione cuiuscumque conditionis personalis ».

[20] *Ibid.*, 14 r.b.

[21] *Ibid.*, 13 r.b: « Nono modo sumitur libertas pro libertate anime quae est exclusiva mortalis peccati».

[22] *Ibid.*, 14 v.a-21 r.a and 22 r.a-22 v.b.

[23] *Ibid.*, 1 r.a.

cised their free will according to the dictates of reason were truly free, those who followed their passions were trapped in the deepest form of servitude. Because the soul was far more precious than the body, Giovanni maintained, the subjection of the rational soul to the passions was greater than the subjection of the body to a master. With reason captive to passion, man's true free choice was lost [24].

Intimately related as contrasting notions of liberty, the first and second definitions of the term offered by the author were difficult to interpret apart from *libertas* as freedom of choice. He defined the first type as follows: « Liberty is the natural faculty of man to do what he pleases unless he be prevented by force or by law ». A second type of *libertas* consisted in the freedom to act « insofar as one's natural powers allow without any restrictions imposed by the positive disposition of the *ius gentium* ». This was a freedom to do whatever the natural instinct urged and was common both to slaves and brute animals [25].

Repelled as were all medieval jurists by the notion that liberty could be limited by force, Giovanni quoted Accursius' interpretation of the first definition, drawn from the *Corpus iuris civilis*. Like Accursius Giovanni read this definition as granting man the possibility of performing any act unless it was forbidden by the *ius gentium* (i. e., the *Digest*'s phrase, « nisi vi aut iure prohibetur », was understood as « nisi vi, id est, iure prohibetur ») [26]. The dispositions of this law, moreover, were reflections of man's reason: the *ius gentium* « est equitas quidam (sic) refulgens in humana intelligentia ex qua effluit dictamen recte racionis » [27]. By contrast the second definition of *libertas* implied no use of reason: it was simply the natural power of every man to do as he wished in so far as he was able. Uncontrolled by reason, man's *libertas* in this sense was identical to that of the beast. Because such a *libertas* gave rein to the passions and sub-

---

[24] *Ibid.*, 22 r.a.

[25] The first type of *libertas* is defined as the « naturalis facultas eius quod cuique facere libet nisi quod vi aut iure prohibetur ». The second consists in the freedom to act « pro possibilitate naturali, circumscripta dispositione iuris gentium positivi » (13 r.a.).

[26] *Ibid.*, 13 r.a.

[27] *Ibid.*, 11 r.a.

jected the rational soul to appetite, this was for man the direst slavery.

When in the first days of the rebellion the insurgents terrorized the population of Bologna into accepting their tyrannical regime and compelled everyone to cry « Long live the people and liberty » against all law and reason, they betrayed their real intentions. They sought a liberty to live like beasts. This in fact was the outrageously prejudiced conclusion of Giovanni's investigation of the people's slogan: « There remains only the freedom to act devoid of any right; and this liberty is bestial and brutal and is a certain form of servitude ... Therefore, when they cry ' Long live liberty ' they are simply proclaiming ' Long live servitude and bestiality ' or ' brutality etc. ' » [28].

The relationship between *libertas* and the law of reason was further developed, however, in the fourth section of the work where Giovanni took up the problem of the best form of government. After investigating which political constitution realized to the highest degree the *bonum commune* and deciding for monarchy, Giovanni discussed the matter of the subject's obedience to the law. Just previously he had spoken of the good prince as « the intermediary between the natural and the positive law » [29]. Good government proceeded from the dictates of natural reason: « Insofar as he (the king) imitates natural reason, to that degree he rules properly; thus, when resting on natural law, the positive law is justifiably binding ». In the good state the virtuous citizen and the virtuous man were the same because the laws were reflections of right reason. They erred who believed that it was servitude to obey the laws and the king. To wish to live without restraint and law was to be more like a beast than a man and to live in true slavery. Rather, obedience to the king and observation of the law constituted not only the safety of the kingdom and the city but it was through this very obedience that subjects became free. Subjection to the just prince insured freedom of choice and allowed freedom of action in conformity with right reason (definitions one and eight). The state ruled by the good prince was by implication truly a govern-

---

[28] *Ibid.*, 14 v.a; Rossi, p. 50.
[29] *Ibid.*, 29 r.b.

ment for the *civis*, the man of free condition (senses three or six) [30].

Because he had already devoted the first and second parts of the tract to a detailed discussion of the papal claims to govern Bologna, Giovanni apparently felt no need to develop the matter more fully when it came to analyzing the seventh meaning of *libertas*: « In the seventh way liberty is considered to be the exclusion of any subjection and of any superiority and this position is held by no one but the Pope » [31]. He must, of course, have been perfectly aware that the cry of the Bolognese for *libertas* meant principally this — independence of papal control — and it is here that the polemical purpose of the work becomes again very evident.

But in setting up political independence as one form of *libertas*, Giovanni reflected the centuries-long controversy regarding the relationship of the various spiritual and temporal powers to one another. Within the area of the temporal, civil lawyers had worked out most detailed analyses of the position of kings vis-a-vis the Emperor. By the end of the thirteenth century lawyers in the service of the French and Angevin monarchs had developed theories to show how their respective rulers were *reges liberi*, i. e., how they were independent of the Emperor [32]. In spite of his statement that only the Papacy was without a superior, Giovanni was prepared to permit the Emperor a great measure of autonomy and, while he promised in his introductory outline to prove in a chapter that « in Italy no popular government is without a superior (acephalum) », he intended to follow that with another designed to discuss « In what way as regards a political constitution it is possible for a

---

[30] *Ibid.*, 31 r.b. G. Tellenbach [*Libertas, Kirche und Weltordnung im Zeitalter des Investiturstreites* in the series « Forschungen zur Kirchen und Geistesgeschichte », 7 (1936), 52] in his description of the medieval concept of *libertas*, based essentially on German documents, concludes similarly that the basic notion of *libertas* in these centuries was linked with the notion of dependence. For criticisms of this idea, see Grundmann, *op. cit.*, pp. 23 ff.

[31] *Ibid.*, 13 r.b: « Septimo modo sumitur libertas pro exclusione cuiuscumque subiectionis et cuiuscumque superioritatis et hec nulli competit nisi pape ».

[32] F. Ercole, *Da Bartolo all'Althusio* (Florence, 1932), p. 77 ff., esp. 85-91; F. Calasso, « Origini italiane della formola ' Rex in regno suo ' etc. », *Rivista di storia del diritto italiano*, III, 2 (1930), 213-259.

popular government to be independent and endowed with liberty »[33]. Thus, he believed in some measure in the possibility of autonomy for a popular government.

While exhibiting a definite conception of *libertas* as 'political autonomy', the writer did not seem to be aware that the battle cry « Long live the people and liberty » might have included a demand for yet another sort of liberty: the liberty of every citizen to participate in the government under which he lived. When the Bolognese professor promised to describe how a « popular government » could be « independent and endowed with liberty », from the structure of his outline and from everything he said in the extant sections we can expect that he would have treated the concept *populus liber* in terms of the categories used to analyze the concept *rex liber*. To post-Enlightenment generations, on the other hand, the slogan has obvious republican overtones: to the modern mind the liberty in question here would involve two concepts of political freedom — not only the liberty of a popular state in relationship to another authority but also the liberty arising from the nature of the popular constitution itself. Granting the overt prejudice of this pro-papal writer, we might easily accuse him of wilfully neglecting to take up this tenth meaning of *libertas* in his account. But before convicting him of this charge, we must first establish to what degree the communal enemies of the Church were themselves able to conceive of a *libertas* peculiarly republican. If it cannot be denied that the Florentines and their allies wanted popular government, nevertheless, had they yet defined any special relationship between the republican constitution and political liberty?

A Roman of the late Republican period would not have disputed the Bolognese lawyer's distinction between liberty as law and liberty as license. Cicero in his defense of Cluentius in 66 B. C. defined the tie between liberty and law in this way: « Legum denique idcirco omnes servi sumus ut liberi esse possimus ». [34]. In his insistence that law must be reasonable and

---

[33] *Ibid.*, 1 r.a; Rossi, p. 32: « Quarto qualiter in plaga italica nullum est populare gubernaculum acephalum. Quinto qualiter politico regimine est populare gubernaculum absolutum, libertate decoratum ».

[34] *Pro Cluent.* 146, quoted from C. Wirszubski, *Libertas*, Ital. trans. G. Musca (Bari, 1957), p. 18. The English original was not available to me.

fairly enforced Giovanni was on common ground with the Roman political philosopher whose works played such a large role in the development of this idea in medieval Europe. But a central aspect of Cicero's concept of laws was lacking in the Bolognese jurist's presentation: that is, Cicero's particular idea of *aequitas*: «The private individual ought to live on fair and equal terms with his fellow-citizens, with a spirit neither servile and abject nor yet domineering » [35]. Where *aequitas* exists there is liberty. A scholar has recently summarized this political concept of the late Roman Republic in this way: « È evidente dunque che ' aequa libertas ' significa eguaglianza di fronte alla legge, eguaglianza di tutti i diritti personali, ed eguaglianza dei diritti politici fondamentali ... » [36]. *Aequa libertas*, therefore, was incompatible with monarchy and possible only in a republic [37]. This does not mean to imply that the term *libertas* had only one meaning in the late Republican period. Men have always exploited the term for their own purposes, cloaking selfish motives with the appeal to liberty. Yet there can be no doubt that the republican definition of *libertas* was at least one of the various meanings and a fundamental one for the period.

The Middle Ages with their monarchical orientation were more directly the heirs of the Roman Empire than of the Republican period, yet the popularity of Cicero, Lucan and Livy kept the symbols and something of the language of republican liberty in circulation. When in 1207 a Northern Italian notary attempted to lend dignity to the manumission of serfs on a particular estate, he put into the mouth of the lord a preamble which at first glance seems to be a reappearance of the concept of *aequa libertas*:

Since Rome, which reigned once as lord and head of the whole world, grew greatly because of three things, that is, equity, justice and liberty, without which no land is able to grow strong nor any mature man able long to live, I, Guido Medici, considering that the condition of the said castle, of the lords and of the *fideles* who dwell there has gone from good to bad and from bad to worse on account of inequity and injustice and servitude and that the castle has now

---

[35] *De officiis*, I. 124, quoted from Wirszubski, p. 24.
[36] Wirszubski, p. 28.
[37] *Ibid.*, pp. 12-14.

been reduced to almost nothing, for the convenience of the aforesaid lords and *fideles* and of the whole castle mentioned above, wish to provide that the situation might improve [38].

The provisions which follow are a disappointment to our expectation. The specific terms of the charter, setting down the rights and duties of the former serfs vis-a-vis their old master had little to do with the opening paragraphs of the act. Yet for the notary there must have been some dim awareness of a connection between the basic terminology used by ancient Romans to describe their glorious freedom and the insignificant act of manumission of serfs he was called upon to rogate.

Something of this same confused memory is reflected in the eloquent praise of liberty found in John of Salisbury's *Policraticus*, VII, 25 [39]. This twelfth-century work, one of the most influential political and moral texts of the Middle Ages, exhibits how in the medieval climate the notion of republican liberty could be distorted beyond recognition. The author began with a celebration of liberty as freedom to reprehend vice. Subsequently, the intimate link between virtue and liberty was established:

because the highest good in life consists in virtue, which alone casts down the heavy and hateful yoke of servitude, the philosophers thought that, if the situation required, one should be prepared to die for virtue, which is the sole cause of living. But virtue does not flourish perfectly without liberty and the loss of liberty is a manifestation that one does not have perfect virtue [40].

---

[38] The passage is found in G. Salvemini, *Studi Storici* (Florence, 1901), p. 3: « Cum Roma, totius que quondam domina et mundi extitit capud, hiis tribus: equitate videlicet, iustitia et libertate multum inoleverit, sine quibus aliqua terra nedum adolere verum etiam adulta diu stare non potest, michi Guidoni Medico consideranti factum Arcis dicte et dominorum et fidelium, qui in ea commorantur, de bono in malo et de malo in peius propter inequitatem et injustitiam et servitutem deduci et ad nichilum fere iam redigi, pro commoditate tam supradictorum dominorum quam fidelium ac etiam totius Arcis pretaxate, quod melius esse placuerit providere ... ».

[39] *Policratici sive De Nugis Curialium*, ed. Clemens C. I. Webb (Oxford, 1909), II, 705 c-709 b.

[40] *Ibid.*, 705 c-d: « ... quia summum bonum in vita constat esse virtutem et quae sola grave et odiosum servitutis excutit iugum, pro virtute, quae singularis vivendi causa est, moriendum, si necessitas ingruit, philosophi

As John proceeded it seems clear that he was speaking of the freedom of the soul from vice: « Although servitude of the person sometimes seems more miserable, the servitude of vice is always more so. What, therefore, is more desirable than liberty? » Yet the first two examples offered as proof of the value of liberty were the actions of Brutus and Cato. Cato took his own life « that he not see Caesar rule » while Brutus caused a civil war « that he might deliver the city from servitude ». After a third example, the suicide of the captured Teutonic women who preferred death to slavery, the remainder of the chapter (about four-fifths of the whole) was devoted to listing one instance after the other of liberty of freedom of speech.

The intimate relationship existing between liberty and virtue, tyranny and moral corruption, was often expressed by authors of the thirteenth century [41]. But the observation was usually worked into a fairly standard treatment of good versus bad constitutions where the three good constitutional forms, monarchy, aristocracy and *politia*, were viewed as fostering the virtue of the members of the community and the three degenerate forms, tyranny, oligarchy and democracy, were presented as encouraging vice. What distinguished a good government from a bad one was not the particular constitutional form but rather whether the regime served the common good [42]. Although all theorists of this century regarded monarchy as generally the best constitution, monarchy's superiority to popular or aristocratic government was judged only relative.

The essential characteristic of tyranny for the Middle Ages was rule against right reason; the utilization of the *res publica* for the benefit of the private individual. Even though by the last half of the thirteenth century theologians like St. Thomas were beginning to distinguish between a tyranny rising from

---

censuerunt. At haec perfecte sine libertate non provenit, libertatisque dispendium perfectam convincit non adesse virtutem ».

[41] St. Thomas, *De regimine principum ad regem Cypri*, I . 3; Jacopo da Varagine, *Chronica civitatis Januensis*, ed. G. Monleone (« Fonti per la storia d'Italia, Rome, 1941, 85), II, 122-3. The same relationship between freedom and virtue or power is behind the preamble to the manumission of serfs above (n. 38) and the Florentine *provvisione* of 1329 below (n. 50).

[42] St. Thomas, *op. cit.*, I, 1; Aegidius Colonna, *De regimine principum*, III, 2 . 2; Jacopo da Varagine, *op. cit.*, II, 117.

misuse of authority originally legitimate and tyranny as a product of usurpation of power [43], nevertheless, at the basis of the distinction lay the universal medieval abhorrence of a government which ruled against law. Bartolus' application of the term 'tyrannia' not merely to the corrupt government of one but to all three degenerate forms merely made explicit an attitude to the classification of constitutions which had been operative in the discussions of political theorists for centuries [44].

It is essential to understand the medieval abhorrence of tyranny and the universally-held notion of a fundamental division between governments of law and tyranny in order to comprehend, at least in part, the inability of the flourishing republican communes of Northern and Central Italy to articulate clearly a republican concept of *libertas*. Contrasting as they invariably did *libertas populica* or *libertà del comune* with *tyrannia* and *signoria*, the communes were drawn to view the contrast in traditional terms of an opposition between good and bad government. Given these categories, they had no further motive for defining more clearly what was meant by the *libertas* which was threatened. 'Popular' liberty, consequently, lost its identity within the larger categorization of 'good government'. What complicated the problem of articulation even further was that, because the two were in fact so intimately related, the *libertas* of the popular constitution was usually confused with

---

[43] St. Thomas, *In sec. libr. Sent.*, dist. XLIV, q. 1, art. 2. Ercole (*Da Bartolo all'Althusio*, p. 300) cites Thomas' distinction only to dismiss it; for Ercole (*Ibid.*, p. 301) the distinction in Thomas is not clear and in the end is reducible to the traditional concept of tyranny *ad usum*. He would like to give Bartolus the credit for making the distinction. Although this interpretation does help to justify Ercole' claim of originality for Bartolus, in my opinion it distorts Thomas' meaning. That Thomas understood by tyranny *quantum ad modum adquirendi* a tyranny resulting from usurpation of power is obvious from his illustration of this category: he cited Caesar who destroyed the liberty of Rome « per violentiam » (Dist. XLIV, q. 2, art. 2, Ad quintum dicendum). This *Distinctio*, incidentally, becomes a *locus classicus* for an analysis of tyranny in late thirteenth-and early fourteenth-century comments on Lombard. Bartolus seems to have been the first civil lawyer, however, to utilize this distinction in a legal treatise.

[44] Bartolus, *De civitate*, I, 4; see, Ercole, *Da Bartolo*, p. 273-4. Aegidius clearly conceived of bad popular rule as tyrannical: a government is called a democracy if the people « non intendit bonum omnium secundum suum statum sed vult tirannizare et opprimere divites » (*De regimine*, III, II. 2).

the *libertas* or independent existence of the commune and it was difficult to isolate the former for analysis.

In speaking of the political mentality of Trecento Florentines, who were the chief defenders of communal liberty in Italy in this period, one historian recently wrote of their meaning of *libertas*:

> In contemporary Florentine usage, it ranged from political independence to republican self-government. As far as Florence and the other free Tuscan republics were concerned, the two coincided, for here political immunity went hand in hand with communal self-government. The full liberties of a free and independent city necessarily included the right to choose its own form of government and if independent government and freedom, ' than which nothing is more precious and more acceptable to mortal beings ' (A. S. F., Signoria, I Canc., *Missive* XI, 49 v), was desirable from outside powers, so was liberty at home [45].

Judging from the ambiguity of most of the texts used to support this statement, however, it is doubtful that the Florentines themselves were as conscious of the distinctions within the word *libertas* as is the modern reader. One of the most recurrent expressions in the public letters of the Florentine Republic in the pre-1370 period was « libertà, popolo e Guelfo » [46] yet it would be difficult to find an explanation of the terminology in the documents. Matteo Villani came closest to defining the phrase when he wrote of Guelfism as the « fondamento e rocca ferma e stabile della libertà d'Italia, e contraria a tutte le tirannie », but neither the expressions « libertà d'Italia » nor « tutte le tirannie » are very helpful for an understanding of popular liberty [47]. In the same way, when Florentines declared in the words of the *Digest* that « libertas inaestimabilis res est » (Dig. 50. 17, 106) or referred to the sacrifice of Cato and other Roman heroes on behalf of *libertas*, the word was almost always employed in an

---

[45] N. Rubinstein, « Florence and the Despots: Some Aspects of Florentine Diplomacy in the Fourteenth Century », *Transactions of the Royal Historical Society*, ser. V, 2 (1952), 29-30. The author gives a large selection of texts from both private and public documents of the Trecento.

[46] See my article, « A Note on Guelfism in Late Medieval Florence », *Nuova Rivista Storica*, 53 (1969), 136, n. 9.

[47] M. Villani, *Cronica*, VIII, 24.

imprecise way. For instance, Dante's praise of Cato as « vere libertatis auctor » in the *De monarchia* II, 5, when read in the context of the whole chapter, becomes more a praise of the ancient Roman as the defender of civil rather than political liberty [48].

I do not wish to imply that many cryptic and ambiguous statements of Florentines in defense of *libertas* were not motivated by republican fervor. My point, rather, is that the practical republican experience had to be filtered through intellectual traditions which usually distorted its articulation. There are a few instances in the *Missive*, the foreign correspondence of the State, where the Florentines demonstrated some awareness of the peculiar nature of republican government: at points they stressed the common ties which prevailed between their republic and neighboring communes arising from the similarity of constitutions. They were aware of the slowness with which popular governments must act when compared with regimes ruled by one man [49]. In one case, after the death of the Duke of Calabria, when Florence once again gained the power to rule herself, a *provvisione* passed by the Councils of the Republic even contrasted monarchy and *libertas*, a basic distinction for the republican conception of the term: « Since liberty, from which is derived each one's power to do what he will, is said to be a celestial gift surpassing the treasures of this earth so that justice, the most perfect virtue, flourishes in the city where it prevails ... it has been provided that the city, the *contado* and the district of Florence is not able nor ought to be subjected in perpetuity ... to any individual ... » [50]. Although the nature of this

---

[48] *Monarchia*, ed. G. Vinay (Florence, 1950), pp. 140-6. The example of Cato was utilized in this chapter to prove two things: « quorum unum est quod quicunque bonum rei publice intendit finem iuris intendit; aliud est quod Romanus populus subiciendo sibi orbem bonum publicum intendit » (p. 142). While the treatment is ambiguous, it seems that Caesar was resisted by Cato because he broke the law and threatened to reduce free men to slaves. The editor of the text writes: « Se proprio occorresse specificare, direi che qui D. pensa essenzialmente alla libertà civile e insiste ... che il cittadino rappresenta per il governante non un mezzo ma un fine » (p. 140, n. 23).

[49] A. S. F., Signoria, I Cancell., *Missive*, XI, 70 v and 117 r.

[50] A. S. F., *Provv.* 25, 51 v-52 r; quoted in N. Rubinstein, « Florentine Constitutionalism and Medici Ascendancy in the Fifteenth Century » in *Florentine Studies* (London, 1968), p. 450, n. 1: «Cum libertas celeste bonum

libertas was not specifically presented as political (« tribuatur unicuique quod velit fatiendi potestas »), the position that any one-man rule was in contrast with such freedom definitely suggests that the authors of this *provvisione* were thinking of *libertas* in some republican sense.

It would be difficult, however, amidst the thousands of references to *libertas* in the public documents of Florence before the 1370's to find another expression approaching the force of this statement of 1329. Perhaps Matteo Villani came closest to the republican sentiments of the *provvisione* when, after a very ordinary statement on Florence's Roman heritage of freedom and her traditional hatred of tyranny, he wrote of Rome's modern descendants: « zelanti di non sostenere quella a tirannia, molte volte per diversi e lunghi tempi apparvono contradi all'imperiale suggezione, intanto che non si poteva in questi popoli sostenere senza sospetto, senza pericolo e senza infamia il raccontamento dell'imperiale nome » [51]. In expressing the Florentine hatred for the « imperiale nome » in general, Villani was in effect making a blanket condemnation of the imperial office as tyranny: the specific acts of individual emperors do not seem to be in question, a factor which would limit the extent of the criticism. But Villani did nothing to develop this idea here or elsewhere.

It is interesting that this republican passage occurs in connection with Villani's reference to Florence's Roman heritage, because the clearest instance of a republican attitude I have been able to find during the period before the 1370's outside of Florence arose in connection with an investigation of the political history of Rome. Elsewhere I have tried to show that the frequent anti-Caesarist remarks in medieval political tracts should not be interpreted as reflecting a commitment to a republican interpretation of Roman history. First of all, if the corpus of a particular writer is examined, it usually appears that he was genuinely ambivalent in regard to the Roman dictator. Secondly,

---

dicatur orbis opes preteriens, et ex ea tribuatur unicuique quod velit fatiendi potestas, ex qua iustitia virtutum perfectissima viget in civitate in qua existit ... provisum ... fuit, quod civitas comitatus et districtus Florentie non possit nec debeat imperpetuum summitti ... alicui persone ... ».

[51] M. Villani, III, 1; see Rubinstein, « Florence and the Despots », p. 31.

almost without exception the criticisms of Caesar were personal and did not lead to a general critique of the institution of the Emperors. The few adverse remarks by Petrarch and Ptolemy of Lucca on imperial government are too vague to be significant [52].

The only statement I have so far found in medieval literature which is unmistakably republican in its criticism of the Emperors as a group and which provides a rationale for the putative superiority of republicanism over monarchy occurs in St. Thomas' *De regimine principum*, I, iv. Relating how the Romans drove out their early kings, Thomas quoted Sallust's observation: « It is almost incredible if we recall how speedily the Roman State grew, when once it had achieved its liberty ». In explanation of this the scholastic theologian wrote:

> For it often happens that men who are ruled by a monarch are slow to interest themselves in the common welfare; since they are of opinion that whatever they do for the common good will in no way benefit themselves, but only serve to enrich whoever appears to control the public interest. But if there is no one person with power over the common interest, they go about the corporate task as though it were their own business and not merely profitable to another [53].

He then applied this principle to the Roman state and concluded that when Rome fell under the power of the Emperors, most of whom were tyrants, it was ultimately reduced to nothing.

In all probability in his conception of the psychological importance of self-government St. Thomas was drawing somewhat on the traditional medieval notion that *aequitas*, *libertas* and *justitia* cause a state to flourish. The manumission charter of 1207, however, in its application of this terminology to the freeing of serfs, manifested the gap which lay between that tradition and its Roman Republican antecedents. In his own interpretation of Roman political events in this passage, on the other hand,

---

[52] See my forthcoming article, « The ' De Tyranno ' and Coluccio Salutati's View of Politics and Roman History », *Nuova Rivista Storica*, 53 (1969). For Petrarch and Ptolemy of Lucca see discussion in H. Baron, *The Crisis of the Early Italian Renaissance*, 2nd ed. (Princeton, 1966), pp. 54 ff.

[53] The translation is from J. G. Dawson, *Aquinas, Selected Political Writings* (Oxford, 1948), p. 21.

Thomas, probably under the influence of his understanding of Aristotle's remarks on political participation [54], brought the conception back to its republican significance. Yet the impact of this observation in an authoritative book was in its turn distorted by the role which it played in the development of St. Thomas' general analysis. He used this historical discussion precisely to show that a government of many fell under the power of a tyrant more easily than did a government ruled by one. The republican interpretation of Roman history, therefore, was buried in a series of arguments designed to prove the superiority of monarchy.

The first Italian and perhaps the first European to integrate this adverse critique of imperial Rome into an assault on the institution of monarchy *per se* was the chancellor of Florence, Coluccio Salutati (1331-1406). Reading certain works by this humanist, one would judge that the Florentine people had at last come to analyze their political sentiments. Already before assuming the post as chancellor, Salutati had indicated an interest in defining the character of popular liberty. In a preamble to a document appointing a commission to rewrite the statutes of Lucca in 1370, Salutati, then chancellor of that commune, explained the reasons behind the revision of the statutes after years of domination by internal and external tyrants [55]. After the destruction of « aurea libertas » in the city « ceperunt leges corrumpi et non pro utilitate populica sed ad quorundam odium pro statuentium voluntate legum approbatarum ordinamenta refigi ». Laws were made during these decades not « ut decuit equabilitate civili sed tirannorum cupidine ». Now with liberty restored, the people of Lucca must be governed « ad equitatem civicam » so that « incipiat oppressus quondam populus equabilitate legum pari conditione vivere et antiqui raptores addiscant

---

[54] In his argument for mixed government, *Sum. Theo.*, I^{a} II^{ae} 105, 1, *ad Resp.*, Thomas wrote: « Respondeo dicendum quod circa bonam ordinationem principum in aliqua civitate vel gente, duo sunt attendenda. Quorum unum est ut omnes aliquam partem habeant in principatu: per hoc enim conservatur pax populi, et omnes talem ordinationem amant et custodiunt, ut dicitur in II *Polit.* (cap. 1, vel 2) ». It would appear that this idea lay behind his remarks on Roman history in the *De regimine principum*.

[55] For the text of this preamble, see my « Coluccio Salutati, Citizen of Lucca (1370-2) », in *Traditio*, 25 (1969), Appendix 2.

ab iniuria resilere ». Although here characterizing the liberty of the Lucchesi as based on uniformity of law and an equal civil status, Salutati manifested no need to go further than this, to generalization and contrast.

Five years later Salutati, as chancellor of Florence and chief propagandist for the Florentine cause, exhibited a similar tendency to give details about the nature and history of republican *libertas* but this time with definite polemical purposes in mind. At times in the *Missive* written for the war government he moved out of the traditional framework of good government versus tyranny to a contrast of popular rule with monarchy. In a message written to the Bolognese in July 1376, after recalling the relationship between virtue and liberty and how the first Brutus had been forced to dissemble until he was ready to expel Tarquin, Salutati made a general attack on the institution of one-man rule: kings were set up for the punishment of men so that « whoever considers himself worthy of being a lord confesses himself to be guilty of the greatest crimes, since it is well-known that lords were to be a punishment not an ornament for cities and the people's burden not their honor » [56]. In November 1377 in a letter to the Romans Salutati, writing in the name of the Otto di Balia, emphasized that ancient Rome was the common ancestor of both Florence and the modern Roman commune. The ancient Romans created their empire fighting for their own liberty and that of their allies. In words which echoed those of Aquinas, Salutati granted that, while some of the emperors had outstanding qualities, under imperial government « vastitatem recepit ytalia et illud imperii culmen effluxit » [57]. Then, focusing on the rela-

---

[56] The following discussion of Salutati's political thought is a summary of some of the conclusions of my article « The ' De Tyranno ' »; the texts referred to here are published in the original in that study.

[57] Aquinas wrote of the Emperors: « Horum autem quidam more regio bonum commune fideliter procuraverunt, per quorum studium romana respublica et aucta et conservata est. Plurimi vero eorum in subditos quidem tyranni, ad hostes vero effecti desides et imbecilles, romanam rempublicam ad nihilum redegerunt » (*De regimine*, I, 4). Salutati in this letter to the Romans (Ricc. 786, 139 r) spoke in a similar way: « Sublata autem sub cesaribus libertate — extollant quicumque volunt laudibus cesarem et usque ad divinitatis honores subliment augustum ... et ceteros quibus volunt lau-

tionship between liberty and greatness, he concluded this section: « Thus the desire for liberty alone brought forth the empire, the glory and all the dignity of the Roman people ». Earlier the same year the Florentine Chancellor in a letter to Bologna developed his notion of « equabilitas » expressed previously at Lucca by defining it as an intrinsic characteristic of states ruled by artisans and merchants. Unlike the nobles, these classes did not boast of their ancestors' achievements nor had they many dependents and extensive family connections to exalt their authority. The middle classes, on the contrary, « ceding power to one another by turns, command when they exercise public office and, when they are private citizens, know how to obey the commands of others without arrogance » [58].

Within the compass of these three letters, consequently, Salutati expressed some essential characteristics defining republican *libertas*. He had taken the traditional idea of the link between virtue and liberty and explicitly presented that liberty as republican. Government of one *per se* was incompatible with true freedom. The traditional contrast between a tyrannical 'government' and a government of liberty where law ruled was, consequently, transformed into the opposition of monarchy to liberty. The criticism of the Roman Emperors, unlike that in Aquinas' *De regimine*, was directly linked to contemporary politics and was used to prove the evils of a government of one man. The antagonism between the feudal hierarchical so-

---

dibus efferant — in ipsorum manibus certe vastitatem recepit ytalia et illud imperii culmen effluxit ». Bruni's general condemnation of the Emperors is modified by a similar concession that some were capable [*Laudatio Florentinae Urbis*, ed. H. Baron (*From Petrarch to Leonardo Bruni*, Chicago, 1968), p. 247].

[58] Medieval commentators on Aristotle's *Politics*, IV, 11 were well aware of the Greek philosopher's position that « the political community administered by the middle class is the best ». Peter of Auvergne in his continuation of Thomas' commentary on the *Politics* (Thomas Aquinas, *In IV libros Politicorum expositio*, IV, lectio X) and Guido Vernani in his analysis of this passage [*Summa librorum Ethicorum, Economicorum et Politicorum*, Bibl. Marciana, Lat. VI, 94 (2492), 103 v] were particularly detailed in their justification of Aristotle's remark. Both Aegidius Colonna (*De regimine principum*, III, 34) and Giovanni da Legnano (*De juribus ecclesiae*, 30 v.b-31 r.a) in their political works repeated Aristotle's emphasis on a large middle class. To my knowledge, however, Salutati was the first to use the peculiar qualities of this group in support of republican government.

ciety and that of the free commune, moreover, was distinctly presented: republican liberty required equality and only the artisan and merchant classes were fitted for this.

Nevertheless, if Giovanni da Legnano in his search for a possible meaning of the phrase « Long live the people and liberty » neglected to analyze the definition of *libertas* which emerged from these public letters of the Florentine Republic, it is unlikely that he did so purposely. Coluccio Salutati himself, the leading intellectual among the anti-papal forces, did not seem to realize the incompatibility of the sense of *libertas* found in these few letters with the more traditional meanings of the term. Whereas a handful of *Missive* celebrated a *libertas* which was antagonistic to any monarchical government, in literally hundreds of others the conflict between the Church and the communes was presented simply as a battle between servitude and liberty. Depending on the letter, it is often possible to interpret *libertas* as referring either to communal autonomy or to the civil freedom of the individual. In Salutati's ordinary descriptions of the evils of tyranny, there was nothing which a devoted monarchist could not have written. His enumerations of the horrors of tyrannical rule were quite traditional except that they were expressed with more eloquence. It is unlikely, therefore, that Salutati himself understood the shout of *libertas* with all its republican implications. For much of the time his mind was still heavily under the influence of the traditional division between law and tyranny as the basic criterion of good and bad government. While disagreeing with Giovanni's specific interpretation of the motive behind the shout, Salutati would probably not have objected to the canonist's basic categorization of the diverse meanings of *libertas* itself.

Nor did Salutati develop his notion of republicanism in subsequent years after the war. He never seemed aware of the need to create distinctions in order to give specific identity to a collection of observations regarding the history and nature of republican government [59]. A large part of the reason behind

[59] Scholars who attempt to interpret the inconsistencies of Salutati's political statements as essentially manifestations of his ability as an orator to say the appropriate thing in the specific situation ascribe to him a clarity of mind regarding various political positions which he did not possess.

his failure to forge a new concept was probably that he was himself a republican only in a limited sense. Like Bartolus, Salutati seems to have considered the appropriateness of constitutional forms in terms of the size of the territory to be governed [60]. The republican form was appropriate for the *civitas* and the *provincia* while the regal constitution was suitable for the Empire. Although he often expressed a deep love of popular government, one should be conscious of this hierarchical conception as a limiting factor. Any government where law prevailed was a legitimate government, a government of liberty; where law does not rule there was tyranny. In his *Invectiva contra Antonium Luschum*, written in the last part of his life, Salutati defined law as « dulce frenum libertatis ». The French, for example, were a free people according to Salutati because the French king enjoyed *regia libertas*, i. e., autonomy, and the free status of French subjects was compatible with the exercise of their king's regal authority. Salutati insisted repeatedly in public and private letters on the distinction between a king and a tyrant.

If we look for the birth of the republican concept of liberty, Salutati is not its author. It is rather to his disciple, Leonardo Bruni, that this credit is due. While almost every fundamental notion regarding republican *libertas* mentioned by Bruni could be found already in the works of the older man, nevertheless, the singularity of Bruni was that he was consciously aware of developing a specific conception of the term. Thus, he achieved a synthesis and a consistency which his teacher did not. Already with the *Laudatio Urbis Florentinae* of 1403/4, at the very beginning of his scholarly career, Bruni had in mind the outlines of an idea of political *libertas* conceived in both constitutional and historical terms which he would develop in numerous works up to the end of his life [61]. The example of the achievements of the Florentine Republic served him repeatedly as a demonstration of what men living in political freedom could accomplish.

---

[60] For Salutati's idea see my « The 'De Tyranno' »; for Bartolus, *De civitate*, l. X.

[61] For a brief analysis of Bruni's republicanism, see N. Rubinstein, « Florentine Constitutionalism », pp. 444 ff. My summary here is based on these pages. The importance of Leonardo Bruni for the development of the republican ideal was first pointed out in the writings of Hans Baron.

For Bruni equality before the law was necessary for true liberty and this was attainable only in a republic. For the proper functioning of a popular state no man should have pre-eminence; « paritas mediocritasque » must prevail among citizens. Once the citizen had the hope of attaining public office and a career was open to his talents, he would be encouraged to develop his abilities to the fullest extent. This did not mean, however, that every resident of Florence was a citizen. Because of the dangers of mob rule or of magnate tyranny, the social classes at the top and bottom of the society had to be excluded from the government. Republican government was an affair of the middle classes.

Bruni's republicanism found its justification, moreover, not only in terms of present-day governments. The author drew for proof of his contentions on the glorious history of the ancient Roman Republic as well. Under the consuls Rome grew to be mistress of the world. Her citizens were virtuous; her government just. With the coming of the Emperors, although some had great qualities, Rome declined and was conquered by other peoples.

As has just been said, none of these individual thoughts was new. But through Bruni's perception of the central notion of republican liberty and the brilliance of his exposition he gave to the popular constitutional form an identity which it had not had in the Middle Ages. Bruni provided a definition by which Florentines could conceptualize what they had long felt to be the distinctive nature of their political way of life. In one sense, his achievement was to separate out the strains of the ancient Roman republican heritage which had been lost in the rich confusion of meanings involved in *libertas* and to recombine the elements of that heritage of ideas into a unified form. In contrast to the wavering, ambiguous usage of Trecento Florentine writers, the works of Bruni and of those he influenced like Cino Rinuccini, Goro Dati and Matteo Palmieri reveal a well-delineated concept of republican liberty [62].

---

[62] While it is possible that some parts of Rinuccini's *Risponsiva* could have been written in 1397, it is certain that others belong to the period after 1406 and still others were probably written after 1408. It is, therefore, fairly safe to assume that the work reflects a knowledge of Bruni's *Laudatio.* See my, « Cino Rinuccini's ' Risponsiva alla Invettiva di messer Antonio Lusco ' », *Renaissance Quarterly*, 1970, pp. 133-49.

NEAL W. GILBERT

THE EARLY ITALIAN HUMANISTS AND DISPUTATION

Seldom has any question been raised about the central aim of the dialogues that Leonardo Bruni addressed to his friend and former classmate, Pier Paolo Vergerio, although serious doubts have been expressed about the date of the dialogues' composition and about the relation of the two dialogues to one another. Literary historians, who have been the most numerous readers of Bruni's text, have usually assumed that Bruni wished to vindicate the literary reputation of the three great Florentine poets and to establish that Dante, Petrarch, and Boccaccio deserve equal consideration with the classics. They have been particularly intrigued by the attitude displayed in the first day's dialogue by Niccolo Niccoli toward the recent poets. Niccoli's bitter attack on the literary reputation of the three Florentines, with its suggestion that Dante's poetry should be « separated from the councils of the learned and left to the wool-weavers and bakers », is so colorful and so outrageous that we tend to remember it long after we have forgotten Niccoli's retractation in the second dialogue. Together with Vespasiano da Bisticci's description of Niccolo's dining habits, this passage has practically created, one might say, the stereotype of the haughty humanist, scorning vernacular literature and the judgments of the ordinary crowd. No matter that Niccolo later spells out in considerable detail his attachment to the literary work of the three poets: we still cannot forget the piquant details of the first day's attack. Perhaps Bruni's readers have also been influenced subconsciously by the words of Niccolo: « I am going to tell you freely what I feel: I beg of you, however, not to spread this around ». As in daily life, we feel an irresistible urge to absorb what follows (the attack on the poets) and to divulge it immediately to our closest acquaintances — in other words, to give his opinion the widest possible diffusion while it is still newsworthy.

For a literary historian, the evaluation of the three Florentine poets is and must remain the most interesting feature of the dialogues. However, when an historian of philosophy reads them, he is more apt to be struck by a topic that is introduced by Coluccio Salutati and presented with considerable warmth of feeling: namely, the utility of *disputation*. If we come to Bruni's dialogues from the reading of later humanists, and particularly northern humanists such as Erasmus, we are shocked to find the leader of Florentine humanism putting in a passionate plea for disputation. Just as surprised are we to find Niccolo, the solitary student who is apparently the prime target for Salutati's charge that the younger men neglect disputation, agreeing wholeheartedly that « nothing can easily be found that contributes more *to our studies* than disputation » [1]. Obviously either our image of the humanists or our image of disputation needs to be altered to fit the Italian scene. As a matter of fact, both images require revision. For the intellectual situation in Italy at the beginning of the fifteenth century differs significantly from the conditions that prevailed later at the University of Paris when Erasmus and Vives developed their lifelong aversion for dialectic. Bruni's dialogues contain a surprising number of clues that can lead us to a better understanding of the attitude of Italian humanists toward dialectic and toward its applications. Once we begin to look through the dialogues for passages that have a bearing on logic or disputation, we find them almost everywhere, but particularly frequent in the first day's discussions. We may even begin to suspect that the initial concern of these talks in Florence, set in the year 1401, was to promote the cause of serious yet relatively informal disputation. And it begins to look as if the issue of the *tres vates* has been introduced simply as an illustration of the sort of discussion Bruni was concerned to promote. To be more precise, the three poets enter the discussion as a footnote, one might say, to Salutati's declaration that in all his life he had found nothing more enjoyable and worth seeking out than « to meet if at all possible *with learned men*, to expound to them things that I have read and thought about and on which I had misgivings, and to seek their judgment

[1] I shall cite Bruni's dialogues from the most accessible edition, that of Eugenio Garin, in *Prosatori Latini del Quattrocento* (Milan-Naples, [1952]), of which « Ad Petrum Paulum Histrum Dialogus » occupies pp. 44-99. This passage occurs at p. 52: « Neque enim facile reperiri posset, ut credo, quod ad studia nostra plus quam disputatio conferat ».

in these matters »[2]. Niccolo, as we have already remarked, has no quarrel whatever with Coluccio's thesis concerning the utility of disputation: in fact, he reinforces it by insisting that to participate profitably in such discussions one must have a certain amount of technical expertise and competence. Niccolo's only objection is that there are not enough learned men around to engage in useful discussion. To explain the dearth of learned men, Niccolo offers two causes: (1) the faulty education of the times, and (2) the loss of classical texts. Salutati, while admitting that the « best arts » have suffered a certain decline[3], nevertheless maintains that singlehanded effort can overcome this obstacle. Nor is the loss of ancient books so great as to be fatal to intellectual development: there are, so Salutati argues, enough books of Cicero and Seneca to teach us all we need to know, or at least a great deal[4]. Niccolo has been quite careful to specify that it is not the quality of men's minds nor their will to learn that is responsible for the scarcity of learned men[5]. It is rather what Vives later was to call the « corruption of the arts », coupled with the irreparable loss of valuable texts from antiquity.

It seems to me quite likely that this theme — the corruption of the arts — formed the original reason for Bruni's directing these dialogues to Pier Paolo Vergerio. Professional education was a life's vocation for Vergerio, and for him this memento of support for training in useful disputation, from the mouth of an admired and respected friend such as Salutati, would have great personal significance. Vergerio had been a teacher of logic at the university of Bologna in 1388-89[6], and had probably also taught logic in Florence at an even earlier age.

---

[2] « ... in omni aetate atque vita nihil mihi gratius fuit, nihil quod aeque expeterem quam doctos homines, si modo potestas data sit, convenire, et quae legerim et quae agitaverim et de quibus ambigerem illis exponere, eorumque in his rebus percontari iudicium ». Bruni, p. 50.

[3] « Sunt enim optimae artes labem aliquam passae ... ». Bruni, p. 66.

[4] Bruni, p. 66.

[5] « Neque enim hominibus ingenia desunt, neque discendi voluntas ... ». Bruni, p. 60.

[6] Vergerio is undoubtedly the « Magister Petrus paulus » appointed « ad lecturam loyce » at Bologna in 1388-89; see U. Dallari, *I rotuli dei lettori legisti e artisti dello studio Bolognese dal 1384 al 1799* (Bologna, 1888), I, 7.

From Vergerio's year of teaching at Bologna we have an exchange of letters which concerns the teaching of logic. Vergerio, a young man of eighteen, writes to an older friend, Santo dei Pellegrini, and expresses the hope that Santo has been able to devote himself to the quiet reading of Cicero and Seneca, who will guide him in his pursuit of the *honestum*. By contrast, Vergerio describes his own life: « I spend day and night in garrulous debate », laboriously pursuing the *verum* [7]. The occurrence of the word « garrulous » immediately tells us that we are dealing with a humanistically-inclined writer who is describing Scholastic disputation. In the humanist vocabulary, Scholastic arguments are always « garrulous » and unproductive. Yet this does not mean that the youthful Vergerio is ready to eliminate dialectic from the curriculum. In his own teaching, he hopes to treat logic as a means rather than as an end in itself, and to make it useful to the orator, the physicist, and even the moral philosopher [8]. Twelve years later, after leaving Florence and going to Padua, Vergerio still held to this ideal of a utilitarian logic, or *ratio disputandi*, which could « easily open the way to all sorts of doctrine » [9]. The subject of disputation, in other

---

[7] « ... ego vero longe a studiis tuis absens, longe otio tuo dispar, noctem diemque garrula disceptatione consumo, texo laqueos, complico sinus, quibus argutum possim interceptare sophistam, miros insuper nature effectus studiosus inquiro ... ». *Epistolario di Pier Paolo Vergerio* (Rome, 1934), ed. L. Smith, p. 13, from Bologna, Feb. 16, 1389.

[8] Santo dei Pellegrini has complimented Vergerio on his style and expressed surprise that he could have retained such a good Latin while surrounded by dialectical battles, and Vergerio replies: « Miraris et tu, mee conditionis non inscius, quomodo garulis sophismatibus circumsessus tantum oratoris gradum scandere et, quod plus dicis, retinere valuerim. Quantus hic gradus sit et quam altus, tu videris, sed tamen non despero, quod, si huic studio intentum me dedero, satis abunde proficiam. Logice quidem discipline, quam aliis trado, ita insisto ut eam michi viam ad alias statuam et non finem, sed plerunque oratorie, cuius eadem ratio est, plerunque etiam et multo studiosius philosophie, non solum ei que naturam rerum ostendit, sed ei quoque in qua omnis recta ratio vivendi consistit ». Vergerio, *Epistolario*, p. 30.

[9] « Proxime huic disputandi ratio adhibenda est, per quam in una quaque re quid verum falsumve sit, facile argumentando quaerimus. Ea, cum sit discendi scientia, sciendique disciplina, ad omne doctrinarum genus viam facile aperit ». Vergerio, « De ingenuis moribus et liberalibus studiis adulescentiae », in *Il pensiero pedagogico dello Umanesimo*, ed. E. Garin (Florence,

words, was one on which Vergerio held firm and lasting convictions. No doubt Bruni knew that this was a topic in which Vergerio would have been very much interested, and this explains why a report of a discussion on the utility of disputation would have been sent to Vergerio at Padua. Bruni, in the prologue to the dialogues, has remarked that hardly a day goes by when Vergerio's absence from Florence is not felt, and especially so on occasions such as one recently when this subject came up. Bruni says that he is going to give Vergerio a description of this *disputation* — serving notice that the discussions are themselves to be regarded as disputations.

Salutati remarks at the outset that he is glad to see Niccoli, Bruni, and Roberto Rossi come out of their rooms and engage in a disputation. Salutati is careful to spell out several times what he means by the word *disputatio*; it is clear that he means to distinguish it from prevailing practices of some sort (it will not be long before Niccoli describes them in the most unflattering terms). « For by the gods what is there that is more helpful for learning about and discussing subtle matters than disputation, where a subject is put in our midst so that many eyes can inspect it in such a way that nothing can be glossed over, nothing be hidden, nothing can escape the regard of all present? » [10]. Salutati goes on to spell out the effects of disputation: it serves to revive spirits flagging from long and solitary study and reading, and to spur us on to more reading and study, whether we win or lose [11]. Salutati says that he had personally gained much benefit from these « discussions or colloquies, which I call disputations », while he was a student at Bologna and later at Florence, where he had the opportunity of engaging the learned Augustinian hermit Luigi Marsili in disputation. When he was just a boy studying grammar at Bologna he used to ask questions of his masters and engage his fellow students in ar-

---

[1958]), p. 132. The last sentence is a variation of the standard medieval definition of dialectic as found, for example, in Peter of Spain.

[10] « Nam quid est, per deos immortales, quod ad res subtiles cognoscendas atque discutiendas plus valere possit quam disputatio, ubi rem in medio positam velut oculi plures undique speculantur, ut in ea nihil sit quod subterfugere, nihil quod latere, nihil quod valeat omnium frustrari intuitum? » Bruni, pp. 46-48.

[11] Bruni, p. 48.

gument[12]. He never gave up this practice; as a mature man, he still loved to make the trip across the Arno to the home of Luigi Marsili, using the more quiet latter half of the trip, from the bridge, to formulate the problem he wished to discuss[13]. Hence Salutati is anxious to urge the practice of disputation upon his « young » hearers (who, in the year in which Bruni sets the dialogues, would have been men in their thirties, with Niccoli the oldest). He recognizes their diligence and devotion to their studies, but finds the younger men lacking in this one respect: they neglect the « use and exercise of disputing »[14]. None of the younger men present denies this charge, and Niccolo even admits that he had heard the advice before, from Luigi Marsili and from Manuel Chrysoloras, although the Greek teacher had not expressed himself so forcefully as Salutati. « Not ours the fault, but that of the times », pleads Niccolo, who goes on to complain about the « perturbation of all disciplines »[15]. It goes without saying that Niccoli and the others are thinking of the « good arts » (including the liberal arts and philosophy (*omnium bonarum artium parens et cuius ex fontibus haec omnis nostra derivatur humanitas*), not of the useful arts or the fine arts. Dia-

---

[12] « ... cum puer adhuc Bononiae essem, ibique grammaticis operam darem, me solitum quotidie vel aequales lacessendo, vel magistros rogando, nullum tempus vacuum disputationis transisse ». Bruni, p. 48. Salutati, it will be recalled, had studied the notarial art at Bologna from 1346, as a young man in his teens.

[13] Bruni, p. 50. On the activity of Luigi Marsili, see Rudolph Arbesmann, O. S. A., *Der Augustinereremitenorden und der Beginn der humanistischen Bewegung* (Würzburg, 1965), pp. 73-119; see especially pp. 80-81, in which Luigi's informal discussion is contrasted with the scholastic disputations held later in the convent of Santo Spirito. Perhaps these disputations, which were publicly announced, were instituted as part of the reform of the *studium* requested by the Signoria of Florence in 1401: see the letter given by Wesselofsky, *Il Paradiso degli Alberti* (Bologna, 1867), I, 334.

[14] « .... in hoc uno tamen vos hebescere neque utilitati vestrae satis consulere video, quod disputandi usum exercitationemque negligitis: qua ego quidem re nescio an quicquam ad studia vestra reperiatur utilius ». Bruni, p. 46. Note the use of the phrase « ad studia vestra »; cf. the pasages cited in n. 1 above: « ad studia nostra ». Salutati obviously wishes to stress the point that dialectic and disputing must not be neglected in *Humanistic* studies.

[15] « Si vero in ea tempestate nati sumus, in qua tanta disciplinarum omnium perturbatio, tanta librorum iactura facta est, ut ne de minima quidem re absque summa impudentia loqui quisquam possit ... ». Bruni, p. 52.

lectic, of course, would enjoy a respectable place among the liberal arts. With regard to the current condition of these arts, we have three positions in this literary work: (1) they are in bad shape (Niccoli); (2) they have suffered a decline (Salutati); and (3) they have just begun to show signs of life in Florence (Bruni, in the prologue) [16]. Salutati and Bruni are not far apart in their positions, it would seem. But as a matter of fact, the divergence between them and Niccoli lies more in the level of competence he demands of the disputer, who will appear hopelessly inept if he does not have complete command of his subject matter, and a knowledge of « consequences, antecedents, causes, effects — in short, of anything that might have a bearing on the subject under discussion » [17]. Far from repudiating the usefulness of what we might call philosophical discussion, Niccolo endorses it and even sets such a high standard for performance that he despairs of successfully engaging in disputation. The background knowledge required for profitable disputation is so organically interrelated that one cannot know even a few things well without knowing many [18]. With regard to general philosophy, Niccolo's complaint is that instead of the fruitful rivalry of four schools such as antiquity witnessed we have what amounts to a monopoly by the self-professed « Aristotelians », who do not even know Aristotle's treatises well. In Niccolo's view — and here he makes a good point — the competition between the Stoics, Academics, Peripatetics, and Epicureans in Greece was profitable because a man who devoted himself to philosophy had to learn to defend his philosophical commitments against attack by members of the other schools. Niccolo observes that Cicero regarded Aristotle as a figure known only « to a very few » philosophers. If this was true in

---

[16] Bruni's position is stated in the prologue to Vergerio: « ... civitas haec florentissima est, tum etiam *optimarum artium* totiusque humanitatis, quae iam penitus extincta videbantur, hic semina quaedam remanserunt, quae quidem in diem crescunt, brevi tempore, ut credimus, lumen non parvum elatura ». Bruni, p. 44.

[17] « Itaque tenenda probe res est, de qua disputare velis; nec ea solum, sed consequentium, antecedentium, causarum, effectuum, omnium denique quae ad eam rem pertinent habenda cognitio ». Bruni, p. 52.

[18] « Omnia sunt inter se mira quadam coniunctione annexa, nec pauca sine multis bene scire quisquam potest ». Bruni, p. 52-54.

Cicero's time, when « every art and doctrine flourished », is it possible that anyone can really expect to know Aristotle well in this « shipwreck of all doctrines », this « penury of learned men? » [19].

The most shipwrecked doctrine of all turns out to be dialectic: « What about dialectic, which is the one art most necessary for disputing? Has it perhaps escaped the general disaster in this attack of ignorance, and achieved a flourishing kingdom? Not at all. For that barbarism that dwells beyond the ocean has launched an attack even on it. And good Lord, what people! Even their names horrify me: Farabrich, Buser, Occam, and other such names, which seem to me to have been taken from the legions of Rhadamanthes. And — leaving aside this joke — what is there, I ask you, Coluccio, in dialectic that has not been disfigured by British sophisms? What is there remaining of that old and true way of disputing that has not been set aside and turned into frivolity and ineptitude? » [20]. This is one of the long line of attacks on British Logicians, which began with Petrarch's letters to Thomas of Messina in the middle of the fourteenth century. We shall return to this topic in a moment, but let us complete the picture of disputation in Bruni's dialogues. When Niccolo ends his diatribe, Salutati points out that Niccolo has just demonstrated by his very speech that it is possible for a man to become good at disputing in these times. In other words Niccolo falsifies his own thesis in the very act of maintaining it. The paradox resembles the well-known Paradox of the Liar, in which Epimenides the Cretan says that he is lying. It is completely in character for Salutati to engage

[19] Bruni, pp. 56-58.

[20] « Quid autem de dialectica, qua una ars ad disputandum pernecessaria est? An ea florens regnum obtinet, neque hoc ignorantiae bello calamitatem ullam perpessa est? Minime vero. Nam etiam illa barbaria, quae trans oceanum habitat, in illam impetum fecit. At quae gentes, dii boni? Quorum etiam nomina perhorresco: Farabrich, Buser, Occam, aliique eiusmodi, qui omnes mihi videntur a Rhadamantis cohorte traxisse cognomina. Et quid est, Coluci, ut haec ioca omittam, quid est, inquam, in dialectica quod non britannicis sophismatibus conturbatum sit? Quid quod non ab illa vetere et vera disputandi via separatum et ad ineptias levitatesque traductum? » Bruni, pp. 58-60.

in this sort of half-serious dig at the school sophisms [21]. When Roberto Rossi objects that Salutati seems to have given away his thesis (the necessity for training in disputation), Coluccio replies that Niccolo presumably would have done even better if he had had the benefit of training in argument. Salutati then disposes of the complaint that the classical authors are lacking, and finally exhorts Niccolo to abandon his defeatist attitude. Niccolo has already admitted (p. 60) that Salutati was able, by his own effort, to rise above the mediocrity of the times and to achieve a wisdom and eloquence equal to or surpassing that of the ancients. Now Salutati returns the compliment and praises Niccolo's « diligence, alertness, and sharpness of mind » [22]. This takes care of the more obvious points of difference, but it leaves an unresolved issue, namely, the statement made by Niccoli to the effect that for a long time no one had achieved eminence in « these studies », that is, in logic, grammar, or rhetoric [23]. It is this statement that leads Salutati to ask, « Have you forgotten Dante, Petrarch, and Boccaccio? » As far as Coluccio is concerned there is no reason why these three men should not be ranked among the ancients by virtue of their « *humanitas* » [24]. The three Florentines are brought into the discussion because they are examples of pre-eminence in « these studies » (meaning, apparently, those that have just been discussed: the *artes sermocinales* together with philosophy). There follows the provocative assault of Niccoli upon the reputation of the *tres vates*, which fails to draw Salutati out. Perhaps this is an illustration of Coluccio's *gravitas*, for, like Socrates, he refuses to contend with an opponent who does not seriously hold the position he presents in debate. But even while putting

---

[21] For an example, see Salutati's letter to Poggio Bracciolini, from 1405, *Epistolario*, ed. F. Novati (Rome, 1905), IV, 126 ff. Salutati was clearly conversant with the trend of school logic in his time, where Petrarch always remained (deliberately) outside its pale.

[22] Bruni, p. 66.

[23] Niccoli: « Quid enim causae dicemus esse, Coluci, quod his tot iam annis nemo inventus sit, qui aliquam praestantiam in his rebus habuerit? » Bruni, p. 60. Since Salutati has rejected the two suggestions as to causes made by Niccolo — perturbation of the sciences, lack of books — it is up to him to offer a better explanation, or to reject the initial statement. The latter, of course, is what Coluccio chooses to do.

[24] Bruni, p. 68.

off this issue for a later time, Salutati expresses his own conviction that the three Florentines were « men adorned with many and the best arts » [25].

With this scene-setting in mind, we can see why the discussion of the three poets takes the form it does: it concentrates on their learning (*multarumque rerum scientia*) rather than on the two other requirements laid down by Niccoli for poets: creative imagination (*fingendi artem*) and elegance of speech (*oris elegantiam*) [26]. When the discussion is resumed, in Roberto Rossi's garden, it focuses on the learning of the Florentine poets. Whether the times of Dante and the other two were more conducive to study, whether the arts of logic, grammar, and rhetoric were in better shape in the previous century, whether the three poets engaged in more learned or illuminating disputation — none of these possible topics is directly debated. Instead we get a digression on the beautiful buildings of Florence (p. 76) and a piece of self-congratulation on the part of the author of the *Laudatio* of Florence before Niccolo begins his retractation. The dialogues seem now to have left their original topic for good, except for Niccolo's final discouraged statement: by comparison with the gifts and achievement of the three great poets, he feels more than ever incapable of competing with the ancients [27]. « ... When I consider the wisdom and elegance (of such ancients as Cicero, Pliny, Varro, and Livy), I, who recognize the limitations of my intellect, am so far from thinking that I can know anything, that not even the most gifted minds seem to be able to learn anything in these times ». Coluccio's preaching has had no effect, and Niccolo is left sunk in his inferiority complex. Has Salutati made a convert to the art of disputation? Hardly, it would seem. Yet even within the discussion of the three poets there are references to logic that deserve our attention.

As for Dante, Niccolo concedes that he may have read the *quodlibeta* of the friars, but does not believe that Dante had even

---

[25] « ... Ego quidem sic sentio, illos fuisse homines multis optimisque artibus ornatos dignosque eo nomine, quod tanto consensu omnium ipsis tributum est ». Bruni, p. 74.

[26] Bruni, p. 84.

[27] Bruni, p. 96.

touched the books of the pagans on which his art depends [28]. The *quodlibeta* were disputations on subjects of the students' choosing in the medieval university. Niccoli must be thinking of Dante's exposure to Scholastic disputations in written form, because he says « *lectitasse* », Dante « had read ». He seems to have in mind the *quaestiones* of the mendicant friars such as Bonaventure and Thomas rather than the secular masters such as Siger of Brabant, whom Dante mentions, apparently in connection with his skill at syllogizing (although nobody really seems to know why Siger is placed in Paradise). In Niccolo's book, exposure of this kind to monkish disputations does not contribute to a man's learning: the tone in which he mentions the *quodlibeta* is not very laudatory (« and other such nuisances »). The other two Florentines, Petrarch and Boccaccio, could hardly be charged with undue enthusiasm for scholastic disputation. Their faults, according to Niccolo, lay rather in the area of rhetoric and in an arrogance that led them to believe that their works were beyond criticism. Niccolo says nothing about the attitude of Petrarch or Boccaccio toward disputation. He does not need to, as a matter of fact, because the position that Niccolo himself has taken corresponds more or less closely to a view to which they would have subscribed.

Let us consider Petrarch's attitude toward dialectic. It is customary to cite one of his letters to Tommaso Calorio as an example of the bitter hostility of all humanists toward logic. These letters do indeed constitute testimony to Petrarch's hostility to *British* logicians [29]. But even in one of these letters Petrarch protests that he is not hostile to all dialectic: he realizes that the Stoics, that « strong and manly sect of philosophers », ascribed great importance to the subject. (How uncomfortable Petrarch would have been if he had been told that the Stoic logic resembled, in important ways, the « Terminist » logic he was condemning!) « I know that it is one of the liberal arts, and

---

[28] « ... verissimum est, Dantem quodlibeta fratrum atque eiusmodi molestias lectitasse, librorum autem gentilium, unde maxime ars sua dependebat, nec eos quidem qui reliqui sunt, attigisse ». Bruni, p. 70.

[29] « Imo vero iam insularum peculiare malus est, si dyalecticorum agmini britannico ethnea nunc novorum Cyclopum acies accesserit ». Petrarch, letter « Ad Thomam Messanensem, contra senes dyalecticos », *Familiares*, ed. V. Rossi (Florence, [1933]), I, 36.

a step by no means useless to those striving for higher things, a not useless equipment for those concerned with the wranglings of philosophers. It stimulates the intellect, signals the way to truth, shows how to avoid fallacies, and finally, if nothing else, renders men prompt and fluent in arguing. *This I do not deny* » [30]. Since this particular letter to Tommaso is so frequently quoted to « demonstrate » that the humanists had no use whatever for logic, I have purposely singled out a passage that stresses the importance of dialectic. As heirs of the classical tradition and of the concept of an education leading to *humanitas* [31], the humanists were bound to admit the respectability of dialectic. Had not Cicero himself endorsed it? We shall not press the point that Boethius — by most humanist calendars an « ancient », with the added advantage of having been a Christian — had also dealt with dialectic and had provided one of the mainstays of medieval logicians, from Abelard on down to Petrarch's time. When the humanists wished to go back to the sources of the dialectical tradition, they went back to Aristotle or Cicero, but not to Boethius [32].

---

[30] « 'Ergo' inquiunt, 'dyalecticam tu condemnas'? Absit; scio enim quantum illi Stoici tribuant, secta philosophorum fortis et mascula; cuius, cum sepe alias, tum in libro *De Finibus* Cicero noster meminit; scio quod una liberalium est et gradus ad alta nitentibus interque philosophorum dumeta gradientibus non inutilis armatura. Excitat intellectum, signat veri viam, monstrat vitare fallacias; denique, si nichil aliud, promptos et perargutulos facit. Hoc ita esse non infitior ». Petrarch, *Fam.* I, 37.

[31] See Hans Baron, « Aulus Gellius in the Renaissance », *From Petrarch to Leonardo Bruni* (Chicago, 1968), pp. 196-215.

[32] When Roberto Rossi, one of the participants in Bruni's dialogues, set out to translate afresh Aristotle's *Posterior Analytics*, he anticipated that he would be asked the inevitable question, « Why Aristotle again? » In his defense he cited the fact that Boethius re-worked the logic of others: « ... si verbosus forsitan dixerit quispiam illorum qui aliena magis quam sua curant, et cur non alia quae nondum nostrae linguae tradita fuerint; aristotelem enim habemus. Cur non platonem? cur non tuchididem? atque alios plures dignissimos latinis partim aut omnino ignotos? ... et cur boetius logicam iam antea alieno labore evigilatam rursus ediderit? » The answer to the critics' question is that Aristotle excelled not just in doctrine but in his presentation, which presumably has suffered at the hands of previous translators: « Sed antecedat merito aristoteles doctrina magnus sed porro doctrine ordine excellentissimus, nam tam et si floruerit disciplina sic tamen pulcherrime cuncta digessit, ordineque mirabili distinxit ut eo maxime ingentem apud omnes gentes gloriam atque aeternum sibi nomen pepererit ».

When Petrarch's letter to Thomas of Messina is quoted, it seems to be assumed often that he is speaking, as a young student, about his studies in the university. Part of this assumption is certainly false: it has been shown that the letters were written at the time when Petrarch began to compile his *Familiares*, about 1350 [33]. And in fact the tone of the letters is not at all what we would expect from a youthful rebel against a course required of him in his elementary studies at the university. For one thing, the defense of Aristotle against his pretended followers is a much more balanced and mature judgment than we would expect from a young man in his teens or early twenties. For another thing, the period about which Petrarch would presumably be writing — the years 1320 to 1326— is far too early for any extensive influence of British logic in Sicily or anywhere else in Italy [34]. To be sure, by 1339, when Boccaccio wrote to Petrarch and extolled him as the equal of the monarchs in each of the arts, including Ockham in logic [35], British logic may well have begun to attract followers in Italy. Or, just as likely, Italian students might have heard that Ockham's logic was the prevailing tendency at Paris. The whole subject cries out for investigation, and until more is known perhaps we should declare a moratorium on the quotation of Petrarch's letter to Thomas.

Roberto Rossi, prologue to his mss. translation of the *Posterior Analytics*, Cod. Marc. Fondo Antico Latino (Zanetti) 231 (1572), ff. 2 v-3 r.

[33] See E. H. Wilkins, *The Making of the Canzoniere, and other Petrarchan Studies* (Rome, 1951), ch. XX, « On the Dates of Certain Letters », pp. 311-45, at p. 312. Wilkins accepts Billanovich's arguments to the effect that the letters of Book I addressed to Tommaso, his fellow classmate at Bologna, are « Componimenti inventati tra il '50 e il '51, per attaccare la serie cronologica dell'epistolario, se pure con numeri radi, fino alla prima giovinezza ».

[34] I put this statement in the most dogmatic terms possible, although I realize full well that such dogmatism is premature. We know very little as yet of the reception of British logic in Italy during the Trecento. If there is anyone who believes in the early date and historical authenticity of Petrarch's letters to Tommaso, I invite him to present evidence concerning Italian followers of British logic in the 1320's.

[35] « ... estque in artibus per excellentiam hiis monarcha: in gramatica Aristarcus, Occam in logica, in recthorica Tullius et Ulixes, in arismetrica iordanizans, in geometria similis Euclidi sive syragusanum sequitur Archimedem, in musica boetizans, et in astrologia suscitat egyptium Ptholomeum. Quid plura? Ut Seneca moralizat, in opere Socratem moraliter insectando, ac in ystoriis scolasticis optimum Commestorem ». Giovanni Boccaccio, *Opere latine minori*, ed. A. Massèra (Bari, 1928), p. 113.

At any rate, Petrarch does not dismiss dialectic as utterly useless: his conclusion, which he asks Tommaso to pass on to the « aged dialectician », is that he, Petrarch, condemns, not the liberal arts, but puerile old men, who waste their time on studies of an elementary and propaedeutic sort when they should have progressed on to better and higher things [36]. Dialectic, then, has its place in the educational scheme for Petrarch, at least officially. He is even capable of condemning disputants for committing the logician's sin of *petitio principii*: « I know certain men who, when the truth or falsehood of some discipline is being discussed, are accustomed to bring into the middle of the discussion the authors [*auctores*, in the medieval sense] of the very same art whose reliability is precisely at issue — which seems to me to be a defect in disputing (*in disputando*), that is, in order to prove what you want, to bring forward what you cannot ... » [37].

Nevertheless, Petrarch was himself temperamentally disinclined to engage in contentious disputation. In the same letter from which the above quotation is taken, Petrarch remarks: « I am not accustomed to dispute of things I know

[36] This is the familiar theme of Time Wasted on Logic, which will reappear faithfully in all future humanist discussions of dialectic. Since we are dealing here with a polemic, it might be well to present some evidence of the sort of thing Petrarch was protesting against. If the reader will consult Paul O. Kristeller's *Iter Italicum* (London, 1963), I, 271, he will find an entry that illustrates the persistence of students of logic in Italy during the early Quattrocento (we then have to make the not unreasonable assumption it reflects conditions in the previous century). He will discover that a certain student, Johannes de Medalis, copied the (Terminist) logic of Peter of Mantua in 1420, and in the previous year, 1419, had copied another work of the same type, Strode's *Consequences*, the latter during his first year as a student at Ferrara. *Seven* years later, behold our student copying, at Padua, more logical works of the very same formalistic sort, by Caietanus de Thienis, Ferrybridge, and Heytesbury (Niccoli's « Buser »). We expect this sort of schedule from twentieth-century students in logic, but Johannes was a medical student ! Should we be surprised that Petrarch distrusted the medical men of his time?

[37] « Scio aliquos, dum de veritate aut falsitate discipline cuiuspiam altercantur, in medium adducere solitos eiusdem ipsius artis auctores; quorum de fide questio est; quod michi non mediocre in disputando vitium videtur; ad probandum quod velis, id afferre quod non possis ... ». Petrarch, letter to Giovanni Dondi (Seniles, XII, 1), *Nel VI centenario dalla nascita di Francesco Petrarca*, (Padua, 1904), p. 46. The letter is dated July 13, 1370.

nothing about (*disputare de incognitis*), as do many people who, while they wish to appear wise, succeed only in revealing how silly they are » [38]. This statement reminds any reader of Petrarch immediately of his encounter with the four Venetian friends, the episode that inspired the invective *De sui ipsius et multorum ignorantia*. We recall how unhappy Petrarch (according to his own account) used to become when the conversation of his friends turned to one of the topics of natural history about which he clearly regarded them (and himself) as ignorant. They were, in other words, disputing *de incognitis*, and Petrarch's invective is an eloquent summary of his feelings in such matters. Nobody can express Petrarch's feelings better than he himself, and so we can appreciate his attitude toward useless argument very well. But — and this is the main point of this paper — we must not make the mistake of imputing Petrarch's temperament to every other humanist, for some of them were by no means so reluctant to engage in argumentative give and take.

No better contrast could be found than in the attitude of Coluccio Salutati: « You know my habits », he writes to a friend who had studied Greek with him, « You know that I am not able to be still, you know how it always pleases (me) to teach what I have learned and how urgently I seek things I do not know, and how much pleasure it gives me *even to dispute of things not known* » [39]. Furthermore Salutati, even as an old man, was still ready to explore areas of Scholastic disputation that Petrarch most certainly never entertained the slightest intention of entering. Writing about 1400, Salutati remarked to a correspondent that he had not been able to find the complete commentary of John Buridan on the *Ethics*, even though he had written to people in Paris [40]. Then, four years later, Salutati writes to Master

---

38 « Non soleo disputare de incognitis ut multi, qui dum videri sapientes cipiunt insipientiam detegunt ... ». Petrarch, letter to Giovanni Dondi, *ibid.*, p. 45.

39 « Scis mores meos, scis quod quiescere non possim, scis quam semper iuverit docere que tenui quamque importune exigam que non novi quamque semper gratum michi sit *etiam de non cognitis disputare* ... ». Salutati, *Epistolario*, III, 131. The letter is addressed to Iacopo Angeli da Scarperia.

40 « *Questiones* optimi Buridani, ultra duas questiones noni libri, licet Parius super hoc scripserim, nunquam potui reperire; dicuntque peritiores eum ulterius non processisse ». Salutati, *Epistolario*, III, 391.

Francesco of Siena and praises the latter's commentary on the *Ethics*, comparing it very favorably with similar commentaries by Thomas Aquinas, Albertus Magnus, Albert of Saxony, Gerardus de Odonis, Henry of Weimar, Walter Burley, and « your » John Buridan [41]. In Petrarch's book such comparisons would have been faint praise indeed, but Salutati is entirely serious [42]. Again, in a much-quoted letter to Peter of Mantua, a logician of the Trecento who has not yet been adequately investigated, Salutati shows a familiarity with the technical apparatus of Terminist logic. Having heard glowing accounts of Peter's talents, he hopes that Peter will master this discipline — wresting philosophical leadership from the British — and go on to devote himself to poetry, « which alone is able to speak of God » [43]. About the intent of this letter it is possible to have divergent views, but I should at least like to suggest that Salutati is not urging Peter to dispose of logic — whatever that would mean — but to master it along with the other arts, so as to be able to achieve significant results in poetry, which, in Salutati's view, is the more important enterprise. The first part of Salutati's hope for Peter — the mastery of British logic — is overwhelmingly

---

[41] Salutati, *Epistolario*, IV, 38.

[42] In the intervening four years, Salutati may have been able to locate a complete copy of Buridan's commentary, or, more likely, he based his judgement on excerpts he had seen. There is a puzzle as to why Salutati found it so difficult to locate a copy of Buridan's commentary on the *Ethics*: it was known in Padua in 1394, when a clerk named Haymo, of The Hague, copied it (See Valentinelli, IV, 72, describing a codex in the Biblioteca Marciana). Furthermore, the Biblioteca Universitaria of Padova has a copy, Cod. 1472, of Buridan's commentary on the *Ethics*, *Politics*, and *Rhetoric*, which was written « in felicissimo studio patavino », and which later belonged to Cardinal Domenico Grimani.

[43] « Gaudebam igitur apud nos emergere, qui barbaris illis quondam gentibus saltem in hoc palmam eriperet, qualem me tibi fama et multorum relatio promittit. cui rei velim incumbas: enuda sophismatum apparentiam; redde nobis rerum noticiam, ut non semper laboremus extremis et in equivoco tum significationum, tum suppositionum aut — quas intelligere minus me fateor — appellationum nemo nos capiat vel confundat ». Salutati, *Epistolario*, III, 318-33. This is one of the few passages I have been able to find in the writings of the early humanists where the technical terms, « suppositio », « significatio », « appellatio » are used in a way that reveals first-hand familiarity with the Terminist tradition.

demonstrated by the extant treatises [44]. Whether Peter of Mantua accomplished anything significant in the way of poetry or humanistic scholarship remains to be seen [45].

Salutati is no more charitable than Petrarch in his judgments concerning professional philosophers, those who « call themselves Aristotelians ». In his treatise *On the Labors of Hercules*, Salutati complains that present-day Aristotelians do not make use of poetical quotations as Aristotle did, but rather seem to scorn poetry. « Indeed I do not admire them but am rather indignant and sad. For although they profess themselves to have reached, through « loyce », to use their corrupt word, the heights of philosophy and to be prepared (for shame!) to discuss all matters in garrulous disputation, yet they neither read nor understand the Aristotelian texts, but seek out I know not what British texts ..., as though our area were not adequate in learning ... » [46]. The cardinal sin of the British-style logicians, in Salutati's eyes, is that they are ready to argue « without books and without the help of texts ». In other words, they are the mirror image of the much-read humanists, who immerse themselves in the classics but do not engage in disputation [47]. The school philosophers are ready to tackle logic, natural philosophy, or metaphysics (« transcendental speculation », in Salutati's terms), and to pronounce definitive judgments — or rather, to relay on the traditions of their masters. The respondents in these

---

44 For example, the logic that occupies ff. 1 r-80 v of Marc. Lat. Cl. VI, 128 (2559). This manuscript, copied in 1424, was bought sixteen years later in Padua by Iohannes Marchanova, who taught logic as well as philosophy at Bologna in the middle of the fifteenth century. Peter's treatise starts right out with a definition of « supposition » and proceeds with an analysis along the lines of Oxford and Paris logic.

45 There remains his exposition of a letter of Seneca in Vat. Lat. 5223; see P. O. Kristeller, *Iter Italicum*, II, 372.

46 « Nam cum per logices, imo (ut corrupto vocabulo dicunt) loyce, et philosophie cacumina volitare se iactent et de cunctis disputatione garrula discutere sint parati (proh pudor !), textus Aristotelicos nec intelligunt nec legunt sed nescio quos tractatus apud ' toto divisos orbe Britannos ', quasi noster eruditioni non sufficiat situs, querunt ». Salutati, *De laboribus Herculis*, ed. B. L. Ullman (Zürich, [1951]), p. 3.

47 « Quos totis lucubrationibus amplectentes sine libris et sine testium adminiculis et dialeticam et physicam et quicquid transcendens speculatio rimatur ediscunt, sive potius edidicisse relictis sui magistri traditionibus gloriantur ». Salutati, *De laboribus Herculis*, p. 3.

disputations are ready in turn to catch the disputant in the net of some sophism, before he has even said anything significant whatever about the subject matter.

These statements of Salutati's accord very well with what Petrarch has to say about professional philosophers in the *De vita solitaria*. This influential work contains several passages contrasting the quiet life of study and meditation with the noisy posturing of the Aristotelians. In his dedicatory letter, for example, Petrarch gives a description of these men, who, « burdened rather than adorned with learning », mix up knowledge, which is a very beautiful thing, with the vilest habits [48]. Petrarch describes these obnoxious pedagogues as delighting in crowds and noise and as preferring to be out in the city streets looking over the « women, the buildings, and even the statues » rather than in with the books. « It would certainly be better to see cliffs and woods, to speak with bears and tigers » than with these men. They carry their educated silliness all around the city like peddlers of old furniture. Again in the second book of *De vita solitaria* Petrarch lashes out at the holders of chairs of philosophy, who claim the title of « philosophers » although they do not deserve it [49]. « I mean the true philosophers, not those whom in my opinion the man who first called them ' chairholders ' labelled correctly. For in the chairs they do philosophize, but in their actions they behave like madmen, laying down precepts for others which they themselves are the first to break and proclaiming themselves the standard bearers of virtue when they are the first to rebel against its rule ». Petrarch

[48] « Sed copia literarum non semper modestum pectus inhabitat, et sepe inter linguam et animum, inter doctrinam et vitam concertatio magna est. De his autem loquor qui, literis impediti et onerati potius quam ornati, rem pulcerrimam, scire, turpissimis moribus miscuerunt, tanta animi vanitate ut scolas nunquam vidisse multo melius fuerit; qui hoc unum ibi didicerunt, superbire et literarum fiducia vaniores esse cuntis hominibus; qui, quieturum libenter Aristotilem ventilantes per compita, cuneatim vulgo mirante pretereunt ... » Petrarch « De vita solitaria », *Prose*, ed. G. Martelloti et al. (Milan-Naples, [1955]), p. 292.

[49] « Philosophos autem dico, non istos quos, qui cathedrarios primum dixit, ille michi proprium rei nomen imposuisse visus est. In cathedris enim philosophantur in actionibus insaniunt, precipiunt aliis preceptisque suis primi obstant primi legibus a se latis derogant, et signiferos se professi primi ordines deserunt primi virtutis imperio rebellant ». *De vita solitaria*, p. 524.

lets up on this severe indictment in order to accommodate one solitude-loving philosopher, namely, Peter Abelard, although he is a little doubtful about Abelard's religious convictions and lack of humility [50]. Had Petrarch ever read any of Abelard's logical works, he would have been still more disturbed, but probably he knew only the *Historia calamitatum*, or the letters.

The document perhaps most frequently cited in connection with Petrarch's views on contemporary philosophers, however, is the invective « On his own ignorance and that of many others », already mentioned. We must stress the fact that none of the four Venetian friends against whom this invective is directed is known to have had any special interest in logic: certainly they did not leave a word of writing that betrays any such interest [51]. From Petrarch's description of their specific interest in philosophy, there is no reason to expect them to be particularly concerned with logic: « They were accustomed to propose either some Aristotelian problem or to bring up something about animals ». When this happened, Petrarch would either keep quiet, or make a joke, or try to divert the discussion, by the provocative device of asking how Aristotle could have known such a thing, since he had no reason (*ratio*) for it, and sense experience (*experimentum*) was impossible [52]. Not a word here

---

[50] *De vita solitaria,* p. 528.

[51] On this confrontation of Petrarch and the four friends, see P. O. Kristeller, « Petrarch's 'Averroists'. A note on the history of Aristotelianism in Venice, Padua, and Bologna », in *Melanges Augustin Renaudet, Bibliothèque d'Humanisme et Renaissance,* IV (1952), 59-65, and « Il Petrarca, l'umanesimo e la scolastica a Venezia », in « *La civiltà veneziana del Trecento* (Florence, [1956]), pp. 147-78. Also see Eugenio Garin, « La cultura fiorentina nella seconda metà del '300 e i 'barbari Britanni' », in *La Rassegna della letteratura italiana,* LXIV (1960), 181-95, and « Cultura filosofica toscana e veneta nel Quattrocento », in *Umanesimo europeo e umanesimo veneziano,* ed. V. Branca (Florence, 1963), pp. 11-30; Lino Lazzarini, « Francesco Petrarca e il primo umanesimo a Venezia », also in the Branca volume, pp. 63-92. Lazzarini observes that the four Venetians were « uomini di cultura, non filosofi di scuola », but argues that the documents concerning two of them reveal their faith « in the doctrine and in the school that the doctrine organized and propagated » (p. 90).

[52] Petrarch here shows, by the way, that he has some familiarity with the fundamentals of school argument in the late Middle Ages. For *ratio* and *experimentum* were the standard grounds for conviction in argument, with *experimentum* replacing the earlier *auctoritas* derived from the rhetorical

of *suppositio*, *ampliatio*, or any of the other hallmarks of Terminist logic [53]. Petrarch actually gives a list of some of the « facts » that his friends liked to discuss: they are old medieval favorites of natural history, such as the *echinus*, a tiny animal that is able to bring a ship traveling at any speed to a halt, even though outside of the water it has no strength [54]. Such a fact would have obvious interest for Venetians, but hardly for logicians.

Later in the invective, in dealing with the doctrine of the eternity of the world, Petrarch makes what is obviously the central charge of the whole treatise: those who accept the tenet (held by Aristotle and « almost all philosophers ») that « out of nothing, nothing can come », are afraid to come right out and attack the Faith, with its belief in creation *ex nihilo*. So these philosophers have adopted an indirect procedure, which consists of disparaging the knowledge of Christians, and calling them obtuse and ignorant. These Aristotelian philosophers are reluctant to show their true colors in public disputation, « not daring to belch forth their errors », and so they take refuge in this patent dodge, to the effect that « for the purposes of the present debate, they are setting aside the Faith » (p. 732).

Now we find something unusual for Petrarch: a specific reference (p. 744) to « contentious Paris and the noisy Street of Straw ». This reference occurs in a listing of Aristotelians that is quite extensive, and which includes even some contemporary Greeks, who cannot understand « our » language, that

---

tradition via Augustine. The same considerations reappear in Petrarch's correspondence during his last years with Giovanni Dondi, a Paduan teacher of medicine.

[53] Nor does Petrarch attack « the moderns » or the « logic of the moderns », although scholars sometimes carelessly assert that he does. Even in 1373 Boccaccio had to write to Petrus de Monteforte and explain that Petrarch never wrote a work « Against the ignorance and arrogance of the moderns ». Evidently Peter had heard Petrarch's invective referred to under that title: « Sub titulo vero quem subsequenter eum scripsisse dicis, scilicet *Contra ignorantiam atque arrogantiam modernorum*, nunquam aliquid legisse recordor ... ». Giovanni Boccaccio, *Opere latine minori*, p. 204. Boccaccio observes that, far from attacking « the moderns », Petrarch went out of his way to praise them, although occasionally he did disparage *himself* « in order that the glory of his contemporaries might increase ». This shows that Boccaccio does not take the term ' moderni ' to refer to a specific school of logicians or philosophers.

[54] Petrarch, *Prose*, p. 712.

is, Latin. But there is no reason to assume that only logicians are making the noise in the Street of Straw, although it is certainly significant that Petrarch singles out, among all the universities known to him, the University of Paris. Petrarch says that his argument is not *against* Aristotle (whom, indeed, he considers to be a very great man) but *for* the truth « and against the foolish Aristotelians who daily impose upon Aristotle », even though they know him only as a name — « ultimately to the scorn, I should hope, of their audience — and who boldly torture Aristotle's statements, even distorting those that are straightforward » [55]. A damaging indictment, but still not directed specifically against logicians. As a matter of fact, it is a general characteristic of Petrarch's remarks on logic and logicians that they are rather vague and not specific. His eulogistic descriptions of the universities of Montpellier and Bologna in the Letter to Posterity stress the prosperity of the cities in question about as much as the condition of the schools [56]. Similarly vague is his description of Paris in 1360 as compared with its flourishing state of earlier years: « For where is that Paris of old, which, while never quite living up to its reputation, still was undoubtedly impressive? Where is the orderly throng of students, the passion for study, the wealth of the citizens, the general enjoyment? Now one no longer hears the clash of disputants but of weapons; one sees the accumulation of arms rather than of books; the air resounds not with syllogisms and lectures but with watchmen and the impact of battering rams upon walls ... » [57]. Compared with wars and pestilence, logic was not so bad after all, we might conclude.

There are, of course, many other allusions to logic and logicians in the works of Petrarch and the other humanists; sometimes they turn up in the most unexpected places. For example, it is surely astonishing that in a work so intimate and personal as the *Secretum* Petrarch should have bothered to insert what is clearly a pointed attack against the traditional Tree of Porphyry, which embodies the (to Petrarch, utterly useless) definition of man as the *animale rationale* [58]. But we have examined, with

[55] Petrarch, *Prose*, p. 750.
[56] Petrarch, *Prose*, pp. 1098-1100.
[57] Petrarch, *Prose*, p. 1110.
[58] Petrarch, « Secretum », in *Prose*, pp. 50-54.

some care, enough passages to give us a sense of the place occupied by dialectic and disputation in the thinking of these early Italian humanists. We may sum up our results by saying that although all of the men involved in any way with Bruni's dialogues were on record as favoring the study of dialectic, they varied considerably in their enthusiasm and interest. Salutati was ready to engage in disputation without too much concern for technical refinements; Vergerio was ready to teach dialectic, probably (I would guess) in pretty much the same spirit. Niccolo, thinking of the learning that reinforced the logical training of the ancients, despaired permanently, it would seem, of profiting from disputation, and took himself out of contention, so to speak. Rossi, essentially only a spectator in the disputations in Florence, was interested enough in logic to translate the *Posterior Analytics*. Bruni surely favored a revival of ancient dialectic and probably on the whole agreed with the middle position of Salutati, with its balance between solitary study and social argument. Petrarch, whose presence can be felt behind the scenes, was unquestionably the least enthusiastic supporter of dialectic, but even he would probably have welcomed the sort of trend that humanists such as Valla, Vives, and Ramus represented in the later Renaissance.

What emerges even more clearly than these observations, which are nothing new, is the vagueness and general imprecision of the knowledge of contemporary logic displayed by these humanists. One gains the definite impression that logic was not much more than a set of horrible names to Petrarch and Boccaccio. Salutati seems to have made an honest attempt to familiarize himself with logical developments, but the attempt obviously failed. We should not blame him too much, for most modern scholars have made even less of an attempt to find out what was actually going on in logic in the Italian Trecento. They seem to have assumed, with little justification, that Petrarch and the other humanists knew what they were talking about, in the sense perhaps that they had been exposed to « British » logic in the classroom. Even this meager assumption should have disturbed someone: why not « Parisian » logic? [59].

[59] A somewhat later humanist, Enea Silvio Piccolomini, complains about « Viennese » logicians — but for an obvious reason: he was writing

I should like to close by suggesting a hypothesis that seems to me to be at least worth exploring. If we can find a group of men who were closely associated with the humanists, and who did have some first-hand experience with Terminist or « British » logic, might our humanists not have derived their impressions from these men rather tham from actual contact with the forbidding treatises or *viva voce* presentation of the subject? Professor Garin has suggested that members of religious orders seem to have shown a great deal of interest in logic. Indeed, when one examines the wealth of manuscripts on logic in Italian libraries that date from the Trecento and early Quattrocento, one cannot fail to be struck by the overwhelming preponderance of clerics and friars. The role of the Augustinian hermits seems to have been especially large in the transmission of Oxford logic, numbering among their members such famous names as Gregory of Rimini and Paul of Venice. We have seen how both Salutati and Niccoli acknowledged the benefit of « disputation » (their style) with Luigi Marsili, who also belonged to this order. Perhaps there may have existed a tension within such an order as that of the Augustinians, between humanistically inclined hermits such as Luigi and eager logicians of the « British » persuasion. Consider the career of Dionigi da Borgo di San Sepolcro, the Augustinian who gave Petrarch his favorite copy of Augustine's *Confessions*. Dionigi has attracted attention primarily because of his pre-humanistic interests [60]. Yet he lectured on the *Sentences* of Peter Lombard, that « much-tortured book », as Petrarch called it, and had written a compendium of logic « according to the doctrine of the most eminent Egidio Co-

---

from Vienna, where Ockhamist logic was strong, in 1450, when the movement was still active. Having praised the kind of logic outlined by Cicero in the *De Fato*, Piccolomini is careful to rule out the endless cavilling of the Viennese, which terminates not in « utility » but in death: « Non tamen hac in re quosdam Viennenses imitatione dignos dixerim; nimis enim multum tempus in sophisticis et cavillosis exponunt argumentis, ut apud eos logice studium non utilitate sed morte terminetur ». Enea Silvio Piccolomini, « Tractatus de liberorum educatione », ed. E. Garin in *Il pensiero pedagogico dello Umanesimo*, pp. 198-294 at p. 286.

[60] See Arbesmann, *Der Augustinereremitenorden ...*, pp. 15-36, with the references given there to the literature on Dionigi.

lonna »[61]. In the German universities, the opposition to Ockhamist logic (sometimes called the « logic of the moderns ») came from adherents to the « way of Thomas and Albertus ». A man like Dionigi, who was teaching theology at Paris in the year 1316-1317, would have been far more likely to know something of Ockhamist logic, and to have resented it, than most of the humanists. And it is likely that Petrarch knew Dionigi first, not at Paris (where Petrarch does not seem to have stayed for any great length of time in 1333), but at Avignon. There both Petrarch and Dionigi would certainly have heard of the notorious Franciscan « heretic » who was incarcerated in a prison of Avignon — hear of him, no doubt, in the most unflattering terms.

If this hypothesis is correct — I am not insisting on Dionigi's role, but on the role of members of religious orders including his order and that of the Franciscans — and others — then we have an explanation both for the emotional fervor and for the imprecision of the humanists' attacks on the barbarous logic from overseas. (By the way, England is as much « overseas » from Paris as it is from Italy, so that even this phrase may have had its origin in some feud within the university of Paris). It might also explain why the incursions of British logic had to be repulsed with such crusading zeal: within the context of a religious order's activities, absorption in technical logic probably made even less sense than it did in the context of medical or legal education, at least in the eyes of the humanists, or humanistically-inclined members. Others, however, were apparently able to reconcile skill in disputing and their religious concerns. One has only to think of the later confrontation of an Augustinian monk named Martin Luther and his adversary John Eck, to realize that disputation did not disappear after the triumph of humanism. And it is just possible that some humanists would have been pleased to see disputation put to serious use.

---

[61] Cited by U. Mariani, *Il Petrarca e gli Agostiniani* (Rome, 1959), p. 34, n. 3: « Compendium Logicae iuxta doctrinam eminentissimi ... Aegidii Columnae ... explanatum per ... Dion. a B. Sanctis ».

JULIUS KIRSHNER

PAOLO DI CASTRO ON *CIVES EX PRIVILEGIO*: A CONTROVERSY OVER THE LEGAL QUALIFICATIONS FOR PUBLIC OFFICE IN EARLY FIFTEENTH-CENTURY FLORENCE *

* I wish to express my gratitude to Professor Peter Herde of the University of Frankfort for his critical reading of my paper. The research for this article was completed during 1968 and 1969 while the author was a recipient of a fellowship from the American Academy in Rome. I wish to thank the Academy for its generous support and Bard College for a leave-of-absence which made it possible for me to work in Florence and Rome. The following abbreviations will be used in the footnotes. *AGN*: *Arte dei Giudici e Notai*; *ASF: Archivio di Stato di Firenze*; *BNF: Biblioteca Nazionale di Firenze*; *Provv: Provvisioni*; *BV: Biblioteca Vaticana*. All references to the *Digest*, hereafter cited as *D*, and to the *Code*, hereafter cited as *C* are found in *Corpus iuris civilis*, eds. T. H. Mommsen, W. Kroll, P. Krueger, and R. Schoell (3 vols., Berlin, 1928-1929).

Before a man could assume office in Renaissance Florence, it was necessary for him to fulfill specific citizenship and tax requirements. These prerequisites, along with others, have been noted by many historians, but have never been adequately explored [1]. How did the statutes define citizenship (*civilitas*, *cittadinanza*) and what was the precise nature of the tax requirements? Answering these questions with precision is difficult. The legal definition of citizenship in the statutes as well as in the works of the legists was in a state of transition, and thus far from clear. Laws which had become hopelessly antiquated were not eliminated from the statute books, even though they were superseded by later legislation. As for taxes, hundreds of laws were enacted dealing with fiscal matters in trecento and quattrocento Florence. A bill which was passed in one legislative session of the councils could be and was frequently abrogated soon after in another session.

With the rise of the Florentine territorial state in the fourteenth century, a new dimension was added to the legal qualifications of officeholding. Certain communities which had succumbed to Florentine domination — Prato (1351), San Gimignano (1353), San Miniato (1369), etc. — were accorded special benefits and privileges by their new masters. Foremost among the privileges was the opportunity to become original Florentine

---

[1] In no way do I mean to imply that the political and social process through which the Florentines obtained office and wielded power has lacked study. The politico-social context of officeholding in Florence has been studied in depth by G. Brucker, *Florentine Politics and Society, 1343-1378* (Princeton, 1962); L. Martines, *The Social World of the Florentine Humanists, 1390-1460* (Princeton, 1963); and his *Lawyers and Statecraft in Renaissance Florence* (Princeton, 1968); and by N. Rubinstein, *The Government of Florence under the Medici* (Oxford, 1966) and « Florentine Constitutionalism and Medici Ascendancy in the Fifteenth Century », in *Florentine Studies, Politics and Society in Renaissance Florence*, ed. N. Rubinstein (London, 1968), pp. 442-462; and see the recent article on politics in the fourteenth century by A. Molho, « The Florentine Oligarchy and the *Balie* of the Late Trecento », *Speculum*, XLIII (1968), 23-51.

citizens and the right to hold office on relatively easy terms [2]. At the same time, hundreds of immigrants in Florence, who had come from central and northern Italy, acquired original Florentine citizenship through statutes enacted on their behalf. These *cives ex privilegio*, as the lawyers called them [3], were usually required to wait from ten to thirty years before they could be elected to public office [4]. Sometimes new citizens were absolutely prohibited from being elected to office [5].

---

[2] See below, p. 234 ff.

[3] The subject of citizenship in the Middle Ages and the Renaissance is in need of a modern monograph; however, see the competent and very useful work of D. Bizzari, *Ricerche sul diritto di cittadinanza nella costituzione comunale* (Turin, 1916). See also, W. M. Bowsky, « Citizenship: The Individual and the State in the Commune of Siena, 1287-1355 », in *Studies in Medieval and Renaissance History*, IV (1967), 193-243. The law concerning *cives ex privilegio* was rooted in the *Corpus iuris civilis* of Justinian. Beyond being born a citizen, Roman law provided that one may become a citizen by manumission, adoption and by privilege of a municipal council. A. Berger, *Encylopedic Dictionary of Roman Law. Transactions of the American Philosophical Society*, Vol. 3, Part 2 (Philadelphia, 1953), 613; H. F. Jolowicz, *Roman Foundations of Modern Law* (Oxford, 1957), pp. 39-43. The influential *Glossa ordinaria* to the *Corpus iuris civilis*, compiled by Accursius between ca. 1210-1228, carried these Roman principles on citizenship forward into the thirteenth century and beyond. Accursius, *ad C.* 10, 39, 3, *Filios* and *C.* 10, 40, 7, *Cives* (Lyons, 1612), II, cols. 76, 78. Dinus del Mugello (d. 1303?) described four ways in which one may become a citizen: « civis fit uno de quattuor modis, scilicet origine, manumissione, electione et adopcione ... »; *ad C.* 10, 40, 6, *Privilegio* in *BV, MS. Borgh*, 374, 232 va. On the same theme, see Bartolus *ad D.* 50, 1, 1, *Municipem* and *D.* 50, 1, 6, *Adsumptio* § *filius*, *Opera omnia* (Venice, 1596), II, 218-219; and a *consilium* of the same jurist, in *Opera omnia*, *ed. cit.*, X, *cons.* LXII, 17 ra-b. See also a *consilium* of Baldus, *Consilia* (Frankfort, 1589), I, *cons.* CCCIXC, 103 vb-104 va; and Angelo da Perugia, *ad C.* 10, 40, 7, *Cives*, published in the *Commentaria ... codicis* of his brother, Baldus (6 vols., Venice, 1577), V, 287 r. See also sources cited below n. 81.

[4] *ASF*, *Provv*, 40, 208-209 r (17 Jan. 1353); *ibid.*, 41, 98 v (20 Oct. 1354); *ibid.*, 58, 91 v (27 Dec. 1370); *ibid.*, 59, 223 v-224 r (19 Feb. 1370); *ibid.*, 60, 26 v-30 r (8 June 1372); *ibid.*, 40 r (19 June 1372); *ibid.*, 80 r-v (29 Aug. 1372); *ibid.*, 61, 132 r-v (13 Sept. 1373); *ibid.*, 64, 53r-v (10 June 1376); *ibid.*, 187 v-188 r (29 Oct. 1376); *ibid.*, 70, 124 v-125 v (30 Oct. 1381). The jurist Baldus (1327?-1400) was made a citizen of Florence in 1359, but was forbidden to hold office for twenty-five years. Bizzari, 28, note 1. I plan to devote a comprehensive study to the fortunes of the *cives ex privilegio* in Trecento and Quattrocento Florence.

[5] *ASF*, *Provv*, 40, 30 v (3 Dec. 1352); *ibid.*, 58, 13 r-15 v (8 June 1370); *ibid.*, 27 r-28 r (21 June 1370); *ibid.*, 173 v (6 Feb. 1371); *ibid.*, 59, 79 r-v

Beginning in the late Trecento the government of Florence attempted to curb these privileges, especially the right to hold office. State action was often spurred by the guilds and sometimes the guilds themselves openly joined the government's campaign against the new citizens. A spearhead in the drive to disenfranchise this group was the guild of lawyers and notaries (*Arte dei Giudici e Notai*). In the early fifteenth century this guild waged a vigorous battle against *cives ex privilegio* hailing from the territories of Florence. A critical moment in this conflict occurred in 1413 when the guild requested the prominent jurist, Paolo di Castro (1360/62-1441) to submit a *consilium* « against the notaries of San Gimignano, San Miniato and others » [6]. Events leading to the *consilium*, the *consilium* itself, and the struggle following it illuminate for us the legal structure of officeholding in early Quattrocento Florence, and provide the focus of our study.

The guild's choice of Paolo di Castro is not surprising.His reputation in Florence had already been secured by a series of lectures on the *Digest* delivered at the *Studio* of Florence between

(21 Aug. 1371); *ibid.*, 61, 98 r-99 r (28 April 1373); *ibid.*, 110 v (26 Aug. 1373); *ibid.*, 65, 286 r-v (23 Feb. 1378).

[6] The *consilium* has been edited: Paolo di Castro, *Consilia* (Venice, 1571), I, *cons.* XXI, 13 ra-14 rb; *Consilia* (Venice, 1580), I, *cons.* XXI, 13 ra-14 rb; *Consilia* (Venice, 1617), I, *cons.* XXI, 13 ra-14 rb. I would like to thank Professor Domenico Maffei of the University of Siena for placing his own copy of the 1617 edition at my disposal. There are hardly any variants among these three editions. The fifteenth-century editions of Paolo's *Consilia* which I have been able to examine do not contain this *consilium.* I have seen the Rome edition of 1473, the Nuremberg edition of 1485, and the Pavia edition of 1486. Unless otherwise indicated, all citations to Paolo's edited *Consilia* will be made to the Venetian edition of 1571. Fortunately, a manuscript copy of the *consilium* has been preserved in a volume of the records of the *Arte dei Giudici e Notai,* which differs significantly from the edited versions. *ASF*, *AGN*, 670, 119 r-126 r. The evidence supporting the fact that the *consilium* was written upon the request of the guild is found in the introduction to the case; *ibid.*, 119 r; « Consilium redditum in favorem artis iudicium et notariarum civitatis et pro civitate Florentie ad instantiam et petitionem... dicte artis per infrascriptos doctores ». The reference to *doctores* si gnifies the nine lawyers of the guild who countersigned Paolo's *consilium*; see below, n. 83. For the quotation in the text on the purpose of the *consilium*, see 119 r of the manuscript (left margin): « In favorem artis contra notarios de Sancto Geminiano et de Sancto Miniato et alios ».

1401-1413 [7]. After 1424, he taught at Bologna (1424-29), Padua (1429-41) and outside of Italy, at the University of Toulouse [8]. It seems that Paolo's prosperous private practice in Florence began in 1413 when he most likely matriculated into the guild [9]. Beyond his career in academic life and private legal practice, Paolo has a special place in the legal annals of Florence. He and another distinguished jurist, Bartolomeo Vulpi da Soncino (ca. 1359-1435), were commissioned by the government to iron out a vast and unwieldy body of conflicting statutes which had piled up since the mid-fourteenth century [10]. Under their guidance, a new redaction of the *Statuta populi et communis Florentiae* appeared in 1415 [11]. Renowned as a specialist in modernizing communal statutes, Paolo was also asked to participate in the reform of the statutes of Viterbo, Fermo, Siena and Lucca [12].

For Paolo, a conflict of laws provided the central element of the case. A variety of legislation and agreements existed — the statutes of the guild, the Statutes of the Captain of the People, ordinary *provvisioni* and treaties — stipulating separate tax and legal requirements directly and indirectly affecting the eligibility of candidates for communal office.

In the redaction of the Statutes of the Captain of 1325, and again in 1355, it was declared that no one could be a consul of his guild or hold any office in the commune unless he was a loyal Guelf, devoted to the Holy Roman Church, and a native

---

[7] For bio-bibliographical information on Paolo di Castro, see N. Del Re, *Sei consigli inediti di Paolo di Castro nei codici Vaticani latini 8068, 8069, 11605* e *Urbinate latino 1132* (Rome, 1945), p. 1 ff.; L. Martines, *Lawyers and Statecraft in Renaissance Florence*, pp. 87, 186, 499-500; D. Maffei, *La donazione di Costantino nei giuristi medievali* (Milan, 1964), pp. 288-290; H. Lange, « Die Rechtsquellenlehre in den Consilien Paul de Castros », *Gedächtnisschrift für Rudolf Schmidt* (Berlin, 1966), pp. 421-440. The pages of F. C. von Savigny, *Geschichte des römischen Rechts im Mittelalter* (reprint, Darmstadt, 1956), VI, 281 ff., remain useful.

[8] Del Re, *Sei consigli*, pp. 14-23.

[9] Martines, *Lawyers and Statecraft* (p. 500) indicates that Paolo began his legal practice in Florence in 1414, but there is no doubt that Paolo was active in the city in 1413. I have not been able to pin down the exact date of Paolo's matriculation into the guild.

[10] Martines, *Lawyers and Statecraft*, pp. 186-187.

[11] *Statuta populi et communis Florentiae publica auctoritate collecta, castigata et preposita, anno salutis MCCCCXV* (4 vols., Freiburg, 1778-1781).

[12] Del Re, *Sei consigli*, pp. 18-19.

of the city or *contado* of Florence. Even if one possessed these qualifications, he could not become an official unless either he or his *antecessor* had inhabited the city or had been enrolled on the registers of the *estimo* for ten years (*allibratus*) [13]. The meaning of *antecessor* was not spelled out, although it probably meant that the residency and tax requirements could be fulfilled by one's paternal grandfather, father and paternal uncles. It must be understood that the Captain's Statute did not necessarily require birth (*nativitas*) in the city or *contado*, but only that a citizen be a native (*originarius*). An original citizen as defined by the legists had three possible meanings: the native land (*origo*) of one's paternal grandfather, father or one's own birthplace [14]. In fourteenth-and fifteenth-century Florence all three definitions were employed in the statutes [15].

A statute of the *Arte de Giudici e Notai*, perhaps issued in the mid-fourteenth century, prohibited any notary from being elected to a communal office, if either he or his father had been listed in the registers of the *estimo* (direct tax) of the *contado*. Notaries who accepted offices in disregard of the prohibition would be fined one hundred pounds *sol. parv.* and would be forced to renounce their offices by the proconsul of the guild. Yet any notary could assume public office, if for five years, he « truly » resided with his family in the city of Florence proper, paid the same real and personal taxes as other citizens and paid his *prestanze* assessments (forced loans). Even after meeting the five year residence and tax requirements, the law continued, notaries could be prohibited from holding office by any statute of the commune [16].

---

[13] *Statuti della Repubblica fiorentina*, ed. R. Caggese, *liber* V, *rub.* LIIII (Florence, 1910-1921), II, 256-257. For the law of 1355, see *ASF*, *Statuti*, 10, *liber* I, *rub.* XLVIII, 25 v-26 r. The Captain's Statute of 1355 also provided « quod quilibet communis, comitatus et districtus Florentie possit sibi eligere notarium ad officia » with the permission of the priors and the colleges. These notaries were required to be Guelfs and *populares*; *ibid.*, *liber* IV, *rub.* LXII, 158 r. This statute was not cited by Paolo di Castro and did not play a part in the legal controversy over officeholding.

[14] Bizzari, pp. 52-53.

[15] See documents cited in notes: 26, 33, 36, 50.

[16] Since the 1344 collection of guild statutes (*ASF*, *AGN*, 749) has been damaged and remains incomplete, it is difficult to determine the exact date of the statute enumerating these requirements. A copy of the statute is conserved, however, in *ibid.*, 670, 120 v-121 r: « Firmatum et statutum est quod nullus notarius, allibratus in comitatu Florentie seu descriptus in

The guild laid heavy emphasis on the distinction between *allibratus* and *prestantiatus*, reflecting a revolutionary development of Florentine taxation in the Trecento. After the frequent imposition of the *estimo* on the city in the first half of the century, direct taxation was normally, though not exclusively, reserved for the *contado* and district of Florence. Instead, the commune relied upon indirect taxes (*gabelle*) and voluntary and forced loans which were interest bearing [17]. By the late fourteenth century, *allibrati* customarily referred to rural folk, while *prestantiati* signified city dwellers.

If in theory *origo* was associated with birth, this legal notion did not discourage the Florentine government from extending original citizenship to a multitude of subjects or awarding them the lesser honor of becoming *comitatenses originarii* of Florence. In the treaty between San Gimignano and Florence of 1353, for example, the men of this subject town as well as from her district and territory were henceforward considered « veri et originarii comitatini et populares Florentie » and were to enjoy the traditional privileges, benefits and immunities attached to their new status [18]. Eager to repopulate the city after the « sweeping

---

extimo comitatus Florentie ipse vel eius pater, possit, audeat vel presumat aliquod offitium ad quod extractus, electus seu deputatus fuerit in civitate Florentie modo aliquo acceptare vel exercere sub pena librarum centum solidorum parvorum dandorum pro una dimidia communi Florentie et pro alia dimidia dicte arti et nichilominus ad renumptiandum tale officium cogatur per proconsulem (*MS*: preconsulem) dicte artis. Verum si quis notarius qui ante acceptationem alicuius officii saltem per quinque annos cum sua familia vere et realiter habitaverit in civitate Florentie et in ipsa civitate ut alii cives civitatis eiusdem onera et factiones communis predicti realiter et personaliter subierit et in libris prestantiarum existentibus in camera dicti communis descriptus fuerit ipsasque solverit, sit et esse intelligatur habilis ad officia communis predicti, nisi aliquam aliam prohibitionem haberet secundum formam ordinamentorum dicti communis ».

[17] See R. de Roover, *The Rise and Decline of the Medici Bank 1397-1494* (New York, 1966), pp. 21-22; M. Becker, *Florence in Transition* (Baltimore, 1968), II, 182 ff.

[18] *ASF*, *Provv*, 40, 138 r (7 Aug. 1353): « Item quod omnes et singuli homines et persone de terra Sancti Geminiani predicti seu eius territorio vel districtus intelligantur esse et sint deinceps in perpetuum veri et originarii comitatini et populares et de populo civitatis Florentie et potiantur et gaudeant et potiri et gaudere possint et debeant omnibus et singulis privilegiis et beneficiis quibus gaudere possunt seu potuerunt quicunque alii originarii comitatini populares civitatis predicte ».

carnage » of the plague in 1348, Florence extended an attractive invitation to its new subjects. If the Sangimignanesi came to Florence with their families and established residency there for six months continuously, they would be treated as « veri et originarii et antiqui cives populares » and would earn the privileges and immunities of original citizenship. Most importantly, they would be granted the precious right to hold office as other original and ancient citizens [19]. Finally, the guildsmen of San Gimignano were allowed to matriculate in any of the guilds of Florence without paying the customary entrance fee [20]. These privileges were denied to families of magnate status [21].

After the rebellious San Miniato al Tedesco was subdued by Florentine conquest in 1369, the citizens of this subject town suddenly became original citizens of Florence. According to the treaty of February 17, 1370, the men of San Miniato were given the benefits and privileges of original citizenship [22]. Unlike the Sangimignanesi, they were not obligated to undergo

---

[19] *Ibid.*: « Eo quoque expresso, addito et declarato quod quicunque de Sancto Geminiano predicto seu eius territorio vel districtus habitaverit cum familia sua in civitate Florentie per sex menses continuos, intelligatur et sit completa habitatione predicta civis popularis et de populo civitatis Florentie donec habitabit in civitate predicta cum sua familia in sua domo propria vel conducta prout habitant alii cives civitatis eiusdem et ipsa habitatione durante pro veris et tanquam veri et originarii cives populares civitatis eiusdem habeantur, tractentur et reputentur in omnibus et per omnia et quoad omnia et gaudea[n]t et potiantur et gaudere et potiri possint et debeant omnibus et singulis privilegiis, beneficiis et immunitatibus ac officiis quibuscunque, quibus gaudent seu gaudebunt vel potiri poterunt quicunque alii et veri originarii et antiqui cives civitatis eiusdem ».

[20] *Ibid.*: « Item quod omnes artifices seu artiste de Sancto Geminiano predicto et eius curia vel districtu, qui volent intrare seu admicti in matriculam seu ad matriculam alicuius artium civitatis Florentie, possi[n]t et debea[n]t per consules eiusdem artis in ipsa et ad ipsam matriculam recipi et admicti sine aliqua solutione pecunie ... ». On matriculation fees, which were regularly higher for foreigners, see A. Doren, *Le arti fiorentine*, tr. G. B. Klein (Florence, 1940), I, 159-162. For the guild of lawyers and notaries, see Martines, *Lawyers and Statecraft*, pp. 28-32.

[21] See document cited in the preceding note.

[22] *ASF*, *Diplomatico*, *San Miniato*, 17 Feb. 1370 (New Style). The treaty has been edited by G. Lami, *Monumenta Ecclesiae Florentinae* (Florence, 1758), pp. 448-460. For the passage on citizenship, see *ibid.*, p. 450. Information and descriptions of the *curia* of San Miniato are found in *ibid.*, p. 459; *ASF*, *Diplomatico*, *San Miniato*, 28 May 1374; *ibid.*, *Carte Corredo*, 24, 70 v.

a period of probationary residency in the capital city unless they intended to enter public life. If they decided to seek office — an office for which only Florentine citizens were eligible — they would then have to furnish proof of six months residency in Florence [23]. As we can see, the legal arrangements forged between the capital city and her subjects were not uniform. Earlier, in 1324, the men of Carmignano had been awarded the privileges of « veri cives » but not those of original citizens [24]. The pact in which Montecatini submitted to Florentine rule in 1330 provided that the Montecatinesi were to be known as « veri cives districtuales et populares et comitatini » [25]. In the case of both Carmignano and Montecatini, eligibility for office was not detailed in the treaties.

These treaties as well as the *provvisioni* conferring original citizenship upon several hundred families had a marked impact upon the internal life of the city. The impact upon matriculation requirements of the *Arte dei Giudici e Notai* offers one excellent example. As we have already seen, any lawyer or notary who was unable to prove that he was a native of the city or *contado* could not matriculate into the guild. Besides this require-

---

[23] Lami, p. 450: « Salvo et excepto ... quod ad officia communis Florentie ad que solum cives Florentini possint eligi vel deputari, nullus eorum possit eligi vel deputari aliqualiter nisi sit vere guelfus et nisi habitaret saltem per sex menses continuos ... cum familia in civitate Florentie in domo sua propria vel constructa, et quod ad probandum de habitatione predicta sufficiat depositio trium testium probantium coram domino potestatis civitatis Florentie ... ». The proviso about Guelfism stemmed from Florentine fears of San Miniato's attachment to the Ghibelline cause, which was very much alive in 1369 and had provoked Florence into a military expedition against the Sanminiatesi. G. Brucker, *Florentine Politics and Society*, p. 238.

[24] *ASF*, *Capitoli-Registri*, 32, 185 r (4 Jan. 1324). Additional copies of this treaty are located in *ASF*, *Provv*, 21, 77 r-78 r; *AGN*, 670, 119 v. On the differences between *veri cives* and *cives originarii*, see below, p. 252.

[25] *ASF*, *Capitoli-Registri*, 32, 171 r (17 Sept. 1330). This act also declared that « omnes de Montecatino, qui nunc iudices, medici, notarii et alii artifices, possint ipsorum artem exercere libere in civitate, comitatu et districtu Florentie et intrare in collegio artium de quibus fuerint vel quas exercerent et se describere et scribi facere in matriculis dictarum artium absque aliqua solutione facienda », *ibid.* Throughout the fourteenth century, the immigration policy of the Florentine government was marked by the preferential treatment accorded to lawyers, doctors, notaries and other skilled *artifices*; Becker, *Florence in Transition*, II, 96 ff.

ment, the matriculant's father had to have resided in the city or *contado* for at least twenty-five years [26]. Such qualifications, the most rigorous among all the guilds in Florence, became less rigid in February, 1371 [27]. From now on, any lawyer or notary who was a « native of the city, *contado* or district of Florence or the lands which had come or would come under the jurisdiction of Florence » was allowed to matriculate into the guild [28]. Also admitted into the guild were lawyers and notaries whose origin lay outside the jurisdiction of Florence, but who possessed the *privilegium civilitatis* [29]. The following year, on October 9, 1372,

---

[26] *ASF, AGN*, 749, 37 v, 38 v: « Et quod (the matriculant) sit vel fuerit civis vel comitatinus Florentie, vel quod saltem sit oriundus de comitatu Florentie, et pater eius habitaverit in ipsa civitate vel comitatu per viginti quinque annos ».

[27] This remark is based on an examination of the fourteenth-century statutes of other guilds. See, for example: *Statuti dell'arte della lana di Firenze (1317-1319)*, ed. A. Agnoletti (Florence, 1940), pp. 84, 100-101; *Statuti dell'arte del cambio (1299-1316)*, ed. G. Camerani Marri (Florence, 1955), p. 67; *Statuti dell'arte di Por Santa Maria del tempo della Repubblica*, ed. U. Dorini (Florence, 1934), pp. 20-24, 208-209, 272; *Statuti dell'arte dei rigattieri e linaioli di Firenze (1296-1340)*, ed. F. Sartini (Florence, 1940), pp. 128, 221, 233-234; *Statuti delle arti dei fornai e dei vinattieri di Firenze (1337-39)*, ed. F. Morandini (Florence, 1956), pp. 24, 79-82; *Statuti delle arti dei corazzai dei chiavaioli, ferraioli e calderai e dei fabbri di Firenze (1321-44)*, ed. G. Camerani Marri (Florence, 1957), pp. 76, 90, 206, 232; *Statuti delle arti dei correggiai, tavolacciai e scudai, dei vaiai e pellicciai di Firenze (1338-1386)*, ed. G. Camerani Marri (Florence, 1960), pp. 33, 50, 94-96; *Statuti delle arti degli oliandoli e pizzicagnoli e dei beccai di Firenze (1318-1346)*, ed. F. Morandini (Florence, 1961), pp. 76, 174-175, 242; R. Ciasca, *L'arte dei medici e speziali nella storia e nel commercio fiorentino dal secolo XII al XV* (Florence, 1927), pp. 31 ff.

[28] *ASF, AGN*, 748, 153 r: « ... quod dominus proconsul et consules dicte artis, qui pro tempore fuerint, non possint, audeant vel presumant aliquem ad dictam artem et collegium recipere vel admittere cuius pater non sit vel fuerit oriundus de civitate, comitatu vel districtu Florentie et seu de terris que venerunt seu venient sub iurisdictione communis Florentie sub pena librarum quinquaginta sol. par ... ».

[29] *Ibid.*: « Et si receptus et matriculatus fuerit cuius receptio et matriculatio non valeat et non teneat, sit ipso iure nulla talis receptio [et] matriculatio, nisi talis receptus et matriculatus seu recipiendus et matriculandus haberet privilegium civilitatis a communi Florentie ». According to Martines, *Lawyers and Statecraft* (pp. 28-29): « During most of the fourteenth century, the guild demanded that the candidate for matriculation, lawyer or notary, be of Florentine origin and that his father have been a resident of the city or county of Florence for at least twenty-five years. This twenty-

the guild announced that lawyers and notaries of the city or *provincia* of Florence, could assume public office if they had lived in the city proper with their families for five years [30]. The modification of the guild's requirements in order to introduce into its ranks men from beyond the walls of Florence was largely due to the need for additional lawyers and notaries to serve in the burgeoning territorial state.

The new citizens also played an influential role in Florentine political life. One has only to remember that the humanist chancellor Coluccio Salutati was a Florentine citizen by privilege and not by birth [31]. As the new citizens gained admission into public office, however, they inspired resentment, indeed scorn, among the conservative elements of Florentine society: the older, patrician families, the *Parte Guelfa* and powerful guildsmen. Conflict between the new men and these conservative forces was vividly emphasized in the chronicles of Giovanni Villani and Donato Velluti and has been re-emphasized in recent histories of Trecento Florence [32]. Neither the new men nor their opponents, it must be underlined, represented homogeneous groups in which their political and social affiliations are always identifiable. Still, a struggle over political power and an emotional, deep-seated distrust of the outsider led to repressive measures (which were analyzed by Paolo di Castro) whose purpose was clearly to sweep the new men from the public offices which they had won.

Despite their commanding position in the government in 1346, for instance, the *novi cives* were upset by a coalition of

---

five year requirement remained in effect throughout the fifteenth and sixteenth centuries ». The documents cited in this and the preceding note demonstrate that there were important exceptions to this requirement, and so does a guild statute of 1415, where either the matriculant, his father or his grandfather could fulfill the residency requirement. *ASF*, *AGN*, 2, 2 v: « Admictendi sint de legitimo matrimonio nati et [qui] habitaverint in civitate vel comitatu Florentie per se vel patrem aut avum per xxv annos ».

[30] *AGN*, 748, 201 v-202 r.

[31] Martines, *The Social World of the Florentine Humanists*, pp. 148-149.

[32] G. Villani, *Cronica*, ed. Dragomanni (Florence, 1844-45), XII, 72, 79, 92; *Cronica domestica di Messer Donato Velluti*, ed. I. del Badia and G. Volpi (Florence, 1914), pp. 242-43; Brucker, *Florentine Politics and Society*, pp. 20-25, 105-127, 202 ff.; Becker, *Florence in Transition*, II, 93-149; Martines, *Lawyers and Statecraft*, p. 44.

older families, the *Parte Guelfa*, and defectors from their own camp. In October, 1346 these forces managed to muster enough votes to push a bill through the councils which disqualified from office any citizen who could not demonstrate that his father, and even more crucial, paternal grandfather, were natives of the city or *contado* [33]. As Brucker has shown, the immediate effect of the law proved devastating, as new citizens were prevented from holding office [34]. Similar provisions were enacted in 1379 during the period of « popular » government. This time a coalition between the leaders of the *arti minori* and their patrician allies pressed for legislation to remove new citizens from the officeholding class [35]. On August 13, 1379 the councils passed a petition « pro parte plurium civium honorabilium mercatorum et artificium », which demanded that those unable to trace their *origo* back to the city or *contado* should not share in the honors of public office. By *origo*, the petition meant that one's father had to be actually born in the city or the *contado*. The law also excluded men from office who had acquired Florentine citizenship *ex privilegio* [36].

The chronicler, Marchionne di Coppo Stefani, related that the law caused an uproar among the *minori* and other groups

---

[33] *ASF, Provv*, 34, 93 v-94 v; Brucker, *Florentine Politics and Society*, pp. 116-119, discusses this law as well as other provisions enacted against the new men.

[34] Brucker, p. 118.

[35] Typical of the demands for disenfranchising this group heard in the meetings of the executive council was that of the patrician Benedetto Alberti: « Provideatur quod forenses non habeant officia et fiat lex talis quod executioni mandetur ». *ASF, Consulte e Pratiche*, 17, 82 v (11 Aug. 1379). For the political affiliations of Benedetto Alberti, see Brucker, p. 391; Becker, *Florence in Transition*, II, 193. Speaking on the same day as Alberti, Angelo da Pino offered a somewhat different solution to the problem: « quod forenses non habeant officia; provideatur cum legibus veteribus, non faciendo novas »; *Consulte e Pratiche*, 17, 82 v.

[36] *ASF, Provv*, 68, 108 r: « Nullus cuius pater non fuerit oriundus et natus de civitate seu tunc tempore, videlicet nativitatis patris de comitatu Florentie vero, proprio et reali seu in civitate aut in tunc vero, proprio et reali comitatu Florentie ... etiam si per formam aut vigorem aliquorum ordinamentorum vel provisionum dicti communis civilitatis beneficium consequutus fuisset aut ipsam civilitatem diceretur prescripsisse aut aliter ipsius civilitatis beneficium pretenderetur habere, possit de cetero extrahi, eligi vel assumi ad officia ... ».

which remain unnamed [37]. Damaged by the law, of course, were the *cives ex privilegio*. Pressures mounted upon the government to repeal the statute [38]. From the 27th to the 29th of August, 1379, the *Signoria* grappled with this issue. Representatives of the guilds (*capitudini*) as well as the nine consuls of the *Mercanzia* were consulted; jurists were requested to help revise the statute [39]. Two central problems faced the policymakers. In the first place, the legal validity of statutes which repealed privileges and rights acquired by treaty was questionable. This view was voiced by the noted jurists, Angelo da Perugia (ca. 1328-ca. 1407), and Giovanni di Ruggero Ricci (ca. 1334-1421) [40]. Secondly, there was confusion over the legal definition of the *contado*. Interpreted in a narrow and traditional sense, the *contado* signified the countryside outside the walls of the city. Given a broader meaning, it might include many of the lands comprising the territory of Florence. This latter definition was put forward by Niccolò Guingi in late August of the same year. Speaking for the *Dodici Buonuomini* in the executive council, he argued that the *contado* ought to include the provinces of Valdinievole, Valdiariane, Valdarno, and other acquired lands [41]. His position was not incorporated into a new statute of September 6, 1379.

---

[37] Stefani, *Cronica fiorentina*, ed. N. Rodolico, *Rerum Italicarum Scriptores*, vol. XXX, Part I (Città di Castello, 1903-1955), rub. 818, p. 346.

[38] *Ibid.*

[39] *ASF*, *Consulte e Pratiche*, 17, 92 r-94 v. Speaking on August 29, Benedetto Alberti declared: « Super lege facta contra forenses, habeantur sapientes communis; et declarent eam et postea conferatur cum capitudinibus et illud quod eis placuerit fiat »; *ibid.*, 93 v. On the 31st of August, Jacopo Ubaldini urged: « Super lege contra forenses, habeant domini duos aut plures de novem mercantie et duo per capitudinem et dicatur eis quod domini intendunt taliter providere quod ipsi sint contenti »; *ibid.*, 94 v. The protocols of the Mercanzia during this crucial period contain no reference to these issues; see *ASF*, *Mercanzia*, 197 (Aug. 1379), no pagination.

[40] This information comes from a second *consilium* of Paolo di Castro on notaries and citizenship in Florence, written in 1421; *Consilia*, I, *cons.* CCLXXIII, 142 v. I have been unsuccessful in locating the opinions of Ricci and Angelo da Perugia on the laws of '79 in the major manuscript collections of *consilia* (Biblioteca Vaticana, Biblioteca Nazionale of Florence, Archivio di Stato of Florence and Biblioteca Classense of Ravenna) or in the editions of Angelo's *consilia*.

[41] *ASF*, *Consulte e Pratiche*, 17, 93 v. A subject city as far away as Arezzo was considered part of the *contado* of Florence; see the *Statuta* of 1415, *ed. cit.*, III, 532-533.

This enactment began by barring from office anyone whose father or elder male kin had not been born in the city or *contado*. The *contado* was broadly defined as those localities which were then subject to the rural *estimo* and the tax on wine sold at retail (*gabella vini ad minutum*) [42]. Although the law was to be enforced even against citizens who had been granted the privilege of citizenship, members of this group whose fathers or elder male relatives originated from any locality within twenty-five miles of Florence and from her district or dependencies were allowed to hold office [43]. Thus far the measure represented a definite retreat from the law of August, since the description of the *contado* and the exemptions outlined covered a substantial part of the population within the territory of Florence. But the restrictive nature of the law was revealed in a separate clause which stated that any native from the district, namely, Valdinevole, Valdiariane, Lower Valdarno, San Gimignano, the communes

---

[42] *ASF*, *Provv*, 68, 120 r: « Quod nullus cuius pater aut alius cuius adscendens masculus et per lineam masculinam non fuerit natus in civitate Florentie aut in comitatu ipsius civitatis, intelligendo ad hoc pro comitatu dumtaxat omnem locum in quo ad presens sit singulariter distributus extimus comitatus Florentie et solvat ad presens vel solitus sit solvere extimum comitatus communis Florentie, et qui non sit exemptus ad presens a solutione gabelle vini ad minutum dicti communis, etiam si tot privilegium civilitatis haberet, nisi ut infra describetur de privilegiis, possit de cetero extrahi, eligi vel assumi ad officia ... ». Because of fragmentary sources, it is very difficult to state with precision the area which formed the *contado* described in the statute. Certainly the smaller towns and rural areas near Florence could be described as the *contado*. For the rural *estimo* in this period, see *ASF*, *Estimo*, 48 (date: 1374). On the *gabella vini ad minutum*, see C. M. de la Roncière, « Indirect Taxes or ' Gabelles ' at Florence in the Fourteenth Century », *Florentine Studies*, pp. 166-173.

[43] *ASF*, *Provv*, 68, 121 r: « Et salvo, expresso et declarato, quod nullo cuius pater aut alius adscendens masculus et per lineam masculinam fuerit de aliquo loco propinquo civitati Florentie per viginti quinque miliaria vel minus aut de districtu Florentie vel de alio loco subiecto ad presens communi Florentie et cui nominatim et cum expressione nominis talis persone cui privilegium tale sit concessum per aliquam provisionem seu ordinamentum dicti communis fuisset hactenus concessum privilegium civilitatis per predictum preiudicium generetur vel fieri possit nec alicui tali privilegio vel aliquibus in ea contentis intelligatur esse vel sit per predictum vel aliquod predictorum in aliquo derogatum vel in aliquo preiudicium factum. Et quodlibet tale privilegium in sui firmitate in omnibus suis partibus persistat prout et quamadmodum concessum fuit ».

of Civitella di Valambra and Bibbiena, the commune and the curia of San Miniato, the Montagna, Poderi and Alpi of Florence could be elected to or selected for office only under specified conditions. They were obligated to live in Florence and pay taxes there as citizens (*ut cives*) for a period of thirty years and be included in the *estimo* imposed on the city in 1379 [44].

The September provision created a climate of suspicion which is illustrated in petitions presented to the government by those whose qualifications for office were now questioned. A typical petition concerned a notary, Ser Alberto. His father had arrived in the city about 1330, where he continued to live up until the time of his death. In Florence he had led a model life: breeding children, paying taxes and serving the state. Ser Alberto himself had held several notarial posts in the Florentine bureaucracy. The petition complained that because of the September provision, Ser Alberto's right to be chosen for or elected to office had been jeopardized and asked the government to certify his citizenship and his rights. On January 13, 1380 the councils voted favorably to approve the petition, declaring that Alberto was indeed a *civis originarius*, who possessed the capacity to assume office as other original citizens [45].

If the legislation of '79 caused consternation among the new citizens, it was rather ineffective in preventing them from entering the government. According to a recent and convincing essay, the years from 1382 to the early fifteenth century witnessed an increase in the entrance of new men into the ranks

---

[44] *Ibid.*, 121 r-121 v. By including San Gimignano in the district, the legislators disregarded the fact that this town had been incorporated into the *contado* in 1353.

[45] *Ibid.*, *Provv*, 68, 226 r (13 Jan. 1380); see also a petition of Ser Taddeo da Montegonzi; *ibid.*, 195 r-v (24 Dec. 1379). A Ser Orlando Giovanni di Piemonte was made a citizen of Florence on November 24, 1379; *ibid.*, 174 v-175 r. He ran into trouble with the communal authorities when he failed to build a house in the city, a requirement in the statute which gave him citizenship.His case went to court and a *consilium*, whose author remains unknown, was read on his behalf. What is important here is that one of the questions in this case was whether or not Ser Orlando could hold office under the regulations imposed by the September law. The lawyer answered in the affirmative. The *consilium* is found in *BV*, *MS. Vat. lat.* 14094, 391 r-393 r.

of officeholders [46]. The tapering off of this trend coincided with the enactment of yet another law establishing very stiff qualifications for office. This provision of October 7, 1404 declared that members of the seven *arti maggiori* and the *scioperati* (rentiers) were to be excluded from the priorate, colleges and all communal offices to which citizens were customarily elected unless they and/or their fathers or any of their male relatives (*consors vel coniunctus*) had previously paid *prestanze* in the city for a period totaling thirty years. A twenty-five year *prestanza* obligation was placed upon the members of the *arti minori* [47]. Due to the constant demand for notaries by the Florentine bureaucratic machine, the notariate was given an exemption from the thirty year requirement imposed upon its guild. This exemption applied to notarial posts normally staffed by non-citizens, for the law stipulated that in the future notaries would have to fulfill a twenty year *prestanza* obligation in order to be elected

---

[46] A. Molho, « Politics and the Ruling Class in Early Renaissance Florence », *Nuova rivista storica*, LII (1968), 408-415.

[47] *ASF*, *Provv*, 93, 100 r-v: « Quod aliquis de membro maiorum artium vel scioperatorum, qui ipse seu cuius pater aut consors seu coniunctus per lineam masculinam non solvit hactenus prestantias in civitate Florentie ad minus per tempus triginta annorum iam complectorum, et aliquis de membro minorum artium dicte civitatis, qui ipse seu cuius pater aut consors vel coniunctus per lineam masculinam non solvit hactenus ad minimum per tempus viginti quinque annorum iam complectorum prestantias in dicta etiam civitate, non possit de cetero habere, obtinere vel quocunque vigore, privilegio seu iure modo aliquo exercere officium prioratus artium et vexilliferatus iustitie et gonfalonieratus societatum populi et duodecim bonorum virorum communis Florentie vel aliquod ipsorum officiorum et seu aliquod aliud officium communis vel civitatis Florentie aut pro ipso communi congruens civibus ipsius civitatis et seu aliquod eligerentur, extraherentur vel deputarentur aut essent soliti extrahi, eligi vel deputari cives seu de civibus dicte civitatis ». According to Molho, « Politics and the Ruling Class », p. 407, there were over 3,000 government offices to be staffed by citizens every year. The Florentine judiciary was always staffed by foreigners. Although Molho's portrait of the officeholding class in this period is excellent, he does not explain why « the momentary expansion of the Florentine body politic » was curtailed in the opening years of the Quattrocento. The precise grouping of forces among the commercial, industrial and banking *haute bourgeoisie* — the dominant political groups at this moment — which pushed the laws of 1404 through the councils, remains to be explained. The protocols of the *Consulte e Pratiche* are silent on these issues.

to notarial offices customarily held by citizens [48]; in other words, the most prestigious notarial offices in the government [49].

The use of the vague words *consors* and *coniunctus* to designate male kin were interpreted very loosely by candidates for public posts, much to the dismay of the government. The legislators moved swiftly to clarify their intentions. On October 31 of the same year, a provision was passed limiting the meaning of *consors* and *coniunctus* to one's flesh and blood: father, paternal uncle and brother (*frater carnalis ex eodem patre*) [50].

Although these rigid requirements contributed to a general contraction of the officeholding class, they were not entirely effective in barring *cives ex privilegio* from office. Members of this group, particularly notaries, contested the relevancy of the laws of 1404 to their privileged status; their contention rested squarely upon the formal treaties made between the capital city and their native towns. Some of the leading lawyers in this period were engaged to argue their case [51]. This legal challenge was successful in pinpointing the weaknesses of the laws and complicating their enforcement. By 1414 several of the major

---

[48] *Provv*, 93, 100 v: «Et quod aliquis, qui sit vel esset in futurum notarius, qui et seu cuius pater vel consors seu coniunctus per lineam masculinam non solvit prestantias in civitate Florentie hactenus ad minus per tempus viginti annorum iam complectorum, non possit deinceps ullo tempore habere, obtinere vel aliqualiter exercere in ipsa civitate aliquod officium notariatus alicuius officii dicti communis Florentie ad quod notarii cives seu de notariis civibus Florentinis solent pro notariis et ut notarii eligi, extrahi vel deputari».

[49] Note that the law attaches the twenty-year *prestanza* requirement to notarial offices staffed by citizens according to custom. Drawing upon guild and electoral records (*tratte*), one may say that in the early fifteenth century the following offices were customarily staffed by citizen-notaries: notaries serving the Signory, the Ten on War, the Monte (the public debt), the Eight on Public Safety, the Treasury, the Ten on Liberty, the Tribunal of the Mercanzia, the officials supervising communal elections, the Six on Arezzo and the Ten on Pisa. *ASF*, *AGN*, 98, no pagination (date: 4 May-31 Aug. 1400); *ibid.*, 99, 151 r-163 v (Jan. 1404, New Style); *ibid.*, 102, 151 r-155 r (Oct. 1412); *Tratte*, 79, 348 v-403 r (date: 1411-1426); *ibid.*, 134, no pagination (date: 1412-1430). On this theme, see Martines, *Lawyers and Statecraft*, p. 13.

[50] *ASF*, *Provv*, 93, 120 v-121 r.

[51] For the lawyers and their arguments, see below p. 246 ff. According to Paolo di Castro some of these cases were actually won; *Consilia*, *cons.* CCLXXIII, 142 ra.

guilds were complaining that the tax requirements were not being observed nor enforced by the officials of the commune, especially in regard to the office of guild consul [52]. Opposition to the thirty year *prestanza* requirement was based on the grounds that the office of consul should not be classified as a communal office, and thus its holders were not subject to the tax requirement. The guilds took steps to remedy the situation. Statutes were enacted by the major and minor guilds on December 21, 1414 which declared « that the office of consul was and is an office of the people and of the city of Florence and the city of Florence is ruled and governed by the guilds » [53]. To make certain that only qualified candidates would be admitted to the consulship, these guilds set up registers to keep track of the *prestanze* paid by their members. Those who failed to meet the tax requirement were disqualified from holding the consulship and *consilia* alleged on behalf of the disenfranchised were to be considered null and void [54].

Because of their great number within the administration of the state, a high percentage of those who would be prevented from holding select offices were immigrant notaries. In the early fifteenth century, about 10 per cent of the notaries functioning in the bureaucracy could trace their origins to San Miniato alone [55]. True, in large measure, these notaries held minor posts in

---

[52] Due to gaps in the sources, complete references for all twenty-one guilds cannot be offered; where registers of guild statutes exist for the year 1414, legislation on officeholding appears without exception. Statutes passed by the individual guilds were uniform in both content and wording. Therefore, it is not an exaggeration to speak of a collective position on officeholding taken by the guilds in 1414. References: R. Ciasca, *L'arte dei Medici e Speziali*, pp. 140-141; *Statuti dell'arte dei Medici e Speziali* (Florence, 1922), pp. 402-405; *Statuti dell'arte di Por Santa Maria*, pp. 435-36; *ASF*, *Lana*, 6, 97 v-99 r; *Calimala*, 5,109 r-110 v; *Cambio*, 5, 127 v-129 v; *Albergatori*, 3, 118 r-119 r; *Corrazzai e Spadai*, 2, 25 v-27 r; *Fabbri*, 1, 84 v-86 v; *Calzolai*, 1, 13 r (a partial copy of the original statute); *Legnaioli*, 4, 23 v-24 r; *Corregiai*, 1, 85 v-87 r; *Chiavaioli, Ferraioli e Calderai*, 1, 103 r-104 v.

[53] *Ibid.*

[54] *Ibid.*

[55] This figure represents a reliable estimate, not an exact number. In 1400 there were approximately 400 notaries in the guild. About 170 notaries were in the administration of the government. In the same year, there were 19 notaries in the guild with « da San Miniato » after their names,

the territory of Florence rather than the more powerful and attractive positions in the city [56]. The purpose of the October laws was not to reduce their number in the administration of the territories of Florence. The central issue was whether or not *cives ex privilegio* could be elected to the major notarial posts traditionally reserved for citizens, even though they had not met the requirements established in 1404.

As we have seen, the *Arte dei Giudici e Notai* commissioned Paolo di Castro to defend the laws of 1404. After reviewing the statutes which had a bearing on the case, Paolo raised three major questions. The first concerned the legal force carried by the statute of 1404 in view of the old Statute of the Captain and the legal requirements of the guild itself. Next, it was asked whether the statute of '79 had been superseded by the later legislation. Finally, in what way was the *privilegium civilitatis* held by the notaries of subject communities to be respected by the government?

To the first question, the jurist applied an old Roman legal principle: when two laws are in conflict, the one which is general in nature is repealed by the law whose scope is specific (*quod generi per speciem derogatur*) [57]. The Captain's Statute, he argued, was general with respect to persons and offices and referred to all guildsmen and every communal office. As the guild statute was binding upon only notaries, it was particular; however, since this statute failed to single out offices under its jurisdiction,

---

all residents of Florence and almost all working for the government. Whether they were first, second or third generation residents cannot be ascertained from the guild records; the same is true for the six notaries « da San Gimignano » and the fourteen « da Prato ». *ASF*, *AGN*, 98, no pagination (May, 1400). By May, 1404 the number of notaries in the guild whose origins could be traced to San Miniato had climbed to 24; the number of Sangimignanesi remained steady at six. *Ibid.*, 100, 17 r (13 May 1404).

[56] In October, 1412 there were 17 notaries « da San Miniato » serving in the territorial state: at Pescia, Barga, Prato, S. Croce sull'Arno, Signa, in the territory of Pisa and Castiglion Fiorentino. *Ibid.*, 102, 155 r-156 v.

[57] *Consilia*, *cons.* XXI, 13 rb. See also Paolo's comments *ad C.* 1, 1, 1, *In primam codicis* ... (Venice, 1568), 2 v. The Roman sources cited by Paolo are found in the *Digest* and *Code*: *D.* 48, 19, 41; *D.* 45, 1, 53; *D.* 45, 1, 19; *D.* 32, 41 § *felicissimo*; *C.* 12, 16, 3. On this theme, see the *consilium* of Angelo da Perugia, *Consilia* (Frankfort, 1575), *cons.* CCCLV, 254 r-255 r. Angelo held the same opinion as Paolo.

it was in part general [58]. The twenty year *prestanza* requirement of 1404, on the other hand, specifically referred to notaries and notarial offices. From this analysis, he concluded that the law of October 6, 1404 takes precedence over the other two statutes with regard to notaries [59].

All the requirements laid down by the Captain's Statute were, he stated, binding upon citizens seeking a guild consulship. Candidates for this office could either be *cives originarii*, that is, of the city proper, or simply citizens of the *contado*, *cives comitatenses*. The distinction between these two grades of citizenship had been sharply etched in Bartolus' (d. 1357) commentary on citizenship, and his formulations were cited by Paolo [60]. Yet, in order to be eligible for a consulship according to the Statute of the Captain, any citizen would have to be *allibratus* or have resided in the city for ten years. Paolo saw a problem here; he observed that *allibratus* referred to *comitatensis*, whereas *prestantiatus* pertained to *civis* [61]. Were candidates then exempt from paying *prestanze*? Even more relevant by the end of the fourteenth century, could citizens be eligible if they had paid *prestanze*, but not the *estimo*? A correct interpretation of the Captain's Statute, he maintained, would permit *cives originarii* who paid *prestanze* for ten years to be candidates for the consulship, though they may not have inhabited the city during that period. It would also allow *cives comitatenses* to assume this post if they had been *allibrati* or had lived in the city for ten years. *Comitatenses* could substitute *prestanze* payments for the *estimo* [62]. The ten year tax

---

[58] *Consilia*, *cons.* XXI, 13 rb; « Secundum vero statutum de v annis est speciale quoad personas non (*MS*: *om.* non) notariorum tantum, sed generale quoad omnia officia communis Florentie ». I have followed the more logical reading of the manuscript; *ASF*, *AGN*, 670, 123 r.

[59] *Consilia*, *cons.* XVII rb.

[60] *Ibid.*; Bartolus, *ad D.* 50, 1, 1, *ed. cit.*, VI, 217 r-v: « ... et sic natus ex cive, ubicumque nascatur, erit civis. Item natus ex comitatensi, ubicumque nascatur, erit civis comitatensis ».

[61] *Consilia*, *cons.* XXI, 13 rb-13 va: « Item (the Captain's Statute) dicit allibratus quod pertinet ad comitatenses, non prestantiatus, quod pertinet ad cives, sed secundum qualitatem personarum sunt verba exaudienda ... ».

[62] *Ibid.*, 13 va: « Sufficit ergo quod si est civis fuerit prestantiatus per annos X, si comitatensis fue[rit] allibratus vel prestantiatus et hoc importat significatio dictorum verborum a quibus non est recedendum ». This passage in the MS is more complete than the edition: « Sufficit ergo quod si

obligation imposed by the Captain's Statute, he continued, was still valid with respect to every office in the commune except that of notary [63]. Paolo did not attempt to reconcile his assertion with the twenty-five to thirty year tax requirements made mandatory by the laws of 1404.

Turning to the office of notary itself, Paolo tackled the problem of what the law of 1404 meant when it spoke of notarial offices customarily held by citizens. Did the legislation intend that only original citizens could assume such posts after meeting the tax requirement? Or could any notary be elected to these offices after paying *prestanze* for twenty years? Paolo explained that the law can be understood in three ways. If one asserts that the legislators had original citizens in mind, then the *comitatenses* — notaries from Montecatini and Carmignano — must be excluded from office, because they were not extended the privileges of original citizenship [64]. As Paolo stated:

... considero quod illi de Carmignano et de Montecatino non fuerunt recepti ad illam civilitatem quam habent originarii cives, sed (*Ed*: et) ad illam quam habent comitatenses; ideo nunquam eam sortiuntur, etiam si per mille annos starent in civitate Florentie, quia verum est dicere quod non sunt originarii cives, nec pro originariis fuerunt recepti, nec per dictam habitationem simplicem possent prescribere dictam civilitatem (*Ed*: civitatem), nisi fuissent tractati et reputati ut originarii per longum tempus ... [65]

The October provisions, it should be remembered, omitted any reference to original citizenship or grades of citizenship. Obviously aware of the contents of the law, Paolo proposed that if according to custom mere citizens as well as original citizens assumed the notarial offices under discussion, then *cives*

---

est civis fuerit prestantiatus per annos X, si comitatensis fuerit allibratus per totalem, licet non habitavit; vel quod habitaverit per X annos, licet non fuerit allibratus vel prestantiatus et hoc importat significatio dictorum verborum a quibus non est recedendum »; *AGN*, 670, 123 r. I have followed the reading of the MS. The difference between the manuscript version and the edition seems to be a result of *homoiteleuton*.

[63] *Consilia*, 13 va.

[64] *Ibid.*, 13 rb.

[65] *Ibid.*, 13 vb; *AGN*, 670, 124 r.

comitatenses should be considered eligible [66]. On the other hand, if custom is not introduced, there is no doubt that all notaries may be qualified, even foreign members of the guild [67]. To Paolo, the criterion of one's eligibility is determined by his fulfillment of the tax requirement. All notaries, foreigners as well as citizens, he therefore concluded, were qualified for office under the October laws if they had paid taxes for twenty years [68].

The statute of October 6, 1404 described these obligatory taxes as *prestanze*. In his analysis of the *comitatensis*' qualifications for office, Paolo apparently went beyond the letter of the law. In the edited version of the *consilium*, Paolo argued:

... nec curo si non solverunt prestantias ut cives, vel reformatio sic dictet, sed sufficit quod solverunt estimum sicut comitatenses, nam et illa sunt onera communis et quod operantur praestantie in civibus, operuntur estimum in comitatensibus, ut sic verba sint intelligenda secundum qualitatem personarum [69].

In the manuscript copy of the *consilium*, the exact opposite position is taken. Here, citizens from the *contado* must pay taxes

... in civitate Florentie et sic requiritur quod solverint prestantias sicut cives, nec sufficeretur soluisse extimum ut comitatenses ... [70]

Based on Paolo's analysis of the Captain's Statute, in which he stated that the terms *allibratus* and *prestantiatus* are respectively related to *comitatensis* and *civis*, it would seem at first that the edition offers a more faithful version of the jurist's thought. In his final conclusion to the case, however, he stated that notaries from the *contado* must pay *prestanze* for twenty years before they can hold office [71].

---

[66] *Consilia*, 13 rb.

[67] *Ibid.*

[68] *Ibid.*, 13 va: « ... et conclusio finalis est quod ad hoc ut notarii, tam cives quam forenses, possint habere officia notariatus, [sed] requiruntur ea quae continentur in reformatione supradicta loquente de annis xx ». Note that Paolo makes no distinction between offices in the city (*instrinsici*) and those outside (*estrinsici*).

[69] *Ibid.*, 13 rb.

[70] *ASF*, *AGN*, 670, 122 v.

[71] The manuscript copy is actually found in a volume of *consilia*, penned between 1388-1436 and housed in the archive of the guild. The differences

Comparing the statute of '79 to the one of 1404, Paolo acknowledged that he was perplexed. The statute of '79 combined both general and particular aims. It was general, because the law lacked reference to individual groups; and particular, because it listed the localities which were affected by the thirty year *prestanza* requirement. Conversely, the statute of 1404 was in part general, for it did not mention specific places. Once more, Paolo followed an opinion of Bartolus: the law which must be obeyed in this case is the one offering the greatest utility [72]. On the surface, the law of '79, with its thirty year tax requirement, would bring more revenue into the treasury. Nonetheless, Paolo insisted, if the twenty year requirement was observed, a greater number of notaries would be induced to pay their taxes in order to qualify for offices. Hence, the twenty year *prestanza* requirement is preferable, « quia plures habilitabuntur ad gubernationem reipublicae, quod est publicam utilem » [73]. Assuredly, Paolo's commitment to republicanism cannot be measured by a single statement conditioned by the imperatives of juridical analysis. He was a staunch and clever defender of oligarchy. As a result, his lovely republican sentiment was not extended to aspirants for public office outside the notariate.

---

between the edition and manuscript are important from an historical as well as a legal angle. We are not dealing here with simple variants, but two separate opinions which, in my view, cannot be solely ascribed to the carelessness of the copyist. It is possible that the scribe who copied the *consilium* attempted to make Paolo di Castro's arguments on taxation more consistent and made changes in order to bring Paolo's thought in line with the law of 1404. Whether or not he acted under instructions from his superiors in the guild is a moot question. According to the guild statutes, all *consilia* read in Florence had to be deposited with the guild under the signatures and seals of their authors. *AGN*, 748, 135 v-136 r (26 Sept. 1369). No doubt, the *consilium* under discussion was registered with the guild, but unfortunately the guild's collection of legal decisions has never been discovered and has probably been destroyed. Hopefully, future discoveries will enable us to establish the text of the *consilium* with more certitude. For Paolo's final conclusion, see below note 82.

[72] *Consilia*, 13 va-b. Paolo cited Bartolus' *Tractatus super constitutione « ad reprimendum »*, *Opera omnia*, *ed. cit.*, X, 103 ra-b§ *non obstantibus*. For a recent treatment of this work see E. Betti, « La dottrina costruita da Bartolo sulla constitutio 'ad reprimendum' », in *Bartolo da Sassoferrato. Studi e documenti per il VI centenario* (Milan, 1962), II, 39-47.

[73] *Consilia*, 13 vb.

The enactment of October '79 was not completely disabled by the later legislation. With the exception of the offices of notary and guild consul, candidates for all other offices were theoretically subject to the thirty-year tax requirement — if they came from the lands specifically named in the law of '79. Now the focal issue was this: what validity did this statute have in relation to the status of the *cives ex privilegio*, the Sanminiatesi and Sangimignanesi? The treaties (*pacta*) with these communities, Paolo ruled, ought to be upheld *de jure*, « quia non potest communitas venire contra contractum et pacta sua » [74]. To buttress his contention, he invoked Cino da Pistoia's (d. 1336/1337) famed commentary on the *lex Digna vox* (C. 1, 14, 4). Cino had demanded that the emperor must not break agreements which he has made with *civitates* under imperial jurisdiction, « quia honestas ligat etiam principem ... et nichil magis debetur homini quam pacta servare » [75]. This opinion, repeated with variations by Bartolus and Baldus, (1327-1400) [76], became an underlying legal principle regulating the relations between the city-state and its subject communities in Renaissance Italy. The principle was warmly endorsed in the fifteenth century by Giovanni da Imola (1367/1372-1436), Francesco Accolti (1416/1417-1488) and Giasone del Maino (1435-1519) [77]. In his own commentary on the *lex Digna vox*, Paolo di Castro reiterated earlier views, stating that the emperor must observe agreements made with his subjects as if he were a private person, and added that these pacts must be observed by his successor [78]. While the statute

---

[74] *Ibid.*, 14 rb.

[75] *Ibid.*; Cino da Pistoia, *ad* C. 1, 14, 4, *Super aureo volumine codicis* (Frankfort, 1578), 26 r. On Cino's doctrine, see R. W. and A. J. Carlyle, *A History of Medieval Political Theory in the West* (6 vols., Edinburgh and London, 1903-36), VI, 14-17, 84; E. Cortese, *La norma giuridica* (2 vols., Milan, 1964), I, 158-161.

[76] Bartolus, *ad C.* 1, 14, 4, *Opera omnia, ed. cit.*, VIII, 21 va; Baldus, *Commentaria super codice* (Lyons, 1545), 55 r.

[77] Carlyle, VI, 153-155.

[78] Paolo di Castro, *ad C.* 1, 14, 4, *In primam codicis ..., ed. cit.*, 26 va-b, « Ultimo, per istam legem determinantur duo. Primo, secundum Cynum quod si princeps facit aliquem contractum cum subditis, debet illud observare et non rumpere vel frangere vel contravenire, sicut quilibet alius privatus, et eodem modo eius successor observare tenetur, quum afficit ipsam dignitatem cuius ipse est administrator. Per hoc etiam determinat Bartolus

of '79 had in fact revoked treaties between Florence and her dependencies, Paolo explained that in point of law this statute was not binding [79].

No uncertainty existed in Paolo di Castro's mind about the binding force of the October legislation over the notaries of San Miniato, San Gimignano and other subject communities, who had become *cives ex privilegio* of Florence. Unlike the statute of '79, Paolo stressed, the enactment of 1404 was not expressly aimed at revoking the privileges held by a particular group of notaries, but touched all notaries. In no way could the statutes of 1404 be condemned for repealing solemn treaties. Logic dictated that the commune's agreements with her subjects must be up-dated, interpreted in the light of early fifteenth-century legislation. In her treaties, Paolo insisted, Florence never intended to convey benefits and privileges to her subjects which were not enjoyed by her own citizens. Similarly, it should never be presumed that Florence loved foreigners more than her own natives [80]. Paolo did not challenge the legal validity of acquired original citizenship, nor the statutory authority of the state to create original citizens. Yet he underscored his case by adopting the position that acquired original citizenship was similar to a fiction or shadow, which surely does not carry a greater advantage in regard to civic dignities than the rights of native born citizens [81]. Above all, the rights of new and old citizens would constan-

---

in l. omnes populi (*D.* 1, 1, 9), quod quando statutum transit in contractu[m] non potest a statuentibus revocari ». See Paolo's commentary *ad C.* 1, 2, 1, *ibid.*, 3 ra, where he argues that privileges conceded « per viam contractus » cannot be revoked.

[79] *Consilia*, 14 ra.

[80] *Ibid.*

[81] *Consilia*, 14 rb; « Hoc presuppositio dico, quod habentes talia privilegia non sunt melioris conditionis, quam illi qui sunt veri cives originarii, sic non possunt dicta officia notariatus habere nisi solverint prestantias per xx annos secundum formam dicte reformationis, sicut nec ipsi veri originarii, et hoc duplici ratione. Prima quia (*Ed*: quasi) fictio, seu figura vel umbra non potest plus operari quam veritas ... secunda (*Ed*: sed) quia dicta privilegia concessa sunt ad similitudinem eorum que habent veri et originarii cives, igitur et secundum communem qualitatem inhaerentem civibus, et cives veri habent cum illa conditione vel qualitate ...; *ASF*, *AGN*, 670, 125 r. In another *consilium* Paolo stated that a « civitas potest facere eum originarium per fictionem, sed non potest per veritatem facere quod non originarius sit originarius ». Cited by Bizzari, p. 53, n. 55. Paolo's notion

tly be redefined by future *constitutiones* and *reformationes* of Florence. Notwithstanding previous statutes and treaties, Paolo concluded, all notaries were obligated to fulfill the twenty-year tax requirement described in the law of 1404[82].

The *consilium* was countersigned and sealed by nine jurists, all members of the guild[83]. Among the lawyers, Bartolomeo Vulpi and Guaspare del Maestro Ludovico Accorambuoni (fl. 1381-1431) lent more than their signatures and seals, as they ventured their own opinions on the case. With regard to the notariate, Paolo di Castro abandoned the requirements for office established by the Captain's Statute and the guild. Since

---

of original citizenship is inextricably connected with the legal principle that original citizenship is ultimately based on birth, a natural process, and cannot be changed by the state except through fiction. As the lawyers declared: « origo non potest mutari ». This principle is firmly rooted in Roman law: *D.* 50, 1, 15 and *C.* 10, 39, 4. We find it expressed in the *Glossa ordinaria* to the *Corpus iuris civilis*, *ad D.* 50, 1, 6, *Adsumptio*, *ed. cit.*, col. 1703. In the fourteenth century, we find it in Bartolus' commentary *ad D.* 50, 1, 1 and *D.* 50, 1, 6, *ed. cit.*, VI, 217 rb-218 va. For Bartolus citizens are divided into two species, original and non-original: « Ita dico, quod civis subdividitur in duas alias species, quia alius originarius ... alius non originarius »; *ad C.* 10, 40, 7, *Cives*, *ed. cit.*, VIII, 21 va. See the remarks of Baldus *ad* C. 10, 39, 3, *Origine* and *C.* 10, 40, 4, *Non tibi*, *ed. cit.*, V, 270 vb. In a *consilium*, Francesco Albergotti (d. 1398) stated: « Considero quod civilitas quaedam est quae non potest induci nisi per naturam, ut civilitas originalis... quaedam est civilitas quae potest induci per constitutionem humanam et ista vere inducitur per statutum ». Cited by W. Ullmann, « De Bartoli sententia: concilium repraesentat mentem populi », in *Bartolo da Sassoferrato*, II, 726, n. 66.

[82] *Consilia*, 14 ra-b: « Concluditur ergo breviter, quod notarii sive sint de civitate sive de comitatu, etiam si de illis 12 terris vel castris supra nominatis (in the law of '79), non possunt consequi beneficia (*MS*: officia) notariatus, nisi solverint praestantias per annos xx secundum formam dicte nove reformationis, non obstantibus quibuscunque aliis statutis loquentibus de aliis temporibus ». *AGN*, 670, 125 v.

[83] *ASF*, *AGN*, 670, 125 v-126 v. The jurists were: 1) Rosso di Andreozzo Orlandi (fl. 1400-1420's), 2) Domenico di Ser Mino (fl. 1413), 3) Jacopo di Bartolomeo Niccoli (ca. 1370-1425), 4) Piero di Leonardo Beccanugi (1377/79-1460), 5) Stefano di Giovanni Buonaccorsi (1353-1433), 6) Federico da Castelcucho (fl. 1413), 7) Bartolomeo Vulpi, 8) Guaspare del Maestro Ludovico Accorambuoni, 9) Guaspare di Barizzi (fl. 1413). Including Paolo di Castro, ten lawyers had defended the laws of 1404 on behalf of the guild. For profiles on most of these jurists, see Martines, *Lawyers and Statecraft*, pp. 482-508.

he was not yet ready to disregard these venerable and traditional requirements, Vulpi attempted to modify Paolo's extreme position. Agreeing with Paolo on the legitimacy of the twenty-year *prestanza* requirement, Vulpi also demanded that before notaries could assume office they would still have to qualify as Guelfs, who were devoted to the Church, natives of the city or *contado* and residents of the city at the time of their election to office [84]. In some respects Vulpi's position reflected contemporary practice, as the guild requirement on residency was still in force, while lip service was still being offered to the requirement on Guelfism [85]. Guaspare approached the case from a different angle. After supporting Paolo's conclusions, he added that if notaries from the *contado* were permitted to continue their administrative duties, even if there was public knowledge that they had not met the twenty-year tax requirement, they should nonetheless be considered qualified for office. By tacitly allowing notaries to remain in office, Guaspare reasoned, the guild had in effect given them a dispensation from the law of 1404 [86]. This brief, interesting opinion was not developed.

With the forthcoming redaction of the *Statuta* in 1415, the jurists were presented with an excellent opportunity to settle the legal inconsistencies on the qualifications for officeholding. Under the direction of Paolo di Castro and Bartolomeo Vulpi, the rubric on the office of guild consul in the Statutes of the Captain (1355) was partially modified [87]. Candidates were no longer asked to prove that they were *allibrati*, but rather that they and/or their ancestors had been *prestantiati* for ten years. Earlier, one could have been eligible for office by fulfilling either the tax or city-residency requirement. Now both the ten year tax and residency requirements were made obligatory [88]. Where the old rubric had been concerned with both guild and communal offices, the new redaction addressed itself to guild offices with one notable exception. The rights of notaries who had become *cives ex privilegio* after October, 1379, including the right to hold

---

[84] *AGN*, 670, 126 r.
[85] See *ibid.*, 2, 4 r; on Guelfism, see below, p. 258-59.
[86] *AGN*, 670, 126 v.
[87] *Statuta, ed. cit.*, III, *liber* IV, *rub.* III, 160-161.
[88] *Ibid.*

office, the redactors wrote, were not to be prejudiced in any way by the present rubric, other communal ordinances or guild laws. Protection was also afforded to the male descendants of these notaries. The assurances and immunities given here were directly related to the controversy over the office of notary and the laws of 1404 [89], and raise an intriguing question: why were they made retroactive to November, 1379? If we recall, the statute of September 7, 1379 had reluctantly given similar assurances to those who had been granted the privilege of citizenship before that date. The immunities of 1415 were designed to offer protection to those made *cives ex privilegio* after the provision of '79. The very fact that the rights of the *cives ex privilegio* had to be protected is an indication of the precarious legal status of acquired citizenship in Florence.

Neither the guild's efforts in 1413, nor the *Statuta* promulgated two years later served to placate the new citizens or to defuse the conflict. Our witness here is Paolo di Castro, who wrote a second *consilium* on notaries and the laws of 1404 [90]. In this *consilium*, Paolo analyzed and attempted to refute the opinions of other jurists who defended the claims of the *cives ex privilegio*. Happily, several of these opinions have survived. They were penned by Antonio da Butrio (ca. 1338-1408), a leading Bolognese jurist and Guglielmo di Francesco Tanagli (1391-1460), a Florentine. Another Bolognese jurist Floriano da San Pietro (fl. 1400) dealt with the problems of the *cives ex privilegio* in Florence, but his *consilia* remain to be discovered, though his arguments and conclusions are reported by Paolo di Castro [91].

The two *consilia* written by Butrio can be dated between 1404 and his death in 1408. They were probably drafted at the request of certain *cives ex privilegio* hurt by the October statutes. In one *consilium*, he treated the problems of the Sangimignanesi.

---

[89] The laws of 1404 may have been interpreted to mean that notaries who were *cives ex privilegio* could not occupy offices customarily held by citizens, even though they had met the *prestanza* requirement.

[90] *Consilia, cons.* CCLXXIII, 142 vb. Some of Floriano's *consilia* have been edited and are found together with his commentary, *In primam et secundam ff. vet* .... (Bologna, 1576), II, 255 r-294 v. Several unpublished *consilia* of this jurist are found in *BV*, *Vat. lat.* 8068, 35 v-36 r, 80 r-81 v; *Vat. lat.* 8069, 383 r-385 v, 124 v-125 v; *Urb. lat.* 1132, 195 r-196 r, 210 r-213 r.

[91] *Consilia, cons.* CCLXXIII, 143 va-143 vb.

For this jurist, the legislators did not repeal the concessions made to the Sangimignanesi in 1353, because they failed to revoke them specifically in the statutes of 1404. In this manner, Paolo di Castro's argument on the specificity of the October laws was turned on its head [92]. Accenting the difference between a treaty and a statute, Antonio maintained that privileges ceded by treaty form a contractual obligation which cannot be broken [93]. The men from San Gimignano who reside in Florence for six months in accordance with the treaty have fulfilled their part of the contract. The Florentine government is obligated, therefore, not only by civil law (*civiliter*), but also has a natural obligation (*naturaliter*) to honor its contractual commitments [94]. The validity of the October measures, Antonio contended, must be doubted « lest the treaties, oaths, and the honor of living in so great a city are destroyed » [95].

Antonio's second *consilium* concerned the Pratesi [96]. When Prato fell under Florentine rule in 1351, the Pratesi became *comitatenses originarii* and the men of Prato who came to live in Florence with their families were awarded the privileges and benefits of original citizens, as well as the right to hold office after six months residency. These privileges were awarded by statute rather than by treaty [97]; in the eyes of the jurists they

---

[92] Antonio da Butrio, *Consilia* (Venice, 1582), *cons.* LIX, 77 rb: « Item quia ab istis dispositionibus generalibus privilegiati censeatur exemptio, ex quo specifica non fit mentio de privilegiis suis ... ». The manuscript copies of this *consilium* are practically identical to the edition. See *BV*, *MS. Vat. lat.* 2651, 371 r-372 v and a manuscript in the Biblioteca Medicea Laurenziana, Florence, *Aedile*, 60, 308 r-v.

[93] *Consilia*, *cons.* LIX, 77 ra: « ... quod ultima reformatio facta per opportuna consilia (6 Oct. 1404) non possit in aliquo detrahere primae concessioni factae hominibus de Sancto Geminiano tum quia non per viam statuti aut privilegii talia sunt, imo per viam contractus, ut patet in privilegio, in quo proponuntur pacta facta et conventiones et iuramenta praestita, etc. ».

[94] *Ibid.*, 77 rb.

[95] *Ibid.*: «Et sic (the October laws) in dubio interpretanda, ne pacta, iuramenta et decus domicilii tantae civitatis rumpantur in non servandis, quod promisit civitas, ... ».

[96] *Consilia*, *cons.* LXXIII, 88 vb-89 ra.

[97] Florence purchased Prato for 175,000 florins from the kingdom of Naples. *ASF*, *Provv*, 38, 183 r-187 r (23 Feb. 1351 Modern Style). For the provision detailing the legal rights of the Pratesi under their new masters, see *ibid.*, 189 r-191 v (28 Feb. 1351 Modern Style).

were dangerously vulnerable to the whims of the Florentine state. In his earlier *consilium* Antonio made a profound distinction between the binding force of a treaty, which was contractual in nature, and that of a simple statute. For him and his contemporaries, a treaty had greater legal weight than a mere statute [98]. This view was reinforced in his second *consilium*, where he accepted the conventional doctrine that the legislator can repeal a right acquired (*ius quaesitum*) by « the positive law of a statute » [99]. According to Antonio, however, the rights acquired by the Pratesi who had come to live and pay taxes in Florence should be respected. Their actions, he explained, transform the terms of a statute into a contract (though not into a privilege) [100]. The tendency to deny the state the right to revoke this type of statute, or any statute which was transformed into a contract, derived from the teaching of Bartolus [101]. Summing up his case, Antonio stated that the requirements for offices set forth

---

[98] This view was expressed by Guglielmo Tanagli and Paolo di Castro, as we shall shortly demonstrate.

[99] *Consilia, cons.* LXXIII, 88 vb. On this doctrine, see U. Nicolini, *La proprietà, il principe e l'espropriazione per pubblica utilità* (reprint, Milan, 1952), 115 ff., 167-171; Carlyle, VI, 15-21, 153-156; E. Cortese, *La norma giuridica*, I, 139-141; for the sixteenth and seventeenth centuries, see F. Oakley, « Jacobean Political Theology: The Absolute and Ordinary Powers of the King », *Journal of the History of Ideas*, XXIX (1968), 339. As his authority, Butrio cited pope Innocent IV, *ad X.* 1, 2, 7 and *X.* 5, 36, 8, *Apparatus super libros decretalium* (Venice, 1578), 2-3, and 223.

[100] *Consilia, cons.*, LXXIII, 88 vb.

[101] See the sources cited above in n. 78. Butrio's views were unquestionably derived from Bartolus' commentary on the *lex Omnes populi* (*D.* 1, 1, 9), where Bartolus stated: « Distingue, aut statutum stat in simplici dispositione statuti, aut transit in contractum, vel quasi. Primo casu per consequens potest statutum simplex revocari... Secundo casu non potest revocari in praeiudicium quasi contrahentis .... » Moreover, Bartolus treated a situation very close to that facing the *cives ex privilegio* in Florence: « Statuto cavetur quod qui venit ad habitandum in tali castro, habeat immunitatem perpetuo: quidam venerunt, nunc civitas vult revocare statutum, et vult ne illi gaudeant immunitate. Certe in praeiudicium earum, qui iam venerunt, non potest revocare. Secus in his, qui nondum venerunt. Nam dictum statutum transivit in contractum, vel quasi contractum, do ut facias, vel facio ut facias, id est, concedo tibi immunitatem ut venias, si aliqui venerunt, ex utraque parte perfectus est contractus ... ». This citation is found in Bartolus' *Opera omnia*, *ed. cit.*, I, 11 ra. Bartolus' teaching soon became a commonplace among the lawyers of the late Trecento and Quattrocento.

in 1404 refer to the future. The Pratesi, whose right to hold office had been acquired and exercised before October, 1404, even though they had not paid taxes for twenty years, must be observed by the Florentine government [102].

Guglielmo Tanagli also defended the *cives ex privilegio*, but the events leading to his *consilium* were quite different. In 1419 the *Arte dei Giudici e Notai* prohibited its members from accepting an office unless they had met the requirements of 1404 [103]. Candidates for office were required to take an oath at the time of their matriculation that they would not accept any office « contra formam statutorum vel ordinamentorum communis Florentiae vel dictae artis » [104]. Notaries who flouted the law were hauled before the court of the Podestà. Sometimes these cases were adjudicated by the *Signoria*. A Ser Niccolò di Berti Martini of San Gimignano had accepted an office contrary to the terms of the statutes and his case was heard by the priors and the colleges on May 3, 1421. This body instructed Tanagli and Alessandro di Salvi Bencivenni (1385-1423), who were then the official legal counselors of the government (*sapientes communis*), to submit a *consilium* on the case [105]. The opinion was actually written by Tanagli and approved by the more prominent Bencivenni.

In the brief to this case we are treated to a concise biography of Ser Niccolò. Besides coming from San Gimignano, he was a loyal Guelf and devoted to the Holy Roman Church. He had lived with his family in the city for many years [106]. From Paolo's *consilium* on this case, we learn that Ser Niccolò had actually been a resident of the city for five years, had paid *prestanze* for three, and had been matriculated into the guild for six. He intended, it was stated, to live in Florence forever, and to pay *prestanze* and all real and personal taxes to which he was subject [107].

[102] *Consilia, cons.* LXXIII, 89 ra.

[103] *ASF, AGN*, 2, 5 v: « Nullus qui non sit habilis secundum ordinamenta et leges factas in anno 1404 ... possit acceptare aliquod officium ... ».

[104] Paolo di Castro, *Consilia, cons.*, CCLXXXIII, 141 vb.

[105] *BNF, Magliabechiano, cl.* XXIX, 187, 227 r-229 v. For biographical information on both lawyers, see Martines, *Lawyers and Statecraft*, pp. 484, 492.

[106] *BNF, Magl., cl.* XXIX, 187, 228 r.

[107] See passage referred to above in n. 104.

Although Ser Niccolò had not paid *prestanze* for twenty years, this short profile tells us that his political and personal credentials were in good order.

Arguing *pro et contra*, Tanagli first wrote that the privileges ceded to the Sangimignanesi by treaty were nullified by the universal provision of October 6, 1404. This point was bolstered by a quote from Bartolus who stated that a *civitas* may rescind a *ius privatum* through one of its general statutes [108]. Quickly shifting to the defense of Ser Niccolò, Tanagli denied that the government had cancelled these privileges, « maxime cum nulla fiat mentio in dicta reformatione ... » [109]. While Bartolus had discussed the power of a *civitas* to strike down a *ius privatum*, Tanagli continued, he had also stated that a *civitas* cannot act *sine causa* [110]. To Tanagli, the action of the commune has no justification and echoing the *lex Digna vox*, the jurist indignantly rebuffed any suggestion that the legislation of 1404

> ... extendit sic ad privilegiatos ex pacto et conventione, sed solum intendit preiudicare et derogare exceptis et privilegiatis ex dispositione dumtaxat ordinamentorum et statutorum communis Florentie [111].

As Antonio da Butrio had done before, Tanagli anchored his case in the exalted, almost sacrosanct status of a treaty.

Beyond these straightforward legal arguments, Tanagli appealed indirectly to the *Signoria* to decide the case in favor of Ser Niccolò:

> Ergo cum non subsit causa nec retro fuerit, non est presumendum nec credendum clementissimum communis Florentie regimen nedum voluisse, sed nec cogitasse, velle privare homines sibi benevolos suo privilegio, maxime cum dictum privilegium fuerit eis indultum in

---

[108] *BNF*, *Magl.*, *cl.* XXIX, 187, 228 v; Bartolus, *ad D.* 42, 6, 21, *Antiochensium* (= *D.* 42, 5, 37), *ed. cit.*, V, 128 ra and *ad D.* 8, 4, 14, *Venditor* § *si constat* (= *D.* 8, 4, 13), *ed. cit.*, I, 186 va.

[109] *BNF*, *Magl.*, *cl.* XXIX, 187, 228 v. This aspect of derogatory clauses was treated by Bartolus in his *Tractatus super constitutione «ad reprimendum»* § *non obstantibus*, *ed. cit.*, 103 ra-b.

[110] *BNF*, *Magl.*, *cl.* XXIX, 187, 228 v; Bartolus *ad D.* [*prooemium*. 1, 2] *ed. cit.*, I, 4 rb.

[111] *BNF*, *Magl.*, *cl.* XXIX, 187, 228 v-229 r.

premium libertatis ex eo quod se subiecerint dicte Florentie, que libertas erat inextimabilis [112].

In the thought-world of early fifteenth-century Florence, the flame of *libertas* signified republican government and a Tuscany free from foreign domination, under the canopy of Florentine leadership and protection [113]. To the less politically naive, *libertas* also meant domination by force, the conquest of Tuscany in the name of liberty [114]. In our case, the medieval legal conception of *libertas* — privilege — offers a more adequate explanation of Tanagli's appeal [115]. In essence, he was imploring the *Signoria* to respect *libertas*, the privileges awarded by Florence to her subjects, the foundation of the Florentine territorial state [116].

In his second *consilium* (1421) and final contribution to the controversy, Paolo di Castro flatly rejected the conclusions of Floriano di San Pietro, Antonio di Butrio and Guglielmo Tanagli. According to Paolo, Floriano wrote that, despite the laws of 1404, anyone who fulfilled the requirements of the Captain's Statute acquired a right to hold office. And by successfully meeting these requirements, he consequently enters into a valid contract with the state [117]. It was true, Paolo admitted, that the state

---

112 *Ibid.*, 228 v.

113 N. Rubinstein, « Florence and the Despots: Some Aspects of Florentine Diplomacy in the Fourteenth Century », *Transactions of the Royal Historical Society*, 5 th series (1952), 21, 30-32; Becker, *Florence in Transition*, II, 202-203.

114 Rubinstein, « Florence and the Despots », p. 33; E. F. Jacob, in his introduction to *Italian Renaissance Studies. A Tribute to the Late Cecilia M. Ady* (London, 1960), p. 28; Peter Herde, « Politik und Rhetorik in Florenz am Vorabend der Renaissance », *Archiv für Kulturgeschichte*, 47 (1965), 167 ff.

115 For the medieval conception of *libertas*, including a rich bibliography, see Herbert Grundmann, « Freiheit als religiöses, politisches und persönliches Postulat im Mittelalter », *Historische Zeitschrift*, 183 (1957), 23-53.

116 After a thorough investigation of the records of the *Deliberazioni dei Signori e Collegi*, *Ordinaria Autorità* and *Speciale Autorità*, I have been unsuccessful in determining what action the *Signoria* took on this case. The records of the *Tratte* from 1421-1425 do not reveal that Ser Niccolò di Berti Martini held an office in these years. Whatever the outcome of the case, its most significant aspect was the defense of Florence's treaty with San Gimignano by two government lawyers.

117 *Consilia*, *cons.* CCLXXIII, 143 ra.

can elevate a foreigner to a full-fledged candidate for office and do this by contract. Yet the Captain's Statute or any statute which prescribes the conditions under which one may be eligible (*habilitas*) for office are never transformed into contracts by simple fulfillment of their conditions. The *habilitas* of citizens and subjects for office exists *prior* to these statutes and flows from citizenship or birth alone, *ex sola civilitate seu nativitate*. Thus the statutes are not transformed into contracts, because in reality nothing is granted or received. The Captain's Statute and the supervening laws of 1404 establish only the terms by which one may exercise his eligibility for office. In complying with these terms, the *habilitas* of citizens and subjects will not be endangered or impeded [118].

In reply to the cases presented by Butrio and Tanagli in defense of the *cives ex privilegio* from San Gimignano, Paolo repeated his plea that Florence had not turned her back on the treaty with the Sangimignanesi. The privilege of citizenship bestowed on the Sangimignanesi in Florence is permanent and like other natives their eligibility for office derives from being citizens. But the way in which eligibility may be expressed is relative to and dependent upon future contingencies. Their demands to be excused from the requirements of 1404 must be cast aside. Indeed, equity demands that these new *cives originarii* observe the laws applicable to all true natives of Florence [119].

This theme was employed by Paolo to combat Butrio's thesis on the rights of the Pratesi. Paolo did accept two juridical assumptions used by Butrio: first, that a *ius quaesitum* grounded on a contract cannot be revoked; and second, that the statute of 1351 granting privileges to the Pratesi can be repealed « be-

---

[118] *Ibid.*: « Si ergo est statutum, quod nisi solvant per x annos non possint habere officia, si vero solverint possint, si recte consideretur tale statutum non dat eis habilitatem ad officia, sed potius illam quam habebant ex sola civilitate seu nativitate restringit ad tempus, scilicet quousque solverint tanto tempore, et completa solutione non acquirunt aliquam habilitatem ex tali statuto, sed eam quam prius habebant et acquisiverant, remanet sine impedimento statuti. Non ergo potest dici, ut ipsi (Floriano di San Pietro and Antonio da Butrio) dicunt, quod solvendo tunc tale statutum transeat in contractum ... » The same logic is applied to the laws of 1404; *ibid.*

[119] *Ibid.*, 143 rb-143 va.

fore a right is acquired, that is, before the Pratesi fulfill their part of the contract » [120]. Conceding the validity of Butrio's assumptions, Paolo rejected his conclusion that the Pratesi who had met the six months residency requirement by October 1404 were exempt from the new requirements. Distinguishing between the privilege of citizenship and eligibility for office, Paolo attacked the idea that the Pratesi possessed a contractual right to hold office,

> ... quia per reformationem editam in ipsorum favorem in anno millesimo trecentesimo quinquagesimo, non fuit eis concessa habilitas ad officia simpliciter, sed solum civilitas ad omnia, sicut si essent veri et originarii cives; unde fuerunt exequati civibus, et per consequens non debent esse melioris conditionis quam cives ... [121]

The arguments of Paolo di Castro carried the day. On June 22, 1421 the councils enacted legislation designed to halt the spreading opposition to the tax requirement attached to officeholding and plug the loopholes in the laws of 1404 [122]. The new law actually served to limit even further the already shrunken pool of qualified candidates for public office. The thirty year tax payment which had applied only to members of the *arti maggiori* and *scioperati* was now extended to include the *arti minori* and the notariate. Taxes to be paid were described as *prestanze* or similar *onera* levied upon citizens in the city proper. Every communal office was subject to the act: those in the city, in the territory, and in a bow to the wishes of the guilds, the office of guild consul [123]. The government of 1404 had side-stepped the thorny legal problems presented by the privileges of the *cives ex privilegio*; the present government attacked these problems head on. Whatever had been ceded or promised to the *cives ex privilegio* concerning their special eligibility for office would no longer be valid — despite the fact that these concessions and

---

[120] *Ibid.*, 143 rb.

[121] *Ibid.* Paolo noted that this had been the earlier opinion of Giovanni Ricci.

[122] *ASF*, *Provv*, 111, 50 v-51 r.

[123] *Ibid.*, 50 v.

promises had been awarded by treaties, privileges and « per viam legis vel ordinamenti quam etiam contractus aut quasi » [124]. In this way, the teachings of Cino da Pistoia on treaties and Bartolus on statutes were rejected, as the legal reasoning of Paolo di Castro was boldly translated into law.

CONCLUSION

In his funeral oration on Nanni Strozzi in 1428, Leonardo Bruni conceived the heart of republican liberty as free access of the citizenry to public office. This condition was the mark of the free people of Florence [125]. While not doubting the integrity of the vision, the legislation of 1404 and 1421 exhibited a different conception of Florentine public life. The honors of public office were now legally limited to those who were able to pay *prestanze* for twenty, twenty-five or thirty years, an extraordinary increase over the ten-year requirement of the Captain's Statute. These stringent requirements helped to reduce the influx of new men entering into the ranks of officeholders [126]. It

---

[124] *Ibid.*, 50 v-51 r: « Predicta (requirements) quoque extendantur atque comprehendant quemcunque etiam quomodolibet privilegiatum seu qui esset vel diceretur de aliquo loco vel terra quantumcunque privilegiato seu in cuius aut eius personarum favorem contra predictorum effectum seu super habilitate ipsorum quoquo modo in totum vel in partem seu aliter tempore submissionis talis loci aut terre seu ante vel postea et tam respectu submissionis quam non vel aliter quomodocunque aliquid provisum seu etiam promissum vel firmatum extitisset et tam per viam legis vel ordinamenti quam etiam contractus aut quasi vel aliter quomodocunque et sub quacunque forma, tenore vel effectu et seu taliter quod provideri seu firmari non possset seu de iure non liceret aut non deberet in contrarium vel aliter quoquo modo, non obstantibus aliquibus repugnantiis, obstaculis, privilegiis aut oppositionibus vel defensionibus quibuscunque ».

[125] H. Baron, *The Crisis of the Early Italian Renaissance* (2 vols., Princeton, 1955), I, 364-365.

[126] The word « helped » or contributed should be underscored, for there is yet no statistical evidence to prove a causal relationship between the laws of 1404 and the reduction of new men entering into office. A telling critique of Bruni's concept of political equality and liberty is offered by N. Rubinstein, « Florentine Constitutionalism », pp. 452-458. According to Rubinstein, « Bruni's claim that there existed in Florence a basic equality in attaining high public office can hardly be taken at its face value ... ».

is in this context that one must judge Paolo di Castro's homage to the principle « equality of the citizens before the law ». This principle, as Bruni proclaimed, was a hallmark of republican liberty. Yet, ironically, in the hands of Paolo di Castro, this lofty republican ideal was wielded as a justification for oligarchy.

On the other side, as we have seen, the cause of the *cives ex privilegio* was championed by jurists in Florence and Bologna. Men like Tanagli were not mere spokesmen for or maleable instruments of official policy [127]. On the contrary, he and other jurists questioned and openly attacked the statutes of '79 and 1404. Nourished by the legal culture of Perugia and Bologna, armed with the *ius commune* or Roman law, every lawyer mentioned in this essay stoutly defended the validity of the treaties between Florence and her dependencies. For the most part, differences existing among these jurists did not arise from a conflict over legal principles, but over the legal consequences of the dynamic and ever-changing policies of the Florentine government. Their *consilia* bear eloquent testimony to a deep respect for citizenship, acquired as well as original, and a willingness to defend the rights of all citizens when trampled by the muddled language of Florentine legislation.

[127] For a different view, see Martines, *Lawyers and Statecraft*, pp. 394-396.

DONALD WILCOX

MATTEO PALMIERI AND THE « DE CAPTIVITATE PISARUM LIBER »

Matteo Palmieri wrote his history of the Pisan war towards the middle of the fifteenth century, probably some time in the 1440's [1]. The *De captivitate Pisarum liber*, which covers the siege and capture of Pisa by Florentine troops in 1405 and 1406, has frequently been neglected in favor of Palmieri's other major endeavors: the *Liber de temporibus*, a valuable chronological manual much praised by contemporaries [2], the *Libro della vita civile*, now important as evidence of Palmieri's civic humanism [3], or the *Città di vita*, with its intimations of neo-Platonism and of daring religious speculation [4]. Nevertheless, the *De captivitate* is worthy of attention, for it illumines the fifteenth-century development of Florentine humanist historiography.

---

[1] It was certainly finished before the death of Neri di Gino Capponi in 1452, for Palmieri includes a letter to Neri in the manuscript. Dati, one of Palmieri's two contemporary biographers, says the work was written before the *De temporibus*, done in 1448. It is impossible to determine a *terminus a quo* with precision, but G. Scaramella, who edited the *De captivitate* for the Muratori series (*Rerum Italicarum Scriptores*), vol. XIX, pt. 2 (Città di Castello, 1904) feels sure it was not written much before 1450. The evidence suggests only that it must have been finished considerably after the death of Gino Capponi in 1421, for his son Neri's *Commentari della guerra o dell'acquisto di Pisa* was certainly not finished by that time. The obvious effect of Bruni on the *De captivitate*, which will be considered shortly, suggests it was not begun until after the publication of the first six books of the *Historia Florentini populi* in 1429. In that case the probable date can be moved up to the late thirties, since during the late twenties and early thirties Palmieri was occupied with the composition of the *Della vita civile* and the beginning of his career in Florentine public service. On Palmieri's life see A. Messeri, « Matteo Palmieri, cittadino di Firenze del secolo XV », *Archivio storico italiano*, ser. V, 13 (1894), 257-340; and L. Martines, *The Social World of the Florentine Humanists, 1390-1460* (Princeton, 1963).

[2] See Vespasiano da Bisticci, *Vite di uomini illustri* (Milan, 1951), p. 303. See also B. Scala, *Historia Florentinorum* (Rome, 1677), p. 19, who uses Palmieri as an authority on dating.

[3] See A. Buck, « Matteo Palmieri (1406-1475) als Repräsentant des Florentiner Bürgerhumanismus », *Archiv für Kulturgeschichte*, 47 (1965), 77-95.

[4] See E. Garin, *Italian Humanism*, Munz tr. (Oxford, 1965), pp. 66-69.

Like most humanist historians, Palmieri relied on one basic source, the *Commentari della guerra o dell'acquisto di Pisa* of Neri Capponi, whose father played a large part in the acquisition of Pisa and probably provided the memoirs from which Neri constructed his commentaries. Though we have almost no information about the exact time when these commentaries were written or even of the precise authorship [5], there can be no doubt that Palmieri used Capponi rather than vice versa. In the first place the accepted fifteenth-century attitude toward the relationship between humanist history and vernacular chronicle is unambiguous [6]. The chronicler collected the facts, which the humanist then turned into « true history ». Vernacular translations could be made of humanist histories for political or social reasons, as happened with Bruni's *Historia Florentini populi*, which was translated by Donato Acciaiuoli at the request of the Florentine Signoria. Because in such a case the fact of the translation would always be clearly noted, the absence of direct evidence to the contrary forces the conclusion that Capponi is the source. Palmieri and Capponi apparently knew each other quite well [7], and one might reasonably expect that Capponi would be willing to provide a factual account of the Pisan war for his more learned friend [8]. In any case Scaramella, who has closely compared certain passages in the *De captivitate* to corresponding sections of Capponi's commentary, clearly shows that Palmieri has smoothed over rough transitions and clarified sequences of events which remain confused in Capponi's work. It is hard to see why Capponi, if he did come later, would introduce confusion where clarity is found in his source. An even more telling piece of evidence is the existence of lacunae in the vernacular commentary where Capponi meant to go back and

---

[5] Scholarly opinion leans to Neri rather than his father Gino. See Scaramella's preface to his edition of the *De captivitate*, p. XII and A. Sapori's article on Capponi in the *Enciclopedia italiana*.

[6] See F. Gilbert's discussion of the relationship between Sanudo and Bembo in early sixteenth-century Venice in *Machiavelli and Guicciardini* (Princeton, 1965), pp. 224-226.

[7] See Martines, *Social World*, p. 196.

[8] Matteo attended Marsuppini's lectures at the Studio (Martines, *Social World*, p. 139) and was reputed for his Latin style (Vespasiano da Bisticci, *Vite*, p. 302).

fill in exact dates or place names. These lacunae are not to be found in Palmieri's history, for the historian has gone to the trouble to research the data missing in his source [9].

Although the problem of Palmieri's sources can be easily resolved, its resolution does not tell much about the structure or significance of the *De captivitate*. In studying humanist history one must consider not only the historian's sources but his models, and here the difficulties are not so easily overcome. The most obvious model is Sallust, for no humanist writing a monograph on a particular war could ignore the historian of the Catilinarian and Jugurthine wars. Palmieri notes in his letter to Capponi a desire to follow the established customs of his predecessors [10], and the opening line of his narrative — « I shall write of the war in which Pisa is captured by the Florentine people » — strongly evokes the manner in which Sallust begins the *Bellum Jugurthinum* [11].

If the impact of Sallust can be plainly established, it cannot be easily assessed. Scaramella insists that the Pisan leader Gambacurta in seeking to overcome his enemies is strongly reminiscent of Jugurtha; that Florence reacts to the news of the fall of the Pisan fortress just as Rome reacts to the defeat of Aulus Albinus; and that the two historians describe two similar political situations in the same words [12]. Not only are these points

---

9 See Scaramella's edition, p. XIV. Matteo does not rely solely on Capponi. In the first place he had to find a source which would have the precise dates and place names which Capponi omits. Moreover, he has added certain military and political events which are not to be found in Capponi at all. Scaramella demonstrates that Palmieri has not used any of the accounts to be found in Sozomeno's history of Pistoia, the chronicle of the Lucchese Sercambi or the memoirs and family *ricordi* of Morelli and Salviati. Instead Matteo has used the *Historia fiorentina* of Pietro Buoninsegni and the *Cronaca* of Ser Nofri to fill in his narrative. With an impressive display of rhetorical art he has woven together the strands of the three vernacular accounts, using the relevant parts of each to shape the story as he wishes it.

10 « Sed cum sit in preceptis usum auctorum precipue esse sequendum », Palmieri, *De captivitate Pisarum liber*, p. 3, lines 6-7.

11 « Bellum scripturus sum in quo Pise sunt a florentino populo capte », *Ibid.*, p. 4, line 19. Sallust begins the *Bellum Jugurthinum*, « Bellum scripturus sum quod populus Romanus cum Jugurtha rege Numidarum gessit », *Bellum Jugurthinum*, trans. J. Rolfe (Cambridge, Mass. & London, 1931), V. [Loeb Classical Library].

12 Scaramella, preface, p. XI.

of similarity too general to be convincing, but such random observations can never establish the manner in which Palmieri uses his model. No more compelling are Scaramella's observations that both historians seek to judge events, to extract moral lessons from the events narrated and to insert orations into their accounts. Such practices are so much a part of all humanist history — both classic and Quattrocento — that in observing them Palmieri is not acknowledging any particular debt to Sallust.

Moreover, the precise moral lessons and basic ethical judgments with which Sallust's works abound are not to be found in the *De captivitate*. None of the Roman historian's basic concerns is present in the work. Sallust's most explicit question, found in the prefaces to both monographs, concerns the relative importance of intelligence and brute force in military operations [13], but Palmieri simply does not direct himself to this question [14]. An even more fundamental theme of Sallust's, found both in the prefaces and the narrative, is that of the moral decadence of his own society [15]. Catiline's and Jugurtha's revolts owe their importance for Sallust to the insight they provide into the growth and effect of moral decay in the Roman people [16]. Not only does Palmieri nowhere suggest that his own age is characterized by moral decay, but he does not relate the problems of internal decadence or vitality to the conduct of the

---

[13] « Sed diu magnum inter mortalis certamen fuit vine corporis an virtute animi res militaris magis procederet. Nam et prius quam incipias, consulto, et ubi consulueris, mature facto opus est. Ita utrumque per se indigens alterum alterius auxilio eget », *Bellum Catilinae*, trans. J. Rolfe (Cambridge, Mass. & London, 1931), I. [Loeb Classical Library]. His prefatory comments in the *Bellum Jugurthinum* apply not only to military history but to life in general.

[14] See below at note 53.

[15] « Verum ex eis magistratus et imperia, postremo omnis cura rerum publicarum minime mihi hac tempestate cupiunda videntur, quoniam neque virtuti honos datur, neque illi quibus per fraudem ius fuit, tuti aut eo magis honesti sunt », *Bellum Jugurthinum*, III.

[16] He says he is writing the war, «primum qui magnum et atrox variaque victoria fuit, dehinc quia tunc primum superbiae nobilitatis obviam itum est. Quae contentio divina et humana cuncta permiscuit eoque vecordiae processit, ut studiis civilibus bellum atque vastitas Italiae finem faceret », *Bellum Jugurthinum*, I. R. Syme, *Sallust* (Berkeley, 1964), has dealt more fully with the historian's intentions. See pp. 138-139 and chapter 11.

war in any meaningful fashion. The outcome of the war does not seem to depend either on the moral vigor of the Florentines or on the moral weakness of the Pisans [17]. In looking to Sallust for guidance, Palmieri has thus not drawn on any of his values or analytical perspectives.

Palmieri looks to Sallust as a source not of ideas but of narrative techniques, and even here his borrowing is quite limited. As Ronald Syme has pointed out, Sallust perfects a number of narrative devices for dealing with a war, for which the annalistic organization adopted by Livy is not wholly apt. He tends to break the chronological order to structure the narrative in terms of themes or to deal with two simultaneous sets of action [18]. Palmieri, in dealing with specific simultaneous events in Florence, in Pisa, in the Florentine camp outside of Pisa and in the Florentine camp at Vico, has occasion to imitate Sallust in order to make his narrative more lucid. Compared with Capponi's account, the events in the *De captivitate*, as Scaramella has observed, are indeed narrated with considerable clarity, and perhaps Sallust's model was a decisive factor. The long introductory section on the history of Rome in the *De captivitate* is strongly reminiscent of Sallust's practice of incorporating long digressions into the narrative, but there are no other significant digressions in Palmieri's work.

This brief survey of Palmieri's *De captivitate* suggests that the author has not made use of Sallust as a model for his history in any meaningful or coherent way. His use of the Roman historian is superficial compared with Poggio Bracciolini's. Poggio's Florentine history, written less than a generation after the *De captivitate*, imaginatively appropriates not only many of Sallust's basic attitudes but also his most important narrative techniques [19]. Yet Palmieri does have a model to guide him in writing of the Pisan war, a model found not among the classical authors but in the very Florentine humanist tradition of which he was a part. The *De captivitate* cannot be understood without realizing the extent to which Palmieri has been influenced by his older contemporary Leonardo Bruni.

---

[17] See below at note 54.

[18] See Syme, *Sallust*, pp. 79-80 and 142.

[19] See D. Wilcox, *The Development of Florentine Humanist Historiography in the Fifteenth Century* (Cambridge, Mass., 1969), p. 144 and pp. 154-167.

While there is no explicit reference to Bruni's *Historia Florentini populi* in the *De captivitate*, Palmieri could be unfamiliar with the work only in the unlikely event that his own history was written before 1429, for it was in that year that the first half of Bruni's *Historia* was published, acquiring immediate fame not only in Florence but throughout Italy [20]. Palmieri was a great admirer of Bruni [21] and during his periods of service on the councils of the commune doubtless associated with the great chancellor. In any case an analysis of the thematic content and organizational structure of the *De captivitate* shows the imprint of Bruni's History to be as clear as that of Sallust's monographs and more profound.

First of all Palmieri, like Bruni [22], avoids any tendency to narrate random events which have no direct significance to his basic analytical perspective and which do not help illumine his understanding of the underlying dimensions of the war. The *De captivitate* opens with an account of the fall of Rome and a summary of Pisan-Florentine relations down to 1405 [23]. This lengthy introduction seeks to bring out causes, to explain how the events being narrated are related to one another. In similar fashion, when Palmieri begins to describe the events surrounding the actual outbreak of hostilities, he digresses to cite the factors underlying these events — the papal schism, the activities of Ladislaus in the south, the anarchy in the north due to the recent death of Giangaleazzo, and the new governments in Padua, Verona and Vicenza [24]. In this way the introductory digression is entirely devoted to political considerations, outlining the interrelated factors which will govern the progress of the war and excluding any irrelevant event. Capponi's introduction presents a striking contrast. The events surrounding the beginning of hostilities are listed together with events throughout Italy and Europe, with no attempt to tie them together

---

[20] *Ibid.*, pp. 2-8.

[21] He praised the *Laudatio* in his *Libro della vita civile*. See Buck, « Matteo Palmieri », p. 87.

[22] For a detailed study of Bruni's historical concerns see Wilcox, *Development*, chapter 2.

[23] Palmieri, pp. 4-5.

[24] *Ibid.*, pp. 6-7.

and show their underlying significance or to single out the political factors determining the course of the impending conflict [25].

Palmieri deals with the military events of the war just as he had dealt with its political background. He dwells less on personal acts of bravery or cowardice than on general preparations for war [26] and broad strategic and tactical considerations [27]. In short, despite his explicit claim that history is nothing more than « celebratio virorum illustrium » [28] he shows the same interest in explaining why battles are fought and won as does Bruni. Finally, Palmieri shares Bruni's interest in institutions and the deliberations of governing councils [29].

The topics which interest Palmieri show that he is clearly similar to Bruni, but this similarity could easily be explained. All of the practices noted above are part of accepted humanist historical theory [30]. Palmieri's agreement with the canons of historical writing found in Cicero and Quintillian and adopted by fifteenth-century theorists is demonstrated by the accurate summary found in the preface to the *De captivitate*. The preface explicitly mentions such topics as debates in council and mi-

---

[25] « Commentari di Gino di Neri Capponi dell'acquisto ... di Pisa », in L. Muratori, *Rerum Italicarum Scriptores* (Milan, 1731), XVIII, col. 1127 A.

[26] See Palmieri, p. 13, lines 10-12, where Florentine preparations after the fall of the Pisan fortress are described, including constitutional measures not to be found in the sources. See also the account of Pisan preparations, p. 14, lines 6-15. He also interrupts the narrative to give numbers and dispositions of troops. See p. 18, lines 15-18 and p. 28, lines 10-16.

[27] See p. 17, line 14 to p. 18, line 2, where Palmieri goes into the means of attacking Pisa. At one point he includes the description of a Florentine war machine, even though none of his sources provides such information (p. 16, lines 16-26). On other occasions he mentions the number of castles surrendered by the Pisans (p. 29, line 27) and alludes to a pestilence in the Florentine camp (p. 16, lines 12-25), although this information cannot be found in the chronicles.

[28] Palmieri, p. 3, line 6.

[29] Military events are often prefaced by constitutional measures (p. 13, lines 14-20); the actual details of voting in the Florentine councils can be found in the *De captivitate* (p. 26, line 27 to p. 27, line 3); he narrates the tactical devices to be used in the siege of Pisa in the form of a debate in the Florentine Signoria (p. 17, line 14 to p. 18, line 2); and finally, the book climaxes with a paired oration before an assembly of Pisans (p. 32, line 15 to p. 34, line 7). In this last case, though not in the others, Palmieri is adopting Capponi's practice.

[30] See Gilbert, *Machiavelli*, pp. 203-235.

litary strategy and clearly states the goal of interrelating events for their didactic value [31].

If the foregoing analysis demonstrates only that both Bruni and Palmieri are humanist historians, a closer inspection of the manner in which each interrelates events reveals a more intimate affinity between the two men. Explaining his choice of subject, Palmieri says he will write of the war between Pisa and Florence, « first because it was great and memorable, then because it was waged with such jealous power, diversity of spirit, indignation on both sides and obstinacy that it contains many things worthy of memory » [32]. Such explicit concern with the psychological aspect of the war, sustained throughout the *De captivitate*, is strongly reminiscent of Bruni's conception of the substance of his own narrative.

In describing the war's background, for instance, Palmieri does not narrate directly the events leading up to open conflict. Instead he explores the animosity between the two cities, noting that the passions generated by the Guelf-Ghibelline feud were fiercest of all in Tuscany and that Florence and Pisa found themselves on different sides [33]. After explaining the origins and strength of the psychological causes underlying the war, Palmieri is not interested in the specific wars which the factional strife has caused but summarizes them in a period dealing mainly with the emotional dimensions of the conflicts [34]. Factional strife

---

[31] « ... historia, que est rerum gestarum magistra, exponit atque demonstrat alacrioresque nos ad rempublicam defendendam et magnas res gerendas facit et ad res improbas segniores. Multa enim sunt que nobis prestat historia, cui non satis est quod factum sit enarrare, sed addere etiam debet, qua ratione, quibus consiliis, quo tempore, per quos et quomodo queque sint gesta; pronuntiare etiam quid senatus decreverit; interponere contiones; regiones interdum pugnamque describere; qui vicerint et quod secutum sit demonstrare; clarorum hominum laudes nequaquam silere et nequiter facta damnare: quod aliud fere nihil est, quam omnium temporum omniumque magnarum rerum summam colligere et unius hominis memorie iudicioque mandare », Palmieri, p. 4, lines 5-14.

[32] « Primum quia magnum et memorabile fuit, deinde quia, emulatione potentie et diversitate animorum utrisque indignantibus, tanta obstinatione gestum est, ut multa memoratu digna contineat », Palmieri, p. 4, lines 19-21.

[33] *Ibid.*, p. 5, line 33 to p. 6, line 4.

[34] « Hinc cohorte inimicitie et divisi animi eo obstinationis vecordieque processerunt, ut alterius alteri inimicos sedulo foverint, et suis tutati sint

alone, however, does not explain the antagonism between these two cities, for Palmieri also notes the pride and vainglory of the Pisans, attitudes fully consonant with the illustrious origins and former great possessions of the city, but sadly discordant with its present state [35]. Only now, after sketching the passions of partisan strife and the jealousy of a decadent power towards its burgeoning neighbor, does Palmieri permit such tangible points of contention as control over Lucca to intrude on the narrative [36]. Throughout his account of the conduct of the war, concrete events are subordinated to psychological considerations just as they are in the introduction [37].

Palmieri, then, narrates as the substance of his history the same intangible and fundamentally psychological dimension which is to be found in Bruni's history. This is hardly astonishing, for this kind of analysis has long been associated with the Florentine tradition of civic humanism, and Professor Baron more than thirty years ago identified Palmieri as one of the men closest to Bruni in thought and feeling [38]. Furthermore the latest student of Palmieri has brought out clearly the dimensions of his civic humanism from an analysis of the *Della vita civile* [39]. As Palmieri in that work bases the health of the state on the educated ethical sense of the citizen, his continued stress on

---

viribus, et sepe inter se seva et plusquam inimica contulerint arma », Palmieri, p. 6, lines 5-8.

[35] « Inerat fastus superbiaque Pisanis, quia olim terra marique potentes Sardiniam, Corsicam et Baleares possederant insulas, et sepe navibus formidabiles potenti navigaverant classe; dedignabantur etiam quia vetustate urbis et antiqua grece originis fama longe Florentinos preibant », Palmieri, p. 6, lines 8-11.

[36] *Ibid.*, p. 6, lines 14-15.

[37] Diplomatic proposals and military events are given full psychological contexts (p. 7, lines 22-23; p. 11, line 1; p. 11, lines 22-31; p. 20, line 7; and p. 29, lines 4-5). Strategic factors are frequently psychological. He dwells on the obstinacy of the besieged Pisans (p. 23, line 29 to p. 24, line 1) as well as the rousing of the spirits of the Florentines (p. 13, lines 10-13). See also p. 18, lines 25-31, where a siege is continued because of its effect on enemy morale, and p. 21, lines 23-24, where the Florentines assault the walls of the city, knowing the state of fear existing within.

[38] H. Baron, « Franciscan Poverty and Civic Wealth as Factors in the Rise of Humanistic Thought », *Speculum*, 13 (1938), 22.

[39] See Buck, « Matteo Palmieri », especially p. 84.

psychological considerations in the *De captivitate* is to be expected.

A study of Palmieri's interests and analytical perspectives has shown that he both accepts the standard canons of humanist historical writing and is a part of the tradition of Florentine civic humanism. As the leading historian and humanist of Florence during the first half of the century, Bruni would certainly have provided an excellent example from whom Palmieri could have acquired the approach which has been observed in the *De captivitate*; but Palmieri's method cannot be positively traced to Bruni without more precise evidence. His use of Bruni's history as a model for his own work becomes unmistakable only upon an analysis of the narrative organization of the *De captivitate*.

In organizing the *Historia Florentini populi*, Bruni faced the problem of incorporating an historical narrative which stressed intangible realities into an annalistic form derived from Livy, who used it for more concrete historical elements [40]. Bruni solved the problem by introducing each year with a generalization which directs the reader's attention to intangible elements and conceptualizations which go beyond the year under consideration. He continues this practice even in the last sections of the work when he could easily use Sallust as a model, because he is narrating a particular war. Sallust avoids periodic dating of any sort and narrates in terms of themes which cross annual boundaries, noting the dates only of important events. Poggio Bracciolini adopts Sallust's mode of organization and uses it for his own ends [41], but Bruni steadfastly holds to the annalistic, Livian form.

Despite the fact that Palmieri's topic calls on him to use Sallust as a model, despite the fact that he introduces his narrative with a Sallustian phrase, and despite the fact that his work covers only a two-year period, the *De captivitate* exhibits not only the annalistic form but precisely Bruni's modification of it. Each of the two years in the *De captivitate* is introduced with a generalization pointing beyond the year and drawing the

---

[40] For a detailed discussion of Bruni's narrative technique, see Wilcox, *Development*, chapter 4.

[41] Wilcox, *Development*, chapter 6.

reader's attention to a psychological state [42]. Palmieri did not find this practice in his source, which in fact gives him any number of concrete events he could have used to introduce the year and which does not organize the material annalistically in any case [43]. Palmieri did not find his mode of beginning the year in Livy, who introduces his year with an important event, usually the consular elections. The only example of such a practice available to Palmieri was Bruni's history, where it is used as an organizational tool. Ironically the short chronological scope of the *De captivitate* makes the annual division useless as an organizational device. In using the *Historia Florentini populi* as a model for his analytical perspectives and ethical judgments, Palmieri has appropriated a narrative technique which is useless for his own ends but which unmistakably stamps Bruni's mark on the *De captivitate Pisarum liber*.

Bruni and Palmieri, then, share a common conception of the nature and function of history and the goal of the historian. History should be didactic, should convey ethical judgments. It should make better men. Furthermore Bruni and Palmieri share common ethical standards and moral values, based on their participation in Florentine intellectual and political life. Nonetheless, in spite of these common goals and values, the two historians have produced histories which are fundamentally different. A closer study of the way Palmieri has analyzed and structured the events of the Pisan war shows that his history in fact lacks the very didactic value which is so central a part of his explicit purpose in writing.

---

[42] « Salutis christiane anno quinto supra quadringentos et mille multum varie et turbulente erant conditiones Italie », Palmieri, p. 6, line 22; and « Adveniente igitur huius anni principio, Florentini ad prosequendum bellum intenti, decem novos decrevere viros, quibus belli gerendi cura inesset », p. 17, line 9.

[43] Where Palmieri had carefully delineated the first year, Capponi simply begins, « Trovandosi Piero di Luna, chiamato Papa Benedetto nella città di Genova, essendosi Messer Giovanni Lamergre detto Buccicaldo per lo Re di Francia governatore di quella città del mese di Giugno ... », Capponi, 1127 A. The chronicler does not note the second year at all (1131 D-1132 E) but mentions the beginning of the military season, the election of the Balìa and the assumption of office of the new government in separate places with no indication that a new year has begun.

The psychological dimension of history for Bruni is intimately related to the institutional history of Florence. The vitality of this relationship determines his acute sense of civic responsibility, which is in turn essential to his civic humanism. History is a means whereby Bruni expresses his feeling that institutions are real only in terms of the psychological needs they serve on the one hand and of the commitments the citizens bring to them on the other. In narrating the history of Florence, Bruni seeks to discover those attitudes and motivations which are ineradicable, which neither the creators of institutions nor their administrators can ignore. He seeks further to show how these basic psychological realities change in concrete circumstances and how they govern the relevance of moral categories. He seeks, in short, a political wisdom founded on a deep understanding of history and of the realities he sees manifested in it.

The search for a deeper wisdom, although an obvious and explicit concern of Palmieri, is not meaningfully carried over into the actual narrative of the Pisan war. The obstinate enmity between Pisa and Florence, for instance, which is the central psychological fact of the *De captivitate*, is neither related to any series of historical events nor interpreted in context with geographical or political causes. It exists from the very beginning, or at least from the start of the Guelf-Ghibelline feud, and does not change. The feud itself is not explained by any concrete circumstances but by the general fact of human greed, a presumed category of human behavior. Palmieri adduces another such category, pride, to explain further the enmity between the two powers, but he explicitly refuses to relate this second feeling to the first, saying simply that it existed in addition to factional zeal [44]. Little can be learned about the conduct of foreign policy from a diplomatic situation conceived in terms of such unanalyzed psychological categories.

In assessing the problems Florence faces in dealing with Pisa, Bruni also first establishes broad categories of behavior which govern the conduct of foreign policy. But he proceeds to explain factional zeal in terms of other basic traits of human nature and to relate it to such factors as geographical proximity. Next he analyzes the particular problems posed by Pisa in terms

---

[44] « Inerat », Palmieri, p. 6, line 8.

of his basic categories and shows how these problems dictate a policy different from what Florence should follow in dealing with other Tuscan powers. Finally Bruni weaves Florence's relations with Pisa into the larger context of general Italian affairs [45]. The concrete events of the narrative convey a coherent policy from which Florentines may analyze other concrete problems. Palmieri, by failing to integrate into the actual events of the war his juxtaposition of an inflexible enmity with such a basic trait as pride, provides no coherent perspective for the reader.

Palmieri's failure is deeper than an unwillingness to analyze his own basic ideals. He does not even seek to use psychological realities to criticize the other dimensions of his work. His characteristic tendency to use moral categories uncritically emerges most clearly in his orations. Bruni uses orations, as the classical historians had done, to show the complex interrelationship between moral values and practical considerations in the conduct of policy [46]. Although Matteo is not insensitive to the complexities of human motivation [47], he devotes his orations wholly to platitudinous and uncritically moralizing sermons. In the first oration of the work the Pisans complain in entirely moral terms of Florentine aggression, castigating human cupidity, quoting the commandment against covetousness and even citing the Pisan success at seizing the garrison as a sign of divine favor [48].

The work concludes with a paired oration similar to this first speech [49]. Gino Capponi, speaking to the Pisans on behalf of the Florentine Signoria, identifies the outcome of the war with the will of God, suggesting that Pisa has fallen either because of its own sins or because of the merits of Florence. He

---

45 See Wilcox, *Development*, pp. 81-90.

46 *Ibid.*, pp. 123-126.

47 He points out, for instance, that the Genoese in helping Carrara against Venice are motivated both by generosity and by the fear that Venice would become too powerful if it took Padua (p. 7, lines 4-5).On a number of occasions he notes the practical motive behind ostensibly moral acts (see p. 16, lines 7-11 and p. 20, lines 2-5).

48 P. 12, line 3 to p. 13, line 9. The oration is copied with few changes from Capponi (1131 C-D).

49 P. 30, line 12 to p. 32, line 12; and p. 32, line 15 to p. 34, line 7.

continues by reciting at length Pisan injustices toward Florence, concluding with a reminder of Florence's generosity in not allowing Pisa to be sacked. The Pisans virtually grovel in reply, admitting their previous nefarious conduct, begging forgiveness of Florence, and repeatedly expressing the captured city's gratitude for Florence's magnanimous treatment. Even the *absolvo te* of the priest is quoted to underline Pisa's unconditioned acknowledgment of its culpability. Both orations, except for the historical recitation of Pisan conduct in the first, which is not related to the other points made in the speech, are virtual translations from Capponi [50]. The orations in the *De captivitate*, except for the most superficial formal similarities with classical form — they are in Latin, and a rough tri-partite division can be discerned — have, then, no profound relation either to their supposed classical models or to those found in the *Historiae Florentini populi*.

Turning to military events, one finds that most of the issues which are so closely and convincingly related to Bruni's general historical conceptualizations, and which predominate in the *Historiae*, are absent from the *De captivitate*. Palmieri does not present, for example, a consistent position on the issue of civilian control of military operations. In one case he attacks civilian intervention into military affairs by associating it with the ignorance of the lowest orders of society [51], and he is certainly sensitive to the value of a competent captain like Sforza [52]. On the other hand he narrates with obvious satisfaction the civilian Gino Capponi's mediation of the quarrel between the same Sforza and Tartaglia [53]. Tactical considerations are psychological in nature but are not developed with the coherence and thoroughness of Bruni. Palmieri does not integrate the significance of chance into his analysis of events. He explains a number of important events, including the fall of Pisa itself, by adducing simply the power of fortune [54]. To say that the fall of Pisa teaches

[50] Capponi, 1142 D-1144 B and 1144 B-1146 E.

[51] « ... plebs omnisque vulgus », Palmieri, p. 16, line 32.

[52] See p. 20, line 16 to p. 21, line 13.

[53] P. 27, lines 5-15.

[54] The fall of Rome (p. 4, lines 28-29); the dispossession of Gabriel Maria Visconti (p. 8, lines 22-23); Gambacurta's overthrow (p. 15, lines 25-26); and the fall of Pisa (p. 27, lines 16-17).

the power of fortune vitiates the entire psychological and political complex of factors which Palmieri has included in the account unless fortune is carefully related to these other causes, and such is not the case. Palmieri in fact makes no attempt to analyze the state of mind of the Pisans in relation to precise events of the war or to its final outcome. Gambacurta seizes power in Pisa in a most high-handed way, calling forth from the historian a series of platitudes on the uncertainty of human affairs and the universal cupidity of mankind [55] but no assessment of the effect of the seizure on the morale of the Pisans and their willingness to resist the Florentines. Instead Palmieri stresses the obstinacy and courage of the besieged. Florence conquers the city in spite of and not because of the attitudes and moral character of the Pisans.

A closer inspection of Palmieri's history has suggested the absence of a synoptical view under which the particulars of the narrative can be subsumed. Palmieri shares many of Bruni's ideas and techniques, including not only a deep interest in psychological factors but even an awareness of the political significance of these factors. He differs from Bruni in not bringing all of the other elements of history together in this psychological dimension and relating the other elements to one another through it.

The analytical weaknesses in the *De captivitate* show far better than the rigor and coherence of the *Historiae Florentini populi* the difficulties facing the humanist historian in mid-century Florence. They also give substance to the comment, found so often among the writings of that century, that history is among the most difficult of tasks. Bruni's personal achievement in writing the *Historiae* has not provided his successors with an easily imitated historical form by means of which they can integrate their ethical concerns and values into a cogent narrative of particular events. It is in the context of Palmieri's attempt to imitate Bruni that the experimentation with other historical forms of such later Florentine writers as Poggio Bracciolini and Bartolommeo Scala is best understood.

---

[55] P. 15, lines 20-25.

GIOVANNI PONTE

ETICA ED ECONOMIA NEL TERZO LIBRO « DELLA FAMIGLIA » DI LEON BATTISTA ALBERTI

Il terzo libro *Della famiglia*, l'*Oeconomicus*, ha richiamato l'attenzione non solo di studiosi di storia letteraria, volti a considerare i suoi pregi psicologici ed artistici, ma anche di studiosi di storia civile ed economica, interessati sia alle opinioni in esso esposte, sia al rapporto fra queste e le condizioni effettive del '400. Già il Villari, a tale riguardo, considera l'opera albertiana « una fedele descrizione dello stato sociale, morale e intellettuale degli Italiani nel sec. XV, quale vanamente cercheremmo negli storici » [1], dopo che il Burckhardt si era limitato a ravvisarvi una trattazione razionale del modo di amministrare la famiglia [2]. Indi il Sombart, studiando l'affermarsi della borghesia dal Medio Evo in poi, fa dell'Alberti un iniziatore del mondo moderno, come teorizzatore del capitalismo borghese del '400, e sostenitore in particolare del principio della « santa masserizia » [3]. Ma, in polemica con lui, il Weber giudica quella dell'umanista una « dottrina da letterati », senza precise novità nel suo stesso razionalismo economico, ristretto a semplice saggezza pratica per conservare il capitale, e inoltre considerato privo di effettiva eticità [4]. La tesi del Sombart viene tuttavia condivisa, fra gli altri, dal Gramsci [5]. A sua volta il Fanfani insiste (in uno sfavorevole confronto con il precapitalismo e il Cristianesimo medievali) sul carattere laico, naturalistico ed utilitaristico dei consigli albertiani circa l'economia, ritenendo pure il l. III *Della famiglia*, per la preferenza ivi accordata al reddito fondiario, una dimostrazione non solo di egoistica « prudenza » negli affari (propria del capitalismo quattrocentesco), ma anche del contemporaneo sviluppo degli investimenti immobiliari a scapito dei

---

[1] *N. Machiavelli e i suoi tempi*, Milano, 1927[4], I, p. 181.

[2] *La civiltà del Rinascimento in Italia*, tr. it., Firenze, 1921, II, pp. 154-8.

[3] *Der Bourgeois. Zur Geistesgeschichte des modernen Wirtschaftsmenschen*, Münich u. Leipzig, 1913, pp. 136-43.

[4] *L'etica protestante e lo spirito del capitalismo*, tr. it., Firenze, 1965, pp. 108-12.

[5] *Gli intellettuali e l'organizzazione della cultura*, Torino, 1953, pp. 34-5.

traffici [6]. Invece il Doren ritiene l'opera albertiana un trattato pedagogico, in cui l'autore insegna a garantirsi contro le attrattive pericolose del mondo [7]. D'altronde, il Luzzatto considera i trattati rinascimentali sulla famiglia e sull'economia domestica semplicemente ispirati a nostalgia per l'antichità, e inadeguati a documentare, nel loro carattere letterario, le condizioni economiche del tempo [8]. E, con indagine più puntuale, il Baron rileva come l'Alberti non condivida la fiducia — propria di Leonardo Bruni e del suo gruppo, e alimentata dalla conoscenza dell'*Oeconomicus* pseudoaristotelico — nelle ricchezze considerate condizione per il pieno sviluppo della vita morale; e insiste sull'impostazione stoica dei libri *Della famiglia*, affermando che tuttavia in essi, secondo l'insegnamento di Seneca, la fiducia nel potere del saggio di resistere alla fortuna e di vincerla prevale

---

[6] *Le origini dello spirito capitalistico in Italia*, Milano, 1934, pp. 109 sgg.; *Cattolicesimo e Protestantesimo nella formazione del capitalismo*, Milano, 1934, pp. 113 e 125. Gioverà ricordare che gli storici dell'economia considerano il periodo migliore per l'Italia quello che comprende il sec. XII, il XIII e la prima metà del XIV: cfr. A. Sapori, *Studi di storia economica*, Firenze, 1955, II, pp. 619-52, e le osservazioni di D. Cantimori, *Studi di storia*, Torino, 1959, pp. 369-78; nonché le discussioni sul divario fra Rinascimento economico e Rinascimento culturale nel vol. *Il Rinascimento: significati e limiti. Atti del III Conv. Intern. Studi sul Rinascim.*, Firenze, 1953, pp. 132 sgg. Le divergenze non mancano, poi, circa una « crisi » del '400 per cui l'economia agricola sarebbe stata preferita a quella industriale e bancaria; così negano una vera e propria decadenza, p. es. H. Baron, *Dekadenz im Italien des Quattrocento?*, in *Bibl. d'Human. et Renaiss.*, XVII, 1955, pp. 421-37, e G. Luzzatto, *Breve storia economica d'Italia*, Torino, 1958, pp. 270 sgg. In rapporto anzitutto alla Toscana, la tesi opposta è difesa dal Fanfani, *Le origini, cit.*, pp. 98 e 142, e da E. Fiumi, *Fioritura e decadenza dell'economia fiorentina*, in *Arch. stor. Ital.*, CXVII, 1959, part. pp. 467-502. Particolarmente cauti i giudizi che si leggono nelle pagine sull'economia medievale, a. c. di M. Mollat, M. Postan, P. Johansen, A. Sapori, C. Verlinden, in *Relazioni X Congresso Internaz. Scienze storiche*, Firenze, 1955, III; cfr. p. 700: « S'il est excessif de parler de ' plein developpement ', il le serait tout autant de parler de ' pleine décadence ' »; p. 702: « ... l'industrie florentine ' classique [quella dei panni fini] était encore pleine de vie et d'activité [nel sec. XV] »; p. 805: « l'Italie ... non contente d'avoir été à la pointe de la ' première renaissance économique ', — celle du XII.ème siècle — aurait inauguré la seconde, tandis que le reste de l'Occident connaissait encore la dépression ».

[7] *Italienische Wirtschaftsgeschichte*, I, Jena, 1934, pp. 657-9.

[8] *Storia economica dell'età moderna e contemporanea*, P. I, Padova, 1950, p. 106.

sul medievale timore per la tentazione della ricchezza, che aveva improntato lo stoicismo del '300 [9]. D'altra parte il Sapori pensa che, con il suo criterio prudenziale, l'autore della *Famiglia* riveli il declino della borghesia mercantile, fattasi nel '400 più meschina e calcolatrice in confronto ai secoli di maggior floridezza economica [10].

Le divergenti opinioni degli studiosi di storia civile ed economica si riflettono variamente sull'atteggiamento di studiosi, soprattutto recenti, di storia letteraria, che rivolgono la loro attenzione alla mentalità dell'Alberti, preoccupandosi di inquadrarla nel suo tempo [11].

La diversità dei giudizi è certamente uno stimolo a riesaminare il problema, a riconsiderare come etica ed economia s' incontrino nel pensiero albertiano. Si può osservare anzitutto che la questione, indubbiamente complessa, presenta più aspetti, e pone quindi più interrogativi: quale significato hanno i singoli personaggi del dialogo, per accertare l'effettivo orientamento

---

[9] *Franciscan Poverty and Civic Wealth as Factors in the Rise of Humanistic Thought*, in *Speculum*, XIII, 1938, part. pp. 24-5.

[10] *Medio Evo e Rinascimento. Spunti per una diversa periodizzazione*, in *Arch. stor. ital.*, CXV, 1957, p. 160; *Studi di storia econom.*, III, Firenze, 1967, pp. 378, 440, 478, 583. Ma nel suo saggio *La famiglia e le compagnie degli Alberti del Giudice* il Sapori precisa pure che Leon Battista nella sua apologia di « casa Alberta » che si legge nella *Famiglia* esprime, non le reali condizioni della casata nel sec. XV, ma quelle dei primi decenni del sec. XIV, con spirito nostalgico (cfr. *Studi, cit.*, II, Firenze, 1955, pp. 1008-11).

[11] Così P. H. Michel (*Un idéal humain au XV.ème siècle: la pensée de L. B. Alberti*, Paris, 1930, p. 319) limita l'importanza attribuita sotto l'aspetto economico dal Sombart ai libri dell'Alberti, pur notando che sono documenti di grande interesse per la storia del capitalismo moderno, e che rappresentano il primo tentativo di sistemare in modo organico un complesso di idee prima presentate empiricamente; M. Petrini (*L'uomo dell'Alberti* in *Belfagor*, VI, 1951, pp. 651-77) ravvisa il carattere borghese dell'umanista — appartenente ad una consorteria in declino — nella sua prudenza nemica del rischio, nel suo « epicureo » desiderio di quiete, nel suo moralismo astratto; A. Tenenti (*L. B. Alberti*, in *I protagonisti della storia universale*, Milano, 1967, V, pp. 281-308) riprende la tesi del « riflusso verso la terra » che si rispecchia nella *Famiglia*; per F. Tateo (*Tradizione e realtà nell' Umanesimo italiano*, Bari, 1967, pp. 279-318) invece il conflitto tra le generazioni, rappresentato nel dialogo del giovane Lionardo e del vecchio Giannozzo, richiama anche ad una « crescente economia monetaria, non più sorretta da una vigile parsimonia nel governo del patrimonio familiare », e ad un distacco tendenziale dall'economia della « villa ».

dell'autore? quale rapporto viene stabilito nel l. III *Della Famiglia* fra la vita politica e quella privata? in quale misura vi è preferenza per la campagna rispetto alla città, per l'agricoltura rispetto all'artigianato e al commercio? sono suggeriti investimenti mobiliari o immobiliari? i precetti sull'economia riguardano solo la condizione degli Alberti, esuli da Firenze nel 1421 (anno cui sono attribuiti i dialoghi) oppure le condizioni, in genere, della borghesia toscana del '400? e quali coincidenze o divergenze si riscontrano da altri che scrissero su problemi economici nei secoli XIV e XV? quale tipo di moralità e di economia risulta, infine, dall'esame dell'opera e dall'accostamento di essa ad altri scritti dell'umanista?

Il problema del carattere e della funzione dei personaggi nel dialogo albertiano è stato studiato di recente dal Tateo[12]. Per lui nella *Famiglia* l'autore, consapevole del divario fra « dottrina » ed « esperienza », e fra le generazioni, non usa la tecnica dell'armonico conciliarsi delle tesi sostenute dai singoli interlocutori, che si riscontra nei dialoghi del tempo, ma si orienta più a definire atteggiamenti mentali che a costruire una conclusione « giusta » in assoluto: nella sua opera si riflette quindi, consciamente, una crisi propria della società del '400, divisa fra giovani umanisti che conoscono teorie ma si smarriscono di fronte alla realtà, e vecchi prudenti, di opposto orientamento. Le osservazioni dello studioso appaiono per certo aspetto positive, in quanto nella *Famiglia* i personaggi sono più complessi, e quindi è più sottile e vario il gioco delle loro tesi, rispetto ad altri testi albertiani anteriori (come sembrano p. es. *Defunctus* e *Deiphira*) o posteriori (*Theogenius*) dove culmina il tipico dualismo fra il saggio e l' infelice, che non sa fare appello alla sua « virtù »; e certo l'Alberti qui comprende meglio che altrove il divario fra astrattezza e praticità, nel suo tentativo di trovare più precisa convalida nella realtà alle sue idee di « letterato », educato sui libri degli antichi; ma d'altro lato sembra eccessivo affermare che egli non giunga ad effettive sintesi, magari abilmente sfumate; e il suo orientamento è, nella sostanza, coerente, al di là delle differenze particolari da libro a libro, da problema a problema. Il personaggio a lui più vicino è Lionardo, di soli otto anni più

---

[12] Il titolo del cui saggio albertiano, inserito nell'opera *cit.* alla n. 11 è: « *Dottrina* » *ed* « *esperienza* » *nei libri della* « *Famiglia* » *di L. B. Alberti.*

anziano, colto conoscitore degli antichi, capace di abilità dialettica e di stringate definizioni: il « letterato » così caro all'Alberti, il giovane umanista che studia le leggi della natura umana, ma che può difettare di pratica conoscenza della vita. Per questo gli sono affiancati Adovardo, e poi Giannozzo: Adovardo, uomo della generazione precedente, è meno colto, ma più ricco di concretezza; il vecchio Giannozzo, escluso dagli studi umanistici, ha in compenso un'esperienza grandissima, la meditata saggezza d'un' intera lunga esistenza. Nel l. I il celibe Lionardo sostiene che, nell'allevare i figli, le gioie dei padri prevalgono sui dolori; Adovardo, per diretta esperienza, dà risalto invece alle sofferenze paterne, ma finisce per convenire con la tesi del più giovane interlocutore, a condizione di averne una conferma pratica [13]; e Lionardo, da parte sua, si dichiara disposto a rinunciare alla sua opposizione al matrimonio: i due atteggiamenti vengono quindi contemporandosi, nell' interesse di « casa Alberta »; le argomentazioni del « dotto » risultano le migliori, ma egli deve convalidarle con il suo esempio concreto. Nel l. II Lionardo domina in modo netto; non solo confuta la tesi di Battista adolescente, secondo cui l'amore — anche moralmente turpe — sarebbe irresistibile nei giovani, ma spiega a lungo come la natura stessa abbia posto, con i vincoli coniugali, le basi per la famiglia, ed abbia orientato questa piccola comunità ad essere popolosa, ricca, virtuosa e onorata. Nel terzo libro l'Alberti s' impegna per moderare e richiamare ai principi d'una perfetta vita quello spirito mercantile ch'era proprio dei suoi « familiari » e che nel *De commodis et incommodis litterarum* aveva rimproverato ai Toscani [14]. Qui è il vecchio Giannozzo a illustrare i retti criteri per l'amministrazione della famiglia, secondo la sua esperienza. Il suo còmpito è analogo a quello del saggio Iscomaco nell'*Oeconomicus* di Senofonte; tuttavia, se si confrontano i due dialoghi, si nota che la preminenza di Iscomaco di

---

[13] L. B. Alberti, *Opere volgari*, a c. di C. Grayson, I, Bari, 1960, p. 80: « Ben son contento stare in quella tua sentenza ch'e' diligenti padri da' figliuoli ricevano vere allegrezze, ma questo più mi piacerà se io vederò che tu dia modo di tutte queste cose come con suttilissimi argomenti così ancora per lunga pruova poterne ragionare ».

[14] Ms. G. IV. 29 della Bibl. Univ. di Genova, cc. 22 r. e v.; G. Mancini, *Vita di L. B. Alberti*, Roma, 1967, p. 73.

fronte a Socrate è più netta che non quella di Giannozzo su Lionardo, i cui interventi sono assai precisi e opportuni, sia per approfondire l'esame dei problemi, sia per integrare criticamente le osservazioni del vecchio; né c' è da stupirsi, poiché l'abilità del « letterato » (che è pur sempre la « coscienza » della famiglia) deve manifestarsi anche di fronte all' « esperto » (come avverrà poi anche nel l. IV, in cui primeggia Adovardo sul tema dell'amicizia); e d'altronde, sappiamo che l'umanista era solito, imitando Socrate [15], interpellare gli « artigiani » per chiarire le proprie idee, completando la sua preparazione intellettuale con le cognizioni pratiche [16].

L'Alberti poteva dunque limitarsi, nei libri *Della Famiglia*, a semplici accostamenti di tesi? In realtà il modo con cui si sviluppano i vari dialoghi attesta che l'autore è consapevole del divario fra teoria e pratica, ma al tempo stesso chiarisce che egli condivide le esigenze dell' Umanesimo in campo pedagogico (tant'è vero che Lionardo domina nei primi due libri, impostati su tale problema), mentre assume un atteggiamento più cauto, accostandosi alle opinioni dell'esperto Giannozzo, sul problema economico (dove l'esempio degli antichi gli appare meno applicabile alle condizioni del suo tempo) [17]. Ma, per comprendere in particolare quale sia l'orientamento albertiano nell'*Oeconomicus*, bisogna considerare le questioni sulle quali gli interlocutori divergono, questioni che del resto hanno interessato maggiormente gli studiosi di economia e di politica (mentre p. es. la delega alla moglie, da parte del « padre di famiglia », delle « minori faccende » relative all'ordinaria amministrazione della casa, sostenuta da Giannozzo e condivisa da Lionardo, secondo un criterio derivato da Senofonte, non propone difficoltà).

---

[15] Riprendendo un famoso giudizio di Cicerone (*Tusc.*, V . 4 . 10) l'Alberti loda Socrate come colui che ha portato la filosofia di cielo in terra; cfr. *Opuscoli inediti:* " *Musca* "; " *Vita S. Potiti* ", a c. di C. Grayson, Firenze, 1954, pp. 45-6.

[16] Sull'abitudine di Socrate, cfr. l'*Oecon.* di Senofonte, VI . 13; circa l'umanista, cfr. la *L. B. Alberti Vita* (in *Opere volgari*, a c. di A. Bonucci, I, Firenze, 1843, p. C).

[17] *Op. volg.*, a c. di C. Grayson, *cit.*, I, p. 165: Giannozzo: « Non avete voi queste cose tutte ne' libri vostri? Eppur si dice nelle lettere si truova ogni cosa. Lionardo: « Così può essere, ma io non mi ricordo altrove averle trovate ».

Differenze d'opinione notevoli si riscontrano anzitutto sul problema della partecipazione alla vita politica, che Giannozzo sconsiglia recisamente (famosa la sua affermazione: « E' si vuole vivere a sé, non al comune ») così che può sfuggire una sua ammissione, tale però da indicare il punto di accostamento alla tesi poi avanzata da Lionardo: « Non ti biasimerò se di te porgerai tanta virtù e fama che la patria ti riceva e impongati parte de' incarichi suoi, e chiamerò onore essere così pregiato da' tuoi cittadini »[18]. Lionardo invece, pur accettando l'aspro biasimo rivolto a chi si lascia trasportare dall'ambizione e dall'autoritarismo, rivela lo spirito dell' Umanesimo civile, affermando sia l' impossibilità di raggiungere la gloria con la vita privata, sia l'esigenza che la « repubblica » sia amministrata dai cittadini migliori[19]. In realtà il dualismo fra le tesi degli interlocutori esprime l'oscillazione dell'Alberti stesso fra il desiderio d'una « repubblica » ben governata e la tendenza — unita ad un senso di sfiducia nella vita politica — all'appartato studio del vero. L'oscillazione si riscontra pure nell' intercenale *Fatum et fortuna*, dove l'esercizio personale delle « bonae artes » è anteposto all'operare nelle comunità statali, perché meglio rispondente al criterio del « bene e beato vivere »[20]; l'umanista cercherà poi di superarla con l'utopia della città platonicamente affidata ai saggi, e con il mito dell' « iciarco ». Qui invece affida a Giannozzo il

---

[18] *Op. volg.*, I, p. 181.

[19] *Op. volg.*, I, p. 183: « Ma neanche quelle republiche medesime si potranno bene conservare, ove tutti e' buoni siano solo del suo ozio privato contenti. Dicono e' savi ch'e' buoni cittadini debbono traprendere la republica e soffrire le fatiche della patria e non curare le inezie degli uomini, per servire al publico ozio e mantenere il bene di tutti i cittadini, e per non cedere luogo a' viziosi, i quali per negligenza de' buoni e per loro improbità perverterebbono ogni cosa, onde cose nè publiche nè private più potrebbono bene sostenersi. E poi vedete, Giannozzo, che questo vostro lodatissimo proposito e regola del vivere con privata onestà qui solo, benchè in sè sia prestante e generoso, non però a' cupidi animi di gloria in tutto sia da seguire. Non in mezzo agli ozii privati, ma intra le publiche esperienze nasce la fama; nelle publiche piazze surge la gloria ... ». Ed è significativo che, fra le raccomandazioni di Lorenzo ai figli Carlo e Battista in quello che appare il suo testamento spirituale, all'inizio della *Famiglia*, sia proprio anche il precetto di acquistarsi fama (*Ibid.*, I, p. 26).

[20] *Prosatori latini del' 400*, a c. di E. Garin, Milano-Napoli, 1952, pp. 650-2; *De re aedificatoria*, IV . 1, ed. Portoghesi-Orlandi, Milano, 1966, p. 269.

còmpito di concludere con una sintesi, che ha carattere di compromesso aperto alle varie possibilità pratiche:

« Così mi piacerà facciate, figliuoli miei, così spero e aspetto farete, e a quello modo acquisterete e conserverete onore assai. Ma bene vi ramento che mai, non dico per acquistare onore, ché per onore si vogliono molte cose lasciare adrieto, ma dico per reggere altri, mai lasciate di reggere voi stessi; per guidare le cose publiche non lasciate però le vostre private. Così vi ramento, però che a chi mancherà in casa, costui molto meno troverrà fuori di casa; e le cose publiche non sovvengono alle necessità private. Gli onori di fuori non pascono la famiglia in casa. Arete cura e diligenza delle vostre cose domestiche quanto al bisogno sarà debito, e alle cose publiche vi darete non quanto l'ambizione e l'arroganza v'aletterà, ma quanto la virtù vostra e grazia de' cittadini vi darà luogo » [21].

Nel suo atteggiamento conclusivo Giannozzo aderisce perciò ad un umanistico principio di « mediocritas »: curare anzitutto quanto è indispensabile, mantenere lo spirito libero da cupidigia, non sottrarsi a maggiori responsabilità quando occorra ed i concittadini lo vogliano. L' intervento di Lionardo è dunque stato utile per temperare l'avversione del vecchio agli oneri politici, motivata da una più ristretta, individualistica e agevole interpretazione dello stesso criterio: « Starsi così, sai, mezzanamente, sempre fu cosa felice » [22].

Un concetto informatore analogo si riscontra pure nella discussione del problema relativo all'attività economica nella quale impegnarsi. Giannozzo, il cui ideale è « una vita quieta senza grave alcuna sollecitudine » [23], non nasconde le sue preferenze per la « villa », di cui tesse l'elogio, non senza ricordi ciceroniani, e con parole che esprimono anche la tendenza di Leon Battista (che dal 1432 godeva d'un beneficio nella pieve di Gangalandi) a vivere nella raccolta pace della campagna. Ma ciò non significa affatto che egli consigli di investire i capitali in proprietà terriere anziché in traffici. Anzitutto, si parla d'una sola « villa », dove lavorano un fattore e vari contadini, non di latifondi. E la sua funzione è quella di garantire alla famiglia i viveri e altri generi

---

[21] *Op. volg.*, I, p. 185.
[22] *Op. volg.*, I, p. 182.
[23] *Op. volg.*, I, p. 179.

di largo consumo a prezzi più bassi, e con sicurezza [24]; se i beni prodotti non si possono « senza grande fatica serbare », si vendono, e si ricomprano al momento conveniente [25]: non è questo il linguaggio d'un grande proprietario terriero, ma di chi mira a soddisfare le necessità indispensabili « secondo natura », di chi cioè si pone solo il problema dell'autosufficienza, — in altri termini — d'un'economia di sussistenza [26]. E quando Lionardo chiede: « Ma a vestire la famiglia onde soppliresti voi? Venderesti voi e' frutti della possessione? ». Giannozzo risponde: « Se quelli m'avanzassino, perché non mi dovessi io farne danari, e in altro spenderli quando bisognasse? Sempre fu utile al padre della famiglia più essere vendereccio che compraiuolo. Ma sappi che alla famiglia tutto l'anno accaggiono minute spese per masserizie e aconcimi e manifatture; e così non raro ti sopravengono dell'altre maggiori spese, delle quali tutte quasi le prime sono il vestire. Cresce la gioventù, apparecchiansi le nozze, anoveransi le dote, e chi a tutte volesse colla sola possessione satisfarvi, credo io, non li basterebbe » [27]. Per fronteggiare le spese straordinarie occorre quindi un'altra attività. E così Giannozzo prosegue: « Però farei d' avere qualche essercizio civile utile alla famiglia, commodo a me, atto a me e a' miei, e con questo essercizio guadagnando di dì in dì quanto bisognasse sopplirei; quello che avanzasse mi serberei per quando accadessino maggiori spese: o servirne la patria, o aiutarne l'amico, o donarne al pa-

---

[24] *Op. volg.*, I, p. 194: Giannozzo. « Darei io modo d'avere la possessione la quale per sè con molto minore spesa che comperandole in piazza fusse atta a tenermi la casa fornita di biave, vino, legne, strame e simili cose, ove farei alevarvi suso pecugli, colombi e polli, ancora e pesce ».

[25] *Op. volg.*, I, pp. 193-4. A questo riguardo, si dimostra molto più pratico Paolo da Certaldo quando consiglia a chi vive di reddito agrario e non sa amministrare bene il suo denaro, di vendere le biade a ottobre, gennaio, e maggio nella misura d'una quarta parte del raccolto ogni volta, e così di fare anche per l'olio e il vino (*Libro di buoni costumi*, a c. di A. Schiaffini, Firenze, 1945, n. 153, pp. 124-5).

[26] *Op. volg.*, I, p. 187. Lionardo. « Prendete voi delle cose quanto pensate vi bisogni, e non più? ». Giannozzo. « Pur qualche cosa più, se se ne versasse, guastasse, perdesse, che non manchi al bisogno ». Lion. « E se ne avanzasse? » Gian. « Penso quale sia il meglio, o acquistarne e servirne uno amico, o vero se pur bisognasse per noi serballa, ché mai alla famiglia mia volsi minima cosa alcuna mancasse. Sempre mi piacque avere in casa tutte le cose comode e necessarie al bisogno della famiglia ».

[27] *Op. volg.*, I, p. 203.

rente, o simili, quali tutto il dì possono intervenire, spese non piccole, non da nolle fare, sì perché sono dovute, sì perché sono piatose, sì anche perché acquistano amistà, nome e lodo. E a me molto piacerebbe a quello modo avere ove ridurmi, e dove contenessi e' miei giovani non scioperati e non oziosi ». Chiede Lionardo: « Quale essercizio prenderesti voi? ». Ed egli replica, sulle generali: « Quanto potessi onestissimo, e quanto più potessi a molti utilissimo ». Lionardo pone una domanda ancor più precisa: « Forse questo sarebbe la mercanzia? ». E Giannozzo spiega: « Troppo; ma, per più mio riposo, io m'eleggerei cosa certa, quale di dì ⟨in dì⟩ mi vedessi migliorare tra le mani. Forse farei lavorare le lane, o la seta, o simili, che sono essercizii di meno travaglio e di molto minore molestia, e volentieri mi darei a tali essercizii a' quali s'adoperano molte mani, perché ivi in più persone il danaio si sparge, e così a molti poveri utilità ne viene » [28].

Risalire da simili osservazioni a una crisi economica del '400, postulare un declino dell'attività mercantile e artigiana, come è stato fatto, non appare sostenibile; Giannozzo riconosce, fra l'altro, che la sua scelta è motivata dal desiderio di « riposo », quello stesso per cui contrapporrà, in sèguito, la « fatica incredibile » del « serbar e' danari » alla « fatica piacevole » del governare la villa [29]; e prevede la possibilità d'un incremento del reddito proprio dalla bottega artigiana [30]; d'altronde, nel l. II Lionardo aveva dichiarato che « in gran traffichi si truovano e' gran guadagni » [31], senza allusioni di sorta a crisi economiche; ma il discorso su questo punto sarà ripreso più oltre. Qui interessa notare come la soluzione sostenuta da Giannozzo (approvata

---

[28] L'opportunità di investire il denaro è poi affermata da Giannozzo (*Op. volg.*, I, p. 248): « Nè in modo alcuno si possono tenere rinchiusi e' danari; e se tu gli tieni serrati e ascosi, sono utili nè a te nè a' tuoi. Niuna cosa ti si dice essere utile se non quanto tu l'adoperi ». Cfr. Paolo da Certaldo *Libro di buoni costumi*, massima n. 356, p. 227.

[29] *Op. volg.*, I, pp. 247-8.

[30] *Op. volg.*, pp. 204-5: « E in questo modo spererei Dio me ne prosperasse, e aspetterei acrescermi non poco concorso alla bottega mia, e fra' cittadini stendermi buono nome, le quali cose non si può di leggieri giudicarne quanto col favore di Dio e colla grazia degli uomini di dì in dì faccino e' guadagni essere maggiori ».

[31] *Op. volg.*, I, p. 147.

da Lionardo, e quindi cara all'autore) risponda ancora una volta all'umanistico criterio del giusto mezzo, per cui il saggio non s'affida alla fortuna, ma agisce con « ragione e modo », senza proporsi mete eccessive, mirando all'essenziale per vivere e bene operare, sommando quindi, per maggior sicurezza, le risorse della villa a quelle dell'artigianato, ma senza mirare a costituirsi grandi patrimoni, secondo l' insegnamento espresso da Seneca in un'opera ben nota all'Alberti, il *De tranquillitate animi* [32]. Le obiezioni di Lionardo, se mai, in questo caso riguardano la preferenza di Giannozzo per la villa come ambiente migliore per l'educazione dei figli; egli osserva che, se è vero che nelle città è più facile la corruzione, ivi « la gioventù impara la civiltà, prende buone arti, vede molti essempli da schifare e' vizii, scorge più da presso quanto l'onore sia cosa bellissima, quanto sia la fama leggiadra, e quanto sia divina cosa la gloria, gusta quanto siano dolci le lode, essere nomato, guardato, e avuto virtuoso » [33]. Le parole di Lionardo non sono prive d'efficacia; Giannozzo non è convinto, ma non insiste; e in sostanza il problema particolare viene qui eluso: « Con tutto questo, Lionardo mio, dubito io quale fusse più utile, allevare la gioventù in villa o nella terra. Ma sia così, abbiasi ciascuna cosa le sue proprie utilità: siano nelle terre le fabriche di quelli grandissimi sogni, stati, reggimenti e fama, e nella villa si truovi quiete, contentamento d'animo, libertà di vivere e fermezza di sanità, io per me così ti dico: se io avessi villa simile quale io narrava, io mi vi starei buoni dì dell'anno, dare'mi piacere e modo di pascere la famiglia mia copioso e bene » [34].

Una conferma del criterio umanistico del giusto mezzo (che ribadisce il precetto della « prudenza », regolarmente espresso dagli autori di « ricordi » dei secoli XIV e XV, concordi nello sconsigliare gli investimenti e soprattutto le speculazioni suscettibili di eccessivo rischio) si ha poi, nell'ultima parte del dialogo,

---

[32] VIII . 9: « Angustanda certe sunt patrimonia, ut minus ad iniurias fortunae simus expositi ... optimus pecuniae modus est, qui nec in paupertatem cadit nec procul a paupertate discedit ».

[33] *Op. volg.*, I, p. 201. Opinione analoga esprimeva il mercante trecentesco Paolo da Certaldo nella sua massima 103: « La villa fa buone bestie e cattivi uomini, e però usala poco: sta a la città, e favvi arte o mercatantia, e capiterai bene » (*ed. cit.*, p. 91).

[34] *Op. volg.*, I, p. 202.

attraverso la discussione sul modo migliore per garantirsi la proprietà e l'uso dei beni economici contro la sorte avversa. Giannozzo (con l'assenso di Lionardo) preferisce i beni immobili poiché, se anche si pèrdono temporaneamente, possono pur sempre ricuperarsi; Adovardo, da poco sopraggiunto, consiglia invece i denari, che permettono di fronteggiare ogni situazione difficile, perché più facilmente conservabili e trasferibili. È facile rilevare che particolarmente su questa discussione influisce la condizione degli Alberti, esuli nel 1421, che quando furono riammessi in città con deliberazioni del 1428, « s'affrettarono a rioccupare le case avite » [35]; ma al tempo stesso il problema è di carattere generale; ed anche in questo caso si giunge ad una sintesi, che viene esposta da Giannozzo: « Così adunque mi piace: non tutti danari, né tutte possessioni, ma parte in questo, parte in altre cose poste e in diversi luoghi allogate. E di queste s'adoperi al bisogno, l'avanzo si serbi pell'avenire » [36].

Ci sembra quindi — concludendo ormai questa parte della nostra ricerca — che l'Alberti (pur non senza oscillazioni ed anche incertezze dovute alla coscienza del divario fra teoria ed esperienza), non rinunci affatto a rivelare i propri atteggiamenti, nell'*Oeconomicus*, attraverso il gioco delle tesi sostenute dai suoi personaggi, ciascuno dei quali esprime un personale orientamento, che corrisponde a determinati aspetti della complessa realtà cui egli si accosta (ciò a prescindere dalla loro effettiva corrispondenza storica ai parenti dell'autore); e ci pare che in genere egli giunga a sintesi ispirate al principio « ne quid nimis » di origine classica, così importante per lui come per gli umanisti.

Un'altra questione ci si presenta, ed è proposta sia da altri passi del dialogo, sia in particolare dall'ultimo che si è ricordato, la controversia sulla convenienza economica della proprietà terriera e dei beni mobili: i libri *Della famiglia* riguardano solo la condizione degli Alberti nel 1421?

---

[35] G. Mancini, *Vita di L. B. Alberti*, p. 69. Per le deliberazioni che revocarono i provvedimenti contro gli Alberti, cfr. L. Passerini, *Gli Alberti di Firenze*, Firenze, 1869-70, II, pp. 346 sgg.

[36] *Op. volg.*, I, p. 250. Il Sapori (*Studi di storia econom.*, *cit.*, II, p. 1005) ricorda che nel '300 gli Alberti solevano investire nei traffici circa metà dei loro capitali, e l'altra metà in beni fondiari e immobiliari; si può quindi osservare che la dottrina umanistica del giusto mezzo confermava, per Leon Battista, una tradizione familiare.

Che l'opera rispecchi l'effettiva condizione e la mentalità degli Alberti in quel tempo, sembra difficile credere: la consorteria, sebbene duramente colpita, non era in condizioni rovinose, se nel 1408 le nozze di Lorenzo, padre di Leon Battista, erano celebrate a Genova con particolare sfarzo; né pare che i consorti rinunciassero a trafficare denaro, per ripiegare — in nome della prudenza — in modo esclusivo sui più sicuri possedimenti terrieri: è significativo che nel 1414 (come l'umanista ricorda nel l. IV) ancora Lorenzo riuscisse a fornire con grande rapidità all'antipapa Giovanni XXIII la cospicua somma di ottantamila fiorini [37]; e sappiamo che Leonardo Alberti divenne banchiere di Martino V [38]. D'altra parte, è noto che i libri primo, secondo e terzo *Della famiglia* furono scritti in Roma tra l'ultimo scorcio del 1432 e la primavera del '34: sarebbe stato logico che allora l'Alberti si riferisse alla situazione di dodici anni prima, mentre la casata era stata riammessa in Firenze e doveva soltanto riavere i diritti politici? Se mai, tutta la dolorosa esperienza precedente dei consorti doveva riflettersi nella *Famiglia*, e l' immaginare che i dialoghi si fossero svolti nel '21 doveva soprattutto richiamare all'esigenza dell'unità e della concordia di « casa Alberta ». Alle cui vicende l'umanista, certo, accenna più d'una volta nel corso dell'opera, preoccupandosi di evitare che si ripetano; tuttavia colpisce il lettore la mancanza di allusioni precise alla situazione politico-economica di Firenze o di altre città, mentre le considerazioni dei personaggi restano più generiche ed universali; anche a proposito dei problemi prima illustrati (partecipazione alla vita politica, preferenza per l'agricoltura o per altre attività, beni mobili e immobili), lo scambio di idee diviene ben presto meno specifico, risponde all'esigenza di risolvere teoricamente problemi che riguardano l'uomo in generale, come, d'altronde, avviene in tutte le opere dell'umanista. Questi si preoccupa d' insegnare ai « familiari » a vincere la sorte avversa, ma al tempo stesso vuole enunciare principi validi per chiunque; e quindi i libri *Della famiglia* assumono un significato più vasto, che la critica, del resto, non ha mai messo in dubbio, ed anzi

---

[37] G. Mancini, *Vita, cit.*, pp. 24, 41 (sulle nozze di Lorenzo), 12 (sul prestito); *Op. volg.*, I, p. 280.

[38] G. Mancini, *Vita, cit.*, p. 66.

ha sottolineato: quello di richiamare al « bene e beato vivere » secondo la retta natura.

Piuttosto, conviene aggiungere che il significato umano di questi dialoghi è superiore alla stessa diffusione che ebbero nel '400, diffusione invero scarsa, poiché (anche per trascuratezza dell'autore) restano pochi manoscritti [39], mentre le prime edizioni a stampa si ebbero solo nel sec. XIX. In pratica — a prescindere dalla sfavorevole accoglienza che ricevettero dagli stessi Alberti [40] — essi suscitarono interesse solo in ambienti di ricchi borghesi fiorentini, dove furono rielaborati nel *Governo della famiglia*, o rifacimento Pandolfini, cui si richiama quello per i Pazzi, e da cui attinse il mercante Giovanni Rucellai entro il 1457 [41]. Nel testo albertiano quegli imprenditori trovavano una trattazione dell'economia che, senza essere sistematica né rispondente in pieno — come si vedrà — alla loro ricerca del profitto, tuttavia considerava i problemi con razionale lucidità, da un punto di vista « terreno », anziché attenersi alle esigenze religiose di Giovanni Dominici (che proprio per Bartolomea Alberti aveva scritto la *Regola del governo di cura familiare*), e certo incoraggiava l'iniziativa individuale; e potevano apprezzare il terzo libro *Della Famiglia* anche per i suoi pregi psicologici ed artistici, per la sua esposizione sorvegliata e attraente, così diversa dalla schematicità di stile e dall' elementarità precettistica dei loro libri di « ricordi », dei loro manuali di tecnica mercantile, di quella stessa *Epistola de gubernatione familiae* attribuita a S. Bernardo, che nel sec. XV fu edita più volte [42].

Un rapido accostamento a testi di altri toscani dei secoli XIV e XV può appunto dimostrare come l'opera albertiana non sia pienamente sistematica, né risponda totalmente alle esi-

---

[39] *Op. volg.*, I, pp. 367-77.

[40] Cfr. *L. B. Alberti Vita, ed. cit.*, I, p. C: « Cum libros de Familia primum secundum atque tertium suis legendos tradidisset, aegre tulit, eos inter omnes Albertos, alioquin ociosissimos, vix unum repertum fore, qui titolos librorum perlegere dignatus sit, cum libri ipsi ab exteris etiam nationibus peterentur; neque potuit non stomachari, cum ex suis aliquos intueretur, qui totum illud opus palam, et una auctoris ineptissimum institutum irriderent ».

[41] Rinviamo in proposito alla nostra recensione a: *Giovanni Rucellai ed il suo Zibaldone. I. Il Zibaldone quaresimale*, a c. di A. Perosa, London, 1960 (in *Rass. lett. ital.*, 64, 1960, p. 473).

[42] Cfr. *GW.* 3960-95. L'opuscolo è oggi ascritto a Bernardo Silvestre o a Giovanni di Paderborn.

genze pratiche della borghesia mercantile del tempo. È già interessante rilevare, a questo proposito, che Giovanni Rucellai, autentico « operatore economico », che dichiarava di avere guadagnato molto nei traffici [43] e che non rinunciava alla proprietà terriera — come del resto era tradizionale nella ricca borghesia toscana [44] — non riprende dal *Governo della famiglia* i passi in lode della « villa », certo non ritenendoli adatti alle sue esigenze; eppure egli trascrive (aggiungendovi suoi consigli particolari ed osservazioni specifiche sulle tendenze economico-politiche di Firenze) i passi sulla « masserizia », sulla « vita civile » (senza tuttavia limitarsi alla tesi di Giannozzo) e sulla prudente ripartizione in ugual misura dei beni mobili e immobili. L'agricoltura è celebrata invece dal Palmieri, sull'esempio del *De senectute* di Cicerone e del *De re rustica* di Varrone; e in lui s'intravede anche una preferenza per i redditi agricoli [45]; ma la tendenza a idealizzare è chiara, tanto più che egli afferma altrove che i maggiori guadagni sono quelli della grande mercatura [46], pur avanzando riserve di carattere morale su questa attività. La trascuratezza del Rucellai per l'esaltazione della « villa », il fatto che fervidi elogi all'agricoltura siano resi non da « operatori economici » del tempo, ma da « letterati » come il Palmieri e l'Alberti, inducono a limitare la tesi d'una rispondenza totale dell'*Oeconomicus* alle condizioni del '400, e ad un « ritorno alla terra » in particolare [47]. Ma non mancano, per indurci a questo,

---

[43] *Zibaldone*, p. 121: « Ne' quali traffichi [mercatura, cambio, partecipazione finanziaria a botteghe artigiane della lana] ò ghuadangnati danari assai, e pel mezzo di tale ghuadangno ò soperito a grandissime spese e massimamente alle gravezze del chomune » (il « ricordo » è del 1473; nel '74 il mercante subì una perdita di 20000 fiorini nella compagnia di Pisa, ma, com'egli dice, per malversazioni altrui).

[44] A. Fanfani, *Le origini, cit.*, p. 98; E. Fiumi. *Fioritura e decadenza della economia fiorentina*, in *Arch. stor. ital.*, CXVII, 1959, pp. 433-6.

[45] *Della vita civile*, a c. di F. Battaglia, Bologna, 1944, pp. 151-3.

[46] *ibid.*, p. 157.

[47] L'Alberti stesso, nel suo opuscolo *Villa*, dove ritiene che sia meglio avere due ville che non una sola, senza però aumentarne ancora il numero (*Op. volg.*, I, p. 360), raccomanda di acquistare la villa con grande oculatezza: altrimenti, è meglio disporre di capitali: « Quello che tu male comprasti una volta, te ne pentirai molte. Sempre potrai spendere il tuo danaio meglio che non potrai vendere il terreno » (p. 359). Il Rucellai raccomanda ai figli non di comprare terreni, ma di operare in città piuttosto che intraprendere traffici in

anche osservazioni d'altro genere. Il problema della scelta del fattore e della sorveglianza da esercitare su lui e sui contadini, già presente nell'*Oeconomicus* di Senofonte, è ripreso dall'Alberti, che in ciò s'incontra con gli autori di « ricordi » del suo tempo, autentici imprenditori preoccupati di non subire inganni [48]. Ed anche la sua condanna, per bocca di Lionardo [49], delle speculazioni disoneste fa pensare alla condanna dell'usura, che troviamo in pagine di mercanti [50]; e ragioni di etica umana e commerciale al tempo stesso ispirano le parole di Giannozzo sul buono e onesto trattamento dei clienti della propria bottega [51]; ma circa il respingere le « furberie » negli affari non altrettanto risoluto era Paolo da Certaldo, un secolo prima, e il pio notaio Lapo Mazzei condannava, da parte sua, la pratica di frodare la gabella, tipica di mercanti del tempo [52]. I precetti albertiani si differenziano dunque dal modo di agire degli « operatori economici » in un periodo in cui si mirava con spregiudicatezza a maggiori guadagni per maggiori spese di prestigio e di lusso rispetto ai secoli precedenti [53].

Ma c'è di più: nel l. III *Della famiglia* manca ogni accenno — in confronto ai « ricordi » contemporanei — ad un problema

---

ambienti lontani (*Zibaldone*, p. 19); egli testimonia inoltre circa la floridezza economica di Firenze dal 1413 al '23 (p. 46) e intorno al 1457 (p. 62); ed esprime un complessivo giudizio ottimistico sul '400 fiorentino (pp. 60 sgg.).

[48] G. Morelli, *Ricordi*, a c. di V. Branca, Firenze, 1956, pp. 234-6; G. Rucellai, *Zibaldone*, pp. 3-8, 19.

[49] *Op. volg.*, I, p. 251.

[50] G. Morelli, *Ricordi*, p. 249; P. da Certaldo, *Libro di buoni costumi*, n. 128, p. 106.

[51] *Op. volg.*, I, p. 204.

[52] P. da Certaldo, *Libro di buoni costumi*, n. 152, p. 123: « Quando comperi biada, guarda che non ti sia empiuta la misura a uno tratto, chè sempre ti calerà due o tre per cento; e quando vendi il fa, e cresceratti la tua biada; ma meglio è la via del mezzo e la ragione: e a quello t'attieni in ogni tuo fatto, e capiterai bene »; L. Mazzei, *Lettere di un notaro a un mercante del sec. XIV*, a c. di C. Guasti, Firenze, 1880, II, pp. 242-4.

[53] La 38° delle prediche tenute a Siena da S. Bernardino nel 1427 illustra più malizie usate dai mercanti; più tardi anche il Pontano parla delle bugie dei mercanti nel *De sermone*, II. 14: « Itaque vix aliquod genus est mercis, in quo non primum sibi locum mendacium pepererit; potissimaque apud mercatores laus est scire et multum et caute fingere. Quo effectum est, ut fides mercatoria, quae antea maxime habebatur integra, nunc fluxa sit admodum ac fragilis ».

assai importante per gli imprenditori fiorentini del sec. XV: la gravità degli oneri tributari, come pure le conseguenti, costanti lamentazioni circa il fiscalismo del Comune. Si potrebbe obiettare che gli Alberti vivevano in esilio, nel 1421; tuttavia, se non altro, il problema dei tributi esisteva anche altrove; e una più precisa conoscenza dell'attività economica avrebbe dovuto indurre il giovane umanista, che si atteggiava a maestro dei suoi congiunti, a non trascurare una questione che indubbiamente aveva particolare interesse, anche da un punto di vista generale. Egli invece, non solo la evita del tutto, ma fa dire ai personaggi che il denaro risparmiato deve servire, fra l'altro, anche per le necessità della patria [54]. Motivi umanistici, etici, prevalgono quindi sulle esigenze di opportunità pratica; e lo conferma il fatto che nella *Famiglia* manca pure ogni richiamo all'esigenza di essere in buoni rapporti con i capi della città, per ragioni di opportunità generale, e per evitare una tassazione eccessiva: precetto che invece ritorna puntualmente in mercanti borghesi che ben conoscevano la « realtà effettuale », come Paolo da Certaldo, il Morelli, il Rucellai [55].

Nell'*Oeconomicus* albertiano — sull'esempio di Senofonte e in accordo con i giudizi espressi in altre opere dall'umanista [56] — si condanna, poi, l'abitudine femminile di usare cosmetici: questione certo interessante in rapporto alla volontà dell'Alberti (e, anteriormente, di Senofonte stesso) di delineare la figura della perfetta « madre di famiglia », ma irrilevante, in sostanza, sotto l'aspetto strettamente economico. Anche questa osservazione ci conferma dunque come sia ampio il significato attribuito dall'autore al termine « economia », intesa come « governo della famiglia », e come la sua opera — che pur intende considerare la realtà — risponda anzitutto ad un'esigenza etica di più vasta

---

[54] *Op. volg.* I, p. 203. L'affermazione di Giannozzo è coerente con la ripresa da parte di Lionardo, nel l. II, di una sentenza di Platone: « ... gli uomini essere nati per cagione degli uomini, e parte di noi si debbe alla patria, parte a' parenti, parte agli amici » (p. 132).

[55] Paolo da Certaldo, *Libro di buoni costumi*, n. 89, p. 99; G. Morelli, *Ricordi*, pp. 274 sgg.; G. Rucellai, *Zibaldone*, p. 9. Nei criteri prudenziali del Morelli rientra poi il lamentarsi sempre di essere in passivo (p. 251).

[56] *Mirzia*, vv. 100-02, in *Op. volg.*, a c. di C. Grayson, II, Bari, 1966, p. 14; *Frottola*, vv. 214-6, *ibid.*, p. 34; *Momus*, a c. di G. Martini, Bologna, 1942, pp. 33-4.

portata. Infatti l'Alberti, dopo avere illustrato il carattere e i còmpiti del « letterato » nel *De commodis et incommodis litterarum*, scrivendo i libri *Della famiglia* si preoccupa di estendere ad una situazione più concreta i principi della sua visione della vita. Lionardo, figura idealizzata di « letterato », è colui che meglio d'ogni altro membro di « casa Alberta » ha meditato sulle pagine degli antichi, e sa riconoscere e definire le leggi della natura applicandole all'attività pratica dell'uomo nell'àmbito d'una comunità piccola, ma affiatata ed efficiente più d'ogni altra. Al tempo stesso, come si è detto, l'Alberti — consapevole del valore insostituibile che ha l'esperienza di chi è vissuto a lungo — affianca al suo « Socrate » due « periti » come Adovardo e, specialmente, Giannozzo, così che dal vario contrastarsi e accordarsi delle loro tesi si chiarisca la soluzione dei problemi relativi alla perfetta famiglia. Tra questi, sono anche i problemi economici; e il punto di partenza per l'esame di tutti è sempre lo stesso: l'affermazione della « virtù » contro la « fortuna ». Il dualismo presentatosi all'Alberti adolescente in modo anche drammatico (se pensiamo a intercenali come *Pupillus* e *Virtus*) negli anni difficili dopo la morte del padre, diviene la premessa ad ogni sua opera successiva; e tutte hanno un'insopprimibile base etica nella loro esigenza di insegnare il « bene e beato vivere », che la virtù umana deve attuare. Per questo, occorre vincere la fortuna: ma non ricercando con ogni mezzo un successo materiale, che non dipende esclusivamente da noi, e che è facilmente transitorio; bisogna invece valersi della retta ragione, e seguire le leggi della natura (non a caso nel l. I *Della famiglia* Lionardo afferma che « non è virtù altro se none in sè perfetta e ben produtta natura » [57], mentre il vizio è « scorretta consuetudine e corrotta ragione, la quale viene da vane opinioni e imbecillità di mente »).

Nel *De commodis* l'Alberti contrapponeva il letterato povero, ma colto, ad altri esponenti della società, lontani dalla virtù; e un'eco di tale atteggiamento è ancora in certe parole di Lionardo — contraddette però da Adovardo — nel finale del l. I *Della famiglia* [58]; ma in sostanza, in quest'opera l'orientamento

---

[57] *Op. volg.*, I, p. 63 (traduce un passo di Cicerone, *De legibus*, I. 8. 25).

[58] *Op. volg.*, I, p. 80. Un'altra pagina sul pregio morale della povertà è nel *Theogenius* (*Op. volg.*, II, pp. 70-1). Ha invece carattere polemico l'elogio

dell'umanista si fa più pratico e comprensivo: chi ha virtù si fonda su quelli che Giannozzo definisce beni propri dell'uomo, a lui concessi direttamente dalla natura, « le operazioni dell'animo, il corpo, il tempo » [59]; agisce usufruendo, a vantaggio suo ed altrui, di quelle cose che in séguito, nel *Theogenius* e nel *Momus* l'Alberti, con gli stoici, chiamerà indifferenti [60], quelle che sono soggette, in varia misura, all'arbitrio della fortuna: fra cui sono appunto le ricchezze. Di esse non ha importanza il possesso, ma l'uso, come l'umanista dichiara più volte: motivo, anche questo, proprio dello stoicismo moderato [61]. Ma il loro retto uso, come spiega Giannozzo, esclude sia l'avarizia, sia la prodigalità, e postula invece la « masserizia », che consiste nella « sollecitudine e cura delle cose », secondo una precedente definizione di Lionardo [62], in « usare e serbare le cose », secondo il concetto di Giannozzo stesso [63]. La « santa masserizia », la retta economia, è dunque una virtù morale; e la ricchezza non è fine a se stessa, da ricercare in assoluto, come non è da respingere a priori: nella *Famiglia* si condannano il lusso e la vita sciope-

---

del mendicante nel *Momus* (*ed. cit.*, pp. 71-2). In complesso nei suoi scritti l'Alberti ritiene che la povertà non sia augurabile, ma che si debba accettare, in caso di necessità, facendo appello alla propria « virtù », che essa stimola — e qui sta il suo aspetto positivo — per mutare la propria condizione.

[59] *Op. volg.*, I, p. 169.

[60] Cfr. Diogenes Laertius, VII . 102; *Op. volg.*, II, p. 61; *Momus*, *ed. cit.*, p. 186.

[61] Cfr. nella dedica al Bruni del l. II delle *Intercenales*: « Divitiarumque usu magis quam copia gaudere sapientem oportet » (*Alcune intercenali ined.*, a c. di E. Garin, in *Rinascimento*, s. II . IV, 1964, p. 128); *Op. volg.*, II, p. 70; e nell'intercen. *Divitiae*: « Divitiarum non possessionem quidem, sed usum, ad consequendam felicitatem conducere arbitror » (*Opera inedita et pauca separatim impressa*, cur. H. Mancini, Florentiae, 1890, p. 176). Ma si vedano anche le *Epistolae septem Epimenidis nomine Diogeni inscriptae*, nell'ed. Mancini ora cit., pp. 267-9.

[62] *Op. volg.*, I, p. 144. Anche in questo caso l'Alberti teorizza in modo più incisivo un'osservazione non nuova; la si trova nell'*Epistola de gubernatione familiae*: « Sed servans doctrinam, raro accusabit fortunam. Raro nam diligentia cum infortunio sociabis, sed rarius a pigritia infortunium separabis » (ed. Brescia, 1494).

[63] *Op. volg.*, I, p. 167 (cfr. p. 176). Il Weber, *L'etica protestante*, p. 109, osserva: « La santa masserizia ... è, in prima linea, un principio dell'amministrazione della casa, non un principio del guadagno ».

rata, che implicano « spese pazze », mentre si ammettono, oltre alle « necessarie », anche talune spese « non necessarie », purché « con qualche ragione fatte » [64], come pure si respinge l'assurda rinuncia degli avari ad usare il loro capitale. Invece si ritiene necessario « serbare a' bisogni » [65], e Giannozzo, dotato di senso pratico più ancora di Adovardo, considera un grave male la povertà [66]. Le parole di Giannozzo nel loro complesso rappresentano, nel l. III, uno sviluppo di precise premesse poste da Lionardo nell'ultima parte del precedente: circa le ricchezze e la loro funzione, egli aveva affermato che importa essenzialmente la libertà dello spirito « virtuoso », la sua superiorità sui mezzi di cui si vale, la consapevolezza dei loro limiti: « ... non sia vizioso l'animo, e non servirà; ornisi di virtù, e arà libertà. Non sia sottoposto l'animo ad alcuno errore, non si sottometta ad alcuna disonestà per avanzare auro, fugga ogni biasimo per non perdere fama, non perda virtù per acquistare tesauro » [67]; ed ancora aveva aggiunto: « Non servirà l'animo adunque per arricchire, né constituirà el corpo in ozio e delizie, ma userà le ricchezze solo per non servire » [68]. Ciò non significa tuttavia amministrare male i beni economici che la fortuna ci offre: Lionardo e Giannozzo concordano su questo; l'uno dichiara: « se adunque nel guadagnare s'adempie le ricchezze, e se i guadagni seguono la fatica, diligenza e industria nostra, adunque l'impoverire contrario al guadagno diverrà dalle cose contrarie, dalla negligenza, ignavia e tardità, li quali vizii non sono in la fortuna, né in le cose estrinsece, ma in te stessi » [69]; l'altro conferma: « Lionardo mio, non faccendo masserizia di quello che usandolo diventa nostro, sarebbe negligenza ed errore. Tanto sono le cose della fortuna nostre sì quanto ella ce le permette, e ancora quanto

---

[64] *Op. volg.*, I, p. 211.

[65] *Op. volg.*, I, p. 167.

[66] *Op. volg.*, I, p. 160.

[67] *Op. volg.*, I, p. 148. Cfr. *De commodis*, ms. G. IV. 29 *cit.*, c. 26 v.: « Mens omni perturbatione vacua contra omnem fortunam victrix perstitit ». Per il motivo stoico, v. Seneca, *Epist.*, 98. Cfr. anche H. Baron, *Franciscan Poverty*, p. 24.

[68] *Op. volg.*, I, p. 149. Cfr. anche L. Bruni, *Human.-philos. Schriften*, hrsg. von H. Baron, Leipzig, 1928, p. 120: « Sunt vero utiles divitiae, cum et ornamento sint possidentibus et ad virtutem exercendam suppeditent facultatem ».

[69] *Op. volg.*, I, p. 144.

noi le sappiamo usare » [70]. Ne deriva un'importante conseguenza, enunciata da Lionardo: « E' primi lodati essercizii, dicono alcuni, sono quegli ne' quali la fortuna tiene licenza niuna, imperio niuno, ne' quali l'animo e il corpo non serve » [71]. Ma l'Alberti gli fa pure affermare che nella grande mercatura, accanto alla fortuna, l'ingegno ha una parte di rilievo [72]; e gli fa respingere, più d'una volta, la tesi che siano « vili » gli « essercizii pecuniari » [73], e sostenere che non sono gloriosi come altre attività, ma che rispondono pur sempre a natura. Qui la cultura dell'umanista si accorda con la coscienza di provenire da una famiglia di ricchi banchieri e mercanti: così avverrà, più tardi, nel *De re aedificatoria*, dove, sia pure in posizione subordinata rispetto ai dotti, anche gli operatori economici sono considerati degni di partecipare al potere [74]. Ma per l'Alberti l'importante resta la libertà dello spirito, condizione indispensabile per vincere la fortuna [75]; e qui c'è da chiedersi se gli imprenditori si preoccupassero altrettanto d'un simile problema. Il suo Giannozzo, che rinuncia ai grandi traffici e preferisce una vita più modesta e tranquilla, si avvicina al saggio vecchio Genipatro del *Theogenius*, un tempo ricco, che ora s'accontenta di quanto gli basta per vivere, e della sua elevatezza morale.

Si è osservato però che l'Alberti enuncia la legge del risparmio, per cui il reddito dev'essere superiore alle spese; ma si è già visto che per Giannozzo l'attività da svolgere deve garantire l'occorrente per le necessità vitali (villa) e per le spese straordinarie (bottega); è vero che egli precisa che il padre di famiglia deve vendere più di quanto acquisti [76]; ma il precetto, oltre a riscontrarsi pure nei contemporanei autori di « ricordi », è pure molto antico, poiché lo enuncia giá un autore a lui noto, Catone

---

[70] *Op. volg.*, I, p. 178.

[71] *Op. volg.*, I, p. 146. In pratica, ammette però Lionardo, la fortuna agisce su ogni iniziativa umana. Sull'argomento si veda lo studio di G. Sasso, *Qualche osservazione sul problema della virtù e della fortuna nell'Alberti*, in *Mulino*, II, 1953, pp. 600-18.

[72] *Op. volg.*, I, p. 147.

[73] *Op. volg.*, I, pp. 141-2.

[74] IV . 1; *ed. cit.*, p. 269.

[75] *Op. volg.*, I, pp. 147-8.

[76] *Op. volg.*, I, p. 203.

il censore[77]. È vero invece che Giannozzo spiega come utilizzerebbe i risparmi eventuali: per « servirne la patria, o aiutarne l'amico, o donarne al parente, o simili, quali tutto il dì possono intervenire, spese non piccole, non da nolle fare, sì perché sono dovute, sì perché sono piatose, sì anche perché acquistano amistà, nome e lodo »[78]. Ma certo egli non destina i profitti a ingrandire l'azienda; e vaghi restano, nel l. II come nel III, gli accenni all'esigenza che la famiglia debba accrescere il suo « avere » e la bottega il suo reddito[79]. In concreto, l'Alberti non si pone affatto il problema di ingrandire la villa o la bottega stessa, mentre un autentico operatore economico avrebbe agito ben diversamente; e così, nella *Famiglia*, viene completamente elusa la fondamentale questione dell'aumento del capitale e del reddito, e del modo migliore per investire il proprio denaro, in rapporto alle circostanze (la discussione sui beni mobili e immobili tra Giannozzo e Adovardo resta troppo generica, e considera soltanto il modo di assicurarsi il capitale stesso).

Si è pure osservato che l'Alberti non riprende più il concetto cristiano, diffuso nel Medio Evo, di dare ai poveri il superfluo. L'osservazione è valida, e si può completare e precisare ricordando l'atteggiamento che verso i poveri l'umanista rivela nel *De re aedificatoria*[80]: essi non debbono vivere di elemosine, ma avere lavoro, o, nel caso di infermità, assistenza costante. Certo l'Alberti segue una morale sostanzialmente « laica », che si fonda sull'esame delle leggi della natura umana, e che intende evitare sia il rigorismo suggerito dalla religiosità medievale, sia l'opportunismo utilitaristico: una morale che vuole rafforzare la virtù dell'individuo nella lotta continua con la fortuna, rendendolo autosufficiente, insegnandogli a usare bene le ricchezze, considerate però mezzi instabili e secondari rispetto alle doti dello animo, alle « artes ». Nella *Famiglia*[81], poi, dedicata ad una con-

---

[77] *De agri cultura*, II . 7.

[78] *Op. volg.*, I, p. 203.

[79] *Op. volg.*, I, pp. 104, 204-5.

[80] V. 8; *ed. cit.*, pp. 367-9.

[81] L'atteggiamento albertiano verso la fortuna è sintetizzato in un passo significativo del l. II (*ed. cit.*, p. 149): « Se la fortuna vi dona ricchezze, adoperatele in lodo e onore vostro e de' vostri, sovvenitene agli amici, adoperatele in cose magnifiche e onestissime. Se la fortuna con voi sarà

sorteria borghese cui egli vuole insegnare a vincere la fortuna, la conquista e l'uso dei beni economici sono considerati specialmente nella loro dipendenza dall'iniziativa morale dell'individuo; ne deriva quindi la condanna dell'« inerzia », con l'elogio dell'« industria » e della « masserizia »; e ancora ne consegue la fiducia che Dio assista chi si impegna, secondo morale, anche nel campo economico: così nel l. II Lionardo loda l'attività degli Alberti perché estesa in Europa, ma soprattutto perché ispirata a principî d'onestà, aggiungendo che, per questo, Dio la favorisce. Il concetto, non nuovo, può far anche pensare, per altro aspetto, ad un'anticipazione di motivi calvinisti, tanto più che in questi dialoghi la povertà — pur se si dice che può dipendere dalla sorte — comincia anche ad apparire un demerito, per quanto può dipendere dall'uomo [82]. Ma anche questi spunti non hanno sviluppi esaurienti, in un'opera come la *Famiglia*, che è ricca di argomenti suggestivi, ma che non è pienamente sistematica. Ciò considerato, non può quindi stupirci che l'Alberti celebri la « liberalità » e la « magnificenza » anziché la « carità », che consigli di valersi della ricchezza per giovare alla patria, o all'amico, o al parente: il senso d'una più precisa solidarietà sociale gli manca, come confermano anche passi del *De re aedificatoria*: avverso ai feudatari e alla « plebe », scettico sulle possibilità dello stato (quando non sia retto da uomini dotti e « prudenti », che si considerino « servi pubblici », come ben di rado avviene), egli in pratica rivolge la sua attenzione prima di tutto all'individuo, e subordinatamente alla famiglia.

Il razionalismo albertiano, si può ormai concludere, presenta aspetti che certo rispondono a tendenze e incoraggiano iniziative economiche della borghesia del '400, in quanto si fonda su esigenze di carattere « terreno », stimola l'operosità indivi-

---

tenace e avara, non però per questo viverete solliciti, nè troppo manco contenti, neanche prenderete nell'animo gravezza alcuna sperando, aspettando da lei più che la vi porga. Spregiatela più tosto, chè facile cosa vi sarà spregiare quello che voi non arete. E se la fortuna a voi toglie le già date e bene adoperate ricchezze, che si dee fare se non portarlo in pace e forte? ».

[82] Per i giudizi di Lionardo, cfr. *ed. cit.*, pp. 144, 147. Circa la tesi albertiana, si noti la divergenza da S. Bernardino da Siena che affermava: « Se vuoi che la tua robba multiplichi, usa di dare limosina » (*Prediche volgari*, a c. di P. Bargellini, Milano, 1934, p. 964).

duale, conferma la bontà di criteri di calcolata prudenza, accetta il sistema economico del tempo, giustifica la grande mercatura, trascura del tutto le ragioni dei salariati. Tuttavia esso non si può considerare in modo assoluto una manifestazione di spirito borghese nel senso di una teorizzazione esclusiva ed egoistica dell'utilitarismo. La sua dottrina, come si è visto, poggia su basi morali, antepone la libertà dello spirito e l'onore ai guadagni, suggerisce di accontentarsi di ciò che basti alle necessità naturali: è la proiezione in campo economico dell'esigenza di virtù propria dell'umanesimo albertiano, intende anzi subordinare l'economia all'etica [83]. In pratica, la prudenza consigliata, il criterio dell'autosufficienza e del giusto mezzo orientano ad una societá borghese costituita da comunità familiari che provvedono anzitutto alle proprie indispensabili necessità, una società onesta e oculata (anche se conosce le spese per motivi di liberalità e magnificenza), che si distingue da quella del sec. XV, per il suo carattere idealizzato [84]. Del resto, anche la città ideale del *De re aedificatoria*, attiva, costumata, e in sé conclusa come un mondo perfetto, si dimostra a sua volta l'utopia d'un umanista d'origine borghese che, per motivi d'universalità, si scosta dai problemi più concretamente immediati della borghesia comunale di primo Quattrocento, e preferisce difendere il suo ideale di letterato (e poi di architetto) che giova agli altri con le sue meditazioni solitarie (seguite da « inaudite invenzioni ») e per questa via consegue la gloria, anziché partecipando direttamente alle iniziative sociali e politiche del momento storico in cui vive.

---

[83] Cfr. P. H. Michel, *Un idéal*, p. 318: « En faisant de la réduction de nos appétits la principale condition de la richesse, Alberti élève l'économie privée à la hauteur d'une question morale ».

[84] Una società, quindi, idealizzata, come è idealizzata « casa Alberta » nelle pagine di Leon Battista. È interessante a questo riguardo una particolare osservazione del Sapori: mentre nella *Famiglia* la consorteria appare concorde e unita fino al tempo dell'autore, invece — come dicono i documenti d'archivio — la situazione era diversa già alla metà del sec. XIV; per cui lo studioso aggiunge: « Chi ha preteso di ravvisare nella prosa del quattrocentista una realtà più vicina è stato tratto in inganno; e se lo scrittore ha favorito quella sbagliata interpretazione lo ha fatto nel tentativo di sollecitare i suoi, che vedeva e sapeva disuniti come gli altri del suo tempo, a un impossibile ritorno al passato » (*Studi di storia econom.*, *cit.*, II, p. 1011).

Anche nel l. III *Della famiglia* appare dunque una costante dello spirito albertiano; e, per spiegare questo carattere, non è necessario pensare a un declino dell'attività economica della Toscana del tempo, e tanto meno cercare le prove di ciò nell'opera dell'umanista: queste, se mai, vanno cercate in altra direzione: nei testi di scrittori meno geniali dell'Alberti e meno importanti nella storia delle idee, ma più di lui legati alla realtà della vita economica, e, meglio ancora, nei documenti d'archivio del secolo XV [85].

---

[85] Mentre questo saggio era in tipografia, sono stati editi i libri *Della famiglia* nella « Nuova Universale Einaudi », a cura di R. Romano e A. Tenenti (Torino, 1969), con un'introduzione densa di concetti. È da rilevare che i due lavori hanno avuto una genesi del tutto indipendente, pur se vari argomenti trattati sono affini; inoltre, accanto a interessanti convergenze, si notano precise diversità anzitutto di metodo (per es. a proposito dell'attenzione da noi rivolta allo stoicismo albertiano e all'influsso dei classici).

Aggiungiamo infine che, per conoscere le idee diffuse nella borghesia mercantile fiorentina e confrontarle con l'interpretazione albertiana, è utile in particolare la lettura del recente volume di C. Bec, *Les marchands écrivains à Florence, 1375-1434*, Paris, 1967.

DONALD WEINSTEIN

THE APOCALYPSE IN SIXTEENTH-CENTURY FLORENCE: THE VISION OF ALBERT OF TRENT

The sixteenth-century text published for the first time here belongs to an old genre, the pseudonymous historical apocalypse [1]. While deriving from a limited number of Biblical and medieval prototypes and drawing upon a conventionalized vocabulary and a stock scenario (e. g. Antichrist, Last Emperor, Angelic Pastor, Conversion of the Jews, World Sabbath), historical apocalypses were nonetheless statements by individuals about real events and problems of their time, and as such they may contain useful information as well as provide insights into attitudes and values. They do not give up their historical truths easily, however. It is the nature of such texts to be misleading about their actual origins and ambiguous in content, and rare is the apocalypse that does not leave its would-be interpreter with some frustrating uncertainties.

The text presented here is a case in point. Purporting to be the account of a vision revealed to a certain Albert, at the time a layman but later a Carthusian monk, in his native Trent in 1436, and to have been dictated by him in Padua in 1490, it is certainly not that but rather a piece of radical political and religious propaganda of early sixteenth-century Florentine origin. Among the « predictions » which can definitely be taken as

[1] I borrow the term from Paul J. Alexander's recent article, « Medieval Apocalypses as Historical Sources », *American Historical Review*, LXXIII (1968), 997-1018. Although primarily concerned with medieval Byzantine texts this is an excellent introduction to the subject of historical apocalypses. For some recent discussions of apocalyptic literature in Florence in the fifteenth and sixteenth centuries see Cesare Vasoli, « L' attesa della nuova era in ambienti e gruppi fiorentini del Quattrocento », *L'attesa dell'età nuova nella spiritualità della fine del medioevo* (Convegni del Centro di Studi sulla Spiritualità Medievale III 16-19 ottobre 1960; Todi, 1962) 370-432; André Chastel, « L'Apocalypse en 1500 », *Bibliothèque d'humanisme et Renaissance, Melanges d'Augustin Renaudet*, XIV (1952), 122-40 and Chastel, « L'Antechrist à la Renaissance », *Cristianesimo e ragion di stato. L'Umanesimo e il demoniaco nell'arte* (Atti del II Congresso Internazionale di Studi Umanistici, Roma, 1952; Rome, 1953), 177-186; Donald Weinstein, « The Myth of Florence », *Florentine Studies*, ed. Nicolai Rubinstein (London, 1968), pp. 15-44.

historical, that is, as having been made *ex eventu*, are the coming of Savonarola to Florence, his preaching and martyrdom there (1490-1498), the invasion of Italy by the French Kings Charles VIII (1494) and Louis XII (1499), the reign of Pope Alexander VI (1492-1503), the military conquests of Alexander's son, Cesare Borgia, Duke Valentino, particularly his invasion of Tuscany (1501), the revolt of Arezzo against Florentine rule (1501), and the concurrent constitutional crisis in Florence which ended with the establishment of the Gonfalonier of Justice as a lifetime office (1502). In short, the historical phase of the vision includes the major Italian and Florentine events of the years 1490-1503, ending with the death of Pope Alexander VI in August of the latter year. At this point vaguer predictions and eschatological fantasies replace historical reporting, beginning with the prediction of the coming of the Angelic Pastor in 1504. This leads me to conclude that the apocalypse was composed, either wholly or in great part, between late 1503 and early 1504 [2].

Not only is it unlikely that a fifteenth-century Albert of Trent composed this apocalypse as the record of a prophetic vision, but apart from the text itself there is no record that such a person ever existed [3]. In other words this is probably an historical apocalypse for which a prophet was invented rather than one assigned to a famous historical person. Both types are found with about equal frequency [4]. We can make one im-

---

[2] My reasoning is that the author would probably not have given such a definite date for an apocalyptic event as important as the coming of the Angelic Pastor unless that date were still in the future. Although I cannot accept a later date of composition than 1503-4 it is suggestive that the copy published here was made in Florence at the end of 1512 (see below), three months after the restoration of the Medici. While there is no direct attack upon the Medici in this apocalypse its piagnone republicanism is implicitly anti-Medicean.

[3] There are entries for Albert of Trent in both *Enciclopedia Cattolica* and Baudrillart's *Dictionnaire d'histoire et de géographie ecclésiastiques*, but neither of them offer any evidence of his existence apart from the sixteenth-century texts of the vision.

[4] Examples of the first type — attribution to persons otherwise unknown: the vision of Fra Antonio da Rieti, widespread in fifteenth-century Italy, printed as *Copia d'una rivelazione che ebbe frate Antonio da Rieta dell'Ordine di Sancto Franceschо de Frati Observanti* (Florence, n. d.); the prophecies

portant identification, however. Of the several Latin and Italian manuscripts of the Albert of Trent vision I have seen in Florentine libraries, one bears the name of a copyist and the date of his transcription. At the end of this Latin text we read, in Italian, the following: « Copied by me, Priest Giovanni d'Angelo di Miglio da Cetica, on the 18th day of December, 1512 ». Giovanni di Miglio of Cetica (a *contrada* in the Casentino district east of Florence) was a secular priest who spent most of his career in Florence, serving first as an official of the foundling hospital of the Innocenti, next as rector of the Church of San Pancrazio, finally, as *governatore*, or *administrator*, of the Augustinian monastery of San Gaggio, on the Via Romana, just south of Florence. There he died in 1540 at the age of sixty-four and was buried. We are told by Giovanni's brother that he was much loved in Florence, that after his death he was found to have been wearing five penitential bands pressed into his bare flesh, and that there were certain other (unspecified) signs of his beatitude [5]. Was the visionary Albert of Trent really the devout priest Giovanni di Miglio? One clue that might seem to link the two is the concern expressed in the text for events in Giovanni's home territory of the Casentino, particularly the prophet's outrage over the Venetian occupation of Monte La Verna, sacred to the memory of St. Francis of Assisi, in 1498. In this connection it is also suggestive that Giovanni's brother Agostino, a Franciscan friar, later wrote a book on the region of Monte La Verna [6]. On the other hand, if Giovanni di Miglio were the author of the apocalypse rather than its mere copyist

---

of Reginaldus Oxoniensis in many mss. Examples of the second type — attribution to famous historical persons: the prophecies and visions attributed to Saint Bridget of Sweden, actually of later date and Florentine in origin (see my « Myth of Florence », p. 35); the various versions of a Book of the Popes attributed to Joachim of Flora. See Herbert Grundmann, «Die Papstprophetien des Mittelalters », *Archiv für Kulturgeschichte*, XIX (1928), 77-138. Still another category would be that of prophecies attributed to famous mythical figures, as the prophecies of Merlin and of the various Sibyls.

[5] Agostino di Miglio, *Nuovo dialogo delle devozioni del Sacro Monte della Verna* (Florence, 1568), 268-9. Once again I wish to acknowledge the help of Signor Ivaldo Baglioni of the Biblioteca Nazionale Centrale in Florence in identifying Giovanni di Miglio.

[6] See n. 5 above. On Agostino see also Luke Wadding, *Scriptores Ordinis Minorum* (Rome, 1650) p. 43.

it is doubtful whether he would have made the errors in the text we shall note below, or that he would have been so vague in « predicting » events between 1503 and 1512.

Whoever the real author was he was undoubtedly Florentine in his loyalties and *piagnone*, as Savonarola's partisans continued to be called, in his political and religious sympathies. He sees events in terms of their effect upon Florence's well-being and he treats Savonarola's prophetic mission and martyrdom as central events in the eschatological drama. He establishes the validity of Savonarola's mission by showing that it was part of the unfolding of the divine program, revealed in the heavens years before Savonarola was born [7], and now proving itself through the fulfillment of the friar's prophecies. According to him the Florentines' enthusiastic response to Savonarola's teachings had saved them from the worst of the *flagellum Dei*, while their subsequent sufferings could be understood partly as punishment for having rejected their prophet.

On the other hand pseudo-Albert was able to maintain a certain independence in both religious and political matters from Savonarola's teachings. He writes in the full awareness of the major upheaval taking place in sixteenth-century Italian politics, and this helps explain his hostility toward most established forms of power and his pessimism about worldly institutions in general. Thus, he abandons one of the cornerstones of *piagnone* doctrine, the traditional French alliance. Whereas Savonarola had come to regard Charles VIII not only as *flagellum Dei* and New Cyrus, but also as New Charlemagne, divine instrument of Florence's protection and of the universal reformation, the author of the Albert of Trent apocalypse can only regard the French king as « monstruosissimus et infidelis », the

---

[7] He was cited to this effect by Gianfrancesco Pico della Mirandola in his biography of Savonarola, *Vita R. P. Fr. Hieronymi Ferrariensis Ord. Praedicatorum* ... ed. J. Quétif (Paris, 1674), I, 151.This was a revised version of about 1530. An earlier, unpublished, version of the biography, written before 1520, does not contain the reference to the prophecy of Albert of Trent, as I have been informed by Professor Giampaolo Tognetti, who kindly checked the manuscript (Florence, Biblioteca Riccardiana 2053) for me. The two versions of Gianfrancesco Pico's biography of Savonarola have been dated by Roberto Ridolfi, *Vita di Girolamo Savonarola*, 2 vols. (Rome, 1952), II, 81.

great betrayer whose coming has plunged Italy into a sea of disasters. With regard to religious matters he is even more outspoken than Savonarola in his attacks upon the scandals of the Borgia papacy and upon Rome as the seat of ecclesiastical corruption. In general his ideas of religious renewal are more openly heterodox than those of Savonarola and the earlier *piagnoni*. He does not hesitate to predict the destruction of the Church (a prediction he attributes to Savonarola himself), although with characteristic inconsistency he also talks of the eventual restoration of Peter to his Church. He beholds, amidst heavenly flames, the coming of a new and correct religion « from the islands of the sea » whose devotees will be clothed in rough pelts. He foresees the leaders of the Church congregating in Florence to receive the « new book » by which the whole of the perfect law will be renewed and he refers to the Eternal Gospel (Revelation 14: 6) that favorite millenarian image of the Joachite Franciscan Spirituals [8]. Whereas Savonarola had not identified himself with a particular class, except, perhaps, in his early preaching, pseudo-Albert is inclined to champion the poor and humble over the rich and powerful. He envisions repeated revolutions against the princes and he sees the people united to regain their strength and overthrow « every tyrannical sect ». His Angelic Pastor is a simple man of the poor.

One puzzling feature of the vision is the prophecy that Venice will share Florence's glorious future. Apart from their admiration for the Venetian constitution [9], Florentines had little reason to feel kindly toward Venice, which, since 1494, had repeatedly violated their territory and leagued with their enemies in her efforts to capitalize on Florence's troubles. Pseudo-Albert, as we have seen, was particularly critical of the Venetian invasion of the Casentino and he foresaw Venice sharing in the

[8] For the literature on the theme of the Eternal Gospel in Joachite thought, as well as for the best bibliography of Joachite scholarship generally, see Morton W. Bloomfield, « Joachim of Flora A Critical Survey of his Canon, Teachings, Sources, Biography and Influence », *Traditio*, XIII (1957), 249-311.

[9] For the best discussion of the admiration for the Venetian constitution in Florence and its influence on Florentine political thought, see Felix Gilbert, « The Venetian Constitution in Florentine Political Thought », *Florentine Studies*, pp. 463-500.

sufferings of the rest of Italy in the coming divine scourges. Nevertheless he predicted that the two lions, Venice and Florence, would eventually join together to recover their lost territories and extend their empires, one on sea, the other on land, even that they would win an ultimate victory over the Eagle (Holy Roman Empire?). This willingness to share the ultimate glories with Venice is a unique feature in the literature of Florentine patriotic prophecies. In a sense it replaces the older Guelf traditions of alliance with the Papacy and with the French descendants of Charlemagne. It must have been born of the same alternation of despair and hope that runs throughout the vision of Albert of Trent. Whatever else she was, Venice was republican, Italian and free. To this Florentine and Italian patriot, hater of the foreign barbarians and of domestic tyrannies, a Venetian-Florentine alliance must have been a last, remote hope. Hence his vision that the two republican lions would arise out of the holocaust, purified and aware of their common ideals, and together redeem their countrymen and all of Christendom.

The mss. I have seen may best be grouped as follows.

GROUP I. 16 th century. Most extensive version. Contains introductory passage describing the vision of an angel holding three vials as well as other passages lacking in the other versions. In this group there are two copies:

C. = Florence, Biblioteca Nazionale Centrale Ms. Capponi 121, fols. 1-10 v. « Dictante ipsomet Frate Alberto Cartusiensis Ordinis. Die xij^{a} Septembris Salutis 1490. Scripsi Paduae ». Latin. At end, in Italian: « Copiata per me Prete Joanni dagnolo demiglio da Cetica. Addi 18 dicembre 1512 ». This is the text published here.

M. = Florence, Biblioteca Nazionale Centrale Ms. Magliabechi XXXV. 1 (Separate codex, 16 leaves) « fra Alberto di Certosa, Profezia o visione avuta a di 10 Aprile 1436. Tradotta dal Latino in volgare ». Italian.

GROUP II. 16 th century. Abbreviated version, begins with invasion of the monstrous infidel (King Charles VIII). In this group there are two copies:

CS. = Florence, Biblioteca Nazionale Centrale Ms. Conventi soppressi (Prov. S. Marco) J. X. 5, fols. 126-131 v. « Profetia del certosino frate Alberto da Trento facta l'anno Mcccc^{o} xxxvi^{o} ». Italian. This codex has been described, and some other parts of its contents published, by Giampaolo Tognetti, « Un episodio inedito di repressione della predicazione postsavonaroliana (Firenze 1509) », *Bibliothèque d'humanisme et Renaissance*, XXIV (1962), pp. 190-9.

P. = Paris, Bibliothèque Nationale Ms. French 828, fols. 217-221 v. « Prophetia fratris Alberti de Trento Ordinis Cartusiensium facta anno Domini 1436 et a me descritta anno 1580 ». Latin.

GROUP III. 18 th century. Fragments. In this group there are two copies:

PA. = Florence, Biblioteca Nazionale Centrale Ms. Panciatichi 117, fol. 302. « Profezie di Fra Alberto da Trento Certosino circa al P. Fra Girolamo fatte nell'anno 1436 ». Italian. Referred to me by Professor Giampaolo Tognetti.

R. = Florence, Biblioteca Riccardiana Ms. Moreni 37, fols. 226 v-238.
fols. 226 v-236 v. Excerpts, included under heading « Profezie fatte, et alcune cose seguite e molte avanti prenunziate dal Padre fra Girolamo Savonarola ». (fol. 224) fols. 236 v-238. « Altre Profezie di fra Alberto da Trento Certosino fatte nell'anno 1436 ». Italian.

In transcribing the text[10], I have made the following changes: elimination of abbreviations; separation of words run together; modernization of punctuation, including use of apostrophes to indicate elisions, and of quotation marks where direct discourse seems intended.

Brackets enclose the passages that make up the text of CS and P. Marginal comments from CS and P are given in the footnotes.

fol. 1 Dictante ipsomet Fratre[11] Alberto Cartusiensis ordinis Die xij^a^ septembris salutis 1490. Scripsi Paduae.

Aspiciens in Celum vidi tres phialas in medio celi et istas habebat Angelus Domini in manu sua. Visio autem mea super phialas fuit die x^a^ mensis Aprilis 1436. Dum adhuc fuissem sine religione vivens. Ego Albertus ex ordine Cartusiensium in patria in qua oriundus sum, videlicet Tridenti. Erat enim Angelus effundens tres phialas. Una autem plena erat aqua, Altera sanguine et altera Igne. Et dixit mihi, « Suspice Celum sursum et numera iudicia Dei et omnes vias non intelliges altissimi sed quae erant a tempore isto usque ad annos novae etatis. Et dixi, « Quid effusio aque? » Et dixit, « Ista est effusio super universum orbem ». Et vidi ab exordio universi quasi omnes creaturas esse deletas a facie terrae. Sed intellige a Millesimo quadringentesimo nonagesimo usque ad Millesimum quingentesimum secundum et postea vide. Et vidi effundere sanguinem super fideles et super Bisantium. Et quasi orientalis plaga effecta obscura infidelibus propter abhominationem. Et insuper vidi effundere sanguinem super europam in regionibus existentibus infra apeninos montes.

---

[10] I wish to thank the following people for assistance: Olga Christides, Marshall Clagett, Felix Gilbert, James John, Paris Legrow, John Lenaghan (who checked the entire transcription), Hans-Georg Pflaum and Antonio Rotondò.

[11] Above the line a phrase very difficult to read. See facsimile. It has been suggested that it might be Greek, but the most likely reading seems to be the one proposed by Professor Felix Gilbert: « Jesus Christus [space] apud apostolum idem ».

et agreppe

Dictavit ipsemet Frater Alberto Cartusiensis ordinis die VII VIII
xxij. septembris salutis. 1490. scripsi Padue

Aspiciens in Celum vidi tres phialas in medio celi et 14
istas habebat Angelus Dni in manu sua. Visio autem mea
super phialas fuit die 7a. mensis Aprilis. 1436. Dum adhuc
fuissem sine religione vivens. Ego Albertus ex ordine
Cartusiensium in patria inqua oriundus sum, videlicet
...idenit erat ...Angelus effundens tres phialas. Una autem
plena erat aqua. Altera sanguine et alia Igne. et
dixit mihi suspice celum sursum et numera iudicia Dei
et ... ... no intelliges altissimi ... q erant atempore isto
usque ad annos nove etatis. et dixi. quid effusio aque et
dixit. Ista e effusio super universum orbem. et vidi abeg or
dio universi quasi omnes creaturas esse deletas afacie terre
sed intellige a m.o iiij nonagiusque ad m.o quingentos. secundum
et ... ... et vidi effundere sanguinem super fideles et
super bisantiu et quasi orientalis plaga effecta obscura
infidelibus propter abhominationem. et in super vidi effundere
sanguinem super europam in regionibus posterioribus infra ape
ninos montes. Vidi undique bella super omnem Italiam Venet

Carolus
... ... mostruosissimus et infidelis nomine non re chrisnianissimus
qui simulata fide pace atque cocordia solo nutu omnem

Firenze, Biblioteca Nazionale Centrale, Ms. Capponi 121, fol. 1.

Vidi undique bella super omnem Italiam[12]. [Veniet monstruosissimus[a] et infidelis, nomine non re Christianissimus, qui simulata fide, pace atque concordia solo nutu omnem/sibi aut pro maiori parte subijciet fol. 1 v
Italiam]. Heu principes Italie quare talem Principem ad dextructionem vestram advocastis? Hic vero inimicissimus fidelium et venetos et serpentes[13] Leonem[14] et claves Petri conabitur evertere. Sed non ab ipso fient hec omnia licet pro maiori parte. In Eneadum urbe non regnabit sed regnum Italiae sibi subijciet, [et in reversione sive post iusto iudicio Dei morietur tanquam delusor fidei[15]. Apparebit insuper destructio et servitus illius Ambrosiani status et dabitur secundo Regi in praedam eo quod fuerit primus omnium malorum causa puniendum, et luctus eius per tempora duraturus erit]. Subijciet sibi galliam iste secundus cisalpinam fere omnem. Iste regnabit similiter adulterata fide et magna fient per eum. Veh Italie. Veh sponse agni. Veh Leoni. Veh Picenis. Veh domui extensi. Veh domui Gonzaghae. Veh Perusinis tirannis. Veh Rome. Veh tibi o sena vetus, in te omnem fere libertatem videmus in servitutem convertere. Veh lucensibus. Veh venetis fidelibus hos substinebit et pericula multa undique evadent. Flagellabuntur et ipsi multa cum abstutia malignantium iusto iudicio Dei propter eorum peccata. Flere Urbinates. Flere a mari usque ad mare[16]. [Et vidi alatum Leonem in partibus Ethruriae quasi prophanantem sachrum Avernae montem. Genuflectatur Franciscus et/invocet canes ad evellendum quasi Leonis alas]. Et post hec fiunt fol. 2
peiora primis[17]. [Nostris temporibus erit abhominatio magna pessima et inaudibilis et ecclesia et sponsa agni adulterabitur. Invadet gregem Domini lupus rapax ab anno 1490 usque ad 1503, vel circa sive parum ultra. Hic ex hispania multa mala inferre videtur fidelibus Christianis. Hic ecclesiam Dei lupanaribus simoniis, adulationibus implebit, et vertetur sacrificium eius in habominationem coram Deo. Hic ad senectam veniens confusibiliter morietur post multorum malorum illationem. Hic magnus prophanator, destructor pecuniis ex latere Christi extractis filiam Dei ecclesiam adulteram quasi possi-

---

[a] Text: « mostruosissimus ».

[12] Left margin: (hereinafter LM) « Carolus VIII rex. » P. « Venuta di Carlo ottavo in Italia ». CS. Right margin: (hereinafter RM) « Re di francia ».

[13] A serpent was a common symbol of Milan. There was a serpent in the Sforza coat of arms.

[14] A lion (marzocco) was a common symbol of Florence, as a winged lion (St. Mark) was of Venice.

[15] P. LM: « la perdita et servitu di Milano ». CS. RM: « Milano ».

[16] P. LM: « Venitiani in Casentino ». CS. RM: « Vinetia Vernia ».

[17] P. LM: « Papa Alexandro sesto ». CS. RM: « Papa Alexandro ».

debit [18]. Hic filios multos qui inter se non sufferentes incedere ab altero convertentur [19]. Interfector iste, sive fratricida, filius iniquitatis et prodictionis, renuet religionem omnem et revertetur ad seculum et erit missus a Diabolo]. Fiet magnus dominus draconem marittimum ligabit et cessabit sibyllare donec solvatur. Hic omnem Emiliam suo subijciet imperio agrumque Picenum et Etruriam pro maiori parte conculcabit. Hic fideles suos interficiet aviditate regnandi. Et sibi bellum ab eo subditi innovabunt [a]. Sed maxima [b] confusio erit istis
fol. 2 v temporibus. Vidi effundere sanguinem de corpore/ phiale, et Angelum arripere gladium. Oh iudicia mea timete omnes populi sub caelo, nam cito est ira dei. [Temporibus praedictis surget Propheta missus ex alto qui divino afflatus spiritu omnem docebit veritatem maxima cum populi iocunditate [20]. Erit eius habitatio in domo florentinorum. Ibi omne eloquium docebit altissimi, multis ieiuniis, castigationibus carnis, populum talem ad Deum conversum. Pro maiori parte dum vivet flagella Dei evitare faciet. Hic ex ordine praedicatorum pro se suisque eliget vitam propheticam. Ipse ex alto loquens, audietur usque ad gentes. Et erit vita eius in secula manens]. Dum vivit haec flagella minatur ibidem. Oculus dexter avulsus erit a [dominio florentinorum [21]. Et si non fuisset hic missus a Deo peiora populo evenissent. [Hic Justus pro veritate morietur in igne in medio filiorum. Erit enim combustus sed antequam moriatur hec venient ibi. Maximam dominii partem non obtinebunt sed erit in predam inimicis eorum [22]. Sed ibidem quinque viri potentes in numero interfectorum sortiuntur. Sextus mala morte ferroque populi furore peribit [23]. Et postea persecutio vertetur in prophetam iustumque Dei missum. Et tandem ad martirium ducetur]. Et antequam moriatur

---

[a] Text: « invocabunt », with « voca » crossed out and « nova » inserted above the line.

[b] Text: « magna », with « gna » crossed out and « xima » added.

[18] CS. RM: « Valentino ».

[19] P. LM: « Il Valentino ».

[20] P. LM: « La venuta di fra Girolamo in Firenze ». CS. RM: « frater Hieronymus de feraria ».

[21] The « right eye » is undoubtedly Pisa, lost to Florence in 1494.

[22] CS. RM: « Sei ciptadini di firenze ».

[23] The five Florentine citizens referred to here were Bernardo del Nero, Niccolò Ridolfi, Lorenzo Tornabuoni, Giovanni di Bernardo Cambi and Giannozzo Pucci. They were accused of plotting the restoration of Piero de' Medici and executed in August, 1497. The sixth man referred to must have been Francesco Valori, leader of the Savonarolan political faction, or Frateschi, who was murdered in revenge for his part in the execution of the five on April 8, 1498.

secreta multa dicet. Et hoc unum inter cetera revelabit videlicet qui
peius Florentinis eveniet post/ mortem eius quam prius hoc non fol. 3
publice dicet, sed familiaribus sibi. Et destructionem Ecclesiae non
tacebit. Post sui obitum maximam confusionem nunctiabit, quae
confusio erit Anno Domini Millesimo quingentesimo secundo ante
obscurationem solis. Et tunc omne gaudium convertetur in luctum.
Confusio iste habebit exordium inter istos menses, videlicet [24] [Martii,
Aprilis, Maii, Junii, Julii, Augusti, sed unum erit quod erit florentia
maxima populorum congregatio. Erit talis effusio sanguinis intus et
extra quod non invenietur locus ubi pes requiescat sine sanguine].
Deprehenditur fere omne dominium quia sinister oculus hoc tempore
evelletur a leone [25]. Et hoc quia non crediderunt prophetam qui
apud suos fideles habetur in maxima veneratione. Post vero hominum
multorum cedem videbitur hic spurius qui sub clave protegitur
laniari, evelli, deleri, a superficie terrae et morietur in maxima tri-
bulatione [26]. Insurgent Duo Leones simul, alatus et simplex, et rugitu
suo atque volatu eius vi reasumet vires et omne dominium suum
cum ceteris membris reasumere videtur. Roma quae erit consueta
malis Flumen sanguine plenum eo tempore horruisti et quasi vidua
tui duces te non poterunt substinere. Omnis Italia conculcabitur quia
potentes in omni parte peribunt./ Omnis Civitas absque consilio fol. 3 v
absque favore deficiet. Hec erunt temporibus illis in partibus mundi.
Reges et Principes mundi punientur a populis iusto iudicio Dei.
Et sic vidi effundere omnem sanguinem. Auferentur dominium a
Florentinis et multi populi congregabuntur et multa effusione sanguinis peracta mortuis ibidem tribus potentibus in armis et belli
ducibus dabitur vexillum volenti. Sed quis erit volens? Novit ipse
Dominus. Eversa insuper premissa libertate [erit magnum excidium
Etruriae a flumine Tiberi usque ad lucensem agrum [27]. Decoriabitur
equus iam liberatus, subiugabitur maiori servitute priori [28]. Sena
flagellorum punitione habita magnates interficiet. Pistorium igne
succendetur [a]. Lucenses in predam dirigentur tyrannidam [29]. Post hec

---

[a] Text: « sucendetur ».

[24] P. LM: « Tumulto di popolo ». Probably refers to the disturbances in Florence in the spring of 1501 relative to the invasion of Cesare Borgia, the revolt of Arezzo and the fear of a Medici restoration.

[25] The « left eye » no doubt refers to Arezzo, which revolted against Florentine rule on June 4, 1501.

[26] The « spurius » referred to here and several more times is surely Cesare Borgia, but the prediction of his death is too vague and inaccurate in description to lead us to suppose that it was made before the event (1507).

[27] P. LM: « Arezo ».

[28] CS. P. LM: « Siena Pistoia Lucca ».

[29] CS. P. LM: « Papa Angelico ».

insurgit homo pauperibus hic colorem nucis avellanae in faciem habens. Hinc inde oculos aspicientes capillos habebit protensos, blanda verba loquens, mediocris stature erit. Hic Dei ecclesiam ad omnem religionem convertere videbitur. Ipse insperato omnia vestimenta sponsae agni restituet. Et erit decus fidelium], sed primo maxima fidelium et infidelium erit ruina bellum, clades et populorum occisio. Et fiet unum ovile et unus pastor. Et caverint populi a iudiciis Dei quae magna minantur. Hec quae diximus erunt in quingentis et duobus et tribus et quatuor annis a cccc° supra Millesimo/
fol. 4 Nonagesimo, nisi placatus fuerit Altissimus sanctorum virorum precibus atque iustorum de quibus dignetur Dominus replere terram quoniam non est qui faciat bonum, non est usque ad unum. [Erit igitur persecutio clericorum in prophetam praedictum et a populis in eos religiosos persecutio vigebit quoniam a seculo non est audita habominatio ipsorum [30]. Erunt quidam nomine observantie opponentes se prophete. Et quia adulterum sanctum nomen tueri conabuntur obtinebunt. Tamen non post multos annos invidentes aliis cognita eorum ypocrisi proijcientur a populis tanquam infames et Dei rebelles [31]. Oh insontes viri et famuli prophete. Nolite timere a facie eorum. Post fiet maxima et universalis persecutio ita quae erit abhominatio in populis religiosos nuncupari et erit maxima strages et rubricantes aquas orbis in flumine Arni ab ortu usque ad finem [32]. O Pisanorum edes omnes fere sanguine et igne cooperientur et dabuntur in praedam atque eternam servitutem]. Erit insuper nova religio mundi confusionem generans. Hec novam insinuat vitam et velut martyres filios multos habebit. Et insurget contra omnem adulterantem clerum. Et erit novissima hominum pessima. Ante igitur omnem excidium Etruriae erit populis pro consilio confusio pro auxilio offensio pro fiducia timor, pro fide fraus, pro libertate servitus
fol. 4 v valida. Dabitur pro pane absinthium, pro lacte fel in potum./ Et erunt multi filii orphani et viduae mulieres apparebunt. Spurius enim ille maximam Etruriae partem conculcabit cum maxima potentum eiusdem regionis admiratione confusione et in pluribus cede. Celi haec omnia minantur sagittis terre motibus multitudine signorum potentorum ac cometarum apparitione. Nam una ad modum Crucis apparebit. Ignee flamme apparebunt ab omnibus mundi partibus. Et multa partes axis ostendent sanguineum rorem et pluviam in partibus Italiae ut mala crudelissima valeant nunctiare in populis. Insuper tria haec sequentur: confusio in principibus; traditio cum fraude in militibus;

---

[30] LM. CS: « persecutione al propheta e seguaci ».
P: « La persequtione contro a fra Girolamo ».

[31] CS. LM: « frati observanti in nome ».

[32] CS. LM: « Pisa ».

desperatione succedente in populis. Et non erit laus cum gaudio, non letitia, sed pro suavi amore et pace odium et insidie parabuntur. Homicidia in proprios sequentur parentes. Et nulla spes salutis erit, nisi conversi fuerint in celum ad patrem omnium rerum qui cuncta [a] ministrat. Et vidi ensem evaginatum super omnem Italiam a predictis temporibus usque ad annos etatis de quibus in alio. Erit sanguinis effusio occidentalium populorum. Nam Italici deiectis barbaris omnem sibi ipsis restituent libertatem. Sed vidi primo gladium evaginatum et erat aspectus Angeli admirabilis qui Canes albos et nigros ad devorandam adulteram ecclesiam mittebat et seviebant in gladio. Et ceciderunt Claves de manu adulteri qui sic derisit legem inreprehensibilem/ et evangelium eternum. fol. 5

[33] [Erit eo tempore mutatio regum multorum in partibus Apuliae atque Italiae innovatio principum. Et postea scisma in ecclesia qualis non visa in seculum fuit. Congregatis ex una parte multis, et ex alia multis, hinc inde clericis in fide confusionem dabunt, quae confusio odibilis in populis universale excidium religiosorum aut pro maiori parte monstrabit]. Tunc temporis indignabitur Altissimus quia adulter adulterabitur pontifex. Et multa adulteria iam commissa voluntate [b] sunt permissa libertati ecclesie in servitutem peccati. Quare haec erunt? Et dixit, « Quia longe est Dominus ab eis. Et non potuerunt resistere iudiciis Dei ».

Omnes concubine libertatem ecclesiae obtinebunt, quousque sit peccatorum consumatio. Nam haec peccata erunt. Potentes, Principes in adulteriam videbuntur, non substinent reprehensionem evangelizantium. Bona peribunt in iudiciis Dei et qui monarchiam habet mattabitur diabolo. Superabitur ab inimicis. Et sui insequentur destruentes potentiam et imperium quia simulata fide adherebunt alteri non Domino.

Erunt ergo in gelido axe confusi et interfecti multi quia defensio fidei facta est offensio. Et sic minati sunt prophetae. Et dixit ad me. Et vidi solem sanguine plenum. Et quod erat in medio restaurabat. Et erunt quatuor mundi partes lumine private./ Et ab fol. 5 v
oriente erat pars sanguinis in sole, ab occidente erat pars sanguinis in sole, a Meridie erat pars sanguinis in sole, a Septemtrione erat pars sanguinis in sole. Et vidi cruentatum Domini sepulcrum et clamabat vox de sepulcro, « Vindica sanguinem meum ». Et dixi, « Non video ». Et aperuit sepulcrum et vidi imperium in servitute perire et cum omni potentia subiectum. Et clamabat vox

[a] Text: « cunta ».
[b] Text: two letters apparently crossed out.

[33] CS. LM: « Puglia Italia Scisma ».

de sepulcro, « Mitte domine manum ». Et misit etiam gladium. Et substulit sceptrum et facti sunt cuncti maligni. Et dixit, « Audi tertiam vocem. Non bibent amplius peccatores sanguinem meum. Heu iudicium Domini. Delebuntur a facie terrae ». Et audivi vocem ab oriente, « Obscurentur oculi eorum ne videant et factum est iudicium magnum in universa terra ». Erunt prodigia in partibus orientis et signa de Celo. Et insurget contra maumettum quidam malignus et obtinebit in parte quia Seductorum princeps apparebit. His temporibus dimicabunt inter se infideles et pontifex infidelium crudelissimam cedem insinuabit. Et sibilabunt ab omni parte hereses, non erit veritas nisi in auro et argento et non habentes infelices erunt. Et sic erit ruina fere omnium infidelium.

Erit ab occidente crudelissimus princeps qui non contentus una morte suorum omnem fere Italiam in damnationem trucidabit. Veniet
fol. 6 igitur visio in omnem Italiam./ Cavete reges. Et dixit mihi, « Ecce,
ecce, ecce. ». Et vidi et non intellexi omnia. Moritur primus, moritur secundus, ecclesie facta est ruina. Oh princeps regum terrae, fulgura, tonitrua, aquae minantur. Et vivit ut maiori confusione periat quam per tonitrua et ignem. Vidi accipere coronam de manu sua de capite ut omni dignitate depulsa, tanquam pessimus ecclesie prophanator moriatur morte crudeli eo quod prophetam deique missum mori non dubitavit. Et clamabat vox de sepulcro, « Interfice sine remedio ».

Vidi inclinatam urbem [34] igne succendi atque comburi. Vidi desolatam sedem agni. Innovantur religiones multe, ut falsam derisionem preteritarum ostendant. Corvini mittunt prophetam et moritur ab igne in medio filiorum. Et vigebit cum mattabitur vivet in libro viventium eo quod non potuerunt delere homines a facie Dei. Columbini erunt ab una parte simul. Et erit idem tempus patrum. Et sicut dilexerunt se patres ita erit filiorum dilectio et amor. Et destruetur quedam simillata lex sub Francisco vigens. Deinde renovabitur ut aquila corvus et columba. Et erit omnium pax una atque doctrina sibilabunt in prophetam multi deridentes Dei arcana. Et a
fol. 6 v morte eius usque ad Pedes decem erit dubia/ sanctitas. Sed tunc cla-
rebit omnibus miraculis et renovatione doctrinae que quidem usque ad tempus erit obscura seculis. Et cum viderint multa experientia dicta eius in omni parte verissima. Et qui insontem virum cum filiis insecuti sunt ad mortem clamabunt et audientur de celo.

[Et audient domini florentini novum de Celo quod nunquam fuit a seculo auditum. [35] In illis igitur temporibus veniet gens antiqua obscura cuius lingua ignorabunt et pre timore pavebunt. Et omnes

---

[34] Probably a reference to Pisa's leaning tower.

[35] LM. P: « Barbari contra fiorenza ». CS: « Nota Firenze ».

timor aprehendet]. Erit initium pestis, et non vigebit propter prophetam omnia eis predicentem. [Et vidi evaginatum gladium super Florentiam. Et vidi piissimam genetricem quasi non posse substinere quia innocentem et iustum interfecerunt. Et mittitur gladius a quatuor partibus civitatis et sanguineum flumen currens ad Mare]. Insurgunt Veneti et omne dominium quasi inrestaurabile admittent a [a] fidelibus et infidelibus vexantur propter eorum superbiam. Tunc erit eis desiderium et cupiditas pacis. Et videbunt se et alios concives quasi destructos esse propter eorum malam iniquitatem. Isti a partibus mundi vexati sunt et alios temptantes absorbentur, non bella, non pecuniae prosunt, quia sic voluit altissimus ut puniat peccata hominum.

[36] [Erit igitur mors prophete unius missi a Deo omnium Civitatum et populorum/ occasio malorum quia deus misit ut illuminaret fol. 7
et obtenebrati sunt propter absentiam eius. Veh vobis humani potentes]. Surgit ab occidente monstrum in natura et multa indicabit populis mala. Alius insurget et peiora dabit, obtento quasi Italiae regno. Moritur ibidem quidam. Multa fient per eum mala iustis et innocentibus populis. Italiae ligurum capi et sine ultione. Sena irruet in potentes eo tempore et non amplius regnabunt tyranni duces quia finem pessimum gustabunt a populis.

[Insuper Florentinis maxima populi confusio vertitur in Principem electum [37]. Et postea humilitas populi severitatem vertitur a deo ut multi magnates habitum transmutent et pauperum vestigia sequentur ut populi furorem evadant. Caveat tyrannus occidentalis in illa civitate, forte cruciabitur tormentis validis quoniam ibi est resolutio belli. Gaudebunt simul pauper et dives et in medio civitatis omni occisione pacta inimicorum [38]. Pulsabunt Campane et Tube cum maxima populi gloria. Erit tunc temporis omnis dominii reintegratio. Et dicetur ab aliis qui sit iste populus Dei atque religionis].

Videant Italici novum/ hominem a ccccc° et iiij° supra M° aut fol. 7 v
parum ante [b] vel circa et audient verba eius quem vidi exire de terra et unum de Celo cui detrahetur a primo, et obtinebit secundus nam iste qui secundo venit videbitur cunctis gentibus propheta sed primus primo obtinebit. Postea conculcabitur nec definitur [c] a nobis quis eorum fuerit electus. Renovabitur doctrina illius innocentissimi quam populi adorabant. Et sicut prius iam mortuus vivet et non erit indubium sanctitas viri.

---

[a] Text: « ad » with « d » blotted out.
[b] Text: « arte ».
[c] Text: « difinitur ».

[36] CS. LM: « La morte del propheta causa d'ogni male ».
[37] CS. LM: « Principe Tiranno oltramontano ».
[38] CS. LM: « Soneranno le champane gloria ».

[39] [Conteritur Perusina Civitas in proprio sanguine. Evellitur funditus princeps quidam Italiae nec revertitur in[a] patriam]. Moritur insuper pax omnium regionum et [40] [signa magna dantur de Celo Florentinis qui conversi ad orationes placatur pro eis Dominus.

Et vidi floridam urbem impiorum in gloria iubilo et letitia]. Et multa mirabilia in obscuratione solis videbuntur illo tempore adeo ut incole mirentur dicentes, « Hec iudicia Domini » cum fient res quae naturam nunquam dedisse visa est ab ortu solis usque ad occasum. Fiet tribulatio in anno secundo et tertio supra mille quingentos [41]. [Caveant a proditione magna domini Florentini quam insidiantur ini-
fol. 8 mici eius quasi Leones ut rapiant et querant ab eis omne/ bonum publice rei. Oh tribulata patria atque vexata, inimici tui domestici tui [42]. Et vidi super ecclesiam evaginare gladium Domini super adulterantem Pontificem fidelium qui potius dextruxit fidem quam edificavit]. Et delebitur his temporibus a facie terrae. Vertitur insuper et cetera. (Hic deest una Pagina). Et vidi convertere domum Juda propter signum celorum imo unum vidi ovile et unum pastorem. Et sic Petrus in sua ecclesia ipsum[b] restituet et regnabit sicut edificator ecclesiae. Et surgent evangelizantes pacem ad fidelium consolationem. Et secta ypocritarum proijcietur in tenebras, eo quae talem et diuturnam derisionem conati sunt ostendere. Et vidi gladium inter solem et lunam et luna superatur a tenebris et facta est occisio magna seculi. Religio nova insurget et non obtinebit Domum. Secunda religio post praedicta tempora ex insulis maris audietur saccis cilicinis vestita quae iusta ritum Domini ambulabit. Et vidi flammas igneas venire de Celo.

[43] [Et vidi unum principem mortuum, quo mortuo, facta est pax universalis], et vidi Dominum sedentem ad iudicandum populos et ambulaverunt infames in perdictionem.

[Magnum edificium Italie vidi subvertere in gentium confu-
fol. 8 v sionem [44]. Omnes uno/ ore clamabant adversus malignum clerum et videbitur illo tempore magna tribulatio [45]. Venientibus Gallis ad deflorandam pulcherrimam Italiam ubi timore predominante in populis libidini et ebrietati inhonestis moribus, vacantes mala morte pro maiori parte morientur omni spe ac pietate depulsa.

---

[a] Text: « im ».
[b] Text: « ipse ».

[39] CS. LM: « Perugia principe ».
[40] CS. LM: « Segni in gloria ».
[41] CS. LM: « Firenze si guarde da tradimenti ».
[42] CS. LM: « Chiesa ».
[43] CS. LM: « pace ».
[44] CS. LM: « clero ».
[45] CS. LM: « galli ».

[46] Ceterum multos indicantur mala ab alemannis quos ut viderint Italici inter se dimicantes maximam victoriam obtinebunt. Et erunt ut prius nominati in armis et moribus. Sed non poterunt hec fieri donec expulsa fuerit de cordibus discordia ipsorum. Videbuntur principes [47] qui subditi nominati sunt. Et peribunt de medio ipsorum barbare nationes adeo ut totus admiretur orbis in omni parte]. Et ille spurius de quo supra erit princeps multa violentia interposita et fient multa mala per eum adeo ut non sit qui habitet in pace. « Cavete [a] oh religiosi viri », facta est vox. Et vidi deponere quasi Dominum celi de Cruce pre dolore o quanta mala minatur altissimus super omnem partem occidentis ad orientem. Et facta est orientalis plaga pessima et maledicta a iudiciis dei. Erunt/ tonitrua multa que fol. 9
maximam edificiorum ruinam insinuabunt. Erunt Civitates maiores confuse.

[48] [Domini Veneti quasi non sint reputantur et fient magni deinde maiores et cum florentinis augent imperium. Et duo Leones vitulum vacce pascentis [49] devorabunt adeo ut non sit qui memoretur amplius. Et erunt duo Leones, unus existens in mari, alter in terris, quasi Dracones. [50] Hec Aquila [51] poterit in eos quia Dominum [b] Deum habebunt inimicorum suorum ultorem. Et obtinebunt post multa bella pacem sempiternam.

[52] Veniet quidam pessimus princeps qui simulata cum ipsis fide occidetur ab eis. Et videbunt Aquilam [53] comburi. Et liliis [54] quasi rare factis reintegrati [c] videbuntur.

[55] Hec habenda est [56] spes florentinis de anno 1502 non pacis neque

---

[a] Text: « h » crossed out.
[b] Text: « in » crossed out.
[c] Text: « au » crossed out.

[46] CS. LM: « Alamanni ».
[47] Followed by « turchi » in P. (fol. 220).
[48] LM. CS: « Vinegia insieme con firenze ». P: « grandezza de Venitiani et Fiorentini ».
[49] The meaning of these animal symbols is not clear. Perhaps the author transformed the grazing steer of the Borgia coat of arms into a grazing cow so that he might endow it with a calf, i. e. Cesare Borgia.
[50] CS. LM: « Aquila ».
[51] Both CS. and P. have « non » here, which makes more sense.
[52] CS. LM: « principe Aquila Gigli ».
[53] An eagle was a common symbol of the Empire.
[54] In this context the Florentine lilies are probably being referred to.
[55] CS. LM: « Fiorentini ».
[56] CS. has here: « Et non debbono ... » P. has « Et non debent ». This makes better sense than the reading of C.

victoriae quia meliora ex alto quam ex humanis habebunt. Deus facit hec quia hec sunt abscondita ab hominibus.

[57] Insuper et erunt congregati omnes fere ecclesiae rectores in inclita urbe florentinorum. Et liber habetur novus in quo renovabitur
fol. 9 v tota lex inreprehensibilis. Jesu Benedicti./ Et dabitur laus et gloria soli Deo.

[58] Lupine edes a Leonibus devorantur ex eo quod exosam habuerunt pacem incole eorum cum ipsis. Florentini nullo modo aliam pacem noverunt [59]. Erunt homines ibi iuvenes et senes utriusque sexus arma spiritualia et temporalia portantes. Pueri fugabunt inimicos].

Et vidi in loco eminentiori Italiae draconem sibilare et igne eius atque veneno principem mori [60]. Quid plura? Cauda sua cinget omnes hereses et secum trahet ad infima terrae. Hec ego vidi solus et non intellexi nisi quod altissimus novit temporibus illis fienda. In populis non habeant fiduciam et in omnibus Principibus sed in Deo.

[61] [Nec super equum [62] equitabit leo post acceptum dominium super eum eo quod non placuit altissimo tempore illo opera humana restitui leoni diadema suum sed omnia vult operari ille altissimus qui omnia novit et condidit]. Veniunt in[a] partibus nostris germanorum gentes, alemanni simul et quasi omnem Asiam invadunt quia super primam solis partem evertitur sanguis quem vidi.

Erit in omni parte orientis gladius acutus anno 1505. Et sic vidi
fol. 10 et audivi iu/dicia Dei que sunt pro illis temporibus parata. Et erunt novissima in gentibus, videlicet ab omni parte Italiae erit mutatio principum, non semel sed pluries. Et erunt populi concordes qui viribus reassumptis omnem tyrannidam sectam desolabunt. Et erunt dies paucissimi felices ad Annos 7 a 4º primo super mille. Et qui solitariam vitam degerint beatiores erunt.

[63] [Ecclesia destruetur maxima cum occisione populorum quia fideles infideles provocant et admissa fide christianorum principum, populi se sine simulatione infidelibus committunt cupientes periculorum evasionem ita quod canes et lupi devorant.

---

[a] Text: « im ».

[57] CS. LM: « Firenze ».

[58] CS. LM: « Siena ».

[59] CS. LM: « Fiorentini ».

[60] The dragon was a very old symbol for Antichrist. On the history of the concept see Wilhelm Bousset, *The Antichrist Legend; a Chapter in Christian and Jewish Folklore* (trans. A. H. Keane; London, 1896). In the prophecies of the period we are concerned with here this was frequently equated with the Turk as well.

[61] CS. LM: « Leone ».

[62] Arezzo was symbolized by a prancing horse.

[63] CS. LM: « Chiesa ».

[64] Deflorabuntur Petri edes sachrae quia sacrificia eorum sunt abhominationes coram Deo.

[65] Cessabunt predicantes et iudicia dei annunctiantes quia Dominus iratus in[a] populis non placatur maledictis et falsis oblationibus].

Insurgunt insuper duo predicantes post silentium et sibilabunt ad devorandam[b] ecclesiam et resarciendam Christi Jesu sponsam. Et erunt in populis beati qui sanctissimis viris adherere poterunt propterea/ Dominus flagellabit multum ut multum iniustis letetur et fol. 10v.
dicat de celo, « Fiat pax in nomine meo ».

[66] [Hoc tempore venient prodigia in urbe Roma, florentiae et Venetiis. Et dabitur signum magnum de Celo ut malum denuntiet et non sit qui in domo Domini requiescat]. Dolent etiam senatos habitantes terrae. Et flabunt venti pestilentes post occisionem multorum. Et non erunt sugentes ubera sine dolore quia non obtinebunt in cunis quietem ... [qui audit intelligat verba ex ore altissimi. Fugiant ad alias nationes qui fuerint sine bello pace et quiete. Restituant corda Deo Celi, terrae et maris et universi orbis. Videbitur in Celo sursum et in terra deorsum omnis tribulatio valida] [67]. Amen.

Copiata per me Prete Joanni d'agnolo de miglio da Cetica Addì 18º dicembre 1512.

---

[a] Text: « im ».
[b] Text: « devorabant » with « ant » crossed out, followed by « dam ».

[64] CS. LM: « Santo pietro ».
[65] CS. LM: « predicanti ».
[66] CS. LM: « prodigii Roma Vinegia Firenze ».
[67] CS. At end: « Finis Christus Maria ».

SERGIO BERTELLI

PIER SODERINI ' VEXILLIFER PERPETUUS REIPUBLICAE FLORENTINAE ' 1502-1512

Per i fondi dell'Archivio di Stato di Firenze (A. S. F.) adotto il sistema di abbreviazioni proposto da P. Ghiglieri, *La grafia del Machiavelli studiata negli autografi*, Firenze 1969: CP (Consulte e Pratiche); Dm (Dieci di balìa, Legazioni e Commissarìe, Missive); Dr (Dieci di balìa, Responsive); SIm (Signori, I Cancelleria, Missive). Indico con B. N. F. la Biblioteca Nazionale Centrale di Firenze, con B. V. la Biblioteca Apostolica Vaticana.

I modi e le forme dell'elezione di Pier Soderini a « doge » della repubblica fiorentina cominciano a venire alla luce [1], anche se non tutto è ancora chiaro. Roslyn Pesman Cooper propende, ad esempio, a vedere nella scelta della sua persona il concorrere dei voti delle classi minori; mentre io vi ho piuttosto visto il convergere dei voti dei vecchi « arrabbiati » (o « disperati ») e dei nemici dei Medici, dando cioè a quell'elezione una coloritura non già « popolare », ma oligarchica — meglio, d'una parte degli Ottimati (Alamanno e Jacopo Salviati suoi sostenitori, Bernardo Rucellai e Lorenzo di Pierfrancesco de' Medici suoi oppositori). A favore di quest'ultima interpretazione mi sembra giochi, soprattutto, l'analisi dei primi atti di governo del Soderini, chiaramente rivolti ad assicurare il gruppo dei Grandi che lo aveva sostenuto, nel senso, cioè, di voler portare avanti quella riforma del Maggior Consiglio che aveva il suo fulcro nella creazione di un nuovo organismo collegiale destinato a sorgere da una ristrutturazione del Consiglio degli Ottanta.

L' idea di un « senato » era già stata d'un altro Soderini, Paolantonio, nei burrascosi tempi savonaroliani. Era stata di nuovo fatta propria da Giovan Battista Ridolfi e presentata nella Pratica del 13 gennaio del 1501 [2]; ripresa e rilanciata ancora una volta da Francesco Pepi e messa in discussione dalla Pratica del 13 gennaio del 1502 [3].

Giovan Battista Ridolfi, nel gennaio del 1500/1501, intervenendo dopo molti altri oratori sulla richiesta posta all'ordine del giorno dal gonfaloniere di giustizia Piero di Simone Carnesecchi, su come, cioè, si potesse « riacquistare la fede per i prestiti al Comune, persa non pagando gl' interessi », diceva: « che chi ha

---

[1] Si v. i recenti saggi di R. Pesman Cooper, *L'elezione di Pier Soderini a gonfaloniere a vita. Note storiche*, in « Archivio storico italiano », CXXV, 1967, pp. 145 ss.; S. Bertelli, *Petrus Soderinus Patriae Parens*, in « Bibliothèque d'humanisme et Rénaissance », XXXI, 1969, pp. 93 ss.

[2] A. S. F., CP 66, cc. 215 ss.

[3] A. S. F., CP 66, cc. 405-407. Cf. anche *Petrus Soderinus* cit., pp. 95 ss.

parlato non li pare habbi monstro i bisogni e pericoli della città sieno quali sono in facto, atteso la città essere disarmata et disordinata, et sanza amici et il remedio sarebbe di havere la amicitia del Re et gente d'arme, et questo non si può fare sanza provedere a danaio, et di fuora si crede più presto la città non voglia che ella non possa et a volere provedere lui stesso si confonde, che bisogna le cose si ordinino, non di meno di poi non passano nel Consiglio Maggiore, e con grave interesse della città, et dixene più ragioni, et che la città ha d' interesse uno 70.000 ducati l'anno, et che nel Consiglio Maggiore sono delle altre cose male facte come è imborsare ciascuno et sanza rispecto se è buono o tristo, pazzo o savio, et però iudicha che a volere provedere a bisogni della Città era chi haveva recordato che il Consiglio Maggiore dessi auctorità del danaio al Consiglio delli 80, era a primordi uno numero di cittadini facto dal Consiglio Maggiore et così delle altre petitioni, et che in questo modo tornerebbe la reputatione drento et fuori: et chi servissi harebbe fede di esser satisfatto, et quando questo non si obtenessi, che la promissione del danaio si observassi per la metà et una più, et alleghò lo exemplo de Vinitiani che hanno il Consiglio dei Pregài et il Consiglio de X, colla agiunta che è uno numero di 30, et questi consigli anchora vinchono le loro deliberationi per la metà et una più, et che loro che hanno il governo antiquo hanno iudicato che in una moltitudine grande non si possa provedere a bisogni della città loro, tanto meno è da stimare la possiamo far noi nuovi etc. » [4].

Dall' intervento si ricava: che il rifiuto della maggioranza popolare a pagare gli interessi sul debito pubblico (a riconoscere, cioè, gli investimenti finanziari degli Ottimati) portava come conseguenza al rifiuto di sostenere con ulteriori prestiti le finanze pubbliche, dal momento che si rivelava una manovra a fondo perduto, priva d'ogni garanzia; che il sistema delle maggioranze qualificate di due terzi significava la paralisi d'ogni iniziativa legislativa; che i « tristi, pazzi », di contro ai « buoni o savi » (cioè di contro agli « uomini da bene ») imponevano l'anarchia e il decadimento dello Stato anche agli occhi delle potenze estere. Ma, soprattutto, il discorso del Ridolfi poneva addirittura in causa la legittimità dei poteri del Consiglio Maggiore, nel senso

---

[4] A. S. F., CP 66, cc. 221 v°-222.

che la riforma avviata dal 1494 non era stata mai portata a termine: gli Ottanta erano « a primordi » un'assemblea eletta dal Consiglio Maggiore. Quel richiamo all' integrità del progetto di Paolantonio Soderini (ché non mi sembra possano avanzarsi altre interpretazioni di questo passo) riveste una eccezionale importanza anche per capire il dibattito politico del periodo savonaroliano.

Occorre, infatti, separare Paolantonio dal Savonarola e rivedere tutti i rapporti degli Ottimati col frate di San Marco. La realtà, soprattutto quella che ci viene incontro dai dispacci di Paolo Somenza a Lodovico il Moro [5], mentre modifica sensibilmente il quadro costruito dal Villari, dallo Schnitzer e da altri, ci conferma sempre più che, anche allora, si trattò d'una lotta ai vertici del potere, tra i diversi gruppi d'una medesima oligarchia. Gli esponenti maggiori: Paolantonio, Lorenzo di Pierfrancesco de' Medici (questi appoggiato da Lodovico il Moro e dai suoi ambasciatori a Firenze), Francesco Valori. Oltre, naturalmente, al gruppo dei medicei, che era però tagliato fuori dalla vita politica di quegli anni, costretto a muoversi nella clandestinità. Una lotta senza esclusione di colpi, iniziata con la disgregazione del gruppo degli accoppiatori del Novantaquattro, proseguita con il volontario esilio di Lorenzo di Pierfrancesco de' Medici e con la messa in ombra di Paolantonio da parte del Valori. Importa, comunque, qui, il rilievo che quel progetto di riassetto costituzionale dello Stato fiorentino che Paolantonio elaborò nel 1494, era considerato ancora valido, almeno da una parte dell'oligarchia fiorentina, proprio perché frenava lo strapotere che il Consiglio Maggiore era venuto acquistando al tempo dell'egemonia di Francesco Valori e dei gruppi savonaroliani.

Per nostra fortuna, possiamo anche individuare chi fossero i sostenitori del nuovo progetto Ridolfi, perché dai verbali di quella stessa Pratica ci risulta che si associarono al suo discorso: Jacopo Nicolini, Tommaso Capponi, Giovanni Formiconi, Agnolo Pandolfini, Piero Guicciardini, Lorenzo Capponi, Alamanno Salviati, Francesco Del Cittadino, Piero Pieri. Da quella seduta scaturì una commissione destinata a rielaborare e a dar forma di legge alle proposte di Giovan Battista e i suoi membri furono: lo stesso Ridolfi, Antonio Canigiani, Piero Guicciardini,

[5] Archivio di Stato di Milano, Sforzesco, 942, 943 e 945.

Bernardo Nasi, Pier Soderini, Bernardo Rucellai, Lorenzo Lenzi, Lorenzo di Pierfrancesco de' Medici, Luca d'Antonio degli Albizi [6]. A chi abbia anche una conoscenza solo superficiale della storia fiorentina di questi anni non potrà sfuggire il significato di questi nomi.

Ad un anno esatto di distanza dalla proposta Ridolfi, la Signoria riprendeva il dibattito sull'assetto costituzionale dello Stato, ponendo ai voti una serie di proposte, tra le quali facevano spicco quella avanzata da Francesco di Chirico Pepi a nome del quartiere di Santa Croce (e che ottenne la maggioranza schiacciante, con cinquantatré voti contro diciotto) e quella di Francesco di Lorenzo Gualterotti a nome del quartiere di Santo Spirito, appoggiata anche da Antonio di Pietro Malegonnelle a nome della pancata di Santa Maria Novella. Del progetto Pepi ho già parlato in *Petrus Soderinus patriae parens*, né qui vi ritornerò. Quanto alla mozione Gualterotti, osserverò che essa allontanava nel tempo una decisione, perché suggeriva che il Consiglio Maggiore eleggesse una commissione di quaranta persone (sottraendo così l' iniziativa alla Pratica!) con l' incarico di redigere la futura riforma, o più progetti « però che a loro parrà », da sottoporre al voto definitivo dell'assemblea popolare [7]. Il voto e il successo del Pepi denotano dunque la volontà della larga maggioranza di tagliare i nodi gordiani; sarà bene anche aggiungere che messer Francesco Gualterotti deve essere considerato un oppositore del gruppo degli Ottimati che votò la mozione Pepi. Cognato del mediceo Lamberto di Giovanni dell'Antella, avendone sposato la sorella Lisabetta [8], piagnone, era stato tra i difensori del convento di San Marco (non si era dunque limitato a firmare, come tanti altri, la petizione ad Alessandro VI!) [9], sarà in futuro tra gli oppositori del Soderini, una volta questi eletto al dogado. Quanto ad Antonio di Piero di Niccolò Malegonnelle, egli era già stato un uomo di rilievo nel periodo mediceo (degli Otto di guardia nel 1486 e 1489, degli Otto di pratica nel 1490, 1492 e 1493, dei Dodici consultori del 1490,

---

[6] P. Parenti, *Historia fiorentina*, B. N. F., II . II . 132, cc. 91 v°-92.

[7] P. Villari, *La storia di Girolamo Savonarola e de' suoi tempi*, II, Firenze 1930, Appendice, pp. III-IV.

[8] A. S. F., CP 66, cc. 385 ss.

[9] Villari, *Savonarola* cit., II, Appendice, pp. XCVI, CII, CLVII, CCLXXVI, CCLXXVII.

1492, 1493 e 1494, dei Cento del 1494, professore di diritto allo Studio), aveva fatto parte del partito del frate, sarà addirittura il candidato dei palleschi nella corsa al gonfalonierato perpetuo [10].

Orbene, proprio i primi atti di governo di Pier Soderini, una volta eletto gonfaloniere perpetuo, furono rivolti a rafforzare — nei limiti che la Costitutione consentiva — il prestigio degli Ottanta, cioè di quell'assemblea che, come dicevo, rappresentava la chiave di volta d'ogni progetto di riforma di quel gruppo oligarchico che aveva abbattuto gli oppositori savonaroliani e che si richiamava all' integrità del progetto di Paolantonio Soderini, affossato proprio dall'ascesa dei frateschi con Francesco Valori. Anzi la scelta di Piero appare come un proposito di riprendere e portare avanti le idee di Paolantonio (scomparso nel 1499), è coerente con l'avanzata di questo gruppo di Ottimati. Il nuovo gonfaloniere, dunque, appena insediato in Palazzo vecchio, il 18 novembre del 1502 convocò il Consiglio degli Ottanta e rivolse loro un discorso programmatico di indubbio significato: « Dixe haverli facti domandare prima per volerli vedere in viso una volta la septimana, et conferire loro quelle cose che sono degne di loro notitia ... », li investì subito dei problemi di politica estera, facendo leggere gli ultimi dispacci degli ambasciatori dalle sedi più importanti, come quello di Francesco della Casa accreditato a Milano presso lo Chaumont d'Amboise, e l'altro di Niccolò Machiavelli inviato al Valentino, nonché un rapporto di Giovanni Ridolfi commissario in quel-l'Arezzo da poco riconquistata. Di più, investì l'assemblea di ben maggiori poteri, invitandola a considerare se era il caso di portare avanti la riforma della magistratura dei Dieci, altro

---

[10] F. Nerli, *Commentarii de' fatti civili occorsi dentro nella città di Firenze dall'anno 1215 al 1537*, Augusta [Firenze?] 1728, p. 92; F. Guicciardini, *Storie fiorentine dal 1378 al 1509*, a cura di R. Palmarocchi, Bari 1931, p. 250. Parlano ancora dell'elezione B. Buonaccorsi, *Diario de' successi più importanti seguiti in Italia et particolarmente in Fiorenza dall'anno 1498 infino all'anno 1512*, Fiorenza 1568, p. 64; L. Landucci, *Diario fiorentino dal 1450 al 1516* a cura di I. Del Badia, Firenze 1883, p. 250 (che è anche l'unico dei cronisti ad appoggiare l'elezione del Soderini: « E quanto bene fu assunto a questa dignità, e quanto bene giudicò el magno Consiglio! Veramente fu da Dio tale opera ... »); B. Cerretani, *Istorie fiorentine*, B. N. F., II . III . 74, cc. 295 ss.; P. Vaglienti, *Cronaca*, B. N. F. II . IV . 42, cc. 132-v°; G. A. Novacola, *Storia*, Bibliothèque Nationale, Paris, MS It. 250, cc. 17-17 v°; P. Parenti, *Historia fiorentina*, B. N. F., II . II . 133, cc. 60-v°.

punto nodale della crisi costituzionale. Un tema, quest'ultimo, che era già stato affrontato dal progetto di riforma di Francesco Pepi: « Apresso, essendo lo officio de Dieci di libertà alla fine, per havere consiglio, atteso le cose vanno atorno, se è da rifarlo et con che conditioni » [11].

Ma, dicevo all' inizio, non tutto è chiaro nell'elezione del Soderini. La crisi costituzionale, come si sa, fu fatta precipitare dal brutale intervento di Cesare Borgia che, proprio al fratello di Piero, al vescovo di Volterra Francesco, presentò l'ultimatum d'una riforma al vertice dello Stato, nella notte tra il 26 e il 27 giugno del 1502. Francesco, in quei giorni, rimasto solo a fronteggiare il Valentino (il Machiavelli, che lo accompagnava, era tornato precipitosamente indietro latore dell'ultimatum) [12], temeva per la sua stessa persona in quell' Urbino rigurgitante di armati e non riuscì a intravvedere che cosa si nascondesse sotto quell'arroganza del duca di Romagna [13]. È però un fatto che le sue missive a Firenze furono tutte a sostegno della politica borgesca, arrivando a dire che de « la amicitia di questo Signore ... si debbe tenerne altro conto che non si è fatto fino a qui »! [14] Nasce in questi giorni quell'amicizia tra i due personaggi, che porterà di lì a poco alla porpora il vescovo di Volterra e che farà di lui, ancora una volta, il difensore di Cesare nei confronti dei suoi concittadini, nei giorni della disgrazia di quegli? [15] Certo è ben strana questa scelta dei Soderini ad incontrare il Valentino nei momenti più drammatici! Insomma, v'era pure una *vox populi* che accusava, sin dall'anno avanti, un gruppo di Ottimati di tramare per un colpo di stato facendo forza sul Borgia. Ed è daccapo sintomatico che venisse inviato ambasciatore a Roma, nei giorni dell'ultimatum di Urbino, proprio Francesco Pepi.

Quel Pepi — e la notizia lo situa meglio politicamente — che come gonfaloniere di giustizia, nel 1499, aveva fatto votare la decima scalata, « una gravezza ingiusta e disonesta ed in gran-

---

[11] A. S. F., CP 67, cc. 85; ma v. anche *Petrus Soderinus*, p. 99.

[12] N. Machiavelli, *Legazioni e Commissarìe*, a cura di S. Bertelli, Milano 1964, p. 270, dispaccio del 26 giugno 1502.

[13] Cf. l'introduzione alla Legazione X, in *Legazioni e Commissarìe* cit., pp. 251-52.

[14] *Legazioni e Commissarìe* cit., p. 306, dispaccio dell'11 luglio.

[15] Cf. in *Petrus Soderinus*, pp. 101-102.

dissimo danno di coloro che avevano entrata di possessione », come la giudicò retrospettivamente il Guicciardini [16]. Una tassazione che ce lo configura in un particolare gruppo oligarchico, di creditori del Comune, come vedremo tra poco a proposito dello stesso Pier Soderini.

Non fu dunque un caso se l'astio popolare si riversò, nel 1501, su Bernardo Rucellai e su Lorenzo di Pierfrancesco de' Medici (che abbiamo visto entrambi membri della «commissione Ridolfi»), su Benedetto di Tanai de' Nerli (uno degli esaminatori del Savonarola) [17], su Alfonso Strozzi (altro esaminatore del frate) [18] e che si dipingessero forche sulla casa di Pier Soderini [19], altro membro della « commissione Ridolfi » e ancor più indiziato per essere stato uno degli oratori del Valentino a Campi, al tempo della sua « passeggiata » per lo Stato fiorentino (gli altri oratori, con lui, erano stati Jacopo de' Nerli e Alamanno Salviati, si noti bene) [20].

Piero di Giovanni Vaglienti, un popolano acceso antisavonaroliano, sotto il giorno 16 maggio del 1501 scrisse nella sua cronaca che, quando Francesco Gualterotti, il vescovo de' Pazzi e Antonio Vespucci (l'amico del Machiavelli cancelliere delle Riformagioni) trattarono con Francisco Troches, inviato del Valentino, stesero un accordo, poi ratificato dagli stessi Gualterotti e Pazzi, con l'aggiunta di Raffaello Acciaioli, « cholla chonchrusione della volontà de grandi e di chi voleva rasetare el ghoverno a sua proposito chon questa forma che al ducha Valentino la Signoria di Firenze li pachassi per 3 anni 300 uomini d'arme e che tutto el sechuito de danni fatti per loro dal dì si partinno di quel di Bologna fusse loro perdonato e chosì a qualunque citadino da quel dì in qua avesse per alchun modo ofeso el pubricho, questo per paura che avevano del popolo che sapiendo la verità della chosa non si levassi e facessi qualche insulto ... » [21]. E il nove maggio,

---

[16] Guicciardini, *Storie fiorentine* cit., p. 194.

[17] Villari, *Savonarola* cit., II, Appendice, pp. CXLV, CXLVIII.

[18] Villari, *ibid.*

[19] Guicciardini, *Storie fiorentine* cit., p. 214.

[20] Le credenziali in A. S. F., SIm 52, cc. 178, con la data del 9 maggio. Si v. anche la lettera dei Dieci a Pier Francesco Tosinghi, in A. S. F., Dm 25, c. 89.

[21] Vaglienti, *Cronaca*, cit., c. 108 v°. Nel secondo incontro, a Barberino, le richieste furono: « in prima reformatione dello stato in uno de tre modi:

parlando dell'ambasceria di Pier Soderini, Jacopo di Tanai de' Nerli e Alamanno di Averardo Salviati, aveva scritto: « niente di mancho io per me sono di parere che fra potenti di quivi e lui », cioè il Valentino, « sia inteligenza e che loro ne sieno molto ben d'achordo e che sapino suo animo e quelo viene a fare e che tuto fanno per dare delle busse al popolo e che sia per fare motivo di mutare a novo modo el ghoverno, perché questo che rengna nonn' è molto loro a grado e stimasi che avanti sieno e XVI di questo, quivi abbi a essere gram chose e novità assai » [22].

A Firenze, in quei giorni, gli animi erano surriscaldati non solo per la passeggiata militare di Cesare Borgia. Più volte il popolo era corso alle armi ed era passata voce di tenersi pronti ad una sollevazione « quando la chanpana grossa del palagio desse 3 tochi », ma sempre i capi dei gonfaloni avevano impedito che si arrivasse allo scontro armato [23]. Una mattina, in piazza, scontrandosi Giovanni Baroncelli con Piero Cambi, il savonaroliano [24] che quand'era degli Otto aveva condannato il figlio del Baroncelli a morte, lo affrontò accoltellandolo [25]. La *vox populi*,

---

o con rimettere e Medici, o ridurre lo stato in pochi, o mantenendo il presente governo nectare qualche cattiva herba, che queste erano le formali parole », A. S. F., Dm 25, c. 94 v°, dispaccio a Pier Francesco Tosinghi del 16 maggio.

[22] Vaglienti, *Cronaca* cit., c. 107. V. anche in Landucci, *Diario* cit., pp. 225-26, dove parlando degli stupri commessi dalle genti borgesche esclama: « Guai a coloro che ne sono stati cagione, e anche a quegli che non ànno punito un tale eccesso, a chi poteva; che si poteva struggere Valentino con più giente che non aveva tre volte. Ma a me non è nuovo quello sanno fare e nostri cittadini; non si curano d'ogni gran male per un lor commodo. E questo s'è veduto più volte, poter vincere e avere un grande onore, non avere voluto, solo per discordia ».

[23] Vaglienti, *Cronaca* cit., cc. 109 v°-110; e v. ancora in Landucci, *Diario* cit., pp. 222-223 dove è detto che il 13 maggio « e signori mandorono un bando che quando e' facessino quegli segni, cioè due colpi d'artiglierie e sei tocchi di campana, in due volte, ognuno atto a portare arme vadi al suo gonfalone; e che niuno porti arme fuori del gonfalone, a pena d'essere rubello. Onde ognuno serrava le botteghe e isgomberava e portava a casa, stimando questa cosa grande pericolo; e ognuno di fuori s'ingegnava di mettere dentro in Firenze ».

[24] Villari, *Savonarola* cit., II, Appendice, p. CCXXIX.

[25] Vaglienti, *Cronaca* cit., c. 110; e in Landucci, *Diario* cit., p. 226, dove è detto che questo figlio del Baroncelli « era un certo bravo che faceva ogni male per contado: e questo caso fece serrare una altra volta le botteghe per tutto ». Il caso è ricordato anche dal Parenti, *Historia fiorentina* cit.

dunque, affermava che il Valentino « era fatto venire per mutare ghoverno », e ciò era corroborato dal fatto che i Signori, prima della partenza degli oratori per incontrarsi col Valentino, avevano fatto radunare i Collegi e dato già l'ordine di suonare la campana per chiamare il popolo a parlamento. Senonché i Collegi non se l'erano sentita di avvallare la proposta della Signoria, per paura della legge del Novantaquattro contro chi convocasse parlamento, cosicché il tentativo di colpo di stato era rientrato [26].

Questa concordanza di notizie nella diaristica dell'epoca fa ancor più risaltare la gravità dell'accusa lanciata in piena assemblea (e non più vociferata per le pancacce o affidata alle pagine d'un diario privato) da Luigi Mannelli in una Pratica del marzo del 1502/3, quando già Pier Soderini era stato eletto al dogado.

Ciò che lascia sconcertati, tuttavia, è il fatto che, in concomitanza con l' irruzione del Valentino per la Val di Marina, apparisse ai confini fiorentini l'odiato Piero de' Medici. Poteva, quel gruppo oligarchico che sognava un parlamento e un rovesciamento di regime, tentare la rimonta politica alleandosi con un Borgia che si dimostrava già legato a Piero de' Medici? [27] A meno di non dar credito alle assicurazioni dello stesso Cesare che, in quella drammatica notte di Urbino, scisse davanti a Francesco Soderini e a Niccolò Machiavelli le proprie responsabilità da quelle di Vitellozzo Vitelli [28]. A meno, ancor più, di non accogliere per veritiera la rivelazione che lo stesso Borgia fece, ancora al Machiavelli, a Imola il 20 novembre del 1502, quando già era risultato palese che razza di rapporti fossero quelli che intercorrevano tra Vitellozzo e lui [29]. In tal caso, l'apparizione del Medici sui confini non sarebbe stata concordata con il Va-

---

[26] Vaglienti, *Cronaca* cit., cc. 109-v°.

[27] Il Buonaccorsi, *Diario* cit., p. 42, dice che allora « dubitossi assai non si volessi gittare in Pisa e per quella via tentare di mettere Piero de Medici in Firenze, il quale era di già partito di Roma col vescovo de Petrucci e venuto a trovare il Duca per fermarsi in qualche luogo a confini della città ... ».

[28] *Legazioni e Commissarìe* cit., pp. 263-64.

[29] *Ibid.*, p. 446: « Tu sai quando noi venimmo con l'esercito in quello di Firenze, veggendo che non gli riusciva quello che desiderava, e che io non vi avevo il capo », Vitellozzo « pensò senza mia saputa di accordarsi con gli Orsini, e scalare Prato una notte, e lasciarmi in preda nel mezzo del contado vostro ... ».

lentino, ma col Vitelli. Vi sarebbe stato, insomma, un complicato gioco di incastri, avente per posta il controllo dello Stato fiorentino.

D'altra parte, ad accentuare i sospetti, sta la vicenda personale di Luigi Mannelli, assai grave. Né depone a suo favore il vedere che, a difenderlo nella consulta convocata dal Soderini per proporre la pena da infliggergli, il 27 marzo del 1503, si alzasse Gioacchino di Biagio Guasconi, che era stato uno dei capi del partito savonaroliano [30]. L'episodio è raccontato incompleto dal Parenti [31], mentre molto più importante è la testimonianza del Vaglienti. Prima di riportarla, però, occorre fare un passo indietro.

Uno dei primissimi atti di Pier Soderini, quando entrò gonfaloniere di giustizia per il bimestre marzo-aprile 1500/1501, fu quello di proporre una nuova tassazione per poter pagare gli interessi del debito pubblico (esattamente, cioè, come il Pepi). Piero, dunque, « chome e' fu entrato provò per via del Chonsiglio di porre danari e prima chominciò a volere metere 3/4 di quintina e una decima e 1/ meza schalata, la quale si faceva chonto gitassi in tutto danari 110 migliaia e più e più volte la misse a partito in el Chonsiglio e mai si vinse, di poi la cimentò per molte altre vie e per insino a dì xv d'aprile per quante volte andassi mai s'otenne, dicevasi per el popolo che perché 'l detto Piero Soderini aveva aver dal Chomune per danari servitonelo che llo faceva per ritrarsi e per fare ritrarre altri suoi amici e quali avevano servito el Chomune a ragione di xiiij° per cento a chapo d'anno » [32].

Fallito il progetto Soderini (e si noti la sua insistenza quasi caparbia di presentare più e più volte ai voti una proposta, che sarà la tecnica che adotterà in modo permanente per stancare l'opposizione, nel suo decennio di gonfalonierato), subentrò a lui Orsini di Jacopo Lanfredini, entrato gonfaloniere nel novembre del 1501. Orsini (è sempre il Vaglienti ad informarcene) subito « tentò una petizione la quale si poteva domandare un zibaldone tante chose in essa si chonteneva e tutte era a danno

---

[30] A. S. F., CP 67, cc. 135 v°-36.

[31] Parenti, *Historia fiorentina* cit., II . II . 133, cc. 91 ss. Il passo è riportato in *Petrus Soderinus*, pp. 93-94 n.

[32] Vaglienti, *Cronaca* cit., c. 105.

del popolo e in aumento de' grandi e di chi aveva prestato danari al Chomune, e per chagione chome pareva loro stare male, volevano ch'el popolo facessi ch'al Chamerlengho di doana e quel del sale fusse ubrighato per sodisfazione de loro chapitali a sodisfalli tenpo per tenpo de danari che pigliavano fermando l' interessi che nne avevano dal Chomune a xiiij° per cento per cinque anni e ch'alle dote delle fanciulle » cioè il Monte delle doti, « de 3, e 4 e 7 per cento di versante delle entrate si rendessi a soldi e lire anno per anno a chi v'aveva danari quella quantità li tochassi ... » [33].

Tutti questi tentativi di ridar fiducia nel debito pubblico, scontrandosi con la pervicace resistenza del Consiglio Maggiore, portavano inesorabilmente ad un contrasto globale, che coinvolgeva non soltanto la politica finanziaria dello Stato, ma la sua politica estera e le sue stesse istituzioni. Il 1501 appare, perciò, per molti versi un anno cruciale per la storia della repubblica, con i pressanti inviti ad approvare nuove tassazioni rivolti successivamente dai vari gonfalonieri di giustizia, da Piero di Simone Carnesecchi a Pier Soderini a Orsino di Jacopo Lanfredini, per non dire del precedente episodio del Pepi. Si può pertanto ritenere che la svolta che condusse al gonfalonierato perpetuo sia stata determinata da un complesso di situazioni, dalle quali emergono soprattutto l'urgenza del pagamento degli interessi del debito pubblico e le pressioni politico-diplomatico-militari di Cesare Borgia che, obiettivamente, venivano in soccorso del gruppo ottimatizio.

Orbene, il discorso di Luigi Mannelli si inserisce in questo contesto, perché fu pronunciato per opporsi ad una nuova proposta di tassazione, con una decima, una quintina e un arbitrio, compensata da una riduzione del tasso d' interesse sulle cedole del Monte delle doti, avanzata dallo stesso Soderini, ora divenuto doge della città. Luigi d'Alessandro Mannelli, dunque, « intorno a ciò propuose molte parole achomodatamente e diceva tochando el vivo a questi che ghovernano dicendo in bighoncia che danari infino a qui spesi s'erano la magior parte gitati via e spesi male e che molte volte ànno potuto riavere Pisa e che mai l'ànno voluta ed eziandio la venuta di Valentino nel chontado nostro quando passò su per il nostro e andò alla volta di Pion-

[33] *Ibid.*, cc. 119 v°-120.

bino, che medesimamente e nostri citadini vi chonsentìno e furono loro che lo feciono venire e che tutto voleva giustifichare chosì etc., in modo 'l deto Luigi fu messo in palagio prigione e esaminato chi lli fé dire e a parole e se questo era di chonsentimento di huomini del suo ghonfalone della Schala, donde lui dice che quando v'andò chiese la bighoncia libera di poter dire quello li pareva e quando venne a l' isamina d'essi huomini non trovò che 2 tale parole li avesino sentito dire, il che fu rimisso in prigione e l'altro dì apresso li fu dato la tortura onde si svenne in sulla gholla e vedesi per le parole sua che tutto fè per fare piacere al popolo e chon chredendo da esso popolo aver favore, ma doveva pensare avanti che venisse a queste parole e di voler fare tale piacere a questo popolo richordarsi delle parole di Messer Giorgio Schali, che disse che chi si fonda in sul popolo, chon riverenza, si fonda in sulla merda » [34].

Come ha già ben messo in luce Roslyn Cooper, lo scontro politico per la riforma costituzionale si accentrava sul trasferimento del controllo finanziario dal Consiglio Maggiore ad un Consiglio degli Ottanta opportunamente modificato. L'arma più forte in mano degli Ottimati, tra il 1499 e il 1502, era stata quella « di sottrarre allo Stato la propria partecipazione attiva », non solo rifiutando la concessione di nuovi prestiti, ma rendendosi ineleggibili « tralasciando il pagamento delle tasse » [35]. Tra quanti finirono « a specchio », cioè in quei registri che prescrivevano i vari divieti di eleggibilità — tra i quali, appunto, il mancato pagamento delle imposte dirette — non a caso troviamo anche Pier Soderini.

Il Pepi, dunque, e Pier Soderini, Giovan Battista Ridolfi, Bernardo Rucellai, Alamanno e Jacopo Salviati, Giovanni e Lorenzo di Pierfrancesco de' Medici, Tommaso e Lorenzo Capponi e tutti gli altri sin qui ricordati, ci appaiono accomunati da una stessa politica, sino all'approvazione della riforma costituzionale, nell'agosto del 1502. Il 22 settembre, al momento delle votazioni in Consiglio Maggiore, questo gruppo di Ottimati si era già scisso. Non esaminerò qui le cause di questa rottura;

---

[34] *Ibid.*, cc. 137 v°-138 v°.

[35] Roslyn Cooper, *L'elezione* cit., p. 149. Erano « a specchio », nel dicembre 1500-gennaio 1501: Lanfredino di Jacopo Lanfredini, Bernardo di Luttozzo Nasi, Alamanno di Averardo Salviati, Jacopo di Giovanni Salviati, Antonio di Vanni Strozzi, Filippo Buondelmonti e Pier Soderini.

dirò solo che essa appare, per molti versi, simile alla frattura verificatasi nel gruppo oligarchico che aveva assunto il potere nel 1494 e che aveva visto l'eclisse di Paolantonio Soderini e il volontario esilio di Pierfrancesco de' Medici, di fronte all'ascesa di Francesco Valori. L'energica reazione al discorso d'opposizione del Mannelli si inquadra, dunque, in un ben preciso contesto e indubbiamente contribuisce, anch'essa, a giudicare l'elezione di Pier Soderini come la vittoria d'un gruppo di Ottimati. Ci avverte, inoltre, di quanta attenzione debba riporsi nello sfruttare i verbali delle Consulte e Pratiche. Il margine di libertà di parola, in esse, era assai ristretto, a meno di non avere un nome altisonante!

Ma il Soderini, dopo un breve periodo volto a tranquillare il gruppo dei suoi sostenitori, si volse ad affermare il proprio potere personale e consortile, seguendo pedissequamente l'esempio dei Medici: dalla nomina del fratello Francesco a cardinale, sino al tentativo di creare degli « homines novi ». Afferma infatti Francesco Guicciardini, all'anno 1504 delle sue *Storie fiorentine*, che il Soderini, « o perché considerassi che se e' metteva el governo delle cose importante nelle mani degli uomini da bene, che loro sendo savi e di autorità ne disporrebbono a modo loro e non seguiterebbono el suo parere se non quanto si conformassino insieme, ed *e converso* che gli uomini di meno cervello e qualità, nelle cose che avessino a trovarsi, si lascierebbono disporre e maneggiare da lui, e così mosso da ambizione, o pure avendo preso sospetto contra ragione, che se gli uomini da bene pigliavano forze, vorrebbono ristrignere uno stato e cacciare lui di quello grado *che aveva acquistato per opere loro* ... cominciò a non conferire ogni cosa colle pratiche, le quali quando si facevano era necessario vi intervenissino e' primi uomini della città »[36]. Un'accusa, per la verità, che risulta troppo generica o che, comunque, pur partendo da un dato reale (la rarefazione delle pratiche convocate dalla Signoria) non ne dà il vero motivo. Più giusto, invece, è l'altro rilievo del Guicciardini, e che, cioè, quando nelle pratiche si giungeva a « qualche conclusione contraria al parere suo », impediva che si mettesse in atto[37]. La sua tecnica, l'abbiamo detto, era quella di proporre e riproporre

---

[36] Guicciardini, *Storie fiorentine* cit., pp. 270-71. Il corsivo è mio.
[37] *Ibid.*

sino alla vittoria le proprie idee, contando sulla stanchezza degli avversari (clamoroso, ad esempio, il caso dell' invio o meno di ambasciatori all' imperatore, nel 1507, discusso in infinite pratiche senza alcun costrutto, sino al colpo di mano dell' invio del Machiavelli).

I motivi della rarefazione delle Pratiche convocate dalla Signoria, invece, sembrano piuttosto da ricercarsi nel progressivo aumentare di poteri del Consiglio dei Dieci, che proprio i « cittadini mediocri » avevano come il fumo negli occhi, tanto da rifiutarne un tempo la rielezione e poi, nel settembre del 1500, mutandone e limitandone i compiti, privandolo della balìa e mutandone la denominazione in quella di « Dieci di libertà e pace ». Già s' è visto come il gonfaloniere perpetuo, nel suo primo discorso davanti agli Ottanta, insistesse al contrario per un loro rafforzamento; e questo rafforzamento fu silenziosamente attuato, sino ad investirli del vero governo della città. Saranno i Dieci, d'ora in poi, a convocare le Pratiche senza più la Signoria (o, comunque, con molta più frequenza e periodicità), mentre si assisterà nel contempo ad una trasformazione della Prima Cancelleria che assumerà sempre più l'aspetto di una alta magistratura (le funzioni del « princeps » del diritto romano). Le funzioni politiche, il governo quotidiano, insomma, nel decennio soderiniano appaiono sempre più accentrate nella cancelleria dei Dieci e nella Seconda Cancelleria (quelle, guarda caso, rette da Niccolò Machiavelli).

Il Guicciardini, ancora, afferma che un altro aspetto della nuova politica soderiniana fu l'allargamento della partecipazione al governo, operata con l' immissione di uomini nuovi nel Consiglio dei Dieci e negli Ottanta, « in forma che quello che e' non conduceva nelle pratiche, conferendolo con questi altri magistrati ... lo tirava el più delle volte a suo proposito » [38]. Un'affermazione che trova riscontro nell'analisi della composizione della magistratura dei Dieci, dal dicembre del 1502 (prima elezione per il nuovo semestre, dopo l'ascesa del Soderini) sino a tutto il 1512. Quel che colpisce, innanzi tutto, è la continuità delle presenze, sino al 1508, di un ristrettissimo numero di uomini e di famiglie, che scompare poi gradatamente e con sempre maggior ampiezza negli anni seguenti, per lasciar il posto a degli

---

[38] *Ibid.*

homines novi i quali, al contrario dei precedenti ottimati, non vengono però mai riconfermati allo scadere dei divieti.

Alamanno di Averardo di Alamanno Salviati, come s' è detto, fu uno dei « grandi elettori » del Soderini. Ebbene: egli è presente tra i Dieci nel primo semestre del 1503, del 1505 e del 1506 e nel secondo semestre del 1508; viene sostituito nel secondo semestre del 1511 e del 1512 da Jacopo di Giovanni di Alamanno Salviati, suo cugino. Né bisogna pensare che, nei periodi di divieto alla rieleggibilità, egli abbandonasse l'attività politica, perché lo troviamo oratore a Ferdinando il Cattolico a Piombino nel Sei, commissario al campo di Pisa nel Nove etc. Jacopo, a sua volta, se non era mai stato prima dei Dieci, lo avevamo trovato oratore al Valentino nel 1503, tra i Gonfalonieri di Compagnia nel 1508/9, tra gli Ufficiali del Monte nel 1509/10 etc.

Francesco di Antonio di Taddeo (già stato gonfaloniere di giustizia nel 1502) appare tra i Dieci nel secondo semestre del 1503 e del 1505, nel primo semestre del 1508, nel secondo semestre del 1509; è sostituito dal fratello Piero nel primo semestre del 1510; riappare nel primo semestre del 1511.

Piero di Francesco del Nero (il cognato di Machiavelli) è tra i Dieci nel secondo semestre del 1505 e del 1507; però nel primo semestre del 1507 vi è eletto Simone di Bernardo del Nero, mentre il fratello, Nero di Francesco, siede tra i Dieci nel secondo semestre del 1508 e nel primo semestre del 1510 e del 1512.

Altri due fratelli presenti tra i Dieci sono i figli di Donato Acciaioli, Roberto (vi siede nel primo semestre del 1507 e del 1510) e Alessandro (che vi siede nel primo semestre del 1508 e nel secondo semestre del 1509 e del 1510). Mentre inoltre Roberto è oratore a Roma nel 1507 e in Francia nel 1510, Alessandro è capitano e commissario di Castrocaro — una carica politico-militare della massima importanza, che implicava il governo della Romagna sotto sovranità fiorentina — nel 1503, e capitano di Volterra nel 1505.

Gioacchino di Biagio Guasconi — già savonaroliano — è anch'egli con frequenza eletto: nel primo semestre del 1503, nel secondo semestre del 1504, nel primo semestre del 1507, del 1509 e del 1510.

Niccolò di Simone Zati siede tra i Dieci sempre nel secondo semestre negli anni: 1504, 1506, 1507, 1509, mentre un suo congiunto, Bartolo di Piero Zati, vi compare nel primo semestre del 1507. Ma Niccolò ha anche moltissime altre cariche in questo periodo soderiniano: è vicario di Scarperia nel 1503, commissario generale di Romagna nel 1504, commissario a Cortona nel 1505, di nuovo commissario generale in Romagna nel 1510/11, podestà di Pisa nel 1511.

Numerosissimi sono, infine, gli eletti per almeno tre volte (fatti salvi i divieti). Tra gli altri troviamo: Niccolò di Alessandro Machiavelli, Gherardo di Bertoldo Corsini, Zanobi di Bartolomeo dello Zaccaria assieme al fratello Francesco (entrambi per le arti minori), Domenico di Bernardo Mazzinghi, Luigi di Agnolo della Stufa, Antonio di Averardo Serristori, Filippo di Andrea Carducci. Due sole volte vengono invece eletti Pier Francesco Tosinghi e Francesco di Chirico Pepi, che pure erano stati altre volte dei Dieci negli anni precedenti il gonfalonierato perpetuo. Il Tosinghi lo troviamo tuttavia tra i Gonfalonieri di Compagnia nel 1504, commissario generale delle Romagne nel 1506, ambasciatore a Roma nel 1510 e dobbiamo ricordare che fu commissario al campo di Pisa nel 1503, in un momento particolarmente importante. Quanto al Pepi, che tanta parte aveva avuto nel mutamento dello Stato, lo troviamo oratore d'obbedienza a Pio III, poi a Giulio II nel 1506, assessore nel Consiglio di Giustizia nel 1508. Senonché, proprio per la posizione preminente sua nel mondo politico fiorentino, finirà per passare anch'egli all'opposizione e lo ritroveremo attivissimo e polemico oratore in tutte le pratiche, assieme a Bernardo Rucellai, ad Antonio Strozzi, a Luca di Maso degli Albizi (altro grande escluso dalla magistratura dei Dieci, nella quale siederà soltanto per il primo semestre del 1504), a Guglielmo de' Pazzi, a Lorenzo di Dietisalvi Neroni, ad Antonio Canigiani etc. Altro grande escluso sarà Giovan Battista Ridolfi, anch'esso presente tra i Dieci solo nel primo semestre del 1504, assieme all'Albizi.

Non bisogna, naturalmente, correre a concludere che tutti i personaggi con più frequenza eletti tra i Dieci fossero della consorteria soderiniana. Tutt'altro, e a farcene avvertiti basterebbero i nomi del Guasconi (a meno che domani non si riuscisse a documentare un suo passaggio dalla parte del Soderini) e il mediceo Luigi della Stufa. V' è tuttavia in quest'elenco già un' indicazione valida: la continuità delle presenze, che implicava continuità anche di governo. Inoltre uomini come i Salviati o i Del Nero sappiamo già, per altre fonti, essere dei soderiniani e può pensarsi legittimamente che, comunque, vi fosse sempre in quella magistratura una maggioranza favorevole al gonfaloniere perpetuo, com' è appunto testimoniato dalla politica che i Dieci condussero per l' intero periodo.

Come prima dicevo, a partire dal 1508 anche questo gruppo di sostenitori del Soderini finisce per essere una minoranza, di fronte ai nuovi eletti. Questi nuovi nomi sono davvero estranei al vecchio gruppo di Ottimati, sono nomi privi di significato. Appaiono i Corbinelli, i Giugni, i Bertolini, i Capponi, gli Alessandri, i Ciacchi, i Morelli, i Martelli, i Basini, gli Spini, i Ricci, i Gondi, i Del Caccia. Compaiono, anche, i Nasi, con Alessandro di Francesco (primo semestre del 1511), a ricordarci degli stretti legami commerciali e finanziari con la Francia. Ma hanno membri delle loro famiglie operanti a Lione anche i Martelli con un Giovan Francesco, i Capponi con Neri, Francesco, Carlo e Simone [39].

Un clima propizio al sorgere di una nuova Signoria si stava dunque formando. Abbiamo così le lodi e l'esaltazione mistico-cortigiana col poema *De rerum primordiis* di Francesco Leoni « marchio Trimontinus » [40] o in questa chiusa d'una lettera che il notaio Mentino di ser Cristoforo di ser Giovanni da Planetto inviava al gonfaloniere il 1º dicembre del 1507:

> Sancte pater patriae Sodorine gloria gentis
> Antique aetatis florida fama tue
> Es tu animo Cesar, forma Paris, actibus Hector
> Iulius eloquio consciliisque Cato
> Te Patres coluere mei tibi servio Princeps
> Adsis mancipio te precor ispe tuo [41].

---

[39] *Capitoli della natione fiorentina habitante in Lione l'anno 1501*, B. V., Reginense 1914, cc. 23-24. Cf. A. Rouche, *La Nation florentine de Lyon au commencement du XVIe siècle*, in « Révue d'histoire de Lyon », 1912, pp. 26 ss.

[40] Cf. in *Petrus Soderinus*, pp. 103 ss. Sarà proprio una coincidenza che, prima dell'epicureo e pagano Leoni, si fosse rivolto al Soderini anche Pier Andrea da Verrazzano coi suoi versi licenziosi? (cf. P. Villari-E. Casanova, *Scelta di prediche e scritti di fra' Girolamo Savonarola ...*, Firenze 1898, p. 495); e che nel 1504 dedicassero la parafrasi di Lucrezio a Tommaso Soderini, nipote del gonfaloniere, Raffaele Franco e Giovan Pietro Machiavelli? (cf. S. Bertelli, *Noterelle machiavelliane. Ancora su Lucrezio e Machiavelli*, in «Rivista storica italiana», LXXVI, 1964, pp. 782 ss.).

[41] B. N. F., Ginori Conti 29, 108/29.

Naturalmente questo è anche il clima propizio a idee tirannicide, come puntualmente accadde nell' inverno del 1510 con Prinzivalle della Stufa, figlio di quel Luigi che abbiamo già trovato per tre volte tra i Dieci di libertà e pace, e che però era stato in gioventù tra gli intimi di Lorenzo il Magnifico (sino ad accompagnarlo, di notte, nelle sue scorribande amorose e a cadere, proprio per questo, in disgrazia per le accuse di una donna, Bartolomea Nasi) [42] e che ai Medici si sarebbe riaccostato nel 1512 e nel 1530 (fu membro delle due balìe che li rimisero in Firenze) [43]. Prinzivalle, giovane di ventisei anni (era nato nel 1484), si trovava in quell'anno a Bologna, dove era anche la corte pontificia. In quell'ambiente, già fortemente ostile al Soderini, maturò il progetto di assassinare il gonfaloniere perpetuo, con l'appoggio del cardinale de' Medici e di Marcantonio Colonna. Rientrato a Firenze per dare avvio alla congiura, Prinzivalle sbagliò al primo colpo, andandosi a confidare con Filippo di Filippo Strozzi, che già ne aveva avute abbastanza, di persecuzioni, per il suo matrimonio con la Clarice di Piero de' Medici, due anni prima [44], per poter desiderare di mettere a repentaglio e beni e vita. Così già il 23 dicembre i Dieci potevano dare un primo avviso della scoperta della congiura al loro ambasciatore presso Giulio II, Pier Francesco Tosinghi, e il giorno dopo tornare a scrivergli dandogli ordine di chiedere udienza al papa e di presentare una formale protesta contro il cardinale de' Medici e contro Marcantonio Colonna, mostrando « quanto eglino habbino manchato et del honore et del debito loro, havendo prima pensato et poi ordinato qui di exeguire un tale effecto ». Ma, aggiungevano, nel presentare la protesta il Tosinghi doveva fare ogni opera per mostrare al pontefice « che in questa materia noi non riconosciamo alchuno motivo di Sua Santità, ma solamente da e

---

[42] Guicciardini, *Storie fiorentine* cit., pp. 77-78; ma v. anche in A. Gherardi, *Nuovi documenti e studi intorno a Girolamo Savonarola*, Firenze 1887, pp. 124-29.

[43] F. T. Perrens, *Histoire de Florence depuis la domination des Médicis ...*, II, Paris 1889, p. 475 n.

[44] In quell'occasione si disse che il Soderini avesse incaricato il Machiavelli di stendere la denuncia agli Otto: cf. L. Strozzi *Vite degli uomini illustri di casa Strozzi*, Firenze 1892, p. 96. La vicenda è narrata distesamente in Guicciardini, *Storie fiorentine* cit., pp. 325 ss. La sentenza degli Otto è pubblicata in P. Villari, *Niccolò Machiavelli e i suoi tempi*, Milano 1913, II, pp. 539 ss.

dua predecti », perché « quando pure egli paressi per la divulgatione che se ne è facta in quel modo che la cosa è, haverne charico et se ne dolessi, monsterràli che non ci è possibile tenere secreto né ritardare il parlare d'uno populo quale tucto si tiene offeso di questo principio; et che se Sua Santità ci è mescolato dentro nasce dal cardinale et Signor Marcantonio predecti, e quali per favorire et dare reputatione alla cosa l'hanno mescolata in questa materia » [45]. Senonché Giulio II prevenne il Tosinghi e fu lui a mandarlo a chiamare. Firenze, gli disse il 26 dicembre, sta già da tempo tramando contro di me sostenendo Francia; ma ora ha passato la misura. « Ma questa che io vi dico toccha ad l'honore della persona nostra, la quale per niente non siamo per sopportare. Io ho inteso per cosa certa, et da chi ha udito leggere le lettere, che il gonfaloniere vostro et quelli vostri Signori hanno scripto ad Parma ad Cyamonte come io mi sono facto capo di una intelligentia per fare amazare il gonfaloniere et per mutare quello stato, con ordine che Cyamonte ne dia adviso al Re, per darmi carico et imputarmi con tutti li principi de Christiani, perché non potrebbe esser cosa più absurda et scelerata, che il capo della Christianità tenessi mano a simili cose. El vostro gonfaloniere et quella Signoria se ne mentono per la ghola ... » (e il Tosinghi aggiunge qui: « usando le formali parole », cioè avverte che cita *ad verbum*), « et non sono per sobportarlo ad nissun modo et ne farò tale demonstratione, che io dimonsterrò ad ogni uno che mi dispaccia ». « Alterandosi sì terribilmente » prosegue il Tosinghi, « che io per me non vidi mai la più infuriata cosa » [46].

Nella stessa giornata, anche il cardinale de' Medici cercò il Tosinghi per giurargli « per l'habito che ho addosso, che di questa cosa io non ne so nulla », anche se riconobbe che « è ben vero che Prinzivalle è stato a casa mia a questi dì, et nelle occorrentie sue di qua lo ho favorito ... ». Avendo per risposta dal Tosinghi che « non si ritorna nella città con questi mezi. Ma col fare et adoperare bene verso quella », rinfacciandogli la denuncia del complotto, fatta da « uno che vi è in luogo di figlio

---

[45] A. S. F., Dm 36, c. 14; ma v. ancora il dispaccio del 1° gennaio, *ivi*, cc. 22 v°-24.
[46] A. S. F., Dr 102, c. 455.

et vi porta amore et reverenza come a padre », cioè da Filippo Strozzi [47].

Intanto Luigi della Stufa, arrestato al posto del figlio riuscito a fuggire, sembrava dovesse essere raggiunto alle Stinche da altri medicei. Il 29 dicembre Pier Soderini si presentava davanti al Consiglio Maggiore, pronunciando una « oratione molto compassionevole di sè e animosa in favore della conservatione dello stato popolare e contro allo intento di chi pensava turbarlo e levarlo di mano al popolo; pianse nel recitare il suo concepto più volte, così mosse a lachrimare il popolo ... exaggerò la invidia e odio contro a Prinzivalle della Stufa e suoi adherenti col mostrare che prima pensorono di amazzarlo in Consiglio, poi di sopra in palazzo, ultimamente quando andava fuori ... Ricorse al popolo sentendosi adversarii molti de primati e quali desideravano mutare stato e tirarlo nelle loro mani ... Apresso vedeva li Octo volti a liberare Luigi o leggermente punirlo sanza altrimenti examinarlo, il che li doleva ... » [48].

Il Parenti, che è sempre ostile al governo soderiniano, aggiunge infatti che la pena inflitta ai della Stufa, padre e figlio (bando di ribelle per Prinzivalle, confino per cinque anni a Luigi nelle campagne di Empoli, dove aveva possessioni), fu mite perché « poterono tanto li amici e parenti di Luigi, ma maxime e malecontenti dello Stato populare, el quale in verità era republica, che indussono li Octo a così determinare » [49]. È un fatto che, alle Stinche, nessuno raggiunse Luigi e che anzi questi, ben presto, ne uscì mostrandosi con fare provocatorio per la città, prima di partire per il confino. Mancò in quei giorni, attorno al Soderini, il gruppo compatto dei suoi consorti, a permettergli di sfruttare l'emozione popolare per rafforzare il proprio potere in forma ancor più autoritaria. Tuttavia è anche certo che altri motivi contribuirono a impedire che si calcasse la mano. Il complotto aveva scoperto troppo: non soltanto il cardinale de' Medici, chiamato direttamente in correo da Filippo Strozzi, ma lo stesso pontefice, se non altro moralmente, come protettore del cardinale Giovanni. Il fosso scavato tra lo Stato fiorentino e Giulio II stava diventando incolmabile, né certo era interesse

---

[47] A. S. F., Dr 102, cc. 461 v°-62.

[48] Parenti, *Historia fiorentina* cit., II . IV . 171, cc. 45-v°.

[49] *Ibid.,* c. 45 v°.

di Pier Soderini (e di suo fratello Francesco) rigirare ancor più il coltello nella piaga. Il 3 gennaio i Dieci scrivevano a Francesco Pandolfini, oratore presso Georges Chaumont d'Amboise: « la dispositione del papa essere peggiorata assai più di quello che la era verso di noi poi che intese resultarli charico del disegno fatto qui » [50], e ancora il Parenti ci informa che « atteso le grandi minacce si ordinò di mandare fanterie ne luoghi nostri più sospecti et advertire i mercatanti di Roma che al più potessino s'allestissino a cagione non fussino usurpati » [51]. La clemenza, dunque, derivava anche da preoccupazioni di politica estera.

Tant' è che il Soderini non si accontentò affatto della sentenza, anche se l'accettò. Ancora il 13 gennaio faceva scrivere, « nomine ser Antonii della Valle », una lettera a Filippo de Rossi per incitarlo, magari con l'aiuto di Bartolomeo della Stufa, figlio naturale di Andrea, a entrare in rapporti con Prinzivalle « et vedere di ritrarre il più puoi, come quando in che modo e con che mezzi disegnava amazzare il Gonfaloniere et quanti et in particulare chi haveva ad trovarsi secho ad tale facto, et amazzato il Gonfaloniere quello disegnavano più oltre, et che fine si havevano proposto in questa cosa et che remuneratione et da chi ne aspectava » e, aggiungeva, « per ritrarre meglio il tucto sarà a proposito ti monstri più presto inimicho del Gonfaloniere che altrimenti ... » [52].

Con tutto ciò, il complotto ebbe ugualmente una conseguenza opposta, come sempre avviene, ai fini auspicati. Il Soderini fece approvare una provvisione che impedisse improvvisi vuoti di potere, nel caso restasse vacante uno dei due maggiori magistrati al vertice dello Stato. La nuova legge stabilì che « ogni qual volta o in tutto o in parte per quale accidente si fussi manchassino alcuno de 2 maggiori magistrati, sempre e restanti havessino auctorità chome interi a ragunar » il Consiglio Maggiore « e rifare tali magistrati manchanti e scambi » [53].

Il regime, all' interno, restava abbastanza forte anche se, nella misura in cui aumentava il potere personale del Soderini,

---

[50] A. S. F., Dm 36, c. 26.

[51] Parenti, *Historia fiorentina* cit., II. IV. 171 c. 46 v°.

[52] *Minutario di lettere scripte per la Excelentia del Gonfaloniere ...*, B. N. F., Ginori Conti 29, 10/a.

[53] Parenti, *Storia fiorentina* cit., II . IV . 171, c. 48.

aumentava anche l'opposizione al suo principato. In questa doppia evoluzione, accanto alla congiura di Prinzivalle, l'episodio più saliente fu forse quello, di due anni prima, della richiesta di investitura da parte di Massimiliano del *vicariatus imperii* sulla città. Mentre l'opposizione — capeggiata dal Pepi — chiedeva il rovesciamento delle alleanze e il passaggio dalla parte imperiale, con un gioco assai pericoloso, data la debolezza congenita del Re dei Romani, il Soderini tastava anch'egli il terreno per un eventuale abbandono della Francia, se la discesa dell' imperatore ve lo avesse costretto, con un grosso colpo che lo avrebbe portato vicino al principato, scavalcando la stessa opposizione [54]. L' impossibilità per Massimiliano di scendere in Italia privò il Soderini di quel riconoscimento giuridico che, per la verità, non era servito nemmeno a Lodovico il Moro a mantenere il potere, ma che pure aveva un rilevante peso sulla coscienza dell'opinione pubblica d'allora.

Quel rovesciamento d'alleanze che non fu possibile operare nel 1507 era tuttavia divenuto impellente tra il 1510 e il 1511. La rottura col papa si era aggravata e per la congiura di Prinzivalle e per l'accettazione dello scismatico e gallicano concilio a Pisa. Un'accettazione voluta dal fratello del gonfaloniere, il cardinale di Volterra, scavalcando tutti gli organi responsabili dello Stato fiorentino, in una fatidica notte in cui a Giulio II venne somministrata l'estrema unzione e il partito dei cardinali francesi sembrò d'improvviso vincente [55]. Erano poi venuti i giorni dello scontro armato tra Francia e Roma e, ancora una volta, Firenze non seppe essere tempestiva. Francesco Vettori, in una lunga pagina autocritica al Machiavelli, il 20 agosto del 1513 gli scriveva da Roma di non aver mai avuto « affectione alcuna alla parte contro a Francia ... et sapete che avanti si ragionasse del Concilio di Pisa, che io sempre teneva la parte francese, perché credevo che con quella Italia havesse a far meglio, et la città nostra s' havesse a riposare ... Et però vedendo poi come ci governamo male in quella materia del Concilio, et quanto i Franzesi si partirono mal satisfatti, cominciai a dubitare che la vittoria loro non havesse a essere la rovina nostra, et che non

---

[54] *Petrus Soderinus* cit., pp. 110 ss.

[55] Cf. l'introduzione alla Legazione XXXIV in *Legazioni e Commissarie* cit., pp. 1372 ss.

pensassero tractare noi come una Brescia; et monsignor di Fois, giovane et crudele, mi faceva più paura, et per questo mi rivolsi. Nondimeno sempre che si ragionava d'accordo con loro, perché mi pareva ci assicurassimo di quel pericolo, lo consentivo et confortavolo. Sono successe poi le cose come sapete ... » [56].

Firenze fu investita dalle truppe di Ramón di Cardona e il Soderini spodestato da Antonfrancesco degli Albizi, Paolo Vettori, Gino Capponi e Baccio Valori. Era un tentativo degli Ottimati di riprendere il potere che, con le proprie mani, avevano consegnato al gonfaloniere perpetuo, ad imitazione dello Stato veneziano, non accorgendosi della diversità di poteri tra il doge e il loro gonfaloniere e dell'equilibrio che sulle isole della laguna veneta si era stabilito all' interno del patriziato. Un tentativo inutile, perché non facevano che aprire la strada al rientro dei Medici, mentre il Soderini attraversava in fuga l' Italia centrale, inseguito da Rinieri della Sassetta, pensando prima di raggiungere Roma, decidendo poi per l'esilio di Ragusa.

---

[56] Machiavelli, *Epistolario*, a cura di S. Bertelli, ... *Opere*, V, Milano 1969, p. 288. Con raccapriccio mi accorgo di aver attribuito queste parole allo stesso Machiavelli nell' introduzione alle sue *Opere*, I, Milano, 1968, p. XXVII.

APPENDICE

Pier Soderini ad Argentina Malaspina, Loreto, 11 novembre 1512. (B. N. F., Ginori Conti 29, 113/23, copia).

A. m. C. Io ti scripsi per ser Domenico, non so se l' harai havuta, di più non ti ho possuto scrivere per non essere stato in luogo accomodato, hor per certo apportatore capitato qui ti significo come per gratia di Dio nostro Signore sono arrivato qui a Santa Maria dell' Oreto con gradissimo mio sinistro, e per il cavalcare e per il sole, il quale mi ha molestato assai, e per questa cagione, e per altro m' è bisognato camminare di notte assai. Io me ne andavo a Roma, come ti havevo significato, ma havendo inteso Rinieri della Sassetta e altri venirmi detro per farmi disonore, e non havendo possuto havere salvocondotta dal Pontefice, che volentieri andavo a Roma, presi questa via e mi sono raccomandato alla gloriosa Madonna, mi indirizzi a prendere cammino più salutifero e più quieto per me che si potessi, m' ha inspirato me ne vadia alla via di Ragugia, come luogo quieto, e sicuro, secondo spero, dove se potrò stare, mi fermerò tanto ch' io veggia se a Roma si potrà star sicuro, e quando sarò in luogo sicuro, e fermo, se vorrai venire sarò contento, e se vorrai restare costì sarò contento, non ho mai havuto novelle di te poi mi partì. Iddio ci conservi sani. Le cose nostre non so come stieno, fa tu quello puoi di buono, che portandomi io bene verso la mia Republica doverrebeno le cose mia essermi aiutate, preservate, perché io mai feci male a nessuno.

De mia panni non credo ve ne sia da potere adoperare, vedrò provedermi di qua. Vorrei Giorgio scrivessi alli sua ci facessino buona compagnia com' è stato fatto a lui, e alli altri di costà. Farai intendere alle mia sorelle sto bene, e dove sono, che ad altri non scrivo. Raffaello faccia quello può di buono, e quando ha qualche danaio lo dia a Giorgio, me li faccia pagare di qua, benché stimo n' harà pochi. Delle cose nostre non posso dirti altro, perché lasciai tempo fa la cura a Raffaello, et hora lascio la cura a te, perché io penso assettarmi se a Dio piacerà a vivere in pace, che sai tu quanto tempo io l' habbia desiderato; ma ben vorrei essere possuto stare in luogo che comodamente tu fussi potuta venire. Dominus Deus provegga lui secondo la volontà sua. Saluta coteste madre e fa fare oratione dando delle elemosine a quelli luoghi pare a te sieno buoni servi d' Iddio. Harò charo intendere del Marchese L[azzar]o quello sia seguito. Madonna Theodosia seguiti co' medesimi favori che l'altra parte, perché tanto attiene a lei quanto Madonna Zaffira. Saluta la fanciullina e la madre. Prega Iddio per me, che m' è stato facto intendere ho più persecutori non posso credere, e non merito. Iddio li disponga al bene. Sai che se io non ti veggo col corpo ti veggo con l'animo. Harei bisogno di qualche servidore fidato, ma che fussi ben fidato, vedi se da casa tua si può haverne nessuno. Né più per questa. Scriverò spesso quanto potrò.

A Santa Maria dell' Oreto, a dì XI Settembre 1512

P. S.

Alla mia charissima consorte
Argentina Malaspina
in Firenze

CECIL GRAYSON

MACHIAVELLI AND DANTE*

* This article is a revised version of a paper read at the Italian Institute, London, on 14 May 1969, during a symposium organized by the Society for Renaissance Studies to celebrate the quincentenary of Machiavelli's birth. I am very grateful to Professor Carlo Dionisotti whose intervention in discussion on that occasion has led me to qualify my earlier conclusions regarding the attribution of the *Dialogo* to Machiavelli. In dedicating this article now to my friend Hans Baron, I am conscious of removing the ground from beneath his feet, as well as my own. If I am right in so doing, I hope he will not mind if we fall together!

We have ample evidence that Machiavelli was a reader and imitator of Dante's *Comedy*. From a public speech of about 1500 to correspondence in 1525 we find him continually quoting Dante and basing several verse compositions on the content, form and language of Dante's poem. He refers to the *Comedy* in the famous letter to Vettori of December 1513 as one of the texts he carried about with him in the « ozio » of San Casciano [1]. On the other hand, we read in the brief but significant *Discorso o Dialogo intorno alla Lingua*, ascribed to 1514-15, a severe criticism of Dante which made Tommasini believe in 1883 that Machiavelli could not possibly have been the author of this work [2]. Although in 1911 Tommasini repeated this argument and added others to support his contention, he failed to shake the confidence of scholars in the attribution of this *Dialogo* to Machiavelli [3]. More recently Ridolfi took up this particular point only to dismiss it with these words: « ... né credo che alle ragioni da addursi contro l'attribuzione del dialogo al Segretario fiorentino possano aggiungersi certe parole dispettose contro il Poeta » [4]. The present occasion is an appropriate one to re-examine the relationship between these two great Florentines, and from this starting-point to re-open the question of the date and authorship of the *Dialogo intorno alla Lingua*, which has long been regarded

---

[1] N. Machiavelli, *Tutte le opere*, ed. G. Mazzoni and M. Casella (Florence, 1929), p. 885. The amorous context (« leggo quelle loro amorose passioni e quelli loro amori », etc.) might suggest the work of Dante he carried was not the *Comedy*, but it must have been, by exclusion, as *Vita Nuova* was not then in print, and it could hardly mean *Convivio* (see below, n. 6).

[2] O. Tommasini, *La vita e gli scritti di N. Machiavelli*, I (Turin, 1883), p. 100 (with reference to the *Allocuzione*, *cit. infra*): « la grande venerazione che in quest'incontro dimostra per l'Alighieri, ci dà argomento a discredere ch'egli mai scrivesse quell'irreverente *discorso intorno alla lingua* da pedantuccio uggioso, che con insufficienti ragioni gli si volle attribuire ».

[3] *La vita*, II (Rome, 1911), pp. 349 ff. See below, nn. 20-21.

[4] R. Ridolfi, *Vita di N. Machiavelli*, 3ª ed. (Rome, 1969), p. 273.

as an important document in the history of the Italian language and in the early « fortuna » of Dante's *De Vulgari Eloquentia*, and more recently as a significant step in the development of Machiavelli's historical ideas [5].

Leaving aside for a moment this *Dialogo*, there is, as far as I know, only one allusion in the certain canon of Machiavelli's works to a work by Dante other than the *Comedy*. It is a reference, in *Discorsi*, I, 53, to a passage from *Convivio* I, which Machiavelli erroneously ascribes to *Monarchia* [6]. It hardly emerges from this example that he was an attentive or retentive reader of either. *Convivio* was in print. *Monarchia* was not, but he could possibly have read it perhaps in Ficino's translation. The case with the *Comedy* is different. Over a period of some 25 years his quotations from the poem and his imitation of it demonstrate an attachment to and in some ways an affinity with Dante that is worth closer study. The quotations begin from the « Allocuzione fatta ad un magistrato » of c. 1500 and extend through the *Discourses on Livy* of c. 1517 and the prologue to *Mandragola* of 1518, to his correspondence with Guicciardini in 1525; they come from all three « cantiche », and are generally cited as illustrations of moral, social and political ideas. Once they are qualified as « versi aurei e divini »; on another occasion introduced with the phrase: « come prudentemente Dante dice » [7]. Machiavelli's imitation of the *Comedy* could be said to begin with the *Primo decennale* of 1504, which, like the *Secondo decennale* of 1514, owes at least its form and some of its expression to Dante.

---

[5] Cf. C. Grayson, « Lorenzo, Machiavelli and the Italian language », in *Italian Renaissance Studies*, ed. E. F. Jacob (London, 1960), pp. 410-432; M. Barbi, *Della fortuna di Dante nel sec. XVI* (Pisa, 1890), pp. 95 ff.; Hans Baron, « Machiavelli on the Eve of the *Discourses*: The Date and Place of his *Dialogo intorno alla nostra lingua* », in *Bibliothèque d'humanisme et Renaissance*, XXIII (1961), 449-476.

[6] *Tutte le opere*, pp. 123-124. The context of *Conv*. I, XI is linguistic. Machiavelli applies the quotation to politics.

[7] The *Allocuzione*, dated 1500-01 by Tommasini, *La vita*, I, 100, quotes *Purg*. X, 73-78 (*N. Machiavelli, L'Arte della Guerra e scritti politici minori*, ed. S. Bertelli [Milan, 1961], pp. 135-37); *Discorsi* I, XI quotes *Purg*. VII, 121-23 (*Tutte le opere*, p. 77); the prologue to *Mandragola* echoes *Inf*. XXXIII, 80 (*ibid*., p. 694); in two letters to Guicciardini of 1525 Machiavelli quoted *Purg*. XX, 86-87 and (incorrectly) *Par*. VI, 134-35 (cf. Ridolfi, *Vita*, pp. 341-2, 345-6).

There is also something of the spirit of moral indignation, as well as the 'terza rima' form and some language of Dante, in the three *capitoli* which Machiavelli wrote: *Dell'ingratitudine* (1509), *Della fortuna* (1512), *Dell'ambizione* (1509 or 1516), all inspired by personal or political events. A much freer assimilation of the model of the *Comedy* is represented by the *Asino*, possibly begun in 1512 and still being written in 1517 [8]. Although the formal imitation of content and expression is closer here than in any other of Machiavelli's works, the spirit could hardly be more different. Here Machiavelli's « smarrimento » « in un luogo aspro quanto mai si vide », from which he is rescued by a sympathetic « duchessa » who takes him into bed before giving him a conducted tour of Circe's animal kingdom, might seem like a parody of the *Comedy*, but I believe this to be unintentional. His satire is aimed at contemporary humanity, not at Dante, whose poem simply provides a convenient vehicle suitably adapted without prejudice or malice. He left his *Asino* unfinished, and at that point he also ceased to attempt major poetry or to imitate Dante.

On this evidence Machiavelli appears as a fairly consistent and somewhat uncritical consumer of the *Comedy*. On the one hand it provides him with a series of apposite moral, social or political quotations, which he implicitly or even explicitly judges favourably. On the other hand it provides him with a model of convenient and at times morally coincident imitation. He feels free and makes free with the poem, as it suits him, to express his own thoughts and feelings. At no point does he seem at all critically engaged with Dante either as a man or as a poet in any unfavourable sense. In his only reference to Dante as a citizen, in *Storie fiorentine* II, xx, Machiavelli merely records his exile without comment [9]. On this showing, if one agrees that the

---

[8] For imitation and echoes of Dante in these works in verse see especially M. Barbi, *Della fortuna*, pp. 297-300, and the Introduction and notes to the following editions: N. Machiavelli, *Operette satiriche*, ed. L. F. Benedetto (Turin, 1920); N. Machiavelli, *Opere letterarie*, ed. L. Blasucci (Milan, 1964); with particular reference to the problems of dating, N. Machiavelli, *Il teatro e tutti gli scritti letterari*, ed. F. Gaeta (Milan, 1965), espec. pp. XVI-XVIII.

[9] *Tutte le opere*, p. 422: « Furono pertanto confinati tutti i Cerchi con i loro seguaci di parte Bianca, intra i quali fu Dante poeta »; no more, no less. The *Storie* were written between 1521 and 1525.

parody of Dante in the *Asino* is unintentional, the references and quotations and imitation of Dante in Machiavelli's works suggest respect and at times admiration for the poet.

Seen in this context the criticism of Dante as a man and a poet in the *Dialogo intorno alla Lingua*, universally attributed to Machiavelli and to the years 1514-15, comes, to say the least, as something of a surprise. It is generally held that the occasion for this work was the communication to Florentine literati by Trissino of the rediscovered *De Vulgari Eloquentia* during one of his visits about that time. The reaction of the author of the *Dialogo* to this treatise and related discussions is not limited to the linguistic implications in an effort to prove to Dante and everyone else that he wrote the *Comedy* in Florentine and not in Italian or a *lingua cortigiana*; it involves the personality of the poet and his relations with Florence, and explains Dante's linguistic views (admittedly misinterpreted) in terms of his political experience and bitterness in exile [10]. The page is worth reading in full: « ... mi fermerò sopra di Dante, il quale in ogni parte mostrò d'essere per ingegno, per dottrina e per giudizio, uomo eccellente, eccetto che dove egli ebbe a ragionare della patria sua, la quale fuori d'ogni umanità e filosofico instituto perseguitò con ogni specie d'ingiuria. E non potendo altro fare che infamarla, accusò quella d'ogni vizio, dannò gli uomini, biasimò il sito, disse male de' costumi e delle leggi di lei. E questo fece non solo in una parte della sua Cantica ma in tutta, e diversamente e in diversi modi, tanto l'offese l'ingiuria dell'esilio! tanta vendetta ne desiderava! e però ne fece tanta quanta egli poté. E se per sorte, de' mali ch'egli li predisse le ne fusse accaduto alcuno, Firenze arebbe più da dolersi d'aver nutrito quell'uomo che d'alcuna altra sua rovina. Ma la fortuna, per farlo mendace e per ricoprire con la gloria sua la calunnia falsa di quello, l'ha continuamente prosperata, e fatta celebre per tutte le provincie del mondo, e condotta al presente in tanta felicità e sì tranquillo stato che se Dante la vedessi, o egli accuserebbe se stesso o, ripercosso dai colpi di quella sua innata invidia vorrebbe, essendo risuscitato, di nuovo morire. Non è pertanto maraviglia se costui che in ogni cosa accrebbe infamia alla sua patria, volse ancora

---

[10] For the misinterpretation of *De Vulgari Eloquentia* see my article cited above, n. 5.

nella lingua torle quella riputazione la quale pareva a lui d'averle data ne' suoi scritti: e per non l'onorare in alcun modo, compose quell'opera, per mostrar quella lingua nella quale egli aveva scritto non esser fiorentina. Il che tanto se li debbe credere, quanto ch'ei trovassi Bruto in bocca di Lucifero maggiore, e cinque cittadini fiorentini intra i ladroni, e quel suo Cacciaguida in Paradiso, e simili sue passioni e opinioni; nelle quali fu tanto cieco che perse ogni sua gravità, dottrina e giudicio, e divenne al tutto un altro uomo; talmente che, s'egli avessi giudicato così ogni cosa, o egli sarebbe vivuto sempre a Firenze o egli ne sarebbe stato cacciato per pazzo » [11].

If it is correct that the *Dialogo* was written by Machiavelli and about that time, it is a pretty startling demonstration of a critical attitude towards Dante nowhere else apparent or implied in his writings. It would mean that it took this *questione della lingua* to unleash severe comment on Dante and the *Comedy*, which Machiavelli otherwise refrained from expressing. There were issues that did not need the prick of *De Vulgari Eloquentia*: e. g. the questions here raised of Brutus, Cacciaguida, the Florentine thieves, « e simili sue passioni e opinioni », not to mention the general issue of patriotism and exile. It is relevant to ask why Machiavelli kept silent on such matters in all his other works [12]. But the criticism of the *Dialogo* extends also to language and style. In the dialogue part of the work the author writes:

« Dante mio, io voglio che tu t'emendi ... tu vedrai come ne' tuoi versi non hai fuggito il goffo, come è quello: *Poi ci partimmo, e n'andavamo introcque*; non hai fuggito il porco, com' è quello: *Che merda fa di quel che si trangugia*; non hai fuggito l'osceno, come è: *Le mani alzò con ambedue le fiche*; e non avendo fuggito questo che disonora tutta l'opera tua, tu non puoi aver fuggito infiniti vocaboli patrii ... » [13]

Is this in character with Machiavelli as we otherwise know him? If we do not exclude the possibility that even he might perhaps

---

[11] *Tutte le opere*, pp. 772-73.

[12] All of these might be expected to arise solely from the *Comedy* and a knowledge of Dante's life.

[13] *Tutte le opere*, p. 775.

have found some of the language of the *Comedy* a little coarse, there is still the extension in that passage that such examples cast dishonour over the entire poem. This is not the impression we have of Machiavelli's views from the other sources noted in his works. I believe that the contrast between the criticism of Dante and the *Comedy* in the *Dialogo* and the general pattern of Machiavelli's attitude towards and use of Dante both before and after the supposed date of the *Dialogo* is sufficient at least to cast doubt not only on the dating but possibly also on the attribution. This is not, of course, sufficient proof that Machiavelli did not write the *Dialogo*; but it cannot simply be dismissed as « certe parole dispettose » which we can overlook in the belief that in all other respects the work is Machiavelli's. I would maintain that this is not the case. In order to advance my argument it is necessary to rehearse briefly the basic evidence to date.

The major source for the *Dialogo* is a MS of 1726 made from a 16th-century MS copied by Giuliano Ricci in 1577 (now lost) [14]. It also bears Ricci's note to the effect that he had received the work from others and had not himself found any such original or draft among Machiavelli's papers; but that he believed the work to be Machiavelli's on the basis of the donor's assurances

---

[14] Three MSS are extant: Bibl. Vat., Rome, Barb. Lat. 5368 (cf. Tommasini, *La vita*, I, 617 ff. and 619, n. 4); Bibl. Naz., Florence, Pal. 815 (copied in 1726) and Misc. Borghini, Filze Rinuccini 22 (16th century, but probably not « del primo quarto del sec. XVI » as Tommasini opines, *La vita*, II, 1041. The text is incomplete, ending at « Tu ti guardi assai bene dai vocaboli fiorentini »; cf. *Tutte le opere*, p. 775). All are descended, according to Casella (*ibid.* p. 728), from the « apografo Ricci ». I regret that I have been unable as yet to study these MSS directly. I am grateful to Dr. John Woodhouse for information about the « Borghini » fragment, which probably found its way into this collection without Borghini's knowledge or even after his time. It is difficult otherwise to explain Borghini's silence about a work on language here bearing the name of Machiavelli. The MS is not in Borghini's hand; it lies in the filza between works of the mid-70s, though this is not necessarily a guide to the actual date of the MS. Dr. Woodhouse, who is currently editing Borghini's writings, tells me there are no allusions to Machiavelli among them (apart from the occurrence of his name in a list of Florentine writers) — a silence which may well be explained by the interdict on Machiavelli's works, though it is questionable whether Borghini would have felt this to inhibit reference to a work on language.

and of a statement by Machiavelli's son Bernardo, then 74, that he recalled his father speaking of such a work and seeing it in his hand [15]. Bernardo was born in 1503, so he was 11 or 12 when, according to present dating, the *Dialogo* was written, and 24 when his father died. So that, half a century later Bernardo's memory at 74 becomes a major prop for the attribution of this particular work to Machiavelli. It was first printed, without name of author, in 1730, and from 1769 as Machiavelli's work [16]. The first real challenge to the attribution came from Polidori in 1852, who among other less substantial items pointed out a contradiction between the *Dialogo* and Machiavelli's *Arte della Guerra* concerning the proportion of auxiliaries in Roman armies [17]. But the case held firm, and was strengthened by Villari and Rajna [18]; while this particular obstacle was then circumvented, and has been ever since by the argument that the *Dialogo* must therefore precede 1520, when, as we now know, Ma-

---

[15] It is worth giving Ricci's note in full (see Rajna's article cited below, n. 18): « Mi è capitato alle mani un discorso o dialogo intorno alla nostra lingua, dicono fatto dal medesimo Niccolò, et se bene lo stile è alquanto diverso dall'altre sue cose, et io in questi fragmenti, che ho ritrovati, non ho visto né originale né bozza, né parte alcuna di detto dialogo, nondimeno credo si possa credere indubitamente, che sia dello stesso Machiavello, atteso che li concepti appariscono suoi, che per molti anni per ciascuno in mano di chi oggi si truova si tiene suo, et quello che più di altro importa è, che, Bernardo Machiavelli figlio di detto Niccolo oggi di età di anni 74: afferma ricordarsi averne sentito ragionare a suo Padre, et vedutogliene fra le mani molte volte ... ».

[16] In 1730 by G. B[ottari], in *L'Ercolano di M. Benedetto Varchi ...*, Florence, pp. 449-67 (the *Prefazione*, p. XXXXIX, describes the author as « Fiorentino giudiziosissimo ... quasi contemporaneo, ma un poco più antico del Varchi »). In 1769, in the edition of Machiavelli's *Commedie, terzine ed altre opere*, Cosmopoli.

[17] *Opere minori di N. Machiavelli*, ed. G. Polidori (Florence, 1852), p. 589. The *Dialogo* (ed. *cit.*, p. 776) says Roman armies were composed of about 12,000 Romans and 20,000 others; the *Arte della Guerra* (*ibid.*, p. 338) says there were about 11,000 of each.

[18] P. Villari, in his *N. Machiavelli e i suoi tempi*, from the 1st ed. of 1877 to the 4th (posthumous) ed. of 1927 (Milan, pp. 399-407) sustained the attribution to Machiavelli with some modification of dating due to the fundamental article of P. Rajna, « La data del *Dialogo intorno alla lingua* di N. Machiavelli », in *Rendiconti Accad. dei Lincei, Cl. di scienze morali*, Ser. V, II (1893), 203-33. See also A. Gaspary, *Storia della letteratura italiana*, trans. by V. Rossi (Turin, 1901), II, 194 and notes pp. 318-19.

chiavelli's greater familiarity with Polybius possibly made him change his mind about Roman armies [19]. Only Tommasini in 1911 tried, but unsuccessfully, to stem this tide of conviction, which Rajna's persuasive article on the dating (1893) had turned into virtual certainty. Tommasini failed not so much because of the relative weakness of his arguments, but on account of his bad presentation of them, and his unlikely conclusion that the author was a supporter of the Medici and a cleric, who got some of his ideas for the work from his friend Machiavelli, sometime between 1519 and 1522 [20].

So the attribution has stayed firm, with some slight shift of date from possibly 1514 to 1515 or even 1516. This discussion about the dating has centered on the need to make the internal details of the *Dialogo* square with Machiavelli's career before 1520 and with the circumstances of the divulgation of the *De Vulgari Eloquentia* in Florence by Trissino. There is, for example, the « vendemmiale negozio » in which the author says the *Dialogo* was written; so it must be an autumn work, and we must know in what year Machiavelli was then in the

---

[19] Cf. H. Baron, « Machiavelli on the Eve of the *Discourses* », pp. 453-55. The argument appears persuasive on the face of it, but see p. 453, n. 3, where Polybius III could have supplied Machiavelli with the same answer several years before VI was available.

[20] Tommasini, *La vita*, II, 349 ff., tries to present arguments on both sides and finally comes up with this strange compromise solution; « Ed è nostra opinione che quel *Dialogo* venisse allora composto (he dates it 1519-22) per dar la soia al cardinal Giulio; e fosse opera, non solo di un mediceo, ma di persona adetta alla curia, e probabilmente un ecclesiastico, amico del Machiavelli, il quale ebbe forse in confidenza a chiedergliene parere, suggerimenti, correzioni ... » The arguments against the attribution to Machiavelli to which Tommasini gives weight are: (1) Machiavelli in other writings refers to his own language as Tuscan, not Florentine, which would put *him* among the « meno inonesti » of the *Dialogo*; (2) the « contrasto manifesto con la sua (M's) ripugnanza a mettere avanti se stesso »; (3) the « sproporzione tra la causa della polemica e l'eccesso dell'invettive da lui usate contro l'Alighieri, eccesso più da inquisitore che combatte un'eresia, che da grammatico »; (4) the violence of criticism of Dante uncharacteristic of Machiavelli and offensive to public opinion of the time. However, in his rather confused presentation of the case Tommasini also refers to the lack of reference by contemporaries and later to this work of Machiavelli, and the unreliability of Bernardo Machiavelli's testimony for this particular dialogue; he also denies Martelli's dependence on the *Dialogo*, but for reasons different from those advanced below.

country. There is the reference in it to a comedy by « uno degli Ariosti di Ferrara », in fact to the prose version of the *Suppositi*; and as Machiavelli knew Ariosto and speaks of him and the *Orlando Furioso* in a well-known letter of December 1517, he could not possibly have referred to the famous poet in that way after 1517; and of course he could not have been writing before 1509 when Ariosto composed that play. On this sort of reckoning we are anyway somewhere between 1509 and 1517, at which point the plot thickens. There is a reference in the *Dialogo* to the courts of Milan and Naples as existing at that time. This will pass for Naples with the Spanish viceroys, but Milan's duke was ejected in September 1515 and was not restored until after 1520. Trissino was in Florence in 1513 and perhaps called there also in 1514 and 1516. Gelli and Varchi confirm the communication by Trissino and discussion of *De Vulgari Eloquentia* in Florence at that sort of time, but are not precisely helpful for the date. The *Dialogo*, however, refers to « la disputa nata più volte nei passati giorni » about language, and depends on a more than superficial knowledge of Dante's treatise; so that we are, on these lines, reduced to the years 1514 (Rajna) or 1515-16 (Baron) [21]. Here a major difficulty arises. In the long passage quoted above, p. 366, the author refers to fortune as having brought Florence « al presente in tanta felicità e sì tranquillo stato » that Dante « ripercosso dai colpi di quella sua innata invidia, vorrebbe, essendo risuscitato, di nuovo morire ». These are strong terms, and it is not easy to find a place for them in Machiavelli's experience at that time. Rajna believed there was no reason why Machiavelli should not say this after 1512 when the Medici were back in Florence and on the papal throne, and he hoped again for employment. Baron is more specific and finds the visit of Leo X to Florence in 1515 « was a most suitable time for Machiavelli to rejoin the stream of Florentine life and believe in tanta felicità e sì tranquillo stato ». But can we really overlook, as Baron suggests, the damning statement about Rome elsewhere in the *Dialogo* « Ma se tu [Dante] parli

[21] For the main arguments here referred to, see the articles cited of Rajna and Baron. For Ridolfi's proposal for a later date (1522-23) see his *Vita di N. Machiavelli*, pp. 510-11, and cf. Baron, « Machiavelli on the Eve of the *Discourses* », p. 455.

della corte di Roma ... io mi maraviglio di te, che tu voglia, dove non si fa cosa alcuna laudabile o buona, che vi si faccia questa; perché, dove sono i costumi perversi, conviene che il parlare sia perverso e abbia in se quello effeminato lascivo che hanno coloro che lo parlano »[22]. I doubt if Leo X would have read this as a compliment, or have been prepared to see it in relation to Dante's time or anyone else's besides his own. Furthermore, autumn 1515 was not at all a good or optimistic time for Machiavelli. His letters to Giovanni Vernacci of 18 August and 19 November are very depressed; in February 1516 he touches bottom (« io sono diventato inutile a me, a' parenti e a li amici »). 1514 would hardly have been better: he was in love that autumn (« non mi diletta più leggere le cose antiche, né ragionare delle moderne »)[23].

---

[22] *Tutte le opere*, p. 776. Baron, « Machiavelli on the Eve of the *Discourses* », p. 455, n. 2, writes: « This, however, is not a censure of conditions characteristic of the curia under any particular pope, but an argument — used in the imaginary debate with Dante — about the general role of Rome in the language development of Italy. If such an historical statement could not have been written in Leo's time because of the inherent offense, (as Ridolfi suggests), one would have to draw the absurd conclusion that for the same reason the fierce condemnation in *Discourses* I, 12 of the political and religious role of the papacy in Italy could not have been written under Leo's pontificate ». I do not think the comparison here made is acceptable. In the context of the *Dialogo* Rome and Florence are seen as linguistically and morally opposed to each other; there is a sharp contrast between the felicity and tranquillity of Florence and the perversity of Rome where « non si fa cosa alcuna laudabile ». It is this contrast which makes the statement unlikely in Leo's time. The situation of *Discourses* I, 12 presents no such contrast. It is worth noting too, in relation to the knowledge, or rather misinterpretation of the *De Vulgari Eloquentia* on the part of the author of the *Dialogo*, that these very words about Rome echo Dante's *own condemnation* of the language of that city (*De Vulgari Eloquentia*, I, XI, 2): « Dicimus igitur Romanorum — non vulgare, sed potius tristiloquium — Ytalorum vulgarium omnium esse turpissimum: nec mirum, cum etiam morum habitumque deformitate pre cunctis videantur fetere ».

[23] Baron, p. 460, refers to these two letters as evidence that Machiavelli was in Florence in the autumn of 1515 and could well have gone to San Casciano for the « vendemmia ». So he might, but the content of the letters is very pessimistic: « ... i tempi, i quali sono stati e sono di sorte che mi hanno fatto sdimenticare di me medesimo » (18 Aug.); « la fortuna non mi ha lasciato altro che i parenti e gli amici, e io ne fo capitale » (19 Nov.). See *Tutte le opere*, pp. 896-97.

It is extremely difficult to overlook these significant comments on the state of Florentine and Roman affairs, even if it is possible by some means or other to make the other references in the *Dialogo* fit in with Machiavelli. These could take us to 1514-15; but the situation in those years simply will not suit Machiavelli or the Florence-Rome position described in the *Dialogo*. It is, however, by no means the only difficulty we have to overlook if we accept the work as written at that time. The more one looks at it, the more the *Dialogo* appears, if written then, as an exceedingly precocious document. We know Machiavelli was in many ways an extraordinary person; but did he possess then the knowledge and insights which this work shows? The author obviously has a rare grasp for that time of the linguistic problems of the vernacular, both general and particular, especially in the matter of vocabulary, phonology and morphology. In 1515 this is way ahead of anything that had been published, — before Fortunio, Bembo and Trissino got into print on the subject. It is not only that the author is familiar with the *De Vulgari Eloquentia* and with current theories for an Italian or courtly language, and can refer confidently to opposing arguments about the determining features of any language, all of which at that date would have to be based on verbal exchanges; he also shows an independence of information and understanding of Italian and language in general that could hardly have been produced simply and immediately, without prior preparation, experience and reflection, by the impact of Trissino and *De Vulgari Eloquentia* in Florence. We ought to ask what evidence of such preparation we have for Machiavelli up to the time it is supposed to have been written. It is true that arguments about the nature and name of the language began from the early years of the 16th century. But, apart from Trissino's visits to Florence, they went on largely outside that city and outside Tuscany. The basic texts which reflect those arguments were all published much later, and it was from these publications that major disputes arose and especially vigorous reactions from Tuscans. It is very strange that at this stage, when there appeared Bembo's *Prose della volgar lingua* (1525) and Trissino's *Epistola de le lettere nuovamente aggiunte* (1524), none of the defenders of Florentine and Tuscan mention Machiavelli as their predecessor. The simplest answer to this silence would be that the *Dialogo* had not then been written. Indeed I would maintain that it could not have been written before 1525 either by Machiavelli or any other Florentine. From that date it fits the contemporary scene; in 1515 it would be an anachronism, which can no longer blandly be accepted on the basis of the kind of arguments about dating hitherto advanced [24].

Among such arguments is the date of one of the earliest replies to Trissino's *Epistola*, — Lodovico Martelli's *Risposta*, published either in December 1524 or early in 1525 [25]. Martelli argues for the Florentine character of Dante's language, and says several things, especially about vocabulary and the language of comedy, that are strikingly similar to passages of the *Dialogo* attributed to Machiavelli. For Rajna and others these similarities constitute an argument for dating the *Dialogo* before 1525. If Rajna were right, Martelli would have known and borrowed from Machiavelli's unpublished work, and gone into print in Florence in 1524-25 when Machiavelli was still alive; and yet no one protested [26]. Is it not more plausible that the boot was

---

[24] I refrain from giving a list of well-known works on the « questione della lingua » which also deal with Machiavelli on the basis of the *Dialogo*; see B. Migliorini, *Storia della lingua italiana* (Florence, 1960), pp. 339 ff. and especially pp. 351-52. So fixed until now has been the idea that Machiavelli wrote the *Dialogo* about 1514-15 that its originality and precocity at that date and in those circumstances have been completely taken for granted (by myself among others), in spite of the fact that they were implicitly if not explicitly recognized. For instance, Gaspary years ago hit the nail on the head when he wrote: « il M. coglie l'aspetto essenziale della questione sull'origine della lingua letteraria, con un'acutezza *di cui nessun altro diede prova in quel tempo* » (*Storia*, p. 194); and more recently F. Gaeta, *Il teatro*, p. XV: « si può dire che esso (the *Dialogo*) rappresenti *un'anticipata confutazione delle tesi esposte dal Trissino stesso nel Castellano* » (my italics). In spite of such views it was not suspected that this precocity might simply be a fiction based on wrong dating.

[25] The first edition bears no date. The colophon reads simply « Stampata in Fiorenza ». But there is no doubt it follows soon after Trissino's *Epistola*. Cf. Rajna, « La data », and also in *Rass. bibl. della lett. ital.*, XXIV (1916), 257-62.

[26] P. Rajna, « La data », p. 206: « Non è possibile che il Machiavelli non tenesse qualche conto delle cose dette da questo suo concittadino e correligionario se avesse scritto più tardi. E chi esamini attentamente la *Risposta* avendo buona cognizione del *Dialogo* ve ne sentirà in più luoghi l'eco. Donde risulta che il *Dialogo* fu composto in ogni modo prima del 1525 ». The probability that this argument might apply equally well in

on the other foot? Martelli at least appears to have thought he was the first. When refuting the existence of the *lingua cortigiana*, he writes: « E qui parrà forse nuovo a costoro che io così risoluto mi opponga a quello ch'ei dicono che ha lasciato scritto Dante nel suo libro *de vulg. eloquio* ». There is an obvious relationship between Martelli's *Risposta* and the *Dialogo* which needs to be examined further [27]. To my mind the evidence points rather to the priority of the *Risposta*, and this order fits too with other considerations.

Towards the end of the *Dialogo*, writing of the way in which Florentine has been diffused through literary tradition, the author states: « Perché ciascuno sa come i Provenzali cominciarono a scrivere in versi; di Provenza ne venne quest'uso in Sicilia, e di Sicilia in Italia; e intra le provincie d'Italia, in Toscana ... » [28].

---

reverse was precluded by the fixation that Machiavelli wrote the *Dialogo* (with what follows about dating),—and *he* could not possibly have borrowed from Martelli!

[27] Tommasini, *La vita*, II, 353 n., plays down the similarities, but they are very noticeable. The following passages of the *Risposta* may be compared with the *Dialogo* in *Tutte le opere*, pp. 773 and 776-77:

p. a III v^0: « Vedansi etiandio alcune comedie di costoro, nelle quali come hanno ad esprimersi gli comici affetti, e gli festivi detti, corettori argutamente delli comuni errori, eglino non usano cotali affetti e cotali detti quali alla Toscana lingua si confanno, ma delli loro ivi seminano, et fanno diversità tale, che recitati non fanno l'uficio alloro destinato, di ammonire movendo a piacevole riso gli ascoltanti. Di questo non è cagione altra cosa, che l'essere poveri dello nervo istesso della nostra lingua ... »

p. a IIII v^0: « Le dittioni pellegrine che divegnono Toscane, non mutano alla Toscana lingua nome, perciò che esse lo mutano et cosi (come è dritto) la parte segue il tutto non il tutto la parte ». Martelli also speaks (p. a VI v^0) of Dante's « sdegno verso la patria » as the motive for his wishing to deprive Florence of the honour of possessing his works; for which cf. *Dialogo*, pp. 772-73.

There are other links to be explored, even in the language used, — and also obvious dissimilarities, especially in Martelli's use of *Convivio* I and his doubts about Dante's authorship of *De Vulgari Eloquentia*, which have no counterpart in the *Dialogo*.

On Martelli's *Risposta* see Migliorini, *Storia*, pp. 352-53, and his article in *Lingua Nostra*, XI (1950), 77-81. But it is not the only aspect of Martelli's works and career worth further investigation, which must move off from Benedetto Croce's article on him in *Poeti e scrittori del pieno e del tardo Rinascimento*, I (Bari, 1945), pp. 274-89.

[28] Ed. *cit.*, p. 778.

Now this is a remarkable statement to make in 1515, for which knowledge of *De Vulgari Eloquentia* was not enough [29]. Even those who knew most about Provençal at that date, and they were very few indeed, were not in a position to give such an assured picture of the historical development of poetry. The point has not gone unnoticed before, but does not seem to have been related to the date and attribution of the *Dialogo* by those primarily concerned with the question. Debenedetti observed in 1911 in his *Gli studi provenzali in Italia nel Cinquecento*: « Non ci aspetteremmo ... un linguaggio così reciso come quello che tiene l'A. del *Dialogo sulla lingua*, pel quale una questione, *sub iudice*, e che non era ancora divenuta argomento non che d'una speciale trattazione, nemmeno di parziali tentativi o studi, è data come risolta »; and he expressed the opinion that those confident words of the *Dialogo* « sembrerebbero almeno in parte giustificate, quando venissero dopo la pubblicazione delle fortunate *Prose* », i. e. after 1525 [30]. Certainly the idea of Machiavelli as a precocious authority in matters Provençal is very striking; and even as a not quite so precocious knowledgeable fellow in the last two years of his life, it is something to give one pause. In 1515 he would be a decade ahead of Bembo in a field of specialization for which we otherwise have no evidence of his interest or activity. When added to the expertise in linguistics of the *Dialogo*, it reveals an unexpected, and I would say an improbable Machiavelli.

There are other things too to make one pause in this *Dialogo*. I will pass rapidly by the statement of the need to recover languages « per il mezzo di buoni scrittori », which as an idea and expression smacks of a later date than 1515. The first editor, Bottari, in 1730, glossed the passage with a reference from Salviati! [31] Let me recall the passage already quoted accusing Dante

---

[29] The only reference to the priority of Provençal in *De Vulgari Eloquentia* is in Bk. I, x, 3: « Pro se vero argumentatur alia, scilicet *oc*, quod vulgares eloquentes in ea primitus poetati sunt ». Dante's presentation alone is not sufficient to justify an assertion in 1514-15 beginning: « ciascuno sa ». For a prevailing view in the late '400 cf. Lorenzo/Poliziano, *Epistola a Federigo d'Aragona*, in Lorenzo de' Medici, *Opere*, ed. A. Simioni (Bari, 1913), I, 6, where the sequence is Sicily, France, Italy.

[30] (Turin, 1911), pp. 166-67.

[31] Ed. *cit.*, p. 456.

of using the « goffo », the « porco » and « osceno », which spoiled the whole poem. Later, speaking of Ariosto's use in the *Suppositi* of the word « bigonzoni », the author of the *Dialogo* adds: « ... e un gusto purgato sa quanto nel leggere e nell'udire dir *bigonzoni* è offeso. E vedesi facilmente, e in questo e in molti altri luoghi, con quanta difficoltà egli mantiene il decoro di quella lingua ch'egli ha accattato » [32]. I find the idea of Machiavelli, endowed with a « gusto purgato », whose ears and eyes are offended by « bigonzoni », and who speaks in terms of linguistic decorum, out of key with the Machiavelli we otherwise know, particularly the author of the comedies; and this is the context of the remark in the *Dialogo*. If written by Machiavelli in 1515, it is a very interesting comment, though little attention seems to have been paid to what would be his first statement on the language and on the nature and function of comedy before he wrote *Mandragola* (1518) and *Clizia* (1525). The recent suggestion that the *Andria* represents an « esperimento di traduzione della comicità terenziana nei moduli del fiorentino parlato, conformemente a quanto, probabilmente nello stesso volgere di tempo, il Machiavelli aveva teorizzato nel *Dialogo sulla lingua* », needs more thorough examination, especially as this is then used to date the *Andria* near 1515 and before *Mandragola* [33]. It is the « gusto purgato » and decorum of the *Dialogo* that make one doubt Machiavelli's authorship in 1514-15, or indeed even later. For a later date, and after 1524 as I have so far been arguing, there is, however, something to be said for a correspondence between the *Dialogo* and the prologue to *Clizia*. Such similarities do not constitute proof of their inter-dependence, for the same ideas exist in common sources, mainly Donatus and Cicero. But, if the *Dialogo* is Machiavelli's, this is the more likely date and place to explore correspondences than ten years earlier [34].

---

[32] *Tutte le opere*, p. 777. If I am correct about the later dating of the *Dialogo*, its author was perhaps using the Roman edition of 27 Sept. 1524 of the *Suppositi*, not the first which was printed in Florence by an unknown printer « non dopo il 1512 » (cf. R. Ridolfi, « La seconda edizione della *Mandragola* e un codicillo sopra la prima », in *La Bibliofilia*, LXVI [1964], 49-55; though it is not clear why the edition is dated before 1512).

[33] F. Gaeta, *Il teatro*, pp. XI-XII.

[34] Compare *Tutte le opere*, p. 662 (*Clizia*) and p. 777 (*Dialogo*), where the list of stock characters corresponds to some extent but is longer in the

While on the subject of comedy I ought at this point to answer the inevitable objection to a late dating of the *Dialogo* arising from the allusion therein to « uno degli Ariosti di Ferrara ». Up to now this manner of referring to the author of the *Orlando Furioso* has been interpreted as a firm date-barrier, 1517, beyond which the *Dialogo* could not have been written [34a]; the assumption being that it was impossible, if not indeed also disrespectful, to refer in this way, after the first edition of the *Orlando* (1516), to its famous author. The assumptions of instant fame and of disrespectful form are open to question not only in 1517 but probably until 1532, by which date it *is* arguable that failure to distinguish Lodovico from the other by no means undistinguished members of his family would not be admissible. To suppose that within that period the phrase « uno degli Ariosti » intends or implies disrespect is not only to disregard the probable historical reasons indicated, but to assume overtones that were not at all necessarily implied. It need not mean that the author of the *Dialogo* either knew who was the author of the *Suppositi* but chose to demote him by imprecision of name, or did not know and was consequently vague. The only truly important factor in the context of the argument is that the author of the comedy referred to is not a Tuscan or Florentine but a Ferrarese; and down to and even beyond 1525 « uno degli Ariosti di Ferrara » would be admissible and do no injustice historically to the writer either of the comedies or the *Orlando*. To assume the opposite overlooks the facts, and results from superimposition of our own later criteria of relative fame and proper appellation which do not suit the times [35].

---

former. For the observations about comedy in these passages and their probable sources, see M. Herrick, *Comic Theory in the Sixteenth Century* (Urbana, 1950), chaps. III, V and VI, 214-22 (in which, however, there is no specific reference to Machiavelli).

[34a] Hans Baron, «Machiavelli on the Eve of the *Discourses*», is an exception to the general opinion on this point. He suggests, however, an explanation which I find difficult to accept, viz. that the author of the *Dialogo* had no need to be precise about this name when addressing Dante who would not know him anyway for obvious reasons of chronology.

[35] The Ariosto family was numerous and well-known in the 15th and 16th centuries, and others besides Lodovico distinguished themselves in letters or politics. See the relative entries in *Dizionario biografico degli Italiani*, vol. IV (Rome, 1962), especially for Alfonso (to whom Castiglione de-

If I am right in my contention that the *Dialogo* was not written before 1525, can it still be regarded as Machiavelli's work? From a strictly practical point of view it would have to have been written by him in 1525 on his return from Venice late in September, or, less likely, in 1526 during his brief October residence in Florence [36]. In either case the reference to the « felicità e sì tranquillo stato » of Florence would have to be taken as comparative with the rest of Italy and in any event as hyperbolical. Furthermore the contradiction with *Arte della Guerra* over the composition of Roman armies forms an obstacle; though it would not be impossible or inadmissible for Machiavelli to change his mind in the direction opposite from the one so far supposed. In this same direction it would be possible to argue a correspondence between the two works in the parallel formula used in both for the switch from narration to dialogue [37]. I would not be too sure, however, that this parallel is sufficiently unique to prove that Machiavelli also wrote the *Dialogo*, any more than do the similarities between this and the prologue to *Clizia* already referred to above.

The really formidable considerations against Machiavelli's authorship are those of interest, knowledge and equipment. If these were, as I have tried to show, improbable and indeed impossible, in 1514-15, they were at least more probable in 1525. From late 1524 to 1530 was *the* period of intense dispute over the question of language, and it is unlikely that Machiavelli remained totally indifferent to it. In fact we know that he did not. The record is not exactly contemporary, but it is close and extremely precise. In his book *In difesa della lingua fiorentina di Dante*, posthumously published in Florence in 1566, Carlo Lenzoni has one of his speakers in the dialogue, G-B Gelli, recount an episode in which, during discussion in Florence soon after

---

dicated his *Cortegiano*) and Gabriele (who completed his brother Lodovico's comedy *I Studenti*). I have to thank Prof. Dionisotti for persuading me that this interpretation of « uno degli Ariosti » is more plausible than my original explanation of it as a probable palaeographic error (*uno* for *L*[co] = Lodovico).

36 Cf. R. Ridolfi, *Vita*, pp. 339 and 366.

37 See *Tutte le opere*, pp. 268 and 774. Even if Machiavelli was unusual in using this formula, the *Arte della Guerra* was in print from 1521, and from then on anyone could have used it.

the publication of Bembo's *Prose*, Machiavelli confounds a Venetian nobleman, named Maffio, by pointing out the absurdity and ridicule which would arise if a Florentine learned Venetian from works of literature and attempted to teach it to the Venetians themselves [38]. This circumstantial and credible account,

---

[38] Ed. *cit.*, pp. 26-27: « Ma che bisogna che io vadia hor faccendo il Catalogo degli scelti, a dimostrarvi quanto sia stata conosciuta, desiderata, & cerca da gli huomini grandi, la predetta urbanità? Se meglio volete vedere la importanza sua; & s'ella si impara da' libri soli: Non vi dispiaccia udire la fine d'un'ragionamento, havuto sin' quando vennon' fuori le prose del Bembo; su'l Cartolaio de' Giunti, da Niccolò Macchiavelli; con un' Messer Maffio Veniziano, che del casato non mi ricorda; ma gentilhuomo da bene, & persona (per quanto si disse all'hora) molto garbata & litterata. S. L. Digrazia Gello caro: perché io ho sempre sentito ricordare il Machiavello, per uno ingegno, (come voi altri dite) molto capresto. GEL. Disputavasi di questa materia medesima, presenti alcuni litterati Fiorentini & forestieri; Et nel più bel del ragionamento, parendo forse al Machiavello, che astutamente gli fusse stato rotto il filo del parlare, così vivo, & così pronto, come egli era di sua natura; continovando più la sentenzia, che le parole, disse. Ditemi digrazia Magnifico Messer Maffio; Se qual si voglia più litterato Fiorentino che ci sia; havesse imparato a parlar Veniziano, in Firenze, in Roma, in Napoli, o simili altri luoghi; da gli scritti de' vostri Poeti & Prosatori, come verbi grazia fanno gl'Italiani, de'l Franzese, & de lo Spagnuolo; Et (per non dire hor' cosa alcuna de la Pronunzia, & vedete pur quanto ella vaglia) vi scrivesse di diverse materie, come occorre spesso di conferire a gli amici: Non conoscereste voi, che egli userebbe molte parole, & modi di dire, fuora dell'uso, & proprietà naturale, della vostra Città? Conosceremolo certamente rispose quel gentilhuomo; & mal' potrebbe egli fare altrimenti. Et non v'increscerebbe per ciò de la semplicità sua, seguitò il Machiavello; se egli fusse oltre a litterato, pur gentilhuomo ancor esso: Et si persuadesse di scriverla come voi altri nativi, od allevati di quella? Mo senza dubio rispose egli; & molto più che d'ogn'altro. Et come non ridereste voi poi, soggiunse il Machiavello; Se egli divenisse tanto ardito; che egli riprendesse i modi vostri del parlare, o dello scrivere; Et volesse darvene precetti; & sottoporvi religiosamente alle parole, modi di parlare, & regole del Giustiniano; & de gl'altr'antichi vostri; più tosto che del Cosmico; o del Cosmico, più tosto che de gl'altri? Et in quella stessa guisa, che nel suo Bruto fa Marco Tullio de gl' Oratori; Volesse ancor giudicare; chi di voi habbia parlato, o parli, più Venizianamente, & meglio? Qui restando sospeso M. Maffio; & pensando forse, o di tornare adietro, o di fare una risposta, che rivolgesse altrove, quello che egli si vedea venire à dosso: il Machiavello, come quelli che con si fatte persone, volse sempre vedere il fin' delle cose, senza dargli più tempo, subitamente soggiunse. Ridereste certo sopra ogni piacevol modo, & non hareste forse rimedio alcuno, à non fare, come Filemone: Ancora che questo Fiorentino, dicesse nelle sue regole, molte & molte cose notabili e buone.

which may be based on Lenzoni's own experience, is clear evidence of Machiavelli's interest and position in relation to the current dispute raised by Bembo's work [39]; and it is all the more significant in that it is the only testimony to his interest in such matters before the attribution to him in 1577 by Ricci of the *Dialogo*. It also contains a phrase similar to one twice used in the *Dialogo* [40]. If the latter is not mere coincidence, it could indicate that Lenzoni knew the *Dialogo* as a work of Machiavelli.

This is an extremely important point. The episode in Lenzoni's work, for all its importance in proving Machiavelli's interest and position in the dispute, does not constitute proof of Machiavelli's authorship of the *Dialogo*; it makes it more probable by eloquently filling the silence that otherwise precedes the emergence of Ricci's MS. There is no doubt, however, that if Lenzoni did know the *Dialogo* and believed it Machiavelli's, he could have no sympathy with its attitude to Dante. As this is fundamental to the argument of the *Dialogo*, it is questionable whether, knowing the work, Lenzoni would think of Machiavelli as an ideal representative of the Florentine point of view. In short the only thing in common between the *Dialogo* and Lenzoni's anecdote is that they both express a view on a similar linguistic issue; beyond this general similarity the substance and arguments are quite different. In this light it is difficult to see Lenzoni's phrase « non potendo più l'Arte che la Natura »

Perché e' sarebbe forza (non potendo più l'Arte che la Natura) che egli, non essendo stato lungo tempo in Venezia a questo fine; e non havendo voluto, esser prima paziente scolare, che prosontuoso maestro: Per non conoscere quanto si converrebbe: vi mettesse di quelle parole, di que' modi di parlare, di quelle superstizioni, & falsi giudizii finalmente, che vi farebbono al tutto fare, lo effetto detto. Ma lasciamo i[l] Machiavello, che aspetta ancor la risposta, da'l Magnifico M. Maffio: Et ditemi voi ... ».

[39] On Lenzoni and his *Difesa*, see Barbi, *Della fortuna di Dante*, pp. 26-30. Lenzoni died in 1551, probably at the age of 45-50 judging by the remarks of Cosimo Bartoli in his *Orazione*, printed at the end of the *Difesa*, (p. [216]): « ... ma a noi quindici o venti anni ancora di vita nel nostro Carlo, sariano paruti assai lunghi, nè tanto di te (i. e. Death) ci dorremo ... parendoci che in quella età, non fusse poi conveniente il biasimarte ... ».

[40] The phrase, toward the end of the passage quoted above: « non potendo più l'Arte che la Natura ». Cf. *Dialogo*, p. 775 (« perché l'arte non può mai in tutto repugnare alla natura ») and p. 777 (« perché gli è impossibile che l'arte possa più che la natura »).

as more than a coincidence with the two similar phrases in the *Dialogo*. Indeed it is more arguable from Lenzoni's silence about the substance of the *Dialogo* and his representation of Machiavelli in this anecdote, that he did not know the work, or at least did not think it to be Machiavelli's. In other words Lenzoni's story gives us one picture, and a welcome one, of Machiavelli's interest in the current disputes; but it is not the same picture as we have from the *Dialogo*, and this testimony gives no real support to the authenticity of the tradition of this text as we have it from Ricci in 1577. At that point Machiavelli's name became attached to this work, not without some reserves on Ricci's part, on the authority of others unnamed whose credentials we do not know, and on the word of an old man who may indeed never have seen or read this particular work. Looked at dispassionately this is a slender thread on which to hang a certain attribution, and it has against it still those unanswered questions about Machiavelli's philological competence and his disposition towards Dante, to be seen now not in relation to 1514-15 but to the last two years of his life. If he did compose it then, we have to set aside the contradiction with the *Arte della Guerra*, and accept a Machiavelli with a knowledge and competence in language and Italian in particular, and in the history of poetry from Provence to Tuscany, remarkable even at that date; a Machiavelli possessed of a « gusto purgato » sensitive in comedy to a word like « bigonzoni », and the severest and most arrogant critic of Dante in the early Cinquecento. We would also have to accept a work in several respects stylistically different from Machiavelli's other writings [41].

It would in any case follow from my argument about dating that the correspondence drawn on the basis of the *Dialogo* by Dr. Baron between Machiavelli's linguistic and historical ideas, bridging the gap between *Principe* and *Discorsi*, would go by the board. Yet the question remains whether, outside that specific chronological context, the *Dialogo* contains passages truly and only characteristic of Machiavelli's historical outlook. Those quoted by Baron are: the movements of people or ideas and

[41] This stylistic difference was noted by Ricci (see note 15 above), and has since been mentioned but not taken seriously. It needs further investigation.

skills from one province or city to another with consequent movement of vocabulary and its assimilation into the language of the new place; language seen in this process of transfer and development as a historical evolution; the corruption of language in time and the need to regenerate it through recourse to the good writers of the past [42]. It is undeniable that in the *Dialogo* language is seen as evolving historically, but is this as Machiavellian as Baron's presentation suggests? The idea of assimilation is in Martelli's *Risposta*, though not developed with the cultural or commercial implications of the *Dialogo* [43]. The regeneration of languages that have been *lost* through decay is not quite the straight parallel with the *Discorsi* Baron maintains: it means a *renovatio ab origine* when the continuity has been completely interrupted, a recovery of what is lost, not a revitalization of the present on the principles of the past. These considerations are not intended to prove that Machiavelli did not write or could not have written such passages, but merely to pose the question whether they could not have been written by someone else after Machiavelli. In short, if we had no external evidence to suggest that the *Dialogo* was by Machiavelli, would we be able to attribute it to him on the basis of such passages as these? Are they in themselves sufficient to counterbalance the other considerations enumerated at the end of the preceding paragraph?

These are questions impossible at present to answer definitively, particularly as there is no other claimant to the authorship of the *Dialogo* now in the field. But it appears from this review that the matter is open to further enquiry. What appears to be no longer open to question is its composition no earlier than 1525, — and probably no later than 1530, judging from the intensely patriotic and republican fervour of the author [44]. The consequence of this chronological shift are admittedly considerable: the loss of what previously seemed a remarkable

[42] Baron, « Machiavelli on the Eve of the *Discourses* », pp. 470-73.

[43] See above, note 27.

[44] See the opening paragraph of the *Dialogo*, pp. 770-71. I infer « republican » from the reference to Brutus. Pre-1530 seems most probable, but I do not exclude entirely the possibility that it could have been written later still, perhaps even in the days of Muzio and Borghini when the linguistic disputes flared up again.

early chapter in the history of Dante's *De vulgari eloquentia*, and the removal from Machiavelli, at the very least, of his claims to linguistic precocity. There is no doubt that the *Dialogo* depreciates in value when moved to later than 1524, and even more when subtracted from Machiavelli; though it would still remain a remarkably incisive document that would do honour to whoever wrote it. Only Dante would perhaps gain by losing Machiavelli as his most aggressive and harsh critic of that period. Or could this not perhaps also be a gain for Machiavelli?

CARLO PINCIN

OSSERVAZIONI SUL MODO DI PROCEDERE DI MACHIAVELLI NEI *DISCORSI**

* Il presente studio è stato scritto mentre l'autore riceveva una borsa Fulbright presso The Harvard University Center for Italian Renaissance Studies a Villa I Tatti.

Vedendo che gli uomini del suo tempo non agiscono e a torto disperano di poter agire come gli antichi agivano, Machiavelli vuol intraprendere un'opera di educazione dell'umanità e scrive i *Discorsi sopra la prima deca di Tito Livio* nei quali insegna a leggere le storie. Un tale programma era originale, e in che misura? Quali erano in proposito le idee del suo tempo? Quali le idee di Machiavelli avanti la composizione di quest'opera?

Con la nuova vita delle città, assistiamo, nella letteratura e nelle arti figurative, a un moltiplicarsi di raccolte di esempi e biografie di uomini illustri: ad uso dei cittadini si raffigurano le azioni da imitare e quelle da fuggire, secondo la vecchia concezione dell'*historia magistra vitae*, e spesso esempi vengono proposti come precetti travestiti: lo scrittore e l'artista « sanno » ciò che è bene e ciò che è male e con un sapiente uso di esempi e della mozione degli affetti insegnano a seguire il primo e a fuggire il secondo. Ma si incontra anche la concezione che una conoscenza non addomesticata di come sono andate le cose sia utile. Così, nel tempo in cui si scrivono cronache di città da parte di cittadini di queste città — mercanti, notai, giudici, cancellieri — si moltiplicano le copie, spesso istoriate, di Svetonio, Valerio Massimo, Livio. Urgeva additare ai cittadini altri esempi che quelli biblici o delle vite di santi. Un cancelliere della repubblica fiorentina, Coluccio Salutati, scrive a Juan Hernandez de Heredia per offrirgli una traduzione dell' Odissea in latino in cambio di un volgarizzamento di Plutarco, che avrebbe resa possibile una sua diffusione tra lettori italiani ignari di grammatica. « Lasciamo agli altri — egli dice — speculare ardui concetti che, una volta appresi, non servono a far l'uomo migliore né più saggio nella vita umana. Studiamo la storia. Essa offre una miniera di esempi all' imitazione di principi e cittadini, insegna a fuggire i pericoli e ad amministrar bene le cose; e l'esempio è più efficace dei precetti. Non c' è vizio o virtù di cui la storia non dia esempi. Vuoi un esempio di giustizia? Ecco Bruto, Torquato, Orazio Coclite, Sicinio, Sergio. Di buoni costumi? Lucrezia, Orithya, Zanobia ». Gli esempi sono tratti per lo più da Valerio Massimo [1].

Ancora Valerio Massimo, poiché dalle storie egli prese esempi di virtù per far gli uomini buoni più che per erudirli, è scelto per le sue lezioni veronesi da Guarino, che era stato pure lui a Firenze. Tra gli scrittori, — dice nella sua prolusione — i più importanti sono gli storici. I filosofi annoiano coi loro precetti, ma chi non s' infiammerà all'esempio di Regolo e di tanti altri? Ciò che è stato serve a conoscere ciò che sarà. Si stimano i vecchi perché videro molte cose e Omero cantò Ulisse « di molte virtù » perché « vide molte cose, uomini, città »; quanto si deve quindi stimare chi conosce la storia, cioè non solo le cose dell'età sua, ma di tante età, diventando così maturo nel giro di pochi anni! Cita Cic., *Or.* II, 36; osserva che nel leggere le storie, più ancora dell'utilità è grande il diletto [2].Della lode ciceroniana della storia come *lux veritatis* Guarino si serve per la sua propria professione di fede nell'alto ufficio dello storico: se non si può dire la verità, meglio tacere [3]. Scrivendo sulla forma di scrivere storie a Tobia dal Borgo, che andava alla corte di Rimini con l'ufficio di storico,

---

[1] *Epistolario di Coluccio Salutati*, ed. F. Novati, II, Roma, 1893, pp. 289-302. Bruto, Sicinio, Sergio, Lucrezia, pur se con diversa conoscenza delle fonti, già per es. in *Ioannis Saresberiensis Policraticus*, ed. C. I. Webb, Oxford, 1909, IV, XI Webb I 273, 21; VI, XVI Webb II, 41, 12; II, XXVII Webb I 158, 1; cfr. H. Liebeschütz, *Mediaeval humanism in the life and writings of John of Salisbury*, London, 1950, pp. 67-73; F. Novati, *Le origini*, ed. A. Monteverdi, Milano, 1926, pp. 432-433; T. E. Mommsen, *Petrarch and the decoration of the Sala virorum illustrium in Padua*, « The Art Bulletin », XXXIV, 1952, pp. 95-116; N. Rubinstein, *Political ideas in Sienese art* ecc., « Journal of the Warburg and Courtauld Institutes », XXI, 1958, pp. 179-207; T. Hankey, *Salutati's epigrams for the Palazzo Vecchio at Florence*, *ibid.*, XXII, 1959, pp. 363-365; D. Marzi, *La cancelleria della Repubblica fiorentina*, Rocca San Casciano, 1910; E. Garin, *I cancellieri umanisti della Repubblica fiorentina da Coluccio Salutati a Bartolomeo Scala*, « Rivista storica italiana », LXXI, 1959, pp. 185-208, poi con aggiunte in *La cultura filosofica del Rinascimento italiano*, Firenze, 1961, pp. 3-37. Ringrazio Miss Lucy Bauer per alcune gentili conversazioni e indicazioni.

[2] K. Müllner, *Acht Inauguralreden des Veronensers Guarino und seines Sohnes Battista. Ein Beitrag zur Geschichte des Pädagogik des Humanismus*, « Wiener Studien », XVIII, 1896, pp. 283-306, a pp. 292-294. La prolusione è del 1426 c.

[3] *Epistolario di Guarino Veronese*, ed. R. Sabbadini, I, Venezia, 1915, pp. 611-612. Cfr. R. Sabbadini, *Il metodo degli umanisti*, Firenze, 1920, pp. 83 e 79.

Guarino dice che le storie — a differenza della poesia — devono sempre dire la verità e devono essere intelligibili a tutti [4].

All'utilità civile mira nelle sue opere il cancelliere Leonardo Bruni. Nella *Historia Florentini populi* riafferma che, se si ritengono più sapienti coloro che hanno visto più cose, tanto più si deve stimare la storia [5]. Nel *De studiis et litteris* dice che è bello conoscere la storia del proprio popolo e quella dei popoli liberi [6]; ma nella dedicatoria del *De bello Italico* afferma che lo storico deve scrivere « tam prospera quam adversas res », giacché si può sperare il meglio, ma si deve scrivere quello che è stato [7].

Un altro cittadino di Firenze, Giovanni Cavalcanti, usa la storia per comporre un libro educativo che manda a Neri di Gino Capponi, del quale esalta le virtù. « Da queste cosiffatte tue excelentie — egli scrive — m'à mosso talento di ridurre delle cose passate et delle odierne al tuo figliuolo presenti in questo mio brieve volume »; e infatti usa accanto ad esempi antichi, esempi tratti dalle sue *Istorie fiorentine* [8]. In polemica con coloro che troppo lodavano l'antichità, Benedetto Accolti, successore di Poggio Bracciolini nella cancelleria fiorentina, professore nello Studio, osserva che non era giusto accusare il suo tempo e quello precedente: nonostante tutto vi erano pur state città libere come Firenze e Venezia, ed era da rammaricarsi piuttosto che esse e i loro grandi uomini non avessero trovato degli storici [9].

In questo tempo un'altra voce del mondo antico sull'utilità delle storie entra in circolazione con la traduzione latina di

---

[4] *Epistolario di Guarino* cit., II, pp. 460-465, n. 796, ll. 102, 223.

[5] L. Bruni, *Historia Florentini populi*, ed. E. Santini, in *Rerum Italicarum scriptores* di L. A. Muratori, nuova ed., XIX, 3, p. 3, 15.

[6] *Leonardo Bruni Aretino Humanistisch-philosophische Schriften mit einer Chronologie seiner Werke und Briefe hg. v. H. Baron*, Leipzig-Berlin, 1928, p. 13.

[7] *Ibid.*, p. 147. Cfr. B. L. Ullman, *Leonardo Bruni and humanistic historiography*, « Medievalia and Humanistica », IV, 1946, pp. 45-61, poi in *Studies in the Italian Renaissance*, Roma, 1955, pp. 321-344, a p. 329.

[8] Firenze, Bibl. Riccardiana, Ms. 2431, c. 1 v; dopo l'ed. parziale di F. P[olidori] in B. Cavalcanti, *Istorie fiorentine*, I, II, Firenze, 1838, sta ora studiando l'opera la signora Marcella Grendler; ringrazio dell'indicazione l'amico Tony Molho.

[9] B. Accolti, *De praestantia virorum sui aevi dialogus*, ed. Bacchini (1689), rist. in *Filippi Villani liber de civitatis Florentiae famosis civibus* ecc., ed. G. C. Galletti, Firenze, 1847, pp. 101-128, a p. 112.

Polibio [10]. In volgare, a Firenze, l'utilità della storia è riaffermata da Donato Acciaioli, nella traduzione delle *Storie* del Bruni commissionatagli dalla Signoria [11]. Più volte i concetti riecheggiano nello Studio fiorentino. Nella sua prolusione al corso sulla *Pharsalia* e sul *De bello civili*, Bartolomeo della Fonte, protetto di Bernardo Rucellai, dice che legger le storie è come aver vissuto al tempo degli antichi, aver assistito alle loro azioni. La lettura di ciò che hanno fatto loro, in bene e in male, ci insegna cosa s' ha da fare noi. E poiché dicono i savi che l'esperienza di molte cose faccia prudenza, chi legge la storia supera facilmente i suoi maggiori: quanto infatti un lungo periodo contiene più esempi dell'età di un uomo, tanto si deve stimare più prudente chi conosce non solo il suo proprio popolo e il suo proprio tempo, ma tutti i popoli di tutti i tempi. La storia — egli osserva — si differenzia dalle altre discipline, nelle quali ragionando si cavano conseguenze dalle premesse: la storia « non rationibus, sed rebus adhibita oratione conficitur » [12]. A sua volta, nella prolusione al corso su Svetonio, il Poliziano ribadisce i medesimi concetti, citando gli esempi di Lucullo che leggeva storie navigando, di Alessandro Severo che consultava gli storici, dell' imperatrice Zenobia. Il desiderio di gloria spinge alle grandi azioni, come si vede nei tempi antichi e — per contrario — in quelli moderni, nei quali, per essere quello mancato, manca la virtù. Passando a dare precetti a chi scrive storie, e insegna per esempi, il Poliziano afferma che lo storico persegue il medesimo fine del legislatore, ma con insegnamenti, non con torture. Plutarco e Svetonio non valgono meno di Erodoto e Sallustio: la biografia ha un alto valore educativo. Di Svetonio loda l' indipendenza. Ricorda l'esempio di Alessandro che strappa il libro bugiardo di mano ad Aristotele che glielo leggeva. Dice che lo storico deve lavorare coscienziosamente, come fa l'arti-

---

[10] *Polybii Historiarum libri superstites e Graeco in Latinum sermonem conversi a N. Perotto*, Roma, 1473.

[11] *Istorie fiorentine di Leonardo Aretino* trad. in volgare da D. Acciaioli, (1473), I, II, Firenze, 1855, 1857, I, p. 47.

[12] B. Fontius, *Orationes in eloquentiam, in historiam* ecc. s. l. a., cc. a 7 v e segg. Nuova ed. parziale e analisi di C. Trinkaus in « Studies in the Renaissance », VII, 1960, pp. 99-105, a pp. 100-101.

giano, dire coraggiosamente la verità, scrivere per i posteri, che sono giudici severi [13].

In volgare, traducendo Appiano dal latino, Alessandro Braccesi, segretario nella cancelleria fiorentina, si rivolge a un pubblico più vasto. Con un andamento che ricorda Cat. 76, attacca il proemio a Giampaolo Orsini [14]:

> Se dalli antiqui scriptori è attribuito non mediocre grado di sapientia a chi ha veduto molte città e cognosciuti e governi et costumi di molti populi et di varie nationi, certamente non piccola obligatione dobbiamo havere alli auctori delle Historie, perché oltre al fare equale la prudentia di quelli che leghono le cose facte da altri alla prudentia di chi ha veduto le città et costumi di molti, sono cagione ancora, che mentre leggiamo li egregii et memorandi facti d'altri, si desta et infiamma nelli animi nostri uno ardore e quasi stimulo alle opere excellenti et preclare per la cupidità della gloria, la quale dopo la morte resta nella memoria de' viventi, et è cosa egregia et utilissima allo uso delle genti la cognitione di varii exempli et casi, conciò sia che da quelli siamo amaestrati in che modo si convenga instruire la vita nostra et con examinare le virtù et vitii alieni et con intendere quello che è suto facto in diversi tempi da varie persone, è facile proporsi la imitatione delle cose migliori. Considerando adunque la historia havere congiunto seco il fructo con la delectatione per la noticia che ha in sé et perché con le cose preterite insegna governare le presenti et prevedere le future, ho giudicato non dovere da quelli, a' quali sono incognite le lettere latine, essere reputata ingrata questa mia exercitatione della traductione di Appiano...

Nei tempi più vicini ai *Discorsi*, da Napoli viene l'*Actius* di Pontano, un dialogo diretto a chi scrive storie. Lo storico dovrà riferire le opinioni e gli intenti di chi agisce, come fanno Livio e Sallustio, dei quali viene mostrato il modo di procedere; dovrà

---

13 *A. Politiani Opera*, Venetiis 1498, cc. [aa VI] - aa X. La *praefatio* è del 1490-91. Sulla tradizione cfr. *Mostra del Poliziano, Catalogo*, a cura di A. Perosa, Firenze, 1955, n° 6. Al seguito il Poliziano dà un saggio di storia della vita e opere di Suetonio, su cui cfr. G. Brugnoli in « Giornale italiano di filologia », X, 1957, pp. 211-220.

14 *Hoc in volumine continentur bellum Carthaginese Syrum Particum et Mithridaticum in vulgari sermone*, Roma, 1502, c. [2]. L'opera fu ristampata da Bernardo Giunta nel 1520, dopo che l'anno avanti era uscita postuma la traduzione del Braccesi *Appiano Alessandrino delle guerre civili dei Romani* ecc. a cura di G. Pandolfini.

riferire « praesagia, auguria, vaticinia, oracula, visiones, sacrificia » [15]. Gli storici meritano lode non meno dei legislatori: per merito loro sappiamo chi primo conobbe Dio, chi fece le leggi, aperse i segreti della natura, trovò le arti e le norme di vita con le quali il genere umano lasciando i boschi cominciò a vivere libero in città e nacquero la pietà e la giustizia [16]. Le storie narrano l'umano incivilimento, dai primordi della società, in tutte le sue manifestazioni: religione e diritto, scienze e arti. Per valutare la posizione di Pontano non sarà forse inutile risalire a un opuscolo scritto mezzo secolo avanti da Poggio Bracciolini. In un dialoghetto, di cui non interessano le conclusioni ma le idee che emergono in chiara formulazione, parlano un medico e un legista. Osserva il legista come i primi uomini, per evitare i danni che gli venivano dal vivere in rapporti di pura forza, si trovarono nella necessità di istituire leggi. Quale necessità, — ribatte il medico — le necessità si cercano per naturale impulso, come il cibo ecc.; le leggi invece furono imposte contro la volontà dei singoli e dei popoli, e bisognò fargli credere, per convincerli, che erano date da Dio, impaurirli. Così fecero Menes, Minosse, Licurgo, Zoroastro, Zamolxis, ma non fece così anche Mosè? e poi Numa, come tutti sanno [17]. Si può osservare che in bocca al legista è messa la teoria epicurea della nascita della società, in bocca al medico una comparazione — che in un minimo necessario innova Diod. I, 94 — tra l'opera di vari fondatori di *leges*. Sembra di poter concludere che al tempo di Machiavelli — scoperti, sulla scia della diffusione di Lucrezio, i legami reciproci nella società di diritto e religione, scienze e arti — si trova espressa l'esigenza di una storia integrale.

I pochi testi fin qui accennati contengono enunciazioni dell'utilità pratica della storia e rappresentano la coscienza diffusa nel pensiero riflesso di una concezione espressa in numerosissimi prodotti del tempo, dalla letteratura alle arti figurative. Secondo tale concezione le storie insegnano per mezzo di modelli offerti

---

[15] G. Pontano, *Dialoghi*, ed. C. Previtera, Firenze, 1943, p. 218, 5-6 e 29. Non mi sembra che in quest'ultima frase si debba ravvisare — col Sabbadini cit., p. 81 — un passo indietro rispetto a Petrarca e Bruni.

[16] *Ibid.*, p. 229, 29-40.

[17] *Poggii Historia tripartita, disputatiuncula secunda*, in *Opera*, 1513, cc. 15 r-20 r, rist. in *La disputa delle arti nel Quattrocento*, ed. E. Garin, Firenze, 1947, pp. 20, 28.

all'imitazione. Nel pensiero riflesso, l'affermazione della superiorità dell'esempio rispetto al precetto è constatazione di una maggior efficacia educativa dell'esempio; ma non soltanto questo. In Salutati la constatazione è diretta contro le speculazioni inutili alla vita civile; analogamente in Guarino; in Poliziano è insieme affermazione del primato delle lettere sul diritto. Come si constata nella vita civile esser naturale l'ambizione, così si nota — come già gli antichi — che la storia soddisfa il desiderio di gloria o, altri osservano con diverse sfumature, quasi il naturale istinto di autoconservazione dell'uomo. Soprattutto diviene di dominio comune il concetto della storia come prolungamento dell'esperienza di vita, « car nostre vie est si briefve qu' elle ne suffit à avoir de tant de choses experience », osserva Commynes, e « plus se veoit de choses en ung seul livre en trois mois que n'en sauroient veoir à l'oeil et entendre par experience vingt hommes de renc vivans l'ung après l'autre » [18]. La riflessione tocca anche il modo di procedere, e si ravvisa una opposizione tra il modo di procedere dello storico e quello di molti altri: la storia, si dice, si confeziona con un discorso applicato alle cose.

Ma coloro che più tale consapevolezza avevano raggiunto, cosa facevano? Tenevano lezioni negli Studi, piene spesso di senso storico. Scrivevano storie nelle quali nuove scoperte balenavano a tratti, tra le preponderanti preoccupazioni stilistiche e retoriche. Scrivevano talora intorno alla disciplina dello storico, in latino, rivolgendosi agli scrittori di storie, anche in questi scritti dando gran parte ai precetti di stile. La produzione ad alto livello era in latino, le nuove tecniche di ricerca e le nuove idee si apprendevano da parte di chi poteva frequentare gli Studi o comunque da cerchie ristrette; la gente comune continuava a consumare esempi intesi nel senso tradizionale. L'uso delle storie in un'opera educativa e in volgare si nota nel Cavalcanti, che faceva quello che sapeva fare, a livello quasi popolare. Non sappiamo di qualcuno che pensasse a scrivere un'opera di altissimo livello in volgare, destinata al più largo pubblico di

---

[18] Philippe de Commynes, *Mémoires*, ed. J. Calmette, Paris, 1924-25, I, pp. 129, 130. Non è forse fuori luogo osservare che nel contesto l'autore si appella all'esperienza fatta stando diciott'anni intorno ai principi per concludere che essa gli ha mostrato che conviene che i principi leggano le storie.

lettori, con l' intento di insegnare a questi infiniti a leggere le storie.

Il risultato è, secondo Machiavelli all'epoca dei *Discorsi*, che al suo tempo gli uomini si dilettano di leggere le storie, ma la lettura non ha conseguenze nella vita pratica. Eppure è chiaro che non si cambiano le cose se gli uomini — molti uomini — non imparano ad agire. Formatosi fuori dello Studio, in letture, conversazioni, nella cancelleria che allarga la sua esperienza delle cose del suo tempo, in missioni al servizio della repubblica, Machiavelli coi *Discorsi* per primo si rivolge ai lettori delle storie, al più vasto pubblico, scrivendo in volgare, con l' intento di insegnare agli uomini come leggere le storie. L' interesse, lasciato il campo dello stile, è rivolto alla sostanza: si tratta di saper leggere e capire le storie, poi anche eventualmente di saperne scrivere; ma l' intento non è insegnare a scrivere storie, ma insegnare ad agire, a cambiare il mondo. Quanto a Machiavelli, quando — essendogli interciso monstrar con altre imprese altra virtù — scriverà storie in proprio, accetterà parte dei precetti che venivano dati agli storici; le *Istorie fiorentine* sono anche un prodotto tipico degli ideali del tempo in proposito. Ma, al di là e nonostante tale carattere, l' importanza delle *Istorie* è nel nuovo modo di leggere le storie che ne sta alla base e che viene insegnato nei *Discorsi*.

Già nel 1500, nella sua legazione in Francia a Luigi XII, Machiavelli, a quanto egli stesso riferisce ai Dieci [19], disse al cardinale di Rouen

che questa maestà si doveva bene guardare da coloro che cercavono la distruzione degli amici suoi non per altro che per fare più potenti loro e più facile ad trarli l' Italia dalle mani; ad che questa maestà doveva riparare e seguire l'ordine di coloro che (vogliono, *cancellato*) hanno per lo addrieto volsuto possedere una provincia esterna, che è diminuire e potenti, vezeggiar li subditi, mantenere li amici e guardarsi da' compagni, cioè da coloro che vogliono in tale luogo havere equale autorità. E quando questa maestà ragguardassi chi in Italia li volessi essere compagnio, troverrebbe che non sarieno né le S. V. né Ferrara né Bologna, ma quelli che sempre per lo addreto hanno cercho di dominarla.

---

[19] Firenze, Biblioteca Nazionale Centrale, *Carte Machiavelli*, I, 17; cfr. N. Machiavelli, *Le opere*, per cura di P. Fanfani, L. Passerini, G. Milanesi, Firenze, Roma, III, 1875, pp. 237-238.

Nel referto di Machiavelli risulta il richiamo fatto nel suo discorso alla lettura delle storie e all'esperienza di cui si ha memoria (« coloro che hanno per lo addrieto volsuto possedere », « quelli che sempre per lo addreto hanno cercho di dominarla »).

La prima enunciazione del luogo comune dell'utilità della storia si incontra in uno scritto pratico, nel quale Machiavelli tratta di quale politica fosse conveniente seguire per la sua città. Stato l'anno avanti ad Arezzo, che si era ribellata ai Fiorentini, Machiavelli scrive una memoria *Del modo di trattare i popoli della Valdichiana ribellati*. La memoria comincia ricordando come Lucio Furio Camillo, vinti i Latini, parlò in senato (Liv. VIII, xiii, 11-18) e come procedettero i Romani in quella circostanza. Riferita la narrazione liviana e considerato di aver sentito dire che la storia « è maestra delle azioni nostre e massime de' principi », Machiavelli soggiunge:

> se alcuno non credesse questo, si specchi in Arezzo l'anno passato e in tutte le terre della Valdichiana, che fanno una cosa molto simile a quella de' popoli latini. Quivi si vede la ribellione e dipoi il racquisto, come qui; ancora che nel modo del ribellarsi e del racquistare vi sia differenza assai, pure è simile la ribellione e il riacquisto. Dunque, se vero è che le istorie siano la maestra delle azioni nostre, non era male per chi aveva a punire e giudicare le terre di Valdichiana pigliare esempio e imitare coloro che sono stati padroni del mondo, massime in un caso dove e' vi insegnano appunto come vi abbiate a governare.

Passa ad analizzare il modo di procedere dei Fiorentini. Lo approva per quanto riguarda Cortona, Castiglione, Borgo San Sepolcro, Foiano; non lo approva per quanto riguarda Arezzo. Loda il giudizio dei Romani e critica quello dei Fiorentini. L'analisi dell'esperienza dal 1498 in poi porta a concludere che se i Fiorentini fossero assaltati, Arezzo si ribellerebbe. L'analisi della situazione attuale porta a concludere giudicando possibile che i Fiorentini vengano effettivamente assaltati [20].

---

[20] *Ibid.*, pp. 366-367. L'esempio antico è ripreso in *D.* II, xxiii, con citazioni dal testo originale, per mostrare quanto i Romani « fuggivano la via del mezzo ». È poi usato l'esempio moderno di Firenze come esempio negativo. Machiavelli insiste nell'analisi del testo liviano e nel raccoman-

Il discorso, come si vede, procede nel modo seguente: narrazione di un esempio tratto da storie lette, affermazione di una similarità della situazione di cui si ha recente esperienza con quella dell'esempio, analisi del modo di procedere diverso seguito nella recente esperienza, consiglio di uniformarsi al modo di procedere dell'esempio, che aveva fatto buona prova. Ossia — se chiamiamo F e R rispettivamente le situazioni dell'esperienza recente e dell'esempio — i fatti sono: situazione R, provvedimento A, successo; situazione F, provvedimento B; e il discorso è che, se è giusta l'assunzione della similarità della situazione F con la situazione R, vi erano buone ragioni perché venisse preso un provvedimento di tipo A, mentre un provvedimento B sembra destinato all' insuccesso.

Si può osservare anzitutto che la posizione dell'esempio al principio del discorso appare dovuta a motivi retorici, al fine della persuasione. La genesi del ragionamento appare diversa: trovandosi davanti a una decisione B, che ritiene sbagliata, Machiavelli procede nel modo seguente: definizione della situazione dell'esperienza recente (F) come caratterizzata dai due fenomeni « ribellione » + « riacquisto »; reminiscenza di una situazione, letta nelle storie (R), caratterizzata dai medesimi fenomeni; assunzione della similarità delle situazioni F e R, che presentano i fenomeni giudicati fondamentali comuni; consiglio. Il comportamento che si critica mediante il ragionamento suddetto è il modo di procedere tenuto nella situazione F nella fase posteriore al « riacquisto ». Infatti, se nella situazione R fu preso il provvedimento A (di natura complessa; scomponibile in provvedimenti differenziati per i diversi ribelli) e questo diede buon effetto, per chi si fosse trovato in una situazione F caratterizzata dai fenomeni fondamentali medesimi della situazione R, era ragionevole prendere un provvedimento di tipo A. Concludendo, sembra di poter ravvisare il fondamento del discorso nell'effetto positivo del provvedimento A, mentre la menzione dell'effetto finale, che gli autori del provvedimento divennero

---

dare: « Questo giudizio debbono i principi imitare »; critica l'opinione di coloro che parlarono in senso contrario nelle deliberazioni a Firenze del 1502. Cfr. *Tutte le opere storiche e letterarie di N. M.* a cura di G. Mazzoni e M. Casella, Firenze, 1929 (d'ora in poi: *Opere*), pp. 175-177.

« padroni del mondo » (ovviamente non per effetto del provvedimento A) sembra da attribuire ad esigenze del discorso persuasivo e non offre fondamento sufficiente per attribuire a Machiavelli la tesi che, poiché i Romani divennero « padroni del mondo », tutti i loro provvedimenti furono senza errore.

Qual è la funzione dell'esempio? L'analisi dell'esperienza dal 1498 in poi — « raccozzato quello che si vide allora, quello che si è veduto poi » e il modo col quale i Fiorentini trattano gli Aretini — basterebbe a criticare il provvedimento preso, giacché « si può sicuramente fare questo giudizio »: che alla prima occasione Arezzo si ribellerebbe e l'effetto dei provvedimenti presi dai Fiorentini non sarebbe raggiunto. L'esempio dei Romani suggerisce in forma persuasiva quale provvedimento s' ha da prendere. Altro è il discorso se ci si chiede qual è la funzione dell'esempio non nel discorso del Machiavelli, ma nel suo pensiero, ossia quanto l'esempio letto nelle storie (R) sia servito in questa circostanza alla comprensione della esperienza (F), quanto a formare la convinzione che il provvedimento B fosse sbagliato. Per quanto non sia facile rispondere, pare si debba tenere che una qualche funzione l'esempio abbia esercitato — e tante volte lo stesso autore testimonia di aver imparato dalle storie come dall'esperienza — quindi che non si tratti di un espediente persuasivo.

Nelle opere di Machiavelli si trovano frequenti enunciazioni della utilità delle storie, proposte di esempi, esortazioni all' imitazione. E quasi sempre sono usati esempi antichi (conosciuti dalle storie) e moderni (conosciuti dall'esperienza). Per quanto siano frequenti gli esempi moderni, sia per l' impegno dell'autore nel giudicare cose di cui ha esperienza, sia per la convenienza di riferirsi a fatti noti all' interlocutore, sembra di poter notare una preferenza per gli esempi delle storie, che consentono per così dire una analisi « in vitro » dei fenomeni. Oltre che essere di tempi non corrotti, e non di tempi corrotti, come Machiavelli giudica quelli moderni.

Nella lettera scritta al Soderini dopo esser stato rimosso dall'ufficio, in un universo pieno di enigmi, cercando di trovare una spiegazione al fatto che spesso i medesimi fini si ottengono con modi di procedere diversi, Machiavelli cita Annibale e Scipione e poi, « giacché non si usa allegare i Romani », diversi personaggi moderni: anche se ritiene vi siano buone ragioni per allegare i Romani, è in grado di procedere servendosi di fatti dell'esperienza recente [21].

Nel *De principatibus* Machiavelli usa gran numero di esempi antichi e moderni e, rivolgendosi in particolare a chi governa, spiega come gli uomini prudenti debbano imitare gli uomini grandi (cap. vi), come si dice che Alessandro Magno imitasse Achille, Cesare Alessandro, Scipione Ciro (xiv), leggere le storie e considerare le azioni degli uomini eccellenti e « questi simili modi ... osservare ». Ricorda anche (xviii) gli insegnamenti dati copertamente ai principi dagli antichi scrittori, « li quali scrivono come Achille e molti altri di quelli principi antichi furono dati a nutrire a Chirone ». Addita ad esempio il modo di procedere del Valentino (vii), Agatocle, Oliverotto (viii), a causa dei loro buoni effetti. Poiché il criterio di giudizio delle azioni è l'efficienza, la funzione dell'esempio è di consentire l'osservazione degli effetti delle azioni e quindi il giudizio. Nei capitoli xii-xxv, che trattano delle offese e difese, si incontrano descrizioni di esempi positivi da seguire e di esempi negativi da evitare; ma segue talora un esempio che fa eccezione, contraddicendo alla conclusione che dalla maggior parte degli esempi raccolti viene tratta. Segue l'esame dell'eccezione. Per esempio, a proposito dei mercenari (xii), esempi positivi: Roma, Sparta, Svizzera; esempi negativi: Cartagine, Tebe, Milano, Napoli; passando poi a esempi che contrastano con le conclusioni, se ne discorre « più da alto ». Per gli aiuti (xiii), esempi negativi Giulio II, Firenze, l' imperatore di Costantinopoli; positivi il Valentino, Ierone, David (con funzione di « figura », cfr. Chirone), Carlo VII; ancora un esempio negativo, i successori di Carlo VII. Per le armi (xiv), es. positivo Francesco Sforza, negativo i successori di lui, ancora es. positivo Filopemene. Ma nei primi undici capitoli, che trattano piú strettamente dei principati, gli esempi rappresentano più spesso tipi che il discorso classifica: Milano presa da Francesco Sforza rappresenta un tipo definito « principato al tutto nuovo », il regno di Napoli preso dal re di Spagna rappresenta un altro tipo definito « principato nuovo come membro aggiunto » (i) ecc. Il modo di procedere del re di Francia, già criticato nella sua legazione, viene portato da Machiavelli come esempio negativo al cap. iii del *De principatibus*,

---

[21] In *Opere*, pp. 878-879.

che tratta della situazione definita « acquisto di stato in una provincia disforme di lingua » ecc. Tale situazione viene esemplificata dal fenomeno contemporaneo più comunemente noto: il Turco in Grecia. Per il modo di procedere in tale acquisto si fa riferimento a quello tenuto in ogni circostanza dai Romani, ma ci si sofferma (« e voglio mi basti ») sul modo da loro tenuto in Grecia. Tornando poi a Luigi XII di Francia, si esamina « se delle cose dette ne ha fatto alcuna ». Si insiste nel mostrare che egli « fece il contrario ». Si isolano cinque suoi errori e un sesto. Si esaminano due discorsi contrari. Si conclude: « Ha perduto adunque el re Luigi la Lombardia per non avere osservato alcuno di quelli termini osservati da altri che hanno preso provincie e volutole tenere ».

Notevole anche il fatto che nella trattazione, con un semplice uso della forma del discorso chiamata preterizione, si tenga conto di esempi, studiati dall'autore, considerati tabù dalla maggior parte di coloro ai quali il discorso è rivolto: i principati ecclesiastici (xi), ai quali poi (xix) viene avvicinato il regno del Soldano, Mosè (vi), come esempio nella trattazione del « principato nuovo acquistato per virtù ». In questi casi la comparazione serve ad allargare la conoscenza col distruggere tabù, rendere osservabili fenomeni solitamente esclusi dall'osservazione: leggendo la Bibbia « sensatamente » si capiscono cose che i più non capiscono, poiché leggono la Bibbia altrimenti.

La trattazione, soprattutto nei primi undici capitoli, presuppone un lavoro di raccolta ed esame di esempi, che vengono usati dove occorre. La loro funzione non sembra tanto persuasiva, quanto analitica. L'eventuale esortazione all' imitazione è giustificata in base all'effetto delle azioni esaminate attraverso gli esempi.

Nel *De principatibus*, dunque, esperienza e lettura delle storie sono usate per una analisi della realtà. Ma al lettore si tende a fornire il risultato dell'analisi, i tipi di realtà già classificati in base a un lavoro precedente, gli esempi ai loro luoghi; per il lettore non esperto non è facile vedere il processo attraverso il quale si è pervenuti ai giudizi, non è facile imparare a fare in proprio un simile lavoro.

Nei *Discorsi* il modo di procedere è in parte diverso. Anche in quest'opera si trova l'uso di esempi « a corroborare » questa o quella opinione. Sulle accuse, per esempio (*D.* I, vii): esempio positivo Roma (Coriolano), esempi negativi Firenze (Valori, Soderini) e gli Etruschi (Arunte); sulle calunnie (*D.* I, viii): esempio positivo Roma (Manlio), negativo Firenze (Guicciardini). Né mancano trattazioni in sé compiute, come quella sulle congiure (*D.* III, vi), che utilizza parte degli « infiniti esempli » ai quali si allude in *P.* xix, quella sulle origini delle città (*D.* I, i), oppure quest'altra, che comincia: « Chi ha osservato le antiche istorie trova come le republiche hanno tenuti tre modi circa lo ampliare » (*D.* II, iv): dove appunto le storie sono date per lette. Ma, a differenza del trattato sui principati, la struttura dell'opera si avvicina a quella di un commentario nel quale i fatti vengano esaminati nell'ordine in cui si trovano narrati nel testo. Seguendo con una certa libertà il testo di Livio, si allena il lettore a soffermare l'attenzione e a meditare su alcuni fenomeni giudicati importanti, istituire comparazioni e via dicendo. Di contro cioè al diffuso modo passivo di leggere le storie degli « infiniti » che « pigliono piacere di udire quella varietà degli accidenti che in esse si contengono »[22], si cerca di sviluppare nel lettore la capacità di osservazione e di fargli tener presente in ogni momento — rompendo il filo della narrazione — tutti i fatti acquisiti per vie diverse che attraverso quel testo. Ogni discorso, si può dire, reca esempi antichi e moderni; nessun discorso è — magari indirettamente — senza esempio, costituendo l'esempio il fondamento del discorso. Tale caratteristica risponde a un deliberato programma che non è di natura stilistica, ma riflette un aspetto fondamentale di una concezione del mondo. Gli esempi antichi e moderni altro non sono che le « cose », i fatti della realtà, né il discorso può avere oggetto diverso. Rispetto all' idea contemporanea dell'utilità della storia, la concezione che sta alla base di tale procedimento sembra rappresentare uno sviluppo per l' identità che vi è stabilita fra esperienza e storia. A questo proposito è notevole la frequenza nelle opere di questi anni e la presenza in testi di rilievo autobiografico di formule che collegano esperienza e lettura delle storie, ossia i due modi di conoscenza. Per limitarci a testi di riflessione dell'autore sul proprio modo di procedere — giacché le opere ne sono piene — leggiamo in alcune lettere:

---

[22] *D*. I, prefazione, in *Opere*, p. 56 b. Avverto che di questa prefazione il Mazzoni dà un testo contaminato.

non avere gustato leggendo né praticando le actioni delli uomini e i modi del procedere loro [23]

non mi diletta più leggere le cose antiche né ragionare delle moderne [24]

lunga esperienza delle cose moderne e continua lezione delle antique [25]

per una lunga pratica e continua lezione delle cose del mondo [26]

per quello che io ho veduto e letto [27]

L' importanza del collegamento appare dall'enunciazione fatta da Machiavelli del proprio modo di procedere nel *De principatibus*. Egli discorre di cose « vere » — antiche e moderne — lasciando da parte le « imaginate » [28]. Esperienza e lettura delle storie forniscono la conoscenza delle cose « vere » e chiudono il cerchio del discorso, dove, a differenza che in Aristotele, non troveranno luogo considerazioni di teorie o progetti del tipo della repubblica di Platone, ma soltanto studio di tutti e soltanto i fatti conosciuti per esperienza o lettura delle storie. Il riso di Alessandro, nel primo dei *Discorsi*, di fronte alle immaginazioni di Dinocrate, è un apologo pieno di significato: a esaltare la prudenza di Alessandro, che aveva acquistato una conoscenza

[23] A Pier Soderini, 1512, in *Opere*, p. 878 b.

[24] A Francesco Vettori, 1514, in *Opere*, p. 894 a.

[25] A Lorenzo de' Medici, 1516?, in Machiavelli, *Il principe, lettera a Francesco Vettori del 10 Decembre 1513, Ritratti di cose di Francia e della Magna, La vita di Castruccio Castracani*, ed. M. Casella, Roma, Milano, 1930 (d'ora in poi *Il principe*), pp. 29-30.

[26] A Zanobi Buondelmonti e Cosimo Rucellai, 1519?, in *Opere*, p. 55 a.

[27] A Lorenzo Strozzi, 1521, in *Opere*, p. 266 a.

Di formule simili nelle opere ricorderò qualcuna. *P.*, xx, in *Il principe*, p. 175: « con esempli che dalle cose antiche e moderne si traggano »; *D.* I, prefazione, in *Opere*, p. 57 a: «la cognizione delle antiche e moderne cose»; *D.* I, xxxix, *Opere* 109 a: «chi considera le cose presenti e le antiche»; *D.* II, xxi, *Opere* 172 a: « se si leggeranno bene le cose passate e discorrerannosi le presenti »; *D.* III, xliii, *Opere* 257 a: « di che si leggono in tutte le istorie vari esempli e ciascuno dì ne' presenti tempi se ne veggono ».

Chiudo con quest'ultima formula, che giova forse a far riflettere su una cosa già evidente di per sé, e cioè che anche dove non si trovano tali formule, il modo di procedere di Machiavelli è sempre il medesimo espresso in queste formulazioni: fatto certamente più importante delle dichiarazioni.

[28] *P.*, xv, in *Il principe*, pp. 129-130.

della natura delle cose, vi si contrappone un progetto immaginato da Dinocrate, che non mostrava di aver fatto capitale di tale conoscenza [29].

Limitato il proprio campo alle cose « vere », lasciando da parte le « imaginate », Machiavelli non intende occuparsi di un aspetto della realtà (la « politica »), ma della realtà. La storia, letta « sensatamente », serve a conoscere la realtà al modo medesimo dell'esperienza. Roma è scelta perché offre l'esempio di lungo periodo meglio documentato e accessibile, e i fenomeni che si vogliono sottoporre ad osservazione sono da osservare in un lungo periodo. Livio costituisce la fonte principale, ma naturalmente Machiavelli usa tutto ciò che dalla esperienza e dalle letture ha appreso.

Il modo di procedere è costituito — volendone dare una semplice descrizione — da due momenti: (a) *narrazione*, ossia una presa di conoscenza dei fatti per mezzo dei testi, seguita da (b) *discorso*, ossia una spiegazione di quei fatti mediante la comparazione con molti altri fatti.

Intento di Machiavelli nei *Discorsi* è richiamare l'attenzione su fenomeni importanti. Il procedimento non segue uno stretto ordine di tempo: di un periodo si osserva un fenomeno e se ne discorre tenendo conto dello sviluppo di tale fenomeno nei periodi successivi, poi a volte si torna sul medesimo periodo di tempo per osservarvi un altro fenomeno. Prendiamo in esame il principio dell'opera:

1 Origini di Roma (cap. i)
1.1 Origini libere di città (ii)
2 Creazione dei Tribuni in Roma (iii)
2.1 Funzione dei tumulti (iv)
2.1.1 La guardia della libertà (v)
2.1.2 Poteva Roma far gli effetti che fece senza tumulti? (vi)
2.2 Tra le autorità dei Tribuni era l'accusa (vii)
2.2.1 Altro sono le calunnie (viii)
3 Ordinatori di Roma: Romolo (ix)
3.1 Chi scelse la tirannide non lesse bene le storie (x)
4 Ordinatori: Numa (xi)

---

[29] *D.* I, 1, *Opere* pp. 58 b-59 a.

4.1 Importanza della religione (xii)
4.1.1 Esempi in cui i Romani usarono la religione (xiii)
4.1.1.1 mostrando sempre di osservarla (xiv)
4.1.2 Esempio in cui i Sanniti usarono la religione (xv)
5 Cacciati i Tarquini Roma divenne libera (xvi)
5.1 Un popolo corrotto venuto in libertà difficilmente vi si mantiene (xvii)

e via dicendo. Discorso delle origini di Roma (1), si tratta della lotta delle classi (2), dei mitici fondatori della città (3, 4), poi ancora di Roma dopo la cacciata dei Tarquini (5) e ogni volta il discorso tiene conto dei fatti successivi utili allo studio del fenomeno del quale tratta.

Soffermiamoci sul punto 2.1.2 (cap. vi): poteva Roma far gli effetti che fece senza tumulti? Machiavelli osserva che si tratta di vedere se in Roma si poteva ordinare uno stato che togliesse via dette controversie. Per esaminare questo, è necessario osservare esempi di repubbliche che senza tumulti sono state lungamente libere e vedere (a) quale stato era il loro e (b) se si poteva introdurre in Roma. Dette caratteristiche si trovano in Sparta e in Venezia. Il governo era che Sparta non apriva la via ai forestieri, Venezia non usava la plebe in guerra. Se il legislatore voleva fare di Roma una città senza tumulti, doveva fare una delle cose fatte da Venezia e da Sparta; ma allora avrebbe tolto ogni ragione dell'ampliare. Allora: se si vogliono gli effetti di Roma, occorre accettare i tumulti; se si vogliono gli effetti di Sparta e Venezia, occorre proibire l'acquistare. Si esaminano le possibilità di attuare la prima alternativa; si esaminano le possibilità di attuare la seconda alternativa; si conclude che sembra più attuabile la seconda.

Come si vede, gli esempi non fungono da modelli di comportamento, ma piuttosto da campioni per l'analisi di fenomeni. Anche se nell'opera si incontrano spesso consigli, questi non prendono il posto dell'analisi. Prendiamo altri esempi di trattazione: *D.* I, xl: creazione del Decemvirato in Roma. Volendo discorrere il Decemvirato, occorrerà (a) narrare tutto quello che seguì per simile creazione, (b) disputare le cose notabili

così per coloro che vogliono mantenere una republica libera, come per quelli che disegnassono sottometterla. Perché in tale discorso si vedrà molti errori fatti dal senato e dalla plebe in disfavore della libertà e molti errori fatti da Appio, capo del Decemvirato, in disfavore di quella tirannide che egli si aveva presupposto stabilire in Roma [30].

Prendiamo *D.* III, vi, delle congiure. Esse sono pericolose ai principi e ai privati; Machiavelli ne parla diffusamente, « non lasciando indietro alcuno caso notabile in documento dell'uno e dell'altro ». L'analisi del Machiavelli, cioè, servirà a chi fa le congiure e a chi le subisce, a chi lavora perché riescano e a chi lavora perché falliscano, o anche a chi vuol capire e desidera che riescano o desidera che falliscano. La trattazione comincia delimitando il campo, con rinvio a un altro luogo dell'opera (*D.* II, xxxii) per fenomeni che non saranno attualmente presi in considerazione. Analisi delle congiure contro un principe. Cause. Pericoli: prima, durante e dopo l'esecuzione. Soggetti: se è uno solo, tendono a zero i pericoli « prima », al massimo quelli « in sul fatto ». Osservazione che soggetti delle congiure sono di solito dei grandi, soprattutto dei grandi troppo beneficati, ma anche dei grandi troppo ingiuriati. Pericoli « prima »: per relazione o per congettura. Rimedi. Pericoli « in sul fatto »: la rassegna lascia per ultimo gli accidenti che, non potendosi prevedere, non hanno rimedio; ma « è bene necessario esaminare tutti quegli che possono nascere e rimediarvi ». Pericoli « poi ». Analisi delle congiure contro la patria. Pericoli: « prima » minori che nelle congiure contro un principe, « in sul fatto » uguali, « poi » zero; tali congiure sono quindi meno pericolose che quelle contro il principe. Difese per coloro contro cui si congiura.

Gli esempi in precedenza raccolti, studiati e classificati, vengono usati nei luoghi della trattazione dedicati ai vari tipi di congiura; la trattazione non sembra che la risultante dell'opera preliminare di raccolta e analisi. Non fa menzione di tutte le congiure note, ma cura che tutti i tipi possibili siano rappresentati e presi in considerazione: la scelta degli esempi risponde a criteri di utilità ai fini dello studio completo del fenomeno, non ai fini di dimostrare una tesi.

A volte un esempio suggerisce una « morale » ed esempi

---

[30] *D.* I, XL, *Opere* p. 110 a-b.

analoghi ne costituiscono una verifica. Prendiamo per esempio *D*. III, xv: che uno e non molti siano preposti a un esercito. Il discorso porta tre esempi (basterebbe in realtà il primo, osserva l'autore, « ma ne voglio addurre altri due »):

1. Ribellione dei Fidenati. Creazione da parte dei Romani di quattro tribuni con potestà consolare. Insuccesso. Creazione di un dittatore.

2. Presa Milano, Luigi XII vuol restituire Pisa ai Fiorentini. Vengono mandati G. B. Ridolfi e Luca degli Albizi; questi non fa nulla finché c'è il primo; tornato il primo a Firenze, mostra le sue virtù.

3. Agrippa, mandato con Quinzio dai Romani contro gli Equi, vuol che Quinzio solo abbia il comando.

Il primo esempio è in sé concluso: situazione, provvedimento A, scacco, provvedimento B. I Romani, ammaestrati dall'esperienza, prendono un diverso provvedimento. Gli altri due esempi ne costituiscono una specie di verifica: (2) i Fiorentini, senza tener conto dell'esperienza dei Romani, prendono il provvedimento A. Un « accidente » converte la situazione facendo vedere quali sarebbero stati gli effetti di un provvedimento B; (3) i Romani prendono il provvedimento A. La prudenza di uno dei comandanti converte la situazione in quella che sarebbe risultata da un provvedimento B.

Machiavelli qui critica la pratica contemporanea ed esorta a tenere il comportamento contrario. Ma l'analisi non appare distorta al fine della convinzione.

I *Discorsi* contengono numerosi riferimenti alla storia di Firenze, soprattutto contemporanea, e ciò è ben naturale dal momento che di Firenze Machiavelli aveva soprattutto esperienza. Ma i Fiorentini costituiscono esempi, non sono i destinatari del discorso più che tutti gli altri. In un preciso momento, vicino al tempo della composizione dei *Discorsi*, Machiavelli scrisse anche un progetto di riforma della repubblica fiorentina. I *Discorsi* invece sembrano l'opera di una vita e il tentativo di educazione che vi si intraprende assai esteso nello spazio e nel tempo. Nella prefazione al primo libro si esprime meraviglia e dolore per il fatto che

> nello ordinare le republiche, nel mantenere li stati, nel governare e regni, nell'ordinare la milizia ed amministrare la guerra, nel iudicare

e sudditi, nello accrescere lo imperio, non si truova principe né republica che agli esempli delli antiqui ricorra [31].

Nelle arti figurative vengono imitati i prodotti dell'arte antica, nel diritto privato e nella medicina non si fa che ricorrere ai giudizi e ai rimedi trovati dagli antichi. Perché dunque le azioni degli antichi regni e repubbliche, dei re, capitani, cittadini, datori di leggi e altri che si sono per la loro patria affaticati sono soltanto oggetto di ammirazione? Sembra per una specie di rassegnazione: « la debolezza de' presenti uomini, causata dalla debole educazione loro e dalla poca notizia delle cose, fa che si giudicano i giudicii antichi, parte inumani, parte impossibili », scrive a un certo punto Machiavelli [32]. Ma nella prefazione al primo libro dice che la causa dell' inattività degli uomini del suo tempo non gli sembra tanto la presente educazione, quanto la poca notizia delle cose, in particolare il « non avere vera cognizione delle storie » [33]. Per questo sceglie come strumento di educazione il discorrere sulle storie di Livio.

Machiavelli scrive con l' intento di essere utile all'azione. « Chi esamina con diligenza le cose passate » può facilmente prevedere in ogni repubblica le future e usarvi rimedi trovati dagli antichi o, « non ne trovando degli usati », altri nuovi. « Ma perché queste considerazioni sono neglette, o non intese da chi legge, o se le sono intese, non sono conosciute da chi governa, ne séguita che sempre sono i medesimi scandoli in ogni tempo » [34]. Negli stessi storici antichi, Machiavelli trovava la esigenza di insegnare comportamenti: gli storici buoni, come Livio, « mettono particularmente e distintamente certi casi, acciocché i posteri imparino come gli abbino in simili accidenti a difendersi » [35]. Ed egli stesso opera in tal modo, convinto che

gli è offizio di uomo buono, quel bene che per la malignità de' tempi e della fortuna tu non hai potuto operare, insegnarlo ad altri acciocché, sendone molti capaci, alcuno di quelli, più amato dal Cielo, possa operarlo [36].

---

[31] In *Opere*, p. 56 b.
[32] *D.* III, xxvii, *Opere*, p. 238 a-b.
[33] In *Opere*, p. 56 b.
[34] *D.* I, xxxix, *Opere*, 109 a-b.
[35] *D.* III, xxx, *Opere*, 242 a.
[36] *D.* II, prefazione, *Opere*, 136 b-137 a.

Ancora più generosamente, Machiavelli sembra pensare che la semplice conoscenza della storia insegni a bene operare onde meritar lode: « è impossibile » che a leggere le storie gli uomini, principi o privati, non desiderino il bene [37].

Machiavelli propone esempi da imitare. Trattando del mantenere un regno ereditario, dice che i principi

> volendo intendere il modo avessono a tenere a fare questo, non hanno a durare altra fatica che pigliare per loro specchio la vita de' principi buoni, come sarebbe Timoleone Corintio, Arato Sicioneo e simili, nella vita de' quali ei troverìa tanta sicurità e tanta sodisfazione di chi regge e di chi è retto, che doverrebbe venirgli voglia di imitargli, potendo facilmente, per le ragioni dette, farlo [38].

Machiavelli sembra credere nella quasi assoluta superiorità dell'esempio di Roma. Nella prefazione al secondo libro dei *Discorsi* si difende dall'accusa di lodare troppo i tempi antichi [39] e in *D.* II, xix ritiene « corrotto » il giudizio dei contemporanei, dice « contrarie alla verità » le loro opinioni, frutto di tempi « corrotti ». « Lucullo con pochi fanti ruppe cento cinquantamila cavalli di Tigrane » e « fra quelli cavalieri era una sorte di cavalleria simile al tutto agli uomini d'arme nostri ». Questo errore è diventato chiaro « dallo esemplo delle genti oltramontane », che conferma quello che della fanteria si narra nelle storie.

> E come e' si vede per quello essere vero, quanto alla fanteria, quello che nelle istorie si narra, così doverrebbero credere essere veri e utili tutti gli altri ordini antichi [40].

Nei *Discorsi* si incontrano forti affermazioni di proprie opinioni da parte dell'autore, perorazioni di giudizi fondati — o che l'autore ritiene fondati — sull'esperienza e la lettura delle storie, discorsi persuasivi, discorsi esortativi, errori di giudizio. Ma il modo di procedere dei *Discorsi* non sembra in alcun modo riducibile a discorso persuasivo. La vecchia idea degli esempi specchi di virtù, come si è visto, aveva lasciato il posto sempre

---

[37] *D.* I, x, *Opere* 74 b.
[38] *D.* III, v, *Opere* 199 a-b.
[39] In *Opere*, pp. 135-136.
[40] *Ibid.*, p. 169 a-b.

più frequentemente a una più aperta concezione dell'utilità pratica delle storie in quanto esse, rispetto all'esperienza di una sola vita, moltiplicano i fenomeni osservabili e quindi le possibilità di conoscenza. La concezione di Machiavelli riconosce una continuità fra la serie di fatti conosciuti dalla tradizione, letta « sensatamente », e la serie dei fatti conosciuti per esperienza diretta. Da questa concezione Machiavelli esorta chi non vi è arrivato a fare il salto: cessare di maravigliarsi, cessare l'ossequio per gli esempi, agire, e convincersi così che egli può agire come i personaggi delle storie. Mosè, Ciro, Teseo: uomini rari e maravigliosi, « nondimanco furono uomini » [41]. Le norme del diritto privato e i rimedi delle malattie, che si impongono come ciò che in determinate circostanze si deve fare, sono stati un tempo inventati da uomini, facendo capitale dell'esperienza. Forse che il diritto pubblico, gli stati, le grandi esperienze collettive appartengono a un altro mondo, non si possono imitare? Col suo discorso esortativo Machiavelli combatte contro lo stato d'animo di chi crede non che vi sono difficoltà oggettive, che si possono studiare, affrontare e alla fine superare, ma che l'azione è impossibile: « come se il cielo, il sole, gli elementi, gli uomini, fussino variati di moto, di ordine e di potenza da quelli che gli erono antiquamente » [42]. Il discorso esortativo — il messaggio di Machiavelli — viene dalla sua concezione dell'unità dell'universo conoscibile, in cui l'uomo opera, identificato nelle cose « vere ».

---

[41] *P.* XXVI, in *Il principe*, p. 204.
[42] *D.* I, prefazione, *Opere* 56 b.

RANDOLPH STARN

FRANCESCO GUICCIARDINI AND HIS BROTHERS *

* My Guicciardini research in Florence during the summer of 1968 was made possible by a faculty fellowship from the University of California at Berkeley, which I am happy to acknowledge here. I am also grateful to Count Francesco Guicciardini and Dr. Gino Corti for opening to me the family archives in the Palazzo Guicciardini.

Francesco Guicciardini, first among his peers, was third among the sons of Piero Guicciardini. Before him came Luigi (1478-1551) and Jacopo (1480-1552); after him Bongianni (1492-1549) and Girolamo (1497-1556).

The simple facts open a complex world to explore. Often as Francesco has been portrayed as the statesman, moralist, and historian, he has rarely been seen in terms of his close relationships with his brothers [1]. It is not for lack of encouragement: many of Francesco's letters are addressed to his brothers; many of his political and economic dealings concerned them. It is not for lack of sources, since Guicciardini papers — letters, account books, literary works — abound in Florentine archives and libraries [2]. Nor is it because the subject is unimportant. Siblings are biological facts, but the ties they create (or fail to create) among themselves reflect in miniature the experience of a society and an age. This is a lesson that Lucien Febvre, Philippe Ariès, and a growing number of historians of the family in early modern European society have driven home. It is a particularly important lesson in Florentine history where the little community of the family traditionally mediated between the individual and the larger community, so much so that Florentine history is often the history of its great families [3]. The

---

[1] The first serious attempt to restore Francesco to his family was a chapter by Alexander Mylonas (whose tragic death in an automobile accident cut short a promising career) in Francesco Guicciardini: A Study in the Transition of Florentine and Bolognese Politics, 1530-1534 (unpublished Ph. D. thesis, Harvard University, 1960), pp. 12-63. Recently Richard A. Goldthwaite has dealt with the economic affairs of the family in *Private Wealth in Renaissance Florence; A Study of Four Families* (Princeton, 1968), pp. 109-157.

[2] See R. Ridolfi, *Gli archivi delle famiglie fiorentine* (Florence, 1934), pp. 95-210; *Le carte strozziane del R. Archivio di Stato in Firenze*, ed. C. Guasti (Florence, 1884), I-II, *passim*; P. O. Kristeller, *Iter Italicum*, I (London/Leiden, 1964), *passim*.

[3] Goldthwaite, pp. 293-303 *et passim*, gives the most recent and most useful bibliography of family studies for Florence and for Italy. See, in gen-

Guicciardini were a great family overshadowed by a great man. A family portrait needs to be drawn, Francesco at the center, but his brothers closely grouped around him.

The brothers Guicciardini had in Piero di Jacopo an Albertian father, the very model of the Florentine patrician and *paterfamilias* [4]. Traditions of class and Guicciardini traditions drew Piero into business, politics, and culture without binding him to any one of them. In business he had the advantage of an only son's undivided inheritance in the usual, balanced Florentine portfolio. It was enough for him not to lose it, to keep the family silk business intact, to accumulate land, to provide for his family. Politics came with patrician wealth and the Guicciardini name. With a father and an uncle in the inner circle of the Medici, Piero began his career near the top and ended it there, a member of the special commission that liquidated the Florentine republican experiment on the return of the Medici in 1512. And yet, during the republic of 1494-1512, Piero had been swayed by Savonarola and became a cautiously active republican. Like the French Abbé, he survived, because he was prudent in the piazza, self-watchful, and, after all, not really a political man. Before he was a politician he was a cultured amateur. He knew his Latin and Greek and the literary lights of Florence. He was one of the three « Petri » to whom Marsilio Ficino addressed his *Apologia*, and he records himself in an oration on justice, a little work on the Florentine electoral scrutiny of 1484, and letters in humanistic script [5]. There is nothing here of the tyrannical, insensitive, or merely incompetent father of great men.

Francesco wrote that his father was the envy of Florentine fathers [6]. He raised his sons « diligentissamente », « without the

---

eral, L. Febvre, « Ce que peuvent nous apprendre les monographies familiales », *Mélanges d'histoire sociale*, I (1942), 31-34; P. Ariès, *Centuries of Childhood* (New York, 1962).

[4] On Piero, see Goldthwaite, pp. 125-132, and the works cited therein.

[5] P. O. Kristeller, *Supplementum Ficinianum* (Florence, 1937), II, 344. The work on the scrutiny has been published by N. Rubinstein, *The Government of Florence under the Medici* (Oxford, 1966), pp. 318-325.

[6] *Ricordo* 39, serie II, *Opere*, ed. R. Palmarocchi (Bari, 1929-1936), VIII, 293.

slightest corruption, frivolity, loss of time »[7]. This meant learning to keep accounts with a sharp mercantile eye. It meant humanistic studies, even soon-forgotten Greek, with Ser Giovanni della Castellina and, perhaps, in the school of Marcello Virgilio Adriani, successor to Poliziano. It certainly meant a heavy dose of religion, for the Guicciardini, children of the *Frate*, were brought up « piously »[8]. There is some suggestion that it also meant a kind of differentiation which matched sons and functions. Alberti had expected the good father to turn each son to the career suited to « the nature of the boy, the name of the family, the customs of the land, to present fortunes, times, and conditions, to the occasion, to the expectations of his fellow-citizens »[9]. Florentine society was not rigid enough to condition strict functional divisions, nor were there laws of primogeniture to enforce them. But the eldest son, Luigi, was the first to be set up in business and in political office; business, proper to a second son, was Jacopo's special calling. Third-born Francesco once considered a career in the Church (a cardinalate no less) and was sent to study law, traditional alternatives of younger sons. It fell to Bongianni to manage the family estate at Poppiano; to Girolamo, twenty years younger than his eldest brother, to take whatever was left. With their diligent upbringing, then, the brothers shared the full, high-tension maze of patrician roles and values, but, within the family, adapted to loose divisions of labor and talent[10]. It was the kind of upbringing that promoted continuity but also continual stress in patrician society.

Piero also educated by his example. His few surviving letters to his sons reveal a kind, but firm, father-figure and set a tone

---

[7] *Oratio defensoria*, *Opere*, IX, 280. On the brothers' education, see Roberto Ridolfi, *The Life of Francesco Guicciardini*, trans. C. Grayson (London, 1967), pp. 1-9.

[8] *F. G. a se stesso* (1513), *Opere*, IX, 99.

[9] L. B. Alberti, *I libri della famiglia*, *Opere volgari*, ed. C. Grayson, I (Bari, 1960), 41.

[10] Mylonas, pp. 19 ff., points out the divisions, but makes them more rigid than they were. Opinion on the intriguing question of correlations between birth order and social parameters is highly inconclusive: see W. D. Altus *et al.*, « Birth Order and Its Sequelae », *International Journal of Psychiatry*, III (1967), 23-37.

of close domestic cooperation the brothers never abandoned [11]. *Ricordanze* written by Jacopo and Francesco on his death in 1513 take the fullest measure of the man and the father [12]. That they are so often conventional is disappointing, but, after all, not surprising or uninteresting: fathers usually compel and live on in their sons in conventions. Both sons agreed about Piero's prudence and goodness. These were his special virtues, according to Jacopo. Francesco elaborated: « He took up few projects and worked on affairs of state slowly and with great maturity, unwilling, except when forced by necessity or his conscience, to speak his mind or his opinions fully in important matters ». (It was the apology of the young and ambitious for their elders.) Piero's second attribute, humanistic traditions behind it, was his learning. Not even the Medici pageants of his youth kept him from studying the humanities, Greek, and a smattering of philosophy, boasted Francesco [13]. « He was ornamented by letters, Latin and Greek », Jacopo added, « and was more than a little accomplished in sacred scripture ». Then there was his piety, described with a Savonarolian glimmer by Jacopo: « in all his affairs he always had before his eyes the honor of God, whom he loved a good deal and for whom he was very zealous ». To Francesco he was a « blessed and saintly soul » who received « all the sacraments of the Church with great devotion, so that one may hope that God has surely taken him into a place of salvation ». Other traits entered at the margins of the portraits. Jacopo recalled Piero's frugal management of his household because of his large family — a quality hardly lost in his sons, large families or not. And beneath the public image Francesco hinted at inner anxieties which may have contributed to his death, « because he was a man who took to heart very much anything that displeased him ».

It is easy to see the society in the father and the father in the sons, too easy perhaps. Ultimately even Guicciardini sons came to terms with their fathers in obscure ways. Francesco

---

[11] *Carteggi di F. Guicciardini*, eds. R. Palmarocchi, P. G. Ricci (Bologna/Rome, 1938-), I, nos. 7-9, 11, 32, 40, 74.

[12] Jacopo's memorial is in A[rchivio] G[uicciardini, Florence], *Libri di amministrazione*, 13, fols. 184 v-185 r; Francesco's in *Ricordanze*, *Opere*, IX, 71-73. I have translated the quotations that follow from these sources.

[13] *Memorie di famiglia*, *Opere*, IX, 49.

wrote that he « loved his father more dearly than men usually love their fathers »; he and his brothers « must be very proud to have been the sons of such a man » [14]. These were emotions Francesco hardly ever expressed, certainly not for his mother or his wife. Elsewhere he recorded filial obedience: when he kept family funds for safekeeping in Ferrara; when he accepted the dictates of his father's conscience and dropped his ambitions for a career in the Church; when he consulted with his father before taking the Florentine embassy to Spain in 1512 [15]. But the loving son was also a defiant son — Alcibiades to himself — who implicated his brothers in his guilt: « all in all [Piero] had more trouble with us than consolation » [16]. Luigi's « debts and disorders » hastened Piero's death [17]. He, Francesco, had only *wished* to defy his father over the ecclesiastical career. The defiance was real enough when, in 1508, he married Maria Soderini against the wishes of his father, who feared the risks of a match with the gonfalonier's family. The marriage was calculated to bring honor and reputation. Francesco was pleased with himself. But guilt nagged at him, linking earthly and heavenly fathers: « I cannot but help having some doubt or scruple that I may have offended God, especially having such a father as mine » [18]. The ambivalence would reappear. Returning from Spain in 1513, the youngest ambassador in Florentine memory, Francesco doused his triumph in scruples: « [Francesco,] up to this day your life and customs have not been worthy of a nobleman, son of a good father, brought up piously, nor of that prudence you judge [to be] in yourself; nor can you persevere in them without the greatest shame, at least to yourself » [19]. In the *Dialogo del Reggimento di Firenze* (1521-25) he cast his father as a shadowy opponent, prudent and philosophical, of Bernardo del Nero, the outspoken aristocrat usually identified as his own spokesman [20]. It is as though Francesco's worldly

---

[14] *Ricordanze*, *Opere*, IX, 72.
[15] *Ibid.*, pp. 54 ff., 69-70; cf. Ridolfi, *Life*, pp. 7 ff.
[16] *Ricordo* 39, serie II, *Opere*, VIII, 293; *Oratio accusatoria*, *Opere*, IX, 211.
[17] *Ricordanze*, *Opere*, IX, 71.
[18] *Ibid.*, p. 58.
[19] *F. G. a se stesso* (1513), *Opere*, IX, 99.
[20] See, esp., R. von Albertini, *Das florentinische Staatsbewusstsein im Übergang von der Republik zum Prinzipat* (Bern, 1955), pp. 100 ff.

gains were offerings and offenses to his father, proofs of his worthiness and protests of independence. The paradox was that the business of justifying himself in the world precluded justification. Guilt, doubt, and reflection hovered beneath honor and reputation. So, perhaps, the roots of Francesco's restlessness, his « pessimism », his preoccupation yet dissatisfaction with form in action and words.

However complex the channels, Piero's legacy to his sons was considerable, and lasting. He left them with a sense of themselves as a family group, « *nostra* linea »[21]. He transmitted the values and roles of Florentine patrician society that the brothers acted out in their own lives. Because of Piero, surely, there was a Guicciardini cluster of character and ideals within patrician norms: their driving concern with honor and reputation; their possessiveness; their self-conscious need to contemplate, or at least to calculate. Their very idiosyncrasies were variations on family themes: Luigi's self-righteousness; Jacopo's willful political independence and his piety; Francesco's will-to-power over past and present; Bongianni's self-sheltering love of solitude; Girolamo's business-like materialism. More tangible, and eminently Florentine, were the legacies of a handsome fortune, Piero's good name, and a head start in the Florentine establishment[22]. Piero saw his three eldest sons suitably married (Luigi to Isabella Sacchetti in 1502, Jacopo to the Bardi heiress Camilla in 1504; Francesco to Maria Soderini in 1508, a good match after all) and the other two grown into young manhood. Before his death Luigi was beginning to overcome a false start in business and to make his way in politics (he was prior for S. Spirito in 1508). The silk company Piero had established with Jacopo was thriving, profitable beyond the returns of his own firm. Francesco was a rising young lawyer and ex-ambassador to Spain. The sons seemed about to deserve the father when Piero died on 20 December 1513[23].

The Guicciardini brothers settled their father's estate four months after his death and once again ten years later. The first

---

[21] See below, n. 52.
[22] See AG, *Spogli*, *passim*; Goldthwaite, pp. 125 ff.
[23] *Ricordanze*, *Opere*, IX, 72-73.

settlement was drawn up on 17 March 1514, from Piero's testament and an informal agreement among the brothers. Liquid assets and income property were divided five ways, leaving each brother about 2,000 florins in movables, chiefly credits with the family silk concerns, and 2,000 florins in land. What remained was to be held in common, according to the provisions of Piero's will: the family palace complex and its furnishings on the left bank of the Arno near the Ponte Vecchio; the villa, with its furnishings, at Poppiano some twenty miles southwest of Florence; an undisclosed but certainly small sum in the Monte; a small and evidently worthless 13 per cent interest in the Montecatini copper mines at Volterra [24]. The second agreement grew out of the rich marriage which, in 1524, Jacopo negotiated for Girolamo with his Bardi sister-in-law. Willing, but as demanding as any heiress (she was probably worth 15,000 florins), Costanza de' Bardi insisted on living in the Guicciardini palace. Luigi was loathe to reduce his quarters there. Francesco admitted that the house would have served *him* very well. The prospect of another property division could not have appealed to Bongianni, content enough to remain undisturbed at Poppiano. But the brothers rose to the occasion, uniting to divide. On 4 March 1524 they reached an agreement on property valued at 4,915 florins. Girolamo and Luigi took the family palace in exchange for payments and shares of the country holdings for the other brothers [25].

That the Guicciardini, and brothers generally in Renaissance Florence, took independent paths with their inheritances is a major thesis of Professor Goldthwaite's recent study of four Florentine families [26]. Jacopo and Girolamo were the family businessmen, while Luigi and Francesco made careers of politics. Bongianni, for his part, lived the life of a country squire at Poppiano. The sociologist of pre-industrial cities would predict as much: « after the elders are gone, brothers generally

---

[24] *Ibid.*, p. 75 *et passim*, and Goldthwaite, pp. 131 ff.

[25] These proceedings are treated in rich detail in several works by Count Paolo Guicciardini: *Cusona* (Florence, 1939), pp. 152-153; *Un parentado fiorentino nei primi del Cinquecento ...* (Florence, 1940); *Le antiche case ed il palazzo dei Guicciardini in Firenze* (Florence, 1952), p. 114.

[26] Goldthwaite, pp. 131-155.

split up and set up independent households »[27]. It is a reminder that Florence was not always the fifth element of Boniface VIII and Florentine historians. But sociologists and historians have also begun to question the classic notion that societies develop from integration to fragmentation, in terms of the family, from extended to nuclear families. The model curve of development has been qualified at both ends: by the realization that nuclear families were the building blocks, and may have been the rule, of societies as traditional as China and Japan; by the persistence of family extension — the notorious mother-in-law, for instance — in industrial society[28]. Consider an early Guicciardini case. On his death in 1294 Tuccio Guicciardini, founder of the family's fortunes, divided an inheritance among his sons which was eventually reconstituted by accidents of death and repurchase[29]. The suggestion (no more, no less) is that the partition of family fortunes was not necessarily a Renaissance phenomenon but a feature of a dynamic urban economy. And yet Tuccio's inheritance *was* reconstituted. If a model applies, it would need to be sufficiently kaleidoscopic to account for centripetal and centrifugal pressures in the family. More than two hundred years later economic interaction among the brothers Guicciardini was still subtle and complex.

The economic activities of Jacopo, Francesco, and Bongianni are particularly well-documented, and, at that, the most revealing of the economic alternatives open to the early sixteenth-century Florentine patrician. Jacopo's portfolio about 1532 has been reconstructed by Goldthwaite from account books nearly complete for 1505-30[30]. There were properties worth about 8,500 florins, some 6,000 florins income-producing,

---

[27] G. Sjoberg, *The Pre-Industrial City, Past and Present* (New York, 1960), p. 177.

[28] See, e. g., M. F. Nimkoff, *Comparative Family Systems* (Boston, 1965), pp. 20 ff.; P. Laslett, *The World We Have Lost* (New York, 1965), pp. 228 ff.

[29] P. Guicciardini, *Cusona*, p. 162.

[30] Goldthwaite, pp. 140 ff. Contrary to the claim (p. 145) that « Jacopo's books do not survive for the period after 1531 » and that « He had liquidated all his local investments » before then, AG, *Libri di amministrazione*, 20, fols. 1-2, contain a balance for 1542 showing profits of 2,404 florins from « mia ragione ». Other post-1531 business accounts survive, if less completely than for the earlier period, in *Libri* 19-20, 26, 29-31; see also AG, *Scritture varie*, 49, no. 2.

and as much as 7,000 florins from his wife's inheritance; investment credits of 2,741 florins, mainly in a silk manufactory first set up in 1502; a furnished city palace (in 1515 Jacopo bought the Benizzi palace next to the « case Guicciardini » for 1,874 florins) valued at 3,076 florins. Jacopo's income between 1513 and 1530 amounted to 14,108 florins from his investments (6,569 florins), real estate (3,987 florins), salaries from business and politics (195 and 636 florins), and the handsome profits from the papal offices in which he substituted for his brother Francesco (2,721 florins). Little sign here of the retreat from business to the land or of the rentier that some historians would like to find in a downgrade Cinquecento. Jacopo's was still the balanced Florentine portfolio; his main source of income was still business, which earned him an impressive 14-15 per cent per annum. Equally impressive, however, were Jacopo's expenditures, 13,514 florins for the same seventeen-year period. Much of this went for his large family of ten children. But after 1532 business put his accounts increasingly on the debit side of the ledger. Beginning in the early thirties, he had sunk most of his capital in a trading company operated by his sons in Flanders. Misfortune followed misfortune: accidental losses, bad debts, intrigue. In 1543 the company went under with debts of 25,000 ducats which were still hanging over the heads of the sons in 1568. If the profitable days of Florentine business were far from over in Jacopo's time, neither were the risks [31].

It was for Francesco to show that the legal profession and high politics could be far more profitable than business. At first there were petty, but prestigious, payments in kind — « a goose at All Saints, a kid at Easter, four pounds of candle-ends for Candlemas, and a joint of veal for St. Giles » [32]. The 300 ducats salary with a daily allowance of three ducats from his Spanish embassy of 1512-13 soon compensated for that, and this was only the beginning. As Governor of Modena (1516) Francesco's salary was 100 florins per month; as Governor of Modena and Reggio (1517-1522) 160 florins. As President of the Romagna (1524-1526) he could hope to earn a princely 4,000

---

[31] Cf. the rival interpretations, bull and bear, of the sixteenth-century Florentine and Italian economies cited by Goldthwaite, p. 235, nn. 1-2.

[32] *Ricordanze*, *Opere*, IX, 57.

florins per annum and as Governor of Bologna (1531-1534) about 240 florins per month. Meanwhile he was investing in business and in land with phenomenal good luck. In 1526 he anticipated liquid assets of 13,000 florins, not to mention the farms and two villas bought for 9,060 florins between 1518 and 1528 that returned about 400 florins annually. This was the Francesco who could describe himself as surrounded « with a houseful of tapestries, silver and servants » and yet, to his own mind, never have enough [33]. At his death in 1540 his estate was worth about 30,000 florins, the political inactivity of his last years notwithstanding. One can almost imagine him calculating the return on the 500 florins his father had spent on his education [34].

Bongianni's economic world was the *piccolo mondo* of Poppiano, of the harvest, the hunt, and the rural society described to his brothers in letters rustic and randomly learned [35]. His bachelor's tastes were modest, even severe, symbolized perhaps by those black and brown capes found among his effects after his death in 1549 [36]. When his estate was divided among Luigi, Girolamo, and Jacopo's three sons, it was worth only 4,821 florins, though he had inherited 4,000 florins from his father and at least 2,000 florins from Francesco [37]. « Sit mihi quod nunc est, etiam minus ... ». Bongianni at least seems to be the Horatian patrician of the more pessimistic historians of the Florentine economy. But would it have been different without Bongianni's ill-health, his retiring nature, his bachelorhood?

For all the divisions and diversities, close economic ties persisted among the brothers. First of all, the ties implicit in their inheritance [38]. Until 1524 the family palace and the villa

---

[33] Ridolfi, *Life*, p. 62.

[34] See Goldthwaite, pp. 134-140; *Ricordanze*, *Opere*, IX, *passim*.

[35] A number of his letters were published by I. Del Lungo, in *Almanacco dell'amico del contadino*, 1887-1893.

[36] AG, *Inventari diversi*, 44, no. 2.

[37] See Goldthwaite, pp. 139-140.

[38] Cf. *ibid.*, pp. 132 ff., where the pull of such ties is greatly underestimated. For Guicciardini property, see A[rchivio di] S[tato di] F[irenze], *Decima Granducale*, 3563, fols. 430 v-433 r (Luigi, Jacopo, Francesco, and Girolamo: joint return on property assessed at 1,149 florins), 187 v-188 r (Bongianni: property assessed at 81 florins). These figures rank the Guicciardini far above the city-wide average individual assessment of 53 florins,

at Poppiano were common property, and from 1514 until 1523 the brothers continued their father's silk business with capital of 6,300 florins as « The Heirs of Piero Guicciardini & Co ». Even after 1524 their interests were not as divided as the mere fact of partition may suggest. Luigi and Girolamo shared the family palace; Jacopo was next door in the Benizzi palace, now part of the Palazzo Guicciardini. Bongianni stated in his tax report of 1534 that he used Girolamo's house when in Florence. As for Francesco, it was largely a matter of circumstances — first the need to live in the lawyers' quarter near the Bargello, then the long absences from Florence — that he lived apart but certainly not isolated from his brothers. No formal division altered the fact that the brothers' patrimony in the countryside lay in the area around Poppiano. Bongianni kept an eye on their property there, and over the years Francesco, Jacopo, and Luigi added to their holdings in the neighborhood. As late as 1534 all the brothers but Bongianni filed a common property tax report. The single accounting presumably worked to their advantage, but a sense of family unity must have entered into it too. Yet, «for some particular reason of his», Bongianni could hold out [39]. Reversing the order, Francesco withheld substantial parts of his estate from his brothers in early versions of his will, but named them his universal heirs in the end [40]. These are revealing comments on the economic relationships among the brothers. They *were* linked at many points; they *could be* independent.

Even their independence could be a family matter, a matter of internal alliances, and rivalries. In families as in politics there are spheres of influence. Among the Guicciardini there was the economic triangle of Jacopo, Francesco, and Girolamo, and, on the other hand, the conservative, squirely alliance between Luigi and Bongianni. The triangle was sealed in an agree-

---

but considerably below the main branches of the city's richest families — Medici, Strozzi, Salviati, Capponi. See S. J. Berner, The Florentine Patriciate in the Transition from Republic to Principato, 1530-1610 (unpublished Ph. D. thesis, University of California at Berkeley, 1969), pp. 5 ff.

[39] Girolamo to Luigi, 22 December 1530, ASF, *Carte strozziane*, ser. I, 59, fol. 186 r.

[40] The final version is in A. Otetea, *François Guichardin* (Paris, 1926), pp. 367-381; cf. Ridolfi, *Life*, p. 330, n. 36.

ment of 1519 by Jacopo, Francesco, and Girolamo to finance the youngest brother for a business venture in Flanders, « Girolamo Guicciardini & Co ». When Girolamo married his Bardi heiress in 1524, the company was reorganized under the direction of Jacopo's son Agnolo and its operating capital increased from 4,500 florins to 7,600 florins, 5,600 of them from the three brothers. (It was this company that failed in 1543). In the twenties Jacopo kept an account for Francesco on his books and was his agent in purchasing the villa of Finocchieto in the Mugello. On several occasions Francesco preferred Jacopo over Luigi to substitute for him as Governor and as President. (Machiavelli's barbed report to the new owner of Finocchieto — « the bottom of a tower is not made otherwise » — did not cut very deeply, it seems). Girolamo had his turn in 1533 when he substituted in Francesco's absence as Governor of Bologna. Already in 1524 Francesco had deposited a very large sum with him to be invested at discretion and paid according to need. When the account was settled on January 1, 1528, it stood at 9,936 florins plus about 2,000 florins profit [41]. If Luigi and Bongianni did not figure in these arrangements, it was partly because neither Luigi nor his brothers forgot that the silk company their father had set up for him had failed where Jacopo's had been highly successful, or, still worse, that his « debts and disorders » had clouded Piero's last days [42]. Luigi had grievances of his own: « Messer Francesco ... thinks more about his own interests than ours »; « Messer Francesco has taken the apple in this affair and the others will have the core and the skin, and worse »; Jacopo was « malign and jealous » [43]. Bongianni could not threaten anyone with success. Over the years he and Luigi corresponded over the details of managing their farms and exchanged the philosophical musings fancied by them both.

---

[41] For the economic relations among the three brothers, see Goldthwaite, pp. 125 ff.; *Ricordanze*, *Opere*, IX, 84 *et passim*; Ridolfi, *Life*, pp. 16-17 *et passim*; AG, *Libri di amministrazione*, 15, *passim*.

[42] *Ricordanze*, *Opere*, IX, 71.

[43] He registered these complaints in letters to his son Niccolò: 15 January 1524 (ASF, *Signori, X, VIII, Legazioni e commissarie*, 73, fol. 37 v); 22 March 1524 (*ibid.*, fol. 46 r); 9 July 1543 (ASF, *Carte strozziane*, ser. I, 98, fol. 256 v).

Bongianni took special care of Luigi's property at Poppiano, and Luigi opened himself to him more than to any of his brothers [44].

Clearly the time had long passed when the extended family was a viable economic unit in Florence (if indeed it had ever been quite so all-encompassing as historians have assumed). The Guicciardini « family » did not exist economically beyond the fraternal group, and, even there, took flexible forms geared to the demands of a still mobile economy. This supports Professor Goldthwaite's thesis, the implications of which may well be as profound and as ramified as he has suggested: forms of economic individualism in the context of divided fortunes and the renewed quest for wealth in every generation; loosening of corporative social and political bonds; forms of architecture, painting, and literature expressive of domestic and dynastic concentration. All this may go a long way to explain the special vitality of society and culture in Renaissance Florence, though we need to know more about non-patrician wealth and, for that matter, patrician wealth beyond Goldthwaite's four great families. Nevertheless, as Tristam Shandy's father liked to ask, « What is the character of a family to an hypothesis? ». It is not quite true, after all, that each Guicciardini brother « took his share and went his own way » [45], and not the least important conclusion to be drawn from their economic experience is that it resists easy conclusions.

Even more than wealth, the Guicciardini name means politics in Florentine history — sixteen gonfalonieri of justice; forty-four members of the signory; a reputation for justice and severity; and, in the person of Francesco, the very epitome of Renaissance politics. Of the family tradition Francesco and his brothers were quite conscious and quite exclusive guardians. From their political careers or their correspondence one would never guess that there were forty-one Guicciardini eligible for Florentine political office in 1525 and no fewer than seventeen in

---

[44] See, e. g., Bongianni's letters to Luigi published by I. Del Lungo, in *Almanacco dell'amico del contadino*, 1887-1893.

[45] Goldthwaite, p. 132.

1531 [46]. Francesco's *Memorie di famiglia* is both the classic expression of a growing interest and faith in family history and a history focused on his own branch of his family [47]. Like the economic radius, the political radius of family interaction rarely extended beyond the five brothers.

In practice the fraternal group was a political power-complex and clearing-house. Favor one of us, Francesco once advised Cardinal Giulio de' Medici, and you will oblige us all [48]. This was a simple matter of propinquity and convenience in part: one's brothers were first in line for political spoils and first to reflect on one's own reputation. It could also be a question of survival when the quick tides of Florentine politics left an individual with no closer allies. Francesco was the center of this political exchange, with his enormous political capital to distribute and defend. He often put in a word for his brothers, and he saw to it that Jacopo and Girolamo substituted for him in his papal offices. During the Medici settlement of the early thirties his efforts were particularly intense and important. It was doubtless partly through his influence that Luigi joined him as a member of the Medicean Senate — only three other families had as many representatives — and that, in 1531, Girolamo was named vicar of Scarperia, official of the Monte, and member of the Eight on Internal Security. At the same time he sheltered Jacopo who had supported the republic of 1527-1530. For all this Francesco saw the proof of his maxim that there were practical advantages in favoring relatives and tolerating their importunities [49]. Under the republic Jacopo defended him from the reprisals of the radical party against patricians in general and the inner circle of the Medici in particular. Certainly it was no fault of Jacopo's that, in 1529, Francesco was declared a rebel *in absentia* and his property confiscated. After the sentence,

---

[46] AG, *Genealogia*, 24, fols. 7 r-8 v. Virtually their only contacts with the larger family group were with their second cousin Niccolò di Braccio: Mylonas, p. 17.

[47] N. Rubinstein, « The 'Storie Fiorentine' and the 'Memorie di Famiglia' by Francesco Guicciardini », *Rinascimento*, IV (1953), 171-225.

[48] *Carteggi*, III, no. 199 (3 May 1520).

[49] *Ricordo* 73, serie I, *Opere*, VIII, 255; cf. Ridolfi, *Life*, p. 82 *et passim*; Mylonas, pp. 25 ff.; F. Guicciardini, *Lettere inedite a Bartolomeo Lanfredini, 1530-1532*, ed. A. Otetea (Aquila, 1927), pp. 113-114, 142-143.

Giuliano Bugiardini: Francesco Guicciardini *(New Haven, Connecticut, Yale University Museum). All photos through the great courtesy of Count Francesco Guicciardini.*

Unknown Artist: Luigi Guicciardini*? (Florence, Palazzo Guicciardini sul Lungarno).*

LVIGI GVICIARDINI

Giorgio Vasari: Luigi Guicciardini *(Florence, Palazzo Vecchio).*

Unknown Artist: Jacopo Guicciardini*? (Florence, Palazzo Guicciardini sul Lungarno).*

Unknown Artist: Bongianni Guicciardini? *(Lucignano Val di Pesa, Villa Guicciardini).*

Maiolica plate with the arms of Girolamo Guicciardini and Costanza de' Bardi in a Della Robbian garland, formerly on their villa at Cusona Val d'Elsa (Florence, Palazzo Guicciardini).

Jacopo did what he could, even if he could only buy his brother's library at auction for safekeeping [50].

Beneath (and within) the practical ties were complexly shared ideals and attitudes. Guicciardini politics and patrician politics were not simply expedient and matter-of-fact. Intensely idealized, family spirit still meant a good deal to the brothers. One of Francesco's deepest wishes was to see his family exalted and its traditions honored [51]. Luigi was more specific, and more to the point, when he pressed the cause of « nostra linea » in the constitutional settlement of 1532 [52]. But even without a sense of family the brothers could rally around a common, and very Florentine, stock of political values. First, or very nearly first, were those summed up in the formula « onore e reputazione », not the mannered virtues of « real » aristocrats in northern Europe, but the public distinctions of the Florentine ruling class. The phrase flowed very readily from Francesco's pen to be elevated, in the *Ricordi*, into a political principle. Jacopo, too, swore that he valued « honor and reputation over possessions », and when he took Francesco's place as Governor of Bologna, Girolamo thought above all of his honor [53]. With their honor and reputation the Guicciardini, good Florentines that they were, also expected « utili », profits. Francesco was notoriously difficult over his salary. It was a matter of principle with him, and hardly less so with Luigi, Jacopo, and Girolamo. The qualifying (and sometimes rationalizing) principle was a sense of civic loyalty, of special responsibility for the destiny of Florence. Tradition, talent, influence, and wealth took their meaning in the context of civic activity; civic obligation, in turn, checked naked self-interest and bureaucratic impersonality. Social psychologists might analyze the results as a tense balance

---

[50] See Ridolfi, *Life*, pp. 201 ff.

[51] Thus the famous lines from the *Memorie di famiglia*, *Opere*, IX, 3: « ... desidero due cose al mondo più che alcuna altra: l'una la exaltazione perpetua di questa città e della sua libertà; l'altra la gloria di casa nostra, non solo vivendo io, ma in perpetuo ».

[52] Luigi to Francesco, 14 October 1531, *Opere inedite*, ed. G. Canestrini (Florence, 1857-1867), IX, no. 87.

[53] Jacopo to Francesco, 7 August 1520, *Carteggi*, III, no. 240; Girolamo to Lanfredini, 11 September 1533, B[iblioteca] N[azionale di] F[irenze], II, V, 28, fol. 95 r.

between self-directed and other-directed values. Under any rubric it was a mainspring of the Guicciardini and, if the extension is allowed, of the patrician political experience in Florence [54].

Political community did not mean political uniformity for the brothers any more than for Florence. There was room for a wide spectrum of patrician political types and styles [55]. At one extreme Bongianni presented the unlikely spectacle of a Guicciardini who never held political office. He was declared eligible in the scrutiny of 1524 but evidently preferred to nurse his delicate health at Poppiano. There is hardly a trace of politics in his correspondence, and his name no longer appears in the scrutiny of 1531. At the other extreme stood Francesco, model *homo politicus*. Jacopo was the family republican who, in 1529, could reprove Clement VII in the name of Florentine liberty. Even the arch-radical Giambattista Busini placed Jacopo among those citizens who were « the ornament and the flower » of the last Florentine republic [56]. Luigi, on the other hand, was a prime target of Busini and other republican historians. He was considered cruel and vindictive, and his execution of his two republican predecessors as commissary at Pisa in 1530 made him a symbol of harsh Medicean reaction, though the evidence suggests that he was acting on orders from Florence [57]. Girolamo, too, was a staunch supporter of the Medici principate, who, in 1552, succeeded Luigi in the Florentine Senate.

---

[54] For these themes in Francesco, see Ridolfi, *Life*, p. 217 *et passim*. Cf. Luigi's many letters in ASF, *Carte strozziane*, ser. I, 59-63, 98; those of Jacopo in *font. cit.*, ser. III, 220, and of Girolamo to Lanfredini in BNF, II, V, 27-28. On patrician political attitudes in general, see the remarkable new synthesis by G. Brucker, *Renaissance Florence* (New York, 1969).

[55] The brothers' political careers, as recorded in the *Tratte* of the ASF and elsewhere, can be followed conveniently in AG, *Spogli*; see also Mylonas, pp. 14 ff.

[56] G. B. Busini, *Lettere sopra l'assedio*, ed. G. Milanesi (Florence, 1861), p. 37.

[57] For contemporary historians and the most recent evaluation of Luigi, see Bono Simonetta, ed., L. Guicciardini, *Del Savonarola* ... (Florence, 1959), pp. 5-32. A letter to Luigi from his son Niccolò, 2 December 1530, goes far to excuse him: « Del Giachinotto si è intesa la executione; che, sendo stato giudicato qui, voi havete facto el resto ... ho poi visto la lettera delli Otto et truovo lo commettono resoluto » (ASF, *Carte strozziane*, ser. I, 59, fol. 185 v).

These Guicciardini divisions reflect and illuminate the larger framework of Florentine politics. That family ties no longer defined a man's politics, as they had 150 years before, is perfectly clear. So too the limitation on applying categories of social class to politics in early sixteenth-century Florence. There are objections enough in the fact that only about 10 per cent of the male population at best was politically enfranchised, and far less politically significant. In a political sense Florence, like most early modern European societies, was a one-class society (or so it may be argued); even the very real economic and social differences within the office-holding class were bridged to some extent by common assumptions and common activities. The particular (and never too obvious) lesson of the Guicciardini case is that political behavior does not necessarily follow the pocketbook or place on the social ladder. At least as important, if the Guicciardini are any indication, were individual differences in temperament and style that the family contained, and sharpened. In 1520 Jacopo was defining what he called his inclination towards « humanity and benignity » in politics in friction with Francesco, an inclination that may have had as much to do with his later republicanism as purely political considerations [58]. Luigi's notorious rigidity and self-righteousness were also schooled, or at least exposed, in the family, the defenses of a man who feels himself outrivaled by his younger brothers [59]. Francesco saw the interplay of family and politics as clearly as anyone when, in 1532, he urged that Luigi be named with him to the new Florentine Senate. Otherwise differences would arise between them, and these, he implied, might put Luigi in opposition to the regime [60].

These were the recurrent patterns, but Guicciardini politics also developed in time with Florentine politics [61]. Like their peers and Florence itself, the brothers were politically amphibious until the experience of the last Florentine republic, alter-

---

58 Jacopo to Francesco, 7 August 1520, *Carteggi*, III, no. 240.

59 See above, n. 43.

60 *Lettere inedite a B. Lanfredini*, p. 139 (16 April 1532).

61 See, in general, Albertini, *Staatsbewusstsein*; V. De Caprariis, *F. Guicciardini: dalla politica alla storia* (Bari, 1950); A. Rossi, F. *Guicciardini e il governo fiorentino dal 1527 al 1540* (Bologna, 1896-1899); C. Roth, *The Last Florentine Republic* (London, 1925).

nately allies of the Medici or the republican opposition. Returning to Florence in 1513, Francesco was appointed to the special commission which dismantled the republican regime he had served as ambassador to Spain. In 1514 Jacopo was composing laudatory verse for Lorenzo de' Medici, Duke of Urbino [62]. In the 1520's Francesco was defending, in the *Dialogo del reggimento di Firenze*, his pet idea of a mixed aristocratic constitution as a trusted servant of Clement VII, while Luigi was approaching the republican opposition which desired to broaden the basis of government. By May 1527 the Guicciardini were at least sympathetic towards the restoration of the republic. The leader of the opposition and new gonfalonier, Niccolò Capponi, was one of their own, an aristocrat, a moderate in internal and external affairs, an advocate of compromise with the Medici. In 1529, however, the radical *Arrabbiati* made their move. Capponi fell in April and with him the attempt to pacify the republic under moderate patrician leadership and to reach an accord with the Pope and the Emperor. Francesco was condemned; Luigi retreated to Pisa in November 1529 and then, after much hesitation, to Lucca, where he joined Girolamo to await the outcome of the siege. Only Jacopo remained to the bitter end. In the autumn of 1530 Francesco, Luigi, and Girolamo returned with the Medici to fallen Florence, while Jacopo, under their protection, took refuge in the country [63]. The Guicciardini had landed on the right political foot again.

But this was the great political watershed for them as for Florence; beyond it lay the Medici principate. There had been little honor and no profit for the Guicciardini under the republic, though they had been called upon often enough to meet the heavy economic burdens of the siege. The radicals had only succeeded in wounding to the core that proud patrician sense of patriotism and responsibility. So the frequent refrain « questa povera città » in all the Guicciardini letters of 1530-31, and a shrill determination that such a disaster should never occur again. The language is of the physician, of surgery and the purge. The radicals and their allies must be excised from the body politic, the brothers agreed, with the exceptions of Bongianni, apoli-

---

[62] *Le carte strozziane*, II, 833.

[63] See Ridolfi, *Life*, pp. 176 ff.

tical even then, and, understandably, of Jacopo. The political fortunes of the family and of the city must rest with the Medici [64]. Only the form of Medici restoration was at issue, and here the Guicciardini were caught between visions of drastic remedies and traditions of patrician independence and authority. Fear of the *popolo* below and a sense of the isolation of Medici and Mediceans above filled Francesco's political discourse of February or March 1531. Luigi set the consequences in historical perspective in a discourse of 1532, arguing that the system of Lorenzo the Magnificent, with its republican façade and oligarchical reality, could not be restored. In Francesco's slightly later discourses and in Luigi's concluding sections, however, there are second thoughts, more reserved and more traditional thoughts. The Medici should rule, after all, in alliance with well-born *amici* patronized and provided with authority in patrician councils of government [65]. « The patriciate did not embrace the concept of absolute rule for the Medici », as the most recent observer of patrician politics notes, « because its members were tied to a previous politics, also because they were sophisticated enough to see that any separation between them and the Medici was extremely dangerous » [66]. It is a classic case of Florentine political tensions between old assumptions and new insights.

Was the charter of the Medici principate in 1532 so far removed from the proposals of the Guicciardini and their peers? The republican tradition, always winning the moral victories lost by the republic, claims as much with its images of tyranny's

---

[64] See Francesco's *Lettere inedite a B. Lanfredini* and his correspondence with Luigi in *Opere inedite*, IX. Girolamo took a troubled and firmly Medicean line in his letters to Lanfredini in BNF, II, V, 28. A moving letter from Bongianni to Luigi described the devastated countryside after the siege: *Almanacco dell'amico del contadino* (1887), pp. 6-8. Profoundly shaken by his experience, Jacopo entered the following *ricordanza* on 19 August 1530: « Et mancò el governo del Consiglio grande et vivere populare; et così permise Dio per la insolenzia degli cittadini maligni et ignoranti et per vivere non populare ma più che tirannico » (AG, *Libri di amministrazione*, 23, fol. 58 r).

[65] Cf. F. Gilbert, « Alcuni discorsi di uomini politici fiorentini e la politica di Clemente VII per la restaurazione medicea », *Archivio storico italiano*, XCIII (1935), 1-24.

[66] Berner, The Florentine Patriciate, pp. 40-41.

triumph over liberty. The other widely held view that Clement VII duped a supine patriciate into its own undoing seems somehow to overrate papal strategy as much as it underrates patrician acumen. Since 1494 patrician theoreticians had envisioned a thorough constitutional reform to clear away the brittle anachronisms, the overlapping and tangled complexities of Florentine government. They wanted patrician assemblies and patrician counselors around the head of state, preferably a Medici, and these they had in the new Dugento, Senate, and Magistrato Supremo. They wanted peace and « law and order », and if the new regime did not bring that blessed state immediately, the tumultuous republican experience had not brought it at all. They wanted, of course, « honor and profit », and obtained them as senators, ambassadors, magistrates, and provincial officials [67].

Certainly the brothers Guicciardini continued to play active political roles, if anything increasing their participation in government. True, Francesco was a special case. After the death of Clement VII in 1534 he could not regain the political heights of a papal favorite and governor. His authority was very great as senator, ducal counselor, magistrate, and as architect of Alessandro's defense before the Emperor in 1536 and Cosimo's « election » in 1537. Even so, he was more vulnerable to his enemies, his rivals, and his own demanding self-esteem. When Cosimo outmaneuvered him in 1537, perhaps he had already decided to retire to the villa at S. Maria a Montici and the *Storia d'Italia* [68]. With Francesco's brothers there were no such ambiguities, and surely they, rather than Francesco, are symbols of patrician standing under the principate [69]. Luigi had risen to the republic's highest office as Gonfalonier of Justice in 1527, but the great age of his political career came with the Medici dukes, so much so that he has been considered the model of the new Medicean patrician-administrator. Under Alessandro and Cosimo he served without a break in important posts in Florentine and Tuscan administration. He was one of the original

---

[67] Cf. *ibid.*, pp. 63 ff., where this line of argument is keenly developed.

[68] See R. Ridolfi, « Francesco Guicciardini e Cosimo I », *Archivio storico italiano*, CXXI (1964), 567-606.

[69] For their offices, see AG, *Spogli*, and Mylonas, pp. 19 ff.

senators of 1532, one of the four counselors of the duke on several occasions, a frequent member of the Eight on External Affairs, and many times the chief ducal official in Pisa, Pistoia, Castrocaro, and Arezzo. Apart from the major posts, he held a very large number of minor offices which testify to the subterranean complexity of ducal administration and to the need, however absolute the duke, to employ the patriciate in the practical affairs of government. Girolamo's career was quite similar after his political apprenticeship, with Francesco's support, under Duke Alessandro. In 1540 he entered the Dugento and in 1552 became a senator. Before his death in 1556 he was several times ducal counselor and a member of the Eight on External Affairs as well as ambassador to the Emperor (1542-43) and the Pope (1550), not to mention his many lesser offices. Even Jacopo, with his republican past, made his peace with the regime. Already in the summer of 1531 and again in 1535 he was named to minor offices as an official on the plague and one of the *conservatores legum*. But the regime was not altogether reconciled to him, nor he to it, until the defeat of the Florentine exiles at Montemurlo in 1537 [70]. The clearest sign of the change was the increasing number of offices he held after 1540 when he, like Girolamo, was named to the Dugento: official of the Monte, two terms with the Eight on External Affairs, vicar of the Mugello. Whatever his private reflections on the republic and the new age of princes, his sons were among the duke's most loyal and enterprising subjects.

Not that the Guicciardini or Florence made the transition from the republic to the principate without profound changes. There were, of course, shifts in political realities and attitudes that the Guicciardini case only begins to suggest. Those constitutional restraints and patrician councils Francesco erected around the young rustic of Cafaggiolo were a house of cards when Duke Cosimo chose to have his way [71]. Francesco was not even spared the posthumous indignity of the duke's inter-

[70] « ... non hanno Jacopo per confidente »: *Lettere inedite a B. Lanfredini*, p. 143 (17 March 1532). Jacopo watched the exiles with moving ambivalence recorded in a letter to Luigi, 12 August 1537, ASF, *Carte strozziane*, ser. I, 60, fol. 165 (transcribed by Mylonas, App., pp. 125-126).

[71] G. Spini, *Cosimo I de' Medici e l'indipendenza del principato mediceo* (Florence, 1945); Berner, pp. 146 ff.

vention in the settlement of his estate in 1540 [72]. Girolamo, in 1541, could be ordered summarily to the Medici villa at Poggio a Caiano for a secret interview with the duke, and Jacopo, in the same period, was obliged to loan large sums to the state [73]. All the while patrician institutions were being restricted in function, convened at the duke's pleasure. The psychological corollary was a sense of release and resignation. In the *Storia d'Italia* Francesco moved from political theory to history, from Florentine to Italian and European history between Habsburg and Valois, from « a vast mass of petty circumstances to a tragic vision of greatness humbled and liberty lost » [74]. Politics receded from Guicciardini letters after 1537, and what remained was largely a chronicle of affairs of court or domestic news or the immediate cares of office. The afflictions of advancing years made themselves felt; the healing image of the countryside and the villa loomed ever larger [75]. These were the symptoms of aging men, but also of the passing of an age.

Beneath Guicciardini public lives were private dimensions defined by the old Florentine ideal of the citizen-scholar and the still older pull of the *vita solitaria e contemplativa*. Francesco filled a sea of papers by himself: his two Florentine histories; the *Storia d'Italia*; the *Ricordi*; the political and autobiographical writings. But the « other » Guicciardini shared this compulsion to write, only to be overshadowed in this too by Francesco. Only two political dialogues by Luigi have been printed since seventeenth- and eighteenth-century editions of his dialogue

---

[72] Niccolò G. to Luigi, 24 May 1540, ASF, *Carte strozziane*, ser. I, 62, no. 117 (excerpts in *Le carte strozziane*, I, 327).

[73] B. Lanfredini to Cosimo, 21 April 1541, ASF, *Mediceo*, 350, fol. 83 v; Jacopo, as a Monte official, loaned Cosimo over 3,000 florins between 1541 and 1543 (AG, *Scritture varie*, 49, no. 2, fol. 4 r).

[74] J. R. Hale, in his fine intro. to F. Guicciardini, *History of Italy and History of Florence* (New York, 1964), p. XLVI.

[75] See, e. g., the letter to Luigi from his physician, G. B. Poltri, 1 June 1540, ASF, *Carte strozziane*, ser. I, 62, no. 120, and the letters from his long-suffering wife Isabella, *Di villa: lettere al marito Luigi negli anni 1535 e 1542*, ed. I. Del Lungo (Florence, 1883). In 1537 Girolamo was writing to Luigi of his plans to pass his time in his villa, « lasciando queste chure fastidiose a chi è prestato da la necessità e dall'ambizione » (13 August 1537, ASF, *Carte strozziane*, ser. I, 60, fol. 248 v).

Il Sacco di Roma appeared (obscured by his younger brother again) under Francesco's name. Many, many more of his writings — literary, political, philosophical, scientific, religious — remain in MS in Florence, inadequately explored, if not unknown [76]. MSS by Bongianni are nearly as numerous and as varied, and all but forgotten [77]. Even Jacopo turned a hand to Latin epigrams at least once and copied Savonarola's prophecies [78]. Of all the brothers only Girolamo was « without letters » [79]. These are minor writers and minor works certainly, but the minor key is still a Guicciardini key, and for that a revealing measure of family and patrician culture, and of Francesco's special genius.

The earliest of the brothers' literary efforts grew out of the humanistic enthusiasms of their youth. It was a time when the *jeunesse dorée* met in the circles of Poliziano and Ficino or of their successors Marcello Virgilio Adriani and Francesco Cattani da Diacceto, especially if their fathers were like Piero Guicciardini [80]. Francesco was not immune to the rage for Latin epistles and epigrams. Even if he had been held in baptism by Marsilio Ficino, his were as self-consciously decorative and as mediocre as any [81]. Soon enough, however, he turned to legal studies (1498-1506) at Florence, Padua, and Ferrara, leaving his brothers to cultivate the muses. Between 1506 and 1508 Luigi was keeping abreast of the festive classicism of the Roman court in correspondence with Giovanni Cavalcanti. He was among the first Florentines to hear of the discovery of the Laokoon at Rome in 1506; for his part, he sent his correspondent information and a drawing

---

[76] See Albertini, pp. 413-421 *et passim*, for one of Luigi's dialogues and Simonetta's ed. of his dialogue *Del Savonarola*. Both contain useful but still very sketchy bibliography. See also F. Gilbert, « Machiavelli in an Unknown Contemporary Dialogue », *Journal of the Warburg Institute*, I (1937), 163-166.

[77] Mylonas, p. 41, cites at least a few of Bongianni's works from BNF, Magl. VIII, 1422.

[78] See R. Ridolfi, *Studi savonaroliani* (Florence, 1935), p. 27.

[79] Remigio Fiorentino, « La vita di F. Guicciardini », in the intro. to Francesco's *Historia d'Italia* (Venice, 1568).

[80] See, most recently, A. De Gaetano, « The Florentine Academy ... », *Bibliothèque d'humanisme et Renaissance*, XXX (1968), 19 ff.

[81] See the Latin letters (1499-1500) to Alessio Lapaccini in *Carteggi*, I, nos. 1-5.

of Etruscan finds near Castellina, receiving a copy of a new comedy from Rome in return [82]. The story that he was the butt of Machiavelli's *Asino d'Oro* is probably apocryphal. But Messer Niccolò did dedicate a *capitolo* on ambition to him (he might have written volumes), and Piero's letters to Machiavelli, one of them evidently forgotten in the Guicciardini archive, reveal that they had been close since 1501 [83]. It was Luigi who acquired Michelangelo's *Pitti Tondo* for the Guicciardini palace from Fra Miniato Pitti and became in later years a friend and patron of Vasari [84]. These claims on culture were recognized officially when, in 1518, Luigi was commissioned to write the Florentine government in Latin on behalf of Leo X and, in 1525, appointed to a three-year term on the governing board of the University of Pisa [85]. Jacopo's literary interest was much more limited; it went far enough, however, for him to write the Latin epigram for Lorenzo de' Medici with a group of young humanists and, in 1523, an eloquent Latin epistle to his nephew on the religious crisis in Germany [86]. But it was Bongianni who came closest to Luigi in the literary byways of the first Medici restoration. In September 1518 he was invited to correspond in Latin with Stephen Philoponus, a rhetorician in the university and a minor, very minor, light of Medicean Florence. The high-flown invitation put him in the company of a number of Florentine youths similarly addressed in a MS now in the Riccardi library. The good rhetorician told Bongianni not to plead « lack of practice

---

[82] ASF, *Lettere artistiche di diversi*, I, 8 a, 16-18, cited in AG, *Spogli*.

[83] « Priegovi sequitiate di tenermi avisato; et dando le lettere a Luigi vengono sicure », Piero wrote to Machiavelli in Borgo S. Sepolcro on 29 November 1501: AG, *Accessioni*, I, no. 6. The letter was given to Count Paolo Guicciardini by Roberto Ridolfi on 14 May 1939. Cf. N. Machiavelli, *Opere*, VI (*Lettere*, ed. F. Gaeta; Milan, 1961), 81, 202 ff., *et passim*.

[84] Luigi's son Niccolò wrote of the arrival of the *tondo* on 16 January 1531 (« non è finita ... pur il viso è quasi finito e bello assai »): ASF, *Carte strozziane*, ser. I, 59, no. 242; cf. no. 110, and *font. cit.*, ser. I, 98, fol. 134v. See Vasari's *Vita di Michelangelo*, ed. P. Barocchi (Milan/Naples, 1962), II, 224 ff.; K. Frey, *Der litterarische Nachlass Giorgio Vasaris* (Munich, 1923-1940), *passim*.

[85] The letter is in BNF, Magl. VIII, 1422, fol. 27; for his university office, see AG, *Spogli*.

[86] *Le carte strozziane*, II, 581-582, 833.

or fear of an unpolished style » and perhaps had the chance to show that his services could remedy that [87].

While classical enthusiasms may be lost, classical educations are only absorbed and molded with demands of time and place. Guicciardini educations met social and psychological motivations in complex tangents. Preoccupations that drove them on in the public world could also drive them in on themselves for relief and enlightenment, and in this private world contemporary problems sought out past models in history and in literature. Francesco's education was a platform from which to survey his contemporaries and himself; his brothers' learning a dense thicket that often shut off their view and cramped their style. But just as Machiavelli had spoken to his Ancients in « curial robes », all the literary Guicciardini — Francesco, Luigi, Bongianni — clothed their literary selves in careful guises. Francesco poses, splendidly self-conscious, pen in hand, the first page of the *Storia d'Italia* before him, in the portrait by Bugiardini [88]. Art shaped the solitude of his most secret writings. To speak to himself he spoke to an audience, an accusing tribunal, in the *Accusatoria* and the *Defensoria*, and the *Ricordi*, far from recording pure experience, fashioned it into principles. With carefully ruled margins, Bongianni wrote prefaces to works he never seems to have written [89]. To introduce a series of rustic dialogues — *Il Ragnatello*, *Le Pecchie* — written in the late twenties and early thirties, Luigi cast himself as the patrician-sage withdrawn from civic life. Ancient predecessors dignified him: Phocion, Themistocles, Camillus, Scipio. His surroundings were Horatian, « my small and delightful villa, where I live alone [and] do not lack occasion, with mind elevated, to consider the marvelous effects of all-wise nature ». If he could not abandon the ungrateful world of activity altogether, learned leisure could keep it at bay [90].

---

[87] Biblioteca Riccardiana, Florence, MS. 911, fol. 63 v. On Philoponus, see M. Cosenza, *Biographical and Bibliographical Dictionary of the Italian Humanists* (Boston, 1962).

[88] See P. Guicciardini, « Iconografia guicciardiniana », in *F. G. nel IV centenario della morte, 1540-1940* (Florence, 1940), pp. 107-115.

[89] E. g., BNF, Magl. VIII, 1493, fols. 284 r-286 r.

[90] BNF, Magl. VIII, 1422, fol. 108 r.

Of course, Guicciardini literary trappings were very different from Machiavelli's curial robes. Whole intellectual histories have been written around the differences between Machiavelli and Francesco[91]. On the one hand, relentlessly brilliant Machiavelli, *popolano*, poet, political theorist; on the other hand, Messer Francesco, aristocrat, agnostic, *the* historian. The distinctions are drawn less crudely now than in the two famous essays written by Francesco De Sanctis more than 100 years ago. The friendship of the two has been retraced; their common assumptions and commitments have been examined. The differences remain, however, as real as Francesco's critical *Considerations* on Machiavelli's *Discourses*. They are partly timeless differences, marvelously produced in one time, between optimism and disillusionment, theory and history, poetry and prose. In time and space they represent the outlooks of different social classes, temperaments, and styles, magnified, like the art around them, to heroic proportions. They also reflect the nearly fifteen years separating the younger (but always older-seeming) Guicciardini from Machiavelli and so parallel the intellectual transition from a Renaissance to a post-Renaissance world. And yet Francesco's mental pilgrimage was not as lonely as he imagined, or as historians have believed; his themes are Guicciardini themes. There are no *Ricordi*, much less another *Storia d'Italia*, from the « other » Guicciardini, but there are elaborate Guicciardini polyphonies around Francesco's central voice.

First of all, on the call for particulars, the sceptical empiricism of Francesco's mature thinking. Even Girolamo, business-bound, could strain to sound like his greater brother: « This predicting of the future, and especially in great affairs, one sees to be fallacious from experience, because very often a third thing may arise that did not appear to merit consideration and yet may change everything; thus he who takes precipitate decisions ... [commits] a kind of madness ... »[92]. There are similar

---

[91] Beginning with two classic essays by Francesco De Sanctis, in *Saggi critici*, ed. L. Russo (Bari, 1957), III. See also U. Spirito, *Machiavelli e Guicciardini* (Rome, 1945), and F. Gilbert, *Machiavelli and Guicciardini; Politics and History in Sixteenth-Century Florence* (Princeton, 1965).

[92] Girolamo to Luigi, 13 August 1537, ASF, *Carte strozziane*, ser. I, 60, fol. 246 v.

injunctions to consider the particular case in the letters of Luigi and Jacopo [93]. In his turn Bongianni resumed a great confrontation. For Bongianni, too, wrote, or began to write, considerations on the *Discourses* of Machiavelli [94]. There are only a few pages of a first draft and, Guicciardini-like, a second draft crabbed with corrections. But this is one of the earliest reactions to Machiavelli, however brief, and it is a wholly Guicciardini reaction. « One can[not] with general discourses include all those particulars without the consideration of which one would be caught in many errors in human affairs. For, while men may descend ... from a common origin and be composed of the same elements, nevertheless, their character, the diversity of time, of place, of habits and customs, diverse accidents, necessities, and occasions make them change frequently in spirit and action ». To which Bongianni added that Machiavelli was guilty of distorting examples « to his meaning ». The key principle of the Legislator was as much at fault as the method. No one, not Philip of Macedon or David or Augustus, could foresee and provide against the flux of human affairs. Bongianni analyzed each case, then turned a Machiavellian point against Machiavelli: « It is necessary that [a prince] proceed sometimes with rigidity and justice, sometimes with more piety and mercy, and sometimes that he extend favor to his friends and sometimes restrict it ». This was the real lesson of antiquity and of the Florentine experience since 1494. « Original foundations are not enough in establishing a city, a province, or a kingdom, but it is necessary that [they] be regulated and ruled continually by the prudence and virtue of whoever governs and rules them ... Time varies and men are mobile and affected by various accidents and occasions, propelled by hope and fear ... ».

These reflections rested on perceptions of realities old and new. Beneath surfaces of harmony, order, and optimism so often used to characterize the Renaissance mentality, a many-sided revolt against abstraction and a sensitivity to historical change had entered into what William J. Bouwsma has called « the

---

[93] E. g., *ibid.*, fols. 11 r, 268 v.

[94] BNF, Magl. VIII, 1493, fols. 287 r-289 v, from which I translate the quotations that follow.

Renaissance view of reality »[95]. Machiavelli had struggled with the two levels in the Renaissance experience and in himself. But Machiavelli did not live through the terrible experiences of 1527-1530 and beyond. Awed, fascinated, fearful, the Guicciardini saw the crisis of Italy through, and the groping sense of a new reality riveted inherited feelings for flux and change. Human affairs were « like a sea driven by the winds » in the famous opening lines of the *Storia d'Italia*. Even in the calm of Poppiano, Bongianni saw an Italy « vilified and suffocated by its own discord, by the condition of the times, by the necessity of things, by celestial influences, or, as some wish, by the just wrath of God ... »[96]. Luigi, between a shudder and a sigh, lamented « this ruined world »[97] which tortured a page of poetry out of pages of Guicciardini prose. Only the thin bonds of friendship kept the world from chaos:

Se nodi d'amicitia non legassino
Le ben partite et compensate some,
Forza fare che corpi abandonassino
Tucto l'ufitio loro, il loco, e'l nome,
Et gl'elementi tutti ritornassino
Sobto l'antico confuso cognome[98].

Where they could, the Guicciardini clutched at themes of certainty. Intense convictions, fragments of faith, burst into erratic counterpoint with the call for the particular and the concrete in their century. Just as often reasoned conviction and consistency were the missing middle ground. Thus the Guicciardini encounter with Savonarola, whose spirit they could never really live into, or out of, their lives. Francesco's religious ambivalence has been noted often enough: on one side, moments of confession, love-hate towards Luther, long notes from Savonarola as late as 1529, the « divine authority » with which the *Frate* was made to speak in the *Storia d'Italia*; on the other

---

[95] W. J. Bouwsma, *Venice and the Defense of Republican Liberty*; *Renaissance Values in the Age of the Counter Reformation* (Berkeley and Los Angeles, 1968), esp. pp. 1-51.

[96] BNF, Magl. VIII, 1422, fol. 243 v, from an essay on Charles V.

[97] *Ibid.*, fol. 141 v.

[98] *Ibid.*, fol. 156 v.

side, bitter anticlericalism, displacement of Providence by Fortuna, and a Christianity decorous, rule-giving, and inevitable [99]. Francesco's brothers have been found on both sides: Jacopo in his Savonarolian *zibaldone*; Luigi *Frateschi*-baiting in his recently-edited dialogue *Del Savonarola*. On the whole, historians and critics have weighed Guicciardini ambivalence towards the cool and conventional or the critical. In the Guicciardini papers, however, the religious question is not so easily resolved, but closer to the core.

The evidence crops up between secular pages, like religion in Guicciardini lives. Following a fragment of a political dialogue there is a preface by Luigi on the differences between ancient and modern popes; after a state-letter in the name of Leo X, a sermon on mercy dated Holy Saturday, 1525; on the scrap of a letter (from Fra Miniato Pitti?) a list of theological works on free will in Luigi's hand [100]. A treatise on the priesthood and two sermons by Bongianni fall between an essay *De unitate et eius scala* and a description (evidently from the *Storia d'Italia*) of the battle of Pavia in 1525 [101]. « Have mercy on me, your ungrateful servant, O God », Luigi preached; « extinguish my iniquity, cancel my grievous errors, annul my incomparable sins »! Bongianni echoed: « Mercy, Lord God, mercy, good Lord, mercy, holy Lord ...; we confess being worthy of every ill ...; unworthy of pity and mercy, we confess meriting Hell and every torment »! Mere rhetoric perhaps; but the language of faith is seldon new, or less convincing for being conventional. It is in any case remarkable *Guicciardini* rhetoric which tapped that religious current Savonarola had opened in Florence and in the Palazzo Guicciardini. And once opened, it spilled from sermonizing into discourse. The primitive Church was like a blinding light, argued Luigi; on the Roman Church it is better to be silent. Before St. Sylvester the Church was ruled by the Holy Spirit; afterwards by Lucifer [102]. For its first 300 years, Bongianni echoed again, the Church proceeded « with the splen-

---

[99] V. Luciani, *F. G. e la fortuna dell'opera sua* (Florence, 1949), pp. 376 ff.

[100] BNF, Magl. VIII, 1422, fols. 11 r-16 r, 22 bis, 29 r-32 v, 147 v.

[101] *Ibid.*, fols. 278 r-303 r.

[102] *Ibid.*, fols. 15 r-15 v.

dor of miracles and of goodness and of doctrine; then, little by little, men began to vary and to expand its ordinances ... »[103]. Only all-mighty and unfathomable God kept the true Church incorruptible, like a jewel, amidst Roman corruption. Savonarola and Luther have clearly made their mark.

But there was no passage from one to the other; there could not be. In the famous *ricordo*, Francesco's career with the papacy, his « particolare », kept him from following Luther; and with Luther or without him it is clear that he was not prepared to relinquish « the laws of the Christian religion in the manner in which they are generally interpreted and understood » (by Italians and Catholics, it is tempting to add)[104]. Luigi's sermon painted the sinful helplessness of man in Lutheran colors, only to let man earn his salvation. Even if it meant a crude literary trick: a divine light flooded the room and redeemed penitent Luigi in a baroque finale[105]. Bongianni, after all, wrote on the dignity of the priesthood, and, in his will, distributed the usual offerings to the religious[106]. Guicciardini religion was anticlerical without the priesthood of all believers, anxious without justification by faith or tridentine reform, fervid without consistency or consolation.

No wonder the Guicciardini, like their contemporaries, were drawn to the occult, even when they resisted the attraction. Medieval traditions and Renaissance precedents lured them on. Sceptical asides on astrologers and a lifelong fascination with astrology: Francesco's case is, again, well known[107]. But Luigi shared his concern, if fewer of his reservations, while Jacopo and Bongianni moved in interested orbits. As early as 1516 a Jewish astrologer was recommended to Luigi from Rome[108]. In July 1526 Jacopo, vice-president of the Romagna and obviously concerned to see if the stars were with him, requested a forecast that Ramberto Malatesta, the strange count of So-

[103] *Ibid.*, fol. 278 v.

[104] *Ricordo* 28, serie II, *Opere*, VIII, 290.

[105] BNF, Magl. VIII, 1422, fol. 32 v.

[106] *Ibid.*, fol. 278 r; AG, *Testamenti*, XXXVII, no. 16.

[107] See Ridolfi, *Life*, pp. 57-63, and, in general, E. Garin, « Magic and Astrology in the Civilization of the Renaissance », *Science and Civic Life in the Italian Renaissance*, trans. P. Munz (New York, 1969), pp. 145-165.

[108] *Le carte strozziane*, I, 137.

gliano, practiced in the art, had prepared for Francesco. Malatesta returned a summary — difficulties and dangers for Italy and the Church, a safe enough prediction — and referred Jacopo to Francesco for the details. Francesco was the expert, Malatesta implied; yet he might have mentioned Luigi [109]. In a Palatine MS in Florence there are thirty-two letters on astrology from Malatesta to Luigi between 1521 and 1531 [110]. Over the years Luigi pressed the astrologer for horoscopes for himself, for Clement VII, and for his family. Count Ramberto begged off on grounds of illness and overwork, tempted with promises of rare mysteries (sometimes already sent to Francesco), recommended astrological manuals (to be borrowed from Francesco), and, less often, gave Luigi what he wanted. Luigi's horoscope, when it came, had the advantage of confirming what he already knew, or hoped: bad luck in his youth but « honors and dignities ... wisdom ... noble magistracies » later; a susceptibility to illness (he was to keep from windy places and « coitu superfluo ») but a life-span beyond middle age, exalted by his country, by women, and by honored friends [111]. It seems a rather small price for the favors the count often requested for himself and for his friends.

Alchemy was at least as fascinating to Luigi and Bongianni, if not to their brothers. The same Palatine MS contains five letters on alchemy to Luigi from a Marchion Cerrono in Venice and Bologna (1534-1539) and another five, alchemical treatises really, from a Lombard priest, Giovanni Bersano, in Cortona (1539-1540). Cerrono's letters are reverent and rambling invitations to speculation on « the most occult writings on physics » [112]. Didactic and erudite, Bersano offered Luigi a full course on alchemy, parrying his insistent questions. His specialty had been Geber, but his studies had convinced him that all true

---

[109] Rambertus Bonatesta (!) to Jacopo, 7 December 1526, ASF, *Carte strozziane*, ser. III, 220, fols. 213-214. On Malatesta, see L. Thorndike, *A History of Magic and Experimental Science* (New York, 1929-1958), V, 220; Cosenza, *Dictionary*. Perhaps he is the mysterious author of Francesco's horoscope whom Ridolfi failed to track down in his *Life*, p. 290, n. 5.

[110] BNF, Palat. 1124, fols. 16-100, *passim*; cf. *I MSS palatini della BNF*, ed. A. Saitta Revignas (Rome, 1955), III, 270-271.

[111] *Ibid.*, fols 42-43 (31 August 1521).

[112] *Ibid.*, fol. 76 r (27 December 1534).

writers on physics had said the same thing in hidden terms: natural processes could be accelerated by certain natural substances. What was important was that any teaching must be tested by experiment. (Luigi wrote « NOTA » in the margin, gullible perhaps, but a good Guicciardini). If Bersano could only *show* Luigi his experiments of more than twenty years ... perhaps there was a « place suitable for a priest » in Florence? [113] Luigi rose to the bait (doubtless with visions of Midas). Those who snicker at alchemy betray their ignorance, he had written his son Niccolò in 1535 [114]. At the same time he had been writing to Bongianni about his contacts with Cerrono and a certain Master Camillo of Arezzo [115]. His plan in 1539 was to persuade Bongianni and, with his aid, the other brothers to put Bersano in the parish church of Poppiano so that he might live « to see with my own eyes and to touch with my own hands the miracles of nature » [116]. As the author of an essay on alchemy, a treatise on mines, and a numerological discourse, Bongianni should have been willing [117]. For some reason, he balked and nothing seems to have come of the project. Nevertheless, in 1542 Luigi was reading Agrippa of Nettesheim and, as late as 1543, was still exchanging alchemical lore with Bongianni [118].

Logically implausible, the combination of classicism, empiricism, Christianity, and the occult was, for the Guicciardini, historically feasible and psychologically true. To isolate any one element or direction alone would be to misrepresent their minds and their age. The configuration must be seen as a whole: the state of strong spirits stranded between Renaissance, Reformation, and Counter-Reform.

Sometime between Francesco's death in 1540 and the summer of 1543, Bongianni Guicciardini drafted a letter to the Emperor Charles V on behalf of the surviving brothers. Caesar's « divine goodness » and « illustrious humanity » have given

---

113 *Ibid.*, fol. 67 v (10 June 1539).

114 ASF, *Carte strozziane*, ser. I, 61, no. 77 (12 September 1535).

115 *Ibid.*, fols. 31, 45.

116 *Font. cit.*, ser. I, 62, no. 16 (4 October 1539); see also nos. 37, 54.

117 BNF, Magl. VIII, 1422, fols. 231 r-234 v, 173 r-180 v, 272 r-273 v.

118 Niccolò to Luigi, 11 December 1542, ASF, *Carte strozziane*, ser. I, 63, no. 45; Bongianni to Luigi, 3 January 1543, *ibid.*, no. 79.

them the courage. They have come to offer him the gift which his representative had told them he desired — Francesco's *Storia d'Italia*:

[And this] is extremely gratifying to us, principally because of the desire to please your Majesty, and, since we are perplexed and doubtful whether to publish these Histories composed by Messer Francesco, our brother, or to keep them secret, because it impelled us to make them known, being [as they are] a thing of great information, written faithfully and with every diligence in the search for truth. Although, prevented by death, [Messer Francesco] could not give them the ultimate ornament and magnificence that histories require, as was his intention and as he would easily have done with his rare genius, ornamented by many virtues and sciences, nevertheless they do not lack useful ornaments and precepts, so that it might have been more in error to keep them secret than to publish them. On the other hand, we were restrained by the fact that they might not correspond to the expectation of his great quality and his last wishes; for even though he did not order it in his testament, he appeared inclined to want them burned, annulled and destroyed, since he knew very well that he had not conducted them to that perfection that he had proposed. Accordingly ... nothing could be more splendid to us [than to present them to] your Majesty, whose authority may silence any slanderer and placate the mind of our brother, if from heaven, where we hope he may be, he should look with disdain on our publishing them against his will in order to satisfy your Majesty and to obey our illustrious lord, Duke Cosimo (to whom he was always devoted), who, having heard your Majesty's wish, has exhorted us to act, putting aside any doubt or scruple ... [119]

It is a remarkable episode — unknown and unexpected in the career of the *Storia d'Italia* before its publication in 1561, but altogether characteristic of the relationships between Francesco and his brothers. The turgid style and submissive

---

[119] BNF, Magl. VIII, 1493, no. 20. The *terminus* 1543 may be adduced from the fact that the Emperor's request had come from « suo castellano », assuming this to be Don Giovanni della Luna, captain of the imperial garrison in Florence until its withdrawal on 3 July 1543: Spini, *Cosimo I*, p. 282. Other new evidence reveals that none other than Duke Cosimo was reading the *Storia d'Italia* in 1541: ASF, *Mediceo*, 351, fol. 26 r; 350, fol. 83 v. In the end, of course, the *editio princeps* was to be published by Agnolo di Girolamo in 1561. Cf. Ridolfi, *Life*, pp. 331-332.

manner are a final measure of distance between them; the sense of fraternal responsibility a sign of enduring ties.

Society is made up of such little communities, *grande histoire* of *petites histoires* which, however small, may be large by implication and, sometimes, in effect. Where Jacob Burckhardt saw only individuals, it has often proved necessary to see groups. Even the proud solitary, Francesco Guicciardini, blends, in many respects, into a family portrait which mirrors, in turn, the texture of his world. One perspective does not replace the other; it is enough for one perspective to render the other problematic, like the Renaissance experience itself.

PAUL F. GRENDLER

THE CONCEPT OF HUMANIST IN CINQUECENTO ITALY

Much scholarly discussion on the meaning and significance of Italian Renaissance humanism has ensued in the past twenty-five years. The works of Hans Baron, Eugenio Garin, and Paul Kristeller demonstrate the important role that the understanding of humanism plays in the interpretation of the Renaissance. These as well as other interpretations involve the understanding of such terms as *studia humanitatis* and *vita civile* because these terms meant much to Renaissance man and were often discussed in the fifteenth and sixteenth centuries. Scholars often employ two other terms as well: humanist and humanism. The latter is a nineteenth-century coinage not yet located in a Renaissance context. Scholars today either use these terms in a general way or define them carefully within the context of their discussions, and do not rest their argument on Renaissance definitions of these terms.

«Humanist» (*umanista* and more commonly *humanista* in the Cinquecento) originated in the Renaissance, and by the second half of the Cinquecento appeared reasonably often and had a fairly clear meaning for Italians. The purpose of this article is to examine the use and understanding of the term humanist in the second half of the Cinquecento with six occurrences and a discourse on humanists, hitherto unnoted.

Two scholars, Augusto Campana and Kristeller, agree that *umanista* denoted one who was involved in the teaching or study of the *studia humanitatis*. Campana has argued that in its original sense, *umanista* qualified a person « as a public or private teacher of classical literature, of the chair of *humanitas* or *humanità* ». He also points to a later, secondary use of the term, as a student of classical learning who was not necessarily also a teacher [1]. Kristeller argues that the term *umanista* originated in the latter half of the fifteenth century « in the slang of university students and gradually penetrated into official usage ». *Umanista* signified

[1] Augusto Campana, « The Origin of the Word Humanist », *Journal of the Warburg and Courtauld Institutes*, IX (1946), 66.

the teacher or representative of the *studia humanitatis*, defined by Kristeller as « grammar, rhetoric, history, poetry, and moral philosophy, and the study of each of these subjects was understood to include the reading and interpretation of its standard ancient writers in Latin and, to a lesser extent, in Greek » [2]. Kristeller adds that individual humanists were interested in other disciplines as well. For Garin, however, a humanist was one who shared the outlook of Renaissance humanism, which is seen as a new vision of man on earth to be found in men of action outside the schools as well as in scholars and teachers. Man was a participant in the *vita civile*, one who dedicated his life in service to city and family, and who accepted earthly values. Garin's definition of humanism puts heavy emphasis on philology and history, but he does not exclude speculative philosophy, including Florentine Platonism [3]. Hence, for Garin a humanist might engage in any activity but was disposed to view man in a certain way.

Campana has located nine Italian uses of humanist in manuscript and printed sources from 1512 to 1588 which support his argument. Kristeller has located the word in a letter of 1490 by the rector of the University of Pisa, and in sixteenth-century university documents of Bologna and Ferrara. In addition, these two scholars have found nine English, French, German, and Spanish references. Garin, on the other hand, adds an example from a document of the *Studio* of Pisa of 1525 in which *umanista* and *Phylosopho* were in close proximity but not interchangeable [4].

I have located five additional occurrences, and noted them in a previous article [5]. In 1540 the Venetian author Francesco

---

[2] *Renaissance Thought: the Classic, Scholastic, and Humanistic Strains* (New York, 1961), pp. 10, 111. Kristeller's views are repeated in other works.

[3] For Garin's view, see *Italian Humanism, Philosophy and Civic Life in the Renaissance*, tr. by Peter Munz (Oxford, 1965), pp. 1-17; *L'educazione in Europa (1400-1600), problemi e programmi* (Bari, 1957), pp. 30-31; *Medioevo e Rinascimento, studi e ricerche*. 2nd ed. (Bari, 1961), pp. 6-7.

[4] Campana, « The Origin of the Word Humanist », pp. 60-73; Kristeller, *Renaissance Thought*, p. 160, n. 61; Garin, *Medioevo e Rinascimento*, p. 7, n. 2. Cf. Marcel Françon, « Humanisme », *Renaissance Quarterly*, XXI (1968), 300-303.

[5] Paul F. Grendler, « Five Italian Occurrences of *Umanista*, 1540-1574 », *Renaissance Quarterly*, XX (1967), 317-325.

Sansovino (1521-83) used the term to refer to an undesignated learned profession. Lodovico Domenichi (1515-64), an author of popular literature, used the term in a book of 1549 to mean grammarians and philosophers who had contact with the classics in schools. Since he included metaphysicians and Platonists within the term his reference supported Garin. In 1554 Sansovino used humanist to refer to a young student of classical Latin. This was the first step in the *studia humanitatis* which led, in the end, to an educated man who lived the *vita civile*. Giovanni Andrea Gilio da Fabriano (fl. 1550-80) in 1564 called humanists those who were expert in etymology with particular competence in Latin. Finally, Sansovino named Lazzaro Bonamico (1479-1552), a champion of Latin who taught at Padua and interpreted Cicero, as a humanist in 1574. On the whole, these references supported the view of Campana and Kristeller.

The first three new occurrences are in the correspondence of the papal nuncio to Venice, Monsignor Giovanni Antonio Facchinetti (1519-91) who later became Pope Innocent IX. Born in Bologna, Facchinetti was nuncio from May 1566 to the end of June 1573. An experienced papal diplomat who served as vicar to Cardinal Alessandro Farnese in Avignon, and governor of Parma after the death of Pier Luigi Farnese, Facchinetti was « molto literato » according to the Venetian ambassador, and his correspondence shows him to have been an able and energetic nuncio [6]. Writing to Rome on August 31, 1566, Facchinetti reported on his inquiry with the Holy Office in Venice concerning Publio Francesco Spinola who was in a Venetian prison. He had learned that the prisoner was « a Milanese, a poet, a humanist, and unfrocked ». (« Egli è un milanese, poeta, humanista e sfratato »). Facchinetti added that Spinola had been in prison for 28 months, was a relapsed heretic because he had abjured heresy more than once in Milan but that he continued to hold various heretical opinions. The zealous nuncio wished to examine his case further because « if anyone can have information on heretics, certainly this man would because as a

[6] *Nunziature di Venezia*, VIII (Istituto Storico Italiano per l' età moderna e contemporanea, Fonti per la Storia d'Italia, 65), a cura di Aldo Stella (Rome, 1963), IX-X.

humanist he read to many here in Venice and associated with many here and elsewhere »[7].

Christened Francesco but adding the Latinized Publio, Spinola was born in Como c. 1520, although later considered a Milanese. After leaving an unidentified religious order and being exiled from Milan, he lived in Bergamo, Brescia, Venice, and Padua, often attached to noble households. On several occasions he taught: in 1560 he began the academic year in Brescia where he interpreted *Pro Milone* and other works of Cicero, and in the following year he supervised the literary education of the sons of the Venetian noble, Leonardo Mocenigo. Then, in or about 1562, he taught the son of the Venetian printer Gabriel Giolito while he worked for four months as a corrector for his press. All his published works were in Latin: in 1558 he completed and published a Latin translation of the psalms begun by Marco Antonio Flaminio; his collected poetry was published in 1563; and in 1562 his method for the correction of the Julian calendar. In July 1564 he was arrested for heresy, and, refusing to recant, he was executed by drowning on January 31, 1567[8].

Concerned with the role which humanists could play in the spread of heresy, Facchinetti returned to the subject in a letter of May 24, 1567, and used « humanist » again. He reported to Rome that due to « the contagion of heresy being born of these humanists and schoolmasters », the Holy Office had resolved to publish a decree enforcing religious loyalty on them[9]. Ever fearful of the expansion of ecclesiastical jurisdiction, the Venetian government protested but in the end the nuncio arrived at an arrangement satisfactory to Rome. He reported in January 1569 that schoolmasters (omitting reference to humanists), would not be able to teach letters, music, arithmetic, or anything

---

[7] *Ibid.*, p. 100. « Et se alcuno può haver notitia d'heretici è verisimile che costui l'habbia perché come humanista ha letto a molti qui in Vinetia et praticato con molti e qui et altrove ».

[8] Pio Paschini, « Un umanista disgraziato nel Cinquecento: Publio Francesco Spinola », *Nuovo archivio veneto*, N. S., XXXVII (1919), 65-186.

[9] *Nunziature di Venezia*, p. 220. « Nascendo la contagione dell'heresia da questi humanisti et mastri di scuola, il tribunale dell'Inquisitione era venuto in risolutione di publicare il decreto ch'io mando qui inchiuso ».

else in Venice, publicly or privately, without examination and approval by the Patriarch [10].

Facchinetti called Spinola a humanist, noted that as a humanist he read to many people, and therefore wished to regulate humanists and schoolmasters. The third reference probably indicates that humanists, like schoolmasters, taught [11]. Since Spinola did teach, as well as comment on Cicero and publish exclusively in Latin, the teaching material of Spinola as a humanist was probably Latin literature. But, it must be added, if Spinola was a humanist because he read and taught the Latin classics, his intellectual interests were not limited to this. He also composed Latin poetry [12], had enough knowledge of mathematics to write on the problem of the calendar, and had a religious interest strong enough to translate the Psalms and to die for his beliefs.

The next occurrence of *humanista* is in a treatise on the education of a prince written in 1571 by Girolamo Muzio (1496-1576) [13]. Born in Capodistria of humble parentage, Muzio made a successful career in the service of many noble houses and as a prolific author of poetry, courtly literature, history, and religious polemic. For the tutor of a young prince Muzio rejected *letterati*, philosophers, medical and legal scholars, and mathematicians, before considering professors of the humanities. These he also rejected because they had a tendency to tyrannize their young charges in their schools [14]. Printed in the margin

---

[10] *Ibid.*, p. 481.

[11] When the nuncio spoke of humanists and schoolmasters, he saw them as similar insofar as heresy emanated from both and he wished to regulate both. Although he did not mention regulation of humanists as such when he returned to the subject in January 1569, it is possible that humanists were included in the decree as teachers of letters.

[12] Facchinetti probably differentiated humanist from poet, as his first statement described Spinola as Milanese, poet, humanist, and unfrocked monk. Since Milanese, humanist, and unfrocked monk refer to different aspects of existence, then poet should also mean a distinct activity.

[13] *Avvertimenti morali del Mutio Iustinopolitano* (Venice, 1572). Some copies carry 1571 as the date. It was not reprinted. Cf. Paolo Giaxich, *Vita di Girolamo Muzio Giustinopolitano* (Trieste, 1847).

[14] *Avvertimenti*, p. 4. « Nè a professori di studii di humanità è da dare cotale impresa, che (per non ne dir altro) essi essendo usati signoreggiare i teneri fanciulli nelle schuole ... ».

as a guide to the content, was *Humanisti*, along with *Philosofo*, *Medici*, *Leggisti*, and *Mathematici*. Muzio went on to cite from antiquity a « maestro di schuola » and a « maestro di lettere latine » who tyrannized their pupils. He concluded that he preferred an honest man of good habits who was experienced in the « things of the world », and who was « accustomed to practice with men and in courts », to any man of learning for the prince's tutor [15].

Whoever added the marginal note — probably the author or an unknown editor — identified a humanist as a professor of the humanities who taught children in a school. The more interesting point is that Muzio did not want a humanist to tutor the young prince because, as he later explained, he wished the boy to be taught « things » not « words ». Muzio was not completely opposed to books, but wanted the boy to learn from them heroic examples and moral doctrines rather than grammatical details [16]. He exhibited a hostility toward humanists to be found in some other Italians in the middle and second half of the sixteenth century [17].

Another use of humanist was by Mambrino Roseo da Fabriano (c. 1500-c. 1584), a prolific historian and translator [18]. In a history of the period 1513-1559, first published in 1562, which was part three of Giovanni Tarcagnota's *Istorie del mondo*, Roseo discussed the damage to scholars wrought by the *Index of Prohibited Books* issued by Paul IV in 1559. Every citizen had to take both Latin and vernacular books to the Inquisition, and Roseo opined that the *Index* was very injurious to the booksellers. Further, no learned man of any profession — doctors, legists, and humanists — was spared this harm [19]. Here humanists were

---

[15] *Ibid.*, p. 5.

[16] *Ibid.*, p. 18.

[17] See Paul F. Grendler, *Critics of the Italian World, 1530-1560: Anton Francesco Doni, Nicolò Franco, and Ortensio Lando* (Madison, 1969), pp. 136-161.

[18] For Roseo, see Romualdo Canavari, « Sulle opere di Mambrino Roseo da Fabriano », in *L'assedio di Firenze di Mambrino Roseo di Fabriano*, ed. Ant. Dom. Pierrugues (Florence, 1894), pp. XI-XLIX; and Francesco Ant. Soria, *Memorie storico-critiche degli storici napolitani* (Naples, 1781-82), pp. 531-33.

[19] *Delle istorie del mondo, parte terza. Aggiunte da M. Mambrino Roseo da Fabriano alle istorie di M. Giovanni Tarcagnota* (Venice, 1585), p. 603. « Fu estimato il danno di questi libri nuovi di librari con i vecchi, che ogni

members of a learned profession comparable to legists and doctors, but Roseo did not elaborate.

A use of humanist in a similar context appeared in the first edition of the *Piazza universale* (1585) of Tommaso Garzoni (March 1549-June 8, 1589). From Bagnacavallo, he studied law and logic at Ferrara and Siena, and later philosophy and theology, taking the habit of the Lateran Congregation of the Canons Regular at the monastery of Santa Maria di Porto in Ravenna in 1566. His major works include the *Piazza universale*, *Teatro de' vari e diversi cervelli* (1583), *L'hospidale de' pazzi* (1586), and *Sinagoga de gl'Ignoranti* (1589). They are storehouses of information on his period and enjoyed great popularity, appearing in many editions, including Spanish, Latin, German, and English translations [20]. The *Piazza universale* is a discussion of all of man's professions including that of the *librari*. The booksellers belonged to a noble profession because, among other reasons, they were always in the company of literate and virtuous persons: theologians, jurists, doctors of medicine, humanists, and so on [21]. As with Roseo, a humanist was a member of a learned profession, comparable to a legal or medical scholar.

In the 1587 edition of the *Piazza universale*, Garzoni added a « Discorso de gli Humanisti », the most extensive discussion

---

cittadino, così volgari, come Latini portava alla casa della inquisizione, di grandissima importanza: ne fu niuno litterato di qualunque professione, che fosse da questo danno essentato, medici, legisti, & umanisti, e d'ogni sorte ». The book appeared in 1562, and was reprinted in 1573, 1580, 1585, 1592, and 1598, always in Venice. The passage remains unaltered in the editions examined (all except 1562 and 1580).

[20] On Garzoni, see Girolamo Ghilini, *Teatro d'huomini letterati* (Milan, 1633), I, 416-17; Jean Pierre Niceron, *Mémoires pour servir à l'histoire des hommes illustres dans la République des lettres* (Paris, 1736), XXXVI, 59-65; Benedetto Croce, « Pagine di Tommaso Garzoni », in *Poeti e scrittori del pieno e del tardo Rinascimento*. 2nd ed. (Bari, 1958), pp. 208-20; and Giuseppe Cochiara, *Popolo e letteratura in Italia* (Turin, 1959), pp. 54-56.

[21] *La piazza universale di tutte le professioni del mondo* (Venice, 1585), p. 846 (sig. GGG 7 v). The signature is added because the pagination is often erroneous. « Per un'altra ragione si dice, che la professione de' Librari sia molto nobile, perché sempre sono in compagnia di persone letterate, & virtuose, di Teologi, di Dottori di legge, di Medici, d'Humanisti, & di molti scientiati ». This quotation occurs in all the other Italian editions. See n. 22.

yet found in the fifteenth and sixteenth centuries [22]. He began by noting that he had tried to embrace all the professions in his book but his attention had been drawn to his previous omission of the humanist, one of the most noble and honored. Garzoni added that he had originally sought to include the humanist under four other professions: grammarian, rhetorician, historian, and poet. But he had become convinced that a humanist is more than this, or rather, a compound of all these. The humanist must have complete knowledge of the disciplines which are the foundation of the profession of *humanità*. In addition, he has lesser knowledge of all the liberal arts, such as mathematics and moral philosophy, and has at his command the principles of all knowledge. In sum, Garzoni continued, the true humanist knows Latin and Greek, and can easily write in both oratory, poetry and prose. He knows every author [23] and from the professorial chair (*cathedra*) can interpret them worthily. Of such perfection or not far from it were Lazzaro Bonamico, Romolo Amaseo, Francesco Robortello, Carlo Sigonio, Fulvio Morato, and others. Garzoni warned against the error and presumption of those who dabbled in the beginning elements of grammar, and then, having taught these principles, arrogantly wished to be called humanists. They profaned the honored name of humanist, they were the reason that the world failed to distinguish between the true and false humanist, and spoke unfavorably of the profession. Garzoni attributed the above definition of the true humanist to Fabio Paolini who was then teaching in Venice, and who had recited in the library of St. Mark an oration concerning the perfect *doctor humanitatis* at the beginning of the academic year.

The five named as humanists and Paolini were scholars of classical Latin and Greek, teachers of the humanities in uni-

---

[22] The first two editions, 1585 and 1586, did not contain the discourse on humanists. Garzoni added it as the 155th and last discourse to the third edition, 1587, and it was then enlarged from 32 lines to 66 lines in five subsequent Italian editions of 1589, 1592, 1595, 1599, and 1601, before disappearing in Italian editions of 1610, 1617, 1638 and 1665, (although it was still listed in their Table of Contents). For the text of the discourse see the Appendix.

[23] Whether Garzoni meant the Latin and Greek classics or all authors is not clear.

versities and similar centers of learning, and authors who wrote on rhetoric, history, and poetry. Lazzaro Bonamico was a well-known teacher at Padua and champion of Latin against the vernacular. Born in Bassano, he taught at Bologna, and later was appointed to read Latin and Greek at the *Studio* in Padua. His few works were published posthumously but he acquired fame as a teacher of eloquence. In Sperone Speroni's *Dialogo delle lingue* Bonamico was the speaker who argued for Latin and, to a lesser extent, Greek, against the vernacular. Francesco Sansovino also called Bonamico a *humanista* in 1574 [24]. Romolo Amaseo (1489-1552) was an esteemed author, scholar, and teacher of the humanities. He held the chair of Greek at Padua, and also taught rhetoric, poetry, and the humanities at Bologna and Rome. Author of Latin orations and translator of Xenophon and Pausanias into Latin, he strongly identified the humanities with antiquity, stressing archeology and linguistics in their study. Like Bonamico, he argued that Latin was the only suitable language for the humanities, although Pietro Bembo maliciously pointed out that he taught the vernacular privately [25].

Francesco Robortello (Udine 1516-Padua 1567) studied at Bologna, held the chair of eloquence at Lucca and Pisa, taught at Venice, and then succeeded Bonamico at Padua where he remained with the exception of a short period of teaching at Bologna from 1557-60. He tried to ascertain the laws of poetry of the ancients in order to teach them to contemporaries. This resulted in his complete commentary on Aristotle's *Poetics* (1548), the first of its kind, which ushered in the age of literary criticism in the second half of the Cinquecento. His other works, all in Latin, included a treatise on writing history (1548), *De artificio dicendi* (1567), *De vita et victu populi Romani* (1559), orations, and *Variorum locorum annotationes* (1549) [26]. Carlo Sigonio (c. 1520-84) of Modena was a famed historian of antiquity and the Italian middle ages as well as a scholar of classical philology.

---

[24] For information on Bonamico and Sansovino's reference, see Grendler, « Five Occurrences », pp. 323-24.

[25] Rino Avesani, « Romolo Quino Amaseo », *Dizionario biografico degli italiani* (Rome, 1960), II, 660-666.

[26] Giuseppe Toffanin, *Il Cinquecento*. 6th ed. (Milan, 1960), pp. 474-79; *Enciclopedia Italiana*, XXIX, 519.

After studying Greek at Modena and further pursuing his studies at Bologna and Pavia, he taught at Modena from 1546 to 1552, Venice from 1552 until 1560, Padua from 1560 until 1563, and then at the *Studio* of Bologna until his death. A pioneer in legal and institutional history, Sigonio used library and archival sources extensively. All of his many works were written in Latin [27]. Fulvio Pellegrino Morato [28] (c. 1500-48) taught *umane lettere* at the court of Ferrara for many years. His publications were in the vernacular as well as in Latin, and included his Latin *Carmen* (1534), a *rimario* of Dante and Petrarch (1528), and a vernacular treatise on the significance of colors (1535). He was also the father of Fulvia Olimpia Morata (1525-55), a Protestant exile known for her Latin poetry and epistles.

Finally, Garzoni attributed the distinction between the true humanist and the grammatical pedant with a smattering of knowledge to Fabio Paolini (Udine c. 1535-Venice 1605). Paolini took degrees in both philosophy and medicine at Padua, but also studied the humanities and Greek under Robortello and Antonio Riccobono. In Venice he first practiced medicine, then c. 1580 became a teacher of eloquence and poetry, lecturing on Cicero's *De Oratore*. From 1589 until his death he held two teaching posts: interpreting Greek at the library of St. Mark, and reading Latin to the members of the *Collegio de' Notai*. He also discoursed on Greek and Arabic medical writers privately in his home. His publications included a commentary on *De Oratore* (1587), a Latin translation of Aesop's fables (1587), commentaries on Vergil (1589), Thucydides (1603), Avicenna (1609), Hippocrates (1604), and a medical work, *De viperis* (1604). The oration to which Garzoni referred exhorted young men to study humane letters and was published as *De doctore humanitatis* in Venice, 1588. Garzoni may have heard the lecture or had access to a manuscript copy [29].

---

[27] *Enc. Ital.*, XXXI, 761.

[28] His name is sometimes spelled Moreto, Moretto, or Moretti. On Morato, see Luigi Ughi, *Dizionario storico degli uomini illustri ferraresi* (Ferrara, 1804), II, 79; *Dizionario enciclopedico italiano*, VIII, 78.

[29] I have been unable to locate a copy of this work. On Paolini, see Gian-Giuseppe Liruti, *Notizie delle vite ed opere scritte da' letterati del Friuli* (Udine, 1780), III, 352-72.

Garzoni's « Discorso de gli Humanisti » appeared in the above form only in the 1587 edition; in 1589 it was enlarged by a 34-line insertion which praised Giovanni Paolo Gallucci (or Galluzzi), 1538 - c. 1621, of Salò. After listing Bonamico, Amaseo, Robortello, Sigonio, and Morato as humanists, the expanded version stated that Gallucci should be included in this group. Not content with grammatical studies in Latin, Greek, and Italian, as demonstrated in his compendium of grammar [30], Gallucci also toiled in logic and rhetoric as evidenced by his *De formis enthymematum* (1586). The insertion continued to name Gallucci's works in various fields: his *De iis, in quibus pueri et adolescentes Veneti erudiendi sunt, ut optime suam Rempublicam administrare valeant* (1586) in moral philosophy, *De usu tabularum* (1586) in natural philosophy, *Theatrum mundi et temporis* (1589) and a commentary on *Joannis Hasfurti ... de cognoscendis et medendis morbis ex corporum coelestium positione* (1586) in mathematics [31]. The versatile Gallucci also translated Albert Dürer's *Della simmetria dei corpi umani* (1591), and possessed a good Latin style as shown by his translation of the *Introductio in symbolum fidei* (1587) of the Spanish religious writer Luis de Granada. Gallucci was able to use spheres, astrolabes, and many other kinds of astrological instruments, and did the woodcuts for his *Theatrum* and translation of Dürer. He also took time from his own studies in order to teach others, and Garzoni opined that this was the true idea of a tutor of the humanities and a man useful to the world. Gallucci was in the process of demonstrating all the doctrines useful to men in a treatise on raising children which he was then writing [32]. The insertion ended there as the original text resumed with the warning against grammatical dabblers.

Gallucci was celebrated in his lifetime as a mathematician, astrologer, and cosmographer who followed the astronomical

---

[30] *La piazza universale di tutte le professioni del mondo* (Venice, 1589), p. 957. The text of the insertion praising Gallucci gave brief titles or descriptions of his works; one can identify them from Giuseppe Brunati, *Dizionarietto degli uomini illustri della Riviera di Salò* (Milan, 1837), pp. 70-72. However, there is no information on a grammar compendium.

[31] The title indicates, however, that this was a book on astrological medicine.

[32] No notice of this work has come to light.

system of Regiomontanus [33]. In addition to the works mentioned, he wrote other treatises in mathematics, astronomy, astrology, and medicine, composed Latin poetry, and translated several works from Spanish and Latin into Italian. He does not resemble the five humanists named by Garzoni in the 1587 version. In short, a man, the bulk of whose scholarly writing was in astronomy and astrology, was termed a humanist, although the insertion did not use the term humanist. As far as the expanded version of the « Discorso de gli Humanisti » was concerned, a humanist was any man of learning who did some work in the *studia humanitatis*, whatever his major scholarly activity.

The authorship of the insertion is unclear. Either Garzoni added the Gallucci material or else it was inserted by an unknown hand in the 1589 edition, possibly after Garzoni's death that June. The edition itself provides no help. It does not list the month of printing, presents no information that a second party prepared it, and the introductory material is exactly the same as in the 1587 edition.

Because of inconsistencies when compared with the 1587 version and other discourses in the *Piazza universale*, it is unlikely that Garzoni wrote the insertion. First, its structure differed from the 1587 edition. In the earlier version, the term humanist was discussed generally with a definition, examples, and an attribution to a source, Paolini, but not with a detailed list of the books of, and extensive praise for, one man. Second, in the 1587 version Garzoni clearly identified the humanist as a scholar and teacher of *humanità*, by which he meant an expert in grammar, rhetoric, history, and poetry, with lesser competence in the rest of the liberal arts, mentioning mathematics and moral philosophy. The insertion added logic, natural philosophy, astrology, painting, religion, and skill with astrological instruments. This was a very eclectic group of intellectual interests, several of which were never included in either the *studia humanitatis* or the liberal arts during the Renaissance. Third, while Bonamico, Amaseo, Robortello, Sigonio, and Morato resembled one another in scholarly interests and careers, they were unlike Gallucci.

---

[33] Lynn Thorndike, *History of Magic and Experimental Science* (New York, 1941), V, 158-60; VI, 60.

Finally, Garzoni's choice of examples was logical and consistent when he discussed other professions. At the beginning of the « Discorso de gli Humanisti », he wrote that previously he had sought to include humanist under grammarian, rhetorician, historian, and poet. In these discourses, Garzoni proceeded as in the 1587 version of the discourse on the humanist. He defined the term by means of Cinquecento treatises, discussed classical examples — which he could omit with the humanist because it was not a profession in the ancient world — and then listed Quattrocento and Cinquecento examples, whom modern scholars recognized as grammarians, rhetoricians, etc. He named Ludovico Dolce, Pietro Bembo, Giulio Camillo, Francesco Alunno, and Francesco Sansovino as modern grammarians; all wrote treatises on vernacular grammar [34]. The Renaissance rhetoricians included Bartolomeo Cavalcanti, Celio Calcagnino, Girolamo Mascher, Cyprianus Soarez, and Cristoforo Barzizza — all of whom wrote on rhetoric [35]. The historians included Leonardo Bruni, Flavio Biondo, Platina, Sabellicus, Collenuccio, Machiavelli, Guicciardini, Giovio, and many others [36]. The poets were Pontano, Vida, Ariosto, Bernardo and Torquato Tasso, Annibale Caro, Pietro Bembo, Claudio Tolomei, Girolamo Benivieni, and others [37]. Garzoni did not include in these four groups anyone so different as Gallucci, nor — to pick three random groups — men known principally as theologians, legists, or astronomers [38]. Each of these received its own discourse. While Garzoni did not differentiate between Latin and vernacular grammarians, rhetoricians, historians, and poets, he had a clear and accurate idea of these disciplines and the men who practiced them. For these reasons, it is very unlikely that Garzoni wrote the insertion concerning Gallucci. Because its purpose was to praise Gallucci rather than to discuss the humanist, it is of little value for the present analysis.

---

[34] *La piazza universale di tutte le professioni del mondo* (Venice, 1601), p. 86.

[35] *Ibid.*, pp. 277-83.

[36] *Ibid.*, pp. 357-59.

[37] *Ibid.*, p. 931.

[38] Incidentally, there is no mention of Gallucci in the discourse on astronomers and astrologers. *Ibid.*, pp. 369-91.

These occurrences show that in the second half of the Cinquecento a humanist was a teacher and scholar of the humanities who often held a university position. He was a professional whose scholarly activity was based on the study of Latin and Greek antiquity. Because the humanities were the foundation of all knowledge, the humanist was a key figure who elucidated basic principles.

There are two minor points. First, the humanist's learned activities were not restricted to the humanities. Several of the six men named as humanists had strong interests in other fields as mathematics and religion, and Garzoni pointed out that the humanist should be acquainted with disciplines outside the *studia humanitatis*. Second, there was criticism of humanists in the second half of the Cinquecento. Muzio did not want humanists to serve as instructors for a young prince because they were classroom tyrants and, by implication, were unacquainted with « things of the world ». Garzoni warned against false humanists who had only a smattering of grammar. Gilio thought that humanists were quarrelsome, and Domenichi satirically pointed out that while humanists successfully pursued their studies in school, at home they were failures as husbands and fathers — again implying that humanists were inept in the real world [39].

Neither Garzoni's discourse nor the other occurrences mentioned involvement in the *vita civile*. Garzoni omits moral philosophy as one of the primary humanities, and the careers of the humanists he named confirm this. Moral philosophy was the humanity most closely allied to the active life because it dealt with man's relations with other men. The humanists named by Garzoni wrote influential works in rhetoric, history, and poetry, but not in moral philosophy. Similarly, they played little or no role in the state nor did they comment on current politics and recent history. Sigonio came nearest to active involvement by serving a prince for a limited time and writing a history of Bologna to 1256. The humanists were seen as professional scholars in disciplines unrelated to the active life.

---

[39] Grendler, « Five Occurrences », pp. 319-23.

With the notable exception of Venice, the ideal of the *vita activa e politica* declined in the Cinquecento [40]. Spanish rule and the growth of absolutist princes necessarily reduced the civic involvement of many Italians. The references to humanist and the humanities in the second half of the sixteenth century support this view. Sansovino, a Venetian, was the only writer noted by Campana, Kristeller, Garin, or myself, who linked a humanist to the *studia humanitatis*, and it, in turn, to the *vita civile*.

The Cinquecento humanist was clearly a professional teacher and scholar whose activities were usually limited to the classroom and study. The definition of Campana and Kristeller is essentially correct. But until more and earlier Quattrocento occurrences of humanist are located, this definition should be restricted to the sixteenth century, especially to the period after 1540 [41]. One hesitates to apply humanist in its Cinquecento meaning to such a figure as Leonardo Bruni who was both a classical scholar and political activist, but never held a university position. After 1540 Gilio did call Bruni, and Benedetto Varchi did term Bruni, Valla, Filelfo, Pontano, Poggio, and others, humanists, i. e., professional men of learning. But this meant that sixteenth-century Italians saw the above figures in the light of their own views, not that Bruni et al., looked at themselves in this way, nor that contemporaries viewed them thus. This is not to say that there were no Quattrocento humanists nor that Italians of that century had no conception of the humanist. In order to understand Renaissance humanists and humanism, the scholar needs to penetrate as much as possible the intellectual, political, and social background. Since Italy changed greatly from the Quattrocento to the Cinquecento, one should be cautious about applying the term with an identical meaning in both centuries [42].

---

[40] Hans Baron, « Secularization of Wisdom and Political Humanism in the Renaissance », *Journal of the History of Ideas*, XXI (1960), 144-45; Grendler, *Critics of the Italian World*, pp. 142, 146-48, 167-70.

[41] The earliest reference located to date is 1490 (by Kristeller) while Campana has found four references from 1512 to 1523/4, and five from 1544 to 1595.

[42] I wish to thank Professor Kristeller for his careful reading of this paper. The fact that I differ somewhat from him does not diminish the value of his comments nor my gratitude.

APPENDIX

This is the text of Garzoni's discourse from *La piazza universale di tutte le professioni del mondo* (In Venetia, Appresso Gio. Battista Somasco, 1587), pp. 956-57, from the Biblioteca Apostolica Vaticana copy. Some accents have been added.

DE GLI HUMANISTI
Discorso. clv.

Io pensava d' haver in questo mio libro abbraciato, e compreso tutte le professioni, & massimamente le più illustri. Ma mi hanno fatto avertito alcuni letterati, ch' io haveva escluso l' Humanista, professione fra le altre nobilissima, & honoratissima. Il quale però io mi credeva haver compreso parte sotto li Grammatici, parte sotto i Rhetori, parte anco sotto gli Historici, & ultimamente se pur vi restava alcuno sotto 'l genere de' poeti. Ma mi dicono, che l' Humanista è un non sò che di più, ò per dir meglio un composto di tutti questi. & che quattro sono come le fondamenta di essa professione d' Humanità: delle quali tutte bisogna ch' habbi intera cognitione quest'artefice: & che per ornamento poi sia tinto di tutte le altre arti liberali, come delle Mathematiche, della Filosofia morale, e finalmente c' habbi li principij d'ogni cognitione, acciò che occorrendo, da per sè possa cavar dalli fonti istessi delle scienze, e servirsi al suo bisogno, non altrimenti che li professori stessi di ciascun'arte. Et voglio insomma che quello sia il vero Humanista, qual sappia, & possa ne l'una, e l'altra lingua cioè latina, e greca, ne l'una & l'altra maniera d'oratione, vërso dico, e prosa scriver commodamente. Intender bene ogni scrittore, & in cathedra poter ogni autore acconciamente, e con dignità interpretare. Tali, o poco lontani da questa perfettione dicono esser stati i Lazari Bonamici, i Romoli Amasei, i Robortelli, i Sigonii, i Moretti, & altri di questa schiera. Là onde si scuopre manifesto l'errore, e la presontione d'alcuni, che quando a pena sono tinti de' primi elementi di grammatica, & insegnano que' principij per non dir pedantarie si arrogano questo nome, & vogliono esser chiamati Humanisti, profanando con la loro prosontione questo nome honoratissimo, dando anco con le lor macchie, & vitii il più delle volte occasione al mondo, che non distingue tra vero, e simulato Humanista di parlar, e sentir sinistramente di questo nome. Autore di tal openione, e difinitione dell' Humanista vero è il Paolini, che legge hora in Venetia, qual nel principio di studio [a] quest'anno hà recitato nella libraria di San Marco una oratione de perfecto Doctore Humanitatis, & in essa hà dimostrato, che tale deve esser il buono, e perfetto Humanista, quale habbiamo detto.

---

[a] Text: stustio

RICCARDO SCRIVANO

INTORNO AL LINGUAGGIO DELLA CRITICA NEL CINQUECENTO

« CAR. Or su vegnamo alla sentenza. ATT. In quanto alla sentenza, a cui appartiene tutto quello, che fa di mestieri al poeta di procacciarsi per mezzo della locuzione; le cui parti sono il provare, il confutare, il negare, l'assentire, far apparire gli affetti, come sono, compassione, ira, timore, e gli altri; e dimostrar la grandezza, e la piccolezza delle cose; dico, che in questa parte l'Ariosto è stato veramente felice; e per questa sola ha cotanto grido, e si ha acquistato il nome di divino. [98] Con questa acconciamente fa egli apparir le cose ed atroci, e piacevoli, miserabili, liete, grandi, e picciole come egli vuole [99]; usando in ciò chiarezza, una delle generali forme di Ermogene, accompagnata dal suo lucido, e dal puro; e semplicità, e dolcezza, tutto che forme speciali del costume [100]; essendo eziandio dolce, e semplice nelle cose gravi [101]; ed adempiendo ciò più con naturale, o divin furore, che con arte molto ricercata [102], si può dire, che in questa parte li ceda il Tasso, e non l'avanzi qualsivoglia volgar poeta. CAR. Ecco che l'Ariosto è pur degno di qualche suprema loda. ATT. Come, signore, non volete che s'onori la verità? CAR. In questa parte della sentenza, che grado di loda daremo al Tasso? ATT. Usando il Tasso modi di dir [104] poetici [105], lontani in tutto dal parlar dell'uso comune, molte volte la sua sentenza non è così chiara come altri vorrebbe, e studiando egli sempre in ciò d'esser breve, e significante nelle voci, non è meraviglia se alle volte oscuro ne diviene. Tuttavolta ciò fa (come nella locuzion vedremo) per dimostrarsi maestro nelle maggior difficultà dell'arte poetica. Però questa sua sentenza, quasi con locuzion laconica, non viene così universalmente lodata. CAR. S'egli adempie quello, che intende di fare, che importa che non sia così chiaro? Dovrebbe almeno appresso il giudizio dei dotti esser lodato, eziandio in questa parte, più dell'Ariosto. ATT. La loda di questa sua cura esquisita dee a lui darsi nella locuzione, e non nella sentenza, poiché ritrovando egli di proprio ingegno nuove metafore, e nuovi modi di dire con voci sempre gravide di sentimento, non può negarseli in ciò la dovuta loda, ma la sentenza, che dalla locuzion risulta [112], formandosi di modi inusitati di lingua, non riesce così grata priva nell'universale di quella dolcezza, ed efficacia, che porta seco la chiarezza del dir proprio, e comune. E quinci è, che il Tasso ricercando troppo l'arte, anzi duretto che no, alle volte divenga » [1].

È questa una pagina del *Carafa ovvero dell'epica poesia*, il dialogo col quale nel 1584 Camillo Pellegrino dava, involontariamente, l'avvio a quella polemica letteraria circa la maggior grandezza poetica dell'Ariosto o del Tasso che sembra sigillare le vicende della cultura letteraria del Cinquecento, trascinando nell'agone letterati, filosofi e scienziati [2]. È anche una pagina che chi s'è occupato della polemica Ariosto-Tasso ha avuto discretamente presente pur nella sua propria prospettiva. Ma essa offre tanti suggerimenti per penetrare nell' intrico fittissimo dell'esercizio e della metodologia critica cinquecentesca italiana, che mi pare non inopportuno riproporla ancora all'attenzione e collocarla anzi al centro di un settore di indagine che, se è stato di necessità avvicinato, non ha avuto il rilievo che merita: voglio dire il maneggio, l'uso e il variare, degli strumenti linguistici di quella critica.

Ricorderò brevemente che questa pagina si colloca quasi al centro del dialogo del Pellegrino. I due interlocutori, il Carafa principe di Stigliano e Giovan Battista Attendolo, hanno fino a questo punto trattato principalmente di quale dei poemi, dell'Ariosto o del Tasso, meriti meglio il titolo di poema eroico. Il Pellegrino non ha dubbi: la *Gerusalemme liberata* ha, sola, pieno diritto a tale titolo perché ha assunto come soggetto una vera

---

[1] C. Pellegrino, *Il Carafa ovvero dell'epica poesia*, in T. Tasso, *Opere, colle controversie sulla Gerusalemme*, a c. di G. Rosini, Pisa, 1827, vol. XVIII, pp. 152-161. Nel testo citato i numeri dal 98 in poi, in parentesi quadre, sono i rimandi delle chiose del Salviati utilizzate di seguito.

[2] Per una minuta descrizione dello svolgimento della polemica si v. B. Weinberg, *A History of Literary Criticism in the Italian Renaissance*, Chicago, 1961, vol. II, capp. XIX-XX, pp. 954-1073. Il W. s'occupa anche della critica intorno all'Ariosto anteriore alla polemica, come necessaria per comprendere non solo la situazione esistente, ma anche i presupposti di molti assunti di essa. La polemica ebbe, come ben si sa, strascichi più tardi, fino a Galilei le cui *Considerazioni intorno al Tasso* e *Postille all'Ariosto* (v. le in *Scritti letterari di Galilei*, a c. A. Chiari, Firenze, 1943) prendono avvio da alcuni dei momenti, e perfino delle battute, della polemica. Del resto il paragone Tasso-Ariosto perdurerà al di là della situazione culturale tardo-cinquecentesca. Cfr. W. Binni, *Storia della critica ariostesca*, Lucca, 1951, e C. Varese, *T. Tasso*, in *I classici italiani nella storia della critica*, Firenze, 1954, vol. I, pp. 466-67.

storia e perché ha rispettato l'unità della favola. L' Ariosto invece ha inventato tutta la materia del *Furioso* e vi ha narrato diverse favole: s'egli, dunque, per qualche aspetto e in qualche luogo può ottenere il nome di poeta eroico, più appropriatamente meriterà quello di eccellente poeta di romanzi, come già furono, seppure da cattivi poeti, il Pulci e il Boiardo. Il Pellegrino accetta così il criterio, già divulgato dal Pigna, dal Giraldi e dal Minturno e praticato da Bernardo Tasso, che, non potendosi giudicare un poema nuovo con regole vecchie, si doveva accogliere la concezione di un poema da collocare nell'ambito dell'epopea, ma distinto dal poema eroico: ed era appunto il romanzo. La discussione verteva fino a questo punto sull' invenzione, la prima delle tre parti della retorica, passata come tale nell'*Ars poetica* oraziana, testo sempre presente a questi critici, come anche ai teorici della poesia, insieme a quelli aristotelici o della tradizione aristotelica, anche se da vari decenni ormai si tendeva ad interpretarlo e integrarlo con l'ausilio di Aristotele riscoperto e riletto con un acuminato esercizio filologico e filosofico [3]. Il discorso sull' invenzione, o sulla favola (secondo la terminologia più frequente del Pellegrino), era la prima parte di una trattazione che avrebbe investito di seguito il costume, la sentenza, l'elocuzione. E a delucidazione della struttura del suo dialogo il Pellegrino scriveva che il poeta « nel suo universale altro non è, che imitator di cose, o d'azioni per mezzo del parlare » e che l' imitazione, « acciocché perfetta divenga, intorno a quattro parti principali conviene, che l' ingegno del poeta perfettamente s'adopri, e ritrovi ed osservi insieme. La prima è la favola, la seconda è il costume, la terza è la sentenza, e la quarta è la locuzione: e queste sono, e non più le parti formali, o di qualità, che Aristotele dice aver l'epopea » [4].

Seguendo puntualmente questo schema il Pellegrino arriva dunque a parlare della sentenza. E se pure egli in parte ha lacerato la struttura delle esposizioni retoriche tradizionali, ponendo sullo stesso piano cose che esse collocavano su piani diversi [5],

---

[3] Cfr. M. T. Herrick, *The Fusion of Horatian and Aristotelian Literary Criticism, 1531-1555*, Urbana, 1946.

[4] C. Pellegrino, *Il Carafa*, pp. 102-103.

[5] Generalmente *costume* e *sentenza* vengono trattati come parti dell'*inventio*; ma si sa quanto queste partizioni e suddivisioni della materia fossero soggette a spostamenti anche notevoli. Nell'*Ars poetica* oraziana, che co-

tuttavia non muta l'ordine di successione, anche perché era ormai consuetudine discutere delle sentenze dopo aver parlato del *decorum* o convenienza, discorso svolto principalmente a proposito del costume, cioè, nell'epopea, dei caratteri dei personaggi. Anche il Piccolomini nella sua illustrazione della *Retorica* aristotelica, apparsa dapprima nel 1565 [6], insieme commento ad Aristotele e proposta filosofica aggiornata alla cultura contemporanea, come ha rilevato il Garin [7], trattava della sentenza dopo il costume e come prima parte dell'enthimema, essendo essa null'altro che un enthimema semplice [8]. Il Piccolomini, il cui minuto commento aristotelico ebbe larga divulgazione e diverse edizioni sullo scorcio del Cinquecento, distingueva poi quattro speci di sentenze. Il Pellegrino, che dà alla sentenza la stessa collocazione, non procede ad ulteriori distinzioni, che non lo interessano veramente come non strettamente applicabili a materia poetica anziché oratoria. Ma in un punto almeno pare aver ben presente il testo piccolominiano: quando, cioè, accenna alla sentenza tassiana come abitualmente espressa « con locuzion laconica ». E il Piccolomini, tra le sentenze non inquadrabili nelle suddivisioni già delineate, discorre di « sentenze laconiche » (o lacedemoniche), cioè brevi o perché prive di metafora o perché miste di metafora fino, magari, all'estremo del parlare enigmatico [9].

Il rapporto che si stabilisce qui tra il testo piccolominiano e quello del Pellegrino è doppio: da una parte si tende a collegare

---

munque restava un modello di organizzazione della materia, per esempio, la *dispositio* o *ordo* restava confusa tra l'*inventio* e l'*elocutio*, e d'altronde del *costume* si parlava dopo l'*elocutio*, in quanto il termine comune di riferimento era il *decorum*. Per la distribuzione delle parti dell'*Ars poetica* si ricorra alla ediz. commentata da A. Rostagni, Torino, 1930.

[6] A. Piccolomini, *Copiosissima parafrase di M. A. P. nel primo libro della Retorica*, Venetia, 1565; *Piena, et larga parafrase nel secondo libro ecc.*, Venetia, 1569; *Piena ecc. nel terzo libro ecc.*, Venetia, 1572. Traggo le citazioni del secondo libro dall'ediz. Venezia, Angelieri, 1597.

[7] E. Garin, *Note su alcuni aspetti delle Retoriche rinascimentali e sulla « Retorica » del Patrizi*, in *Testi umanistici sulla retorica*, Roma-Milano, 1953, p. 30.

[8] A. Piccolomini, *Copiosissima parafrase* lib. II, cap. XXI, p. 294: « Gli Enthimemi non sono altro che sillogismi fatti per lo più di cotai materie; ne segue che tolta via la forma, e la legatura di così fatti sillogismi, le propositioni che erano o conclusioni o premesse, e principij in essi, fatte libere dalla forma del sillogismo, che le teneva insieme, vengon a rimaner sententie ».

[9] A. Piccolomini, *Copiosissima parafrase*, p. 305.

intimamente sentenza (o alcune speci di essa) ed elocuzione, a considerare cioè in generale una pura astrazione la sentenza presa per se stessa e non vestita di elocuzione; dall'altra il sentimento che, se la sentenza è troppo poco sostenuta dall'elocuzione, finisce col divenire oscura, smarrirsi nell'enigmatico.

Già questi elementi avvisano di un fatto rilevante: non si può parlare nel Cinquecento di dottrina poetica senza l'appoggio di una utilizzazione capillare e profonda di dottrina retorica. In quest'ultima, sentenza ed elocuzione, non solo per ragioni di esposizione, ma proprio per una questione di principî, venivano rigidamente separate: a queste ragioni di principio il Pellegrino è sensibile, ma tende ugualmente a collegare, come del resto il Piccolomini che poneva delle relazioni precise tra uso della sentenza e uso della metafora, sentenza e locuzione, e, quando dice che la sentenza « risulta » dalla locuzione, non commette un' imprecisione dovendo dire invece che essa « si manifesta » per mezzo della locuzione, ma intende affermare che la forza concettuale della sentenza deriva in gran parte dalla forza espressiva della locuzione.

Ma la pagina è interessante anche perché contiene il solo appunto che il Pellegrino fa al Tasso, posponendolo in ciò all'Ariosto. Il che non accade, come può apparire dalla battuta dell' Attendolo, « come, signore, non volete che s'onori la verità? », per desiderio di apparire giusto e cavalleresco nei confronti del poeta ch'egli ha assunto come antagonista del suo Tasso; accade invece per ragioni diversamente precisabili. Prima di tutto ciò gli consentirà, come dice di seguito, di mostrare l'eccellenza del Tasso nel campo ch'egli considera non solo capitalissimo ma decisivo per l'arte poetica, cioè la locuzione, e particolarmente l' invenzione di nuove metafore e di nuovi modi di dire. Soprattutto però è questa la via per affermare che l'eccellenza del poeta non può in nessun modo risultare dalla forza razionale delle sentenze, che insomma la poesia non è questione di razionalità nuda e cruda. L'Ariosto è migliore del Tasso proprio dove non risulta cosa d' importanza ai fini della poesia essere migliore: e lo è in forza sì di una chiarezza, che è certo merito del poeta perseguire ed ottenere, ma mai a scapito del suscitare affetti e meraviglia. Quella chiarezza infatti l'Ariosto ottiene con un « dir proprio, e comune » che comporta sempre il rischio di divenir banale e non poetico, anche se da questo vistoso rischio l'Ariosto generalmente si salva. Ciò risulta evidente nel seguito del dialogo. Dopo aver detto che certe oscurità e falli della *Gerusalemme* sono dovuti al fatto che il Tasso, per le sue vicende biografiche, non ha potuto dare al poema l'ultima mano [10], brevemente riprende il discorso sulla sentenza, ma per dire:

« CAR. Siccome nella parte del costume avete fatto, perché non recate anche nella sentenza alcuno esempio ne' poemi dell'Ariosto, e del Tasso? ATT. Non ho bisogno d'esempj, essendo la cosa chiarissima: leggete l' isola d'Alcina descritta dall'Ariosto, ed il giardino d'Armida descritto dal Tasso, e vedrete la facilità del dire nell'uno, e la troppo cultezza nell'altro »; e dopo aver riferito gli esempi soggiunge: « Vedete i concetti dell'Ariosto facili, e vestiti per lo più di voci chiarissime e dolci; e quelli del Tasso per lo più traslati, e vaghi di sensi esquisiti » [11].

Si vede bene che, se sinceramente avverte un rischio di oscurità e di durezza nel Tasso, tuttavia non può tacere della « cultezza » del suo poeta, della ricchezza dei suoi traslati, dell'aspirazione ai « sensi esquisiti » e, perfino, della sua abilità nella brevità della sentenza, come di seguito dichiara.

Questa pagina, insomma, appare decisiva per più ragioni nel discorso del Pellegrino: in primo luogo perché rivela come nel suo uso si vengano spostando, cioè caricando di più complessi significati, i termini abituali della retorica, strumenti indispensabili nella discussione intorno alla poesia; in secondo luogo perché mostra come le ragioni di gusto sono sostenute validamente da ragioni culturali; le quali, in terzo luogo, sono fondate su di un'aperta utilizzazione del rapporto retorica-poetica e quindi sul movimento complessivo che queste discipline e in genere la cultura cinquecentesca hanno compiuto o vanno compiendo. Come sostegno di quest'ultimo fatto, basterà sottolineare il ri-

---

[10] C. Pellegrino, *Il Carafa*, pp. 161-63. Non v'è dubbio che per questa via il Pellegrino trovava un altro modo per dar credito al suo poeta. Del resto in questo luogo non citava esempi di sentenze manchevoli, oscure o durette, ma ricordava invece due errori di memoria scusati col fatto che certi versi del manoscritto del poema erano stati eliminati lasciando invariati i rimandi di altri canti.

[11] *Ibid.*, pp. 165 e 167.

ferimento ad Ermogene di Tarso, il dotto retore del secondo secolo [12], che aveva cercato di ordinare le linee di sviluppo della retorica classica greca e latina: un riferimento usufruito non senza il Bembo come intermediario, come indica l'uso di termini sentiti in tipica dimensione bembesca, « chiarezza », « semplicità », « dolcezza » [13].

Nella prospettiva generale della situazione culturale di quegli anni questa pagina del Pellegrino ha però il suo vero risalto solo quando sia messa in rapporto alle puntuali risposte che Leonardo Salviati pubblicò come « Chiose della Crusca » [14]. È infatti alla luce del dibattito che suscitò che quel passo del *Carafa* si può intendere nel suo significato di nodo di tutta la trattazione e di momento cruciale dell'organizzazione del discorso del Pellegrino. Sono, queste, cose che il Salviati avverte acutamente e per questo le sue chiose si fanno qui più brevi e principalmente sottolineano le contraddizioni dell'avversario. Coerentemente,

---

[12] Cfr. L. Radermacher, in Pauly-Wissowa, *Real-Encycl.*, VIII, 1, coll. 865-877, e in generale B. Riposati, *Problemi di retorica antica*, in *Introduzione alla filologia classica*, Milano, 1951, pp. 666 e 783.

[13] Si presenta qui la necessità di un discorso sull'influsso della retorica classica sul Bembo, nel complesso abbastanza trascurato dalla critica bembesca: discorso che qui non è possibile che accennare. Si dovrà però almeno osservare che nel campo estetico il termine platonismo rinascimentale resta sempre molto vago. In tale campo la cultura rinascimentale si richiama ai neoplatonici, largamente influenzati da Aristotele. Il quale, in fondo, con la *Retorica-Poetica* s'era sforzato di dare dignità alle rispettive materie, classificandole e rilevandone la natura filosofica. Le teorie umanistico-rinascimentali sull'arte erano fondate su una sintesi platonico-aristotelica (dignità della poesia come regolatrice delle passioni, ecc.). Nelle scuole umanistiche ciò dipendeva interamente da Orazio. Il problema dell'imitazione, come si presenta dal Poliziano al Bembo, è un'elaborazione umanistica consistente nell'imitazione dei classici. Non c'è dubbio che in Bembo è presente l'ideale del *poeta perfetto* oraziano non del *poeta demens*: di qui i suoi criteri di grazia, piacevolezza, gravità e chiarezza. Più tardi, quando si comincia a spiegare Orazio con Aristotele, si cerca in sostanza una maggior precisione scientifica, cioè filosofica dell'arte. Ecco dunque la necessità di dare una maggior consistenza e una precisione più circostanziata al linguaggio che si usa, con una catalogazione, anche, degli strumenti a disposizione per l'indagine sull'arte.

[14] Il titolo con cui apparve in pubblico la prima volta è: *Degli Accademici della Crusca Difesa dell'Orlando Furioso dell'Ariosto. Contra 'l Dialogo dell'Epica poesia di Camillo Pellegrino*, Stacciata prima, Firenze, 1584. Cito dall'edizione Rosini delle *Opere* del Tasso, cit.

del resto, al suo atteggiamento generale, che è fondato sulla convinzione di essere miglior conoscitore della lingua toscana e, anche per questo, più preciso interprete della tradizione culturale umanistico-rinascimentale: di essere insomma, come fiorentino, miglior linguista nel giudicare dei poeti italiani, e di essere, ancora come fiorentino, miglior filologo nella lettura dei testi classici. Osserva dunque il Salviati:

[98] « Questo non può essere vero, che la sentenza mal vestita di locuzione possa piacere all' universale. Prendasi pure qualsivoglia concetto piacevolissimo, che se non è espresso felicemente con parole, non piacerà mai alla più parte delle persone. Nel Furioso sono i concetti bellissimi a meraviglia, distinti, chiari, e perfettissimi in ciascun genere; ma con tal favella manifestati, che pajono ancora più perfetti, che non sono, e più belli » [15].

Già qui il Salviati fa ben di più che osservare una contraddizione interna alla valutazione del Pellegrino circa la sentenza ariostesca: la contraddizione cioè che è nel credere che si possa rivestire con locuzione imperfetta una sentenza perfetta; contraddizione del resto più che altro apparente, in quanto il Pellegrino intendeva porre l'accento su una corrispondenza piena, coerente e tale da soddisfare sia il lettore dotto sia il largo pubblico del *Furioso*, tra chiara sentenza e chiara elocuzione, merito davvero senza ombre solo quando si considerasse una locuzione chiara migliore di una locuzione ricca di traslati, di metafore, insomma suscitatrice di mirabile. Il Salviati, in realtà, si vale qui di una semplificazione del linguaggio retorico-poetico, parlando della sentenza semplicemente come concetto, o contenuto, e di locuzione come favella, o linguaggio. Così, mentre coglie la vera sostanza del discorso del Pellegrino, provvede immediatamente, sia pure con qualche velo per non dar troppo spicco all'osservazione dell'avversario e alle conseguenze che ne deriverebbero, a rintuzzarla, affermando che la coerenza dell'Ariosto era totale, ma non a un grado basso, bensì ad un livello altissimo. E non si creda che il Salviati, usando quei diversi termini, intendesse uscire dal preciso, ma non chiuso per lui, campo della pratica dotta del discorso sulla poetica: quella semplificazione

---

[15] L. Salviati, *Chiose*, in Tasso, *Opere*, p. 152.

era concettuale solo nella misura in cui riusciva a far capire più immediatamente la sostanza di pensiero della tradizione critica. Si trattava solo, dunque, di cogliere più precisamente il significato di ogni singolo termine di questa ottenendo una miglior comprensione dei fatti indagati. Atteggiamento da umanista, che crede che la conoscenza degli antichi filologicamente fondata sia una conquista di ordine filosofico. Situazione molto interessante, sia per capire il senso del suo discorso nel seguito delle *Chiose*, sia per determinare il significato della sua posizione nella cultura di quella svolta storica, oltre che nella contingenza della polemica. Inoltre egli si preparava il terreno per colpire più a fondo l'avversario. Nella chiosa seguente afferma infatti:

[99] « Questo autore scambia, e confonde, non accorgendosene, in questo ragionamento, più d'una volta la sentenza con la favella » [16].

E questa osservazione è fondamentale. Il Pellegrino, di fatto, ha una nozione precisa della distinzione da fare tra sentenza ed elocuzione, anche se ne ha discorso ponendole sullo stesso piano. Ma egli, s' è visto, costantemente tende a rendere la locuzione assolutamente indispensabile al poeta, mentre non gli pare altrettanto della sentenza. Il risultato è di rendere sempre più indissolubile la sentenza dalla locuzione: così verrà molto diminuito il merito che ha riconosciuto all'Ariosto e prevarrà, nella valutazione complessiva del poeta, il merito del Tasso. Al Salviati, come s' è detto, non sono affatto sfuggiti questi intendimenti, insomma il giuoco costruttivo del discorso del Pellegrino. E tali intendimenti ribatte con l'asserzione della necessità di una rigida separazione concettuale di sentenza e locuzione. Avverte cioè che non a caso il Pellegrino aveva voluto discorrere di sentenza sullo stesso piano della favola o invenzione e della locuzione o linguaggio, oltre che del costume: e si richiama quindi ad una più esatta lettura della *Retorica* aristotelica e non solo ad una maggior fedeltà di scuola a quest'ultima. Egli non è infatti meno del Pellegrino avviluppato nella discussione cinquecentesca su retorica e poetica: ma i suoi testi di riferimento sono sostanzialmente diversi. Intanto ben più del Piccolomini ha importanza per lui la trattazione retorica di Bernardo Cavalcanti, di qualche

---

16 *Ibid.*, pp. 152-53.

anno anteriore a quella del Piccolomini, ma non meno di questa ispirata da una pretesa filosofica, autentica del resto [17]. Senonché, mentre nel Piccolomini aveva parte la sua educazione padovana e speroniana, con una spiccata tendenza a collocare la retorica in un rapporto concreto con tutto il sapere filosofico, e cioè con la dialettica prima e la poetica finalmente, in Cavalcanti, vecchio repubblicano, la retorica manteneva il suo vivo rapporto con la politica.

In questo senso il libro cavalcantiano della *Retorica*, che parrebbe in conflitto col processo così avanzato del pensiero europeo del Cinquecento rappresentato dal Vives e dal Ramo, era in verità un'opera molto bene organizzata, risultato di una attiva meditazione dello svolgimento della dottrina retorica da Aristotele ai suoi tempi. E, secondo la principale istanza del Cavalcanti, gran parte della sua opera era rivolta ad una minuta trattazione della vita civile, del peso cioè, del significato e delle direzioni agibili dalla retorica nella vita politica, come si può vedere nel secondo libro della *Retorica*, che riguarda l' invenzione e cioè la materia della retorica e i « capi » in cui si articola. La struttura del trattato s'appoggiava quindi in buona parte alla linea standardizzata delle opere retoriche: nel libro III parlava delle « probazioni », distinguendole in artificiose e non artificiose; delle prime parlava subito, con esposizione assai ampia, muovendo dagli argomenti (membro, forma, materia, luoghi, soluzioni degli argomenti) per passare alle sentenze; delle seconde parlava nel quarto libro, facendo seguire il discorso, amplissimo, sul costume, concetto del quale seguiva la storia all' interno della retorica da Cicerone in poi. Nel quinto libro, quindi, trattava dell'elocuzione, della disposizione e infine di una delle parti minori dell'oratoria, cioè la pronuncia o modo di recitare. Una struttura che contaminava chiaramente e volontariamente Platone e Aristotele, assumendo dal primo il concetto che la retorica ha da rispecchiare il vero e dal secondo la possibilità di considerare la retorica un'arte: una contaminazione però che si realiz-

---

[17] B. Cavalcanti, *La retorica, divisa in sette libri*, Pesaro, 1559. Gli ultimi due libri sono dedicati ad opportuni esempi di oratoria fondati sulla precedente trattazione. Sulla figura del Cavalcanti e sul significato della sua esperienza poco s'è studiato: si v. principalmente i rimandi del Weinberg agli scritti di critica letteraria del Cavalcanti e l'ediz. delle *Lettere edite e inedite*, a c. di C. Roaf, Bologna. 1967.

zava in un momento avanzatissimo del suo processo di svolgimento.

In quella struttura è già interessante l' inversione nella trattazione del costume e della sentenza: inversione che conseguiva pianamente alla stessa definizione di sentenza: « La sentenza — diceva infatti — è una determinazione non di cosa particolare, ma universale, e non perciò di qualunque cosa, ma delle cose, circa le quali sono l'attioni humane, che sono da eleggere, o da fuggire nell'operare »[18]. Dove, a parte il costante richiamo, da vecchio repubblicano come s' è detto, ad una concezione della retorica come arte della persuasione al bene, è indicativo che un po' tutta l' invenzione, e dunque la sentenza che ne è parte (essendo una sottodivisione delle « probazioni »), sia destinata ad un fine morale e trovi il suo momento culminante nell'attenzione al costume. Ma anche dove discorre del modo di trovare le sentenze si capisce perché sia detta esplicitamente la connessione di queste ultime col costume: « Noi potremo agevolmente trovare le sentenze, se noi riguarderemo a quelle cose, che appartengono a i costumi, e all'opinione dell' huomo, e che accaggiono in questa vita humana, e, se il particolare ridurremo all'universale »[19]. Ma a parte le ragioni di tale collocazione, basta questa ultima ad indicare come per il Cavalcanti la sentenza avesse una sua dimensione concettuale assolutamente certa e ben definibile e articolabile. Ma v' è di più. Secondo le normali concezioni dell'arte retorica (si ricordino le definizioni del Piccolomini) il Cavalcanti considera le sentenze parti d'enthimemi e aggiunge che gli ornamenti atti a trattar le sentenze sono le interrogazioni, le similitudini, le comparazioni, che le sentenze devono essere « accomodate » alle cose e alle persone (si tratta cioè del consueto richiamo alla « convenevolezza » o *decorum*), che si possono porre sentenze per concetti, che ci si deve guardare dalle sentenze comuni.

Mi par chiaro da dove il Salviati traesse sostegno per la sua rigida separazione di sentenza ed elocuzione; e si badi che certamente la *Retorica* cavalcantiana era un testo a lui ben noto, non

---

[18] *La retorica*, p. 170.

[19] *Ibid.*, p. 173. A questa collocazione non ostava del resto l'*Ars* oraziana che del costume trattava dopo il capitolo sull'elocuzione e sotto il concetto di *decorum*, ragionando cioè di stile conveniente ai caratteri: *Ars poetica*, vv. 114-118, che ha appoggio in Arist., *Rhet.*, II, 7, e *Poet.*, XV.

solo perché radicato, com'egli stesso è, nella recente tradizione fiorentina, ma anche perché fondato su una concezione totalmente umanistica della cultura, concezione che aveva al centro l' idea di una funzione civile, politica della cultura. Naturalmente non era senza profonde differenze che tale concezione circolava nel repubblicano Cavalcanti e nel mediceo Salviati: il quale aveva poi ben chiara la nozione di una funzione politico-culturale che doveva essere assolta dalla, pur privata, ma fortemente protetta, Accademia della Crusca [20]. Comunque sia di ciò, mi pare da sottolineare particolarmente il fatto che anche il Salviati, come il Pellegrino, non potevano non valersi (e non semplicemente sottintendere) delle conquiste e, come che sia, degli strumenti della retorica nel discorrere di poesia. Se poi egli ben capiva che nella poesia si dovevano prendere in considerazione altri strumenti che nella retorica, altri ornamenti cioè pertinenti alla locuzione, tuttavia era lontano dal credere che della sentenza non si potesse discorrere separatamente se non in modo astratto: era proprio su questo che si fondava nel distinguere, per semplicità di discorso, ma con effetti consistenti per tutto il susseguente svolgimento del pensiero intorno alla poesia, di un'opposizione-relazione di contenuto-concetto e di favella-elocuzione. Lo metteva su questa strada lo stesso riferimento del Cavalcanti ad un tipo di « concetto posto come sentenza » che poteva apparirgli perfino come la vera sentenza dei poeti, semplice, razionale, comprensibile a tutti, anche se non comune. E naturalmente neppure gli mancavano per questo gli appoggi nel tessuto più tipico della retorica classica: basti pensare ai vv. 128-131 dell'*Ars poetica* dove vien condotto un confronto tra *ordo-elocutio* da un lato e *inventio* dall'altra in merito ad argomenti nuovi, basandosi Orazio sul consueto testo di Neottolemo di Pario, confortato in questo caso da Filodemo [21].

---

[20] Per le vicende della fondazione e organizzazione dell'Accademia della Crusca ancora fondamentale è C. Marconcini, *L'Accademia della Crusca dalle origini alla prima edizione del vocabolario*, Pisa, 1910; ma certo si sente la necessità di uno studio fondato su una più articolata prospettiva storico-politica.

[21] Cfr. Philod., *De poem.*, l. V, col. 10, ll. 33 sgg. e col. 9, ll. 5-9. Neottolemo sostiene che la forma è più importante del contenuto: opinione cui Filodemo s'associa aggiungendo però che « non devesi neanche separare la forma dal contenuto ».

Appare dunque abbastanza chiaramente a questo punto che, se il Pellegrino e il Salviati erano costretti a concordare circa la necessità di agganciare lo studio della poetica a quello della retorica, cosa che del resto, anche semplicemente sulla base dell'*Ars* oraziana, nessuno metteva in discussione [22], tuttavia sul modo di concepire la retorica, di utilizzarne la lezione, di usufruire delle trattazioni di essa prodotte nel corso del Cinquecento, v'era tra di loro una consistente divergenza: divergenza che non poteva non essere connessa con la concezione della poetica e della poesia che dalle loro particolari impostazioni essi derivavano.

Ma di questo dirò tra poco. Occorre prima riflettere su alcune altre chiose che il Salviati oppone al testo del Pellegrino e che sono fondate su riferimenti culturali assai complessi. Con la chiosa 100, « Ecco ch'egl' intende della locuzione », egli non solo ribadisce l'accusa di confusione tra sentenza ed elocuzione ma mostra di rifiutare l'applicabilità delle « generali forme » di Ermogene a tutte le singole parti della retorica: per lui semplicità e dolcezza, in quanto sono attributi della locuzione, non possono essere riferiti alla sentenza e tanto meno al costume, di cui nel luogo in questione il Pellegrino fa cenno. È una prova ulteriore dello sforzo del Salviati di riportarsi ad un'accurata, filologica interpretazione del testo aristotelico e di rifiutare le arbitrarie costruzioni degli interpreti anche più antichi: nell'utilizzazione degli appoggi offerti dalla tradizione della discussione intorno alla retorica Pellegrino e Salviati divergono, dunque, sensibilmente, come s' è detto. In questo senso, cercando cioè di mantenere il senso e la portata della dottrina aristotelica, è rilevante la chiosa seguente:

[101] « Nelle cose gravi è l'Ariosto dolce, e semplice, quanto è richiesto, perciocché niuno al par di lui diede mai più il convenevole a ciascheduna forma del favellare ».

---

[22] Negli studi sulla poetica cinquecentesca, va detto, non s'è sempre tenuto conto a sufficienza delle necessarie connessioni con la retorica, per la difficoltà forse di aver presente l'intrinseca dimensione unitaria della cultura cinquecentesca, l'insistita fedeltà alle divisioni classiche nell'organizzazione di essa, riflesse prontamente nella scuola. Utili sono in questo senso gli studi di P. O. Kristeller, *Renaissance Thought, The Classic, Scholastic and Humanist Strains*, New York, 1961.

Nel trattare le sentenze, le « cose gravi », essendo la gravità un attributo tipico della sentenza [23], l'Ariosto è, quanto altri mai, dolce e semplice, perché nessun poeta ebbe come lui il senso preciso del *decorum*, o convenevole. In questa distinzione il Pellegrino non aveva un atteggiamento diverso dal Salviati, per la verità: ma s' è visto quale rischio per il Pellegrino era insito nella semplicità delle sentenze. Per il Salviati al contrario semplicità, in quanto attributo della locuzione, tornava in chiarezza, vero attributo di essa. E in una chiosa successiva, la 128, al Pellegrino, che aveva avanzato l' idea che « la bontà, e la virtù della locuzione, primieramente consiste in muover gli affetti, e in

---

[23] Per le chiose citate qui e di seguito [100, 101, 102, 128], v. L. Salviati, p. 153 e 182. Quasi mai nel corso delle avanzate discussioni cinquecentesche sulla poetica e retorica la sentenza è scompagnata dalla gravità. Tuttavia alla determinazione di questa associazione si giunge attraverso fasi diverse, connesse con la ripresa della ricerca retorica al di là del testo oraziano. Basti scorrere i seguenti rimandi che ricavo da citazioni offerte dal Weinberg, *A History*: essi testimoniano come si verifichi, intorno agli anni della riscoperta di Aristotele (della *Poetica*, cui corrisponde però un rinato interesse per la *Retorica*, specie come ausilio alla comprensione dell'*Ars* oraziana, cfr. Herrick, *The Fusion*), una svolta sensibile, come accade del resto di un po' tutta la materia in discussione. Nel commento a *Quinti Horatii Flacci Poemata*, Milano, probabilmente 1518, p. CXXXVI, Giovanni Britannico da Brescia dice: « est enim elocutio: ut docet Cicero in rhetoricis idoneorum verborum et sententiarum ad inventionem accomodatio »; dove principalmente risulta una stretta connessione tra sentenza e parole adatte all'elocuzione. Si verifica insomma una sorta di ambiguità nell'assegnazione della sentenza all'invenzione: ed è l'atteggiamento di Mario Equicola che nel *Libro de natura de amore*, Venezia, 1525, p. 319, dice che « l'invenzione ... senza ornamento è una massa d'oro che non risplende » e aggiunge che l'ornamento si ottiene con squisite sentenze. Dal canto suo Gian Giorgio Trissino nella traduzione del *De vulg. eloq.*, Vicenza, 1529, b VIII, dichiara che uno degli elementi dello « stilo tragico » è la gravità delle sentenze. Tre anni dopo G. B. Giraldi Cintio nella *Lettera a Celio Calcagnini super imitatione*, datata appunto al 1532 nell'ediz. dei suoi *Poemata*, Basilea, 1540, pp. 199-207, si chiede a proposito di Cicerone: « quis sententiarum pondere gravior? ». Ormai l'associazione gravità-sentenza non mancherà più sia in testi che accentuano il valore morale della sentenza, come Fr. Filippo Pedemonte, *Ecphrasis in Horatii Flacci Artem poeticam*, Venezia, 1546, c. 36 (la filosofia morale « tragoedias comoediasque gravissimis sententiis, et ad recte vivendum appositis replevit »), sia in quelli che ne evidenziano il significato puramente retorico come F. Robortello, *In librum Aristotelis de arte poetica explicationes*, Firenze, 1548, pp. 41-50, dove semplicemente viene parafrasato Aristotele anche a proposito delle sentenze come elementi delle parti qualitative.

generar meraviglia, e diletto », ribatte: « La bontà, e la virtù della locuzione consiste principalmente nella chiarezza, e nella brevità, e nell'efficacia. Il muover le passioni, e la meraviglia è impresa della sentenzia. Il diletto, comune all'uno e all'altro ». È caratteristico che ambedue si trovavano in ciò assai lontano dalla concezione del Bembo, che sotto questo aspetto aveva largamente accettato le « generali forme » suggerite da Ermogene. Infatti il Bembo decisamente applicava la gravità all'elocuzione, scrivendo nelle *Prose*: « Due parti sono quelle che fanno bella ogni scrittura, la gravità e la piacevolezza; e le cose poi, che empiono e compiono queste due parti, son tre, il suono, il numero, la variazione, dico che di queste tre cose aver si dee risguardo partitamente, ciascuna delle quali all'una et all'altra giova delle due primiere che io dissi. Et a fine che voi meglio queste due medesime parti conosciate, come e quanto sono differenti tra loro, sotto la gravità ripongo l'onestà, la dignità, la maestà, la magnificenza, la grandezza e le loro somiglianti; sotto la piacevolezza ristringo la grazia, la soavità, la vaghezza, la dolcezza, gli scherzi, i giuochi, e se altro è di questa maniera » [24]. Ambedue rifiutano non già le cose che venivano attribuite alla gravità, ma, appoggiandosi alla tradizione retorica sia pure nei loro diversi modi, la possibilità di riferire tutte queste cose all'elocuzione. Ma se su di un piano concettuale il Pellegrino non era in posizione diversa dal Salviati, nella concretezza dell'esercizio critico tutto ciò gli appariva ben più intimamente legato che non al suo avversario: e ciò conseguiva dalla sua convinzione di fondo che la vera pietra di paragone tra i poeti fosse l'elocuzione. Anche qui dunque assistiamo ad un maneggio comune di linguaggio critico, ai cui singoli termini però sono creati di volta in volta diversi rapporti e quindi diversi spazi, se non ancora in modo esplicito, almeno certo come tendenza di base del valore semantico.

Ma, come dicevo, la trama culturale su cui si appoggia il Salviati è ancora più complessa. Nella chiosa 102 egli scrive: « L'apparir cotale è suprema loda, e supremo d'ogni artificio ». È un'affermazione che un po' sbalordisce in questo contesto, perché in fondo altro non è che la ripresa del concetto della

---

[24] P. Bembo, *Prose della volgar lingua*, lib. II, cap. IX, ed. a c. di M. Marti, Firenze, 1961, p. 321.

« sprezzatura », cioè che nulla è più bello di quello che, essendo difficilissimo e fabbricato con molta arte, appare poi semplicissimo e naturale. Il Pellegrino aveva con la sua frase voluto accennare al fatto che l'Ariosto era senza vere regole, cioè senza le classiche regole della retorica-poetica, anche se veniva definendo nuove regole per un nuovo tipo di opera letteraria. Con ciò faceva un diretto riferimento alla concezione platonica del poeta pervaso da divino furore, anche se certamente egli aveva nel contempo in mente (come a porre un interno limite alla sua dichiarazione che suona positiva) la contrapposizione che concludeva satiricamente l'*Ars* oraziana tra il poeta perfetto e il « poeta demens », contrapposizione che approdava alla conclusione che al vero poeta occorre « avere il dono dell'entusiasmo divino, ma sapersi anche sottoporre a tutte le fatiche, a tutte le prove, a tutte le correzioni dell'arte » [25]. Ma il Salviati non era affatto disposto a concedere qualcosa alle implicazioni limitative che si trovavano nella sentenza del Pellegrino e nel ribattere a queste ultime prima ancora che alla lettera del testo che discuteva, che in fondo puntava semplicemente sulla mancanza, voluta, del rispetto delle regole antiche da parte dell'Ariosto in accordo con la sua idea dell'assegnazione del *Furioso* a un nuovo genere di poesia, egli si valeva liberamente di un' impostazione culturale-letteraria tipicamente manieristica: segno di quanto questa forma di sensibilità, fondata però su un ricco tessuto culturale, fosse penetrata nella mentalità corrente del secolo avanzato, anche in un intellettuale il cui maggior vanto era di agganciarsi con pienezza di autenticità alla tradizione più alta, per lui, dell'umanesimo, quella filologica cioè, che gli appariva anche la base per essere vero e buon filosofo.

Tale disposizione viene ancora ribadita nella chiosa 104 (« E qui pur si vede, ch'egli scambia la sentenza con la locuzione, e non se n'avvede: perché della locuzione, e non della sentenzia, son questi difetti, che e' dice ») [26] e non già perché tema il Sal-

---

[25] A. Rostagni, ediz. comm. dell'*Ars poetica*, cit., p. 118.

[26] L. Salviati, p. 154. Del resto lungo tutto il corso delle *Chiose* il Salviati torna con spietata insistenza su questa accusa di confusione rivolta al Pellegrino. Si v., per esempio, i seg. luoghi: Chiosa 112, « La sentenza non risulta dalla locuzione, ma si manifesta per lei », p. 161; Chiosa 120, « Non è sentenza, in mal'ora, ma locuzione: perché la sentenza in parecchi di questi luoghi, nell'un poeta, e nell'altro è la stessa, e solamente per la

viati che non si sia capita la diversità della sua posizione dal Pellegrino, ma perché ciò gli consente di provare come tutto il discorso di quest'ultimo non verta più sulla sentenza, e cioè indirettamente sull' invenzione, ma sull'elocuzione. E nelle sue chiose seguenti egli decisamente, anche se il momento nel testo del Pellegrino non è ancora a fuoco, si volta a discorrere di fatti attinenti la locuzione. Nella chiosa 105, relativa ai modi di dir poetici, afferma infatti:

« L'Ariosto gli usa più poetici, che non fa il Tasso, ma con tanta maestria, che a chi gli legge pajono belli sì, e vaghi oltre modo, e leggiadri, ma naturalissimi, e senza punto di sforzamento: in guisa che non ci sembra, che altrimenti si potessono dir bene quelle cose, da chi le dicesse daddovero. Il Goffredo allo 'ncontro non ha né belle parole, né bei modi, a mille miglia, quanto il Furioso: e sono l'une, e gli altri, oltre ogni natural modo di favellare, e con legatura tanto distorta, aspra, sforzata, e spiacevole, che udendole recitare ad altrui, rade volte s' intende, e ci bisogna prendere il libro in mano, e leggerle da per noi; essendo elle tali, che non basta il suono, e la voce, ma per comprenderle bisogna veder la scrittura, e qualche volta non è assai » [27].

È certo un passo gustoso, e la critica non ha mancato di sottolinearlo e citarlo. Ma è anche assai più che gustoso. Era un metter le mani avanti, ad anticipare una risposta a quello che il Pellegrino trattava di seguito, un prevenire il lettore che avesse letto il *Carafa* insieme alle *Chiose*. L'atteggiamento del Salviati è ora il seguente: poiché il Pellegrino porta, dall' interno, il discorso sulle sentenze verso la locuzione, col sottinteso che in questo campo nessuno potrà rivaleggiare con la mirabile opera del Tasso, discutiamo pure di questa e si vedrà che la locuzione tassesca è manchevole, debole, innaturale, sforzata ecc. Se invece il discorso si fosse voluto mantenere nel campo più veramente pertinente, cui le chiose precedenti avevano portato, avrebbe dovuto ad un dipresso essere il seguente: il Pellegrino ha affermato che l'Ariosto è poeta senza regole in quanto crea un nuovo

---

diversità delle parole si fa diversa », p. 169; Chiosa 148, « Le parole non formano la sentenza, ma la palesano. Il formarla tocca al discorso, o allo 'ntelletto », p. 197.

[27] *Ibid.*, p. 155.

tipo di poesia che non si può chiamare eroico; per lui il Tasso, invece, e con maggior dominio delle intrinseche difficoltà della poesia, accetta le regole e, rispettandole, riesce ad una vera, grande poesia. Ebbene, risponde il Salviati, no: l'Ariosto rispetta le regole, e con grande ispirazione e con dominio perfetto al punto di nascondere quelle regole, fa grande poesia; il Tasso invece restringe quelle regole in un corpo meschino, contraffatto, disforme, cosicché, come nell' invenzione non fa poesia ma semplicemente storia, così nell'elocuzione è sgarbato e sbagliato. Al di là della lettera della discussione circa il Tasso e l'Ariosto v' è tutta una diversa conformazione della cultura dei due contendenti: diversa conformazione che non vuol dire presenza di due distinte culture, bensì piuttosto diversa collaborazione ad un corpo unico, diverso atteggiamento all' interno della stessa cultura.

La posizione del Salviati, in particolare, è ulteriormente definibile attraverso alcuni luoghi dell' *Infarinato primo*, la risposta ch'egli diresse contro l'*Apologia* del Tasso nel 1585 [28]. Qui varie cose, che nelle chiose scritte in nome della Crusca erano solo accennate e sottintese, vengono fermamente dichiarate: e, per esempio, al Tasso che insinua che l' invenzione, propriamente parlando, è piuttosto parte che riguarda l'oratore anziché il poeta (segno che il Tasso, dal canto suo, aderiva all'ormai assodato rapporto retorica-poetica e solo cercava un proprio spazio di movimento tra questi termini) egli oppone che il poeta è l' inventore della favola e non degli ornamenti, secondo l'esigenza più autenticamente aristotelica che poeta è colui che imita e quindi invenzione e imitazione sono la stessa cosa. Sono proprio queste decise prese di posizione che mostrano fino a che punto poteva arrivare l' interesse del Salviati per la sostanza filosofica del discorso aristotelico su retorica e poetica: naturalmente accade anche che l' *Infarinato primo* dà l' impressione di una maggior freddezza polemica, di una minore vivacità del discorso rispetto alle *Chiose*, che con esso concordano tuttavia pienamente come qualità del discorso soprattutto per la fitta rete di rimandi e sostegni culturali. A questo proposito penso che sia utile portare l'attenzione su alcuni luoghi precisi dell'*Infarinato primo* e, tanto per cominciare, sulla frase (degli « Av-

---

[28] T. Tasso, *Opere*, a c. di G. Rosini, cit., vol. XIX, pp. 57-307.

vertimenti dello stampatore a chi legge » che sono dovuti certamente alla penna stessa del Salviati) in cui il Tasso viene accusato di comportarsi nella sua risposta in forma di dialogo « con dialettici ravvolgimenti » [29], di abusare cioè di gratuiti, facili, ovvii sillogismi ricavati dai modelli della vecchia scolastica. Il Tasso, dunque, valendosi dei modelli della dialettica scolastica e nominalistica, mostra il fondamento arretrato della sua cultura, mostra di non aver appreso nulla dalla lezione umanistico-filologica: il Salviati è ancora l'umanista che si gloria, ora, nella situazione culturale dell'avanzato Cinquecento, di riportare tutto al vero Aristotele, alla giusta comprensione dei suoi testi. Al Tasso, che ha detto che « l'offizio de' retori è dire il vero », egli replica duramente:

« Di grazia non ci fate il Platonico addosso. L'uffizio de' retori è d' insegnar la retorica: e se per *de' retori*, intendete degli oratori, l'uffizio degli oratori è di parlare in maniera, che sia acconcia a persuadere. Il dire il vero semplicemente tocca al filosofo, e specialmente al divino. All'oratore, e al dialettico non mica semplicemente; ma quando accade, che sia lo stesso, che il lor proponimento particolare: secondoché anche il verisimile, che impresa spezialissima è del poeta, con esso vero può accordarsi, e anche a esso poeta non esser tolto, se, non ostante la verità, ad ogni modo v'abbia luogo la invenzione » [30].

Questo passo si può comprendere solo se si tenga conto della discussione umanistico-rinascimentale sui rapporti tra dialettica, retorica, e quindi poetica, della quale il Salviati ha certo sicura notizia. Punto di partenza potrà essere l' introduzione di Poliziano al suo corso su Quintiliano [31] in cui mostra come si connettano retorica e dialettica, traducendo quella semplicemente le argomentazioni di questa e fondandosi sulla concezione di una doppia dialettica, una tutta terrena, « strumento, di cui l'uomo si vale a coordinare i propri ' discorsi ' », e una suprema che « se ne sta beata, *in se considens*, e lascia che la logica propriamente detta si affanni tra proposizioni e raziocinii, fra regole e teo-

---

[29] *Ibid.*, p. 71.

[30] *Ibid.*, p. 93.

[31] Cfr. *Prosatori latini del Quattrocento*, a c. di E. Garin, Milano-Napoli, 1952, p. 800 sgg.

remi » [32]. Retorica e dialettica, osserva il Garin, s' incontravano appunto nel momento in cui si realizzava il distacco della logica dalla metafisica.

La vicenda del rapporto tra dialettica e retorica, come ha mostrato il Garin, passava in seguito attraverso alcuni interventi salienti. Quello di Rodolfo Agricola, prima di tutto, nel *De inventione dialectica*, che faceva della retorica il momento espressivo della dialettica, giungendo così a combinare dialettica e retorica ed assegnando alla prima interamente l'*inventio*, cioè la determinazione dei « loci », e alla seconda l'*elocutio*, o ornato. Era questa una problematica tutt'altro che ignota nella cultura cinquecentesca italiana, anche se con ben maggior vigore essa fu affrontata soprattutto dal Vives e dal Ramo, da quest'ultimo soprattutto portata lucidamente ad una situazione di profonda rivoluzione contro la logica antica, in una visione unitaria dell'esercizio della filosofia che si traduceva in una precisa confi-

---

[32] E. Garin, *Note su alcuni aspetti delle Retoriche rinascimentali ecc.*, cit., p. 17. A questo fondamentale studio di coordinazione della discussione su dialettica e retorica rimando per tutti i riferimenti che seguono. Va anche ricordato che punto sicuro di riferimento per il rapporto retorica-dialettica era la terza parte del *Fedro*, dove Platone, discutendo se la retorica fosse o no un'arte, mostrava chiaramente prima quali dovevano essere i metodi della dialettica [« SOCR. Credimi, Fedro, io sono innamorato di queste cose, delle suddivisioni e delle riunificazioni, per essere in grado di parlare e di pensare. E se ritengo che qualcun altro sia capace per sua natura di abbracciare l'unità che è naturalmente nel molteplice, lo seguo, ' tenendo dietro alla sua traccia, come quella di un dio '. E ancora quelli capaci di far ciò — dio sa se dico bene o male — li chiamo finora ' dialettici ' », L 266 b-d; cito da Platone, *Opere*, Bari, 1966, p. 779], quindi come la retorica non sia definibile senza la dialettica (ivi, 269 a-e), e infine concludeva sull'indissolubile connessione di verità e retorica [« SOCR. Fino a che non si conosce la verità sul soggetto di cui si parla o si scrive e non si è in grado, poi, di definirlo in se stesso e avendolo definito non s'è appreso come dividerlo nelle sue specie, fino a che è divisibile; se in seguito, dopo l'analisi fondata sullo stesso metodo, della natura dell'anima, non si scopre per ciascun aspetto di questa natura il tipo di discorso che gli è adatto, e su questo non si costruisce e si ordina il discorso, con uno stile tutto screzi e comprendente tutti i toni dell'armonia per un'anima complessa e con uno stile lineare per un'anima semplice, —no, fino a questo momento non si sarà in grado di trattare l'oratoria a regola d'arte, per quanto è umanamente possibile, né al fine di insegnare né al fine di persuadere, come tutto quanto s'è detto prima ci ha dimostrato »; ediz. cit., p. 794]. Sui limiti della retorica come arte altro riferimento d'obbligo era anche alla prima parte del *Gorgia*, 447 a-461 b, cioè alla discussione tra Gorgia e Socrate.

gurazione del processo conoscitivo attraverso grammatica, retorica, dialettica e che si attuava in un rinnovato ordine degli studi dell'università francese. A questo profondo rinnovamento il Ramo dedicava, con precisa disposizione, tutta la sua opera, da quella di grammatico a quella di dialettico o logico, conscio soprattutto della stretta « relazione che passa tra le forme elementari dell'espressione linguistica, e la possibilità di costruire una scienza della logica articolata e perfetta » [33].

Ma anche in Italia aveva accolto questa attribuzione dell'*inventio*, e anche della *dispositio*, al campo della logica-dialettica lo Speroni nei dialoghi sulle lingue e sulla retorica, assegnando invece a quest'ultima lo studio delle parole [34]. Retorica e dialettica venivano così collegate nello sforzo di elaborare un pensiero che uscisse dal chiuso dell'esercizio che ne avevano fatto le scuole e si prospettasse come concreto processo di indagine che avesse a disposizione un linguaggio proprio, bene individuato e logicamente soddisfacente.

Una via diversa aveva invece seguito il Cavalcanti, che, come s' è visto, aveva cercato di ridare, se non autonomia, certo completezza filosofica e civile alla retorica. Il Cavalcanti, cioè, accettava interamente l'esigenza, già dichiarata apertamente dal Poliziano e coltivata da tutta la cultura successiva, di una dialettica tutta umana, strumento concreto di sapere mondano e questa configurava, anche in lui agendo esplicitamente un'esigenza culturale umanistica di miglior adesione alla lettera dei grandi filosofi dell'antichità, nella prima parte della sua *Retorica*: infatti, come s' è detto, la sua trattazione dell'*inventio* si articolava poi in una serie di « capi » che non erano nella sostanza che i « loci » che l'Agricola considerava il campo d'azione dell'*inventio* assegnata alla dialettica. Anche nelle sue motivazioni politico-ideologiche il Cavalcanti recava del resto la stessa convinzione che sosteneva la sua esigenza filosofica, quella cioè di un'adesione profonda alla cultura e al mondo umanistici.

Nel suo modo di accostare retorica e dialettica, apertamente palesato nella replica al Tasso citata di sopra, il Salviati s'appog-

---

[33] Per il Ramo, in questa prospettiva, si v. C. Vasoli, *Retorica e dialettica in Pietro Ramo*, in *Testi umanistici sulla retorica*, cit., pp. 95-134. La citaz. cui rimando è a p. 114.

[34] S. Speroni, *Dialogo delle lingue. Dialogo della retorica*, Venezia, 1542.

giava ad alcuni momenti dell'antica discussione ed aderiva, nel fondo, alla posizione che il Cavalcanti aveva cercato di definire. Non già per spregio verso Platone si rifiuta di essere annoverato tra i platonici. È che per lui la vera concretezza del pensiero è di assegnare ad ogni cosa la sua parte e la retorica è perfettamente definita in se stessa quando si afferma ch'essa è l'arte di persuadere. Al filosofo divino, cioè al teologo, spetta di dire il vero e questo potrà fare semplicemente, senza ritrovati retorici: ma al dialettico e all'oratore spetta il compito di ben persuadere e di ben ragionare, e non di fare ciò semplicemente ma con l'ausilio degli strumenti che sono propri delle loro discipline, tutti precisabili e definibili anche nelle relazioni vicendevoli di queste ultime. Il vero costoro lo diranno ogni volta che esso coinciderà col loro particolare proponimento. La stessa cosa accade al poeta, il cui campo è il verisimile, e il vero potrà egli assumerlo come suo solo quando coinciderà col verosimile.

In questo rigore la sollecitudine principale del Salviati è di ordine filologico, anche se questo, umanisticamente, coincide naturalmente coll'ordine filosofico. È per questa ragione, sostenuta da quelle motivazioni storico-culturali del resto, che sovente si ha l' impressione che il Salviati afferri o almeno accosti una condizione filosofica attiva, vasta, complessa, esercitata in particolare a cogliere il significato filosofico di Aristotele e non il solo valore classificatorio, anche se nella pratica le classificazioni aristoteliche di retorica-poetica appaiono nel Salviati più rigide: il che accade in quanto egli le concepisce come gli strumenti razionali della filosofia aristotelica.

A sostegno di quanto ora si dice potrebbero valere non poche pagine dell'*Infarinato secondo* [35] e soprattutto quelle in cui discute della possibilità, ch'egli rifiuta, di determinare un diverso genere di poesia quale sarebbe il romanzo. Ma basterà richiamarsi ad un' interessantissima pagina dell'*Infarinato primo*, nella quale il Salviati riprende e chiarisce dal suo rigoroso punto di vista la discussione del rapporto, o conflitto, tra « regole dell'arte » e

---

[35] La *Risposta dell'Infarinato secondo* è il testo che il Salviati opponeva alla *Replica* del Pellegrino alle *Chiose* andate in pubblico sotto il nome della Crusca. Mi servo anche per questo testo dell'ediz. delle *Opere* del Tasso a c. di G. Rosini, cit., vol. XVIII: si v. in particolare la lunga « risposta » alla « replica » XX del Pellegrino, pp. 25-31.

« regole della lingua ». Occorre, per aver chiare le ragioni dell' intervento del Salviati, rifarsi per un momento al *Carafa*, là dove il Pellegrino per bocca dell'Attendolo cercava di organizzare il discorso verso l'obiettivo che gli stava a cuore e che era, come nelle parole che seguono si può vedere, il nuovo in tutte le parti che concernono la poesia. Discutendo dunque, ancora nella fase iniziale del dialogo, della invenzione o favola, scriveva il Pellegrino allargando subito il discorso alla locuzione:

« Non diremo, come alcuni dicono, che la volgar poesia non ha come serva da sottoporre il collo al giogo della greca, e della latina, che dir ciò a me pare una vanità: poi che non si toglie al poeta la libertà di ritrovar di proprio ingegno nuove favole, nuovi concetti di sentenza, nuovi modi di dire, con nuovi ornamenti di locuzione: avendo in questa parte ogni lingua licenza di servirsi della proprietà sua, e molte volte di quello, che non le regole, o la ragione, ma l'uso confermato da' buoni scrittori le apporta innanzi »[36].

Per il Pellegrino è del tutto consumata la concezione umanistica che vera poesia è solo o principalmente la classica e che la poesia nuova dovrà conformarsi a quella: ammettendo, anzi sostenendo, che la poesia di romanzo non è inquadrabile nelle antiche regole già valide per la poesia greca e latina, ne consegue che nuove favole, nuove sentenze, nuovi modi di dire e, infine, nuove locuzioni saranno necessarie perché quella novità sia vera e concreta. È evidente che in tutto ciò è l'atteggiamento che di massima si può dire bembesco ad essere scartato. Ma poiché la mente del Pellegrino ha come chiaro obbiettivo principale di affermare che ciò che fa veramente il poeta è la locuzione, è spontaneamente su quest'ultima che insiste: osservando appunto che nella locuzione, insomma nella lingua (e si badi al passaggio che si determina nel linguaggio tra locuzione e lingua, reso necessario dal fatto che l'espressione « locuzione » sembra troppo ristretta alla pratica della poesia e l'espressione « lingua » sarà invece più ampia), le regole non potranno sovrastare alle proprietà intrinsiche di una lingua che è invece fondata sull'uso dei

---

[36] V. la citaz. completa in C. Pellegrino, *Il Carafa*, cit., pp. 16-17. Per le parti utilizzate dal Tasso e quindi dal Salviati si v. l'ediz. cit. dell'*Apologia* e dell'*Infarinato primo*, pp. 154-55.

buoni scrittori. E dunque l'eredità umanistica a questo proposito della lingua è ancora in qualche modo valida pure pel Pellegrino perché la lingua dei poeti sarà basata sui modelli offerti dai grandi poeti del passato. In tutto ciò il Pellegrino rilevava un contrasto che non sapeva o non gli interessava di sanare in quel momento determinando un qualche nuovo rapporto: ma il Salviati è appunto tale contrasto che torna a rilevare quando obbietta (chiosa 14):

« L'uso, e l'arte bisogna, che s'accordino, volendo, che siano vera arte, e vero uso ».

L'arte cui si riferisce il Salviati è l'arte della lingua, naturalmente, cioè l' insieme delle regole che definiscono le proprietà di una lingua: è proprio quest'arte che sta a cuore al Salviati come accademico della Crusca. E non se ne considera custode semplicemente sulla base di una sua più ampia conoscenza della lingua fiorentina o toscana, volgare insomma, ma perché egli anche ne ha ben valutato e capito le ragioni filosofiche che ne sostengono le strutture. Pure il Tasso è ben conscio che il discorso qui cade sulla lingua e le sue regole quando risponde:

« Qual chiamate vero uso? SEGR. Il buono. FOR. Questo meglio intendo: e buono è quello dei buoni. Ma s' io concederò, che l'arte non sia costante, mi parrà che non sia buona, perché l' incostanza è rea, e s'ella non è buona, non è vera. Come farem dunque per accordar sempre l'arte vera coll'uso vero? SEGR. Io non vedo il modo, e vorrei, che mi fosse dimostrato. FOR. Peravventura l'arte non si muterà; ma l'uso mutandosi, cercherà quanto sia possibile di non allontanarsi dall'arte; ma questa è cosa più difficile in effetto, che in apparenza ».

Anche per il Tasso, come per il Pellegrino, e come per lo stesso Salviati, l'uso dei buoni scrittori non è da mettere in discussione: si tratta del margine consueto di eredità umanistica che l'educazione di fondo classicistica di tutto il secolo conserva. Ma non è questo il punto interessante della battuta tassiana e dell' insieme del discorso. Questo sta invece nel fatto che il Tasso considera le regole, qualunque regola, a qualunque disciplina, materia, campo applicata, fissa: se no, non si potrà considerare vera regola. Se le regole sono fisse, l'uso della lingua, che resta la sola variabile, sarà quello che si dovrà mutare per farlo aderire alle regole. E la difficoltà di ciò deriverà dal fatto che si dovrà nello stesso tempo tener conto dei buoni scrittori: e dunque è all'abilità, alle conoscenze, all' ispirazione stessa del poeta che è affidato il sapersi regolare nel superare questa difficoltà, questo contrasto tra regole della lingua, o arte della lingua, e uso linguistico. Ma nel ribattere al Tasso il Salviati scopre una concezione ben più articolata, che non si capisce se non si mette in relazione con il fondamento logico, dialettico (della nuova dialettica, che per lui, da umanista-filologo, non è tanto una novità quanto una riscoperta della vera dottrina degli antichi, non una rivoluzione come appare, per esempio, al Ramo, ma invece un' intuizione più profonda del sapere che gli antichi avevano posseduto e semmai una rivolta contro la cultura scolastica medievale) che egli possiede. Per lui le regole della lingua non si possono mettere sullo stesso piano delle regole che sorreggono le altre branche del sapere, la cui filosoficità è applicabile a ogni diversa formazione storica. L'aspetto filosofico della lingua sta nella sua mutabilità: e non sarà pertanto solo l'uso a mutare, ma anche le regole della lingua. Ma si legga la pagina cui mi riferisco e si vedrà chiaramente l'avanzata posizione del Salviati in questo momento della discussione:

« Il Pellegrino prende l'*arte*, per le *regole di essa arte*, come si piglia molte fiate in ciascuna lingua da tutti i buoni autori. E di quell'arte intende, che dà regola alle favelle, né ad altro significato per conseguente le parole della Crusca, che gli rispondono, si convengono appropriare. Dice adunque la Crusca, che l'usanza delle favelle colle regole delle medesime bisogna che sian d'accordo, se vere regole, e vera usanza sien degne d'esser chiamate. La vera usanza, cioè, che vera usanza nomar si possa, e la più comune de' migliori: le vere regole nelle lingue, cioè a cui di regole in esse lingue veramente convenga 'l nome, quelle sono, e non altre, che son prese da tale usanza, e formate secondo quella. Onde se da' più, e migliori introdotta fosse altra usanza, il che nelle lingue, che vivono nella voce del popolo, senza fallo può avvenire; quella di prima, usanza più non sarebbe, ma trasporterebbesi cotal nome in quella che succedesse: e in tal caso eziandio le regole sarebbe bisogno che si mutassero, e s'accordasser coll'ultimo uso: e non facendolo, veraci regole non sarebbon da riputare. E tanto suonan le parole della risposta, che bene è anche pervenuta alle nostre orecchie questa profonda filosofia, che quelle cose, che capiscon definizione, non si posson mutar giammai: ma le regole de' linguaggi, non essendo elle massimamente, come non sono, di necessità fondate sulle ragioni, come quelle dell'arti cui dicono *facitive*, né di definizione, né d'altra cosa che la somigli, non potrebbono esser capaci ».

Tutto il discorso punta decisamente a mostrare come le regole della lingua non siano strumenti da collocarsi sullo stesso piano delle regole delle arti « facitive », tra cui è la poesia, cioè per il Salviati, stretto alla norma aristotelica, l'arte di imitar per mezzo del verisimile. Naturalmente sarebbe assai facile imputare a questa impostazione delle gravi carenze proprio nell' ordine filosofico e anche si potrà avvertire che in qualche modo ambiguo è il comportamento del Salviati, come se le ragioni della polemica lo inducessero ad un ricorso all'astuzia, ad una certa improvvisazione di argomenti. E certo si potrà dire che giuoca in lui una avversità preconcetta verso coloro che pensano di poter dare una destinazione diversa, loro propria, alla lingua; che pensano addirittura che il Tasso meriti il nome di grande e vero poeta proprio per il possesso di quella lingua che il Salviati, da cruscante e da fiorentino, pensa di possedere invece in esclusiva. Ma queste sono le venature caduche del suo atteggiamento. Che, *bon gré mal gré*, si mostra ben più complesso: la sua convinzione di umanista-filologo, che primo compito dell' intellettuale è riportare i testi che si discutono e su cui ci si esercita, di cui ci si vale, alla loro autenticità, compito che investe, e qui sta l'allargamento di fatto della tradizione umanistica, Aristotele non meno di qualsiasi altro autore classico, si completa con una percezione della problematica filosofica che l' Umanesimo ha svolto. E in questa problematica filosofica egli inserisce il particolare problema della lingua, che in questa pagina noi potremo dire valersi di una prospettiva che è propria della linguistica.

Non diremo invece che tutti i problemi del rapporto dialettica-retorica-poetica siano da lui individuati con la stessa forza e neppure investiti con gli stessi strumenti di indagine. Ma non sarebbe questo un chiedergli troppo? Un'altra osservazione va fatta invece su un luogo della pagina riferita. Quando egli osserva che mutando l'uso, e mutando secondo le esigenze della lingua parlata, dovranno mutare anche le regole, egli non intende assumere semplicemente la concezione democratica fiorentina di cui era stato sostenitore più vistoso il Varchi [37]. Egli intende piuttosto mettersi dinanzi alle lingue nella realtà del loro determinarsi, come mostra il peso ch'egli riconosce comunque all'uso dei buoni scrittori. Ed è dunque su un equilibrio tra uso parlato e tradizione scritta che si fonda la sua attività di linguista nel seno stesso della Crusca: ed è l'equilibrio che in genere regge le sue tante osservazioni alla lingua del Tasso sparse nelle Chiose, nell'*Infarinato primo* e nell'*Infarinato secondo*.

Credo che a questo punto sia lecito trarre qualche conclusione dall' insieme del discorso che ho fatto. In tutta la polemica il Salviati è soprattutto interessato alla difesa di un patrimonio di cultura che è sostanzialmente quello umanistico, ma che a lui appare approfondibile, allargabile, usufruibile, anzi assolutamente necessario al progresso della cultura, come la storia più recente a livello filologico e a livello filosofico ha del resto mostrato. Il Pellegrino invece, e proprio per questo fa del Tasso il suo poeta e il suo viatico, si muove su un terreno assai diverso. Abbastanza estraneo alla tradizione umanistica filologico-filosofica, egli ha tuttavia acquisito i nodi dei problemi e con essi la terminologia della discussione culturale cinquecentesca. Ha ben chiari in mente i nodi e le ragioni con cui e per cui vanno assegnati dei limiti alla concezione bembesca, dà tutto il rilievo necessario agli studi rinnovati nel corso del secolo intorno ai testi aristotelici, maneggia con precisione gli elementi della stessa tradizione esegetica aristotelica antica e moderna. Ma la sua formazione è restata piuttosto retorica e soprattutto degli strumenti retorici si serve nel cercare di conseguire i suoi obbiettivi; mentre il Salviati ha raggiunto una diversa concezione della retorica quale la tradizione fiorentina gli ha offerto. Si badi al fatto che veri, accreditati elementi filosofici il Pellegrino non li maneggia mai, o solo dall'esterno. Se per il Tasso, nel quale urgono anche problemi spirituali complessi e una sofferta visione del mondo, è indispensabile pervenire ad una fusione aristotelico-

[37] Cfr. B. T. Sozzi, *Aspetti e momenti della questione linguistica*, Padova, 1955, pp. 87-91. E in questo volume si v. il capitolo, *L. Salviati nella questione linguistica cinquecentesca*, pp. 103-173, interessante soprattutto per la formazione del Salviati. Su Varchi e Salviati v. anche M. Vitale, *La questione della lingua*, Palermo, 1960, pp. 57-61, e B. Migliorini, *Storia della lingua italiana*, Firenze, 1960, pp. 356-59.

platonica [38], una cosa che per il Salviati non è neppure in discussione tanto è ovvia [39], e non perché non rilevante, ma perché tale fusione è la stessa storia della cultura dall'antichità ai tempi presenti, per il Pellegrino di veramente importante c' è solo la novità. Nuova invenzione di strumenti retorici, cioè invenzione

---

[38] Cfr. U. Bosco, *La religiosità del Tasso*, in « La Rassegna della letteratura italiana », I, 1955, pp. I-II, e E. Mazzali, *Cultura e poesia nell'opera del Tasso*, Bologna, 1957.

[39] Che il rapporto Platone-Aristotele fosse sentito dal Tasso in modo particolarmente pressante non vuol dire che lo fosse comunemente altrettanto nella cultura del Cinquecento. Né, mi pare, si trattava per il Tasso di una sintesi da operare tra tradizione umanistica, di ispirazione platonica, e cultura cinquecentesca, di rinnovato interesse per Aristotele. In lui quel problema assumeva una tensione assolutamente personale: e coloro stessi che, come il Patrizi, sul finire del secolo si appellano a Platone contro Aristotele sono sospinti da un diverso tipo di esigenze, anche se la condizione tassesca non è loro sconosciuta e per certi aspetti, quelli politici ad esempio, non è neppure lontana dalla loro. La conformazione platonico-aristotelica della cultura cinquecentesca, non foss'altro che per la base classicistica su cui si fonda e su cui viene esercitata, era rilevata per esempio dal Bruno, che non si opponeva ad Aristotele e all'aristotelismo in nome di Platone, ma in nome di un sapere più antico, primigenio, come rivela il suo richiamo a Pitagora. Per le condizioni generali del rapporto platonismo-aristotelismo non possiamo qui che rimandare ancora a P. O. Kristeller, *Renaissance Thought*, cit. E, per tornare alla dimensione corrente del rapporto Platone-Aristotele nella cultura cinquecentesca, potrà servire questa battuta del Guastavini, che nel 1588 si prese l'incarico di difendere l'*Apologia* del Tasso contro l'*Infarinato primo* con una *Risposta all'Infarinato* (v.la in T. Tasso, *Opere*, a c. di G. Rosini, cit., vol. XIX; la battuta in questione è a p. 94). Richiamandosi alle parole del Tasso (v. nota 30) sull'« offizio de' retori » e alla conseguente replica del Salviati, dopo aver detto che « l'ufficio del retore non è già di insegnar la retorica, ma di vedere in ciascheduna cosa quello, che sia acconcio a persuadere » (che è, nei riguardi del Salviati, un conflitto di parole, in quanto con « insegnare » non intendeva certo semplicemente ammaestrare, ma prima di tutto indagare, scoprire), aggiungeva: « Ch'esso [il retore] debba difendere il vero, non solo di Platone, ma d'Aristotile fu sentenza, il quale su questo la prima utilità della retorica fondò: e tutto che dica, tal facoltà esser facoltà de' contrarj, si dichiarò però espressamente, non per fare ambedue le cose, che il male non si dee mai fare; ma per conoscere come sta il negozio; e per potere sciogliere, se alcuno se ne servisse, lo stesso afferma ancora del dialettico ». Ora, come si vede da questo luogo, un accordo tra Platone ed Aristotele è del tutto ovvio pel Guastavini. Il quale si fondava sugli spunti intorno alla retorica della ricordata terza parte del *Fedro* e intorno alla poesia, e alla competenza circa il giudicarne, dell'*Jone* (testi ben noti, del resto, a tutti i disputatori) e pianamente collegava questi testi alla *Retorica* aristotelica. In

di un nuovo linguaggio poetico, e quindi invenzione di nuove favole, di nuove sentenze, di nuovi concetti poetici. Non è un caso che in seguito egli si dedichi allo studio e alla trattazione del *Concetto poetico*[40]. È che egli si trova su una via che porterà al barocco e dà il suo contributo alla particolare lettura barocca del Tasso stesso. Ma quello che importa qui rilevare è che dall' interno della retorica-poetica il Pellegrino intendeva far scaturire la novità. Quella novità che dava fastidio al Salviati, il quale in una delle *Chiose*, la 124, al Pellegrino che, tutto entusiasta della novità, affermava, appoggiandosi a Giulio Camillo Delminio, l' ingegnoso distruttore della retorica che sarà poi l'autore fondamentale, ed esaltatissimo, del Patrizi pronto a rifiutare tutta la retorica classica in nome di un ritorno puro e semplice al Platone avversario della retorica (*Gorgia*) e della poesia (secondo libro della *Repubblica*), che Cicerone doveva la sua grandezza soprattutto all'aver trovato « nuovi traslati, nuove metafore, nuove frasi, e nuovi modi di dire », rispondeva con mossa umorosa:

> « Costui l' ha con questi nuovi. La importanza consiste nell'usar bene i vecchi ».

Ma, si badi, Salviati non era semplicemente il conservatore, l' intellettuale donferrantesco arroccato sulle vecchie posizioni. La sua cultura era fondata su una larga percezione dello svolgimento delle vicende quattro-cinquecentesche ed era capace di aperture notevoli, complessa sempre, anche quando non veramente capace di soluzioni.

In sostanza, dunque, il rapporto che storicamente si può stabilire è assai complesso: i vivissimi contrasti di disposizione culturale che esistono tra i due e che sostengono le loro diverse ragioni di gusto, le fonti di cui si servono e la diversa valutazione della tradizione che si è formata intorno alle fonti primarie, quelle classiche cioè, contrasti che ho cercato di delineare in queste

---

ciò non faceva che riprendere un atteggiamento del Piccolomini espresso nell'*Instrumento de la filosofia*, Roma, 1551. Coincidenza di testi col Pellegrino rimarchevole, se non sbalorditiva; e non tale perché l' impostazione era del tutto comune alla più larga cultura cinquecentesca.

[40] C. Pellegrino, *Del concetto poetico*, in A. Borzelli, *Il Cavalier Marino (1569-1625)*, Napoli, 1898, pp. 325-59 (il Borzelli lo assegna all'anno 1598).

pagine per certi aspetti, non sono ancora l'opposizione di due culture, una innovativa, l'altra conservativa. Se di un tal contrasto si potrà parlare, ciò sarà possibile solo più tardi, quando il barocco si opporrà volontariamente al rinascimento e darà un senso particolare alla già sorta polemica dei moderni con gli antichi [41]. E anche allora appariranno inconsumabili gli enormi materiali che una tradizione culturale che aveva la sua matrice nella classicità aveva accumulato. E tuttavia quella discussione, portata avanti su posizioni obiettivamente diverse, è tutt'altro che priva di significato: non solo perché, come tutta la discussione critica e filosofica del tempo, ci dà la misura storica concreta di quelle vicende culturali, ma soprattutto perché dal suo seno nascono gli strumenti di linguaggio che consentiranno il passaggio a nuove condizioni. Strumenti che, se non per tutti, almeno per alcuni, e il Salviati è tra questi, non possono che essere fondati su ragioni filosofiche.

È infatti nella specifica sede del linguaggio che si vengono coagulando esigenze nuove: e abbiamo per l'appunto assistito, anche semplicemente nelle poche fasi del dibattito polemico che s' è cercato di mettere a fuoco, ad un processo di dilatazione o di restringimento, di scivolamento o di spostamento del valore semantico di certe parole e infine di sostituzione delle vecchie con delle nuove parole, che non è giuoco gratuito, ma ben giustificato all' interno del processo, perché le nuove parole hanno col vecchio anche un nuovo significato, una diversa portata. Nelle sue linee generali il linguaggio della critica è il risultato di un'operazione di fusione di retorica e poetica: questa operazione non avviene però a freddo o in laboratorio; avviene nel vivo della pratica culturale e comporta una rimeditazione continua di tutto l' insieme della cultura e come non si può discutere della poetica senza valersi della retorica, così non si può discutere di questa senza valersi della dialettica, cioè della logica. La natura filosofica del problema della critica nel Cinquecento è pertanto evidente: diversamente vengono a presentarsi in questo tempo i rapporti tra dialettica, retorica e poetica e quando una soluzione linguistica affiora è generalmente perché una diversa disposizione o intuizione filosofica si è affacciata.

---

[41] Cfr. G. Margiotta, *L'origine italiana de la querelle des anciens et des modernes*, Roma, 1953.

Il linguaggio della critica del Cinquecento, in tale prospettiva, appare a volte come un vero e proprio linguaggio tecnico: ma in realtà accade che il suo stesso processo di svolgimento lo sottrae continuamente al chiuso cerchio di una tecnica. Mi par dunque che si potrà per esso accogliere piuttosto la definizione di linguaggio speciale, come ha fatto il De Mauro [42] per il linguaggio della moderna critica d'arte, perché esso di fatto combina espressioni che vengono da una larga tradizione, che si sforza di essere precisa ma che lo è solo nella misura in cui può chiarire veramente le condizioni della propria discussione, con espressioni che trae da altre discipline, variamente connesse con essa, che in fondo non può fare a meno della tradizione di un sapere totale, ed espressioni nuove derivate dalla lingua comune o comunque generate da nuove esigenze. Se parecchie delle parole che la critica letteraria cinquecentesca usa sono dei « termini », in realtà la maggior parte di esse sono tali solo nell'aspirazione

---

[42] Mi riferisco all'interessante studio di T. De Mauro, *Il linguaggio della critica d'arte*, Firenze, 1965: soprattutto al secondo capitolo, *Linguaggio comune, linguaggi speciali e linguaggi formalizzati*, che si conclude con questo passo assai fertile di suggerimenti per il lavoro che qui si propone: « Tra i due poli opposti costituiti dall'uso corrente di una lingua storica (è questo che chiamiamo linguaggio comune o ordinario) e dall'uso di una lingua formalizzata, come grado intermedio non basta inserire soltanto l'uso di una terminologia combinata con le comuni parole di una lingua storica. Vi è, più vicino al linguaggio ordinario, ciò che si suole chiamare impropriamente una ' lingua speciale ', ossia, più esattamente, l'uso speciale di una lingua, l'uso che si crea nell'ambito di gruppi che si formino, per ragioni culturali o economiche ecc., in seno a una comunità linguistica: il carattere speciale degli usi linguistici risulta soprattutto da fatti lessicali, ossia particolarmente frequenti di certe parole o di certe accezioni di talune parole, ma può talora risultare anche da qualche particolare atteggiamento stilistico, cui i membri del gruppo cercano di uniformarsi nel parlare ». Su quest'ordine di problemi si v. G. Devoto, *I fondamenti della storia linguistica*, Firenze, 1960. E c'è un altro suggerimento da derivare dal saggio del De Mauro, il quale osserva, p. 22, che « la filosofia del linguaggio è restata per molti secoli bloccata sulle posizioni di Aristotele e degli aristotelici », che intendevano la lingua come « il riflesso specularmente fedele delle nostre conoscenze del reale, e queste sono a loro volta riflesso dell'organizzazione della realtà in generi, specie e individui ». Ora, quello che accade nell'esercizio critico del Cinquecento, come in tanti altri campi del sapere in quel tempo, è di mettere in dubbio che le « connotazioni dell'anima » e « le cose » siano le stesse per tutti come sosteneva Aristotele. Colle cose variano quelle connotazioni, ma ambedue poi variano indipendentemente.

di chi le adopera. Accade insomma che tutte quelle espressioni, derivate dalla tradizione culturale o dalle lingue comuni o nuove, hanno una plurivalenza semantica assai vasta. L'analisi del linguaggio dei critici del Cinquecento appare non solo la via da seguire per spiegare i vari aspetti dell'arco semantico del loro vocabolario tecnico-estetico, ma anche la chiave per capire la civiltà che rappresentano, la natura dei giudizi che esprimono, la consistenza delle idee che propongono. Col che intendo presentare, più che altro, come ben si capisce, una prospettiva di lavoro.

Gli interventi intorno alla critica letteraria del Cinquecento non sono scarsi e non da ieri: sono tanto abbondanti anzi che il radunarli costituirebbe una considerevole bibliografia. Essi, tuttavia, si possono considerare disposti in tre fasi: una prima, principalmente descrittiva, che svolse un grosso lavoro di indagini e di raccolta di dati e di materiali e che ebbe corso fino al principio di questo secolo; una seconda, che quei materiali cercò di ordinare in una prospettiva che non potè essere che quella della preestetica, degli avvertimenti confusi ed incerti della nuova scienza estetica; una terza, vagamente neopositivistica, che s' è preoccupata soprattutto di sottrarsi alle ipoteche idealistiche, che ha ricercato nuovamente i testi, li ha ordinati in una prospettiva più completa e più esatta, ma che ha finito col risolversi in un nuovo descrittivismo, più attendibile, ma sempre manchevole in quanto, per enormi che siano i materiali radunati, resta sempre chiuso in determinati campi e si lascia sfuggire, per forza di cose, la frequenza veramente determinante dei rapporti, influenze, condizionamenti reciproci di quei campi. È proprio alla determinazione di questi che un nuovo impegno si deve richiamare.

J. R. HALE

THE FIRST FIFTY YEARS OF A VENETIAN MAGISTRACY
The *Provveditori alle Fortezze* *

* I should like to acknowledge Professor William Bouwsma's and Professor F. C. Lane's care in reading a draft of this essay. I owe much, too, to the habitual kindness and the searching eye of Dr. Paolo Selmi. Any errors that remain are, of course, my own.

> Per certo se con giusto giudicio si vorrà andar considerando con quanta grandezza, con quale illustre apparato, e regale spesa siano state molte fortezze dalla Republica in questi tempi fabricate, e che per quanto comporta la diversa usanza di tempi faranno queste a quelli più famosi edificij presso all'antichità paragonate, troverassi, che per respetto così della spesa, come della grandezza dell'opera, non minor laude di magnificenza devono haversi i Vinetiani acquistata di quella, che si dia a gli antichi Romani ....
>
> (Paolo Paruta, *Historia Vinetiana*)

After its recovery from the sickening defeat at Agnadello, the Venetian government adopted a generally defensive and neutral posture in international affairs. Commercially, this meant the guarding of its sea lanes with no attempt to extend them by force. Territorially it meant that the medieval concept of a border, something flexible, responsive to the losses and gains of inheritance and war, changed towards that of a frontier enclosing a changeless homeland. Encircled by two active enemies, the Turks in the east, the Austrian archdukes in the north, and two potential ones, Spanish Milan in the west and the papacy in the south, Venetian neutrality had perforce to be armed. Venetian diplomacy, moreover, dedicated to an active policy of sowing discord among these enemies and distracting them by bringing pressure to bear on their potential adversaries from England and France to Persia, required a strong base to give it credibility. The sixteenth century, therefore, saw a marked increase in the attention Venice paid to its fortifications.

The chief new works undertaken were: in the east, Candia (Herakleon), Canea (Khania) Corfu and Zara (Zadar); against the north, Peschiera and Verona; in the west, Bergamo and Brescia; in the south, Legnago. But because of the effects of weather and ground subsidence, and because of pressure to revamp old fortifications 'alla moderna', less costly work was carried out intermittently at — to box the compass once more — Cephalonia, Famagosta, Suda, Spinalonga, Dulcigno, Budua, Novigrad, Trau (Trogis), Cattaro (Kotor), Sebenico (Sibenik); Capo d' Istria, Treviso, Cadore, Marano, Anfo, Chiusa; Crema and Orzinovi. Venice itself acquired the Lido forts of S. Andrea and S. Niccolò and a defensive system at Chioggia. The list could be considerably extended if it were to include fortifications like Naxos and Padua, where improvements were discussed and prepared, but not carried out.

These are the sites that were the major preoccupation of the period with which this essay is concerned, the fifty years between 1542 and 1592. But already in the years since Agnadello the burden of static defense had been growing too heavy for the crowded agenda of the *collegio*. The absence, too, of a connecting link between site works and the *collegio* led to delays and misunderstandings. An attempt to counter this difficulty was made tentatively in 1527, when a senator was elected to act as a contact between the *collegio* and the work going forward at Legnago. Foreshadowing the work of the *fortezze* magistracy, the duty of this individual, who was given no title, was to remain in Venice and see to the execution of all orders relating to the fortifications [1]. Administrative problems were thrown into especially high relief by the widespread reconstruction work needed after the Turkish war of 1537-1540, especially up the length of the Adriatic from Corfu to Zara. The problem was all the greater for the administrative disarray in which the coastal towns had been left and an economic plight which led them to plead for relief from taxation. In 1542 the senate acted as it traditionally did when one of its spheres of competence was swelling to unmanageable proportions: it released the pressure by creating a new magistracy.

After drawing attention to the fact that fortresses are « as everyone knows very well » the foundation of the state, and citing the unprepared condition in which Corfu had had to face the Turk, the decision of September 25th laid the blame for past inefficiency on the lack of a body specifically concerned with fortification and the pressure of other business on the *savii*

---

[1] Senato, Deliberazioni, Terra: Registri [S. D. T. R.], 24, f. 161 v. All documents cited are in the Archivio di Stato, Venice.

of the *collegio*. Two senators were therefore to be elected annually with the title of *provveditori delle fortezze* [2]. Their responsibility, which extended to both *Terra* and *Mar*, was to ensure that fortresses (the term included town walls and citadels as well as isolated strong points) were adequately maintained. The *provveditori* were limited in their freedom of action. They had to refer the orders they gave to the *savii* of the *collegio* who could countermand them, though only after explaining their reasons to the senate.

To keep themselves informed they were to be present when *rettori* reported on their terms of duty and they were to receive reports on matters concerning fortifications and stores from other returning officials — castellans, for instance, or *provveditori in terra ferma* — whose duties had kept them in touch with fortified places. On the sixth of October the first two *provveditori* were elected by the senate and *zonta*: Alessandro Contarini and Filippo Cappello.

The lack of continuity caused by having both *provveditori* quit office at the same time was corrected in 1551 [3]. At the election in October of that year the *provveditore* chosen with the fewer votes was to remain in office only for six months; thereafter the terms of office were to overlap. The same decision spelled out the period of disqualification before a man could be re-elected — equal to the number of months he had held office — and laid down penalties for a *provveditore* who accepted another commission before his term was completed [4]. Two later pieces of legislation stressed the importance of the magistracy. In 1566 it was coupled with the magistracies *all'Arsenale* and *all'armar* as being one of the key organs elected by the senate, and, with them, its officers were to be chosen before the balloting took place for other posts. It was further decided that a man could be appointed no matter what other post he already

---

[2] See Appendix. 'Alle fortezze' only became standard form in the seventeenth century; before that they were referred to as *provveditori alle*, or *delle*, or *sopra le fortezze*. The Latin form was *super fortilitiis*.

[3] S. D. T. R., 37, ff. 154 r-155 r, 6 July.

[4] Re-elections were common, helping sustain the continuity of administration. Thus Alessandro Contarini was reappointed in 1544, 1547, 1549 and 1554. Antonio Cappello, first elected in 1550, served again in 1552, 1556 and 1558.

held, unless it were that of *conservatore delle leggi* and as long as he was not a member of the *collegio* [5]. In March 1579 the council of ten had introduced new accounting procedures as part of a general re-allotment of funds among the magistracies [6]. A counter-signature was now required before *fortezze* money could be disbursed. The indisposition of one of the *provveditori* could (and repeatedly did) hold up the business of the office, and in 1580 it was decided that henceforward there were to be three *provveditori*, two holding office for a full year and one for six months [7]. Finally, the importance of the magistracy was once more stressed in 1585, when it was laid down that a *provveditore* could only leave his post for that of ambassador or *provveditore generale*, or were he appointed to the *collegio* [8]. Like other legislation of the period, this reflects the strain on the restricted membership of the senate caused by the multiplication of offices and the principle of rotation.

While the Venetian constitution could throw out new limbs at need, it was less good at putting them to effective use. The policy of appointing amateurs to specialist duties, and for only a short period, meant that while their responsibilities were heavy, there were continual checks on their freedom of action. These checks were particularly hampering in the case of the *provveditori alle fortezze*. Partly this was due to the large sums involved. Control over expenditure was kept in the hands of the senate and the ten not only so that the spending of the state's annual income could be kept under review, but because the imposition of special taxes and labour services in the territories affected by works of fortification involved political decisions; they touched on the perennially nervous relationship between Venice and the *terra ferma* and its overseas possessions. Politics, as well as purely military decisions were involved in two further respects. Military engineers might decide that the best way of defending a town was by building a citadel within it; the inhabitants might interpret this as a threat to their own liberty. (This

---

[5] S. D. T. R., 43, f. 74 v, 3 October.

[6] See below, p. 526.

[7] Provveditori alle Fortezze [P. F.], 2, f. 29 r, 31 January. (All dates in this essay are modernized).

[8] S. D. T. R., 56, ff. 70 v-71 r, Oct. 2.

issue led to no action being taken on the proposal to build a citadel in Padua in the 1540's.) And the responsibility of the *provveditori* for military security had to be balanced against the ten's responsibility for political security, which led them to send out inspectors of their own and to correspond directly with *capitani* about the ability of a town's defenses to keep out spies and malcontents [9].

The *provveditori* were, in effect, a committee of the senate, and they suffered to some extent from the rivalry between senate and ten that was to lead to the constitutional friction of 1582-83 and the redefinition of that council's powers. In a decision supplementary to that setting up the *fortezze* magistracy, the senate had noted that « the chief fortresses of the state are under the control of our council of ten, as are the most important and necessary artillery and munitions; the provision of money, moreover, is for the most part determined by that council ». To establish a line of communication for the *provveditori* between discussions concerning ' senate ' fortifications and those of the ten, it was decided that one of the *savii del consiglio* and one of the *savii di terra ferma*, who had access to the meetings of the ten, should be responsible for liaison in matters of fortification between the ten and the *collegio* and thus keep the *provveditori*, who sat with the *collegio* when their duties were discussed, and the senate informed. Similarly one of the *savii agli ordini* was entrusted with reporting any discussion in the ten dealing with fortification in the *Mar* zone. It was possibly on the insistence of the ten, and certainly to the detriment of the clarity with which the duties of the *provveditori* had just been defined, that the three *savii* were entrusted with the « specific charge of ensuring that all our fortresses are provided with the things appropriate and necessary to them » [10]. While the implication is that the *savii* were to check the allocation of guns, powder, foodstuffs and other supplies, the planning of fortifications was at all stages involved with quarters for garrisons and with food and arms stores; the *savii* thus amounted to a body shadowing the *provveditori* at every point of their duties.

---

[9] E. g., Consiglio di Dieci, Deliberazioni [C. D. D.], Secreta: R., 1539-46, ff. 107 v, 165 v, 72 r, and C. D. D., Comune, R., 62, f. 103 r.

[10] S. D., Secreta, R., 62, f. 59 v-60 r.

The ten continued to order cannon directly from the *patroni* of the arsenal and have them transported to fortresses with only a rare stipulation that a copy of the inventory should be sent to the *provveditori*. They continued to receive reports on the state of artillery and of powder stores direct, and give instructions without reference to the *provveditori* even when repairs and alterations supervised by their magistracy were going forward. As a result, there was no one office that could give a clear overall account of a fortress's state of readiness.

On the other hand, the ten appear only to have maintained control over the full range of operations involved in planning and arranging for the execution of fortifications in the case of those within the *dominante*, those of immediate concern to the protection of the city itself. In 1543 the council asked for advice on the fortification of Chioggia from the duke of Urbino, Michele Sanmicheli, and Antonio da Castello, interviewed them, and gave orders for the work to be carried out — only then entrusting the organization of the labour force to the *provveditori*. The single note of dissent to this procedure was sounded by Antonio Priuli, who proposed that the matter should be postponed and raised at a later time « in the *consiglio de' pregadi* [senate], where other matters concerning fortifications are discussed » [11]. The decision to fortify the Lido had already been taken in 1534 and subsequently dropped. It was therefore appropriate that the council of ten should take the initiative again in 1543, and had it not been divided on the issue of which fort should be begun first, S. Andrea or S. Niccolò, it would doubtless have acted as it did at Chioggia. As it was, the controversy was referred to the *collegio* with the intervention there of the three *capi dei dieci* and the *provveditori*. The decision to build S. Andrea first (on the designs of Sanmichele and Castello) and then S. Niccolò (according to the duke of Urbino's model) was then taken by the ten [12], and at least until 1579 they continued to make the decisions affecting these fortresses « important above all others » [13]. After 1542, apart from their interest

[11] C. D. D., Secreta, R., 1539-46, f. 91 r. The money was sent to the *podestà* of Chioggia by the ten; the *provveditori*, however, were to be accounted to for its disbursement.

[12] *Ibid.*, f. 101 v and 104 r-v.

[13] C. D. D., Comune, R., 34, f. 164 v.

in the *dominante* forts, and a few additional works [14] for which the council had allocated money before the creation of the *fortezze* magistracy, the ten appears to have surrendered its initiative in proposing fortifications, though it continued to answer letters about defense works sent directly to the *capi* without consulting the *provveditori*, particularly when too much sharing of responsibility might lead to the leaking of secrets « to the ears of the Turk » [15].

Thenceforward the *collegio* remained the principal locus where information was gathered and projects planned before being passed to the senate for decision and to the *provveditori* for execution. Information about the state of fortifications came from *rettori* and castellans, local *provveditori*, *sindici*, and *provveditori generali*: any of those officials, that is, whose commissions, roving or stationary, called for reports on military preparedness. Occasionally a community would raise a question, like the repair of its walls, directly. Those reports and suggestions were addressed — when in written form — most frequently directly to the doge, whose secretariat diverted them to the *collegio*, rarely to the doge and the *signoria*, and fairly commonly to the *savii* ' dell'una e dell'altra mano'. As the *signoria* and the *savii* normally made up part of the *collegio*, these addresses all led to the same place. On receipt of information the *collegio* discussed it. Commonly more information was called for at that point, in writing were the informants *en poste*, personally in the case of recently returned officials or when, say, engineers could be reached who had experience of the site in question. This was the point, too, at which models and drawings were discussed, the doge himself sometimes intervening. The *collegio* might ask for oral opinions to be put in writing; experts could ask permission to speak again at a later meeting: these few days represented, in fact, a crucial point in the process of decision-making, for they culminated, after a vote had been taken, in the making of a specific recommendation to the senate [16].

The *collegio's* ' bill ', as it were, was sponsored in the senate by the three *savii* — one from each *mano* — responsible for in-

---

[14] E. g., Cerigo, *ibid.* 62, ff. 115 v-116 r.

[15] Secreta, Materie Miste Notabili, 1, (Asso = Naxos, 1577).

[16] For the role of the *collegio* v. *ibid.*, 1 and 2, *passim*, but with special reference to Crete and Cyprus.

forming themselves about fortification matters [17]; and the 'bill' was supported by the reading of passages from reports and, if necessary, by the production of models. As far as it is recoverable, discussion in the *collegio* appears to have been primarily technical. In the senate the recommendation was discussed against the general background of the current financial and political position. Either it was approved, and orders given for its implementation, or — and this is true of most proposals involving large expenditure, especially on the *terra ferma* [18] — doubts were expressed which led to control of the investigation being taken over by the senate. From this moment it was that body which determined the supplementary fact-finding procedure, electing, it may be, a special investigatory commission from its own members, writing to officials on the spot and summoning new engineers. While the *collegio* might be asked to digest the fresh information and report back its findings, the senate was henceforward the directing agency until a firm decision had been reached.

Before seeing what part the *provveditori* played in this decision-making structure, there is a further body to be considered which had a short life, but was highly characteristic of the politico-administrative mentality of the Venetian patriciate. Little more than a month had elapsed since the setting up of the *fortezze* magistracy when another body was created to deal with fortifications: the *collegio sopra le fortezze* [19]. The senate decision drew attention to the complexity of the issues involved in the planning of new fortifications for Zara, and the number of persons from whom expert advice had to be sought. A body of twenty-five senatorial 'nobili nostri' who were familiar with

---

[17] They are sometimes named; e. g., P. F., 2, ff. 92 r, 102 r, 108 r.

[18] 'Mar' decisions were straightforward in that they were directed against a traditional and openly acknowledged enemy, the Turk, and involved labour, the provision of which was, in the main, welcomed rather than resented. 'Terra' decisions led to speculation and resentment on the part of Venice's neighbours, and frequently involved local protest based on legal precedents, 'hard times' or resentment at being keyed in more firmly to Venetian political-military domination. See, though for a later period (the 1630's), my « Francesco Tensini and the Fortification of Vicenza », *Studi Veneziani* (1969).

[19] So-called in S. D. T. R., 33, f. 127 v, Oct. 6, 1544. Up till then they were referred to simply as the 'XXV nobili'.

the subject was to be elected. A majority vote of this body, together with the 'normal' *collegio* was to be « as firm and binding as if it had been taken in this council » — i. e. the senate [20]. The new *collegio* was reconvened to discuss reports on Padua in the following year. In 1544, because of the difficulty of getting together the necessary quorum of twenty, the membership was enlarged to thirty [21]. In 1547, because a series of reports on Padua, Verona and Legnago had revealed that due to faulty organization certain works had been begun without careful planning while others had been left incomplete, the senate ordered that in future no work was to be undertaken until a model or drawing had been passed as satisfactory « either by this council or by the *collegio nostro sopra le fortezze* » and that works so licensed were to be completed before others were commenced [22].

This, to my knowledge, is the last reference to this new *collegio*. Trouble with the quorum suggests one explanation, the fact that it did not in practice prevent an overlap with the senate suggests another [23]. Designed to cut down a very time-consuming aspect of senatorial work without deputing a zealously guarded legislative function to a chiefly advisory body, the *collegio*, the new body's failure demonstrates the disinclination of senators to delegate power over issues involving large sums of money or to accept decisions (as opposed to recommendations) which incorporated the votes of non-senators. From 1547 the senate relied on the election of *ad hoc* bodies of *provveditori generali* [24] to report back to the *collegio* when works on a large scale

[20] Senato, Deliberazioni, Mar: Registri [S. D. M. R.], 26, f. 145 r, Nov. 2. The record of the first meeting is headed « In Collegio cum additione xxv nobilium habente autoritatem consilii rogatorum ». And in addition to the two colleges the following are noted as attending: *consiliarii*, *capi della quarantia*, and one of the *provveditori*. Twenty-three members of the *collegio sopra le fortezze* are listed. Thirty-nine votes were cast in all and one minority opinion recorded. *Ibid.*, f. 149 r-v, Nov. 31.

[21] S. D. T. R., 33, f. 127 v, Oct. 6.

[22] *Ibid.*, 34, ff. 182 v-183 r, Feb. 3.

[23] S. D. M. R., 28, f. 164 v, May 29, 1546, where the senate amends a *collegio* decision in light of fresh information from Zara.

[24] The number varied. Two were appointed to visit Bergamo in 1585, four to inspect Brescia (together with Savorgnan) in 1588, three to advise on the proposed new fortified town of Palmanova in 1592. P. F., 2, f. 41 r; *ibid.*, 60; S. D. Secreta: Registri, 89, f. 82 v.

were under consideration. In 1587, still in pursuit of that elusive goal, a total expert oversight of fortifications, it appointed Giulio Savorgnan ' sopraintendente general di tutte le fortezze del stato nostro così da terra come da mar ' [25].

The creation of the *collegio sopra le fortezze* throws into relief, however, the restricted nature of the role the *provveditori alle fortezze* were expected to play in the making of decisions. They were present at meetings of the *collegio* when fortifications were discussed, as they were when the senate discussed them. Very rarely they were sent to discuss plans on the spot [26]. The records of *collegio* and senate meetings are such that only dissident opinions are noted, and then only infrequently. No *provveditore* is cited as advancing a minority view. Their role was not to argue, but to assemble records, provide information and to administer and put into effect decisions proposed and ratified by others. Inevitably, as their files thickened and as the precedents they established became part of the routine administration of building projects, their magistracy increased in stature, but still as a provider of services. Indeed, as its efficiency grew in this respect, the *provveditori* were called upon less and less frequently for their advice [27].

Essentially the *provveditori* were building contractors, responsible for the most costly aspect of the state's public works programme. As such they were involved in a policy of retrenchment in government spending which spanned the second half of the sixteenth century. Already in 1540 the *savii sopra la mercantia* had been instructed to conduct a purge of public officials throughout the *terra ferma* [28]. In 1558 garrisons on the *terra ferma* were cut down, in 1560 it was the turn of those on the Dalmatian coast [29]. In 1564 the *provveditori* were made responsible for a

---

[25] P. F., 2, 49 r.

[26] Both were ordered by the senate to go to Padua, Legnago and Verona with experts of their own choosing in 1546; one was sent to Peschiera in 1549. S. D. T. R., 34, f. 166 v; *ibid.*, 36, f. 132 v.

[27] At least, in the marginal notes which record attendance in senate registers and *filze*, they appeared less frequently from the late 1560's and very seldom from the late 1570's.

[28] The principles behind this purge long continued to be invoked. E. g., S. D. T. R., 53, f. 4 r, March 7, 1580.

[29] *Ibid.*, 41, ff. 113 r-114 r; S. D. M. R., 35, f. 10 r and 51 r ff.

second purge of officials — accountants, building subcontractors, carpenters, masons, storekeepers — who were no longer essential to the fortification work then going forward. Within two months all such officials were to turn up in Venice to be interviewed by the *provveditori* (six months in the case of those in the *Mar* jurisdiction) and with their help the *collegio* was to determine who would be retained and who would be fired [30].

This order was sent to *rettori*, but it was above all on these individuals that the *provveditori* were expected to check. Within months of the establishment of their magistracy they were being called upon to make sure that *rettori* did not spend the money sent to them for fortifications on anything other than walls, ditches and gun emplacements — « as has been done until now by many of our representatives » — and to be especially vigilant that public money was not spent on personal display, such as the putting up by *rettori* or *provveditori sopra le fabriche* [31] of their own coats of arms or names on gates or bastions. The *provveditori* were to check the accounts of all *rettori* or *provveditori sopra le fabriche* returning from duty, and were there any discrepancy between the record in the *fortezze* office of the sums which they had been licensed to spend and their actual expenditure, the *provveditori* were to refuse to issue the receipt (*bolletino*) without which they were left without voting rights [32]. Consequent legislation in which the *provveditori* were involved supports the view that the patricians who served as *rettori* and in other positions of responsibility outside the city were not always ideal public servants. It was deplored that they were prone to leave their posts without permission [33], that they handed out more jobs than were strictly necessary [34], that they made contracts with individuals for lime and stone without inviting bids and accepting the lowest [35], that they ordered more material than they could afford so that the *fortezze* office was plagued with unpaid bills [36]. In the inspection of public accounts throughout the

[30] S. D. T. R., 45, f. 45 v-46 r; 63 r ff.; 76 r ff.; 83 v.
[31] Officials responsible on the spot for a particular building programme.
[32] S. D. T. R., 32, 113 v ff.; 197 r.
[33] *Ibid.*, f. 113 v.
[34] *Ibid.*, 36, f. 6 v.
[35] *Ibid.*, f. 110 r.
[36] *Ibid.*, f. 170 r.

terra ferma made in 1547 by the *sindici inquisitori*, a number of other fraudulent practices were turned up [37], and where a flood of regulations had failed, the government tried the opposite approach by nearly doubling the *rettori's* allowances. This was in 1549 [38]. Complaints continued to flow in. The *rettori* were paying for lime without checking to see whether it had been watered (it was bought by weight) en route from the furnace [39]. They were even taking personal advantage of the difference in the rate of exchange between Venice and the Levant [40]. In many cases the *rettori* were merely guilty, of course, of a lack of vigilance, as when forged requests for money were made in their name [41], but complaints about their mis- or overspending were constant, and the *provveditori* were used as one of the chief means of controlling it.

From 1543 all payments to *rettori* for fortifications had to be authorized by the *camerlengo de commun* responsible for the *fortezze* account with his signature countersigned by one of the *provveditori*. *Rettori* were to send monthly statements to the *fortezze* office and if a *rettore*, on returning from duty and being denied a *bolletino*, wished to justify himself to the senate he could only do this when the senate had obtained the opinion of the *provveditori* [42]. From 1555 *rettori* were subject to similar checks by the *provveditori* on the grain store it was their responsibility to preserve against an emergency, and on building materials, even though these had been acknowledged on receipt in a note describing quality, quantity and condition on arrival. Thus any discrepancy between the money and materials sent to a *rettore* and the accounts he brought back at the end of his term of duty, could lead to deprivation of voting rights until the discrepancy was made good. And the penalty for not sending monthly accounts — the form of which was carefully spelled out — to the *provveditori* was dismissal and a five hundred ducat

---

[37] *Ibid.*, f. 53 r.

[38] *Ibid.*, f. 160 v-163 r.

[39] S. D. M. R., 31, ff. 122 v-123 r.

[40] *Ibid.*, f. 52 v.

[41] *Ibid.*, f. 97 v. On May 16, 1551, the *camerlenghi di comun* were instructed to keep specimens of *rettori*'s hand-writing so that forgeries could be detected.

[42] S. D. T. R., 32, ff. 174 v-175 r.

fine, half of which was to go to the arsenal and half to the *fortezze* office [43].

A handful of examples will show how difficult it was to enforce the letter of this efficiency-economy drive. In 1551 Niccolò Rimondo, on his return from a period as *conte* of Traù was refused his *bolletino* because he was unable to account for twenty-five ducats that had been sent in the early days of his office. He claimed that he had not received it; the *collegio* accepted his case (represented to them by the *provveditori*) and the sum was charged to his predecessor. In 1561, Gian Domenico Manoleso, ex-castellan of the Castel Vecchio of Verona, was short forty-four *stara* of grain, claiming that the loss was due to damp. As three keys were needed to get into the store (the others held by the *capitano* and the storekeeper) the claim was allowed. In 1565, Piero Emo, returned from being *provveditore sopra le fabriche* at Legnago, could not account for 320 ducats worth of timber. So much timber, however, had been rushed to shore up a collapsed *cavaliere* that the storekeeper may well have been confused. The senate ordered the *provveditori* to give him the benefit of the doubt and make up the loss from *fortezze* funds. Paolo Zorzi returned in 1566 from his post as *capitano* of Candia without any certified accounts. He was given his *bolletino* on payment of an 800-ducat security and eight months in which to have them sent to Venice. In 1573 returning — and accountless — *rettori* from Corfu, Tine and Micone, were excused because they pleaded the dislocating effects of the recent Turkish wars [44]. These cases (which are, I think, reasonably representative) reveal the nervous financial mood which prompted the economy regulations rather than the existence of peculation on a large scale.

The *provveditori's* office [45] was itself run with a minimal and poorly paid staff. It started with an accountant to record monies paid from the *fortezze* account at the *cecca* into the working account at the office, and the sums forwarded and the goods and salaries paid for from that. He was also responsible for checking the monthly statements sent in by *rettori*. Elected by

---

[43] S. D. M. R., 33, ff. 27 v, 35 r, 56 v-57 r. Accounts had to be sent in monthly by *Rettori di Terra*, every four months by *Rettori di Mar*.

[44] P. F., 20 (1), f. 37 v; *ibid.*, f. 47 r; S. D. T. R., 45, ff. 134 r-v; P. F., 20 (1), ff. 51 v-52 r; *ibid.*, f. 96 r.

[45] The records do not show where in Venice it was located.

the *collegio* and paid fifty ducats a year from the *fortezza* account [46], he was assisted by a clerk whose salary of twelve ducats a year came from the same source [47]. For the part-time services of a notary in the chancery the account was charged twenty-four ducats a year [48], a sum which was slightly raised in 1547 by which time the need for his services had risen to a point at which « he needed almost always to have his pen in hand » [49]. In 1562 the accountant, Stefano Spiera, was given an assistant bookkeeper (at one ducat and sixteen grossi a month), because of the increasing load of his work. Traditionally in Venice jobs like clerkships and overseerships in the building trades were handed down from father to son. When Alvise Stella resigned from being clerk in 1553 at the age of eighty, the *provveditori* replaced him with his son. But for the younger man the salary, which had risen to twenty-four ducats a year, was no longer enough. He soon handed it to *his* son, but he, too, found it insufficient. Ten years later, in 1565, Zamaria Dalla Piazza was making the same complaint that the salary was too low for such a « heavy and insupportable » job. Initiating a new dynasty of resignations, he was succeeded by his son [50].

In 1589 the establishments of all magistracies were challenged by an inquiry into government spending conducted by *revisori sopra la scansation delle spese superflue*. By this time, besides an accountant and his assistant and a clerk, the *provveditori* had acquired an overseer whose duty was to inspect the materials — timber, nails, clamps and so forth — purchased by the office and sometimes to inspect construction work on the spot. His salary was fifty ducats a year. Since the council of ten had handed over to the *provveditori* responsibility for the maintenance of S. Andrea and S. Niccolò, they had appointed a custodian to the former, and a foreman to the latter, whose chief job was to see that the mud excavated from the canals of Venice was used to consolidate the land surrounding the fort. The *provveditori* managed to persuade the *revisori* that all these posts were ne-

[46] S. D. T. R., 32, Jan. 30, 1543.
[47] P. F., 20 (1), f. 3 r.
[48] *Ibid.*, f. 3 v.
[49] *Ibid.*, f. 21 r.
[50] *Ibid.*, ff. 40 v, 44 r, 49 r.

cessary [51]. The total wages bill of the office was under 350 ducats per annum.

While suggestions for the repair or modification of fortifications most commonly came from the reports of *rettori* or *provveditori generali* and thus came before the *collegio* in the first instance, *rettori* (or representatives fulfilling similar functions under another name) increasingly wrote to the *provveditori* directly [52], as did various public-spirited individuals [53]. Such suggestions were referred at the discretion of the *provveditori* to the *collegio*. Until a decision had been reached by that body and the senate, the *fortezze* office functioned as an archive for the relevant drawings and models [54] and the *provveditori* kept in touch with the engineers and captains who were investigating the situation on the spot, sometimes summoning them to a conference in Venice the results of which would be duly reported in the *collegio*.

Once a decision had been made to proceed, the relevant documentation which had remained in the hands of the *collegio* or senate for the purpose of debate was transferred to the *fortezze* office [55]. A local construction hierarchy was then set up on the spot. Commonly this was supervised by the *capitano* [56] or his

---

[51] P. F., 2, ff. 91 r-92 v and P. F., 36 (1), April 16, 1590. The custodian of S. Andrea got 10 ducats (reduced by the *revisori* from 12) a month; the foreman at S. Niccolò, 6.

[52] E. g., P. F., 36 (4), Dec. 7, 1590.

[53] « I am making so bold [to give an opinion on Verona, in September 1583] both for the zeal I bear towards the illustrious signory of Venice, my patron, and because I have found in the books of the Romans that they listened to anyone, however humble, who spoke to them of matters of concern to the republic ». Anon., P. F., 37 (4), f. 149 r. In 1556 a crank, Joan. Battista de Lion, wrote to say that he had discovered a fatal flaw in the defenses of Padua. Michele Sanmicheli, who was sent to investigate, wrote a report of contemptuous rebuttal. P. F., 65 (1).

[54] The archivio of the *fortezze* survives, unfortunately, in a maimed form. There are very few drawings from this period and no models. I cannot trace the ' cattastico modelli e dissegni ' cited in an inventory of 1798, P. F., 69 (5). The *fortezze* office obtained a part-time curator of models and drawings in 1566, S. D. T. R., 46, f. 17 r. It is not clear how long he served there.

[55] E. g., when, after long discussion, the senate decided to go ahead with plans for improvements at Brescia in 1591, the copy of the minute was endorsed « Le scritture sono state mandate all'offitio delle fortezze ». P. F., 2, f. 110 r.

[56] Occasionally, as at Sebenico, the *capitano's* salary was charged to the

equivalent. Alternatively a *provveditore* was appointed by the *maggior consiglio* to take charge. In peace time the engineer responsible for the plans stayed on the site long enough at least to see the trace drawn (possibly with the aid of a local surveyor) and returned to check progress from time to time, in war time — or indeed when many projects were going forward simultaneously — the engineer could be out of touch with his work for long periods. The actual work programme was organized by a site overseer (*proto*), with deputy foremen in charge of the masons, carpenters and blacksmiths. He directed the labourers (raised by local authorities on the orders of the senate) and was assisted in keeping a labour roll, an inventory of materials received, and a record of work performed, by one or two bookkeepers [57].

The *provveditori* sent drawings and models (in *gesso* or wood) to the site to act as guides during the absences of the engineer, and they also supplied overseers and specialist craftsmen if these could not be recruited locally. The demand came particularly from overseas, where local craftsmen were not familiar with Venetian construction techniques and where there was a shortage of trained overseers and bookkeepers [58], but the *provveditori* also provided trained personnel for works on the *terra ferma* and in all cases their ratification of locally-made appointments was necessary [59]. Most frequently, these jobs were filled by transfer, or by a relation of a man known to the *provveditori*, but occasionally they were advertised by a written announcement displayed « on the Rialto steps » [60]. The *provveditori* were also responsible for sending small change (*sesini*) for the labourers'

---

fortifications while work was proceeding on them. S. D. M. R., 33, f. 157 v, 29 Sept. 1557.

[57] P. F., 2, f. 26 v and 20 (1), f. 3 r for examples from Zara and the Lido. Salaries for these posts varied from 3-11 ducats per month, depending on the amount of work involved and responsibility.

[58] E. g., S. D. M. R., 30, f. 29 r; P. F., 2, f. 8 r and 10 v; S. D. M. R., 35, f. 164 r, and P. F., 20 (1), ff. 31 r-v for examples from Corfu, Cattaro and Candia.

[59] P. F., 20 (1), ff. 40 r and 49 r (Peschiera); *ibid.*, f. 45 v (Legnago). The files kept on such men — P. F., 36 (1), 14 Feb. 1596 — have disappeared. Where really large sums were involved, the *collegio* itself would appoint a bookkeeper: S. D. T. R., 37, f. 17 r (Peschiera).

[60] P. F., 20 (1), f. 139 v. Copy of advertisement for a *proto* in 1585.

weekly pay and could use their judicial powers to settle labour disputes [61]. Meanwhile the bookkeepers on the site reported on the arrival of all supplies to the *provveditori's* accountant, who was required by law to mark these receipts against his record of goods dispatched, and they furnished the *capitano* — or, rather, an accountant from the local *camera* — with the details he was expected to send month by month to the *fortezze* office.

On the *terra ferma* building supplies were usually obtained by the *capitano* or *provveditore* in charge; the *provveditori* were normally only concerned when operations were under their direct supervision; thus they bought Istrian stone for S. Andrea. Within the *stato de Mar*, however, their activities in connection with the purchase and dispatch of supplies were considerable. From Capo d' Istria to the Aegean they were responsible for keeping fortified places equipped with timber (mainly planks of various sizes), bricks, nails, angle-irons and clamps (and pigs and bars of iron for forging on the spot) and with tools, especially picks and shovels. These materials were sent not merely for fortifications, but for constructing and repairing quarters for troops and food and munition stores. Orders for the purchases were given by the senate or, more rarely, the council of ten, in the light of requests made by *rettori*, the costs — in which freight charges figured largely [62] — being worked out with the advice of the *fortezze* office. The *provveditori* then bought and sent the goods, obtained receipts for them [63], dealt with complaints [64] and with the consequences of vessels being sunk,

---

[61] I know of only two examples, however. In one they threaten a recalcitrant subcontractor with a 25-ducat fine, three months in prison and three « squassi della corda »; in the other they insist that a galley loaded with *fortezze* supplies sail in spite of the vessel's being the subject of private litigation: P. F., 20 (1), ff. 57 r, 60 r.

[62] The space occupied by timber made these charges high. Some examples (chiefly from P. F.): freight charge 421 out of a total of 4,506 lire, 114 out of 658 ducats (Zara); 620 out of 3,212 lire (Sebenico); 651 out of 8,145, 1,271 out of 9,663, 700 out of 4,177 lire (Corfu); 780 out of 2,387, 500 out of 1,330 ducats (Candia); 680 out of 2,228 lire (Zante).

[63] One of the difficulties of keeping track of these supplies is suggested by an order of 1575 which specifies that the receipt should be enclosed in a wind- and water-proof cover. P. F., 2, f. 21 r.

[64] E. g., a cargo of bricks which en route from Treviso to Zara were largely « reduced to powder », *ibid.*, f. 41 v.

diverted by storms or having their cargoes forcibly unloaded at ports of call where the local authorities were themselves desperate for supplies.

The *provveditori* were occasionally called upon to dispatch materials other than building supplies, from guncarriages, powder and shot to medicines and boots, caps, and cloth for soldiers' uniforms. But what added more heavily to the administrative burdens of the *provveditori* was their responsibility for victualing. « Fortified places cannot truly be said to be fortified », as a senate preamble put it in 1547, « unless they are provided with an adequate food supply » [65]. Before this date victualing had been organized on an *ad hoc* basis, *rettori* reporting to the *collegio* or the council of ten and receiving from them money for purchases and licenses for the sale of stocks threatened by damp. From 1547 this procedure was rationalized, a lump sum being allocated to the *fortezze* account (though with a separate accounting procedure) and the *provveditori* were empowered to negotiate directly with *rettori* and introduce an accounting procedure parallel to that used for construction work. *Rettori*, at the end of their term of duty, had to satisfy the office on this score, too, before the *provveditori* could supply them with a *bolletino*; the procedure applied both to *Terra* and *Mar* [66]. This meant that the *provveditori* inherited part of one of the more complex areas of governmental administration, for the state granaries, in Venetian territory as elsewhere, were involved not only in the socially nervous business of price-fixing, but were subject to pressure in times of dearth and could not, therefore, be managed merely in terms of military preparedness [67].

The original brief to the *provveditori*, to ensure that fortified places were defensible for at least a year ahead, now involved making sure that a starving population would not force a garrison to surrender. For the people as a whole this was almost exclusively a matter of grain for bread, and grain, from wheat to millet, was thus the *provveditori*'s chief concern. But they were

[65] S. D. T. R., 35, f. 41 v.

[66] See esp. S. D. T. R., 35, f. 33 r., 36, f. 108 r. The account was called the « a comprar vettuarie per le fortezze » and from the point of view of overall budgeting remained a sub-account of the *cassa delle monitioni*.

[67] See P. F., 36 (1) for some of the problems involved.

also responsible, within this overall concern, for the detailed diet of the garrisons themselves [68]. As itemized by one of the government's most trusted advisers in military matters in the 1540's and 1550's, the duke of Urbino, this included, besides grain of various sorts for bread: beans, rice, oil, salt, cheese, salt meat, fish, vinegar, wine, and wood for fuel [69]. From 1552, moreover, the *provveditori* were entrusted with obtaining enough hand-and horse-driven mills to grind flour for garrisons [70]. This soon involved them in the installation and maintenance of water mills as well [71].

Assistance in the planning of fortifications, the supply of building materials and grain: while these were the major concerns of the *provveditori*, they were far from exhausting the list of their duties. They were responsible for — or at least their aid could be invoked for — the water supply of fortified places, and thus with the construction of wells [72] and indeed with fountains if to bring water meant a temporary breaching of a city wall [73]. If a town wished, for the convenience of trade, to open new gates in its walls and thus weaken the defenses, it had to obtain permission from the *provveditori* [74]. They were concerned with the design, supply and installation of defensive chains across rivers for riparian fortresses [75]. Where town ditches were filled with running, as opposed to stagnant water, there was a demand to use it for irrigation purposes by individuals farming outside the counterscarp and *glacis*; it was for the *provveditori* to supervise this and determine the charges [76]. They might be called on to provide equipment and trained men for dredging work at fortified sea ports [77]. The council of ten was reluctant to allow

---

[68] S. D. T. R., 36, ff. 189 v-190 r.

[69] P. F., 37 (4), f. 72 r, Dec. 16, 1551.

[70] S. D. T. R., 38, f. 159 v and S. D. M. R., 32, f. 53 r. They had formerly been instructed to provide mills only from time to time, e. g., for Legnago in 1547, S. D. T. R., 35, f. 40 r.

[71] *Ibid.*, 41, f. 119 r (Padua); P. F., 2, f. 33 r (Traù).

[72] E. g., P. F., 36 (1), 9 Mar. 1588 (Corfu).

[73] *Ibid.*, July 9, 1594 (Asola).

[74] E. g., *ibid.*, June 12, 1551 (Capodistria).

[75] S. D. T. R., 41, f. 68 v (Chiusa), f. 120 r-v (Verona), P. F., 37 (4), Apr. 13, 1593 (Legnago).

[76] P. F., 2, f. 60 v (Legnago).

[77] *Ibid.*, ff. 34 r, 37 r, 87 v (Canea, Zara, Candia).

markets to be held inside certain fortifications because of the security risk of an influx of strangers; even markets held outside the walls were not looked on with favour, so local communities petitioned for them via the *provveditori* [78]. As well as being responsible for the building of garrison quarters within fortifications the *provveditori* could be asked to construct them outside, as when in 1572 they were charged with providing transit accommodation on the Lido, near the S. Niccolò monastery, for troops en route for, or returning from, overseas [79].

The earth-shifting, labouring work on a fortification was deputed through a quota system to neighbouring territories charged by the senate with supplying so many men for so many months, the details having been worked out by the *collegio* with the *provveditori* [80]. This system led to loud complaints, especially from the territories farthest away and least likely to benefit personally from the work, and especially in harvest time when men were reluctant to leave the land. These complaints were referred, in the first instance, to the *provveditori*. Again, part of the costs of major fortifications were charged against other towns on the theory that the strengthening of any one part of the Venetian dominions was for the benefit of the whole. This also led to protests, and it was the duty of the *provveditori* to investigate them and, indeed, to call the senate's attention to towns that were defaulting on these unpopular payments [81].

Unpopular, too, was the *provveditori*'s responsibility to advise against granting building licenses where the internal functioning of a fortification might be impeded (especially near gates

---

[78] *Ibid.*, f. 65 r; P. F., 36 (1), Mar. 22, 1590 (Legnago and Peschiera).

[79] Troops in transit had formerly been billeted in monasteries within the city — and this order was the result of the monks' protests. P. F., 2, f. 2 v and 104 v-105 r.

[80] E. g., S. D. T. R., 51, f. 47 v (Bergamo).

[81] E. g., *ibid.*, 32, ff. 162 v-163 r (Vicenza behind with payments for Corfu). There are numerous examples in P. F., 36 (1), *passim*. Earth-shifting was allocated on the basis illustrated by these two cases: Bergamo — figures refer to *perteghe* — work divided between the Bergamasco (5,000), Bresciano, including Asola (5,000), Veronese (2,000), Vicentino (2,000), Cremasco (1,000); Verona — Veronese (7,000), Colognese (500), Vicentino (3,500), Bergamasco (3,500), Bresciano (5,500). P. F., 2, f. 24 r and S. D. T. R., 33, ff. 23 v-24 r.

and munition stores)[82] and to prevent any building or planting from interfering with its external functioning. In spite of heavy penalties[83], buildings had been erected outside town walls which impeded the field of fire from battlements or ramparts. One of the earliest duties of the *provveditori* was to ensure that *rettori* carried out the order to clear away all buildings within half a mile of the walls, and any building or any planting of trees or crops that could block the operation of platforms for cannon or gun emplacements in the flanks of bastions[84]. In 1551 this legislation was repeated and strengthened. If returning *rettori* could not prove to the *provveditori* that ramparts, curtains, bastions and ditches were free from any impediments, they could be denied voting rights[85]. This legislation proved extremely difficult to enforce. In peace time the *glacis* of a fortification was a standing temptation to plant and cultivate, especially to those citizens who had owned the land before it was taken over by the state. The ramparts and the earthen tops of bastions tempted soldiers from the garrison to grow fruit and vegetables there. A more thunderous version of the law of 1543 and 1551 was issued in 1588, repeating the need for sworn and witnessed testimony from *rettori*, and empowering the *provveditori* to impose a fine of fifty ducats on anyone contravening the order[86].

Another issue in which the *provveditori* were involved and which brought public and private interests into conflict was corcerned with riparian property rights. In 1565, for instance, the Adige flooded and damaged the fortifications of Legnago. The *provveditori* were sent by the senate to inspect the course of the river and the streams that ran into it and report any construction that had altered the water flow — mills, weirs, fish-traps, and the like[87]. So many were discovered that the senate decided to elect a panel of twelve from among its members to formulate specific proposals, restricting eligibility to those who

---

[82] E. g., P. F., 36 (1), July 16, 1584 (Verona).

[83] In 1512, a year in prison and 200 ducats fine. S. D. T. R., 18, f. 24 r.

[84] *Ibid.*, 32, f. 118 v, Feb. 15, 1543. The order repeats one of Nov. 1513.

[85] Minute of decision of *maggior consiglio* (26 June) in P. F., 1. The returning *rettore* had to bring a declaration to this effect countersigned by his successor and by an official of the *camera*.

[86] P. F., 2, ff. 72 v-73 r.

[87] S. D. T. R., 45, f. 167 r.

did not possess property, nor were related to anyone who had property in the area « between the Po and the Bacchiglione or in the Veronese, Vicentino or Colognese »[88]. That was on February 19, 1566. Four days later, however, it was noted that « because the number of interested parties turned out to be so great, the election could not be made », and it was decided to try again, excluding only those who owned land themselves, or were the fathers, sons or nephews of those who did[89].

This, of course, is but one aspect of a problem which increased in magnitude during the course of the sixteenth century. As more and more of the senatorial class acquired land in the *terra ferma* it became more difficult to pass legislation in the interest of the state itself. The *fortezze* records have already suggested that the *rettori*, who came from this same class, showed some inclination to protect the *terra ferma* from the full rigour of regulations emanating from Venice. A final example of the *provveditori's* ' occasional ' functions throws an interesting pencil of light on the interrelationship between the legislative and executive functions of the *ceto dirigente*.

The authority of the *provveditori* had not proved sufficient to enforce the senate's order to *rettori* of January 1543, that they should not divert *fortezze* money to the repair and decoration of their own *palazzi*. They had, moreover, been plagued by requests for money for this purpose, and in 1585 the senate moved to put teeth into their original order. *Rettori* were to be deprived of voting rights if they could not satisfy the *provveditori* on this score and all proposals to spend public money on *rettori*'s own residences had to be approved by the *collegio* and senate. The sums involved were, in fact, never large, but the fact that the issue had a considerable symbolic importance is evidenced by the provision that assent to such requests had to be passed — unusually — by a five-sixths majority in both bodies[90].

---

88 *Ibid.*, f. 217 v.

89 *Ibid.*, f. 218 v.

90 *Ibid.*, 56, f. 86 r. The distribution list for the promulgation of this law gives a useful view of what were considered to be the key *fortezze* on the *terra ferma*: Padua, Treviso, Peschiera, Verona, Orzinovi, Bergamo, Brescia, and Crema, and overseas: Zara, Sebenico, Cattaro, Corfu, Candia, Canea, Spinalonga, Suda, Grabusa. By 1589 the necessary majority had been chan-

The duties of the *fortezze* magistracy frequently involved cooperation with other magistracies. Before timber could be felled permission had to be obtained from and trees selected by either the *patroni all'arsenal* or the *savii alle acque*; the *savii* had to be consulted when water courses were changed for the cleansing or filling of wet ditches. The *savii alla mercanzia* had a general oversight of salaries during work on fortifications. Victualing led to cooperation with the *provveditori alle biave*. Artillery was supplied by the *provveditori all'artiglieria*; they employed munition storesmen and in some places, but not all, were responsible for the fabric of powder magazines. The closest relations were with the *patroni all'arsenale*, from whom the *provveditori* on occasion borrowed craftsmen and overseers and obtained a large part of the material and supplies they dispatched to their fortresses [91]. The two magistracies were sometimes charged to work together on some aspect of defense works, such as the installation of a chain « in all secrecy » between the Lido forts [92].

Inventors who approached the government in the hope of selling some new way of defending or constructing fortifications were referred to the *provveditori*, who interviewed them, examined models and drawings and, if the ideas seemed practicable, arranged trials before making recommendations. The inventions submitted during the period covered by this essay were not impressive [93]; a new method of making lime, an unspecified weapon proposed by an ex-slave of the Turks, a way of fixing the chain in the Peschiera channel, devices for strengthe-

---

ged to four-fifths, but it is interesting that the names of the *savio* of the *consiglio* and the *terra ferma* with special responsibility for *fortezze* issues were — against the common practice — entered in the records of these decisions. P. F., 2, ff. 95 r (Asola), 96 v (Oderzo), 97 r (Cittanova), f. 108 v (Lendinara).

[91] The procedure varied. Normally the *provveditori* approached the *patroni* for materials stored in the arsenal. Sometimes the *patroni* were ordered to dispatch supplies without reference — on occasion even without sending an inventory — to the *provveditori*. Sometimes an order was broken down between them, as in 1578 when the *provveditori* were given money to buy nails and timber for Budua while the *patroni* were made responsible for tools, wheelbarrows, barrels and a « great bell ». S. D. M.: Filze, 72, Oct. 5.

[92] C. D. D. Secreta, R., 1539-46, ff. 96 r-v.

[93] P. F., 36 (1), *passim*.

ning walls. Only one, so far as I know, was adopted [94], though not all were written off as peremptorily as were certain « secrets » as « problematical, impossible and incapable of success ». But this was another aspect of the *provveditori's* function which could invoke cooperation with, or at least reference to, other magistracies. Battista Scarpa, for instance, claimed to have an infallible method of securing the Lidi which he refused to reveal to the *provveditori*. If the doge (i. e. the *collegio*) nevertheless resolved to give him a trial, the *provveditori* suggested that it should be entrusted to them together with the *savii alle acque* [95].

Far more important was the role of the *provveditori* in the selection of military engineers. As in other levels of the building trade, preference was given to dynasties; thus in addition to the great military architect, Michele Sanmicheli, whose services they inherited, the *provveditori* also employed his son, Zuan Hieronimo, and his nephews, Alvise and Bernardino Brugnoli. Other men either approached the government directly or were recommended by *provveditori alle fabriche* or *in terra ferma* who had employed them on a temporary basis. In either case the *collegio* asked the *provveditori* to take up references and interview them. Thus, petitioning for permanent employment, Giovan Battista Bonhomo of Brescia had enclosed testimonials which praised his work at Zara and Corfu and the *provveditori* contacted three ex-*capitani* of Zara to confirm them. They also requested candidates to bring models and drawings; in one case an applicant was told to draw the Lido forts. They then reported back to the *collegio*. Because, after Sanmicheli, he was the most outstanding of the sixteenth-century Venetian military engineers, their report on the Florentine Bonaiuto Lorini is worth quoting. « We summoned him before us and he showed us drawings and other designs in his own hand from which, and from his accompanying remarks, we could see clearly that he is professionally competent, quick to apprehend, of solid and mature judgement in his replies and suggestions, and, lastly, full of excellent and useful new ideas » [96]. They supported his request

---

[94] Bonaiuto Lorini was granted a patent in 1580 for « edificii per lui ritrovati da cavar canali et fossi et terrapienar le piazze delle fortezze, et per portar polvere et ogn'altra cosa ». S. D. T. R., 53, f. 5 r.

[95] *Ibid.*, Aug. 4, 1578.

[96] On these interviews, P. F., 31 (1), *passim*. For Lorini's, Jan. 18, 1581.

for a *condotta* also because there were then only three engineers who were employed on a permanent basis: Bonhomo, Francesco Malacreda, and Zenese Bresciano.

The government, indeed, was extremely grudging in its employment of permanent military engineers. Three of four was the usual number, at a salary which began between 120 and 200 ducats a year and normally leveled off at between 280 and 340. Requests for increases were usually supported by the *provveditori* who were reluctant to lose the few men on whose services they could always rely, but they frequently led to close or adverse votes in the senate or council of ten. An attempt to raise Malacreda's salary from 340 to 400 ducats was turned down four times by the latter body [97]. The motive for keeping the engineer corps so small was doubtless primarily one of economy, but the design and supervision of fortifications was not entirely dependent on them. Many designs were submitted by high ranking *capi di guerra* in the Venetian service, like the duke of Urbino or Marcantonio Martinengo, for whom the planning of fortifications was one of the talents expected of the well educated, all-round soldier. Much of the bread-and-butter work of supervision and the provision of working drawings was carried out by engineers employed often for long periods, but always on the basis of one job at a time, men whose earnings varied between sixty and 144 ducats a year. It was not a satisfactory system. The high ranking amateurs had many other duties. The part-time engineers lacked authority and prestige. The few professionals had constantly to be switched from one site to another and, moving between the *terra ferma* and the fortresses overseas, were sometimes out of reach for months at a time. The cost of correcting mistakes and rebuilding walls and bastions that collapsed from the lack of consistent expert supervision far outweighed the money saved by keeping the corps small and added considerably to the administrative burden of the *provveditori* [98].

---

[97] C. D. D. Comune, R., 33, f. 48 v; 34, f. 164 v. Even Sanmicheli had had trouble in getting his traveling expenses reimbursed: P. F., 20 (1), ff. 10 v and 14 v.

[98] E. g., S. D. T. R., 39, ff. 192 r-v (Orzinovi); *ibid.*, 44, f. 44 r and 45, f. 156 r (Peschiera).

This is not the place in which to treat the financing of Venetian fortifications in any detail. The raising of money from taxation and from cameral dues remained complex even after the « nova regolatione » of 1579 [99]. This reform purported to ensure a steady annual income of some thirty thousand ducats for the *fortezze* account. The actual income was more like twenty-two thousand. Fortifications were expensive. Between 1543 and 1546, 7, 332 ducats were spent on one bastion alone at Verona; the bastion at the Campo Marte there had cost 20,416 ducats by 1574 [100]. *Provveditori* returning from Asola complained regularly about the old-fashioned state of its fortifications; simply to improve them, it was estimated, would cost sixty thousand ducats. Figures between one hundred and one hundred and fifty thousand ducats were quoted for Cerines in Cyprus [101]. Neither of these schemes, nor many of the others that were proposed, were undertaken. Yet by the end of our period, mainly thanks to extensive works from the mid-1580's at Bergamo and Brescia, the *fortezze* office had run up a debt of one hundred and fifteen thousand ducats at the *cecca* [102]. The *provveditori* had no say in the apportionment of public monies to the *fortezze* account; any disbursement from it of more than one hundred ducats had to be approved by a three-quarters majority in the *collegio*. Their responsibility was for seeing that the sums granted for fortifications were spent carefully and accounted for exactly. In an atmosphere of almost continual cheese-paring they spent far more time checking their accounts, dealing with protests about labour allocations, and harassing local *camere* to pay their dues than in discussing those ideal geometrical forms which in the eyes of all Europe had coupled the name of Italy with the art of fortification.

It is, of course, arbitrary to close this sketch of the *fortezze* magistracy in 1592. At the beginning of the next year the senate proposed « in the name of the Holy Ghost and for the benefit

---

[99] Printed in *Bilanci Generali della Repubblica di Venezia*, vol. 1, part 1 (Venice, 1912), pp. 605-606, from C. D. D., Zecca, R., IV, ff. 22 v-23 r.

[100] P. F., 37 (4), ff. 26 r and 132 r.

[101] P. F., 36 (4), Dec. 20, 1589; Secreta, Materie Miste Notabili, 1 (unfoliated, undated, but apparently 1558).

[102] P. F., 2, f. 104 v. This was in July 1591. Further borrowings were necessary in the next months, *ibid.*, ff. 113 r-v and 118 r-v.

not only of ourselves but the Christian Republic as a whole to construct a *fortezza reale* in the *patria* of Friuli » [103]. This proposal set in motion the most grandiose public works operation ever undertaken by Venice, the construction of the fortress town of Palmanova. But the implementing team decided on by the *savii* of the *collegio* and three *ad hoc provveditori generali* who had inspected and chosen the site did not include our magistrates. At its head was Marcantonio Barbaro (who had not been a *provveditore alle fortezze*); subordinate to him, with responsibility for construction work, was Marcantonio Martinengo; Giulio Savorgnan was to act as general adviser; there was to be a site engineer, a secretary and an accountant [104]. The role of the *fortezze* office remained, as it was to continue, that of a subordinate factotum, arranging supplies, querying traveling expenses and, eventually, helping in the government's prolonged attempt to persuade families to settle within the giant harmonies of this most rationally designed of fortresses, least rationally located of towns.

---

[103] S. D., Secreta, R., 89, f. 82 v, Jan. 29. The actual decision was not confirmed until Oct. 19. *Fortezza reale* = a fortification entirely in the ' modern ' style.

[104] *Ibid.*, ff. 137 v-138 v.

APPENDIX: THE FOUNDING DOCUMENT

S. D. Secreta, R., 62, ff. 59 r-v

[Sept. 24, 1542]

Sono di tal qualità li tempi presenti che sì come alla giornata si vede non solamente per ragion di guerra, over per forza di arme, ma etiamdio con fraude si cerca di occupare le città et loci che non sono ben guardati et moniti, al che dovendo quelli che sono al governo di questa republica, con ogni suo spirito et diligentia attender et proveder che tali disordini non seguino nel stato nostro, il fondamento del quale, come a tutti è notissimo, sono le fortezze sì da mar come da terra, le qual in molti loci, perchè non hanno quelle provisione et cose che necessariamente per la summa importantia di esse doveriano haver, potriano in diversi modi pericolare con grandissimo danno et interesse della signoria nostra, sì come in manifesto pericolo stete la importantissima fortezza nostra di Corfù al tempo che l'armada del signor Turcho se li presentò sotto, il che tutto procede perchè questo cargo, che è di savii del collegio, per le molte et continue occupatione non può esser essequito secondo che ricerca il publico bisogno, et etiam per non esser ditto cargo particolarmente applicato ad alcun magistrato di questa nostra città; et però:

L'anderà parte che non derogando all' auttorità di savii del collegio nostro, siano eletti per scrutinio di questo conseglio doi honorevoli zentilhomini nostri che siano del corpo di esso conseglio de pregadi et zonta et de là in suso, eccettuando quei del collegio per le ragion ditte, con titolo de proveditori delle fortezze, sì da mar come da terra, i quali siano per un anno, et in suo loco se debbi elezer altri successive di tempo in tempo, et possino esser tolti de ogni loco et officio etiam continuo, et con pena nè possino refutar sotto pena di ducati 500 oltra le altre pene comprese nell'ultima parte contra li refudanti; habbiano auttorità di aricordar, procurar et proveder che tutte le fortezze nostre et terre che a loro paresse esser de importantia siano fornite delle cose opportune et necessarie alla conservation di esse al meno per uno anno, et in questa materia possino in nome della signoria nostra scriver di fuora a chi serà bisogno et ricever lettere et metter le parte che li parerano in questo conseglio, cosi uniti come separati, a beneficio di esse fortezze, ben però che le lettere et parte siano prima vedute et ben considerate per li savii del collegio nostro, li quali se ben fusseno de altra opinione non li possino impedire salvo con deliberation di questo conseglio, il qual non possi esser negato alli preditti proveditori sempre che in tal materia lo rechiederano; et siano etiam obligati ditti proveditori essequir quanto più presto li serà possibile tutte le deliberation di qualunque conseglio nella detta materia; et acciochè li ditti dui proveditori habbiano bona informatione de ogni cosa, sia etiam preso che alle relation delli rettori nostri si debbano ritrovar presenti in collegio, et da tutti essi rettori, capitanei, proveditori, castellani et altri ministri che venirano de cadaun loco nostro li sia dato una nota particolare delle cose che bisognerano, a fine che possino far le debite provisione, et il presente capitolo sia aggionto in tutte le commissione a ziò habbino a essequir quello; dechiarando che la elettion delli detti dui nobili sia fatta il mese di ottobre da poi fatte le zonte, et così successive de anno in anno.

105

[no adverse or doubtful votes]

R. BURR LITCHFIELD

OFFICE-HOLDING IN FLORENCE AFTER THE REPUBLIC

I.

The evolution of Florence under the Medici Grand Duchy has received little attention from Renaissance historians. The sixteenth to eighteenth centuries are a dark age in Tuscan history, when new institutions prepared the region for its subsequent history, while there were also tenacious survivals from the past. The political crises that led to the establishment of the Duchy in 1530, and to the consolidation of the new regime after Cosimo I's accession to power in 1537, permanently altered the Republican constitution. Cosimo preserved the independence of the Duchy, enlarged it to include the territory of Siena, and his successors continued as an indigenous dynasty until their extinction in 1737, when they were replaced by the Hapsburg-Lorraine and Tuscany became a semi-dependency of Vienna. Under the Medici, the institutions of the Republic changed as authority was concentrated in the person of the Duke. The city state was partly transformed into a regional state. The older system of self-government by Florentine citizens in the councils and magistracies of the capital was replaced by the administration of a hierarchy of bureaucratic functionaries appointed in the name of the Duke. This bureaucratization of the state became permanent and remained after the incorporation of Tuscany into the Savoy Monarchy in the 1860's [1].

---

[1] The collection and elaboration of material used in this essay was assisted by a grant-in-aid from the American Council of Learned Societies (IBM-GIA-66). I am also grateful for the assistance of the Computation Center of Brown University. The bureaucratic element of the Renaissance state is discussed suggestively in F. Chabod, « Y a-t-il un Etat de la Renaissance? » in *Actes du colloque sur la Renaissance* (Paris, 1958) pp. 57-74. See also P. J. Jones, « Communes and Despots: the City State in Late-Medieval Italy » in *Transactions of the Royal Historical Society*, 5th Ser. Vol. 15 (London, 1965) pp. 71-96, and L. Martines *Lawyers and Statecraft in Renaissance Florence* (Princeton, 1968) pp. 387-476. In this essay, the term « bureaucracy » is assumed to have the meaning and characteristics assigned in the

Yet the new structure of institutions obscures the long continuity of the fifteenth-century Republican elite. The Medici Dukes never freed themselves from this class, nor did the new bureaucratic functionaries of the Duchy supplant its political influence. Two centuries after the fall of the Republic, Florence was still ruled by a citizen aristocracy, whose way of life had come increasingly to resemble that of noble aristocracies north of the Alps.

It is difficult to identify the patricians of the fifteenth century with precision, since many Florentines qualified for inclusion in the lists from which office-holders were selected at different levels, and the citizens of the Republic were divided by political faction. Yet the electoral procedures for the three highest executive committees, the *Tre Maggiori*, conceded a special prominence to a group of families that was distinct from the general populace. The committees included the *Gonfaloniere di Giustizia* and eight priors of the *Signoria*, and the twelve *Buonuomini* and sixteen *Gonfalonieri* of the *Collegi*. The members were renewed through a complex procedure every few months [2]. Qualification for the *Maggiori* depended partly on wealth, since most of the places were reserved for families inscribed in the major guilds, and partly on family connections, since another criterion was previous occupancy of the offices. Important families were admitted to the scrutinies of office-holders as *benefiziati* from one generation to another. Florentines who did

---

definition of Weber (H. H. Gerth and C. W. Mills, eds., *From Max Weber* [New York, 1958] pp. 196-204). These characteristics include: clear areas of administrative specialization, a definite hierarchy of authority, records, fixed rules, and trained, appointed, permanent functionaries. Weber's type does not correspond fully to the practice of Florence under the Republic, since although the administrative functions of a bureaucratic state were well developed from the fourteenth century, the form of administration was not truly bureaucratic in a Weberian sense. The personnel of the Republican magistracies and councils was not permanent, and the independent jurisdiction of different magistracies was such that a hierarchal chain of administrative authority had been only partly achieved. The type corresponds somewhat better to the practice of the Medici Duchy and to the system that emerged as a result of the eighteenth-century reforms.

[2] N. Rubinstein, *The Government of Florence under the Medici, 1434-1494* (Oxford, 1966) pp. 1-67. See also his « Florentine Constitutionalism and Medici Ascendancy in the Fifteenth Century » in N. Rubinstein, ed., *Florentine Studies* (London, 1968) pp. 442-462.

not qualify for the *Maggiori*, if they were enfranchised at all, were relegated to the scrutinies for the lesser magistracies and for the provincial judgeships. It has been estimated that the number of males eligible for all offices in a given year was 2,000 to 2,500, in a total population of 50,000 to 60,000, although this number may have risen to from 3,000 to 4,000 under the more egalitarian practices of the Savonarolian Republic, and the popular regime of 1527 [3]. The highest offices of the Republic were filled from a relatively small number of families, and the size of the office-holding class may be less important than the frequency with which relatively few family names appeared among the successful candidates. During the fifteenth century, some 700 family names appear in the important office of prior, but of these a more limited group of 380 names appears four times or more, and 150 names appear ten times or still more frequently [4]. The more prominent clans, with their different branches, included such early arrivals in the city as the Acciaiuoli, Altoviti, Capponi, Medici, Ridolfi, Salviati, Strozzi and others. Enriched through banking and commerce, chief actors in the city's political life, patrons of its culture, these formed the cadres of the patrician elite. They had preserved the liberties and independence of Florence for more than two centuries.

What happened to these families after 1530? The best work on the first years and new institutions of the Duchy, by Antonio Anzilotti, was written sixty years ago [5]. Anzilotti traces the consolidation of the new regime: the great reform of the constitution in 1532, the rise to power of Cosimo I, and the creation of an entourage of *auditori* and *segretari* in new offices that permitted him to establish his own authority in the city and extend it through the countryside. Anzilotti assumes the Ducal regime greatly weakened the influence of the Republican elite by over-

---

[3] Martines, *Lawyers and Statecraft*, pp. 388-89.

[4] Names of priors from the *Priorista Grifoni*, published in G. M. Mecatti, *Storia Genealogica della Nobiltà e Cittadinanza di Firenze* (Naples, 1754) pp. 321-410.

[5] A. Anzilotti, *La Costituzione interna dello Stato fiorentino sotto il Duca Cosimo I de' Medici* (Florence, 1910). See also his *La Crisi Costituzionale della Repubblica fiorentina* (Florence, 1912) pp. 126-148. Anzilotti's conception is further developed in D. Marrara, *Studi giuridici sulla Toscana medicea* (Milan, 1965) pp. 33-55.

riding the guarantees of 1532 through which the established families had intended to preserve their influence. Their demise was hastened by a gradual decline of the urban economy. « In his ascent to power, rich Florentine families were ruined and their property was confiscated ... After the first struggle with the great families, no economically strong class challenged the affirmation of princely absolutism, but a new aristocracy appeared, raised up through the beneficence of the Prince, and grouped itself around him » [6]. With the establishment of the Ducal regime, the patricians of the Republic were progressively relegated to decorative places at the court, and political power passed to the new bureaucracy, made up of outsiders to Florence and creatures of the Duke, who became, in effect, the new governing class of the Principate.

It is true that under Ducal rule the great families among the *benefiziati* of the fifteenth century completed their transformation into a court nobility. Rudolf von Albertini has traced the corresponding changes in Florentine historical and political thought [7]. At the court, the sons of old families were soon submitting formal proofs of noble lineage for admission into the equestrian order of St. Stephen, which Cosimo founded in 1562. Under his successors, the regulations excluding feudal nobles from offices in the magistracies were withdrawn. The Strozzi, Ridolfi, Niccolini, Pucci and others soon acquired fiefs in Tuscany or elsewhere, which made them equal to the surviving feudal nobles of the *contado* [8]. Scipione Ammirato expressed the self-image of the aristocracy in his collection of genealogies of prominent families printed in 1615. « If one looks well at great Republics, as was that of Florence, it will be seen that its families had no reason to compare themselves slightingly to [seigneurs, barons, counts, marquises and the like] ... for although they had no seigneuries and had not lived in quite such a cavalieresque manner as is usual in the court of a king or a great prince (for public order under the Republic would

[6] Anzilotti, *Costituzione interna*, p. 154.

[7] R. von Albertini, *Das Florentinische Staatsbewusstsein im Übergang von der Republik zum Prinzipat* (Bern, 1955).

[8] P. Neri, « Sopra lo stato antico e moderno della nobiltà toscana » in G. B. Neri-Badia, *Decisiones et Responsa Juris* (Florence, 1776) pp. 598-99, *et passim.*

not permit such inequalities of titles or manners of living), yet they have been *Gonfalonieri di Giustizia*, *Priori*, *Commissari* of the Ten of War, in the *Balie*, and in other similar positions, hardly inferior to seigneurs with authority over non-noble persons ... » [9].

After the 1560's, when Anzilotti's study ends, it becomes difficult to trace this development further. Riguccio Galluzzi, in the eighteenth century, who is still the best historian of the Medici Duchy, also describes the establishment of the Medici absolutism, and the names of important Republican families continue to figure prominently in his history up to its conclusion in the 1730's [10]. Others give more attention to the Dukes and their court than to the functionaries of the regime [11]. Was the old aristocracy, and its tradition of civic liberty, thus truncated in the sixteenth century? Or did the Medici Duchy serve as an instrument of continuity?

II.

Two series of documents from the Florentine archives help to shed light on this question. The first consists of the documents relative to a law in 1750, under the Hapsburg regency for Francis Stephen, that defined the legal status of the patricians and helps to measure the continuity of families from the Republic [12]. The qualifications for admission to offices in the magistracies appear not to have changed very much after 1532, for although matriculation in the guilds no longer affected political rights, a distinction continued to be made between families

---

[9] *Delle famiglie nobili fiorentine di Scipione Ammirato, parte prima* (Florence, 1615) « A lettori ».

[10] R. Galluzzi, *Storia del Granducato di Toscana* (Florence, 1822), 10 Vols.

[11] See the standard histories by A. von Reumont, *Geschichte Toskanas seit dem Ende des florentinischen Freistaats, 1530-1859* (Gotha, 1876-77) Vol. I, R. Caggese, *Firenze dalla Decadenza di Roma al Risorgimento d'Italia* (Florence, 1912-21), Vols. 2-3 and A. Panella, *Storia di Firenze* (Florence, 1949), pp. 199-269.

[12] The law is printed in L. Cantini, *Legislazione toscana raccolta ed illustrata* (Florence, 1800-08) Vol. XXVI, p. 231 ff. The *provanze di nobiltà* and *libri di oro* are in the *Archivio di Stato, Firenze, Archivio della deputazione sopra la nobiltà toscana*.

who qualified for a select group of important offices, and families who did not. In practice, the *benefiziati* for the *Maggiori* of the Republic became the *benefiziati* for the highest magistracies of the Duchy. Political standing continued to reflect social rank, but newcomers were progressively admitted to the scrutinies for offices. The law of 1750 attempted to regulate rank by creating an honorific nobility with two distinctions. Old families who could present proofs that their ancestors had been eligible for the *Maggiori* of the Republic before 1530 were designated as « patricians ». Families possessing some title of nobility of more recent establishment in the city were designated, with few exceptions, as mere « nobles ». Other families habilitated for offices retained political rights as non-noble « citizens ». The patricians were registered in *Libri di Oro* which, along with the accompanying proofs of nobility, identify the eighteenth-century descendents of the fifteenth-century elite. It is clear that many old families had disappeared from the city by the eighteenth century, or no longer counted as aristocrats, and a few newer families passed as patricians, but a sizeable number of old families remained. By 1760, when the registration was substantially complete, 311 families had presented proofs of patrician status and 77 more qualified before 1800, a total of 388 families of old standing in the city who were still prominent at the end of Medici rule. Most of the family names can be located in the Republican priorates, and the proofs of nobility contain authenticated genealogies which make it possible to identify individuals in each generation from the late fifteenth century up until the 1860's [13].

The second source consists of five comprehensive lists of offices and office-holders in the Ducal bureaucracy at different dates between the sixteenth and late eighteenth centuries [14].

---

[13] Families were counted by application for recognition of noble status. Of the 311 families registered as patricians in 1760, the names of 253 had appeared as priors of the Republic, 26 more were ancient families or had been *magnati*, nobles technically disqualified from office-holding, at the time of the Republic, and the remaining 32 were newcomers after the early sixteenth century of sufficient standing to be assimilated into the older group, and passed as patricians through membership *per giustizia* in the Order of St. Stephen.

[14] The list for 1551 is published in A. D'Addario, « Burocrazia, economia e finanze dello Stato fiorentino alla metà del Cinquecento » in *Ar-*

They range from a list of offices, but without the incumbents, that was prepared for Cosimo I in 1551, to an anonymous, but detailed, list dated 1604, and then three lists prepared by the personnel of the *Tratte* and the *Segreteria di Stato*. One was drawn up under the direction of Niccolò Arrighi, who was employed in the *Tratte* in 1685, and contains series of office-holders beginning in the sixteenth century and ending in 1695. The second was made about 1765, but shows the office-holders of the regime under the last Medici Duke, in 1736. The third is a very complete list of offices and office-holders in 1784, and was drawn up in the midst of the administrative reforms of Peter Leopold. These lists provide the names of functionaries in the central Ducal administration in Florence. Some political offices of the court are included, although ambassadorships, offices and troops of the *Bande*, and functionaries in Siena, which preserved its own institutions and was ruled separately under a Governor, are not included. The names are those of appointed permanent functionaries, and not of the rotating members of the Florentine magistracies, or the chief justices of provincial towns, whose names can be found in separate registers of the *Tratte* [15]. Taken singly, the lists provide a cross-section of the central Ducal bureaucracy at these different dates, from the Secretaries of State and the *auditori*, *segretari* and *provveditori* of the different magistracies and bureaus, down through the intermediary *ajuti*, *ragionieri* and *scrivani*, even so far as the *custodi* and *donzelli* who swept the stairs and did errands in the *Uffizi*, the *portalettere* of the post office, and the guards and *facchini* of the customhouse stations at the city gates, and they show the changes in time both of offices and of personnel. Taken together, the lists pro-

---

chivio storico italiano (1963). For 1604, *ASF.*, *Manoscritti*, F. 233, anonymous list dated « 1604 *a giugno* ». For 1695, *Miscellanea Medicea*, FF. 696, 697, « Teatro di grazia e giustizia ovvero formulario dei rescritti a tutte le cariche che conferisce il Serenissimo Granduca di Toscana per via dell'Uffizio delle Tratte, illustrato ... da Niccolò Arrighi ... ». Filza 696 contains notices of offices within the city of Florence, Filza 697 contains notices of offices in the *Contado*. For 1736, *Archivio di Gabinetto*, F. 123, « Relazione degli uffizi e degli impiegati del governo di Toscana divisa in tre parti ». For 1784, *Archivio di Gabinetto*, FF. 127, 128, 129 « Portate e Ruoli degli Impiegati ». The *Archivio di Stato* contains further lists of office-holders, mostly for the eighteenth century.

15 *ASF. Tratte*, registers of *intrinsici* and *estrinsici*.

vide the names of some 5,700 men who were the successive holders of from 200 to 500 appointed positions beginning in the sixteenth century, and the names of nearly all office-holders toward the end of Medici rule.

The increasing number of permanent functionaries under the Duchy emerges from these lists with great clarity. Tuscany was acquiring a more regular bureaucracy. Already in the fifteenth century, the magistracies, in which citizens had held office for only brief terms of a few months, had been surrounded by a number of subaltern functionaries, *cancellieri*, *segretari* and *notai*, including the great humanist chancellors of the *Signoria*, whose tenure of office had been more permanent than that of the citizen magistrates [16]. The administration of the Republic had depended partly on a professional staff. The permanent functionaries increased considerably in number and importance after 1532, although their ascendency over the old committees was not complete until the eighteenth century. The Medici preserved the magistracies of the Republic, of which the members now shared responsibility with an increasing number of permanent officials. The reform of 1532 had created two new general councils, the Senate of 48 and the Council of 200 of which the members were appointed for life, it replaced the *Signoria* with a revolving executive committee of Senators, the

---

[16] For a description of the professional staff of the Republic in the *Signoria* and *Riformagioni*, see D. Marzi, *La cancelleria della Repubblica fiorentina* (Rocca S. Casciano, 1910). No study of the staff of the remaining magistracies of the Republic exists. N. Rubinstein « The beginnings of Niccolò Machiavelli's career in the Florentine Chancery » in *Italian Studies* XI (1956) 72-91, gives full particulars of the conditions of Machiavelli's appointment and tenure of office as second chancellor of the *Signoria* between 1498 and 1512. He was elected to office by the Council of Eighty, from among other candidates, for an initial two-year term, which was then renewed yearly. The greater permanence that offices had acquired by the mid-seventeenth century is clear from the following formula of appointment as *Sotto Cancelliere* of the *Magistrato Supremo* (the office corresponding to Machiavelli's old one) in 1695: « Essendo restata vacante la carica di sotto Cancelliere del Mag/to de Clar/mi L. T. e Consiglieri, S. A. S. elegge per nuovo Sotto Cancelliere il Dott/re N. N. per stare a beneplacito dell'A. S., e con tutti gli emolumenti, provvisioni et obblighi soliti, nel modo che haveva il suo antecessore, et il Seg/rio delle Tratte ne faccia passare il partito nel med/mo Mag/to de Clar/mi L. T. e Consig/. » (*ASF. Miscellanea Medicea*, F. 696, p. 261).

Magistrato Supremo, and the other magistracies continued in roughly their old form. The members were selected in specified proportions from the Senators, members of the 200 and citizens who qualified for offices, by the two councils, through the Secretary of the *Tratte*, or from among the eligible candidates by the Duke [17].

Yet under Cosimo I the jurisdiction of the magistrates was progressively limited by new officials, Ducal *auditori*, *segretari* and lesser functionaries. Cosimo supplemented the *Magistrato Supremo* with a second executive committee, the *Pratica Segreta*, including the *Auditore Fiscale*, the *Auditore* of the *Riformagioni*, the *Depositario Generale*, and others whom he freely appointed and who served as an intermediary link between himself and the councils and magistracies [18]. As the reins of authority tightened in the hands of the Prince, the number of subaltern permanent positions also increased. Table I, which follows, shows the number of places in the citizen magistracies and in the more permanent appointed positions at successive dates between 1551 and 1784. The offices have been grouped according to administrative function: (I) the upper councils of state, (II) the general administration, (III) the law courts, (IV) the finances and Ducal domaine. The figures reported are only approximate since some offices have been excluded from consideration, and the lists themselves are not entirely complete [19]. However, in 1551, when

---

[17] Cantini, *Legislazione toscana*, Vol. I, pp. 5-7. The electoral procedures are described in *ASF. Tratte*, F. 1101, « Registro legale ossia repertorio di massime relative alle tratte ed a tutti gli uffizi ».

[18] Anzilotti, *Costituzione interna*, pp. 41-53, *et passim*.

[19] The offices considered, with the dates of the lists in which they appear, are as follows. The lists from 1551 and 1604 are not entirely complete. The list from 1551 omits the *Pratica Segreta*, *Depositeria Generale*, *Abbondanza* and *Sanità*, and the list from 1604 omits the *Segreteria di Stato*, *Consulta* and *Riformagioni*. The number of these offices, 10 magistrates and 20 functionaries in 1551, and 17 functionaries in 1604, has been estimated. To insure uniformity, the personnel of the Guilds, the *Opere* di *S. Maria del Fiore* and *Or S. Michele*, the *Bigallo* and the *Studio Fiorentino* have been omitted from all the lists, as have menial jobs at the lowest level, such as *donzelli*, *garzoni*, *tavolaccini* and *facchini*, and offices exercised outside of Florence in the *Dogana* and *Gabella del Sale*.

(I) *Upper Councils of State: Segreteria di Stato* (1551-1784), *Magistrato Supremo* (1551-1784), *Pratica Segreta* ([1551]-1784), *Segreteria di Guerra* (1695-1784), *Segreteria di Finanza* (1784).

Table I: Temporary places in the magistracies, and permanent appointed offices, in the central Ducal administration of Tuscany, 1551-1784.

	1551		1604		1695		1736		1784	
	M	O	M	O	M	O	M	O	M[a]	O
I. Upper Councils of State.	21	15	21	19	21	22	21	30	—	65
II. General Administration.	33	36	32	62	34	81	34	102	—	67
III. Law Courts.	47	21	47	35	39	41	39	33	—	40
IV. Finances and Domaine.	37	117	37	204	54	222	54	272	—	343
	138	187	137	320	148	366	148	437	—	525
TOTALS	325		457		514		585		525	

M. = Places in Magistracies; O. = Permanent Offices.

([a]) The *Tratte* was suppressed in 1782, and in 1784 the rotating positions in magistracies had disappeared.

(II) *General Administration: Otto di Pratica* (1551), *Cinque del Contado* (1551), *Nove Conservatori del Dominio Fiorentino* (1604-1736), *Camera delle Comunità* (1784), *Tratte* (1551-1736), *Riformagioni* (1551-1784), *Archivio* (1604-1784), *Pupilli* (1551-1784), *Abbondanza* ([1551]-1736), *Grascia* (1551-1736), *Sanità* ([1551]-1736), *Cacce e Pesche* (1695-1736), *Posta Generale* (1695-1784).

(III) *Law Courts: Ruota Civile* (1551-1784), *Otto di Guardia e Balia* (1551-1736), *Supremo Tribunale di Giustizia* (1784), *Consulta* ([1604]-1784), *Mercanzia* (1551-1736), *Onestà* (1551-1604), *Conservatori di Legge* (1551-1736), *Stinche* (1551-1736), *Casa di Correzione* (1784).

(IV) *Finances and Domaine: Fisco* (1551-1784), *Depositeria Generale* ([1551]-1784), *Soprassindaci* (1695-1784), *Monte Comune* (1551-1784), *Monte di Pietà* (1551-1736), *Agenzia di Presti* (1784), *Gabella e Monte del Sale* (1551-1736), *Monte Redimibile* (1695-1736), *Gabella dei Contratti* (1551-1736), *Decima*

some of the new functionaries of the Duchy had already emerged, the number of permanent positions in these different branches of administration was approximately 187. The largest increase in time took place between 1551 and 1604, when the number of positions increased by 133, or by 71 per cent. By 1736, the number of positions had increased by another 117, or by an additional 62 per cent. The number of offices in the magistracies increased somewhat in the seventeenth century and then remained the same, although as time went on more of these places were filled through appointment by the Duke, rather than through the old system of selection through the *Tratte*.

The expanding bureaucracy seems symptomatic of the new hierarchy of command, and of a somewhat greater extension of the scope and powers of government. One important change was the emergence of the Secretariat of State, which at first was only the secretary of the Duke. The list from 1695 provides a series of names beginning with Lelio Torelli, the jurist and confidant of Cosimo I, in 1546 [20]. The secretariat did not become a separate administrative council above the *Magistrato Supremo* until the beginning of the Hapsburg regency in 1739, but the Ducal secretaries had long been important personages. In 1695 there were two Secretaries of State and a Secretary of War, and in 1736 the three secretaries were aided by ten assistants [21].

The personnel of the central law courts changed least, while the personnel of the finances and the Ducal domaine increased considerably, and new offices appeared in the area of general administration. The appellate jurisdiction of the *Ruota Civile*, the civil court that originated in 1502, was extended outside of the city during the 1530's and 1540's, although the civil competence of the *auditori* of the *Ruota* did not replace the criminal jurisdiction of the old Republican magistracy, the *Otto di Guardia e Balia*, which survived, under the tutelage of the *Auditore Fi-*

(1551-1736), *Decima ecclesiastica* (1695-1736), *Dogana* (1551-1736), *Zecca* (1551-1736), *Farine* (1604-1736), *Amministrazione generale I* (1784), *Amministrazione generale II* (1784), *Amministrazione generale III* (1784), *Lotti* (1784), *Capitani di Parte Guelfa* (1551-1736), *Scrittoio delle Fortezze e Fabbriche* (1695-1784), *Scrittoio delle Possessioni* (1736-1784), *Tribunale delle Regalie e Possessioni* (1784), *Magona* (1695-1784).

[20] *ASF. Miscellanea Medicea*, F. 696, pp. 865-67.

[21] *ASF. Archivio di Gabinetto*, F. 123 pt. 1, cc. 666-667.

scale, until 1777 [22]. The *Mercanzia*, the commercial tribunal, and the *Consulta*, a new court in 1600 which received and reviewed petitions addressed to the Duke, completed the principal ordinary courts of the capital [23]. Justice remained mostly in the hands of the *Vicari* and *Podestà* of provincial towns, who were nonetheless Florentines, although the surveillance over these local officials by the central administration increased. The two Republican magistracies that had supervised provincial justices were joined into one in 1559, the *Nove Conservatori del Dominio Fiorentino*, with extended authority over the *Contado* [24]. The considerable increase of personnel in the fiscal administration resulted from an increasing dependence on indirect taxation and from the creation of new *Monti* of the state debt. A Ducal tax on mills, and the office of the *Farine* to administer it, was introduced in 1552, while the number of petty officials concerned with the collection of tolls, the tax on stamped paper, and the salt tax, that continued from the Republic, also grew [25]. Tuscany was becoming further plagued with small exactions that went to the Ducal treasury or to share-holders in the state debt. In addition to the old *Monte Comune* and the *Monte di Pietà*, a *Monte* on the salt tax was erected during the seventeenth century, and a *Monte Redimibile*. By the 1730's, interest payments on the debt accounted for about one-quarter of the Ducal revenues [26]. The Ducal domaine acquired a separate administration. What had been the public domaine of the Republic, roads, fortresses and public buildings, came under the direction of the *Capitani di Parte Guelfa* in 1549. This old magistracy continued to function until 1769, although a separate bureau of buildings and fortresses was created in the sixteenth century,

---

[22] On the *Ruota* see Anzilotti, *Costituzione interna*, pp. 83-129, on the *Otto*, G. Antonelli, « La magistratura degli Otto di Guardia di Firenze » in *Archivio storico italiano* (1954) pp. 3-39.

[23] Galluzzi, *Storia del Granducato di Toscana*, VI, 104. Some judicial functions were also exercised by magistracies in the general administration and finances, and the *Magistrato Supremo* functioned as a high court of equity.

[24] Anzilotti, *Costituzione interna*, pp. 55-81.

[25] *ASF. Miscellanea Medicea*, F. 696, pp. 347-89, 391-415, 447-470, 609-637.

[26] *ASF. Archivio di Gabinetto*, F. 123, pt. 2, cc. 79 ff.

and was augmented by yet a third bureau for the Ducal estates [27]. Other offices appeared in the general administration, among them the *Archivio Generale* in 1569, and the *Uffizio della Posta*. The origins of the Post Office are uncertain, although it first appears to have been a concession farmed out to a private individual, that was later administered by the state. The names of some of the officials are recorded from the 1620's, and by 1784 there were 29 permanent employees whose salaries cost the fisc 8,144 *scudi* yearly, or about 2,000 English pounds sterling at the current rate of exchange [28].

The change in the system of administration was carried forward by the Medici, but was not completed by them. It was not until after the Restoration, in 1815, when the Senate was not reinstated after its suppression by Napoleon, that the Duchy was entirely ruled through a hierarchy of permanent functionaries, and even then there were exceptions in municipal government [29]. At the end of Medici rule, the Council of 200, the Senate, and the magistracies of the capital, which still accounted for a large number of positions, remained from the old system of guaranteed participation by Florentines, and the last general scrutiny that enabled citizens for offices was held in 1758 [30]. These survivals largely disappeared as a result of the eighteenth-century Hapsburg reforms. Judged from eighteenth-century Hapsburg standards of administrative efficiency, the overlapping jurisdictions of councils, magistracies, citizens and functionaries caused multiple delays and inconveniences. As one of the regents for Francis Stephen wrote to Vienna in 1739: « The government of this place is a chaos almost impossible to disintangle, it is a mixture of aristocracy, democracy and monarchy ... » [31]. As well, both the Regents and native reformers saw correctly

---

[27] *ASF. Miscellanea Medicea*, F. 696, pp. 437-44, *Archivio di Gabinetto*, F. 123, cc. 618-33, 650-659.

[28] *ASF. Miscellanea Medicea*, F. 696, pp. 771-76, *Archivio di Gabinetto*, F. 123, cc. 632-644, *Archivio di Gabinetto*, F. 129, No. 41.

[29] See A. Anzilotti, *Decentramento amministrativo e riforma municipale in Toscana sotto Pietro Leopoldo* (Florence, 1910) and A. Acquarone, « Aspetti legislativi della Restaurazione toscana » in *Rassegna Storica del Risorgimento* (1956).

[30] *ASF. Tratte*, F. 1114, « Squittinio generale per l'anno 1758 ».

[31] Quoted in N. Rodolico, *La Reggenza Lorenese in Toscana, 1737-1765* (Prato, 1908), p. 41.

that the reservation of offices for Florentines protected vested interests in the Capital. The reforms began with the finances in 1741, and were extended to every part of the administration under Peter Leopold, after 1765 [32]. Enlightened despotism created a far more efficient and autocratic system than Cosimo I and his successors had been able to put into operation. The reforms effected considerable changes. Between the time of the lists of 1736 and 1784, the temporary positions in the magistracies disappeared and the number of aristocratic Florentines in appointed positions of the bureaucray also diminished sharply. Superfluous offices were combined, jurisdiction was further centralized, the total number of functionaries decreased, regulations assured better competence in office, and salaries were somewhat augmented.

III.

The continuity of the period between the fall of the Republic and the end of Medici rule is revealed still further by the men these lists show to have been the office-holders of the Medici state. When the names of office-holders are compared with the genealogical information about patrician families provided by the law of 1750, it becomes clear how well aristocratic Florentines adapted themselves to the practices of the Duchy, and how consistently old families had made their way into important offices of the Ducal regime.

The continued prominence of the patricians was foreseen in 1532 when the life-members of the Senate were assured a dominant place in the magistracies and upper councils of state. This body had perhaps been intended to provide the aristocratic element in a mixed constitution, and its members were consistently recruited at the upper levels of the social hierarchy. Of the 650 men appointed as Senators between 1532 and 1782, 85 per cent came from families who proved patrician status under the terms of the law of 1750, and the surnames of other Senators

[32] The legislation is summarized in detail in *Governo della Toscana sotto il regno di sua maestà il re Leopoldo II* (Florence, 1790), see also A. Zobi, *Storia Civile del Granducato di Toscana* (Florence, 1850-55) Vols. 1-2, *passim.*

had appeared frequently as priors of the Republic, although their families had disappeared from the city, or had become extinct, before the eighteenth century [33]. Under the Medici, 28 members of the Capponi clan were senators, as were 20 Strozzi, 12 Guicciardini, 11 Niccolini and 10 Salviati. The Senators, in their red-trimmed robes, took precedence at public functions, met collectively to assent to some types of Ducal legislation, moved from one position to another in the magistracies, and also appeared frequently in the important permanent offices of state [34].

For it was not only in the magistracies that the patricians continued to exert an important influence. It seems very likely that Cosimo I, in the establishment of his own authority, had attempted to contain the Florentine aristocrats in the Senate, and to make use of non-patricians and non-Florentines in the key permanent offices of state. The newcomers, men like Jacopo Polverini, from Prato, a justice of the *Ruota*, who was *Auditore Fiscale* in 1543 and *Auditore* of the *Riformagioni* and of the *Magistrato Supremo*, Francesco Vinta, from Volterra, who became *Auditore* of the *Riformagioni* in 1555, and Lelio Torelli, from Fano, who was the first secretary of the Duke, *Auditore* of the *Nove*, and finally a Senator in 1571, were jurists and foreigners maintained for their loyalty to the Duke and their independence of political entanglements in the capital [35]. Yet, under Cosimo, high appointed offices had also been occupied by members of old families. Considering their standing in the city, and the places they soon occupied at the court, it was difficult to exclude patricians from important offices, and it was probably inevitable that they would eventually preempt influence over appointment to the lesser positions. At any event, in 1604, members of patrician families not only dominated the rotating positions in the magistracies, but were also well established in the appointed positions of some, although not all, branches of the bureaucracy, and the control of offices by Florentine aristocrats increased thereafter.

---

[33] Senators from Mecatti, *Storia Genealogica*, pp. 147-227 and from *ASF. Tratte*, F. 91. Extinct families include such names as Dell'Antella, Del Bene, Del Caccia, Serragli.

[34] On the functions of the Senate, see *ASF. Consulta*, F. 454.

[35] Anzilotti, *Costituzione interna*, pp. 44-46, 158-59.

Table II shows the number and percentage of office-holders in appointed positions of the bureaucracy who belonged to families proving patrician status under the law of 1750. The table groups office-holders according to administrative function, and distinguishes the more important and highly-paid positions from the intermediary and less lucrative ones. The identity of office-holders in 1551 is unknown, in 1604 some members of important old families who had disappeared from the city before 1750 have not been counted as patricians, and in the remaining lists some individuals whose family affiliation is uncertain have also been counted as non-nobles [36]. In 1604, under Duke Ferdinando I, members of patrician families occupied one fifth of the appointed positions in the central offices of the Ducal government. This proportion increased to one-quarter in 1695, under Cosimo III, and to nearly one-third in 1736, under Gian Gastone. Considering only the more responsible and important positions, the first Secretaries of State, and *auditori*, first *segretari* and *provveditori* of different bureaus, the proportion of patricians was more than one-third in 1604, increased to two-thirds in 1695, and to three-quarters in 1736. If Cosimo I had attempted to free Florentine government from the influence of an oligarchy, under his successors this oligarchy reasserted itself. By the early eighteenth century, in comparison with systems of administration elsewhere, political influence in Florence was exercised by a rather small group. There were more nobles in office in the central administration of Tuscany than in the central administration of Piedmont, although one assumes that Florentine offices were less dominated by aristocrats than the magistracies of Genova, Lucca or Venice [37].

Significantly, the aristocracy penetrated least into the administration of justice, and this fact may have had much to do

---

[36] For instance, in 1604, Filippo dell'Antella was employed in the *Gabbella dei Contratti* and in the *Farine*, while Donato dell'Antella was *Soprassindaco* of the *Nove* and *Soprintendente delle Fortezze* in the *Capitani di Parte*. Two members of the Serragli family were also employed in the *Farine*. *ASF. Manoscritti*, F. 233.

[37] G. Quazza, *Le Riforme in Piemonte nella prima metà del '700* (Modena, 1957) I, 94-95, for the period 1713-42, estimates a proportion of 15.8 per cent nobles in the upper sectors of the Ducal administration of Piedmont, and 1.5 per cent nobles in the median and inferior sectors.

Table II: Participation of Patrician Families in appointed offices of the central Ducal administration of Tuscany, at different levels, 1604-1784.

	1604			1695			1736			1784		
	UPPER P IO	INTERM P IO	TOTAL P IO O	UPPER P IO	INTERM P IO	TOTAL P IO O	UPPER P IO	INTERM P IO	TOTAL P IO O	UPPER P IO	INTERM P IO	TOTAL P IO O
I. Upper Councils of State.	3 9 33%	0 6 0%	3 15 19 20%	8 10 80%	0 5 0%	8 15 22 53%	14 16 88%	1 13 7%	15 29 30 52%	5 19 26%	8 46 17%	13 65 65 20%
II. General Administration.	2 5 40%	10 43 23%	12 48 62 25%	6 8 75%	16 64 25%	22 72 81 31%	8 9 89%	17 90 19%	25 99 102 25%	2 6 33%	5 54 9%	7 49 67 12%
III. Law Courts	0 4 0%	0 15 0%	0 19 35 0%	3 12 25%	0 16 0%	3 21 28 11%	2 12 17%	3 15 20%	5 27 33 19%	0 14 0%	2 26 8%	2 40 40 5%
IV. Finances and Domaine.	5 9 56%	30 158 19%	35 167 204 21%	12 14 86%	45 190 24%	57 104 222 41%	15 16 94%	66 249 27%	81 265 272 31%	10 17 59%	33 268 12%	43 285 343 15%
TOTALS:	10 27 37%	40 222 18%	50 249 320 20%	29 44 66%	51 275 22%	90 319 366 28%	39 53 74%	87 367 24%	126 420 437 30%	17 50 34%	48 387 15%	65 437 525 15%

P. = Patricians; IO. = Identified Office-Holders; O. = Offices.
Percentages are Patricians of Identified Office-Holders.

with the internal quiet and stability of Medici rule. Under the Republic, first with the *Podestà* and later with the justices of the *Ruota*, the law courts had been entrusted progressively to foreign jurists, who could stand above private interests and factions in the city, and this practice continued under the Duchy [38]. The justices of the *Ruota*, and later of the *Consulta*, were not Florentine aristocrats and were frequently promoted to other key offices, such as that of the *Auditore Fiscale*, the *Auditore* of the *Magistrato Supremo* and the *Segretario* of the *Otto di Guardia e Balia*, which were generally held by non-nobles. The patricians were more prominent in the upper councils of state and in the finances and the Ducal domaine, which is indicative of their social standing and close ties with the city's banking and commercial interests. All the first secretaries of the Dukes were patricians after the appointment of Giovanni Battista Gondi by Ferdinando II in 1641 [39].

One is tempted to conclude that the Medici Duchy had some very similar features to princely absolutisms elsewhere, which instead of levelling the aristocracies that confronted the regime, came to a compromise with them, either by using nobles as bureaucrats, or by ennobling families who rose to prominence in the service of the dynasty as a new *noblesse de robe*. The first of these two alternatives, rather than the second, was more

---

[38] In 1695, the *auditori* of the *Ruota* were described as « ... forastieri di nazione, e ben versati nelle materie legali, che nel suo principio si conducevano da Priori di Libertà e Gonfaloniere di Giustizia per un solo triennio, a fine che con una lunga dimora in detta carica non perdessero la neutralità supposta per ben giudicare in persona straniera e divenissero con la continua familiarità e domestichezza con i cittadini parziali d'alcuno dei litiganti ed egualmente sospetti che i cittadini medesimi. Presentemente per giusti motivi costumasi da Ser/mi G. Duchi di tollerarli in detta carica fino che venga la congiuntura di promuoverli ad altre o più lucrose o più confidenti e riguardevoli ». (*ASF. Miscellanea Medicea*, F. 696, p. 831).

[39] Alessandro de' Cerchi, who owed his own advancement in the bureaucracy to Gondi's patronage, reported Gondi's appointment in the Cerchi family history as follows: « Non si era veduto mai sino a quel tempo da Ser/ Padroni confidare un ministerio cosi geloso a Gentiluomini Fiorentini, e segretari anche inferiori erano pure [allora] sudditi dello stato, ma non mica nati nella Città Dominante, sicche in persona del Gondi avendo la nobiltà nostra dato principio al godimento di questo pregiabilissimo onore, et egli subito avuto mira di fare seco participi anche i compatriotti, e introdurgli nelle vacanze che seguissero ... ». (*ASF, Carte Cerchi*, F. 167, c. 81).

typical of Florence, where bureaucratic office did not confer legal status. Although a certain number of families of justices in the law courts, and court favorites, eventually received patents of nobility from the Medici, or recognition as nobles from the Hapsburgs, these families were relatively few [40]. The best entrance to political office under the Medici Duchy, as it had been under the Republic, appears to have been birth into a family with established standing in the city.

IV.

One wonders about the quality of administration under this system in which the great families of the capital continued to have such a large part. The lists of office-holders provide some additional information in this regard about the succession of individuals into particular positions, and about fees and salaries.

Tuscan administration under the Duchy may have lacked some of the worst abuses of Lombardy or the Kingdom of Naples, which were under Spanish rule. The Duchy was little disturbed by wars during the Medici period, and there were no serious internal revolts. Yet one of the problems of absolute government in early modern Europe was a tendency toward the infeudation of the state. In outlying areas where central authority did not penetrate effectively there was a tendency to preserve old feudal jurisdictions and to create new fiefs for noble families who might take over the entire administration of a previously independent commune, appoint the local justice, collect taxes and fees, appoint the parish priest and assume administration of the commons. A type of infeudation could also infest a bureaucracy when the central authority lost the power to appoint office-holders, sold offices, or made offices hereditary for the persons who had purchased them. When this happened, func-

[40] For instance the families Curini, Luci and Maggio rose to prominence through the courts. However, although Francesco Vinta's sons Paolo and Belissario had brilliant administrative careers in the late sixteenth century, and the Concini enjoyed honors from the Dukes for three generations before their extinction in 1636, none of the *auditori* of Cosimo I planted permanent roots in the city.

tionaries became increasingly independent and there were inevitable problems.

There was some infeudation in Tuscany under the Medici in the creation of new fiefs. The number of Ducal fiefs increased in the early seventeenth century, although infeudated communes were less numerous than in other regions of Italy. Of the 47 Ducal fiefs existing in 1749, 19 had been created between 1620 and 1650, and 24 were in the possession of Florentines [41]. The Medici were reluctant to relinquish control over local administration. Nor are the Dukes known to have sold offices. Patronage was clearly exercised in appointments to offices, through the Court, the Senate and the Secretary of the *Tratte*, and there may have been a private sale of offices, but venality was not institutionalized. Since the lists from 1695 and 1736 show who the previous incumbents in positions had been, it is possible to assess the extent that offices had tended to become possessions of individual families. Although high positions in whole sectors of the bureaucracy were held by Florentine aristocrats, and some individuals had more than one, it was very seldom that the successive holders of an office had the same family name.

Still, the prevalence of upper-class Florentines created problems in the administration of the Duchy and, despite the efforts of Cosimo I, helped to perpetuate the subordination of the countryside and provincial towns to the capital that had originated with the first expansion of the city state. The bureaucracy served the interests of Florentines. The problems emerge, in part, from consideration of the nature of salaries. The official salaries, the *provvisioni* paid from public revenue, were quite small, and office-holders anticipated additional revenue from fees, or *incerti*, that were calculated as a part of their eventual gain. The *incerti* generally consisted of a participation in fees for the expedition of business, and their exaction must have created considerable temptation to increase the amount of paper work, to send supplicants helplessly from one office to another, and to solicit gifts [42]. The Ducal administration became a type of *cosa nostra*

---

[41] Zobi, *Storia Civile*, Vol. I, *Appendice di Documenti*, *ASF.*, *Riformagioni*, F. 288.

[42] For this problem in Lombardy, see F. Chabod, « Stipendi nominali e busta paga effettiva dei funzionari dell'amministrazione milanese alla

for well-born Florentines who furthered the interests of their own dynasties. One small example seems indicative of administrative procedure. In 1749, Cerchio di Alessandro de' Cerchi, from the great family of the fourteenth century, being a Senator of Florence, was serving a term of office in the *Magistrato Supremo*, of which one of the functions was the resolution of disputes involving inheritances. He was to decide the case of the heredity of the Usimbardi, another old family, which had become extinct. The will provided for the passage of the patrimony to a family nominated by the court. « Thus our Senator Cerchio and Senator Jacopo Guidi, who were to make the nomination, thought best, the first to nominate the son of the second ... and the second [the son] of the first ... ». At this point one of the Ducal *Auditori* intervened, so that the Usimbardi patrimony went neither to the Cerchi, nor to the Guidi, but to a third patrician family, the Alamanni [43]. These problems were confronted by the Hapsburg reforms.

This continuity of the old elite seems a key to many aspects of the social and political life of Florence under the Medici. The continuing close relationship of old families to political power helped to assure both their own survival and the persistence of other aspects of the fifteenth-century scene. The old form of the urban economy, with its wool and silk shops and commercial ventures, in which aristocratic families were the principal investors for generation after generation, did not disappear in the sixteenth century, but continued, along with the guilds, the old economic regulations, and the old pattern of patrician investment, despite a decrease in the volume of activity and a gradual shifting of investments from business to land. Indeed, the continuity of families led to a concentration of wealth, and to the accumulation of large estates, so that, by the eighteenth century, in their way of life, such great families as the Corsini, the Salviati, the Rinuccini or the Corsi truly resembled noblemen from England and France. The persistence of old families is also related to a continuity of taste and culture in the seventeenth- and eighteenth-century city. The patricians

---

fine del Cinquecento » in *Miscellanea in onore di Roberto Cessi* (Rome, 1958), II, 187-363.

[43] *ASF*, *Carte Cerchi*, F. 167, c. 314.

preserved an artistic heritage that was little endangered by the arrival of wealthy newcomers who wanted to tear down the old palaces and build new ones in their places, in a different style. The manuscripts, chronicles, records and erudite compilations that still today reveal the history of the Renaissance city were preserved in the old palaces by the families themselves, or by *letterati* employed by them, for the purpose of discovering and preserving the traces of their own family origins.

Finally, what did Florentines think about the state and their relationship to it? It seems clear that Florentine government after the Republic was a « monarchy », rather than the « mixed monarchy » that the architects of the reform of 1532 had perhaps intended, since the Duke was the primary source of new legislation, and the prerogatives of the Senate and the magistracies were exceedingly limited [44]. But within this monarchy, a persistent tradition of legality, open government and public participation continued in a curious way. It was still present in the eighteenth century when the extinction of the Medici re-opened the question of the liberties and independence of the Florentine state [45]. The Republican interpretation of Machiavelli, which culminated in the edition of his works that was published under the patronage of the De Ricci family in 1782, was linked to this heritage [46]. The eighteenth-century commentators based their interpretation of their great ancestor on the *Discourses* rather than on the *Prince*, that is, they saw Machiavelli as an apologist for Republics rather than for Despotism. The patricians in the new offices of the Duchy recalled that their distant origins were Republican ones.

Yet the memory of Republican liberty was a divided one.

---

[44] Yet the Duchy was sometimes characterized as a « constitutional » monarchy in the eighteenth century. Lorenzo Cantini, *Vita di Cosimo de' Medici* (Florence, 1805) pp. 24-25, thought the settlement of 1532 created « ... una monarchia costituzionale, che ... può dirsi irregolare, perché venne divisa la suprema podestà fra il principe, ed i magistrati della Repubblica, i quali restarono nel loro primo essere tanto riguardo alla loro elezione, che alla loro autorità ... e non soffrirono altra variazione che quello di riconoscere per loro capo, e presidente, il nuovo principe ... la di cui volontà nel governo non era libera, ma soggetta all'approvazione dei magistrati ».

[45] Note particularly the interesting work of M. Rosa, *Dispotismo e libertà nel settecento, interpretazioni « repubblicane » di Machiavelli* (Bari, 1964).

[46] G. Procacci, *Studi sulla fortuna di Machiavelli* (Rome, 1965) pp. 372-386.

On one hand, some patricians now thought the liberties of Florence were guaranteed by the independence of the Duchy, by the reform of 1532, which assured their participation in the magistracies of the capital, and by the Duke, whose grace opened their way to participation in bureaucratic office [47]. Their view of policy was to continue the old practices of the Medici regime. But not all Florentines shared this aristocratic conception of the state. Some, both among the patricians and the newcomers in the bureaucracy, remembered a more open type of liberty from the distant Republic. They saw correctly that the reform of 1532, and Medici rule, had subverted this liberty in the interests of a small elite [48]. For them, with the advent of the Hapsburgs, and in the dawning awareness of the Enlightenment, the first steps toward the recovery of their more ideal conception, seemed for a time to be cooperation with the Hapsburg reforms.

[47] G. Giorgetti, « Stefano Bertolini, l'attività e la cultura di un funzionario toscano del sec. XVIII, 1711-1782 » in *Archivio storico italiano* (1951).

[48] See N. Carranza, « Polemica antimedicea dopo l'istaurazione Lorenese » in *Bollettino storico pisano* (1953-54), Rosa, *Dispotismo e libertà*, pp. 27-48, and A. Anzilotti, « Le riforme in Toscana nella seconda metà del secolo XVIII; il nuovo ceto dirigente e la sua preparazione intellettuale » in his *Movimenti e contrasti per l'unità italiana* (Milan, 1954) pp. 133-180.

ERIC COCHRANE

THE FAILURE OF POLITICAL PHILOSOPHY IN SEVENTEENTH-CENTURY FLORENCE: LORENZO MAGALOTTI'S « CONCORDIA DELLA RELIGIONE E DEL PRINCIPATO »

Thanks to the recent labors of Hans Baron, Eugenio Garin, and Nicolai Rubinstein — to mention but three of the more prominent students of Renaissance Florence — the contribution of Florence to the tradition of Western political philosophy has at last been fully recognized. Civic humanism, as this particular contribution is usually called, has been shown to have flourished in two successive periods: from 1402 to about 1450 and from 1495 to about 1532. It has been rescued from the accusation of being mere rhetoric or an academic exercise, particularly by Baron and Delio Cantimori. And its genesis has been minutely analyzed, most notably by Gennaro Sasso and Sergio Bertelli, in terms of the psychological and intellectual make-up of its authors and of the special historical circumstances in which they lived.

At the same time, some efforts have been made to account for the rapid demise of political philosophy in Florence after the consolidation of the Medici Principate in 1537. When those citizens who had always governed the city and written about its government were permanently excluded from positions of political responsibility, they had little choice, according to Vittorio de Caprariis [1], but to turn « from politics to history ». Those of them who preferred exile to silence soon lost sight of the intimate connection between theory and practice upon which the work of their predecessors had always been based; and they soon wandered off toward the Utopias that, according to Luigi Firpo, became common all over Italy in the age of Lodovico Agostini and Tommaso Campanella. Those of them who submitted to Cosimo I's categorical moratorium on constitution writing were unable to conceive of a kind of government different from the *comune* they had experienced or the *polis* they had read about. None of them ever thought of extending his

[1] De Caprariis, *Francesco Guicciardini: Dalla politica alla storia* (Bari, 1950). See also the last chapter of Felix Gilbert, *Machiavelli and Guicciardini: Politics and History in Sixteenth-Century Florence* (Princeton, 1965).

reading to the Codex of Justinian, which Cosimo's legal advisor, Lelio Torelli, was just then making palatable to men of letters. None of them ever thought of extending his « experience » to the internal changes then taking place in Milan, in the Papal States, and even in Spain, as well as in Tuscany. Hence, none of them was ever induced to provide what was most needed at the moment: a theoretical justification and theoretical guidelines for the sort of bureaucratic, authoritarian, centralized *Rechtstaat* that Cosimo was building in Florence and that others were to build all over Europe in the next two centuries [2]. The realization that the Medici alone could save them from another Spanish occupation and a tacit guarantee of an undisturbed monopoly of the municipal magistracies reconciled the patriciate to the new regime. A half century of peace, a period of almost unprecedented economic prosperity, and a fairly rigid enforcement of equality before the law reconciled the plebeians as well. And the personal popularity of all the grand dukes from Ferdinando I on eventually led all classes to believe that the basic problems of political life had been solved once and for all. Discontent thus gave way to contentment. Criticism degenerated into politically innocuous scandal stories. History retreated into detached erudition. And political philosophy dwindled into empty eulogies of princes and rhetorical appeals for a crusade against the Turks. The best that the new regime could elicit in the way of a theoretical framework was Scipione Ammirato's none-too-rigorous version of *ragion di stato* [3]. And the last two representatives of the Renaissance political tradition, Paolo Sarpi and Traiano Boccalini, went completely unnoticed, except for a couple of anodine warnings to the Venetians about the political expediency of submitting to the whims of God's vicar [4].

What still remains to be explained is why political philosophy was not revived in Florence when the conditions that suffocated

---

[2] See my « The End of the Renaissance in Florence », *Bibliothèque d'humanisme et Renaissance*, XXVII (1965), 7-29. I discuss this question much more fully in Chapters I and II of my forthcoming history of Florence after the Renaissance.

[3] On Ammirato's *Discorsi sopra Cornelio Tacito*, see Rodolfo de Mattei, *Il pensiero politico di Scipione Ammirato* (Milan, 1963).

[4] One such pamphlet is by Giovan Battista Strozzi, friend and sometime patron of Galileo. See his *Orazioni ed altre prose* (Rome, 1635).

it disappeared. After the turn of the seventeenth century, indeed, economic prosperity gradually yielded to a long-term depression. Investments abroad were decimated by bankruptcies in Spain. Wool and silk production shrank before foreign competition and tariff barriers. And when the crisis of 1619-20 precipitated an unfavorable *conjoncture* all over Europe [5], Tuscany was transformed from a predominantly industrial and commercial country into a primarily agricultural one. At the same time, the public treasury was drained by the plagues of 1631 and 1633. It was completely emptied by the War of Castro in 1643-44. And it then devoured the private capital of the citizens through a forced conversion of the *luoghi di monte* at a much lower interest rate [6]. Worse yet, the prestige of the ruling house was tarnished by its inability to protect Galileo from the Holy Office and to make good its claim to the Duchy of Urbino. The personal popularity of its individual members suffered an irreparable blow in 1670 with the accession of the morose, haughty, bigotted, narrow-minded Cosimo III [7]. Worst of all, the Medici gradually lost the one trump card that had been most effective a century earlier in reconciling proud republicans to their rule: their promise to preserve the independence of the state. They became ever less able to resist Imperial demands for money and troops, Papal demands for the extension of ecclesiastical property, and the demands of certain religious orders for financing the conversion of India and Germany. When Cosimo's sons refused to follow the heroic example of their father in begetting children from a detestable wife, the end of the dynasty, and therefore of the only possible deterrent to the territorial ambitions of the great powers, appeared to be imminent.

The time was ripe, then, for reassessing a regime that had existed, *de facto* rather than *de jure*, for over a hundred years and that had remained practically unchanged in its structure and institutions since the death of its founder. Similar reassessments,

---

[5] See the two articles by Ruggiero Romano published respectively in *Annales E. S. C.*, VII (1952), and *Rivista storica italiana*, LXXIV (1962).

[6] Guido Pampaloni and Romolo Camaiti in *Archivi storici delle aziende di credito*, Vol. I (Rome, 1965).

[7] On Cosimo III, see Harold Acton, *The Last Medici* (London, 1932), and the relevant chapters in the still standard *Istoria del Granducato di Toscana* by Riguccio Galluzzi (Florence, 1781).

after all, were then taking place in Naples with Francesco D'Andrea, in France with Bossuet, and in England with John Locke; and the birthplace of modern political philosophy seemed called upon to make a contribution of European significance to the solution of what was to some extent a European problem.

Fortunately, Florence had at least one citizen who was prepared to respond to the call: Lorenzo Magalotti [8]. Magalotti had been born, in 1637, into one of the oldest and most respected families of the city, one which had the additional advantage of being closely related to Pope Urban VIII. He had been educated at the Collegio Romano and at the University of Pisa « with all the ornaments of chivalry [becoming to] a noble and well-bred patrician » of the mid-seventeenth century [9]. He had been appointed, in 1660, as secretary of the Accademia del Cimento, and he had thoroughly digested the scientific method which, as he explained in the preface to the *Saggi di naturali esperienze* [10], had recently become more empirical and less able to admit theses not drawn from a minute examination of concrete phenomena. He had been nominated a gentleman at the granducal court at the age of 22, and he had acquired such a thorough knowledge of the operation and the personalities of the Tuscan government that he was charged, in 1670, with drawing up a list of prospective office-holders for the new grand duke [11]. He had developed an elegant, witty, rich prose style, one that eventually earned him honors as a precursor in Arcadia and the rank of a linguistic authority in the fourth edition of the *Voca-*

---

[8] The most comprehensive modern biography is Stefano Fermi, *Lorenzo Magalotti, scienziato e letterato* (Florence, 1903). More information in Walter Moretti, « Lorenzo Magalotti e il suo secolo », *Atti e memorie ... La Colombaria*, XXI (1951), 213-307. Still more in Chapter IV of my forthcoming history of Florence (n. 2, above).

[9] Vincenzo Viviani, quoted by Angelo Fabroni in his introduction to Magalotti's *Lettere familiari* (Florence, 1767).

[10] The most recent edition is that of the Domus Galileiana (Pisa, 1957); another was published by Enrico Falqui in 1947. The Accademia del Cimento has been unfortunately neglected by historians. W. E. K. Middleton of Vancouver is presently working on a monograph that may help fill the gap. In the meantime, the most abundant source of information is Giovanni Targioni Tozzetti, *Notizie degli aggrandimenti delle scienze fisiche accaduti in Toscana nel corso di anni LX del secolo XVII* (Florence, 1780).

[11] Archivio Ginori-Venturi, Florence, Nos. 136 and 251 A.

bolario of the Accademia della Crusca (1729-34). He had made several extensive trips abroad. He had learned to speak Latin, Spanish, French, and English fluently and to get along in Portuguese, Dutch, and Swedish. He had met the most important political, as well as cultural, personages in all the countries he visited and had put down the information they furnished him, together with his own penetrating observations, in hundreds of personal letters and several official reports [12]. Moreover, he had read the political as well as the historical works of Machiavelli, which Antonio Magliabechi, the founder of the first Florentine public library and the dean of seventeenth-century Italian scholarship, gathered together while compiling a complete bibliography. And he learned how to apply what he read to current political problems from none other than Henry Neville, the diehard Cromwellian who spent three years in Italy after being released from the Tower and who published an English translation of Machiavelli's works at London in 1675 [13].

Yet when Magalotti attempted to respond to the call, in the years following his precipitous return to Florence in 1678, he soon became aware that something was missing. For one thing, his preparation was really not as thorough as he thought it to be. His position as court gentleman, and later as privy counsellor, gave him ample opportunity to stand around observing people in the antechambers of Palazzo Pitti; but it never invested him

---

[12] Many of the letters from abroad are published by Falqui in Magalotti, *Scritti di corte e di mondo* (Rome, 1949), though the bulk of his correspondence is still in manuscript. The trip through Spain is recorded in an official diary published by Angel Sanchez Rivero (Madrid, 1933). Anna Maria Crinò's edition of the voyage through England has just been published by Edizioni di Storia e Letteratura in Rome. The official reports to Cosimo III from England, France, and Sweden have now been edited by Walter Moretti as *Relazioni di viaggio* in the Laterza « Scrittori d' Italia » series (Bari, 1968). Crinò has found some errors in Moretti's edition after examining another manuscript in the British Museum; her findings will soon be published by the Accademia della Crusca.
On Magalotti's literary style in historical context, see Walter Binni, « La formazione della poetica arcadica e la letteratura fiorentina di fine Seicento », in his *L'Arcadia e Metastasio* (Florence, 1963).

[13] Giuliano Procacci, *Studi sulla fortuna del Machiavelli* (Rome, 1965), pp. 255 ff. See also, Anna Maria Crinò, *Fatti e figure del Seicento anglo-toscano* (Florence, 1957) and *The Popish Plot* (Rome, 1954).

with even the shadow of responsibility [14]. His experience as a diplomat taught him to play billiards at Bonn and to escort the Spanish ambassador to his carriage in Vienna [15]; but since Tuscany was too small a power to be included in any important negotiations, it taught him nothing about how the Franco-Dutch War was actually brought to an end. Similarly, the Accademia del Cimento had trained him to describe the particular. But for political as well as for scientific reasons, it had become so radically empirical in methodology that it actually discouraged him from passing from the particular to the general. Indeed, the Accademia persistently refused to use the forbidden formula « The Earth moves », even though all its observations of Saturn presupposed just that conclusion. It refused to say anything about the composition of matter, even though Alessandro Marchetti showed that Galileo's projectiles made sense only in terms of Lucretius' atoms [16]. And it hesitated to reject categorically the theory of spontaneous generation even after Magalotti's drinking companion, Francesco Redi, had polluted the atmosphere of five royal villas with the rotting flesh of a hundred different walking and crawling creatures [17].

When observation was incapable of producing laws, then science lost its purpose. And when the scientific method was applied to political phenomena, political philosophy lost its purpose too. It is not surprising, then, that Magalotti was as insensitive to institutions, which could not be seen, as he was sensitive to the peculiarities of individual people, who were all too visible. His report on England gave one page to the House of Commons (in the Moretti edition), as compared to thirty-nine pages of « portraits » of court personalities. Single bits of information acquired an almost ridiculous degree of

---

[14] A reflection of his disappointment with court life is his poem on the canary: *Canzonette anacreontiche* (Florence, 1823), p. 15.

[15] Letter to Marucelli, 10 November 1675, Archivio di Stato, Florence, Mediceo 4412.

[16] See Niccola Carranza, « Antonio Magliabechi e Alessandro Marchetti », *Bollettino storico pisano*, XXVIII-XXIX (1959-60), 393-446.

[17] See Carlo Alberto Madrignani, « Il metodo scientifico di Francesco Redi », *La Rassegna della letteratura italiana*, LXV (1961), 476-500, and Pietro Franceschini, « Il secolo di Galileo e il problema della generazione », *Physis*, VI (1964), 141-204.

certainty — like the one he picked up from some prejudiced Britons about the « ignorant, weak-headed » Irish [18]. And the nearest thing to a general rule (*massima*) he dared advance, even though it was *massime* that he pretended to be looking for, was that the behavior of women at the English court refuted the Tuscan proverb: « Who won't pay the whore pays the doctor » [19].

For another thing, Magalotti lacked a point of reference. Machiavelli had gone to France and had written the *Ritratto delle cose di Francia* for the purpose of enabling his government to formulate a more effective foreign policy. Magalotti went to Granada, Lisbon, Leiden, Hamburg, Stockholm, and elsewhere for the purpose of amusing himself, recruiting new members for the Accademia del Cimento, buying books for Cardinal Leopoldo de' Medici, and distracting Prince Cosimo from his marital difficulties. What he wrote, then, might have been amusing. But it was never intended to be useful — not even the long chapter on the economic conditions of Sweden, which only proved that Italians had no hope of ever doing business there [20]. The men he met, similarly, might tell him much about their countries, and he advised the grand duke to contact Francesco D'Andrea the moment he arrived in Florence for a report on « the true conditions of the present constitution of this kingdom [of Naples] » [21]. But nothing they said ever encouraged him to look more critically at what went on in his own country.

Empiricism aside, moreover, Magalotti could conceive of only one legitimate form of government: one in which all power rested in the hands of a single prince and in which physical force was rendered unnecessary by the moral force of the Catholic religion. That was exactly the kind of government that existed in Tuscany. Hence the role of a Tuscan political philosopher

---

[18] Moretti, *Op. cit.*, p. 114. However, Magalotti's analysis of recent class changes in England, which seems to have come right out of James Harrington's *Oceana* of 1659, corresponds to positions still held by many historians today. See Stuart J. Woolf, « La trasformazione dell'aristocrazia e la Rivoluzione inglese », *Studi storici*, X (1969), 309-34.

[19] Moretti, p. 68: « Chi non paga la puttana, paga il medico ».

[20] *Ibid.*, p. 283.

[21] Magalotti to Apollonio Bassetti, 11 August 1671, in Salvo Mastellone, *Francesco D'Andrea, politico e giurista* (Florence, 1968), p. 48.

consisted simply in observing the flaws in those governments that differed in structure from the Tuscan model. Spain, Magalotti discovered, suffered from pride and superstition, which could be overcome by an injection of true Christianity [22]. Sweden suffered from the excessive independence of its senate; and it could be cured only by educating its kings abroad and then having them bolster their military power by the conquest of Denmark. England suffered from a division of authority between king and subjects; and since a plurality of religions had already infected all its classes with creeping atheism, nothing could be done to prevent an interminable civil war. But Tuscany suffered from nothing except the boredom of its courtiers and the excessive piety of its prince, neither of which was really worth while correcting.

To some extent this a-critical attitude was not wholly unjustified. Tuscany may have lost much of its wealth and most of its international prestige; but at least it was spared the wars that tore apart the rest of Europe during the seventeenth century. The grand duke may occasionally have indulged in apparent acts of violence — as he did one night in 1681 when he shipped two gentlemen off without trial for a lifetime imprisonment in the dungeons of Volterra [23]. But everything the grand duke did was considered to be just by definition; and at least the laws he promulgated, arbitrary and contradictory though they might be, were equally binding on all his subjects. Graft and corruption were kept to a minimum, as most foreign visitors remarked with amazement [24]; and one tiny indiscretion in the Salt Office was enough to send secret agents as far as Venice in search of the culprits [25]. Offices were filled by election or appointment, not by purchase or inheritance; and fees for administrative services were posted publicly to keep Tuscany free of the effects of venality and low salaries that plagued even the best-governed states of the age. Princes, cardinals, and ministers had to pay the same customs duties as « the least of the inhabitants of the

---

[22] Magalotti to Leopoldo, 16 November 1668, in Falqui, *Lettere di corte e di mondo*, p. 34.

[23] «Bidosso, o vero Diario di Francesco Bonazini», Biblioteca Nazionale, Florence, Mag. XXV. 42, *sub dat.* 17 April 1681.

[24] Neville in Crinò, *Fatti e figure*, p. 193.

[25] «Bidosso, o vero Diario di Francesco Bonazini», 22 November 1677.

city », as the French envoy was shocked to discover [26]; and judges in the criminal courts were strictly enjoined to recognize no class distinctions among defendants or witnesses [27].

Hence, Magalotti occasionally grumbled. But it never occurred to him, or to any of his compatriots, to complain or criticize. Not until Cosimo III had ruled for another thirty-five unglorious years did Giuseppe Averani, a law professor at Pisa, begin to wonder about the value of current policies regarding ecclesiastical property [28]. Not until the Medici dynasty had finally died out, leaving behind a « chaos prèsque impossible à débrouiller », did Averani's brilliant pupil, Giulio Rucellai, begin to apply his teacher's doubts in the form of legislative reforms [29]. Not until after 1765, when the entire administrative structure was overhauled in accordance with the principles of the Enlightenment, did anyone turn to Machiavelli in search of the bonds of society that absolutism had failed to forge. And Machiavelli's complete works were at last published in Florence in 1782, over a century after Magalotti had talked about them with Neville [30].

Still, there was one more reason why Magalotti failed as a political philosopher. Like most of his Tuscan contemporaries, he never managed to discover a vocation — a profession, that is, to which he could fully commit himself without any misgivings about its moral or practical value. Orazio Rucellai Ricasoli wrote philosophy — and put his friends to sleep reading it aloud to them — without ever feeling himself a philosopher [31]. Carlo Dati studied Greek texts without ever being able to justify his antiquarian lore as anything but a pleasant

---

[26] Archives of the Ministère des Affaires Etrangères, Paris, Toscane 15, fols. 177-82.

[27] Law of 21 August 1700 in the collection of Tuscan laws at the New York Public Library.

[28] See the biography by Niccola Carranza in *Dizionario biografico degli Italiani*.

[29] See Franco Venturi, *Settecento riformatore: Dal Muratori al Beccaria* (Turin, 1969), pp. 299 ff.

[30] Procacci, *Op. cit.*, pp. 372 ff., and Mario Rosa, *Dispotismo e libertà nel Settecento: Interpretazioni « repubblicane » di Machiavelli* (Bari, 1964).

[31] See Augusto Alfani, *Della vita e degli scritti di Orazio Rucellai Ricasoli* (Florence, 1872).

pastime [32]. Francesco Redi wrote poetry without being a poet, attacked traditional medicine without being any more than a part-time physician, and made remarkable discoveries in microbiology while insisting that he was but a dilettante of the sciences. But while his friends laughed, Magalotti worried. For he had read enough of Ignatius of Loyola, John of the Cross, Francis de Sales, and Pascal to know that he did have a vocation and that God expected him to find out what it was. He therefore tried law, astronomy, scientific essay writing, art criticism, travel literature, and poetry [33], one by one, all without success. He then tried diplomacy [34]; and that proved so unrewarding that he suddenly fled from Vienna without filing his papers, closing his house, or even informing his superiors. In the early 1680's he tried theology. And theology might have turned out to be the right choice — to judge from the quality of his *Lettere contro l'ateismo* [35] — had his own theological conclusions not dragged him into still another one: mysticism. Only after six months of mental torture in the cloister of the Chiesa Nuova in Rome had almost deprived him of his sanity did he finally give up. And he spent the remaining years of his life doing what he admitted to be a mere frivolity, namely, concocting perfumes, which is what he was still best known for as late as 1968 [36].

Thus Magalotti's attempt at political philosophy was undertaken with all the seriousness of a search for a vocation; and sometime between the late 1670's and the early 1680's — after he had given up diplomacy, that is, and before he had taken

---

[32] Antonio Minto, *Le « Vite dei pittori antichi » di Carlo Roberto Dati e gli studi erudito-antiquari nel Seicento* (Florence, 1953).

[33] On Magalotti's literary works, see now G. Güntert, *Un poeta scienziato del Seicento: Lorenzo Magalotti* (Florence, 1966).

[34] Selections from his diplomatic correspondence were published by Cesare Guasti in *Giornale storico degli archivi toscani*, IV (1860) and V (1861).

[35] *Lettere familiari ... contro l'ateismo* (1 st ed., Venice, 1719; more recently that of Venice, 1821, with notes by Domenico Maria Manni). The numerous variants among the several extant manuscript copies will have to be resolved by a future editor. See the positive judgment of this work by Giorgio Spini in *Ricerca dei libertini* (Rome, 1950).

[36] See Giovanni da Pozzo's review of Moretti in *Belfagor*, XXIV (1969), 237-44. A recent edition of the *Lettere odorate* is the one by Falqui (Milan, 1943).

up theology [37] — he sat down to write the *Concordia della religione e del principato*, a treatise that was intended to be much more comprehensive than the title might suggest. He read through the works of many of his predecessors, from Xenophon to Pierre Nicole. He kept adding to his prospective table of contents until it covered everything from courtiers to commerce. He wrote out a first draft of the second chapter and parts of several others. He had his secretary — the one man in the world who could read his execrable handwriting with any facility — copy out many of the pages. He then went back over his text, crossing out some passages, adding others, and tacking on slips of paper with sealing wax. Finally, he collected a mass of quotations to be inserted later under the appropriate chapter headings.

Yet what he had written turned out to be far beneath his usual high standards. His sentences were impossibly complex, with subjunctives and relative clauses piled on top of each other to the point of incomprehensibility. The various subjects were so scrambled about that it was often impossible to perceive a logical progression from one to the other. The argument frequently wandered off into blind alleys — as it did most notably in the passage on the Trinity, when he was almost forced to admit oligarchy as the best form of government. Discretion overtook him whenever he seemed to be making an explicit reference to a current situation, and he quickly retreated into vague generalities. His vast « experience » in political affairs was omitted completely, and his « reading » was reduced to those few authors most remote from the practical question he posed: Aristotle, Jerome, Thomas Aquinas, Erasmus, and Bacon. That left Machiavelli with no other function than that of being a model for Bartolommeo Vagelli's second-rate medallions [38]. Finally, Magalotti came to the conclusion that political philosophy as a discipline had never, and could never, amount to anything but pedantry. All it could do was design governments

---

[37] An approximate date is furnished by the reference in the second passage reproduced below to the treatise of Pierre Nicole, which was first published in 1670. This passage, then, must have been written « about » (the wording is imprecise) ten years later.

[38] Angelo Maria Salvini letter of 20 October 1708, in *Prose fiorentine* (Venice, 1738), part. III, Vol. I, p. 161.

for « states bordering on Plato's Republic ». It could never affect the real course of affairs: that was the business of princes. And princes, being « gentlemen in the state of glory », never bothered, and did not need to bother, with what was ostensibly written on their behalf [39].

Magalotti thus realized that this quest for a vocation had even less promise than the others. He therefore put the manuscript away; and no one saw it again until Stefano Fermi began preparing his complete bibliography of Magalotti's works at the turn of the twentieth century [40]. Publishing the whole document would be a waste of paper. But publishing at least a few of the more important pages will serve at least a negative purpose. It will destroy the myth created by Magalotti's disciples in the first decades of the eighteenth century and accepted by all those scholars recently who have looked at the title page while only glancing at the text: the myth, that is, according to which the treatise was a mine of political wisdom [41]. It will reveal it to be what it actually was: not a neglected monument in the history of political philosophy, but a manifestation of the inability of even the best intentions to overcome historical circumstances unfavorable to the production of such a monument.

---

[39] Below, p. 576.

[40] Fermi, *Bibliografia magalottiana* (Piacenza, 1904).

[41] See the Elogio by Giuseppe Averani in his *Lezioni toscane* (Florence, 1744-61).

I reproduce the text of MS Ashburnham 1207, with the kind permission of the Biblioteca Laurenziana of Florence and with help on a few of the more illegible words from my good friend Salvo Mastellone. Walter Moretti has described the table of contents on p. 402 of his edition of Magalotti's *Relazioni di viaggio* (Laterza), along with the titles of his other writings on related subjects. I have written out abbreviations and have left the original punctuation, except where modernization is necessary for clarity. I have respected Magalotti's cancellations. But I have put his marginal additions between slant lines (/) and additions to the additions between double slant lines (//).

CONCORDIA DELLA RELIGIONE E DEL PRINCIPATO Fol. 1

Indice de' Capi [1] 2

Proemio. P°: Che cosa debba chiamarsi nel Principe Devozione. 2°: Dell' Educazione del Principe. 3°: Degli amici del Principe. 4°: De' Servitori intimi. 5°: De' favoriti. 6°: De' Ministri di stati. 7°: De' Ministri che soprintendono alla giustizia. 8°: Dell'obbligo che hanno i Principi di consigliarsi. 9°: Del discernimento nell'elezione de' Teologi. 10°: Del pubblico esercizio della pietà [2]. 11°: Dell'uso della carità, e del modo di sovvenire a' poveri. 12°: Come, e con quali persone, e vizi debba il Principe usar la clemenza, o il rigore. 13°: Del riserbo nell'ascoltar chi riporta, e de' pregiudizi delle prime impressioni. 14°: Del grand'accorgimento nel descernere i Buoni dagl' Ipocriti. 15°: Della delicatezza con cui ha a avviarsi agli scandali segreti. 16°: Dell' invigilare che non s' introduca l'ozio, e de' mezzi conducenti a questo fine. 17°: Del Premio, e dell'uso della liberalità [3]. De' mezzi da conciliarsi l'amore e 'l timore. 19°: De' diversi modi

[1] As indicated above, this table of contents has already been published, with only minor variants, by Moretti, *op. cit.*, p. 402. The chapter headings are on separate lines in the original.

[2] The entire title is crossed out in the original, but nothing is substituted.

[3] Two words follow in the margin but have no bearing on the title.

che hanno a tenersi con la Nobiltà, e con la Plebe. 20º: Dell'obbligo di sostenere il decoro, e la maestà. 21º: Della convenienza di non trascurar l'occasioni lecite d'ampliare il proprio stato. 22º: Della guerra. 23º: Del commercio. 24º: Delle feste, degli spettacoli, e altri pubblici divertimenti, e della caccia.

Della necessità d'esser ben informato delle cose esterne.

Tra Pº e 2º aggiungere un capitolo [:] Che cosa sia veramente l'esser Principe [4]. Quanto diverso da quel che apparisce agli occhi degli sciocchi.

3 [Another table of contents, crossed out with a single horizontal line].

4 [Another, still rougher version of the table of contents, written on a different kind of paper and inserted into the bound volume].

8 PROEMIO

9 CHE COSA SIA VERAMENTE ESSER PRINCIPE E CHE COSA SIA IL PRINCIPATO

10 CHE COSA SIA L'ESSER PRINCIPE. Cap. 2

Noi ci protestammo nel Proemio di quest'opera di voler formare un' idea di Principe che fosse inimitabile; e a dir' il ver, e' ci venne fatto di parlare della devozione in una forma / che piacerà a Dio, che non siamo fatti stimar tanto semplice / di credere che generalmente il debole della maggior parte de' Principi sia l'esser troppo devoti, e che il maggiore scoglio, che s' incontri con essi, sia un eccessivo attaccamento agli esercizi di pietà, e di religione. Sia per tanto con lor buona grazia il dichiararci, che in tanto ci siamo un poco riscaldati a mostrar di volergli ritirar dal troppo, in un genere, nel quale essi per l'ordinario anzi soglion difettar nel poco, in quanto abbiamo voluto assicurarci, che non ci abbiano ad allegare a sospetto di non intendere quanto basti il lor mestiero, benissimo sapendo come molti di loro con la scusa di non poter far tutto, si dispensano dal fare anche il poco, / pretendendo così d'occultar la fiaccola / d'una somma infingiardaggine / dietro il velo / d'un poco di maggior difficoltà. No, no; noi conosciamo assai bene i Principi; e crediamo di poter dire senza iattanza d' intendere assai meglio del lor mestiere, e del modo cui e' lo praticano che non ci intendiamo della vita spirituale, e però si compiacciano, anzi che di istimarci per la nostra presente *dabbenaggine* [5], saperci grado della nostra discrezione, già che per non aver a passar con essi per troppo indiscreti, non ci siamo curati d'avventurarci a passar con altri per poco pii; nel che abbiamo fatto come chi vuol divider con tutta puntualità cavalleresca due che

---

[4] This turns out actually to be the first chapter in the text. The *Proemio* is missing, whatever Magalotti suggests to the contrary in the first lines of what he calls *Cap. 2*.

[5] Underlining by the author.

si battono, che per non insospettire l'estraneo, o men conosciuto,
porta la punta della spada all'amico. Sperando per tanto, che la Re- 10 v
ligione, come discreta non abbia a essersi offesa da noi per un simil
modo di procedere, sicura che il nostro fine non è stat'altro, che il
non renderci sospetti al Principato, col quale vorremmo pur vedere
se potessimo aver fortuna di metterla d'accordo, così vogliamo ancora
sperare, che questo in correspondenza d'un tratto così pieno d'equità,
e d' indifferenza, non ricuserà la nostra mediazione, e che dopo aver
accettato e applaudito la parte del nostro arbitrio, che (diciamo così)
affligge la Religione, non vorrà declinar poi quella, che potesse non
interamente piacere a lui, il che quant'egli pur tentasse di fare, ci
rendiamo sicuri, che il suo Padrino, che è l'ottimo Principe, piglierà
sopra di se il metterlo alla cagione. E che / ben lontani dall'accordarsi
i Principi a interpretare sinistramente la nostra dottrina e dire « Cognatio eorum simul quiescere faciamus omnes dies festos Dei a terrâ », si suporranno (?) a cambiar [6] talmente in zelo, in carità, in beneficenza // verso i loro sudditi // quel che non possono pagare a Dio in orazione ... [7] che ciascheduno di essi possa dire [:] « Respicite quoniam non mihi soli laboravi, sed omnibus exquirentibus disciplinam », e che altri possa dir di fatti che « Iddio immutavit tempora, et dies festos ipsorum, et in illis dies festos celebraverunt ad horam » [8].

Facciamo ben da principio: Per Principe non intendiamo qualunque possiede stati. Principe chiamiamo Ciro, non Divo Augusto, non Sardanapalo. Ma noi la pigliamo troppo lunga. Lungo, e superfluo sarebbe ancora il cominciare a formare il carattere del Principe per contrapporre a quel del Tiranno, oltre che non è nostra intenzione lo scrivere di questa materia per acquistarci concetto d'aver
detto assai, facendoci pagar la compiacenza di credere d'aver a passar 11
per eruditi dal tedio, e dalla nausea di chi legge. Di queste cose vi son pieni tutti gli scritti di politica, e di morale, nè noi professiamo di scrivere a persone alle quali così fatti minuzzamenti possano arrivar nuovi. E poi come il Principe s'avesse a conoscere per via di contrarii, non occorrebbe star a perder il tempo, e la fatica, essendo il Tiranno una sorta di / fiera così indomita e feroce / che ognun la conosce senza che altri si metta a farne la notonomia. E poi di Tiranni veri Tiranni in oggi non è più la moda; o sia che il rispetto della religione abbia posto un freno alla perversità degli uomini qual non arriva mai a porre la superstizione, e che si sia tanto raffinata l'arte che si trovi la via

[6] Crossed out in very light ink. But the correction has faded away. The passage quoted is Ps. 73: 8-9.

[7] Two lines are crossed out.

[8] Magalotti identifies the quotations: *Ecclesiasticus*, XXXIII 18, and 9; but he puts the citations in reverse order.

di far le medesime cose / con manco rumore / e come suole dirsi per
proverbio, con più utile e *meno* [9] pompa. Posto dunque, che noi non
vogliamo star a repeter cose già dette da altri, e che dall'altro canto
non vogliamo arrogarci l'autorità di riformare il mondo con formare
il Principe sopr'un modello affatto nuovo, ci contentiremo di rica-
varlo da un idea antichissima, che ne formò lo Spirito Santo, quando
volle formare il carattere di Dio, allora ch'egli cominciò (diciamo
così) materialmente a regnare: Impercioche quantunque sia verissimo,
che il Regno di Dio è regno di tutti i secoli, par tuttavia da osservare,
che sin tanto ch' Egli non venne all'atto della creazione non si poteva dir ch' Ei regnasse, se il regnare [10] suppone una cosa su la qual
s'eserciti la superiorità, e il dominio. Perché non essendo allora nulla
11 v altro che Iddio, o più tosto, altro che Dio e 'l nulla, se con tale stato
la Divinità potesse rozzamente adombrarsi per qualche similitudine
con alcune di quelle cose che noi intendiamo / (con tutto che quella
somma // e felicissima // individua unita renda impropriissimo, e
insufficientissimo quel concetto ancora) / più tosto che per Regno,
si spiegherebbe forse meglio per una specie di severissima Oligarchia
Aristocratica, tra le tre Divine persone dove non cadendo per la
loro perfettissima uguaglianza né superiorità, né inferiorità, si come
non si poteva trovare chi fosse suddito, così non si poteva né anche
ritrovare chi fosse Re. Onde dice l' Evangelista, parlando di quel
tempo nel quale era Iddio il Verbo, e che il Verbo era appresso Iddio,
e che Iddio era il Verbo, che non c'er'altro che Vita e Luce, e che
innanzi che di queste ne fosse fatto quel che fu fatto, queste erano
in lui ed erano lui medesimo. Ma quando poi mediante la Creazione
ad extra gli piacque di formarsi un' Imperio degno di lui, / e che /
prese / per diversi / il trattamento, e le qualità di Re, / allora / lo
Spirito Santo per bocca di David ce lo descrive con queste parole [11]:
Il Signore regnò (perché a Dio è l'istesso il voler una cosa e il farlo) [,]
si vestì la Maestà, si vestì la Fortezza, e s'accinse, cioè prese l'attività, e con quest'arredo di regali attributi / fondava / la terra che
non possa (?) commuoversi. / Fu da allora preparato il Seggio, che
era dal principio de' secoli. / Ora questo / e non altro / vogliamo
noi che sia il carattere del nostro Principe [:] Maestà, Fortezza, e
14 Attività [12], le quali si come in Dio furon sempre regolate dalla soa-

[9] Magalotti's underlining. *Manco* is written just above, but *meno* is not crossed out.

[10] These two words are crossed out in very light pencil, and «di quel regnare» is written almost invisibly above them.

[11] Two lines in Latin are crossed out.

[12] Between ff. 11 v and 14 r are inserted two slips of paper marked respectively 13 and 14 (the numeration is posterior). The texts as altered by

vità, e dalla sapienza, che in tanto non vennero espresse dal Profeta[,] in quanto non erano di quegli attributi che cominciassero, non a essere, che tutti vi furon sempre, ma a raffigurarsi più visibilmente in Dio allora ch' Ei cominciò a regnare, così nel Principe conviene, che quei primi tre [,] cioè la Maestà, la Fortezza, e l'Attività siano sempre misurati con la Pietà, e la Prudenza, che son tra gli uomini le subalterne di quel che si chiama, ed è santità e sapienza in Dio. Della prima abbiamo già parlato a bastanza, mostrando in che maniera debba usarsi dal Principe. Della seconda [,] essendo impossibile il darne precetti universali come dell'altre virtù, essendo ella più tosto che virtù, la maestra e la reggitrice delle virtù. Basterà che se ne ravvisino le proporzioni nel ragionar che faremo non soltanto de' tre su detti attributi, ma di tutto quello ancora, che ha correlazione al carattere di quel Principe che è nostro intendimento il formare [13]. [...]

[DELL'EDUCAZIONE] [14] 70

Quando il caso, che m'accennate si dia, bisogna ch' io intenda meglio, se i libri de' quali mi domandate hanno a servire per una istruzzione, o hanno a esser letti per suo studio dal personaggio commessovi. Io risponderò in tutt'e due i casi. Se il 2º, bisognerebbe prima sapere di molte cose: i suoi anni, il suo genio, la sua capacità, e poi sopra tutto la pianta, su la quale vi sarà stato dato ordine dall'architetto maggiore d'andare alzando questa fabrica. Se il Pº, voi sapete ch' io non son letterato, e che ci saranno benissimo 200 Autori tutti adattabilissimi all'uso intento, de' quali io non saprò ne meno il nome. C' è Institutio Principis d' Erasmo di Roterdam, ci sono i Simboli del Sahavedra, c' è la Scuola della Verità del Juglares, ci sono delle cose del Tesauro, e più di fresco l' Educazione del Principe stampata in circa 10 anni sono a Parigi da Monsieur Nicoles in franzese. Ma io ve ne dico quattro, e ce ne saranno le migliara. Non dubito, che in tutti non ci siano delle cose buone, e che il vederli non sia utilissimo, se non altro l' Istruzzione di S. Tommaso al Re di Cipra,

---

the author read as follows: 12. Che la felicità del Principe consiste nel render felici gli altri, e che per render felici gli altri convien far servire il temperamento all'esigenze del Principato, non il Principato all' inclinazione del temperamento. 13. Trattato 2º. Del Principato. Ragionamento Pº. Della Maestà Esteriore. Cap. Pº. Che cosa sia l'esser Principe.

The rest of the text here reproduced is written on a separate sheet fixed onto the original with wax seals.

[13] From here on the handwriting changes. This chapter ends at f. 55.

[14] Only scattered notes precede this passage, which in turn is probably only a note to be included in an eventual text of the chapter. The passage appears to be a letter; but given Magalotti's penchant for writing in an epistolary form, the recipient is probably imaginary.

quella di Sinesio ad Arcadio giovanetto, e la Ciropedia di Xenofonte
70 v mi farebbon mentire. Ma che io approvi lo sposare o questo, o quello
Istruttore di Principe, e mettersene a formare uno sopra un modello
stampato; o, questo no; perché questo è un mestiero, e in tutti quelli
che scrivono, quel del Pedante è per lo più quel che prevale; e cre-
dendo io, che quel, ch' ha da prevalere nel Principe abbia a essere il
Cavaliere, e pochi cavalieri (intendo di professione, non di nascita)
avendo costumato in tutti i tempi di scrivere precettivamente, però
escludo un così stretto attaccamento agl'autori, i quali per lo più
formano idee di Principi, che non si trovano se non ne' paesi adiacenti
alli stati della Repubblica di Platone. Io stimo, che il fonte più sano
degl'ammaestramenti d'un giovane Principe sia il sapere, l'esperienza,
e il giudizio di chi l' ha in cura, e che questo sappia adattare il lavoro
alla qualità del legname, che ha tra mano, intendendo per legname,
non tanto l' indole, quanto la fortuna, i tempi, le congiunture, i vicini,
e sopra tutto lo stato del sistema universale. Tal massima è buona per
il Delfino, che non è buona per il Palatino di Simmeren, e all' incontro
quando si vuol attender l' indole, tal concetto grande era adattabile
a un Castruccio Castracani, che non valeva niente per un di quelli
71 sgraziati Re degl'Assiri, o de' Medi. Ho detto assai; e perché in voi
concorrono tutte le parti più desiderabili per tant'uffizio, basta che
v'accomodiate a far il maggiore capitale sopra di voi medesimo, e
sto per dire, che quando non sapeste farne altro, formatelo Cavaliere,
e vedrete, che vi verrà formato ottimo Principe, non essendo altro
a mio credere il Principe, che la natura del Cavaliere, lasciatemi dir
così, nello stato della gloria [15].

---

[15] The other pages allotted to this chapter in the bound manuscript volume are blank.

JOHN A. TEDESCHI

FLORENTINE DOCUMENTS FOR A HISTORY OF THE *INDEX OF PROHIBITED BOOKS* *

* The inspiration and model for this article is provided by Antonio Rotondò's valuable edition of Inquisitorial correspondence preserved in the Bologna and Modena archives: « Nuovi documenti per la storia dell' 'Indice dei Libri Proibiti' (1572-1638) », *Rinascimento*, ser. 2, 3 (1963), 145-211. For bibliography and a general discussion of the work of the Congregation of the Index the reader is referred to Rotondò's introduction and to his forthcoming essay « La censura ecclesiastica e la cultura italiana dal XVI al XVIII secolo ».

In the transcription of the letters I have not broken up the following frequently encountered abbreviations: Ill.mi (Illustrissimi), R.mi (Reverendissimi), Sig.ri (Signori), R. V. (Reverentia Vostra), V. R. (Vostra Reverentia), SS.ri (Signori), P. V. (Paternità Vostra), V. P. M. R. (Vostra Paternità Molto Reverenda), N. S. (Nostro Signore).

From the documents which once formed a part of the archive of the Florentine Inquisition, I have selected for publication the twenty-eight surviving letters addressed to the Inquisitor of Florence by various cardinals of the Congregation of the Index [1]. They span a short period of little more than a decade, from March 1592 to September 1606. The letters confirm the impression which has emerged from recent studies of the devastating effects on Italian culture of Roman censorship practice [2]. They illustrate both the plight of the intellectual and the enormous difficulties encountered by Rome in its ambitious and unrealistic program of controlling what could be written, printed and read in that part of Europe which remained under its jurisdiction. The result was unmitigated confusion. Authors suffered interminable delays in the often vain hope that overworked

---

[1] The four codices surviving from the archive of the Florentine Inquisition are preserved in the royal library at Brussels, MS. II 290. Their contents are summarily described in J. Van Den Gheyn, *Catalogue des Manuscrits de la Bibliothèque Royale de Belgique*, IV (Brussels, 1903), pp. 84-86. Rapid surveys of the collection are G. Biagi, « Le carte dell' Inquisizione fiorentina a Bruxelles », *Rivista delle biblioteche e degli archivi*, 19 (1908), 161-168 and M. Battistini, « Per la storia dell' Inquisizione fiorentina (documenti inediti della Biblioteca Reale di Bruxelles) », *Bilychnis*, a. 18 (1929), 425-448. The Brussels manuscripts are obviously a part of the material removed from Vatican and Italian archives at Napoleon's orders in 1810. After his fall the bulk of the Inquisitorial documents were sold to Parisian paper merchants as scrap. Among the codices that survived, several were acquired by Trinity College, Dublin, one by the Bibliothèque Nationale, Paris and the present four by the Brussels library. The sorry affair is narrated by A. Mercati, *Il sommario del processo di Giordano Bruno* (Vatican City, 1942), pp. 3-5.

[2] In addition to Rotondò's « Nuovi documenti », see P. Prodi's description of its effects on Bolognese university life and on the career of Carlo Sigonio in Prodi's excellent *Il Cardinale Paleotti (1522-1597)*, II (Rome, 1967), chapter XII, « Riforma religiosa e cultura ». Paul Grendler has completed research for a study on « The Roman Inquisition and the Venetian Press, 1550-1600 ».

revisori would approve the publication of their writings [3]; university professors were cut off from new developments in their disciplines [4]; and booksellers and printers were ruined financially as a result of prohibitions which ranged from Ariosto to Zasius [5].

The Florentine documents illustrate both the reigning confusion and the efforts to correct it. The first letter, for example, attempts to settle the question as to whether provincial inquisitors could issue permits to read heretical literature [6]; another, the uncertain status of the writings of Jean Bodin. Several of the letters are concerned with the complications and embarrassment ensuing from the premature helter-skelter publication of the Index of Clement VIII, which had to be suspended while some last minute additions and revisions could be made [7].

The letters reflect the increasing severity of Roman censorship. Writers or specific classes of writings which had been partially tolerated in the Tridentine Index of Pius IV became totally prohibited. This was the fate of the Talmud and of Scripture in translation [8]. The printed catalogue of the Oxford and

---

[3] Fra Damiano Rubeo, in the service of the *Maestro del Sacro Palazzo*, once confidentially urged a theologian who had just written *De praedestinatione* to have his treatise published in Venice. There was no chance for its publication in Rome where there was an enormous backlog of material to examine. Rotondò, « Nuovi documenti », p. 157 (letter of 25 April 1576).

[4] Shortly after the publication of the Index of Paul IV (January 1559), the city of Bologna sought for its university a blanket permission to use prohibited books which were not directly concerned with religion. The request was eventually refused. The best that could be obtained was the occasional license granted to individual professors to consult specific books. Cf. P. Prodi, *Il Cardinale Paleotti*, II, 237.

[5] Among the works prohibited were Bembo's *Rime* and Guicciardini's *Historia*. Cf. P. Prodi, *Il Cardinale Paleotti*, II, 240 f.

[6] The provincial inquisitors' own rights in this matter had not been easy to determine. See, for example, the letter sent to the Bolognese inquisition by the Holy Office in Rome (24 November 1572): « Quanto a quello poi che V. R. domanda, se uno inquisitore ha licentia di legere libri prohibiti, li dico che molte volte se n' è raggionato tra questi Signori in Congregatione, et sempre si è detto di sì, ch' hanno licentia, però quando importa il bisogno dello Officio et non altramente ». Bologna, Biblioteca Comunale (Archiginnasio), MS. 1860 f. CI.

[7] Letters 5-8.

[8] Letter 5.

Cambridge University libraries was proscribed [9], and, as we shall see below, a work of historiography. A request by a Florentine literary academy for permission to possess copies of works by Boccaccio, Machiavelli and Lodovico Castelvetro for the purpose of preparing expurgated editions was peremptorily refused [10]; a decade or two earlier similar efforts had been tolerated by the church [11].

The topic of several letters is the projected *Index Expurgatorius* [12], which, if successfully completed, would have permitted

---

[9] Letter 17.

[10] Letter 24. Since the Index of Paul IV, Machiavelli had been one of those authors « quorum scripta omnino prohibentur ». By the end of the sixteenth century license to read him was extremely difficult to obtain and was refused to individuals of high rank: in 1610, for example, to Baron de Fucariis, the imperial ambassador in Venice. In the same year a certain Cesare di Pisa, alias Astrologhino, was arrested, tortured and convicted because copies of Machiavelli and Bodin had been found in his possession. G. Procacci, *Studi sulla fortuna del Machiavelli* (Rome, 1965), pp. 317 ff, 327. A decree of the Roman Inquisition issued 4 October 1600 denied permission to Baccio Valori to place a copy of the *Discorsi* in the Medici library. A. Sorrentino, *Storia dell'Antimachiavellismo europeo* (Naples, 1936), p. 117.

The literary critic Lodovico Castelvetro, suspected as the translator of two works by Melanchthon, was condemned as a contumacious heretic by the Roman Inquisition on 20 November 1560. His writings were proscribed first by the Index of Pius IV. Cf. H. Reusch, I, 153 f. (cited in n. 1 to the texts).

On the prohibition of Boccaccio, see A. Sorrentino, *La letteratura italiana e il Sant'Uffizio* (Naples, 1935), Ch. V, « Il Boccaccio ».

[11] An expurgated version of Machiavelli was prepared by two of his grand-sons during the pontificate of Gregory XIII. They would not publish it, however, with Rome's condition that it should appear without Machiavelli's name, or with a substitute. Cf. G. Procacci, *Studi sulla fortuna del Machiavelli*, pp. 317 ff. As for Boccaccio, a commission under Vincenzo Borghini was established in Florence in 1571 to correct the *Decameron*. The project was undertaken with papal blessing. The *Maestro del Sacro Palazzo*, Tommaso Manriques, and the confessor of Pius V, Eustachio Locatelli, selected the passages requiring expurgation. As they were completed, chapters were sent to Rome for approval. The new authorized edition was published by the Giunta in Florence in 1573. In June of the same year the new *Maestro del Sacro Palazzo*, fra Paolo Costabili, ordered that it be removed from circulation. A fine example of confusion in Roman censorship practice. Cf. Rotondò, « Nuovi documenti », p. 152, n. 5. Other expurgated editions followed, Lionardo Salviati's in 1582 and Luigi Groto's in 1588. See, on the entire question, A. Sorrentino, *La letteratura italiana e il Sant'Uffizio*, Ch. V.

[12] Letters 10-13.

entire libraries of prohibited books to circulate, though subject to the prescribed expurgations. The cardinals of the Index hoped to enlist the services, as correctors and expurgators, of trusted men of letters and theologians. The Florentine inquisitor was repeatedly asked to assist in their recruitment. Eventually, one solitary *Index Expurgatorius* [13], containing corrections for a mere fifty books, appeared. A reason for the failure of the plan may have been the uncooperative attitude of Italian scholars who would not participate in the required mutilations. Such a state of affairs seems to be reflected in a brief note hastily scribbled by the Florentine inquisitor at the foot of a letter (n. 22, dated 23 March 1602), enjoining him to constant vigilance in the control of the city's presses and to be more zealous in the matter of forwarding expurgations of prohibited books to Rome: « Adì 13 di Aprile si risposa che in quanto alla stampa, non si mancava. In quanto alla censura, che s'aspettava da Roma, non essendo qui chi voglia tal con ... » [14].

The Congregation of the Index regularly communicated to the provincial inquisitors the titles of recently banned works toward which they should exercise special vigilance. On 2 July 1600 the Florentine inquisitor was warned that a copy of Philipp Camerarius' *Operae Horarum Succisivarum sive Meditationes Historicae* (Nuremberg, 1599) had been confiscated in Rome [15]. The book had been condemned « per esser perni-

---

[13] See n. 18 to the documents.

[14] This crucial word is unfortunately partly illegible. But the sense of the note seems clear enough to me: that there was no one in Florence who would undertake the work of censorship.

[15] Letter 15. Philipp Camerarius, jurist, philologist and man of letters, was the son of Joachim Camerarius, many of whose writings he edited. During a student journey to Italy the younger Camerarius suffered imprisonment by the Roman Inquisition. The episode is the subject of J. G. Schelhorn's « Relatio vera et solida de captivitate romana, ex falsa delatione orta, et liberatione fere miraculosa Philippi Camerarii et Petri Rieteri », included in Schelhorn's *De vita, fatis ac meritis Philippi Camerarii* (Nuremberg, 1740). More light has recently been shed by P. Paschini, « Episodi dell' Inquisizione a Roma nei suoi primi decenni », *Studi romani*, 5 (1957), 285-301.

The *Meditationes* grew from one « centuria » to three in subsequent editions. It was translated into French by Simon Goulart as *Les meditations historiques* (Lyons, 1610) and into English by John Molle, entitled first *The Walking Librarie* (London, 1621) and, in later issues, *The Living Librarie.*

tioso ». Ordinarily we would be left to guess what in a book of historical meditations should have been found objectionable. Fortunately, in this instance, we know the reasons for the prohibition. It has been possible for me to consult the *Correctio* or list of expurgations drawn up for Camerarius' book [16]. Works by arch-heretics which dealt with religion did not receive this attention. These were totally prohibited and could not be owned or read under any circumstances. Lists of expurgations were prepared for a less dangerous class of literature. Though Camerarius was a Protestant, he was not as notorious as Calvin or Luther, all of whose works were prohibited, and he had written on a non-controversial subject. His book would be temporarily suspended until authorities could examine it and recommend what expurgations, if any, were required [17]. This was the theory. In practice, very few suspended books were permitted to circulate [18].

The Camerarius expurgations would be applied in the brutal form of ink erasures on the text, or they would be incorporated

---

[16] The *Correctio* was acquired by Antonio Rotondò from a Modenese bookseller and presented to me in December 1968. This document in four leaves begins: « Correctio libri, cuius tit. est, Operae Horarum Succisivarum, sive Meditationes Historicae, per Philippo Camerario auctore, Norimberga, 1599, in 4° ». Then follow the list of prescribed expurgations with precise page references: « In cap. 62 p. 288 deleantur verba ista qua sunt circa medium ' Quoniam autem de hac donatione ', slz. Constantini usque ad fin. capitis; totum n. tendit ad ostendendum donationem Constantini Imper. factam D. Sylvestro, fabulam esse ». Presumably, the archive of the Inquisition in Rome which houses the papers of the now defunct Congregation of the Index contains many similar documents. The Camerarius *Correctio* is the only one that I have ever seen.

[17] See the clarification issued by the Congregation of the Index to certain doubts which had been raised by the Bolognese Inquisitor (1583): « I libri sospesi con questa ragione si sospesero, acciò che, venendone per le mani, non si permettessero se non corretti, sendoli trovati dentro errori; però quelli non sono tali assolutamente prohibiti. Ogni inquisitore però debbe fare in quelli la sua diligenza et revisti et ispurgati darli, né permettere in quel mentre che i librai li vendano, se non dopo fatta la censura; ispurgati, sì ». Rotondò, « Nuovi documenti », p. 163.

[18] *Il Cardinale Paleotti*, II, 237: « Ma questa regola rimase in realtà lettera morta perché gli esami e le correzioni da parte degli inquisitori e delle facoltà teologiche procedevano con estrema lentezza o non erano permesse da Roma, spesso con il deliberato proposito di ritardare la diffusione di quei libri ».

into a new printed edition, in the slight eventuality that one should be undertaken in Italy. It seems to have been the customary procedure for the local inquisitor to round up all available copies, introduce the expurgations and then make restitution to their owners [19]. There is no certain way to determine whether the Camerarius *Correctio* was prepared in Rome by a *revisore* attached to the Congregation of the Index or by one of the provincial Inquisitions. We know that expurgations drawn up in Rome were copied and circulated to the outlying officials [20], and we also know that the latter possessed the authority to carry out the corrections themselves [21]. Due to the extreme rarity of documents of this kind (the archive of the Inquisition in Rome remains closed to scholars) its contents deserve to be mentioned.

The most frequently recommended cancellations for the *Meditationes* concern laudatory references to heretics (Beza, Bullinger, Vermigli, etc.) or to prohibited authors (Erasmus, Machiavelli). Another expurgation slices off a quotation from Johannes Aventinus which attacks begging throughout history and the nefarious consequences of its practice by the mendicant orders. To be excised is Robert Gaguin's insinuation that in France the public good had invariably suffered when clergy became embroiled in affairs of state; Eusebius' reflection that the persecutions suffered by Christians under Diocletian were the result of strife and jealousy among bishops; an allegation

---

[19] See, for example, the letter (2 October 1603) from Cardinal Borghese to the Inquisitor of Modena communicating the corrections prescribed by the Congregation of the Index for the recently published study of St. Thomas by the Jesuit Francisco Suarez: « Pertanto V. R. farà diligenza di raccogliere o dà librari o da altri tutti i volumi del detto 4° tomo che in cotesta sua giurisditione si trovassero et gli corregga secondo la sopradetta forma et così corretti poi gli restituisca a' padroni, ordinando a gli stampatori et librari che, in caso che si facesse di nuovo stampare, si debbono regolarsi secondo l' istessa correttione prescritta di sopra ». Rotondò, « Nuovi documenti », p. 179.

[20] See the document cited in n. 17. Rome's answer to the Bolognese query (« Se si può havere tutte le correttioni fatte in Roma particolarmente di queste opere infrascritte ... ») is « Le correttioni de i libri fatte fin qui in Roma si daranno. Ben è vero che essendovene alcune longhe et bisognando tempo assai a ricavarle, saria bisogno di uno che non havesse altro da fare che rescriverle ... ». Rotondò, « Nuovi documenti », p. 164.

[21] In several letters, as we have noted, the Florentine Inquisitor is asked to send to Rome expurgations compiled in Florence.

of papal avarice attributed to a distant patriarch of Constantinople; and the ancient tale that a hairy monster had been born to the mistress of Pope Nicholas III. The four pages which are to be deleted at the end of chapter 58 are an eloquent plea for religious toleration, with a reminder that men of different faiths have successfully co-existed and of Augustine's pronouncement that only God was lord over men's consciences. Several pages in which the history of the exposure of the « donation of Constantine » is related with great fairness and objectivity are to be deleted, as well as a reference to priests possessed by the devil, and that Roman Catholics in Transylvania in very recent times had been idolatrous in their worship of sacred images. In a passage where Ariosto is said to have attributed the invention of artillery to a monk, the word « monachus » is to be inked out. A derisive reference to a priest as « sacrifico cuidam » is to be replaced by the more respectful « presbitero vel sacerdote ». Finally, a lament that human superstitions had frequently been exploited by priests (« a sacrificulis ») for their own ends and for personal enrichment is to be erased.

How carefully did the *revisore* carry out his task? It is obvious that the list of expurgations was compiled in great haste. In view of the mountains of books for which this process had to be repeated, this is not surprising. The *revisore* did not trouble to identify the mysterious « I.B.B.M.O. » appended to a long prefatory letter of commendation addressed to Camerarius. The initials belong to Giovanni Bernardino Bonifacio, Marchese d' Oria, a patron of many men of letters, one of the few Italian noblemen to apostatize from the Catholic church in the sixteenth century. Names of countless other Protestants overlooked by the expurgator include those of Girolamo Donzellini, Philippe de Mornay and Thomas Erastus. A long disquisition on Lorenzo Valla and his research into the « donation of Constantine » is left intact although, as we have noted, a discussion of this subject occurring elsewhere was deleted.

A cursory comparison of the method employed by the Italian *revisore* with the corrections made to the *Meditationes* in the Spanish *Index Expurgatorius* (Madrid, 1667) yields this tentative conclusion. Although the latter is clearly more severe and wide-ranging in its mutilations, it is also more consistent and, in some way, more intelligent. The Italian document is content simply to cancel out obnoxious names. It prescribes the deletion of Beza's name but allows the accompanying epigram by Beza to stand. The Spanish Index recognizes that the threat to the faith is not in the name of a man but in his work. It removes both. Or, as in numerous other instances (where the document follows its name-erasing policy) it adopts a more sophisticated procedure. It leaves both an epigram and its heretical author's name, deleting only such complimentary attributes as « elegantissimus » and « praestantissimus ».

Fragments from the dispersed archives of the Inquisition are all that we have available at present for studying certain aspects of the developing culture and institutions of the Counter-Reformation. I have thought it appropriate to publish them here because they help to detail the closing of that freer period to which Hans Baron has devoted a lifetime of study. With the outlawing of Boccaccio and Machiavelli the Renaissance had ended in Italy.

1. (T. II f. 163)

Reverendo Padre. Questi miei Ill.mi et R.mi Sig.ri Cardinali Generali Inquisitori Colleghi hanno ordinato che si scriva à tutti li Reverendi Inquisitori et se gli commandi espressamente, come con la presente si fa alla R. V., che non ardiscano ne presumano in modo alcuno dare licentia di tenere ò leggere libbri prohibiti, perchè essi Inquisitori non hanno auttorità di dare simili licentie, ne la trovaranno nelle patente loro, et per ciò V. R. doverà senz'altro astenersene per l'avvenire, et rivocare quelle c' havesse forse concesse per il passato.

Con questa occasione si fa intendere a V. R. come sin dell'anno 1591 per ordine della felice memoria di Gregorio XIIII fu prohibita la *Republica* di Giovanni Bodino in qualsivoglia lingua che si trovasse, o fusse stata tradotta, come opera ripiena di errori et impietà ancorachè si dicesse di essere stata corretta et emendata. Per il che V. R. farrà diligentia et ordine espresso che non se ne legga, ne se ne tenghi alcuna e trovandosene le facci tutte brugiare. Et appresso sono state prohibite tutte le altre opere sue sino che siano reviste o espurgate dalla Sacra Congregatione sopra l' Indice de' Libbri Prohibiti, et anco la *Demonomania* [1]. Per il chè ella le sospenda tutte sino ad altro ordine, ne permetta che si vendano ò concedano. Ne questa essendo per altro, la saluto et il Signore la conservi nella sua santa gratia.
Di Roma a XI di Marzo 1592.
Di V. R., come fratello

Il Cardinale di Santa Severina

2. (T. II f. 164)

Reverendo Padre. Da questi Ill.mi et R.mi SS.ri Cardinali Generali Inquisitori miei Colleghi è stato ordinato che V. R. non ardisca in modo alcuno di conceder licenza a qualsivoglia persona di leggere libri prohibiti, non havendo gl'Inquisitori particolari questa autorità;

---

[1] On the prohibition of Bodin's writings, see H. Reusch, *Der Index der verbotenen Bücher*, 2 vols. (Bonn, 1883-1885), I, 417, 537 and J. Hilgers, *Der Index der verbotenen Bücher* (Freiburg i. Br., 1904), pp. 422, 521, 536 ff. Cf. n. 11 below.

et che faccia conservar la presente negli atti di cotesto Santo Ufficio, acciochè in ogni evento quest'ordine possa esser nota ai successori di lei. Con che la saluto, et alle sue orationi mi raccomando.
Di Roma, a VIII di Agosto MDXCII.
Di V. R., come fratello

Il Cardinale di Santa Severina

3. (T. II f. 154)

Molto Reverendo Padre come fratello. In Fiorenza è stato stampato hora da Filippo Giunta un volume di diverse sorti di Versi latini d'un Gio. Battista Pinello Genovese. Et perchè senza mia notitia et saputa me l' ha dedicato con un' Epistola latina, et altri versi sussequenti, et mandatomelo dopo ch' è stato stampato, et havendo visto in quei versi molte adulationi lontane et contrarie all'animo mio, et essendo anco l'opera cosa da giovane come la P. V. potrà vedere, però alla ricevuta di questa, la P. V. senza perderci tempo farà subito precetto a quel libraro che non la divulghi, ne ne dia fuori copia veruna, et cosi avvertirà che si faccia, ch' intanto ho scritto al Giovanni Battista auttore dell'opera che se ne venga à Fiorenza, et faccia levare l' Epistola et versi dedicati a me, et indrizzi poi l'opera, a chi li parve, ch' io resto sodisfatto della sua buona volontà [2]. Per il quale mando

---

[2] There is no more than a passing mention of G. B. Pinelli in M. Giustiniani, *Gli scrittori liguri* (Rome, 1667), pp. 340-342 and G. Tiraboschi, *Storia della letteratura italiana*, VII[4] (Modena, 1792), 1438. By A. Oldoino, *Athenaeum Ligusticum, seu syllabus scriptorum Ligurum* (Perugia, 1680), p. 331, Pinelli's talents are rated rather cautiously: « quare inter aetatis nostrae summos poetas non ultimum obtinuit locum. ». And C. Jannaco, *Il Seicento* (Milan, 1963), p. 377 names him in a long string of « commediografi, che si ricordano a titolo di documentazione ».

The work which had aroused the cardinal's ire is the *J. B. Pinelli Carminum liber primus* (*-tertius*) (Florence: Junta, 1594). According to the *Catalogue* of printed books in the British Museum (vol. 190, col. 320), the colophon is dated 1593. Pinelli recalls this sorry episode in a later edition of his poetry, *Carminum Libri IIII ad illustrissimum D. D. Iacobum Auriam* (Genova, 1605), p. [3] of dedication: « Tibi haec nostra, Iacobe, prodeunt. O ne ingrata quae in vestibulo potissimum. Porto minima damus, verum tua. Tua arbos, tui fructus, in hisce quae potiora, tibi, aut tuis scripta. Florentino prelo superioribus annis expressa, ut ut reconcinnata, quae postmodo tui patris in laudes typis in patria commisimus, adnexa. Iam tibi coniunctim omnia quicquid hinc ablegatum, nostrum haud esto ».

la lettera a V. P. che ce la potrà far tenere quanto prima con darmi avviso del seguito. Et la gratia di Dio sia con lei.
Di Roma li XXX di Ottobre 1593.
Di V. P. M. R., come fratello affettuosissimo

Cardinale Pinello [3]

4. (T. II f. 115)

Molto Reverendo Padre. La Santità di N. S. dopo molte consultationi della S. Congregatione dell' Indice, havendo tenuto molti giorni appresso di se l' Indice [4] che si manda a V. R., dopo haverlo Sua Beatitudine in tante occupationi voluto rilegere, et considerare con la sua pastoral diligenza tutte le cose che potessero impedire la debbita essecutione, l' ha rimandato alla Congregatione, commettendo che si publichi, et così in essecutione dell'ordine di Sua Santità si è publicato in Roma, et lo mandiamo col medesimo ordine a V. R. che lo faccia publicare et esseguire ove s'estende la sua giurisditione, come ricerca l' importanza del negotio, con partecipazione di Monsignore Nuntio, facendo mandar ad essecutione quanto è scritto nell' Instruttione [5] et nelle Regole [6] che si danno per l'espurgatione dè libri per tener lontana, come conviene all'officio suo in tutti i modi, la pestifera contagione dell' heresia, et essendo molto nota a Sua Santità et alla Congregatione la pietà et il zelo dell' honor del Signore Iddio di V. R.

---

[3] A note, probably in the Florentine Inquisitor's hand, at the bottom of the page states (in my interpretation) that he has communicated the order to Giunta, the printer, who has promised to keep him informed of developments: « Et così esseguirà et me ne darà avviso ».

[4] The Index of Clement VIII is fully discussed in H. Reusch, *Der Index der verbotenen Bücher*, I, 532-549 and J. Hilgers, *Der Index*, pp. 536-538. The full text of the Index is reprinted in H. Reusch, *Die Indices Librorum Prohibitorum des sechzehnten Jahrhunderts* (Tübingen, 1886), pp. 524-578.

[5] An important addition to the Clementine Index are the Instructions prepared for the use of individuals responsible for the prohibition, expurgation and printing of books, « Instructio eorum, qui libris tum prohibendis, tum expurgandis, tum etiam imprimendis diligentem ac fidelem, ut par est, operam sunt daturi ». H. Reusch, *Die Indices*, pp. 529-535. An abridged English version of these Instructions is in H. Brown, *The Venetian Printing Press* (London, 1891), pp. 144-147.

[6] The ten « Regulae » drawn up by the Tridentine fathers and first published in the Index of Pius IV (1564) set down the guidelines for Roman policy in the control of printing and the prohibition of books. They are printed in Reusch, *Die Indices*, pp. 247-251. Cf. J. Alberigo, et al., *Conciliorum Oecumenicorum Decreta* (Freiburg i. Br., 1962), p. 773.

non se le scrive con più parole, tenendo per fermo che userà la solita sua diligenza in questo negotio di servitio di Nostro Signore Dio, dal quale le pregamo il colmo della sua santa gratia.
Di Roma il dì 27 di Marzo 1596.
Di V. P. M. R., come fratelli

Il Cardinale di Verona
Il Cardinale di Terranova
(Two illegible signatures)

5. (T. II f. 137)

Reverendo Padre. Perchè il Segretario della Congregatione sopra L' Indice de' Libri Prohibiti si trova haver mandato a V. R. L' Indice stampato senza haverne fatta parola in questa Sacra Congregatione della Santa Romana et Universale Inquisitione, non si sono messi in esso Indice alcune particolari dichiarationi che concernono L' Indice di Papa Pio quarto di felice memoria, fatti da Papi successivi e dalla detta Sacra Congregatione dell' Inquisitione. Perilchè Sua Santità mi ha espressamente commandato ch' io debba scrivere a V. R. come fo con la presente, che non havendo publicato il detto Indice insino adesso, sopra seda a publicarlo insino à nuovo ordine; et havendolo publicato avverta, che Sua Santità non ha inteso, ne intende di derogar ne innovar per il detto nuovo Indice cosa alcuna de' decreti et regole contro di questa Santa Inquisitione, e della Beatitudine sua, ne de' suoi predecessori, ma che si osservino inviolabilmente; et se bene la quarta regola del detto Indice di Pio quarto concede che gli ordinarii et Inquisitori possano dar licenza di tener Biblie volgari, Evangelii et altri libbri della Sacra Scrittura [7], nondimeno dal tempo di Pio quarto istesso in qua questa Santa Inquisitione ha prohibiti tali libri, et la lettione ò ritentione loro, et così anco i Compendii, et Sommarii della Biblia, et Sacra Scrittura, ò sia del Testamento vecchio, ò nuovo in lingua volgar. Per questo V. R. non dia tale licenza, et se per avventura, l' ha data, la revochi.

Et perchè nel sopradetto Indice di Pio quarto, si concedeva la espurgatione de' libri del Thalmud [8], per questo nuovo Indice [9] [non

[7] Regula IV in Reusch, *Die Indices*, p. 248.

[8] The Index of Pius IV prohibited the Talmud (Thalmud Hebraeorum ejusque glossae, annotationes, interpretationes et expositiones omnes), permitting it, however, if the name was deleted (si tamen prodierint sine nomine Thalmud et sine injuriis et calumniis in religionem Christianam, tolerabuntur). H. Reusch, *Die Indices*, p. 279.

[9] A special separate section in the Index of Clement VIII provides

è] mente di Sua Santità di approbar tal cosa, ma che restino dannati questi et altri libri di Ebrei secondo la sua Bolla et Constitutione « contra libros et impia scripta Hebraeorum » [10]... che sia inviolabilmente osservata, non ostante altra carta in contrario.

Et se bene in questo Indice nuovo si trova per errore sospesa *La Republica* di Giovanni Bodino in sino che sia espurgata, nondimeno non si ha da espurgare altrimente; ma si debba tenere per condannata, come fu da Papa Gregorio XIIII in qualsiasi lingua e stampa, si come ancora la sua *Demonomania* è stata condannata dalla Santità del Nostro Signore [11]. Onde l'una et l'altra opera si hanno da tenere per dannate. Per le ... et le dette cose, et altri particolari se cinformaranno (?), et poi le ... darà avviso a V. R. Intanto la saluto, et alle sue orationi mi raccomando.

Di Roma, a XXVII di Aprile 1596.

Di V. R., come fratello

Il Cardinale di Santa Severina

6. (T. II f. 116)

Molto Reverendo Padre. Con l'occasione del novo Indice mandato di ordine di Nostro Signore dalla nostra Congregatione à publicarsi in tutto il Christianesimo son state mosse certe difficultà d'alcuni Vescovi et Inquisitori per l'osservatione d'alcune Constitutioni Pontificie et Decreti delli Ill.mi Sig.ri Cardinali della Congregatione del Santo Officio fatti per il passato in materia dei libri, perilchè volendo

---

for the absolute prohibition « De Thalmud et aliis libris Hebraeorum ». Reusch, *Die Indices*, p. 536. Cf. n. 12 below.

[10] Clement VIII's Bull had been issued on February 28, 1592 « Contra Haebreos, tenentes legentesque libros Thalmudi, & alios hactenus damnatos, aut blasphemias, & contumelias in Deum, & Sanctos continentes ». *Bullarum Privilegiorum ac Diplomatum Romanorum Pontificum amplissima collectio ... opera et studio Caroli Cocquelines* ... V[1] (Rome, 1751), 428-429. Cf. W. Popper, *The Censorship of Hebrew Books* (New York, 1899), esp. pp. 90 ff.

[11] The original intention of Clement VIII's Index was to prohibit Bodin's *Daemonomania* wholly and the *De Republica* and *Methodus* until such time as they could be properly expurgated. Reusch, *Die Indices*, p. 559. This conditional prohibition was made absolute for all of Bodin's works by a late addition to the Index. *Ibid.*, p. 537 and n. 12 below. The prohibition was later relaxed in the case of the *De methodus*. An expurgated version was authorized in the *Indicis Librorum Expurgandorum* issued at Rome in 1607 by the Master of the Sacred Palace, Giammaria Guanzelli of Brisighella. In the Bergamo, 1608 edition, the expurgations to be applied to the *Methodus* occur at pp. 499-501.

dar à tutti compita sodisfatione Nostro Signore ha ordinato alla nostra Congregatione dell' Indice, che si mandino l' incluse osservationi [12] et dichiarationi conforme alle quali si publichi et osservi l' Indice da tutti, et nella nova impressione che si farà in Roma il tutto se inserisca nell' Indice. Sichè V. P. con il suo santo zelo et prudentia attenda a far osservar l' Indice, et alla giornata occorrendo nove difficultà conforme alla Constitutione di Sua Santità posta nell' Indice, si darà piena sodisfatione dalla Congregatione nostra a tutti di quanto sarà ricercata in servitio di Nostro Signore Iddio, dal quale li prego il colmo della sua santa gratia.
Di Roma a li II di Maggio 1596.
Di V. P. M. R., come fratello

Il Cardinale di Verona

7. (T. II f. 138)

Reverendo Padre. Dopo che ho scritto a V. R. quel che occorreva intorno al nuovo Indice de' libbri prohibiti già stampato, la Santità di N. S. ha fatto rimediare a quel mancamento che vi era con una osservatione di due fogli sopra alcuni capi che si mandano qui alligati [13]. Et si hanno da porre ne' volumi già stampati dopo le Regole dell' Indice di Pio Quarto di felice memoria et avanti la nuova instruttione per quei che hanno da espurgare ò prohibire i libbri. Perchè per quei che si hanno da stampar di nuovo, si proveder à meglio ne' luoghi proprii. Et in questo modo, conforme alla mente di Sua Beatitudine, V. R. potrà fare publicare et osservare il predetto Indice. Intanto la saluto, et alle sue orationi mi raccomando.
Di Roma ai X di Maggio MDXCVI.
Di V. R., come fratello

Il Cardinale di Santa Severina

8. (T. II f. 139)

Reverendo Padre. Dopo che ho scritto a V. R. quel che occorreva intorno al nuovo Indice de' libbri prohibiti già stampato, la Santità

---

[12] The last-minute corrections and revisions to the Index sent out with the present letter provided for the revision of Rules 4 and 9 in the Index of Pius IV, and the total prohibition of the Talmud, the writings of Bodin and the Book of Magazor. They were included in subsequent editions of the Clementine Index as an « Observatio ». Reusch, *Die Indices*, pp. 536-537.

[13] See n. 12.

di N. S., quanto à i volumi già stampati e mandati di quà, ha fatto rimediare a quel mancamento che vi era con una osservatione di due fogli o carte sopra alcuni capi che si mandano quì alligati; et si hanno da porre ne' detti volumi già stampati dopo le Regole dell' Indice di Pio Quarto di felice memoria, et avanti la Instruttione fatta di nuovo per quei che hanno da espurgare, o prohibire i libbri. Et di più ha fatto mutare, o aggiugnere ancora alcune altre parole nella seconda pagina o faccia della detta Instruttione, et per questo ha fatto ristampare tutto il primo foglio di essa Instruttione, e lo pur si manda alligato con questa a ciò che si levi quel primo ch'era nell' Indice mandato, et in luogo di esso si ripona quest'altro ristampato di nuovo, et che poi il predetto Indice si possa far publicare et osservare in questa maniera [14]. Perch'quanto a quei che si hanno da stampar di nuovo si proyederà appresso ne luoghi proprii. Con che la saluto, et alle sue orationi mi raccomando.

Di Roma, a XII di Maggio MDXCVI.

Di V. R., come fratello

Il Cardinale di Santa Severina

9. (T. II f. 117)

Molto Reverendo Padre come fratello. Hanno preso grande ammiratione questi Ill.mi SS. miei Colleghi che sia stampato in Firenze doppo la publicatione dell' Indice, la *Diffesa di Silvestro Facio intorno lo sputo di sangue* [15], senza osservarsi quello che ordina l' Indice nel S. V. de librorum impressione [16], non si specificando la licentia de' superiori, che hanno permesso il libro, come altre volte in Firenze solevano fare gl' Inquisitori, et non apparendo l'approvatione di chi habbi rivisto quel libretto, con osservare quanto nel S 2 [17] si comanda.

Et se tutte queste cose da N. S. ordinate nel' Indice si fussero osservate, non haverebbe causato qualche disordine questo libretto. Et da qui avanti sarete più cauto in dar' le licentie, e deputare li cor-

---

[14] These late revisions are explained in J. Hilgers, *Der Index*, pp. 536-538.

[15] S. De Renzi, *Storia della medicina in Italia*, III (Naples, 1845), 577. Cf. G. Veneroso, *Risposta alla querela sotto nome di Difesa intorno allo sputo di sangue* (Ferrara, 1597).

[16] The responsibility of Bishop and Inquisitor in the proper licensing of a book for the press is the subject of paragraph 5 under the rubric « De impressione librorum » in the *Instructio* introduced in the Clementine Index. Reusch, *Die Indices*, p. 535.

[17] Paragraph 2 under the rubric « De impressione librorum » of the *Instructio*. Reusch, *Die Indices*, p. 534.

rettori de libri, con esprimere sempre la licentia del' Ordinario del' Inquisitione, e la fede del' Revisore, uno o più che siano stati, conservandosi l'essemplare authentico nel'Archivio da tutti sottoscritto. Con che fine mi raccomando alle sue orationi.
Di Roma li 27 di Gennaio 1597.
Di V. P. M. R., come fratello

Il Cardinale (illegible)

10. (T. II f. 118)

Molto Reverendo Padre come fratello. Hanno distribuito questi Ill.mi SS. miei Colleghi in varie Religioni et Università gran quantità di libri da espurgare per poter quantoprima publicare L' Indice Espurgatorio[18] tanto universalmente desiderato. Et essendo una delle principali Inquisitioni la vostra, aspettano haver notitia di molti libri dannati e sospesi, che per prima fussero in cotesta Inquisitione, overo nel'essecutione del' Indice si fussero scoperti, o alla giornata se n' havesse cognitione, con mandare anco nota delle spurgationi altre volte fatte che costì si trovano, et di quelle che attualmente si van' facendo conforme al novo Indice. Con che fine alle vostre orationi mi raccomando.
Di Roma li 10 di Marzo 1597.
Di V. P. M. R., come fratello

Il Cardinale di Verona

11. (T. II f. 119)

Molto Reverendo Padre. Desiderano questi miei Ill.mi Sig.ri della Congregatione dell' Indice, che con diligentia attenda all'esecutione di quello, con dare aviso dell'espurgatione dei libri, qual con l'aiuto

---

[18] The Roman church finally brought out one volume of this Index: *Indicis Librorum Expurgandorum in studiosorum gratiam confecti. Tomus primus in quo quinquaginta auctorum libri prae caeteris desiderati emendantur. Per Fr. Jo. Mariam Brasichellen. Sacri Palatii Apostolici Magistrum in unum corpus redactus, et publicae commoditati aeditus* (Rome, 1607). It was reprinted at Bergamo the following year, twice in the eighteenth and once in the nineteenth century. Nothing, beyond the first volume, was published. Bodin, as we have seen (n. 11), was among the expurgated authors. Cf. H. Reusch, *Der Index der verbotenen Bücher*, I, 549-559. The Spanish church was more successful in issuing Indices with expurgations. See, for example, *Tres Indices Expurgatorios de la Inquisición Española en el Siglo XVI* (Madrid, 1952).

di varii Consultori va facendo, mandandone copia autentica, et nota dei libri sospetti che alla giornata va scoprendo, con essar molto vigilante nei libri che si stampano, et avisar tutte le dificultà che occorrono. Con che fine alle vostre orationi mi raccomando.
Di Roma il dì 22 di febbraio 1598.
Di V. P. M. R., amorevole

Il Cardinale di Verona

12. (T. II f. 120)

Reverendo Padre. Desiderano questi miei Ill.mi Sig.ri della Congregatione dell' Indice che mandi nota de' libri prohibiti e sospesi che si ritrovano nell' Offitio et appresso li Vicarii in diversi luoghi della sua giurisdittione, e che seguiti nel censurare libri con l'aiuto de' varii Consultori, con mandar copia autentica conforme all' Indice delle Censure. Con che fine alle sue orationi mi raccomando.
Di Roma ai 6 d'Agosto 1599.
Di V. R., amorevole

Il Cardinale di Terranova

13. (T. II f. 121)

Reverendo Padre. Quantoprima mandarete nota alfabetica de tutti libri sospesi, ò prohibiti, che si ritrovano nella vostra Inquisitione, overo appresso librari, et anco di tutti quelli che si ritrovaranno appresso tutti li vostri Vicarii in altre città, e quanto al censurar libri si darà rimedio per effettuar quanto si desidera. Con che fine alle vostre orationi mi raccomando.
Di Roma a 22 di Settembre 1599.
Di V. R., amorevole

Il Cardinale di Terranova

14. (T. II f. 122)

Reverendo Padre. Aspettano questi miei Ill.mi SS.ri la nota de' libri prohibiti, ò sospesi, che si trovano appresso li suoi Vicarii, et anco copia delle censure, che si ritrova, con la nota delle licenze, che ha dato di legger libri, et attenda a far eseguir L' Indice come si conviene, et alle sue orationi mi raccomando.
Di Roma li 3 di Dicembre 1599.
Di V. R., amorevole

Il Cardinale di Verona

15. (T. II f. 123)

Reverendo Padre. Sapendo quanto sia il suo valore, et quanto habbi zelo dell' servitio d' Iddio, non mi stenderò in ricordarli, che attenda all'essecutione dell' Indice, havendo particolar cura nella stampa, e scoprendo alla giornata libri pernitiosi, ne dia aviso, confidando che sarà vigilante, e darà conto del tutto a questi miei Ill.mi SS.ri della Congregatione dell' Indice, a quali sempre sarà grato ogni suo aviso, et hauran gusto di veder alcuna censura de' libri sospesi. Et capitando costì un libro intitolato, *Opere succisive seu meditationes historicae Philippi Camerarii*, stampato in Norimberga [19], sappiate che per esser pernitioso, è stato dannato. Con che fine alle sue orationi mi raccomando. Di Roma, li II di luglio 1600.
Di V. R., amorevole

Il Cardinale di Verona

16. (T. II f. 149)

Reverendo Padre. È venuto fuora un libro in ottavo intitolato *Rerum memorabilium iam olim deperditarum et contra recens, atque ingeniose inventarum libri duo a Guidone Pancirolo Juris Consulto clarissimo italice primum conscripti, nec unquam hactenus editi, nunc vero, et latinitate donati, et notis quamplurimis ex Jurisconsultis, historicis, poetis, et Philologis illustrati per Henricum Salmuth*, Ambergae typis Forsterianis MDIC [20]. Et perchè si è osservato che nelle note del detto Henrico si contengono molte heresie et errori gravissimi, sebene Guido Pancirolo autore del libro fu cattolico, come è il testo del libro, questi miei Ill.mi et R.mi Sig.ri Cardinali Generali Inquisitori Colleghi hanno prohibite le note fatte dal sopradetto Henrico Heretico, con ordine che per l'avvenire non si possano tenere, ne leggere, e hanno ordinato che Vostra Reverentia publichi et notifichi la prohibitione delle sudette note non solamente in cotesta città, ma anco la faccia publicare negli altri luoghi de' suoi Vicarii in modo tale che per la prohibitione non venga notato il Pancirolo, persona Cattolica, ma solamente le note del sudetto Henrico Salmuth heretico [21]. Et non comporti che per l'avvenire alcuno ardisca

---

[19] See Introduction, pp. 582 ff.

[20] Guido Panciroli (b. Reggio Emilia, 1523-d. Padua or Venice, 1599) was a distinguished jurist who taught successively at Bologna, Padua and Turin. The *Rerum Memorabilium*, an encyclopedia of technology from antiquity to modern times, was first condemned by an edict issued at Rome by the *Maestro del Sacro Palazzo* on 2 May 1601. J. Hilgers, *Der Index*, p. 418.

[21] Heinrich Salmuth, the translator and editor, was a jurist and syndic of Amberg. He was the son of the celebrated Lutheran theologian of the

di tenere et leggere il libro con le sudette note, ma usi in ciò ogni diligenza necessaria. Ne questa essendo per altro la saluto, et il Signore la conservi nella sua Santa gratia.
Di Roma a IX di Maggio M.DCI.
Di V. R., come fratello

Il Cardinale di Santa Severina

(on the verso, the subscriptions of Florentine booksellers)
Noi Filippo Giunti habbiamo ricevuto la sopra detta intimatione dal Molto R.do P. Inquisitore di Fiorenza questo dì 16 di Maggio 1601.
Io Giovanni ... ho ricevuto la detta intimatione per Cosimo Giunti dal Molto R.do P. Inquisitore di Fiorenza questo dì 16 di Maggio 1601.
Io Salvestro di Domenico Magliani ho ricevuto la detta Intimatione dal Molto R.do P. Inquisitore e prometto osservarla. E in fede ho scritto di mia propria mano questo dì 16 Maggio 1601.
Io Filippo di Lionardo Mondicelli libraro ho ricevuto la detta intimatione dal Molto R.do P. Inquisitore di Fiorenza questo dì 16 di Maggio 1601.
Io Bartolomeo Ruoti libraro ho ricevuto la detta Intimatione dal Molto R.do P. Inquisitore e prometto osservarla, e in fede ho scritto il dì sopradetto.
E io Girolamo di Jacopo Franceschi [h]o ricevuto la presente intimatione questo 16 sopradetto di propria mano.
Io Bartolomeo ... [h]o ricevuto dal R.do P. Inquisitore la sopradetta intimatione questo dì sopradetto.
Io Alessandro di Zanobi Camerini libraro ho ricevuto la detta intimazione questo dì sopradetto.
Io Bartolomeo Francesco ho ricevuto dal R.do P. Inquisitore la sopradetta intimatione questo dì sopradetto.
Io Piero di Ventura Bassini ho riscevuto la medesima intimatione.

17. (T. II f. 150)

Reverendo Padre. Da questa Sacra Congregatione della Inquisitione è stato prohibito il libro intitolato *Ecloga Oxonio Cantabrigensis distributa*

---

same name. C. G. Jöcher, *Allgemeines Gelehrtenlexicon*, IV (Leipzig, 1751), col. 70. Salmuth's commentary takes up a much larger part of the book than Panciroli's text. It would have been found objectionable by the Roman Inquisitors for numerous complimentary references to such heretics and condemned authors as Melanchthon, Bodin, Joachim and Philipp Camerarius; and for such a statement as Melanchthon's that printing could be considered a divine gift, coming as it did at a time «ut renascentis

in libros duos, quorum prior continet catalogum confusum librorum manuscriptorum in illustrissimis bibliothecis florentissimarum Academiarum Oxoni et Cantabrig., posterior catalogum eorundem distinctum et dispositum in quatuor facultates. Omnia haec opera et studio T. J. novi Collegii in Academia Oxoniensi socii et utriusque Academiae in artibus magistri. Londini impensis Georg. Bishop et Jo. Narson [i. e. Norton], 1600 [22]. Et in subscriptione epistolae legitur nomen auctoris per extensum, Thomas James. Però ne do avviso a V. R. a fine ch'ella faccia publicare la prohibitione con ordinare ai librari et à ciascuno che haverà il detto libro che lo debbano consegnare sotto quelle pene che a lei pareranno convenienti. Et non essendo la presente per altro, stia sana et il Signore la conservi nella sua Santa Gratia.

Di Roma a gli VIII di Giugno MDCI.

Di V. R., come fratello

Il Cardinale di Santa Severina

Verso: Signatures of booksellers as above.

18. (T. II f. 151)

Reverendo Padre. Essendo venuto a notitia della Santità di N. S. che in un libro del Padre Tomaso Saiglio Gesuita, intitolato *Thesaurus Litaniarum* [23], si contengono 365 sorti di litanie, et che in un'altro

---

in Ecclesia sincerioris doctrinae ». (p. 591). I have used the second edition (Amberg, 1608).

[22] The condemnation of the *Ecloga* was contained in the Edict published at Rome on June 1, 1601. J. Hilgers, *Der Index*, p. 418. Thomas James (1573?-1629) was the first librarian of the Bodleian library and the present work is simply a catalogue of books and manuscripts at Oxford and Cambridge. One wonders whether the Inquisitors knew that James earlier had published a translation into English of *La Cantica di Salomò* by the heretic Antonio Brucioli (*Commentary upon the Canticle of Canticles* [London, 1598]: S. T. C. 3928). James went on to compose several anti-Catholic books, including an edition of the Roman Index: *Index Generalis Librorum Prohibitorum a Pontificiis, una cum editionibus expurgatis vel expurgandis ... in usum Bibliothecae Bodleianae ... designatus per Tho. Iames ...* (Oxford, 1627). It is not listed in G. Bonnant, « Les Index Prohibitifs et Expurgatoires contrefaits par des protestants au XVIe et au XVIIe siècle », *Bibliothèque d'humanisme et Renaissance*, 31 (1969), 611-640. Cf. *Dictionary of National Biography*, X, 658-660.

[23] The writings of the Belgian Jesuit, Thomas Sailly (b. 1558), are listed in C. Sommervogel, *Bibliothèque de la Compagnie de Jésus ... nouvelle édition*, VII (Brussels, Paris, 1896), coll. 403-407. The *Thesaurus Litaniarum ac Ora-*

libro intitolato *Thesaurus Sacrarum pretium sive litaniae variae*[24], come in altri libretti si contengono diversi modi di litanie, la Santità Sua ha sospesi per hora i sudetti libri, & l'uso delle sopradette litanie, et solo ha eccettuate le ordinarie che sono nel Messale et nel Breviario, et le litanie in honore della Madonna Santissima di Loreto, volendo Sua Beatitudine appresso fare quella deliberatione, et risolutione, che conviene sopra la diversità et numero delle sudette litanie[25]. Però V. R. non manchi di notificare la sospensione a tutti i librari, Vicarii Episcopali, et suoi particolari ne' luoghi sottoposti alla sua giurisdittione, et a tutti quelli che sarà di bisogno, et faccia in maniera che si osservi la mente et volontà di Sua Beatitudine, dando avviso di quanto haverà poi esseguito. Ne questa essendo per altro, stia sana, et il Signore la conservi nella Sua Santa gratia.
Di Roma a XVI di Giugno MDCI.
Di V. R., come fratello

Il Cardinale di Santa Severina

Verso: Signatures of booksellers.

19. (T. II f. 152)

Reverendo Padre. La Santità di N. S. ha prohibito il trattato del Dottor Pietro Antonio Pietra Piacentino intitolato *De iure quaesito per Principem non tollendo, seu de potestate Principis*, Venetiis apud Damianum

---

tionum Sacer. Cum suis adversus Sectarios Apologiis Opera P. Thomae Sailly Presbyteri Societatis Jesu editus (Brussels, 1598) is no. 7 in his catalogue. Sommervogel notes: « cet ouvrage a été mis à l' Index, le 7 août 1603, à cause de certaines litanies non approuvées ». Cf. A. de Backer, *Bibliothèque des écrivains de la Compagnie de Jesus. Supplement*, III (Louvain, Lyons, 1876), coll. 469-472, esp. 470: « ... c'est qu'on a jugé à propos de s'en tenir aux litanies anciennes, qui se trouvent dans le Bréviaire, et autres livres qui servent à l'office de l' Eglise ». In his *Thesaurus Precum et Exercitiorum Spiritualium* (Antwerp, 1609), p. [4] of preface, Sailly explains that the objectionable litanies in the earlier version had been inserted without his knowledge.

[24] It is unlikely that this is also by Sailly. Neither Backer nor Sommervogel attribute to him a work with this title. And the decree issued at Rome, 7 August 1603, prohibiting the *Thesaurus* lists it as an anonymous writing. This and similar decrees are published as an appendix to the *Index Librorum Prohibitorum Alexandri VII ... iussu editus* (Rome, 1664), p. 295.

[25] Clement VIII's *Breve*, « Cum in Ecclesia », introducing the revised Roman Breviary was issued on 10 May, 1602. J. Hilgers, *Die Bücherverbote in Papstbriefen* (Freiburg i. Br., 1907), p. 20.

Zenarum 1599 [26] perchè in esso si contengono espressamente molte propositioni hereticali. Però lo fo sapere a V. R. à ciò che ella publichi Editto sopra la prohibitione di tal libro, con farsi consegnare da librari, et anco dalle persone particolari li volumi che ne havessero appresso di se, con prohibire espressamente, che per l'avvenire niuno possa tenere, ne leggere il detto libro sotto le pene statuite contra quelli che tengono libri prohibiti. Onde ella alla ricevuta di questa esseguisca il presente ordine ne' luoghi soggetti alla sua giurisdittione, et lo notifichi dove, et à chi sarà di bisogno. Et dia avviso della essecutione. Intanto la saluto, et alle sue orationi mi raccomando.
Di Roma a VII di Luglio MDCI.
Di V. R., come fratello

Il Cardinale di Santa Severina

Verso: Signatures of booksellers [27].

20. (T. II f. 153)

Reverendo Padre. Havendo la Santità di N. S. fatto un Decreto da osservarsi in materia delle Litanie [28], ne mando a V. R. l'alligata copia in stampa, acciochè ella lo faccia publicare in cotesta città, & per maggiore commodità ne faccia stampare ancora alcuni essemplari conformi, et gli distribuisca tra gli Ordinarii, et Preti delle Chiese

---

[26] A portion of an identical letter, sent to the Inquisitor of Modena, is published by Rotondò, « Nuovi documenti », p. 173. According to L. Cerri (*Memorie per la storia letteraria di Piacenza in continuazione al Poggiali* [Piacenza, 1895], pp. 176 f.), Pietra was compelled to appear personally before the Roman Inquisition to answer charges arising from his book, which was burned in his presence. Due to his advanced age (in 1599 he would have been 87 years old according to Cerri) he was condemned only to salutary penances. It is impossible, without having seen a copy of Pietra's treatise, to identify the « propositioni hereticali » which led to its condemnation. Cerri merely informs us that Pietra had been addressing himself to the problem of the relationship of a prince to the private property of his subjects. For the printer, Damiano Zenaro, this was not the first time that one of his books had been confiscated and burned. Cf. G. Pesenti, « Libri censurati a Venezia nei secoli XVI-XVII », *La Bibliofilia*, 58 (1956), 27.

[27] One of the Florentine booksellers subscribed to the notification of prohibition with these words: « Io Cosimo Giunti ho ricevuto la retroscritta notificatione sotto pena del Arbitrio questo dì detto (11 July, 1601). In botega ce ne uno quale si è consegniato al Padre Inquisitore ».

[28] Cf. H. Reusch, *Der Index der verbotenen Bücher*, II, 73.

Cathedrali Collegiate et Parochiali, et tra i Conventi, Monasterii di Regolari, et Oratorii di Compagnie, et altri a chi sarà bisogno, a ciò che ne habbiano notitia, et osservino quanto è mente et ordine di Sua Beatitudine. Et non essendo la presente per altro, la saluto et alle sue orationi mi raccomando.
Di Roma a XX di Ottobre MDCI.
Di V. R., come fratello

Il Cardinale di Santa Severina

21. (T. II f. 155)

Reverendo Padre. Si è inteso che alcuni Ginevrini, ò de' paesi convicini hanno portato in Italia Bibbie stampate in Ginevra, che contengono molte parole, et note d' heretici, et le hanno distribuite fra i librari et persone particolari, ancorchè in esse Bibbie falsamente sia notato che siano stampate in Lione [29]. E potendo di ciò succedere gravissimi danni et pregiuditii alla Santa fede Cattolica, la Santità di N. S. ha ordinato che V. R. usi ogni essatta et possibil diligenza per ritrovare se fin hora siano state portate et distribuite simili Bibbie costì et da chi; et che per l'avvenire ella invigili, come ricerca la gravità del fatto, et dia in ciò gli ordini necessarii acciochè non vi siano portati tali libri, et trovando che ve ne siano proceda contro i transgressori con ogni rigore et secondo sarà di giustitia, confidandosi ch'ella per la parte sua non mancarà di esseguire quanto sarà di bisogno per corrispondere con gli effetti alla mente et ordine espresso da Sua Beatitudine. Ne questa essendo per altro, saluto V. R. et alle sue orationi mi raccomando.
Di Roma a XXIII di Febraro MDCII.
Di V. R., come fratello

Il Cardinale di Santa Severina

---

[29] The forgery of Lyons on the title-pages of books actually printed in Geneva was a practice which infuriated many French printers and resulted in a number of royal proclamations intended to check this illicit activity. By the substitution of imprints, Geneva's printers obviously hoped to obtain a freer circulation for their merchandise in Catholic Europe. Antoine Blanc, formerly of Lyons, who was received as *Bourgeois* of Geneva in 1585, frequently employed this device, as when, for example, he printed the *Catalogus Testium Veritatis, qui ante nostram aetatem Pontifici Romano atque papismi erroribus reclamarunt* ... MDXCVII Ex typographia Antonii Candidi, Lugdun. See, on this whole subject, J. Baudrier, *Bibliographie Lyonnaise*, XII (Lyons, Paris, 1921), 468-500.

22. (T. II f. 124)

Molto Reverendo Padre. Aspettano questi miei Ill.mi Sig.ri haver relatione del progresso che si è fatto in osservanza dell' Indice con l'aiuto del Ordinario et di varii Consultori circa la censura de' libri. Et sia vigilante circa la stampa de libri in non admettere cosa, se ben frivola, che sia contro le Regole dell' Indice, et habbi particolar cura in ciò alle cose di menantarie. Con che fine alle sue orationi mi raccomando.

Di Roma a dì 23 di Marzo 1602.

Di V. R., amorevolmente

Il Cardinale di Verona

23. (T. II f. 125)

Molto Reverendo Padre. Restano questi miei Ill.mi Sig.ri della Congregatione dell' Indice molto maravigliati in veder la negligentia, che si usa circa le stampe, e tanto maggiore quanto che più volte è stato scritto che si usi ogni diligenza et si stia vigilante, et con tutto ciò è comparso un *Giardino de Madrigali* stampato in Rimini di Mauritio Moro [30], quale si è prohibito di espresso ordine di N. S. per contenere molte obscenità, et una *Praxi Episcopale* di Monsignore Thomasso Zerola [31], Vescovo di Minori, stampata in Venetia, nella quale essendo alcuni gravi errori, e perciò si prohibisce, che non si venda, ò legga, sinchè non sia publicata la Censura. Però V. R. non mancarà di publicare la prohibitione dell'uno, e dell'altro libro, e con maggior di-

---

[30] Edict of condemnation issued in Rome, 14 December, 1602. J. Hilgers, *Der Index*, p. 418. The *Catalogue* of printed books in the British Museum (vol. 164, col. 646) lists *I tre giardini de' Madrigali del Costante, Academico Cospirante, M. Moro vinetiano* (Venice, 1602). That Moro was in sacred orders results from the title of another book, *Rappresentatione del figliuolo prodigo del Rev. P. D. Mauritio Moro, novamente dal detto in ottava rima composta* (Venice, 1585). Only a passing reference to Moro in L. Ughi, *Dizionario storico degli uomini illustri ferraresi*, II (Ferrara, 1804), 80.

[31] The *Praxi Episcopale* was condemned by Edict issued on 14 December, 1602. J. Hilgers, *Der Index*, p. 418. The two parts which comprise the work were originally issued separately, 1595 and 1598, and subsequently as one work in 1599 and 1602. Cf. G. Sbaraglia, *Supplementum et castigatio ad scriptores trium ordinum S. Francisci, A. Waddingo aliisve descriptos* ... III (Rome, 1936), 140. Zerola served as Bishop of Minori from 1597 until his death in 1603. P. B. Gams, *Series episcoporum ecclesiae Catholicae*, 2nd ed., (Leipzig, 1931), p. 898.

ligenza invigilare circa la stampa, e' libri novi, et che vengono di fora, con dare aviso di quanto alla giornata andrà scoprendo di errore ne i libri. Con che fine alle sue orationi mi raccomando.
Di Roma a 20 di Dicembre 1602.
Di V. P. M. R., amorevole

Il Cardinale di Terranova [32]

24. (T. I f. 157)

Reverendo Padre. In risposta della lettera di V. R. delli 4 di Decembre le dico, che questi Ill.mi e R.mi Sig.ri Cardinali miei Colleghi non hanno voluto conceder licenza al Regente dell'Accademia de' Spensierati [33] di tenere e leggere l'opere del Macchiavello, Boccaccio e Castelvetro ad effetto di correggerle, e farle ristampare di nuovo ...
Di Roma li 12 di fabraro 1605.

Il Cardinale Borghese

25. (T. II f. 140)

Reverendo Padre. Questi Ill.mi et R.mi Sig.ri Cardinali Generali Inquisitori miei Colleghi stimando necessaria ogni diligenza che si

---

[32] Note added at foot of page: « Alli 3 di Gennaio 1603 si pubblicorno gli editti della prohibitione delli 2 sopradetti libri per la città, et per lo stato alli Vicarii del Santo Offitio ».

[33] This is certainly one of the more obscure academies in Florence. Its existence in not recorded in E. Cochrane, *Tradition and Enlightenment in the Tuscan Academies* (Chicago, 1961) or by G. Prezziner, *Storia del pubblico Studio e delle società scientifiche, e letterarie di Firenze*, 2 vols., (Florence, 1810). M. Maylender, *Storia delle Accademie d'Italia*, V (Bologna, 1930), 237-238 cites a document « I Capitoli riformati degli Accademici Spensierati col parere dell'Accademia delli Conservadori, l'anno 1607 », preserved in the Biblioteca Nazionale, Florence (Cod. Cl. VI, n. 163); and he furnishes the names of three Spensierati: the poet Pier Girolamo Gentile (1563-1640), the jurist Fabbrizio Mattei of Forlì and P. A. Canonieri. E. Benvenuti publishes « Un curioso manifesto satira degli Accademici Spensierati », *Rivista delle biblioteche e degli archivi*, 22 (1911), 15-17 and describes the academy as « il prodotto più genuino di quello scetticismo e di quell'umorismo che nacque, si puo dire, con gli spiriti bizzarri fiorentini », p. 15). One wonders what part, if any, was played by Pietro Andrea Canonieri, a leading exponent of « Tacitism » and the *Ragion di Stato*, in the Spensierati's proposal to prepare an expurgated edition of Machiavelli's writings. *Tacitismo* has been defined succinctly as « uno sforzo di controriformizzare il pensiero del Machiavelli ». G. Toffanin, *Machiavelli e il Tacitismo* (Padua, 1921), p. 6.

possa fare in materia delle stampe, per quel che tutto dì si prova per esperienza, mi hanno commesso, ch' io avvisi V. R. a dovere stare vigilante, et usare ogni diligenza possibile per se stessa, et per mezzo di persone dotte, zelanti, et pie nel rivedere li libri, et altre operette, o historiette, che alla giornata si stampano costì, acciochè non contengano cose prohibite conforme alle Regole dell' Indice, nè conceda licenza di stamparsi, che prima non siano reviste con ogni accuratezza. Non manchi ella dunque di sodisfare in ciò al debito suo, et notifichi la presente a' suoi Officiali ne' luoghi dove si stampa, facendo anco sopra tutto conservare gli originali, che si approvano, et danno alla stampa acciochè si veda se in essi viene commessa alteratione alcuna, et sempre apparisca da chi siano stati revisti, et approvati i libri, et opere, che si stampano. In questa maniera con l'osservanza inviolabile del presente ordine verrà à provedere al beneficio publico, et ella non potrà essere notata di trascuraggine ò negligenza, dove al contrario, oltra la mala sodisfattione potrebbe ancora dar occasione di farsene risentimento con suo poco honore. Et il Signore la conservi.
Di Roma, a XXIX di Aprile MDCV.
Di V. R., come fratello

Il Cardinale Borghese

26. (T. II f. 165)

Reverendo Padre. Sebene altre volte è stato ordinato, et prohibito a gl' Inquisitori che non diano licenze di tenere et leggere libri prohibiti, tuttavia alcuno Inquisitore non ostante tal prohibitione s' è ingerito in dar tal licenze. Però questi Ill.mi SS.ri Cardinali miei Colleghi hanno ordinato che di nuovo si faccia sapere à ciascuno Inquisitore che per l'avenire non ardisca in modo alcuno dar licenza à qualsivoglia persona di tenere et leggere libri prohibiti. Il che serve a V. R. acciochè a suo tempo ella così osservi et faccia osservare da suoi Vicarii, registrando la presente ne' libri di cotesta Inquisitione per informatione de soccessore. Et stia sana.
Di Roma li 15 di Aprile 1606.
Di V. R., come fratello

Il Cardinale Arigoni

27. (T. II f. 141)

Reverendo Padre. Mando a V. R. un'essemplare dell' Editto fatto da questa Sacra Congregatione in materia de' libri e scritture, si stam-

pate, come manoscritte sopra l' interdetto et potestà del Papa [34], acciò lo faccia publicare in latino et volgare in tutti li luoghi che conoscerà necessarii della sua giurisdittione potendoli far ristampare anco bisognando. E stia sano.
Di Roma li 30 di Giugno 1606.
Di V. R., come fratello

Il Cardinale Arigoni

28. (T. II f. 142)

Reverendo Padre. Sebene per l' Editto publicato a' mesi passati [35] sono prohibiti li libri e trattati circa le censure et interdetto di N. S. con la Republica di Venetia, ne' quali si contengono propositioni scandalose, scismatiche, erronee, et heretiche respettive, con tutto ciò sono stati prohibiti alcuni altri libri venuti a luce, ò che si publicaranno per l'avenire sopra l' istessa materia, purchè meritano le sopradette note e censure come vedrà dall'allegato Editto [36] V. R., acciò lo faccia publicare in cotesta città, et ove conoscerà essere di bisogno ne' luoghi della sua giurisdittione. E stia sana.
Da Roma li 23 di Settembre 1606.
Di V. R., come fratello

Il Cardinale Arigoni

---

[34] The edict against Venice was issued on 27 June. Its contents are summarized in a second edict of 20 September (« fuerint expresse prohibiti nonnulli libelli, & scripturae typis mandatae, & evulgatae, occasione censurarum, & interdicti S. D. N. in Rempublicam Venetam ») published as an appendix to the Index of Alexander VII, p. 299. (Cited at n. 24 above). Rotondò, « Nuovi documenti », p. 183 indicates the existence of two copies of the rare 27 June edict in the Modena archive.

[35] The edict of 27 June.

[36] The edict of 20 September (see n. 34 above) prohibited books hostile to the papacy and siding with Venice which had appeared since the publication of the 27 June edict.

CHARLES G. NAUERT, JR.

PETER OF RAVENNA AND THE «OBSCURE MEN» OF COLOGNE: A CASE OF PRE-REFORMATION CONTROVERSY*

* The author wishes to express his appreciation to the American Philosophical Society of Philadelphia and the Research Council of the University of Missouri for grants which supported the research on the general study of which this article is part.

The catastrophic breakdown of the medieval church during the years after 1517 occurred amidst storms of angry polemic and bloody persecution that make the sixteenth century one of the most conflict-ridden periods in human history. The generous and optimistic hopes of reforming humanists like Erasmus and More ended in cruel disappointment; and that great boon to the spread of enlightenment, the art of printing, became the medium by which pamphleteers and polemicists made the sixteenth century the most ideologically divided and intellectually turbulent, perhaps, until our own [1]. But the outpouring of tracts and the angry exchanges by controversialists which marked the age of the Reformation, like most other things in human history, had their precursors. The appearance of a prophetic figure like Martin Luther profoundly modified and immeasurably deepened the current of religious controversy. Nevertheless, there was already a heritage of issues, controversial habits, and perhaps even party alignments which formed a background for the new spiritual upheaval. Older ways of conducting religious disputes, and pre-Reformation ways of thinking about reform of church and society, persisted for a generation at least. New issues and new lines of division became evident only slowly; and for a long time, many men experienced difficulty in comprehending just what these new issues and divisions were, or even that they were new.

Thus the conflicts that divided men before Luther's spectacular appearance, and the ways in which men conducted themselves as controversialists, helped to shape the way in which men understood — or misunderstood — the spiritual crisis of the Reformation. This relationship is obvious enough, taken as an abstract proposition. And at least one of the pre-Reformation conflicts, that between the German humanist Johann

---

[1] Lucien Febvre and Henri-Jean Martin, *L'apparition du livre* (Paris, 1958), pp. 432-443.

Reuchlin and the theological faculty of the University of Cologne, has long been regarded as a prelude to the Lutheran Reformation, particularly because of the way in which the most striking controversial publication of the affair, the *Epistolae virorum obscurorum*, appealed from constituted authority to general public opinion and also launched destructive attacks that passed far beyond the original issues and tended to undermine respect for the old ecclesiastical institution as a whole. Yet these conflicts as a general phenomenon have been of secondary or incidental interest to modern scholarship; and such fundamental questions as the causes and nature of religious and ecclesiastical disputes, the methods used to conduct them, and the alliances and enmities which they fostered, have hardly been asked, much less answered.

The result of this neglect is that important aspects of the religious and intellectual situation on the eve of the Reformation are not well understood, and that many current generalizations about the relationships between humanists and scholastics, or between both of these groups and the Lutheran movement, are open to question. For example, the humanists themselves, especially after the outbreak of the Reuchlin affair, tended to interpret the conflicts in which they were involved as simple encounters between humanistic enlightenment and scholastic obscurantism; and though modern scholarship has tended to undermine this view, it still persists. The real situation in the intellectual world of the early sixteenth century was much more complex. Humanists and scholastics did not always behave like mortal enemies. Even in the most conservative centers, such as Cologne, there were partisans of the newer intellectual currents [2]; and when conflicts did break out, people sometimes divided in ways that are hardly consonant with the notion of unmitigated hostility between a camp of entrenched, unbending conservatives and a rival camp of bold, innovative humanistic challengers. Thus a fresh look at these literary (and sometimes judicial) contests should contribute significantly to a better

---

[2] Hermann Keussen, *Die alte Universität Köln: Grundzüge ihrer Verfassung und Geschichte* (Veröffentlichung des kölnischen Geschichtsvereins, 10) (Cologne, 1934), p. 195; Charles G. Nauert, Jr., *Agrippa and the Crisis of Renaissance Thought* (Urbana, Illinois, 1965), pp. 10-14, 69.

understanding of the age, even though the controversies themselves, regarded as isolated events, may often seem of minor importance.

As a particular case of pre-Reformation conflict, the encounter between the Italian law professor Peter of Ravenna [3] and the theological faculty (the « obscure men » of the Reuchlin case) of the University of Cologne has several points of special interest. It illustrates an apparent disharmony between the views of a leading Italian scholar and the dominant figures at Germany's most influential and most conservative university. It seems on first sight to pit spokesmen for the new intellectual force of humanism (Peter himself, Hermann von dem Busche, and Ortwin Gratius) against the dominant figures of scholastic conservatism at Cologne (Gerardus Zerbolt van Zutphen and Jacob von Hochstraten). And thus it obviously constitutes a prelude to the more famous incident that set the Cologne theologians at odds with Johann Reuchlin and his defenders among the German humanists. The parallel was quickly seen by contemporaries like the authors of the *Epistolae obscurorum virorum* [4] and Agrippa von Nettesheim [5]. Modern scholarship has also noted the parallel [6]. Even the cast of characters is strikingly similar, though one, Ortwin Gratius, has changed sides.

---

[3] Peter was probably born about 1448 and at an early age won great fame for his prodigious memory. His treatise on the art of memory, the *Phoenix*, has been studied recently by Paolo Rossi, *Clavis universalis: Arti mnemoniche e logica combinatoria da Lullo a Leibniz* (Milan, 1960), pp. 27-30, and Frances A. Yates, *The Art of Memory* (London, 1966), pp. 112-114, and *passim*. The most extensive modern biographical studies are by Eisenhart, « Petrus Ravennas », *Allgemeine deutsche Biographie*, XXV, 529-539; by R. Chabanne, « Pierre Ravennas », in Raoul Naz, ed., *Dictionnaire de droit canonique*, VI, col. 1484-1497; and by Heinrich Heidenheimer, « Petrus Ravennas in Mainz und sein Kampf mit den Kölner Dunkelmännern », *Westdeutsche Zeitschrift für Geschichte und Kunst*, XVI (1897), 223-256. Peter's family name is usually given as Tommai, but this name is not certain.

[4] Second series, no. 20 and 50, in Eduardus Böcking, ed., *Ulrichi Hutteni ... Operum supplementum* (2 vols.; Leipzig, 1864-1870), I, 220, 265. Henceforth cited as Böcking, *Supplementum*.

[5] Agrippa, *De beatissimae Annae monogamia, ac unico puerperio...* (N. p., 1534), fols. M5 r-M6 v. Reuchlin himself likened his case to the Cologne theologians' persecution of Peter of Ravenna and other jurists in letters of 31 August 1513 to Jacques Lefèvre d'Étaples and 1 November 1518 to Cardinal Achille de Grassi, both cited by Heidenheimer, pp. 251-252.

[6] Keussen, p. 195; H. J. Liessem, *Hermann van dem Busche: Sein Leben*

The story of the conflict between Peter of Ravenna and the Cologne faculty is rather simply told. After a long and successful career as professor of law at several Italian universities (most recently, Padua), Peter was persuaded by Duke Bogeslav X of Pomerania to come to his territorial university at Greifswald as professor of both laws and as reformer of the university. After teaching there successfully for five years (from his matriculation on 24 April 1498 to April of 1503)[7], he left on account of a plague that cost him the death of a beloved daughter, and went, on the urging of the Elector Frederick the Wise of Saxony and his brother Johann, to the new University of Wittenberg. There he lectured for a number of years (3 May 1503 to summer, 1506), perhaps as a professor law and perhaps not: there is no record of his having matriculated, though his son Vincentius became rector in 1504 and held the chair of civil law from 1504 until his resignation toward the end of 1506. Vincentius then returned to Italy, but the father and his wife Lucretia went to Cologne, somewhat before the son's departure, out of fear of the plague that disrupted the university in the summer of 1506[8].

The appearance of a mature and celebrated teacher from the famous law schools of Italy, a man at least as famous for his prodigious memory and his treatise on the art of memory (the *Phoenix*) as for his many publications in the field of jurisprudence, was a great event even in an important university like Cologne; and Peter's friend Ortwin Gratius reports (probably with some exaggeration) that his first public lecture was packed to overflowing and received warm applause. The Cologne city

---

und seine Schriften (Programm des Kaiser-Wilhelm-Gymnasiums zu Köln. Ostern 1884-1889) (Cologne, 1884-1889, 2 vols.), I, 54; Dietrich Reichling, *Ortwin Gratius, Sein Leben und Wirken: Eine Ehrenrettung* (reprint ed.; Nieuwkoop, 1963, from ed. Heiligenstadt, 1884), p. 27.

[7] Th. Pyl, « Petrus von Ravenna », *Baltische Studien*, XX (1864), 530-534. Peter served twice (1498 and 1501) as rector at Greifswald, and his son Vincentius also served twice (1499 and 1502). *Cf.* Eisenhart, *ADB*, XXV, 531-532.

[8] Chabanne, in Naz, VI, col. 1488-1490; Eisenhart, *ADB*, XXV, 532-534. The eighteenth-century biographer Carl Christian Gercken, *Ad historiam Petri ac Vincentii Ravennatum corollarium* (Dresden, 1773), concluded that Peter did not hold a professorship at Wittenberg, but reversed this judgment in his later *Fata Petri Ravennatis per Germaniam* (Dresden, 1777).

council hastened to secure his services by naming him professor *extraordinarius* of both laws (at only a small salary, as his enemies later were careful to point out) [9]. His matriculation occurred on 3 August 1506, and the customary fees were remitted *ob reverentiam personae* [10]. Peter's lectures at Cologne covered not only topics in civil and canon law but also matters of religion and morals; and his remarks on his departure suggest that he had pupils from the arts faculty as well as from law [11]. His teaching at Cologne, as previously at Greifswald and Wittenberg, seems to have attracted large numbers of students and to have won him the friendship of a considerable number of persons in the law and arts faculties, and also among the well-to-do patriciate that ruled the city. Ortwin Gratius, Peter's closest friend and apologist, after listing the various princes who were his patrons or who sought to be — Duke Bogeslav of Pomerania, Frederick the Wise of Saxony, the Emperor Maximilian I [12], the King of Denmark, and the Dukes Magnus and Balthasar of Mecklenburg — provided a catalogue of those persons at Cologne who were special friends of the Italian jurist: Andreas de Venroed, apostolic protonotary and provost of St. Cunibert at Cologne, a doctor of canon law who later (1512) became rector of the university; the jurist Petrus Antonius de Clapis; Johannes Potken, provost of St. Georg and a humanist; Johannes de Burse, a Premonstratensian; Johannes Fastardi Bare de Busco, doctor of laws and rector in 1504; Geraldus Systorp de Kempen, doctor of laws and rector in 1506; Johannes de Graes (Ortwin's own

---

[9] The chief contemporary source for Peter's career in Germany is Ortwin Gratius, *Criticomastix*, printed as an appendix to Peter's *Alphabetum aureum* (Lugduni, 1511), fols. A3 v-B4 v. The record of his disciplinary hearing of 6 March 1507, printed by Franz Joseph von Bianco, *Die alte Universität Köln und die späteren Gelehrten-Schulen dieser Stadt* (Cologne, 1855; 2 vols. in 1), I, 404, mentions his small salary.

[10] Keussen, p. 195; Bianco, I, 846.

[11] Peter's *Testamentum*, or farewell address, of Palm Sunday (16 April), 1508, printed in his *Compendium breue et pulcherrimum in materiam consuetudinum feudorum* (Coloniae, 1508). Henceforth cited as *Compendium breue*. For mention of his pupils, fol. K4 r.

[12] There is some uncertainty about when the Emperor received Peter at court and heard his exploits of memory, but Eisenhart, *ADB*, XXV, 531, and Chabanne, in Naz, VI, col. 1486-1487, think that he spent the period 13 February-13 March 1498 at the imperial court at Innsbruck while en route from Venice to Greifswald.

uncle and guardian, pastor at Deventer); the young humanist and poet Remaclus Florenate; two *Bürgermeister*, Gerhard von Wessel and Gerhard Wasserfass; Johann von Reidt; Johannes Rinck, who had Peter's portrait painted and kept it in his house; his brother Hermann Rinck; and many others in the university and in the city council. Of less eminent but no less enthusiastic friends, Gratius lists the young English law student William Harris; two other students, Johannes Schudherynck de Nuscia and Johannes Riphan de Weter; and the *fiscalis* of the Archbishop of Cologne, Urbanus de Viersen [13]. Other friends not included in Gratius' catalog were Gratius himself; Agrippa von Nettesheim; the wandering humanist Hermann von dem Busche, who returned to Cologne in 1507 or early 1508 and apparently is the author of the *Eulogium* of Peter printed in the latter's *Compendium breue et pulcherrimum in materia consuetudinum feudorum* and signed « H. B. P. » [14]; the scholastic theologian and inquisitor Servatius Vanckel [15]; and the literary editor for the Quentell publishing house, Walther Tanger von Herzogenbusch [16].

But although Peter of Ravenna had friends and admirers in Cologne, he also had enemies who found scandalous things in his teaching and writing and who spoke, wrote, and acted in order to prevent him from spreading his ideas in the university. Shortly after mid-February of 1507, the faculty of theology decided to denounce to the whole university certain of his teachings; and on Saturday, 6 March, the entire faculty was convoked to hear a complaint brought by « certain wise and venerable masters of arts and professors of sacred theo-

---

[13] Gratius, *Criticomastix*, in *Alphabetum aureum*, fols. B8 v-C1 v. Even after his controversy, Peter always avowed his love for Cologne and its university; e. g., *Testamentum*, in *Compendium breue*, fol. K4 r; *cf.* his *Valete*, *ibid.*, fol. C6 r. Peter in his *Notabilia quaedam dicta*, in *Alphabetum aureum*, fol. CLXXXIII r, mentions having given legal advice to Reidt, who was later much interested in university reform, according to Keussen, p. 197.

[14] *Compendium breue*, fol. A1 v. This identification was made by Heidenheimer, pp. 228-229. According to Liessem, I, 28, the abbreviation for « Hermannus Buschius Pasiphilus » was a regular signature used by Busch and appeared on the title-page of his *Flora* (1508).

[15] *Valete*, in *Alphabetum aureum*, fol. D3 r.

[16] He wrote a *distichon* for the title-page of *Alphabetum aureum*; *cf.* Reichling, pp. 22-23.

logy » against certain doctrines taught by « the venerable and distinguished man, master Peter of Ravenna, U. I. D. » [17] A book of extracts from the records of the theological faculty shows that its action of mid-February concerned the issue that later became the chief subject of the pamphlet controversy, Peter's contention that German princes who refused burial to the bodies of penitent condemned criminals and kept them exposed on the gallows were guilty of mortal sin [18]. The charges, as presented to the entire university faculty by one of the theologians, were that through these teachings « many scandals had arisen in the university and that more were to be feared » [19]. The theologians demanded that prompt remedy be provided, and added that « in the books which he published under his name, certain printed sayings were read which were scandalous and offensive to pious ears, especially to young students » [20]. After deliberation by each faculty separately, it was agreed that Peter should be required to appear with his principal critic (presumably Jacob von Hochstraten, though the record does not specify) before a commission made up of the rector, the entire law faculty (to which he had appealed), and a deputy from each of the other three faculties [21]. At this hearing, Peter was informed of the articles charged against him, and admonished that however he might undertake to defend them, « nevertheless they were new and unheard of, and too extraordinary, and hardly consonant with law and reason, but offensive to pious ears and extremely tumultuous and scandalous ». He was warned « to abstain from further teaching of these doctrines, publicly or privately, by word of mouth, by writing, by printing, or otherwise », and was instructed to revise and correct the works containing them. « Otherwise, proceedings would be taken against him, and he would be dealt with as the law provides ». If he wished to defend his statements and to discuss their truth or falsity, this would be allowed, provided he did so in a scholastic manner, « that

---

[17] Printed by Bianco, I, 404-406.

[18] Paris, Bibliothèque Nationale, MS. Nouv. acq. lat. 2165, fol. 4 r.

[19] Bianco, I, 404.

[20] *Ibid.* The reference to scandalizing young students probably means that his joking statement that Italian students could not live without whores was already being used against him.

[21] *Ibid.*, I, 404-406.

is, in the form of a scholastic disputation, showing conclusions containing his opinion, to which he or another would respond, with some [doctors] presiding over the disputation and others opposing, according to the ancient and laudable custom of the aforesaid university ... ». If he should wish to defend his conclusions in writing, this also would be allowed, but only with the proviso that he should communicate his writings to the rector of the university and to none other, and should not further publicize them without authorization by the rector [22].

This stark demand for total conformity or, failing that, for confinement of the debate within the authorized circles of the university, was nothing remarkable in a medieval university, for these bodies claimed extensive rights of discipline over their members. As in any university of the age, Peter at his matriculation had sworn to observe its statutes; and at Cologne these provided explicitly that doctors, licentiates, and bachelors who had taken their degrees elsewhere must swear obedience to the dean of the faculty [23]. Whatever he may have thought about the wisdom of the demands imposed upon him, Peter, a thoroughly conservative academician who well understood the rules of academic life, did not deny the faculty's right to impose discipline. He replied that at the command of the rector and the university, he would abstain from his accustomed teaching of these and similar doctrines. He also promised to revise his books, though he claimed that the errors were not his work but were the fault of the printers [24]. He was then dismissed « with peace and friendship » [25], and the theologians promised to desist from their attacks on him.

Although such strict disciplining of an elderly and famous professor may have seemed somewhat unusual even then, this type of control was not unprecedented at Cologne. In fact during 1496, when the theological faculty was engaged in passing one of several statutes that made belief in the Immaculate Conception obligatory for all its members, two Dominicans (the order had traditionally opposed the doctrine) were required to swear to

---

[22] *Ibid.*, I, 405.
[23] *Ibid.*, II, 56-57.
[24] *Ibid.*, I, 406.
[25] *Ibid.*

uphold it before the university licensed them to teach. One of these was none other than « Frater Jacobus de Hochstraten Dominicanus » [26]. Thus Hochstraten himself, Peter's sharpest and most persistent critic, had faced the same sort of disciplinary requirement and had submitted.

Unfortunately for the tranquillity of himself and of the university, however, Peter of Ravenna was convinced that he had been the victim of a cabal of presumptuous and insincere persons motivated by jealousy of his fame and popularity [27]. While he was willing to make a formal act of submission, he deeply felt that his teaching was true. Still more, he felt that it was holy and that its contrary was an evil doctrine misleading princes into mortal sin and inflicting unnecessary und unjustifiable misery on penitent and religiously reconciled criminals, not only in this life but (much more important) in Purgatory by denying them the spiritual benefits of Christian burial. He felt required by conscience to continue to oppose the German custom of denying church burial to criminals who had shown contrition and had received the sacrament of penance [28].

Keen personal resentment against Hochstraten also forced Peter to continue defending the condemned views. The Ravennan had made his submission to the university when directly confronted by its authority. He felt strongly, however, that the point at issue was fundamentally a question of law, not of theology [29], and that whereas he was a professionally competent lawyer and « a veteran doctor » [30], Jacob (though doubtless a learned theologian) was so ignorant of the law that « he hardly knows the difference between the Clementines and the *Liber Sextus* », and yet presumed to interpret the laws and in doing

---

[26] Paris, Bibliothèque Nationale, MS. Nouv. acq. lat. 2165, fol. 4 r.

[27] Peter to Gratius, *Alphabetum aureum*, fol. C4 v; *Valete, ibid.*, fol. C8 r; and *Compendium breue*, fol. K4 r: « Semper enim inuidit glorie mee. et omnia facit que tendant in denigrationem nominis mei ». Gratius, *Criticomastix*, in *Alphabetum aureum*, fols. A3 r, B5 v, also attributes the attacks to foolish personal spite and envy.

[28] *Valete*, in *Alphabetum aureum*, fol. C8 r: « et si aliter dicerem vel scriberem, facerem contra conscientiam que non potest aliquo modo deponi ».

[29] *Notabilia quaedam dicta*, in *Alphabetum aureum*, fols. CLXXXII v-CLXXXIII r.

[30] *Valete*, in *Alphabetum aureum*, fols. C5 v, C6 r, and especially C8 r.

so, grossly distorted them[31]. This sense of offended personal and professional pride found clear expression at a later stage in the debate when Peter, promising to write a further reply to Hochstraten's tracts, added: « For I shall reply in such a way, shall write in such a way, that he will recall that I am a man. He does not know the character of the Italians, who do not tolerate insults »[32].

Driven by this combination of conviction and resentment, Peter continued to defend the censured doctrines, if not in his public lectures, then certainly in his writings. In the summer of 1507 he brought out a revised edition of his *Compendium iuris canonici*, and added to it a restatement of his opinions[33]. In the eyes of Peter's critics, this renewed publication of his views constituted a breach of the agreement made the preceding spring; and while the documents do not make clear just what formal disciplinary measures, if any, were taken[34], an exchange of controversial pamphlets ensued. Sometime late in 1507 or early in 1508, Hochstraten published (probably at the press of Johannes Landen) a short tract, *Iustificatorium principum alamaniae ... dissoluens rationes clarissimi utriusque Iuris Doctoris et Equitis Magistri Petri Rauennatis quibus principum iudicia carpsit*[35]. At

---

[31] *Dicta notabilia extrauagantia*, in *Alphabetum aureum*, fol. CLIII r, and Preface to *Compendium breue*, fol. A2 r: « cum vix adhuc discernat que sint Clementine et qui sit Sextus liber, voluit iura interpretari ... » Since the latter passage speaks of Peter in the third person, it may be not his work but that of his English friend William Harris, who wrote the dedication to the Emperor Maximilian, or of Hermann von dem Busche, who supplied a prefatory poem.

[32] Peter to Gratius, in *Alphabetum aureum*, fol. C4 v: « Ita enim respondebo: ita scribam vt me virum esse meminerit [.] ignorat naturam italorum qui sibi verba dari non patiuntur ».

[33] Heidenheimer, pp. 225-226; Eisenhart, *ADB*, XXV, 536; Chabanne, in Naz, VI, col. 1492-1493. The edition of *Compendium juris canonici* I have seen (Parisiis, 1521, in the Bibliothèque Ste. Genevieve at Paris), does not contain the additions made in 1507.

[34] Leonard Ennen, *Geschichte der Stadt Köln* (Cologne, 1863-1880, 5 vols.), IV, 99, states that the theological faculty renewed its earlier censure but gives no evidence or specific details; Reichling, pp. 25-26, states that the university suspended him from lecturing but cites no evidence.

[35] Probably printed at Cologne by Johannes Landen in 1508. Both of the two copies in the Bibliothèque Nationale at Paris are bound with his *Defensio scholastica*, which seems to have the same type faces and which

about the same time, Peter was on the point of publishing his popular dictionary of legal citations, *Alphabetum aureum*; and to the end of the main text he added three brief appendices as a sort of preliminary reply, entitled *Dicta notabilia extrauagantia*, *Allegationes in materia consuetudinum*, and *Notabilia quaedam dicta*. Parts of these retorted directly to the *Iustificatorium* (which he had just seen), [36] parts dealt more generally with points of law involved in the debate, and parts concerned entirely unrelated legal questions.

There is no proof that Peter's former pupil Agrippa von Nettesheim was literally accurate when he wrote that the Cologne obscurantists had driven the famed Italian jurist out of the city, and Peter himself claimed that the city council paid him an entire year's salary though he taught for only half the year [37]. But in the tightly knit community life of a medieval university, to be the focus for such deep animosities must have made life difficult. His open rebellion against the university by continued teaching of the censured doctrines must have offended many who had once been friends; and there is clear evidence that many former friends in Cologne broke with him after the dispute became a matter of public literary polemic. Perhaps he was even forbidden to continue lecturing in the university [38]. Although he continued to express his love and respect for Cologne and its university, he finally decided (despite the pleas of Gratius, Harris, and other loyal friends) to depart. Whether this decision was entirely voluntary or under compulsion is not certain. His departure by boat for Mainz occurred on the Thursday after Easter (i. e., on 27 April), 1508.

But while he was preparing to leave, the literary polemic continued. Apparently his enemies had tried to blacken his name by insinuating that he was a man of no family or established position at home, and that his departure from Venice and his subsequent travels in Germany proved that he was an unstable, rootless adventurer, unable to hold a job, a man unworthy of

---

carries publication data. Henceforth these two works are cited as *Iustificatorium* and *Defensio scholastica*.

[36] *Alphabetum aureum*, fol. CLII v.

[37] Agrippa, *De beatissimae Annae monogamia* ..., fols. M5 r-M6 v; Heidenheimer, pp. 241-242.

[38] Reichling, pp. 25-26, thinks so.

respect [39]. The reply to these slanders was the work of the young arts professor Ortwin Gratius, who on 1 March 1508 dedicated to Peter his tract *Criticomastix*. Writing this defense of Peter was an act of considerable boldness, for Gratius was an impoverished and very junior master in the *bursa* (college) Kuyck whose *regens*, Gerardus Zerbolt van Zutphen, was second only to Hochstraten among the opponents of the Italian. Gratius denounces the insinuations made against Peter's character and learning and in defense not only praises his recently published *Alphabetum aureum* but also emphasizes the high honors conferred on Peter by many noble princes and by the Cologne city council. He catalogues some of the multitude of learned and influential persons at Cologne who had become Peter's friends. The major portion of the *apologia*, however, is a detailed narrative of Peter's career between his departure for Germany in 1498 and his arrival at Cologne in 1506. This account is designed to scotch the dishonorable insinuations against Peter's past career, by making it clear how widely he had been honored, and by what excellent and highly placed men. He concludes with a plea from himself and other friends that Peter should stay in Cologne, and writes a glowing praise of the city and of its university as an excellent place for a scholar to live. Significantly, perhaps, in view of his later desertion from Peter's cause, Gratius confines his argument to denouncing in general terms the jealousy and malevolence of Peter's enemies. He does not discuss the issues of the controversy, nor does he make a specific endorsement of Peter's viewpoint [40]. Peter wrote a reply expressing thanks for this defense, and added the treatise, plus Ortwin's letter of dedication and his own letter, to his *Alphabetum aureum* [41].

But the Ravennan, whose combative nature had been aroused and who (despite the pleas of Gratius and others that he should remain) had already decided to leave Cologne and eventually to return to Italy [42], was not the man to let others carry the whole burden of his defense. In his note of thanks for *Criticomastix*, he

---

[39] Gratius, *Criticomastix*, in *Alphabetum aureum*, fols. A3 r, A6 v.

[40] His failure to do so has been noted by Reichling, pp. 27-28.

[41] I have seen only the Lyon, 1511, edition of this book, but it seems that the Cologne edition of 1508 must have appeared early in the year and then have been reissued with the appended materials.

[42] Peter to Gratius, in *Alphabetum aureum*, fol. C4 v.

said that he would not leave the city until he had replied to Hochstraten. The first real tract that Peter devoted to the conflict was entitled *Valete cum perpetuo silentio ad clarissimum theologie professorem magistrum Iacobum de Alta platea ordinis predicatorum Petri Rauennatis Iuris vtriusque doctoris de Bassa platea.* Although the tract repeats and expands Peter's arguments based on civil and canon law, and offers rebuttal of the arguments used in Hochstraten's *Iustificatorium* (which, Peter has heard, was really the work of several persons) [43], it is characterized more by satirical attacks on Hochstraten and his allies, and by angry denunciation of their malevolence and their ignorance of the law, than by systematic presentation of juridical or theological arguments. As a strictly scientific investigation of the subject being debated, Peter's work cannot bear comparison with the orderly series of nine scholastic *quaestiones* which constitutes Hochstraten's *Iustificatorium.* But he was not writing a scholarly reply: he was writing an angry polemic, designed not to conduct an argument within the limited circle of scholars, but to appeal to the fairness and decency of all educated men. Toward the end of his tract, though he promised that he would say no more on this subject in Cologne, he threatened that if he lived to see Italy again, he would republish his own and his critics' works and so make their ignorance and malevolence known in that country [44].

At the very end of his *Valete,* as a further illustration of how his enemies twisted and distorted his words, he mentioned one of the two lesser questions on which he had been attacked: his statement, made in jest, that « students cannot live without whores — I am speaking of Italians, however, not Germans » [45]. One can imagine the class chuckling as the foreign teacher carefully assured his German law students that of course only Italian students, not German ones, consorted with prostitutes. The jest was made as an amusing illustration of a serious principle of law: that a landlord who rents to a person of a given trade or profession cannot evict the tenant for engaging in the acti-

---

[43] *Valete,* in *Alphabetum aureum,* fol. C5 v.

[44] *Ibid.,* fols. C7 v, C8 r.

[45] I quote not Peter but the charge made by Hochstraten in *Defensio scholastica,* fol. D4 v. *Cf. Valete,* in *Alphabetum aureum,* fol. C8 v.

vities customarily associated with his trade. Just as a landlord who rents to an artisan cannot object at law if his renter conducts his customary trade on the premises, so a landlord who rents to students cannot evict them for bringing lewd women onto the premises, for that is an activity habitually associated with the trade of being a student. Peter, who was famed for his memory (in Italy he had been nicknamed « Pietro dalla Memoria ») [46], and who had written the most popular treatise of his age on the art of memory [47], doubtless used the jocular example to fix a basic legal principle in his students' minds. He complained (and with considerable justice) that Hochstraten's use of this illustration was clear evidence that his enemies were eagerly searching for every word which they could twist into the basis for an attack on him [48]. The second minor charge levied against Peter, that he had taught that princes had no right to impose the death penalty for simple theft, was more honestly germane to the principal issue and was actually the substance of what Peter had taught [49].

Despite Peter's evident bitterness, his final public oration at Cologne, which took place in the Minorite church on Palm Sunday (16 April), 1508, contained no hint of his controversy and abounded in expressions of love for Cologne and the university. It took the form of a « Testament », really a farewell address in the form of a will, in which Peter, explaining that he had embraced the rule (meaning the lay Third Order) of St. Francis and so had no gold or silver to bequeath, willed instead to his heirs a collection of pious counsels and spiritual benefits. The designated heirs of his spiritual treasure were « the most celebrated city of Cologne, which loved and honored me in the beginning, the middle, and the end », and also « the most celebrated University of Cologne, in which there are most learned theologians, most excellent jurisconsults, most expert doctors

---

[46] Pietro Paolo Ginanni, *Memorie storico-critiche degli scrittori ravennati ...* (Faenza, 1769, 2 vols. in 1), II, 420.

[47] Yates, p. 112.

[48] *Valete*, in *Alphabetum aureum*, fol. C8 r.

[49] Hochstraten mentioned this question at the end of *Iustificatorium*, fol. D4 r, but did not take either it or the question about Italian students up until he published his *Defensio scholastica* some months later (the edition is dated 8 May 1508).

of medicine, and most acute masters of arts » [50]. There is not the slightest trace of satirical intent. Peter constitutes his son Vincentius, who now lives at Rome in the service of the Cardinal of Santa Sabina, as executor, with instructions to use his influence at the Curia in behalf of any Cologne citizens who need his help [51]. The oration closes with a plea for forgiveness if by word or deed he has offended anyone in Cologne, and with a request that all persons, and especially the secular and regular clergy in the large audience, should pray for the safe return of himself and his wife Lucretia to their fatherland. Although some of the pious sentiments which constitute Peter's « legacy » might have seemed pertinent to his controversy with the theologians (such as Biblical injunctions against the sin of envy or to love one another), there is not even an oblique reference to his troubles in Cologne, not the slightest hint that Peter has suffered because his enemies failed to exercise these virtues in his behalf. The message of the « Testament » is one of reconciliation.

In the eyes of his critics at Cologne, however, Peter had broken the promise of silence made a year earlier; and since Hochstraten's *Iustificatio* had elicited only further arguments and bitter invective, it was now necessary to respond more fully and to demonstrate the scandalous nature of a viewpoint which in effect stated that the princes of Germany (and by implication their spiritual advisers) were living in a state of mortal sin because they denied burial to executed criminals. Two treatises were prepared, one by Hochstraten, *Defensio scholastica principum almanie in eo quod sceleratos detinent insepultos in ligno ... contra nouissimum opus clarissimi vtriusque iuris doctoris et equitis aurati Magistri petri rauennatis*. This work, which contained appendices dealing with Peter's attack on use of the death penalty for simple theft and with his joking remarks about Italian students, came off the press of Johannes Landen at Cologne on 8 May 1508, just a few days after Peter left that city. The second work was by Gerardus Zerbolt van Zutphen, *Tractatus de cadaveribus maleficorum morte punitorum ad considerationem Alemanniae Principum*

---

[50] *Compendium breue*, fols. K3 r-K4 r.
[51] *Ibid.*

et aliorum Judicum. It is apparently even rarer than Hochstraten's *Defensio scholastica*, and I have not located a copy [52].

The *Defensio scholastica* complains bitterly against the disorganization, the misquotations from the *Iustificatorium*, and the unscholarly invective tone of Peter's *Valete*, and resumes his stance of defending German princes against accusations of mortal sin regarding burial of condemned criminals. This book has the form of a point-by-point rebuttal of the arguments used by Peter. The counter-arguments are partly theological and partly juristic in nature. Aside from the complaints against Peter's avoiding the issues and lapsing into invective unworthy of a scholar [53], the work is relatively moderate in tone; and it avoids personal attacks except for the repeated accusation that Peter has distorted Hochstraten's words on certain questions. The only clearly tendentious part of the tract is the section that tries to make a serious charge out of Peter's rather flippant remarks about Italian students [54].

This book was by no means the last shot of the theologians, and Peter's departure from Cologne did not end the controversy. When he came to Mainz at the end of April, 1508, he decided to settle there for a time, since he was finishing work on his manual of feudal law, *Compendium breue et pulcherrimum in materia consuetudinum feudorum*, for the Cologne publisher Quentell, who brought it out that same year, probably in the summer. In addition, as Peter or one of his friends stated in the preface, he intended to stay near Cologne until he had replied again to Hochstraten; and it is probable that disturbed conditions in Italy on account of the wars would have made an immediate journey home impossible in any case [55].

Once again, this time in a less eminent university, Peter's eloquence, learning, and gifts of memory made a favorable impression. A few days after his arrival, he lectured in the Carme-

---

[52] Heidenheimer, pp. 235-240, also was unable to find the book and cited it only from the reference in Panzer, *Annales*, VI, 364.

[53] *Defensio scholastica*, fols. A1 v-A2 r, D4 v.

[54] *Ibid.*, fols. D4 v-E4 v.

[55] *Compendium breue*, fol. A2 r; *cf.* Peter's own words on fols. H4 r and K4 r, where he threatens to write against « another holy father », probably Zerbolt. On the effect of military operations in Italy, Eisenhart, *ADB*, XXV, 537, and Chabanne, in Naz, VI, col. 1493.

lite church before a large crowd of scholars, including the papal legate, Bernardino Carvajal, Cardinal of Santa Croce. He won great applause and was quickly appointed professor of canon law at the University of Mainz, where he taught for a little less than a year [56].

But controversy followed Peter to Mainz. In his own account of his favorable reception there, he remarked that everyone approved his first oration « except one theologian, who, however, was not from Mainz », and added that « one may presume that this was Brother Jacob von Hochstraten, Dominican, who either was in the city that day or arrived a few days later » [57]. Peter went on to say that he made this assumption because since Hochstraten had always envied his fame and tried to besmirch his reputation, he must have been the outside critic on this occasion. Whatever the aim of this particular visit by Hochstraten to Mainz, there can be no doubt that the theological faculty at Cologne did attempt to start a judicial process against the Italian scholar before the archiepiscopal court at Mainz, for on 10 September the general vicar of the archdiocese, Theodericus Zobel, wrote a letter to the dean and theological faculty at Cologne acknowledging receipt of their letter denouncing Peter of Ravenna. Zobel expressed a desire to fulfill the faculty's demands, but would promise only that he would reserve judgment until he had had a chance to confer with Peter himself, and then would « without doubt do whatever seems to be our duty » [58]. Whether this attempt to prosecute Peter had any further effect is unknown; but the attempt certainly was made. Apparently Peter stayed in Mainz until early 1509, when he and his wife moved to Worms and he gave lectures before the judges of the *Reichskammergericht*, in his own residence and in the choir of the church of

---

[56] In the summer of 1508, the student Johannes Sorbillo wrote into one of his books a memorandum that he had heard Peter's course in canon law at Mainz. See Theodor Muther, *Aus dem Universitäts- und Gelehrtenleben im Zeitalter der Reformation: Vorträge* (Erlangen, 1866), p. 117. *Cf.* Heidenheimer, pp. 223-256, and especially pp. 252-254 for references to Peter's residence at Mainz from the contemporaries Reinhart Noltz of Worms and Johannes Butzbach. Peter's own account of his experience at Mainz is in *Compendium breue*, fol. K4 r.

[57] *Compendium breue*, fol. K4 r.

[58] Printed by Liessem, I, 27, n. 2.

St. Lorenz [59]. On the last day of February, 1509, he was received as an *advocatus* before the *Reichskammergericht*; and later that year, his former pupil at Cologne, Adolphus Eicholtz, visited him at Worms while on his way to study at Bologna [60]. There is no later direct evidence on Peter's life; and since he was a very old man by sixteenth-century standards, it is likely that he died not long afterwards, perhaps at Worms. Some biographers conclude that since his former friend Gratius wrote a *distichon* favoring Hochstraten's third work against Peter, the *Protectorium*, Peter must still have been living in 1511 when that book was published [61]. But at the very end of this same tract, Hochstraten mentions having heard a report of his adversary's death. Ortwin's *distichon* may have been written for the original text of the main portion of the *Protectorium*, which is dated 20 June 1509; and the verses may then have been retained as a sort of public recantation when the book was printed (or reprinted) in 1511 [62]. In a letter of 1518, Johann Reuchlin attributed Peter's death to sorrow over the attacks by « this monster » Hochstraten, but named no date or place [63].

But Peter lived long enough to write one final tract against his critics. The Mainz historian Heidenheimer during the last century discovered in his city a book entitled *Prima pars egregij et salutiferi*[*s*] *operis celeberrimi juris vtriusque doctoris Petri Rauennatis contra Gherardum de Zutphania et fratrem Jacobum Theologie professores* [64]. According to Heidenheimer's description, the satirical and polemical elements already found in Peter's earlier works must have been even more pronounced here; and the parallel to the satirical tone of the *Epistolae obscurorum virorum*

---

[59] Heidenheimer, pp. 252-254.

[60] Muther, p. 125, cites the archival record of his reception but is uncertain whether this could be the same person, since he is unaware of the other evidence for Peter's moving to Worms in 1509. On Eicholtz's visit, see P. S. Allen, in a note in his *Opus epistolarum Erasmi*, III, 390 (no. 866).

[61] *E. g.*, Heidenheimer, p. 252.

[62] The *distichon* is on the title-page of *Protectorium*. Hochstraten's reference to Peter's death is *ibid.*, fol. C4 r.

[63] Böcking, *Supplementum*, II, 450.

[64] I have been unable to locate a copy and hence must rely on the rather extensive summary given by Heidenheimer, pp. 234-240. The book had no indication of place, publisher, or date, but Heidenheimer attributes it to Johann Schoeffer of Mainz and dates it in the late summer of 1508.

was even more obvious. Peter draws an imaginary picture of a cabal of Cologne theologians who, having gained only public obloquy by the first work which they brought out under Hochstraten's name, now conspire once more against the Ravennan. Motivated by jealousy of Peter and by fear lest their failure to silence him might allow the jurists to replace them as the dominant element in the university, the obscurantists decide that since they are unable to destroy the Italian's fame among learned men, they should publish two works aimed at ruining his reputation among the people, who are gullible enough to think that because the theologians publish charges against a man, there must be something dangerous about him. But unlike Peter, whose writings are so popular that printers come, money in hand, begging for his works, the obscurantists know that no printer will take their works unless they pay him the costs of publication. Finally, with great reluctance, the miserly Dr. Gerardus agrees to give two gulden out of his hoard. Then an upright theologian protests against their conspiracy, but they drive him out. The result of the conspiracy, as thus depicted by Peter, is the two tracts *Tractatus de cadaveribus maleficorum* by Gerardus and *Defensio scholastica* by Hochstraten. Now speaking in his own person again, Peter announces his intention to issue a twofold reply, the first part (the one under discussion) aimed mainly at Gerardus, and the second (probably never completed) directed against Hochstraten. The rest of the completed part, the *Prima pars*, restates his views on burial of criminals, and then lists some seventy *ineptiae* he has found in the tract of Gerardus.

The final work of the controversy was Hochstraten's *Protectorium principum Alemanie de maleficis non sepeliendis contra Rauennatem* (probably not printed until the author had collected endorsements from faculties other than his own and had prepared the copy for the edition of 1511) [65]. Although the book contains

---

[65] The title-page of the Cologne edition of 1511 reads: *Ad Reuerendissimum dominum Bernardinum presbyterum Cardinalem Dyaconum tituli sanctae crucis Editio tertia ab eximio sacre Theologie et bonarum artium professore Magistro Iacobo de Hoechstraten. ordinis predicatorum. Iam heretice pravitatis Inquisitore. In defensionem principum Almanie compilata. contra clarissimum vtriusque iuris doctorem dominum Petrum Rauennatem. Plurimorum clarissimorum virorum in diuino pariter et humano iure doctissimorum testimonijs et signaturis approbata.* The true title of this tract, in short and usable form, appears at the end,

a dedicatory epistle from Hochstraten to Cardinal Carvajal (dated 28 May 1510) and a letter to the author from an unnamed theologian (dated 1508), both of which denounce Peter, the tract itself is once again a rather impersonal piece in the manner of traditional scholastic discourse, though it presents a larger number of juridical arguments than its two predecessors. Hochstraten summarizes Peter's position in four points and then composes a *quaestio* containing the main issue, « Whether princes of Germany and rulers of cities sin mortally when they deny the bodies of condemned criminals to those who request them for burial ... » [66]. He presents a brief positive argument (Peter's viewpoint), emphasizing the spiritual suffering of a longer term in Purgatory that the souls would have to undergo because they were deprived of the spiritual benefits of a funeral. Then Hochstraten argues the negative case (his own) in thirty numbered paragraphs.

The 1511 *Protectorium* also contains several appendices. The first, dated 1510, discusses a related question raised by the Ravennan during their earlier exchanges, whether even criminals who die impenitent (*i. e.*, not reconciled to the Church) should be granted « canine burial » (simple interment without ceremony and not in consecrated ground). At the end of this section, Hochstraten asks how a man so learned as Peter could have fallen into such patent errors. His solution is that having once ardently embraced one fundamental error, Peter was led inexorably into other false conclusions [67]. Next, mindful of his own earlier char-

---

on fol. C4 v, which is a sort of second title-page: *Protectorium principum Alemanie de maleficis non sepeliendis contra Rauennatem*. Despite the use of the phrase « editio tertia », there is no evidence of any earlier publication, and I assume that the phrase results from the fact that this was the author's third publication against the Ravennan. At the end of the main treatise, on fol. B5 v, there appears: « Finit editio hec anno gratie. M.CCCCC.IX. Mensis Iunij. die. XX ». But this notation may well refer only to completion of the manuscript. The colophon at the end of the entire work, in the 1511 edition, does not say « Finit editio ... », but « Impressum Colonie anno. M.CCCCC.XI. &C. » Incidentally, the phrase « editio tertia » has led several authors (*e. g.*, Reichling, pp. 26-27) to assume that the *Iustificatorium*, the *Defensio scholastica*, and the *Protectorium* represent three editions of the same work. They do not: though subject and viewpoint are of course the same, the three books differ greatly.

[66] *Protectorium*, fol. A2 v.

[67] *Ibid.*, fol. B6 v.

ges that Peter had often distorted his words in quoting them, Hochstraten offered a table of references giving the places in Peter's writings where the passages he himself had quoted could be found [68].

But the most interesting part of the book is a series of endorsements from theologians and jurists. Apparently Hochstraten had sent his manuscript around, to the law faculty at Cologne, to the theological and law faculties at Louvain, and to the jurists in the law courts at Utrecht and Liége. He scrupulously pointed out that only the main treatise written in 1509, not the appended little work on burial of impenitent criminals, was covered by the endorsements [69]. Peter had challenged Hochstraten to cite modern authorities, especially jurists, as he himself had cited modern and older theologians on his side [70]; and his antagonist here took up the challenge. He gave no individual endorsements from members of the Cologne theological faculty, since, he said, that body as a whole had condemned Peter's view at the very beginning of the conflict in 1507, a condemnation which he quoted. The individual endorsements from outside of Cologne are of considerable interest, including from the Louvain theological faculty the chancellor of that university, Adrian of Utrecht (the future Pope Adrian VI), and from the Louvain faculty of laws a prominent friend of humanists, Jerome Busleiden, whose will provided for the foundation of the famous *Collegium trilingue* at Louvain [71].

Far more significant, however, is the list of endorsements from inside Cologne itself, for if Peter of Ravenna lived long enough to learn of it, he must have found it unsettling to his conviction that many learned and influential men in Cologne sympathized with his cause. Those who endorsed the Dominican friar's final attack on Peter included Theodoricus Wichwael, Bishop of Cyrene and coadjutor of the Archdiocese of Cologne, who was generally friendly to the new learning; Petrus Sultz of Cologne, then (1509) rector of the university and licentiate

---

[68] *Ibid.*, fol. C1 r.

[69] *Ibid.*, fol. B5 v.

[70] *Valete*, in *Alphabetum aureum*, fol. C8 r.

[71] For these endorsements from outside Cologne, *Protectorium*, fols. C2 r-C4 r. They are dated in 1509 and 1510.

in theology; Gerardus Systorp de Kempen, Christianus de Conresheym, Petrus de Clapis, Heribertus de Blisia, Robert von Reidt, Iudocus de Erpach, and Ludolphus Gravie, all of them doctors of law; the licentiates Jacob Faber and Heinrich von Wyldeshusen; and Bishop Johannes Lampier, confessor of the Archduke Charles [72]. Systorp and Clapis figured in Gratius' list of Peter's friends; Reidt may well have been a relative of his friend Johannes von Reidt; and Bishop Theodoricus was a person who normally would have sympathized with a spokesman for humanism, and a good friend of Peter's admirer Agrippa von Nettesheim. Since the verses by Gratius on the title page of the *Protectorium* also mark a public declaration of support for Hochstraten by Peter's closest friend and most outspoken defender, it seems clear that the university had closed ranks against the troublemaker from Italy.

Except for occasional passing references by critics of academic obscurantism like Johann Reuchlin, Agrippa von Nettesheim, and the authors of *Epistolae virorum obscurorum*, the controversy between Peter of Ravenna and the Cologne theologians ended with the publication of Hochstraten's *Protectorium* in 1511. Probably Peter was already dead. But what is one to make of the whole affair? What was it all about? Most modern writers, observing the clear evidence of Peter's intense piety and uncompromising support of papal authority and of traditional practices like prayers and indulgences for souls in Purgatory, have accepted the explanation offered by Peter and his friends: that the critics were motivated by jealousy of Peter's success and by hatred of « good learning » — that is, of humanistic studies [73]. A few ultra-Catholic historians, unmindful of the Ravennan's piety and orthodoxy, have assumed that Peter really was a dangerous man, if not quite a heretic [74]. This view, however, is seldom accompanied by any analysis of the issues of the case; it is enough that the Italian jurist criticized the Cologne theologians. There have been suggestions that rivalry between religious orders was a factor, since Hochstraten was a Dominican

---

[72] *Ibid.*, fols. C1 v-C2 r.

[73] Heidenheimer, pp. 254-255; Eisenhart, *ADB*, XXV, 536-537; Muther, p. 124.

[74] A. Esser, « Petrus Ravennas », *Wetzer und Welte's Kirchenlexikon*, 2. Aufl., IX, col. 1935-1937; Reichling, pp. 22-28.

and Peter was affiliated with the Third Order of the rival Franciscans [75], but this explanation is unlikely. In fact, the Ravennan stated with evident sincerity that he had always revered the Dominicans, that the Dominican saints Peter Martyr and Vincent, as well as St. Thomas Aquinas, were his patron saints, to whom he had daily recourse in prayer, and that on this account he deeply regretted having to oppose a Dominican [76]. A third explanation suggested by historians is that Peter was resented as a foreigner, especially when he presumed to utter denunciations of a widespread German legal custom and to accuse German rulers of mortal sin [77]. While one must not read nineteenth-century German national sentiment back into this earlier period, it is well established that there was throughout pre-Reformation Germany much anti-foreign sentiment, directed especially against Italians. Of the three traditional explanations of Peter's troubles, therefore, personal jealousy probably had some effect but was hardly the reason why former friends turned against him; Dominican hostility to a Franciscan tertiary probably had no influence; resentment against a foreigner who criticized German customs and German rulers probably did play an important part and will be discussed further.

As for obscurantist hatred of humanism, it (and with it, the obscurantism of Cologne) has been exaggerated. Besides, it remains to be proved that Peter of Ravenna really was a humanist. Professionally speaking, he was a jurist, not a professor of humane letters. While he defended his citation of Roman historical authors in his sermons (he had not quoted poets, he pointed out, because the laws forbade this practice to Christian orators) [78], the use of classical citations was hardly a novelty in the medieval university. Significantly, on the one occasion when he referred to the work of destructive critical humanism

---

[75] Gercken, *Fata*, p. 30, who alludes to the struggle between the two orders over the Immaculate Conception. Peter, however, nowhere mentions the Dominicans' tradition of hostility to the doctrine. *Cf.* Ginanni, II, 156-157, and Eisenhart, *ADB*, XXV, 536.

[76] *Valete*, in *Alphabetum aureum*, fol. C5 v. His eldest son was named for the Dominican St. Vincent.

[77] This viewpoint is strongly expressed by Reichling, p. 25: « stand es dem *Ausländer* zu, öffentlich *deutsche* Einrichtungen und *deutsche* Gebräuche anzutasten ...? » (His emphasis.).

[78] *Dicta notabilia extrauagantia*, in *Alphabetum aureum*, fol. CLXXXII r.

in questioning received traditions, he was uncompromisingly hostile: certain « bad Christians », he wrote, deny the Donation of Constantine, but this is because they read only pagan historians and neglect religious writings [79]. Though young humanists like Gratius admired him on account of his eloquence, his learning, and his prodigious memory, Peter's deep Franciscan piety and his traditionalism on all matters pertaining to religion were obvious to all; and in no sense could he have been mistaken for a radical and destructive humanist like Ulrich von Hutten, for example.

The main issues of contention between Peter and Hochstraten involved certain debatable points of law and theology. On the civil law governing burial of executed criminals, the Italian jurist argued that the principal text in the *Pandects* (Lib. XLVIII, tit. XXIIII, *De cadaveribus punitorum*) established as a general rule that bodies of criminals must be delivered to relatives seeking them for burial, and that exceptions to this rule might be made only in the case of criminals executed for monstrous crimes (*lèse-majesté* was the only case explicitly authorized in the text). He claimed that in reality, Roman law refused burial only when the offense subjected the criminal to a form of execution that involved destruction of the body, as by burning. Even then, he added, the law provided that the remains should be collected and interred. In addition to the text of the *Pandects*, his chief authority was the famous medieval jurisconsult Baldus, who had argued from the Biblical parallel in Deuteronomy 21 : 22-23 that since Hebrew law required that the body be removed from the gallows and buried before sundown, it was wrong to leave criminals exposed on the gallows. On this civil-law point, Hochstraten emphasized not the words of Ulpian that « bodies ... must not be denied », but rather the statement that permission must be sought, and that the text specifically mentioned that in some cases permission was refused. He denied that *lèse-majesté* was the only case where denial was authorized, and showed that in other cases (as in execution of parricides by enclosing them in a leather bag with noxious beasts and throwing them into water) Roman law did not require burial.

---

[79] *Ibid.*, fol. CLVIII. The reference must be to the famous treatise by Lorenzo Valla.

But being trained as a philosopher and theologian rather than as a jurist, he emphasized mainly an abstract but not inconsiderable argument: that the real governing principle must be the welfare of society, and that if a local ruler decided that the death penalty alone was not enough to extirpate a certain crime, he had the right to add further penalties, such as exposure of the body to public view, in order by the horror of the sight to deter others from similar crimes. Returning to the field of jurisprudence, he argued that the law providing for hanging of highwaymen at the scene of their crimes in order to deter other potential offenders implied that the bodies must be left hanging for a long time; and that in the case of traitors, the law certainly did add penalties beyond mere execution. In fact, it attainted even the innocent children of the guilty party and also confiscated his property. Turning to the argument of Baldus, he minimized Baldus' authority and charged that Peter's reliance on Deuteronomy 21 was a case of judaizing heresy: that is, the granting of current legal force to the requirements of the old Jewish law. Whereas Peter argued that the text in Deuteronomy 21 was essentially moral in nature, resting on a principle of natural law, and hence still binding, his German foe argued that the passage was part of Hebrew legal practice and hence was abolished, with the other ceremonial and judicial laws, at the time of the Incarnation.

There were also issues in the interpretation of canon law. Peter of Ravenna claimed that church law laid down an absolute requirement that all penitent Christians be given burial. Hochstraten agreed that church law did not prohibit burial of executed criminals who had been reconciled to the Church, but he argued that the canons involved were permissive only, not prescriptive. Church law required a Christian ruler to permit a condemned criminal to receive the sacrament of penance, but the friar denied Peter's argument that burial was therefore also required. He also pointed out that during an interdict, the Church denied burial even to innocent persons (a point to which Peter replied that this was a temporary denial only, and that in any case it was an act of the Pope, who had a degree of authority not allowed to local secular princes). Likewise, church law denied burial — permanently and in all cases — to penitent persons who died of wounds received in tournaments, precisely for the purpose of deterring others from an evil practice. In both the fields of canon law and civil law, therefore, the German Dominican granted princes much discretionary authority, while Peter regarded the laws as binding absolutely and would authorize few if any exceptions.

The two antagonists also divided sharply on one theological issue. Peter argued that the canon law had required burial of penitent Christians in all cases because without the spiritual benefits conferred by church burial, the soul would undergo an unnecessarily long period of punishment in Purgatory. These spiritual effects of non-burial were what made Peter especially severe in denouncing errant rulers as cruel and guilty of mortal sin. They had a right and duty to take a criminal's life in the cases provided by law, but no right to add further penalties that would delay the soul's release from Purgatory. Burial was « almost a sacrament », and the requirement to grant the sacrament of penance (necessary for the criminal's salvation) also inescapably implied the granting of burial. In reply, Hochstraten followed two lines of theological argument. The first and more important was that Peter exaggerated the spiritual benefits of burial, which was quite different from a sacrament since it was in no wise necessary for salvation. All or nearly all the spiritual benefits of a funeral derived from the prayers said for the soul of the deceased and the alms offered in his behalf; and these prayers and alms could be offered by his friends and relatives even if the body was kept on the gallows. In fact, Hochstraten once argued, the pitiful sight of the body on the gallows might elicit more prayers for the soul than would be offered during a funeral, so that it was hard to judge whether burial or exposure was more conducive to the welfare of the soul [80]. The second line of argument was that even if the soul did stay longer in Purgatory as a result of the prince's refusal to permit burial, the penalties suffered in Purgatory were justly due, so that the prince was guilty of no offense against the condemned person [81].

One other major issue divided the two controversialists: the battle for jurisdiction between the fields of law and theology.

[80] *Protectorium*, fols. A5 v-A6 r; *cf. Iustificatorium*, fols. C3 v-C4 r.

[81] The arguments summarized in this and the two preceding paragraphs are repeatedly stated in the tracts of Ravenna and Hochstraten cited above.

Although both men presented arguments and cited authorities from both fields, Peter claimed that the argument was essentially over a point of law, and so that he was the professionally qualified expert while Hochstraten was an unqualified person intruding on a point outside his competence. On the other hand, the Dominican friar argued that since a question of mortal sin was involved, the dispute rightfully belonged to the field of theology. It would be interesting to know just what Peter's colleagues on the Cologne law faculty thought and said privately on this issue. Perhaps the fact is of no significance, but when the Cologne jurists wrote their individual endorsements of Hochstraten's *Protectorium*, each one of them inserted a limiting clause reserving the right to teach otherwise if the opposite opinion prevailed in the future: *salvo iudicio semper saniori* [82].

Obviously, these and certain lesser differences of viewpoint provided sufficient material for a debate among scholars, and perhaps even (if the theological faculty had not been so vastly more powerful at Cologne than the law faculty) for a jurisdictional clash between faculties. What they really fail to explain is the bitterness of the dispute and the eventual abandonment of Peter by many of his Cologne friends. Peter's standpoint was not all radical. He was himself deeply religious and fully loyal to traditional religious practices. He flatly rejected the sort of aggressive humanism that subjected traditional beliefs and doctrines, such as the Donation of Constantine, to destructive criticism. He was more vigorous than his Dominican foe in asserting the superiority of clerical — especially papal — authority over the authority of secular princes. He based his argument on generally received authorities; and it was Hochstraten in the case of Baldus and the legal commentators and glossators, not his lay opponent, who made light of the views of writers whose opinions were generally accepted as definitive. Just as Peter's whole career in the field of law avoided innovation and stayed within the medieval juristic tradition [83], so the authorities he relied on were traditional and respectable. Perhaps it was

---

[82] *Protectorium*, fols. C1 v-C2 r.

[83] Roderich Stintzing, *Geschichte der populären Literatur des römisch-kanonischen Rechts in Deutschland am Ende des 15. und im Anfang des 16. Jahrhunderts* (Leipzig, 1867), p. 148.

necessary, in order to discredit his views, for Hochstraten to charge him with a tendency to « judaize » (because of his reliance on Deuteronomy 21) and to make much of his flippant joke about Italian students; and for the university in its 1507 condemnation to stigmatize his views not only as « suspect », « scandalous », and « false » (which to the scholastic mind of his time they may have been) but also as « new » and « unheard of » (which they certainly were not). But the extreme nature of the response remains surprising.

One must make large allowance for native resentment of a foreign scholar who dared to make serious charges against German legal practice and German princes, for Hochstraten in his pamphlets comes back repeatedly to the notion that it is scandalous to level charges of mortal sin and cruelty against noble German princes and prelates, many of whom are even honored by the Church as saints [84]. Peter, he thinks, behaves irrationally when he labors to impute major guilt to innocent and virtuous rulers, while he tries to lighten the justly merited penalties of criminals. Each of Hochstraten's tracts is labelled a justification, a defense, or a protection of German princes. The bad impression which Peter's criticism made was probably magnified by the broader charges of social injustice contained in his *Valete*, for instead of sticking to the question of burial of criminals, he argues that it seems incomprehensible that German law punishes simple theft with execution and even with refusal of burial under the pretext of defending the general welfare, while two crimes much more un-Christian and disruptive of society than the theft of a goose or a hen, fornication and adultery, are punished hardly at all unless forcible rape is proved. He recalls having seen a German adulterer punished with only two hours in the stocks, where he spent his time joking with passers-by, while he had seen a mere boy of fifteen suspended from a yoke and then perpetually banished for a small theft [85]. Venetian practice, he notes, is quite different and far more just. Thus despite all his conservatism, his declared admiration for Germans and for Cologne, and his explicit denial that Italians were

---

[84] *Protectorium*, fol. B4 v.

[85] *Valete*, in *Alphabetum aureum*, fols. C6 r-C7 r.

better than Germans [86], Peter did subject German customs to a degree of criticism that important people, both in the university and in the secular world, may have resented. The insinuations against Peter as a rootless adventurer, to which Gratius replied in his *Criticomastix*, probably do reflect some resentment against the foreigner who put himself forward as critic.

Peter's turning from the narrow issue of burial of criminals to the broader aspects of crime and punishment also reflects another trait which goes even further to explain the bitterness of the attack on him and the gradual alienation of many of his friends. The medieval university was a privileged, self-conscious, and tightly knit corporation with very definite rules of procedure and of propriety. When Peter's attacks on German princes were first denounced in 1507, he was offered an opportunity to defend himself. But he was warned that he must conduct his defense in proper scholastic manner and that if he wrote in his defense he might communicate these writings only to the rector and might not publish them outside the university without the rector's permission. When he chose instead to submit, he promised to keep silence on this issue, to abstain from teaching or publishing his censured views, and to correct his books. He was expected to keep these pledges not for a time but permanently, just as Hochstraten had been expected to keep his oath to defend the doctrine of the Immaculate Conception. A member of a medieval university was under discipline. But Peter of Ravenna broke that discipline and his promise to keep silence; at least his critics felt he did. Not only did he resume defense of his censured opinions, but also he published that defense in books that circulated outside the university. Further to deepen the offense, his *Valete* and his subsequent works were quite unscholastic — that is, unscientific and unscholarly. Hochstraten said so bluntly in his second and third tracts. Peter's works were suasive in nature and polemical in tone. He was addressing himself not just to his peers at Cologne as

---

[86] Peter's disclaimer is in *Valete*, *Alphabetum aureum*, fol. C6 r. Pyl, pp. 153-158, notes evidence that Peter was resented as a foreigner (a highly paid one) by some of the native doctors at Greifswald. But though there was some resentment, there was no controversy. *Cf.* Eisenhart, *ADB*, XXV, 532-533.

he ought, but to the whole Latin-reading public of his day, and was threatening to spread his attacks all over Germany and even to Italy. He denigrated his critics as vain and presumptuous; he engaged in personal attack on his enemies, accused them of dishonorable conspiracy, and even passed along a rumor — he had heard it both at Cologne and at Mainz, though he gave it no credence — that Hochstraten had a mistress [87]. He depicted Zerbolt as both a miser and a drunkard. His contempt for Hochstraten and his kind is expressed again and again, nowhere more concisely, perhaps, than in this word-picture of Hochstraten and Zerbolt:

> And the two of them in a hundred words utter a hundred lies. And after they have written their absurdities, they sit sprawled out and spit all around, and look back at passers-by with eyes raised up to see whether anyone, amazed at their most profound learning, is looking at them. But all persons who are not suspect hold them in derision, and these blind men, deprived of all intelligence, defending cruelty, do not perceive that the world pays them no heed [88].

Peter did indeed, as others have pointed out [89], do much to create the scurrilous interpretation of the Cologne *Dunkelmänner* that later found its full development in the *Epistolae virorum obscurorum*.

Thus by the end of 1508, and perhaps some months earlier, Peter seemed obviously guilty of several offenses: he had slandered the princes of Germany and their spiritual advisers; he had broken his pledge to maintain public silence; he had gone outside of academic channels by having his tracts printed and by writing them in a way that cast aside the rules of academic discourse and appealed in a polemical way to general public opinion; he had cast aspersions on the learning, the intelligence, the integrity, and even the moral character of some of his col-

---

[87] *Compendium breue*, fol. H4 r.

[88] *Ibid.*, fol. K4 r: « et ambo in verbis centum dicunt mendacia centum. Et postquam suas ineptias scripserunt large sedent et rotunde spuunt, incedentesque per viam respiciunt oculis elatis. an aliquis in illos conuertit oculos. stupens de sua profundissima scientia. Sed omnibus non suspectis sunt in derisu. nec aduertunt excecati et omni intellectu priuati crudelitatem defendentes. quod a seculo non fuit auditum ».

[89] Reichling, p. 27; Heidenheimer, pp. 244-246.

leagues. In short, he was threatening the very existence of the university as a tightly knit corporation whose members were subject to discipline. Of course a good defense could be made for much that he did, and against the malevolence of his critics. But given the mentality of the late medieval university world, his defiance and contentiousness must have made his conduct seem unprofessional, improper, even scandalous to many men who at first had been favorably disposed to him. The desertion of his cause by former friends and their willingness to endorse Hochstraten's final attack on him are not surprising. Even the « betrayal » by Gratius, his warmest defender, is not extraordinary. Gratius had to make his career within the university, for he was very poor. Furthermore, even in his *Criticomastix*, he had expressed glowing pride in the city and the University of Cologne. This was his *alma mater*, and he was proud of her. While he had admired Peter himself, he had no particular enthusiasm for the cause which his friend was upholding, and hardly even alluded to it in the defense of Peter that he wrote. He was a university man to the very core; and though somewhat more reluctantly and more slowly than others, he rallied to the university when loyalty to the institution became the real issue. As for Hochstraten, this same determination to uphold the university and to drive out a person who was causing dissension may explain why he felt justified in making so much of Peter's joke about Italian students, and why he denounced Peter's views as not only false but also scandalous, unheard-of, and perhaps heretical.

Two important forces that were at work in the pre-Reformation intellectual world are thus well illustrated in the affair of Peter of Ravenna at Cologne. One is the powerful sense of corporate solidarity and institutional loyalty that drove conservative-minded men together and made them demand that the individual either conform or be destroyed. The second important force is the tendency of certain individuals, driven by conviction, or ambition, or perhaps diabolic inspiration, to find, in the printed polemical tract and in the appeal to a growing body of educated public opinion, a means of kicking over the traces and transferring a controversy out of the university and into the wider world. Peter of Ravenna died too soon, and the issue was too insignificant, for this emergent clash between corporate conservatism and individual freedom of opinion to develop very far. But the case does suggest the presence of tendencies leading toward not only the scandals and conflicts of the Reuchlin case that followed soon after, but also the far greater upheavals of the Age of the Reformation.

LEWIS W. SPITZ

HUMANISM IN THE REFORMATION

In a precocious *Jugendarbeit* published many years ago Hans Baron emphasized that in Germany the humanistic ideas streaming in from another cultural world fused in multi-faceted forms with enduring indigenous views [1]. He had made a bold beginning in Reformation studies with an impressive monograph on Calvin's conception of the state and the confessional age [2]. But soon he was drawn to that other cultural world, the Italian Renaissance, driven by political circumstances, but also, one may suppose, responding to the Nietzschean *Sehnsucht nach dem Süden*. He left behind an array of major historical problems concerned with the cultural impact of the Italian Renaissance upon the North and of humanism upon the Reformation still not resolved by historians.

Thanks to the debate over periodization and the concept of the Renaissance, that « most intractable child of historiography », the relation of the Renaissance to the Middle Ages is now much better understood than its relation to the period which followed. On very basic questions the discussion of this problem has not progressed much beyond the polar positions taken by Wilhelm Dilthey and Ernst Troeltsch in their classic exchange many decades ago about the place of the Reformation in the total sweep of history. Dilthey viewed the Renaissance and the Reformation as twin sources of modernity. The Reformation was the religious expression of the Renaissance [3]. Troeltsch argued that the Reformation was a revival of otherworldly religiosity, antithetical to the artistically ennobled naturalism of the Renaissance as well as to the secularized, scientized culture

---

[1] Hans Baron, « Zur Frage des Ursprungs des deutschen Humanismus und seiner religiösen Reformbestrebungen », *Historische Zeitschrift*, CXXXII (1925), 413-446, 446.

[2] Hans Baron, « Calvins Staatsanschauung und das Konfessionelle Zeitalter », *Beiheft I der Historischen Zeitschrift*, 1924.

[3] Wilhelm Dilthey, « Auffassung und Analyse das Menschen im 15. und 16. Jahrhundert », *Gesammelte Schriften*, II (Stuttgart, 1940), 1 ff.

of modernity. The Reformation rooted in deep veins of popular religious belief proved to be the stronger movement, institutionally formative and sociologically more productive than the elitist and aristocratic Renaissance. The Renaissance, as Troeltsch read history, went underground like a stream to emerge once again in the Enlightenment [4]. The power of the Reformation and of the Catholic resurgence was not purely negative or corrosive of humanist values. Rather, Troeltsch conceded, through weakening, refraction and adaptive transformation the Renaissance « became a world culture and permeated all the pores of high society ».

Scholars have long since brought the Burckhardtian retrospective vision of the Renaissance into sharper focus, bringing out the genuine religious concerns of the Italian humanists. It is time for a closer look at the course of humanism as a cultural force in the Reformation era, a re-examination replete with implications for the question of the interrelatedness of the two historical movements. Such a look reveals that the magisterial reformers and their epigoni in subsequent generations responded positively to the cultural treasures of Renaissance humanism. They did not merely reluctantly accommodate them or craftily assimilate them, but rather gladly embraced, enthusiastically sanctioned, and energetically promoted them in publications and through education. To document and analyze adequately the nature of this affirmative response on the part both of mainline Protestant intelligentsia and the reformed Catholic intellectual world would require a small shelf of books. The more modest aims of this paper are rather merely to illustrate the enthusiastic reception by the reformers of humanist learning in its major disciplines, to sketch the course of humanism in its variegated developments, and to take note of its final dispersion in subsequent decades and centuries.

---

[4] Ernst Troeltsch, « Renaissance und Reformation », *Gesammelte Schriften*, IV (Tübingen, 1925), 261-296. H. A. Enno Van Gelder, *The Two Reformations in the Sixteenth Century* (The Hague, 1961), represents this badly dated Erasmus - to - the Enlightenment viewpoint.

I.

THE RECEPTION

The Renaissance humanists opposed to the badly maligned scholastic learning not a new systematic philosophy but rather a body of learning designed to teach men how to lead the good life. They had an incredible faith in the power of the spoken and the written word, in rhetoric and literature. True eloquence could be derived only from the « harmonious union between wisdom and style » [5]. They drew upon ancient classical and patristic literature as an almost inexhaustible source of precepts and models. They embraced the liberal arts and the classical and biblical languages. They developed an approach to education designed to transmit these arts effectively and to direct the young to lives of private and civic virtue, as well-rounded persons fully developed physically, mentally, and spiritually. They cultivated grammar, rhetoric and poetry in conscious opposition to the former emphasis in the schools upon formal dialectic. They contributed in important ways to the development of a sense of history and wrote substantial histories, even though there were definite limitations to their theory and practice of history [6].

As a corollary of this new sense of history they reoriented the study and application of law in a way quite at variance with the commentaries of the medieval glossators. They emphasized the importance of moral philosophy, very often a Ciceronian stoicism or ethical Paulinism tinged with Platonism. Their social philosophy stressed responsibility toward the body politic, whether civic humanism in a republican sense, or princely government in a traditional sense.

They cultivated a knowledge of the Biblical texts and the ancient Christian writers as the sources for true religion. They were Christocentric in theology, although seldom expressly Christological in the sense of a Pauline soteriology. These

---

[5] Hanna H. Gray, « Renaissance Humanism: The Pursuit of Eloquence », *Journal of the History of Ideas*, XXIV, no. 4 (October-December, 1963), 497-514, 503.

[6] See Felix Gilbert, « The Renaissance Interest in History », Charles Singleton, ed., *Art, Science, and History in the Renaissance* (Baltimore, 1967), pp. 373-387.

phrases characterize the mainstream of that complicated and multi-faceted phenomenon given the generic name of Renaissance humanism. Its protean nature came into play as it adapted itself to the cultural situation in non-Italian Europe, but its characteristic features remain identifiable.

During the first two or three generations of the European Reformation movement the major intellectual and cultural emphases were not so much passively assimilated and formally transmitted as they were enthusiastically embraced and promoted. There were admittedly individual cultural atavists and anti-intellectual sects ready to jettison secular culture along with the world itself. But with respect to humanist culture, the stance of the main-line reformers was positive. The cultivation of humanist learning became together with other mundane vocations a « sphere of faith's works ». While such a development might in retrospect seem predictable for a movement which sprang up in a university setting and within the communion of the very church which had been the mother of universities, a difference in leadership, Muentzer instead of Luther, Amsdorf instead of Melanchthon, Farel instead of Calvin, might well have sent the revolution spiralling off onto an anti-intellectual or at least unhumanistic course. A successful proletarian revolution might have brutalized culture and wiped out the hard-won refinements of centuries. Wars might have broken out sooner, before the cultural transition from Renaissance to Reformation had been effected. There are many unprofessional questions that might be asked which reduce the self-evident and predictable quotient to near zero. The counsel of the 19th-century English historian James Froude is still valid: « To look wherever we can through the eyes of contemporaries, from whom the future was concealed ».

Young Philipp Melanchthon delivered the keynote address in his inaugural lecture at Wittenberg University « On Improving the Studies of Youth » (1518). A brash, bright young man, Melanchthon demeaned medieval culture, berated the sophists, and transmitted to Protestantism the humanist *fable convenu* about the Dark Ages [7]. He called for a revival of the « letters of reborn

---

[7] Melanchthon « De corrigendis adolescentiae studiis », *Melanchthons Werke in Auswahl*, III, *Humanistische Schriften*, Richard Nürnberger, ed. (Gütersloh, 1961), 29-42, also in the *Corpus Reformatorum*, XI, 15 ff. The earliest

culture ». He urged the cultivation of the whole humanist curriculum including rhetoric above all, Greek and Hebrew letters, history, philosophy, and science. He pledged that he would devote himself to teaching with all of his energy and talent. Melanchthon was more fortunate than Sir Charles Firth at Oxford in our century, who suggested publicly that certain reforms were in order in the university and suffered a boycott for two decades as his reward. For in Luther Melanchthon found a ready ally, a bit surprising considering that Melanchthon had not been Luther's choice for the chair. Luther himself took the initiative in effecting the humanistic reform of the university curriculum at Wittenberg. Under Melanchthon's influence, Luther's interest in humanistic studies and his competence in them grew, especially during his later less pressured years. For all his interest in theology, Melanchthon remained a professor in the arts faculty to the end of his career. He returned to the theme of the glories of classical culture and the value of the ancient languages again and again in subsequent decades [8].

In 1557 a certain Bartholomäus Kalkreuter of Krossen delivered an academic address at Wittenberg praising humanist learning and the prince of the humanists, Desiderius Erasmus himself. The great Erasmus, he declaimed, does not need to be lauded any more than Hercules or Cyrus. The youth should be encouraged to study his useful writings, to consider his virtues, and to reflect upon his great talent. Bartholomäus praised his keen sense of discovery, his insight and perspective in choosing his subject-matter and his sentences, the richness of his expression, the brilliance of his pictures, the beauty and spirit of his presentation with which he so distinguished himself that it could appear as though the graces themselves had from all sides strewn

---

extant selection from Melanchthon on the *artes liberales* is an oration he delivered in 1517 « De artibus liberalibus » in which he stressed the importance of the quadrivium and singled out the study of history and poetry for special emphasis. Heinz Liebing, « Perspektivische Verzeichnungen », *Zeitschrift für Kirchengeschichte*, III (1968), 290-292, discusses the way in which Melanchthon, and other reformers, transmitted the humanist conception of the Dark Ages to Protestantism.

[8] E. g., Melanchthon, « Oratio de studiis linguae Graecae », *Melanchthons Werke in Auswahl*, III, *Humanistische Schriften*, 134-148; *CR*, XI, 855 ff., and many similar orations. Cf. Carl S. Meyer, « Melanchthon as Educator and Humanist », *Concordia Theological Monthly*, XXXI (1960), 533-540.

his speech with flowers. His virtues, his diligence, patience in need, modesty, and beneficence were evident in his life. He was led by divine grace to do his edition of the New Testament. He contributed greatly to the re-awakening of the Greek and Latin languages. « Since, therefore », Bartholomäus concluded, « Erasmus possessed a great power of genius and many outstanding virtues, and since he in the highest degree promoted the language study necessary to the church and the state, we wish to preserve his memory in a thankful heart, to read his literary monuments, and to acknowledge him gratefully » [9]. The special charm of this encomium of Erasmus and of Erasmian humanism is that a sixty-year-old professor had prepared it for Bartholomäus to deliver. Twenty-one years after the death of Erasmus the titular head of the Lutheran movement, Philipp Melanchthon, paid this tribute to Erasmus, the great Christian humanist [10].

Melanchthon's inaugural address and the many orations, treatises, prefaces, and editions which he produced during the decades which followed sanctioned the liberal arts and validated humanist culture for the learned world. Melanchthon was the commanding figure in a sizable army of *literati* who advanced the cause of humanist learning in the Reformation movement. Peter Mosellanus, the little man who had been Luther's choice for the position which Melanchthon received on the insistence of Frederick the Wise, delivered a powerful address at Leipzig

---

[9] *CR*, XII, 264-271, cited in Karl Hartfelder, *Philipp Melanchthon als Praeceptor Germaniae* (Berlin, 1889), p. 118.

[10] For the Erasmus-Melanchthon correspondence documenting their continued good relations and periodic contacts, see Emil Walter, ed., « Erasmus und Melanchthon I. Briefwechsel zwischen Erasmus und Melanchthon », *Einladungsschrift des Herzoglichen Karls-Gymnasiums in Bernburg* (Bernburg, 1877). Heinrich Bornkamm states expressly that Melanchthon arrived in Wittenberg as an Erasmian, « Melanchthons Menschenbild », Walter Elliger, ed., *Philipp Melanchthon* (Göttingen, 1961), 76-90, 78. For a bibliography of the extensive recent literature on Melanchthon as a humanist, see Peter Fraenkel and Martin Greschat, *Zwanzig Jahre Melanchthonstudium. Sechs Literaturberichte (1945-1965)* (Geneva, 1967), 72-77, « Humanismus, Philosophie, Wissenschaften »; 150-158, « Melanchthon als Humanist und Mann der Wissenschaft ». Worthy of special mention are Adolf Sperl, *Melanchthon zwischen Humanismus und Reformation* (Munich, 1959) and Wilhelm Maurer, *Der junge Melanchthon zwischen Humanismus und Reformation*, I, *Der Humanist*, II, *Der Theologe* (Göttingen, 1969).

University, *An Oration Concerning the Knowledge of Various Languages which Must be Esteemed*[11]. Mosellanus made a deep impression on the Leipzig students in the short time he lived. Andreas Althamer, for example, who became a reformer in Brandenburg-Ansbach, was inspired at Leipzig by Mosellanus and the English Graecist Richard Croke[12]. The historic moment came for Mosellanus when he delivered the oration on *The Right Method of Disputing* before the Eck, Carlstadt, and Luther debate in Leipzig in 1519[13]. The day the sickly but spirited Mosellanus died, Melanchthon and Joachim Camerarius were present and grieved deeply over his loss.

Joachim Camerarius (1500-1574) became one of the greatest classical scholars of the century. Educated at Leipzig, Erfurt and Wittenberg, he taught Greek and history at the Nuremberg gymnasium for several years. He assisted Melanchthon in preparing the evangelical Augsburg Confession in 1530. Duke Ulrich of Wuerttemberg directed him to reorganize the University of Tübingen. In 1541 he helped to reform the University of Leipzig, where he devoted the remainder of his life to classical scholarship. A prolific author of more than one hundred fifty works, he did translations into Latin of many major Greek authors such as Homer, Theocritus, Demosthenes, Sophocles, Lucian, and others. A life-long friend of Melanchthon, he wrote the best contemporary biography of the reformer. Two of his public addresses are particularly representative of the ongoing enthusiasm for classical learning combined with evangelical conviction, the *Oration on the Study of Good Letters and the Arts and of the Greek and Latin Languages* and the *Oration Concerning the Cultivation of Piety and of Virtue by the Studies of Good Arts*[14].

---

[11] Mosellanus, *Oratio de variarvm Lingvarum cognitione paranda Petro Mosellano Protegense Avthore Lipsiae in Magna Ervditorvm Corona pronunciata* 2nd ed., (Basel, 1519).

[12] Theodor Kolde, *Andreas Althamer der Humanist und Reformator in Brandenburg-Ansbach* (Erlangen, 1895), p. 4.

[13] *De Ratione disputandi, praesertim in re Theologica, Petri Mosellani Protegensis oratio*, republished in V. E. Löscher, *Vollständige Reformations-Acta und Documenta*, III (Leipzig, 1720), 567-578; German translation, Walch, ed., *Luthers Sämmtliche Schriften*, XV, 998-1015.

[14] Joachim Camerarius, *Oratio de studio bonarum literarum atque artium et linguae graecae ac latinae* (Leipzig, 1542); *Oratio de cultu pietatis ac virtutis studiis bonarum artium* (Leipzig, 1545).

The Swiss Reformation followed a similar development. True to his early conditioning, Ulrich Zwingli in Zurich went the farthest among the major reformers in fusing humanist thought and evangelical teaching. His famous treatise *Of the Upbringing and Education of Youth in Good Manners and Christian Discipline* was in the best humanist pedagogical tradition, though with a more earnest stress on religion, to be sure [15]. « Rank, beauty and wealth are not genuine riches, for they are subject to chance », Zwingli concluded. « The only true adornments are virtue and honor ».

In Geneva Calvin, a young French humanist converted to the evangelical movement, founded the Academy, later to become the University of Geneva. The twenty-seven weekly lectures offered included three on theology, eight on Hebrew writings, three on Greek ethics and five on Greek orators or poets, three on physics or mathematics, five on dialectics or rhetoric. Calvin's colleague and successor as head of the movement, Theodore Beza, a professor of Greek, delivered the *Address at the Solemn Opening of the Academy in Geneva*, praising the good arts and disciplines [16]. Calvin delivered the concluding remarks at the ceremony. Mathurin Cordier (1480-1564), Calvin's own Latin teacher, was the author of Erasmus-like colloquies and Latin instruction books. Living out his days in Geneva, he was in many respects a model of the evangelical humanist pedagogue. Another less well-known advocate of the *pietas litterata* was Claude Baduel (1491-1561), for many years a humanist professor at Nîmes, who went to teach at Geneva. A friend of Johannes Sturm of Strassburg and for a brief time a student of Melanchthon in Wittenberg, he was dedicated to the two great loves of his life, beautiful language and a gospel in harmony with the new learning [17].

---

[15] *CR*, LXXXIX, 526 ff., translated in G. W. Bromiley, ed., *The Library of Christian Classics*, XXIV, *Zwingli and Bullinger* (London, 1953), 102-118.

[16] *CR*, XLV, 542-548. See Paul-F. Geisendorf, *Théodore de Bèze* (Geneva, 1967), pp. 105-109, on Beza as Greek professor and the founding of the Academy.

[17] N. J. Gaufrès, *Claude Baduel et la Réforme des Études au XVI*[e] *Siècle* (Paris, 1880), p. 288. Two treatises typical of his dual emphases are Claudius Baduellis, *De Ratione Vitae Stvdiosae ac Literatae in Matrimonio collocandae et degendae* (Lyons, 1544); *De Morte Christi Meditanda, ac contemplanda oratio* (Lyons, 1543).

Never in history, except perhaps in our own time, has so much been written on educational theory and practice as in the age of the Renaissance. The volume increased during the Reformation and the note of urgency grew even more intense. The reformers went beyond the humanist elitist conception, urging universal compulsory education, promoting secondary school education in the classical gymnasium, and declaring the vocation of the teacher to be divine like that of the preacher. Luther's *Address to the Municipalities* and other educational treatises are well-known. Melanchthon's role as *Praeceptor Germaniae* in promoting secondary schools with a classical curriculum was of tremendous importance. Typical of many similar expressions was his *Oration in Praise of a New School, Delivered at Nuremberg in an Assembly of Very Learned Men and Nearly the Entire Senate* (1526). This school still survives and the statue of Melanchthon standing in front seems to be saying: « For what else brings greater benefits to the whole human race than letters? No art, no work, not, by Hercules, the very fruits born of the earth, not, finally, this sun, which many have believed is the author of life, is as necessary as the knowledge of letters » [18]. The greatest of all Protestant educators was Johannes Sturm, who administered the model gymnasium in Strassburg and wrote an impressive array of books on education, all developing his ideas on the nobility of classical letters and the humanist program of education [19]. The intellectual community remained international, as it had been before the Reformation, and surprisingly cohesive. Sturm, for example, was in close contact with Roger Ascham,

---

[18] *Oratio Philippi Melanchthonis in laudem novae scholae, habita Noribergae in corona doctissimorum virorum et totius ferme Senatus (1526)*, Richard Nürnberger, ed., *Melanchthons Werke in Auswahl*, III, *Humanistische Schriften*, 64; also, *CR*, XI, 106 ff.

[19] Two titles must suffice, the treatise *Nobilitas literata, liber unus* (Strassburg, 1549) and the *Scholae Lavinganae* (Lavingae, 1565), illustrating his curricular planning. The best monograph remains Walter Sohm, *Die Schule Johann Sturms und die Kirche Strassburgs in ihrem gegenseitigen Verhältnis 1530-1581* (Munich and Berlin, 1912). It would require a sizeable bibliography to list Sturm's treatises or the flood of titles from the humanist reformers. Hermann Busch (1468-1534), for example, wrote the *Vallum humanitatis* (Cologne, 1518) pleading for including the thorough study of the classics in the educational system. Erasmus called the treatise « opus eruditum, acutum et expolitum ».

great English educator and tutor of Queen Elizabeth. Ascham praised Sturm for successfully combining example with precept and even named an unlucky son after him [20].

Not only were the lines of contact and influence international, but they were also interconfessional, for the lines were not drawn clearly until the second half of the century. Thus Sturm praised very highly the great learning and good judgment of Conrad Heresbach, who once delivered an oration at Freiburg in praise of Greek letters. A volume published in 1551 included the address of Heresbach, the treatise of Sturm on the education of princes, and two letters of Ascham and Sturm on the English nobility [21]. Heresbach remained a Catholic although he was associated with the problematical Archbishop Hermann von Wied of Cologne, and although a cleric, he eventually married.

The humanists reemphasized the classical definition of man as a living being having the power of speech. The reformers saw regenerate man as having the power of the Living Word. Their emphasis on the written and the spoken word of the Gospel (*Verbum evangelii vocale*) coincided neatly with the humanists' stress upon the verbal arts, upon grammar, rhetoric, and poetry. Melanchthon's own grammar was only one among many. « Much ruin happened to the church », he commented, « through the decline of grammar » [22]. Many composite volumes on grammar illustrate both the continuity and the European character of the tradition. Thomas Linacre's study of the structure of the Latin word, for example, was republished a number of times together with Joachim Camerarius's book on the art of grammar and figures of speech, accompanied by a letter of Melanchthon commending Linacre's extraordinary knowledge of Latin syntax [23].

---

[20] See *Rogeri Aschami Epistolarum Libri Quatuor. Accessit Joannis Sturmii, aliorumque ad Aschamum, anglosque alios eruditos epistolarum liber unus* (Oxford, 1703). See also the thorough study of Ascham's life and works, Lawrence V. Ryan, *Roger Ascham* (Stanford, 1963).

[21] *Clarissimi Viri Conradi Heresbachii Ivreconsulti de laudibus Graecarum literarum oratio: olim Friburgi in celeberrimo conuentu & Doctorum & Procerum, habita. Ioan. Stvrmii de edvcatione Principum: ad illustrem Principem Gulielmum, Ducem Iuliacensium, Cliuensium, etc., Rogeri Aschami et Ioannis Sturmij Epistolae duae, de nobilitate Anglicana* (Strassburg, 1551).

[22] *Grammatica Philippi Melanchthonis Latina* (Leipzig, 1560).

[23] *Thomae Linacri Britani de emendata strvctura Latini sermonis libri VI ...* (Leipzig, 1556); also 1564, 1580. Camerarius wrote voluminously on gram-

Such a keen interest in grammar and language did they maintain that a knowledge of all three languages, Latin, Greek, and Hebrew, a very rare achievement in the 15th century, became almost a commonplace among men of learning in the 16th and 17th centuries.

Rhetoric, the pursuit of eloquence, was the vital center of humanist learning. Melanchthon expressed his unconditional acceptance of humanist rhetorical theory and undertook to refine it even further in work of his own. Representative of his many tributes to rhetoric was his *Encomium on Eloquence or Declamation on the Absolute Necessity of the Art of Speaking to Every Kind of Study* [24]. He wrote his own volume on rhetoric and in his *Loci Communes*, or commonplaces, he applied the topical approach to theology, eliciting extravagant praise from Erasmus for his effort [25]. Scholars such as Camerarius carried on the rhetorical tradition on the university level, writing on rhetorical theory and commenting on the orations of Cicero [26]. Educators such as Johannes Sturm impressed the importance and centrality of rhetoric upon the gymnasium students even before they reached the arts faculty at the university [27].

The cultivation of poetry persisted through the century, for the *literati* felt as did the humanists the special power of poetry in evoking as well as expressing refined emotion, especially religious feeling. Eobanus Hessus was revered and honored

---

mar, Latin and Greek, as, for example, his *Commentarii utriusque linguae* (*graecae et latinae*)... (Basel, 1551), and on many other subjects.

[24] *Necessarias esse ad omne studiorum genus artis dicendi, Philippi Melanchthonis declamatio* (*sive: Encomium eloquentiae*), Richard Nürnberger, ed., *Melanchthons Werke in Auswahl*, III, *Humanistische Schriften*, 44-62; also, *CR*, XI, 50 ff.

[25] *Philippi Melanchthonis de Rhetorica libri Tres* (Wittenberg, 1519); *Loci communes rerum theologicarum seu hypotyposes theologicae* (Wittenberg, 1521).

[26] The Rhetoric of Camerarius was enormously successful and appeared in many later editions, *Elementa rhetoricae* (Basel, 1541); again in 1551, 1564, etc. See also his *In partitiones ciceronianas commentatiunculae* (Strassburg, 1560); *In Marcum Tullium Ciceronem annotationes* (Lyons, 1562), and other works.

[27] Typical of many such works are Johannes Sturm, *De amissa dicendi ratione libri duo. Eiusdem, De Literarvm Lvdis Recte Aperiendis, Liber vnvs* (Lyons, 1542); *Ioannis Sturmii De vniversa ratione elocutionis rhetoricae libri IIII* (n. p., 1576?).

with a biography from the pen of Camerarius [28]. The Leipzig savant tried his own hand at turning Greek verse into Latin [29]. The literature on poetry remained voluminous. An interesting example, because it is relatively little known, is Micyllus's three books on metrics [30]. Religious poetry abounded from Clement Marot's version of the Psalter to the Calvinist poets later in the century. But except for the work of Johannes Secundus Everaerts in the Netherlands and a few others, poetry as frankly sensuous or erotic as the *Amores* of Conrad Celtis became a rarity [31].

Leonardo Bruni and other Italian humanists had assigned first place to history for its pragmatic value in moral instruction and in providing vicarious experience to statesmen and citizens. Whatever their shortcomings in their own historical writing and in their failure to teach history professionally on the university level, the humanists still held history to be of great value and contributed to the development of historical consciousness as a reflection of their sense of distance from the ancient past. The reformers were driven by their polemical situation into the serious study of ecclesiastical history. They also adopted the humanist pragmatic interpretation and exploitation of secular history. Luther regretted that he had been forced as a student to spend years on dialectic and had had no opportunity

---

[28] *Narratio de H. Eobano Hesso, comprehendens mentionem de compluribus illius aetatis doctis & eruditis uiris, composita a Ioachimo Camerario Padebergensi* (Nuremberg, 1553).

[29] Cf. such representative works as his *Commentarius explicationis primi (et secundi) libri Iliados Homeri ... conversio in Latinos versus*, 2 vols. (Strassburg, 1538-1540); *Commentatio explicationum omnium tragoediarum Sophoclis, cum exemplo duplicis conversionis* (Basel, 1556); *Theokritu eidyllia ... Theocriti idyllia. Hoc est parva poemata, XXXVI. Eiusdem Epigrammata XIX ... per H. Eobanus Hessem et Joachimi Camerarij scholia non inerudita accessere* (Frankfort, 1545); *Ekleta georgika, sive opuscula quaedam de re rustica* (Nuremberg, 1596); *Elegia hodoiporike Metallaria ad Philippum Melanthonem*, 2 vols. (Basel, 1557), and many others.

[30] Jacobus Micyllus, *De re metrica libri tres, cum praefatione Philippi Melanchthonis* (Frankfort, 1539). Micyllus published many elegia, epithalamia, and other varieties of poetry.

[31] Johannes Secundus Everaerts (1511-1536) was the greatest of the 16th-century Dutch Neo-Latin poets, famous for his *Basia*, *Epigrammata*, and *Odae*. On Calvinist poetry see the old volume by Prosper Tarbé, *Recueil de poesies Calvinistes (1550-1566)* (Reims, 1866).

to read the historians and poets. As the years progressed and pressure relaxed, however, Luther did read the historians. He wrote prefaces to the historical works and editions of Galeatius Capella, Lazarus Spengler, Georg Spalatin, Robert Barnes and others.

Melanchthon wrote his *Chronicon* and the famous prefaces to Caspar Hedio's and Johann Cuspinian's histories [32]. Johann Sleidan with his *Commentaries on the Condition of Religion and the Republic under Charles V* (1555), and Flacius Illyricus with his *Catalogue of the Witnesses of Truth* (1556) and the *Magdeburg Centuries* (1559 ff.) developed further a distinctively Protestant historiography [33]. Camerarius did a Latin edition of Thucydides and his own histories. Late in the seventeenth century a Lutheran classical scholar named Cellarius fastened the term *medium aevum* upon historiography.

The reformers generally endorsed the humanist approach to law and supported a lofty conception of its dignity and divine sanction. The lesson of history for the interpretation of law was not lost on them. Just as many humanists had been converts from legal studies to the liberal arts, so many reformers, not the least of them Luther and Calvin, moved from the law to the gospel, but respect for the law remained [34].

The central concern of the reformers in their drive to the sources was, of course, religious. In the return to the Scriptures and the preoccupation with the witness of Christian antiquity, they often followed a trail blazed by the humanists. The Leipzig debate, the Sacramentarian Controversy, the dispute with the left-wing spiritualists, all threw them back upon historical evidences in the patristic writings. While Scripture remained the *norma normans*, the church fathers testified to the *primum et verum*. The modest beginnings in patristic studies made by Italian hu-

---

[32] For the *Chronicon's* preface and dedicatory epistle, see *CR*, IX, 531-538, XII, 712-720; preface to Hedio's chronicle, *CR*, III, 877-884; preface to Cuspinian's *Chronicle*, Robert Stupperich, *Der unbekannte Melanchthon* (Stuttgart, 1961), pp. 182-191.

[33] For a compact collection of prefaces, see Heinz Scheible, *Die Anfänge der reformatorischen Geschichtsschreibung. Melanchthon, Sleidan, Flacius und die Magdeburger Zenturien* (Gütersloh, 1966).

[34]. Cf. *Philippi Melanchthonis De Legibvs Oratio*, Theodor Muther, ed., (2 nd ed., Weimar, 1869); also, *CR*, XI, 630 ff.; Guido Kisch, *Melanchthons Rechts- und Soziallehre* (Berlin, 1967).

manists such as Ambrogio Traversari or Lorenzo Valla and the tremendous contributions made by such northern humanists as Erasmus were carried to new heights by Protestant and Catholic scholars in the centuries which followed [35]. Luther contributed a preface to Georg Major's *Lives of the Fathers* [36]. Melanchthon composed a « little patrology » in which he offered counsel as to « the discernment with which Augustine, Ambrose, Origen, and other teachers ought to be read » [37]. The confessions were buttressed with a *Catalogus Testimoniorum* of the fathers, and the dogmaticians such as Chemnitz, the « second Martin », had a most impressive knowledge of patristic sources.

Theology proper was the heart of the matter. Was it possible to hold to Luther and Calvin's evangelical position with their anthropology and their radical conception of justification by God's grace alone and still take seriously the cultural mission of humanism and its religious implications? The common view of man in the Renaissance was based upon the stoic-Ciceronian popular philosophy which predicated a dualistic compound of body-soul, reason-will, higher and lower impulses. The ethical life was achieved through control of the passions. Medieval thought had taken this dualism for granted, but with the renewed emphasis upon Aristotle, the ethical life was seen less as the control of passions toward quiet and rest, and more as the subduing of passions by active virtues. These were first of all the natural virtues, but then preeminently the theological virtues of faith, hope, and charity. In humanism Ciceronian anthropology predominated once again, with powerful Platonic impulses

---

[35] Charles Stinger of Stanford University is currently investigating Traversari's contribution to the revival of Christian antiquity. See Hanna H. Gray, « Valla's *Encomium of St. Thomas Aquinas* and the Humanist Conception of Christian Antiquity », Heinz Bluhm, ed., *Essays in History and Literature* (Chicago, 1965), pp. 37-51. A brief but valuable article is Robert Peters, « Erasmus and the Fathers », *Church History*, XXXVI, n. 3 (September, 1967), 254-261. Still of interest, though biased, is Pontien Polman, *L'Élemént Historique dans la Controverse religieuse du XVIe Siècle* (Gembloux, 1932).

[36] Georg Major, *Vitae Patrum, in usum ministrorum verbi ... repurgatae. Cum praefatione Martini Lutheri* (Wittenberg, 1544).

[37] *CR*, XX, 703 ff. A study which could serve as a model for others is Peter Fraenkel, *Testimonia Patrum. The Function of the Patristic Argument in the Theology of Philip Melanchthon* (Geneva, 1961).

added. The reformers basically took this philosophical anthropology for granted. Luther, for example, had a high regard for « natural man », whose reason is the loftiest creation of God. But standing in the presence of the holy God, man is as nothing, in every way dependent upon God's grace and mercy. The way in which humanism developed in the Reformation until its gradual dispersion was determined largely by the kinds of response given to the question of man's relation to God posed so unequivocally by Luther. Could secular culture be so related to religious faith as to maintain an authenticity of its own without capitulating entirely to otherworldliness? Could mankind sustain the intense evangelical faith of the reformers over a longer period of time without compromising with the demands of secular culture or natural religion?

II.

DEVELOPMENTS AND DISPERSION

The Reformation sealed the fate of humanism, but humanism helped to determine the destiny of the Reformation. The great divide came with Luther's publication of *The Babylonian Captivity of the Church* in 1520, for then the older humanists could see that the evangelical cause was not the same as theirs, and turned away. But it was this very treatise that prompted so many of the younger humanists to join Luther's movement [38]. Luther as an evangelical leader was uncompromising in his stand on the big questions of God, man, and the Word. His two major con-

[38] A number of articles are concerned with the historic place of German humanism and its encounter with the Reformation. See Gerhard Ritter, « Die geschichtliche Bedeutung des deutschen Humanismus », *Historische Zeitschrift*, CXXVII (1923), 393-453; Paul Joachimsen, « Der Humanismus und die Entwicklung des deutschen Geistes », *Deutsche Vierteljahrsschrift für Literaturwissenschaft und Geistesgeschichte*, VIII (1930), 419 f.; Otto Herding, « Probleme des frühen Humanismus in Deutschland », *Archiv für Kulturgeschichte*, XXXVIII (1956), 368 ff.; Bernd Moeller, « Die deutschen Humanisten und die Anfänge der Reformation », *Zeitschrift für Kirchengeschichte*, LXX (1959), 47-61; Lewis W. Spitz, « The Third Generation of German Renaissance Humanists », *Aspects of the Renaissance. A Symposium*, Archibald Lewis, ed. (Austin, 1967), pp. 105-121, where the author toys with the utility and futility of social science generation theories.

frontations were with giants much under the influence of humanism, with Erasmus, who could not concede the impotence of man *coram deo*, and with Zwingli, who insisted upon a tropological interpretation of the words of institution of the Sacrament. Luther's radical either/or, the whole man (*totus homo*) either in a state of sin or in a state of grace, the paradox of the *simul iustus et peccator*, and the offense of a literal interpretation of the Scriptures were too much for his opponents. But these dramatic debates by no means tell the whole story of humanism in the Reformation.

Luther favored humanist learning as a noble form of worldly culture. Of a basically generous nature, he recommended various works of Erasmus in later years. But on the fundamental teaching on justification he would brook no concessions or compromise. Nor would the followers of Flacius Illyricus, the watchdog of orthodoxy, later dogmaticians and gnesiolutherans. But beyond Luther a variety of syntheses between evangelical religion and humanism emerged on a broad spectrum from Zwingli to Bucer, Melanchthon, and Calvin. Beyond Zwingli were the evangelical rationalists, men such as Servetus, Socinus, and Castellio. That leading Anabaptists had enjoyed a humanist education has been fully appreciated only in recent years. Erasmian or humanist « spiritualism » and moralism made itself evident not only in « Puritanical » individuals but also in various sects. Within Lutheranism Georg Major played an important role as a representative of a mediating position in theology. The Erasmian and Melanchthonian element in his thought was an important component [39]. Within Calvinism the « Nicodemites » had their ardour tempered by humanist palliatives. Humanist influences were widespread throughout Protestantism during the sixteenth century. And not merely Protestantism, for thanks to the influences emanating from the writings of Vives, Sadoleto, Suarez, and the *ratio studiorum* of the Jesuits, it remained a vital force within Catholicism, where the conflict with the dogmatic tradition was not extremely acute [40].

---

[39] A neat example taken from among his many titles is Georg Major, ed., *Rhetorices Philippi Melanchthonis et copiae Erasmi tabulae* (Nuremberg, 1561).

[40] The literature on Jesuit education is enormous, but a recent work merits special mention because it explores substantive matters such as the

Humanist impulses were not only widespread horizontally on a European scale, but reached down vertically through the centuries. Where humanist influence was strong, it nourished tendencies toward universalism or at least toward latitudinarianism, especially in the Netherlands and England, and fostered an irenic spirit. This influence was already in evidence at the Colloquies of Worms and Regensburg, where the « Erasmian » churchmen labored for a doctrinal formula which would make reunion possible. It was an important element in the makeup of the great irenicist Georg Calixtus and informed the whole Helmstedt group in the seventeenth century [41]. The grand design of Leibniz for the reunion of Christendom was in part a product of the humanist synthesist approach to religion. Fused with distinctively Enlightenment emphases, this learned humanist tradition influenced even the writing of church history toward impartiality and a pragmatic interpretation in Johann Lorenz Mosheim and the Goettingen school, although, to be sure, their new approach was in part merely a reaction against the confessional polemics of the preceding decades. The Prussian Union of the Lutheran and Reformed confessions enforced by Frederick William III in 1817 was politically motivated, but in part was a reflection of a religious mentality informed by the humanist-rationalist tradition. The humanist thought-world was still in evidence among the ecumenical and irenic churchmen of the nineteenth century [42].

---

theological anthropology of the Jesuits, which makes it a study particularly germane to the problem of humanism and religion under discussion here, Mabel Lundberg, *Jesuitische Anthropologie und Erziehungslehre in der Frühzeit des Ordens (ca. 1540-ca.1650)* (Uppsala, 1966).

[41] See Hermann Schuessler, *Georg Calixt: Theologie und Kirchenpolitik. Eine Studie zur Ökumenizität des Luthertums* (Wiesbaden, 1961) on his Helmstedt background, his Aristotelian philosophy, Lutheran theology, humanist view of history, ecumenical efforts and failures.

[42] Ragnar Holte, *Die Vermittlungs-theologie. Ihre theologischen Grundbegriffe kritisch untersucht* (Uppsala, 1965), attributes the attempt to bridge naturalism and supernaturalism and the union efforts of the Lutheran and Reformed churches to Schleiermacher's immediate influence and to the effects of rationalism. But a much bolder approach to 19 th-century irenicist and ecumenical efforts relating them to the humanist historical inheritance is the work of Manfred P. Fleischer, *Katholische und lutherische Ireniker unter besonderer Berücksichtigung des 19. Jahrhunderts* (Göttingen, 1968). See also

In broad and sweeping strokes the role of humanism in the Reformation can be sketched roughly like this. Where a certain confession dominated, whether Lutheran, Calvinist, or Catholic, humanist learning was cultivated in the schools, in gymnasia and in the universities. Where it was transmitted in this academic way, it was preserved longer than where it remained a matter of a few individuals or groups. The various confessions, the Catholic somewhat more easily than the Protestant, gave an important place to humanist culture and gave it a positive role to perform in the worldly sphere. But this humanist learning insinuated itself also into the religious thought of the *literati* and in due course influenced theological developments and ecclesiastical policy. Where the Reformation owed very much to secular government, as in England, it was subject to its wishes in education and culture, often very favorably inclined toward the classical inheritance.

A gradual but significant « foreign element » was added to the humanist educational formula during the course of the sixteenth century, the revival of Aristotle. Ever since Leonardo Bruni had translated the *Nichomachean Ethics*, it had been a basic text for humanist moral philosophy. Melanchthon thought that it could be used profitably together with Aristotle's natural scientific treatises without the reintroduction of his formal dialectic and metaphysics. But promoted by such Aristotelian polymaths as Jacob Schegk of Tübingen in the second half of the century, Aristotle returned as a servant of Protestant scholasticism. A similar development took place within Calvinism, where Peter Ramus fought back against Aristotelianism in the name of a single rhetorical method [43]. In Catholicism, where the Council of Trent had given special approval to Thomas, the Aristotelian revival was an almost predictable development.

---

his article, « Lutheran and Catholic Reunionists in the Age of Bismarck », *Church History*, XXXVIII, no. 1 (March, 1969), 43-66.

[43] Peter Petersen, *Geschichte der Aristotelischen Philosophie im Protestantischen Deutschland* (Leipzig, 1921), describes 1530-1690 as the period of the dominance of Aristotelian philosophy. Neal Gilbert, *Renaissance Concepts of Method* (New York, 1960), discusses in the third chapter the influence of humanism on methodology in the university curriculum. Walter Ong, *Ramus: Method, and the Decay of Dialogue* (Cambridge, Mass., 1958), offers the best analysis of Ramist topical logic and the importance of its visualist approach to knowledge for modern science.

But the new Aristotelianism did not eliminate the standard humanist disciplines of grammar, rhetoric, poetry, moral philosophy and languages any more than Aristotle in his day completely obscured Socrates and Plato. The balance achieved between religious concern as such and the cultivation of classical learning in « confessional humanism » resulted in a strength and stability which lasted into modern times, no small achievement for so fragile a thing as higher culture. Wisdom at length gave way to empirical science and technology, but still cries out for a redress of grievances [44].

To return, then, to the question which Hans Baron left to us so many years ago. It should be quite clear even from this brief survey, with its proofs more suggestive than definitive, that the central thesis of Ernst Troeltsch is quite as untenable as is that of Wilhelm Dilthey. The Renaissance and the Reformation did not constitute the clear and evident division of European culture into its classic pagan and Christian components. The Renaissance lived on through humanism into the Reformation and beyond it into modern times. The evangelical humanists felt the continuity of the classical tradition from the Italian Renaissance down to and including themselves. In the preface to the *In Vitam Beati Rhenani*, addressed to Christoph of Wuerttemberg, Johannes Sturm spoke of the succession of learned men from the time of Lorenzo Valla « to our own time ». Moreover, the evangelical and the Catholic humanists alike assumed that there was a natural connection between classical learning and religious faith. They could quite agree with Coluccio Salutati's reply to the criticisms of Giovanni Dominici: *Connexa sunt humanitatis studia, connexa sunt et studia divinitatis, ut unius rei sine alia vera completaque scientia non possit haberi.* Just as Italian humanism fused in the North in multifaceted forms with enduring indigenous views, so northern humanism in the Reformation combined with a great variety of religious con-

[44] See the brilliant article by Heinz Liebing now of the University of Geneva, « Die Ausgänge des europäischen Humanismus », *Geist und Geschichte der Reformation* (Berlin, 1966), pp. 357-376. The author owes much to Professor Liebing not only for his writing in this field but for stimulating conversation at the *Institut für Spätmittelalter und Reformation*, Tübingen, in the summer of 1969.

victions from Luther to Zwingli, with Melanchthon in the middle.

It seems appropriate to allow Melanchthon the closing words, from his *Encomium on Eloquence* [45]:

« Therefore I do not cease to exhort you to the study of elegance and of those arts without which the other disciplines cannot be maintained except very miserably, for it is fitting that public need should receive something from you. For where barbarity vitiates the more serious disciplines, the ethics of the people are also usually endangered. For it is much more true that ethics are made out of learning than what Plato wrote, out of the songs of musicians. I have spoken ».

[45] Melanchthon, *Encomion eloquentiae* (1523), Richard Nürnberger, ed. *Melanchthons Werke in Auswahl*, III, *Humanistische Schriften*, 62.

GERALD STRAUSS

THE COURSE OF GERMAN HISTORY: THE LUTHERAN INTERPRETATION

Cicero's remark that « to be ignorant of what happened before you were born is to remain forever a child » [1] was not merely a ubiquitous commonplace in the sixteenth century. It summarized the reflections of many thoughtful men on their past, notably in a country as preoccupied with its destiny and its problems as Germany. Political and moral maturity could scarcely be attained without an awareness of one's history. But what *was* that history? Did the numberless events of the distant and recent past coalesce into a meaningful pattern? Was there, in the grand unfolding of the divine will which was history, room for the distinct development of a particular nation? That development having been grasped and related, what bearing did it have on the present? These questions, though remaining largely implicit, impelled much of the historical writing done in Germany in the sixteenth century.

While a coherent pattern of national history emerged only in the second half of that century, German historical scholarship was vigorous from its beginnings. Partly in the interest of self-discovery, partly to dispel the general ignorance concerning Germany which, it was thought, prevailed in the world, German literary men devoted much of their time to the elucidation of their nation's past. The story of this endeavor has been often told. Professional scholars and amateurs, national enthusiasts and local patriots, produced a mass of source publications, critical studies, historical investigations and descriptions on the full range of subjects relating to ancient and medieval Germany. The result was a spate of works of considerable merit and great utility, extending from the local chronicles of Sigismund Meisterlin written in the 1450's to Beatus Rhenanus' *Three Books on Germany* of 1531 — a high point in German antiquarian scholarship — to large-scale descriptions of country and people such as Sebastian Münster's *Cosmography* of 1544, in whose crowded

[1] Cicero, *Orator, ad M. Brutum*, 34, 120.

pages the ambition to discover and set down what could be learned about ancient and modern Germany seemed to have reached fulfillment [2].

Special problems received the largest share of attention: the question of boundaries, particularly the western borders of the Empire in medieval and recent times; ancient survivals into the present — place names, foundations, regional customs; tribal names, languages, the modern consequences of the migrations; the whole question of the relationship of the German heartland to the Holy Roman Empire. Ancient Germanic society, especially in its military and religious aspects, remained an endlessly fascinating subject. Biographies had to be written, inscriptions and coins collected. Description and chronicling — a kind of stock-taking of the country's natural and spiritual stores — engaged the fervor of scholars and writers caught up in the zeal of their nascent national consciousness. A thousand years of neglect had to be made good, whole chapters of obloquy expunged from the pages of printed history. Complaints, denials, accusations concerning shabby historical treatment at the hands of jealous foreigners were incessantly reiterated. Laments and accusations persisted as a stereotype in German historical writing throughout the century and lent it an air of tension and a polemical, often aggressive tone. But there must also have been felt the satisfaction of a job well done. By and large, the ambition of German intellectuals to describe their country and bring its history « from the shadows into the light of day » (as they said) [3] had, by the second half of the century, been accomplished.

Satisfactory in scholarship, often excellent in description and characterization, these works represent a substantial scholarly and publicistic achievement. It cannot be said, however, that they express or reflect a coherent view of German history. As interpretive history they offer little food for thought. No attempt

---

[2] See Gerald Strauss, *Sixteenth-Century Germany, its Topography and Topographers* (Madison, Wisc., 1959) for a discussion of this topic and references to the literature.

[3] For example, Reuchlin, writing in the preface to Johann Nauclerus' *Memorabilium omnis aetatis et omnium gentium chronici commentarii* ... (Tübingen, 1516), III recto: Nauclerus has brought to light again « et gesta et literas Germanorum, quae multos iam annos in tenebris et situ delituerant ».

was made to find in German history a recognizable process of development or a meaningful historical pattern. Apart from inscrutable divine purpose, only the caprice of human volition was recognized, producing isolated actions and reactions in discrete situations.

The evidence suggests that at least some contemporaries hoped for something better. German history, it was said, equal to, and even surpassing, that of Greece and Rome, called for a major historical talent to tell it justly. If only a new Thucydides were to arise to record the wars against Rome or the exploits of the Hohenstaufen! Many an industrious compiler prefaced his own modest effort with apologies for its lack of breadth, and expressed the heartfelt wish for the appearance on the scene of a historian of vision and power [4]. He may have thought of style, proportion, form when calling upon such a man. But some writers, at least, seem to have been aware that compendia and chronicles were no longer enough, that the historian preparing to take on a great subject should draw meaning from, and give shape to, the recital of events. The discipline of history was no longer the preserve of the learned. It was a favored interest of the laity as well as of the scholarly community. Most works first written in Latin were translated into German, and from the 1530's on an increasing number of writers composed their histories in German or produced them in two languages, vernacular versions usually being longer and richer in color and personality [5]. Historical evidence was also seen to have practical value. Political and constitutional crises often revealed historical documentation as an invaluable ally to negotiation [6],

---

[4] E. g. Huldreich Mutius, *De Germanorum prima origine* ... (Basel, 1539), preface. The more elegant the work's style, the easier to fulfill its purpose of enlightening men of learning in Italy and elsewhere. Mutius himself was retained by the Basel professor Eustathius Quercetanus to turn his large collection of German chronicles and documents into a Latin history to be addressed « ad Graecos et Latinos » (A recto).

[5] See Melanchthon's preface to Kaspar Hedio's translation of Johann Cuspinian's *de Caesaribus ... opus: Ein ausserlessne Chronica von Julio Caesare ... bis auf Carolum Quintum* (Strassburg, 1541).

[6] E. g. the guilds of Cologne, following their successful rebellion against the city government in 1513, demanded that an archive be established. Jacob Wimpheling, *Germania* (Strassburg, 1501, dedication) argues that the ge-

and authorities were being urged to ensure the survival of essential records and preserve the memory of important events [7]. This apparent growth in historical consciousness, coinciding as it did with persistent uneasiness over the political problems facing the country, suggests that a comprehensive interpretive synopsis of the course of German history would have been warmly received.

In the event, German historiographers were slow and tentative in their response. Unable or unwilling to stray from the well-paced tradition of adapting and extending older chronicles, they made it clear that the desired synthesis would not be drawn from the sources themselves. Until well past the middle of the sixteenth century, historiography in Germany remained chronicling. The inherited form was flexible enough to accommodate a few idiosyncratic departures. But a commitment to a responsibility other than that of enumerating events in the order in which they happened was required before a chronicle of facts, with or without comment, could turn into history.

A few among the chronicles attained the rank of paradigms, their authority being preserved by new editions and imitations. For much of the sixteenth century the model par excellence was the chronicle of Johann Nauclerus (or Verge, his family name), a teacher of law at the University of Tübingen in the 1470's. From about 1480 until his death in 1510 Nauclerus labored on the book that made his reputation, a world chronicle extending from the Creation to the year 1500 [8]. Though apparently encouraged by the Emperor Maximilian [9], Nauclerus made few concessions to either national or dynastic history. His book records

---

neral historical ignorance prevailing in Germany enabled Louis XI to press his claims to the German lands west of the Rhine.

[7] E. g. beginning in 1482 the election capitulations of the Archbishops of Mainz obliged incumbents to establish archives for all important political documents (Bayerisches Staatsarchiv Würzburg, *Mainzer Domkapitel Urkunden*, Libell 5, 6, etc.). Wimpheling, *Germania*, Book II, urges the Strassburg Council to cause records to be kept of every memorable event in the affairs of city, territory, and Empire, « so that future generations may be mindful of these things ». *Tutschland Jacob Wympfflingers* ... (Strassburg, 1648) Cii recto.

[8] *Memorabilium omnis aetatis et omnium gentium chronici commentarii a Ioanne Nauclero ... digesti in annum salutis MD* (Tübingen, 1516).

[9] Ernst Joachim, *Johannes Nauclerus und seine Chronik* (Göttingen, 1874).

the deeds of the peoples of Europe, or rather of their sovereigns, with nearly equal weight given to all the nations. More important than any single group is the papacy, a continuing institution and the connective thread leading the chronicler through the centuries [10]. Apart from the Church, Nauclerus' theme is the instability of temporal things. Perhaps it was in response to an increased concern with German history that he devotes a little more than their share of space to the affairs of the Empire [11], but his manner of reporting them permits no distinction between his own country and others. Germans deserve detailed attention as the bearers of the imperium. But their history is no less transitory, nor is it more immediate to the chronicler, than the fate of ancient Rome.

Nauclerus' chronicle was acclaimed from the moment of its appearance in 1516 [12]. Erasmus praised the author as a meticulous and honest collector of facts [13], still the best criterion for success as a historian. More important: Nauclerus continued to exert an influence through those who imitated or, in at least one case, copied him. He was an important source for Johann Carion's chronicle in the 1530's. Huldreich Mutius' German history of 1539 is, despite its claim to have been drawn from all the old chronicles and other sources its author could put his hands on [14], for the most part lifted from the pages of Nauclerus and his follower Nicolaus Baselius [15]. Mutius' book is an efficiently written chronicle of political events, but it advances no argument and urges no interpretation, unless it be the by now obligatory patriotic sentiments that invade the narrative

---

[10] Or rather of the history of the sixth age. Nauclerus' historical scheme is that of the six World Ages, each divided into generations. The sixth age begins with the birth of Christ.

[11] German history proper is contained on pp. 105-304 out of 495 pages. Roman history, for example, takes up 123 pages.

[12] It seems to have circulated in manuscript before publication. Cf. Ernst Joachim, *Johannes Nauclerus*.

[13] In his prefatory epistle to the 1516 edition of the Chronicle. See above, note 8.

[14] *De Germanorum prima origine, moribus, institutis, legibus et memorabilibus .... ex probatioribus Germanicis scriptoribus in Latinam linguam translati* ... (Basel, 1539).

[15] For an examination of Mutius' sources, see K. E. H. Müller, *Die Chronik des ... Huldreich Mutius* (Prenzlau, 1882).

whenever the subject permits them[16]. As long as the historian's job was served by a bare recital of events, Nauclerus, and others like him, continued to be appreciated. In 1568 he was still the model for Laurentius Surius, a Carthusian monk in Cologne who sought to oppose the « poison of wicked, perverted teachings introduced by historians in order to mislead the common man »[17], by setting plain facts against the lies of Lutheran historians and by chronicling the events of his own time in the pedestrian manner of Nauclerus[18]. Actually, Surius argues a good deal, but in conception and arrangement his book is entirely derivative. Events — important or trivial as the case may be — are placed side by side in unbending succession, suggesting nothing other than the passage of time and the good or evil intentions of their instigators.

There are other examples of such survivals into the later sixteenth century. The so-called Ursberg Chronicle, compiled by the prior of the Premonstratensian monastery of Ursberg during the reign of Frederick II, was first printed in 1515[19] and again in 1537, at which time Melanchthon added a short preface, praising the author's skill in portraying the whole sweep of human history, and stressing the importance of gaining an understanding of the great changes in history[20]. The Ursberg Chronicle probably attracted attention as an early example of partisan anti-papal historiography[21]. It was reprinted several times in the sixteenth century[22] and was one of the chief sources

---

[16] E. g., pp. 160-1.

[17] Laurentius Surius, *Commentarius brevis rerum in orbe gestarum ... ex optimis quibusque scriptoribus congestus* (Cologne, 1568). A German translation, by Heinrich Fabricius, appeared in the same year: *Kurtze Chronik oder Beschreibung der vornembsten händeln und Geschichten ...* (Cologne, 1568). The words quoted are from the translator's preface, A II verso.

[18] See Surius' own statement, *Commentarius ...*, A IIII recto.

[19] In Augsburg, from the one surviving manuscript of the entire work in the possession of Konrad Peutinger. An earlier edition of part of the work had been printed at Augsburg, c. 1474.

[20] Cf. Melanchthon's preface to the Strassburg edition of 1537, II verso.

[21] Melanchthon's preface to the Ursberg Chronicle in Kaspar Hedio, *Ein ausserlessne Chronik ...* (Strassburg, 1543) CCIII recto.

[22] Strassburg, 1540; Basel, 1569; Strassburg, 1609. There is a critical edition: Oswald Holder-Egger and Bernhard von Simson (eds.), *Die Chronik des Propstes Burchard von Ursberg* (*Scriptores rerum Germanicarum in usum scholarum*) (Hanover and Leipzig, 1916).

of medieval history for the Magdeburg Centuries. To David Chytraeus it was, as late as 1564, the most useful and penetrating of the old chronicles [23]. In 1539 the Strassburg preacher Kaspar Hedio turned out a German translation, and in 1543 he added to it other chronicle material in order to bring it up to date [24]. Interestingly enough, there is less spirit in Hedio's contribution than in his thirteenth-century source. Apart from an occasional bit of sniping in the direction of Rome, Hedio recites events one after the other without transitions or interpretation.

How hard it was to breathe new life into a dated form is shown by chronicles of institutions and places where new and exciting things were happening. Neither the monastic reform movement, nor the surge of urban culture in the fifteenth and sixteenth centuries found adequate historiographical expression in the work of local historians, and this despite the influence of humanist ideas and techniques on historical thought [25]. German humanist historians were probably too deeply immersed in disputes over special problems to gain the distance required for the synoptic view. The problem of the Empire loomed too large for German writers to make their way around the subject without expending a great deal of time and energy on such politically acute, but historiographically subsidiary, debating points as the *translatio imperii*, the election rights of pope and emperor with respect to each other, the devolution of the sovereign's authority to lesser rulers, imperial and curial reform, and the many other politically sensitive issues that were inseparable from the Empire as an institution, especially as a legal institution [26]. Few writers, indeed, seem to have been inclined to heed the summons for a German Thucydides to seize the facts of

---

[23] *De lectione historiarum recte instituenda* (Wittenberg, 1564), 1 recto.

[24] Kaspar Hedio, *Ein ausserlessne Chronik von Anfang der Welt bis auff das iar ... 1543 ...* (Strassburg, 1543). Hedio had been responsible for the 1537 Latin edition, to which he also added new material.

[25] Paul Joachimsohn, *Zur städtischen und klösterlichen Geschichtsschreibung Augsburgs im 15. Jahrhundert* (Bonn, 1895), pp. 33-49. *Id.*, *Die humanistische Geschichtsschreibung in Deutschland I: Die Anfänge. Sigismund Meisterlin* (Bonn, 1895).

[26] For a good summary of this « problem of the Empire » and a sketch of its background, see Morimichi Watanabe, *The Political Ideas of Nicholas of Cusa ...* (Geneva, 1963).

national history and place them in context. So experienced a historical scholar as David Chytraeus, who had been a student of Melanchthon's and lectured on history at the University of Rostock in the third quarter of the sixteenth century, where he wrote numerous works on chronology and methodology as well as chronicles of Prussia and Saxony and a documentary history of the Augsburg Confession, evinced no interest in the interpretation of German history [27]. Even opinionated and committed men like Sebastian Franck and Johannes Aventinus failed to venture into general interpretations. Aventinus, like most world chroniclers before him, was mainly intent on showing that the Holy Roman Empire was not likely to escape the fate which had overtaken Persia and Macedon. His interest is no more confined to German history than it is — despite the title of his major work, the *Bavarian Chronicle* — to his home province. His concern is for humanity, human society, the human condition. Unhistorical in his mental habits, he used history as a vehicle for advancing his passionately held and forcefully argued opinions [28]. No more do we find a consistent interpretation in Sebastian Franck's *German Chronicle* of 1538, a work whose title [29] leads one to expect a national history and whose expressed intention of « pointing out the true kernel and main themes of our history » [30] raises hopes of an attempt at interpretation. In fact, Franck is content on most points to quote Nauclerus and Hartmann Schedel. He, too, wants to see German history take its rightful place [31]. But he has no use for the patriotic trumpeting of one's own national virtues [32] and thinks it foolish

[27] Of Chytraeus' many works, see especially *Chronicon Saxoniae ... ab anno 1500 usque ad MDXCIII* (Leipzig, 1593) and its German translation (Leipzig, 1597); *Historia der Augsburgischen Confession ...* (Rostock, 1576), and *De lectione historiarum recte instituenda* (Wittenberg, 1564). On Chytraeus' historical lectures and his immense correspondence on historical matters, see Detloff Klatt, « Chyträus als Geschichtslehrer und Geschichtschreiber », *Beiträge zur Geschichte der Stadt Rostock*, V (1909), 4-202.

[28] On Aventinus' mind and methods, see Gerald Strauss, *Historian in an Age of Crisis: The Life and Work of Johannes Aventinus* (Cambridge, Mass., 1963).

[29] *Germaniae chronicon: Von des gantzen Teutschlands, aller Teutschen Völcker herkommen ... von Noe bis auf Carolum V* (Frankfurt am Main [?], 1538).

[30] *Ibid.*, AA III verso.

[31] See the conventional statement, *ibid.*, AA II recto.

[32] *Ibid.*, LXXXI recto; CCXXIV verso; etc.

to concentrate on the deeds of a single segment of humanity. In writing a German history he merely wished to redress the balance overthrown by chauvinistic historians of other countries.

Aventinus and Franck are immensely attractive writers. Their compelling personalities emerge strongly from their books, making them a joy to read. But as historians they represent no gain on so jejune an exercise in chronicling as Schedel's *liber chronicarum* of 1493, a work which, because of its usefulness as a compendium and attractiveness as a piece of book making, cast a prolonged spell on sixteenth-century historical writing. A thoughtful thumbing through of Schedel's *Nuremberg Chronicle* (as it is usually called) [33] reveals some interesting clues to the reasons for the current indifference to interpretive history. Content to think within a historical framework which could not help but drain historical actuality of life and pertinency, Schedel added neither point nor direction to the chronological, biographical, and descriptive fragments of which his chronicle is composed. Human history is biography. Even the city descriptions for which Schedel's chronicle is famous are biographies. A picture attracts the eye; essential facts are registered. Events are more interesting as vignettes, illustrated by woodcuts, than as pieces in a consecutive narrative. There is no development. Sacred and secular history occur apart from each other, their segregation made visually evident on facing pages. To be sure, Schedel's *Chronicle* reflects the smug self-assurance of Nuremberg's well-to-do bourgeoisie, as it does the cautious commercial policies of its publisher, Koberger. The great problems of world and national history remained largely beyond its narrow horizon, and in this respect the work is akin to most municipal chronicling, which tended to concern itself only with those events of external history that pertained directly to the main preoccupations of the city [34]. In the case of Schedel's chronicle, its very popularity as a work of historical reference and edification suggests that its author's conventional habits by no means misrepresented the general trend of historical thought in the early decades of the sixteenth century. Even where stronger

---

[33] Hartmann Schedel, ... *Buch der Croniken* (Nuremberg, 1493).

[34] Cf. Heinrich Schmidt, *Die deutschen Städtechroniken als Spiegel des bürgerlichen Selbstverständnisses im Spätmittelalter* (Göttingen, 1958).

convictions and a keener grasp of political problems showed up the inadequacy of conventional procedures, the inherited pattern remained largely intact.

Of this tenacity of received ideas and methods Jacob Wimpheling's treatise on German history is a particularly interesting example. Often spoken of as the first work on German history written from the national point of view [35], the *Epitoma Germanicarum rerum* of 1505 was, indeed, published to provide Germans with a first introduction to their national history [36] and to demonstrate the continuity of that history from antiquity through the medieval centuries, the age of Carolingians, Hohenstaufen, and other imperial dynasties being revealed as a time of high deeds, and a fitting succession to the heroic migration period. In relating the deeds of medieval emperors, Wimpheling conveys the excitement of discovery. His is the first German history, the only serious attempt so far to put to rest the lingering notion that Germany has no history, indeed, that Germans are unworthy of having a history at all. Identifying himself on the first page of his work as an Alsatian [37], and thereby adding urgency to the discussion of problems of territorial and political sovereignty [38], he passes quickly over the ancient tribes to the crucial questions of the origins of Charlemagne [39] and the transfer of authority from the Carolingian to the Saxon dynasties [40]. On this important point, the transmission of the imperial title, Wimpheling was well briefed with arguments, being about to prepare Lupold von Bebenburg's *Tractatus de*

---

[35] Paul Joachimsen, *Geschichtsauffassung und Geschichtschreibung in Deutschland unter dem Einfluss des Humanismus* (Leipzig and Berlin, 1910), p. 66.

[36] I use the Basel edition of 1532, p. 315.

[37] *Ibid.*, p. 315.

[38] On these points see, in addition, Wimpheling's *Germania* (Strassburg, 1501), Book I, written against Louis XI's (then the dauphin) contention that ancient Gaul, and therefore modern France, extended to the shores of the Rhine. For counter arguments, see Thomas Murner's *Germania nova* of 1502.

[39] *Epitoma*, chapter 9 « De Carolo magno primo Germanorum imperatore ... et de inhumano facinore Gallorum modernorum ». Also chapter 22 with its massing of evidence to show that Charlemagne and his father were ethnically German.

[40] *Ibid.*, chapter 22 « De defectione stirpis Caroli magni in Gallis; deque indignatione Gallorum in electorum institutionem ». Especially p. 330.

iuribus regni et imperii for the press [41]. But these tasks of demonstration having been accomplished, the remainder of his narrative relapses into chronicle, a mere recital of deeds and wars succeeding the arguments so vigorously pressed before. Having indicated the point of departure of German national history and identified the direction in which events and agents were moving, he was content, for the rest, to report salient events, only occasionally lacing the recital with references to national accomplishments and appeals to his countrymen to crown their history by seizing the leadership of the Christian crusade against the Turks.

Wimpheling's limitation to an epitome suggests that he intended nothing more at the time than a first try at national history. As such the book was a success and, more important, a signpost. For although lacking erudition and patience for the sustained practice of the historian's craft, Wimpheling was driven by a powerful motive for writing and propagating history: his enlistment in the Alsatian resistance to French political and cultural encroachment. History as a weapon for contending a vital interest, history as a means of gaining support for a noble cause — here was a task for the practicing historian which, though hardly new, was bound to make him cast a critical look at historiographical ideas and procedures no longer adequate to the imperatives of the day.

When a coherent interpretation of the course of German history did emerge after the middle of the sixteenth century, it came not as a result of redoubled efforts by the chronicler, nor in consequence of the transplantation to Germany of humanist ideas. Chroniclers, while accustomed to taking the long view, were too deeply enmeshed in their infinite world of petty details, while humanist scholars, though their source criticism and their pursuit of questions of origin and derivation were vital and fruitful, were not by their outlook impelled toward a reassessment of the whole course of German history [42]. Nor

---

[41] Originally written in 1340, the *Tractatus* was published in Strassburg, 1508.

[42] For a somewhat different view, see Paul Joachimsen, *Geschichtsauffassung* ..., in which it is argued that humanism precipitated the decisive break with medieval traditions of historiography in German historical scholarship. See especially pp. 74-77, 104-5.

did the great undertaking of the *Germania illustrata*, whose objective it was to portray Germany in her present condition, ever turn to the task of giving shape to, and making sense of, the historical events of the preceding ages. The many territorial and local descriptions which were the fruit of the impetus given the *Germania illustrata* idea by Celtis and his colleagues in the first decade of the sixteenth century, are essentially eulogies of the splendor of Germany and of the good life being lived there. They tended to avoid risky questions of interpretation. Sebastian Münster, one of the ablest among the descriptive guides to the German scene [43], stoutly proclaimed his desire to remain above political and other controversies in order to perform his task without injuring person or party [44].

Münster was, in any case, and along with most of his fellow writers on human affairs, much too conscious of the inadequacy of his knowledge and the fallibility of his judgment [45] to display the kind of self-confidence needed for the job of interpreting history. No such lack of self-assurance troubled those who were eventually to accomplish this task. Historical reassessments have always coincided with turning points in history, and have been closely associated with the movements responsible for them. In their sweep and scope these historical interpretations reflect the movement's uncompromising confidence and self-absorption. It would be astonishing if the Lutheran Reformation had not brought about a searching review of German history, or if it had failed to produce a consistent interpretation of the course of that history. Although not important to the movement as a source of self-knowledge, history was of evident value as a weapon in the struggle against religious and political oppo-

---

[43] Münster's *Cosmographia* (published Basel, 1544; I use German version of 1545 and Latin version of 1550) covers, of course, the entire world. But the bulk of the book, pp. 189-591 out of 818 pp. in the 1545 edition, is taken up by the third book on Germany. Münster states it as his principal objective to « emphasize the German nation as much as possible ... ». *Cosmographia* (Basel, 1545), a VI recto.

[44] *Ibid.*, preface, a VI recto.

[45] Karl Heinz Burmeister (ed.) *Briefe Sebastian Münsters* (Ingelheim, 1964), *passim*. Nearly every one of Münster's surviving letters shows the man's respect for facts, his passion for bringing as many facts as possible into his possession, his desire to avoid controversy at all costs, and the sense of his own fallibility.

nents. With Melanchthon showing the way, and his son-in-law Caspar Peucer to execute the design, the themes and arguments advanced by earlier writers were joined into a coherent body of historical opinion. The resulting historical portrait of Germany — a country besieged, despoiled, violated, her guileless, trusting people defrauded by sly foreigners — is not a pretty one, but as a tool of propaganda it had great power, negatively as a means of identifying the enemy, positively as an instrument for rallying popular support.

The ability of history to sway opinions had, of course, long been recognized. Wimpheling and Aventinus had utilized it for this purpose, the latter with considerable skill. Of the careworn portrait of Germany arising from Peucer's *Chronicle* in the 1570 's, every line and wrinkle had been drawn before. The power of history to personalize and dramatize the great issues and controversies was evident to all. No one having read Johann Stumpf's tragic chronicle of the reign of Henry IV was likely to remain unaffected by its scenes of perfidy, filial treachery, and popular inconstancy [46], nor fail to agree with Stumpf that the struggle between the unfortunate emperor and the overweening pope was the beginning of the Empire's time of troubles, the end of which was not yet in sight [47]. The facts of history had often before been seized as weapons of attack and defense. But never had the entire course of German history come under such pointed review. Now, however, writers and publishers in the service of the Lutheran Reformation applied to the entire course of German history the lessons drawn from earlier fragmentary examinations of events and personalities, creating for the first time an interpretation of German history which made it possible to grasp both its scope and its essence.

A fundamental lack of interest in the intrinsic processes of history prevented the first generation of Lutheran historians from abandoning the traditional scheme of world monarchies, or from consigning to the rubbish heap such transparent and already exposed, but nonetheless useful, forgeries as the false

---

[46] Johann Stumpf, *Keyser Heinrychs des vierdten ... fünftzigjärige Historia ...* (Zurich, 1556).

[47] A point also made in Stumpf's main work, *Gemeiner loblicher Eydgnoschaft ... Beschreybung* (Zurich, 1548) ff. 49 v-50 r.

« Berosus » of Annius of Viterbo. Frequent protestations notwithstanding, it was not so much historical truth that counted; what mattered was the utility of historical exemplification, and the impact of historical argument. In its general outline the course of German history as seen in Wittenberg was accurate enough, based as it was, for the most part, on well established facts and much-debated points of view. But the Wittenberg authors did not primarily seek the critical approval of the scholarly community. Their appeal was to a wider public and their purpose to teach or, more properly, indoctrinate.

Melanchthon's role in the production of Johann Carion's world chronicle of 1532 has by now been clearly established [48]. Carion, a professional astrologer and mathematician, had drawn up some notes and reflections on world events and taken them to Melanchthon, whose respect for the science of astrology and its practitioners seems to have prompted him to revise a manuscript singularly conventional and lacking in form. Carion's brief chronicle and its various translations and continuations [49] therefore reflected from its first edition Melanchthon's historical ideas, as these are known to us also from his various prefaces and univerity lectures [50]. Though too brief to press any of its arguments conclusively, the little chronicle mirrors not only Melanchthon's views on history, but also the spirit in which history, and particularly German history, had been written since the beginning of the sixteenth century. Every incident is introduced as an *exemplum*. Emperors represent virtue, France

---

[48] See Robert Stupperich, « Geschichtliche Arbeit und Geschichtsbetrachtung », in *Der unbekannte Melanchthon* ... (Stuttgart, 1961), pp. 72-84, for a discussion of the literature on this point. Most informative: Gotthard Münch, « Das Chronikon Carionis Philippicum », *Sachsen und Anhalt* I (1925), 199-283.

[49] *Chronica, durch Magistrum Johan Carion vleissig zusamen gezogen* ... (Wittenberg, 1532). New editions Wittenberg, 1533, 1538, 1549; Augsburg, 1533, 1540; Magdeburg, 1534; Frankfurt, 1546; continued by Johann Funck, Frankfurt, 1555. All these in German. Latin translations 1537, 1539, 1550, 1555. Other editions and translations are listed by Georg Theodor Strobel, *Miscellaneen* ... VI (Nuremberg, 1782), 159-206. I cite according to Wittenberg, 1532.

[50] On Melanchthon's historical ideas see Robert Stupperich, *loc. cit.* and Attilio Agnoletto, « Storia e non storia in Filippo Melantone », *Nuova rivista storica* 48 (1964), 491-528, with bibliography.

and the papacy the powers of greed and envy whose machinations (« *Praktiken* ») have plunged Germany into ruination [51]. Hope is confined to the expectation of the world's end, which cannot now be more than a few generations away [52].

That a much more comprehensive, detailed, and polemical survey of German history than this should have transformed the later versions of the *Chronica Carionis*, despite the Lutheran belief in the imminence of Doomsday and the consequent irrelevance of temporal history, cannot be due to anything other than the nature of the Lutheran movement as a struggle. Melanchthon had strong convictions about the power of history to teach by example, not only how to act in given situations, but also how to relate one's own strivings to the great currents of world history. This explains the great importance he attached to general history — « whole chronicles » (as he put it) « from beginning to end » [53]. History was an invaluable aid to his theological pedagogy. As revised by Melanchthon in 1558 and 1560 (as far as Charlemagne) [54] and continued by Caspar Peucer through the reign of Maximilian [55], the so-called Chronicle of Carion in its long Latin and German versions of 1572 and 1573,

---

[51] 129 verso; 149 recto; 151 recto; 163 recto and verso, and *passim*.

[52] 169 recto and verso.

[53] See Melanchthon's preface to Kaspar Hedio's translation of Cuspinian's *de Caesaribus atque Imperatoribus Romanis opus* ... of Strassburg, 1541, reprinted in Robert Stupperich, « Geschichtliche Arbeit », pp. 183-91. For an ill-tempered and anti-Protestant, but not inaccurate, review of Melanchthon's attitude to history, see Richard Fester, « Sleidan, Sabinus, Melanchthon », *Historische Zeitschrift*, 89 (1902), 11-12.

[54] Printed in *Corpus Reformatorum* XII. For a discussion of Melanchthon's version of the *Chronica*, see Gotthard Münch in « Das Chronikon », pp. 258-75.

[55] Peucer completed the Latin version of the *Chronica Carionis* with the publication of part V (Wittenberg, 1565, to the death of Maximilian). All parts together appeared in 1572. This last edition was translated into German: *Chronica Carionis ... vermehret und gebessert durch Herrn Philippum Melanchthonem und Doctorem Casparum Peucerum* (Wittenberg, 1573). Peucer's difficulties in Wittenberg did not begin until 1574, when he was tried and imprisoned. The Elector August of Saxony sought, despite his theological antipathy to Peucer, to persuade him to complete the *Chronica* with a final part on contemporary affairs. But Peucer resolutely refused to comply while in prison and under suspicion, and the last section of the chronicle was never written. See Caspar Peucer, *Historia carcerum* ... (Zurich, 1605), pp. 302-3.

though preachy and obtrusively pedantic in its parade of book learning, advances an absorbing and, in its total impact, stirring interpretation of the course of German history. Nothing in Melanchthon's various pronouncements on history suggests that he himself had taken a special interest in German history. But Peucer, who was invited by the academic senate of the University to carry on Melanchthon's lectures and continue the chronicle [56], turned the narrative decisively in that direction. So completely did German history come to dominate the final versions of what had started out as an epitome of a world chronicle that, from the fourth book (the beginning of Peucer's authorship) onward, the discussion of other countries and peoples is confined to occasional notes on « conditions in England » and « conditions in Poland » [57].

German history proper begins at a point when a great change in the structure of the Roman Empire divided the western from the eastern regions. First among the new western rulers were the German Franks who « conquered the occidental empire and, through their wisdom and manly deeds, maintained and continued it in Germany » [58]. The appearance and character of German lands and peoples, as portrayed in Peucer's description of the country at the time of Charlemagne (pp. 411-44), reveal the might now in the hands of Germans, though the discussion of the extent and privileges of their conquest is set against a backward glance to the fate of ancient empires. The ups and downs of history, the reader is reminded, should admonish him, even as pride in his own country swells his breast, that life is but exile and the future can bring only calamities. The claims of conscience thus satisfied, Peucer proceeds to the question of Charlemagne and of the imperial title (pp. 451 ff.). Of the legitimacy of this title there are many proofs. Charles won it by conquest and the right of war, and it was bestowed on him by the Roman nobility with the approval of the eastern emperor. Charles was not created emperor by the pope, who has neither

---

[56] See the documents printed in Georg Theodor Strobel, *Miscellaneen*, VI (Nuremberg, 1782), 190-91.

[57] A great deal of space is, of course, given to the Church. But secular history in Peucer's version of Carion's *Chronica* is the history of the Holy Roman Empire.

[58] I cite according to *Chronica Carionis*... (Wittenberg, 1573), p. 409.

the right nor the power to dispose over the kingdoms of the world. A long look at Charles' public and private life suggests a man of exemplary virtues, in sum « one of the truly good and wholesome monarchs through whom God chooses to reign » (p. 470). But the ensuing swift breakdown of the Carolingian empire illustrates the nature of human history and furnishes scores of « examples, which rulers would be wise to take as a warning to themselves » (p. 490).

Meantime the papacy had usurped the rule of the Church and subverted the traditional supremacy of the emperor over the pope into a papal hegemony [59]. Glancing back over the fifteen hundred years since the coming of Christ, Peucer finds an uninterrupted growth in papal power and a corresponding decay of everything else (p. 511). During the first five hundred years of this long span of time truth remained ascendant, but the succeeding half millennium saw the battles of truth against lies, heresy, and superstition become ever more violent as vice gained on virtue, the wicked felt their strength, and the good grew feeble. « In the last five hundred years », he concludes, « idolatry, superstition, and ambition have grown ripe in the Church. Of its erstwhile discipline nothing is left but a shadow ». The papacy is not seen here as a historical phenomenon, as it is in the work of another Protestant historian, Johann Sleidan [60], who shows how the steady growth and success of papal power must be explained as the result of stealth and the ruthless, single-minded pursuit of the politics of domination. Melanchthon and Peucer saw Rome as a supernatural force. It simply exists; no one is to blame for having allowed it to arise, but everyone must see it as an admonition to heed the judgment of God on men's sins (p. 537).

Wicked power requires a victim for the perpetration of its mischief, and this is the role in which the German nation sees itself cast. Papal designs and Italian intrigue cause « *Empörung*

---

[59] The reversal of the traditional relationship of emperor and pope was generally accepted as the source of all German troubles with the Church. Cf. Sebastian Münster, *Cosmographia* (Basel, 1545), ff. 49 v-50 r; 62 r; 69 r and v.

[60] Especially in *Oration an alle Stende des Reichs. Vom römischen Nebenhaupt, im Keisertum erwachsen* (1542), printed in *Bibliothek des litterarischen Vereins in Stuttgart* CXLV (Tübingen, 1879).

und Aufrur » to break out again and again (p. 571). This is the background of German history during the middle ages. Heroic efforts were required to withstand assaults unleashed from Rome, but even though Germany could boast her share of determined rulers, her history records more defeats than victories. The reign of Henry IV is a climactic moment in this struggle, as well as one possessing the peculiar character of one of history's *fatales periodi* in which great mutations occur in human affairs (pp. 634 ff.). The Church's transformation of itself into a secular monarchy having been consummated [61], fundamental alterations were bound to throw the Empire into turmoil, as « the sovereignty and majesty of imperial dignity were undermined by papal cunning and, ultimately, destroyed and brought into the utmost contempt » (p. 641). Stopping at nothing, the popes did not rest until they had crushed the German emperors into docile subjects, « torturing them cruelly and steeping them in disgrace ». A mere shadow now of her former autonomy, Germany had been irretrievably altered into « an alien shape and condition » (« *ein gar frembde gestalt und form* » p. 641). With no object other than the extension of their hegemony over Germany by means of fomenting dissension and civil war, the popes and other « arrogant Italians » succeeded in ruining the country through « the shedding of noble German blood », « the extirpation of the most distinguished of her princely houses », and « the subversion of her ancient laws and customs » (p. 642). Now and then a handful of stalwart men struggled to their feet, but it was no use. The pope's power was too vast now, and the common rabble too blinded by superstition (p. 643) to reverse the Roman triumph.

Why did emperors and princes acquiesce in this destruction of the nation's manhood? Peucer raises the question in anticipation of protests from even the most resigned believers in God's inscrutable direction of events. True to the by now customary stereotype of the naive and artless German whose simple piety left him naked to Latin cunning, the very virtues of the

---

[61] Approximately 1000 years having passed since the apostles first began to preach, the Church was about to enter its « third period of 500 years during which its doctrines, discipline, and organization were to take on a new shape ». *Chronica Carionis* ..., p. 634.

German character are shown to have brought on his undoing. « Not because of terror or timidity », did the emperors succumb, « nor through any flinching in the face of danger, painful though it must have been to gaze upon the pitiful ruination of their fatherland, the gruesome massacre of their subjects, and the terrible destruction of so many of their truest and dearest friends. The main cause of our sovereigns' reticence in the face of provocation was their unswerving love of the Christian faith, which made them unwilling to offer resistance to the popes. This is the principal, indeed almost the only, reason why pious German emperors submitted to the popes » (pp. 721-22).

Under the sign of papal tyranny nothing went right. At best the country could patch its divisions and muddle through its difficulties (p. 775). After the death of Frederick II, the last monarch to rise to self-defense against the pope, « everything went to rack and ruin » (p. 811). What follows — not only in national, but also in regional and local history — is unrest, invasions, civil strife, a story of general disintegration. Instances of public and individual corruption proliferate. The revival of studies and letters, brought west by refugee scholars from Constantinople (p. 1044) is a bright note, as is the introduction of printing into Germany, for to these is due the cleansing of Christian doctrine and the renewal of religion (p. 1046). But the human story continues in gloom. We are assured that the Roman Empire will last to the end of time (and « prophecy and soothsaying » confirm the belief [p. 776]). But might not the imperium be once again transferred to another people? Peucer thinks not. Only the Turks stand as a possible successor, and they do not constitute, he thinks, a civilization (p. 776), But the nagging doubt, by no means mere rhetoric in the historical thought of the time, made the backward glance over the course of German history a peculiarly poignant experience.

This picture of German history was the generally accepted one in the Protestant historical literature of the later sixteenth century. It is implicit, where not explicitly affirmed, in regional descriptions and local chronicles [62]. Older works brought up

---

[62] For a comprehensive, though superficial, survey of the literature of regional and local historiography in Germany, see Franz X. von Wegele, *Geschichte der deutschen Historiographie* (Munich and Leipzig, 1885), pp. 143-78; 372-464.

to date or translated carried insertions or addenda to make them fit the pattern [63]. There is, to be sure, a counterpoint, namely the hope, or expectation, of a brighter destiny for the pitiful figure of wasted and impotent Germany. Without in any way altering the impression conveyed by the historical retrospect, this interpretation sees Luther's Germany as a risen and steeled nation which, having regained the light of true religion, and shed the blindfolds of her Roman slavery along with the ignorance of her own history, now serves God's purpose in the world. Sleidan puts this point of view forcefully, not in his best known work, the *Commentaries* of 1555, in which it is implicit, but in his *Address to the Estates of the Empire* of 1542, a no-holds-barred polemic, republished several times in the later sixteenth century. Look at our history, he says, learn from it and be proud of it. Barbarians at first, we have grown polished and refined. Victimized throughout the centuries by ruthless pontiffs and foreigners we were conditioned by adversity. « And as if to offer proof that God has chosen us to accomplish a special mission, there was invented in our land a marvelous, new, and subtle art, the art of printing » [64]. This opened German eyes, even as it is now bringing enlightenment to other countries. « Each man became eager for knowledge, not without feeling a sense of amazement at his former blindness » [65]. The cultural and religious renewal now in evidence in Germany is sure indication of other blessings to come.

Germany as a nation with a divine mission was another stereotype in historical literature. Matthias Flacius, chief historian and administrator of the Magdeburg Centuries, points to the presence of a small band of German warriors in the army with which Caesar defeated Pompey as a sign that God had, from the beginning, destined the Germans as possessors of the Empire [66]. Some writers saw a German mission of suffering,

---

[63] E. g. Basilius Faber who, in 1582, translated into German Albert Krantz's *Saxonia* of 1520, apologized for his author's deficient understanding of papal and imperial affairs. Albert Krantz, *Saxonia ...* (Leipzig, 1582), f. IIII r.

[64] Johann Sleidan, *Oration an alle Stende ...* (see note 60, above), p. 79.

[65] *Ibid.*, p. 80.

[66] *De translatione imperii Romani ad Germanos* (Basel, 1566); *Von Ankunfft des römischen Keysertums an die Deutschen* (Ursel, 1567), d 3 recto. In the

like that of ancient Israel. Indeed, much that was written in Germany at the time carries overtones suggesting an image of Germany as sacrificial victim [67]. Others could not believe that the Empire of Charles V was all shadow and no substance. « I conclude », writes Sleidan, « that never in her history has our German nation stood as high. Who knows, she may be the greatest in the world » [68].

Sleidan's confidence — or near-confidence, for he catches himself up short with a reminder that nearest the top one is also closest to one's downfall — arose from the conviction, gained in a half century's successful endeavor to portray Germany's riches and splendors, that the country's position in the world was solidly based on natural and man-made wealth. Matthias Quad summarized this belief at the beginning of the next century in a book appropriately titled *Teutscher Nation Herrligkeit* [69]. The optimistic, not to say boastful, view of German society given by Quad had been present throughout the second half of the sixteenth century. It gave voice to what was, no doubt, a genuine and widely-held sense of pride and gratitude. But it is an unreflective strain, not only because materialistic and quantitative, but because it is unhistorical. It never posed the real question: why had the Empire's splendid physical and human resources not been translated into strength, unity, and order? Why were calls for an end to strife and a healing of divisions fated to remain plaintive rhetoric? No informed and candid reply was given to the question until Pufendorf supplied it in 1667. Meanwhile the historical retrospect provided in Peucer's chronicle fashioned an integrated view of history which not only explained much that had been confusing in the distant and recent past, but also generated that sense of aggrieved self-righteousness which is so useful to an embattled movement.

The circulation of the *Chronica Carionis* in Peucer's final

Centuries themselves, the arrangement of material is too schematic to permit proper presentation of the course of German history. Affairs in the Empire come up at the beginning of Chapter 16 of each century.

[67] See my forthcoming collection *Manifestations of Discontent in Germany on the Eve of the Protestant Reformation*.

[68] Johann Sleidan, *Oration an alle Stende ...*, p. 81.

[69] Cologne, 1609.

redaction has never been precisely investigated [70], but all indications suggest that it was widely used in the Protestant world as a text for university lectures and as a teaching book in schools and for the instruction of young princes [71]. It was frequently republished, not only in Wittenberg, but also in Geneva, Lyons, Frankfurt, Rostock, and Dordrecht [72]. Its view of the course of German history must have been passed on to at least a generation of people called upon to understand the place of their country in the political and religious world of their time. No doubt, brooding speculations on disintegration and demise were, in any case, more congenial to the religious mood of the sixteenth century German than visions of eminence. The persistent image of Germany as long-suffering victim may therefore be yet another piece of evidence of that country's intense and honest religiosity.

---

[70] For some evidence, see Gotthard Münch, « Das Chronikon », pp. 276-83.

[71] See also Franz Schnabel, *Deutschlands geschichtliche Quellen und Darstellungen* (Leipzig and Berlin, 1931), pp. 45-6.

[72] For editions and translations see Georg Theodor Strobel, *Miscellaneen*, VI, 159-206. The *Chronica Carionis* is still given as a source for general world history in Johann Christoph Gatterer's *Handbuch der Universalgeschichte* I (Göttingen, 1763).

EUGENE F. RICE, JR.

THE PATRONS OF FRENCH HUMANISM, 1490-1520

During the last decade of the fifteenth century and the early decades of the sixteenth Jacques Lefèvre d' Etaples, Josse Badius Ascensius and Guillaume Budé successfully introduced in Paris an approximation of the educational and cultural program of Italian humanism. The transplantation to an alien environment of a program largely shaped by the intellectual and social needs of that two and a half per cent of citizens who manipulated the levers of capitalist command in Florence and Venice required skillful adaptation and a protective and receptive audience. Who were the patrons of humanism in France, and more particularly in Paris, during the crucial phase of its reception?

The source that best answers this question is the dedicatory epistle. Few books were without one. A list of the people to whom Lefèvre, Badius and Budé, Josse Clichtove, Charles de Bovelles, Gérard Roussel and François Vatable, Robert Fortuné, Guillaume Cop, Guillaume Parvy, Valerand des Varennes and their colleagues, friends and students addressed their editions, commentaries, treatises, verses and textbooks is a directory of the names and conditions of the men actively interested in their work [1].

It will hardly surprise a twentieth-century historian to learn that Parisian humanists dedicated more books to each other than to anyone else. The second largest group of dedications, which it is undesirable to separate too neatly from the first, went to faculty colleagues, students and friends at the university. A third group, only very little smaller than the second, was received by members of the regular and secular clergy: a Car-

[1] I have used about 300 dedicatory epistles: roughly half are included in my forthcoming book, *The Prefatory Epistles of Jacques Lefèvre d' Etaples and Related Texts*; another important group is the dedications of Josse Bade printed by Philippe Renouard, *Bibliographie des impressions et des oeuvres de Josse Badius Ascensius, imprimeur et humaniste (1462-1535)*, 3 vols. (Paris, 1908; photographic reprint, New York, Burt Franklin, 1964); the rest are scattered in original editions of works published by Parisian scholars before 1520.

thusian novice, the abbess of Faremoutiers, canons of the chapter of Notre-Dame, the royal confessor, the bishop of Paris or the abbots of Cluny and Saint-Germain-des-Prés. (Again the categories overlap. Some clerics were of course humanists and many more were teachers or students at the university). Influential laymen — officers of the crown and magistrates of the sovereign courts — received the fourth and smallest group of dedications. Only three members of the old nobility appear on the list: two were bishops, the third, Pierre d'Aumont, second son of Jean d'Aumont, lieutenant governor of Burgundy, and of Françoise de Maillé, dame de Châteauroux, was a student in the faculty of arts. Virtually no merchants or merchant-bankers appear either, no one, that is, currently engaged in international commerce or exchange and deposit banking on more than a local scale. (The exception is a man in the book trade, the publisher Jean Petit). Nor did humanists dedicate their books to retail merchants, manufacturers, shopkeepers or artisans. The king received a handful of dedications. Louis XII had a humanist physician and a humanist historiographer. But royal patronage of humanism became important only after 1520. Until then it was an intellectual movement confined to some among the masters and students of the university's faculty of arts, the higher echelons of the city's secular and monastic clergy, and the proliferating corps of royal officers, notably the magistrates of the Parlement of Paris.

Only a minority of these men were persons of power, wealth and influence who supported humanists in tangible ways: with pensions or ecclesiastical benefices, by employing them in their households as Latin secretaries or tutors for their sons and nephews, by subsidizing the publication of their books and paying handsomely for dedications. Colleagues or students in the faculty of arts were rarely patrons in this stricter sense; nor were fellow humanists — although a scholar like Guillaume Parvy, because he was the king's confessor, could act as an avenue to patronage. Patrons in the strict sense were almost invariably important royal officers, lay or ecclesiastical. The same surnames recur in both categories. What is constant is a group of families: the Bourrés, Ganays, Doucets, Huraults, Hacquevilles, Ruzés, Beaunes, Briçonnets, Berthelots, Ponchers, Guillarts, and Duprats.

The brothers Jean and Germain de Ganay, the most important patrons of art and letters in Paris between 1490 and 1508, are good early examples of the type. Jean de Ganay corresponded with Ficino and Aleander. In 1496 David Ghirlandaio sold him a mosaic of a seated virgin and child in the style of the late Florentine Quattrocento (now in the Musée de Cluny). Germain de Brie was his Latin secretary. Charles de Bovelles wrote him letters on mathematics and philosophy, while Fausto Andrelini celebrated in verse each of his promotions. Budé dedicated to him his *Annotations on the Pandects*, Lefèvre d' Etaples his edition of the *Arithmetic* of Jordanus, Guillaume Parvy an edition of Aquinas's *De regimine principum*. His younger brother Germain was even more enthusiastically devoted to the new intellectual fashion. In the preface to his commentary on Terence of October 1492 Guy Jouvenneaux has described Germain de Ganay's *litterata convivia*, where Parisian lovers of the « good and humane arts » ate well, drank well and sometimes spoke Greek. Lefèvre reported incidents from these gatherings in his commentaries on the *Organon* (1503) and on the *Politics* (1506). Badius Ascensius called them Germain's *triclinia* and was still praising them and his host in 1508. The circle of his humanist patronage, friendship and correspondence was exceptionally large. He received dedications from almost every humanist in Paris and corresponded with Ficino, Trithemius, Cornelius Agrippa of Nettesheim, Francesco da Diacceto and Lascaris. He was, as Guillaume Cop wrote of him, « another Maecenas » and in the « opinion of not only France but also of learned Italy, *optimarum litterarum asylum* » [2].

The Ganays came from the Charolais. The first member of the family who can be identified in records more reliable than fictive genealogies is a late fourteenth-century Jean de Ganay. He served the Burgundian dukes as *procureur* in the *bailliages* of Auxerre and Autun. In the fifteenth century the family split into two branches: one remained at Charolles in Burgundy, the other settled in Bourges and served in the royal administration of the *bailliage* of Berry. The brothers Ganay belonged to the branch of Charolles, grandsons of Jean I and sons of Guillaume I de

---

[2] *Pauli aeginetae praecepta salubria Guilielmo Copo Basiliensi interprete* (Paris, Henri Estienne, 4 April 1510), sig. a, v, v.

Ganay, the duke of Burgundy's pensioned lawyer at the Parlement of Paris and Cour du Trésor. In 1461 he became an *avocat du roi*, remaining in the royal service after the reincorporation of the duchy into the royal domain by Louis XI [3]. He trained both of his sons in the law. Jean II made a brilliant legal and administrative career. He became fourth president in the Parlement of Paris in 1490, accompanied Charles VIII to Italy in 1494, where his activities can be followed in Commines and Guicciardini's *Storia d'Italia*, and took a prominent part in the diplomatic negotiations with Pope Alexander VI in December-January 1494-1495 and in the peace negotiations after Fornovo. Charles VIII appointed him Chancellor of the Kingdom of Naples, but he returned to France with the king. By 1506 he was first president of the Parlement. When in January 1508 Louis XII made him Chancellor of France, he reached, as Budé put it in the preface to his commentary on the *Pandects*, « the pinnacle of public office, a magnificence achieved as a reward of personal merit rather than as a gift of fortune » [4]. His brother did almost equally well as an ecclesiastic: *conseiller clerc* in the Parlement of Paris (1485), canon of Notre-Dame of Paris (1486), canon of Saint-Étienne of Bourges (1492), dean of Beauvais (before 1494), president of the Court of Requests (28 June 1496), bishop designate of Cahors (August 1509) in opposition to Guy de Châteauneuf, the candidate elected by the chapter, but victoriously bishop in fact and law on 4 May 1511. He became bishop of Orleans in 1514 and died in 1520, the last of the Charollais branch of the Ganays [5].

---

[3] Christopher Stocker, *Offices and Officers in the Parlement of Paris, 1483-1515* (Unpublished PhD. dissertation, Cornell University, 1965), a valuable book to which I owe many biographical details about the Ganays and other families connected with the Parlement.

[4] Ernest de Ganay, *Un Chancelier de France sous Louis XII: Jehan de Ganay* (Paris, 1932); G. Dupont-Ferrier, « Les avocats à la Cour du Trésor de 1401 a 1515 », *Bibliothèque de l'Ecole des Chartes*, XCVII (1936), 66-67; *Gallia-Regia, ou état des officiers royaux des bailliages et des sénéchaussées du 1328 à 1515* (Paris, 1942-1954), I, 378.

[5] A. Renaudet, *Préréforme et Humanisme à Paris pendant les premières guerres d'Italie (1494-1517)*, 2nd ed. (Paris, 1953), p. 150 and *passim.*; H. Stein, « L'Imprimeur Orléanais Jean Asselineau et l'entrée de l'évèque Germain de Ganay en 1514 », *Revue des Bibliothèques*, XLI (1935-1936), 14-22; Jean Le Maire, « Les Fouilles de la Cathédrale Sainte-Croix d'Orléans

In 1505 Lefèvre d' Etaples dedicated a commentary on the *Corpus Hermeticum* to Guillaume Briçonnet, bishop of Lodève (1472-24 Jan. 1534). Within three years the Briçonnets had succeeded the Ganays as the most important patrons of Lefèvre and his circle and more generally of Parisian humanism. When Lefèvre retired from active teaching at the collège Cardinal Lemoine in 1508, Briçonnet, who had succeeded his father as abbot of Saint-Germain-des-Prés the year before, gave him rooms in the abbey and a pension. Here — and in the office of the printer Henri I Estienne — Lefèvre gathered around him a group of younger collaborators and during the next ten years produced a series of remarkable works: the *Quincuplex Psalterium* of 1509, dedicated to his patron's father, Cardinal Guillaume Briçonnet; in 1512 his commentary on the Pauline epistles, dedicated to the bishop of Lodève, in partial return, he wrote, « for the innumerable benefits which you have heaped upon me for so long, and continue to heap on me still, and especially for the particular support you give my studies »; in 1514 the great edition of the complete works of Nicholas of Cusa, dedicated to Denis Briçonnet, bishop of Toulon and Saint-Malo, brother of the bishop of Lodève; in 1517 an edition of Euclid's *Elements* dedicated to François Briçonnet, *receveur général des finances* and *maître de la Chambre aux deniers du roi*, one of two sons whom Pierre Briçonnet, knight of the Order of Saint-Michel and general of the finances of Languedoc and of France, had earlier entrusted to Paulo Emilio, royal historiographer, for tutoring in Latin and history and to Lefèvre for instruction in moral philosophy; and, finally, in 1518 the *Contemplationes Idiotae* of the fourteenth-century mystic Raymundus Jordanus, dedicated to Michel Briçonnet, son of yet another Guillaume, seigneur of La Kaérie in Touraine and a councillor in the Parlement of Paris, and himself a member of the household of Marguerite of Angoulême and bishop of Nîmes. In 1515 the bishop of Lodève brought another bishopric into the family, that of Meaux; and on his return from Rome in 1518, took up residence in his diocese and

(1937): mort, obsèques et sépulture de Germain de Ganay », *Bulletin de la Soc. arch. et hist. de l'Orléanais*, XXIV (1940-1943), 80-87, 111-113; P. O. Kristeller, *Studies in Renaissance Thought and Letters* (Rome, 1956), pp. 51-54, 96-97, 126-127, 314, 316, 321.

began to reform it. He made Lefèvre his vicar general *in spiritualibus*. To help him educate the parish clergy, improve preaching and evangelize the laity, Lefèvre called on many of the younger members of his circle: the Hellenist Gérard Roussel, for example, and François Vatable, later to be among the first *lecteurs royaux* in Greek and Hebrew. Briçonnet supported the learned preachers generously, spending 900 livres in 1521, 700 in 1522 and 600 in 1523. He was precisely what Vatable called him: « a most distinguished patron of humane letters » [6].

The Briçonnets were spectacularly successful, but otherwise typical of the social milieu of humanist patronage. They began as merchants of Tours, where from early in the fifteenth century the family had been prominently active in municipal finance and government. The five sons of Jean I Briçonnet made their first fortune in the management of the royal and household finances. The king appointed Jean II *élu* at Tours and in 1464 receiver general of Languedoc; a younger brother, also named Jean, receiver of the *taille* and *aides* for Tours, Chinon and Loches and receiver general of Languedoeil; André, royal notary and secretary, *argentier* of the household, and head of the *deniers des coffres*, a department of the *Chambre aux deniers* in the household finances. The next generation moved into every branch of the

---

[6] Many documents about Briçonnet's reforming activities at Saint-Germain-des-Prés and Meaux appear in Guy Bretonneau, *Histoire généalogique de la maison des Briçonnets* (Paris, 1621), pp. 132-224. The best guide to the admirable correspondence with Marguerite of Navarre (Paris, BN., ms. n. acq. fr. 11495) is Pierre Jourda, *Répertoire ... de la correspondance de Marguerite d'Angoulême* (Paris, 1930). See also BN. ms. fr. 6528 (Briçonnet's trial) and ms. lat. 12838 (his will); Ph. - Aug. Becker, « Les idées religieuses de Guillaume Briçonnet, évêque de Meaux », *Revue de théologie et des questions religieuses*, IX (1900), 318-358, 377-416; Renaudet, *Préréforme et Humanisme*, *passim*. and *Le Concile gallican de Pise-Milan* (Paris, 1922), *passim*., but esp. pp. 311, 374, 518, 584; M. Mosseaux, *Briçonnet et le mouvement de Meaux* (Unpublished thesis, Paris, 1923; copy in the Bibliothèque de la Société de l'Histoire du Protestantisme français, Paris); Lucien Febvre, « Le cas Briçonnet », *Au coeur religieux du XVIe siècle* (Paris, 1957), pp. 145-161; *Dictionnaire de biographie française*, VII (1956), 286-287; R. J. Lovy, *Les Origines de la Réforme française, Meaux, 1518-1546* (Paris, 1959); Stocker, *op. cit.*, pp. 192-201, 277-279, 284-286, 290-291, 295, 298-300, 306-308, 313-315; Henry Heller, *Reform and Reformers at Meaux: 1518-1525* (Unpublished PhD. dissertation, Cornell University, 1969), pp. 21-49, which contains a detailed and persuasive re-examination of Briçonnet's entire career.

royal administration: financial, legal and ecclesiastical. They held a host of diplomatic assignments and special commissions. They moved into offices in the *bailliages* and *sénéchaussées*; entered the Parlements of Paris, Toulouse, Dijon and Rennes; became treasurers at the Cour du Trésor and presidents of the Chambre des Comptes; collected taxes everywhere in the kingdom; occupied lucrative benefices in the church. Guillaume Briçonnet, father of the bishop of Lodève and Meaux, was the youngest son of Jean II, treasurer of France, and Jeanne Berthelot. He built an enormous personal fortune as *général des finances* of Languedoc under Louis XI and as Charles VIII's principal councillor. On the death of his wife, Raoulette de Beaune, daughter of a family as rich and ambitious as his own, he took orders and began a second spectacular career in the church: bishop of Saint-Malo (1493), cardinal (January 1495), part of the spoils of the Neapolitan campaign, bishop of Nîmes (1496), archbishop of Reims by open pressure and simony (1497), abbot of Saint-Germain-des-Prés (1504). He died in 1514, a diplomat, administrator, financier, who had spent his life at the center of great affairs, *oraculum regis, regni columna* [7].

These examples could be multiplied. Louis Ruzé, *conseiller de ville* in 1500, *conseiller au Parlement* in 1511, and *lieutenant civil au Châtelet* or subprefect of Paris, was a friend of Budé and Josse Bade, encouraged Greek studies, and supported younger scholars. Like the Briçonnet, the Ruzé were a mercantile family from Tours. Charles VII used them to collect the *taille* and *aides* in Le Mans; Louis XI appointed three of them to the Parlement of Paris. Their descendants served Louis XII and Francis I with continuing profit and distinction [8]. Etienne Poncher, royal

---

[7] For the sources and literature see the articles by M. Lecomte in *Dictionnaire d'histoire et de géographie ecclésiastiques*, X (1938), 676-682; Claude-Henriette Bassereau, « Jean Briçonnet l'Ainé et Jean Briçonnet le Jeune, bourgeois de Tours et financiers au XVe siècle », *Positions des thèses*, *Ecole Nationale des Chartes* (1951), pp. 15-19; Stocker, *Offices and Officers*, *passim.*; and articles by R. Limouzin-Lamothe in *Dictionnaire de biographie française*, VII (1956), 285-288.

[8] Renouard, *Badius Ascensius*, II, 534 and III, 174, 190-192, 199; L. Delaruelle, *Répertoire analytique et chronologique de la correspondance de Guillaume Budé* (Paris, 1907), pp. 10-11, 33; *Opus Epistolarum Des. Erasmi*, ed. P. S. Allen (Oxford, 1910), II, 402; E. Jovy, *François Tissard et Jérôme Aléandre* (Vitry-le-François, 1900-1913), fasc. III, pp. 12-13.

orator, *conseiller clerc* in the Parlement of Paris (1485) and Chancellor of the duchy of Milan between 1504 and 1511, bishop of Paris (1503) and archbishop of Sens (1519), was among the warmest supporters of the literary, educational and reform program of Badius, Lefèvre and other humanists. His family was also from Tours. Two generations of *grenetiers*, receivers of the *taille* and *aides* and members of the Cour des Monnaies lifted the third generation to the episcopacy and the sovereign courts [9]. During the 1520's Josse Clichtove's most useful patrons were several members of the Guillart family. In the fifteenth century they had been bourgeois of Orléans, members of the « Corporation of Merchants Frequenting the River Loire », *fournisseurs* of the dukes of Orléans, and treasurers of the counts of Maine. When Duke Louis became King Louis XII, the Guillarts prospered with him, serving him and his successors in financial offices, the Parlement of Paris, and as bishops of Tournai, Chartres, Châlons-sur-Saône, and Senlis [10]. By the late 1520's the Chancellor Antoine Duprat, his sons and brother, the bishop of Clermont, were receiving almost as many dedications as the Briçonnets a decade earlier. For four generations the Duprats had been wine and cloth merchants, money lenders and royal officers in the Auvergne. The future Chancellor, Antoine V, was the first to abandon trade. He studied law, served the crown as *lieutenant du roi ès bailliage* in Montferrand, councillor in the Parlement of Bordeaux and later in Paris. In 1511 Jean Petit published his codification of the customary law of his native province. During the first twenty years of the reign of Francis I he was the most powerful man in the kingdom after the king, accumulating wealth, titles and offices, both lay and ecclesias-

---

[9] Renouard, *Badius Ascensius*, II, 135, 146, 271, 317, 475; III, 84, 388; Renaudet, *Préréforme et Humanisme*, *passim.*, but especially pp. 14-15, 348-353, 438-443; Allen, II, 454; Emile Ganelle, *Le Tombeau des Poncher et Jacques Bachot* (Lille, 1923); and Monique Garand-Zobel, « Etienne Poncher, évêque de Paris, archevêque de Sens (1446-1525) », *Positions des thèses, Ecole des Chartes* (1954), 61-71.

[10] *Catalogue des actes de François Ier*, I, 404, no. 2149; 447, 2366; 653, 3424; II, 406, 5781; III, 10, 7491; IV, 755, 14510; V, 167, 15527; 444, 16958; VIII, 575, 32255; B. Hauréau, *Histoire littéraire du Maine*, IV (Paris, 1852), pp. 196-197; P. S. Allen, « Hieronymus Balbus in Paris », *English Historical Review*, XVII (1902), 421-423; Allen, II, 150 and IV, 527-528; Maugis, *Histoire du Parlement de Paris* (Paris, 1916), III, 115, 119, 148.

tical (he was left a widower in 1508) on a scale paralleled earlier only by the Briçonnets [11].

Claude de Seyssel's *Monarchie de France* helps us situate these patron families more securely in the social hierarchy of early sixteenth-century France. He distinguishes three principal classes of men: the nobility, the *peuple gras* or *état moyen*, and the *peuple menu*. Earlier generations of Ganays, Briçonnets, and Duprats belonged to the *peuple gras*. More specifically, they belonged to that section of the *état moyen* « qui se veulent excerciter en autre chose que leurs ménages et marchandises ». Gradually abandoning the commerce and money lending in which they had made their earliest fortunes, they became financial and judicial officers.

Seyssel defines the position of these officer families even more precisely. They were social climbers, not only from *marchandises* to *offices*, but also from *état moyen* to the nobility. The nobility, Seyssel tells us, remains the order highest in dignity and power, « so much so that members of the second estate are trying constantly to penetrate it » [12]. Unlike Commines, who pilloried the Briçonnets as parvenus, Seyssel encouraged the king to ennoble middle class men in order, first, to replenish an estate continuously depleted by war and poverty and, second, to encourage members of the *état moyen* in virtuous, loyal service to the king and *chose publique* by this hope of social ascent. He pictures, indeed, an exceedingly mobile society, a mobility useful because « chacun se contente de son état et n'a occasion de machiner contre les autres, sachant que par bons moyens et licites il y peut parvenir ». And this in fact happens today: « La facilité y est telle que l'on voit tous les jours aucuns de l'état populaire monter par degrés jusques à celui de noblesse; et au moyen état, sans nombre » [13].

The social history of families like the Ganays, Briçonnets and Duprats confirms Seyssel's testimony. They had begun

---

[11] Marcellin Boudet, « Documents sur la bourgeoisie dans les deux derniers siècles du Moyen Age: les Du Prat », *Revue de la Haute Auvergne*, XXVIII-XXXII (1926-1931); Albert Buisson, *Le Chancelier Antoine Duprat* (Paris, 1935); *Dictionnaire de biographie française*, XII (1968), 503-505.

[12] *La Monarchie de France*, I, 15, ed. Jacques Poujol (Paris, 1961), pp. 123-124.

[13] *Ibid.*, I, 17, p. 125.

their ascent from *peuple menu* to *état moyen* in the fourteenth century. By the middle of the fifteenth their members were rich merchant-bankers, experienced in municipal government and finance, men of « prud' hommie, souffisance, notabilité et avoir ». Such men were useful to the king. They lent him money. They managed his household finances. He employed them in the immensely difficult and lucrative collection and administration of the direct and indirect taxes of the crown. Gradually they abandoned their *marchandises* and devoted themselves entirely to royal service, in judicial and ecclesiastical offices as well as in the financial administration. They became the nucleus of a fourth estate, the corps of royal officers. In return for their services to the commonwealth, the « grace et privilège du Prince » rewarded them. The king gave them offices which automatically conferred nobility: the first presidency of the Parlement of Paris, for example, or the Chancellorship. He granted or sold them patents of nobility. He created a Bourré, a Poncher, a Briçonnet and a Duprat knights of the Order of Saint-Michel.

As part of the same process officers bought noble land, especially near Paris where property was changing hands rapidly around 1500. Of sixty-five parishes south of the city in which laymen held the principal seigniory, fifty-two changed hands one, two, three, even four times between the late fourteenth century and the middle of the sixteenth [14]. As older seigniorial families sold out, officer families bought their properties. Jean de Ganay, for example, bought the barony of Persan in 1490 and a year later did homage for it to the duke of Orleans, the future Louis XII. He bought the fief of Roussets in 1510 and the seigniory of La Buissière in Gâtinais in February 1512, just before his death [15]. Ennobled in 1464, Jean Guillart, lawyer, notary, and financial officer, bought the seigniory of Epichelière at Soulingé-sous-Vallon in the province of Maine and built a chateau. He left house and title to his son Charles, fourth pre-

---

[14] Yvonne Bézard, *La Vie rurale dans le sud de la région parisienne de 1450 à 1560* (Paris, 1929), pp. 68 ff.; Guy Fourquin, *Les Campagnes de la région parisienne à la fin du Moyen Age* (Paris, 1964), pp. 465-474.

[15] Léon Mirot, *Inventaire analytique des hommages rendus à la Chambre de France* (Melun, 1932-1945), fasc. II, p. 308, nos. 3152-3153; p. 316, no. 3248; Ernest de Ganay, *Jehan de Ganay*, pp. 66-70.

sident in the Parlement of Paris. Charles' elder son André inherited the property; the younger, Louis Guillart, became a bishop. Between 1509 and 1522 the Ponchers acquired the seigniories of Micy, Lésigny, Limours, Brie-Comte-Robert, La Ferté-Alais, Tournan, Moret, Torcy and Crécy [16]. The son of the chancellor, Antoine VI, was lord of Nantouillet, Précy and Maucreux and Baron of Thiers and Thoury-sur-Allier. The Briçonnets began accumulating seigniories early in the fifteenth century. They acquired Guyancourt by marriage, then bought the seigniories of Glatigny near Versailles and Villedombe-près-Saclay. By 1520 the family had lands in the Ile-de-France, in Brittany, near Tours, around Bordeaux and elsewhere [17].

They consolidated their properties and furthered their careers by intermarriage. Briçonnets married Berthelots, Bohiers, Ponchers, Groliers and Beaunes. The Chancellor Duprat was the son of Jacqueline Bohier. Jacques de Beaune, baron of Semblançay, the celebrated financial minister of Francis I, was married to Jeanne Ruzé. Gilenne Berthelot was the wife of Jean Ruzé. Wherever one probes, the pattern is likely to resemble this one: In 1522 Gérard Roussel dedicated his new translation of Aristotle's *Magna Moralia* to François Bohier. François was a younger son of Thomas Bohier, financial officer, baron of Saint-Cirgues and builder of the chateau of Chenonceau, and Catherine Briçonnet, a sister of the bishop of Lodève and Meaux. He and his elder brother Antoine were educated by a humanist tutor, Remigius Rufus Candidus. Antoine, a royal treasurer, married Anne Poncher and inherited his father's lands and titles (seriously encumbered by debts). Later in the reign of Francis I he was to become a royal chamberlain, member of the *Conseil privé* and lieutenant general of Touraine. Early destined to an ecclesiastical career, François studied civil and canon law. He was *canonicus primarius* or *praepositus* of Chartres in 1515-1516 when Remigius and Josse Bade dedicated to the two brothers [Pseudo-] Lull's *In Rhetoricen Isagoge* and Quintilian's *Institutio oratoria*. In 1522 he was dean of Tours and in 1535 succeeded his uncle Denis Briçonnet as bishop of Saint-Malo. He maintained his patronage

---

[16] Mirot, I, p. 35, no. 384; p. 51, nos. 367-368; p. 111, no. 1249; p. 157, no. 1760.

[17] Mirot, I, p. 206, nos. 2314-2316; Bézard, p. 76; Fourquin, p. 472.

of letters in his maturity and himself translated into French Cusanus' *Coniectura ultimis diebus mundi* [18].

Intermarriage was the more natural because these families had common geographical origins. They came from the Loire valley and the region south to the Auvergne. The chateaux of the Loire are concentrated in the same area and for the same reason. Expelled from Paris by the English and Burgundians, Charles VII spent most of his reign close to the Loire. After his coronation Louis XI settled at Plessy-lez-Tours. Under Charles VIII and Louis XII the court was ordinarily at Amboise or Blois. In an age and kingdom where the accumulation of great wealth was still inseparably tied to physical access to the monarch's person, the king's presence for so many years in their vicinity was a wonderful opportunity for the mercantile families of Tours, Orleans, Blois, Bourges, and Issoire. They seized and developed it with profitable skill.

The great officer families of the reigns of Charles VIII, Louis XII and Francis I were an exceptionally homogeneous group. By the decades between 1490 and 1520, when some of their members were the patrons of the humanists of Paris, their wealth was invested in land and offices; they looked to the king for honor and advancement (parents schooled their children to gain and merit royal favor and threatened idlers with remaining « en casanier dans la poussière ») [19]; their profession was commonly the law or the church, or both; they were legally nobles.

The intellectual interests of Guillaume Budé or Lefèvre d' Etaples suggest no obvious reason why these officer families encouraged humanism — in spite of the fact that Budé himself belonged to one: his family was ennobled in 1399; his father,

---

[18] De la Chenaye-Desbois et Badier, *Dictionnaire de la noblesse*, III, 383; Eubel, III, 248; Renouard, *Badius Ascensius*, II, 413; III, 45, 197, 210, 471-472; Ch. de Mecquenem, « Antoine Bohier: abbé de Saint-Ouen (de Rouen), abbé commendataire de Fécamp et d'Issoire, archevêque de Bourges (1515-1519), cardinal (1517) », *Mémoires de la Soc. hist., litt. et sci. du Cher*, 4e ser., XXXIII (1922), pp. 1-47, which contains two useful tables tracing the relationships among Bohier, Briçonnet, Berthelot, and Beaune; *Dictionnaire d'histoire et de géographie ecclésiastiques*, IX (1937), 513; *Dictionnaire de biographie française*, VI (1954), 781-783. Other useful genealogical tables in Alfred Spont, *Semblançay* (? - *1527*). *La bourgeoisie financière au début du XVI*[e] *siècle* (Paris, 1895), Appendix.

[19] Bretonneau, *Maison des Briçonnets*, p. 45.

like his grandfather before him, was a royal notary, secretary, treasurer, *garde des Chartes du roi*, and owned very substantial properties in the Ile-de-France. Humanists reformed the curriculum of the arts faculty by « purifying » instruction in logic and putting greater emphasis on literature and mathematics; by paraphrases, commentaries and new translations they restored Aristotle's philosophy to its original eloquence and meaning (or so they believed); they encouraged the study of Greek and an historically more sophisticated reading of the Latin classics; they worked for religious reform and a purer, simpler piety by publishing the mystics and the Church Fathers and by returning to the Biblical text in its original languages; they popularized historical studies in first editions of medieval histories of the French monarchy, editions and translations of classical historians, and learned investigations of Roman antiquities and the historical development of the civil law. To be sure, a rhetorical training had professional relevance for royal councillors, lawyers, churchmen, and diplomats. This is one reason why Briçonnets and Duprats gave their children a humanist education; and why a noble of more ancient lineage, Jacques d'Amboise, bishop of Clermont, put Clichtove in charge of the education of his nephews. But there was no inherent affinity between humanism and the interests of this particular social group. The humanist program was politically, socially and economically neutral. Like the several varieties of Protestantism, humanism appealed to men of diverse social origins and for reasons dependent on local and temporal circumstance. Lutheranism at different times and places attracted peasants, artisans, merchants, knights, princes, and kings. Similar circumstantial links, which must be studied locally and individually, connect the humanist program with its social carrier.

In Paris in the early sixteenth century the link between humanism and the bureaucratic nobility was, I suggest, the need of « new men » for cultural ideals distinct from those of the group with whom they shared and competed for power, the older nobility. Distrusted and patronized by the traditional aristocracy, envied and resented by the *moyen état*, nobles, but not *nobles d'armes et de race*, their recent bourgeois extraction known to all, the social position of the « new men » was ambiguous. A flattering dedication was a *tuba famae*. Legitimate pre-eminence in the republic of letters helped legitimize an earned preeminence in the wider republic of men. A humanist education inculcated a self-confident dignity independent of both office and birth and helped bridge the gap between legal nobility, the reward of service, and acceptance as a gentleman.

But even if we agree that social insecurity and group rivalry predisposed « fourth-estate » families to support humanists, it remains noticeable that clerical members were more active patrons than laymen (which suggests that the traditional function of bishops to encourage scholarship and learning continued to be an important motive of patronage) and that although almost all patrons were members of officer families the reverse is not true. Only a small minority were actively interested in humanistic studies. Clearly individual inclination and taste directed patronage as effectively as social position predisposed it. Nor did members of the fourth estate retain their quasi monopoly of patronage for long. Soon the king, then members of the military aristocracy became patrons of humanism. By the end of the reign of Francis I it had become the function of a humanist education not only to make gentlemen out of merchants, but to make courtiers out of nobles, moulding them both to a common end of service in the sovereign territorial state.

SAMUEL KINSER

IDEAS OF TEMPORAL CHANGE AND CULTURAL PROCESS IN FRANCE, 1470-1535 *

* The research for this paper was carried through with the aid of a Newberry Library Grant-in-Aid and a Northern Illinois University Summer Research Grant. I wish to express my thanks to these institutions for their valuable help. Miss Katherine Davies of Edinburgh first directed my attention to the ideas of culture in Budé's *De Asse*, and her own as-yet-unpublished work on the book has been of inestimable aid. Without Professor Kiffin Rockwell's expertise I should have many times despaired of unravelling Budé's figured style.

In the last fifty years a number of historians have traced the growth in popularity of the idea of progress. Today this idea — that man's activities, or the laws of temporal change which determine those activities, are such that human existence steadily improves — is perhaps less attractive and less convincing than it was when intellectual historians first became interested in it. Those who in the course of European history have held that time is cyclic, fluctual, or statically repetitious may well appear to us as something other than the more or less benighted precursors of the Condorcets, Comtes, and Spencers whose progressive views triumphed in the nineteenth century. And many of those who have recorded this triumph may now appear to us to have assumed the truth of the idea that time is progressive as the basis for their own investigations. By making that assumption, they predetermined who would play the hero in their writing, and how the hero would sweep to victory along a unilinear path of development, before they ever set pen to paper [1].

Most students of the idea of progress point to modern science as the enterprise which did most to achieve the ascendancy and unfold the meaning of human progress [2]. This explanation,

[1] I have in mind primarily such recent surveys of the subject as Sidney Pollard's *Idea of Progress* (London, 1968) and Charles Van Doren's *Idea of Progress* (New York, 1967). Neither author appears to be aware of the research which has been accumulating on the ancient and medieval history of the idea. More important, the conceptual framework of their books as well as of their model, J. B. Bury's classic *Idea of Progress* (London, 1920), is even narrower than that employed by such earlier students of the subject as Jules Delvaille in his *Essai sur l'histoire de l'idée de progrès jusqu'à la fin du XVIIIe siècle* (Paris, 1910) and Hubert Gillot in his *La querelle des anciens et des modernes en France* (Paris, 1914).

[2] I paraphrase Bury, *op. cit.* (New York: Dover paperback edition, 1955), p. 351: «In achieving its ascendancy and unfolding its meaning, the Idea of Progress had to overcome a psychological obstacle which may be described as the illusion of finality ... The illusion of finality is strong ... It is science, perhaps, more than anything else — the wonderful history of science in the last hundred years — that has helped us to transcend this il-

however, may well be as circular as that which constructs a line of historical development in accordance with the very thesis which is being investigated. If, for example, scientific activity is habitually structured in such a way that it can only be carried on in a cumulative manner, each man's work contributing to the next man's in a progressive fashion, it would not be surprising to find scientists or writers about science concerned with ideas of progress. If, conversely, much non-scientific activity can only be carried on in a non-cumulative manner, each man's work throwing light on the next man's without either repeating it or adding to it in any simply definable way, it would be reasonable to expect non-scientists — men concerned with ethical or esthetic problems, for example — to develop concepts of time reflecting the non-cumulative character of their work and interests.

The progressive notion of time to which most men subscribe now is a consequence not so much of new scientific insights into some true and universal nature of time as it is of a change in the relative prestige of cumulative activities, such as most scientific and technological research is, vis-à-vis non-cumulative activities such as painting, oratory, or philosophy. In ancient and medieval times such non-cumulative activities were held to be more important than scientific or technological enterprises. The opposite is true today. The non-progressive versions of time to which most men subscribed before the nineteenth century were affirmed not on the basis of a balanced judgment of all kinds of human activity in all times and places, but rather on the basis of limited knowledge of such times, places, and kinds of activity. The limitations of knowledge were supplied by presumption: it was presumed that certain kinds of activity were more important or fundamental than other kinds, and that over long periods of time their pattern would be the same as that for the limited periods with which the writer was acquainted. These same limitations of knowledge obtained

---

lusion ». Bury sees the emergence of a theory of progress as occurring for the first time in the seventeenth century because « There can be no certainty that knowledge will continually progress until science has been placed on sure foundations. And science does not rest for us on sure foundations unless the invariability of the laws of nature is admitted ... The philosophy of Descartes established this principle ... » (*ibid.*, p. 66).

and these same presumptions were made by progressivist writers who, as we now know, existed in ancient, medieval, and early modern times as well as since the time of Fontenelle. But these progressivist writers were not very influential before the nineteenth century, in spite of the « rise » of science. Not science but scientism — ideological commitment to the investigation and management of nature as the most important or fundamental human activity — is responsible for the belief in progress prevalent today. Conversely, ideological commitment to the investigation and management, or at least propitiation, of infinite, eternal forces beyond nature had much to do with the juxtaposition in ancient, medieval, and early modern times of a realm of being in which time is static or even non-existent to a realm of becoming in which temporal changes occur continuously and chaotically or rhythmically and repetitiously.

However men regard the temporal continua in which they exist (I say continua and not continuum because for Augustinian Christians as well as for philosophical Platonists man exists in at least two intersecting yet distinct temporal perspectives simultaneously, one natural and finite, the other supernatural, infinite, and — insofar as it is thinkable — « timeless »), they do so on the basis of belief, not demonstration. There is no way for men to determine objectively the general character of human time. We do not live long enough, nor do we experience enough kinds of human activity, to be able to measure their mutual relationships and to sum up their general character. A leap of faith must be made, and for most men, the direction of that leap is determined by the general character of the culture in which they live. If we wish to understand why the idea of progress has been so popular in the nineteenth and twentieth centuries, we might well reflect upon the tendency in our culture to believe that scientists and technicians have a better grasp of and more control over the terms of our existence than anyone else.

The cultural climate of opinion largely determines one's notions of time; conversely, one's ideas of time influence one's vision of culture. Temporal conceptions must therefore be related to the cultural conceptions of those propounding them, if they are to be explained and understood. No man is an advocate of progress and nothing more. He is first of all a believer in certain kinds of human activity as more important than other kinds and then a believer in the progressive character of the more important kinds. On these bases he has made an inductive leap, a leap of faith, to assert that other kinds of human activity are either unimportant, if non-progressive, or are carried along in the wake of the main stream of human activity, partaking of its progressive character in greater or less degree. And he has made a second leap to assert either that because the short-range changes in human activity are progressive, the long-range changes will also be so, or that although the long-range changes in human activity are progressive, various short terms of time may be non-progressive.

If we were to identify in each man's writings the two leaps just mentioned — the movement from assertions about kinds of activity to assertions about the general character of the temporal development of culture, and the movement from assertions about limited periods of time to assertions about long or even infinite periods of time — the history of the idea of progress would acquire a very different form and meaning from that generally accepted now. Such a history would show, I think, that the broader and more complex a man's concept of culture is, the less likely he will be to see either a simply progressive or simply repetitious pattern in time [3]. The complexity of his notions of time will be proportionate to his awareness of and interest in diverse forms of human activity. And his awareness and interest will be by and large proportionate to the opportunities and outlets available to him for observing and participating in such activities. That is why it is particularly important for students of the idea of progress to establish when and how the walls between differing intellectual disciplines, between national traditions, or between theory and practice, are broken down. For the crumbling of traditional compartments of activity multiplies the possibilities of looking at human experience in new ways. My purpose in this paper is to illustrate this truism with reference to the temporal ideas of Philippe de Commynes (ca. 1447-1511), Guillaume Fichet (1433-ca. 1478), and Guillaume Budé (1468-1540).

---

[3] I use the word culture in the anthropological sense, as the ensemble of symbol-making and symbol-using activities of man.

These men, who wrote in the period between 1470 and 1535 in France, have not been previously cited in histories of the idea of progress. Up until now scholars have maintained that it was only in the later sixteenth century that Frenchmen liberated themselves from excessive adulation of antiquity, asserting their own cultural worth and temporal uniqueness. Du Bellay's *Deffence et illustration de la langue françoyse* (1548), Rabelais' *Cinquiesme Livre* (1564), Bodin's *Methodus ad facilem historiarum cognitionem* (1566), and above all Loys LeRoy's *De la Vicissitude ou Variété des choses* (1575), have been cited as key documents on the literary side of this process of liberation. The praise of modern technological ingenuity and cultural accomplishment in these works, however, was anticipated in a number of ways by Guillaume Budé, whom we shall study here, and by such other early sixteenth-century writers as Claude de Seyssel, Symphorien Champier, Christophe de Longueil, Robert Gaguin, Tixier de Ravisy, and Geoffroy Tory. New ways of thinking about the relationships between past, present, and future, and between literature, technology, theology, and morality begin to emerge about 1500 in France, not a half-century later. A militant modernism emerges almost *pari passu* with that desire to see antiquity reborn which we associate with the Renaissance. By the 1540's ideas both of *imitatio* and *aemulatio*, of renovation and innovation, were commonplace in France: a new cultural pattern, a new climate of opinion had been established [4].

---

[4] Franco Simone, in his « La coscienza storica del rinascimento francese e il suo significato culturale », *Convivium*, XXII (1954), 151-169, the study closest to my own in its theme, still concludes (p. 161) that French humanists before 1550 were not sufficiently aware of their own originality and were too closely tied to their Italian instructors, even though he cites some of the figures mentioned in the text here as modernists, and others also whose claims to inclusion in the modernist ranks are not well supported by the quotations he offers. A. C. Keller, « The Idea of Progress in Rabelais », *Publications of the Modern Language Association*, LXVI (1951), 236, sees the beginnings of French progressivist ideas in Rabelais' *Tiers Livre* (1546) and *Cinquiesme Livre* (1564), which show « ... a shift in emphasis so marked that the conservative traditional humanist of the first two books has become in the last three a forerunner of Bacon and a herald of the values of the seventeenth and eighteenth centuries ». Keller assumes (1) that « conservative traditional humanists » — that is, writers interested in rebirth — are hostile to ideas of progress, and (2) that ideas of progress only arise from observations of scientific or technological changes. These observations,

This new climate of opinion did not by any means cover all of France. The ideas of time and culture of Philippe de Commynes, which are concerned neither with cycles of rebirth nor with progress, probably remained characteristic of the majority of thinking Frenchmen throughout the sixteenth century. Commynes' *Memoirs* were published in twenty-two French editions before 1600, and in sixteen Latin and Italian translations. Not even Rabelais, let alone Budé or Fichet, could boast of such international popularity [5]. Although Commynes' popularity is certainly not attributable merely to his view of temporal change, that view should help us to remember that partisanship either for ancients or moderns was probably characteristic of only a small group of people in the sixteenth century.

Among that small group were artisans and practical men like Ambroise Paré and Jacques Cartier, as well as the learned men of letters mentioned earlier. Edgar Zilsel and others have emphasized the importance of the sub-group to which Paré and Cartier belonged among early champions of progress. They have not noticed that the « craft » of philologists like Fichet and Budé was changed by the invention of printing in ways parallel to those which changed the crafts of barber-surgeons and navigators following the introduction of gunpowder and the compass. What had been a hit-and-miss affair, guided by rules of thumb, was not only in the case of dressing gunshot wounds and navigating ocean-going ships but also in the case of publishing texts becoming a science, a methodologically

---

however, may be made by non-conservative, non-traditional humanists as well as by artisans and scientists, as Keller maintains in his « Zilsel, the Artisans, and the Idea of Progress in the Renaissance », *Journal of the History of Ideas*, XI (1950), 235-40.

[5] See Ferdinand Van der Haeghen, *Bibliotheca belgica*, V (Brussels, 1890), no. 161 ff., for a complete list of these editions and translations of Commynes' *Memoirs*. Budé's works were not reprinted until the nineteenth century, after the appearance of the *Omnia Opera* (Basel, 1557), with these exceptions: *Annotationes in... Pandectarum libros*, 1566; *Epistolae graecae*, 1567, 1574; *De Asse*, 1562, 1692, 1695; *De Contemptu rerum*, 1624; *De Philologia*, 1696. Fichet's *Rhetorica*, as well as his prefaces to Barziza's works, received only one printing. The publication and influence of Rabelais' works is studied in Maurice de Grève, *L'interprétation de Rabelais au XVIe siècle* (Geneva, 1961).

definable field of activity with general rules and certain conclusions precisely derivable from those rules [6].

The changing perspectives which new inventions offered were not, however, always grasped and utilized, as we shall see in our consideration of the ideas of Guillaume Fichet. Fichet, who with Jean Heynlin was primarily responsible for the introduction of printing to France and whose praise of the invention and its uses borders on extravagance, retains ideas of time and culture characteristic of a class of thinkers found in medieval times — a class different from that to whose ideas Commynes gives voice, but nevertheless, like Commynes and unlike Budé, a class which was traditional in its social origins, institutional commitments, and ideological expressions.

What has been most conspicuously lacking in studies of concepts of progress is a careful consideration of causation. A naive quotation-mongering has prevailed; wrenched from their contexts, these quotations serve preconceived theories very well — the continuity (or discontinuity) of intellectual tradition, the progressive (or anti-progressive) character of certain kinds of work. Such foreshortened methodology is of little use in explaining either the still-compartmentalized thinking of Commynes and Fichet, or the new syntheses realized by Budé. There are three contexts which must be considered in interrelated fashion if we are to explain why the walls erected by thought about time and culture crumble in Budé's case and stand erect in Fichet's and Commynes'. The first is the context of form and meaning expressed in the particular piece of writing in which a given quotation occurs: the intention of the work as a whole, its general structure, previous uses of the same words and metaphors, and so on. The second is the context of cultural institutions and ideas in which the particular writing was composed:

---

[6] Paré's new surgical methods are generally held to have arisen out of his treatment of gunshot wounds. See the articles by A. C. Keller mentioned in note 4 and Edgar Zilsel, « The Genesis of the Concept of Scientific Progress », *Journal of the History of Ideas*, VI (1945), 325-349. Both Paré and Cartier are mentioned by Simone, *op. cit.*, while Keller and Zilsel cite only Paré. Unlike Keller and Zilsel, Simone does not subscribe to the notion that progressivist ideas required the underpinning of science and technology.

the libraries, personal acquaintances, educational institutions, publishing houses from which the author receives the material about which he writes and to which he communicates his finished work. The third is the context of social forces influencing the writing: the author's means of support (both physically and psychologically) during composition, the audience he desires for his work, and the action which he hopes to inspire in that audience as compared with one's own estimate of the probable reaction to his writing. An exhaustive analysis of these three aspects of the sources of a written work is of course impossible to carry through, since information about many of the factors involved is lacking. But the three aspects must at least be distinguished and pondered, even if they are not systematically considered and explicated, as they will not and cannot be in the present essay.

Unlike historians of more thoroughly studied and better recorded times, students of fifteenth- and early sixteenth-century France cannot claim either statistical probability or even a complete survey of existing sources as a basis for their assertions. Like those whom we shall quote, we will make a number of poorly substantiated leaps in thought in the course of our discussion. These leaps, however, are those of conjecture and not of conviction, for this inquiry is conceived of as suggestive rather than definitive, offering not so much new conclusions as new hypotheses. Its purpose is thus to imitate the example of the scholar whom we honor with this publication by re-opening and widening the basis of discussion of a problem which, as he pointed out ten years ago, is central not only to our estimate of Renaissance culture but also to our understanding of the way in which that culture is related to our own « modern », « scientistic » age [7].

I.

« ... What is new in the ... *modern* age is the understanding that the critical present is at the same time the beginning of a completely new period in human history ... Individuals [since

[7] H. Baron, « The *Querelle* of the Ancients and the Moderns as a Problem for Renaissance Scholarship », *Journal of the History of Ideas*, XX

about 1750] have been pressed to identify themselves with the causes peculiar to the time into which they were born. Indeed, a new kind of loyalty is accepted, a loyalty to the moment in which we live »[8]. Individuals in the fifteenth century, rather than identifying themselves as living in a unique moment, thought of themselves as living in a unique era — the Christian era — and in that sense every fifteenth-century man was a firm believer in progress. To the extent that he was aware of pre-Christian forebears, he felt superior to them.

Living as he did on this plateau of Christian superiority, fifteenth-century man's sense of time and culture was radically split in a way that modern man's is not. Fifteenth-century man's sense of these things was built on discontinuity, on the shattering difference between the general situation — his presence somewhere in the immeasurable era of full revelation, of absolute spiritual truth which was to last from Christ's first coming to His second — and the particular situation in which he found himself in this moment or that of his physical existence. The immensity and immeasurableness of Christian man's spiritual situation pressed upon and tended to level out every effort to give meaning, form, and contour to the peculiarities of biology, society, or psychology which he observed in himself or his fellows. The plateau of time and culture upon which he found himself appeared to be extraordinarily flat. Every irregularity observed in the landscape shrank to insignificance as soon as one raised one's eyes to the sky above. The obsession of Christian poets with the fleeting quality of love, of youth's bloom, indeed of every quality of life whether in bloom or decay, is partly a consequence of this contrast.

Modern man, too, lives fleetingly, with a deep sense of the inconsequentiality of the instants through which he lives. But this sense is not conditioned by belief in an immense realm of static, supernal truth within the soul and beyond the moon; it arises rather from uncertainty about what will happen next. Modern man lives precariously, from moment to moment, with

---

(1959), 6. That « modernism » and « scientism » are connected is my assertion, not Professor Baron's.

[8] Richard Koebner, « Semantics and Historiography », *Cambridge Journal*, VII (1953), 142. The italics are Koebner's.

no assurance that anything which he has built up to now may not be destroyed utterly in the next instant. He knows that he is not in entire command of either his body or spirit, but he believes that no one else is either. His triumphs and disasters, physical or spiritual, are his alone to suffer or enjoy. He lives in an expanding nothingness, spun out of his own creativity and his own destructiveness. If time or culture exist for modern man, it is because he has built them up for himself, moment by moment. Modern man is committed to viewing time and culture as possessing continuity — that is, as being historically explicable — at the same time as he knows that he can never prove that they do possess it and that he may himself in the next moment lose not only his faith but his very existence through some unforeseeable catastrophe. Fifteenth-century man was committed to viewing time and culture as being discontinuous — that is, as being a mystery, whose rises, falls, advances and recessions are explicable only by revelation — at the same time as he took for granted that the rhythms of his personal existence, the continuity of his daily experience, were in some absolute way guaranteed by God above. The mixed views, the seemingly contradictory assertions of Commynes, Fichet, and Budé about time and culture cannot be understood unless we keep in mind their unspoken assumptions and ours — their sense of living in a vast if mysterious landscape of venerable traditions, revealed truth, and inconsequential details, our sense of living in and among tottering skyscrapers of human ingenuity, erectable and demolishable in a day.

Philippe de Commynes, a minor Burgundian nobleman whose sense of opportunity and psychological acuity compensated for his lack of formal education, wrote the memoirs of his political experience in French because he knew no Latin. He seems to have been only superficially acquainted with either pre-Christian or Christian history, to judge from the infrequent and vague references in the *Memoirs* to men and events preceding his own time by more than two generations. Commynes had translations of Livy, Valerius Maximus, and Josephus transcribed for his library, however, and he tells us in a passage of the *Memoirs* written about 1489 that « one of the surest means to make a man wise is to have him read ancient history and learn how to conduct and guard himself and how to manage his affairs wisely, according to histories and examples of our ancestors. For our life is so short that it cannot give us the necessary experience in so many matters »[9]. The wisdom in governing affairs of which Commynes speaks is political wisdom. The context in which these words appear is that of King Louis XI's fear of imprisonment by Charles the Bold, Duke of Burgundy, during his interview with Charles in the duke's town of Péronne in 1467. In the sentences just before those which we have quoted, Commynes criticizes Louis for coming to Péronne at the duke's invitation: « It is great folly for a prince to put himself in the power of another, especially when they are at war; and it is to their advantage if they have studied history in their youth. They can thus realize what happens in such assemblies and how some of the ancients committed great frauds ... »[10].

The movement from criticism of a particular political maneuver to advice about the uses of ancient history is sufficiently large. But the next step which Commynes takes is even larger. Not only is life too short to afford anyone sufficient political experience to make him wise, but « we are diminished by age and we do not live as long as men did in former times; neither are our bodies as strong, and similarly our faith and loyalty to one another have been weakened ». These assertions are probably derived from two passages in II Esdras, an apocryphal book whose words were often cited in support of the theory that the world was slowly decaying[11]. They embody Commynes'

---

[9] *Mémoires*, ed. J. Calmette and G. Durville, I (Paris, 1924), 128-129. All translations of authors quoted in the text are mine, unless specified to the contrary in a footnote. This edition of the *Memoirs* will be henceforth quoted thus: Calmette, I, 128-129.

[10] Calmette, I, 128.

[11] Cf. Calmette, I, 129 (« Joinct aussi que nous sommes diminuez d'aage, et que la vie des hommes n'est si longue comme elle souloit ny les corps si puissans, semblablement que nous sommes affoibliz de toute foy et loyaulté les ungs envers les autres ») with II Esdras 5: 54-55 (« Considera ergo et tu, quoniam minores statura estis prae his qui ante vos, et qui post vos quam ut vos, quasi iam senescentes creaturae et fortitudinem iuventutis praetereuntes ») and with II Esdras 14: 16-17 (« ... Quantum enim invalidum fiet saeculum a senectute, tantum multiplicabuntur super inhabitantes mala. Prolongabit enim se magis veritas et appropinquabit mendacium ... »). I quote the text given by G. H. Box, *The Ezra-Apocalypse* (London, 1912), pp. 331 and 360. II Esdras, or « fourth Ezra », or « the apocalypse of Ezra », was copied as part of most Vulgate codices of the Bible during the Middle

broadest generalization about the character of time to be found in the *Memoirs*. What is interesting about these assertions is the apparent need which Commynes felt to bolster a very limited and obvious piece of reasoning, the necessity of supplementing one's personal experience through reading, with a lugubrious commonplace about the increasing debility of man. This commonplace, attacked some forty years later by Juan Luis Vives in the name of the principle that nature « always remains equal to herself, and not rarely comes forward more strongly and powerfully than in the past ... », is characteristic of a culture which saw improvement in man's condition in very different terms from those in which humanists like Vives did [12]. Progress for Commynes does not lie in recognizing, let alone encouraging the presumptuous notion that « [the human race] should daily progress in arts, disciplines, virtue, and goodness » [13]. On the contrary, the only hope of improving human affairs lies in recognition of the wickedness of « the great » and the weakness of « the small », and in understanding God's consequent need to restrain the one and make up for the other both in this life and the next.

The ideal human state is one of equilibrium, in which each man can enjoy his property without threat from others. Commynes was a radical although largely unconscious materialist

---

Ages, although it was never accepted as canonical. It was frequently commented upon by Biblical exegetes (see Box, *op. cit.*, pp. 62-63, note e, and p. 309, note w, for some references; see also R. F. Jones, *Ancients and Moderns* [Berkeley, California: paperback edition, 1965], p. 279, n. 1, for some seventeenth-century uses of it).

[12] The sentence in which this phrase appears is as follows: « .. Neque enim effoeta est jam vel exhausta natura, ut nihil prioribus annis simile pariat: *eadem est semper sui similis, nec raro tamquam collectis viribus pollentior, ac potentior*, qualem nunc esse credi par est robore adjutam et confirmatam, quod sensim per tot secula accrevit ». See Vives, *Opera omnia*, VI (Valencia, 1785; reprinted London, 1964), 6. Italics indicate the words translated in the text, taken from Foster Watson's translation of Vives' *De tradendis disciplinis*. See Vives, *On Education*, tr. F. Watson (London, 1910), p. 8.

[13] Ibid., p. cv, a translation from Vives' *De causis corruptarum artium*, published together with *De tradendis disciplinis* in 1531. See Vives' *Opera omnia*, VI, 39: « ... Et qui ex illis fuerunt boni viri, haud dubie manum quoque illis porrexerunt, quos altius videbunt ascensuros quam quo ipsi pervenissent; *hoc enim judicabant e re esse generis humani, ut in dies artibus, disciplinis, virtute, ac probitate proficeret* ... » (italics are mine).

who systematically interpreted qualitative distinctions in quantitative terms. Thus, political order had for him only one *raison d'être*, the materialistic one of ensuring peace and security to men and their possessions. Commynes' career as diplomat, spy, privy councillor, and accused traitor had convinced him that this peace and security were constantly threatened by the plots of one prince or another. Lesser men, too, may seek to seize « castles, furniture, a field, a pool, a mill, depending on each person's rank ... » [14]. Thus neither reason, nor fear of God, nor love of their neighbor stop men from their plotting, and consequently God is obliged to « beat us with many rods for our bestiality and wrong-doing » [15]. Since « the small » are punished sufficiently by their superiors, God concentrates on « the great », setting up a « contrary » to each prince, « to keep him in fear and humility » [16]. A balance of power results which, however, is kept in perpetual imbalance by the phenomenon which concerns us here, the ever increasing debility of men. It is debility which accounts for sin ultimately, for if men really believed that they would be punished for their misdeeds they would never commit them [17]. And the lack of faith among Commynes' contemporaries seem to derive from their physical inferiority in comparison with men of former times, if the conjunction « and similarly » which connects Commynes' comment on the physical with that on the moral charac-

---

[14] Calmette, II, 224. See my Introduction to the new English translation of the *Memoirs*, I (Columbia, South Carolina, 1969), 3-20, for details of Commynes' biography, and pp. 44-58 for a lengthier discussion of Commynes' moral and religious beliefs.

[15] Calmette, II, 212-213: « Or fault donc conclure que la raison naturelle ny nostre sens ne la craincte de Dieu ny l'amour de nostre prochain ne nous garde point d'estre violentz les ungs contre les autres ny de retenir l'autruy ou de l'autruy oster par toutes voyes qui nous sont possibles ... Ainsi doncques est vray que Dieu est presque forcé ou semons de monstrer plusieurs signes et de nous battre de plusieurs verges, par nostre bestialité et par nostre mauvaistié, que je croy myeux ».

[16] Calmette, II, 207-208: « Au fort, il me semble que Dieu n'a créé en ce monde ny homme ny beste à qui il n'ayt fait quelque chose son contraire pour le tenir en humilité et en crainte ».

[17] See the long tirade in Calmette, II, 224-225, which expresses this conviction. This passage is quoted and commented upon in my edition of the *Memoirs*, I, 51-53.

teristics of man is interpreted causally [18]. Whether or not physical decay causes or merely parallels spiritual decay — and Commynes' materialistic set of mind in other respects supports a causal interpretation [19] — the world is certainly getting worse morally. As proof of this, Commynes asserts that « the cruel and sudden punishments which Our Lord has laid upon the great in the last thirty years » outnumber all those occurring during the preceding two hundred years [20]. It would seem that as the world wanes God, in order to keep in balance the sin and its retribution which increasing lack of faith brings about, must increase his punishments of those at the apices of the power structures which Commynes sees everywhere.

One dimension of Commynes' thinking about human time is thus moral; in this dimension the world appeared to be in continuing decline, a decline visible not only in terms of the « cruel and sudden punishments » of God but also in terms of man's physical debility. A second dimension of Commynes' thinking about human time is political: in this dimension the world appeared to be in continual flux. « ... The things of this world are not very stable » [21]. « ... Neither enemies nor [one's own] princes are always similar [in behavior], even when the situation is, [but] still it is good to be informed of by-gone affairs » [22].

Note that Commynes couples an assertion about the fluctual behavior of men here, as in the quotation with which we introduced discussion of the *Memoirs*, with an assertion about the value of supplementing personal experience by reading about the past. Such reading seems to be defensive rather than a means to control the course of events. Commynes believed that knowledge of the past might teach a man to « manage his

---

[18] See the quotation in note 11.

[19] See my edition of the *Memoirs*, I, 51-55.

[20] Calmette, III, 300.

[21] Calmette, I, 209, in speaking of a dynastic change in England: « ... C'est la première foiz que j'euz jamais congnoissance que les choses de ce monde sont peu estables ».

[22] Calmette, I, 230, in speaking of negotiations between Louis XI and Charles the Bold: « Car, combien que les ennemys ny les princes ne soyent point tousjours semblables, encores que les matières les fusent, si faict-il bon estre informé des choses passées ».

affairs wisely » [23], but not that it would enable him to change human nature, political or moral.

The controlling assumptions in Commynes' ideas of time and culture are that political activity is the most important kind of human activity, and that political activity involves constant wrongdoing by the « great » who rule over the « small ». These assumptions derive from Commynes' measurement of politics and morals against static standards. In the moral sphere the standard is one of absolute faith in the idea that if one is violent, perfidious, or cruel towards others, one will be punished by God. In the political sphere the standard is one of absolute peace and security within a state and absolute equilibrium of power between states. What, then, is the relationship between these two spheres, these two standards, and the assumptions about time and culture derived from them?

Commynes assumes that society is naturally hierarchical; he never questions the division of men into a few « great » and many « small » people [24]. Social power implies rights of government in Commynes' eyes and, conversely, rights of government or political power imply rights to high social status. Commynes recognizes no non-material means to the attainment of social and political power — he is almost completely blind to Louis XI's increasing reliance on legally trained bureaucrats — and no non-material ends for that power, such as Dante's notion that polities are formed to realize the intellectual potentiality of man [25] or the humanists' notion that political achievements, like literary ones, are undertaken with a view to making those who perform them famed and glorious. For Commynes all human activities are dedicated to material ends; religion itself is spoken of in the *Memoirs* almost exclusively as a sanction for material order. As we have seen, politics also should function exclusively to make peace, security, and equilibrium permanent and absolute. But in fact, because of men's bestiality and wrongdoing, politics serve men as the prime means of effecting social and economic change. Political activity is therefore the most

---

[23] See the quotation from Commynes on pp. 714-715 above.

[24] See my edition of the *Memoirs*, I, 48-49 and 72-74, for substantiation of this point.

[25] *De Monarchia*, I, ch. 3.

important kind of human activity not only because it offers the most opportunity to men to prevent change but also because it is the arena in which most change is attempted. The « wise » prince will be able to thwart such attempts, Commynes believes, but even if the attempts are thwarted, equilibrium without and peace and security within will have been upset. Perpetual flux is thus the norm in the world of politics.

Worse still, as the wise prince maneuvers to survive, he involves himself in perfidies, cruelty, and violence. These immoralities will inevitably be punished by God, as they were in Louis XI, Commynes' hero, and in Charles the Bold, Commynes' nostalgically remembered boyhood prince, and in almost all the other lords whose careers Commynes traces in his *Memoirs*.

Unlike Machiavelli, Commynes did not advocate the lying, cheating, and bribing which he praises upon occasion as having preserved this or that prince from ruin or failure. Political solutions are not the same as moral ones, but they are not unrelated either. Commynes, rather than box off the public world of subterfuge and treachery from the private world of conscience, fell back upon the notion that men's capacity to be good was failing, which in turn was caused perhaps by the senescence of the race itself. He was thus able to praise politically and condemn morally the same actions. The ceaselessly fluctuating world of political activity is situated in Commynes' eyes on an inclined plane. That inclined plane represents the moral activity of men, and it is inclined downward. For those who felt — and feel? — like Commynes the plateau of Christian time and culture is slowly sinking toward universal wreck.

II.

Guillaume Fichet published in 1471 a summary of the precepts of rhetoric which he advocated in his teaching of that subject at the University of Paris. In the preface he compares the studies carried on at Paris with those pursued in ancient Athens, declaring that the latter's glory does not at all exceed that of Paris in the zeal with which all the arts are pursued, with one exception: the art of rhetoric is and has been neglected. « Up to now no one has emerged at Paris », concludes Fichet,

« who like Plato, Aristotle, Isocrates, Theophrastus, and many other Athenians, might at length have understood and taught rhetoric together with all philosophy » [26].

Fichet's comparison of Paris and Athens echoes a commonplace with a long medieval history, the so-called *translatio studii*. After the Romans brought the « study of wisdom » from Greece to Rome, said Vincent of Beauvais (ca. 1190-ca. 1264) in one version of the commonplace, Alcuin brought it to Paris [27]. The notion that learning had been transferred from one place to another without any essential alteration was consonant with and perhaps reinforced the ideal of stasis and equilibrium which was related, as we have seen with respect to Commynes, to the Christian's sense of human weakness and transgression. Amid the turmoil and turpitude of this world the learned tradition, preserved and passed on from generation to generation, represented an element of stability and continuity, a banner of truth held high above the vicissitudes of time. The truth which it protected was, of course, the same as that to which Commynes looked as a measure of the choices with which the possession of power confronted rulers. The university, where scholars passed on the « study of wisdom », was an ecclesiastical institution, and as such its knowledge was dedicated to showing the unchangeable absoluteness of Christian verity, not to adding to or changing it.

The concept of time implied by Fichet's words, therefore, is one of restoring a continuity partially broken by the neglect

---

[26] Unlike Commynes' works, Fichet's are difficult to obtain. I shall quote in the notes almost all of the Latin originals of the translations in the text. « Quo fit ut, tametsi Parisiorum Lutetia locum inde mortuis Athenis nulla parte laudis inferiorem sit studio reliquarum artium assecuta, nemo tamen ad hanc usque memoriam Parisii emersit, qui ut Plato, ut Aristoteles, ut Ysocrates, ut Theofrastus, ut Actici quidem alii quam plurimi, rhetoricam cum omni philosophia tandem aliquando sciret ac doceret ». Pierre Champion has reprinted this preface from Fichet's rare *Rhetorica* in facsimile form in his *Les plus anciens monuments de la typographie parisienne* (Paris, 1904), no. 22.

[27] « Hoc itaque monasterium post hoc, ut dictum est, donante Carolo, suscepit regendum Alchuinus scientia vitaque praeclarus, qui et sapientiae studium de Roma, Parisius [sic] transtulit, quod illuc quondam e Graecia translatum fuerat a Romanis ». Quoted by Etienne Gilson, *Les idées et les lettres* (Paris, 1932), p. 184, from Vincent's *Speculum historiale*, Book 23, ch. 173 (Venice, 1494), f. 308 v.

of rhetoric and the concept of culture implied by that temporal ideal is religious. When Fichet says that he wishes rhetoric taught together with « all philosophy », he means that he would like all knowledge consonant with Christian dogma to be professed in a persuasive manner rather than to be offered with the « bare words » of logic alone [28]. For Fichet, as for Commynes, as for every Christian since doubting Thomas, the basic problem of culture is how to make men believe, how to persuade them to « have faith ». In the institutional context of the medieval university that problem had from the twelfth century onward taken the form of rivalry verging on warfare between what might anachronistically be called the Department of Comparative Literature and the Department of Philosophy and Religion. The Department of Comparative Literature maintained that appeal to the heart as well as to the head was necessary, and that eloquence, that is, Christian wisdom set forth rhetorically, was the best means to that end. The Department of Philosophy and Religion maintained that appeal to the head would move the heart, and that logic, the demonstration of necessary truth, was therefore the best ally of Christian wisdom. The late medieval phase of this perennial warfare between those pursuing the « art » of persuasion and those pursuing the « science » of disputation was conditioned not only by the intellectual tendency to reduce the complicated relationships between academic disciplines to a hierarchy with theology at the top, but by the material difficulty of instructing a large number of students with only a small number of manuscript books. Outlines, schemata, and logical demonstrations are efficient ways of conveying much knowledge in brief form when

---

[28] « Nam de philosophia quidem illa quae de moribus aut rerum natura est deque sacris litteris disputare, disputata nudis verbis perscribere plerisque nostratibus commune, idque feci facioque ut caeteri ». This sentence is from a letter by Fichet to Bessarion quoted by Franco Simone, « Guillaume Fichet retore ed umanista », *Memorie della reale accademia delle scienze di Torino*, LXIX (1939), series 2, part 2, 24. The full letter is reproduced in Champion, *op. cit.*, nos. 18-20. Fichet makes the same point in the sentence following that quoted in note 26 from the preface to his *Rhetorica*: « Quin hi [i. e., Parisian professors] quidem nuda rerum cognitione contenti ... minimopere student eloquentie ». Simone, *op. cit.*, pp. 17 and 24-25, emphasizes Fichet's contrast between rhetoric as an ornamental and persuasive instrument and logic as a spare, hard discipline.

books are scarce and expensive. Not the least of the reasons why Cornificius won and Noël Beda lost their respective skirmishes was that John of Salisbury possessed no printing press. Lefèvre d' Etaples and his friends, who did possess that weapon along with others recently acquired, were able to shift the battlefield from the crowded lecture halls of a religious institution to the less ideologically defined turf and more spacious perspectives of bookstall, study, and salon.

To the importance of printing not only in changing the relative prestige of literature and logic but in altering the bases of cultural and temporal expectations we will return. Here we may observe only that within the context of the Parisian university system, its purposes, and its material means, Fichet's lament about the relative neglect of rhetoric is perfectly explicable. Fichet and his opponents shared the same purposes and the same material means. It was only the intellectual means about which they disagreed, and this disagreement, which might be said to be as old as the arguments between Socrates and the sophists and as new as those between protagonists of C. P. Snow's « two cultures », has not only a long history but a double one, at least since the rise of Christianity. For the arguments between logicians and rhetoricians invariably raised the question of pagan contamination. The traditional answer given by rhetoricians to this question was that the cultivation of eloquence was not primarily directed at understanding the non-Christian sentiments expressed so beautifully and convincingly by their beloved *auctores*. It was rather a training in stripping this « wealth » of persuasiveness from pagan « Egyptians », as St. Augustine put it, and in applying it to Christian propositions [29]. Etienne Gilson has maintained that this method of picking and choosing among pagan utterances is the *leitmotiv* of « Christian humanism » and may be traced backwards from Fichet and his friend Gaguin to Nicolas de Clamanges (d. 1437), John of Sali-

[29] See Augustine's *De doctrina Christiana*, 2 . 40 . 60. Strictly speaking, Augustine developed the metaphor not in relation to the eloquence of the pagans but in relation to those ethical and religious teachings in which they seemed to anticipate Christian doctrines. Augustine's words, however, became a kind of general license applied by Christian humanists to justify their references to pagan authors in almost all respects, as Martin Grabmann has indicated, *Mittelalterliches Geistesleben*, II (Munich, 1936), 9-18.

sbury, Alcuin, and Saint Augustine [30]. All of these men, like the classicizing artists of the Middle Ages to whom Erwin Panofsky has drawn attention, felt little compunction about dividing form from meaning if it served Christian ends [31]. I say « little » and not « no » compunction, because these men were not unaware of how difficult if not impossible it is to separate form from meaning without distorting both, and thus all of them devoted effort to « reintegrating » (Fichet's term) past models of eloquence as well as to despoiling them for Christian purposes [32].

The difference between medieval humanists like Fichet, Clamanges, or Augustine and Renaissance humanists like Budé, Rabelais, or LeRoy is not so much the character of their convictions as it is the difference in the social and institutional means by which those convictions were expressed. Not the amount of interest in ancient culture, not the amount of « objectivity » or historical-mindedness or secular-mindedness which they brought to classical studies, but rather the diversity of outlets and opportunities for developing interest, objectivity, historical-mindedness and secular-mindedness is what differentiates these two groups of literary scholars most clearly. Certainly, as Gilson maintains, there is a remarkable continuity of intellectual tra-

---

[30] Gilson, *La philosophie au Moyen Age* (Paris, 1952), p. 753.

[31] See Chapter 2 of Panofsky's *Renaissance and Renascences in Western Art* (Stockholm, 1960).

[32] In a prefatory letter to Gasparino Barziza's *Epistolae*, the first book published in Paris (1470), Fichet addresses his friend Heynlin, associated with him in introducing the printing press, in the following manner: « Magnam tibi gratiam Gasparinus debeat, quem pluribus tuis vigiliis ex corrupto integrum fecisti. Maiorem vero coetus doctorum hominem quo non tamen sacris litteris (quae tua provincia est) magnopere studes, sed redintegrandis etiam latinis scriptoribus insignem operam navas » (Champion, *op. cit.*, no. 1). The context indicates that Fichet means by « reintegrating » merely the verbal restoration of texts made « corrupt » by careless scribes. In order to make texts whole again philologically, however, scholars were forced to « reintegrate » the texts with the surroundings, verbal and non-verbal, in which they were written. The key idea is expressed in the prefix « re- »: Fichet does not intend merely to « integrate » Latin writers with present-day concerns; he wishes to « reintegrate », to place the text back in the earlier context of the concerns of the author when he wrote, for only thus can he begin to discover the words which the author, and not the later copyist, wrote down. Such an intention leads on to understanding the meaning as well as the form of the words in terms of their original rather than present-day context.

dition regarding the use and ends of classical studies from St. Augustine's times to those of Budé and Erasmus. But this continuity must be seen in relation to the discontinuity of cultural life during the same period. Educational institutions, manuscript repositories, conventions of patronage, patterns of communication and exchange of ideas, were repeatedly broken down or swept away after short periods of efflorescence, making it necessary to begin anew, to restore once more texts corrupted or reduced to remnants by the disruption of monastic, scholastic, or courtly life. The vehicles of cultural development are not the same as those of social, economic, or political development. But they are dependent upon the latter, just as the latter are dependent upon a flow of ideas and upon many varied types of educational training in order to develop.

The question as to why rhetoric, and the classical authors acknowledged as masters of rhetoric, had not been as diligently pursued as « all philosophy » cannot be answered simply by examining the institutional and ideological conditions of study in Paris in 1470 or earlier. Social, economic, and political factors, too, shaped a culture developing in fits and starts. When bread and leisure became more plentiful and more dependable, classical studies began developing in a more cumulative fashion. As a result, Renaissance humanists, though no less devoutly Christian than earlier classical scholars, were less single-minded ideologically. The society in which they lived offered them new and steadily more diversified ways of exploiting their love of ancient literature.

« I feel great satisfaction, most learned Robert », declares Fichet in a letter to his friend Gaguin which was published as a preface to Gasparino Barziza's *Orthographiae liber*, « when I observe how the Muses and all aspects of eloquence, which an earlier era ignored, flourish in this city » [33]. When he first came to Paris, Fichet continues, orators and poets were « rarer than the phoenix ». No one studied Cicero assiduously, no one knew how to compose poetry according to metrical rule, and those

---

[33] Champion, *op. cit.*, no. 5: « Magna me voluptas capit, eruditissime Roberte, quum Musas et omnes eloquentiae partes, quas prior aetas ignoravit, in hac urbe florere conspicio ». Barziza's *Orthographiae liber* (Paris, 1470) was the second book issued by the Paris press, according to Champion.

at the University of Paris had fallen into a rustic sort of speech through lack of use of pure Latin style. « But our days are marked by far better signs, since all the gods and goddesses, as poets say, are favoring the arts of speaking well every day more and more » [34].

The generalization which Fichet makes here is more limited than the broad comparison between Paris and Athens cited earlier. The « earlier era » of which Fichet speaks is that of the years around 1450 as compared with those around 1470 — scarcely a generation apart [35]. These are years during which Fichet lived and worked almost continuously in Paris. His words about them express an assessment of personal experience rather than an opinion inherited from others, as the commonplace mentioned earlier does. The change which Fichet sees as having taken place at some unspecified time between 1450 and 1470 is growing « every day more and more ». Progress is being made in « the restitution of the studies of humanity » [36]. The word « restitution » warns us that, whatever Fichet thinks about the progressive character of recent times, his long-range notion of the temporal phases through which the *studia humanitatis* have passed is one of ups and downs. The immediate goal for his

---

[34] *Ibid.*: « Nam ut me primum adolescentibus annis Boico ex agro Lutetiam contuli, idque Aristoteleae disciplinae causa, mirabar sane oratorem aut poetam, phoenice rariorem Lutetia tota inveniri. Nemo Ciceronem, uti plerique nunc faciunt, nocturna versabat manu, versabat diurna; nemo carmen fingebat legitimum, nemo fictum ab alio caesuris noverat librare suis, desuefacta siquidem a latinitate schola Parisiensis ad sermonis rusticitatem omnis pene deciderat. At lapillo longe meliore dies nostri numerantur, quippe quibus di deaeque omnes, ut poetae loquuntur, bene dicendi artes in dies magis magisque aspirant ».

[35] J. Monfrin, « Les lectures de Guillaume Fichet et de Jean Heynlin ... », *Bibliothèque d'humanisme et Renaissance*, XVII (1955), 11, shows that Fichet arrived in Paris in 1449 or 1450. « Prior aetas » (see note 33) seems to me necessarily to refer to Fichet's arrival because of the conjunction « nam » which introduces the following sentence (see note 34).

[36] Having illustrated his assertion that the Muses have returned to Paris by enumerating examples, including works by Gaguin himself, Fichet returns to the main subject of his letter in the following words: « Non enim est huius temporis de tuis studiis, praesertim ad te scribere. De studiorum humanitatis restitutione loquor. Quibus (quantum ipse coniectura capio) magnum lumen novorum librariorum genus attulit ». Champion, *op. cit.*, no. 6.

time with respect to the *studia humanitatis*, it seems, is that of equalling, not surpassing, the ancients.

This does not mean that Fichet was incapable of recognizing innovations which would aid in the study of good letters. Gutenberg was « the first », Fichet tells us, who brought letters and scholars closer and more fruitfully together, and he should be deified just as were Bacchus, the inventor of wine, and Ceres, inventor of the plow. « And so I praise our era more than the earlier one, since I see that knowledge of writing and of speaking skillfully will be pursued as swiftly as possible not only by means of studying but by means of books. Thus renown, which may fly far and wide throughout the world, will not be lacking to anyone of our countrymen, unless indeed they neglect their own advantage » [37]. In this concluding sentence of his prefatory letter Fichet returns to the differences between 1450 and 1470, after assimilating Gutenberg to the ranks of those divinities who have benefited man with their inventions.

Both in his letter to Gaguin and in his letter to Heynlin, Fichet relates the present to the past by contrasting the two periods rather than by regarding one as developing out of the other. The initiation of the second period is, even in the case where only twenty years are involved, not seen as historically conditioned or otherwise explicable than by the efforts of a godlike inventor. In the first case, Fichet uses a phrase describing superstitious Roman religious practices which he cannot have meant to be taken literally (« at lapillo longe meliore dies nostri numerantur ... »). In the second case, he treats the coming of printing as the work of one great man, Gutenberg, a method of handling innovation which was employed throughout ancient and medieval times in a thoroughly non-historical manner [38]. Fi-

---

[37] *Ibid.*, no. 12: « Quocirca magis aetati nostrae, quam superiori quidem illi congratulor, quandoquidem video cum studiis, tum libris artificiose scribendi dicendique scientiam assecutum iri quam plurimos. Neque nomen (quod longe lateque volitet per orbem) defore quibusque nostris hominibus modo ipsi sibi non prius defuerint ».

[38] Denys Hay, *Polydore Vergil* (Oxford, 1952), pp. 53-64, shows that Polydore's book, *De inventoribus rerum* (first published in part in 1499), follows such ancient and medieval writers on the same theme as Pliny, Isidore, and Guglielmo da Pastrengo (*De originibus rerum*, written about 1350) in regarding each aspect of culture, each tool, each human skill, as having originated once only in time, in the inventive brain of one man. This gene-

chet saw that at least technical innovation might occur and that conditions of study might improve, but the larger framework within which such improvement and innovation might take place was apparently of little interest to him.

Fichet's lack of interest in the implications of innovation may reflect a naturalistic assumption that culture, like animals and plants and the seasons, changes cyclically. Such an assumption may certainly be inferred from his statements about changes in vocabulary at the end of the preface to his *Rhetorica*: « My opinion will always be the same as that of Horace, who believed that just as forests change their leaves with each year's decline, and the earliest drop off [39], so with words the old race perishes and, like the young of human-kind, the new-born bloom and thrive. Many terms that have fallen out of use shall be born again, and those shall fall that are now in honor, if usage wills it, in whose hands lies the judgement, as well as the right and rule of speech » [40]. Unlike the passage where Fichet speaks of the new enthusiasm for classic studies as a « restitution » which presumably need take place only once, changes in language are here conceived as periodic and repetitive. Old words which have lost the strength which they had when « new-born » will be « born again ». Fichet does not use a verbal form of the word « renaissance » for purposes of contrasting his own period with other ones. Rather, his thought seems to be that at any given time some words are being reborn, others are flourishing, and still others are dying. The process of linguistic change is seen as a rotational process in which no space of time is like any other in its verbal usages, and yet none is superior to any other either. This cyclic process is spelled out at even greater length in Fichet's source,

---

ralization needs some qualification (see, e. g., Polydore's chapter on architecture, *op. cit.*, III, ch. 7, in which, following Vitruvius, Polydore traces the slow early growth of architecture, attributing its improvement to social needs, not individual geniuses), but it is in the main true.

[39] Fichet is quoting Horace's *Ars poetica*. In a footnote to this line in his edition of the *Ars poetica*, H. R. Fairclough says that « In Italian woods, as in Californian, leaves may stay on the trees two or even three years. Only the oldest (*prima*) drop off each autumn ». Horace, *Satires, Epistles and Ars poetica* (Cambridge, Mass.: Loeb Classical Library, 1926), p. 455, note d.

[40] Fichet's words, which appear in Champion, *op. cit.*, nos. 27-28, are, except for the first clause, a combination of vv. 60-62 with vv. 70-72 of Horace's *Ars poetica*. I have used the Loeb translation quoted in note 39.

Horace. Both the uniqueness of each era's mode of speech and the inevitability of change and destruction of that mode, no matter how great its « glory and glamour », are more emphasized by Horace than by Fichet [41].

In terms of the quarrel between ancients and moderns which has emerged in Western culture each time that certain writers have been canonized as classical and to be imitated, Fichet should be counted one of the moderns. But that quarrel, which had already been prosecuted fiercely in Italy for two generations, seems scarcely to have existed in later fifteenth-century France in the field of literary studies [42]. Fichet's lack of interest in the implications of his assertions, his abbreviation of his source's comments both in favor of innovation and in opposition to long-range progress, is at least as significant as the opinion which he expresses.

Franco Simone, in the most extended and important study of Guillaume Fichet's thought which has yet appeared, says that he, like his predecessor Clamanges and his successor Gaguin, is « one who suffers in existing conditions and yearns for better times; he has the impression of being in the shadows, searching for light » [43]. This is to attribute to Fichet an uncertainty about the character of his own times which his words do not reveal. That uncertainty is not Fichet's but ours, and it stems primarily from our efforts to relate Fichet, as Simone does, to what went on culturally before and after he lived, rather than to what went on socially, politically, and economically at the same time as he

---

[41] See *ibid.*, vv. 46-69. A parallel passage occurs in Horace's *Epistles* II, 2, 119.

[42] H. Baron, *The Crisis of the Early Italian Renaissance* (Princeton, 1955) chapters 13 and 15, and Giacinto Margiotta, *Le origini italiane de la querelle des anciens et des modernes* (Rome, 1953), have traced the quarrel in fifteenth-century Italy. John F. d'Alton, *Roman Literary Theory and Criticism* (London, 1931), pp. 266-354, offers the most detailed exposition of the quarrel among Roman writers. Many scholars have dealt with the medieval history of the *topos* as it was applied to literature, most prominently Gilson and E. R. Curtius. But of course the commonplace occurs in non-literary fields as well — technology, logic, medicine, music, theology — from the ancient Greek period onward. H. Baron, « The Querelle ... » (see note 7 above) provides the most useful survey of the fifteenth-and sixteenth-century uses of the topos. See also August Buck, « Aus der Vorgeschichte der Querelle des anciens et des modernes in Mittelalter und Renaissance », *Bibliothèque d'humanisme et Renaissance*, XX (1958), 527-541.

[43] Simone, « Fichet ... », p. 42 (see note 28 for citation of this article).

lived. The '50's, '60's, and '70's of the fifteenth century were not halcyon times. During this period France was never free from the possibility of a revival of the devastations of the Hundred Years War, as the reader of Commynes' *Memoirs* knows. In 1465 Paris was besieged by the troops of the Burgundian duke and his allies in the War for the Public Good against Louis XI. In 1475 a huge and well-equipped English army disembarked at Calais, threatening to overrun the whole of the kingdom. Only after the unexpected death of Charles the Bold in 1477 and the consequent end of the threat of Burgundian-English joint enterprises against France could men look forward with some confidence to years of uninterrupted peace. During all this period reconstruction from the devastations of the Hundred Years War, which ended more or less officially with the capture of Bordeaux from the English in 1453, was hampered by the threat of renewed invasions and by the heavy taxation policy of Louis XI.

There was, in short, little reason for any kind of overarching optimism about life in the third quarter of the fifteenth century. François Villon's preoccupation with death is no personal obsession. It would have been rather strange, almost quixotic, if either Fichet or Commynes had expressed broad new optimistic or progressive conceptions of time or culture in this situation. Oppressed by the larger political and social conditions of their time, struggling with the traditional difficulties besetting cultural life in such uncertain circumstances, both men were understandably conservative as far as general ideas are concerned. Limited in their interests, they were effective only within narrow institutional situations. But events which took place in their time, events in which they not only participated but about which they reported, caused the narrow institutional situations patterning their thought to burst open and expand enormously. And so we who study their works today, having in mind what happened later to the movements in which they were involved, may be tempted to search their words for a sense of their historical situation at the « beginning » of the « modern era » of culture which they did not and could not have [44].

---

[44] I place « beginning » and « modern era » in quotation marks merely to indicate that the definition of beginnings, like that of modernity, is relative

Commynes saw and reported upon the rationalistic calculation and centralizing zeal of Louis XI, qualities which were extremely important in the rebuilding of national political power [45]. Fichet recognized the importance of printing as a means of eliminating perpetually corrupt manuscript texts and of providing students with extended examples of literary eloquence [46]. Printed books freed literature from the chains of the monastic, collegiate, or ducal library, helped introduce new procedures into the classroom, and gave a powerful impetus to the philological comparison of textual variants. National political power offered new means of gathering and investing resources — cultural as well as economic, human as well as natural — which had been sacked up and buried, stymied, stunted, or simply destroyed during the preceding period of disunity and disruption. But Fichet and Commynes saw only the new means and not the new ends. Commynes, though he reported upon the invasion of Italy in 1494, one of the first great manifestations of the nation's new power, saw it as a dangerous throw-back to the foolish, grandiose schemes in which his former master Charles the Bold had indulged, rather than as a forecast of glories to come. Commynes' point of view, formed during the days of feudal rivalry between the dukes of Burgundy, Brittany, Normandy, and their various allies vis-à-vis Louis XI, was not useful in the new political situation, and so he remained out of power, after an embassy to Venice whose results did not please Charles VIII, until his death in 1511. Fichet, after supervising together with his friend Heynlin the selection of books

---

to the standpoint of the person defining the historical situation about which he is writing. Few historians any longer maintain, like Burckhardt and Michelet, that there was some absolute beginning to some absolutely modern period of human existence.

[45] See my edition of the *Memoirs*, I, 57-58, for substantiation of this assertion.

[46] According to James Wadsworth, *Lyons, 1473-1503* (Cambridge, Mass., 1962), p. 20, Fichet's claims for printing are not original. They repeat ideas first voiced in 1457 by Fust and Schoeffer, Gutenberg's successors in Mainz. Wadsworth offers no citations to prove his assertion. See the beginning of Fichet's letter to Heynlin, prefacing Barziza's *Epistolae*, partially quoted in n. 32, as well as his extended praise of printing in the letter to Gaguin, prefacing Barziza's *Orthographiae liber* and partially analyzed in the text here.

to be printed at Paris between 1470 and 1472, surrendered to the cabals of those at the university who felt threatened by the rising popularity of literary studies and left for Rome, where he received preferment from the curia and died in obscurity. He too could not envisage the utterly new framework outside the university and outside the clerical estate in which his doctrines were destined to develop. He, like Commynes, saw the future either as a difficult and, in the best of cases, not unflawed return to the past, or as a wearisome extension of the present. He therefore remained institutionally bound to the church and its framework of studies, just as Commynes found it impossible to cast off the static, hierarchical modes of regarding society within which he had matured and prospered. Each of these men allowed what was apparently most important to them in a subjective sense — political calculation in the case of Commynes, rhetorical polish in the case of Fichet — to be tested by and subordinated to what was apparently most important to them in an objective sense — divine retribution in the case of Commynes, Christian dogma in the case of Fichet. Fichet and Commynes placed their faith in ideals of Christianity which they did not entirely understand, and thus they were unable to connect their faith in these ideals with what interested them most personally. In both men awareness of short-range change thus scarcely affected their convictions about the long-range character of time or culture. Neither man made the large leaps of which we spoke at the beginning of this paper.

III.

Guillaume Budé is the first great student of the classics in France who was in no way dependent upon the church or its associated institutions for his livelihood. Son of a well-placed royal lawyer, he was dependent instead upon the central power of the monarchy for his wealth and prestige. It is Budé who, in response to a different personal, social, and institutional situation, brings together the impulses to political and cultural renewal, the one and the other of which Fichet and Commynes recognized separately; and so it is not surprising to find in him ideas of time and culture which involve giant leaps, compared with the generalizations of his predecessors. The reasons for these leaps are of course compositional and personal, traditional and thematic, as well as social and national, as we have emphasized in our introduction. None of these reasons can be traced here in the detail which Budé's difficult and complex work demands. We shall emphasize the social and the national because these factors contrast most sharply with the statements of Commynes and Fichet, while being aware that we thus present an incomplete view of Budé's work [47].

There is an inner connection between the expansionist policies of Charles VIII, Louis XII, and Francis I, and the influx of new blood into bureaucracy and army after the end of the Hundred Years War. The responsiveness of the nobility to these projects of foreign adventure is strikingly different from the apathy with which they regarded the attempts of Charles VII and Louis XI to rid France of the English and Burgundians. That responsiveness shows the results of Louis XI's patient detachment of the middle and lower ranks of the nobility from their traditional overlords by means of royal pensions and writs of appeal from local courts. For the first time in a century men had an alternative other than that of choosing between rival feudal factions. The increasingly royalist attitudes of the nobility under Louis XI's successors show that, whatever may have been their sense of loyalty or its ideological components, they did recognize the purely quantitative and strategic advantage of the king, now that France was free of foreign armies. The vastness and variety of opportunities for advancement under royal auspices, as compared with those under anyone of lower rank, were beginning to impress themselves upon everyone.

If, in this new political situation, Guillaume Budé emerged as the archhumanist of France, the very incarnation of that cultural movement which gave direction to French developments in the arts and sciences throughout the sixteenth century, it was not simply because of his scholarly achievements. The Budés,

---

[47] I am preparing a longer study of Budé's concepts of time and culture entitled « Budé and Historicism ». As we shall see, Donald Kelley makes a number of points relevant to our subject in his « Guillaume Budé and the First Historical School of Law », *American Historical Review*, LXXII (1967), 807-34.

like the L' Hospitals or the de Thous later in the century, were *gens de robe*, members of that large circle of families who entered the royal bureaucracy via the practice of law in the fifteenth century. The movement of these families from the merchant aristocracy in French cities to national positions of power was, from the point of view of its consequences for sixteenth-century culture, the most important change in French society after the end of the Hundred Years War [48]. For this new class needed new ideas to support and justify its anomalous place between the older estates of nobility and commoner. It is not surprising, therefore, that Guillaume Budé, one of the scions of this newly rich and newly powerful class, was observed and listened to assiduously. Budé's notions of culture grew steadily more popular not only because of what he said but because of who he was. The power of humanism in French cultural life and the progress of Budé's career seem almost to go hand in hand.

If, then, many minds during Budé's lifetime were fascinated by Greek and Roman authors, while earlier intelligences found less matter in these texts and more in the intricacies of scholastic logic, it is because the social ambience, economic opportunities, and political goals in the society in which these minds applied themselves showed certain subjects to be less and less relevant to life at large and other subjects more so. Between 1480 and 1580 the proportion of French men of letters supported by church patronage rather than by other means dwindled by more than thirty percent. Most of the change in proportion is a result of state support, usually in the form of a legal or bureaucratic post of some kind. This change is accompanied by a corresponding shift in literary subject-matter, a shift away from religious toward secular and classical themes [49].

---

[48] Bernard Guenée, *Tribunaux et gens de justice dans le bailliage de Senlis à la fin du moyen âge* (Paris, 1963), has emphasized the extent to which new families who became powerful in sixteenth- and seventeenth-century politics and culture pass from *petit bourgeois* status to the ambiguous position of *noblesse de robe* in the two generations following the end of the Hundred Years War. The cause of this, Guenée maintains, was the expansion of royal bureaucracy at this time.

[49] These are the preliminary results of my study, « Men of Letters and Patronage: A Correlation between Sources of Support and Subject-matter in the Writings of 1150 Frenchmen Living between 1450 and 1600 ».

Lay rather than clerical, nationally-minded rather than provincial in political awareness, the typical French man of letters after 1550 has, as we would expect, different notions about time and culture from those of his predecessors. It was between the 1470's and the 1510's that these notions first emerged. It was then that the closed atmosphere of concern with philosophy versus rhetoric, permanent moral and religious values versus fluctuating human concerns and desires, began to open and to stimulate new kinds of comparisons and contrasts.

This process of opening or enlarging cultural horizons was gradual, and it proceeded in two directions, toward Christian reform and toward national glory. Not that the two directions were always or even usually separated; on the contrary, the moral enthusiasm which moved Robert Gaguin, Jacques Lefèvre d' Etaples, and their friends, was interwoven with nationalistic pride, just as the latter was founded in a sense of religious righteousness. France, to Frenchmen, embodied the best of Christianity. The most Christian King was descended from Charlemagne, protector of the faith. He was destined, as the royal physician Jehan Michel asserted in a set of prophetic discourses published shortly before Charles VIII invaded Italy, to lead the French hosts to Jerusalem. Charles VIII himself seems to have thought of the Italian expedition as a first step in a crusade which would liberate Constantinople [50].

Themes of anti-Italianism, Christian reform, and revival of the classics are inextricably interwoven in the history of the humanist movement in France, and in each of Guillaume Budé's major works. For French humanism, like Italian humanism, began as a rejection of recent and even contemporary traditions of culture in the name of older, broader traditions which were felt to fit present and future needs more fully. In Italy's case those older traditions were above all Roman, although they

---

[50] Margaret Mann, « Autour du Paris d'Erasme », in *Mélanges offerts à M. Abel Lefranc* (Paris, 1936), p. 114, reports Michel's prediction. The furor of national enthusiasm which, she asserts, filled Paris in 1494-95 is poorly documented. Counter-evidence is offered by Maulde La Clavière, *Histoire de Louis XII*, Part I, Volume III (Paris, 1891), 8 ff. A study of public opinion about politics and of alleged French « nationalism » is badly needed for the period 1490-1560. Maulde speaks of Charles VIII's projects, *ibid.*, III, 2, 8, 14, etc.

were also by implication Greek, since Greek forms of thought molded those of Rome from an early date. Italy's cultural traditions, insofar as they were Roman and Greek, fostered a view of foreigners as *barbari*. Hence, the revival of antiquity implied a sense of superiority to those northern Europeans who, within the medieval and Christian framework of culture, had been only too often conquerors as well as religious comrades.

France's recent past was feudal, disunited, and inglorious, but only several centuries ago it had been, although still feudal, nevertheless united and grand, a radiating center of Christian power. In contrast to Italy, whose soil was filled with the works of Roman grandeur, France's national heritage, Greek, Roman, Celtic, Germanic, Christian, was so complex that it could not speak with a single tongue. The contrasting traditions rooted in her past made France a cultural hybrid, and this was an advantage for French humanists. It gave them a freedom in relation to their antecedents and contemporary rivals which Italian men of letters did not have — the freedom of an inferior, perhaps, but still the freedom to borrow without betrayal and to reject without remorse [51].

It is not surprising, therefore, that Budé did not regard the classical past *en bloc*, as many Italian humanists did. To such Italians the only blemishes to be discovered in the course of study of antiquity were due to medieval barbarity; beyond the vale of gloom which Petrarch, Biondo, and others agreed in calling the « dark » ages, the light of ancient wisdom shone pure and whole. But for Frenchmen, such a simplified scheme of history had less appeal. No splendorous light shone for them from beyond a barbarian abyss, for most of their past lay « buried », to use a figure of which Budé was to make signal use, down in

---

[51] The stifling pressure of Italians' allegiance to their classical ancestors is emphasized by Baron, *Crisis* ..., chapter 14, and especially by Margiotta, *op. cit., passim.* Margiotta assumes throughout his book that those Italians who spoke in favor of the *volgare* and in praise of modern achievements were guilt-ridden exceptions in a generally classicistic climate of opinion. This assumption is combatted by Baron, *Crisis* ..., pp. 533-534. Italians certainly freed themselves quickly from bondage to the past but not so quickly from a sense of their superiority as the only legitimate heirs to and guardians of that past.

that very valley [52]. To Budé every nation's history, except that of the divinely chosen Hebrews, represented a gradual development in which the direction of change was not necessarily always upward. This Budé showed first in respect to the codification of ancient Roman law. Not only had medieval commentators like Accursius or Bartolus misinterpreted the historical meaning of Roman laws, Budé showed in his *Annotations to the Pandects* (1508), but so had the ancient codifiers, such as Justinian's minister Tribonian. Tribonian and others had taken Roman law to be a single, consistent whole, when in fact, as Budé demonstrated, it had developed inconsistently over the course of a thousand years in many different historical contexts, each of which needed to be distinguished [53].

Budé developed this same concept of Roman antiquity as a series of historical developments with differing institutions and slowly evolving ways of life in his *De Asse*, written between 1508 and 1514. He did more in this book, however, than show how the *as*, the basic unit of Roman coinage, changed in value over the centuries. He theorized about the meaning of these changes in a number of digressions which make explicit the ideas of time and culture embodied in his work on the *Annotations*. These ideas reflect both a new consciousness of the implications of his philological analysis of ancient law and that new sense of the political importance of the humanist movement

---

[52] See the long quotation from Budé's *De Philologia* (Paris, 1532) on p. 743. The « burial » of their past does not mean that Frenchmen did not try to supply themselves with a noble and impressive history. The obscurity of France's origins was a severe handicap in a culture in which political and social legitimacy was based on aristocratic blood lines. Medieval French chroniclers fabricated a glorious Trojan ancestry for their kings, thus setting up a situation akin to that of Italian greatness and fall. But this explanation, because it rested so completely on assertion, was rejected in the course of the sixteenth century by French scholars, as George Huppert has shown in « The Trojan Franks and their Critics », *Studies in the Renaissance*, XII (1965), 227-241. Even before the demolition of the Trojan theory, the notion of the ancient grandeur of the Celts was replacing it. As we shall see, Budé appealed to this grandeur as a weapon against the overweening Italians. The Celtic movement in sixteenth-century France needs thorough study; the sources for such a study are ample.

[53] See Kelley, « Guillaume Budé ... », 818-822 (full citation in note 47), for substantiation of this point. Some Italian scholars — Valla, Poliziano — carried on the same anti-Tribonian polemic, as Kelley points out.

which we mentioned earlier. Upon discovering that Pliny had made mistakes in calculating the relative worth of different sorts of Roman coins, for example, he says:

> I for my part do not believe that the authority of Pliny, nor that of any man whatever among the ancients, should be held so sacred as to make us forget that there always has been and always will be a perfectly immediate power of [discerning] truth in the form of good and equitable judges ... It seems to me an absurd vow with which learned men of our time have bound their judgment and that of posterity when they hold that the bare name of antiquity should be venerated as a deity. I think that in fact the men of antiquity were men like ourselves. And they sometimes wrote about things which they little understood [54].

Several pages later Budé shows how Cicero misinterpreted Aristotle's concept of entelechy. He then goes on to attack the pretensions of Ciceronians who regard their master as an unsurpassable model to be imitated. Quintilian, a sort of « second Cicero », says Budé, called the Latin language merely the « disciple and imitator of Greek ». Quintilian showed that Cicero's forcefulness was due to his imitation of Demosthenes, his copiousness to study of Plato, and his pleasantness to the influence of Isocrates. Therefore, concludes Budé, to call Cicero a model who cannot be equalled is like saying that Protogenes, when he makes a copy of Apelles' painting of Venus, has made something more excellent than the original. Such an assertion would appear « either dishonest or ridiculous » [55].

Men of every age make errors, but every age also possesses good and equitable judges capable of discerning those errors and finding out the truth for themselves. Imitation of others' achievements is slothful; the Latins deserve nothing but scorn for merely being « actors » in a drama for which the Greeks wrote all the script. « Greece enriched the Latins not only with

---

[54] *De Asse* [Paris, 1532], ff. 4 v-5 r. (The leaves of this edition are numbered with Roman numerals, but I shall use Arabic numerals in my footnotes to refer to them). Budé's works having recently been reprinted, I shall offer only the most important or problematical of his Latin phrases in my notes.

[55] *Ibid.*, f. 7 r. This is the first major attack on Ciceronianism by a non-Italian, so far as I know.

[cultural] disciplines, but even with her very words ... », Budé insists [56].

Budé's attack on Roman imitators is motivated by present-day concerns more than by a desire for historical accuracy. He was striking at the claim of contemporary Italians to represent, as inheritors of Roman culture, an unsurpassable model for others. But he was also holding up to ridicule the claim of « certain Frenchmen » that « only Italians are capable of eloquence and poetry ». This claim ran counter to Budé's hopes for the future of French letters and, indeed, to a sense of his own importance. « If our ancestors during the past one hundred years », says Budé, « due to an indolent veneration for antiquity, had not dared to try anything new, we should be wanting in good part the present-day illustriousness of letters ». Lorenzo Valla was one such modern Hercules who « wrested truth from monsters », Budé continues, « ... and although I don't consider myself to be armed with weapons [lit., lionskin and club, in reference to Hercules] like his [Valla's] notable commentaries ... I too seem in my own mind to be engaged right now in the defense of truth with some assurance. I wish that everyone — and especially the French — were so minded, seeing that foreigners are already striving with the ancients for literary glory » [57].

Budé is equivocal in this passage: although he asserts that new things have been accomplished — and by Italians — he does not claim that these innovations place modern men on a higher level than men of antiquity. Moreover, in the preface to *De Asse*, Budé expresses the familiar interpretation of his time as the rebirth of something previously in existence: Varro

---

[56] *Ibid.*, f. 7 v: « Ingrati profecto est animi cum Graecia latinos non modo disciplinis, sed etiam suis verbis locupletaverit: eaque adhuc teneant, nec beneficium nos, nec debitum agnoscere ». The metaphor about Latins being mere actors in a Greek drama occurs in the sentences just following this one.

[57] *Ibid.*, ff. 132 v-133 r. I quote Budé's curious metaphor concerning Hercules on f. 133 r: « Equidem etsi leonino me tergore clavaque munitum esse cum eius notae commentatoribus non sentio, ut cuiusvis aerumnae Herculem futurum me profiteri confidam, in umbraculis mecum ipse domesticis, non in campo sub magistris antiquitatis exercitatus, nunc tamen semiermem saltem fidutiam ad veritatem tuendam afferre mihi videor. Itaque omnes esse animatos, praesertim Francos cupio, quandoquidem externi quoque iam cum antiquis literarum gloria certant ».

tells us that all the arts were discovered and perfected within the space of a thousand years, he says, without offering any criticism. All these fine things, however, which were invented by the ancients or adopted and adapted to their use, either fell into disuse through « the declining state of things », or were neglected by « heedlessness ». They became so « defiled by the deposit of ages », that posterity had to rediscover them for its own purposes. The diligence of learned men in carrying on this process of rediscovery, Budé concludes, has achieved so much in two generations that « antiquity seems almost to have arrived among us » [58].

Budé seems to want two things, both the restoration of antiquity just as it was and also the addition of new truths about antiquity and perhaps about other things as well. As to whether this makes or would make the moderns superior to the ancients, he expresses no opinion, but seems to imply that it is enough if we can equal their deeds. Certainly it would make the moderns different from the ancients. Budé can in no case be claimed as an exponent of *imitatio*.

Budé's curious mixture of ideas of rebirth and restoration with those of innovation and originality is nicely expressed in one of the concluding phrases of the preface to *De Asse*. He describes his purpose in writing about the Roman coinage system thus: « I am the first, I believe, to have undertaken to restore this aspect of antiquity ... » [59]. What Budé is asserting is that the act of restitution is itself a novelty. There is a creativity involved in the historian's ability to make something long dead come alive again: it is not a repetition of an action once performed but unfortunately forgotten, nor is it merely the restoration of a monument « defiled by the deposit of ages ». Budé's

---

[58] *Ibid.*, unnumbered first page of the preface: « Inde artium omnium consummatio, quas Varro intra mille annos repertas et absolutas fuisse tradit, cum varias scilicet usus meditando excuderet artes, ut inquit Homerus alter. Verumenimvero res multae praeclarae ab antiquis vel inventae, vel usurpatae, et in eorum usu positae, ita vel aevi situ squalidae, vel incuria temporum neglectae, vel rerum inclinationibus diu desitae fuerunt, ut iterum inveniendas in usum suum easdem posteritas habuerit. Quare virorum acrium doctorumque diligentia tantum una et altera aetate effectum est commentando, ut antiquitas propemodum interpollata in usum linguae Latinae ad nos pervenisse videatur ».

[59] *Ibid.*, unnumbered second page of the preface.

work results in the addition of entirely new knowledge to the sum of knowledge which his contemporaries had about antiquity: he has written something new about something old. Budé here expresses an idea — only half-consciously, to be sure — which lies at the heart of the historian's faith, an idea which makes the historian uncomfortable with any version of temporal change which regards human development as a unilinear process which moves in a direction which is always away from what has already happened, the « past », toward what may or should happen, the « future ». For the historian the way forward is to a very large degree the way backwards, since — in Santayana's phrase — « those who do not know the past are condemned to repeat it ». Delving into the past drives a wedge into the future because it is only by knowing what has been done that one can know what remains to be done and what tools and materials are at hand to accomplish it.

Once again the interrelatedness of ideas of time and of culture emerges. Budé tells us that he has been able to achieve this new thing, the understanding of a previously unknown aspect of ancient times, only by means of a special method. *De Asse*, he says, is a work which is « greater » and « more elaborate » than his *Annotations* because it could not be composed simply by studying one kind or group of « disciplines » or « crafts » such as jurisprudence. To achieve understanding of the Roman coinage system required use of every methodological tool available which « pertains to the interpretation of antiquity ». « Every type of good authority » among either Latin or Greek writers had to be searched through, analyzed, and « clarified » in the course of the work [60]. The fact that Budé envisaged philological and historical work as « encyclopedic » not only in aim but in methodological amplitude enabled him to break down the barriers to understanding a subject which, as he discovered, required analysis of a system of state finance which had evolved over hundreds of years. Nothing less than an attempt to understand the whole nexus of political and economic forces in the Roman republic and later in the far-flung empire would do. Demarca-

---

[60] *Ibid.*: « Nunc alteram lucubrationem grandioris incepti operosiorisque profero: non in unum genus illam quidem editam, aut disciplinarum, aut artium: sed in universum pertinentem ad antiquitatis interpretationem, et per omne prope genus auctorum probiorum utraque lingua patentem ».

tions of subject-matter and analytic approach which had been previously established necessarily gave way. Budé's purpose in *De Asse* led him to new, more encompassing conceptions of the way in which different disciplines are related and that in turn led him on to a new and more encompassing idea of ancient times.

IV.

Our discussion of Guillaume Budé's *De Asse* has offered some examples of interaction among the three aspects of causation which I have suggested are relevant to the study of shifts in climates of opinion. Budé's purpose and his method in this book, both of which he thought were new, led to a breakdown of some of the compartments in terms of which Fichet and Commynes regarded past and present events, and this opened up for Budé new ways of understanding temporal change and cultural process. Budé's social position and personal contacts, his independence of the traditional source of patronage for learning and culture — the church — and his status as an officer of the crown, led him to respond to events and ideas in his time in a special way and, vice-versa, led others to respond to his achievements in new ways. Finally, the movement toward greater stability and prosperity in day-to-day life within France and toward national expansion abroad allowed new cultural developments to proceed not only unimpeded but even stimulated by the general conditions of life and work. In this concluding section I would like to indicate how, under the influence of all these factors, Budé developed further his notions of time and culture to the point where we can discern in one of his later works the main features of the most important and systematic treatise connecting time with cultural development which was written in sixteenth-century France, Loys LeRoy's *De la Vicissitude ou Variété des Choses*.

Most secondary literature refers to Budé as a classicist who fostered the prestige of antiquity rather than as one who believed in modern superiority [61]. Nothing in Budé's two early works,

---

[61] See, e. g., A. C. Keller, « Idea of Progress ... » (full citation in n. 4), p. 240, where he attempts to explain the development of Rabelais' ideas

the *Annotations* and the *De Asse*, from which we have quoted so far, belies this opinion, for while Budé urges rivalry with ancient men, and points out that nothing intrinsic prevents modern men from « doing something new », he does not assert that that newness — the achievements of Valla, or of himself in restoring knowledge of the Roman coinage system — places modern times on a higher plane than antiquity. In his *De Philologia* (1532), however, Budé moves very close to taking this further step toward the ideas of time as progressive and culture as cumulative. *De Philologia* is written in the form of a dialogue between King Francis I and Budé. Budé puts the following speech into the mouth of the king:

> I think that Divine Providence is an architect who arranges mortal affairs as follows: he prescribes and commands something new to be designed by his workers and artisans in art and nature, in which they apply themselves to one and the same thing in each age, so that each age may be distinguished, and just as life may be more abundantly furnished from day to day, so also it may be from age to age. But there are certain fated inundations over works both of nature and of art by which things invented for the use and trade of men are carried away, while meantime other kinds of things arise which until then, because of the fated order, were buried in the depths of the secrets of nature.
>
> Recent centuries have brought forth unheard-of things, however, which antiquity, however ingenious, never ... suspected, such as fire-making machines of war ... and ingenious Mars' weapons of destruction ... On the other hand, recent times brought forth printing, a great aid, it seems to me, in awakening and raising the reputation of your letters, which lay so long neglected and dead.
>
> I think many other things, too, in either category, which will be important in the future, have been set down in the deep secrets of nature, which must be brought to light each in its own time. Nor indeed do we see all things which were buried in those earlier floods

---

about modern achievements: « ... Rabelais' changed attitude toward ancient authority coincided with the death ... of four of the leading scholars of Europe ... two of whom — Erasmus and Budé — were the very life-givers of his enthusiasm for ancient learning. Important signs of a new independence among scholars began to appear precisely in the period 1534-46 during which these old-line scholars died and during which Rabelais adopted a new philosophy ». In contrast to other scholars, D. Kelley, *op. cit.*, p. 824, calls Budé a partisan of the « moderns ».

as yet emerging nor to a certain extent even known to exist, even if our age moves every stone, as they say, and dares everything, and strives to dig and carry out the submerged objects [62].

One year before the appearance of *De Philologia* Budé's friend Vives, whom he had met in 1519, published his *De disciplinis* with its ringing appeals to man's natural capacity « daily [to] progress » [63]. It is unlikely that Budé had a chance to read Vives' book before composing his own, and in any case the differences between the notions of time and culture of the two are as striking as the similarities. They deserve more careful and detailed analysis than can be given here, where we can only note that while nature in Vives' book is a human power, ready to aid the individual in creating all manner of new things if he only tries — an attitude characteristic of Budé too in the *De Asse* — nature in the speech of Francis I quoted above is a superhuman force controlled by Divine Providence both in its burials of past inventions and in its bringing forth « unheard-of things » [64]. The sense that God's hand hovers over history, omnipresent in Commynes but present only in a highly rhetorical form in Fichet's account of Gutenberg's « divine » invention of printing and scarcely present at all in Budé's earlier musings about the course of time, here re-emerges in a very ingenious form. This idea of the indirect control which God exercises over history by means of the ordered unfolding of nature is developed by LeRoy in his book *On Vicissitude*.

The influence of Budé's ideas on LeRoy's thought is easy to trace. LeRoy accounted himself a student and friend of the great humanist and published a biography of him in 1540 just after Budé's death. LeRoy's *Life of Budé*, unlike his later *On Vicissitude*, reflects Vives' ideas and Budé's in almost equal measure. For example, in the *Life* the uniqueness of modern man

---

[62] *De Philologia*, f. LXVI r.

[63] See p. 716 and notes 12 and 13 above. *De causis* ... and *De tradendis* ... are two parts of Vives' larger work, *De disciplinis*.

[64] Cf. Vives, *Opera omnia*, VI (Valencia, 1785), 5: « ... Ut quod olim veteres illos scriptores fefellit, non id factum humani ingenii vitio, sicut nonnulli arbitrantur, sed illorum ostendam; ideoque nationes attuli petitas ex natura, non e divinis oraculis, ne ex philosophia in theologiam transilirem ... ». Translated by F. Watson, *op. cit.* (see note 12), p. 7.

is asserted not in reference to new inventions such as printing and cannons [65], but rather, like Vives, in reference to the discoveries — the lands, seas, and species of men unknown to the ancients in the New World [66]. Like Budé in the *De Asse* as well as like Vives, LeRoy asserts without offering examples or explanation that modern men are not inferior to the ancients in genius, while some are equal to them in learning and even superior to them in eagerness and industry [67]. Finally, the sense that times condition men, that certain ages are fated to restore letters or to bring other innovations, expressed in the speech of Francis I by Budé, is given in embryonic form in the preface to LeRoy's *Life of Budé*. It must not be thought that great orators like Demosthenes and Cicero, philosophers like Thales or Aristotle, or poets or medical writers emerge at random, says LeRoy.

Rather there is a certain power which takes counsel for the human race, and bears and nourishes such men, so that they either invent the arts necessary to living well and blissfully, or polish and perfect the discoveries of others. And in our age, when all the good arts have

---

[65] It is interesting to note that Rabelais couples printing with artillery in *Pantagruel* (chapter 8), published in November, 1532, one month after the royal privilege granted Budé for *De Philologia*. This same pair of inventions recurs in Du Bellay's *Deffence et Illustration de la langue françoyse* (I, chapter 9), published in 1549. Henri Chamard points out this triple occurrence in his edition of the *Deffence* (Paris, 1904), p. 117, n. 1. Although Rabelais corresponded with Budé, it is unlikely that he saw the text of *De Philologia* before his own work was printed. Perhaps a still earlier source of the coupling than Budé's *De Philologia* will be discovered some day.

[66] *G. Budaei viri Clarissimi Vita* (Paris, 1540), pp. 47-48: « Quandoquidem non solum ea quae densissimis ignorantiae tenebris obducebantur, in lucem velut ab inferis revocata sunt, sed quae veteribus fuerant penitus obstrusa, nova maria, novae terrae, ac species hominum, viae coeli pelagique nunquam antea ne fando quidem auditae, nova sydera patefacta nobis, multae artes repertae priscis incognitae saeculis, religio in pristinam vindicata dignitatem ». Vives' praise of the geographical and anthropological discoveries of modern navigators occurs in *op. cit.*, VI, 5, just preceding the quotation given in note 64 here. These two passages in Vives can easily be misinterpreted if the religious concerns which he expresses in the same paragraphs are disregarded.

[67] *Budaei ... Vita*, p. 6: « Quod si ad huiusce nostri seculi felicitatem animum convertere velimus, sine dubio comperiemus nostros homines antiquis ingenio non inferiores, multos doctrina pares, studio autem et industria longe superiores: nec minoris aestimandos, nisi caecitate quadam animi eorum laudi et gloriae invidere, quam favere mallemus ».

begun to emerge again, nature has renewed herself out of the darkness of earlier times and has brought forth many men renowned in every virtue and discipline, among whom it is marvellous to observe how much Budé especially excells ... [68].

There is more of nature mysticism here than in Budé's words; not Divine Providence but « a certain power ... bears and nourishes » great men. Unlike Vives' assertion that nature is « always equal », nature here « renewed herself » after a kind of hibernation period. The power of nature, it seems, is cyclic, not constant. This conception is amplified and systematized in LeRoy's *On Vicissitude* where, however, it is integrated with the plans of God. For LeRoy's cyclic theory in this work is founded on the idea which we have seen underlying Commynes' *Memoirs*, that God disciplines the world morally by equalizing pleasure and pain « so that each nation has in turn a part in happiness and unhappiness, and none becomes proud through too long prosperity » [69]. In contrast to Commynes' work, where God intervenes directly, God's balancing of one nation and one age against another is instrumentalized in LeRoy's book by the growth-and-decay rhythms of nature.

This moralistic balancing principle comes out even when LeRoy emphasizes the innovating features of his own time: printing, the compass, and cannons are three things with which antiquity has nothing to be compared, he declares in the tenth book of *On Vicissitude*. Yet balancing these innovations are evils peculiar to our time: not only wars, high prices, famines, and plagues, but an unheard-of disease which God has obviously sent to punish human lubricity — syphilis — and new heresies like that of Luther.

---

[68] *Ibid.*, p. 5.

[69] *Vicissitude*, f. 63 r: « Toutefois quant à moy ie croy que Dieu soigneux de toutes les parties de l'Univers octroye l'excellence des armes et des lettres ores en Asie, ores en Europe, ores en Afrique, establissant le souverain Empire du monde, l'une fois en Orient, l'autre en Occident, l'autre en Midy, l'autre en Septentrion, et permettant la vertu et le vice, vaillance et lascheté, sobriété et delices, sçavoir et ignorance, aller de pays en pays, honorans et diffamans les nations en diverses saisons: à fin que chacune ayt en son tour part à l'heur et malheur, et que nulle enorgueillisse par trop longue prosperité ... ». I have used the Paris 1583 edition.

For just as we have seen that at the times in the past when mutations of human things have occurred and nature has made her greatest efforts, extreme evil has been coupled with excellent virtue, and extraordinary calamities have accompanied great felicity, so now one could not imagine any sort of misfortune or vice which is not found in this century along with the good fortune of good letters which have been revived and of the arts which have been restored [70].

Besides being aware of the technological uniqueness of modern times and regarding culture as a variable, easily disrupted development over long periods of time, Budé and LeRoy shared a third idea: both of them felt that the patronage of princes was a prime factor in achieving cultural greatness. According to LeRoy's *Life of Budé*, Greece under Alexander and Rome under Augustus produced many great men partly because of the favorable climate — note again LeRoy's tendency to naturalistic explanation — and partly because achievement was rewarded with honor. The fall of letters in Greece and then in Rome and all Italy was solely due to the neglectfulness, capriciousness, and envy of those who ruled over affairs [71]. It is interesting that this point is not made in *On Vicissitude* where, on the contrary, the fall of letters is attributed to human laziness, long wars, and barbarian tyranny [72]. Thus, LeRoy's explanation of the fall of letters in *On Vicissitude* is sociological while his earlier explanation in 1540 is political. Budé's explanations, like LeRoy's first view, are political, and they are associated with that polemic which Budé carried on against the lovers of Italian learning in his own day.

Budé was a less vehement proselytizer for the moderns than LeRoy: he was never sure just how superior his age was to others

---

[70] *Ibid.*, f. 219 r.

[71] *Budaei ... Vita*, p. 45: « Quid postea artes eaedem in Graecia sunt extinctae? in qua et natae, et altae, et ad summum perductae intra mille annos fuerant? quid Roma cesserunt, totaque Italia? quid exulatum ad Arabas discesserunt? quid tam multis annis inscitia grassante inter mortuae iacuerunt? an aliunde id factum, nisi ex sordibus, morositate, invidia illorum, qui civitatibus, et amplissimis regnis, atque imperiis praefuerunt? ».

[72] *Vicissitude*, f. 33 r: « Par mesme ordre et vicissitude pareille les disciplines estans petites au commencement augmentent peu à peu et montent à leur perfection où apres que sont parvenues dechoient tantost, et finablement [perissent] par la paresse des hommes, ou par la calamité des guerres longuement continuees, ou par la tyrannie des Barbares ».

which had preceded it. But he was sure of the necessity for Frenchmen to show their superiority, and this perhaps helped make his scattered comments on the greatness of his own time and on the French potential for further greatness more effective than LeRoy's systematized remarks in stimulating French achievements in the sixteenth century. Let us look once more, in conclusion, at the political context of Budé's championship of the moderns.

Budé dedicated *De Asse* to the « genius — or Minerva — of France » [73]. His purpose, like LeRoy's, was to stimulate by his work the further restoration of letters — but not just by anyone. During the previous one hundred years the Italians, first among Latin peoples, had the chance to sharpen their pens on the whetstone of ancient eloquence; now the French have the opportunity to emulate both ancient and modern Italian writers in all things [74].

Some Frenchmen — unnamed — maintain that their countrymen are unsuited to letters, in contrast to the Italians, whose sky and soil make even infants wail eloquently and poetically [75]. But if eloquence and humane studies have not hitherto been greatly celebrated in France it is not due to climate or the gentle Gallic nature — thus Budé rejects in advance the biologizing of LeRoy — but rather to the boorishness and even wickedness of certain important administrators. These men are so ignorant that they do not know Strabo's testimony that the Gauls — that is, ancient Frenchmen — who lived near Marseilles, a Greek colony in ancient times, very quickly acquired Greek letters. But if the Gauls were formerly well-fitted for literature, who can deny that modern Frenchmen may aspire to the same success and that eloquence may once again enjoy public honor? If only due rewards are established, oratory and poetry will return to France [76].

«O tempora! O mores!» exclaims Budé in another digression in the *De Asse*: France, once looked upon both by herself and by others as the leader of Christendom, is now degenerate, a

---

[73] *De Asse*, unnumbered last page of preface.
[74] *Ibid.*, f. 13 r.
[75] *Ibid.*, f. 12 r.
[76] *Ibid.*, ff. 19 r-v.

helpless infant not even capable of coping with her own problems, whether in acting or in speaking about them [77]. Far from viewing the pursuit of letters as a contemplative activity, removed from public life, Budé argues that great actions are inseparable from great thoughts and vice versa. « As if nature had established dissension between heart and hand. I think that in fact the powers of [men's] spirits wax strong in both respects [heart and hand] when those spirits are properly formed by doctrine and training ». This is especially true of those peoples « whose natures are endowed with every talent », Budé continues. Strabo is witness that such are the natures of the Gauls, and « experience teaches the same thing ». The history of the Greek and Roman empires provides a further argument in favor of this idea. For these empires were « acquired and retained no less by cultivating the spirit than by exercising the body. For indeed Pallas and Minerva were thought of as the same deity, and power of judgment and decision was held to inspire a Martian spirit both in armored breasts and in [men's] hearts, whether they were Roman or Greek » [78].

Whereas LeRoy is content to use without explanation the medieval commonplace of the parallel rise and fall of achievements in arms and letters [79], Budé here suggests an inner connection between intellectual and physical achievements. He carries it further in a discussion of the classical virtues of wisdom and prudence, maintaining that the first is inseparable from the second and that the second in turn governs all other virtues in human life. Pursuers of wisdom, therefore, are the only ones

---

[77] *Ibid.*, f. 14 v.

[78] *Ibid.*, f. 19 v. I quote the beginning and end of this difficult passage: « Quasi vero natura dissidium inter cor et manus ingenerarit. Ego vero in utranque partem vires animorum valere puto quum recte animi ipsi formantur doctrina et institutis ... Quippe idem numen Palladis et Minervae, et Martios animos loricatis pectoribus et togatis [i. e., Roman] praecordiis aut palliatis [i. e., Greek] vim iudicandi censendique inspirare creditum est ».

[79] *Vicissitude*, f. 33 r: « ... Ne s'entredelaissans gueres la puissance et sapience: mais ordinairement faisans bonne compagnie l'une à l'autre. Comme j'ay observé depuis trois mille ans estre advenu cinq ou six fois en certaines saisons, trouvant l'excellence des armes et des lettres avoir esté premierement en Egypte, Assyrie, Perse, et Asie la mineur: Consequemment en Grece, Italie, et Sarasmesnie ».

capable of raising France from her present cultural inferiority. The only thing they require to re-establish in France, as in Italy, the splendor of arts and letters of twelve hundred years ago is the favor of kings and princes.

Budé saw the cause of letters as a political problem, not as a moral or natural one. He wrote a treatise for Francis I in 1519 which was later entitled « On the education of a Prince » — a collection of proverbs with commentary, the only French book he ever consented to write [80] — in which the virtue of « liberality » turns out to be the chief virtue of princes, and is illustrated in proverb after proverb. After playing an important role in convincing the king to appoint the royal lecturers who formed the nucleus of the future Collège de France in 1529, he was still not satisfied and when he wrote the *De Philologia*, he proposed a vast new program of subsidies for scholars and a research center which, he says, he would like to have called the « Museum ». He threatens the king that if he does not carry out this restoration of letters, he, like so many of the great French kings of medieval times, will be forgotten because of the lack of eloquent records of his activities.

Budé's continuing search for patronage from the state, his direct and bold appeals to the king — his letters report many such ventures — stand in stark contrast to the procedures of Fichet and Commynes. We possess the letters which Fichet wrote to the persons receiving presentation copies of his *Rhetorica:* dukes, counts, cardinals, and archbishops are among those to whom he sent copies, but not the king of France. While making allowance for the unscholarly if not antischolarly tastes of Louis XI, one cannot help but notice the difference between the feudal world to which Fichet relates his cultural endeavors and the monarchical world to which Budé relates his. Writing to the count of Geneva, Fichet asks the prince to accept the *Rhetorica* as a gift from his « subject », whom the love of learning has « exiled » far from his native home in the count's territories [81].

---

[80] He did not consent to having it published. Budé apparently wrote this little book with one purpose only in mind: gaining the ear of a king who knew no Latin. The book remained in manuscript until after his death, when it was published in adulterated form in 1547.

[81] Champion, *op. cit.*, pp. 15-16, gives the list of men to whom Fichet sent presentation letters and paraphrases Fichet's letter to the count. The

Commynes addresses his *Memoirs*, in a prologue which has been preserved, to Angelo Cato, an Italian physician in attendance at the French court who, Commynes hoped, would dress up his work in Latin so as to make it acceptable to the world of scholars. Cato died before Commynes completed the *Memoirs* and he apparently could never bring himself to publish it or even to offer it to anyone else [82]. No such humility restrains the hopes and ambitions of Budé:

> Since we see in our age letters restored to life ... what forbids us from hoping that new Demosthenes, Platos, Thucydides, Ciceros, Livys, and other writers of the same note or almost equal to them may soon spring up among us, not so much imitators of these ancient men as their emulators?... In my opinion, the last difficulties in bringing to completion the restoration of ancient wisdom have been destined for this time. For so many men pursue studies, and this age is so fertile in genius, and such good fortune has attended the dissemination of books in Latin and Greek, that we have nothing for which we could desire except that of a certain hope of reward. For who embraces the arts, studies, or virtue itself, if you eliminate all recompense? [83]

Here, together with his sense of the political character of the development of culture, Budé expresses that double feeling about the past which we have noted again and again in his work. He appears at the same time eager to restore «ancient wisdom» and confident that his time will produce new Platos and Ciceros. Budé concludes this particular passage thus: « Indeed this age seems not only to have restored to life ancient things, which had long since perished and been lamented, but to have brought out every last quality of things, both in the arts and in nature » [84]. In this passage at least it is clear that Budé saw the restoration of

---

original of this letter has not yet been published, and thus the words in quotation marks in the text here may be Champion's, not Fichet's.

[82] The *Memoirs* were first published eleven years after Commynes' death. No manuscript which can be dated before Commynes' death has ever been found, although several others dating probably between 1520 and 1550 have been preserved.

[83] *De Philologia*, f. LXV v.

[84] *Ibid.*, f. LXVI r: « Adeo haec aetas non modo res priscas, desitas et deploratas, vitae restituisse, sed et artibus et naturae ultimas operum notas videtur excussisse ».

antiquity not as an end in itself, and not even as an all-important spur to new achievement. Rather, he saw it as part of a much larger movement toward an all-inclusive, cumulative perfection which had almost been reached in his time. It is this vision of cumulative progress which King Francis rejects in the long speech quoted earlier [85].

The king sees no imminent consummation in the arts or in nature. Each age, though unique in possessing such novelties as printing or gunpowder, is yet unable to build upon this uniqueness. For the « inundations » which separate one age from the next are so destructive that even the greatest industry and the boldest genius imaginable cannot restore what has been washed away. And if the past cannot be restored, it cannot be built upon. Mankind cannot, therefore, be said to be approaching perfectibility.

In spite of these arguments King Francis' interlocutor, the « Budé » who speaks in *De Philologia*, replies to the king with the same optimism as he had expressed before, tempering it just enough to make it consistent with his plea for royal patronage:

> In truth, sir, life seems to require few things, or perhaps nothing, by which it could be made better equipped, provided that good letters in both languages receive the last touch of restitution, something dependent above all upon your kindness, as I think I have sufficiently said and taught before. Thus, although I could not say that nothing, yet almost nothing would be lacking by which life could be made more holy, more moral, and more in keeping with the dignity of the name of Christian [86].

Budé's ideas of temporal change and cultural process are fluctuating and inconsistent, like the two incompatible views of innovation which he puts into the mouths of the two characters

[85] The sentences which occur just before Budé's conclusion, quoted in note 84, expand upon the perfection which Budé felt his age had achieved: « Quid vero fieri hoc tempore desperemus, quod olim factum fuerit? Etenim quid memoria nostra et parentum non inventum est, quid non editum et proditum, ad vitam iuvandam et ornandam, aut ex antiquitate relatum? Quod utinam ad vitam commodius agendam atque elegantius, non etiam ad onerandam luxu et delitiis ac pene obruendam multa naturae et artibus inventio actuosa extudisset et excudisset ».

[86] *Ibid.*, f. LXVI v.

in *De Philologia*. Budé's fluctuation and inconsistency in this particular case might be explained as resulting from his literary purposes in the dialogue. It is true that Francis I's pessimistic assessment of past and future is appropriate to a patron reluctant to grant funds for philological studies on the vast scale proposed by Budé. Conversely, Budé's praise of present-day attainments is appropriate to someone anxious to awaken in the king a desire to finish up, by means of patronage, a task already almost completed. But the words of both men range far beyond these utilitarian purposes. They pronounce judgment upon the whole history of man, suggesting that the author was perhaps expressing in outer, literary form a dialogue which he had previously held with himself—a dialogue in which he, like his characters in *De Philologia*, had been unable to come to a conclusion.

But if Budé's inconsistency is sometimes a result of an inconclusiveness in his own mind, it is at other times a result of conflicting aims. A signal example of this is hinted at in the last phrase of the speech from *De Philologia* just quoted: while Budé's earlier speeches in that work have urged the king to further French glory through scholarly subsidies, this one points out the advantages accruing to Christian life. We have already mentioned the dual impulse toward cultural change characteristic of early sixteenth-century France. Men sought to reform and perfect Christianity and to achieve national glory at the same time. In *De Asse* the two ideals are assumed to be so compatible, if not identical, that the pronoun « we », employed without qualification, sometimes means « we the French » — including those ancient Gauls who defeated in battle the Romans (that is, Budé's rivals, the Italians) — and sometimes « we the chosen people of God » — including the ancient Jews who, as Josephus reports, invented many things which Egyptian writers ascribed to non-Jews « out of malice and prevarication »[87]. The confusions which result from this double meaning of « we » are manifold. For example, while Budé asserts in certain passages, as we have seen[88], that all the arts had their origin in Greece, he maintains at the same time that all the ancients except the Jews, and later the Christians, were in error about the central truths of life.

---

[87] *De Asse*, f. 118 r.

[88] See p. 738.

Greek and Roman historians must be corrected by « us » — the Christians — who possess sacred uncorrupted history, he says. We may wonder at the felicity of our times, — « we who have been born when the world is already declining » — for they are times in which we may discern « both far forwards and backwards ... what things are, what things have been, and what things, soon to happen, may linger on » [89]. Here Budé echoes Commynes' conviction of secular decline while at the same time calling his age happy and worthy of wonder because of the opportunities it affords for understanding past, present and future.

The variety and the frequency of these strange combinations of temporal and cultural ideas suggest that Budé never developed a general theory of history such as Le Roy tried to do in his *On Vicissitude*. Budé seems to have been less concerned about the consistency of his thought than he was about its comprehensiveness. And indeed his varied comments upon ancient and modern times, Christian and pagan traditions, and French and non-French societies, exhibit most impressively the speculative freedom and breadth of interest which awareness of their complex past typically gave to French humanists [90]. Nowhere in the works of Budé which we have examined do we find a partisanship which excludes one point of view because of the zeal with which another is being argued.

The conflict which arose in early sixteenth-century France between the claims of ancient and modern culture — a conflict which often enough took place not between men but rather within the minds of thoughtful men such as Budé — was not without significance simply because it produced no long-lived formulae or because only passing references to science and technology can be found. The new ideas of time and culture

---

[89] *Ibid.*, ff. 120 r-120 v. I quote from 120 v: « Caeterum admirari temporum nostrorum felicitatem, qui mundo iam vergente nati, tamen longissime prorsum retrorsumque cernimus (ut Maronianus ille Proteus) quae sint quae fuerint quae mox ventura trahantur ».

[90] See, p. 736. The unique breadth of French sixteenth-century historical thought was pointed out long ago by Robert Flint in his *History of the Philosophy of History* (New York, 1894). It is emphasized in chapter 1 of J. G. A. Pocock's *The Ancient Constitution and the Feudal Law* (Cambridge, 1957), and is one of the central themes in Donald Kelley's book on sixteenth-century French historiography, *The Foundations of Modern Historical Scholarship* (New York, 1970).

which appear in this period have complex relations to earlier and later notions of these entities, relations which can only be explained by observing the continuing interaction, as Hans Baron has always insisted, of socio-political with intellectual and cultural forces. The significance of these ideas is larger than that suggested by the traditional historical themes of the development of the idea of progress and the origins of the Renaissance. For these ideas raise the question of man's ability to control, conserve, or simply to sustain his humanly-created, time-bound and time-binding, mode of life.

As men grew more aware of the possibilities open to them, they lost some of that confidence in the abiding quality of things which had sustained an earlier age. The way ahead might be the way backwards, in spite of all one's efforts and historical skill. Facing that possibility, Budé — or rather, his fictional counterpart in *De Philologia* — looked confidently into the abyss of the future, King Francis less so. We who face that same possibility recognize the author of *De Philologia*, the man who envisaged both « King Francis' » and « Budé's » ways of looking at things, as a « modern »: not because he shares our assumptions or our conclusions, but because his sense of past and future, of science and craftsmanship and nearly every other form of cultivating « spirit » and « virtue », is no longer whole, secure, and neatly boxed. Budé's sense of these things, like ours, is mixed, vacillating, rich, and torn.

GEORGE HUPPERT

THE IDEA OF CIVILIZATION IN THE SIXTEENTH CENTURY

The word « civilization », an eighteenth-century coinage in both French and English, was created as a prime weapon in the linguistic arsenal of the Enlightenment. In the vocabulary of the *philosophes*, this was a proud word. They spoke of civilization as a « long and difficult work of liberation » and took the view that « as civilization extends on earth, wars and conquests will disappear ». Civilization was the opposite of savagery, but it was also more than that, for the word *police* had served for sometime to describe the condition of a complex, urban and sophisticated society. Voltaire, who never used *civilisation*, makes the distinction between *peuples policés* and *sauvages*, as does Turgot. *Police*, in Voltaire's age, referred to a society's constitution — its politics, laws, administration, military and fiscal organization — and the use of the word presupposes that the society in question had reached a high degree of development in all these respects, that Reason, in short, had transformed the customs of the people from a savage state to a *policée* condition.

But where philosophic writers wished to describe the comparable progress of Reason in the realm of morality and culture, the word *police* was not adequate. It became necessary to add *civilisé* to *policé*, as when Voltaire writes of the Egyptians' progress toward civilization: « Les Egyptiens ne purent être rassemblés en corps, civilisés, policés, industrieux, puissants, que très longtemps après tous les peuples que je viens de passer en revue ».

Lucien Febvre, in a justly famous essay written forty years ago, argued that the word *civilisation* was born in mid-eighteenth century — and not before — because the very idea it was meant to convey was new in mens' minds. In his view, philosophical writers like Voltaire and Turgot were in need of a noun which would describe the condition of a people at once *policé* and *civilisé* [1]. In explaining the creation of the neologism *civilisation*

[1] The quotations and interpretations in this paragraph are a summary of the relevant portion of Lucien Febvre's « Civilisation: evolution d'un mot et d'un groupe d' idées » in *Pour une histoire à part entière* (Paris, 1962),

(there were very few words ending in -ation), E. Benveniste argues plausibly enough that the word which the *philosophes* were hunting for had to designate not only the state or condition of being civilized, but also the process of becoming civilized. *Civilisation* described « a universal gradation, a slow process of education and refinement » in man's condition, leading him from his original savagery to his present way of life. As Benveniste — I think rightly — concludes, this amounted to « not only an historical view of society, it was also an optimistic and resolutely non-theological interpretation of the evolution of society » [2]. The idea of civilization as understood in the eighteenth century clearly implied the rejection of the traditional Christian view of human decline, as expressed, for example, in the medieval theories of the Four Monarchies or of the Seven Ages of human history. The idea of civilization, in short, was inseparable from the idea of progress.

Now, if the word *civilisation* is clearly a new arrival in the eighteenth century [3], the same cannot really be said of the idea of civilization, in spite of Febvre's and Benveniste's erudite arguments. Febvre himself suspected that the concept may have been much older than the word. After all, Voltaire did get along without *civilisation* and managed to express the idea by combining *police* with other words such as the adjective *civilisé* and the verb *civiliser*. How long had the idea existed before the word? Could not the old noun *civilité* have served the purpose for earlier writers? This is the clue which Febvre followed, but as he did not launch a full-scale investigation, he did not happen to find what he was looking for. As this is precisely what I did find, I offer the results of my own inquiry here as a sequel and conclusion to Febvre's *sondage*.

Civilité is an old word. Febvre found it in Robert Estienne's dictionary of 1549 where it means urbanity, the condition of being civil, urbane, courteous. In Furetière's dictionary of 1690

---

pp. 481-528. The Voltaire text is on p. 497. This essay first appeared in the *Première Semaine Internationale de Synthèse* (Paris, 1930), II, 1-55.

[2] E. Benveniste, « Civilisation », in *Éventail de l'histoire vivante: hommage à Lucien Febvre* (Paris, 1953), I, 47-54.

[3] In addition to the essays of Febvre and Benveniste, see also J. Moras, *Ursprung und Entwicklung des Begriffs der Zivilisation in Frankreich (1756-1830)* (Hamburg, 1930).

it still has no other meaning. It is defined as « Manière honnête, douce et polie d'agir, de converser ensemble ». The meaning Febvre was looking for is not recorded in the dictionaries — which is to say that *civilité* could not have been used in the sense of civilization very widely. This, however, should not surprise us. If we are right in assuming that the modern concept of civilization is an ideological weapon of the Enlightenment, we are not likely to find it expressed very frequently before the eighteenth century. The logical place to look for it is in the writings of *philosophes avant la lettre*, early representatives, that is, of the philosophy of the Enlightenment.

Here again, Febvre knew what he was doing. He looked into Descartes' *Discours de la Méthode* and found the adjective *civilisé* used in the modern sense — as opposed to the then current sense of « polite », « well-mannered », « courteous » [4]. As for the noun *civilité*, used in the sense of the modern *civilisation*, Febvre found no trace of it. What must have persuaded him to give up the chase is that the seventeenth—and eighteenth—century writers do seem unanimous in confining the meaning of *civilité* to « good manners ».

One has to look elsewhere. One has to go back to the time before the conventions of courtly language and of orthodox sentiments triumphed — to a time, that is, which preceded the successes of the Counter Reformation in France. One could begin by following Joseph Niedermann in his pursuit of the changing meaning of the words *cultura*, *civilitas*, and *humanitas* in Renaissance thought [5]. Niedermann notices Jean Bodin's use of the noun *humanitas*, for example. Bodin, when he is writing in Latin, uses *humanitas* to refer to the way of life of a society which has achieved a high degree of formal culture (*disciplinae*) and reached, at the same time, a fairly complex development of its laws and its government. Such societies Bodin contrasts with « barbarous » societies. When Bodin is writing

---

[4] Febvre, « Civilisation », p. 491, citing Descartes. Febvre also cites Montaigne's use of the adjective « *civilisé* », but the example is not persuasive for Montaigne was speaking of a person, Adrian Turnèbe, when he described him as having « quelque façon externe qui pouvait n'estre pas civilizée à la courtisane ».

[5] Joseph Niedermann, *Kultur: Werden und Wandlungen des Begriffs und seiner Ersatzbegriffe von Cicero bis Herder* (Florence, 1941).

in French, he uses *humanité* and *civilité* in a sense which is distinct from the common usage. This is the case, for instance, when he is citing Cicero to the effect that « la civilité & courtoisie a pris sa naissance en l'Asie mineure & en a rempli toute la terre » [6]. To say that here, in a text of 1577, *civilité* is used to express the modern conception of civilization may be going too far. It is, one might counter, an isolated case, and Bodin, after all, is merely translating Cicero. The same reservations can be invoked against Niedermann's other example, which he found in Calvin (1541) who wrote of « les peuples les plus rudes et plus eslongnez de civilité et humanité » [7]. Calvin was also translating Cicero. I could add a third example, also an early one (1542) and also an instance of translation. Louis Meigret, in his translation of Polybius, wrote: « L' Histoire commencera sur la fin de ce que Siconius ha laissé par escrit. Or estoient avãt ces tems ci les affaires du monde sans civilité » [8]. I am inclined to think this a clearer instance because of the context. But there is no need to build on such slender foundations.

The verb *civiliser* and the adjective *civilisé* were both acquiring a new meaning in the fifteen-sixties, at least among some philosophically-minded writers who, as we shall see, had certain things in common. Niedermann observes this transformation in a text of 1568, Louis Le Roy's *Politiques d'Aristote*, in which the author writes of « les pais les plus temperez et civilisez ». There is no question, in this instance, of a person being civilized in the sense of courteous. Rather, as Niedermann observes, « Das Volk ist hier civilisé » [9]. While Calvin may have used the word in the same sense, he was quoting Cicero and his use was quite isolated. With Le Roy we are on much firmer ground. Walter von Wartburg notes Le Roy's use, also in 1568, of the verb *civiliser* to mean « transforming from a primitive, natural condition to a more advanced one by means of moral, intellectual and social culture » [10].

---

[6] Jean Bodin, *Les six livres de la Republique* (Paris, 1577), I, 767.

[7] *Institution de la religion chrestienne: texte de la première édition française (1541)* ... (Paris, 1911), Vol. I, p. 4.

[8] Louis Meigret, *Les Cinq premiers livres des histoires de Polybe* (Lyon, 1558), p. 2.

[9] Niedermann, p. 70.

[10] *Französisches Etymologisches Wörterbuch* (Tübingen, 1949).

In Le Roy's vocabulary, *civil, incivil, civilisé, civiliser* are words clearly associated with a general theory of historical evolution identical with that of the eighteenth-century philosophical writers. « If we consider », he writes in 1568, « all the ancient past of which some memory remains, we will find that the regions which we now occupy were inhabited until about 3000 years ago by people as rude and incivil as the savages discovered by the Castilians and the Portuguese some time ago » [11]. In his last and most ambitious work, published in 1575, Le Roy developed his theory of the growth of civilization fully. Here he used the noun *civilité* in the very title of the book: *De la vicissitude ou varieté des choses en l'univers, et concurrence des armes et des lettres par les premieres et plus illustres nations du monde, depuis le temps ou a commencé la civilité, & memoire humaine iusques à present.*

Le Roy is by no means our star witness. It is reasonable to begin with him, since Niedermann and Wartburg already attracted our attention to this author. There are earlier texts, however, and clearer, quite indisputable, instances of the use of *civilité* in the sense of civilization. Before we take a close look at these, it might be worth our while to examine the general context in which the idea of civilization was born. For an early exposition of a rationalist theory of the origins of civilization, we might turn to Guillaume Paradin who, in the preface to his *Cronique de Savoye* (Lyon, 1552) argues that the usefulness of historical study lies in its being able to provide answers to questions such as the following:

« By what instinct or inclination were men moved for the first time — considering how rude, how barbarous, how incapable of friendship they are — to assemble together in bands, to live near each other, to communicate with each other, to go about their business together? How did they reach the conclusion that they ought to endure one of their number to command them, that laws should be devised to ease the lot of the good and give them security and peace as well as inspire terror in the

---

[11] Louis Le Roy, *De l'origine, antiquité, progrés, excellence et utilité de l'art politique* (Lyon, 1568), p. 12: « Si[nous]voulons considerer toute l' antiquité dont il[nous] reste quelque memoire, nous trouverons les habitans iadis és pays ou nous demourons, avoir esté avant trois mille ans, autant rudes & incivils, que sont les sauvages nagueres descouvers par les Castillans & Portugalois ... ».

bad and provide for their punishment? [How did they reach the decision] to let themselves be locked up inside of common walls all under one lock and key — and other such matters concerning human company and society? »[12] Paradin does not happen to use *civilité* in his published works but his assumptions about the origins of civilization are those of Le Roy or Voltaire. For that matter, they are also the assumptions of Cicero. When such views are boldly expressed by a sixteenth-century Christian, they are inevitably in conflict with orthodox interpretations of history. Rationalist and secular theories of the growth of civilization go hand in hand with an exaltation of the powers of historical study. Paradin's historicism, indeed, comes close to being blasphemous. Not only does he affirm that « History is the climax and goal of all philosophy » (« l' histoire est le comble de toute Philosophie ») but he describes historical knowledge as « a window which, once opened, makes the entire past visible, almost like Divine Providence, for whom everything is simultaneously present ». (« Laquelle estant ouverte, descouvre tout le passé; quasi comme une divine providence, a laquelle toutes choses sont presentes »)[13].

Calvin, Meigret, Paradin, Le Roy among the older men, Bodin, perhaps, among the younger ones. Where would one find men who think like that in the fifteen-sixties? We are looking for a man of the younger generation who has had a classical education and has studied Roman law, preferably under Cujas or Alciati. A Frenchman who belongs to the magisterial class, who has an extraordinary interest in historical study, who writes in French and is self-conscious and deliberate in his use of the language. A man whose religious opinions might be rather free, a man, at least, for whom Moses is not the only model of historiography. A man who is enthusiastically a modern, who

---

[12] Guillaume Paradin, *Cronique de Savoye* (Lyon, 1552), A 2 v.: « ... par quel instinct ou inclination furent premierement les hommes tant rudes, tant barbares & incapables d'amitié, meuz à s'assembler par trouppes, habiter les uns pres des autres, communiquer & contracter de leurs communs affaires: finalement amenez à ceste raison, d'endurer l'un d'entre eux sus eux Seignorier, establir des loix au soulagement, asseurance & repos des bons, terreur & punition des mauvais; se souffrir enfermer dedens mesmes murailles sous une seule clef & autres choses concernans la compaignie & societé humaine ».

[13] Paradin, *Cronique,* A 1 r. and A 3 r.

embraces the « defense and illustration of the French language » as a worthy goal for scholars, who glories in the achievements of his *siècle*: the discovery of the New World, the invention of printing. A man in short whose mind wanders freely in the past but who prefers the present.

In 1560, in Paris, one of the most likely candidates to fulfill all these conditions is Estienne Pasquier [14]. Let us open the first book of his *Recherches de la France*, just published. No mistake about it. We find him writing of his ancestors, the Gauls, and disputing with Caesar over their condition: Caesar is made to admit that among all the barbarian peoples, the Gauls are « reputez de conditions civilizées le possible » [15]. As to the Franks, Pasquier is eager to point out that contemporary evidence makes much of their « *civilité et justice* » [16]. Pasquier's use of *civilité* is probably the earliest clear use in the sense of civilization. « The Franks », he writes, « were not a rustic people; unlike some barbarian nations, they were *civilisez* and *poliz*, according to Roman customs » [17]. Elsewhere he writes that Italy, on the eve of the Goths' coming, was « denuée d'une commune civilité » [18]. Pasquier is not using *civilité* in the common meaning of « good manners ». Obviously, *civilité* is what the Romans had and the barbarians had little of.

What we need now, to finish off this demonstration, is to find a writer very much like Pasquier in all respects but who, in addition, might have the advantage of being unusually verbose. Someone, that is, who is likely to explain the obvious. For if everyone in Pasquier's circle knew what he meant by *civilité*, Pasquier would not bother to define the word. No sensible man would.

In the Sieur de la Popelinière (more simply, Lancelot Voisin) we have our man. La Popelinière, the author of a really first-rate and much imitated history of contemporary French affairs, was

---

[14] See Huppert, « Les recherches d'Estienne Pasquier », *Annales* (*E. S. C.*). January-February (1968), 69-105.

[15] The references here are to the 1572 edition *Des Recherches de la France*, *Livres Premier et Second* (Paris, 1572) f. 11 r., in which the text of Book I is identical with that of the first edition of 1560.

[16] *Ibid.*, f. 16 r.

[17] *Ibid.*, f. 16 v.

[18] *Ibid.*, f. 17 r.

also the author of books on geography, naval and military science, and other such diverse matters. Like Pasquier, Le Roy, Bodin, and the overwhelming majority of the French intellectuals of his time, he had received an excellent classical education (under A. Turnèbe) and had spent some time at the university studying law. His historical interests ranged widely, far beyond the normal confines of political history. His conception of an ideal history amounted to a demand for the creation of a comparative history of civilizations. This view he spelled out, in particular, in three treatises published together, the *Histoire des Histoires*, the *Idée de l'Histoire Accomplie* and the *Dessein de l'Histoire Nouvelle des François* (Paris, 1599).

These books of La Popelinière's are something very special. What makes them suitable for our purposes is that the author was a compulsive explainer. The reason for this, I believe, is that he was a maverick and an outsider. Unlike Pasquier, for example, La Popelinière never did find a comfortable niche in the charmed circle of the Paris magistrature. Instead he claimed nobility, and commanded troops for a short time. He was a Protestant, but he was condemned by his own leaders as too sympathetic to the Catholic cause. In his attitude toward intellectual authority and tradition he was a true Don Quixote tilting against windmills. Emphatically a Modern — even a Futurist, one might say — he denounced all past efforts at writing history as puerile and gave the ancient Greek and Roman historians very low marks in his survey of the history of historiography which was, incidentally, the first such book ever written. I think it was because he never belonged to a particular intellectual circle, but only to a « rare troupe », as he put it, of his own imagining, that he always felt the need to explain what he meant. This problem of communication is a handy accident for us. La Popelinière treated his contemporaries as rather obtuse, for he was writing, as he explained, to be understood by posterity. When an inspired pedant like La Popelinière uses a word in a new-fangled way, he is sure to define his usage. Here he is, explaining his use of the adjective *civilisé* in 1599.

« The Greeks », he writes « had already been civilized for a long time ». Here he must pause to explain what he means by civilized: « civilized, that is to say governed and organized according to certain political forms rather than living in a savage state as do so many of the peoples of whom we have discovered some in America and on the African coasts and who are without letters or writings. For civilized peoples cannot get along without letters or writings » [19].

La Popelinière defines *civilité* very clearly. It is the opposite of *ruralité*. La Popeliniére was of the opinion that the Phoenicians taught the Greeks the rudiments of civilization. The Greeks, before their contact with the Phoenicians, were « still rural and without *civilité* » The Phoenicians tutored the Greeks to the point where they became accustomed to a « social and political life by means of letters, arts and sciences » [20].

Clearly, *civilité* is not only a certain sophistication in one's manners, but some sort of winning combination of government, laws, social organization and culture. It is even more than that: there is a superior kind of morality which is found among civilized nations. This is clear in La Popelinière's description of the civilizing mission of the Greeks in Italy and Sicily, where they had to pull the natives away from their « half-savage customs » and impose on them a way of life « closer to the duty of humanity » [21].

Civilization, then, is not a simple process. It involves, first of all, the use of writing, but it means also a way of life which is neither « rural » nor « austere », it implies a certain degree of deliberation and rationality (as opposed to mere tradition) in the formulation of the people's *police*, it implies the use and furthering of letters, of arts and of the sciences and, finally, a morality superior to tribal tradition, true *humanitas*. Furthermore, La Popelinière does not view civilization as a God-given

---

[19] *Histoire des Histoires*, p. 82: « ... les Grecs estoyent ia long temps civilisez, c'est à dire gouvernez & maintenuz sous certaines formes d'estats Politics: ne vivans à la Sauvagine, comme tant de peuples, d'ont nous avons descouvers partie, tant en l'Amerique que costes d'Afrique, sans lettres ny escrits. Or les peuples civilisez, ne se peuvent passer de lettres ny d'escrits ... ».

[20] *Ibid.*, p. 13: « ... façonnerent les Grecs qu'ils y trouverent encor ruraux & sans civilité: pour s'accomoder à une vie sociale & politique par le moyen des lettres, des Arts & sciences ... ».

[21] *Ibid.*, p. 67: « ... de leurs façons demy sauvages, pour les policer par forme de vivre plus approchantes du devoir d'humanité, que ne faisoyent les meurs austeres & façons rurales d'ont à l'advis commun ils avoyent usé iusques alors ».

bounty mysteriously vouchsafed to chosen peoples, but rather as a man-made historical process which can be studied and understood. Civilization is an evolutionary process. All civilized societies, he assumes, had been at some earlier time as savage as the American Indians were in his day.

The question of the origins of civilization was for La Popelinière, as for Bodin and Le Roy, the primordial question. The Italians were civilized by the Greeks, the Greeks by the Phoenicians, and so on, until the beginnings of this most important of all events become lost in the darkness of time. The ancients who were so much better placed to pursue this question failed in this regard as in so many others. « For, as is well known, even the most famous Greeks — Solon, Democritus, Empedocles, Pythagoras — if he is to be counted a Greek — Lycurgus, Plato and others — none of them went beyond Babylon, the Euphrates and Egypt ». The failure of the Greek philosophers to collect information about the origins of civilization, La Popelinière thought, may have been due to the fact that the Orient was closed to the Greeks before Alexander's conquests, or it may be that the Greeks lacked courage, or means, or perhaps their discoveries have been lost [22].

Fortunately, all is not lost. La Popelinière's ambitious goal is « the right and entire knowledge of men, both inside and out » [23]. To achieve this, he proposes a comparative study of civilized and savage peoples. This would require prolonged field work and scientific expeditions to the New World to be financed by the Dutch Estates. What he hoped to find was an answer to the question: what are the precise differences between « civilized peoples and those whom we call, rather improperly, savage peoples? » [24]. The final use of such information, should

---

[22] This is La Popelinière's argument in his letter to Scaliger, dated January 4, 1604. This letter was published in *Epistres françoises des personnages illustres et doctes à M. Joseph Juste de la Scala*, Jacques de Rèves, ed. (Amsterdam, 1624), pp. 303-307. The letter has been reprinted by Corrado Vivanti as an appendix to his article « Le scoperte geografiche e gli scritti di Henri de la Popelinière », *Rivista storica italiana*, LXXIV (1962), 225-249.

[23] *Letter to Scaliger*, « Il faudroit donques buter à la droicte et entiere cognoissance des hommes, soit au dedans, soit au dehors » (Vivanti, p. 248).

[24] *Ibid.*, « ... ès peuples civilisez et ceux qu'on appelle assez improprement sauvages » (Vivanti, p. 247).

it be obtainable, would be, in effect, the discovery of the nature of man. This is, one might argue, a pagan question: evidently, any Christian ought to know the answer already. La Popelinière's anthropological enthusiasms seem to belong in the eighteenth century, together, that is, with the invention of the idea of civilization. But his views are, in fact, quite plausible in the sixteenth century. La Popelinière is no *homme moyen instruit* in his time, but he is not absolutely alone either, as we have seen. The idea of civilization, as it will be understood in the eighteenth and nineteenth centuries by the *philosophes* and their heirs, is already part of the mental equipment of some sixteenth-century intellectuals, who use the noun *civilité* to express it. These men have a good deal in common. They also have much in common with the eighteenth-century *philosophes.* Their classical and legal studies, the religious conflicts they were surrounded by, and which they could regard with a certain amount of detachment, their social position astride the bourgeoisie and the nobility — all this predisposed men like Pasquier as well as men like Voltaire (or La Popelinière and Condorcet, Le Roy and Montesquieu) to view the nature and destiny of man more with the eyes of Cicero than with those of Augustine. The fundamental questions remained the same: what is man? Where does he come from? Where is he going? Men who had no confidence in theology, and who saw themselves as descendants of Hellenic rather than Hebrew culture, learned to frame the old, powerful question in an entirely new way. Modern man, they thought, is the product of civilization: he comes, via a long and dolorous path, from savagery; and he goes where civilization will lead him, perhaps to Utopia.

DONALD R. KELLEY

HISTORY AS A CALLING: THE CASE OF LA POPELINIÈRE

Nowhere in this temple
Are the works of God concealed.
It is to man in the center
That they are best revealed[1].

So one 16th-century French humanist expressed the view that man's unique « dignity » brought him not only immortality but also an ideal perspective from which to survey the world. In particular, as François Baudouin argued, « The study of history is the one way we can ascend to that knowledge of divine and human things, thus to see our haughty spirits as in a mirror and to gain some perspective on [*circumspiciamus*] what has been done in the world ... ». These were not new ideas, of course, but they were being given a new epistemological twist at this time. It was beginning to dawn upon some scholars that man's dignity involved a crucial ambiguity, that he was obliged to attend not one but two temples — that, in short, there was a fundamental distinction between God's creation and the world of man's own making. In precisely the same way that Vico would later distinguish between the *verum* and the *factum*, Baudouin marked off nature (*res naturales*) from the sphere of human action (*res humanae*) [2]. In the latter « ampitheater », he conti-

---

[1] Guy du Four, Sieur de Pibrac, *Les Quatrains* (Paris, 1574), no. 8:

« Il ny a coin si petit dans ce temple,
Ou la grandeur n'apparoisse de Dieu.
L'homme est planté justement au milieu,
Afin que mieux par tout il le contemple ».

It may be noticed that man's superiority to the animal world, expressed in this medieval commonplace, rests not only upon reason but also upon history; see, for example, the preface to Henry of Huntingdon's *Historia Anglorum*: « Historia ... maxime distinguat a brutis rationabiles ... ».

[2] *De Institutione historiae universae et ejus cum jurisprudentia conjunctione* (Strasbourg, 1561), opening and closing paragraphs. Almost identical language is used by J. J. Grynaeus, « De Historia in universum » (Zurich, Zentralbibliothek, MS B. 130).

nued, man was a performer (*actor*) as well as observer and critic (*spectator* and *judex* or *interpres*). Nature might be understood through reason and contemplation, but humanity had to be viewed in terms of memory and temporal sequence (*ordinibus temporum*). The significance of this argument, it seems to me, is that for the first time the historian's field of inquiry has been defined in explicitly philosophical terms. In this way history attained a certain intellectual parity with other established professions.

In more concrete ways, too, the study of history was coming of age in the 16th century. Through its reception into the university curriculum and through the various « methods » devised by Baudouin, Bodin, and others, history was transformed from a badly defined literary genre into a recognizable — if still badly defined — academic discipline. It was promoted literally from an « art » to a « science ». For some humanists, in fact, it outranked philosophy itself. « As the soul is nobler than the body », declared Pomponio Leto, « so history surpasses other bequests and offers the most authoritative part of wisdom, for in it may be found an imitation of life ».[3] Not only had history begun to invade and to inform the more established disciplines, including law, theology, and philosophy, not to mention literature and historiography itself, but it had begun to appear, at least in the eyes of some scholars, as the actual *source* of these disciplines [4]. Here are some of the assumptions underlying the various attempts to restore, or to recreate, the plenitude of history, most conspicuously in the « designs » of history proposed by Louis le Roy and Bernard du Haillan, in the « researches » of Etienne Pasquier, and in such humanist *summae* as Le Roy's *Vicissitude of Things in the Universe* (1575), Christophe Milieu's *Writing of Universal History* (1547), and perhaps Polydore Vergil's *Inventors of Things* (1499 and later editions) [5]. To judge

---

[3] Pomponius Laetus, *Opera ... varia* (Mainz, 1521), f. II r (letter to Francesco Borgia).

[4] P. Droit de Gaillard, *Methode qu'on doit tenir en la lecture de l'histoire* (Paris, 1579), p. 552: « Et pour dire en un mot, toutes disciplines ne prennent pas leur source ... que de l' histoire, comme d'une fontaine tresabondante ».

[5] C. Milieu, *De scribenda universitatis rerum historia* (Basel, 1551), proposed a threefold division, corresponding to natural history, social and

from such works the intellectual imperialism of history was unmatched since the triumph of Aristotelian philosophy in the 13th century.

But there is another factor in the establishment of history as an independent field of study that has not been sufficiently appreciated. This is the impulse provided by the ecclesiastical controversies of the 16th century. As Hans Baron has argued, the historical perspective of 15th-century Italy was shaped as much by political conflict as by « archeological enthusiasm », in Burckhardt's phrase. A similar view must be taken of 16th-century historical thought, which likewise became involved in the *vita activa* — and in a still more fundamental « crisis », namely, the Protestant Reformation. From the beginning this conflict, which of course had a social and national as well as an ideological dimension, was expressed in fundamentally historical terms; that is, as a clash not merely of religious values but of distinct historical « traditions ». Consequently, history was not merely a weapon of controversy but the characteristic mode of thought in which Protestants and Catholics expressed their differences. It was the Protestants, of course, who took the lead in the attempt to make a reevaluation — or perhaps transvaluation — of Christian antiquity and its later tradition [6]. It is no accident that the first chairs of history were set up in Protestant universities and devoted specifically to ecclesiastical studies, nor that the first comprehensive handbook of historical method, that of Baudouin, was inspired by the Protestant conception of « universal history ». The eventual result of the demands of religious polemic — together with the interest it aroused and the subsidization it provided — was to transform the investigation of history into a major scholarly industry.

By the end of the 16th century, in short, history was recognized not only as a distinct mode of thought but as a most demanding profession. From at least some enthusiastic students it elicited not only scholarly allegiance but a kind of religious

---

economic history (*historia prudentiae*), and the history of arts and sciences (*historiae sapientiae*). Le Roy's « Proiect ou dessein du royaume de France » appeared in his *Exhortation aux françois pour vivre en concorde* (Paris, 1570); cf. B. Du Haillan's *Promesse et desseing de l'histoire de France* (Paris, 1571).

[6] A prime example is Flacius Illyricus, *Catalogus testium veritatis* (Basel, 1556).

devotion; and it may be suggested that, because of its ideological function, it had become not only a science but a calling.

Of those who were « called » at this time, no one better illustrates the heritage and the ideals (I will not add, the accomplishments) of modern historical scholarship than Lancelot Voisin, Sieur de la Popelinière. In 1599 La Popelinière published a remarkable work which was at once the last of the 16th-century handbooks of historical method and the first comprehensive history of historiography and which illustrates all of the themes I have introduced [7]. Yet this *History of Histories*, together with the *Idea of Perfect History* and an ambitious « Design for the New History of the French », was still-born, not to say misbegotten. It is perhaps not surprising that La Popelinière should have been neglected in the 17th century, when historical knowledge was going out of fashion; but even in the history-haunted 19th century, when Bodin was resurrected as a father of historical methodology, his disciple La Popelinière was practically unknown. Gabriel Monod, one of the few to appreciate his significance as part of a *nouvelle vague* of French historical writing, tried to persuade Augustin Renaudet to take up the subject for his thesis, but that young man (fortunately for students of humanism and pre-reform) had other things on his mind, and in fact it is only recently that La Popelinière has attracted attention [8]. Yet, as one of his few 19th-century readers justly remarked, « La Popelinière has his place among those, who *helped* to bring historical literature from a rude and indiscriminate superstition, to the more philosophic position which it occupies in modern

[7] *L'Histoire des histoires* (Paris, 1599), published with the separately paginated *L'Idee de l'histoire accomplie*, followed by « Le Dessein de l'histoire nouvelle des François ». I take this « histoire accomplie » to be equivalent to Bodin's « historia consummata » and to Baudouin's « historia perfecta » or « integra ».

[8] Beginning with Herbert Butterfield, *Man on his Past* (Cambridge, 1955), appendix I. Most important are the articles by G. Wylie Sypher in the *Journal of the History of Ideas*, XXIV (1963), 41-54, and XXVI (1965), 353-68, and by Myriam Yardeni in *Revue d'histoire moderne et contemporaine*, XI (1964), 109-26, whose bibliographical references I shall not repeat. Cf. Lucien Febvre, « Un historien de l'humanisme: Augustin Renaudet », *Bibliothèque d'humanisme et Renaissance*, XIV (1952), x, and G. Monod, « De progrès des études historiques en France depuis le XVIe siècle », *Revue historique*, I (1876), 5-38.

times » [9]. Whatever its novelty and whatever its influence, La Popelinière's provoking and badly written treatise, brimming with opinions and half-baked ideas, was an incomparable illustration of the exalted status which history was beginning to claim for itself in the 16th century.

Soldier, diplomat, man of letters, La Popelinière was one of the most interesting and unconventional authors of the later 16th century [10]. Opinionated, bursting with ideas and projects, he was also one of the least successful. In 1577 La Popelinière's characteristic indiscretion got him involved in a duel, and he received a wound in the face as a result. After this he retired from military service to what he hoped would be a quiet life of literature. He was fascinated with maritime affairs and wrote two books on different aspects of this subject: *The Three Worlds* (1582), dealing with the discoveries of the past century and the revised physiognomy of the earth, which now consisted of the Old World, America, and « Australia », as he called Antarctica; and *The Admiral of France* (1584), a pioneering essay in comparative institutional history. It was his *History of France*, however, that produced most of his fame, that absorbed his energies, and that eventually changed the course of his life. The indiscretions committed by La Popelinière in this book had a still more disastrous effect upon his career, causing him to lose favor first with his party, the Huguenots, and then, more irreparably, with Henry of Navarre. Nor did any of his later writings, the *History of Histories* or even the laudatory *History of the Conquest of Bresse and Savoy* (1601), restore him to the king's good graces. La Popelinière kept his vision of historical truth but, it would appear, little else. In 1608 he died, as Pierre de l'Estoile cynically remarked, « of a disease common to men of learning and virtue, that is, of misery and of want ». [11]

---

[9] Note in the copy of the Houghton Library at Harvard, signed « C. Francis 1857 ».

[10] The only satisfactory biography is Sypher's dissertation (Cornell, 1961), in which many of the documents concerning La Popelinière's career and the « crisis » discussed below have been transcribed. A few of these have also been published in the appendix of Agrippa d'Aubigné, *Histoire universelle*, ed. A. de Ruble, I (Paris, 1886), 371 ff.

[11] *Journal de l'Estoile pour le règne de Henri IV*, ed. L.-R. Lefèvre and A. Martin, II (Paris, 1958), 412.

La Popelinière's « idea of history » was not a theory recollected in tranquillity; it was an ideal forged and tested in the course of a deep personal crisis that furnishes an almost archetypal illustration of the dilemma of the contemporary historian. It was widely assumed, as one of La Popelinière's better known countrymen remarked, that « the only good histories are those written by men who themselves managed or participated in the events ... » [12]. But in the midst of a bloody and fratricidal conflict how could a man rise above passion and partisanship? How could one who was at once spectator, actor, and critic achieve a truly historical perspective? La Popelinière's solution to the problem was simple and radical. Machiavellian, some might say, although La Popelinière himself, as the author of a conventional Calvinist « Anti-Machiavel », would have been shocked at the notion [13]. Professional, is perhaps a better way of putting it; for what he did was to establish a purely historical standard, dispensing altogether with value judgments. Evangelical, one might add; for he seemed to regard history, and to preach its saving graces, with an almost religious fervor. From the earliest version of his book, *The True and Whole History of these Recent Troubles of France and Flanders* (1571), La Popelinière addressed himself to a strictly unadorned account of the civil wars without any attempt at suppression or rationalization. It was a noble dream. But if this was proper for the writing of history, it was no way to run a war; and this is where La Popelinière's own troubles began.

L'Affaire La Popelinière was set off in 1581 with the publication of his *History of France*, which he had the temerity to dedicate to Henry III and to Catherine de Médicis. The attack was begun by a minister in La Rochelle, and in the summer the case was taken up by the national synod of Huguenot churches held in that city, where La Popelinière's book had appeared [14]. Among various minor indiscretions were certain uncalled-for

---

[12] Montaigne, *Essais*, ed. F. Strowski and F. Gébelin, II (Bordeaux, 1919), 116.

[13] « Contre Machiavel », in Bibliothèque Nationale, Paris, Manuscrits, Fonds français, vol. 20787, f. 19 v.

[14] B. N., MSS, Collection Dupuy, vol. 744, ff. 230-68 (« Lettres et memoires touchant l' Histoire de Lancelot du Voisin, Sr de la Popeliniere ») contains the documents concerning this episode, which Sypher discusses fully.

remarks about the cruelty of his former commander François de la Noue, who indeed had become an intransigent since St Bartholomew (and who was now a prisoner in the chateau of Limbourg). La Popelinière had also in several passages spoken not unfavorably about the Catholic « faith » (before Luther's time), and he had suggested that the Calvinists were not wholly blameless in preparing the way for the religious wars. It was the implied criticism of the Huguenot party, of course, that brought down upon his head the wrath of its leaders. The issue seemed so serious that Henry of Navarre himself took notice of it. « Messieurs », he wrote to the magistrates of La Rochelle in June, « I have learned that ... a certain Popellynyere, who lives at present in your city, has produced a book against the reformed religion and also against those of our house » [15]. Five weeks later the synod condemned La Popelinière and his book and insisted upon a public retraction. This, with some qualifications, they received three years later (February 1585), when « L. Voesin » signed a prepared statement of submission [16].

Not without a struggle, however. In the intervening years La Popelinière had been making frantic efforts to justify himself, denying that he had sold his pen to the Guises, protesting his fidelity to the reformed religion and to the house of Navarre as well as to historical truth, or rather denying that there was any difference between them. He wrote first to Theodore Beza in Geneva. « We have the same goal of illustrating God's glory by the clear truths of His doctrine in true accounts of the deeds of His church », (a reference to the *Ecclesiastical History* attributed to Beza), although being « far from your calling », he added, « I do not work as fortunately as you do » [17]. But he affirmed his sincerity and accuracy. The reason he had dedicated his book to the King and the Queen Mother, he explained, was in order to influence Catholics as well as his fellow reformers and so to give the work a bi-partisan character. In reply, Beza thanked him for his fraternal sentiments and remarked that he, Beza, had more to learn than to teach in such matters, though

---

[15] *Ibid.*, f. 248 r (3 June 1581).

[16] *Ibid.*, f. 255 r. The condemnation by the synod (9 July) appears on f. 254 r, and it has been printed in Haag, *La France Protestante*, IX (Paris, 1859), 530-31.

[17] *Ibid.*, f. 235 r-236 r (15 Jan. 1581).

he did not deny the attribution of the work mentioned. He made only two criticisms, that La Popelinière had not denounced vigorously enough the massacres of Vassy and St Bartholomew, and that he had falsely praised the wicked apostate François Baudouin, who twenty years before had learned how dangerous it could be to criticize Calvinism in the name of a historical ideal. All La Popelinière had said was that Baudouin was « learned and eloquent », but perhaps Beza detected a more reprehensible sympathy between the two authors [18].

With Henry of Navarre and the Prince of Condé, La Popelinière took a different tack. He admitted that he « might have written too briefly or unclearly and so have given material to men of bias or of weak understanding », but he protested his continued good faith. « Sire », he pleaded, « my only intention has been to represent to posterity the praiseworthy deeds of your predecessors ... And if those of your party do not write down what you and others have done, the Catholics will write to their own great advantage and to the detriment of the reformers » [19]. Elsewhere he elaborated on this argument that competition with the Romanists extended also to posterity, and he used one of the favorite examples of his generation. « Who does not see that the same causes and similar events have affected us in France as those whom our ancestors called Albigensians, Beggars of Lyon, Waldensians, Beguines, and others whom until now we have regarded as abominable heretics and rebels? This is due to the absence of a true history of the events and circumstances in which they took up arms against the Catholics for the defense of their religion, which was not different from our own. On the other hand, the Catholics wrote many books which were in no way contradicted ». It was La Popelinière's historical vocation even more than his Huguenot allegiance, in short, that had led him to and sustained him in his life's work.

---

[18] *Ibid.*, f. 237 r, referring to the *Histoire de France* (La Rochelle, 1581), f. 269 r, mispaginated and cited by Beza as « 299 ». Baudouin was attacked in two separate *responsiones* by Calvin in 1562, one by Beza in 1563, and again by Beza in the *Vie de Calvin* and in the *Histoire ecclésiastique*, where he is styled « apostat renommé ». In general, see my article on Baudouin in *Journal of the History of Ideas*, XXV (1964), 35-57.

[19] *Ibid.*, f. 240 r (undated) and f. 238 r (12 Aug. 1581), the latter (to Condé) published in *Bulletin historique et philologique* (1892), pp. 250-51.

This passage appears in what was La Popelinière's most serious attempt to defend his position at this time, a relatively formal, though unpublished, « Response for History », which may indeed have been a draft of his statement to the magistrates of La Rochelle [20]. It is remarkable how this little manifesto, though written in the heat of a disastrous law suit, parallels or even prefigures the more mature evaluation of the nature and purpose of history that appeared in La Popelinière's *Idea of History* some fifteen years later, when he could afford to take a more serene view of the historian's role. A comparison of La Popelinière's apologetic writings with his more theoretical work provides an interesting illustration of the ideological basis not only of his own thought but, to some extent, of historical scholarship in general.

Running contrapuntally through La Popelinière's work are two fundamental themes: fidelity to truth and, in a general sense, civic humanism. On the one hand the historian was set apart from other men of letters because of his concern for literal and factual truth; on the other hand he was superior to the philosopher because of the public services that he, like the rhetorician, could perform. Unfortunately, these two themes were not quite in harmony. Since history was, in La Popelinière's phrase, « une chose publique », it was inherently controversial and open to partisanship. Royal or municipal historiographers were hired as official propagandists, not as irresponsible gossips, and even a free-lance writer like La Popelinière recognized his public obligation (*devoir*). Like Baudouin he wanted not only to serve his country, he hoped also to remain, as he put it to Beza, « in conformity with the traditions of the Christian church ». At the same time history had to be written « for the profit of human society » [21]. This was difficult enough; for some people he would always be *trop Huguenot*, La Popelinière admitted, for others *trop Catholique*. What made the task impossible was La Popelinière's fanatical allegiance to historical truth. His dilemma, in other words, was to reconcile his role as « actor » with that

---

[20] B. N., MSS Fr., vol. 20297, ff. 458 r-463 v, entitled « Responce pour l'histoire ».

[21] « Responce », f. 458 r; *Histoire des histoires*, p. 26, and *Idee de l'histoire*, p. 47.

of « spectator ». « They are three and four times blessed », Baudouin had declared, « who descend into that lower arena » [22]; but as he and La Popelinière found out, there might be a curse awaiting them as well. It was for this reason that La Popelinière, again like Baudouin, expanded his perspective — not only to encompass earlier traditions but to focus upon « posterity », as the most appropriate audience for his work. So La Popelinière's view of history became at once more comprehensive and more detached.

This detachment was reinforced by, if it did not actually stem from, La Popelinière's growing alienation from his comrades. The ministers of La Rochelle, as he told a friend during his time of troubles, had condemned his book after a bare two hours' perusal and « in the style of the Spanish Inquisition ». They had set up a « papacy » more tyrannical than that of Rome, and they were hypocrites as well. « What would they say », he asked, « if they saw the secret memoirs I have that would make them blush? » — not, he added, that he would publish such scandals out of vindictiveness [23]. He did not deny that there were some lapses in his history, but after all this was only human weakness; Beza himself had allegedly made something like seventy-nine errors in his own book. Anyway, the important thing was that La Popelinière was fair-minded. A generation earlier Martin Bucer had warned Calvin himself about the dangers of bias: « We judge as we love », he wrote, « but we love as we please ». Baudouin, who as Calvin's former secretary had had access to his correspondence, noted this remark and later used it against Calvin, as if it were a personal rebuke. Now La Popelinière, attacked in much the same way as Baudouin had been, recalled this statement in his « Response » in order to justify the frankness of his history [24]. Like Baudouin, he sought a standard of judgment that transcended « passion » and « party », and so he took his stand upon « conscience ».

---

[22] *De Institutione historiae universae*, p. 2.

[23] B. N., MSS Dupuy, vol. 744, f. 263 r-v, to « Mon frere ».

[24] « Responce », f. 462 v. Cf. Baudouin, *Responsio altera ad Joannem Calvinum* (Cologne, 1562), p. 40. The incident is discussed — and the attack upon Baudouin renewed — by Emile Doumergue, *Une Poignée de faux* (Lausanne, 1900), pp. 104-15.

Of course every historical writer knew the Ciceronian « first law of history », to tell the whole truth and nothing but the truth. But La Popelinière thought that he had discovered something new. « I have practiced a new means of representing the design and actions of both factions », he explained to Beza, « being neutral and indifferent to the two parties, as befitting the historiographer ». In his *Idea of History* La Popelinière later stated this rule in a more generalized form. « One of the most certain premises of a good historian », he wrote, « is to leave the praise and blame of men to the merit of their actions, which he must represent faithfully » [25]. Above all one should never try to act as both prosecutor and judge, as his enemies had done. It was necessary to investigate the behavior of men, but always in terms of the intention and consequences (*la volunté, puis le bien et le mal qui en venoit*). Again La Popelinière later generalized this requirement by demanding that the historian seek out *la cause, le progres, bonne ou mauvaise issue* [26]. What is more, such judgment should always be made in the context of the particular time and conditions and not in an abstract or dogmatic way. This is why it was the business of the historian, not the philosopher or the theologian, to establish the sequence of cause and effect in human affairs.

It was in this way, led by the logic of his own argument and pushed by the objections of his opponents, that La Popelinière came to his view of history as an independent and indeed sovereign discipline. He emerged from his crisis with a particularly deep conviction that history was superior to theology, at least to that « scholastic theology » that divided Protestants and Catholics. Despite its pretensions, such « positive theology » was only a « human science » — and at that less certain than history. La Popelinière acknowledged that history dealt with « accidents », but he denied that this gave any grounds for « pirrhonisme ». On the contrary, the concern of history for incontrovertible facts made it more secure than other « human traditions », which rested upon mere « opinion ». The very fact that history had to be understood in terms of times and circumstances (*selon*

---

[25] « Responce », f. 462 v; *Idee de l'histoire*, p. 324, and *Histoire des histoires*, p. 413.

[26] « Responce », f. 458 v; Histoire des histoires, p. 52.

le tems, les personnes et les affair[*es*] *des hommes*) made it more reliable and more useful than either philosophy or political science (*la police*) [27]. Such indeed was the way in which history as a mode of thought was distinguished, that it represented the actions of men « according to the times, the places, their causes, progress and results ». Echoing Bodin, La Popelinière concluded that history was « above all arts and sciences » [28].

La Popelinière did not win his case, but for the rest of his life he continued to gather evidence, to devise arguments, and to seek support for his conception of history. After 1585, as part of his scholarly crusade, he embarked upon a vast program of reading in historical writers of all ages and societies. This included not only historiographers but political writers such as Seyssel and Machiavelli, philologists such as Guillaume Budé and Joseph Justus Scaliger, and the authors of the so-called *artes historicae*, such as Baudouin, Milieu, and above all Bodin. In general La Popelinière sided with the « moderns ». He was a militant, and indeed defensive, advocate of the vernacular, and he was contemptuous of those « fonder of antiquity than of reason ». This included both the philological tradition, whose celebrated « encyclopedia » he regarded as an inflated and disorganized « mélange of sciences », and most historians, who tended to have an « excessive respect for their predecessors » [29]. He complained in particular about the French tradition of royal historiographers (Robert Gaguin, Paolo Emilio, Guillaume du Bellay, Denis Sauvage, Du Haillan, and Jean de Serres), partly, it may be suspected, because he hoped for some such position himself in order to subsidize his projects. In any case it was to remedy this unfortunate situation — the fact that the French had no histories except rehashes of old chronicles — that La Popelinière offered to the public his own « idea of history ».

---

27 « Responce », f. 460 r; *Idee de l'histoire*, p. 36, *Histoire des histoires*, « Avant-discours », and *Histoire de la conqueste des pais de Bresse et de Savoye* (Lyon, 1601), p. 9. For a contrasting view of the « sciences humaines » and their inferiority to theology, see the remarks of La Popelinière's enemy and one time captain, François de la Noue, *Discours politiques et militaires*, ed. F. E. Sutcliffe (Geneva, 1967), p. 603.

28 *Histoire des histoires*, p. 461; cf. Bodin's *Methodus* in *Oeuvres*, ed. P. Mesnard (Paris, 1951), p. 113.

29 *Idee de l'histoire*, pp. 1, 197; cf. his defense of the vernacular in *L'Amiral de France* (Paris, 1584), « Avant-discours ».

The foundation for this, the oldest of a long line of « new histories », was a hastily assembled yet carefully planned history of historiography. In this work La Popelinière offers not only critical comments upon practically all published historians down to his own day, but an interesting and ingenious periodization of the development of historical literature. He recognized a pattern of four « seasons », that is, four levels of historical consciousness and expression [30]. First came a period of « natural history », that is, oral tradition and superstition (such as Germany described by Tacitus, Gaul by Caesar, or Mexico by Sebastian Fox). Next, a period of « poetic » history (in Moses, for example, or Homer), which lasted until the establishment of a rational chronology (the Olympiads or the founding of Rome). « It is evident », wrote La Popelinière in an interesting anticipation of romantic theories of the origins of history, « that the poets were the first historians » [31]. This is followed by « continuous history », which means simple chronicles and annals, unilluminating but at least faithful to the facts. Finally comes a kind of civilized history characterized by the addition of eloquence to the narration of facts and consequently by consideration of cause and effect. This stage of history arises with the growth of human arts and sciences (beginning in Greece with Herodotus, in Rome in the 4th century) and lasts until the decay of civilization, coinciding roughly with the end of political dominion. Every nation moved through such a cultural cycle, La Popelinière believed, and so did its historiography.

For the first time, La Popelinière thought, a fifth stage was about to be reached, namely his own « perfect history ». No historian, ancient or modern, not even his predecessor « La Bodiniere », had ever achieved the synthesis of knowledge, eloquence, and philosophy necessary for this. After laying down the rules for his « new history », La Popelinière went on to redefine its form and content. He proposed a simple five-stage periodization (ancient, Roman, Germanic, and Frankish Gaul, and modern France), and pointed out the crucial importance of the problem of racial origins [32]. In the second part of his

[30] *Ibid.*, p. 137.
[31] *Idee de l'histoire*, pp. 362-64.
[32] *Histoire des histoires*, pp. 25, 33, 49, 155, and esp. 66.

« Design », in fact, he presented a thorough, though by no means original, critique of the theory of Trojan origins. As for the content, La Popelinière, like some of the « new historians » of our own century, took the position that nothing human was alien to it. With Gaillard he believed that « all the arts, sciences, and other human inventions derive from history ». In addition, there must be consideration of the geography of France, the forms of government, the crown, various institutions, offices, legal organization, social classes, and religion [33]. For this purpose the historian should ransack all available primary sources, and above all the archives, though all too often, he added, these had been closed to public view.

How « new » was La Popelinière's new history? It is obvious that his views derive in general from the rhetorical conception of history revived by the humanists. This includes both the claim that history was, by virtue of its concreteness and social utility, superior to philosophy, and the hope that it would encompass all human activity. Despite his dismissal of the « long-winded » discourses of Baudouin and Milieu, La Popelinière remained well within the genre of the *ars historica* — and none more long-windedly so.

In one respect, perhaps, he helped to change this relatively sheltered tradition. He was even more aware than his model Bodin of the geographical basis of history and, especially, of the significance of the « new horizons of the Renaissance ». Near the end of his life he conceived a mad scheme for a kind of anthropological expedition to Africa and America designed, again, to extend the scope of history (*rendre l'histoire de particuliere generale*) and to perfect it (*afin de nous approcher de la perfection de l'histoire*) [34]. But, although he wrote to the great Scaliger in order to get

---

[33] *Idee de l'histoire*, pp. 269 ff., 358 ff. The latter passage has been translated and discussed by George Huppert, « The Renaissance Background of Historicism », *History and Theory*, V (1966), 48-60.

[34] La Popelinière's two letters to Scaliger appear in Jacques de Rèves (ed.), *Epistres françoises de personnages illustres et doctes, a Monsr. Joseph Juste de la Scala* (Harderwyck, 1624), pp. 151-53 (9 Jan. 1601) and 303-7 (4 Jan. 1604). The second letter has been reprinted in the valuable article by Corrado Vivanti, « Le Scoperte geografiche e gli scritti di Henri de la Popelinière », *Rivista storica italiana*, LXXIV (1962), 225-49. More generally, see the remarks of Geoffroy Atkinson, *Les nouveaux Horizons de la renaissance française* (Paris, 1935).

financial support from the Estates General of Holland, nothing more came of this enterprise than of his design as a whole. And his impact was even slighter than his accomplishment. None of the later propagandists for a « new history », neither James Harvey Robinson nor, curiously, Voltaire, bothered to read his work. If La Popelinière was « called », he was obviously not, from this point of view at least, one of those chosen.

Yet La Popelinière deserves better of that posterity to which he had devoted so much of his life. Like Bacon he had tried to open up a new road to knowledge; and if, like Bacon, he was more interested in pointing the way than in making the trip himself, he nonetheless illustrates a significant phenomenon in the history of thought, namely, history's declaration of independence from other disciplines, especially from philosophy, theology, law, and political science. For this reason his ideas must be distinguished from the more influential work of Bodin. As La Popelinière himself wrote of his distinguished predecessor, « Since the method of understanding and organizing something consists in comprehending and arranging its parts, and since history consists rather in truth and its order, it seems to me that he should have taken time to order or to illuminate particular history rather than to digress so on universal history » [35]. This is why Bodin's book was, in La Popelinière's opinion, a « method of law » rather than of history. To La Popelinière, on the other hand, history had no superior in temporal things. It was as much a « profession » as law itself and as such had its own distinctive mode of thinking [36]. The « method » of history, in fact, followed the pattern of human experience; that is, it proceeded according to the succession of times and the variety of circumstances, and it sought to reproduce the plenitude of the human past.

It may be true, as one of La Popelinière's intellectual descendants (and few readers) remarked, that his work was « less a method for studying history than judgments on historians » [37]. Certainly, in keeping with his autobiographical preoccupations, he was more interested in the character of the historian than in the teaching of history. Yet it is precisely here, it seems to me, that

---

[35] *Idee de l'histoire*, p. 29.

[36] « Responce », f. 458 r, « la profession de l'histoire ».

[37] Lenglet du Fresnoy, *Methode pour etudier l'histoire* (Paris, 1729), I, IX.

his major significance lies. What he offered in fact was a kind of « mirror for historians », an idealized description that deserved to be set beside those conventional pictures of the prince, the courtier, the ambassador, the citizen, the artist, and perhaps most revealingly Bacon's « man of science » [38]. Ideally, the historian had himself been literally « in the midst of things », an actor as well as an observer, and so epitomized the humanist view of man as poised between the world of experience and the world of ideas. At the same time, while the historian derived substantial benefit from his two-fold role, he had also to cut himself loose from particular sects and authorities, whether political or doctrinal. Only then could he become, in La Popelinière's phrase, a truly « contemplative historian ».

Finally, La Popelinière laid great emphasis upon the moral duty of the historian (*le devoir d'un vray historiografe*). Not that he maintained a Calvinist interpretation of history, but he does seem to have transferred the emotional energy of his faith to his profession, so that it became a deadly serious cause, almost a crusade. The reason he had struggled so intensely against censorship of his work was that he found it shocking to silence « a public person like the historiographer », as he called himself, « pushed by God for the common good, of which he is the faithful recorder » [39]. Indeed, what La Popelinière had done was to transmute his « first calling », as he called his religious belief, into a historical form; as Beza, the theologian, labored to extend the faith, so La Popelinière, the historian, labored to preserve the memory of the deeds of the faithful. Later, of course, this program was broadened and even detached from its original ideological context, but La Popelinière continued to believe that « the principal goal and true purpose of history is to bring not pleasure but profit to everyone » [40] — that Clio

---

[38] See M. E. Prior, « Bacon's Man of Science », *Journal of the History of Ideas* », XV (1954), 348-70. The parallel between Bacon and La Popelinière has been drawn out — very far out — by Sypher in the second of his articles (see note 8).

[39] B. N., MSS Dupuy, vol. 744, f. 263 v.

[40] *Idee de l'histoire*, p. 306, echoing Cicero's « esse utilitatem in historia, non modo voluptatem » (*Brutus*, 228). The phrase « duty of the historiographer » appears often, e. g., B. N. MSS Dupuy, vol. 744, ff. 242 r, 244 v, 264 r, 266 r.

was not so much a muse as a missionary. The Protestant view of a « calling », according to the famous formulation of Max Weber, required one to labor in a single-minded and above all methodical fashion for the benefit of the whole community. La Popelinière's conception of history owed more than a little to the Protestant ethic, it seems, if not to the spirit of capitalism.

In such *chiaroscuro* tones, then, La Popelinière painted his portrait of the complete historian. He was at once the involved participant and the disinterested observer, the omnivorous autodidact and the duty-bound professional, the *uomo universale* and the man with a calling.

WERNER L. GUNDERSHEIMER

THE CRISIS OF THE LATE FRENCH RENAISSANCE

The *Oxford Universal Dictionary* offers definitions of the word « crisis » that would appear to have escaped the attention of some recent historians who have used the term as an interpretive tool. In pathology, a crisis is defined as « the point in the progress of a disease when a change takes place which is decisive of recovery or death; also, any marked or sudden change of symptoms ». In figurative use, crisis means « a turning point in the progress of anything; also, a state of affairs in which a decisive change for better or worse is imminent ». I have intentionally borrowed the title of this paper from Hans Baron's celebrated *Crisis of the Early Italian Renaissance*, and I have done so with the greatest sense of respect and obligation, because I believe that he is one of the few scholars who have spoken in recent years of historical « crisis » without debasing the coinage of the English language [1]. In writing of the Florentines' response to their imminent conquest by the Milanese under Giangaleazzo Visconti in 1402, Dr. Baron was able to make a strong case for the idea that in both politics and culture, the turn of the fifteenth century in Italy coincides with a turning point, a period of change « which is decisive », to return to the language of the dictionary.

For scholars interested in problems of periodization, the *renaissance des lettres et des beaux arts* in France has long been an engrossing subject for discussion. The traditional view has it that nothing of great significance happened before Francis I's return from Italy in 1515 [2]. A modified interpretation of this view traces the stirrings of French interest in Italian humanism

---

[1] *The Crisis of the Early Italian Renaissance*, 2 vols. (Princeton, 1955); rev. one-vol. ed. (Princeton, 1966), esp. pp. 443-4, where the author discusses the use of the term « crisis » in historical writing.

[2] For the historiography of the concept of the French Renaissance, see Wallace K. Ferguson, *The Renaissance in Historical Thought* (Cambridge, Mass., 1948), pp. 257-68; Franco Simone, *Il Rinascimento francese* (Turin, 1961), esp. pt. II: « Nuovi contributi alla storia del termine e del concetto di 'Renaissance' »; and the useful survey by H. Hornik, « Three Interpretations of the French Renaissance », *Studies in the Renaissance*, VII (1960),

and art to Charles VIII's invasion of the peninsula in 1494, and its aftermath. More recently, Franco Simone and others have attempted to show that Italian influences exerted a powerful hold on the thought and style of many French writers from the time of Petrarch, and that French humanism developed gradually and steadily from the fourteenth century on [3]. While accepting these findings, it might be worth observing that the scale of public demand and royal patronage is so much greater in the sixteenth century that it appears to produce a change in kind, not merely in degree. I have tried to develop these views elsewhere, and I mention them here only by way of observing that whereas the origins of the French Renaissance have occasioned interesting and fruitful debate, its end has not [4]. One looks in vain for treatments of this subject in Wallace K. Ferguson's admirably thorough work, *The Renaissance in Historical Thought* [5].

Yet, various opinions have been offered and, surely, many writers have assumed an answer to this question for the purpose of setting chronological limits to books and articles. But it is now high time to try to answer the question positively, in terms of evidence drawn from a large number of fields of human activity. I have tried to do this, and have come to the conclusion that there was a crisis of the late French Renaissance. Before explaining that view, it will be useful to examine some of the other prevailing notions on the end of the French Renaissance.

43-66 (reprinted in W. L. Gundersheimer, ed., *French Humanism, 1470-1600* [London & New York, 1969], pp. 10-47).

[3] Simone's contribution here is best sampled in his early work, *La Coscienza della Rinascita negli umanisti francesi* (Rome, 1949), and in the important articles reprinted as Part I of *Il Rinascimento francese, op. cit.*, « Tradizione medievale e influenze italiane nella formazione del rinascimento francese ».

[4] Gundersheimer, *French Humanism*, pp. 9-18.

[5] The section called « Problems of the Northern Renaissance », pp. 253-57, deals exclusively with issues concerning the origins of the movement, as does the section specifically devoted to France. Some historians of French literature attempt to deal with the problem in terms of their special interest, but they usually follow the divisions of individual reigns. Thus A. Tilley, *The Literature of the French Renaissance* (Cambridge, 1885), detected two phases, the second of which ran from 1547 to 1594, and was described as « the full flood (p. 42) ». This method arbitrarily ignores all other types of historical change.

I.

In 1959, H. R. Trevor-Roper published an important article called « The General Crisis of the Seventeenth Century », in which he argued that between 1640 and 1660 many European countries passed through a critical period which brought to an end « the state and society of the European Renaissance » [6]. He quoted the English preacher who told the House of Commons in 1643 that « These days are days of shaking ... and this shaking is universal: the Palatinate, Bohemia, Germania, Catalonia, Portugal, Ireland, England » [7]. France, England's great and powerful neighbor, is not included in the catalogue, but Trevor-Roper means to include France in all of his generalizations on the Renaissance. Central to his theory is the idea that the sixteenth century was more or less monolithic, that there could not have been a crisis before the 1640's. Earlier revolutions are not decisive, they are not turning points; « even in France Henry IV takes up, after a period of disturbance, the mantle of Henry II » [8]. « From the end of the fifteenth century to the middle of the seventeenth century we have one climate, the climate of the Renaissance; then, in the middle of the seventeenth century we have the years of change, the years of revolution; and thereafter, for another century and a half we have another, very different climate, the climate of the Enlightenment » [9]. Obviously, then, the argument refers to culture as well as political institutions. Trevor-Roper claims that « the great representatives of the European Renaissance are universal but unsystematic. Leonardo, Cervantes, Montaigne, Shakespeare take life for granted: they adventure, observe, describe, perhaps mock; but they do not analyze, criticize, question » [10]. It is hard to imagine that any serious reader of Montaigne would maintain that he neither

---

[6] The article first appeared in *Past and Present* (1959), no. 16. I have used the reprint in Trevor Aston, ed., *Crisis in Europe, 1560-1600* (New York, 1967), pp. 63-102.

[7] *Loc. cit.*, p. 63. The speaker was Jeremiah Whittaker, and the date was 25 January 1642-43.

[8] *Loc. cit.*, p. 66.

[9] *Ibid.*, p. 67.

[10] *Ibid.*, p. 73.

analyzes nor criticizes and the same is true of Leonardo for that matter. And if the Renaissance is unsystematic, what does one make of Piero della Francesca and Alberti, of Machiavelli, of Ramus, of Bodin, of Copernicus, Vesalius, Paré? Do they not analyze, criticize, question? Or are they not « great representatives? ». As for the state, Trevor-Roper maintains that « the Renaissance State — up to and beyond 1600 — expands continuously without as yet bursting its old envelope. That envelope is the medieval, aristocratic monarchy, the rule of the Christian prince » [11]. Does this characterization really fit Henry III, secluded in his circle of *mignons* while the realm of the most Christian king ground to its knees under the burdens of religious war? Does it really apply to Henry IV, whose political achievements depended directly upon his pliability in matters of religion? And what was the great crisis in mid-seventeenth-century France? The Fronde, says Trevor-Roper. What a tempest in a teapot was the Fronde! Compared to the devastating sixteenth-century religious wars, waged over four decades, it was a mere skirmish [12].

There is no doubt that Trevor-Roper's essay was a brilliant and suggestive contribution to many general questions of periodization in the seventeenth century, and that its principal inadequacies relate to France, which may be viewed as an exceptional case. Roland Mousnier has already exposed the errors in Trevor-Roper's argument in relation to French social, political, economic, and institutional history [13]. It would seem that Mousnier views

---

[11] *Ibid.*, p. 73.

[12] *Ibid.*, p. 94. Here, Trevor-Roper shows that to some extent he regards France as a special case, but the qualification is mild: « Midway between completely unreformed Spain and completely reformed Holland lies what is perhaps the most interesting of all examples, Bourbon France. For France, in the seventeenth century, was certainly not immune from the general crisis, and in the Frondes it had a revolution, if a relatively small revolution. The result was, as in Spain, a victory for the monarchy ». I think the Frondes are more accurately understood as uprisings than as revolutions. In fact, Trevor-Roper (p. 95) lists some of the major changes in French institutions and administrative practices that antedate these uprisings, without ever acknowledging what drastic modifications this implies toward his basic position.

[13] In *Past and Present*, No. 18 (1960), reprinted in Trevor Aston, ed., *Crisis in Europe, 1560-1660*, as « Trevor-Roper's ' General Crisis ': Symposium », pp. 103-11.

the accession of Henry IV and the end of the religious wars as the turning point of the French Renaissance. There is much to be said for this view. The Treaty of Vervins (1598) brought France to a relatively durable internal peace, Henry IV restored the monarchy, introduced new mercantile and fiscal policies with the aid of his brilliant and tireless minister, Sully, embarked on a great program of construction in Paris, and in general cultivated that image of benign autocracy that smart kings — whether they breathed the climate of Renaissance or Enlightenment — liked to show the world. It retains the century as the turning point, thus satisfying that primitive instinct we have to celebrate according to the decimal system, because we have ten fingers. Thus Mousnier's approach corresponds with that of many textbooks, which, to add to the general confusion, tend to respect the century as a unit.

If, however, we use as our indicators evidence taken from cultural as well as political and institutional history, it emerges that the French Renaissance ends well before the beginning of the seventeenth century. In fact, I think it is appropriate to talk about post-Renaissance France after 1575, and to understand the period from 1570 to 1575 as one of crisis, when decisive changes seem to take place, even though some of these are not resolved until the reign of Henry IV. While realizing that all attempts at periodization must partake to some extent of arbitrariness or simplification, let us examine some of the evidence on which such an unconventional point of view has been formulated.

II.

Between August of 1570, when the Peace of St.-Germain brought new concessions to the Protestants in the wake of the third religious war, and August of 1572, when the Massacre of St. Bartholomew's Day set off another round of civil strife that was to last for more than two decades, the crown enjoyed the luxury of being able to concern itself with foreign policy [14].

---

[14] J. W. Thompson, *The Wars of Religion in France, 1559-1576* (Chicago, 1909), p. 422.

While all Europeans rejoiced at the great international victory over the Turkish fleet off Lepanto, French Protestants and moderate Catholics alike hoped that in their realm a *modus vivendi* had been reached, and that the urgent business of building up the nation would supplant the passionate strife that had been tearing it apart. This was a period of peace propaganda, some of it indebted to Erasmus' *Querela Pacis* [15]. There seems to have been a moratorium on the most scurrilous and partisan forms of pamphleteering. It was a moment of optimism after bleak years of conflict. In the summer of 1572, it suddenly ended [16]. The massacre polarized France as none of the previous atrocities had done. Moderate Catholics had to cope with a profound sense of collective guilt, while the more zealous faction which was to shape the Catholic League of the 1580 's glowed with satisfaction [17]. The decapitated body of Protestant France writhed in shock and pain, and above all, disillusionment. Optimism withered. Protestant political thought, now shunning Calvinist doctrines of obedience to magistrates, was swiftly radicalized, to use a term now fashionable. Open rebellion, even tyrannicide, came to be justified on religious grounds [18]. All of the arguments that do-

---

[15] On this aspect of French pamphleteering, see James Hutton, « Erasmus and France: The Propaganda for Peace », *Studies in the Renaissance*, X (1963), 103-27; W. L. Gundersheimer, *The Life and Works of Louis Le Roy* (Geneva, 1966), pp. 76-9, which discusses Le Roy's important tract, *Exhortation aux Francois pour vivre en concorde et jouir du bien de la paix*; also, the splendid volume by V. De Caprariis, *Propaganda e pensiero politico in Francia durante le Guerre di Religione, I: 1559-1572* (Naples, 1959), pp. 440-59.

[16] De Caprariis, p. 460.

[17] De Caprariis, p. 461, notes the favorable impression made upon many French Catholics by the reprisals used by the Duke of Alba in the Low Countries several years before the Massacre. Many believed this was the only way to deal effectively with the problem, as is shown by the present example from a letter of Villars, quoted by De Caprariis: « ... il est temps d'en uzer ceste façon, si vous voulez vous deffere de ceste vermine. Cela fera panser aux autres à leurs consciences ... A ce que je puys panser, il faudra uzer de la force, si l'on veult estre hobey ... ».

[18] J. W. Allen, *A History of Political Thought in the Sixteenth Century* (London, 1928), p. 308: « Now, for the first time, attacks of extreme violence were made in print on the King personally. It was declared that his assassination would be just and laudable. Wild projects circulated on paper ». Cf. De Caprariis, p. 468, who speaks of the resulting Huguenot political ideology as constituting an authentic revolutionary force [« un'autentica forza rivoluzionaria »].

minate the English political controversies of the next century appear here in the 1570's [19]. Thus, in the political life of France, the massacre was a turning point. The deathblow that it dealt to the slender remaining growth of Renaissance optimism can be traced in many ways.

Following the death of Charles IX in 1574, Henry, the Duke of Anjou, fled the Polish crown to which he had been elected, and returned to France as Henry III. The last glimmers of the hopeful spirit I have been describing appear at the beginning of his reign, in works such as Le Roy's *Vicissitude*, which is also full of foreboding [20]. But even these qualified expectations were disappointed, and there is a kind of grim irony in the fact that Jean Bodin's *Six Livres de la République* (1576), which propounded influential arguments in favor of absolute monarchical sovereignty, and was dedicated to Pibrac, the young monarch's loyal aide, appeared in the reign of an absolute royal incompetent [21]. This irony is compounded by Bodin's loss of Henry's favor as a result of his support of negotiation, rather than war, as a means of dealing with the Protestants. Bodin's subsequent withdrawal from political life, his turning to the production of relativistic works on theology, demonology, and natural philosophy [22] suggest the same kind of rejection of a humanistic commitment to the world's work that one sees in other ways in Montaigne and Charron, in the rise of Stoicism and Epicureanism, and in the apocalyptic rhetoric and fulsome martyrologies of Agrippa d'Aubigné.

Of Henry III more should be said. His coming to power at what I take to be a critical moment was greeted with hope, for

---

[19] Much evidence of this may be found in J. H. M. Salmon, *The French Religious Wars in English Political Thought* (Oxford, 1959).

[20] For an analysis of Le Roy's *Vicissitude*, see now my *Life and Works of Louis Le Roy*, pp. 95-129.

[21] On the problem of royal incompetence and sixteenth-century theories for explaining and dealing with it, see E. M. Peters, « *Roi Fainéant*: The Origins of an Historian's Commonplace », *Bibliothèque d' humanisme et Renaissance*, XXX (1968), 537-47, esp. p. 547.

[22] M. J. Tooley observes, in the introduction to her abridgment of *Six Books of the Commonwealth* (Oxford, n. d.), p. XIII, that « Judging by his writings at this time [1580's and after], however, his withdrawal from politics went deeper than a mere change of scene and occupation. There was also an intellectual withdrawal ».

as a youth he had shown much promise for good. But upon assuming his royal powers, he soon began to show signs of what N. M. Sutherland, with serene understatement, has called « a disequilibrium not far removed from insanity », and to emerge as what the late James Westfall Thompson called « a mountebank, a roisterer, a dabbler in philosophy, a religious maniac, and a moral pervert » [23]. We need not assume that the French found these years disillusioning. A Venetian ambassador describes their parlous state: « ... i francesi, per ambizione e per avarizia, sedotti ed ingannati con vane speranze, sono concorsi precipitosamente alla propria rovina ... » [24].

Henry's court was a center of literary, as well as behavioral preciosity, and there is much evidence to suggest that after 1575, French literature may be most accurately characterized as post-Renaissance. In a learned and intriguing study entitled *Metaphysical, Baroque and Précieux Poetry*, Odette de Mourgues has discussed significant changes in the form and content of French poetry after 1575 [25]. At the risk of over-simplifying, though I

---

[23] *The Wars of Religion in France*, p. 513; N. M. Sutherland, *The French Secretaries of State in the Age of Catherine de Medici* (London, 1962), p. 189. Of the many good sources for the character and reign of Henry III, the best is the *Mémoires-Journaux* of Pierre de l'Estoile, which may be sampled in the edition of Brunet, Champollion, *et al.* (Paris, 1875-96), or, more conveniently, in the one-volume abridged translation by Nancy L. Roelker, *The Paris of Henry of Navarre: Pierre de l'Estoile* (Cambridge, Mass., 1958).

[24] E. Albèri, ed., *Le Relazioni degli ambasciatori veneti al Senato durante il secolo decimosesto*, Ser. I, vol. IV (Florence, 1860), p. 453. Hereafter « *Relazioni* ».

[25] Oxford, 1953. In addition to the very persuasive and elegantly presented arguments given by Mme. de Mourgues, much evidence exists to confirm our judgment that the period 1570-1575 is a turning point for the literature of the French Renaissance. Wherever one looks, the work of scholars tracing particular genres or styles gives new confirmation. Thus, M. R. Jung, *Hercule dans la littérature française du XVIe siècle: De l'Hercule courtois à l'Hercule baroque* (Geneva, 1966), p. 187: « Dans la deuxième moitié, on n'avait qu'à exploiter, qu'à amplifier, qu'à mettre en valeur ce que les décennies antérieures avaient préparé », in the interpretation of the Hercules motif. It lost its spontaneity, its style, and the invigorating impact of new and original applications (p. 191): « Les dernières décennies du XVIe siècle ont vu se propager les histoires d'Hercule un peu partout — on les retrouve jusque sur les salières, sur les monnaies, les armures, les bannières. Mais ce qu'elles ont gagné en terrain, elles l'ont perdu en substance. C'est déjà le déclin ». The same is true for the French eclogue, as seen by A. Hu-

hope not overstating, a complex argument, I think it is fair to state that these conclusions emerge from her work: (1) That what might be defined as essentially Renaissance characteristics in the work of Ronsard, Du Bellay, and others of the *Pléiade* are rejected by the new generation of poets that emerges in the 1570's and 1580's, in favor of the types of poetry cited in her title; (2) that in poetry in general, Renaissance optimism gives way to what the author calls Late Renaissance pessimism, or what I would like to call post-Renaissance despair; (3) that whereas the poetry of the middle of the century is in many ways boldly innovative, of wide appeal, and is written by great artists, that of the end of the century tends to be either conventional or *recherché* in form, of much more limited appeal, and written by skillful poets of the second rank [26].

Without quibbling over the categories which Mourgues uses, or how she applies them to individual authors, it will be useful to look in greater detail at the work of at least one of the poets she treats, Agrippa d'Aubigné. On stylistic grounds, Mourgues presents him as a baroque poet, and I find nothing to object to in that. However, it is the content of d'Aubigné's thought that seems to me to yield the most useful insights on the end of the French Renaissance.

The greatest of French Huguenot writers was born in 1552, and raised in the optimistic, secularistic ambiance of the Renaissance, despite his Calvinist education, and his early commitment to the Protestant cause. He received advice from Ronsard, and wrote a *canzoniere*, significantly between 1570 and 1573, which he dedicated to Diane Salviati, the niece of Ronsard's Cassandre. In 1575 the poet began work on his masterpiece, *Les Tragiques*, that powerful and variegated work that appeared in print in 1616 [27]. If Agrippa's *canzoniere*, *Le Printemps*, expres-

---

lubei, *L'Eglogue en France au XVIe siècle* (Paris, 1938), Pt. IV, chs. 17-18, pp. 600-95, esp. pp. 670-71: « La période tourmentée qui va de la mort de Charles IX à la fin des Valois constitue donc pour le genre une époque d'imitation ». The interpretation offered by A.-M. Schmidt, *La Poésie scientifique en France au XVIe siècle* (Paris, 1938), pp. 357-59, is also compatible with this approach.

[26] *Ibid.*, pp. 31, 88, 116, 138.

[27] I have used the edition by A. Garnier and J. Plattard, *Les tragiques, édition critique avec introduction et commentaire*, 3 vols. (Paris, 1932). Hereafter « *Tragiques* ».

ses the concerns and uses the forms typical of the *renaissance des lettres*, *Les Tragiques* speaks the language of withdrawal, disillusionment, pessimism toward the world. Of its seven books, the first, *Les Misères*, is the most historical [28]. Here, even allowing for the author's partisan view of events (which also colors his interminable and comparatively pedestrian *Histoire Universelle*), a general sense of despair and resignation appears.

Madame de Mourgues has characterized d'Aubigné's works as huge frescoes, and the reader of *Les Misères* is bound to agree. In one memorable passage, France is described as a desolate place, made of cinders, and as a mother nursing two infants that fight at her breasts, injuring her and one another in the process. This and many other passages are full of blood imagery, and a content analysis of the work would probably turn up an astounding frequency of words like « sang » and « sanglans ». Though a monarchist, the poet could write:

> Les Rois, qui sont du peuple & les Rois & les peres,
> Du troupeau domesticq sont les loups sanguinaires [29];

He describes the horrors and atrocities of the wars in excruciating, agonizing detail. But he goes beyond the recitation and dramatization of the horrible when he writes of the paradox of such decline amidst such learning:

> France, tu es si docte & parles tant de langues!
> O monstreueux discours, ô funestes harangues!
> Ainsi, mourans les corps, on a veu les esprits
> Prononcer les jargons qu' ils n'avoient point apris.
> Tu as plus que jamais de merveilleuses testes,
> Des cerveaux transcendans, de vrais & faux prophetes.
> Toi, prophete, en mourant du mal de ta grandeur,
> Mieux que le medecin tu changes ton mal-heur [30].

---

[28] de Mourgues, *op. cit.*, characterizes d'Aubigné as a Baroque poet (p. 86), and describes his works as being analogous to huge frescoes (p. 101). Without becoming enmeshed in the terminological issues with which she has dealt, it is worth remarking that her observations seem very just.

[29] *Tragiques*, I, 11. 197-8.

[30] *Ibid.*, 11. 633-640.

And with the endless brutality of war, there comes a gradual change in human nature:

On void perir en toi la chaleur naturelle,
Le feu de charité, tout' amour mutuelle ... [31];

Much of the blame for all of this is laid at the feet of the Guise family and of Catherine de' Medici, whom Agrippa describes as a Jezebel, and compares to Nero [32]. The anti-Medicean, anti-Italian, and anti-court sentiment here is not uncommon in French Protestant polemics, and it seems almost gratuitous to observe that if the late Renaissance in France was primarily (though not exclusively) a phenomenon of the court and its immediate surroundings and dependencies, it is not surprising, given the court's debasement, to witness cultural as well as political deterioration in the 1570's and 1580's. In his second book, *Princes*, d'Aubigné gives us some glimpses into the interaction between politics and culture at the court; and focuses on all kinds of vice, lubricity, bad faith, ruses, and betrayals. Henry III's taste for masquerades is well known, and the poet evidently conceives of this in terms of an entire style of life:

... au milieu des massacres sanglantes,
Exercices & jeux aux desloyaux tyrans,
Quand le peuple gemit sous le faix tyrannique,
Quand ce siècle n'est rien qu'une histoire tragique,
Ce sont farces & jeux toutes leurs actions;
Un ris sardonien peint leurs affections;
Bizarr' habits & coeurs, les plaisants se desguisent ... [33]

How perfectly that one line summarizes the poet's view of the world, « Quand ce siècle n'est rien qu'une histoire tragique ». Few Frenchmen between 1575 and 1595 disagreed. Agrippa d'Aubigné does not conceive of his own time as a period of cultural renascence, and it would be strange indeed if he did.

---

[31] *Loc. cit.*, II. 653-4.
[32] *Loc. cit.*, II. 747-852.
[33] *Tragiques*, II, II. 203-209.

So far as the testimony of experienced political observers is concerned, d'Aubigné's view is thoroughly corroborated. An impressive series of Venetian ambassadors, for example, comment sadly on the decline of a great people. As early as 1562, the ambassador Michele Soriano saw the handwriting on the wall in a truly prophetic report to the Senate, in which he observed that three principal dangers threatened France: (1) the decline in the fear of God, which leads to disobedience of the laws and magistrates, and relativism in interpreting Holy Scripture; (2) the erosion of law and order (« la polizia e l'ordine del governo »), leading to the decline of all constituted authority and the overthrow of an entire way of life (« la mutazione dei costumi e del modo consueto di vivere »); (3) the division of the populace, whence come seditions and civil wars. Soriano says that these things have not reached major proportions, but that he fears very much that they will [34]. His successors confirmed his gloomy forebodings. In 1582, Lorenzo Priuli writes that anyone who knew France earlier would marvel at the total transformation from order, tranquillity, prosperity, and peace to chaos, confusion, poverty and civil war [35]. By 1600, Francesco Vendramin sees the country slowly beginning to heal itself, ruled at last by an able king [36].

III.

Someone might well be tempted to inquire, on the basis of the previous remarks, whether there was not a well-developed

---

[34] *Relazioni*, pp. 105-49, esp. pp. 137-8. His general evaluation of the present condition of France is summarized (p. 147) in the following sentence: « E chi vuol comparare lo stato presente del regno a quello de' tempi passati, che soleva essere tanto formidabile ai maggiori re e imperatori del mondo, lo trova tanto debole e tanto infermo, che non ha niuna parte in sè che sia sana ».

[35] *Relazioni*, pp. 407-49. Priuli, writing two decades after Soriano, speaks of the same great transformation, comparing the present with the recent past (esp. pp. 407-08): « Ma chi vede la catastrofe di questa tragedia, voglio dir chi considera lo stato presente delle cose tanto diverso dal passato, convien con gran ragione meravigliarsi; ... pare che tutte le cose siano messe in grandissima confusione ».

[36] *Relazioni*, pp. 453-67.

tradition of Renaissance pessimism about such things as human nature, war, and the like, which I have conveniently neglected. That there was such an intellectual tradition, deeply ingrained in Western thought, is undeniable. It is equally obvious that in the period from 1500 to 1600 it frequently found expression, both in the conventional Pauline and Augustinian rhetoric of theologians and Christian humanists, and in the secularized, but analogous vocabulary of what might be called « Renaissance minds », such as Machiavelli's, Guicciardini's, Aretino's, Le Roy's. I do not wish to classify as « Renaissance » only that which is redolent of optimism or naiveté, or to consign the most acute perceptions of less hopeful observers trained and guided by the classics to some sort of counter-renaissance insurgency [37]. The movement could contain such variety up to a certain point, on the one condition that the optimistic side continued to flourish. For the belief in a rebirth of culture was a humanistic act of faith, partaking of the nature of a perception, a program, and a self-fulfilling prophecy [38]. The tensions between despair and optimism in such authors as Machiavelli and Le Roy, the tensions between skepticism and belief in men like Henry Cornelius Agrippa and Jean Bodin, hold them within the framework of Renaissance debates on man, God, and society. It is when this tension disappears, when the old battles no longer seem worth fighting, when optimism becomes the charming or stupid irrelevancy of an earlier generation, that I think one should be prepared to speak of the Renaissance as a thing of the past. And, allowing for minor exceptions, it seems to me that this transition takes effect in France after 1575.

---

[37] This seems to be the general approach of Hiram Haydn, *The Counter-Renaissance* (New York, 1950).

[38] It seems quite clear by now that both Italian and French humanists conceived of their own social and intellectual roles in terms of partaking in such a revival, even if as individuals they stressed the vernacular languages, and the possibility of superseding the ancients. Still useful here are the articles by H. Weisinger, « The Renaissance Theory of the Reaction Against the Middle Ages as a Cause of the Renaissance », *Speculum*, XX (1945), 461 ff.; « The Self-Awareness of the Renaissance as a Criterion of the Renaissance », *Papers of the Michigan Academy of Sciences, Arts and Literature*, XIX (1944), 661 ff.; and other articles by the same author listed in the extensive and useful bibliographical essay on this subject by F. Chabod, *Machiavelli and the Renaissance* (London, and Cambridge, Mass., 1958), pp. 201-47.

After all, the thinkers of late sixteenth-century France are no strangers to classical learning, but few could be called « Renaissance humanists ». Bodin's flight from the world has already been cited. For others, the newly discovered lands and people provided endless fascination, and another form of escape [39]. Montaigne, though steeped in classical learning and secluded in the provinces, often takes the detached, ironical stance of the man of knowledge who knows too much to be sure of anything. Stoicism, in its late sixteenth-century reincarnation, may be viewed perhaps as a personal religion, an escape from discredited confessionalism, as well as an antiquarian revival. What has been called a « renaissance » of Stoicism could also be interpreted as a kind of rejection of the values and assumptions of the previous revival of learning [40]. The Epicureanism of Gassendi and his circle reflects yet another form of escape, this time into materialistic philosophy, scientific theorizing, and finally, a new set of ethical norms [41]. On the darker side, there is a great revival of witchcraft, mysticism and related arcana [42].

---

[39] G. Atkinson, *Les Nouveaux horizons de la Renaissance française* (Paris, 1935).

[40] As shown by L. Zanta, *La Renaissance du stoicisme au XVIe siècle* (Paris, 1914). Montaigne has occasionally been regarded as « post-Renaissance » in basic intellectual orientation, on the strength of his refusal to be bound by classical norms and precedents, and the essential past-mindedness of earlier humanism. Thus, F. Chabod, *Machiavelli and the Renaissance*, p. 199: « This fundamental change of attitude finds its supreme expression outside Italy, to wit, in the writings of Montaigne, who not only ridicules the traditional distinction between 'barbarian' and 'non-barbarian' ('chacun appelle barbarie ce que n'est pas de son usage', *Essais* I, 31), but even goes so far as to place the so-called 'savage' races on a higher plane than those normally regarded as 'civilized', asserting that the former are closer to 'nature' and that 'ce que nous voyons par experience en ces nations là [i. e. the peoples of America], surpasse, non seulement toutes les peintures dequoy la poesie a embelly l'age doré ... mais encore la conception et le desir mesme de la philosophy' (*ibid.*) ».

[41] A useful introduction to the subject in general is D. C. Allen, *Doubt's Boundless Sea: Skepticism and Faith in the Renaissance* (Baltimore, 1964). On Gassendi and his circle see T. Gregory, *Scetticismo ed empirismo: Studio su Gassendi* (Bari, 1961); B. Rochot, *Les travaux de Gassendi sur Epicure et sur l'atomisme, 1619-1658* (Paris, 1944); R. Pintard, *Le libertinage érudit dans la première moitié du XVIIe siècle* (Paris, 1943).

[42] For evidence of this, see, for example, J. L. Blau, *The Christian Interpretation of the Cabala in the Renaissance* (New York, 1944). Quite recently,

The greatest single act that served to bring about a renewed sense of human possibilities in France was Henry of Navarre's expedient rejection of Calvinism and espousal of the Gallican Church. A perfect, politically motivated act expressing in itself a kind of escape into religious relativism, it was also the deed that redeemed France. Similarly in his subsequent political style, Henry IV foreshadowed the absolutist policies of his Bourbon descendants, just as the artists and intellectuals of his reign seem to sense their own distance from the beautiful epoch of Francis I and Henry II, and begin to align themselves with the styles, techniques, interests, methods, and attitudes of the age of Molière, Descartes, and Pascal. By 1589 a new age would begin. The last of the Valois had been removed from the scene through an assassination sanctioned by the latest Catholic political thought. But the French Renaissance did not expire with him. In most important ways, its time had come a decade and a half before.

F. Secret has delved more deeply into Christian Cabalism in a series of important works, and H. R. Trevor-Roper has written interestingly of late sixteenth-century witchcraft, in *Religion, the Reformation and Social Change* (London, 1968).

WILLIAM J. BOUWSMA

GALLICANISM AND THE NATURE OF CHRISTENDOM

Over forty years ago Lucien Febvre insisted on the crucial importance of distinguishing between *religious* and *ecclesiastical* history, between powerful spiritual movements related to the major currents of European social and political development and the particular events and institutional forms through which, almost incidentally, they may find expression. The Reformation, in Febvre's perspective, was thus a movement of European scope that brought into focus, in areas destined to stay Catholic as well as in those that broke away from the medieval church, tendencies that had been gathering force for centuries. The problem for the historian, he suggested, was to identify these forces and then to show how they operated in various situations and were modified by local conditions [1].

Although his brilliant essay was directed finally to explaining the origins of the Reformation in France, Febvre confined his attention largely to the sources of French Protestantism, which, as it turned out, failed to win over more than a minority of Frenchmen. But the general impulses behind the Reformation were often as effective among Catholics as among Protestants, as Febvre was well aware; and a better illustration of his point may perhaps be found in Gallicanism, which bridged the centuries before and after the Reformation proper, and which was attractive to generations of Frenchmen, among them not only personages of evident gravity, learning, and intelligence, but also in many cases men close to the center of public life.

Gallicanism has not been very positively regarded by historians, nor has it been closely associated with the problems posed by either the Reformation or the Renaissance. Standard general histories of France have viewed it largely as a dimension of politics, and it has suffered from the same distaste attached

---

1 « Une question mal posée: les origines de la réforme française et le problème des causes de la réforme », first published in the *Revue historique*, CLXI (1929), and included in *Au coeur religieux du XVIe siècle* (Paris, 1957), pp. 3-70.

to other aspects of the Old Regime [2]. On the other hand historians who have studied Gallicanism systematically have tended to see in it little more than an incoherent bundle of currents of opposition to the Holy See, based on an ignorance of history and defective theology, and animated by a selfish indifference to the larger needs of the Christian community [3]. For both Gallicanism emerges as, in a rather precise sense, a transparent species of ideology, an elaborate mask for the special interests of crown and class. Students of ecclesiastical rather than of religious history (in Febvre's sense), its major historians, have assigned it only a limited significance even in the history of the church. Thus, in a manner ironically reminiscent of recent insistence that the revolution at the end of the eighteenth century was a national achievement, Victor Martin maintained that Gallicanism, native in origin and utterly self-absorbed, was « a movement specifically French ». « Exported outside the kingdom », he declared, « it quickly died or was radically transformed » [4].

Martin was obviously asking precisely the sort of question that Febvre had called on historians of the Reformation to reject, and this paper will not pursue Martin's question by arguing that Gallicanism had a large influence beyond the borders of France. I think that it had, in fact, some external effect, though the problem of what constitutes an « influence » and why a movement of thought exerts influence under some conditions but not others is in any case more complicated than is some-

---

[2] A good example is the treatment by Ernest Lavisse, *Histoire de France*, VII (Paris, 1905), Part I, 387-400, Part II, 14-37.

[3] An extreme, though not altogether unrepresentative example of this view is M. Dubruel, « Gallicanisme », *Dictionnaire de théologie catholique*, VI, Part 2 (Paris, 1924), cols. 1096-1137; see, for example, cols. 1108-1109: « Ces théories sont des constructions factices imaginées pour justifier des résistances aux développements théoriques et pratiques de la primauté de Pierre », etc. Among the most important recent works on the subject are Joseph Lecler, « Qu'est-ce que les libertés de l'Église gallicane », *Recherches de science religieuse*, XXIII (1933), 385-410, 542-568, and XXIV (1934), 47-85; Aime George Martimort, *Le Gallicanisme de Bossuet* (Paris, 1953), with massive bibliographies; and the magisterial works of Victor Martin, *Le Gallicanisme et la réforme catholique* (Paris, 1919), *Le Gallicanisme politique et le clergé de France* (Paris, 1929), and *Les origines du Gallicanisme* (Paris, 1939).

[4] *Origines du Gallicanisme*, I, 39.

times supposed. The primary interest of Gallicanism lies rather in what it reveals about the concern of pious Frenchmen, like other Europeans, to redefine Christianity and the idea of Christendom, and thus to bring religious life into a closer correspondence with the changing structures of European society. From this standpoint Gallicanism can hardly be viewed as a narrowly national movement; the more Gallican Frenchmen were, the more emphatically they affirmed their membership in a larger European community. Thus it should hardly be surprising to discover that Gallican theorists were sometimes well aware of their affinities with men elsewhere; and, conversely, both as a practical and a speculative posture, Gallicanism was an object of general European interest, among Catholics as well as Protestants.

Although Gallicanism can be traced back at least to the fourteenth century and perhaps earlier [5], achieved a political climax of sorts in the later seventeenth century, and may be discerned again lurking behind the Civil Constitution of the Clergy and even later, the most significant chapter in its venerable history for the purposes of this paper was the heroic age of Gallican speculation extending from the end of the Council of Trent to the ministry of Richelieu. During this period Gallicanism enjoyed its maximum freedom from royal control, and it was therefore most spontaneous and responsive to a variety of contemporary impulses, both positive and negative. Notable among the latter was the challenge of the Counter Reformation, during these years in its most militant mood and resolved to impose on Catholic Europe the whole pattern of universalist, hierarchical, and theocratic values elaborated by the papal theorists of the thirteenth and fourteenth centuries. This theoretical system had now been given concrete application in the decrees of Trent, whose significance was as much symbolic as practical [6]. Gallicanism, during this period, saw itself clearly as the major obstacle, in France and perhaps in all Europe, to a reactionary offensive stemming from Rome.

During this period, in addition, although the case of Edmond Richer shows that Gallicanism still found vigorous spokesmen

---

[5] *Ibid.*, I, esp. 29 ff.; Lecler, pp. 388-395.

[6] For the Council of Trent as a stimulus to Gallicanism, see Lecler, pp. 542 ff.

among the clergy, its major champions came from the relatively independent magistracy, a group peculiarly fitted by its cosmopolitan culture as well as its specialized training to respond creatively to the general needs of the age [7]. That the Gallican leadership in these years consisted so largely of lawyers deserves some emphasis [8]. Supported by the prestige of imperial Rome and dedicated to the practical requirements of the *vita activa*, the civil law had long ignored the constraints of theology, and lawyers had perhaps earlier than any other social group insisted on a practical independence from ecclesiastical supervision; as early as the thirteenth century it was said that a good jurist was necessarily a bad Christian [9]. Legal training was thus particularly calculated to nourish a sense of the dignity of the lay estate and the prerogatives of the secular power.

Much of what was most significant in the Gallicanism of the later sixteenth and early seventeenth centuries may be associated with attitudes traditional among lawyers. Fundamental among these was an assumption that the entire institutional order was pluralistic rather than unitary; in both Italy and France lawyers had early accustomed themselves to working within a framework composed of a congeries of particular states rather than an all-inclusive system, and thus they had long opposed the directive claims of the papacy. Their concern with clearly defined spheres of activity and established procedures gave them a certain bias towards constitutionalism, and the same tendencies nourished a spiritual conception of the church. Legal study had also relied heavily on a species of historical research potentially applicable to revealing the evolution of institutions through time. Guillaume Budé had already exhibited something of this interest in France during the earlier sixteenth century;

---

[7] A systematic study of this group, its social and political backgrounds and its culture, is badly needed. There are scattered suggestions in René Pintard, *Le libertinage érudit dans la première moitié du XVIIe siècle* (Paris, 1943), and George Huppert, *The Idea of Perfect History: Historical Erudition and Historical Philosophy in Renaissance France* (Urbana and Chicago, 1970).

[8] It may be observed that the general importance of lawyers in the political and cultural history of the Renaissance is now receiving increased attention, for example in Myron P. Gilmore, *Humanists and Jurists* (Cambridge, Mass., 1963), and Lauro Martines, *Lawyers and Statecraft in Renaissance Florence* (Princeton, 1968).

[9] Martin, *Origines du Gallicanisme*, I, 137-138.

and it was destined to develop during succeeding generations into an increasingly sophisticated historicism. This tendency among the Gallican magistrates combined with a professional interest in the relation between law and the immediate needs of time and place to produce a type of mind notable for its openness, its flexibility, and its resistance to dogmatic rigidities in all aspects of human experience. The Gallicanism of the lawyers during this period can therefore enlarge our understanding of the later Renaissance in France as well as of the Reformation.

Fundamental to Gallicanism in every period of its history was the assumption that Christendom properly consisted not of a unified, hierarchically organized system, but of discrete and parallel entities [10]. This was taken to mean not only the independence of rulers from ecclesiastical supervision but also the legitimate existence of separate and independent states. As early as John of Paris (to whose authority later Gallicans appealed), Frenchmen had argued for a pluralistic political order [11]; and by the later sixteenth century Gallicans simply assumed that, since traditions and problems differed widely throughout Europe, it was essential that institutions should vary locally, and that they should be locally and flexibly administered. Above all they were persuaded that what was appropriate for Italy was by no means necessarily suited to France [12]. They were immediately concerned with the organization of the church,

---

[10] In this connection cf. Edmond Richer, *De la puissance ecclésiastique et politique* (Paris, 1612), p. 11: « ... non donc la seule puissance est de Dieu: il y en a de mediocres & d'inferieures: & comme ce que Dieu a conioint ne doit estre separé: aussi ne se doit on aproprier, ce qu'il a attribué à ceux qui nous sont adioincts ... ».

[11] For John of Paris see Otto Gierke, *Political Theories of the Middle Age*, tr. Frederic William Maitland (Cambridge, 1900), p. 20 and n. 61. Richer appealed to his authority, p. 48.

[12] There is a witty reflection of this attitude in Paolo Sarpi, *Istoria del Concilio Tridentino*, ed. Giovanni Gambarin (Bari, 1935), II, 250, which quotes the bishop of Valence as observing that « it would be a great absurdity to watch Paris burn when the Seine and Marne are full of water, in the belief that it was necessary to wait to put out the fire for water from the Tiber ». See also, in this work, the remarks attributed to the French chancellor at Poissy (II, 300). On the general point see Martimort, pp. 106 ff.

but this concern had a more general relation to the structure of European politics.

In its application to the church, the substitution of numerous parallel authorities for an arrangement in hierarchy led to a marked bias for the separate and independent authority of bishops [13], and even some tendency to insist on the independent, divinely-bestowed authority of each individual priest [14]. Their larger concern with local needs was also basic to Gallican hostility (most eloquently expressed in the pamphlets of Saint-Cyran, in this matter a close ally of Gallicanism) towards the regular clergy, international rules governing administrative affairs being themselves generally suspect [15]. This feeling was, of course, most vigorously directed against the Jesuits. The same interest was basic to Gallican support for conciliarism, one of the constants in the history of Gallicanism, equally shared by magistrates and theologians [16]. The council was superior to the pope in their view, however, for practical as well as theoretical reasons, a fact of some interest for appraising the Gallican mind. Gallicans preferred councils because many heads are better than one and because the needs of the church are not single and general but plural and particular, the needs of individual churches and individual churchmen which can only achieve satisfactory expression in an assembly [17]. The principle

---

[13] Cf. Martimort, pp. 19-20, 76 ff. The same kind of episcopalianism was prominent in Saint Cyran; cf. Jean Orcibal, *Jean Duvergier de Hauranne, abbé de Saint-Cyran, et son temps* (Paris, 1947), pp. 353-354.

[14] As in Richer, p. 10. Cf. p. 18, where Richer insists also on the participation of priests in church councils.

[15] Cf. Orcibal, pp. 35 ff., and Martimort, pp. 21-22.

[16] On the general point see Martimort, pp. 41 ff. For some particular expressions of conciliar sentiment, cf. Pierre Pithou, *Les Libertez de l'Eglise Gallicane* (in his *Opera* [Paris, 1609], pp. 511-533), p. 522; Jacques Leschassier, *De la liberté ancienne et canonique de l'Eglise Gallicane* (Paris, 1606), pp. 29-30; Richer, pp. 18-23.

[17] Cf. Richer, p. 18, on the superiority of a council: « ... & celà se iuge en partie par inspiration divine, partie par la lumière naturelle: veu que plusieurs yeux voyent plus loing & aperçoivent mieux qu'un seul: & il n'a esté concedé de Dieu ou de Nature à un seul d'estre sage, de peur qu' l ne s'en eslevast ... ». There is an interesting parallel here with the defense of royal rule through councils in Philippe de Commynes, *Mémoires*, ed. J. Calmette and G. Durville (Paris, 1924-1925), I, 103.

may be partly a feudal residue, partly a reflection of Aristotle; but the realities it reflected were those of the fragmented modern world.

The limited role in the church that Gallicans attributed to the pope was a corollary of these views; they saw the church as a constitutional apparatus properly governed by duly established machinery according to general laws and set procedures. The pope was no longer, for them, the apex of a hierarchy, the church's ultimate point of contact with the divine authority claimed for the whole, but hardly more than *primus inter pares*, the president of a college in which no member was essentially higher or lower than another since each was appointed directly by God. Gallican theorists considered the pope neither infallible in matters of doctrine nor broadly competent in the administration of the church [18]; they were utterly opposed to the doctrine of a papal *plenitudo potestatis*. No element in the pope's authority could be regarded, in their view, as unlimited; to the extent that he ruled the church, he did so as a constitutional monarch, and resistance to him was legitimate on conventional constitutional grounds [19]. On this point the connections between secular and ecclesiastical thought seem unusually close [20]. For the Gallican writers, however, the church, itself a congeries of particular churches, had not one but many constitutions: a universal constitution based on natural and divine law as implemented by the general council, but also a series of local constitutions based on local traditions and needs. « In France », declared Pithou, referring specifically to the church but certainly invoking a larger set of political conceptions, « absolute and

---

[18] Martimort, pp. 23 ff. on the general point.

[19] Cf. Charles Faye, *Discours des moyens pour lesquels messieurs du clergé ... ont declaré les Bulles Monitoriales ... nulles & injustes* (Paris, 1591), in *Traitez des droits et libertez de l'Eglise Gallicane*, ed. Pierre Dupuy (Paris, 1731), I, 98-99, which denies that the pope is universal bishop and insists on the limits of his authority in France. For the same point, see Guy Coquille, *Autre discours*, in his *Oeuvres* (Bordeaux, 1703), pp. 192-196; Pithou, pp. 522-526; Richer, pp. 7-9, 14, 17, 22-23, 29.

[20] This tendency may be viewed as an application to the church of the general resurgence of French constitutionalism in the later sixteenth century, as noted by William Farr Church, *Constitutional Thought in Sixteenth Century France* (Cambridge, Mass., 1941), pp. 74 ff.

infinite power has no place but is contained and limited by the canons and regulations of the ancient councils of the church received in this kingdom »[21]. The Gallican liberties may thus be understood as an elaborate parallel to the fundamental laws of France, and the Parlement of Paris was felt to be the proper guardian of both[22].

The pluralistic vision of the institutional order and the constitutionalism of the Gallican magistrates were directly related to a conception of the church that distinguished sharply between its mystical and spiritual dimension and the external and administrative framework through which the church operates in specific situations. If they gave special attention to the latter, it must be remembered that they were lawyers, professionally engaged with the definition of legal rights in concrete situations which they had to take into account. But as Christians in a period of deepening piety, in which they participated, they were aware that faith had other and more profound dimensions[23]. And as Christian lawyers, they were faced with the problem of coordinating the particular institutional and local realities with which they were in regular professional contact and the inescapable fact that Christianity in some sense also transcended the local scene, that the church was in some sense (if not in what was a regular part of their own experience) a universal and single body.

Like many of their contemporaries in other parts of Europe, Catholic as well as Protestant, they did so by sharpening the distinction between the spiritual and temporal realms and limiting the church to the former[24]. It is, indeed, not entirely clear

---

[21] *Libertez de l'Eglise Gallicane*, pp. 513-514.

[22] On the general point cf. Martimort, pp. 84 ff. See also Martin, *Gallicanisme et la réforme*, pp. 350, 353, for examples of parlementary condemnations (to the distress of Rome) of heresy. For a typical assertion of the responsibilities of the clergy in ecclesiastical matters, cf. Leschassier, pp. 31-32. Leschassier argues that the defense of the church « est le plus grand honneur qui puisse estre en la main de iuges souverains, que de rendre à l'Eglise la sainctеté de ses anciens reglemens ».

[23] On this point see Martimort, pp. 97-98.

[24] As in Richer, pp. 29-32, who here makes a general Gallican point with particular sharpness.

what functions they were disposed to allow to the spiritual power; they were not systematic theologians in most cases, and perhaps it is best to speak rather of tendencies than of a mature theory of the church. Among these tendencies was an inclination to regard as the true church only what was immutable and therefore vulnerable neither to the vagaries of time nor to their own professional attention. Whatever history or the law could touch, whatever could be affected by the things they knew best, appeared to them as profane and tainted, as therefore not the true body of Christ, which by definition was spiritual, holy, subject to no shadow of turning.

This conclusion is difficult to demonstrate. No Gallican, as far as I am aware, quite said as much, and it must be deduced as the assumption underlying numerous general pronouncements. Here, for example, is a proposition of Jacques Leschassier, one of the most scholarly of the Gallican magistrates: « Among the political laws of the church, the divine or apostolic is the eternal and perpetual, the others are temporal and provisional, made for human and temporal reasons; and the church tends, by its duty and according to the opinion of all good Christians, to the restitution of the apostolic law » [25]. The attitudes to history and reform suggested by this statement will concern us in a moment; here what should be noticed is its appeal to an ideal model from which every historical accident must somehow be shucked away. Among such accidents Leschassier clearly included not only all political dominion and property but rights of disposal over every temporal thing, which he explicitly denied either to the pope or to any clerical body. Pithou took much the same position, and the order of his argument implied (though it did not make explicit) the view that much and perhaps all the external administration of the church belonged to the temporal power. Thus he first denied the pope any general authority over temporal matters in France, and then he insisted that it belonged to the king to call national ecclesiastical councils responsible for the discipline of the clergy [26]. There appears to have been a sense in which the Gallican liberties did not prop-

---

[25] *Liberté de l'Eglise Gallicane*, p. 31.

[26] *Libertez de l'Eglise Gallicane*, pp. 514 ff. Pithou's list of actions prohibited to the pope is remarkably comprehensive.

erly concern the spiritual « estate » at all, but only (to apply a distinction of Richer) the « government » [27].

This position too had important implications for the role of the pope; the spirituality of the church as well as its decentralization severely limited his authority. It meant that the pope had no right to interfere in any way with political affairs or to call temporal magistrates to account [28]. On this the Gallican magistrates, with their keen sense of the dignity of the lay condition as well as their concern as lawyers to maintain the rights of the crown, felt strongly; and whenever it arose they came into action. Many Gallican treatises were occasional, called into existence by efforts to assert papal authority over rulers. Pius IV's summons to Jeanne d'Albret to appear before the Holy Office produced the *Mémoire* of Du Mesnil; Gregory XIV's attack in 1591 on the rights of Henry of Navarre to the French throne resulted in works by Coquille, Fauchet, and Faye [29]; the assassination of Henry IV (so widely attributed to a Jesuit and therefore papalist plot) was shortly followed by the treatise of Richer and certainly helps to explain Richer's wide support [30]; Pierre Pithou composed a history of the interdict, the device by which popes had long sought to impose their authority on rulers, and now a potential danger to France [31]. Although these men did not deny the right of the pope to excommunicate kings as individuals, they consistently rejected the alleged political implications of such action; they denied the pope's authority to depose any ruler or to release his subjects from obedience [32].

---

[27] Richer attacks papalists because they « confondent l'estat de l'Eglise avec le gouvernement » (p. 39).

[28] Martimort, pp. 62-63, on the general point. Cf. Pithou, p. 513, and Leschassier, p. 29.

[29] Coquille, *Discours des droits ecclesiastiques et libertez de l'Eglise de France*; Claude Fauchet, *Traicté des libertez de l'Eglise Gallicane*; Faye, as cited above, note 19. The two first works are also in Dupuy, I, 70-86, 190-210.

[30] Cf. Leopold Willaert, *Après le concile de Trente: la restauration catholique (1563-1648)* (Paris, 1960), I, 387.

[31] *De l'origine et du progrès des Interdicts ecclésiastiques*, included in Dupuy, I (separately paged).

[32] On the general point, Martimort, pp. 66-67. Cf. Pithou, p. 518; Faye, 99 ff.; and *Maintenue et Defense de Princes souverains et Eglises chrétiennes, contre les attentats, usurpations et excommunications des Papes de Rome*, printed in *Mémoires de la Ligue* (Paris, 1601-1604), IV, 374-616.

The large supervisory role Gallicanism assigned to the crown in the national church had several sources, among them the idea that his authority was derived directly from God (a belief much facilitated by the general denial of hierarchy) and the long tradition that saw the king as no mere layman but an ecclesiastical functionary bound by sacred oath to defend the church from all its enemies, notably including those in Rome [33]. At the same time there had been a strong tendency from an early point for Gallican theorists to emphasize that the church consisted of the whole congregation of believers, laity as well as clergy [34]; and this view too implied the special responsibility of the king as primary layman. Finally, the distinction between the church's spirituality and its institutionality suggested parallel leadership, and Gallican theorists were prompt to attribute the direction of the institution to the crown. The duty of the king, as Leschassier remarked, was « not to baptize and to preach, but to provide for baptizing and preaching and to guard the rights of the church » [35]. Popes deceived themselves, declared Le Jay, if they supposed that they alone were concerned with the harmony of the church, a responsibility that devolved also on kings and princes [36]; and Leschassier explained that it was above all to be exercised through their « sovereign judges », the « natural and legitimate protectors of the ancient law » [37]. Thus through a series of venerable conceptions the Gallican magistrates, at once pious and practical, managed to combine the most transcendent ideal for the church with practical accommodation to the world as they knew it.

The obvious contrast between this ideal and the contemporary church of their own experience cried out to them (as to other religious reformers) for explanation, and to this task they brought the techniques for the historical study of law at work

---

[33] See on this point the classic work of Marc Bloch, *Les rois thaumaturges: étude sur le caractère surnaturel attribué à la puissance royale, particulièrement en France et en Angleterre* (Strasbourg, 1924); Martimort, p. 83.

[34] Martin, *Origines du Gallicanisme*, I, 33; Lecler, p. 392.

[35] *Liberté de l'Eglise Gallicane*, pp. 30-31, appealing to the authority of Charlemagne and Constantine.

[36] *Le tocsin* (Paris, 1610), p. 31.

[37] *Liberté de l'Eglise Gallicane*, p. 33.

in France and, under the influence of Jacques Cujas, already evident in the transition from the more systematic and general *mos italicus* to the more specific and historically oriented *mos gallicus* [38]. Gallicanism thus participated fully in the broader movements that made of this period the first great age in French historiography [39]. But while some secular historians in France were moving toward an idea of progress, the Gallican historians of the church proposed a return to ancient and even primitive models; they sought an antidote to history [40].

The Gallican view of church history thus resembled the vision of the European past shared by both medieval religious reformers and Renaissance humanists. In this perspective an original perfection had been succeeded by a long degeneration that had coincided precisely with the medieval centuries, and this in turn would be followed by a restoration in which, at least among humanists and Gallicans, the contemporary flowering of philological scholarship (as the key to grasping the whole pattern) would play the essential role. But Gallicanism, through its contact with legal study, was as a program of reform more concrete than medieval reformism or humanism. It perceived that change in the church (as in the law) responded to specific historical circumstances, and it was therefore concerned not merely with a general educational and spiritual revival but also with the actual structure of institutions and their modes

---

[38] Cf. Julian Franklin, *Jean Bodin and the Sixteenth Century Revolution in the Methodology of Law and History* (New York, 1963) and, more generally, J. G. A. Pocock, *The Ancient Constitution and the Feudal Law* (Cambridge, 1957), pp. 1-29.

[39] As a number of scholars are now showing us. In addition to the works of Huppert and Franklin, cited above, see Werner L. Gundersheimer, *The Life and Works of Louis Le Roy* (Geneva, 1966); Samuel Kinser, *The Works of Jacques-Auguste de Thou* (The Hague, 1966); Franco Simone, *Il Rinascimento francese: studi e ricerche* (Turin, 1961); George W. Sypher, « La Popelinière's *Histoire de France*: A Case of Historical Objectivity and Religious Censorship », *Journal of the History of Ideas*, XXIV (1963), 41-54, and « Similarities Between the Scientific and the Historical Revolutions at the End of the Renaissance », in the same journal, XXVI (1965), 353-368; Donald R. Kelley, « *Historia Integra*: François Baudouin and His Conception of History », *Journal of the History of Ideas*, XXV (1964), 35-57, and « Guillaume Budé and the First Historical School of Law », *American Historical Review*, LXXII (1967), 807-834.

[40] On the general point see Lecler, pp. 547 ff.

of operation. Its historical analysis was also sharper. It had not only a general theory but also an interest in the actual processes and stages of historical change; the technical defects in its scholarship, which were those of its time, and the distortions stemming from its preconceptions should not be allowed to obscure these substantial merits.

A favorite Gallican text, cited by Pithou as a kind of summary at the end of his own major treatise, came from the book of Proverbs: « Pass not beyond the ancient bounds which thy fathers have set »[41]. The verse was more than a conservative slogan. It was an invitation to historical scholarship: the health of the church, it suggested, depended on a clear definition of the limitations on ecclesiastical action and organization established by the early church. For lawyers this implied the need for a systematic reconstruction of ancient canon law; and therefore, in contrast to earlier Gallicans, who had appealed to ancient practice merely in general, the Gallican magistrates of the seventeenth century made a serious attempt to describe it in specific detail. They published a series of canonical collections antedating Gratian, but they were chiefly interested in the practice of the first five centuries when, as they believed, popes were properly submissive to the temporal power and the church universal consisted of a federation of local churches, all respecting each other's autonomy and mutually related through general councils convened by emperors[42].

The most erudite among the Gallican students of the early church was probably Leschassier, whose *De la liberté ancienne et canonique de l'Eglise Gallicane* argued that the church had possessed an « ancient and common law », an antique *codex canonum* originated by the apostles, formulated through councils, and clearly recognized at Ephesus and Chalcedon, that had generally guaranteed « ancient and canonical liberty »[43]. For Leschassier

---

41 *Libertez de l'Eglise Gallicane*, p. 533. The text is Proverbs 22: 28.

42 For a typical discussion of how much of antiquity could serve as a model for the contemporary church, see *Lettre de Monseigneur le cardinal Du Perron. Envoyé au Sieur Casaubon en Angleterre* (Paris, 1612), pp. 22-25. On the general interest of the Gallican magistrates in the study of ancient canon law, see Martimort, pp. 90-91.

43 Lecler, pp. 554-557, gives a general account of Leschassier's views.

this ancient instrument for the defense of the church against « servitude » (i. e., centralization) had supplied the model for the more specific liberties of the Gallican church; the ancient church, he believed, had recognized papal authority only *legaliter et regulariter*, legally (according to Roman law) and canonically [44]. But it was all too obvious that, even in France, the original liberty of the church had not survived. The loosely federal constitution of the first centuries had collapsed under pressure from Rome, and thus the Middle Ages assumed a distinct identity.

This vision of the past is significant in several ways. It invested the autonomy of the Gallican church with the sanction of antiquity, and at the same time it depicted the Gallican liberties as rooted in the universal liberty enjoyed by the entire church during the first centuries of its existence, not merely in peculiar and shifting local conditions. As an argument for reform it had, therefore, a very general bearing. It was both (in a precise sense) radical and dangerous. It is also of considerable historiographical interest. By recognizing that even in France the ancient liberty of the church had disappeared, it implies a break with the myth of national continuity so inhibiting to the emergence of the Renaissance consciousness in northern Europe. It also suggests a concern to identify the crucial elements, moments, and discrete stages in a long and general historical process of subversion and recovery in which (in contrast to the polemical historiography of contemporary Protestantism) the essential causes were natural and all too human rather than diabolical.

Their conception of the church as essentially spiritual helped the Gallican magistrates to take this cool view of its history, for a visible institution whose career is punctuated by distinct events and phases was for them not properly the church at all, and it could therefore be discussed like any other earthly phenomenon. The Gallican treatment of the historical church was in this respect much like that of their Venetian contemporary, Paolo Sarpi [45]. Thus Coquille attributed the success of papal claims to temporal authority to the inherited prestige of ancient Rome,

---

[44] Pp. 9, 25.

[45] On Sarpi's vision of church history, see my *Venice and the Defense of Republican Liberty: Renaissance Values in the Age of the Counter Reformation* (Berkeley, 1968), esp. pp. 571 ff.

only by historical accident the see of Peter [46]. For Charles Faye earlier popes had been generally submissive to secular authority, and the relationship between popes and emperors had been proper until the time of Hildebrand. But then, « finding that this violent remedy profited the church, that institution exchanged its ancient humility for pride, cruelty, and tyranny, fastened papal attention on temporal concerns, and brought scandal that caused schism and heresy » [47]. Leschassier associated the rise of ecclesiastical tyranny directly with internal developments in canon law, which had been compelled to express the « worldly greatness » that had penetrated the church. Under papal auspices the ancient code of the church universal had been gradually replaced by a specifically Roman canon law from which articles protecting local liberty were systematically excluded. He considered the process well under way with the code of Dionysius Exiguus and essentially completed by Gratian and his followers. After Gratian Christendom (except for the magistrates of Paris) entirely forgot « that the church had ever had any other law than this » [48].

Not every Gallican admitted that even the church in France had shared in the general eclipse of liberty. Charles Faye, for example, claimed that she had remained twelve hundred years the same, without any alteration in her « laws and form of establishment and police ». In this respect he believed that the French church had been unique; every other church had changed for the worse [49]. But Leschassier knew better; he was explicit that in spite of staunch resistance, the Gallican church had fallen into the same « miserable servitude » as the rest of Christendom. From this condition she had only been rescued by Saint Louis, but that ruler's assertion of the autonomy of the French church against Innocent IV had begun a steady recovery that was still continuing in Leschassier's own time. In his conception, therefore, there had already been three phases in the

---

[46] *Devis entre un Citoyen de Nevers, & un de Paris*, in *Oeuvres*, I, 200: « Quand la Ville de Rome commandoit à tout le monde, le Pape étant élû à Rome étoit reconnu Souverain ».

[47] *Discours*, p. 100.

[48] *Liberté de l'Eglise Gallicane*, pp. 16 ff., 27.

[49] *Discours*, pp. 103, 115.

history of the church in France: an ancient era of freedom, an intervening period of tyranny, and a new age of freedom. The first and third were qualitatively identical: « ... the ancient and the modern ... are one same liberty measured differently ». The ancient was based on the code of the church universal, while « the modern is contained in the ordinances of our kings, in their concordats and in the judgments of their sovereign courts; and this second liberty has been introduced by necessity, as subsidiary to the first ». Modern Gallicanism was the ancient church universal reborn in one nation, and thus the model as well for ecclesiastical reform everywhere [50].

The Gallican magistrates contemplated the accomplishments of Trent and the various reforms sponsored by Rome in the light of these conceptions. In their view these developments pointed not to the true *reformation* of the church but rather to a universal extension and consummation of that *deformation* so successfully prosecuted by the medieval papacy. Genuine reform, they believed, could proceed only along the lines marked out by Gallicanism; a reformed Christendom meant, for them, a collection of autonomous units modeled on France. As Leschassier declared, « The modern councils, which contain the servitude of the church, must yield to the ancient, which contain its liberty, since this is a common canonical and ancient right » [51].

These rather summary remarks about the attitudes and content of Gallicanism should be enough to suggest why the works of Gallicans were of considerable interest to other Europeans, not only because Gallicanism presented itself as a potential ally against the pope but for more positive reasons. Gallicanism suggested that a certain undogmatic spiritual unity was consistent with the political pluralism required by the emerging identities of particular states. It associated dogmatic rigidity with the corrupt medieval past, and Gallican writers occasionally took a remarkably broad view about the definition of Christian belief [52]; for Catholics Gallicanism offered a real alternative to

---

[50] *Liberté de l'Eglise Gallicane*, pp. 4-8.
[51] *Ibid.*, p. 30.
[52] For example, Faye, *Discours*, p. 105, which quotes Augustine in support of the proposition that a man sincerely concerned to know the truth

the restrictive and often uncongenial orthodoxies required by the papacy. Basic to this attitude was also an intellectual style (among the Gallican magistrates if not necessarily among their theological allies) that also made their position widely attractive. Precisely during a time when the Roman reform movement sought to reinvigorate rational and systematic modes of thought, denounced or tried to control free historical investigation, and took an increasingly dim view of the new science, the Gallicanism of the magistrates sought truth in the concrete and empirical world, worked towards increasingly sophisticated techniques of free historical investigation and analysis, and accepted the autonomy of science as well as of politics; a sympathetic interest in the new astronomy was only one reflection among others of the remarkably open attitude to all human experience that characterized the Gallican magistracy [53]. Gallicanism thus brought into focus tendencies central to a whole generation of Europeans.

It should be clear, then, why lines of communication were open between Gallican leaders and like-minded men, perhaps especially government officials, in other parts of Europe; and they operated in both directions. Gallican writings occupied a prominent place in the Calvinist Melchior Goldast's monumental *Monarchia S. Romani imperii* (Hanover and Frankfort, 1611-1613) [54]. They were also read in England, occasionally in English translation [55]; and conversely the oath of allegiance that the Gallican Third Estate proposed to impose on the realm at the Estates General of 1614 was modeled on the Anglican oath of James I [56].

---

cannot be considered a heretic. Cf. Coquille's favorable treatment of Luther, *Devis*, p. 204.

[53] Cf. Ludwig von Pastor, *The History of the Popes*, tr. Dom Ernest Graf (London, 1898-1953), XXV, 300. See too Sarpi's *Lettere ai Gallicani*, ed. Boris Ulianich (Wiesbaden, 1961); these letters deal repeatedly with scientific interests.

[54] In addition to numerous teatises by older Gallican writers such as Gerson and John of Paris, Goldast included works of Richer, Leschassier, Louis Servin, and other contemporary Gallicans.

[55] For example, Richer, *A Treatise of Ecclesiasticall and Politike Power* (London, 1612).

[56] See Martin, *Gallicanisme et la réforme catholique*, pp. 367 ff.

The connections between Gallicanism and Venice, as another Catholic power, are, however, particularly instructive. After several decades of withdrawal from European affairs, the Serenissima, still regarded as a major state, was during the later sixteenth century drawing closer to France, whose recovery after the Religious Wars she welcomed as a make-weight on the Italian peninsula to Spain. An interest in French thought accompanied thoughts of political alliance, and both were mediated by ambassadors like Philippe Canaye, who, although forbidden direct contact with the Venetian patriciate, communicated with its more important members through such influential personages as Paolo Sarpi [57]. The mentality of this group, among which Galileo spent his most happy and fruitful years, is suggested by its interest in such works as the essays of Montaigne and Francis Bacon. It was cosmopolitan, skeptical, generally suspicious of both the motives and the results of intellectual system-building, and in politics resolved to defend the autonomy of the secular world and the absolute independence of the Republic [58].

Venetian interest in Gallicanism was notably stimulated by the papal interdict of 1606-1607 and the tense years following that traumatic event. The Venetians helped Canaye himself to recognize the larger importance of Gallicanism. Possibly a bit misled by Venetian flattery, he wrote home from Venice: « The greater the effort to stifle our Gallican liberties, the more they are studied and embraced by all nations, so that here they are described as a law of nations necessary to the conservation of every kind of state » [59]. Such prominent Gallicans as Leschassier and Louis Servin were induced by the Venetian ambassador in Paris to compose treatises in behalf of Venice, whose cause against Rome was discovered to be much the same as that of France [60]; and Sarpi, who had long been interested in the doc-

---

[57] For Sarpi's contacts with Gallican leaders, see Ulianich's long introduction to his edition of the *Lettere ai Gallicani.*

[58] See, in general, Gaetano Cozzi, *Il doge Nicolò Contarini: Ricerche sul patriziato veneziano agli inizi del Seicento* (Venice, 1958), esp. pp. 1-52.

[59] Letter to Hotman de Villiers, Oct. 12, 1606, in his *Lettres et ambassade* (Paris, 1635-1636), III, 233.

[60] Leschassier, *Consultatio Parisii cujusdam de controversia inter sanctitatem*

trines of Cujas, busied himself in securing copies of Gallican treatises to circulate among the Venetian leaders [61]. In these works the Venetians found, if not novel arguments, valuable support for their general insistence that the autonomy they required for themselves represented the legitimate and historic organization of the church universal.

But here too the exchange moved in both directions, in spite of the complacency of Canaye. Gallicans admired and found encouragement in Venetian resistance to Rome, and they read the Venetian treatises with as much avidity as the Venetians read theirs. The magistrates of Paris followed the Venetian interdict with deep interest, collecting and passing around each scrap of news, and reacting with varying degrees of enthusiasm to the Venetian pamphlets as they reached Paris. For Pierre de l' Estoile, Paolo Sarpi, the leading Venetian theorist, was a kind of saint [62]. Nor did the impression that the Venetian interdict left in France die quickly. The papal nuncio in Paris noted with alarm a year after the interdict came to an end how much encouragement « the contumacy of the Venetians » still gave to the French. In his view it continued to justify and to excuse « the faults and errors » of the French, among whom « papal jurisdiction is almost completely destroyed » [63]. After the assassination of Henry IV, the author of the famous *Anticoton* praised Venice for expelling the Jesuits. If France had been equally wise, he meant to imply, the king would still have been alive [64].

Viewed in this broader context, therefore, Gallicanism takes on a new and larger meaning. Religious thought has a unique capacity to bring into focus fundamental changes in the whole

---

Pauli V et Sereniss. Rempublicam Venetam, ad virum clariss. Venetum, and Servin, *Pro libertate status et reipublicae venetorum Gallo-franci ad Philenetum epistola*, both printed in Paris in 1606.

[61] See his *Lettere ai Gallicani* and his *Lettere ai Protestanti*, ed. Manlio Duilio Busnelli (Bari, 1931), passim.

[62] On the general point see his *Mémoires-Journaux*, ed. G. Brunet (Paris, 1875-1896), VIII, 254 ff.; on Sarpi, p. 255.

[63] Roberto Ubaldini to Cardinal Borghese, Aug. 5, 1608, in « Per l'epistolario di Paolo Sarpi », ed. Pietro Savio, *Aevum*, X (1936), 74, n. 1.

[64] (Paris, 1610), pp. 46-47. This work is now generally attributed to César de Plaix.

range of human values and attitudes which may find only partial expression in other aspects of human activity. And Gallicanism reveals, perhaps more generally than any other development in the religious history of France during the later medieval and early modern periods, how fully France participated in the spiritual and cultural crisis of the Renaissance and Reformation.

THEODORE K. RABB

A CONTRIBUTION TO THE TOLERATION CONTROVERSY OF THE SIXTEENTH CENTURY: SANDYS'S « A RELATION OF THE STATE OF RELIGION »

In the last year of the sixteenth century, after a three-year trip around the Continent, Edwin Sandys wrote a brief book recording his impressions of the various religions he had encountered during his lengthy Grand Tour [1]. The son of an archbishop of York, well versed in law after more than a decade of study at Oxford and the Middle Temple, Sandys was a perfect example of that recurrent phenomenon: the intelligent English gentleman speaking his mind about the important issues of the day. At the time, however, there seemed no great likelihood that he would have anything of consequence to say. For nobody could have foreseen that this 38-year old of few accomplishments would soon achieve considerable prominence: a knighthood within four years, and leadership of the House of Commons and the Virginia Company shortly thereafter. In 1599 he appeared to be no more than a worthy member of the Establishment, middle aged by Elizabethan standards, and with nothing of note to show for himself. At best one might have expected a prosaic work, of minor concern to his contemporaries or to posterity. In fact, it contained the first indication of those abilities that were to make so resounding an impact on the House of Commons: in particular, his skill in the reasoned analysis of intractable problems. The future Sir Edwin's work deserves consideration, not merely as a milestone in his intellectual development, but primarily as an important contribution to the current discussions of religious toleration — important enough to attract the interest of such diverse figures as Paolo Sarpi and Hugo Grotius [2].

---

[1] The editions of the work are discussed in Theodore K. Rabb, « The Editions of Sir Edwin Sandys's *Relation of the State of Religion* », *The Huntington Library Quarterly*, XXVI (1963), 323-336. The dates of the Grand Tour are established in *idem.*, « The Early Life of Sir Edwin Sandys and Jacobean London » (unpublished Ph. D. dissertation, Princeton, 1961), pp. 28-30.

[2] See Rabb, « Editions », p. 323 and pp. 335-336; also Gaetano Cozzi, « Sir Edwin Sandys e la *Relazione dello stato della religione*, » *Rivista storica italiana* LXXIX (1967), 1096-1121, which includes an excellent analysis

I.

Sandys called his book *A Relation of the State of Religion, And with what Hopes and Policies it hath beene Framed, and is maintained, in the severall States of these Westerne Partes of the World* [3]. It would be difficult to improve on the title for a one-sentence description of the work, with the exception that Protestantism was left for a second volume which was never completed. Unfortunately, the title also gives a foretaste of Sandys's style, which was rarely felicitous and often unclear. He had a fondness for subsidiary clauses (usually in parentheses) that made his sentences long and confusing, and he liked to pack as many facts as possible into every overloaded sentence. Most of the book was given over to a detailed account of Roman Catholic practices, with the result that the presentation always remained sober and methodical. Memorable phrases are non-existent, and even metaphors are few and simple. The treatise was the product of an academic mind, more concerned with content than with form.

In most editions *A Relation* was about 200 quarto pages long, and from the fourth edition it was divided into sixty short chapters, corresponding to the main topics, which provide an easy guide to the structure of the work. First came an introduction, which served as a dedication to Whitgift in the fourth and later editions. Here Sandys stated that the purpose of his travels had been to observe the religions of Western Europe in

---

of the notes Paolo Sarpi added to the book — published in the Italian and French translations. About half of Cozzi's article is devoted to a survey of the contents of Sandys's book. Like a number of authors, he stresses the Irenicism, but he does not appear to have consulted the British Museum copy of *A Relation* ... (cited in note 48, below), on which an important part of the present paper's analysis rests. Moreover, his main concern is to give an overview of the entire contents of the book — an intention that he fulfills admirably — and not to concentrate on the various aspects of Sandys's theory of toleration, which is the chief object of this article. Cozzi quotes (pp. 1096-1097) two brief mentions of Sandys by other Italian scholars, but neither of these is more than a passing reference, and need not be pursued further here. The principal remaining literature is given in note 27, below.

[3] From 1629 (the fourth English edition), the book bore the title *Europae Speculum, or A Relation* ... References will be to this edition, the first to be paginated.

order to discern what possibilities existed for unity, at least among the reformed Churches. He added that he intended to restrict himself only to those matters which « may seeme most necessarie for our Countrie to be knowne » [4]. The first forty-two chapters dealt with various aspects of Roman Catholicism; six chapters then discussed religious conditions in Western European countries; and these were followed by a one-chapter estimate of the strength of the Papacy, three chapters on the restoration of Christian unity, seven chapters covering the Jews and the Greek and Russian Churches, and a last chapter which promised treatment of the reformed religions at a later date. The long section on the Roman Catholics was the most thorough, dealing with their beliefs and practices, their government, and the means they used to increase their power. By contrast, the surveys of the various countries were brief estimates of the relative strengths of their religions; and the section on unity discussed some popular plans for the reconciliation of Christianity. The final chapters described Judaism in a tone of mild bewilderment, replete with reasons for the Roman Catholics' failure to convert the Jews; and then outlined the beliefs, structure, and difficulties of the Greek and Russian Churches.

Apart from its omission of Protestantism, the book certainly succeeded in its avowed purpose. By so doing, it provided its readers with as full and accurate an account of its subject as was available. Moreover, its preoccupation with Catholicism and reconciliation was an emphasis that was well suited to the tastes of its English audience. For modern readers, however, and for an insight into the personality of its author, the main interest lies in Sandys's tolerant statements about Catholics and Jews, and in his remarkable discussion of the possibility of reconciliation among Christians.

II.

Comments about differing religious beliefs at the end of the 16 th century must be viewed within the context of an intolerant age, when men were fighting for their faith and had

---

[4] *A Relation*, p. 2.

little but vituperation for their opponents. Typical of the times were some of the other books that were published in the same year as Sandys's: *The Downefall of Poperie*, *The Popes Funerall*, *The Woefull Crie of Rome*, *A Declaration of Egregious Popish Impostures*, and *The Unlawfulness and Daunger of Tolleration of Diverse Religions in One Monarchie* [5]. Sandys had no such illusions about Papal power or the prospects for Christian unity: in Rome he heard no woeful cry and saw no imminent downfall. Nor did he condemn the Catholics on all sides. By present-day standards he might seem heavily biased, because he stated his basic position unequivocally when he introduced « the Romane Religion » as the faith which, of all others, had « most manifoldly declined and degenerated » from early Christianity [6]. Such a comment, together with descriptions of Catholic ceremonies as « childish ... and unsavory », revealing « sillinesse », and causing « disgrace and contempt », were only to be expected from an English Protestant [7]. What was surprising was that Sandys also had so many good words to say for the Catholics.

From the first he stated plainly that little was wrong with the Papists' doctrines and beliefs. His quarrel was with their ceremonies, superstitions, and methods of aggrandizement — notably their intolerance. Yet even in the midst of disapproval he found much that was worthy of commendation. He declared, for instance, that the Catholic custom of praying three times a day at the ringing of a bell was a practice that could be « recommended to the imitation of all worthy Christians » [8]. Nor did he disagree in principle with the use of gorgeous and magnificent displays in order to glorify God, since « this outward state and glorie being well disposed, doth engender, quicken, encrease and nourish, the inward reverence and respectfull devotion which is due so soveraigne Maiestie and power » [9]. He also

---

[5] *A Short-Title Catalogue of Books Printed in England, Scotland & Ireland and of English Books Printed Abroad 1475-1640* (London, 1946), numbers 1819, 1825, 1833, 12882; and *A Transcript of the Registers of the Company of Stationers of London 1554-1640*, ed. E. Arber, Vol. III (London, 1876), p. 287.

[6] *A Relation*, p. 3.

[7] *Ibid.*, p. 3.

[8] *Ibid.*, p. 5.

[9] *Ibid.*, pp. 9-10.

admitted that « much good matter both of faith and pietie [was] eloquently delivered » in Catholic sermons, and that in principle both Lent and Confession were fine institutions. The latter he considered « a great meanes to bring men to integritie and perfection » if it were restored to its « primitive sinceritie » [10]. But its observance at the time led him to conclude that he was « farre from their understanding, who blaze so much the severitie of the Romane Religion », because « praesupposing the truth of their doctrine as ... practised; for a man that were desirous to save his Soule at his dying day, and yet deny his Body no wicked pleasure in his life time, [there was] no such Church as that of Rome » [11].

In general, Sandys tended to find merit in Catholic customs and ideas, but to disapprove of their implementation. Nonetheless, there is little reason to doubt that he sincerely attempted to live up to his own stated principles: « I choose rather to commend the vertue of an enemie, than to flatter the vice or imbecilitie of a friend » [12]. He pointed out commendable Roman practices on a number of occasions, and when he found fault with them he rarely used the violent language that was so common in his day. At worst, he employed adjectives such as « unsavory ». Since the book was characterized by its temperance, its derogatory passages tended to be mild and short.

If anything, Sandys's attitude towards the Catholics seemed to be one of begrudging admiration for their ability to maintain their strength and meet the challenge of Protestantism. He disliked many of their methods, but he had to acknowledge that they achieved their intentions. He even thought that, but for the frequent change in Popes, the Catholics would have mastered the world [13]. With disarming frankness he openly admitted that their policies of « feare and constraint » for some, mainly in Italy, and great elasticity for others, such as friars [14] or new believers (whose every « fancy may be satisfied » once loyalty was established) [15], were highly effective in generating loyalty.

---

[10] *Ibid.*, pp. 7 and 10.
[11] *Ibid.*, p. 17.
[12] *Ibid.*, p. 10.
[13] *Ibid.*, p. 27.
[14] *Ibid.*, pp. 8 and 22.
[15] *Ibid.*, pp. 34-35.

This hold over the people was then skillfully maintained: by popular, magnificent, and colourful ceremonies, by attractive music, by intolerance of all « doubt or question » [16], by sagacious dispensations, and above all by the maintenance of « the ignorance of the Laietie [which] was the chiefest and surest sinew of their greatnesse and glorie » [17]. Sandys also noted that the Catholics were quick to adopt from the Protestants useful methods of aggrandizement, such as disputations and a greater stress on education. All in all, he regarded them as a formidable power, expert in the use of propaganda, backed by great families and nations with vested interests in Church offices, and in the enviable position of being able to call on the capable, dedicated and huge reserve of manpower that was gathered in the various religious orders. Moreover, the Catholics were united, and Sandys therefore believed the Turkish threat to be the only « bridle which holds in the Papacie » from attacking the Protestants [18]. He felt that the Pope's advantages would outweigh his difficulties in the long run, especially as the people of Southern Europe, the bastion of Catholicism, seemed to be richer and cleverer than their merely stronger Northern counterparts.

This analysis of Catholicism was no jeremiad: it was simply a careful attempt to indicate as fully and accurately as possible the attitudes and strengths of the Catholics. Whenever Sandys considered praise, admiration, or a plea for imitation to be appropriate, he did not hesitate to give his opinion. Possibly the most remarkable of his compliments were those that he reserved for two of the Popes themselves. Sixtus V he called « one of the worthiest Popes ... and of a mind most possessed with high and honourable enterprises » [19], who « was redoubted as a Prince of great worth and Spirit » [20]. Even more striking was the estimate of the reigning Pope, Clement VIII. Sandys regarded Clement as a man who was calm, competent, « devout in his way, and thinks without doubt that he is in the right » [21]. He even discounted the derogatory rumors about Clement's

[16] *Ibid.*, p. 25.
[17] *Ibid.*, p. 34.
[18] *Ibid.*, p. 193.
[19] *Ibid.*, p. 136.
[20] *Ibid.*, p. 149.
[21] *Ibid.*, p. 151.

early life, and added that the Pope was a humble and thrifty man. Furthermore, he conceded that Clement had been a good Prince, having converted Henry IV, gained Ferrara, and made peace between his two major allies, Spain and France. Sandys concluded with the startling sentiment that « this Pope [is] both good Man, good Praelat, and good Prince. And so I leave him, wishing his dayly encrease in all parts of true goodnesse » [22].

Remarks such as these undoubtedly later gave High Commission sufficient cause for ordering the burning of the book, despite its obvious and basic antipathy towards Catholicism [23]. For Sandys's statements could not be taken as evidence of affection for the Papists. Rather, they were reflections of the moderate and reasonable outlook of their author. If confirmation is sought, one need only turn to some of Sandys's comments on the Jews. Here too, although he regarded their religion as « somewhat strange », he thought they had « very honourable and holy » opinions about God, and « very exquisite » views which were « neere unto truth » about Man [24]. On other matters, especially their morality, they were « to be commended », and those that he had met had been « of singular vertue and integritie of mind » [25]. These opinions were not the result of any particular sympathy for the religion that was under discussion. Sandys at one point recorded (as an example of Catholic mistrust of theological discussions) that in Italy he had been « halfe threatned for no other fault than for debating with a Jew and upholding the truth of Christianitie against him » [26]. He had obviously come into contact with a number of Jews, and his attitude towards Judaism was not merely a nostalgic recollection of the people of the Old Testament. Tolerance in such matters was not a question of sentimentality or conviction, but the product of a peculiarly dispassionate mind.

---

[22] *Ibid.*, p. 156.
[23] See Rabb, « Editions », pp. 325-329.
[24] *A Relation*, pp. 222-23.
[25] *Ibid.*, p. 226.
[26] *Ibid.*, p. 117.

III.

Equally restrained was Sandys's examination of the possibility of reconciliation among the major Christian Churches. This is the part of the work that has drawn the principal attention of modern scholarship — first from J. W. Allen, whose excellent presentation of Sir Edwin's views is the best summary available, and later from W. K. Jordan and Joseph Lecler [27]. They have treated *A Relation* as an episode in the toleration controversy of the sixteenth century — which it was — but one must also try to understand Sandys's position in light of the careful analytic bent that was characteristic of everything he wrote (including his later parliamentary speeches). It was a systematic, reasoned investigation unique in its times.

The book's special qualities are best appreciated if one realizes that the background against which it was written can be summed up as chaotic religious violence. The Edict of Nantes had been issued only the year before, but there was nothing to indicate that a significant reduction in the tension between Protestants and Catholics was imminent. After all, Ferdinand of Styria had only just begun a career of intolerance and repression that was at least as merciless as anything witnessed in Philip II's Spain. Advocates of reconciliation were unmistakably an embattled minority, not even united among themselves. Some still wished for a return to complete unity — though after the failure of leaders like Bucer, Contarini, and Melanchthon earlier in the century, they should have had few illusions. Nonetheless, the possibility of a *via media*, or at least acceptance of a common core of belief (with differences viewed as non-essentials),

---

[27] J. W. Allen, *A History of Political Thought in the Sixteenth Century* (London, 1928) — in the second edition (1941), Sandys is discussed on pp. 241-246; W. K. Jordan, *The Development of Religious Toleration in England*, Vol. I (Cambridge, Mass., 1932), pp. 367-371; and Joseph Lecler, *Histoire de la tolérance au siècle de la Réforme*, Vol. II (Paris, 1955), pp. 346-349. See too the Cozzi article cited in note 2 above. Before Allen, Sandys does not seem to have figured at all in the literature — see, for example, Johannes Kühn, *Toleranz und Offenbarung* (Leipzig, 1923): I am indebted to Hans Baron for bringing this book to my attention. The most recent study, Henry Kamen's *The Rise of Toleration* (New York, 1967), does not mention Sandys.

did not seem totally utopian: the Union of Brest-Litovsk in 1596 had established just such a compromise, and Bodin's *Heptaplomeres* suggested that all the world's faiths could be joined together in this fashion. By the 1590's, however, most of the moderates were simply *politiques* — advocates of tolerance for the sake of political peace. The only two previous writers whose direct influence can be traced in Sandys's book — Michel de l' Hôpital and Richard Hooker — were both representatives of the *politique* approach, and he clearly shared their hopes [28]. But he also had his own contribution to offer: taking the developments of the century to their logical conclusion, he abandoned the search for unity. His detached analysis of contemporary proposals for reunion brought him to the conclusion that co-existence and mutual respect were the sole feasible goals for men of good intentions. His own comments about Catholicism not only provided an example of the attitude he was recommending, but also help us understand the kind of atmosphere he sought as a remedy for Europe's ills.

The most noticeable contrast between Sandys and his predecessors is the restraint in his language. Sixteenth-century propagandists for tolerance made frequent pleas for calmness, but were usually anything but calm. They were dealing with a subject charged with emotion, and they felt deeply and personally involved in the issues — Roland Bainton has aptly dubbed Castellio « The Remonstrator » [29]. It was as protagonists that they wrote, not as observers, and some (for example Bucer, Contarini, l' Hôpital and Melanchthon) tried to implement their beliefs by public action. Where Sandys differed was in his dispassionate attitude toward the problem. He presented himself,

---

[28] He refers to the « The worthie Chauncellour » de l'Hôpital, and endorses the Frenchman's advocacy of moderation. Allen, Jordan, and Lecler all tie their analyses of Sandys closely to their interpretations of Hooker, rightly stressing that Edwin was a long-time pupil and friend of the great theologian. There can be no mistaking the parallels in their outlooks: the attachment to leniency and restraint, the pragmatism, and even the final resignation to God's will (see below, notes 39 and 46). The purpose of the present paper, however, is to isolate those features of *A Relation* that are unique, and not merely reflections of contemporary schools of thought.

[29] R. H. Bainton, *The Travail of Religious Liberty* (New York, 1958), Chapter 4.

not as someone who was taking sides, but as an objective investigator who was looking into a complex question and weighing the various answers that had been offered. The outlook was typical of the man, and it gave his presentation the unusual quality of a detached enquiry.

The tone that was to be adopted was foreshadowed in the introduction to the book. Sandys stated quite plainly that one of the purposes of his investigations had been to discover « what possibilitie and good meanes of uniting at leastwise the severall braunches of the Reformed professours » could be found; but he added that he considered « unitie universall bee more to be desired than hoped » [30]. He had hopes, but little expectation, of unity. Recent events in France he viewed with an incredulity that prevented him from expecting other countries to follow suit. The achievement of Henry IV had been so exceptional that Sandys regarded « France beyond all hope of man reuinited in it selfe » [31]. For Western Europe in general he saw little prospect of reconciliation, since the two major sides were too intolerant and stubborn to attempt any compromise.

The pessimistic attitude and disapproval of intolerance were recognized by Allen, Jordan, and Lecler as the bases of Sandys's position. In adopting this outlook, Sandys, according to Jordan, « stood almost alone in the breadth of his view of the religious situation in Europe » [32]. Yet it was not so much the all-embracing quality of his approach as the cast of mind in which it was framed that chiefly distinguished him from his contemporaries. The most remarkable impression left by the section of some twenty quarto pages that was devoted to a discussion of unity is its almost coldly analytical treatment of an exasperating and disappointing subject.

Sandys started with the proposition that there was « such a proportion of strength on both sides, as bereaveth the other of hope ever by warre to subdue them » [33]. Unity could be forced solely by Time, and then only after « great alterations ». Consequently there remained only five proposed means of achieving

---

[30] *A Relation*, p. 2.
[31] *Ibid.*, p. 48.
[32] *Religious Toleration*, p. 367.
[33] *A Relation*, p. 194.

unity: by the « Unitie of Veritie, or Unitie of Charitie, or Unitie of Perswasion, or Unitie of Authoritie; or Unitie of Necessitie » [34]. The first, some thought, could be achieved by calm mediation, since there was agreement on fundamentals and many people wanted peace. This type of « common-core » proposal Sandys dismissed because it found too little acceptance. The second approach, a kind of moderation, was based on charity, and would be successful, according to its proponents, because an end had to be put to the quarrels which gave « wicked joy » to non-Christians. It would involve a lessening of obstinacy on both sides, with the Catholics giving up some of their ceremonies, and the Protestants showing greater charity by ceasing to think that « they are then rightest, when they are unlikest the Papacie » [35]. Revisions and accommodations of this sort would establish a « common-core » unity on basic matters, such as a Confession of Faith, the Liturgy and Church government, while less important beliefs would be left to the theological quibbles of the Schools. But Sandys once again considered success unlikely, though he admitted that this type of accommodation was much more acceptable and promising than the others.

The third proposal was for complete unity, achieved by persuasion, and reached when one side collapsed; this he discounted as highly improbable. The fourth, also for complete unity, but now established by higher authority, was expected to come from a General Council or from the action of Princes. With regard to such schemes he saw « sundry difficulties so great, that they draw to bee next neighbours to so many impossibilities ». In particular, he pointed to « the untractableness of the Papacie » and sarcastically remarked that « they dreame of an old world, and of the heroicall times, who imagine that Princes will break their sleeps for such purposes » [36]. He therefore concluded that, since the long period of opposition had « formalized » the split, this particular proposal for unity was « an honested-harted desire, but no probable dessein » [37]. Finally,

---

[34] *Ibid.*, p. 194.
[35] *Ibid.*, p. 197.
[36] *Ibid.*, pp. 201 and 205.
[37] *Ibid.*, p. 206.

if one expected necessity to force unity, there was such danger only from the Turk; and here Sandys wisely noted that « Empires are not then always at theyr strongest, when at theyr biggest » [38]. He dismissed the Sultanate as « a dying monarchy » concluding that, despite Christian disunity, the Turks presented no fearful threat. The problem of unity, therefore, « must I leave and recommend it to God » [39].

The method Sandys used was to present each proposal in turn, to discuss its shortcomings, and to give cogent reasons for its probable failure. There were no emotional harangues or pleas; recriminations were only mild; and there were none of the usual dramatic calls to conscience, Scripture or the wrath of the Almighty, except perhaps for the final quiet resignation to God's will. There could be no doubt that he was sincere when he stated that « for my owne part, the greatest desire I have in this world, is to see Christendome reconciled ... and that without the ruine and subversion of eyther part ... and thinke any kind of peace were better than these strifes, which did not prejudice that higher peace between God and mens consciences » [40]. But he obviously considered this desire to be no more practical than the proposal for reaching unity by authority: a « speculative consideration, which ... experience doth need to rectifie » [41]. The whole problem was presented in a scholarly, critical manner, with each proposal examined and found wanting.

The only suggestion which Sandys acknowledged to be profitable was, typically, the advocacy of calmer and more charitable attitudes. Here he proudly pointed to the Reformation in England which, he said, had been « brought in with peaceable and orderly proceeding » [42]. However, such good fortune was

---

[38] *Ibid.*, p. 207.

[39] *Ibid.*, p. 215. Cf. Hooker's conclusion: « How sober and sound soever our proceedings be in these causes, all is in vain which we do to abate the errors of men, except their unruly affections be bridled ... We have used all other means, and ... We have laboured in vain ... there is no way left but this one, ' Pray for the peace of Jerusalem ' », in Richard Hooker, *Works*, ed. J. Keble, Vol. III (Oxford, 1841), pp. 464-465. See above, note 28, and below, note 46.

[40] *A Relation*, p. 201.

[41] *Ibid.*, p. 206.

[42] *Ibid.*, p. 214.

rare, because an all-pervasive intolerance determined the more usual situation of restless disunity. As a first step he recommended that there be more contact between the two sides, because disagreements and disputes are « made calm by entercourse, by parlie they are reconciled, by familiaritie they are extinguished » [43]. Peace would be immeasurably closer if only people sought « whatsoever goodnes appeares in any man » and could « love whatsoever in [an enemy] hath resemblance of vertue » [44]. Sandys portrayed the intractability of the two sides, and their refusal to communicate with each other, as a disease which tainted all efforts towards compromise [45].

A Relation depicted an unhappy situation, but pessimism was not remarkable among discussions of this subject. What was unusual was the accuracy, detachment, and analytic method of the presentation, repeatedly tied to ethical rather than religious considerations. And in one major respect Sandys's treatment was virtually unique: he offered no solution to the problem. He did advocate greater tolerance and charity, which might eventually result in peace between the two sides. But he made this suggestion with little hope of implementation: the proposal seemed to be a piece of fatherly advice, not a plausible remedy. Furthermore, although charitable tolerance could be a panacaea for religious ills, and a worthy aim in itself, it could not on its own restore unity. At most Sandys was recommending a means of lessening strife, and even here he hardly expected success. Where the central problem, reunion of Christianity, was concerned, he certainly had no solution, for he had nothing more positive to offer than the hope that Divine Providence would « effect those things which to mans witt may seeme impossible » [46].

Jordan concluded that « Sandys' magnificent ideal broke down when he was obliged to discard one means of securing it after another » [47]. This interpretation is based on the supposition that the five means of achieving unity were put forward as Sir Edwin's own solutions to the problem. In fact, however, these

---

[43] *Ibid.*, p. 107.
[44] *Ibid.*, p. 110.
[45] *Ibid.*, p. 75.
[46] *Ibid.*, p. 216. See above, notes 28 and 39.
[47] *Religious Toleration*, pp. 370-71.

various « solutions » were presented by Sandys in his role as investigator, not advocate. These were not his own answers to the problem. On the contrary, they were being cited as the most important and popular of the many proposals that had circulated throughout the century. For corroboration that Sandys did not put them forward as his own answer, one can turn to the corrections (made in his own hand) in the copy of the first edition of the book that is now in the British Museum. Clearly marked on the pages that outlined the different types of unity are quotation marks, placed at the beginning of each line in the margin [48]. Only one meaning can have been intended: these were not Sandys's own solutions, but those of his contemporaries. He had examined them and found them wanting, but he had no alternative of his own to offer.

IV.

The seventeenth century, an age when religious passions and violence gradually subsided, seemed to regard *A Relation* as a tract for the times. The book went through fourteen editions, two reissues, and three translations between 1605 and 1687. At first, in 1605, it encountered suppression — three editions were needed in that one year, but the Court of High Commission ordered all copies seized and burned. Yet as time passed its humane message and calm tone aroused increasing interest until, by the end of the century, the restraint it sought had gained sufficiently wide acceptance to render further editions unnecessary [49].

If the subsequent history of his treatise is any indication, Sandys in 1599 was disclosing for the first time that ability to capture attention and crystallize a viewpoint which was to be so strikingly apparent during his parliamentary career after 1604. Moreover, he was demonstrating that sober discourse had a place — a vital place — even in so contentious and inflammatory

---

[48] Copy of the 1605 edition in the British Museum (Catalogue Number C. 28 f 8), the five pages from the page preceding signature T to the page following signature T 2.

[49] See Rabb, « Editions », *passim*.

an issue as religious toleration. And he came to a conclusion (that co-existence was desirable for its human qualities), which was novel in its own day and held its appeal for nearly a century. If one relates this conclusion to its underlying motive — that the basic virtues of charity, concentration on man's better side, and peace, should be the Europeans' supreme considerations, even in disagreements over faith — one realizes that Sandys placed the entire controversy within an ethical, non-theological framework, and that this, too, was a foretaste of the future. It would be easy to exaggerate the importance of *A Relation*, because it can hardly be considered a major influence in intellectual history. But the respect and interest it aroused justify the assessment that it was not only a significant landmark in the history of toleration, but also a revealing indicator, both of the direction moderate opinion was moving, and of the feelings of a sizeable body of contemporary opinion. If the present paper has succeeded in fleshing out the accounts of Allen, Jordan, and Lecler, it has also, hopefully, indicated why Sandys fully deserves the honored place they have given him in the history of religious toleration during the sixteenth century.

INDEX OF NAMES

Stampato nel mese di novembre 1970
nello Stab. Tip. già G. Civelli - Via Faenza, 71 - Firenze
per conto di G. C. Sansoni S. p. A.